COUNTRIES OF THE WORLD
INFORMATION SERIES

Information CHINA

(IN THREE VOLUMES)

And Nation Shall Speak Peace unto Nation

COUNTRIES OF THE WORLD
INFORMATION SERIES

Information Bulgaria
Information China

In preparation:
Information Czechoslovakia
Information Hungary: 2nd Edition
Information Mongolia
Information Poland
Information Romania

Information CHINA

The Comprehensive and Authoritative
Reference Source of New China

Volume 2

Compiled and Translated by

The Chinese Academy of Social Sciences

Edited for Pergamon Press by
C V James

PERGAMON PRESS

OXFORD · NEW YORK · BEIJING · FRANKFURT
SÃO PAULO · SYDNEY · TOKYO · TORONTO

U.K.	Pergamon Press plc, Headington Hill Hall, Oxford OX3 0BW, England
U.S.A.	Pergamon Press, Inc., Maxwell House, Fairview Park, Elmsford, New York 10523, U.S.A.
PEOPLE'S REPUBLIC OF CHINA	Pergamon Press, Room 4037, Qianmen Hotel, Beijing, People's Republic of China
FEDERAL REPUBLIC OF GERMANY	Pergamon Press GmbH, Hammerweg 6, D-6242 Kronberg, Federal Republic of Germany
BRAZIL	Pergamon Editora Ltda, Rua Eça de Queiros, 346, CEP 04011, Paraiso, São Paulo, Brazil
AUSTRALIA	Pergamon Press Australia Pty Ltd., P.O. Box 544, Potts Point, N.S.W. 2011, Australia
JAPAN	Pergamon Press, 5th Floor, Matsuoka Central Building, 1-7-1 Nishishinjuku, Shinjuku-ku, Tokyo 160, Japan
CANADA	Pergamon Press Canada Ltd., Suite No. 271, 253 College Street, Toronto, Ontario, Canada M5T 1R5

Copyright © 1989 Pergamon Press plc

First edition 1989

Library of Congress Cataloging in Publication Data
Information China: the comprehensive and authoritative reference source of new China/compiled and translated by the Chinese Academy of Social Sciences: edited for Pergamon Press by C. V. James.
p. cm.—(Countries of the world information series)
Bibliography: p.
Includes indexes.
1. China. I. James, C. V. (Caradog Vaughan) II. Chung-kuo she hui k o hsüeh yüan. III. Series.
DS706.I5 1988 951—dc19   88–19603

British Library Cataloguing in Publication Data
Chinese Academy of Social Sciences
Information China: the comprehensive and authoritative reference source of New China.
1. China
I. Title   II. James, C.V.
951.05'8

ISBN 0–08–034764 9

Printed in Great Britain by A. Wheaton & Co. Ltd, Exeter

CONTENTS

VOLUME TWO

Contents of Volume One   ix
Contents of Volume Three   xii
Colour Plates   xvi
Facsimiles of Ancient Maps   xvi
Geographical and Historical Maps   xvii
The Transliteration and Pronunciation of Chinese   xviii

Part IV: The National Economy

1. Introduction   443
The Economy in Semi-Colonial and Semi-Feudal China   443
The Contemporary Socialist Economy   444
The Guiding Principles for the Economy of the New Democracy   444
The Three Years of Restoration (1949–1952)   444
Socialist Transformation and Construction 1953–1957 and the Establishment of
    a Socialist Economy   448
Detours: Experiments, Consolidation and Advance in the Eight Years
    1958–1965   452
The Damage Caused to the Economy during the Cultural Revolution
    (May 1966—October 1976)   454
The New Historical Period for Developing Modern Socialism   457
The Achievements of the Thirty-Six Years 1949–1985   462
The Organization and Function of the National Economic Administration   465
The Evolution and Present State of the Economic Structure   469
Daily Economic Development and Average Economic Level per capita   473

2. The Restructuring of China's Economic System   475
Spreading the Reform from Country to Town   475
Working Out the General Programme for Overall Urban Reform   476
The Profound Change in Economic Structure Brought About by Reform   477
Economic Co-operative Ventures at Home and Abroad   481
Macro-Economic Management   482
Building a Socialist Economic System with Chinese Characteristics   484

3. Agriculture   488
The Development of Agriculture in New China   488
A Turning Point in the Development of Agriculture   490
The Development of Agriculture since the Third Plenary Session of
    the Eleventh Central Committee of the CPC   491
New Policies Benefiting the Development of the Rural Economy   493
Reform of the Rural System   496
The Prospects for Agriculture in China   508

4. Industry   511
Industrial Production and Construction in New China   511
The System of Industrial Management   512
The Structure of Industrial Departments   514
The Regional Distribution of Industry   515
Technological Progress in Industry   517

The Metallurgical Industry   520
The Chemical Industry   523
The Machine-Building Industry   525
The Electronics Industry   533
The Building Materials Industry   537
The Textile Industry   539
Light Industry   542
The Food Industry   546

5. Communications and Transport   550
    Rail Transport   550
    Highway Transport   554
    Inland River Transport   558
    Coastal Transport   561
    Marine Shipping   563
    Civil Aviation   564
    Pipeline Transportation   567
    Future Developments   568

6. Energy Resources and the Energy Industry   569
    Resources   569
    Achievements in Energy in New China   571
    The Quantity and Structure of Energy Consumption   576
    The Shortage of Energy Supply and its Causes   578
    Energy Development Strategy   578
    Objectives and Measures for Energy Development During the Seventh
        Five-Year Plan (1986–1990)   579
    Conservation of Energy   582

7. Posts and Telecommunications   583
    A Historical Survey   583
    The Current Situation   584
    Problems and Prospects   585

8. Commerce and Services   587
    Commerce in Ancient Times   587
    Modern Commerce   587
    Contemporary Commerce   588
    Mode of Operation of Chinese Commerce   589
    Types of Chinese Commercial Enterprise   591
    Catering and Service Trades   592
    Reform of the Commercial and Service Management System   595
    Prospects for the Development of China's Commerce and Service Trades   598

9. Enterprises   600
    Enterprises in Old China   600
    Enterprises in the People's Republic   600
    Types of Ownership   600
    Classification of Industrial Enterprises According to Size   602
    Management of Enterprises through the State   602
    Managerial Reform and its Development   603
    The Leadership System in Enterprises   605
    The Operation and Management of Enterprises   607
    Business Funds Established in Enterprises   608
    Political Parties in Enterprises   609
    Mass Organizations in Enterprises   609

10. Urban Construction   611
    Population Centres in Urban China   611
    The Development of Chinese Cities   611
    Urban Planning   612
    Public Utilities   614
    Urban Housing Construction   617
    New Cities   618
    The New Tangshan—a City Built out of Earthquake Ruins   619
    Urban Greening and Scenic and Historical Places   620

11. Finance and Banking   624
    Circumstances under the Kuomintang Government   624
    Circumstances in Revolutionary Bases under the Communist Party of China 624
    Financial System and Achievements of New China   625
    Financial Management and the Reform of the System   628
    Banking Achievements and the Reform of the Banking System   630
    China's Banking System   633
    Management of International Banking   635
    Auditing   638
    Insurance Business   639

12. Prices and Price Control   641
    General Information   641
    Price Control Organizations and Terms of Reference   646
    Forms of Pricing   646
    Price Supervision and Inspection   647
    Reform of the Price System and Price Control   648

13. Labour and Wages   650
    Labour Resources and Structure   650
    Management of Labour and Wages   651
    Urban Employment Policy   651
    Ways to Create Job Opportunities   652
    Labour Employment   653
    Wage Systems   653
    The Wage System for Enterprises   654
    The Wage System for Government Institutions and Offices   656
    Welfare Benefits   656
    Industrial Health and Safety   657
    Major Labour Protection Systems   657
    Vocational and Technical Training   658
    Prospects   659

14. Family Planning and Population Policy   661
    Changes in Population Reproduction Patterns   661
    Analysis of Factors in Changes in Population Growth   662
    Characteristics of Changes in Population Reproduction   664
    Population Policy   664
    Progress in Establishing Special Organizations and Training Family
        Planning Workers   667
    Prospects   669

15. Tourism   670
    The Development of the Tourist Industry Today   671
    The Nature and Variety of China's Tourist Resources   672
    Major Tourist Areas   676
    China's Tourist Routes   711
    Notice to Persons wishing to Travel in China   713
    Regions of China Open to Foreigners   715
    Applying for a Visa; Customs Regulations   717
    Currency Regulations   718
    Flying to China   720
    Climate and Clothing   722
    Foreign Airlines in Beijing   724
    Distances in China   725
    China Tourist Offices   726
    Procedures for Alien Entry into and Exit from the
        People's Republic of China   726

16. Prospects for the Next Two Decades   729
    Major Tasks and Strategic Steps for Economic Development in the
        Seventh Five-Year Plan   729
    Objectives for Economic Development   730

Objectives for the Development of Science and Technology, Education
    and Other Social Programmes 732
Capital Construction in the Seventh Five-Year Plan Period 733
Import and Export 733
Living Standards and Social Security 734
Perspectives for further Economic Structural Reform 735

Part V: Foreign Trade and Foreign Economic Relations

The Development of Foreign Trade 739
The Administrative Bodies of Foreign Trade and Economics 740
Embassies and Commercial Departments of the People's Republic of China
    in Foreign Countries 743
Organizations Dealing with Foreign Trade 751
Enterprises Dealing with Foreign Trade 755
Utilization of Foreign Capital and Introduction of Foreign Technology 763
Special Economic Zones and Open Coastal Cities 769
International Engineering Contract and Labour Service Co-operation
    and International Aid 779
Balance of Payments and Exchange Control 783
Prospects 787
Provisions of the State Council of the People's Republic of China for
    the Encouragement of Foreign Investment 788

Part VI: Living Standards and Social Welfare

Living Standards 793
Social Welfare 805

Part VII: The Armed Forces

General Information 817
The Birth and Growth of the People's Liberation Army 818
Leading Military Bodies, Services and Arms, Military Educational Institutions 832
Military Training 839
Political Work in the Armed Forces 840
The PLA's Mass Work 843
Logistics 845
The Chinese People's Armed Police 847
The Militia 848
The System of Military Service 849
Science and Technology and the Defence Industry 850
The Modernization of National Defence 851

Part VIII: Sport

A Brief Outline 855
The Sixth National Games of the PRC 860
Sport for the Masses 867
National Traditional Sports 871
Improving Athletic Performance 873
Sports Organizations, Personnel and Facilities 888
Looking Forward to the Future 895

Part IX: Medicine and Health

General Information 899
The Network of Medical and Health Services and the Public
    Health Campaign 902
Public Health 905
Maternity and Child Health 908
Traditional Chinese Medicine 911
Medical Research 915
Pharmacy and Medical Apparatus 918
International Medical Co-operation and Exchange 920
The China Red Cross Society 922
Mental Disorders: their Treatment and Prevention 925
Future Prospects 929

VOLUME ONE

Foreword	xix
Preface	xxi
The Organization and Structure of *Information China*	xxii
Editorial Staff of *Information China*	xxv
Acknowledgements	xxvii
Chronology of Chinese Historical Periods	xxix
Dates in the Text	xxix
Abbreviations	xxx
Weights and Measures	xxxi
Currency Exchange Rates	xxxi
Chinese Names	xxxii
The National Flag, Emblem and Anthem of the People's Republic of China	xxxix

Part I: China: Land and People

1. Introduction	3
The Administrative Division of China	4
2. The Economic Geography of China	6
North China	7
North-East China	13
East China	18
Central-South China	27
South-West China	33
North-West China	38
3. Population	44
China's Three Population Censuses	46
Breakdown of China's Population by Age	47
The Urbanization of the Chinese Population	48
Family Patterns in China	49
4. Geological Structure	51
Geotectonic Setting and Topographic Features of China	51
Platforms of China	52
Geosynclinal Regions of China	53
The Epi-Continental Sea and Marginal Sea Basins of Eastern China	53
The Deep Fractures of China	54
A Brief Review of the Plate Tectonics of China	55
5. Geography and Topography	57
Mountainous Areas	57
The Four Great Plateaux of China	59
Plains	59
Basins	60
Deserts and *Gobi*	60
6. Mineral Resources	62
General Situation	62
Major Resources	63
7. Climate	67
Drought	67
Waterlogging	67
Frost	72
Cold Wave	72
Typhoon	72

8. Water   73
   Rivers   73
   Lakes   74
   Sea   75
   Underground Water   76

9. Soil   77
   Features of Soil Distribution   77
   The Main Soil Types   77
   The Geographic Regions of Soils   81

10. Vegetation   84
    The Geographical Distribution of Vegetation   84
    The Main Forest Regions   86
    Other Kinds of Vegetation   90

11. Fauna   93
    Vertebrates   93
    The Ecogeographic Communities of Terrestrial Vertebrates   96
    Aquatic Animals   98

12. Nature Reserves   100
    Nature Reserves Protecting All-round Ecological Systems   100
    Nature Reserves Protecting Precious Zoological Resources   102
    Nature Reserves Protecting Rare, Precious Plants and Peculiar
       Types of Vegetation   104
    Nature Reserves and National Gardens for the Protection of Scenic Spots   105
    Nature Reserves Protecting Unique Geological Sections and Special
       Types of Landform   105
    Nature Reserves Intended to Protect Coastal Environment
       and Natural Resources   106

13. Scenic and Historical Places   107

14. Spoken and Written Languages   119
    The Four Stages of Development of Han Chinese   120

15. Environmental Protection   126
    The Development of Environmental Protection in China   126
    China's Achievements and Experiences in Environmental Protection   129
    Protection of the Natural Environment   133

Part II: The History of China

1. Ancient China (From pre-historic times to 1840)   141
   Primitive Society   141
   Slave Society   142
   Feudal Society   144

2. Recent China (1840–1919)   180
   The Opium Wars   180
   The Peasant War of the Taiping Heavenly Kingdom and the
      Second Opium War   182
   The Sino-French War (1883–1885)   188
   The Sino-Japanese War (1894–1895)   188
   The Reform Movement of 1898 and the Yihetuan Movement   193
   The Revolution of 1911   197
   The Rule of the Northern Warlords   206

3. Modern China (1919–1949)·   211
   The May 4th Movement   211
   The Founding of the Communist Party of China   213

The First Revolutionary Civil War   215
The Second Revolutionary Civil War   222
The War of Resistance Against Japan   228
The Third Revolutionary Civil War   235
The Birth of New China   240

4. Contemporary China (1949-   )   243
   The Period of Rehabilitation of the National Economy (1949–1952)   243
   The First Five-Year Plan (1953–1957)   246
   The Ten Tortuous Years (1957–1966)   249
   The Turbulent Decade of the Cultural Revolution (1966–1976)   253
   The New Era of Socialist Construction (1976-   )   256
   The Thirteenth National Congress of the Communist Party of China   262
   The New Standing Committee Members of the Political Bureau of the CPC 269
   Two Profiles   273
   Appointment of Li Peng as Acting Premier   274
   Change of Status of Hainan Island   274

5. Famous Historical Figures   275

6. Archeology and Cultural Relics   331
   Important Archeological Finds   331
   Historical Relics   342
   Important Historical and Cultural Cities   345

7. Chronological Record of the Major Events in Chinese History   349

Part III: Sociopolitical Structure and Legal System

Summary   381
The Constitution   384
The System of People's Congresses   389
The President of the People's Republic of China   393
The State Council and Subsidiary Organs   393
The Central Military Commission   395
The Local People's Governments at Different Levels   395
The Chinese People's Political Consultative Conference   397
The Communist Party of China   401
Democratic Parties   404
Social Bodies   409
Legislation   411
Judiciary   413
The Adjudicative System   419
Lawyers   422
Notarization   424
People's Mediation Committee   426
Organs and Policy of Reform Through Labour   428
Rehabilitation through Labour and Work-Study Schools   431
Comprehensive Control of Social Order   433
Law Concerning Foreign Economic Relations   435
Prospects   440

VOLUME THREE

Part X: Education

An Overview   933
Pre-school Education   944
Primary Education   947
Secondary Education   949
Vocational and Technical Education   951
Higher Education   953
Adult Education   959
Special Education   963
Teachers and Teacher-training   965
Educational Research   967
The Reform Drive and Prospects for the Future   970
Specialisms in Chinese Universities and Colleges Open to Foreign Students   973
Chinese Universities and Colleges Open to Foreign Students for
   Short-term Courses   979
International Exchanges   979

Part XI: Science and Technology

An Historical Review   985
Basic Policies and Strategies for Development in the Present Age   993
Major Achievements in the Present Age   995
The Present Situation and Strategies for the Development of
   Bourgeoning Technology   1009
Scientific and Technological Organizations and Contingents   1022
The Reform of the Scientific and Technological Structure   1027
Foreign Co-operation and Exchange   1031
Prospects   1032

Part XII: Philosophy and the Social Sciences

Historical Retrospect   1041
Major Achievements in New China   1044
Main Disciplines   1049
International Exchanges   1053
Specialized Institutions and Academic Organizations   1055
Prospects   1058

Part XIII: Literature and the Arts

1. Ancient Literature   1063
   Early Oral and Classical Literature   1063
   Philosophical Trends   1067
   Stages of Development   1070
2. Modern and Contemporary Literature   1073
   Literature of the May 4th Period   1073
   Proletarian Revolutionary Literature   1075
   Literature After 1949   1079
   New Epoch Literature   1080
3. Theatre   1083
   Traditional Opera   1083
   Modern Drama   1087

4. Cinema   1092
   From 1896 to the 1940s   1092
   From 1946 to 1966   1094
   A New Epoch   1099
   The Lessons of Experience   1100
   Styles and Types in the New Epoch   1102

5. Fine Arts   1110
   Sculpture and Painting   1110
   Calligraphy   1121

6. Architecture   1123
   The Main Features of Ancient Chinese Architecture   1123
   Types of Ancient Architecture   1126

7. Music   1136
   Music in Ancient China   1136
   Music of the New Democratic Revolutionary Period   1139
   Music in Contemporary China   1141
   The Music of Minority Nationalities   1149
   Publishing, Recording and Research   1150

8. The Dance   1153
   Folk Dances Rooted in the Life of the People   1153
   The Professional Dance Art of New China   1155
   Prospects   1162

9. Acrobatics   1164
   Acrobatics as a Form of Entertainment   1164
   Acrobatics in the People's Republic   1167

10. Oral Story Telling (Quyi)   1174
   Origins and History   1174
   Quyi in New China   1176

11. Arts and Crafts   1178
   Origins and History   1178
   Arts and Crafts in New China   1178

Part XIV: Cultural Facilities

   Libraries   1189
   Museums   1198
   Archives   1204

Part XV: Mass Media

   Press Agencies and Newspapers   1215
   Books and Periodicals   1224
   Radio and Television   1231

Part XVI: Nationalities

   General Information   1247
   The Distribution of China's Minority Peoples   1248
   Joint Efforts Toward a Unitary Multinational Country 1253
   Socio-Economic Patterns in Old China   1255

Written and Spoken Languages   1258
Religion   1261
Culture   1263
Habits and Customs   1269
Policies on Minority Nationalities   1276
Economic, Cultural and Educational Development   1284
Prospects   1287

Part XVII: Religious Beliefs

The Religious Beliefs of Nationalities in China   1291
Polytheistic Worship and Primitive Religions   1301
New China's Policy on Religion   1305
Institutes and Publications   1307

Part XVIII: Foreign Policy and External Relations

China's Foreign Policy   1311
China's External Relations   1314
Relations Between the Communist Party of China and Political Parties in
    Other Countries   1356
Associations   1360

Part XIX: Overseas Chinese Affairs

Overseas Chinese Nationals and People of Chinese Origin   1365
Historical Relations Between Overseas Chinese and China   1371
Policy Concerning Overseas Chinese Affairs   1374
Offices of Overseas Chinese Affairs at National and Provincial Level   1380
Federations of Returned Overseas Chinese at National and Provincial Level 1382

Part XX: "One Country, Two Systems" and the Unification of the Motherland

One Country, Two Systems   1387
Hong Kong   1387
Macao   1391
Taiwan   1392

Appendixes

1. Chronological Systems and Calendars of China   1401
2. Chinese Festivals and Holidays   1404
3. Chinese Food and Drink   1410
    Chinese Food   1410
    Tonic Food   1415
    Tea   1416
    Chinese Alcoholic Liquors   1418
4. Postage Stamps in China   1421
5. Climatic Data   1423
6. Time Differences   1424

China in Figures   1427

Further Reading   1565

Indexes   1571

COLOUR PLATES

Colour illustrations are thematically organized into colour sections.
Each colour section presents a series of numbered Plates.

Volume 1	Plates 1– 4	General Survey
	Plates 5– 8	Flora and Fauna
	Plates 9–16	Scenic and Historical Places
	Plates 17–24	Facsimiles of Ancient Maps
	Plates 25–32	Archeology and Cultural Relics
Volume 2	Plates 33–36	Industry
Volume 3	Plates 37–44	Literature and the Arts
	Plates 45–48	Nationalities and Religious Beliefs
	Plates 49–52	External Relations

Facsimiles of Ancient Maps

Plate 17   A Topographic Map of the South Changsha State, Western Han Dynasty (206 BC–AD 25) (before restoration)

A Topographic Map of the South Changsha State, Western Han Dynasty (206 BC–AD 25) (after restoration)

Plate 18   The Garrisons of South Changsha State, Western Han Dynasty (206 BC–AD 25)

Plate 19   The Wutai (Five Platforms) Mountains in the Five Dynasties Period (907–960)

Plate 20   China and her Neighbours, Song Dynasty (960–1279)

Yu's Trace, Song Dynasty (960–1279)

Plate 21   The Map of Territory Postscripted by Yang Ziqi, Ming Dynasty (1368–1644). Detail

General Map, from the Enlarged Territorial Maps, Ming Dynasty (1368–1644)

Plate 22   Astronomical Map, Song Dynasty (960–1279)

Plate 23   Map of Pingjiang, Song Dynasty (960–1279)

Zheng He's Navigation Map, Ming Dynasty (1368–1644)

Plate 24   Secret Map of Unified Territory (Atlas of the Chinese Empire), Ministry of Internal Affairs of the Qing Dynasty (1644–1911). Fragment

Territorial Changes and Strategic Passes of Different Dynasties, Qing Dynasty (1644–1911)

GEOGRAPHICAL AND HISTORICAL MAPS

A map section at the end of each volume contains geographical and historical maps relevant to the volume concerned.

Volume 1   Map 1.1   Administrative Divisions
            Map 1.2   Population

            Map 1.3   Relief
            Map 1.4   Mineral Resources

            Map 1.5   Climate (1)   & Map 1.6   Climate (2)
            Map 1.7   Vegetation

            Map 1.8   Western Han Dynasty
            Map 1.9   Tang Dynasty

            Map 1.10   The Silk Road
            Map 1.11   Zheng He's Expedition to the "Western Ocean"

            Map 1.12   The Revolution of 1911
            Map 1.13   The Northern Expedition

            Map 1.14   The Long March of the Red Army
            Map 1.15   The General Counter-Offensive from Bases in the Occupied Areas
                       during the War Against Japanese Aggression

            Map 1.16   The Three Decisive Campaigns and Crossing the Changjiang
                       River Campaign in the War of Liberation
            Map 1.17   Timetable of the Liberation of China

Volume 2   Map 2.1   Distribution Pattern of Crops
            Map 2.2   Animal Husbandry and Fishery

            Map 2.3   Industry (1)
            Map 2.4   Industry (2)

            Map 2.5   Railways
            Map 2.6   Air Routes

Volume 3   Map 3.1   Nationalities

THE TRANSLITERATION AND PRONUNCIATION OF CHINESE

Various systems have been used at different periods to transliterate Chinese characters into Latin script as an aid to comprehension and, especially, pronunciation. Most common before the founding of the People's Republic of China (PRC) was the Wade-Giles system, but in 1958 the People's Government promulgated its scheme for the Chinese Phonetic Alphabet, which adopted 26 Latin letters as the basis of a system of romanization to popularize the standard Chinese pronunciation *Putonghua*. This system was formally adopted in September 1977 by the United Nations Third Conference on the Standardization of Geographical Names, and since 1 January 1979 it has replaced Wade-Giles and other conventional systems as the norm for the romanization of Chinese personal and geographical names in diplomatic documents of the PRC. In August 1982 the International Standardization Organization (ISO) stipulated that the Scheme for the Chinese Phonetic Alphabet—*Pinyin*—would be the international standard for the transliteration of Chinese documents. It is therefore observed in this book. Note also the following:

1. Since tone marks are omitted, certain conventions are adopted to distinguish between homophones in geographical names: e.g., Shanxi and Shaanxi.

2. To avoid confusion between syllables followed by other syllables *beginning* with the vowels a, o, e, an apostrophe is used to divide them; e.g., Xi'an, Chang'an, Yan'an.

3. Apart from Tibetan, Mongolian, Korean and Manchu, which have their own conventional forms of romanization, the names of other minor nationalities are transliterated according to the "Romanization Code of Chinese Minor Nationalities", which was authorized as the national standard in December 1982.

The following table illustrates how sounds (represented by symbols of the International Phonetic Alphabet) are rendered in Pinyin and how this differs from the Wade-Giles system.

International Phonetic Alphabet Symbol	Pinyin	Wade-Giles
Initial Consonants		
[p]	b	p
[pʻ]	p	pʻ
[m]	m	m
[f]	f	f
[t]	d	t
[tʻ]	t	tʻ
[n]	n	n
[l]	l	l
[k]	g	k
[kʻ]	k	kʻ
[x]	h	h
[tɕ]	j	ch
[tɕʻ]	q	chʻ
[ɕ]	x	hc
[tʂ]	zh	ch
[tʂʻ]	ch	chʻ
[ʂ]	sh	sh
[ʐ]	r	j
[ts]	z	ts
[tsʻ]	c	tsʻ
[s]	s	s

International Phonetic Alphabet Symbol	Pinyin	Wade-Giles
Vowels or Phonemes Following Consonants		
[a]	a	a
[o]	o	o
[ɣ]	e	
[ai]	ai	ai
[ei]	ei	ei
[ɑu]	au	au
[ou]	ou	ou
[an]	an	an
[ən]	en	en
[aŋ]	ang	ang
[əng]	eng	eng
[uŋ]	ong	ung
[ər]	er	rh
[i, ɿ, ʅ]	i (yi)	i (yi), ih, u
[ia]	ia (ya)	ia (ya)
[ie]	ie (ye)	ieh (yeh)
[iɑu]	iao (yao)	iao (yao)
[iou]	iou (you)	iu (yu)
[iɜn]	ian (yan)	ien (yen)
[in]	in (yin)	in (yin)
[iɑŋ]	iang (yang)	iang (yang)
[iŋ]	ing (ying)	ing (ying)
[yŋ]	iong (yong)	iung (yung)
[u]	u (wu)	u (wu)
[ua]	ua (wa)	ua (wa)
[uo]	uo (wo)	uo (wo)
[uai]	uai (wai)	uai (wai)
[uei]	uei (wei)	uei (wai)
[uan]	uan (wan)	uan (wan)
[uən]	uen (wen)	un (wn)
[uɑŋ]	uang (wang)	uang (wang)
[uəŋ]	ueng (weng)	ung (wng)
[y]	u (yu)	u (yu)
[ye]	ue (yue)	ueh (yueh), uo
[yɜn]	uan (yuan)	uan (yuan)
[yn]	un (yun)	un (yun)

Note: Forms in round brackets in columns 2 and 3 represent the spelling of vowels forming individual syllables.

PART IV

THE NATIONAL ECONOMY

1. INTRODUCTION

CHINA is a vast country, rich in mineral resources, water, forest, grassland, wasteland, beach and ocean. It has other advantages in developing its economy: China is not only one of the world's most famous, civilized, ancient countries; it was also one of the earliest countries to have a developed economy and technology. According to unearthed metal historical relics, as early as about the year 2,000 BC both metal and stone instruments were used in China. In the Shang dynasty (16th century–11th century BC) the technique of smelting and casting bronze reached a very high level. At the end of the Spring and Autumn period and at the beginning of the Warring States period (around 480 BC), the Chinese grasped the technology of smelting iron. In the Han dynasty (206–220 BC) the technology of smelting and casting iron and forging and smelting developed further. Ancient China's agriculture, animal husbandry, water conservancy projects, textile, architecture, transportation, commerce and foreign trade were also developed. From the ruins of an ancient ore-smelting site at Tonglushan, Daye, in Hubei province; the Han dynasty iron-smelting ruins at Guxingzhen at Zhengzhou in Henan; the Dujiangyan water conservancy project built by Li Bing in about 256–251 BC, during the Warring States period at Chengdu in Sichuan; the Grand Canal and the "silk road", it can be seen that in ancient China the scale of production was large, technology was sophisticated, and trade and economy were highly developed.

The Economy in Semi-Colonial and Semi-Feudal China

In the short space of time between the 1760s and the 1830s, Britain, France, the United States and Japan successively completed the Industrial Revolution and stabilized the capitalist system. But China was still a feudal society with backward technology and a stagnated economy because of the centralized feudal rule, which lasted more than 2,000 years, and the closed-door policy of the Qing dynasty government. After the Opium War in 1840, China's closed door was forced open by the big powers. However, China did not turn into a capitalist country: it gradually became a semi-colonial and semi-feudal society. From that time to 1949, the historical process was one of the appearance, formation, development and collapse of a semi-colonial, semi-feudal economy. The semi-colonial, semi-feudal economy in modern China (1840–1949) had the following characteristics:

● The invading powers used military and political pressure to force China to sign unequal treaties and controlled China's financial and economic lifeblood. Some seized parts of China's territory, plundered its resources and obtained indemnity. Some forced China to open trading ports, seized the right of navigation on China's rivers and opened concessions. Large amounts of foreign commodities were sold in China and the big powers controlled the country's finance, markets, railways, and customs and excise.

● The countryside was under the rule of feudalism. Landlords and rich peasants, who accounted for less than 10% of the rural population, possessed more than 70% of the land while poor and middle peasants, accounting for 90% of the rural population, possessed less than 30% of the land. The peasants with not enough land or none at all had to rent land from the landlords, and to turn half of their crops over to them, besides paying exorbitant taxes and miscellaneous levies. Although they laboured all the year round, they did not have enough to wear or to eat. They lived a hard life.

● Bureaucrat capitalism monopolized major departments of the national economy. China's bureaucrat-capitalist class, with the state power in their hands, extorted a large amount of wealth from the people through heavy taxes and levies. According to statistics, before China was liberated in 1949, their wealth was 20 billion US dollars. Their fixed assets in industry and transport accounted for 80% of that of the whole country, and they had almost a total monopoly of railways, highways and air transportation.

● Under the oppression of imperialism, feudalism and bureaucrat capitalism, China's national capitalism could hardly develop. Many national capital enterprises were on the brink of bankruptcy or semi-bankruptcy. In 1949 there were only 123,000 national capital industrial enterprises in China, with a total of 1,640,000 workers and staff.

● China's productive forces were fettered by the semi-colonial, semi-feudal system. For a hundred years China's economy was always in a confused and backward position. In 1936 modern industry accounted for only 10% of China's national economy: there were 3 million industrial workers, accounting for 0.6% of the country's population. In old China the highest annual outputs of major industrial products were: steel, 923,000 tons (1943); raw coal, 61.88 million tons (1942); electricity, less than 6 billion kWh (1941); cotton cloth, 2.79 billion metres (1936). During the War Against Japanese Aggression and the Civil War launched by the Kuomintang, industry was greatly damaged. Heavy industry declined 70% and light industry declined 30%. The structure of industry was illogical; light industry accounting for more than 70% and heavy industry accounting for less than 30%. The heavy industry consisted mainly of excavating and processing, which produced primary raw materials. There were few machine producing enterprises. The distribution of industry was not proportionate, being concentrated mainly in the North-East and the coastal cities. Agriculture in old China remained stagnant. The highest annual grain output was 150 million tons (1936) and the highest annual cotton output was 849,000 tons (1936). Later their output declined greatly. Even coastal cities had to import much wheat and rice every year, and half of the cotton used in textile mills was imported.

● The finance was weak, confused and on the brink of collapse from financial deficit, unfavourable trade balance, commodity shortages and inflation. Market prices sometimes rose several times a day. The labouring people became poorer and poorer, struggling for existence on the brink of hunger and death. After visiting old China, some Western scholars said that the majority of Chinese "had actually been on the verge of abject poverty for a long time."

The Contemporary Socialist Economy

In 1949 the People's Republic of China was founded, and when the economy had been restored and developed, and the socialist transformation carried out, a socialist economy gradually took shape. For more than thirty years the socialist economy experienced a hard and tortuous road, advancing by trial and error. After overcoming various difficulties, China is now carrying out a reform of its economic system.

The Guiding Principles for the Economy of the New Democracy

In order to liberate the productive forces and turn old China into an independent and prosperous New China, the Chinese Communist Party led the Chinese people in a protracted, tortuous struggle against imperialism, feudalism and bureaucrat capitalism. The aim of the struggle was to establish a new democracy, a socialist system in China, and finally to turn it into a prosperous and happy communist society. During the Second Civil Revolutionary War (also called the Land Revolution 1927–1936), the War Against Japanese Aggression (1937–1945) and the Third Civil Revolu-

tionary War (also called the Liberation War, 1946–1949), the Chinese Communist Party led the people in establishing revolutionary bases called Soviet areas, border areas and liberated areas. The economy which appeared and developed in these areas was designed mainly to guarantee the needs of the revolutionary war. It consisted largely of agriculture and a handicraft industry: there was hardly any modern industry. The sectors of the economy included public, co-operative and private economy, a combination which formed the embryo of China's new-democratic economy.

In 1940, in his *On New Democracy*, Mao Zedong pointed out that semi-colonial, semi-feudal China had no other choice but take the road of new democratic revolution, and in *The Current Situation and Our Tasks* (1947), he set out the three guiding principles for the economy of China's new democratic revolution: confiscating the land of the feudal class and giving it to the peasants; confiscating the bureaucrat capital and transferring it to the new democratic country; protecting national industry and commerce.

The socialist state-owned economy, the semi-socialist co-operative economy, the private capitalist economy, the individual economy and the national capitalist economy which was based on co-operation between the country and individuals, were the five main economic sectors of the People's Republic, making up the new democratic economic system.

The road from new democracy to socialism, which the Chinese Communist Party stipulated for China's economy, conformed to China's situation at that time and the objective law of development. In September 1949 it was reaffirmed in the *Common Guiding Principle of the Chinese People's Political Consultative Conference*. It successfully promoted the restoration of the national economy and the realization of the socialist transformation.

The Three Years of Restoration (1949–1952)

Initial difficulties

After the founding of the People's Republic of China, the new government faced grave financial and economic difficulties. First, because of the reactionary rule of the Kuomintang government and the Civil War, the national economy was seriously damaged. Compared with 1936, total industrial output value in 1949 had declined by 50%: the total output value of agriculture by 20%; and the output of sugar, grain and cotton by 51%, 24.5% and 48% respectively. Second, because of enemy blockade, materials were in short supply. When the People's Government took over Shanghai, rice stocks were enough for only half a month, and coal for five to seven days. The cotton in the textile mills could last only one month. Third, finance was in difficulty and income fell short of expenditure. Up to the end of 1949, the People's Government had to provide food and clothing for 9 million people (including several million former KMT military and civil personnel). In 1949, some 120 million *mu* of land were inundated (15 *mu* = 1 hectare) – 28 million *mu* seriously – and seven million people needed immediate relief. In the cities, the number of unemployed reached 4 million. Money was needed for military expenditure and for repairing railway tracks. Total expenditure in that year, if converted into millet, was 28.8 million tons, while revenue was only 15.15 million tons. Fourth, speculation was rife and prices rocketed. Speculators seized the opportunity to raise prices four times – in January, April, July and November. This affected the whole-sale price index of every large liberated city. If the wholesale price index in December 1948 was 100, it reached 5376 in November 1949. In February 1950 another rise in prices made it more than twice as high as at the end of 1949. At that time, some foreigners predicted that New China's "financial and economic difficulties would never be overcome." A Japanese economist said, "Restoration is no easy thing. It seems that the Anshan Steel and Iron Factory (in Liaoning) is good only for cultivating sorghum." However, the People's Government of New China put their faith in the workers, peasants, intellectuals and patriots, and within little more than three years they completed the arduous task of reorganizing and restoring the national economy.

The abolition of the imperialists' privileges, confiscation of bureaucrat-capital and the establishment of a state-owned economy

To establish new production relations, New China's first and foremost task in the economy was to abolish the imperialists' economic privileges in China, confiscate bureaucrat-capital and establish and strengthen a state-owned economy so as to keep the economic lifelines in the people's hands.

China abolished all the unequal treaties (including the economic clauses) which the imperialist powers had forced her to sign and took back tariff autonomy and the control of foreign trade and foreign exchange. The imperialists' privilege of raking in high profits through unequal trade with China and tariff preference was abolished. In the early period of New China, there were very few factories, mines or properties (most of them had been evacuated) owned by foreign monopoly capital in China. They were allowed to exist temporarily, under supervision. The legitimate interests of small factories and small shops run by foreign residents were protected. On 16 December 1950, when the Korean War broke out, the US government announced that it would take control of China's public and private property in the United States. On 28 December of the same year the Chinese government was forced to order that all property

belonging to the US government and US enterprises be controlled and checked, and that their bank assets be frozen. On 30 April 1951, when the British government announced that it would take part in the Korean War, the Chinese government gave the order to requisition the property of Britain's Asian Kerosene Corporation, but in general, China did not confiscate US and British property in China, but requisitioned, managed, purchased and controlled.

The People's Republic of China confiscated the enterprises belonging to the KMT government and bureaucrats: these comprised 2,858 factories and mines, with 1,290,000 workers and staff. In transportation, China confiscated more than 20,000 kilometres of railway tracks, more than 4,000 locomotives, 4,000 passenger trains, 47,000 goods trains, more than 200,000 tons of ships and 30 ship and bus repairing factories. The 12 planes belonging to the former China Aviation Corporation and Central Aviation Corporation, which had left for Hong Kong earlier, revolted and came back to the mainland. In finance, New China took over the Central Bank, the Bank of China, the Transportation Bank, Chinese Peasants' Bank, the Central Trust Bureau, the Bureau of Postal Remittance, the Co-operative National Treasury and more than 2,400 local banks. The new government also took over a dozen monopoly trade corporations, such as the Fuxing Corporation, Fuhua Corporation, Tea Corporation of China, Salt Corporation of China, Silk Corporation of China, Edible Oil Corporation of China, Import and Export Corporation of China, Changjiang Sino-American Industry Corporation, etc. Because of appropriate policy and measures during the process of turning the thousands of bureaucrat-capital enterprises into state-owned enterprises, losses were minimized. Social and production order was quickly restored. Later, state-owned enterprises carried out democratic reforms, production reforms and wage reforms. The government encouraged people to present production tools, set new records in production and put forward rationalization proposals. Outmoded conventions and bad customs such as searching the workers were abolished. The workers and staff became masters of the country. Factories carried out movements to raise output and economize on materials, and conducted labour competitions. Every enterprise set up a social labour security system, a free medical care system for workers, and other welfare systems. The standard of living of workers and staff was improved along with the development of production. These measures aroused workers' and staff members' enthusiasm for production: many model workers, such as Ma Wanshui (leader of an advanced tunnelling team in the Long-yan Iron Mine in Hebei), Ma Hengchang (a new record-setter in the engineering industry in Heilongjiang), Meng Tai (an old worker at the Anshan Steel and Iron Plant, who loved the plant as much as his home) and Hao Jianxiu (a woman textile worker in

Qingdao, Shandong, who invented an advanced method of production) appeared all over the country. They led all workers in fulfilling quotas ahead of schedule and in overfulfilling the production tasks of the restoration period.

Land reform and individual economy

One of the main tasks of the new democratic revolution was to abolish China's 2,000-year-old feudal system. Before the People's Republic was founded in 1949, 120 million rural inhabitants (27% of the rural population) had carried out land reform. In 1950 the People's Government issued the *Land Reform Law of the People's Republic of China* and land reform was carried out in the newly liberated areas from the winter of that year. By August 1952, except in Taiwan and some minority nationality regions, land reform was completed. More than 300 million peasants, who had previously owned little or no land, obtained 46 million hectares of land, and this accounted for 46.5% of the arable land in China: 60–70% of the rural population benefited from the land reform, the success of which totally destroyed the exploiting feudal system and aroused the peasants' enthusiasm. Agricultural production went up rapidly: in 1952 total agricultural output value increased 26% over 1950. Then, in accordance with the wishes of peasants, the Government led them on the road of mutual aid and co-operation. By 1952 there were more than 8 million mutual aid groups for agricultural labour and 4,000 primary agricultural co-operatives in China. Within three years the Government invested 700 million yuan in strengthening 42,000 kilometres of dykes and began to harness the Huaihe, Yihe, Shuhe, Yongding, Daqing and Chaobai rivers by building 358 irrigation projects. The Government extended agricultural credits, provided the peasants with fertilizer, new types of farm implements and pesticide and purchased agricultural and sideline products at a reasonable price in order to help the peasants with production.

In the cities, the Government organized handicraftsmen and developed handicraft workshops to improve technology and to raise efficiency. By 1952 there were 3,280 handicraft production co-operatives in China and 3% of the handicraftsmen (218,000 people) worked in them. Their output value was 246 million yuan, accounting for 3.4% of the total handicraft output value.

Finance and economics, prices, industry and commerce

The People's Government policy for capitalist industry and commerce was to make use of their positive role, which was favourable to the national economy and people's livelihood, and to limit their negative role, which was unfavourable to them. In the liberated cities, the Government protected private industry and commerce. However, in 1949, when the national economy was still in difficulty, some speculators cornered the market, manipulated prices and sold gold, silver and foreign currency for profit, so the Government issued stipulations banning the free circulation of gold, silver and foreign currency. Shanghai sealed up the centre for speculation – the "stock exchange" – and arrested more than 230 of the leading figures who had been sabotaging the finance. Similar measures were taken in Wuhan and Guangzhou. At the same time, the State tightened its control over private financial operations. The tumult of financial speculation subsided temporarily. The State also tightened its grip over the market, factories and businessmen were registered, and commercial transactions were brought under strict control. The State used its power to control market prices and banned speculation and panic purchasing. Since revenue and expenditure were not balanced and the speculating capital was disturbing the system, prices soared. After careful preparations, the Financial Committee under the State Council of the Central People's Government decided to launch an attack on speculating activities. Military and Government organizations cut down their expenses and major goods were assembled in big cities. For example, before 25 November 1949, 30,000 tons of grain were transferred from the North-East to Beijing and Tianjin, which prepared 350,000 bolts of cloth and 5,000 pieces of yarn; Shanghai prepared 1,100,000 bolts of cloth and 28,000 pieces of yarn; and Hankou prepared 300,000 bolts of cloth and 8,000 pieces of yarn. On 20 November, all the trading companies in every big city began to raise their prices until they were the same as those on the black market. Beginning on 25 November they sold the goods in great quantities for ten days and prices went down by 30–40%. This gave speculation capital a heavy blow and shocked industrial and commercial circles in Shanghai.

However, this price stability was only temporary. To solve the inflation problem completely, it was necessary to realize a balance of revenue and expenditure, to bring the various local financial and economic organizations left over by the war under the unified management of the State, and to centralize the funds and materials of the nation to facilitate unified control and keep expenditure within the limits of income. At the beginning of 1950 the State issued ten thousand portions of bonds in kind (i.e., bonds whose nominal value is calculated in terms of material objects such as food, coal, etc.) to make up the deficit. In March of that year the State Council promulgated the *Decision on Unifying National Financial and Economic Affairs*, demanding the unification of financial and economic management, the consolidation of revenue and expenditure planning to achieve balance, and the stabilization of prices. There were three main tasks for the unification of financial and economic management:

first, to unify national revenue and expenditure, the accounts of major national income had to be settled daily at the state treasury, to answer major national expenses and guarantee military supplies and economic recovery; second, to unify national material distribution, the main materials, such as food, yarn, cloth and industrial products, were distributed by the State, in order to bring the market under control; third, to unify national currency management, the cash of various enterprises, organizations and the army was brought under the centralized management of the Central People's Bank in order to reduce the amount of circulation on the market. Having realized these unifications, the Government cut down administrative expenses, strengthened taxation management and market control, cracked down on speculation and profiteering, established state-owned and co-operative commerce and created favourable conditions for commodity circulation. Remarkable effects were produced within one year. In 1950 the national revenue and expenditure approached balance and in the next year there was a small surplus. From March 1950 prices began to fall and tended to become stable. If the wholesale price index of March 1950 is taken as 100, the number became 75 in April, 85.4 in December, 92.4 in 1951 and 92.6 in 1952. This put an end to the galloping inflation that had lasted more than ten years in old China.

Beginning from June 1950, the State took measures to reorganize industry and commerce and to help the privately owned enterprises through the transition period. These measures included the readjustment of public–private, labour–capital and production–sale relations, with the regulation of the relations between state-owned and private industry and commerce as the key point. The State maintained the necessary production of privately owned industrial enterprises by enlarging its processing and purchase orders and giving appropriate preferential treatment in the distribution of raw materials; it created a good sale for the products of private industry by enlarging the purchase of agricultural products, promoting the exchange between urban and rural areas and managing the exportation of industrial products; it combined the efforts of both state-owned and private units to speed up the capital turnover of private enterprises by providing loans; and it eased the tax burden for private enterprises by reducing the items of merchandise tax from 1,136 to 358. As for private commerce, speculation was forbidden but freedom was given in prices (regional price difference and the difference between wholesale and retail sale prices) and the range of management. Labour–capital contradictions were dealt with and solved by negotiation, provided that the democratic rights of the workers were guaranteed and production promoted, and workers were exhorted to raise the production rate and to make efforts to tide over the difficulty and develop production. Instead of acting blindly, production and sale planning was

adopted in various trades, so that through negotiation the amount of production was determined according to quotations on the market, and trades not meeting social needs or in overproduction were made to change. Thanks to these regulation measures, many private enterprises began business after the latter half of 1950. The market became brisk and the trade volume increased. There was a flourishing of capitalist industry and commerce by the year's end. At the end of 1951, to fight against encroachment on the interests of the State, the movement against the three evils (corruption, waste and bureaucracy) and then the movement against the five evils (bribery, tax evasion, theft of state property, cheating on government contracts and stealing economic information) were successively launched, cracking down on unhealthy tendencies and evil practices and protecting the law-abiding capitalist industry and commerce.

The results of the economic reorganization, rehabilitation and development

By the end of 1952 the national economy of New China was firmly established, forming the economic structure of new democracy. It withstood the Korean War and foreign blockade and embargo, reached and surpassed historical peaks in many economic quotas, and started several important construction projects. In a word, great achievements were made in the transformation of production relations and the development of productive forces (see Tables 1 and 2).

During the three years 1950–52, key projects of capital construction and their investment were as follows: 0.7 billion yuan in irrigation projects, including the first phase of the project of bringing the waters of the Huaihe under permanent control, the flood-diversion project for the Yangtze and Jinjiang rivers, the irrigation project for diverting the course of the Yellow River and the construction of the Guanting Reservoir in Beijing; 1.77 billion yuan in communications projects, including the Laibin–Munanguan, Chengdu–Chongqing and Tianshui–Lanzhou railways, with a total length of 1,263 kilometres; and other projects such as the opening of the seamless tubing mill and the heavy rolling mill in the Anshan Steel Plant, and housing construction with a floor area of 14.92 million square metres.

As the above statistics indicate, the socialist state-owned economy was established and developed rapidly, gaining dominance in industry, communications, foreign trade and finance; the entire national economy recuperated and exceeded former historical peaks; construction was started in field irrigation works, railway transportation and housing for staff and workers. From then on, the economy of New China entered the new period of large-scale socialist transformation and construction.

Table 1: Major Quotas for the National Economy in the Rehabilitation Period

Quotas	Unit	Previous highest peak before Liberation		1949		1952	
		Amount	Year	Amount	Ratio to the previous highest peak (%)	Amount	Ratio to the previous highest peak (%)
Industrial output	0.1 billion yuan	281	1936	140	50	343	122
Agricultural output	0.1 billion yuan	408	1936	326	80	484	119
Yield of major products:							
Satin	10,000 tons	44.5	1933	32.7	73.5	65.6	147.4
Clothing	0.1 billion m	27.9	1936	18.9	67.7	38.3	137.3
Sugar	10,000 tons	41.0	1936	20.0	49.0	45.0	110
Raw coal	0.1 billion tons	0.62	1942	0.32	51.6	0.66	106.5
Crude oil	10,000 tons	32.0	1943	12.0	37.5	44.0	137.5
Electric energy production	0.1 billion kWh	60.0	1941	43.0	71.7	73.0	121.7
Cement	10,000 tons	229	1942	66.0	28.8	286	124.9
Sulphuric acid	10,000 tons	18.0	1942	4.0	22.2	19.0	105.6
Soda ash	10,000 tons	10.3	1940	8.8	85.4	19.2	186.4
Caustic soda	10,000 tons	1.2	1941	1.5	125	7.9	658.3
Metal cutting machines	10,000	0.54	1941	0.16	29.6	1.37	253.7
Steel	10,000 tons	92.3	1943	15.8	17.2	135	146.3
Food	10,000 tons	15,000	1936	113.18	75.5	16,392	109.3
Cotton	10,000 tons	84.9	1936	44.4	52.4	130.4	153.6
Peanuts	10,000 tons	317.1	1933	126.8	40.0	231.6	73.0

Table 2: State Investment in Capital Construction in the Rehabilitation Period

	1950	1951	1952	Amount	Total proportion in the national expenditure in three years
Capital Construction investment (0.1 billion yuan)	11.34	23.46	43.56	78.36	21.4

Socialist Transformation and Construction, 1953–1957, and the Establishment of a Socialist Economy

At the end of the rehabilitation period, though reaching or surpassing historical peaks, China's economy was still backward. The per capita national income was only 104 yuan in 1952. Modern industry contributed only 21.3% of the total output value, and heavy industry supplied only 35.5% of the industrial output. The proportions of state-owned, individual and private capitalist economy in the national revenue were about 19%, 72% and 7% respectively.

The general line for the transitional period and the First Five-Year Plan

At the end of 1952 the Central Committee of the Chinese Communist Party advanced the general line for the transitional period according to Mao Zedong's proposal: "from the founding of the People's Republic of China to the completion of socialist transformation is a transitional period. For the general line and main task of the transitional period, the State must bring

about, in a fairly long period, step by step, the socialist industrialization of the country, and accomplish, step by step, the socialist transformation of agriculture, handicrafts and capitalist industry and commerce." In September 1954 the general line was stipulated by the First Session of the National People's Congress and laid down in the first *Constitution of the People's Republic of China.*

From the spring of 1951, directed by Zhou Enlai and Chen Yun, the General Committee of Finance and Economy began to draw up the First Five-Year Plan (1953–1957) for the development of the national economy, which set the basic task in the spirit of the general line: to concentrate the main efforts on the construction of 694 large and medium-sized industrial projects, with the 156 projects designed with Soviet aid as their nucleus; to develop agricultural producers' co-operatives with partial collective ownership, and handicraft producers' co-operatives, thus laying the preliminary foundations for the socialist transformation of agriculture and handicrafts; and to place capitalist industry and commerce in the main in the orbit of the many forms of state capitalism, thus laying the foundations for the socialist transformation of private industry and commerce. The First Five-Year Plan also stipulated a series of specific targets: 42.74 billion yuan of total investment in capital construction during the period, with industrial investment taking up 58.2% of the total and heavy industry 88.8% of the industrial investment; an average yearly growth rate of industrial and agricultural output of 8.6%, with 14.7% for industry, 17.8% for heavy industry and 4.3% for agriculture; a 33% increase in the average income of workers and staff in five years, and a doubling of purchasing power in rural areas.

The socialist transformation of agriculture

The land reform destroyed the feudal bonds and raised the economic and political position of the agrarian people, realizing the ideal of "land to the tiller". To lead the peasants along the road of collectivization, the Party Central Committee promulgated the *Resolution on Mutual Aid and Co-operation in Agriculture* in 1951 and the *Resolution on the Development of Agricultural Producers' Co-operatives* in 1955. In July 1955 Mao Zedong delivered the report *On the Co-operative Transformation of Agriculture*. Under the principles of voluntary participation, mutual benefit, demonstration of typical cases and state aid, the co-operative transformation of agriculture went through three successive stages: the mutual-aid team, the elementary agricultural producers' co-operative and the advanced agricultural producers' co-operative.

In the mutual-aid team, with private management retained, the participants worked together through an exchange of labour forces and through a charged supply of draught animals and farm tools for exchange or public use. This form was based on individual economy, but it already contained an embryo of socialist economy. Its productivity was generally higher than that of families farming on their own.

The elementary agricultural producers' co-operative was a semi-socialist economic form of partial collective ownership, with lands put together as investments and under unified management. Land, draught animals and heavy farm tools were owned by individual peasants but handed in to the co-operative for collective use, and draught animals and farm tools could be purchased by the co-operative. The co-operative's net income from agricultural and sideline products was distributed as follows: tax; accumulation fund (for purchasing public means of production) and public welfare fund (for the welfare of its members); and payment for the contribution of labour, land and other means of production, distributed among the members. The yield of agricultural crops per land unit of these co-operatives was generally higher than that of mutual-aid teams. The elementary co-operative played an important part in the socialist transformation of agriculture.

The advanced agricultural producers' co-operative was a socialist economic form based on collective ownership of the means of production. Land, draught animals and farm tools no longer belonged to individual members, but became the public wealth of the co-operative. Draught animals and farm tools were sold to the co-operative on a voluntary basis and under the principle of mutual benefit. There were still privately owned properties, such as basic requirements of everyday life, small patches of land, a small amount of trees, cattle, domestic fowls, light farm tools and tools for household sidelines. After deducting tax, public accumulation fund and public welfare fund, the co-operative's income was distributed among the members in proportion to the labour contributed in terms of both quality and quantity. In June 1955 the number of advanced co-operatives was only 500, including 40 thousand rural households. By the end of 1956 the number had increased to 107 million – 87.8% of the total rural households. At that time the advantages of the mutual-aid teams and elementary agricultural producers' co-operatives had not yet come into full play; therefore over-hasty transition to the advanced co-operative form, coupled with the violation of the principle of voluntary participation and mutual benefit in many areas, constituted a serious error.

The socialist transformation of the individual handicraft industry

According to the 1953 statistics, people engaged in handicrafts totalled 19.3 million, with an output of 10 billion yuan. Like individual peasants, the individual handicraftsmen were labourers with a small private property. But the handicraft industry belonged entirely to the commodity economy, requiring the purchase of raw materials and other means of production and the sale of all products. Accordingly, the socialist transformation of the individual handicraft industry took several successive forms, including the supply and marketing team, the supply and marketing co-operative, and the semi-socialist and then socialist producers' co-operatives.

The co-operative transformation of the handicraft industry developed gradually, from small scale to large, and from the elementary form of supply and marketing co-operation to the advanced form of production co-operation. By the end of 1955, the number of co-operative members had increased from 220 thousand in 1952 to 2.2 million, making up 27% of employed persons in the whole nation. In 1956 there was an all-trade or all-area upsurge of the co-operative movement in the handicraft industry, with some people forming production co-operatives directly and leaving out the supply and marketing co-operation period, and by the end of the year, co-operative members had reached 92.2% and their output 93%.

China's handicraft industry displayed traditional features in many of its varieties. In his article *Hastening*

449

the Socialist Transformation of the Handicraft Industry Mao Zedong said, "Many good things in the handicraft industry must not be done away with. Wang Mazi and Zhang Xiaoquan's knife and scissors should not be done away with in ten thousand years." He also highly praised some handicraft products, such as cloisonné enamel, glass grapes produced by five women of the Chang family (a handicraft family in Beijing famous for blowing glass grapes) and the roast duck. However, not enough attention was paid to these instructions in later practices, and the pace of co-operative transformation was too fast.

The socialist transformation of capitalist industry and commerce

The national capitalists of New China played both a positive and a negative role in the national economy and people's life. In view of this dual role the People's Government adopted a policy of utilizing, restricting and transforming the capitalist economy; i.e., under the principle of "consideration to both the state and private economy and benefit for both labour and capital", to utilize the positive role of capitalist industry and commerce, allowing it to develop to a certain extent, and to restrict its negative role, transforming it gradually into socialist economy under the policy of redemption and in a peaceful way. The mode of transformation was buying out rather than confiscation. Two steps were taken to achieve this purpose: the first was a change from capitalism to state capitalism, and the second was a change from state capitalism to socialism.

State capitalism had elementary and advanced forms: at the lower level of state capitalism, which was formed in the first period after Liberation, capitalist firms in industry processed materials supplied by the Government, produced on government orders, or sold all their goods to the Government for marketing, and those in commerce acted as sales agents for state commerce. In processing, ordering and marketing, state-owned units signed contracts with the state capitalism and provided it with contacts, guidance and control. The State monopolized the purchase of major commodities concerning the national economy and the people's life. The state-owned commerce let private retail shops handle retail business on commission, and the capitalists got their profit from wholesale and retail sale price difference and commission. In this elementary form, the socialist economy established external connections with private enterprises through contracts, and the internal affairs such as production and management were still under the control of the capitalists. The proportion taken up by these industrial enterprises in the total output value of private and state capitalist industry was 56% in 1952, 62% in 1953, 79% in 1954 and 82% in 1955. In commerce, the proportion taken up by private or co-operative shops acting as commission agents or conducting

wholesale purchase and retail sale in the turnover of private commerce amounted to 17% in 1954 and 45% in 1955.

The advanced form of state capitalism was based on joint state-private ownership. Its characteristic was that the socialist economy not only established external connections with private enterprises, but also penetrated into their internal structure. The joint state-private ownership first existed only in individual enterprises and then embraced whole trades. Early in 1949 a few enterprises under joint state-private ownership emerged. For example, in some private enterprises property belonging to bureaucrat-capitalism or enemy and puppet concerns was confiscated and became the state share. The second step was joint state-private ownership embracing all trades. In the latter half of 1955, all-trade joint ownership was accomplished in nine trades in Beijing, such as flour, electrical machinery and the medical industries; 13 trades in Shanghai, such as cotton spinning, mechanized shipbuilding and steelmaking; and eight trades in Tianjin, such as rubber and tobacco production. In October 1955 Mao Zedong invited leaders of the All-China Federation of Industry and Commerce to a symposium, urging the industrialists and traders to follow the socialist road. Chen Yun delivered a report on the overall state plan for the transformation of the capitalist industry and commerce, advancing the redemption policy in the form of fixed interest. (In joint state-private enterprises, means of production were subject to the unified management and utilization of the State; therefore state ownership was practically realized. However, to buy out the privately owned means of production, the State paid a dividend to the capitalists with a fixed interest. When establishing joint ownership, the private share was checked and ratified, and the annual interest rate was set at 5%, regardless of industry or commerce, large or small, profit or loss, and the difference of trades. The fixed interest was first announced as payable for seven years, and was then extended for three more years (it actually lasted for ten years.) In November of that year (1955), the Central Committee held a meeting on the transformation of the capitalist industry and commerce, and then the Seventh Session of the Seventh National Congress, at which the *Draft Decision on the Transformation of the Capitalist Industry and Commerce* was promulgated. In 1956 there was a nationwide upsurge in the establishment of joint state-private ownership in all trades. At the end of 1956 the number of joint state-private enterprises, workers and staff and their total output value took up over 99% of the former private industry. The private shares in these enterprises were valued at 2.4 billion yuan (1.7 billion for industry, 0.6 billion for commerce and 0.1 billion for communications). From the beginning of 1956 the State paid 1.14 million private shareholders about 165 million yuan as fixed interest every year. Meanwhile, all those previously engaged in the management of capitalist enterprises were assigned work by the Government on the principle of "assigning jobs according to their abilities and granting appropriate preferential treatment".

Laying a basis for socialist industrialization

With the victory of the three socialist transformations, China overfulfilled its First Five-Year Plan, thus laying an initial basis for socialist industrialization.

Investment in capital construction centring on heavy industry totalled 55 billion yuan, surpassing the target by 15.3%. There was particular growth in China's heavy industrial departments embracing energy resources, iron and steel, non-ferrous metal, the chemical industry and machinery.

During the First Five-Year Plan period China's economy grew at a fast pace. The annual growth rate was 11% for the total output value, 18% for industry, 4.5% for agriculture, 12.9% for light industry and 25.4% for heavy industry. The proportion of industry in the total industrial and agricultural output rose from 41.5% in 1952 to 56.7% in 1957, and that of heavy industry in the industrial output from 35.5% to 45%. In these five years commodity circulation was expanded, prices remained stable, and there was an obvious rise in the living standard of the people, especially of the workers and peasants.

The initial formation of the organizational and managerial systems of the economy

In these five years, along with the development of socialist transformation and construction, the organizational and managerial systems of the centralized state economy were basically established.

The large districts were abolished and replaced by a managerial system consisting mainly of central departments. Centralized management was adopted in capital construction, goods and materials, labour, wages, prices, finance and trade. State monopoly of purchase and sale (purchase and supply according to the state plan) was implemented for products such as food, cotton, cotton cloth and edible vegetable oil.

Modelled after the Soviet Union, a highly centralized planning and management system was set up, employing mainly administrative measures and centring on the circulation of materials and goods. In January 1952 the Central People's Government set up the State Planning Committee as the supreme organization for drafting national plans. A planned economic system was formed from above to below, and the proportion of mandatory state plans continuously increased. Directed by the state plan and financial administration, state enterprises built up their internal systems of management but still lacked decision-making powers and vitality. Agriculture and the handicraft industry were not granted adequate decision-making powers either, and the production

responsibility system was not fully carried out. This economic system had played its positive role in history, but with the advancement of the socialist cause some of its defects unsuited to the development of productive forces became more and more apparent. It was a rigid system with an over-centralized management.

Investigation into ways of socialist construction

China's economic construction had no precedents to refer to and basically followed and modelled itself on the Soviet Union. But with different national conditions, China had to avoid repeating the old paths and detours trodden by the Soviet Union, but had to proceed from actual conditions and look for her own road to socialist construction.

On 25 April 1956, after hearing reports by the state departments, Mao Zedong delivered his speech *On the Ten Major Relationships*, in which he expounded the correct handling of the relationships between accumulation and consumption, heavy industry, agriculture and light industry, the construction of the economy and national defence, the industry of coastal and inner areas, central government and local governments, production units and individual producers, learning and innovation, etc. He pointed out that it was necessary to learn from the achievements of all nationalities and countries, but that indiscriminate imitation should be avoided. This report summed up the experience of socialist construction in the past and pointed out the direction for future development.

In November 1956 the Eighth National Congress of the Communist Party of China was convened. The Congress clearly pointed out that the principal contradiction in the country was no longer that between the working class and the bourgeoisie, but that between the rapidly growing economic and cultural needs of the people and the inability to meet such needs. Therefore the main task of the people of the whole country was to concentrate their efforts on developing the social productive forces to meet the growing economic and cultural needs of the people, and to transform China from a backward agricultural nation to an advanced industrialized country. The decision of the Eighth National Congress was correct and pointed out a new road for China's socialist construction.

In February 1957, at a Supreme State Conference, Mao Zedong delivered his speech *On the Correct Handling of Contradictions among the People*, demonstrating in theory the basic contradictions in the socialist society and the method of solving them. He divided the contradictions in socialist society into two categories: those between the Chinese and their enemies and those among the people. He thought that in China the large-scale, mass class struggle, like a violent storm, was basically ended, and that the main task in the future was to handle the contradictions among the people correctly, to unite the people in exploiting nature and developing culture and the economy. Many other Party leaders also summed up past experiences in the various fields of socialist construction and put forward theoretical conclusions suited to the practical situation.

Academic investigations were pursued in ideological and theoretical circles. Professor Ma Yinchu advanced his theory on population control, and Sun Yefang put emphasis on the function of the law of value. It was proved in practice that these academic investigations were suited closely to the national conditions of China and were highly original.

Detours: Experiments, Consolidation and Advance in the Eight Years 1958–1965

In looking for the proper way of national construction, the Chinese leaders and economists displayed their courage and wisdom in seeking the truth, both in theory and practice, and in many questions they approached or grasped the right answer. But for unexpected setbacks, China's economy would have achieved more remarkable results.

The adoption of the general line, the Great Leap Forward and the people's communes

In May 1958 the Second Plenum of the Eighth National Congress of the Chinese Communist Party was held. It pointed out the necessity of transferring the Party's emphasis more heavily on to socialist construction. The plenum approved the general line put forward by Mao Zedong at a meeting in Chengdu in March of the same year: "going all out, aiming high and achieving greater, faster, better and more economical results to build socialism". The general line reflected the pressing, universal demand of the Chinese people of various nationalities to overcome the backwardness of the national economy and culture, and incorporated the positive results of past investigations into a new way of building socialism. Its shortcomings were that it overlooked objective economic laws and overemphasized the exertion of subjective initiative regardless of the existence or absence of the necessary conditions and of objective possibilities.

Due to the lack of experience in socialist construction and inadequate understanding of the laws of economic development and of the basic economic conditions in China, and also due to the fact that Mao Zedong and many leaders, both at the top and in the grass roots, had become smug about past successes and were impatient for quick results, the Party Central Committee and the People's Government – without careful investigation and prior experimentation -- rashly initiated the Great Leap Forward and the movement for rural people's communes after the formulation of the general line. This caused flagrant "Left" errors, marked by high targets, blind directions

and proneness to exaggeration and egalitarianism, and brought severe setbacks to the national economy.

The Great Leap Forward, centring on large-scale iron and steel-making, advanced unrealistic targets. The steel production index for 1958 was first set at 6.24 million tons, but in August it was decided that steel output was to double the 1957 sum, reaching 10.70 million tons. In fact, steel output in the first eight months of that year was only 4.50 million tons, which meant that 6.20 million tons had to be produced in the period from September to December. To attain the unrealistically high index, other trades and professions had to make way for steel, and all efforts were concentrated on steel production. Many "small earth heaps" (small furnaces which the masses used in smelting iron and steel by indigenous methods) were built, and over fifty million people went to fell wood in the mountains, collect minerals and set up smelting furnaces on the spot. A large proportion of the products was actually useless iron slag. The Great Leap Forward and the large-scale steel-making movement caused a tremendous waste of labour, materials and wealth. The quality of products declined; the consumption of raw materials and fuel increased; and there was a severe imbalance in the national economy. Soon Mao Zedong and the Party Central Committee recognized some of the errors in the Great Leap Forward, and in a meeting held in Wuchang in November proposed to reduce the construction scale, cut down the predicted 1959 index and stop the large-scale steel-making, and took some readjustment measures. All these exercised a temporary restraint on the Great Leap Forward. But the "Left" ideology in the economy was not done away with. In July and August 1959 an enlarged meeting of the Political Bureau of the Party Central Committee and the Eighth Plenary Session of the Eighth Central Committee of the Communist Party of China were held at Lushan in Jiangxi province. The Lushan meeting was first meant to rectify the "Left" errors, but in fact it extended them, launching a struggle against "Right deviation". Therefore the Great Leap Forward emerged again in the first half of 1960 and brought more difficulties to the national economy.

In August 1958, at a meeting at Beidaihe, the Party Central Committee promulgated the *Resolution on Establishing People's Communes in Rural Areas*, which brought about a nationwide upsurge in the people's commune movement. The movement was over-hasty in the transformation of ownership (from small collective to large collective ownership, or even to state ownership), resulting in an egalitarian system in which poor and prosperous brigades shared equally and the reward was the same for good and bad labour. This egalitarian practice ignored actual conditions and deprived the peasants of their proper rights. It was a heavy blow to the initiative of the peasants and caused a marked decline in production. Economic organizations and authorities at the basic level were amalgamated; family plots, cattle, domestic fowls and other family sidelines of the commune members were transferred to public ownership, and fairs and trade markets were banned.

The problems in the commune movement were soon recognized by the Chinese leaders. At a meeting in Zhengzhou in November 1958, Mao Zedong proposed to rectify these errors. From December 1958 to March 1959 the Party Central Committee passed its decisions and regulations demanding that management and accounting should be at three levels (the commune, production brigade and production team) with the production team as the basic unit. To rectify "Left" errors, the principles of exchange at equal value and distribution according to work were emphasized. However, with the movement against "Right deviation" after the Lushan meeting in 1959, "Left" ideology gained ground once more. The "Left" influences on the people's commune movement caused severe setbacks in the rural economic situation, which had been favourable before 1956. Some peasants starved because of the sharp output reduction from 1959 to 1960.

The first readjustment of the national economy

In the Great Leap Forward, the people's commune movement and the movement against "Right deviation" from 1958 to 1960, the transformation of production relations went beyond the level of the development of social productive forces, and the growing speed of production and construction far exceeded objective possibility and the power of the nation. This caused setbacks in China's economy. In the autumn of 1960 the Soviet government suddenly informed China of its decision to withdraw the over one thousand Soviet experts from China and to scrap several hundred contracts. This, coupled with natural calamities of the time, brought China's economy into great difficulties and caused serious losses to the nation and the people.

The major manifestations in the difficult period from 1959 to 1961 were as follows: there was a sharp decline in the production of agriculture, light industry and heavy industry. The average yearly decline rate of agricultural output was 10.7%. Grain output in 1959 was 30 million tons less than the previous year, and in 1960 the output was 143.5 million tons, dropping to the level of 1951. From 1958 light industry declined for three successive years. Heavy industry had also declined sharply up to 1961; in the four years from 1958 to 1961 finance was in the red, with a total deficit of 18.03 billion yuan; there was confusion in management and a general decrease in economic benefit; the market was in short supply. People found it difficult to make a living and did not have enough food and clothes.

In the winter of 1960, the Party Central Committee and the People's Government began to rectify the "Left" errors, and in January 1961 decided to carry out a policy of "readjustment, consolidation, filling out and improvement". This marked the first great change in guiding ideology after the launching of all-round socialist construction. The policy put emphasis on readjustment, especially the rehabilitation of the economy. The main task was "overcoming difficulties, rehabilitating agriculture and industry, and striving for a basic improvement in the financial and economic situation".

The major readjustment measures adopted at the time included: readjustment of production relations in rural areas and the rehabilitation and consolidation of agriculture. In rural people's communes, a three-level economic system was adopted, with the production team as the basic accounting and management unit. Family plots were returned to commune members, the management of family sidelines was encouraged, and the rural fairs and trade markets were restored. State purchase quotas were cut down to give the peasants a breathing space and at the same time state aid to agriculture was increased; resolute retrenchment of capital construction and the production of heavy industry. Capital construction investment was 38.4 billion yuan in 1960, and was reduced to 12.34 billion yuan in 1961 and to 6.76 billion yuan in 1962; Temporarily stopping, shutting down, merging, transforming and consolidating industrial enterprises with a shortage of raw and processed materials, or having high cost, low quality and unfavourable economic effects; Retrenching workers and staff, and reducing the 26,000,000 urban population; Strengthening the centralized management, getting rid of the deficit and stabilizing the market, bringing back to centralized management some of the powers formerly left to local authorities, such as the issuing of money, the management of important materials and goods, and the planning of capital construction, and retrenching financial expenditure and money put into circulation; consolidating and strengthening management in all trades and professions. Many rules and regulations were formulated concerning agriculture, industry, commerce, research organizations in natural sciences, and institutes of higher learning. These played an important part in readjusting the economy, restoring normal management, raising the level of management and developing science and technology.

Through the joint efforts of the Chinese people, economic readjustment achieved remarkable results. At the end of 1962 the decline of production in agriculture, light industry and heavy industry came to an end; finance was balanced; market prices fell to a certain extent and people's livelihood began to improve. From 1963 three more years were spent in economic readjustment, and in 1965 the task was fulfilled. Different economic departments achieved stable and balanced development on the new basis. The industrial and agricultural output, national income, revenue and output of major products surpassed those of 1957. Moreover, many economic and technical quotas reached historic peaks during the 1965–1966 period, bringing a new prosperity to China's economy.

New achievements and the "saddle shape" curve

The history of economic development between 1958 and 1966 displays setbacks as well as rehabilitation and advance. This tortuous economic curve is called the "saddle shape", since it looks like a horse's saddle, first declining and then rising to a greater height.

Figure 1 shows the change in industrial and agricultural output, national income and revenue from 1957 to 1966. Figure 2 shows grain and steel yields between the same dates (see page 463).

Figure 1: The Change in Total Output and Other Quotas from 1957 to 1966

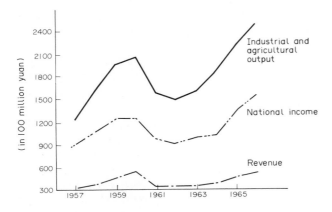

The Damage Caused to the Economy during the Cultural Revolution (May 1966 – October 1976)

Early in 1965, the Third National People's Congress announced that the nation had basically readjusted its economy and was ready to enter a new period of development, enabling China to gradually become a powerful socialist country with modern agriculture, industry, national defence and science and technology. Before it was possible to carry out this programme, however, a number of political careerists, such as Lin Biao, Jiang Qing, Kang Sheng and Zhang Chunqiao, took advantage of the Cultural Revolution that had been initiated and led by Mao Zedong in May 1966 and the nation slid into turmoil – almost civil war. The chaos continued for ten years until the "Gang of Four" of Jiang Qing, Zhang Chunqiao, Yao Wenyuan and Wang Hongwen was smashed. Altogether, the Cultural Revolution caused China to suffer its biggest setbacks and losses since the foundation of the People's Republic in 1949, and took its economy to the verge of collapse.

The paralysis and disintegration of the economic system

Pressurized by attacks on "capitalist-roaders" and by exhortations to "seize power", the work of management bodies, senior personnel and economic planners in charge of the nation's economy was brought to a standstill. For instance, the State Economic Commission responsible for industry, transport and communications ceased to function, along with central and local government offices in charge of economic work; the State Planning Commission almost came to a halt and numerous officials were labelled as "capitalist-roaders" and dismissed from their posts, while their "rebel" opponents – who did not understand production at all – took their place and allowed production to fall into an anarchic state. In addition, factions were formed inside the enterprises, where they argued with and attacked each other, causing more losses to production. As a result, the State Council was forced to set up a "business team" to do the work of the State Economic Commission, but even then it proved difficult to enforce orders and prohibitions and to take command of the situation.

The spread of "Left" deviation

The slogan "take class struggle as the key link" dominated all enterprises and the economy as a whole, causing a reversal of the achievements in socialist construction of the previous seventeen years. The correct theory that the development of production relations should correspond to that of productive forces, and that socialism should strive to expand its social productive forces was repudiated as a revisionist theory, while the theory of continuing the revolution of the means of production was boosted. Regardless of the level of development of rural productivity, the "Gang of Four" trumpeted about "poor transition" (i.e., even though productivity levels were low, the system of collective ownership was forced to transform itself into that of the "ownership by the whole people"). Individually owned businesses and rural markets which had been regarded as a necessary supplement to a planned economy were abolished as "remnants of capitalism." The economic macro-control that had been adopted by the State was then dismissed as a system of outmoded rules, regulations and conventions shackling the revolution; essential managerial regulations enterprises were regarded as "interfering, strangling and oppressive" and were abolished. Commodity production and commodity exchange in socialist conditions were refuted, and a series of economic managerial theories such as the law of value, distribution according to work and economic results were all labelled remnants of capitalist forces. In addition, professional intellectuals were all repudiated and dismissed from their posts as "counter-revolutionary academic authorities", while the slogan of anti-science, "the more knowledge one has, the more reactionary one will become", was proclaimed far and wide. The study and introduction of foreign scientific and technological achievements was criticized as the "philosophy of servility to things foreign" and "doctrine of trailing behind at a snail's pace." Furthermore, veteran leaders, good at the management of economy, and theoreticians such as Chen Yun, Bo Yibo, Deng Zihui, Sun Yefang, Ma Yinchu, Xue Moqiao and Xu Dixin, etc., were all wilfully criticized and repudiated, and some of them were even put in gaol.

The damage to the economy

After the rejection of correct guidance for the economy and the systematic sabotage of regular economic organizations and managements, industrial and agriculture production were almost at a standstill or even regressed. The decline in national economic results was the centralized reflection of the state of the nation.

Along with the rise and fall of the turbulent Cultural Revolution, the national economy was seriously damaged three times: first in 1967 and 1968, during the beginning of the Cultural Revolution, the economy fell back. Calculated against a constant price, the gross industrial and agricultural output value and the national income in 1968 dropped 13.4% compared with 1966, and the state revenue (based on the fixed price in the same year) decreased 35.3%; second in 1974, during the movement to "Criticize Lin Biao and Confucius", Jiang Qing directed her spearhead at Premier Zhou Enlai, who was then in charge of national economic affairs. As a result, the national economy stagnated and the total output value of industry and agriculture and the national income increased only 1.4% and 1.1% over the previous year, and the state revenue actually dropped by 3.3%; and third, at the end of 1975, during the movement called "Criticize Deng [Xiaoping] and Counter the Right Deviationist Trend to Reverse Correct Verdicts". When economic construction slid into turmoil once again, the gross output value of industry and agriculture in 1976 increased by only 1.7% compared with the previous year, and the national income and state revenue dropped 2.7% and 5% respectively. In a word, during the ten years of the Cultural Revolution the total output value of industry and agriculture and the national income increased by an average of 7.1 and 4.9% a year, both below the annual average growth rate of 8.5% and 6.2% respectively in the years from 1953 to 1966.

The rapid growth of population and low level of national income

Owing to the fact that governments at all levels slackened their efforts to control the size of the family, the population of China grew greatly, increasing by 190 million in ten years, a number equalling the population of Japan and France put together. The annual mean growth was 2.3%. Thus, most of the newly increased national income had to be used to offset consumption by the newly-born population. The national income per capita fluctuated over a long period between 210 and 260 yuan, with an average growth of 2% a year only (calculated on a constant price). If the dubious nature of some of the statistical figures is taken into consideration, the national income per capita did not rise at all, in fact, and even dropped at some points during the ten years.

The ratio between accumulation and consumption

The programme of the Fourth Five-Year Plan (1971–75) set unduly high quotas. For instance, the programme stipulated that some 35.00–40.00 million tons of steel would be produced by the end of 1975. As a result, the total number of workers and staff, the total amount of wages and the sales volume of grain topped the state plan and the market was in short supply, so that the State had to once again simplify its work force and cut the urban population. Due to the enlargement of the scale of capital construction, the proportion of accumulation in national income rose sharply from 23.2% in 1969 to 32.9% in 1970, and 34.1% in 1971. Afterwards, the proportion remained above 31%. In the seven years from 1970 to 1976, the proportion averaged 32.6%. Owing to the higher accumulation, people's consumption was squeezed. For instance, the average wage of workers and staff in enterprises run by the State dropped by 6%. At the same time, the ratio in agriculture, light industry and heavy industry was in serious imbalance. The proportion taken by heavy industry in the total amount of investment accounted for 54.5% in the Third Five-Year Plan period (1966–1970) and 52.1% in the Fourth Five-Year Plan period (1971–1975), an increase of 15.8% and 13.4% respectively over the First Five-Year Plan period, during which stress was put on the development of heavy industry. As a result, large quantities of funds, materials and labour forces in other enterprises and trades were taken away by the development of heavy industry, leading to the slow progress of agriculture, light industry, the building industry, transport and communications, as well as mining, so that for a long time, the production of consumer goods lagged behind social demands, commodities fell short of demand and circulation was held up. For instance, cotton cloth increased by an average of only 1.9% a year, and grain only 3%; furthermore, the yields of cotton and oil-bearing crops even dropped. Moreover, imbalance could be also found in handling the relations between coastal areas and inland, and between construction for national defence and economic construction. Of course, it was necessary to build an indispensable inland industry so as to improve the distribution of industry throughout

China, and it was essential to ensure the proper development of the industries concerned with national defence. However, during the Third and Fourth Five-Year Plan periods, undue emphasis was placed on preparation against war and on inland construction. As a result, investment in inland construction was as high as 66.8% and 53.5% respectively. Some constructions went in for so-called "location by mountains, decentralized and concealed"; thus production conditions were overlooked and funds wasted.

Quotas of major economic outputs declined, financial deficits rose for four years and enterprises ran at serious losses. Although a certain growth was achieved in the total amount of national income during the ten years of the Cultural Revolution, it was obtained by depending chiefly on more investments, increased work forces and high consumption of energy and raw materials. The situation all too often arose when there were no work quotas set for enterprises, no cost accounting, no one ready to assume responsibility, high consumption of unit-product and the production of poor-quality products or even overstocked goods that nobody wanted, as well as appalling waste. According to statistics for 1976, one-third of the enterprises in the country ran at a loss. Financial deficits occurred in four of the ten years. State expenditure in these years exceeded revenue by a total of 1.9 billion yuan.

Promised but not delivered

Owing to the high rate of accumulation, capital construction exceeded the State's financial and material resources, the returns on investment dropped, and popular consumption had to be cut down. During the ten years, consumption levels of food and clothing were almost totally static; some items were even reduced. Compared with 1966, the consumption per capita in 1976 was: grain increased from 190.5 kg to 191.5 kg – an increase of 0.5%, which was lower than the figure in 1952; edible vegetable oil decreased from 1.75 kg to 1.6 kg – a drop of 8.6% – 0.95 kg lower than in 1956, the peak year; pork rose from 7.05 kg to 7.25 kg – an increase of only 2.8%; and cotton cloth from 6.66 metres to 7.9 metres – an increase of 18.5%. As for housing, there was no precise investigation; however, statistics in 182 cities in 1978 showed that the average housing per capita was 3.6 square metres of floor space, which was lower than the figure of 4.5 square metres of floor space in 1949. This indicated that the Chinese people had sacrificed their own interests and welfare in order to bring about growth in the national economy.

Attempts by Zhou Enlai and Deng Xiaoping to reverse the trends

Zhou Enlai, Premier of the State Council, found himself in an extremely difficult situation throughout the Cultural Revolution but always kept the general interest in mind and bore the heavy burden of office without complaint, striving in all possible ways to counter the wanton damage to the national economy inflicted by Lin Biao and Jiang Qing. In the early days of the Cultural Revolution, he demanded firmly that departments in charge of industry, communications, finance and trade at all levels should set up their mechanisms for guiding production, stand fast at their posts and persist in production.

After the smashing of the Lin Biao counter-revolutionary clique in September 1971, Zhou Enlai – with the support of Mao Zedong – took charge of the day-to-day work of the Central Committee. He presided over the national planning conference held at the end of the same year and the beginning of the next, in which the national economic plan was discussed and drawn up. In view of the situation of turmoil existing in the management of enterprises at the time, this meeting stipulated that managerial regulations for enterprises should be restored and strengthened.

In October 1972, the appropriate economic departments under the State Council convened a meeting in Beijing for the purpose of strengthening economic accounting and putting an end to the losses incurred in enterprises. This meeting emphasized that enterprises should be consolidated, managerial regulations adhered to and economic accounting strictly implemented. Soon after the end of the meeting, the document *Stipulation on Adhering to Unified Planning and Strengthening Economic Management* was drafted under the guidance of Zhou Enlai, to be submitted for discussion and approval to the national planning conference which was to be held in January of the next year. Unfortunately, this document failed to be adopted because of opposition by the representatives from Shanghai, manipulated by Zhang Chuanqiao. Even so, the document exerted an active influence on practical work. At the same time, Zhou Enlai – with the approval of Mao Zedong – withstood the pressure by Jiang Qing and her associates, who opposed the expansion of technological exchanges with foreign countries. Zhou approved the import of 1.7-metre hot-rolling and cold-rolling plants from Japan and West Germany in 1972 and 1973, which were later installed in the Wuhan Iron and Steel Plant, and dozens of complete sets of large-scale chemical fertilizer and several of comprehensive coal-cutting machines – all of which played an important role in accelerating the transformation of China's heavy industry.

At the national planning conference in 1973, Zhou Enlai criticized the "Left" deviation errors pursued in rural areas by the "Gang of Four", such as "extending the people's communes and merging production teams", "expropriating small private plots" and "poor transition". The efforts of Zhou Enlai and the Chinese people enabled the national economy to achieve a favourable turn in 1973 – the year in which the total social output value reached 477.6 billion yuan, the total output value of industry and agriculture went up to 396.7 billion yuan, and the total national income totalled 231.8 billion yuan – an all-time high. In the same year, steel output registered 25.22 million tons, crude oil 53.61 million tons, cloth 8.71 billion metres, grain 264.94 million tons, and cotton 2.562 million tons – all the highest since the founding of the People's Republic. Unfortunately, late in 1973 the "Gang of Four" launched a campaign to "criticize Lin Biao and Confucius" with their spearhead aimed at Zhou Enlai, so that the favourable conditions which had just arisen were once again thrown into confusion.

In December 1974 Zhou Enlai was seriously ill and Deng Xiaoping – with the support of Mao Zedong – took charge of the day-to-day work of the Central Committee and the State Council. He set his hand to the consolidation of the economy in all fields and began systematically to correct the errors of the Cultural Revolution. First he solved the problem of railway transport, which was then seriously disrupted because of the trouble made by factionalist forces and was causing harm to industrial and agricultural production as well as to the cities. The Central Committee worked out the *Decision on Strengthening Railway Work*, which produced an instant effect, so that the daily volume of freight handled on the railways rose to an all-time high and the rate of running on schedule was also greatly improved. The whole situation on the railways changed considerably. Then Deng Xiaoping paid special attention to iron and steel production, and through a month of consolidation the steel output per day surpassed the average level of the annual plan.

Under the guidance of Deng Xiaoping, the State Council drew up the draft *Questions on Accelerating the Development of Industry*. This was an important regulation for consolidating China's industry, which put forward a series important principles and policies to restore and develop it. Unfortunately, this regulation was strangled by the Jiang Qing counter-revolutionary clique before it became a formal document.

After one year's consolidation, China's national economy began to rise from standstill and decline, and in 1975 a new high tide appeared in the economic field. The total output value of industry and agriculture increased 11.9% over the previous year: agriculture rose 4.2% and industry went up 15.1%. Some major products and output, such as grain, raw coal, steel, crude oil, generated energy, cotton yarn and cloth, increased by more than 10%. The volume of rail freight reached 867.46 million tons, or an increase of 12.7%, and the retail volume of social commodities went up 127.1 billion yuan – an increase of 9% over the previous year.

However, the good times did not last long. Mao Zedong could not accept Deng Xiaoping's systematic correction of the errors of the Cultural Revolution and triggered the campaign to "Criticize Deng [Xiaoping] and Counter the Right Deviationist Trend to Reverse Correct Verdicts." Affairs were once again turned upside down, and consolidation was regarded as "restoration of capitalism". After Zhou Enlai died of cancer in Beijing in January 1976, Deng Xiaoping was dismissed from his posts in the Party and the Government. As a result, the "Left" deviationist errors – which had been under correction – were again restored and spread; the political situation – which was becoming stable and united – was again plunged into turmoil; and the economic situation – which had been taking a turn for the better – was once again exacerbated.

In July 1976, a shatteringly violent earthquake destroyed the whole city of Tangshan in Hebei. Natural and man-made calamities drove the national economy into a predicament even worse than before.

The achievements of the mass struggle

During the Cultural Revolution, the Party and the people went through countless difficulties to combat the "Left" errors and actions of the "Gang of Four". Under trying conditions, they kept up their efforts in production and other fields of work, doing their best to minimize the harmful effects of the Cultural Revolution. During this period, China's economy sustained terrible losses. In spite of this, advances were made in grain production, industry and transportation, capital construction and science and technology. New railways and the Yangtze River Bridge at Nanjing were completed; a number of large enterprises using advanced technology were put into operation; a hydrogen bomb was successfully tested; man-made earth satellites were launched and retrieved; new hybrid strains of long-grained rice were developed and popularized, etc. Needless to say, none of these successes can be attributed in any way to the Cultural Revolution, without which China would have scored far greater achievements.

The New Historical Period for Developing Modern Socialism

The victory won in overthrowing the Jiang Qing counter-revolutionary clique in October 1976 enabled China to enter a new historical period of modern socialist construction. However, in the two years up to December 1978, when the Third Plenary Session of the Eleventh Central Committee of the CPC was held, the Party had been advancing its work haltingly, due to the "Left" errors in the ideological guidelines for the economy. The Third Plenary Session of the CPC put an end to this situation and made the strategic decision to shift the focus of work to socialist modernization. It marked a crucial turning point of far-reaching significance in the history of the Party.

The continuation of "Left" errors

With the overthrow of the "Gang of Four", cadres and masses enthusiastically plunged into their new efforts. Industrial and agricultural production was fairly swiftly restored. However, the long-standing "Left" errors in economic work had not been cleared up, so that mistakes in violation of objective economic law and impatience for quick results in economic work were still common.

In August 1977, the Eleventh National Congress of the Chinese Communist Party was held. This congress played an active role in exposing and repudiating the crimes of the "Gang of Four" and in mobilizing the whole nation to build a powerful, modern country. However, due to the limitations imposed by the prevailing historical conditions, it did not correct but reaffirmed the erroneous theory "take class struggle as the key link" and the other policies and slogans of the Cultural Revolution. At the same time, unrealistic tasks and impractical targets were put forward owing to the overestimation of the potential of the economy, which had just taken a favourable turn, and the demand for breakneck speed in construction. For example, by the end of 1985, steel output was required to be 60.00 million tons and crude oil output 200.5 million tons, and 120 large-scale projects were planned to be built or rebuilt during the years 1978 to 1985. In addition to that, 14 large-scale heavy industrial bases were scheduled to be formed. Thus, the total planned investment in capital construction from 1978 to 1985 equalled the sum total in the past 28 years. As a result, the rapid increase of investment in capital construction, which far exceeded the limits of the country's financial and material resources, aggravated the imbalance in the national economy. Owing to the fact that undue stresses were placed on the production and construction of heavy industry, people's living standards were not improved as much as they should have been.

A historic turnabout

In December 1978, the Third Plenary Session of the Eleventh Central Committee of the CPC was held. It marked a crucial turning point of far-reaching significance in the history of the Party since the birth of the People's Republic. This session decided on the guiding principle of emancipating the mind, using the brain, seeking truth from facts and uniting as one in looking forward to the future. The session re-established the Marxist ideological, political and organizational line.

The principal economic decisions made by the Third Plenary Session of the CPC were:

– To discard the slogan of "take class struggle as the key link", which had become unsuitable in a socialist society, and to shift the focus of work to the economic construction of socialist modernization;

– To reform the structure and system of management of the economy, which concentrated power unduly, and to enlarge the enterprises' initiatives in management; to act according to economic law and attach importance to the law of value, integrate ideological work with economic sanctions and bring cadres' and workers' productive enthusiasm into full play;

– To solve the problem of serious imbalance in the national economy and formulate the decision to accelerate the development of agriculture;

– To make active efforts to promote equal and mutually beneficial economic and technical co-operation with other countries on the basis of independence and self-reliance, and to strive for the introduction of foreign advanced technology and equipment;

– To devote major efforts to strengthening the scientific and educational work needed by the modernizations;

– To improve the people's living standards, step by step, on the basis of the development of production.

This session pointed out the orientation for the development of national economy.

Readjustment of the national economy

With the overthrow of the "Gang of Four", China's national economy was restored and developed very fast. However, serious imbalances between major sectors were not changed completely due to the damage done by the Cultural Revolution over ten years. Chaos in production, construction, circulation and distribution was not eliminated. A series of problems in popular welfare, in both urban and rural areas, neglected for many years, remained to be solved. Capital construction was too large in scale, with undue investment.

The serious imbalance between major sectors manifested itself in several important ways:

– *Extreme backwardness of agriculture over a long period of time.* In 1978, the average volume of grain owned per capita was little higher than that in 1957, while the average volume per capita of cotton, peanuts, and oil-bearing crops was lower than in 1957. During the three years from 1976 to 1978, some 13.25 million tons of grain were imported. In 1978, the State spent $US 2.1 billion on the import of grain, cotton, edible oil, and sugar – nearly 20% of total imports.

Investment in agriculture, light industry and heavy industry was irrational. Among the investments in capital construction as a whole, those in heavy industry had always been too high, while those in light industry and agriculture were very low. This is shown in Table 3 (the total investment amount in various departments of the national economy is taken as 100):

Table 3: Total Investments in the National Economy

	First Five-Year Plan period	Second Five-Year Plan period	1963–1965	Third Five-Year Plan period	Fourth Five-Year Plan period	1976–1978
Investment proportion in heavy industry (%)	36.1	54.0	45.9	51.1	49.6	49.6
Investment proportion in light industry (%)	6.4	6.4	3.9	4.4	5.8	5.9
Investment proportion in agriculture (%)	7.1	11.3	17.7	10.7	9.8	10.8

Table 3 shows that the proportion of investment in light industry was always low, and that in the period from 1976 to 1978 it was lower than that in the periods of the First and Second Five-Year Plans. As a result, light industry lagged behind over a long period, and light industrial products were in very short supply.

– *Shortages in the energy industry and communications.* At that time, China was short of 10 million kW of generated energy, and as a result 20% of the nation's industries could not bring their productive capacity into full play. The gap in the coal industry was even wider, the oil industry lacked reserves, and communications fell far short of freight volume growth. Railway carrying capacity in some key junctions could only meet the needs of 50–70% of the total demand.

– *Imbalance between accumulation and consumption.* In the years 1976 and 1977, the accumulation rate was over 30% and in 1978 it rose to 40.7% Capital construction became more and more over-extended: the number of large and medium-sized projects under construction increased from 1,400 in 1977 to 1,700 in 1978, resulting in poor returns on investments. By contrast, the proportion of investment in welfare facilities such as housing dropped. As for consumption, peasants' average income from the collective increased little, while the average wage of workers and staff in state-run enterprises decreased from 652 yuan in 1965 to 644 yuan in 1978.

– *Increase in expenditure of foreign exchange.* By the end of 1978, twenty-two agreements had been concluded for absorbing complete sets of items from abroad, with a planned total investment of $US 56 billion, of which $US 12.3 billion was foreign exchange, exceeding the limits of the country's financial and material resources.

– *Poor economic results in enterprises.* In 1978, one-third of the nation's enterprises had not restored their normal sequence of production, and 24.3% of the state-run industrial enterprises which had independent

accounting were running at a loss – to a total as high as 3.75 billion yuan. Twenty-one of the 38 major items of the consumption quota in key industrial enterprises had not been restored to their previous highest level. Some 13 of the 30 principal quality quotas among the major industrial products were lower than their previous best. Low quality and unsaleable goods overstocked were worth a total amount of 10 billion yuan. In view of all this, the State Council decided that the national economy must be readjusted within three years.

In April 1979, the State formulated the principle of readjusting, restructuring, consolidating and improving the national economy. However, the problem of imbalance was not solved at its roots due to the fact that some departments and regions had an incorrect understanding of the decision and took only ineffective measures to carry out the principle, although the situation in 1979 and 1980 did take a favourable turn.

At that time, various dangers were concealed within the national economy: Investment in capital construction was out of control, and in capital construction directly arranged by the State it was not cut back, while in capital construction run by localities, departments and enterprises it increased to far too high a level; consumer funds rose too quickly, due to purchasing price increases for agricultural and sideline products, over-employment, the raising of wages and granting of bonuses. The arrangement of accumulation and consumer funds exceeded the national revenue for the same period; expenditures in capital construction and in other projects arranged by the State exceeded its revenues, giving rise to a large financial deficit, which in turn led to the printing of more money. In the years 1979 and 1980, national deficits approached 30 billion yuan. The issuing of extra money led to further currency devaluation in the market place. In 1979, retail prices rose 1.9% over the previous year, and they went up a further 6% in 1980.

To change the situation as soon as possible, the

Chinese government decided by the end of 1980 that the national economy should be further readjusted from the year 1981. Major requirements put forward by the State Council were: on the one hand, to cut down investment in capital construction on a large-scale, reduce expenditures for national defence and administrative expenses, and decrease financial expenditures; and, on the other hand, to accelerate the development of agriculture and light industry, increase the production of consumer goods and open up new sources of revenue.

Benefits resulting from this readjustment included:

– *Successful cutting down and control of the scale of capital construction.* Investment in national capital construction dropped from 55.8 billion yuan in 1980 to 44.2 billion yuan in 1981 – a decrease of 20.7%, of which the investment directly arranged by the State decreased from 34.9 billion yuan to 25.1 billion yuan – a decrease of 28%. This was a key step toward ensuring that the national economy should regain the initiative after its state of passivity. The accumulation rate of national revenue dropped from 31.5% in 1980 to 28.3% in 1981.

– *Strengthening of financial and credit administration, reducing financial deficits by a big margin.* In 1981, the State Council formulated the *Decision Concerning the Balance between Financial Revenue and Expenditures and the Strict Management of Financial Administration*, and the *Decision Concerning Feasible Strengthening of Credit Management and the Strict Control of the Issuing of Currency*. As a result, the state financial deficit decreased from 12.7 billion yuan in 1980 to 2.5 billion yuan in 1981 and the amount of newly issued currency was also less than in the previous year.

– *Reduction and regulation of orientation of heavy industry.* Also, major efforts were devoted to developing agriculture and light industry, and the ratios of agriculture, light industry and heavy industry were readjusted. Among the total output value of industrial and agricultural production in 1978, agriculture accounted for 27.8%, light industry 31.1%, and heavy industry 41.1%. By 1981, agriculture rose to 32.5%, light industry increased to 34.7% and heavy industry dropped to 32.8%. In 1982, agriculture went up to 33.6%, and light industry remained at 33.4%.

A new strategy for economic and social development

After the Third Plenary Session of the Eleventh Central Committee of the CPC, with the ideological guideline of emancipating the mind and seeking the truth from facts, China began to sum up its experiences further – to draw lessons in its economic construction and to feel its way toward a new strategy yielding a better economic return, as opposed to its traditional, lopsided strategy of seeking the growth of industrial output value – in particular, the heavy industrial output value.

On 31 November–1 December 1981, Premier

Zhao Ziyang made a report, *The Present Economic Situation and the Principles for Future Economic Construction*, at the Third Session of the Fifth National People's Congress. He explained formally the new strategy of economic and social development as: "to start from China's reality, to blaze a new trail in our economic construction for the attainment of better economic results, so that people might get more benefits." Premier Zhao held that "the crux of the problem is to do all we can to get better economic results in the areas of production, construction and circulation. On economic returns, he put forward ten principles: Accelerate the development of agriculture by relying on correct policies and on science; Give prominence to the development of consumer goods industries and further adjust the service orientation of heavy industry; Raise the energy utilization ratio and promote the building of the energy industry and transport; Carry out progressive technical transformation of key units and make the maximum use of existing enterprises; Carry out the all-round consolidation and necessary restructuring of enterprises by groups; Raise more construction funds and use them thriftily through improved methods of acquisition, accumulation and spending; Persist in a policy of opening up to the outside world and enhance China's capacity for independent action; Actively and steadily reform the economic system and realize the initiative of all concerned to the full; Raise the scientific and cultural level of all working people and organize strong forces to tackle key scientific research projects; Proceed from the concept of everything for the people and make overall arrangements for production, construction and the people's livelihood. This series of new strategies was diametrically opposed to the old practice of high accumulation, high speed, inefficiency and less improvement in the people's living standards, formed under the long-standing guideline of "Left" thinking. This new strategy promoted an all-round development of the economy, science and technology, education, culture and society during the Sixth Five-Year Plan period.

Building socialism with Chinese characteristics

In September 1982, the Twelfth National Congress of the Communist Party of China was convened. Deng Xiaoping pointed out in his opening speech that China should blaze a path of its own and build socialism with Chinese characteristics. Hu Yaobang put forward in his report *Create a New Situation in All Fields of Socialist Modernization* that the general objective of China's economic development in the two decades between 1981 and the end of this century – while steadily working for more and better economic results – was to quadruple the gross annual value of industrial and agricultural production, from 710 billion yuan in 1980 to 2,800 billion yuan in the year 2000. This general objective showed no divergence from what Deng Xiaoping has put forward many times since 1979–that China will reach a high level of prosperity by the end of this century, when the gross national product per capita will be $800. This is the first goal in China's economic and social development. The second goal put forward is that China will approach and catch up with advanced countries in her economy and technology in the year 2050.

In order to realize these strategic goals, China must make improvement of economic results its central task and go a step further with the policy of invigorating the domestic economy and opening up to the outside world, accelerating the restructuring of the national economy as a whole so as to build socialist modernization with Chinese characteristics.

A new pattern of economic structural reform

The Third Plenary Session of the Eleventh Central Committee of the CPC stressed the imperative need to raise productive forces by a big margin for China's socialist modernization. This naturally involves changing in many ways the relationships of production and superstructure that do not suit the development of productive forces, and also changing all unsuitable managerial modes and forms of ideological manoeuvre. In June 1981, the Sixth Plenary Session of the Eleventh Central Committee of the CPC once again pointed out that there was no fixed model for the development of socialist productive relations, and stressed that major efforts should be devoted to developing socialist commodity production and exchange of commodities so as to create a specific form of productive relations that would suit and stimulate the development of productive forces.

A major breakthrough was first effected in the rural areas by the widespread institution of the contracted responsibility system based on the household and linking remuneration to output, and by the implementation of a series of other reforms. These measures have served to greatly emancipate the productive forces in the countryside, and the rural economy is becoming specialized, commercialized and modernized. In the cities, the reform has centred on invigorating enterprises, and varying degrees of reform have been effected in the areas of planning, finance, taxation, pricing, banking, commerce, labour and wages. As a result, the urban economy has thrived as never before. The capacity of enterprises for transformation and development has gradually increased. The socialist market has continued to expand. Diverse forms of ownership and modes of business operation have developed remarkably and lateral economic ties of various types have gradually been strengthened. Many changes have been made in the mechanism of the entire economy, changes that have helped to invigorate it. They have also helped heighten the enthusiasm and stimulate the initiative

of workers and other employees. Since the implementation of the Party Central Committee's *Decision on the Reform of the Economic Structure* promulgated in October 1984, the outline of a socialist economic structure with Chinese characteristics is becoming increasingly clear and the future is growing more and more bright. The petrified economic structure characterized by excessive and rigid control has been replaced by a vigorous new version appropriate to the planned development of a commodity economy based on public ownership.

With distinct Chinese characteristics, the new pattern demonstrates: on the question of the ownership, the tendency of seeking blindly for public ownership – the higher the degree of public ownership, the better – is discarded, and diverse forms of ownership and modes of management are encouraged while maintaining the predominance of public ownership; on the structure of economic decision-making, over-concentration of power in state administrative organs and enterprises, which dampened initiative, is replaced by a system in which ownership is appropriately separated from management rights, and enterprises are operated at multiple administrative levels of State, enterprises and workforce; on the question of economic regulating system, the practice of rejecting the market mechanism and relying mainly upon mandatory state plans and administrative measures adopted in past years has been discontinued and is replaced by extending the scope of guidance in planning and increasing the use of economic levers and market mechanisms to regulate the economy; on the question of the relationship of economic results, the tendency to ignore the interests of enterprises, the collective and the workforce, as well as egalitarianism in distribution, is replaced by the policy that consideration is to be given to the interests of the State, enterprises (the collective) and individuals and by the policy of distribution according to work done; and on economic organization, the tendency of not defining the duties of administrative organs and enterprises and depending mainly on subordination and dividing economic relations into vertical strips and squares is replaced by establishing an economic system with a criss-cross network by relying mainly on the lateral ties, with central cities in the pivotal role.

Theoretically, this new pattern has been established on the basis of the three important breaks with traditional theory.

Firstly, the break with the traditional ideas of setting planning economy against commodity economy, to affirm that the full development of a commodity economy is an unavoidable stage in developing the social economy; and to clarify that the planned socialist economy is a commodity economy planned on the basis of public ownership. For a long time, people did not recognize that the means of production was a commodity, and that the law of value also played a role in regulating the production

461

fields, so that they paid no attention to the circulation fields or to tertiary industry. This led to a high speed national economy which was yielding poor economic returns. Practice has taught the function of the market and the importance of strengthening the macro-control and management in a planned way. The target for China's economic reform is that the macro-economy should be controlled firmly and well, while the micro-economy should be opened and enlivened, resulting in control without rigidity and enlivenment without confusion.

Secondly, the break with the outmoded notion that socialist enterprises could only be managed directly by the State, and could not run independently or assume sole responsibility for profits or losses, and clarification that the ownership of socialist enterprises owned by the whole people can be appropriately separated from the management rights. The enterprise should become the genuine economic body, with a fair degree of independence, and it should become the producer and manager of a socialist commodity, with the ability to reform and develop independently and to become a legal person with certain rights and obligations.

Thirdly, the break with the habitual belief that functions could not be divided between administrative organs and enterprises, and that the state plan was law, clarifying that they should in fact be divided and that the functions exercised by government organs in economic management should change from mainly direct control to mainly indirect control. The state plan is not an immutable instruction; a planned economy does not mean taking the plan as mandatory. Of course, some mandatory plans related to the national economy and people's livelihood have to be guaranteed; however, most of the guidance plans can only be realized by relying on economic levers.

In the Seventh Five-Year Plan period (1986–1990), China will put its restructuring of the economy in first place so as to lay the foundation for the establishment of these new patterns.

The policy of opening to the outside world

This is a fundamental national policy which has remained unchanged over a long period of time. China's policy of opening to the outside world also demands that various regions, cities and departments should open to each other at home. This is an indispensable national policy for developing productive forces, not merely an expedient measure.

In its past history, China did not entirely close itself to international intercourse, but carried out its policies of opening to the outside world during its powerful and prosperous era. For instance, in the Han dynasty and Tang Dynasty, China kept close ties with Japan, Korea and South-East Asia and dispatched its envoys to western Asia (including those areas west of present-day Xinjiang). The Silk Road to the Middle-East and Europe is world-renowned, and in those days foreign trade was flourishing. The People's Republic of China proclaimed on its founding day, 1 October 1949, that China would do business with both socialist and capitalist countries. However, China's economic relations with foreign countries did not develop as might have been desired owing to internal and external causes. Later, influenced by "Left" thinking, the policy of self-reliance was set against the expansion of trade with foreign countries, making China a semi-closed or entirely closed country. Fortunately, things were quite different after the year 1978. Thanks to the policy of reinvigorating the domestic economy and opening to the outside world which is now being carried out in China, four special economic zones were established in Shenzhen, Zhuhai, Xiamen and Shantou, and later 14 cities were opened further to the outside world, namely, Dalian, Qinhuangdao, Tianjin, Yantai, Lianyungang, Nantong, Shanghai, Ningbo, Wenzhou, Fuzhou, Guangzhou, Zanjiang, Qingdao and Beihai, as well as Hainan Island. All this made China's coastal areas become the foremost regions opening to the outside world.

China's economic policy of opening to the outside world will remain unchanged for a long time to come – a decision made on the basis of objective needs. As Deng Xiaoping has stated, the Chinese are wholeheartedly devoted to the modernization programme and are striving for a peaceful international environment to conduct international exchanges and to carry out the policy of opening to the outside world so as to realize their goal set for the year 2000. For the next 50 years, China will continue this policy and will even surpass its present target of approaching the level of the developed countries. Deng Xiaoping declared that China's policy of opening to the outside world will remain unchanged to the end of this century and will continue well into the next.

China's policy of opening to the outside world will not only promote the development of China's economy and benefit the world economy, but will also contribute to safeguarding world peace.

The Achievements of the Thirty-Six Years, 1949–1985

Thirty-six years have elapsed since the birth of the People's Republic of China in 1949. The Chinese people, led by the Communist Party of China, are working hard to make the country strong, and have endured plain living and a hard struggle in order to accomplish achievements in China's socialist construction and economic development that were not even vainly hoped for in old China. Especially since the Third Plenary Session of the Eleventh Central Committee of the CPC, the State has put the building of socialist modernization in first place and blazed a new path in its work on the economy, with the yielding of higher economic results as its centre. All this has made the Sixth Five-Year Plan period the best period since the founding of the People's Republic, and the national economy is now full of unprecedented vitality.

The development of the national economy

According to statistics in 1949, old China's total social output value (i.e., the sum total of the output value in the five material production fields of agriculture, industry, the building industry, transport and communications and commerce) registered only 55.7 billion yuan. The total output value of its agricultural and industrial production was 46.6 billion yuan, and national income (i.e., the sum total of the net output value of the five material production fields) was 35.8 billion yuan only, while in the year 1985, China's total social output value reached 1,630.9 billion yuan, the total output value of industrial and agricultural production 1,333.6 billion yuan, and the national income (net output value created within one year) registered 682.2 billion yuan – an increase of 25.7 times, 26.2 times and 12.9 times respectively over the year 1949. (See Figure 1). During the Sixth Five-Year Plan period, the national economy grew at an average rate of 10% a year; such a high growth rate has seldom been seen even during the golden age of economic development in advanced industrial countries since World War II. As for the production of material objects, in 1985 the output of many products surpassed several times over the sum total for several decades in old China. For instance, steel output in 1985 was 46.79 million tons, six times the total output (7.60 million tons) from 1898 to 1948. In 1985, the output of coal, cotton yarn, cotton cloth, bicycles, sewing machines, cement, grain, cotton and rapeseed ranked first in the world; meat, peanuts, tea and TV sets – second; chemical fertilizer, sulphuric acid, the total production volume of energy, and soya beans – third; steel – fourth; chemical fibre and generated energy – fifth; and petroleum – sixth.

Figure 2: Comparison of China's Grain and Steel Yields from 1957 to 1966

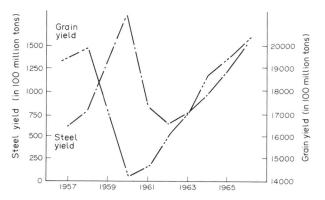

Social reproduction capacity

From 1950 to 1985, investment in fixed assets in the units under the ownership of the whole people reached 1,449.8 billion yuan, of which investment in capital construction registered 1,078.7 billion yuan and in renewal and transformation and other measures 371.1 billion yuan. Some 4,000 large and medium-size projects and several thousand small-size projects, as well as various buildings and houses with an area of more than 2.7 billion square metres of floor space were built. The first phase project in the Baoshan General Steel Plant in Shanghai (with an annual production capacity of three million tons) was completed and went into operation in 1985. In thirty years and more since the birth of New China, the Chinese people not only made full use of 1.5 billion *mu* of cultivated land, but reclaimed a vast wasteland with an area of 33 million *mu*. In addition, rivers such as the Yellow River, Huaihe, Haihe, Luanhe, Zhujiang (Pearl River), Liaohe, Yangtze and Songhuajiang have all been brought under control to varying degrees. Rebuilt and newly-built dykes, protective embankments in lakeside areas and sea walls amount to 170,000 kilometres in length. Principal water conservancy projects can withstand any of the floods which occur once every twenty or forty years. Much geological prospecting has been done in the three decades: Chinese geologists have found practically all the more than 140 kinds of useful minerals known to the world. It has been proved that China is one of the few countries in the world endowed with a fairly complete range of minerals in sizeable reserves. By the end of 1985, its verified coal reserves were 769.18 billion tons, which can be worked for 800–900 years if calculated according to the excavated output in 1985. China's proved iron reserves amounted to 496.41 billion tons, and petroleum reserves in China are especially rich. The country leads the world in non-ferrous metals, such as tungsten, zinc, lithium, rare-earth metals, titanium, vanadium, molybdenum, mercury and tin. In addition, China is rich in rare metal reserves, such as thorium, uranium, beryllium, niobium and germanium, needed in building up national defence and in economic construction. The large-scale construction has rapidly expanded the productive capacity of China's industry, agriculture and transport, and considerable improvements have been also made in productive technical equipment. The country has made numerous kinds of large-scale technological equipment and successfully established its advanced, world-level nuclear industrial bases, space-flight industrial bases and designed and manufactured satellites and space rocket devices, as well as the large-scale Gezhouba Key Water Control Project, by introducing a quantity of advanced technical equipment and production parts from abroad, on the one hand, and by depending on its own strength, on the other hand.

The distribution of productive forces

In old China, the distribution of regional economy was quite illogical, and 70% of the country's industry was distributed in the coastal areas of East China, while the vast hinterland and minority nationalities areas had few or no modern industries at all. The total output value of industry produced in North-West and South-West China and in Inner Mongolia, which occupy 69% of the country's total land, accounted for only 9% of the nation's total industrial output value. To change such irrational distribution of the economy, the People's Government adopted a series of important measures in investment, finance and technology. Along with the development of the economy in the coastal areas, investment was heavily allocated to the inland economy, especially in the developing of capital construction in minority-inhabited areas. Many industrial bases have now been newly built in the hinterland and minority areas. Major examples include natural gas, chemical industry, iron and steel and machinery industrial bases in Sichuan; non-ferrous metal and chemical industrial bases in Yunnan; coal, non-ferrous metal and chemical industrial bases in Guizhou; coal, chemical, metallurgical and machinery and power industrial bases in Shaanxi, Gansu and Ningxia; coal, metallurgical and chemical industrial bases in Anhui; coal, non-ferrous metal and machinery industrial bases in Henan; metallurgical, machinery, chemical and power industrial bases in Hunan and Hubei; and machinery, petroleum, chemical and light industry and forest industrial bases in Heilongjiang and Jilin. Some 100 railways were built between 1950 and 1985, three-quarters of which are located inland, adding some 30,000 km open to traffic, including the routes Chengdu–Chongqing, Baoji–Chengdu, Lanzhou–Xinjiang, Baotou–Lanzhou, Chengdu–Kunming, Xiangfan–Chongqing, Jiaozuo–Zhicheng, Zhicheng–Liuzhou, Taiyuan–Jiaozuo, Guizhou–Guangxi, Hunan–Guizhou, Turpan–Korla and Yanzhou–Shiqiushuo, etc. By the end of 1985, railway services were available in every province, autonomous region and municipality throughout the country, except the Tibetan autonomous region, and railway mileage in minority areas registered 12,495 km – an increase of 8,984 km as against 1949. Highways in China reached 254,083 km, or an increase of 242,688 km over 1949, of which, those leading directly to Tibet include the Sichuan–Tibet highway (formerly known as the Xikang–Tibet highway), the Qinghai–Tibet highway, the Xinjiang–Tibet highway, and the Yunnan–Tibet highway, as well as quite a number of highways built within the autonomous region. All this created an important prerequisite for the acceleration of economic development in the remote border areas.

The improvement in economic results

During the Sixth Five-Year Plan period, China began to shift its strategy of development from attaching importance to speed to improving economic results, and gradually moved on to a new course, in which economic results were regarded as central. The targets of economic results in this period were considerably improved over those of the Fifth Five-Year Plan period. This was visible in the following facts: during the Sixth Five-Year Plan period the average growth rate of national income and revenue caught up with the average growth rate of total output value. The average growth rates were about 10%, as opposed to the previous situation of "sharp increase in output value, with a lower increase in national income and revenue, and even in nominal income." National income created by each field of social labour increased by an average rate of 6% annually if calculated according to the constant price the same year; energy consumption per unit declined year by year. In 1985, the consumption of energy on 10,000 yuan of national income dropped by 23.4% as compared with 1980. Because of the rise in energy utilization, national income increased by about 30 billion yuan a year; economic results targets rose greatly in various enterprises and industrial trades, agriculture, commerce, transport and the building industry, if compared with those during the Cultural Revolution and the Fifth Five-Year Plan period. Taking the state-run industry as an example, profits and tax submitted to the State in 1985 increased by 14.3% over the previous year, higher than the 12.9% of the growth rate in total output value. Energy consumption reduced or saved per year equalled 30 million tons of standard coal. Energy consumption per 100 million output value dropped from 65,000 tons in 1984 to less than 60,000 tons in 1985. In the same year, the productivity of labour increased 9.4% over the previous year, 5% over the scheduled figure. It was the best year in the Sixth Five-Year Plan period. Among the increased industrial output value, 74.6% was due to the growth in the productivity of labour. Meanwhile, circulating funds speeded up in turnover and the number of enterprises running at a loss was reduced year by year to less than 10.7% in 1985. A gratifying achievement was that the number of advanced enterprises yielding better economic results was increasing rapidly. For instance, the Capital Iron and Steel Corporation had increased its profit at an average progressive rate of more than 20% for six years running. National revenue reversed its downward trend and showed marked and steady growth in the period 1983 to 1985. Towards the end of the Fifth Five-Year Plan period, there was a fairly big deficit in revenue, totalling nearly 30 billion yuan for 1979 and 1980. In the following plan period, however, increased revenue was brought in through expanded production and circulation and improved economic efficiency. Domestic revenue rose by 12.5 billion yuan in 1983, 25.29 billion yuan in 1984, and 36.45 billion yuan in 1985, with a total of 186.64 billion yuan for the year, thus balancing the budget.

Of the five previous plan periods, the fifth had seen the biggest increase in revenue: 26.96 billion yuan more in 1980 than in 1975. The increase during the sixth period, however, was still higher: revenue in 1985 increased by 78.12 billion yuan over 1980, or 2.9 times the volume of the fifth Five-Year Plan period. Meanwhile, funds outside the budget increased by a big margin, too, and reached 140.0 billion yuan in 1985. Together with the budgetary funds, the state revenue totalled 320 billion yuan, double the figure for 1980.

The improvement in material and cultural living standards

In old China, the economy was backward and people very poor. Since the founding of the People's Republic, the problem of clothing and food for the one billion Chinese people has been basically solved through the great efforts made by the People's Government, resulting in its becoming self-supporting in grain and more than self-sufficient in cotton. Especially since the year 1979, the long-standing "Left" errors that determined that attention was paid only to construction, not to the improvement of the people's welfare were overcome and emphasis was placed – along with the development of production – on the improvement of living standards, for the 800 million peasants in particular. Policies of encouraging some people to become prosperous sooner than others and a series of corresponding measures were adopted by the Government; for instance, raising the purchase prices of agricultural products, readjusting wages and restoring bonuses. As a result, a marked improvement has been made in living standards, both in urban and in rural areas. According to 1985 statistics the average net income per peasant approached 397.6 yuan, an increase of 197.7% over the figure of 133.5 yuan in 1978. The proportion of poor households who had an average net income of no more than 100 yuan per capita declined from 33.3% of the country's total peasant households in 1978 to 10% in 1985. Workers' living standards have improved, too. The average annual wage per worker under ownership by the whole people increased from 614 yuan in 1978 to 1,142 yuan in 1985 – an increase of 87%. Due to the growth of employed population, the number of workers and staff members reached 123.58 million and the number of family members supported by one worker (including the worker himself) decreased from 3.29 persons early after Liberation to 1.74 in 1985.

During the Sixth Five-Year Plan period, the living standards of the people improved more than at any other time since the founding of the People's Republic. This is illustrated by the following facts: First, the incomes of both urban and rural residents increased enormously. Adjusted for price rises, the annual per capita net income of rural residents went up by 13.7%

and that of urban workers and other employees and their family members by 6.9%, and 36.48 million people were newly employed in the cities and towns. Second, the consumption level of both urban and rural people was raised rapidly, with notable changes in pattern. Diet improved, clothing became more varied and sales of durable consumer goods – especially TV sets, washing machines, radio-cassette recorders and refrigerators and other household electrical appliances – all grew rapidly. Third, housing conditions improved. During the Sixth Five-Year Plan period, more than 650 million square metres of floor space were built in cities and towns, and 3.2 billion square metres in rural areas. Fourth, savings deposits of both urban and rural residents increased by a wide margin, reaching 162.26 billion yuan by the end of 1985 – four times the figure for 1980. Average savings deposits per capita were 155.2 yuan, or some 650% over the figure of 21.9 yuan in 1978. With the improvement in material welfare, notable progress has been made in cultural living standards also. Taking higher education as an example, there was total enrolment of 1.703 million in regular colleges and universities in 1985, as against 1.144 million in 1980. Initial successes have been achieved in restructuring middle school education. There has been rapid growth in vocational and technical school education, and good progress has been made towards universal elementary education. Different types of adult education programmes have been initiated throughout the country on an unprecedented scale.

The Organization and Function of the National Economic Administration

China is a socialist country with a vast territory and a huge population, and its economy is still backward and uneven. How to establish a system of economic administration suited to China's conditions so as to promote its productivity is a question which is still under study but is being resolved step by step. Since the founding of the People's Republic, changes have taken place several times in the economic administrative system. During the mid-1980s, the administrative system of the economy was engaged in restructuring the old pattern into a quite new one. Below is a broad outline of its history and an analysis of the situation up to 1985.

The characteristics of the past administrative system

Since the birth of New China, a combined administrative system has been exercised by the central, unified leadership and local regional administration, with the former as the dominant factor. During the years of the Great Leap Forward movement and the Cultural Revolution, attempts at change were made: large numbers of enterprises directly under the Central Government were put under regional administration, together with the transfer of power to the lower levels. However, all this failed, and control again returned to the Central Government, because over-transfer had led to the system running out of control. It was said that "control leads to rigidity; rigidity to relaxation; relaxation to disorder; and disorder to restriction." Before the change from the old economic system to the new pattern, such characteristics as the following could be seen, though sometimes obscured by slogans:

– Governments at all levels administered enterprises directly through their departments in all trades and professions, leading to a tendency not to differentiate duties as between administrative organs and enterprises or rights as between ownership and management;

– Economic management departments under governments at all levels could be roughly divided into two categories – comprehensive departments indirectly administering enterprises, and professional departments administering enterprises more or less directly;

– Overlapping systems of State departments and local governments in the administration of enterprises, led to a tendency for departments and regions to be interlocked but still separated. As a result, enterprises were deprived of initiative.

The organizing of an economic system under the State Council

The organ in charge of economic management under the Central People's Government, that is, the State Council (which was called Government Administration Council before 1954), has always occupied an important place. In the early days after the founding of the People's Republic, the Government Administration Council subordinated the Central Finance and Economy Commission, which was in charge of national finance and economics in addition to the Heavy Industry Ministry, the Trade Ministry and fifteen other departments of finance and economics, accounting for 47% of the total departments under the administration of the Council. After the Government Administration Council was renamed the State Council, the departments in charge of finance and economics always made up 55% of the total number of departments under the State Council, though changes and readjustments were conducted several times among ministries, commissions and bureaux. Since the Third Plenary Session of the Eleventh Central Committee of the CPC in 1978, the focus of national work has been shifted to socialist modernization, so that the proportion taken by the departments in charge of finance and economics had further increased to 67% by the year 1980. In the spring of 1982, some

overlapping organs with similar professional roles were merged and reorganized – the original 96 ministries and commissions under the State Council were reduced to 62, of which organs in charge of economy were reduced from 66 to 42. However, the proportion of these departments among the newly-established organs remained unchanged.

By the end of 1985, the State Council commanded 68 ministries, commissions, directly-affiliated bureaux, national corporations and research centres, which can be roughly divided into seven categories:

1. Comprehensive administrative organs of the national economy, namely, the State Planning Commission, the State Economic Commission, the State Commission for Restructuring the Economic System, the State Science and Technology Commission, the Commission for Science and Technology and the National Defence Industry, the State Bureau of Statistics, the State Bureau of Patents, the State Bureau of Standards, and the State Bureau of Measures. With the exception of the State Bureau of Statistics, the above-mentioned bureaux are directly subordinated to the State Economic Commission, and their functions and powers are as follows: the *State Planning Commission* is responsible for working out the annual plan, the five-year plan and the long-term plan for the national economy and social development according to the line, principle and policies for economic affairs formulated by the State Council; the *State Economic Commission* is in charge of carrying out the line, principle and policies on economic affairs and supervising the implementation of the annual national economic plan, coordinating and resolving questions related to the economic and technological activities arising in various departments of agriculture, industry, transport and communications, finance and monetary matters, and domestic and foreign trade, as well as organizing and conducting the technical transformation of enterprises and the restructuring of the economic system; the *State Science and Technology Commission* is responsible for administering national scientific and technological work, studying policies on science and technology, putting forward important questions of science and technology for joint research with the State Planning Commission and the State Economic Commission, and organizing and coordinating scientific and technological forces to tackle key problems.

2. Comprehensive professional managerial and supervisory organs in charge of national financial and monetary matters, labour and prices, namely, the Ministry of Finance, State Auditing Administration, the People's Bank of China, the Industrial and Commercial Bank of China, the Agricultural Bank of China, the Bank of China, the People's Construction Bank of China, the People's Insurance Company of China, the State General Administration of Foreign Exchange Control, the China International Trust and Investment Company, the Ministry of Labour and

Personnel, the State Bureau of Prices, the General Bureau of Industrial and Commercial Administration and the State General Customs Administration.

3. Professional ministries and bureaux in charge of the production and manufacture of goods and materials in the fields of agriculture, industry, transport and building materials, consisting of the Ministry of Agriculture, Animal Husbandry and Fishery, the Ministry of Forestry, the Ministry of Water Resources and Electric Power, the Ministry of Urban and Rural Construction and Environmental Protection, the Ministry of Geology and Mineral Resources, the Ministry of the Metallurgical Industry, the Ministry of the Machine-Building Industry, the Ministry of the Nuclear Industry, the Ministry of the Aeronautics Industry, the Ministry of the Electronics Industry, the Ministry of the Ordnance Industry, the Ministry of the Astronautics Industry, the Ministry of the Coal Industry, the Ministry of the Petroleum Industry, the Ministry of the Chemical Industry, the Ministry of the Textile Industry, the Ministry of Light Industry, the Ministry of Railways, the Ministry of Communications, the Civil Aviation Administration of China, the Ministry of Posts and Telecommunications, the State Bureau of the Building Materials Industry, and the State Pharmacological Administration.

4. National professional corporations directly subordinated to the State Council, including the China Shipping Industry Corporation, the China Petroleum and Chemical Industry Corporation, the China Automobile Industry Corporation, the China Non-ferrous Metal Industry Corporation, the China Ocean Petroleum Corporation, the China Tobacco Corporation and the China Silk Corporation.

5. Circulating and administrative organs of commercial, tourist and material trades; namely, the Ministry of Commerce, the Ministry of Foreign Economic Relations and Trade, the State Bureau of Travel and Tourism, the State Bureau of Goods and Materials and the State Reserve Bureau.

6. Administrative and research organs in the service of economic construction, including the State Bureau of Meteorology, the State Bureau of Oceanography, the State Bureau of Seismology, the Chinese Academy of Science and the Chinese Academy of Social Science.

7. Advisory bodies and research institutions on national economic problems, consisting of the Centre for Research on the Development of Economic Technology and Society, under the State Council; the Centre for Research in Economic Laws and Regulations, under the State Council; and the Centre for Research on the Development of China's Rural Areas.

The administrative organs of the economy under local government

Under the leadership of the State Council, local people's governments at all levels are the executive organs of local state power, as well as the local organs of state administration. Local people's governments exercise their responsibilities through a provincial governor (mayor or chairman of an autonomous region), county magistrate, district head or township head (head of a town). Local governments at the levels of province (autonomous region) and county are in charge of the administration of their economic construction and financial affairs. Functional organs for the administration of economic affairs similar to the ministries and commissions set up by the State Council are established at the corresponding levels, such as the provincial (municipality or autonomous region) planning commission, economic commission and commerce department and country planning commission, economic commission and commerce bureau. The various economic functional organs of local governments work under the unified leadership of the people's governments at the corresponding levels, as well as under the leadership and business guidance of the departments responsible for the work under the State Council. By the end of 1985, the administrative organization of the economy on the three levels of central government, province and county had been established in 29 provincial people's governments (except Taiwan, and including five autonomous regions, and three municipalities directly under the Central Government), and in 2,046 people's governments at county level.

The characteristics of China's economic administrative organs

The above-mentioned government organs, research institutes and economic bodies in the management of the economy directly under the State Council were set up successively during the reform of the state structure started at the beginning of 1982. This system should not and cannot remain unchanged. According to the plan that top priority should be given to economic structural reform during the Seventh Five-Year Plan period, the State will establish a new, socialist macro-economic management system by gradually changing from mainly direct to mainly indirect control in its management of enterprises. In this process major reforms will certainly be conducted in management organs, from the central to the local governments. The orientation of the reform is to bring about a gradual change from an economic management system controlled mainly by administrative measures to a management system indirectly controlled by improved economic and legal measures, supplemented by the necessary administrative measures according to the principle that duties should be divided between administrations and enterprises and that organs should be simplified and powers transferred to lower levels, with the macro-economic control combined with the reinvigoration of the micro-economy. This change of function makes it imperative for departments in charge of overall economic management, inspection and supervision to be better staffed and for departments of professional economic management to be appropriately merged or streamlined.

The *Constitution of the People's Republic of China* adopted on 4 December 1982 by the Fifth National People's Congress at its Fifth Session stipulated clearly and definitely (Section III of Chapter Two) the characteristics, composition, function and powers (including the functions and powers on economic management) and the system of responsibility. The fundamental points of the stipulation are as follows:

The State Council – that is, the Central People's Government of the People's Republic of China – is the executive body of the highest organ of state power; it is the highest organ of state administration. The State Council is composed of the following: the Premier, the Vice-Premiers, the State Councillors, the Ministers in charge of ministries, the Ministers in charge of commissions, the Auditor-General and the Secretary-General. The Premier has overall responsibility for the State Council, and the Ministers have overall responsibility for the ministries and commissions under their charge. Executive meetings of the State Council are composed of the Premier, the Vice-Premiers, the State Councillors and the Secretary-General of the State Council. The Premier convenes and presides over the executive meetings and plenary meetings of the State Council.

Among the functions and powers exercised by the State Council, those related directly to economic construction are: to draw up and implement the plan for national economic and social development and the state budget; to direct and administer economic affairs and urban and rural development; to conduct foreign affairs and conclude treaties and agreements with foreign states, and to direct and administer the building of national defence, etc. The State Council establishes an auditing body to supervise the revenue and expenditure of all departments under the State Council, of the local governments at different levels, of the state financial and monetary organizations, and of enterprises and undertakings. Under the direction of the Premier of the State Council, the auditing body independently exercises its power to supervise, through auditing in accordance with the law, subject to no interference by any other administrative organ or any public organization or individual.

The functions of economic management organs at different levels under the State Council

According to the above-mentioned regulations and requirements of the reform of the economic structure, government organs at all levels managing the economy should no longer devote their energy to assigning quotas, approving construction projects and allotting funds and materials. Instead, they should do overall planning, formulate policies, organize coordi-

nation, provide services, use economic means of regulation and exercise effective inspection and supervision. In short, there are three basic functions:

1. *Decision-making, planning and coordination.* Overall strategic decisions, such as strategic goals, emphases and steps in national economic and social development, and the line, principles and policies for developing the national economy are mainly formulated by the Central Committee of the CPC, the National People's Congress and the State Council, while the State Planning Commission, State Economic Commission and State Science and Technology Commission and related departments are responsible for drawing up the draft of the national economic and social development plan, especially the long-term plan (ten years or more), mid-term plan (five-year) and the annual plan – including the plan for exploiting natural resources, technological transformations and the development of intellectual resources, as well as some key projects, particularly the construction plan for energy, communications and the raw materials industries. All these must be examined and approved by the National People's Congress before they are put into practice by the State Council. In managing the economy, government organs must often harmonize the various kinds of economic contradictions arising in localities, departments and enterprises and their economic relations. Government organs also have the power to appoint and remove cadres within a prescribed scope, and to administrate in matters related to external economic and technological exchanges and co-operation. In exercising these functions and powers, the first and second categories mentioned above play a leading role; the third, fourth and fifth categories also play an important role in their own fields: while the sixth – and especially the seventh – categories (newly-emerged organs in the 1980s) take effect as assistants, consultants and sources of information and advice.

2. *Inspection, supervision and control.* Indispensable macro-economic control must be conducted along with the reinvigoration of enterprises. To ensure the fulfilment of the State's strategic goals and long-term plans, to adhere to correct economic principles and policy and to guarantee that enterprises and economic activities are in keeping with socialist targets and the interests of the whole, it is very important for the State to conduct strict but flexible inspection, supervision and control. The major objectives of these are: to ensure the steady, continuous and co-ordinated development of the national economy, increasing in a proportionate and planned way; to protect the property under the ownership by the whole people against damage and appropriation, and to crack down firmly on those offenders who seriously sabotage the economy; to punish and deal with any contraventions of financial discipline and regulations; to intervene and correct any tendencies toward decentralism, selfish departmentalism and lack of vision, and to

exercise regular and effective supervision and control of those key items which are of vital importance to the nation's economy and the people's livelihood, such as the balance of the State's revenue and expenditure, balance of revenue and expenditure of foreign currency and trade, balance of credit, issuing of banknotes and gold reserves, the scale of total investment in fixed assets, balance of goods and materials of major means of production and subsistence (such as grain, coal, oil, power and steel, etc.), national production quotas, margin of growth of wages, welfare and consumer funds, as well as prices and quality of major products. Corrupt practice in the past was characterized by excessive and rigid control, on the one hand, and by mainly depending on administrative measures and direct control in the management of enterprises, on the other hand. Enterprises were not adept at using economic means and legal measures for indirect control, and economic operations were not good at shifting the focal point of planning to the full use of economic policies and economic levers, such as prices, tax revenue, credit, interest rates, exchange rates and wages, in overall management and macro-regulation. Similarly, the important role played by banks in economic control and regulation was also ignored. Since the 1980s, China has begun to pay attention to administering its economy by economic measures. For instance, the means of investment in capital construction and the allocation of circulation funds has been changed from allocation by the State to loans granted by banks; adjustment of prices for some products and industrial products in short supply on the market; change of energy policy, using coal instead of oil, and implementation of the policy of payment for energy resources partly in kind and partly in cash; and regular spot checks on product quality, etc., etc.

3. *Service, research and advice.* A state organ in a socialist country like China is an organ serving the people. One of its most important functions is to make a contribution to the development of social productivity, to the progress of grass roots units and enterprises, to the prosperity of the country and to the happiness of its people. In order to carry out this function in practice, the state organ should ensure a basis of investigation and study in order to collect and disseminate economic information quickly and accurately, and should encourage enterprises to act vigorously on their own initiative. State organs should also analyze and study important problems of the national economy in order to identify new situations, propound new solutions to its problems and sum up past experience so as to draw up policies and measures which accord with the actual situation. They should become good assistants and consultants and lead enterprises on to the road to yielding better economic results. In other words, China's organs of management of the economy are changing from the pattern of depending on administrative decree, direct control and administrative routine towards a new pattern of study of the economic realities, indirect control and service.

Eight principal functions of government organs managing the economy were put forward in the *Decision on the Reforms of China's Economic Structure* adopted by the Central Committee of the CPC in October 1984, which indicated the orientation of reform for the years to come. Government organs managing the economy must: formulate the strategy, plans, principles and policies for economic and social development; work out plans for the exploitation of natural resources, for technological transformation and for the development of intellectual resources; coordinate the development plans of localities, departments or enterprises and the economic relations among them; arrange for the construction of key projects, especially those in energy, transport and the raw and semi-finished materials industry; collect and disseminate economic information, learning to use means of regulation of the economy; work out economic regulations and ordinances and supervise their execution; appoint and dismiss cadres within a prescribed scope; administer matters related to external economic and technological exchanges and co-operation; etc.

The Evolution and Present State of the Economic Structure

After the founding of the People's Republic in 1949, China did a great deal to transform its backward and lopsided economic structure and achieved great successes, despite the many setbacks: first, the establishment of a socialist economy dominated by public ownership, or by state ownership; second, the establishment of an independent and fairly complete industrial system and national economy system; third, a certain improvement in the regional economic structure and technological structure; and fourth, through the restructuring and reform started at the beginning of the 1980s, considerable progress in the composition of ownership, the relation between accumulation and consumption, and the composition of and relation between the means of production and means of subsistence, which developed gradually towards coordination. However, along with the profound reform and development of the economy, some essential readjustments and improvements are still needed in China's economic structure to remove the anomalous features.

The composition of the ownership of the means of production

From the birth of the People's Republic to the late stages of the First Five-Year Plan period, New China made fruitful efforts in the thorough transformation of the structure of feudal and semi-colonialist ownership inherited from old China. Not only were feudal land ownership and bureaucrat capital ownership abolished, but also the wide-scale agricultural individual ownership and individual handicraft industrial ownership were transferred to the collective. The nationalist capitalist industry and commerce were also gradually transferred to ownership by the whole people. This revolutionary transformation of ownership conformed to the law that the relations of production should suit the development of productivity, and enabled China's economy to develop at an unprecedented speed. However, certain problems, such as acting with undue haste and producing an unduly unitary system, were encountered in the course of the socialist transformation of agriculture, handicraft industry and capitalist industry and commerce. During the movement for a Great Leap Forward and for rural people's communes, rural areas throughout the country stirred up a "communist wind", and went blindly in pursuit of "bigger in size and of a more developed socialist nature". Small collectives were impatient to become big collectives, while collective ownership was transformed into ownership by the whole people; as a result, the development of the productive forces was hindered and damaged to a certain degree. During the Cultural Revolution, "Left" errors were spread unchecked, and the "Gang of Four" trumpeted about "poor transition". Attention was paid only to the development of the state-owned economy, while the collective-owned economy was underrated and weakened, the individual economy rejected and abolished, and private plots and country markets eliminated in pursuit of a unitary system. All this damaged the development of productive forces and the interflow between city and country. Since the Third Plenary Session of the Eleventh Central Committee of the CPC, the State has gained the initiative in setting things right and has readjusted its unduly unitary ownership structure by looking closer at economic realities. Household-contracted responsibility for annual output is promoted in rural areas, and at the same time individual economy is permitted and developed appropriately in both urban areas and the countryside. Thanks to the implementation of the policy of opening to the outside world and absorbing foreign funds and technologies, a number of enterprises run by joint venture with foreign enterprises, or by co-operation, as well as wholly foreign owned enterprises have mushroomed. According to statistics, by the end of 1985 enterprises belonging to this type reached some 6,000, with an investment totalling $US 16.08 billion by foreign firms. In addition, a combined economy with various kinds of ownership has gradually evolved in industry, commerce, transport, the building industry and service trades, in both cities and rural areas; ownership by the whole people, collective ownership, private ownership and foreign funds can exist within an enterprise or group of enterprises. During the Sixth Five-Year Plan period, various forms of ownership and diversified businesses emerged in the reform of the economy and may be characterized in the following ways. First, taking public ownership as the dominant factor: ownership by the whole people is the leading factor of a socialist economy, but collective ownership is also an important component, so the development of collective ownership is encouraged. According to statistics, the number of workers and staff in enterprises under collective ownership in cities and towns rose from 24.25 million in 1980 to 33.24 million in 1985. Second, the individual economy in cities and towns is connected with socialist ownership, as opposed to the individual economy connected with capitalist ownership, and this plays an important role in the development of production, facilitating popular prosperity and increasing needs of employment, so that it has become a necessary and useful supplement to the socialist economy and is therefore supported. By the end of 1985 the number of individual producers had reached 4.50 million. Third, since it is also a useful and necessary supplement to China's socialist economy to utilize foreign funds and attract foreign firms to set up joint venture enterprises, co-operative enterprises and wholly foreign owned enterprises, their interests should be protected. Fourth, a new economic form of great future value is that of a flexible and varied combination based on voluntary participation, mutual benefit and common development among enterprises owned by the whole people, the collective and individuals, and the economy with foreign funds – especially lateral economic ties or the economic operation of share capital within an enterprise. Fifth, China will continue to promote its varied forms of ownership and diversified management with the prerequisite of upholding public ownership as the leading factor in order to suit the development of productive forces. Pluralistic structures of ownership will make production relations better suited to the needs of the development of productive forces.

The distribution structure of national income – accumulation and consumption

In the period 1950–85, the national income increased at an average rate of 7.6% a year. However, progress was uneven, sometimes smooth and sometimes slow. Moreover, the distribution structure of the national economy was not coordinated during this period. Serious imbalances were caused three times owing to the excessively high accumulation rate. The initial stage, during the First Five-Year Plan period, was successful, with an average share of accumulation of 24.2%, but the years from 1958 to 1960 caused the first imbalance in the national economy. The average share of accumulation was as high as 39.3% and in 1959 even rose to 43.8%. As a result, an imbalance between consumption and accumulation appeared and the national economy had to be readjusted for the first time so that the accumulation share dropped to 15%

from 1961 to 1962, and went up to 22.7% from 1963–65. From 1970 to 1978, the average share of accumulation in the national income was 33.1%. It was 34.1% in 1971 and 36.5% in 1978, which caused the second and third imbalances in 1970–1973 and in 1978. In 1979 it was still 34.6%. After the second readjustment in 1981, the average share of accumulation dropped to 29.0% from 1981 to 1983, which was well balanced. However, it once again went up to 31.2 and 33.7% owing to the excessive haste, in 1984 and 1985, especially in the fourth quarter of 1984. Only when timely measures were adopted by the Government to control the scale of investment in fixed assets did the share of accumulation come under control. During the Seventh Five-Year Plan period, the share of accumulation will be controlled within 30%. The excessively high accumulation was usually caused by too much investment in fixed assets, especially the large investments in capital construction. For instance, the first imbalance in the national economy was caused by the Great Leap Forward in 1958, when investment in capital construction rose sharply from 14.3 billion yuan in 1957 to 26.9 billion yuan in 1958, and from 49.07 billion yuan in 1959 and 38.87 billion yuan in 1960, which was obviously much too high for a poorly developed country like China. During this period, the proportion of financial revenue accounted for 40.6% of the national income, while that of the expenditure on capital construction made up 55% of the financial expenditures, resulting in an imbalance in the national economy and difficulties in the welfare of masses. In 1962, investments in capital construction had to be cut down to 7.126 billion yuan – a decrease of 21.2% of the figure 9.044 billion yuan in 1953. However, in 1970 the scale of investment in capital construction once again expanded under the slogan of strengthening inland construction, building up the defence industry and doubling the industrial output value. Thus, investment in capital construction rose from 20.1 billion yuan in 1969 to 31.3 billion yuan in 1970 – an increase of 55.6%, and it again went up to 34.1 billion yuan in 1971. Financial revenue from 1970 to 1971 accounted for 35.2% of the national income, while the expenditure on capital construction occupied 44% of the financial expenditures. From then on, both expenditures and accumulation share were still high. Some unrealistic slogans and targets were put forward in the so-called "new great leap forward" which prevailed in 1978, such as attempting to build ten oilfields as large as the Daqing Oilfield and ten iron and steel plants as big as the Anshan Iron and Steel Plant. As a result, investment in capital construction in that year reached as high as 50.1 billion yuan – an increase of 31% over the previous year. And in the same year, the financial revenue accounted for 37.2% of the national income, while expenditure on capital construction occupied 40.7% of total financial expenditures. Due to the unchecked accumulation funds, consumption funds were

squeezed away. Thus, people's living standards did not improve but declined.

It is important to keep these historical lessons in mind. Too high an accumulation share will cause the national economy to become strained and people's living standards to drop, resulting in a vicious circle in the economy. Eventually, the accumulation rate has to be brought down. Therefore the scale of investment in fixed assets should be under control and the accumulation rate should be no more than 30%. If this is achieved, the national economy can be developed continuously, steadily and in a well-balanced way. Of course, as the accumulation funds are controlled, the consumption funds should be prevented from excessive expansion. In 1984 and thereafter, the phenomenon of consumption funds running out of control arose because bonuses were recklessly allocated by some enterprises and the total volume of wages exceeded the growth of productivity. Fortunately, no serious losses were created thanks to the realization of what was happening and its speedy correction. An important economic strategic problem is to handle the ratio between accumulation and consumption cor-

Table 4: Changes in the Ratio Relations Between Accumulation and Consumption in National Income

Year	National income (100 million yuan)	Consumption (100 million yuan)	Accumulation (100 million yuan)	Accumulation rate (%)
1952	607	447	130	21.4
1953	727	559	168	23.1
1954	765	570	195	25.5
1955	807	622	185	22.9
1956	888	671	217	24.4
1957	935	702	233	24.9
1958	1,117	738	379	33.9
1959	1,274	716	558	43.8
1960	1,264	763	501	39.6
1961	1,013	818	195	19.2
1962	948	849	99	10.4
1963	1,047	864	183	17.5
1964	1,184	921	263	22.2
1965	1,347	982	365	27.1
1966	1,535	1,065	470	30.6
1967	1,428	1,124	304	21.3
1968	1,409	1,111	298	21.1
1969	1,537	1,180	357	23.2
1970	1,876	1,258	618	32.9
1971	2,008	1,324	684	34.1
1972	2,052	1,404	648	31.6
1973	2,252	1,511	741	32.9
1974	2,291	1,550	741	32.3
1975	2,451	1,621	830	33.9
1976	2,424	1,676	748	30.9
1977	2,573	1,741	832	32.3
1978	2,975	1,888	1,087	36.5
1979	3,356	2,195	1,161	34.6
1980	3,696	2,531	1,165	31.5
1981	3,905	2,799	1,106	28.3
1982	4,290	3,054	1,236	28.8
1983	4,770	3,358	1,421	29.7
1984	5,661	3,895	1,766	31.2
1985	7,273	4,820	2,453	33.7

Note: This table is calculated in accordance with the year prices.

rectly. Chinese leaders and economists have realized clearly from past experience that disasters will certainly happen in the economy if the scale of investment in fixed assets is too great, if there is excessive expansion of consumption funds, and if the accumulation funds are out of control.

Table 4 (above) shows the distribution structure of national income, by years.

The composition of industries

This refers to the structural relations between the industrial departments of the national economy and in the interior structure of these departments. New China has achieved great successes in the transformation and reconstruction of the backward and extremely haphazard composition of industries left by old China. It has now changed from a backward agricultural country to a fairly advanced agricultural and industrial country. A complete industrial system and national economic system has been gradually established. For instance, in 1936, before Liberation, modern industry accounted for only 10% of the national economy, and in 1949 industry occupied 30% of the total output value of industrial and agricultural production, of which modern industry comprised 17% only. However, in 1985 industry made up 53.7% of the total social output value and 65.7% of the total output value of industry and agriculture, most of which was from modern industry. The ratio between the net industrial output value and agricultural output value was 1:5 in 1949 and 1:1 in 1985. Heavy industry was very weak in old China, accounting for 26.6% in 1949, while it had risen to 53.3% by 1985. Obviously, China has realized its industrialization and laid the foundation of its heavy industry. The change in the proportion of industry and heavy industry is shown in Table 7.

However, the development of agriculture, light industry and tertiary industry was ignored whilst undue emphasis was given to the expansion of heavy industry, leading to their backwardness over a long period. The production of grain was given priority, to the neglect of forestry, animal husbandry, fishery, sideline occupations and rural areas industry. In heavy industry, undue emphasis was for a time put on the development of iron and steel; the processing and manufacturing industries developed unchecked, with little improvement in quality and technology, while at the same time both the energy and mining industries were ignored. As for the national economy, not only were agriculture and light industry ignored, but transport, telecommunications, commerce and service trades were also overlooked. This one-sidedness of the industrial structure caused imbalances in the national economy that required years of readjustment. For instance, in the three years of the Great Leap Forward, agriculture decreased at an annual average rate of 8.2%, while on the other hand heavy industry increased at an average annual rate of 49.4%, resulting in a serious imbalance in the national economy. From 1976 to 1978, heavy industry increased at an average progressive rate of 14.9%, while light industry and agriculture increased at an annual average rate of 12.5% and 5.2%, respectively. Obviously, this is out of all proportion. Meanwhile, the proportion of commercial and transport total output value in the social total output value was 11.6% and 3.7% respectively in 1957; however, it dropped to 5.2% and 2.9% in 1980, being the weak link in the national economy. It is important for China to strengthen its energy industry, transport and telecommunications, commerce and service trades in the readjustment of industrial structures during the 1980s.

Since the readjustment started in the beginning of the 1980s, the industrial structure has been getting

Table 5: Proportions of Industrial and Heavy Industrial Output Value

	1949	1952	1957	1962	1965	1970	1975	1980	1985
Proportion of industrial output value in the total industrial and agricultural output value	30%*	43.1%	56.1%	61.2%	62.7%	66.3%	69.9%	69.2%	65.9%
Ratio between net industrial and agricultural output value	18:100	34:100	60:100	68:100	79:100	97:100	113:100	117:100	100:100
Proportion of total heavy industrial output value in the total industrial output value	26.4%	35.5%	45%	52.8%	48.4%	53.8%	55.9%	52.8%	53.3%

Note: *of which modern industry accounted for 17%.

472

better results. The proportion of agriculture in the total output value of industry and agriculture rose from 27.8% in 1978 to 34.3% in 1985 and that of light industry in the total output value of industry went up from 43.1% in 1978 to 46.7% in 1985. During the Sixth Five-Year Plan period, the annual average growth of agriculture reached 11.7% – not only higher than the annual average increase rate of 3.5% from 1953 to 1980, but also higher than the figure of 4.5% during the First Five-Year Plan period and 5.1% in the Fifth Five-Year Plan period. Such speed has seldom been seen in the history of the development of agriculture in the world. During the Sixth Five-Year Plan period, light industry increased at an average rate of 12% a year, being higher than the figure of 6.6% of heavy industry.

Within the agricultural structure, the proportion of plantation in the total output value of agriculture dropped from 67.8% in 1978 to 49.8% in 1985, whilst the proportions of forestry, animal husbandry, sideline occupations and fishery rose appropriately from 32.2% to 50.2%. In 1985, the proportions of the total output value of industry, building industry, transport and commerce in the total social output value in rural areas reached 42.9%–an increase of 6.4% over the previous year.

Inside heavy industry, the proportion of the total output value of mining rose by 1–2% in 1978. Considerable progress was made in the energy industry: in 1983, the total productive volume of energy reached 712.63 million tons of ideal fuels, being an all-time high, second only to the United States and the Soviet Union, and in 1985 it went up to 855.38 million tons of ideal fuels – an increase of 20% over 1983. Within the composition of energy, the proportion of raw coal dropped from 95% in the 1950s to some 70% in the 1980s, while the proportion of crude oil rose from 1–2% to more than 20%. In addition, the proportion of hydropower and natural gas also increased.

Inside light industry, the proportion taken up by the output value created by the products which take farm produce as their raw materials dropped from 87.5% in 1952 to 67% in 1985, while the proportion of those which take industrial products as their raw materials rose from 12.5% to 33%.

Changes have also taken place in the structure of import and export commodities. In 1985, the total volume of import and export trade reached $69.6 billion. From 1952 to 1985, the proportion of primary products in the total export volume dropped from 83.4% to 50.6% and those of industrial finished products rose from 16.6% to 49.4%. The proportion of primary products in the total import volume dropped from 18.7% to 12.5%, and those of industrial finished products rose from 81.3% to 87.5%.

Such a change of industrial structure is the result of the strategic shift carried out on the economic front since the beginning of the 1980s, and is also a consequence of the readjustment and reform of the economy. Improvements have been made in the situation in which people were in pursuit of output value and speed of development, concentrating on the expansion of heavy industry and plantation in a lopsided view which overlooked the development of agriculture, light industry and tertiary industry. The industrial structure is being straightened out and is developing rationally.

Although considerable achievements have been made, with a good beginning in the readjustment of China's industrial structure, relations within the industrial structure have not been straightened out completely and a number of weak links still exist. During the Seventh Five-Year Plan period, China will continue to keep its overall growth in agriculture; to emphasize the improvement in the internal structures of various circles under the prerequisite of promoting the stable development of light industry; to accelerate the development of the energy and materials industry and to control the growth of ordinary processing industry properly. Top priority will be given to the development of transport and telecommunications. China will devote its major efforts to developing the building industry and accelerating the expansion of tertiary industry so as to open up new products, new production fields and newly emergent industries. By the end of 1990, the proportion of tertiary industry will increase from 21.3% in 1985 to 25.5%. The output value of the consumer goods industry will rise 40% over 1985, the total volume of energy will reach 99.1 billion tons standard coal, the total freight volume will be 9.4 billion tons and the total volume of postal and telecommunications business will register 5.0 billion yuan. By that date, fundamental changes will have taken place in the structure of industry.

Daily Economic Development and Average Economic Level per capita

By the end of 1985, the total volume of China's average daily economic development was much higher than in 1952. For instance, in 1952 China could produce 180,000 tons of raw coal, 1,200 tons of crude oil and 3,700 tons of steel a day, while in 1985, it could produce 2.33 million tons of raw coal, 340,000 tons of crude oil and 130,000 tons of steel a day – or several dozens times and even more than 200 times the 1952 figures respectively. Output of some products ranks first in the world. However, China is a country with a population of more than one billion. Its level of average wealth and products possessed per capita is still low. For instance, the Gross National Product (GNP) per capita was only 748 yuan and the steel output per capita 45 kg.

Table 6: Wealth Created in China in a Day (calculated according to price in the same year)

	1952	1985
Social total output value (100 million yuan)	2.78	44.70
Total output value of industry and agriculture (100 million yuan)	2.22	36.50
Agricultural total output value (100 million yuan)	1.26	12.50
Industrial total output value (100 million yuan)	0.96	24.00
Gross National Product (GNP) (100 million yuan)	–	21.60
National income (100 million yuan)	1.61	18.70
Financial revenue (100 million yuan)	0.50	5.10
Total volume of energy production (10,000 tons)	13.35	34.35
Raw coal (10,000 tons)	18.08	238.9
Crude oil (10,000 tons)	0.12	34.25
Generated energy (100 million kwW)	0.20	11.36
Steel (10,000 tons)	0.37	12.8
Automobiles	0	1198
Cloth (10,000 metres)	1,049.32	4,019
TV sets (10,000 sets)	0	4.57
Of which: Colour TV sets (10,000 sets)	0	1.14
Grain (10,000 tons)	44.9	103.86
Oil-bearing crops (1,0000 tons)	1.15	4.32
Pork, beef and mutton (10,000 tons)	0.93	4.82

Table 7: Daily Consumer Volume

(consumer volume of agricultural and sideline products includes supply volume on markets and the volume of peasant self-produce and self-use; grain here means trade grain, and consumer volume of industrial products means the purchasing volume of residents in the same year)

	1952	1985
Total consumer volume of residents in both urban and rural areas (100 million yuan)	1.19	11.6
Consumer volume per capita (yuan)	0.21	1.1
Grain (10,000 tons)	30.81	72.5
Pork (10,000 tons)	0.92	4.0
Edible vegetable oil (10,000 tons)	0.33	1.5
Daily necessity cloth (10,000 metres)	889.99	3,325
Supply volume of bicycles (sets)	900	85,000
Supply volume of sewing machines (sets)	300	30,000
Supply volume of wrist-watches (retail)	1,100	160,000
Supply volume of washing machines (retail)	–	30,000
Supply volume of TV sets (retail)	–	59,000
Supply volume of refrigerators (retail)	–	6,027.4
Supply volume of tap water for daily life in cities (10,000 tons)	–	1,443
Supply volume of liquefied petroleum gas for daily life in cities (ton)	–	1,685
Supply volume of coal gas for daily life in cities (cubic meter)	–	435

Table 8: Daily Circulating Volume and Service Volume in China

	1952	1985
Turnover volume of goods (100 million tons/kilometre)	2.09	49.6
Of which: Goods turnover volume by railway (100 million tons/kilometre)	1.65	22.26
Total retail volume of social commodities (100 million yuan)	0.76	11.79
Number of passengers transported by various means of transport (10,000 person – time)	67.17	1,553.68
Of which: Passengers transported by railways (10,000 person-time)	44.80	307.15
Total number of passengers transported by bus and trolley bus in cities (10,000 person-time)	–	7,042
Posted letters (10,000 pieces)	221.64	1,281.64
Telegrams (10,000 pieces)	3.30	60.2
Completed residence of workers and staff (square metres of floor space)	3.68[1]	26.2
Published books (10,000 copies)	216.44	1,827.4
Published magazines (10,000 copies)	54.79	761.37
Newspapers published by province-level or above (10,000 copies)	441.10[2]	5,473.97

[1] Figure in 1953.
[2] Including those published by prefectures.

Table 9: Daily Changes in Social Population

	1952	1955
Newly employed population in cities and towns (10000)	–	2.23
Birth population (10,000)	5.77 (40/minute)	5.1 (35/minute)
Deaths	2.65 (18/minute)	1.9 (13/minute)
Married couples (10,000)	–	2.3
Divorced couples	–	1,255

Table 10: Average of Major Economic Targets per capita

	1952	1985
Total social output value per capita (yuan)	178.41	1,568.11
Total output value of industry and agriculture per capita (yuan)	142.38	1,282.26
National income per capita (yuan)	103.53	655.44
GNP per capita (yuan)	–	757.66
Grain output per capita (kg)	288.13	364.52
Cotton output per capita (kg)	2.2	3.99
Output of pork, beef and mutton per capita (kg)	5.95	16.93
Raw coal output per capita (kg)	116.01	838.43
Crude oil output per capita (kg)	0.77	120.09
Generated energy per capita (kWh)	12.83	394.89
Steel output per capita (kg)	2.37	44.99
Cloth output per capita (metre)	6.73	14.11
Savings deposits per inhabitant (yuan)	1.51	156.01

2. THE RESTRUCTURING OF CHINA'S ECONOMIC SYSTEM

AFTER the founding of the People's Republic of China in 1949, the country went through a democratic reform which changed fundamentally the semi-feudal, semi-colonial economic system of old China. During the First Five-Year Plan period (1953–1957), the initial centralized and unified economic system of socialism took shape. Later, several changes were made in the economic system during the Great Leap Forward period (1958–1960), the Economic Readjustment period (1961–1965) and the Cultural Revolution period (1966–1976). However, the economy never really broke with the old pattern, which was carried out through the administration.

In December 1978 the Third Plenary Session of the Eleventh Central Committee of the Communist Party of China was held, and this raised the curtain on the reform of China's economic structure. Within the past few years the reform has achieved great things, attracting worldwide attention.

Spreading the Reform from Country to Town

Since 1978, China has concentrated its efforts on remedying the disproportion in the national economy, from which it suffered serious dislocation. The economic restructuring started first in the countryside and scored great achievements in a very short time. China adopted a series of policies and measures designed to enable farmers to recuperate and diversify and to encourage them to develop production in various forms. These include increasing the purchase prices of agricultural products and by-products by a big margin, and rehabilitating family plots, household sideline production and country fair trade, in order to lighten the farmers' burden. In carrying out these policies and measures and satisfying the farmers' strongly expressed wishes, a production responsibility system of agriculture in various forms has been established in vast rural areas, with the household-contracted responsibility system as the main element. The responsibility system has related farmer's earnings to their working results, motivated them toward greater production and raised their efficiency. On the basis of this development in the rural economy, part of the sideline production has begun to separate off from agriculture, and many farmer households engaged in specialized production have thus appeared. With the development of agricultural production according to the principles of voluntary participation and mutual benefit, farmers have organized various economic entities, such as seed companies, foodstuffs companies, agricultural machinery services and promotion centres for the new technology. Township enterprises engaged both in processing agricultural products and by-products and in serving agricultural production have also emerged. Therefore China's traditional economy of self-support and semi-self-support in rural areas has begun to disintegrate, while the rural economy is moving towards specialization, large-scale commodity production and modernization. A state of prosperity and continuous increase of production has prevailed in the rural areas. The output of grain, cotton, oil bearing crops and other farm produce has doubled and redoubled. Chinese farmers, who lived in poverty for hundreds of years, have become prosperous in a very short time.

With regard to restructuring the urban economy, which involves a wider range of issues and is more complicated than the rural economy and provides most of the state revenues, a more prudent and safer policy is followed. The urban reform begins with the expansion of the decision-making powers of enterprises, which leads and promotes the reform in other fields. This is a great change from past practices of periodically delegating managerial powers to enterprises. In 1978, Sichuan province made the first experiments in providing some industrial enterprises with added decision-making power. In May 1979 the State designated the Capital Iron and Steel Complex in Beijing, the Shanghai Diesel Engine Plant, the Tianjin Bicycle Factory and five other enterprises experimental units. By 1980, the number of experimental enterprises in China had increased to 6,600. At the very beginning, these experimental enterprises put into practice the system of retaining a portion of the profits. In the meantime, they were given some rights in production planning, product marketing, use of funds, appointment and dismissal of cadres, employment of workers and staff, and the handing out of rewards and penalties to them. Since the end of 1982 these experiments – in which profits may be replaced by taxes, and both taxation and profit sharing are provided – have been made in over 450 state-owned enterprises. This taxation system, comprehensively implemented in October 1984, helps to correct the economic relationship between the State and enterprises. At the same time, in order to find a way to improve the economic relationship between workers and staff and the enterprises in which they work, the economic responsibility system with contracted jobs as the main element combining responsibility, authority and benefit is implemented inside these enterprises. That is to say, the economic responsibility undertaken by enterprises toward the State and society or the norms set by the State is to be fulfilled at the different levels of workshops, groups and individuals. A system of personal responsibility has also been established. The economic interests of enterprises are made closely linked to the improved performance of the enterprise and the working results of workers and staff. The principle of rewarding the diligent and good and punishing the lazy and bad, and of giving more pay for more work, is applied fully. The system of piece rate wages and rewards is restored. Thus, when the two types of relationships are handled satisfactorily – the relationship between the State and enterprises and the relationship between enterprises and their workers and staff – renewed vitality appears within the enterprises.

In accordance with the need to reinvigorate enterprises and the economy, and together with the reorganization of enterprises, a system in which the director or manager assumes full responsibility is gradually being put into practice. While the director assumes full responsibility, the system of congresses of workers and staff members and other mechanisms of democratic management must be improved within enterprises. Outside enterprises, with the readjustment of the system of production, enterprises should develop various forms of economic and technological partnership and co-operation transcending trades and regions. Various forms of ownership and management will also be established. Experiments in reform are also being made to varying degrees in such other economic systems as those of circulation, planning, finance, prices, monetary matters, wages, science and technology, and education. In order to probe a way toward economic reform in cities and give a full role to cities as centres, a number of big and medium-sized cities and towns have been chosen as experimental points for comprehensive reform. Great efforts have been made in building up open economic networks of different sizes with big and medium-sized cities and towns as their backing. Such urban reform has been repeatedly explored and tested, so that economic life has been invigorated to an extent unknown for many years. It has also laid the basis for further development of overall urban reform.

Working Out the General Programme for Overall Urban Reform

1984 was the year when the emphasis in economic affairs was shifted from readjustment to reform. The stress of the economic restructuring also began to shift from country to town.

Urban reform has yielded marked results in recent years. However, a number of restrictions are still imposed on it, and the reform measures are only local and not sufficiently thorough. Defects in the present urban economic structure that seriously hinder the expansion of the production forces have yet to be eradicated. Enterprises are still short of vitality. All this has produced sharp contradictions within the economic situation as a whole.

Incompatibility with the demands of the growing rural economy

With the overall growth of the rural economy, the commodity rate of farm produce has increased greatly. The income of farmers has doubled and redoubled. In the past, farmers strove only to have enough to eat and to clothe themselves. Now they are beginning to buy high- and medium-grade goods and to build new houses. Township enterprises and multiple undertakings have been developed. Outdated production equipment and traditional ways of ploughing have gradually been replaced by advanced equipment and modern techniques. All this has placed more and higher demands on the cities, including the urgent need to unclog the channels of distribution between town and country; to expand storage, processing, transport and market outlets for agricultural products and by-products; to provide more and better manufactured goods and varied means of production and to provide funds, technology, personnel and information. The former systems of production and distribution in cities cannot suit the needs of the new situation, since they were formed under circumstances when the commodity exchange between town and country and other economic ties were not very well developed.

Inhibition of further growth of the urban economy

China's cities exert a decisive influence on the whole national economy. As at 1985, about 82.4% of the fixed assets of independently accounting industrial enterprises, 77% of the total number of workers and staff, and 87.3% of the total industrial output value were concentrated in the cities, and over 90% of state revenues came from tax and profit delivered by the cities. Cities are the economic, political, scientific, technological, cultural and educational centres where

China's production forces develop, and they provide the State with its main source of revenue. But since the economic structure of cities is seriously irrational, the enthusiasm, initiative and creativeness of enterprises and their workers and staff members have, as a result, been seriously dampened and the huge potential of China's urban economy is far from being fully tapped. The economic effectiveness of urban enterprises in production, construction and circulation is still very low.

Unsuitability for further opening to the outside world

The adoption of the policy of opening to the outside world represents a great change in the direction of China's economic construction. To accelerate the progress of modernization, China has an urgent need to develop its import and export trade and to import foreign investment and advanced technology. Cities are the gateway to the foreign world. China's cities, in particular, are mostly located in the coastal areas on key water and land communication lines. The urban economic structure and administrative systems must be made advantageous to developing the import and export trade; to absorbing foreign investment, advanced technology and experience of management; to developing various forms of Sino-foreign economic entities and enterprises exclusively owned by foreigners; to co-operation with foreign centres of economy, technology and culture, as well as friendly contacts between peoples. But China's original highly-centralized systems bound the feet of enterprises and cities. The system of foreign trade, in particular, did not suit the changes in international markets, where the supply of commodities surpassed demand and competition was very fierce.

Inability to give impetus to science and technology and to catch up with the technological revolution

Under the present economic structure, science and technology are not closely connected with production and construction. Enterprises lack the decision-making powers, material conditions and economic motives which could bring about a great advance in technology. Various systems of management impose heavy restrictions on enterprises: they need to renew their equipment, to improve technology and to develop new products; they have no source of funds, no source of raw materials, no channels for selling their products and cannot get preferential treatment in prices and taxes. If such an economic structure does not undergo a fundamental change, enterprises will find it hard to conduct production on the basis of advanced technology, and the gap between China and developed countries in the economy and in technology will become bigger and bigger.

Because of all this, it is now an extremely urgent task for China to shift the stress of the reform from country to town and to accelerate the economic restructuring with the emphasis on cities.

The Third Plenary Session of the Twelfth Central Committee of the Chinese Communist Party held in October 1984 analyzed the current economic and political situation in China, summed up the experience, both positive and negative, in socialist construction, particularly that of reform of the economic structure in the urban and rural areas over the past few years, and decided "to go a step further with the policy of invigorating the domestic economy and opening to the outside world, and to accelerate restructuring of the national economy as a whole, with the focus on the urban economy, so as to create a new, better situation for China's socialist modernization." The session adopted the *Decision of the Central Committee of the Communist Party of China on the Reform of the Economic Structure.* The decision, a programmatic document to China's economic restructuring, expounds the theoretical basis of China's economic restructuring, points out the basic direction of the reform, and sets the nature, aims, tasks and basic orientation. The session drew up a strategic plan for the reform: China's economic restructuring – with the focus on cities – thus began in a comprehensive way. In 1985 alone the readjustment in prices, wages and the organization of agricultural production was achieved.

The Profound Change in Economic Structure Brought About by Reform

Reviewing the seven years from 1979 to 1985, China's economic restructuring has changed the way of delineating the limits of authority between the Central Committee and local areas. The restructuring seized hold of the central issue, which will strengthen the vitality of economic units. The economic restructuring spread out from country to town, gradually moving from extending the decision-making powers of grassroot units to transforming the upper institutions of administration; from production to circulation and distribution; and from micro-economy to macro-economy. The reform has broken down the conventions which bound people's minds for so long, as well as the irrational patterns of management. It has surpassed any reform on the historical record, both in depth and in width.

After the economic restructuring in the past seven years, profound changes have taken place above all in the following fields:

– *In the system of ownership*: In the past seven years, China has broken from top to bottom with "Left"

477

ideas and the unitary system of the public ownership, especially the system of the ownership of the means of production by the whole people, correcting the mistaken ideas that the higher the level of socialization, the more advanced, and the larger the scope of management, the better, and correcting also the mistaken practices of discriminating against, squeezing out and cracking down on collective and individual economies. On condition that the economy owned by the whole people must take the lead, a policy of guidance, encouragement and protection is adopted to stimulate active development of the collective economy in town and country, to develop the individual economy appropriately, and to encourage – within certain limits – the establishment of Sino-foreign joint ventures, jointly-operated enterprises and enterprises owned exclusively by foreigners. In order to enliven the economy, China is also expanding its horizontal ties and, in line with local conditions, promoting diversified economic entities jointly operated by the units of different systems of ownership. Statistics show that of the gross industrial output value, the collective economy accounted for 19% in 1979 and had risen to 27.7% in 1985. The system of individual ownership grew out of nothing: it made up 0.4% in 1985. Other types of industry (including co-operative ventures) between ownership by the whole people and collective ownership, between ownership by the whole people and individuals, and between collectives and individuals, Sino-foreign co-operative ventures, operations by overseas Chinese and commercialists and industrialists from Hong Kong and Macao, and industry exclusively owned by foreign investors also grew out of nothing. In 1985, they accounted for 1.4% of the gross industrial output value. Among labourers in both town and country, workers and staff members from enterprises owned by collectives were 22.74 million in 1979 and 32.24 million in 1985; individual labourers rose from 0.32 million to 4.50 million. The proportion of workers and staff from enterprises with collective ownership, and individual labourers in the gross labour force rose from 23.1% to 29.4%. By the end of 1985, Sino-foreign joint ventures had reached over 2,343; jointly-operated enterprises over 3,822; and the enterprises exclusively owned by foreigners over 121. Most of the workers and staff members from collective enterprises newly established in recent years and individual labourers are engaged in tertiary industry. Of the total turnover from the retail trade, the proportion of collective ownership rose from 7.4% at the end of 1978 to 37.2% at the end of 1985. The individual economy and the turnover to non-agricultural residents by farmers accounted for 2.1% at the end of 1978 and had risen to 22.1% by the end of 1985. It is thus clear that China's system of ownership is changing gradually from the basic unitary public ownership to a common development of many and varied forms of ownerships, with the socialist public ownership as the key factor.

At the same time, the economy of public ownership itself is also being constantly improved and perfected. In the light of the different conditions in various enterprises, a system containing several forms of management is adopted in order to benefit the development of production. A diversified economy centring on the system of contracted household responsibility is put into comprehensive practice in rural areas. Enterprises with collective ownership have gradually resumed their original characteristics, including independent accounting, assuming sole responsibility for profits and losses, and democratic administration. A form of stock company is also adopted. Supplying and selling co-operatives in rural areas have also resumed the original nature of collective ownership. In enterprises with ownership by the whole people, apart from expanding their decision-making powers and implementing various forms of the economic responsibility system, several kinds of management – such as the contracted system, transfer and leasing to the collective or individuals – are also conducted in small commercial and industrial units, and some of them change over to collective ownership. In enterprises of the building trade, a system of investment and payment partly in kind and partly in cash and a contracted system of inviting tenders are carried out. The contracted responsibility system is also implemented within the building trade, and the State has applied the overall responsibility system for outputs to the oil and coal industries. As the decision-making power of enterprises owned by the whole people is expanded and with the separation of ownership from the right of management, more and more experiments in reform are being made in the management of enterprises.

China's reform of the structure of ownership and the diversity of management have made production relations much more suited to the development of the production forces, playing a key part in invigorating China's national economy in recent years.

– *In the decision-making powers of economic units*: There were several major defects in the original economic structure in China: Economic units at the grass roots level were not acknowledged as producers and managers of socialist commodity production; and the State exercised excessive and rigid control over these units, so that enterprises lost their proper rights and economic interests. Taking this as the key link, the reform started with simplification of the administration and expansion of decision-making powers, as well as breaking absolute egalitarianism in distribution in order to enliven the economy of the grass roots units and promote reform of the administrative structure in every field.

A system of contracted household responsibility by which remuneration is linked to output has been introduced in rural areas. The state monopoly for the purchase and marketing of agricultural products has been done away with, while a system of fixed quotas for purchasing has been implemented. All this aims to expand the decision-making powers of farmers in production and management.

The economic restructuring in cities also started with the expansion of the decision-making power of enterprises. Since 1979, the State Council has issued some ten successive documents about the reform of enterprises, which have clearly stipulated the responsibility, authority and benefits, so that the decision-making power of enterprises in production and management has been notably expanded. In respect of planning, on condition that the mandatory tasks allocated by the State are fulfilled, enterprises are allowed to plan their own production according to supply and demand in the markets. A diversified economy with one trade as the basis can also be carried out. In respect of purchase and sale, enterprises have the right to purchase equipment and raw materials in the market place, sell their own products excluded from the plan of purchase and, within certain limits, to negotiate prices with purchasers or to fix the prices themselves. In respect of applying funds, the portion of profits retained by enterprises has been increasing year by year; enterprises are allowed to use the fund for developing production as a depreciation fund or for heavy repair in general, and they may also issue bonds to raise funds by themselves. In respect of personnel affairs, persons in charge of enterprises are chosen and appointed by way of examination and interview, democratic election, invitation of applications for jobs and self-recommendation. Enterprises can appoint and dismiss middle-level cadres independently without having the approval of higher authorities; they can admit workers and staff members through examinations of their own; some small enterprises owned by the whole people can choose their proper way of management on the basis of actual conditions. Special measures for decreasing regulation tax and increasing the depreciation rate of fixed assets can be adopted in large and medium-sized enterprises to lighten the social burden and strengthen their vitality. The reform in the past few years has changed the role of enterprises from subsidiary bodies of administrative departments to relatively independent managers of commodity production. Some of them have become enterprises of both production and management, or enterprises of management and expansion.

In addition to the measures adopted to expand their decision-making powers, the vitality of enterprises is also strengthened in two other aspects. One is to regulate the proportions of the relations of distribution between the State and enterprises and to do away with the method of unified purchase and unified payment by the State to enterprises owned by the whole people, regardless of cost, profit and loss. Through successive trial implementations of an enter-prise fund system, a system of retaining a portion of profits and a responsibility system for profit and loss, the general replacement of profit delivery by taxes has finally been decided on as the basic form for dealing with the relations of distribution between the State and enterprises; in this, enterprises do not have to turn over profits to the State after they have paid their taxes according to law. The system ensures both the stable growth of state revenues and the continuous increase of the profits retained by enterprises. In 1980, the profits retained by independently accounting industrial enterprises made up only 9.2% of the total profits, excluding the taxes paid to the State. By 1985, the proportion increased to 31.6%. Another feature is to apportion the relations of distribution within an enterprise and to break the egalitarianism in distribution among workers and staff. Enterprises decide on the amount of wages and bonuses for their workers and staff members according to the performance of enterprises and the contribution of workers and staff to it. They apply the principle of distribution according to work, giving more pay for more work, rewarding the diligent and good, and punishing the lazy and bad. For instance, in 15% of large and medium-sized enterprises, experiments are made to establish wage levels by relating the total wages of workers and staff to the taxes and profits turned over to the State. In coal-mines, workers are paid according to tons of coal they are responsible for; in building enterprises, workers are paid according to the output value they produce. The State controls the situation only by collecting an appropriate amount of tax on the above-norm bonus from them. Piece rate wages can be adopted in enterprises or in posts where conditions permit.

With the extension of the decision-making power of economic units at the grass roots level and the break with egalitarianism in distribution, great changes have taken place in China's enterprises. They no longer ask for instructions from higher authorities for everything they do; they are no longer ignorant about markets; and are no longer unconcerned about finding a good market for their own products and about their profit and loss. They have begun to pay close attention to market demands, involved themselves in finding markets for their own products and cultivated the sense of management, sense of markets, the sense of competition and the sense of profit and loss that a manager of socialist commodity production should have. As a result, the economic efficiency of enterprises has been universally increased.

– *In the system of markets:* China formerly had only a highly-centralized economic system, excluding the use of markets: it did not have a financial market, a technological market or a labour market, and even the commodity market was incomplete and underdeveloped. Under such circumstances social and economic life became unavoidably rigid. The reform of the past few years has made China's leaders more and more aware that if importance was given to commodity production alone, disregarding reform in circulation, or if attention was paid only to the extension of the decision-making powers of enterprises and to the breakdown of egalitarianism in distribution, while overlooking the establishment of a complete and open socialist market system containing all kinds of essential factors of production, then all that had been said about intentions to invigorate enterprises, to bring the market into full play and to establish an economic system full of vitality would be only empty talk. Therefore, a multiple reform, with many aspects, is being carried out in order to establish and perfect the marketing of socialist commodities: various forms of economy are being developed in order to break the monopoly of having only one economic form. The collective and individual commerce, catering trade and service trade are being fostered particularly, and the country fair trade has come into bloom, so that an initial improvement in the structure of commerce has been achieved. The socialist commerce has changed from one market, one channel of distribution and one economy monopolized by the State, to diversified economy with the state-owned economy in the lead and with various ways of management and many channels of distribution.

The varieties and amount of commodities under the direct control of the state plan will gradually be reduced so as to expand the regulation of markets. In 1979, 188 commodities were listed in the plan of the Ministry of Commerce: they were reduced to 23 in 1985. The variety of means of production allocated by the State was 256 in 1980 and reduced to 23 in 1985, of which the proportion allocated by the State also decreased notably. The proportion of steel dropped from about 60% to 55.4%; of timber, from about 80% to 35.2%; of coal, from 53.7% to 47.3%; and of cement, from 33.9% to 19%. Machinery and motor-driven products except automobiles, conductors and boilers for industrial use can be freely purchased or sold.

The state monopoly on purchase and marketing of manufactured goods for daily use, the state monopoly on purchase, and the purchase of agricultural products and by-products assigned by the State will be abolished step by step. Ties between the administrative regions and systems of ownership will be broken and various flexible ways of purchasing and marketing will be applied, including planned purchase, ordered purchase, chosen purchase, selling on a commission basis, self-sale and long-distance transportation and sale by collective units or individuals.

State-owned commerce and supply and marketing co-operatives are still the mainstay of commerce, but trade warehouses, wholesale markets, farm free markets, jointly-operated shops and united enterprises of agriculture, industry and commerce have recently emerged. Various forms of trade centres, in particular, have been established in cities and in collecting and distributing centres for agricultural products and by-products. Sale is conducted without considering objective laws, geographical localities or whether it is public or private. Anyone interested in wholesale or retail can go to trade centres to buy and sell freely, provided they have business licences or have completed other legal formalities.

Industrial means of production may now circulate as commodities. By the end of 1984 nearly 700 means of production service corporations and more than 320 means of production trade centres were open in China. Many enterprises set up their own sales departments, selling their own means of production. There are a few goods which are distributed by the State and cannot be exchanged between enterprises and regions until after the enterprises have completed the quotas the State assigns them. Goods which were formerly supplied according to the state plan are now supplied in more flexible ways: some are supplied to everyone who wants them; some to those who need them badly; some to those who have the coupons for them; some to those who need them to form a complete set of equipment.

A new system has been adopted to break the barriers between cities and the countryside. In the past the cities and the countryside did not have any contact: in the cities, commodities were supplied by state-run shops, and in the countryside they were sold by supply and marketing co-operatives. Now state-run commerce can go to the countryside and supply and marketing co-operatives, and peasants can go to the cities and open shops to sell their products. The wholesale system of commerce has also been changed, and national wholesale departments and provincial wholesale departments have merged into wholesale corporations in cities.

To establish a complete socialist commodity market and make the most of the law of values, China has done a lot in the area of price reform, which is considered one of the most important issues in the reform of the economic system. In the first place, she reformed the price system, which reflected neither value nor the relation of supply and demand. The prices of some commodities are no longer fixed by the State: some have been raised and others lowered.

– Since 1979 there have been several raises in the purchase prices of farm and sideline produce, livestock products, aquatic products and forest products, and adjustments in the price parities between them. Purchase prices in 1984 were 17.5% higher than in 1980. In urban areas the prices of grain and edible oil remained unchanged; in the countryside the price of grain was raised so that it was the same as its purchase price.

– In 1985 the prices of meat, egg, aquatic products and vegetables were no longer fixed by the State, but the State gave every urban resident a subsidy. This is the most difficult step in the price reform, but the results are satisfactory. The output of these non-staple foods has increased and the State's subsidies on them have been reduced. Although the retail price index in 1985 rose by 8.8%, it was lower than the rate of increase in the incomes of urban and rural residents. Markets remained stable and prosperous.

– Since peasants' income increased considerably, the State changed its low-price policy for agricultural means of production, but the price increase is not as big as that for non-staple foods and hardly affects the peasants' income. It accelerated the production of means of production for agriculture.

– In 1982 the State no longer fixed the price of coal produced in small coal mines run by villages and towns. After they had completed their quotas, state-run coal mines could sell the extra coal at a higher price. The State regulated regional price differences of coal, and price differences between different qualities of coal. The price of a ton of coal rose from 22 yuan in 1982 to 31 yuan in 1985. These measures accelerated coal production.

– In 1985 the State loosened its grip on prices of heavy industry means of production which were not included in its production plan. This accelerated the production of those products, reduced their reselling and raised the prices of fuel and raw materials, which had been comparatively low.

– The State raised the fares of railway transport and water transport. In 1985 the State again raised the price of short distance railway transport to ease the heavy burden on it.

– In order to give enterprises an incentive to improve the quality of their products, the State used floating prices for some products in machine, electronics, chemistry, metallurgy and building materials industries. For some durables, good quality products command higher prices, while poor quality products fetch lower prices. These measures have improved China's unreasonable price system to a certain extent. Second, to reform the over-centralized price-management system, China gradually reduced the scope of the State's unified prices and gave local authorities and enterprises more power to decide prices. In 1980 the prices of 113 agricultural and sideline products were decided by the State, but the figure has now dropped to twenty-five. Even the twenty-five products can be sold at negotiated prices after their producers have finished the tasks stipulated in their contract with the State. In 1982 the prices of 85 manufactured goods for daily use (accounting for 75% of sales) were decided by the State, but the figure has now dropped to 37 (accounting for 30% of sales). The prices of almost all small commodities are no longer controlled by the State. The means of production controlled and distributed by the State are still sold at planned prices, but the means of production at the disposal of enterprises and the extra after completion of the state production plan can be sold at floating prices, negotiated prices or free prices. China's policy is to gradually reduce the proportion of prices planned by the State and to increase the proportion of market prices, so that the gap between planned prices and market prices will become narrower and finally be unified at a reasonable level. Prices which are under the guidance of the plan are subject to change according to the relation of supply and demand. China's price reform is proceeding steadily.

On the whole, after the reforms of the past few years China's socialist market system is taking shape. The market for means of subsistence (including agricultural and sideline products and manufactured goods for daily use) has been established and is going well. The market for means of production is beginning to enlarge, but the proportion of means of production that goes into the market is comparatively small. Markets for technology and finance are in a period of experiment. The market for labour (to stimulate reasonable mobility of the labour force, within certain limits) is budding. Adjusting the function of the law of values to China's production and demand is becoming more and more important.

Economic Co-operative Ventures at Home and Abroad

The development of a commodity economy requires breaking down the barriers between regions and countries and turning the closed economy into an open economy. Therefore, the policy of opening to the outside world will be China's fundamental long-term policy. China is actively developing economic co-operation and technological exchanges with foreign countries. At the same time different regions in China are now open to each other to stimulate economic co-operation between regions and enterprises. The opening policy is an important part in the reform of China's economic system.

In opening to the outside world, China has switched from the backwardness of closing its doors to a forward-looking policy of making good use of international exchanges on the basis of self reliance. It has developed economic and trade relations with over 170 countries and regions, and the number of countries and regions that have friendly exchanges of visits with China is even greater. In 1980, special policies and flexible measures were adopted in Guangdong and Fujian provinces to develop economic relations with foreign countries, and special economic zones were established in Shenzhen, Zhuhai, Shantou (Guangdong province) and Xiamen (Fujian province). In 1984, the 13 coastal cities of Dalian, Qinhuangdao, Tianjin, Yantai, Qingdao, Lianyungang, Nantong, Shanghai, Ningbo, Wenzhou, Fuzhou, Guangzhou, Zhanjiang, Beihai as well as Hainan Island were opened up, and some of the policies used in special economic zones were applied also to them. In 1985 the Government opened three triangular zones: the

Yangtze river delta, the Zhujiang (Pearl River) delta, and a triangular area in southern Fujian. Now, the population in the open areas exceeds 100 million and the gross value of their industrial output accounts for more than half the gross value of China's industrial output. Attempts have been made to reform the system of foreign trade, which is no longer managed by foreign trade departments alone. Local governments and enterprises have been given more power to trade with foreign countries. A number of local and specialized import and export trade corporations were established and a few very big enterprises are allowed to do business with foreign countries directly. Foreign currency earned from export is shared between the State and the producer. According to the principle of independence, equality and mutual benefit, China has formulated about 200 laws and regulations on foreign trade. Steps have been taken to improve the environment for the investment of foreign capital and to bring in foreign capital in various forms. By the end of 1985 foreign capital used by China came to more than $38 billion, including loans, investment by foreign merchants and compensation trade. There has been a breakthrough in bringing in advanced technologies: by the end of 1985 China had brought in more than 14,000 technologies, many of which represented the international level of the end of the 1970s and the beginning of the 1980s. Some of them are key equipment. China's volume of export rose from 28th place in the world in 1980 to 16th place in 1985. China will continue the policy of opening to the outside world, quicken the reform of the foreign trade system in order to use more foreign investment, introduce advanced technology, and increase exports to suit the needs of modernization.

In the past, China's economy was controlled by a vertical, closed administrative system which inhibited the lateral economic ties the commodity economy required. Now things are different: many places have broken the barriers between different departments, districts, trades and systems of ownership and developed economic and technological co-operation and exchange with each other. According to incomplete statistics, by the end of 1985, co-operative ventures between different districts and departments had exceeded 50,000 items. They included the exchange of commodities, funds, technology and personnel. Some were one-off operations, some short-term and some long-term. They took the form of materials exchange, compensation trade or technological guidance. In some cases integrated complexes were established with large and medium-sized enterprises as the backbone, producing famous brand name and good-quality products which accorded with the demands of specialized production; therefore they have great prospects. The advantages of lateral economic co-operation are that the exploitation of resources, the utilization of funds and the disposition of productive forces are rational. Profits are higher. They can make

the structure of enterprises more rational and raise the level of technology and management.

In recent years, in order to bring into full play the economic function of large and medium cities, China has made a comprehensive experiment with reform of the economic system in 61 cities, including Chongqing, Changzhou, Shashi and Wuhan, aiming to give more power and responsibility to cities which will act as intermediaries between the State and enterprises in organizing and managing the economy, so as to break down the barriers between different departments and regions, between cities and countryside and between different systems of ownership; to organize the economic activities of enterprises rationally; to promote the economic and social development of the towns and neighbouring countryside; to form an open economic network with large and middle cities as bases, according to economic law. At present, it is planned to organize the following economic zones: the Yangtze River Delta economic zone (with Shanghai as the centre, including Shanghai, Suzhou, Hangzhou, Ningbo, Wuxi, Changzhou, Nantong, Shaoxing, Jiaxing, Huzhou and the neighbouring towns and countryside); the Shanxi economic zone (including Shanxi, the western part of Inner Mongolia, northern Shaanxi and western Henan); the North-East economic zone (with Shenyang as the centre, including Liaoning, Jilin, Helongjiang and the four eastern leagues of Inner Mongolia); the Zhujiang (Pearl River) delta economic zone (including Guangzhou, Foshan, Jiangmen, Shenzhen, Zhuhai and the neighbouring towns and countryside); and a Southern Fujian economic zone, a Beijing–Tianjin–Tangshan economic zone, a Xinjiang economic zone, a Xi'an economic zone and a Wuhan economic zone are under consideration. The establishing and development of these economic zones will play an important role in the development of China's economy. In order to give free rein to the function of cities, China has also carried out the reform of designating cities to lead counties. By the end of 1985, 129 large and middle cities had put into practice the new system under which 571 counties were controlled by 129 cities.

Macro-Economic Management

In China in the past the State organized and managed the economy by directly issuing administrative decrees and fixing mandatory production targets. This reduced the enthusiasm of enterprises and labourers. In recent years various reforms have been introduced, with the following aims:

– *Separate the responsibilities and functions of government and those of enterprises.* In principle, governments at every level do not directly control enterprises. With the exception of a few enterprises which must be controlled by an economic department of the Government, all enterprises will gradually be controlled by cities. Departments will only exercise trade management over enterprises. The major functions of departments are: to formulate the strategy, plan and policy of development, formulate a plan for resource exploitation, technology transformation and intelligence exploitation; coordinate relations between regions, departments and enterprises; plan priority construction; formulate economic laws and supervise their implementation; employ economic regulating measures to control foreign economic and technological activities; appoint and remove cadres, etc. Cities do not interfere in enterprises' production, supply and marketing except to plan, coordinate, serve and supervise economic activities. Enterprises must register with cities, pay taxes and accept supervision from cities. The Ministry of the Engineering Industry and the Ministry of the Electronics Industry were ahead of other ministries in delegating enterprises to cities; almost all enterprises belonging to the two ministries have been delegated. Other ministries are doing the same.

– *Reorganize enterprises and manage them through economic organizations.* When the national economy was readjusted according to the principle of co-operation among specialized departments, some regions and departments established a host of specialized corporations, general factories and integrated complexes. They can be roughly divided into the following types: first, enterprises producing the same products and with familiar techniques were organized and coordination was carried out among specialized departments; second, in order to make comprehensive use of resources, enterprises concerned were organized into a joint corporation under unified leadership, management and accounting; third, co-operation between a region's techniques and technology at its base; fourth, co-operation in funds, labour forces, equipment and technology; fifth, industrial enterprises co-operating with enterprises of commerce, material and foreign trade in business; sixth, co-operation in designing, construction, supplying of set equipment, transporting, importing and exporting. The reform has played an effective role in making the industrial structure more rational, in raising the extent of comprehensive use of resources and in raising economic efficiency.

– *Improve planned management, reduce the scope of mandatory planning.* In 1984 the State Council issued "temporary stipulations on improving the planning system", which reduced the number of industrial products that must be produced according to the National Planning Commission's mandatory planning from 123 kinds in 1980 to 60, down from 40% of the total industrial output value to 20%. The minimal investment for a construction project which must be approved by the National Planning Commission was raised from 10 million yuan to 30 million yuan. The stipulations also said that only Central Government, ministries, provinces, autonomous regions and muni-

cipalities directly under the Central Government have the power to issue mandatory planning. Simultaneously they increased the scope of guidance planning and market regulation.

– *Reform the fiscal and taxation systems.* In order to gradually reform the old fiscal management system of unified revenue and unified expenditure, in 1980 China adopted the measure of "dividing revenue and expenditure, every level being responsible for its own", in order to make local governments increase revenue and economize on expenditure. In 1985, as profits were substituted by taxes, China decided to adopt a new fiscal system of "dividing tax categories and checking revenue and expenditure, with every level being responsible", so as to arouse the enthusiasm of local government and ensure a steady rise in central revenue as well. China's old taxation system was far from perfect. Since there was only a single tax category, it was almost impossible for taxes to play the regulatory role as an economic lever. In recent years, China has taken several measures to increase tax categories, readjust tax rates and achieve a balance between revenue and expenditure. By 1985, state-owned enterprises had to pay the following taxes: income tax, product tax, value-added tax, salt tax, business tax, resource tax, house property tax, land tax, tax for using cars and ships, city construction tax and bonus tax. There were also tax categories for collective enterprises, private enterprises and individuals. To suit the development of foreign trade and the economy, the State issued an *Income Tax Law Concerning Chinese–Foreign Joint Ventures*, an *Individual Income Tax Law* and an *Income Tax Law Concerning Foreign Enterprises*. These reforms strengthened its indirect control over the macro-economy.

– *Reform the bank system.* The old bank system was highly centralized: such economic levers as credit, settling accounts and interest rates were inhibited from playing their roles. Recent reforms have established a bank system in which the functions of government and enterprises are separated. It is a system with the People's Bank of China at the head and with the four specialized banks (the Industrial and Commercial Bank of China, the Agricultural Bank of China, the Bank of China and the People's Construction Bank of China) as the mainstay, and with other monetary organizations (including insurance companies, credit co-operatives, investment companies, trust companies, lease companies, etc.) as subsidiary organizations. The People's Bank of China is the central bank which issues money. It is the State's institution for controlling the monetary business of China. It has no direct relation with enterprises. It is responsible for macro-planning, distributes credit funds, regulates the circulation of money and promotes the rational development of the national economy. The Bank of China is the only foreign exchange bank designated by the State. It raises foreign exchange through various channels, on liberal terms, to support domestic economic construction. At present, its foreign exchange is used mainly on new projects of energy and transport, and on middle and small-sized enterprises with short-term technological transformation projects which will bring in foreign exchange. Second, in the past only circulating credit was extended; now fixed credit is extended, too. According to the stipulation by the State, bank loans instead of financial allocation will be provided to those fixed assets investment projects which are able to pay them back. All the circulating funds of newly built, state-owned enterprises come from bank loans. This reform can make enterprises use the money more carefully, improve their business management and focus attention on the efficiency of investment. Third, interest rates are allowed to play a regulatory role. In the past, interest rates had few grades and there was not much difference between them. Moreover, interest rates remained unchanged for a long time. From 1979 to 1985 China raised the interest rates of deposit four times and readjusted the interest rate of bank loans twice. Within certain limits, a differential interest rate, a floating interest rate and interest-deducted loans were used. This played an important role in speeding the circulation of the funds of enterprises and in developing the national economy proportionately. Fourth, in other reforms, China started various trust business. While bank credit predominates, commercial credit, trust credit and folk credit also exist. The function of banks was enlarged. In the past banks extended loans only according to mandatory planning; now banks extend various kinds of loans and engage in various monetary business.

– *Better economic legislation.* By the end of 1985 the National People's Congress, its standing committee and the State Council had issued 327 economic laws, legislative measures and documents which had legal effect. More than 3,000 courts have been set up for economic cases. All the economic departments belonging to the State Council have set up organizations of economic law. China is quickening the construction of the economic law system in order to suit the demands of reform and opening to the outside world.

These reforms have brought about a series of significant changes: China's economy has begun to change from a rigidly planned system to a vigorous commodity economy; although socialist public ownership is still the main element, other systems of ownership have appeared which overlap and develop together; the self-sufficient and semi-self-sufficient agriculture is changing into specialized, commercial and modern agriculture; enterprises are changing from subsidiary bodies of administrative organizations to socialist commodity producers and managers; the single channel, multi-link, closed circulation system is becoming a multi-channel, less-linked, open system; the closed-door policy has changed to the policy of opening to the outside world; macro-management is changing from direct administrative control to indirect control with economic levers; the traditional natural economy idea and "Left" ideas are changing into ideas of creativity, efficiency, business and competition. Because of the reform of the economic system and these changes, China's national economy has entered the most vigorous new period since the founding of the People's Republic. China's economy has kept rising at a rapid and steady speed and the people's life has improved. In reforming its economic system, China has no precedent to go on but has made considerable achievements and won the support of the Chinese people and of public opinion throughout the world.

On the whole, the reform of China's economic system has had a preliminary success, but there are many problems left to solve. In many places measures to expand the decision-making power of enterprises are not adopted. Enterprises, especially large and medium-sized state-owned enterprises, have to pay too many taxes and there are many irrational burdens on them, so their vitality is weak and they cannot compete under roughly equal conditions. Economic relations between the State and enterprises need to be further adjusted. Enterprises do not really enjoy full power of management or bear complete responsibility for profits and losses. Since China's price system is not rational enough and barriers between different departments and regions still exist, competition cannot be fully launched. A perfect market system has not yet been established: the financial market, technological market and labour market are in the embryonic stage. The function of the market is largely limited. In macro-management, the regulatory function of economic levers has not been fully performed. Measures for indirect control and economic legislations are not yet perfect. The work of checking and supervision still lags behind. Inefficient and overstaffed organizations exist. What their powers and responsibilities are is not clear. The reform programme must continue in order to solve these problems.

Building a Socialist Economic System with Chinese Characteristics

From 1979 to 1985 China experienced seven years of reform of its economic system. After the seven years practice and theoretical research, its future course has become clear:

The theoretical basis of the reform

From its experience of reform in practice in the past few years, China has demonstrated for the first time that a socialist economy is a commodity economy planned on the basis of public ownership. It must conscientiously follow and use the law of value and pay proper attention to the important function of economic levers and market regulation. Because the commodity economy is an unavoidable stage in the development of a socialist economy, it is only when the commodity economy is fully developed that the economy as a whole can actually be invigorated and all enterprises encouraged to raise their efficiency, do business flexibly and suit the demands of a complicated and changing society. This cannot be achieved by administrative measures and mandatory planning alone. While confirming that a socialist economy is a commodity economy, the State will guide, regulate and exercise administrative control over economic activities to avoid and overcome the lack of vision brought about by the commodity economy, so that the national economy remains vigorous and develops in correct proportions.

The thesis that a socialist economy is a commodity economy planned on the basis of public ownership is the theoretical basis for China's reform of its economic system. The primary task in China's economic reform is to establish a lively and vigorous socialist economic system to suit the needs of the development of a commodity economy planned on the basis of public ownership. This is a new system with Chinese characteristics.

The nature of the reform

China is a socialist country: reforming its economic system does not mean changing the socialist system. While upholding the socialist system, China must reform those features in its economic management system which hinder the development of productivity and establish a new system which will promote development. The reform, carried out step by step in a planned and orderly way, is the self-perfection and development of the socialist system. The aim of the reform is to accelerate the development of productivity, to make China into a prosperous country and to bring its people a rich and happy life.

The reform will establish a lively and vigorous socialist economic system which will accelerate the development of productivity. The system will be different from China's previous rigid, socialist economic system and the pure market economy system in capitalist countries. It is a system with Chinese characteristics.

The blueprint for the reform

According to the *Decision on the Reform of the Economic System*, the blueprint for China's economic reform includes the following measures:

—Abolishing the practice that the higher the extent of public ownership, the better. China will establish a structure with public ownership as the main element, consisting of various kinds of ownership and ways of management.

—In the past, administrative organizations made all the economic decisions, and enterprises had little decision-making power. Now the power of ownership and the power of management are separated. Centralized decision-making and decentralized decision-making are combined. The State, an enterprise and an individual labourer can all make decisions within certain limits of their own.

—In the past, China used mandatory planning and administration to regulate the economy. Now the State manages enterprises mainly through indirect control, i.e., by economic and legal measures, and also by certain necessary administrative measures.

—In the past, egalitarianism in the distribution of income overlooked the interests of enterprises and labourers. Now consideration is given to the interests of the State, the collective and the individual. In this way, Central Government, local government, departments, enterprises and labourers can all be motivated.

—In the past, there was not a clear distinction between the responsibilities and functions of government and those of enterprises. There were barriers between different regions and different enterprises. Now a clear distinction is drawn between the responsibilities and functions of government and those of enterprises; lateral economic ties have been developed and a criss-cross economic organizing network established, with big cities as pivotal points.

In addition, a sensitive information system and a scientific and effective supervision system are to be set up.

Some principles of the reform

According to the practice of the past few years, to realize the above blueprint China must adhere to some basic principles in its economic reform. They are as follows:

- *The ownership and managerial power of state-owned enterprises must be separated.* This will enhance their vitality.

- *All enterprises must have decision-making powers in management.* They will then work efficiently as socialist producers and distributors of commodities, each enjoying relative independence and full power of management and bearing complete responsibility for profits and losses, so that they will have the power of self-accumulation, self-transformation and self-development.

- *A planned system which combines unity with flexibility must be established.* Through an overall balance in the plan and economic measures, the State controls

485

important economic activities while letting unimportant ones drift. It must gradually reduce the scope of mandatory planning in favour of guidance planning and let the market play the regulatory role.

– *The price system must gradually be revised.* This must be done in accordance with production development and the State's financial ability, while ensuring that the common people get a steady rise in their incomes. There must be a systematic readjustment of irrational prices according to exchange at equal value and the relationship between supply and demand. At the same time, there must be a gradual reduction in the proportion of goods whose prices are set by the State and an increase in the scope of floating prices and free prices, so that prices will flexibly reflect changes in labour productivity and the relationship between supply and demand.

– *Various economic levers, and legal and administrative measures should be used to regulate economic activities.* This will combine invigorating economy with macro-regulation and control.

– *A clear distinction must be drawn between the responsibilities and functions of government and those of enterprises.* This should accompany streamlining administration and delegating more power to lower levels. The government apparatus must play the correct role in controlling the economy. In principle, government departments will no longer run and manage enterprises directly.

– *The cities must play their full role as centres.* To do so, they must gradually establish open economic networks of varying dimensions around them, especially large and middle cities.

– *More competition between enterprises must be encouraged.* All enterprises will be subject to direct consumer comment and testing on the market. Superior enterprises will survive, while inferior ones will be forced out of business.

– *Various forms of economic responsibility system must be established.* In these systems, responsibility, power and interest are correlated and the interests of the State, the collective and the individual are unified. Workers will earn more if they work more.

– *A unified, strong and efficient direction and management system must be adopted.* Enterprise directors (managers) must be responsible for the production. At the same time, China must perfect the workers' representatives congress and other democratic management systems. Workers' unions and the workers' representatives congress should play their role in examining and approving important decisions of enterprises, supervising administrative officers and safeguarding the workers' legitimate powers and interests.

– *Workers' wages and bonuses must be related to the economic efficiency of their enterprises.* The wages of workers and staff in government institutions should be connected with their responsibility and achievement. Enterprises must appropriately increase the

workers' pay differential, so that hard-working and skilled workers are rewarded, while lazy and unskilled workers are punished. There should also be a difference in payment between mental labour and manual labour, between complex labour and simple labour, between skilled labour and unskilled labour, between heavy labour and non-heavy labour.

– *Some areas, enterprises and individuals should be allowed and encouraged to become prosperous first through their own hard labour.* At the same time, China should guard against wide discrepancies in income and gradually achieve prosperity for all members of society.

– *While keeping public ownership as the main element, China must develop various forms of ownership and management.* Economy with ownership by the whole people is the guiding force in a socialist economy; the collective economy is also an important component, and the individual economy is a necessary and useful supplement. The enterprises owned by the whole people can be managed by the State, the collective or by share, or turned over to collective or individual management, by contract or lease.

– *China should maintain the policy of opening to the outside world.* It must reform its foreign trade system according to the principle that the enthusiasm of every department is aroused and action taken with respect to foreign countries is co-ordinated. It must actively increase economic and technological exchanges and co-operation with foreign countries, continuing to manage special economic zones and to open further coastal ports to foreign countries, making use of foreign funds, attracting foreign merchants to engage in joint ventures or co-operative enterprises or to launch ventures exclusively with their own investment.

– *Barriers between different regions, different trades and different enterprises must be broken down.* They must open their doors to each other. According to the principle of making the best possible use of favourable conditions, in various forms, mutual benefit and developing together, China will promote lateral economic ties between different regions, trades and enterprises and develop economic, technological co-operation between them.

– *China must appoint and actively foster a large number of economic management cadres who are revolutionary, young, well educated and professionally competent.* In carrying out the reform, the steps taken must be active and steady. If something is known to be wrong, it will be reformed. If there is uncertainty, experimental tests will be conducted first. Easy steps will be taken before more difficult ones. After each step, the experience gained will be reviewed and used to maintain steady progress.

To quote Deng Xiaoping, "We must take the current favourable opportunities to explore our road unswervingly. At the same time we will find the problems and resolve them. We will make every effort to succeed in the reform in not too long a time."

Top priority has now been given to reform, which the Chinese government and people are actively promoting in accordance with *Resolution of the Central Committee of the Chinese Communist Party on the Reform of the Economic System* so as to lay the foundation for a vigorous socialist economic structure with Chinese characteristics by 1990 or soon after.

3. AGRICULTURE

OLD China relied on agriculture for its existence, but its agriculture was very backward. The distribution of cultivated land was extremely inequitable: over 70% of the land was in the hands of landlords and rich peasants who constituted less than 10% of the rural population, while peasants who made up more than 90% of the rural population owned less than 30% of the land. The landlords and rich peasants, by virtue of the huge areas of lands they owned and feudal privileges they enjoyed, cruelly exploited and suppressed the mass of peasants. The landlords rented out their land to peasants who lacked land or owned no land at all. The latter would give half or even 70 or 80% of their produce to the landlords as rent in kind. This, plus the exploitation of usurious loans and exorbitant taxes and levies, left the peasants little gain after a year's hard work. They struggled for their existence in poverty and on the verge of death all the year round.

The feudal land system severely hindered the development of China's agriculture and the successive years of war also brought about great damage to China's agricultural production. On the eve of the founding of the new China, the grain output was 113.18 million tons and the yield of cotton was 0.444 million tons, amounting to only about 75% and 52% of the peak annual yield of the old China (1936). Agricultural production went from bad to worse and the rural economy was depressed.

The Development of Agriculture in New China

The development of New China's agriculture passed through roughly four periods between 1949 to 1978:

The period of land reform (1949–1952)

After the founding of New China in October 1949, the People's Government immediately started to lead the whole nation in restoring the national economy. In agriculture, stress was laid on two aspects of work: the first was to adopt a series of policies and measures to support agricultural production; the second was to carry out land reform in the newly-liberated areas following the land reform in the formerly liberated areas.

In December 1949, the Ministry of Agriculture convened a national conference which determined that the major policy in agriculture was to bring about its recovery. By granting agricultural loans, providing manure, newer types of farming implements and pesticides, buying agricultural produce at rational prices, etc., the State supported and helped peasants to develop production. To change the conditions for agricultural production, the Government organized peasants to build irrigation works: in the spring of 1950 alone, 300 million cubic metres of earth was moved in these projects. All these policies provided favourable conditions for the recovery and development of agriculture.

In June 1950, the Government promulgated the *Land Reform Law of the People's Republic of China*. In the winter of the same year, a large-scale land reform movement began to get underway. The landlords' lands and other means of production were confiscated to various extents in stages and distributed among the peasants. By the end of 1952, the land reform was more or less completed except in Taiwan and some of the minority nationality areas. People who had taken part in the reform, plus those in the previously liberated areas where land reform had already been carried out, accounted for over 90% of the total rural population. The reform had distributed 46 million hectares of land among those who lacked land or owned no land at all, satisfying the peasants' age-old desire to own land, and at the same time exempting them from about 35 million tons of grain in rent each year and various other extra burdens attached to the land.

The land reform greatly aroused the peasants' enthusiasm for production, liberated the productive forces in the countryside, and gave great impetus to the recovery and development of agriculture. During the three years from 1950 to 1952, the gross agricultural output value increased progressively by 17.8%, 9.4% and 15.2% respectively. The output of grain and cotton in 1952 reached 163.92 million tons and 1.304 million tons respectively, surpassing the output of 1936, the year that recorded the best harvest in old China. With the growth of production, the peasants' income showed an increase of 30% in 1952 over 1949.

The period of co-operative transformation of agriculture (1953–1957)

The practice of leading the peasants in taking the path

to shared wealth for all by mutual aid and co-operation had begun in the revolutionary base areas long before the founding of the new China. However, at that time stress was laid on encouraging the peasants to form seasonal or year-long mutual aid groups and the practice was not widespread. It was after the founding of the People's Republic of China, particularly after the land reform, that the co-operative transformation of agriculture was put forward as a historic task that had to be completed.

To ensure the healthy development of the movement for the co-operative transformation of agriculture, the Party's Central Committee adopted important resolutions which advocated the co-existence of the various forms of co-operation, such as the mutual aid groups, elementary agricultural producers' co-operatives, and advanced agricultural producers' co-operatives, and put forward the principle that the movement should be pushed forward energetically but prudently and steadily in accordance with the principle of voluntary participation and mutual benefit.

The co-operative movement to transform China's agriculture was originally planned for completion within 15 to 20 years. However, it was actually completed within six years (1951–1956). By the end of 1956, 118 million peasant households had joined the agricultural producers' co-operatives, accounting for 96.3% of the country's total peasant households; of these, 107 million joined the advanced agricultural producers' co-operatives, amounting to 87.8% of the country's total.

During the same period, new-type animal-drawn farming implements, chemical fertilizer, pesticides and fine varieties of crops were popularized and water conservancy projects were undertaken in many regions, bringing about a distinct improvement in the conditions for agricultural production. This, plus the launching of the patriotic emulation drive for good harvests across the countryside, brought steady growth in agricultural production. During the five years from 1953 to 1957, agricultural production increased at an average annual rate of 4.5%. The grain yield of 1957 reached 195.05 million tons, an increase of 19% over 1952; the output of cotton in 1957 increased by 25.8% over 1952, to reach 1.64 million tons; and the output of other agricultural products also increased by a considerable margin.

During the later stage of the movement for the co-operative transformation of agriculture, an erroneously unrealistic and rash advance was attempted. The movement was conducted in too impatient and rash a manner, with its lack of variety in the forms of co-operation, and in violation of the principle of joining the co-operatives on a voluntary basis. Co-operatives were formed with great difficulty in some places where conditions were not ripe, and their management and administration were in a state of chaos. These problems had not been properly resolved when

the movement for setting up people's communes was initiated.

The period of setting up people's communes and adjustment (1958–1965)

In August 1958, the Second Session of the Eighth Congress of the Communist Party of China adopted the general line for socialist construction ("to go all out, aim high and achieve greater, faster, better and more economical results in building socialism") and a series of related basic points. At the same time, as a result of the over-impatience in the guiding ideology which called for quick results and neglect of objective economic laws, the "Great Leap Forward" movement and the movement for setting up people's communes were blindly launched. During the short period of several months from August 1958 to the end of the same year, 740,000 agricultural producers' co-operatives were merged into over 26,000 people's communes, which consisted of 99% of the total peasant households in the country.

In their early days, the rural people's communes were very large organizations that integrated government administration and economic management. On average, a commune owned 4,500 hectares of land, with 20,000 to 30,000 people in 4,600 households, about 44 times as much as the average agricultural producers' co-operatives in 1957. In some places a commune was even larger, consisting of a whole county. Within the commune all the means of production belonged to the commune, which directly arranged production and allocated the labour force. The commune organized the labour force into platoons, companies, battalions and regiments, and conducted "large formation warfare". An egalitarian supply system and semi-supply system for consumer goods for individuals were practised within the commune. Commune members all had their meals in collective canteens and the slogan "eat for nothing" was advanced. The houses and furniture of commune members could be appropriated gratuitously by the commune. In some places a slogan was put forward which called for the elimination of commodities and currency. All this shows that the people's commune movement, instead of correcting the mistakes that had occurred during the later stage of the co-operative transformation of agriculture, went further down the wrong road and dampened the enthusiasm of the broad masses of commune members. These mistakes, plus mistakes such as the campaign "to go all out with steel and iron", over-high production targets and over-high state purchase quotas, brought about the continuous decline of China's agricultural production after 1959 by a large margin, at an average annual rate of 9.7%. By 1961, gross agricultural output value was lower than that of 1952. Grain production declined sharply from 200 million tons of 1958 to 170 million tons of 1959. Grain output in 1960 was a mere 143.5

million tons, even lower than that in 1951. Cotton production in 1961 was also lower than that of 1951.

From 1959 to 1962, the basic accounting units of the communes, i.e., units that had their rights of independent management, were adjusted a number of times. First, the people's commune was replaced by the production brigade as the basic accounting unit, which was more or less equivalent to the advanced agricultural producers co-operative. Then its position as the basic accounting unit was assumed by the production team, which was more or less equivalent to the former elementary agricultural producers co-operative. In 1962, the Tenth Plenary Session of the Eighth Central Committee of the CPC adopted the *Regulations Regarding Work of the People's Communes (Revised Draft)*, known as the "Sixty Regulations", and established the commune system which integrated government administration and economic management and had its three-level ownership by the commune, the production brigade and production team, with the production team as the basic accounting unit. Management and administration were strengthened and the principle of "distribution according to work" was stressed. At the same time, the private plots were returned to the peasants, country fairs resumed, loans and material supplies given to the countryside increased, the amount of grain purchased by the State was reduced and the purchasing prices for grain and other agricultural products were raised. In this way, errors made during the people's commune movement were corrected to some extent; since the basic accounting unit was smaller and the household sideline production was resumed, the peasants had more say in managing their production. They became more enthusiastic for production, and agricultural production recovered quite quickly.

By 1965, agricultural production had on the whole recovered to the level of 1957. From 1963 to 1965, the total agricultural output value increased at an average annual rate of 11.1%.

The period of the Cultural Revolution (1966–1976)

Initiated in 1966, the Cultural Revolution severely lashed the Chinese economy, which had only just recovered. The previously formulated, effective policies, such as those which allowed the peasants to preserve private plots, the production team to assume sole responsibility for its profits or losses as an independent accounting unit, country fairs to resume and the farm output quotas to be fixed for each household, as was the practice in some production teams, were criticized as a programme to restore capitalism. Even management on the basis of fixed production quotas and a diversified economy was denounced as being capitalist in nature, and the principle of material gains was labelled as revisionism. In short, a series of correct policies and measures that

had been adopted during the period of readjustment were once again criticized; the errors that had been corrected prevailed again; and "Leftist" policies increased rather than decreased. In addition, the "Gang of Four", vigorously preaching that "we would rather have socialist weeds than capitalist seedlings", pursued a policy of "taking grain as the key link," which played havoc with the practice of developing a diversified economy according to local conditions and brought serious consequences in both practice and ideology.

Only because the collective economy bore sole responsibility for its own profits and losses, unlike the "iron rice bowl" principle which prevailed in state-owned enterprises, and the broad masses of commune members and cadres at grass roots level resisted "Leftist" efforts did China's agriculture manage to maintain an average annual growth rate of 3.8% during the Cultural Revolution. However, it should be noted that this growth was mainly the reflection of the growth of grain production, which was achieved at the expense of industrial crops and the development of other kinds of production.

In general, during the 30 years from 1949 to 1979, China's agriculture developed considerably. The total agricultural output value of 1979 was 158.4 billion yuan (158,400 million yuan), an increase of 270% over that of 1949. The average annual increase rate was 46%, which was rather high compared with the economic growth rates of other countries.

The output of major agricultural products also increased quite quickly. The grain output rose from 113.18 million tons in 1949 to 332.12 million tons in 1979; cotton from 0.444 million tons to 2.207 million tons; and oil crops from 2.564 million tons to 6.435 million tons. This can be said to be a significant achievement. However, as the above analysis shows, China's agriculture had trodden a tortuous path. If there had not been the two upheavals of the people's commune movement and the Cultural Revolution, and if the agricultural economic system had been more rational, China would certainly have achieved much more.

A Turning Point in the Development of Agriculture

The Third Plenary Session of the Eleventh Central Committee of the CPC opened up the road for the vitalization of China's agriculture.

China entered into a new historical period of development after the "Gang of Four" was smashed in October 1976. In December 1978 the Communist Party of China convened the historically significant Third Plenary Session of its Eleventh Central Committee, which decided to shift the stress of the Party's work on to socialist economic construction for China's modernization. Thereafter, China's rural economy commenced its transition from a self-supporting or semi-self-supporting economy to a commodity economy, and from traditional agriculture to modern agriculture. To conform with this profoundly significant strategic transition the plenary session discussed and adopted *Resolutions on Certain Problems For Accelerating the Development of Agriculture (Draft)* and *Regulations Regarding Work in Rural People's Communes (Draft for Trial Implementation)*. These two documents, like later documents concerning the responsibility system in agricultural production, stipulated a series of policy measures and economic measures to accelerate the development of agriculture and created the necessary conditions for its revitalization.

This major change of direction has brought about rapid development of agriculture. From 1981 to 1985, agricultural production grew at an annual rate of 11.7% and the output of agricultural products increased correspondingly.

The Development of Agriculture since the Third Plenary Session of the Eleventh Central Committee of the CPC

Crop cultivation

During the 29 years from 1950 to 1978, the output of grain increased by an average of 6.6 million tons a year, cotton by nearly 60,000 tons a year and oil crops by 90,000 tons a year, while during the seven years from 1979 to 1985, the output of grain, cotton and oil crops increased by an annual average of 10.6 million tons, 280,000 tons and 1.5 million tons respectively.

Artificial pollination in a peach garden in a suburb of Shijiazhuang, Hebei.

Not only has China, whose cultivated land accounts for only 7% of the world's total farmland, solved the problem of feeding and clothing one-quarter of the world's total population, but it has begun exporting large amounts of grain, cotton and other farm products. At present, farm products for exporting in large quantities include maize, soybean, cotton, peanut kernels, peanut oil, rapeseed, oranges, apples, tea, etc. Moreover, several famous kinds of Chinese specialities, such as longan, litchi and Hami melon, are exported to Hong Kong and Macao.

Animal husbandry

In 1985, the output of pork, beef and mutton was 17.60 million tons, twice as much as that of 1978 (8.563 million tons); the output of wool was 180,000 tons – an increase of nearly 29% over that of 1978. The amount of livestock was also greater to differing degrees. At the end of 1985, there were 330 million live pigs available, a 10% per cent increase over 1978. China leads the world in the number of pigs raised and the output of pork. Every year China has large numbers of pigs, cattle and sheep; large quantities of frozen beef, pork, mutton and rabbit meat; and a large amount of goatskins available for export. Breakthroughs have been made in developing the production of poultry and eggs. The output of fresh eggs in 1985 reached more than five million tons, an increase of 23.9% (1.03 million tons) over 1984.

In recent years, new advances have been made in the preparation of pasture. In 1978, there were only 800,000 hectares of artificial pasture and improved pasture; by 1983, such grazing lands had expanded to 3.35 million hectares, a three-fold increase compared with 1978. In addition, the area of fenced grazing land reached 3.29 million hectares. Therefore the total area of China's artificial grazing land was 6.64 million hectares, preliminarily ending the situation whereby the speed of grassland preparation lagged behind pastural ageing. At the same time, the mixed feed industry was developed. Before 1978, there was only

Alxa Prefecture in Inner Mongolia is an area of camels.
(Photo by Yang Shenhe)

491

A section of terracing in the North-West China/North China/North-East China shelter-belt in Shanxi.

The ocean fishing fleet of the Aquatic Products Integrated General Company of the Ministry of Agriculture, Animal Husbandry and Fishery of China starting off from a fishing port at Zhanjiang, Guangdong, to fish in the West African fishing zone. *(Photo by Chen Xuesi)*

one mixed feed factory in China in production and its annual output was about 10,000 tons. In 1984, China produced nine million tons of mixed feed of various kinds. These developments will have a favourable effect on the further development of animal husbandry.

Forestry

Forestry has developed considerably in recent years. The output value of forestry rose to 14,640 million yuan in 1985 – an increase of 76% over 1978. From 1981 to 1985, a total of 28.72 million hectares were afforested and the quality of the afforestation improved generally. The first phase of the project of building the shelter-belt system across the "three northern regions", which was acclaimed as the "green Great Wall" and traverses 12 provinces, autonomous regions and municipalities directly under the Central Government, was completed in 1985 at a cost of 1.7 billion (1,700 million) yuan, afforesting a total area of six million hectares and increasing the afforested areas in the regions from 4% to 5.9% of the total.

Fisheries and aquiculture (the aquatic industry)

China's output of aquatic products in 1985 was 7.05 million tons, an increase of 50% over 1978, of which 4.20 million tons were marine produce and the other 2.85 million tons came from fresh water aquiculture.

During the past several years, the development of China's aquatic industry has manifested itself in two main aspects: one is that the fishery resources of coastal waters have been to a certain extent restored because of the strengthening of the administration and management of fishing in coastal waters, the strict delimitation of fishing seasons and fishing zones, and the setting of appropriate limits on the size of catches; the other is that aquiculture has been vigorously

developed. Not only have the coastal shallow waters and ocean beaches been further exploited and made use of, but freshwater fish-farming has also been actively developed. The waters of large lakes and reservoirs have begun to be utilized and fish-farming in ponds has been extended from the south of China to the north. Freshwater fish-farming has begun to good effect in northern provinces and autonomous regions such as Heilongjiang and the Inner Mongolia autonomous region. Of the aquatic produce, prawns enjoy quite a high prestige as a speciality of China and also as a traditional export commodity. Moreover, live pond fish, eels, shellfish, frozen shellfish and other kinds of fish are exported in various quantities each year.

A bumper harvest of prawns bred in coastal waters at Handagang Farm in Hebei province. *(Photo by Liu Zhiwei)*

Township enterprises

Since 1979, China's township enterprises have developed considerably. By 1985 their number had reached 1.57 million, employing 41.52 million people, compared with 28.26 million employees in 1978. Their total output value in 1985 was 182.7 billion (182,700 million) yuan, up 320% over that of 1978. Of this, 131.1 billion (131,100 million) yuan came from rural industrial enterprises, a 300% increase over that of 1978.

The living standards of the peasants

Since the Third Plenary Session of the Eleventh Central Committee of the CPC, there has been notable improvement in the living standards of the peasants. The average net income of a peasant in China in 1985 was 397.6 yuan, double that of 1980, with an average annual increase of 41.3 yuan during these five years – seven times as much as the average annual increase during the previous 23 years. In 1985, peasant households with a per capita income of less than 200 yuan accounted for 12.3% of the country's total peasant households, while five years before such households had made up 61.6%; those with a per capita income of 200 to 500 yuan made up 65.4% of the total in 1985, while such households amounted to only 36.8% in 1980; in 1980, those with a per capita income of over 500 yuan constituted 1.6% of the total, while in 1985 peasant households with a per capita income of over 500 yuan accounted for 22.3% of the total peasant households. In addition, 2.3% of the peasant households registered a per capita income of over 1,000 yuan.

The composition of the peasants' food cereals has changed. Coarse food grain (such as maize, sorghum and millet) was available in the past for eating, but now fine food cereals (flour and rice) account for 85% of the total. High quality consumer goods, such as TV sets and tape recorders, ownership of which peasants once regarded as being out of the question, have begun to enter their homes. In recent years, many peasants have built new houses and their living conditions have improved markedly.

New Policies Benefiting the Development of the Rural Economy

Lessening taxation in the countryside

For many years the Chinese government's agricultural taxation policy was not to tax production increases. Since the Third Plenary Session of the Eleventh Central Committee of the CPC, agricultural taxes have been reduced in accordance with different conditions to accelerate the development of agriculture. In 1979, a total of nearly 2.37 million tons of fine cereal (flour and rice), equivalent to 750 million yuan, was remitted in agricultural taxes. The lessening of agricultural taxes has undoubtedly played a positive role in the recovery and rehabilitation of China's agriculture, which was plagued during the Cultural Revolution.

Raising purchasing prices for farm and sideline produce

After the founding of the People's Republic of China, the People's Government raised the purchase price of

Table 1: Output of Main Agricultural Products

Product	Unit	1949	1952	1957	1978	1984	1985
Grain	million tons	113.18	163.92	195.05	304.77	407.31	379.11
Cotton	million tons	0.444	1.304	1.64	2.167	6.258	4.147
Oil crops	million tons	2.564	4.193	4.196	5.218	11.91	15.784
Sugarcane	million tons	2.642	7.116	10.392	21.116	39.519	51.549
Flue-cured tobacco	million tons	0.043	0.222	0.256	1.052	1.543	2.075
Tea	million tons	0.41	0.082	0.112	0.268	0.414	0.432
Pork, beef and mutton	million tons	2.2	3.385	3.985	8.563	15.406	17.607
Pigs available at the end of the year	million	57.75	89.77	145.9	301.29	306.79	331.40
Draught animals available at the end of the year	million	60.02	76.46	83.82	93.89	108.39	113.82
Aquatic products	million tons	0.45	1.67	3.12	4.66	6.19	7.05

Source: *Statistical Yearbook of China*, 1986, pp. 180, 181, 188, 194.

farm and sideline products many times, which to some extent narrowed the pricing "scissors differential" between industrial and agricultural products inherited from old China. However, because of the neglect of agriculture in the Party's guiding ideology, particularly because the production cost of agricultural products increased every year while their purchasing prices remained basically unchanged during the decade or so after the mid-1960s, the problem of inequitable price parities between industrial and agricultural products was not solved and for a long period the income of agriculture was too low. This had a directly unfavourable effect on the development of agriculture.

In March 1979, the Chinese government decided to raise the purchase prices for farm and sideline products by a big margin. The price for state-purchased grain was raised by 20%; the price for grain beyond the state-purchase quotas rose by 70%; the price increase rate for cotton and oil crops was respectively 15% and 25%, and 65% and 75% for cotton and oil crops beyond the state-purchase quotas; the price for live pigs went up by 26%; prices for cattle, sheep, eggs, beet, sugarcane, hemp, ramie, silkworm cocoons, timber from the south, mao bamboos, milk, some traditional Chinese medicines, and the major aquatic products went up by appropriate margins. On average, purchase prices for 18 of the major farm and sideline products rose by 24.8%, which cost the State an extra 10.8 billion (10,800 million) yuan in 1979 – the biggest margin since the founding of New China. In 1980, purchasing prices for cotton, jute, and rosin were raised in succession at a cost of more than 900 million yuan; in addition, the producer price for timber in the north-east and Inner Mongolia was raised by 30% in 1980. In 1981, the purchasing price for soybean was raised by 25% over the previous year, which alone added 230 million yuan to the peasants' income.

If 100 is taken as the purchasing price index for farm and sideline products in 1978, by 1985 it had risen to 166.8. The rise in prices boosted peasant enthusiasm for developing production and selling their produce. For instance, the State purchased 60.095 million tons of grain in 1979 – up 9.37 million tons over the previous year; 1.505 million tons of edible oil – up 0.40 million tons over the previous year; and 135 million pigs – up two million pigs over the previous year.

Allowing some peasants to become rich sooner and helping the poor

For a long time, the principle of "common riches for all" was regarded as meaning that "everybody ate from the communal pot" and pay was equal, regardless of working performance or the efficiency of management. No difference in the degree and speed of acquiring wealth was allowed. This practice of absolute egalitarianism severely suppressed the peasants' initiative in production and hindered the increase of social wealth, making "common riches for all" an empty slogan in the end.

After the Third Plenary Session of the Eleventh Central Committee of the CPC, the Chinese government, considering it a normal phenomenon and an objective law that some people walked a little faster while others walked relatively slower on the road to affluence, permitted and encouraged a section of the peasants to become rich first. Only by allowing some people to become rich early can the others be brought along to become rich also, and the goal of "common riches for all" be finally achieved. Therefore, the policy of allowing some people to get rich first and the principle of "common riches for all" complement rather than contradict each other.

In recent years, the disparity in peasant incomes has become greater. In particular, some specialized households (able persons in the countryside) have much higher incomes than ordinary peasant households. However, their wealth has been built up against a background in which the overwhelming majority of the peasants have also increased their incomes and are gradually improving their living conditions.

Judging from the peasant households that have become rich, most have done so by working hard. These households have expended more labour on their production activities, mastered more skills and more advanced technology, and been more capable in management and administration. That is why they achieve better economic results and receive higher incomes. Allowing such people to become rich first arouses people's enthusiasm to learn from advanced experiences, gives great impetus to the improvement of production technology, management and administration and economic results, and hastens the peasantry along the road to "common riches for all".

While allowing and encouraging some peasants to become rich early, the Chinese government pursues positive policies to help the remote areas, minority nationality regions and peasant households with special difficulties. Unlike in the past, while a basic livelihood is still guaranteed, government policy has changed from providing pure relief to helping them develop production, particularly commodity production, to eradicate poverty and develop the means for their becoming wealthy. At present, 2,100 counties – 90% of the country's total, and 50,000 townships – 60% of the country's total, are doing the work of helping the poor. By the end of 1985, nearly 100,000 economic entities and integrated economic entities had been set up to help the poor. These economic entities, in their diversified forms, are mainly engaged in small projects in line with specific local conditions. With less investment but quicker returns and high efficiency in ridding the poor of their poverty, they have achieved good social as well as economic results. Of the 9.5 million poor households that received help, five million have emerged from poverty and have enough food and clothing. On the whole, the work of helping the poor has achieved initial success across the country. Peasants in the eastern part of China are well-off, while those in the western part of China are relatively poor. However, development of the western rural areas has been accelerated in recent years. The net per capita income for peasants in the western part of China rose by 14.9% in 1985 over the previous year, compared with an increase of 9.4% for peasants in the eastern part. The disparity between the income of peasants in the eastern part of China and that in the western part will be gradually reduced.

Readjusting the rural economic structure

Before the founding of the new China, China's rural economy consisted mainly of agriculture, with little commerce, industry, communications and transportation, and service trades. The major component part of agriculture was crop cultivation, with a total output value amounting to 85% of the agricultural production, while in crop cultivation, grain production played a major part, with the area for grain cultivation coming close to 90% of the total crop growing area. Although New China recorded remarkable achievements in agriculture after 1949, the historically formed single-product structure, which laid too much stress on grain production, was not thoroughly changed. In 1978, the total output value of agriculture accounted for 69.5% of the total rural output value; crop cultivation accounted for 67.8% of agricultural production; grain production accounted for 79.7% of crop production. Such a proportion was extremely irrational. Since different regions have their own specific conditions, special resources and special local products, too much stress on grain production resulted in the failure to make full and rational use of these resources and give full play to the unique advantages of various localities. It is therefore one of the important economic policies of the Chinese government to readjust the rural economic structure, change the situation of single-grain production and help rationally apportion the various rural economic sectors in an effort to bring about their harmonious development.

After 1979, the various parts of China made an initial readjustment to the rural economic structure. The readjustment centred mainly on three aspects. The first was to readjust the ratios of crops cultivated: on the basis of maintaining grain production above a certain level, the areas for the growing of industrial crops were expanded. The second was to vigorously accelerate the development of forestry, animal husbandry and fisheries, and try to coordinate their growth with that of agriculture. The third was to gradually shift the surplus labour force to these second and third industries.

As a result of several years of effort, China's rural economic structure has changed in a number of ways:

– Firstly, *the ratios of crops grown have changed*. In 1985, areas for cereal crops were 108.85 million hectares, a fall of 11.74 million hectares from 1978, while areas for industrial crops reached 22.38 million hectares, an increase of 7.94 million hectares over 1978. The proportion of grain production in overall crop cultivation fell to 66.2% in 1985 from 79.7% in 1978. These changes within the ratios of crops cultivated brought about a big increase in the output of grain and major industrial crops. Grain output in 1984 increased by 743.44 million tons over that of 1978; of the major industrial crops, cotton output increased by 90% and oil crops by 200% over 1978 – sufficient to meet social needs on the present consumption level.

– Secondly, *the inner structure of agriculture has changed*. The proportion of crop cultivation in the total agricultural output value (including that of village-run industries) fell from 67.8% in 1978 to 50% in 1985, while the proportion of forestry rose from 3% to 3.8%, animal husbandry from 13.2% to 14.5%, fishery production from 1.4% to 1.8%, and sideline production from 14.6% to 30.1%.

– Thirdly, *the proportion of the various sectors of the rural economy has changed*. The proportion of agricultural production in the total rural output value fell from 69.5% in 1978 to 57.1% in 1985, while the proportions of other sectors increased, with industry rising from 19.1% to 27.6%, commerce from 3.3% to 4.2%, the building and building material industries from 6.5% to 8.1%, and communications and transportation from 1.6% to 3.0%.

However, judging from the composition of the labour force, there are still nearly 100 million able-bodied peasants who need to be reallocated to non-agricultural economic sectors. In 1985, the rural labour force engaged in agriculture accounted for 81.9% of the total rural labour force while the remaining 18.1% were engaged in non-agricultural production – 10.4% in secondary industry and 7.7% in tertiary industry.

The Yuhua Electric Fan Factory is a rural enterprise in Shunde county, Guangdong province, which produces 23 million electric fans of several varieties annually.
(Photo by Liu Yusheng)

Developing township enterprises and supporting agriculture with industry

The so-called township enterprises include industrial and commercial businesses formerly set up by the communes, production brigades and production teams, as well as co-operative enterprises, joint-stock enterprises, individual household-businesses and private enterprises which the peasants have newly set up. Since the Third Plenary Session of the Eleventh Central Committee of the CPC, the Chinese government has attached great importance to the development of township enterprises, regarding their development not only as an important facet of readjusting the rural economic structure and a strategic measure to vitalize China's rural economy, but also as the road China must take to break the old pattern of urban–rural dichotomy, integrate urban and rural areas into an organic whole and build socialism with Chinese characteristics. Since 1978, the Government has adopted a series of preferential policies to support the development of township enterprises. For example, it now adopts a tax-free or low-tax policy for township enterprises in accordance with different conditions, turns over farm and sideline products suitable for rural processing to township enterprises, extends urban industries to rural areas in a planned way and vigorously develops urban–rural associations. In recent years, township enterprises have been developing rapidly and already show several signs of the significant role they play:

– Firstly, *they provide employment for a large surplus of the rural labour force.* For example, if the 41.52 million workers in township enterprises (35 million of them have been employed since 1979) were employed in state-run enterprises, a single worker would require a state investment of 24,000 yuan, and the total number would involve a state investment of 1,500 billion (1,500,000 million) yuan. Township enterprises provide a way out for the large surplus of rural labour force without the State spending a cent.

– Secondly, *they help narrow the differences between town and country and between industry and agriculture.* Having peasants running industrial, trading and other businesses has raised the rural economic level and peasant incomes by a large margin. This is gradually reducing the difference between town and country and between industry and agriculture.

– Thirdly, *they have improved the peasants' cultural quality.* To survive and develop in an environment of fierce competition, township enterprises require large numbers of technicians and managerial personnel. This need means that the peasants have intensified their efforts to improve their cultural and managerial levels.

– Fourthly, *they have supported and accelerated the development of agriculture.* Township enterprises have not only increased the peasant incomes, but have also provided a steady flow of funds for the development of agriculture. During the three years from 1979 to 1982, township enterprises provided eight billion (8,000 million) yuan as funds for agriculture. In different regions there are various forms by which rural industry supports agriculture. In some cases, a certain proportion of the enterprises' profits is earmarked for farmland capital construction or for farming machinery, chemical fertilizer, etc.; in other cases, the profits drawn may be granted to farmers, particularly those engaged in grain cultivation. At a time when purchasing prices for some agricultural products are rather low, such practices can reduce the disparity between the income of those engaged in industry and the income of those engaged in farming and, moreover, benefit the development of agriculture.

Developing rural credit

In March 1979, the Chinese government decided to set up the Chinese Agricultural Bank to meet the needs of money circulation in the countryside. At the end of the same year, the balance of the loans the State granted to the countryside was 12.29 billion (12,290 million) yuan and it rose to 35.26 billion (35,260 million) yuan in 1985.

The rural monetary organizations (mainly credit co-operatives) have undergone rapid development in recent years. By the end of 1985, there were more than 410,000 such organizations, which have business contacts with 80% of the peasant households, and the balance of saving deposits reached 72.5 billion (72,500 million) yuan while the balance of various loans on credit rose to 40 billion (40,000 million) yuan, being increases of 166% and 390% over 1980. Of the saving deposits, private deposits of peasants were 56.48 billion (56,480 million) yuan, an increase of 380%, with the average of per capita deposits being 85.2 yuan. Of the remaining sum of the loans, 19.4 billion (19,400 million) yuan was granted to peasant households, an eleven-fold increase over 1980; loans given to township enterprises reached 16.44 billion (16,440 million) yuan. During the five years from 1981 to 1985, the total sum of various kinds of credit extended by the credit co-operatives reached 201.6 billion (201,600 million) yuan, accounting for 62% of the total sum of agricultural credits; the recall rate was rather high, reaching 92.7%.

The growth of agricultural funds has improved the circulation of funds and not only given strong support to agricultural production, but also given impetus to the readjustment of the rural economic structure and the development of commodity production.

Reform of the Rural System

The adoption of an output-related system of contractual responsibility

The output-related system of contractual responsibility is an effective form that the Chinese peasants have created in practice to organize co-operative production. During the later stage of the movement for the co-operative transformation of agriculture, and also during the economically difficult period from 1959 to 1961, successive systems emerged in the countryside, such as the fixing of farm output quotas for each household, the fixing of work loads for each household and the "three fixings and one award" system (the fixing of output quotas, work loads and production cost, and the granting of an award for output in excess of output quotas) and demanding of compensation for shortfalls. Besides, responsibility systems such as contracting for a particular piece of work and payment according to work finished were widely practised. Practice has proved that to adopt a variety of responsibility systems in the collective economy is beneficial for the development of agricultural productive forces.

However, for a long time these types of responsibility system were often criticized as "capitalism" and were not fully implemented. Since the Third Plenary Session of the Eleventh Central Committee of the CPC at the end of 1978, which restored the Party's tradition of seeking truth from facts and proceeding from actual conditions, the various responsibility systems, particularly the output-related system of contractual responsibility, have been put into practice across vast areas of China.

The output-related system of contractual responsibility means that the co-operative economic units, in order to bring the peasants' initiative into play, contract their business projects to individuals, households or groups. The two sides then sign a contract and the contractor has full rights of independent management and owns and commands all the products or income except the part to be turned in according to the contract. Since the contract is based on output, the system is termed the "output-related system of contractual responsibility". Since the contractor assumes sole responsibility for his profits or losses under the condition that he fulfils his task of turning in the fixed amount of produce, he is in fact responsible for the management. So the system is also called the "contract responsibility system of management."

The output-related system of contractual responsibility has several different forms. One is contracting for specialized trades and paying according to output. Under the unified management of the production team, the peasants are given different work in different specialized trades in accordance with their expertise and ability and the nature of the trades. The fixed production quotas in farming, forestry, animal husbandry, sideline production, fishery, industry and commerce are contracted to specialized groups or households in line with the principle of benefiting production and management. Payment is then decided according to production output. There are several forms of payment: the contractor is completely

responsible for his profits or losses, except that he has to turn in the fixed production quotas; payment is determined according to the fulfilled output quotas fixed in the contract; payment is decided according to the output value or profits the contractor has produced; production quotas are fixed for each household, i.e., the production team or co-operative contracts the arable land to the households according to the number of family members and able-bodied persons, and these households will turn in the quotas fixed in the contract to both the State and collective and retain the rest.

The output-related system of contractual responsibility, particularly the household contractual responsibility system, is the basic form that has emerged from the various systems across the country. At present, the form whereby the household operates as the basic economic unit is practised in most areas, except in a few comparatively developed regions and some suburbs where the system of unified accounting and distribution on the level of what is equivalent to the former commune or production brigade still exists. To further consolidate and stabilize the household contract responsibility system, the Chinese government has extended the period for the contractor's use of the contracted land, generally by 15 to 20 years. In some places, special licences have been issued to ensure the long-term use of the land by contractors, which has dispelled their misgivings. They enthusiastically put labour and manure or fertilizer into the land; they level the land, pool money to dig wells, vie with each other to buy small tractors and draught animals and increase the investment in their farming.

The output-related contractual responsibility has thoroughly eliminated the drawbacks of the old rural economic system and its advantages are obvious:

– Firstly, *the peasants' right of independent management and collective ownership is maintained.* The status of the collective economy as commodity producers is really valued. Since the production team contracts the various items of production to production groups and signs legal contracts which stipulate the rights and responsibility of the two parties, the right of independent management of both sides has been actually defined and cannot be flagrantly interfered with by higher authorities.

– Secondly, *it provides greater internal motivation for the development of production.* The output-related system of contractual responsibility guarantees the contractor's right of independent management, on the one hand, and on the other hand it links the contractor's income more closely to his gain in production, thus eliminating the absolute egalitarianism in distribution within the collective economic unit. A contractor is not only an able-bodied peasant, but also a production manager, so he can really pay attention to the quality of his farm work and to the whole process of production and every link in his managerial chain, knowing that he is his own master. He will try by every possible means to adopt measures which can help increase his output and income. Therefore, not only can the intelligence and wisdom of the labourer be brought into play, but his enthusiasm for learning science and technology can be aroused.

– Thirdly, *it has pushed forward the reform of the rural system as a whole.* When the contractor has finished the contracted task, he can engage in certain production projects or establish another enterprise either alone or in co-operation with others, thus opening up various ways for co-operation and coalition at various levels and in different contexts. This makes it necessary to change the old rural administrative system and also provides the conditions necessary for the change.

The increase in specialized households and the development of economic coordination and co-operation

Specialized households and co-operative coalitions emerged after the output-related system of contractual responsibility came to be practised in the countryside. At first, the specialized households were mainly those that specialized in grain production. Those engaged in other trades developed without giving up grain production, so they were actually "two-trade" households that had not broken away from the state of "small-scale peasant economy", in which "every family tills some land and every household engages in every trade by itself". The Chinese government attaches great importance to the specialized households emerging in the countryside and adopts policies which actively support them. Since 1982, the households that have contracted farmland or specialized in other trades and households of independent management have mushroomed. There is an increasingly greater variety of specialized households engaging in ever expanding business areas at increasingly higher levels of specialization. In many places specialized villages have emerged, which engage in different trades and which have different features. There are, for example, villages specializing in raising milk cows, grain production villages, and even villages which specialize in making sofas. In some places, specialized towns and fairs have arisen. One outstanding and spectacular feature is the rapid development of specialized households engaged in exploiting natural resources. Some contract to afforest barren hills; others to cultivate and exploit small river basins. They move out to barren hills, ocean foreshores, mountain slopes, lakes and ponds, and set up numbers of small nurseries, orchards, farms and fisheries, thereby fully exploiting and utilizing the natural resources of various regions. The State and governments at various levels give them appropriate aid through the formulation of policies (e.g., prolonging the contract validity periods, giving preferential treatment to contractors in profit distribution and providing technology free of charge), taxation and credits.

A peasant factory in Puyi county, Hubei province which makes 500 kinds of fans and chopsticks which are sold to over 30 countries, including the USA, Italy and Japan.
(Photo by Li Yifang)

The emergence and development of specialized households has promoted the development of commodity production and the division of labour and trades. The more the division of labour and trades develops, the more specialized households will feel the shortage of pre- and post-production services, funds, technology and labour. In many places the specialized households have formed new co-operative relations and various types of economic coalitions amongst themselves, in accordance with the need to develop production. They set up joint corporations and various types of service businesses to meet their needs of service and self-service. They also establish various kinds of economic coalitions with factories, commercial businesses or technological research institutes, which are run by the State, collective or individuals, to meet their need to expand production and enhance economic results.

At present, the specialized households and the economic coalitions they form are the basic patterns of the specialization and socialization of China's rural commodity production and embody the significant reform of the basic rural economic organizations.

The relaxation of control and the invigoration of circulation

The reform of the system of farm product circulation is an extremely important aspect of the reform of China's rural economic system. The state monopoly and the single channel for purchasing and marketing were the two major features of the circulation system for rural produce before the reform. With the development of the output-related system of contractual responsibility in the countryside, the original means and channels of purchasing and marketing became increasingly unsuitable. The Chinese government took timely measures, in accordance with the specific Chinese circumstances, for the gradual reform of the circulation system of agricultural products.

First and foremost, a diversified economy has been pursued, varied economic sectors have been given support and encouragement, and different channels of circulation and services are being opened up. Since 1979, great changes have taken place in the circulation channels of agricultural products, as can be shown by the following achievements: markets for agricultural products have been restored and developed, and wholesale markets characterized by free trade on a small scale have emerged; township industrial and commercial businesses in agriculture, fishery, animal husbandry and forestry have organized the processing and marketing of agricultural products in order to link production with marketing and to simplify work procedures; supply and marketing co-operatives in rural areas have been reformed and commercialized in forms of peasant co-operation, thus increasing the co-operatives' popularity among the masses, promoting a democratic work-style in administration and strengthening flexibility in management; new co-operative businesses and households specializing in purchases and sales have developed in the countryside.

Secondly, the scope of state monopoly and assignment for purchase has been gradually narrowed and the variety of market regulation increased. The Chinese state monopoly for purchasing and marketing was implemented in 1953. Agricultural products were

divided into three categories: for the first category, which included grain, cotton and oils, a system of state monopoly of purchases was adopted; a system of state assignment for purchases was applied to the second category, which consisted of tobacco, sugar, tea, pigs, chickens, eggs, Chinese medicinal herbs and vegetables grown on city outskirts; a third category was allowed by the Government to be freely marketed. Regardless of the extent to which the state monopoly for purchase and the state assignment for purchase might differ, for peasants they were, in fact, compulsory tasks. In 1985, the Government decided that the policy could no longer be applied to peasants, except with regard to a handful of products. According to this decision, state commercial departments now order grain and cotton from peasants through contracts between the two parties; and products beyond the quota can be placed at the peasants' disposal. As for the second category of products, peasants can sell them on the free market. With the cancellation of the state monopoly for timber purchases from collective forests, timber markets have been opened and the policy of purchases and sales on a negotiated basis has been implemented. All Chinese medicinal herbs can now be purchased and marketed freely except for a few varieties which must be placed under strict control in order to protect natural resources.

The separation of commune management from government administration

The people's commune, which in the past adopted the system of "integrating government administration with commune management", was a grass roots organ of state power as well as a collective economic organization of peasants. In January 1983, the Chinese government decided to gradually separate commune management from government administration and restore the township system in order to provide economic organizations and political power with their own independence and let them have their own roles and functions.

In general, the township system is set up on the basis of the original commune jurisdiction, though certain communes with too much jurisdiction were formally divided into smaller township administrations. In addition to their responsibility for civil administration, public security, judicial work, culture, education, and sanitation, township administrations – which function as state power at the grass roots level – should lead in economic construction, although they must not become engaged directly in the collective economy. Their tasks are: to supervise and organize the implementation of the entire township's economic and social welfare plans, formulated by the township people's congress; to handle economic statistical work and engage in administration; to supervise enterprises in executing state policies and decrees, fulfilling economic contracts and paying

Hefei Popular Science Association of Anhui sells books about agricultural technology in the countryside. They are warmly welcomed by peasants. (Photo by Fu Zhenxin)

taxes; to safeguard the legitimate economic rights and interests of legal economic entities, and to clamp down on illegal economic activities and criminals.

Township economic organizations are set up according to the needs of production development and the aspirations of the peasants. These organizations – as distinct from those of the past, when only one economic form was pursued from the higher to the grass roots level – are various in form and scale. Among them, some are based on the range of original communes or production brigades, while others are different in form. Regardless of location within or outside a township, these organizations are economically legal and independent from each other, without administrative subordination. Among the many economic forms, businesses engaged in agriculture, industry and commerce are a new organizational form with several types.

One type is the complex which combines economic integrated businesses and specialized households in the countryside. These complexes have developed from state-run farms and are engaged in agriculture, industry and commerce. They are characterized by the fact that after the combination, the ownership and the original relation of subordination remain unchanged. The complexes only give part of their profits to the co-operators in return for their raw materials. Some of them have adopted a policy of sharing processing and marketing profits with peasant households according to the shares they have bought.

Another type is the specialized company which combines other township businesses through contracts and establishes a production chain from processing to marketing.

In 1984, the work of separating business management from government administration and the setting up of township administrations was fundamentally completed. The successful reform owed much to the output-related system of contractual responsibilities, which gives peasants powers of decision in management and renders the direct interference of state power in management unnecessary.

The reform of state-run farms

Since the founding of the People's Republic of China in 1949, state-run farms have developed by leaps and bounds, although they are not yet in an economically satisfactory state. Before the Third Plenary Session of the Eleventh Central Committee of the Communist Party of China most state-run farms had long been deficit-ridden. During the ten-year Cultural Revolution (1966–1976), their deficits amounted to 3.19 billion yuan. Besides being hindered by "ultra-left" ideas and political upheavals, state-run farms also suffered from over-centralization, rigid management and the system of "every one eating from the two big communal pots" (i.e., every state-run farm ate from the state's big pot and every worker ate from the

farm's big pot). These factors accounted for the financial losses of state-run farms.

Table 2: State Farms before 1978

	1952	1978
Number of farms	562	2,067
Acreage under cultivation	377,000 hectares	4,284,000 hectares
Number of workers	359,000	5,140,000
Grain output	225,000 tons	6,485,000 tons
Cotton output	5,000 tons	74,200 tons
Pork output	200 tons	144,100 tons
Milk output	900 tons	271,100 tons
Fleece output	500 tons	12,900 tons

Source: *Statistical Yearbook of China, 1986,* p. 211. China Statistics Publishing House.

With the implementation of the output-related system of contractual responsibility, which takes households as production units, agriculture has been invigorated and production has accelerated. While constantly adjusting and perfecting the rural co-operative economy, the Chinese government carefully studied and absorbed the successful experience of the output-related contractual responsibility system in the countryside, and began to reform the managerial system of state-run farms. In 1979 it decided to enlarge the managerial decision-making powers of state-run farms on the basis of reforming the leadership system. In the light of this decision, state-run farms had the power to formulate sowing plans and determine ways to innovate technically and to practise management by adapting measures to local conditions. They also gained the power to allocate their own funds, initiate welfare work and formulate specific policies of rewards and penalties in accordance with the stipulations made by the authoritative departments responsible for the work. Being responsible for their financial affairs, state-run farms assign tasks to brigades under their leadership by deciding their personnel numbers, output, costs and profits, and they reward those that have overfulfilled their tasks. The first year the reform was carried out, the farms on the whole made up deficits and gained profits. 1980 saw bumper harvests despite natural disasters, and gained profits of 600 million yuan.

However, the 1979 reform went only part of the way to solving the problems of over-centralization, rigid management and the system of every farm eating from the State's "big pot". The problem of every worker eating from the brigade's "big pot" remained unsolved and the initiative of workers had not been fully tapped.

In 1982, continued reform of state-run farms was under way. The farms began to fix output quotas for

The Dujiang Weir in Guanxian county, Sichuan province, built in 256 BC, can irrigate 460,000 hectares of fields. It is also a famous scenic spot.

each household and person instead of each brigade. Households became the basic management units. In August 1983, the system of two-strata management was pursued, that is, state-run farm management and family farm management co-existed. The system facilitated the development of family farms, and of farms jointly run by several families, called family-combined farms. Up to 1985, the number of family farms and family-combined farms on more than 2,000 state-run farms increased to 940,000. All these family farms and family-combined farms conducted independent accounting.

The maintenance of good relations between state-run farms and family farms is the key to bringing into play the initiative of both farms and workers. Now state farms and family farms apply the system of unified management and decentralized management. State farms engaged in planting are responsible for the programming and utilities of land, the plan of planting of major crops, the distribution of varieties, facilities irrigation and the protection of plants. While acting under the unified management of state farms, family farms and family-combined farms can make independent decisions on production targets, measures to increase production, purchases of production means, division of labour, arrangement of working hours and internal distribution of revenues. After turning over the profits stipulated by the State and

state farms, family and family-combined farms can keep the remaining income in accordance with their contracts.

Family and family-combined farms are basic accounting and distribution units assuming sole responsibility for their profits or losses. Being legal entities, they can open bank accounts, apply for loans, raise funds and hire a number of workers. They also have the power to sign economic contracts, handle surpluses after fulfilling contracted tasks and expand by depending on what they have accumulated. In Heilongjiang, where there are many state farms, 130,000 family and family-combined farms contracted for 1.4 million hectares of arable land in 1985 – about 84% of the state farms' whole area. With their own accumulated funds of 40 million yuan, the family and family-combined farms bought more than 2,700 giant tractors, 200 harvesters and 430 automobiles. In 1985, despite natural disasters, the state farms in the province made a profit. This demonstrates the vitality of the system of two-strata management.

The application of technology in agriculture

Irrigation construction and water and soil conservation

Water is the lifeblood of agriculture. The Chinese government has always attached great importance to

501

irrigation in its economic construction. Since the founding of the People's Republic of China in 1949, the number of large and medium-size reservoirs in China has increased from 10 to 2,700, and irrigation and drainage power has risen from 120,000 horse-power to 78 million horsepower. At present, the area under irrigation in China stands at 44,036,000 hectares. Although this accounts for less than half of China's arable land, irrigated land produces two-thirds of the country's total grain output. Large-scale irrigation projects reduce the damage to agriculture from natural disasters. In the past few years, the lastest technology and special techniques have been applied to the harnessing of rivers and to irrigation projects.

– China can now use computers and optical facilities to interpret water and soil conservation data, e.g., on the evolution of river mouths, lakes and river courses, and in engineering geology, as shown by the following achievements: the analysis of the geological structure of the Three Gorges Dam in the Yangtze river; the interpretation of Modaomen shallow sea topography in the Zhujiang (Pearl River) estuary; the investigation of water loss and soil erosion; the investigation of the area flooded by fresh water on the Three Rivers Plain and the investigation of saline-alkali land on the great bend of the Yellow River. The application of **remote sensing** technologies provides an ideal basis for the comprehensive harnessing of great rivers, large lakes, wide-range droughts, floods and saline-alkali land, because of its speed, efficacy, effectiveness in all-weather conditions and its wide scope.

– The **harnessing of small river basins** controls water courses and tributaries within a certain range of river basins, thus rationally using natural resources through the utilization of comprehensive techniques.

In areas characterized by loess ravines and hilly land, biological measures (such as planting weeds, shelter forests and rotating weeds and crops) go hand in hand with engineering measures (such as building medium and small silt arresters, and water storage projects). At the same time, the harnessing of smaller streams is integrated with the harnessing of slopes, so as to set up successive terraces for soil protection and detention. These also serve to keep reservoirs in the river basin clear at all times. In this way, increased production can be guaranteed.

In areas of ravines and debris, four measures for soil protection are taken: terraces are levelled and afforested; terraces are edged with trees and weeds, and terrace borders are erected; slopes are levelled and weeds are planted along them; and silt arresters are constructed at the bottom of ravines.

In river areas, arbors and shrubs are planted to consolidate river banks, and projects are constructed to retrench channels, expand sandy areas, divert flood waters for irrigation and lead silt from ditches and slopes to riverine sands.

Soil improvement

The massive construction of irrigation projects and the strengthening of water and soil conservation create conditions for soil improvement. During the past 36 years, 4.569 million hectares of saline-alkali land – about 59.4% of the total saline-alkali land in the country – have been harnessed. In southern China half of the 7.3 million hectares of low-yield waterlogged

Piping water from the Yellow River to irrigate farmland.

Grassland has been greatly improved at Ergun, Inner Mongolia. Seeding and harvesting of herbs are mechanized.

fields and 6.67 million hectares of poor red-loam and loess-loam have been transformed. In addition, 6.7 million hectares of sloped fields have been terraced. Soil improvement on a large scale has increased soil fertility and laid a favourable foundation for high and stable yields.

– The major technical measure to transform low-yield waterlogged fields is **draining.** Three types of draining are used – horizontal, vertical and biological. Horizontal draining is conducted through open drains and underground pipes; vertical draining, also called shaft draining, describes the combination of irrigation and draining through wells; biological draining refers to the transpiration of forest belts. In Quzhou city, in Zhejiang province, the original grain output per hectare was 2,250–3,000 kilograms, but since the city spent three to four years transforming its 6,000 hectares of waterlogged fields, the grain output per hectare has now increased to 7,500 kilograms. By installing open drains and shafts, Shenushi village in the Hebei county of Cang has tackled droughts, waterlogging and alkalization in a comprehensive way. As a result, the grain output per hectare in the village has increased by 52%, from 3,000 kilograms to 5,000 kilograms, and the village has eliminated poverty. In 1983, the method of drilling underground holes with machinery to drain waterlogged fields was popularized in Shanghai and provinces such as Zhejiang and Jiangsu, where waterlogging is more serious. This method is also helpful for soil improvement. Surveys show that compared with the conventional method of digging ditches, the new method enhances soil oxidation and activation by increasing soil nitrogen by 5.1%, quick-acting phosphorus by 8.4%, and quick-acting potassium by 28.8%, while reducing

ferrous content by 71.3%. This favours the growth of rice and green manure crops.

– An important measure for protecting soil and achieving high yields in agriculture is to greatly promote the production, utilization and efficiency of **organic fertilizer.** From 1978 to 1985, the application of fertilizer in China increased from 8.84 million tons to 17.76 million tons; the production of farm manure developed while techniques in applying fertilizer improved.

In the South, about three million hectares of paddy fields retain water during winter. In December 1983, the Chinese government popularized Sichuan's techniques of growing green duckweed in paddy fields during the winter in a bid to increase organic fertilizer and fodder.

From autumn to spring, one hectare of paddy field in Sichuan produces 7.5 tons of duckweed on the average. The highest hectare yield is 30 to 37 tons. One hectare of fresh duckweed can fertilize two to three hectares of fields, so green duckweed can boost the output of both rice and dryland crops. In general, the first and second yields of a product one year can be increased by more than 10% to 5% respectively once green duckweed is applied to the fields. The average per-hectare output of rice can be augmented by over 750 kilograms, while the average per-hectare output of maize, wheat and rapeseed can be increased by 450 to 600 kilograms. Sweet potato output is increased by about 1.8 tons if green duckweed is applied. Two hundred kilograms of fresh green duckweed equals or exceeds one kilogram of urea. Fresh duckweed can also be used as fodder. After animals have eaten it, their droppings can be placed on the fields as green manure. Green duckweed therefore can greatly in-

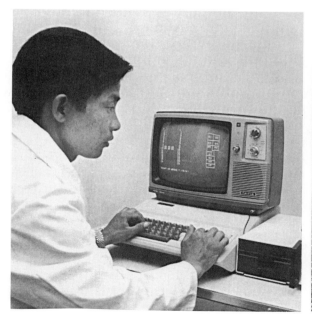 

Computers are used to control sprinkling irrigation in vegetable fields at Changzheng, Jiading county, Shanghai. *(Photo by Liu Zhongyang)*

A canal diverting the water of the Tuo river for irrigation in Sichuan province.

Factory-like production of rice seedlings in a village in Wuxi county, Jiangsu province.

crease organic fertilizer, make up for the lack of chemical fertilizer and reduce costs.

In the North, an effective way to solve the deficiency in high-quality organic fertilizer is to greatly develop **dryland green manure.** With large tracts of unused hills, slopes and disused fields, the north has favourable conditions for growing dry green manure crops such as sweet clover, sesbania, mung bean, lucerne, ormosia grass and false indigo. There are various methods for growing these crops: rotation of grain and manure crops, intercropping of grain and manure crops, interplanting and multiple cropping of short-period manure crops, and planting manure crops in orchards and vegetable fields.

– The **techniques of applying mixed fertilizers** involve an adequate mixture of such nitrogenous fertilizers, phosphates and potash and the proper application of these fertilizers in the light of experiments conducted into soil nutriment and crop conditions. The Hubei Province Soil and Fertilizer Station has developed a technique of applying mixed fertilizers according to soil conditions, cropping and fertilizer effects. While fixing the output quota in accordance with soil quality and the amount of fertilizer in accordance with output, the station mixes organic fertilizers with mineral fertilizers, macro-elements with micro-elements, and nitrogenous fertilizer with phosphate and potash fertilizers. This method has achieved good results.

In general, the scientific techniques of applying mixed fertilizers, which have been applied during recent years, can augment production output by more than 15%.

Variety improvement

During recent years, great progress has been made in the improvement of crops, livestock and fish. Variety improvement has always been one of the major popular features of China's agricultural technology. In 1985 there were 2,548 seed stations and companies, 2,271 variety breeding farms and 669 livestock

breeding stations in China's countryside. A great number of fine varieties are bred yearly. Many of them have achieved good economic results after being put into production.

In crop breeding, improved varieties of rice, wheat, corn, cotton and peanut bean have been developed and popularized in recent years. For instance, a new hybrid **rice,** well known at home and abroad for its high yield, has been introduced throughout China, and hybrid varieties of rice have contributed to the increase of China's output in recent years. *Yuanfeng-zao* – a rice variety cultivated through atomic radiation – is characterized by its early maturity, high yield, fine quality and adaptability. It is ideal for planting in southern China, where three crops are cultivated a year. It has been sown on over one million hectares every year since 1980.

Varieties of **wheat** have also been repeatedly upgraded. A new variety, *Jinghua No. 1*, which has been cultivated in recent years, was grown on 80,000 hectares in 1985 in all parts of China. This crop yielded an income of 20 million yuan.

China's **cotton** varieties have been repeatedly upgraded as well. High yielding and fine quality *Lumian Cotton Seed No. 2* and *No. 6* (two improved varieties of *No. 1*) have been cultivated. China has also cultivated new varieties of antigen "52–128" and "57–681" which produce a better quality of anti-fusarium wilt and antibiotic broad-spectrum, compared with similar varieties in the United States and the Soviet Union. This provides an excellent resource in the fight against cotton wilt, which is a global headache for cotton growers.

China has also brought out dozens of new varieties of cotton seeds with anti-wilt quality from the above two antigen varieties.

In **vegetable** cultivation new varieties have been developed, yielding finer quality cucumber, tomato, eggplant, sweetbell red pepper, and Chinese cabbage. Seven improved varieties of cross-breed cabbage were cultivated during the country's sixth five-year period (1981–1985). These form a series of cabbage seeds

A bumper wheat harvest on Henan plain.

that mature earlier, normally or later. These varieties feature fine quality and high yield and have been popularized nationwide.

As for animal husbandry, improved breeding has also upgraded the quality of China's livestock. Over half the **pigs** now sold in markets are from improved cross-breed hogs, and 35.5% of China's **sheep** are from finewool, betterwool or improved sheep. Three million, or 4% of all of China's **cattle** have been improved through cross-breeding. The spotted milk cows number some 300,000. In beef production, China has brought in a variety of cattle which can been fattened to 400 kilos in 140 days.

In recent years, market demand has stimulated the

A Tibetan herdsman at Donghu Sheep Breeding Farm in Qinghai. He looks after a flock of sheep and has reached the goal of "more than one hundred lambs per one hundred female sheep".

raising of low-fat hogs, which are 56–60% lean. In some parts of China, half of the pigs raised are this type of hog.

China is also using artificial insemination to improve its livestock. The application of this technique is becoming more widespread. This can only lead to better cuts of meat on the Chinese dinner table.

Control of plant and animal disease and pests

Plant and animal disease and pest control is another major project. In the 1950s China eliminated the ferocious Asiatic migratory locust and cattle plague. In 1965, wheat rust was all but brought under control. By 1985, China already had 14,694 stations to disseminate agricultural technology and 7,689 veterinary stations in rural areas.

The popular adoption of modern advanced technology and improved methods of combating plant and animal diseases and pests have led to an overall control of these diseases and pests. This was achieved by the production and application of highly effective, mildly poisonous and non-lingering farm chemicals.

Successes have already been made in research on some key scientific projects. For example, scientists are using the natural enemies of plant pests to control the cotton aphis and their work has produced some impressive results. In addition, research work has been done to improve the ecology by providing shelters and means of propagation for pests' natural enemies. Study of the biology, ecology and protection of the pests' enemies has also been conducted.

– The **pallas** (spotted ladybird) is the main natural enemy of insects and pests. However, affected by nature and human factors it reproduced too slowly to fulfil the demand for pest control. Now, thanks to the application of the new techniques and with the propagation and release of ladybirds, the pine scale pest can be satisfactorily controlled.

– The development of a versatile new **aphicide** is important for many reasons: it is highly effective, it leaves no residue, it protects the pests' natural enemies, and it is safe for humans and livestock. Application over a large area has proved that this insecticide can kill 80% of citrus red mite, rust mite, the cotton aphis and apple red mite. In some places, it has proved 95% effective. Farmers in Taizhou prefecture, in Zhejiang province, successfully controlled red mites by spraying the aphicide over 3,300 hectares of orange groves. Moreover, no traces of the chemical remained in the fruit.

– A notable advance in the use of **vermicides** is signified by a new helminthic which cures animal parasitic diseases. Practice has indicated that the medicine is quite effective in eliminating nematode, cestode and liver fluke in cattle, horses, pigs, sheep and poultry without any negative reaction.

Fishing and the upgrading of aquatic cultivation

China leads many countries of the world in its technology of fresh water cultivation of aquatic products. With thousands of years experience in the cultivation of fresh water plants, animals and fish, China has learned many high-yield techniques. In southern China's Guangdong, Jiangsu and Zhejiang provinces, half a million hectares of land are devoted to raising fish. Fish raising and silkworm raising are conducted simultaneously: the fish are raised in ponds which have mulberry trees planted on their banks. The leaves of the trees and the silkworm excrement are used to feed the fish. The fish faeces enrich the soil in the ponds, which in turn is the best fertilizer for the trees and the adjoining rice paddy fields. The by-products of the mulberry trees, the fish and the silkworms are effectively utilized in an ecologically sound cycle of cultivation. Nowadays, it is not uncommon to find fish farms in Guangdong, Jiangsu and Zhejiang yielding 7.5 tons of fish per hectare. In 1985, one fish pond in Wuxi city, in Jiangsu province, yielded 38.5 tons of fish per hectare. For several years, certain countries in the Asian Pacific region have sent specialists to China to learn the techniques of fresh water aquiculture.

Furthermore, in the late 1950s China cultivated its own fish fry, including black carp, grass carp, silver carp and variegated carp, the four main pond fish in China, under artificial conditions – a world first. This provided a vital lesson in breeding fish in fresh water.

This was an advance from the past practice, whereby fish cultivation had to rely totally on natural fries in the Yangtze river and Zhujiang (Pearl River). Many of these fry died during the costly transportation.

China also pioneered fish raising in paddy fields; some farmers now produce fish and rice in the same field, while others alternate fish and rice every six months.

Grouper breeding in net chests at Bao'an county, Guandong province.

When fish and rice plant live symbiotically, paddy fields can yield more rice because the fish help to eliminate pests and rack the soil. The paddy fields are an excellent environment in which to breed small fry, which in turn are very much needed by the large fish farms, lakes and reservoirs. Fish cultivators can earn several tens of yuan more in profit from each hectare of paddy rice. Paddy fields where fish are raised now total approximately 540,000 hectares. It is anticipated that the number of hectares of land devoted to fish production will be doubled during China's Seventh Five-Year Plan period.

China has also succeeded in artificially breeding river crabs. The technology is now widely applied in more than ten provinces, municipalities and autonomous regions.

China is also breeding ocean plants like laver kelp and sea tangles, ocean fish and crustaceans like oysters and prawns. The progress made in the development of artificial breeding of these products has greatly stimulated marine aquiculture.

The application of modern farming machines

Farmers in old China relied on simple, hand-made tools and beasts of burden. After 1949, the Government set great store by the application and upgrading of farm implements. Early in the 1950s tractor stations were set up experimentally, with the purpose of spreading the use of tractors. At the same time, irrigation and drainage products were manufactured and popularized while the use of farm chemicals was widely adopted. Implements to broadcast farm chemicals were manufactured and introduced on a large scale.

China thus took a big step towards semi-mechanization in agriculture. With the nationwide practice of the rural household responsibility system, millions of Chinese farmers are now purchasing farming machines and advanced implements, which is something unprecedented. In 1985, the total farming mechanical power was approximately 284 million horsepower, an increase of 125 million over that of 1978, and equivalent to 172 times that of 1957.

In 1985, there were 852,000 large and medium-sized tractors and 3.82 million small tractors, increases of 53% and 179% respectively over those of 1978. The number of loading lorries also soared from 74,000 to 430,000. With the increasing number of tractors, China has accelerated the mechanization of its agricultural system.

In 1985, 34.44 million hectares, 30% of China's total arable land, were ploughed by machines. In 1985 there were 78.25 million horsepower of farming, irrigation and drainage machines, a 19.3% increase over 1978 and 139 times more than in 1957. 44.04 million hectares of China's land could be irrigated and 24.63 million hectares (55.9%) of the irrigated land was machine irrigated.

Since the founding of New China, machines have also been gradually introduced in the animal husbandry, forestry and fishery industries. In 1985, there were 12,000 grass cutters, 1.087 million fodder grinders, 18 million shearing machines and 10 million milking machines in China. The fishing industry now has 4.992 million horsepower of motor-powered boats. More cold freezers have been installed to improve the capacity for keeping poultry and aquatic products fresh.

In recent years, satisfactory results have also been gained in planting seeds and grass and in aerial chemical spraying for forestation and farming purposes.

With its vast territory and rich crop varieties, China requires a diversity of farm machines to meet the needs of different methods of farming in various areas. Consequently, machines suited to local conditions have been designed and built. For instance, machines for tilling the soil are produced in North-East China, while wind-powered electrical generators are made in the Inner Mongolia autonomous region to satisfy the nomadic herdsmen on the grasslands. Inner Mongolia also produces the 2 BFC-1 tractor sowers suitable for use in both hilly and flat areas. This kind of machine is not only able to sow seeds of corn, bean, sorghum, millet and other crops, but can also be used for ploughing, sowing, fertilizing and tilling.

Farm machine institutions are researching and experimenting with new methods of rice transplanting and with machines for processing agricultural products to meet farmers' demands.

The development of meteorology

China's meteorology has developed to keep pace with economic construction. China is frequently visited by natural calamities and unfavourable climatic conditions, both of which have an enormous effect on agriculture. Therefore, it is vital for agricultural production that quick and precise weather forecasts are available.

There were only 101 meteorological stations or observatories in 1949 and the instruments and equipment were often outdated. By the end of 1985, the number of meteorological stations had increased to 2,635 and constituted a complete modern monitoring and communication system. Now there is at least one scientific research observatory for weather forecasting in every province and minority autonomous region and in the municipalities of Beijing, Tianjin and Shanghai.

The provincial observatories mainly research methods of forecasting adverse weather conditions which affect a local area. They also study the regularity of calamities and are searching for ways to combat frost, storm and other calamities and to artificially make rain.

Meteorologists and weather specialists were in short supply in the early 1950s. To solve the problem, a lot of specialists in weather observation, weather forecasting, communications and information services were trained in special programmes and on-the-job training. Since 1955, vocational schools and institutes of meteorology have been set up to train specialists in the field. In some universities and colleges, departments of agricultural meteorology have also been set up.

The past few years have witnessed achievements in agricultural meteorological research. The study of the utilization of agricultural climate resources has contributed to an increase in agricultural production.

Much experimentation has been conducted in methods of altering adverse weather conditions. For instance, researchers have launched special rockets to help turn clouds into rain. In 1982, many parts of China were hit by serious disasters. Thanks to timely and precise weather forecasts, much time was gained to help combat these disasters and avoid losses. Many local weather stations and meteorological observatories have made a point of offering their services for agricultural production. Some have been active in spreading popular scientific knowledge on meteorology by providing information and weather forecasts to rural households. This has proved to be of great benefit to rural farm production.

A large hothouse for raising vegetables in Shanxi province.

507

In the Guangxi Zhuang autonomous region, meteorological departments have succeeded in forecasting freezing temperatures in early spring. This has helped farmers prepare for and combat cold snaps. Consequently, only a small amount of rice seedlings rotted. On six occasions, weather stations and observatories in Qinghai province have accurately forecast snowstorms in March and April, ensuring herdsmen enough time to protect their animals. As a result at least 900,0000 livestock were saved in the prefectures of Yushu, Hainan and Guoluo.

The present work on dividing regions according to their climatic conditions will greatly assist the development of agriculture.

The Prospects for Agriculture in China

A long-term aim is to modernize China's agriculture and then its economy as a whole, so that China will have an agricultural base with brilliant prospects:

– China will rank as an advanced agricultural nation;

– China will apply the latest technology to agriculture and integrate technology with traditional practices to form a technological structure with Chinese characteristics;

– China will coordinate the various branches of its agricultural development;

– China will have a diversified rural economic system which will include state, collective, private and mixed ownership, in which public ownership will take the lead;

– China's rural economy will vigorously and effectively unify economic, social and ecological results;

– China will have a new generation of farmers with a better knowledge of science and management;

– China's rural areas will be transformed into a new type of prosperous socialist countryside with a picturesque environment;

– The rural economy will be more closely associated with that of cities, and differences between town and country will be effectively reduced.

This is the profile for a contemporary rural economy with Chinese characteristics. The realization of these objectives will be a process taking 70 to 100 years.

The objective for the year 2000

Experts at the Institute of Rural Development at the Chinese Academy of Social Sciences anticipate that the total agricultural output value by the year 2000 will be 500,000–540,000 million yuan, 1.3–1.43 times more than in 1980. The net output value of agriculture will be 350,000–70,000 million yuan. The rural GNP (Gross National Product) will reach 900,000–1,000,000 million, about five times the 1980 figure of 198,400 million, and the GNP from the agricultural industry will amount to 370,000 to 400,000 million yuan, a 160–170% increase over 1980. The GNP for rural industries and tertiary industry will increase 8.6 times and 7 times respectively. The branches of agriculture—farming, forestry, animal husbandry and fisheries will witness a boom and the principal agricultural products will receive a big boost as well. By that time, grain output will total 500 million tons; cotton, five million tons; and oil crops, 21.5 million tons.

Experts also predict that by the year 2000 the population of China will reach 1,250 million, with 780 million rural residents. The rural labour force will be 450 million, with half engaged in agriculture and the other half in non-agricultural activities.

By the turn of the century, farmers' living standards will improve dramatically. The income per capita in the countryside will jump to 765 yuan. Currently, of every 3.7 yuan spent, 2.7 comes from city dwellers, but by the year 2000 they will spend only 2 yuan of every 3.

Targets for the Seventh Five-Year Plan period (1986–1990)

By 1990, the total rural output value of agriculture (including that of village-run enterprises) will be 490,000 million yuan, an increase of 120% over 1980.

The total output value of the farming industry will increase from 141,530 million yuan in 1980 to 273,300 million in 1990. This is an annual increase of 2.1%. The output value from forestry will increase from 9,450 million yuan in 1980 to 25,000 million, an annual increase of 10.8%. The output value of animal husbandry will jump from 33,960 million to 71,300 million yuan, an annual increase of 6.9%. Fishery output will increase from 3,808 million to 8,400 million – a growth rate of 7.7%; sideline production, from 33,480 million to 172,700 – a 12.7% annual rate of increase.

Principal agricultural products per capita

By 1990, China's principal products from agriculture, animal husbandry and fisheries will not only supply the country but will also be exported.

The output of grain is planned to reach 425 million to 450 million tons, i.e., 400 kilos per person. The output of meat, eggs, milk and aquatic products will be 22.75 million, 8.75 million, 6.25 million and 9 million tons respectively, some 20.4, 7.8, 5.6 and 8 kilos per person.

The Chinese will enjoy an obviously higher level of nutrition compared with 1980. The daily protein intake per person will increase from 66.4 grammes in 1980 to 70.3, and fat intake, from 29.9 to 44.1.

Further reform of the rural economic system

The aim is to practice a system of multiple ownership

A modern earthless vegetable-growing factory has been set up in Beijing. More than 20 varieties of vegetables are grown without any earth in the hothouse. *(Photo by Yu Huiru)*

with public ownership as the leading element. State and collective ownership will play the main role, with private ownership playing a supplementary role. Associations among various forms of ownership will be energetically promoted.

Perfecting the rural collective economic system

The system of contracted household responsibility by which remuneration is linked with output will continuously be improved. The relations between township government and economic co-operative organizations which are financially strong should have the Party organization separated from government organs, and enterprise management separated from government.

The accumulations and property left by the original people's communes should also be properly handled. Setting up ownership should be in line with local conditions and people's wishes. In some places where the household responsibility system is practised, a unified management may sometimes be practised and information services may be offered to meet the needs of production. At the same time, to increase their income, farmers will be encouraged to have their contracted land recontracted to better farmers, so the land will be concentrated gradually in the hands of more eligible farmers.

Specialized households will be backed continuously by the Government. Various kinds of service, co-operation and association will be promoted on the basis of family management.

Farmers will be allowed to set up their markets as well as credit co-operatives, to improve the rural marketing and banking system while continuing to reform the systems of rural marketing and supply and credit co-operatives. In short, a complete system of rural co-operatives and associations will be established to unify farmers in the socialist economy.

Setting up a comprehensive organic market system

Doing away with the previous system of the state planned purchasing and marketing of agricultural products marked the second step in China's rural reform. The first step was characterized by the implementation of the farm production responsibility system and has broken the time-honoured "big pot" (all eat from the same pot, regardless of contributions). This has brought the farmers' initiative into play and paved the way for new development of the rural commercial economy. However, this requires a smooth circulation of commodities and agricultural products. This means that only by creating a satisfac-

509

tory marketing system can the rural commercial economy be boosted smoothly.

During the Seventh Five-Year Plan period, the contracted purchasing system will be improved, with contracted purchasing proportions being reduced while the proportion of purchases according to market price will be increased.

The principal aim for the coming rural reform is to set up and develop the commercial market. This first requires that new commercial forms should be sought and levels in managing the market should be up-graded, while the regulation of the market should be perfected. The establishment and development of the market for key elements of production will involve the freer flow of capital, working force, and means of production and technology. In this flow, a market will accordingly emerge. Endeavours will be made to encourage the labour force to circulate in coming years, and conditions will be created for an obvious outflow from agricultural production. A financial market will be established to raise money from farmers for the projects which can bring better economic results.

Technological policy and the "sparking plan"

To develop China's agriculture, a practical economic policy should be worked out and investment be enlarged. It is also indispensable to study and work out a technological policy to suit China's specific conditions. The policy should contain the following points:

– Modern advanced science and technology should be integrated with China's traditional technologies. China needs to introduce improved varieties and techniques of cultivation, and plant disease and pest control from countries and regions which are scientifically and technologically advanced in agriculture. China should also make full use of its traditional techniques, which still require study for better application. For example, the techniques of non-irrigated cultivation, multi-crop planting, proper utilization of land as well as intensive and meticulous cultivation, biological control of pests and the treatment of livestock with Chinese traditional medicine and acupuncture.

Mechanical techniques should be applied along with biological techniques, with the latter predominating. The application of technical methods in crop breeding, irrigation and capital construction on farmland is aimed at yielding more output per hectare. Highly effective farming machine tools can raise labour productivity tremendously and reduce wastage of labour. Thus, the application of biological techniques in China is of great importance, since the over-large population is burdened by a shortage of cultivated land.

4. INDUSTRY

Industrial Production and Construction in New China

INDUSTRY in old China was extremely backward. Its dominant features were low production level, few modern industrial establishments and backward economic management. Industrial production was restored and grew very rapidly after the founding of New China.

Beginning in 1953, China entered a period of large-scale construction of its national economy. Proposals were then advanced that the country should carry out socialist industrialization step by step over a fairly long period of time. Industrial construction centred on the 156 Soviet-aided key projects started during the First Five-Year Plan period. A number of basic industries that were necessary to the state industry and had been lacking or had had a very weak foundation, such as power, coal, petroleum, iron and steel, non-ferrous metals and basic chemistry, were established. Industrial plants making large metal-cutting machine tools, power generating equipment, mining equipment, automobiles, tractors and aircraft were also established, thus laying a preliminary foundation for socialist industrialization.

In 1958 the Great Leap Forward movement was launched in China. It was carried out under the guiding thought of attempting to accomplish too much too soon, an attempt that far exceeded the then national power to sustain. It was also conducted under the guiding policy of taking "steel as the key link", laying stress on one thing (steel) to the neglect of all others. Finally, it led to the serious imbalance of the different sectors of the national economy. In the subsequent several years, a policy of "readjustment, consolidation, filling out and raising of standard" was put into effect. Industrial production began to show an upturn in 1963 and took a turn for the better across the board by 1965.

The Cultural Revolution was launched in 1966. For ten long years, industry suffered serious setbacks and losses. The different sectors of the national economy were again seriously out of proportion.

The upheaval of the Cultural Revolution ended in 1976. Industrial production had a relatively quick recovery. However, the different sectors of the national economy became even more dislocated because of the underestimation of the heavy losses caused by the Cultural Revolution, the eagerness to

obtain quick results and the demand for unduly high targets.

In December 1978, the Third Plenary Session of the Eleventh Central Committee of the Communist Party of China (CPC) made a strategic decision to shift the focus of the work of the Party to the construction programme for socialist modernization. The Party Central Committee proposed that a policy of "readjustment, restructuring, consolidation and improvement" of the national economy be enforced. It was only then that industrial production took a sound path toward stable development.

On the whole, China's industrial production and construction has advanced quite quickly in the past more than 30 years, despite fluctuations on several occasions. Between 1950 and 1985, the growth rate of China's industrial production averaged 12.8% each year, exceeding the growth rate of the world's major industrially developed countries in the same period.

China has established an independent and fairly integral system of industry in the course of construction in the past more than 30 years. The fate of China, whose industry depended on foreign countries and was fragmentary and extremely backward in the old days, has undergone a fundamental change:

– *The number of industrial enterprises and the amount of industrial fixed assets have increased tremendously*

The value of industrial fixed assets in the whole country increased from 14.92 billion yuan in 1952 to 688.6 billion yuan in 1985, while the value of fixed assets of industrial enterprises owned by the whole people grew to 595.6 billion yuan. The former registered a 45-fold increase while the latter a 39-fold increase as compared with 1952.

– *Many new industrial departments have been established and new products made*

Over the past more than 30 years, a number of traditional industrial departments that were non-existent in old China have been set up. These include industries making metallurgical and mining equipment, power generation equipment, oil refineries, new types of machine tools, automobiles, aircraft, locomotives and ships, as well as high alloy steel and

511

non-ferrous metals. Furthermore, some new industrial departments, such as petrochemicals, electronics, space navigation and nuclear power, have been established.

– Industrial productive capacity and output have increased rapidly

The following is a breakdown of the output of China's major industrial products in 1985: cement, 145.95 million tons; cloth, 14.67 billion metres – both ranking first in the world output; coal, 0.87 billion tons – ranking second in the world output; sulphuric acid, 6.764 million tons – as against 8.17 million tons in 1984; chemical fertilizer, 13.22 million tons – as against 14.60 million tons in 1984 – both products ranking third in the world output; steel, 46.76 million tons – ranking fourth in the world output; crude oil, 125 million tons and power generating capacity, 410.7 billion kWh – placed sixth and fifth in the world output respectively.

– The industrial workers' technical equipment has markedly improved and labour productivity has increased greatly

In 1985 the fixed assets of all the industrial enterprises owned by the whole people averaged 15,612 yuan per worker and funds held by him amounted to 14,689 yuan each, a 4.4-fold and 4.1-fold increase over 1952 respectively. This shows that the workers' technical equipment has noticeably improved. Labour productivity in industrial enterprises owned by the whole people came to 15,198 yuan per worker in 1985, a 4.04-fold increase over 1949. Between 1950 and 1984, the increase in industrial output value due to improved labour productivity in state-owned industries amounted to 389.11 billion yuan, accounting for 79.9% of the total increase in industrial output value in the period. Labour productivity per worker in state-owned industrial enterprises further grew to 15,198 yuan in 1985 – up 8% from the previous year. Table 1 (below) indicates the improvement of technical equipment of workers' and labour produc-

tivity in industrial enterprises owned by the whole people.

There are, however, still quite a few problems in China's industry. They are mainly: low level of management and operation of industrial enterprises, low technical level, imperfect harmony between departmental structure and product structure and poor economic returns. China is taking measures to solve these problems.

China's goal is to achieve industrial modernization. In conditions of constant improvement of economic returns, China will strive to secure a stable, sustained and well-coordinated growth of industry so that by the end of this century, the gross industrial output value will quadruple the 1980 figure; that the amount of major industrial products will top the list of world output; that the technical level of various trades and professions can attain the advanced level achieved by the industrially developed countries in the late 1970s or early 1980s; and that China can make major progress in industrial modernization and meet as much as possible the needs of the people for a prosperous material and cultural life.

The System of Industrial Management

Several changes in the system of industrial management have been made since the founding of New China. However, inadequate attention has been paid to the economic relationship between the State and the enterprises because of the failure to understand that the socialist economy is a planned commodity economy, because of the denial of the positive role of the principle of material benefit and the principle of distribution according to work, and because of the practice of regarding the enterprises as an appendage to the state organizations. The reforms conducted several times mainly laid emphasis on readjusting the limits of authority of the central and local administration. This explains the failure to attain a real improvement in industrial management.

In 1979 China adopted the policy of "readjustment, restructuring, consolidation and improvement". To deal with the problems existing in the system of

Table 1: Improvement in Technical Equipment and Labour Productivity

| Year | Workers' technical equipment | | Labour productivity (yuan/per worker per year) | Labour productivity index (1952 as 100) |
	Value of fixed assets held by each worker (yuan)	Funds held by each worker (yuan)		
1949			3,016	72.1
1952	2,918	2,878	4,184	100.0
1957	4,473	4,416	6,362	152.1
1965	8,401	8,379	8,979	214.6
1978	10,501	10,763	11,130	266.0
1984	14,393	13,238	14,070	336.2
1985	15,612	14,689	15,198	363.2

Note: Labour productivity is calculated in terms of constant prices of 1980.

industrial management, a series of experiments in reform at selected units have been carried out. Below are some of the main reform measures that have been introduced since 1979.

– The expansion of decision-making powers of the industrial enterprises

The experimental work of expanding the decision-making powers of the industrial enterprises at selected units was begun in 1978. Fairly good results were reported in all these experiments. On this basis, the State Council enacted the *Provisional Regulations on Extending the Decision-Making Powers of the State Industrial Enterprises* in May 1984, giving such enterprises due power in the following ten aspects:

On the condition of ensuring the state plan and the contract for the supply of goods to the State, the enterprises may themselves make arrangements for production and operation; they may sell a portion of the products they are entitled to keep for themselves, products in excess of the planned quota, new trial-produced products, products which the purchase and sales departments do not purchase, and dead stock; they may fix – within certain limits – the prices of the industrial means of production at their own disposal; at the time of placing orders for goods, they have the right to choose units supplying those materials for unified distribution by the State; they have the right to use funds they retain as their share according to the ratio prescribed by the departments in charge, and may invest in external undertakings any production development funds in which they do not have immediate use; they have the right to let or transfer with compensation any surplus and idle fixed assets; they have the right to fix the structural establishment and recruit personnel within the fixed quota of personnel; the director (manager) is empowered to appoint or dismiss middle-level administrative cadres, to reward or penalize staff members and workers, to advertise for technical and administrative personnel and recruit workers and select the best of the applicants; on the condition of implementing state regulations, the enterprises are empowered to select the forms of wages and distribute bonuses, and in accordance with state regulations, the enterprises are empowered to participate in or organize inter-departmental and inter-regional joint operation, organize co-operative efforts in production or distribution of products. In September 1985 the State Council approved the provisional regulations about certain questions on increasing the vitality of large and medium-sized state-owned enterprises, and defined in more explicit terms several policy measures about increasing the vitality of these enterprises. These measures are: to put a proper limit on the scope of mandatory plans and give the enterprises a certain flexibility with respect to the mandatory targets handed down by the State; to systematically and

progressively reduce or waive regulatory taxes on advanced enterprises with better economic returns and with high regulatory tax rates; to permit enterprises, mainly large ones or those bringing out products with famous brand names, to break down the limits of ownership and undertake economic partnership and co-operation transcending trades, regions and urban and rural areas; to give some large enterprises the right to conduct foreign business operations directly; on the condition of ensuring the fulfilment of the state plans, enterprises may diversify products and operations. All this creates good external conditions for large and medium-sized enterprises to improve their management and operation.

– The institution of a comprehensive economic responsibility system in the industrial field

The economic responsibility system in the industrial field has developed on the basis of carrying out experiments in the expansion of the decision-making power of the enterprises at selected units; it is a continuing and profound process of expansion. There are two fundamental links in this system: one is the introduction of the economic responsibility system in enterprises by the State. This links the distribution of profits with the good or bad economic performance of the enterprises, handles the relationship between the State and enterprises properly and helps to resolve the problem of making no distinction between well-run and badly-run enterprises. The second link is the introduction of the economic responsibility system within the enterprises. This links the personal responsibility, the criteria of progress checking and economic returns, with the income of the staff members and employees, ensures proper handling of the internal relationship of the enterprises, and resolves the problem of making no distinction between employees who work well and those who work badly. The introduction of the economic responsibility system has further carried out the principle of distribution according to work, effectively brought into full play the initiative of enterprises and their staff workers and employees, encouraged the enterprises to improve their management and operation, and obtained notable results.

– The substitution of tax payments for profit delivery

This is the switch from profit delivery to tax payments by the enterprises. Since 1980 experiments in this work were first made in more than 400 industrial enterprises, and on the basis of the results of these experiments at selected units, the State Council decided as from 1983 to put into practice the first step in replacing profit delivery with tax payments, namely, a system of simultaneous existence of profit delivery and tax payments. Its specific measures are: all profit-making large and medium-sized state-owned enterprises, on the basis of the profit they have made, should pay a revenue tax at a 55% tax rate. As to their after-tax profits, the enterprises deliver a part of them to the State and retain a part for their own use at a level fixed by the State. According to the different circumstances of the enterprises, four measures are used to handle the part of profit for delivery to the State – payment according to a rate of progressive increase, a fixed ratio, a regulatory tax or a fixed quota. All profit-making, small, state-owned enterprises should pay income tax according to the 8-grade above-quota progressive tax rate on the basis of the profits thay have made. After paying tax, these enterprises shall be responsible for their own profits and losses. From enterprises with fairly large after-tax profits, the State may collect certain contract fees or have them deliver a portion of their profits to the State according to a fixed amount of money.

Next, a decision was made by the State Council to take the second step in replacing profit delivery with tax payments as from 1 October 1984 and to extend this practice to all enterprises in 1985. The main content of the second step is to divide the original industry and commerce tax into a product tax, a value added tax, a salt tax and a business tax in the light of the different tax payers, to improve the income tax and the regulatory tax and to introduce a resources tax and some other taxes until the completion of the transition from the simultaneous use of profit delivery and tax payments to the substitution of tax payments for profit delivery. After-tax profits are to be retained by the enterprises for their own use.

The purpose of substituting tax payments for profit delivery is to fix the relationship between the State and the enterprises in financial distribution by means of taxation, to ensure the steady growth of state revenues and to provide the necessary conditions for enterprises to exercise their decision-making power so that they will gradually attain independence in their management and operation and be responsible for their own profits and losses.

– The restructuring of the managerial systems of the departments and advancing to management by trades

It is necessary to restructure the managerial systems of the departments in accordance with the principle of separating the functions of Government and enterprises, streamlining administration and instituting decentralization. In August 1984 China began with the reform of the managerial system of the machinery industry. The State Council decided that apart from the departments of the defence industry, all independent machinery plants directly under the various ministries of the State Council should be placed under organizations at a lower administrative level and, in principle, under those in the cities. After reform, the Ministry of the Machine-Building Industry will become a functional department of the State Council

to administer the overall management of the mechanical industries and trades throughout the country, and mainly to administer the principles and policies related to the machinery industry, work out overall planning, strike a comprehensive balance, organize, coordinate and supervise services and exercise control over the mechanical professions and trades. Meanwhile, reforms have also been conducted by organs of industrial management in some provinces and autonomous regions. In general, these organs no longer manage or operate enterprises directly. Instead, such management will gradually be taken over by city governments.

The Structure of Industrial Departments

The structure of the industrial departments in old China was deeply stamped with the brand of a semi-feudal and semi-colonial structure. It was featured by an extremely lopsided development: industry made up a very small proportion in the national economy. Heavy industry was extremely backward; the processing industry lagged far behind the mining industry; the machine building industry had a very weak foundation. Both the light and heavy industrial departments were fragmentary and heavily dependent upon foreign countries.

Since the founding of New China, tremendous efforts have been made to develop the manufacturing industry and various new industries to fill the gaps in China's industry. The lopsided industrial structure in old China has been radically changed within a quite short period of time through the following measures:

– The establishment of a complete structure of industrial departments

Chinese industry is now composed of many and different categories of industrial departments. From the top downward these industrial departments have formed an independent and fairly integral industrial structure.

– A change in the structure of major industrial departments

The following is a breakdown of the proportions of the total output value of major industrial departments in the total industrial output value in 1952: textiles and food, ranking first and second respectively, their combined output value accounting for 51.6% of the total industrial output value; next came the machinery industry, with only 11.4%; metallurgy and chemicals followed, accounting for 5.9% and 4.8% respectively; electricity, coal and petroleum combined to make only 4.2%. However, a marked change has taken place in the structure of industrial departments in the course of large-scale economic construction. The machine industry leapt to first place in 1985, accounting for

Table 2: Comparative Proportions of Heavy and Light Industries

Item	1949	1952	1957	1965	1975	1978	1980	1985
Total industrial output value	100	100	100	100	100	100	100	100
Of which:								
Light industry	73.6	64.4	51.7	50.4	43.3	42.7	47.0	49.6
Heavy industry	26.4	35.6	48.3	49.6	56.7	57.3	53.0	50.4

26.9% of the total industrial output value (30% in 1971), up 15.5% on 1952. Next came the textile and food industries, accounting for 15.3% and 11.5% respectively. The total output value of these two departments dropped by 24.8% as compared with 1952. The chemical and metallurgical industries ranked third and fourth, accounting for 11.2% and 8.0% respectively, an increase of 6.4% and 2.1% over 1952. The three energy departments, petroleum, electricity and coal, added up to make 10.1% – up 5.9% from 1952.

– A fundamental change in the proportions between light and heavy industries

In 1949, the gross output value of heavy industry was 26.4% of the gross national industrial output value, while that of light industry came to 73.6%. A fundamental change has taken place in the proportions between light and heavy industries thanks to the development of construction in the 30 years or so after the founding of New China. In 1985 the proportion of light industry to heavy industry in the national economy was 49.6 to 50.4, a fairly coordinated development between the two. See Table 2 above.

– A considerable change in the proportional relations within heavy and light industries

Within heavy industry in old China the manufacturing industry was very weak and the processing industry lagged far behind the mining industry. By 1985, the proportion of manufacturing industry had gone up to 53.0% and that of the mining industry and raw and semi-finished materials industry had dropped to 11.5% and 35.5% respectively. The proportion of the output value of the energy industry in the total output value of heavy industry rose from 12.4% in 1952 to 20.4% in 1985 and its proportion in the total industrial output value went up from 4.2% in 1952 to 10.3% in 1985. Energy production was originally confined to coal only, but now there are various kinds of energy, with coal as the main item. The output of coal accounted for 96.7% of the total energy output in

1952. By 1985 it had dropped to 72.8% while the proportion of crude oil, natural gas and hydropower was 20.9%, 2.0% and 4.3% respectively.

In light industry, the pattern of raw materials has improved visibly. In 1952, the output value of products using agricultural products as raw materials made up 87.5% of the total output value of light industry. Starting from the mid-1950s, China began to pay special attention to developing light industries using non-agricultural products as raw materials. Efforts were made to develop chemical fibre, plastics, synthetic detergents, synthetic fatty acid, electronics and other new industries. This brought about a change in the situation in which most light industries had long depended on agriculture for the supply of raw materials. In 1985, the proportion of light industry using agricultural products as raw materials fell to 67.0% and that of light industry using industrial products as raw materials went up to 33%. The output of light industrial products using industrial products as raw materials, such as bicycles, sewing machines, watches, TV sets, tape recorders, cameras, washing machines and refrigerators, increased rapidly.

The Regional Distribution of Industry

The regional distribution of industry in old China was utterly irrational. This chiefly finds expression in the following aspects:

– More than 70% of industry was concentrated in the eastern coastal areas, which accounts for less than 12% of the country's territory

With the exception of a few cities on the Changjiang (Yangtze) river such as Wuhan and Chongqing, the vast interior regions virtually had no modern industry to speak of. The industrial output value of the vast regions of South-West China, North-West China and Inner Mongolia, which make up 68% of the country's land, accounted for only 9% of the national total. The rich mineral resources of these regions had not been exploited and used, and basic industries were virtually non-existent.

The National Economy

– The development of industry in individual regions was extremely unbalanced

In North-East China, for instance, heavy industry, mainly mining and munitions industries, developed lopsidedly. In the coastal areas south of the Shanhaiguan pass, textile and other light industries were developed one-sidedly, while heavy industry was very backward.

– Industry was concentrated in a small number of cities

These were chiefly Shanghai, Tianjin, Qingdao, Guangzhou, Wuxi, Shenyang, Anshan and Dalian. Urban economy was divorced from rural economy. Meanwhile, industries concentrated in a few cities were attached to different imperialist countries, most of the equipment and raw materials relied on imports and there were no organic ties in the economy between various cities.

After the founding of New China, attention was paid to the rational distribution of industry. While the role of the original industrial bases in the coastal areas was brought into full play, new industrial bases were set up in the vast hinterland. During the First Five-Year Plan period, the stress of construction in the coastal areas was laid on building the north-east industrial base centred on the reconstruction and expansion of the Anshan Iron and Steel Company; in the inland areas, the stress was laid on building the central China industrial bases centred on the Wuhan Iron and Steel Company and the North China industrial base centred on the Baotou Iron and Steel Company; industrial construction also started in South-West and North-West China. The rate of increase of the total industrial output value in the inland areas reached an average annual rate of 20%, surpassing that of the coastal areas.

During the Second Five-Year Plan period and the period of readjustment (1959–1965), the existing heavy industry base in North-East China became stronger and more consolidated with the opening of the Daqing oilfield. In North China the metallurgical and coal industries further developed and industrial

bases and key enterprises were reinforced, such as the Shanxi energy base and coal, power and non-ferrous metals enterprises.

Changes in the proportions of the total industrial output value of the inland and coastal areas are shown in Table 3.

Through more than 30 years of readjustment, remarkable changes have taken place in the distribution of China's industries and tremendous achievements have been scored in this respect:

– Old industrial areas have been strengthened and transformed and large numbers of new industrial cities, bases and areas have been built and expanded

In the coastal areas, great efforts have been made to strengthen and transform the industrial area along the Shanghai–Nanjing railway with Shanghai as its centre, the industrial areas in the central and southern parts of Liaoning, the Beijing–Tianjin–Tangshan industrial area, the Zhujiang (Pearl River) Delta industrial area, with Guangzhou as its centre, and the Shandong industrial area along the Jiaoji and Yanqing railways, with Jinan and Qingdao as centres. These areas have become quite advanced and strong comprehensive industrial bases. In the inland areas, vigorous efforts have been made to build and expand the Wuhan industrial area, the Heilongjiang industrial area, the central Hunan industrial area with Changsha and Zhuzhou as centres, and the central Henan industrial area with Luoyang and Zhengzhou as centres, as well as a large number of industrial cities such as Jilin, Changchun, Taiyuan, Xi'an, Baoji, Lanzhou, Chongqing, Chengdu, Dukou and Guiyang and new, comprehensive or specialized industrial bases.

– The distribution of industries in the coastal and inland areas has gradually become rationalized

Between 1952 and 1985, the growth rate of the number of industrial enterprises, the number of workers and staff, and the amount of fixed assets in the inland areas surpassed that of the coastal areas. By the end of 1985, the number of industrial enterprises in the inland areas had reached 243,200 and that of the

Table 3: The Proportion of Coastal Areas in Total Industrial Output

Item	1952	1957	1965	1975	1980	1984	1985
Absolute figure of total industrial output value (100 million yuan)	343.3	783.9	1,393.9	3,218.8	4,992.4	7,029.9	8,294.5
Of which:							
Coastal areas	238.1	516.7	879.1	1,963.3	3,070.1	4,202.6	5,003.5
Inland areas	105.2	267.2	514.8	1,255.5	1,922.3	2,827.3	3,291.0
Proportion of total industrial output value (%)	100	100	100	100	100	100	100
Of which:							
Coastal areas	69.4	65.9	63.1	61.0	61.5	59.8	60.3
Inland areas	30.6	34.1	36.9	39.0	38.5	40.2	39.7

coastal areas was 220,400, accounting for 52.5% and 47.5% of the country's total industrial enterprises respectively. The amount of industrial fixed assets of state enterprises in the inland areas stood at 367.29 billion yuan while that of the coastal areas was 321.30 billion yuan, accounting for 53.3% and 46.7% of the national total respectively. The number of workers and staff of state-owned industrial enterprises in the inland areas was 28.292 million persons, while that of the coastal areas was 27.268 million persons, accounting for 50.9% and 49.1% of the national total respectively. The steady growth of the material and technological foundation of the industries in inland areas made it possible for the growth rate of the industrial output value and the quantity of products in these areas to exceed those of the coastal areas by wide margins, and their proportions to rise continuously. In 1985, the total industrial output value of the inland areas reached 329.10 billion yuan, an increase of 39.8 times that of 1952, faster than the 23-fold increase in the coastal areas. The proportion of the gross industrial output value of inland areas in the national total rose from 30.6% in 1952 to 39.7% in 1985. Compared with 1952, the changes in the proportion of the output of several major products in the inland areas in 1985 were as follows: coal rose from 56.1% to 76.0%; electricity from 36.4% to 50.9%; steel output from 14.2% to 43.5%; cement from 20.7% to 48.5%; cotton yarn from 18% to 41.4%; the output value of the machine-building industry increased from 24.1% to 37.5%. Starting from scratch, the output of chemical fertilizers, bicycles, TV sets, refrigerators and washing machines in 1985 increased to take up 61.2%, 21.1%, 24.6%, 19.8% and 28.5% of the national total respectively. The development of industries in the inland areas greatly improved the regional distribution of China's industries.

– *The economy of minority nationality regions has developed rapidly*

As China attaches great importance to industrial growth in the national minority regions, industry in the five autonomous regions has developed swiftly. In the Inner Mongolia autonomous region, the Baotou industrial base centred on the Baotou Iron and Steel Company has been set up; in the Xinjiang Uygur autonomous region, the Karamai oilfield has been built together with a number of non-ferrous metal and textile enterprises; in the Ningxia Hui autonomous region, the Helan Mountain coal base and the Qingtongxia hydropower station have been built; in the Guangxi Zhuang autonomous region, sugar-refining, linen and machine-building industries have been set up; in the Tibet autonomous region, a number of medium-sized and small power generation, building materials, machine-building, woollen textile and leather plants have been built. By 1985 the gross industrial output value of these five autonomous

regions had reached 31.49 billion yuan, an increase of 57 times that of 1952; its proportion in the country's total industrial output value rose to 3.8% from 2.0% in 1952. The amount of fixed assets of state-owned industrial enterprises reached 39.474 billion yuan, which represents an increase of 135.2 times compared with 1952; its proportion in the national total rose to 6.6% from 1.6% in 1952. The number of workers and staff of state-owned industrial enterprises came to 2.326 million, an increase of 34.5 times over 1952; its proportion in the national total rose to 6% from 1.6%.

– *Township industry has developed swiftly, gradually improving the distribution of industries between town and country*

Since the founding of New China, the development of township industry has gone through three upsurges: at the end of the 1950s, in the beginning of the 1970s and in the beginning of the 1980s. By 1985, through development, readjustment and consolidation, there were 854,000 township enterprises, (239,000 township-run industrial enterprises and 615,000 village-run industrial enterprises) with a total of 27.817 million workers and staff and a gross income of 145.9 billion yuan. In 1985 township industry processed 46.6 million tons of grain and ginned 980,000 tons of cotton. It produced 227.79 million tons of coal, accounting for 26.1% of the country's coal output, and 630,000 tons of phosphate fertilizer, accounting for 36% of the country's total output. It also produced 29.05 million tons of cement, 2.19 million tons of machine-made paper and paperboard and 550 million metres of silk fabrics, accounting for 19.9%, 24% and 38% of the country's total output respectively. Its output of bricks, lime, sand and stones and medium-sized and small farm implements made up 75–90% of the total output in the country. The output of iron ore, pyrite ore, edible vegetable oil and other products makes up a large proportion of the country's total output. The output value of the township industry of Beijing, Tianjin and Shanghai doing processing work or turning out accessories for big industrial enterprises accounts for 60–80% of the total output value of township industry of the three cities. They can produce parts and accessories and auxiliary equipment as well as high quality precision products. Today township industry has become an important component part of the diversified undertakings of China's rural areas. It is of far-reaching importance to speeding up the economic and cultural development of the rural areas, making full and rational use of the rural labour force and raising the standard of living of the peasants.

Technological Progress in Industry

The technological level of industry in old China was extremely low. To change this backward state inherited from the past, New China made strenuous efforts in various fields and set up a series of new branches of science and technology and industrial departments, e.g., for semiconductors, computers, electronics, automation, atomic energy and jet propulsion technologies. In the early 1960s and 1970s, China imported large engineering projects, whole sets of equipment and new technologies for the petro-chemical, metallurgical, energy, engineering and electronics industries. They played an important role in the building and development of the chemical fertilizer, chemical fibre, plastics, synthetic detergent, electronics and other new industries and in improving the technologies of the metallurgical, energy and machine-building industries.

Since 1980, China has stressed the improvement of economic performance as the focus of economic construction. In industrial construction, the principle of taking technological transformation as the chief means to secure expanded production has been adopted in place of the practice of building new enterprises to achieve the purpose. This has pushed ahead technological transformation in industry. Funds allocated for the updating of equipment, technological transformation and other measures have increased year by year, from 14.3 billion yuan in 1981 to 17.1 billion yuan in 1982, 20.7 billion yuan in 1983, 22.5 billion yuan in 1984, and 35.1 billion yuan in 1985. At the same time, the work of technological import was stepped up. During the period of the Sixth Five-Year Plan, more than 10,000 foreign technologies were imported, some of which were advanced technologies and key equipment up to the international level of the late 1970s and early 1980s. Through technological import, joint ventures with Chinese and foreign investment and joint operation, the technological level of many industrial enterprises and trades improved visibly.

Through more than 30 years' work, China's industrial technology has achieved marked progress and laid the technological foundation for the country's socialist modernization. Its major achievements find expression in the following aspects:

– A number of new industrial departments at advanced or fairly advanced levels have been set up

These include the aviation, electronics, petrochemical, nuclear and space navigation industries. At present, China not only can produce large numbers of black and white and colour television sets and tape recorders but can also produce large and medium-sized computers and micro-computers. The successful manufacture of the extra-big *Yinhe* (Milky Way) computer which can make over 100 million calculations indicates that China's computer technology has entered a new stage. The manufacture of atomic bombs, hydrogen bombs and nuclear submarines, the launching of carrier rockets and the launching and accurate recovery of man-made earth satellites sym-

bolize the huge progress of China's industrial technology. In July 1984 China launched an experimental communication satellite which succeeded in reaching its geostationary position. This shows that China is able to produce all kinds of raw and semi-finished materials for making satellites and has attained a new level in launching, monitoring, synchronously reaching geostationary positions, and other space technologies and has joined the front rank in the world in this field. China's space navigation industry has entered the international market by providing a service to other countries in launching satellites.

– Tremendous changes have taken place in the technological conditions of existing industrial departments

Each department is now in possession of a number of up-to-date technologies and items of equipment which have played a decisive role in raising the quality of products and expanding their varieties. For instance, the technological conditions of the metallurgical industry have gone through great changes. Now the industry boasts such new equipment as a 2,580-cubic-metre blast furnace and top combustion stoves. A huge blast furnace with a capacity of 4,000 cubic metres has been built and commissioned at the Baoshan Iron and Steel Company. The capacity of the top-blowing oxygen converter has reached 150 tons, and the technology of continuous casting is being popularized. Following the import of the highly automatic 1.7-metre rolling mill by the Wuhan Iron and Steel Company, the Benxi Iron and Steel Plant also installed a 1.7-metre rolling mill designed and made by China itself. The breakthrough in the technology of ore dressing of low-grade red hematite has raised the ratio of ore concentrate from 58% to 63%, and the recovery rate from 64% to 75%. With the rising level of technology, the varieties of iron and steel have increased correspondingly.

The machine-building industry is now able to provide large advanced equipment, such as the 30,000-ton die-forging hydraulic press, numerically controlled machine tools and precision machine tools including the precision raster display jig boring machine with a 2×3 metre working table and the leading screw grinder which can grind 5 metre-long lead screws. The shipping industry has developed from making repairs to designing and building big ships. Today China can build 25,000-ton cargo ships, 50,000-ton oil tankers, ocean-going surveying ships and all kinds of warships and auxiliary vessels. With the growth of the shipbuilding industry, the ship checking technology has attained international level. A successful trial flight of the large *Yun*-7 plane has been made. The production capacity for whole-set equipment has increased considerably. China can now produce 2,800 mm aluminium plate cold rolling

A 1.7-metre rolling mill in the Wuhan steel factory in Hubei province. *(Photo by Wang Xiangsen)*

mills, iron and steel complexes with an annual output of 1.5 million tons, coal washing plants with a capacity of 3 million tons, oil refineries with an annual output of 2.5 million tons, and whole-set equipment producing 300,000 tons of synthetic ammonia and 240,000 tons of urea, as well as 330,000-volt high tension power transmission and transforming equipment, 200,000 kW and 300,000 kW internal cooling thermal power generating units and 225,000 kW mixed-flow hydraulic electrogenerating units. A 170,000 kW low water head power generating unit has been installed at the Gezhouba hydropower station and is operating satisfactorily. Transformation of ordinary machine tools and industrial kilns with micro-electronics technology and the wide application of the technologies of hot spraying (welding) and electric spraying have all achieved marked economic results.

In the oil industry China has mastered the technology of drilling 3,000 metre deep wells and has drilled a number of extra-deep oil wells exceeding 6,000 metres. It has begun to master the skill of drilling offshore deep wells and inclined wells and has developed the new oil refining technologies of catalytic cracking of lift legs, multiple-metal reforming, hydrogeneration refining and dewaxing of molecular sieves.

In the building materials industry, an experimental production line using the pre-calcining process which turns out a daily output of 700 tons of clinker cement has successfully gone into operation. The output is double that of the rotatory kiln of the same specifica-

tion and saves more than 30% of energy. This enables China's cement making technology to attain the advanced international level of the 1970s. A production line for float glass has been set up and commissioned. The application of aluminium silicate refractory fibre has conserved large quantities of energy.

In the textile industry, the wide application of airstream spinning, jet weaving and new printing, dyeing and finishing technologies has improved the quality of the products and increased their colours and designs. The complete set of equipment turning out 15,000 tons of terylene short fibre annually and their processing technology are up to international level today.

– The level of mechanization has risen steadily

The production equipment of all industrial departments has increased substantially and their quality has also improved enormously. In many industries, mechanization has replaced heavy manual labour. In coal extraction, the backward production method of haulage by man and horse has generally given way to mechanization or semi-mechanization. The number of coal cutters in state-owned coal mines has increased steadily. By 1985, 45% of coal extraction in large and medium-sized state-owned coal mines had been mechanized. High temperature, high voltage power generating units made up of 48% of the total number of power generating units.

The level of power equipment is another major gauge of technological progress. In 1984, power consumption by industrial departments exceeded 280 billion kWh, 61 times that of 1952. The average power consumption of each worker and staff member came to 5,400 kWh in 1984, an increase of more than six times that of 1952.

— Tremendous progress has been made in the work of standardization

By focusing on setting standards for consumer goods, energy conservation, machinery and electrical appliances and products for foreign trade, the work of standardization has been steadily pushed ahead. By the end of 1985, state standards had been set for 7,569 industrial and agricultural products.

The pace for adopting international standards has also been stepped up. By the end of 1985, international standards or advanced standards abroad had been adopted for 2,196 of the 7,569 products for which national standards had been set, making up 29% of the total; 782 products, or 10% of the total, had reached the international level at the end of the 1970s and the beginning of the 1980s. The two combined to make up 39% of the total. The adoption of international standards has promoted the technological progress and improvement of product quality of Chinese enterprises.

The areas covered by national standards have become increasingly more extensive. Most of the national standards formulated before 1980 were technological standards for traditional industries. During the Sixth Five-Year Plan period they were extended to new technologies and modernized management. By the end of 1985, 21 of the national standards were in the field of nuclear technology, 370 were for information technology and 395 for exploitation and comprehensive use of energy. This promoted the application of new skills and technologies and the introduction of modernized management.

While the formulation and revision of national standards were stepped up, various departments and localities made greater efforts to work out or revise standards for specialized trades and for enterprises. By the end of 1985, various departments in the country had formulated more than 17,000 specialized (ministry) standards and nearly 120,000 standards for enterprises had been set by various localities.

To bring into full play the role of standardization, improve the quality of products fundamentally and achieve the best social economic effect, attention has been paid in the past few years to the formulation of whole sets of standards and the work of connection and coordination between the standards has been strengthened. This was designed to link up scientific research, production, circulation and use organically and technologically so as to ensure concerted production and construction.

A national standard system with the national standards and specialized standards as the main body and local enterprises standards as a supplement has now taken shape in China. More than 80% of the products turned out by enterprises at county level and above have standards to go by.

Although China's industrial technology has gained striking advances, for one reason or another technological progress in industry as a whole has been rather slow and in many aspects it lags behind industrially developed countries. This finds expression conspicuously in the following aspects: backward technology and equipment, low efficiency and huge consumption; few varieties of products, poor property and low quality; little technological reserves, weak capacity of development and slow rate of technological updating. China is now adopting the necessary measures to solve these problems.

MAJOR INDUSTRIAL DEPARTMENTS

The Metallurgical Industry

China's ancient smelting technique has a long history. As early as 2,500 years ago, iron implements were produced and used. But it was not until 1890 that China started building its first modern iron and steel plant, the Hanyang Iron Works. The subsequent development of the industry was still very slow. Steel output in 1943, the peak year of this product in old China, was only 923,000 tons. Later, the industry suffered repeated damage. By 1949, when the entire mainland was liberated, there were only seven blast furnaces, 12 open-hearth furnaces and 22 small furnaces operating, with an annual output of merely 158,000 tons of steel and 250,000 tons of iron.

A profound change has taken place in the metallurgical industry since the founding of New China:

— The metallurgical industry has built a fairly large infrastructure

Investment of capital construction in this industry amounted to 92.29 billion yuan between 1953 and 1985, accounting for 16.8% of the total industrial investment and occupying the first place for investment in the industrial sector.

The construction of China's metallurgical industry began with the construction of the Anshan Iron and Steel Company. By the end of the 1970s, the Anshan

Company had become the country's largest base of steel products, with an annual output of approximately seven million tons of steel and five million tons of rolled steel. During the First Five-Year Plan period, the Qiqihar Steel Plant was built in Heilongjiang province. Work on the construction of the new Wuhan Iron and Steel Company and the Baotou Iron and Steel Company also began. The latter two iron and steel complexes first turned out iron in 1958 and 1959 respectively. The Wuhan Complex has an annual capacity of four million tons of iron, four million tons of steel and 4,180,000 tons of rolled steel. The Baotou Company now has an annual capacity of eight million tons of iron, 2.43 million tons of steel, 2.70 million tons of iron and 1.10 million tons of rolled steel.

Some other enterprises that have undertaken technical transformation have also become an important force in the iron and steel industry. An example is the iron and steel enterprises under the Shanghai Metallurgical Bureau: in the whole of 1957 they could only produce 520,000 tons of steel, but in 1985 they had an annual production capacity of five million tons of steel and 4.20 million tons of rolled steel. They have become the second largest steel base in the country, next only to the Anshan Company, capable of turning out many varieties of high quality rolled steel.

In 1964 the Chinese government decided to establish an iron and steel industry base in the hinterland, at Panzhihua in Xichang, Sichuan. The base was established in the first half of the 1970s after arduous efforts and many difficulties. The new iron and steel complex has the capacity to produce 6.50 million tons of iron ore, 1.93 million tons of iron, 1.50 million tons of steel and 1.10 million tons of rolled steel a year. It is a large iron and steel complex designed by China and installed with Chinese-made equipment by successfully applying the technique of separating iron from vanadium, titanium and cobalt.

Since 1979 China has concentrated its efforts on building the largest iron and steel complex in the country, the Baoshan Iron and Steel Complex near Shanghai. Its main equipment is imported from abroad and has the following characteristics: high-powered equipment; new techniques, low consumption of energy and a high degree of automation. When the complex is completed, it will be able to produce 6.5 million tons of iron, 6.7 million tons of steel, 4.22 million tons of rolled steel and 1.22 million tons of commercial billet a year. The first stage of the project was completed in 1985. The project has been put into operation.

A number of iron and steel companies have been established, renovated or expanded since the founding of New China. They include the Benxi Iron and Steel Company, the Capital Iron and Steel Company, the Fushun Steel Plant, the Dalian Steel Plant, the Xiangtan Steel Plant, and the Kunming Iron and Steel Company. A number of key metallurgical enterprises have also been established, such as the Maanshan

The sulphuric acid shop in Guixi copper smeltery in Jiangxi province. *(Photo by Xiong Zhuoran)*

Wheel Tyre Plant, the Yunnan Tin Company, the Silver Non-Ferrous Metal Company, the Jiangxi Copper Company, the Zhuzhou Smelting Plant and the Zhengzhou Aluminium Plant. China's metallurgical industry, especially the ferrous metal industry, has grown on a large scale after more than 30 years of construction. By the end of 1985, there were 7,200 metallurgical enterprises, including more than 20 large iron and steel complexes.

– There has been a steady rise in the level of technical equipment

The level of technical equipment of China's metallurgical industry has greatly improved over the past 30 years and more. In old China the largest blast furnace had a volume of only a little over 900 cubic metres, the capacity of the biggest open-hearth furnace was 150 tons, and that of the largest electric furnace was only five tons. There was also a very low level of mechanization and automation in mining and steel rolling. But in 1984, there were 25 blast furnaces with a volume of more than 1,000 cubic metres each. The blast furnace at the Anshan Iron and Steel Complex has a volume of 2,580 cubic metres and the modern blast furnace at the Baoshan Iron and Steel Complex that went into operation in 1985 has a volume of 4,000 cubic metres and is computer-controlled. In steel melting, there are 11 open-hearth furnaces, each able to process 500 tons a day. The biggest top-blown oxygen converter can process 150 tons. The large top-blown pure oxygen converter at Baoshan can process 300 tons.

With the improvements in techniques and equipment in steel smelting, the proportion of steel tapped by different processes has changed. Compared with 1952, the proportion of steel by open-hearth process dropped from 81.8% to 28% in 1984, that by electrical process rose from 10.5% to 20.8% and that by converter process increased from 7.7% to 51.2%. The proportion of steel tapped by continuous casting has steadily increased. In steel rolling, the Wuhan Iron and Steel Company imported a 1,700 mm strip steel cold, hot rolling machinery unit in the 1970s. The Benxi Iron and Steel Company was installed with Chinese-made 1,700 mm strip steel hot rolling machinery unit. Greater progress has also been made in modernizing the technical equipment in the fields of mining, ore dressing, sintering, coking, ferro-alloys smelting and refractories.

– There has been a considerable increase in output value and production, expansion of varieties and improved quality

The total output value of the metallurgical industry in 1985 reached 66.4 billion yuan, a 36-fold increase over 1952. It registered an annual growth rate of 11.6%, accounting for 8.2% of the total industrial output value. Iron output reached 43.84 million tons; steel, 46.79 million tons; and rolled steel, 36.93 million tons; or 22.7 times, 34.7 times and 33.8 times the output of 1952 respectively.

The types of steel have increased in number alongside the increase in output.

In the early days of New China, there were more than 100 types of steel and over 400 specifications of rolled steel. Now China has the capacity to produce over 1,000 types of steel, including high alloy steel and precision alloy steel, as well as more than 20,000 specifications of rolled steel. The proportion of such products as steel plate, tube and strip steel rose from 12.3% in 1952 to 36.2% in 1983. According to the characteristics of China's natural resources, an alloy steel series has been set up by taking advantage of the rich supply of tungsten, molybdenum, vanadium, titanium and rare earth. The proportion of alloy steel reached 6.9% in 1984 and that of low alloy steel came to 13%. The quality of products has also improved: for high-speed tool steel it has approached international standards. In addition to self-sufficiency in supply, they have been made into cutting tools and drills for export. New key metallic materials needed for the national defence industry and high technology includ-

ing the making of atomic and hydrogen bombs, missiles, submarines, rockets and communication satellites are mainly supplied at home.

– The siting of the iron and steel industry has been improved

About 90% of the iron and steel output in old China was concentrated in the north-eastern part of the country. The output of steel and iron in North-East China in 1943 accounted for 94.5% and 88% of the national output respectively. By 1952, steel output along the coastal areas accounted for 85.8% of the national output, of which 70% was in the north-east and only 3.8% in the south-west and north-west. China took note of this irrational distribution of the iron and steel industry and made steady improvements. While renovating and expanding the iron and steel plants along the coastal areas, China has successively built the Baotou Iron and Steel Company, the Wuhan Iron and Steel Company and the Panzhihua Iron and Steel Company and expanded the Taiyuan Iron and Steel Company in the interior. These large iron and steel complexes produce more than one million tons of steel a year each. In the interior, key iron and steel enterprises whose annual steel output stands at below one million tons include the Chongqing Iron and Steel Company, the Jiuquan Iron and Steel Company, the Xiangtan Iron and Steel Works and the Chengdu Seamless Steel Tubes Plant. A number of important special steels plants have also been built or expanded at Qiqihaer in Heilongjiang, Chongqing and Jiangyou in Sichuan, Guiyang in Guizhou, Daye in Hubei, Wuyang in Henan, Xi'an in Shaanxi and Xining in Qinghai. Meanwhile, attention has also been paid to giving full scope to local initiative, and many local small and medium-sized iron and steel works have been built. There are iron and steel enterprises in all the various parts of the country except the Tibet autonomous region. In 1985 the proportion of steel output in the coastal areas dropped to 56.5%, and that in the north-east plummeted to 24.4%. It was 12.3% in the north-west and south-west, including 8.4% in Sichuan. The output of iron, steel and rolled steel from the small and

Table 4: The Increase in the Total Output Value and the Output of Major Products of the Metallurgical Industry

Item	Unit	1952	1957	1965	1975	1980	1984	1985
Total output value of metallurgical industry	100 million yuan	20.2	60.0	149.5	288.3	430.3	579.4	664.0
Of which:								
Ferrous metals	100 million yuan	13.9	41.8	106.7	193.8	298.9	400.9	444.3
Non-ferrous metals	100 million yuan	6.3	18.2	42.8	94.5	131.4	178.5	219.7
Iron ore	10,000 tons	429	1,937	3,149	9,694	11,259	12,670	
Pig iron	10,000 tons	193	594	1,077	2,449	3,802	4,001	4,384
Steel	10,000 tons	135	535	1,223	2,390	3,712	4,347	4,679
Rolled steel	10,000 tons	106	415	881	1,622	2,716	3,372	2,693
Ferro-alloys	10,000 tons	1.7	10.5	33.9	76.9	99.4	127.5	149.4

medium-sized enterprises in the localities accounted for 20–30% of the total national output. This is of far-reaching significance in promoting the development of the local economy.

– The problems and prospects of development

China's metallurgical industry still cannot meet the need for national economic development, despite its great achievements. There is a great gap in technical level as compared with the advanced level of the industrially developed countries. Products are mostly destined for use in capital construction of heavy industry, while those for use in light industry and in the civil building industry are fewer in quantity. Energy consumption is high, exceeding the sustaining capacity of the national economy. The use of new techniques in production is inadequate. There is disproportion in the internal relationship between ferrous and non-ferrous metals.

China is taking measures to make a readjustment and solve the above-mentioned problems as quickly as possible. During the Seventh Five-Year Plan period, China plans to restructure and build a number of key iron and steel and mining projects, so that their main equipment will reach the advanced level attained by the developed countries in the late 1970s. In regard to non-ferrous metals, further efforts will be made to exploit aluminium, lead, zinc and copper mines, in that order of importance, and to make arrangements for the production of tin, a favourable export item, and other products in short supply. Efforts will be made to increase the capacity for the production of steel, rolled steel, iron and iron ores, as well as aluminium oxide and electrolysis of aluminium.

The Chemical Industry

The chemical industry in old China had a very weak foundation. There were a small number of chemical plants in some major cities such as Dalian, Tianjin, Shanghai, Nanjing, Guangzhou, and Chongqing. For example, the Yongli Ammonium Sulphate Plant in Nanjing and the Yongli Alkali Factory in Tianjin. Except for a few plants making basic chemicals and fertilizer, most of these plants produced paints, dyestuffs, drugs and rubber by processing imported raw materials. In 1949, only 40,000 tons of sulphuric acid, 88,000 tons of soda and 6,000 tons of fertilizer were produced. The output value of chemicals amounted to 177 million yuan, accounting for 1.6% of the total industrial output value in the country. Since the founding of New China, the chemical industry has achieved noted successes:

– The output of the chemical industry has increased quickly

From 1953 to 1985, the total output value of the

off

chemical industry increased by an average annual rate of 16.4%, a growth rate next only to that of the oil industry. It amounted to 92.67 billion yuan in 1985, when its proportion rose to 11.2% of the total industrial output value of the country, ranking fourth in output, next only to the machine-building industry, the textile industry and the food industry.

– The construction of the chemical industry has been proceeding on a fairly large scale, and its siting has become more and more rational

China has paid great attention to the capital construction of the chemical industry. From 1953 to 1985, the State invested 58.27 billion yuan in it—10.5% of the total industrial investment, which was less only than the investment in the metallurgical, power, machine-building and coal industries. During this period, China laid special emphasis on the import of chemical technology. The amount of foreign exchange spent on this by the Ministry of Chemical Industry was one-quarter of the State's total foreign exchange expenditure for the import of technology. This proportion rose to one-third if the chemical projects imported by the textiles and light industries are also taken into account.

In the construction of the chemical industry, China has built many new plants, while renovating and restructuring the existing ones in the coastal areas. Among the major projects built since the founding of the PRC are the Sichuan Chemical Plant, the Luzhou Natural Gas Chemical Works, the Jilin Chemical Industrial Corporation, the Xixiashan Chemical Fertilizer Plant, the Anqing General Petrochemical Plant, the Taiyuan Chemical Industry Corporation, the Nanjing Chemical Industry Corporation, the Dalian Chemical Industrial Corporation, the Tianjin Soda Plant and the Yanshan General Petrochemical Corporation.

Considerable efforts have been made to develop the chemical industry in the interior, while giving full scope to the operations of the chemical industrial bases in the coastal areas. Chemical enterprises have been established in the interior provinces and autonomous regions, including Tibet. The proportion of the output value of the interior chemical enterprises in the total national chemical output value rose from 17.3% in 1952 to 37.3% in 1985. Sichuan ranked fifth in the output of chemicals in the country. Taking advantage of the abundant resources of natural gas and phosphorus available, the province laid stress on increasing the production of nitrogen and phosphate fertilizer. In 1985 Sichuan's chemical fertilizer output reached 1,352,000 tons, topping the list of fertilizer producers in the various parts of the country. At the same time, the province has also energetically increased the production of sodium chloride, sulphuric acid, soda, dyestuffs, coating, natural gas, organic chemicals, rubber products and chemical equipment. Sichuan has

Table 5: The Growth of the Chemical Industry

Item	Unit	1952	1957	1965	1975	1980	1984	1985
Sulphuric acid	10,000 tons	19.0	63.2	234.0	484.7	764.3	817.2	676.4
Soda	10,000 tons	19.2	50.6	88.2	124.3	161.3	188.0	201.1
Caustic soda	10,000 tons	7.9	19.8	55.6	128.9	192.3	222.2	235.3
Chemical fertilizer	10,000 tons	3.9	15.1	172.6	524.7	1,232.1	1,460.2	1,322.2
Of which:								
Nitrogen fertilizer	10,000 tons	3.9	12.9	103.7	370.9	999.3	1,221.0	1,143.8
Phosphate fertilizer	10,000 tons	—	2.2	68.8	153.1	230.8	236.0	176.0
Agricultural chemicals	10,000 tons	0.2	6.5	19.3	42.2	53.7	29.9	21.0
Ethylene	10,000 tons	—	—	0.3	6.5	49.0	64.8	65.2
Plastics	10,000 tons	0.2	1.3	9.7	33.0	89.8	118.0	123.4
Synthetic rubber	10,000 tons	—	—	1.59	5.67	12.3	17.4	18.1
Tyres	10,000 tyres	42	88	232	700	1,146	1,569	1,926
Chemical pharmaceuticals	10,000 tons	0.01	0.22	1.05	3.05	4.01	5.35	5.85

become one of the important bases of the chemical industry in China.

China has practised the policy of simultaneous development of large, medium-sized and small chemical enterprises. While establishing a group of large key enterprises and building a dozen main bases of chemical industry, the State has set up many small chemical enterprises. These small enterprises account for 40% of the fixed assets of the chemical enterprises owned by the whole people. They occupy a high proportion of the output of certain principal products. For example, 77% of paint; 50–60% of fertilizer, calcium carbide and dyestuffs; 40–50% of pyrite, phosphorus, sulphuric acid and tyres; and 20–30% of agricultural chemicals, plastics and caustic soda.

— *The necessary chemical departments have been established*

After more than 30 years of construction, China has virtually all the necessary departments of the chemical industry. There are 19 departments: chemical ores, petrochemicals, coal chemicals, acid base, inorganic salts, chemical fertilizers, agricultural chemicals, organic materials, synthetic resin and plastics, synthetic rubber, synthetic fibre monomer, sensitivity materials and magnetic record materials, dyestuffs and intermediate, coating and pigment, chemical reagents, catalyst and solvent as well as auxiliaries, new chemical materials, rubber products and chemical equipment.

China has all along attached importance to chemical fertilizers and agricultural chemicals in planning the industry. To accelerate the development of the fertilizer industry, China has built small and medium-sized nitrogen fertilizer plants, and in addition it has imported 13 sets of advanced equipment capable of producing 1,000 tons of synthetic ammonia and 1,600 tons of urea per day. Meanwhile, it has also increased the production of phosphate fertilizer. There are phosphate fertilizer plants in all the provinces, municipalities and autonomous regions except Tibet. There

were more than 3,000 fertilizer enterprises in 1985 with an annual output of 13.22 million tons of fertilizer. Of this total output, 86.5% was nitrogen fertilizer; 13.2%, phosphate fertilizer and 0.2% potash fertilizer. On the average, the amount of locally made fertilizer applied to every hectare of land in China has increased from 4.5 kilograms in 1952 to upwards of 150 kilograms at present. There are more than ten varieties of fertilizer, including urea, ammonium nitrate, ammonium bicarbonate, ammonium chloride, ammonia water, liquid ammonia, ammonium sulphate, calcium superphosphate, fused calcium-magnesium phosphate, ammonium phosphate, potassium chloride, potassium sulphate, micronutrient and decayed plant acids. There are more than 400 enterprises making agricultural chemicals, and an integrated system of making farm chemicals, from synthesis to processing, has been formed. In 1980 some 537,000 tons of pesticides were produced. To prevent pesticide pollution of farm crops, poultry, domestic animals, aquatic products and environment, energetic efforts have been made in the past few years to increase the production of organic phosphate, phrethrin and other farm chemicals that are effective but carry low residual toxicity, while reducing or halting the production of pesticides with high residual toxicity, such as HCH and DDT. The total output of pesticides has declined year by year. Only 211,000 tons of pesticides were produced in 1985.

Soda and caustic soda are raw materials vital to the chemical industry and necessary for the development of the light and textile industries. The number of plants making these two raw materials has increased considerably since the founding of New China. There were 26 soda plants and 184 enterprises making caustic soda in China at the end of 1984, in which year China produced 1,880,000 tons of soda – ranking fourth in the world output, next only to the United States, the Soviet Union and Britain, and 2,220,000 tons of caustic soda – fifth in world output, next only to the United States, Federal Germany, Japan and the

Soviet Union. The quality of Chinese-made soda attained world standard as early as the 1920s. *Hongsanjiao* (Red Triangle) soda won a gold medal at an international fair held at Philadelphia in 1926. Soda kept its top quality after the founding of the PRC: the *Hongsanjiao* soda of the Tianjin Soda Plant, *Gonglian* soda of the Dalian Chemical Industrial Corporation, and *Zili* (Self-Reliance) soda of the Qingdao Soda Plant each won state gold medals for a top quality product. The Tianjin Chemical Plant, the Shenyang Chemical Plant, the Dagu Chemical Plant and the Quzhou Chemical Industrial Corporation won state prizes for their quality solid caustic soda. The *Tiangong* (Excellent Workmanship), *Dongfanghong* (The East is Red) and *Hongsanjiao* solid caustic sodas sell well at home and abroad and receive a "pass without examination" certificate.

Synthetic materials is a new chemical industrial branch. China started making synthetic fibre, synthetic rubber and plastics from coal in the 1950s. The output increased rapidly with the development of the petrochemical industry in the 1970s. In 1983 China produced 390,000 tons of synthetic fibre monomer, 169,000 tons of synthetic rubber and 1,121,000 tons of plastics. Home-made synthetic rubber, which is used to make rubber products, accounts for more than one-third of the total consumption. Polyethylene, polypropylene and polyvinyl chloride are widely used to make packing materials, electrical appliances, furniture, parts and accessories for everyday industrial articles and motor vehicles and aircraft. Their use in the building industry has just begun. High molecular synthetic materials have also been used to make hydrocephalus drain equipment, artificial larynxes, artificial skin, artificial heart valves and other artificial organs.

The chemical ores industry has also developed rapidly: there were 241 enterprises in 1984. Of these, the key chemical mines are the phosphate mines at Jinping in Jiangsu, Jinxiang in Hubei, Kaiyang in Guizhou, Xinghe in Sichuan, Liuyang in Hunan and Jingzhong in Hubei; pyrite mines at Wude in Guangdong, at Xiangshan in Anhui, at Zhangjiagou in Liaoning, at Yangquan in Shanxi, at Longyou in Zhejiang and Yuntai in Jiangsu; boron mines at 501 Yingkou, at Kuandian and Fengcheng in Liaoning; two vanadium mines at Pingyang in Zhejiang and Lujiang in Anhui, and a lime mine at Yushan in Hebei. Construction is going on in many other chemical mines. In 1983 China produced 11,638,000 tons of phosphate, 7,355,000 tons of pyrite and 378,000 tons of boron. The output of potassium was small, equivalent to 20,000 tons of potassium chloride. The output of limestone and serpentine could meet the needs of production.

The problems and prospects of development

The main problems confronting China's chemical industry are: disproportion in the internal relationship of the industry, backward technology and outdated equipment in many chemical enterprises, poor integration of science and technology with production and poor economic returns. That is why the chemical industry cannot keep pace with the development of the national economy. There is also the problem of undue emphasis on key projects in the development of the chemical industry. From 1953 to 1980, accumulative investments in the capital construction of the chemical fertilizer and pesticide projects amounted to 23.95 billion yuan, accounting for 57.3% of the total investment in the chemical industry. This was mainly used to develop the nitrogen fertilizer industry, which showed the lack of overall planning which, in turn, affected the development of other enterprises and products and resulted in the irrational structure of the industry and product mix.

During the Seventh Five-Year Plan period, China will lay stress on readjusting the fertilizer mix, increase the production of soda and other basic chemicals, develop the production of fine chemicals and open up new areas of production of chemicals. At the same time, energetic efforts will be made to develop the three major synthetic materials and increase the capacity for the production of ethylene, resins, synthetic rubber and synthetic fibre.

The Machine-Building Industry

The foundation of the machine-building industry in old China was extremely weak. From 1865, when the government of the Qing dynasty established the Jiangnan Manufacturing Bureau in Shanghai, up to the eve of the founding of the PRC, there were only a few small machinery plants in some coastal cities. These plants mainly did repair and assembly work and could only produce simple machines and electrical products. In 1949, 1,600 metal-cutting lathes, 140,000 sets of ball bearings, 10,000 horsepower internal combustion engines and 700 tons of mining equipment were produced.

Thanks to the efforts made over the past 30 years since the founding of New China, the machine-building industry has grown in size, from doing repairs to manufacturing, from copying to self-designing and from making ordinary products and single machines to making certain high-grade, precision and advanced products and complete sets of equipment. It has developed rapidly and won great achievements:

– The steady expansion of the machine-building industry

From 1952 to 1985, the State invested altogether 80.53 billion yuan in the construction of the machine-building industry. Newly added fixed assets amounted to 61.4 billion yuan. A total of 804 large and medium-

Table 6: The Output of the Various Products made by the Machine-Building Industry

Product	Unit	1952	1957	1965	1975	1980	1984	1985
Mining equipment	10,000 tons	0.18	5.29	4.0	19.61	16.25	25.81	31.4
Metallurgical equipment	10,000 tons	0.02	1.38	1.74	8.21	4.1	4.97	
Petroleum equipment	10,000 tons	—	0.59	1.29	6.32	5.71	12.23	16.69
Chemical equipment	10,000 tons	0.1	0.72	3.42	7.59	6.98	9.30	11.39
Power generating equipment	10,000 kW	0.6	19.8	68.3	496.5	419.3	467.4	563.0
Forging equipment	10,000 units	0.11	0.29	0.75	4.47	4.85	4.81	
Metal cutting lathes	10,000 units	1.37	2.8	3.96	17.49	13.36	13.35	16.72
Motor vehicles	10,000 units	—	0.79	4.05	13.98	22.23	31.64	43.72
Tractors (over 20 hp)	10,000 units	—	—	0.96	7.84	9.77	3.97	4.50
Walking tractors	10,000 units	—	—	0.36	20.94	21.79	68.86	82.25
Internal combustion engines	10,000 units	4	69	279	2,348	2,539	4,072	5,547

sized projects went into operation, of which the most important machine-building industrial enterprises are: No. 1 Motor Vehicle Works at Changchun City, No. 2 Motor Vehicle Works at Shiyan City, the Luoyang Bearing Plant, the Luoyang Tractor Plant, the No. 1 Heavy-Duty Machinery Plant at Qiqihar, the Harbin Steam Turbine Plant, the Harbin Boiler Plant, the Harbin Electrical Machinery Plant, the Wuhan Heavy Machine Tools Plant and the Lanzhou Petrochemical Machinery Works. By 1985 there were 111,000 machine-building industrial enterprises with a vast contingent of scientists, researchers, designers and technicians as well as technical workers. The total output value of the machine-building industry amounted to 223.5 billion yuan in 1985 – 107 times the amount in 1952. The machine-building industry occupies one of the most important positions in the entire industrial sector. Its output value accounts for more than one-quarter of the total industrial output value.

– The increase in the variety and output of products of the machine-building industry and the marked improvement in quality

By the end of 1985, China's machine-building industry was making 129 major products and 1,030 minor products and had 53,000 items of products. It is capable of making main engines up to fittings and necessary accessories and parts to form complete sets of equipment. Many of them are important precision products and sophisticated machinery. For many years this industry has provided certain high standard equipment for national economic construction and defence. About 85% of the equipment owned by the basic industrial departments is made in China.

China has adopted international standards with regard to the quality of products of the machine-making industry. The Ministry of the Machine-Building Industry applied 6,857 state and ministry standards at the end of 1985. Of this total, 3,000 standards (44%) were up to international standards. Many enterprises have organized production according to state standards. By the end of 1985, 26% of the engineering products attained the international level of the 1970s and early 1980s. For example, 57 kinds of meters have attained the integration of machinery and electricity. Their performance, reliability and quality have attained the advanced level of the early 1980s.

China's machine-building industry has attained a certain international status. In 1985 its output value was equivalent to 90 billion $US, or about 4% of the gross world output value of the same industry. Its place in world output moved up from 20th before Liberation to the present 7th, next to the United States, Japan, the Soviet Union, Federal Germany, France and Britain. Its output of walking tractors has increased so fast that it ranks first in the world output. Its output of motor vehicles has moved up from about 20th in the 1970s to the present 12th. Its metal cutting lathes rank 4th in terms of output but 10th in terms of output value. Its output of power generation equipment and ball bearings ranks 6th.

– A fairly comprehensive machine making system has been established, with nearly all the necessary departments

Under the Ministry of the Machine-Building Industry there are 10 departments, covering more than 100 branches. Each branch has a number of major enterprises with better working conditions and a stronger technical force to undertake the serial production of quality goods. Together with a large number of small and medium-sized enterprises, these backbone enterprises have initially formed an integrated manufacturing system. The following is information about several principal branches:

Machine tools and forging equipment

Old China could only make simple machine tools, whose highest annual output was only 5,400. But in 1985 a total of 167,200 metal cutting machine tools were made in China, a 31-fold increase compared with the peak annual output in pre-Liberation years. China began making high-grade precision machine

A computer-controlled production line with numerically controlled machine tools, industrial robots and auto-conveyers, designed by Beijing Machine Tools Research Institute. *(Photo by Li Anbao)*

tools in 1958: it now has the capacity to produce over 130 types of such tools and 2,000 lathes a year. Some of these products have attained advanced international level. Research on numerically controlled machine tools began in 1958 and products were turned out in 1961. After importing and absorbing advanced foreign technology, China joined the ranks of the world's foremost producers of numerically controlled machine tools in 1980. Vertical lathes made by the Beijing Precision Machine Tool Plant, the horizontal lathes made by the Qinghai No. 1 Machine Tool Plant, the numerically controlled lathes made by the Changcheng Machine Tool Plant and the numerically controlled external grinders of the Shanghai Machine Tool Plant have been installed in Japanese FANUC automatic plants. Each lathe operated by an industrial robot forms a processing unit itself.

There are 500 kinds of forging presses. Many new products were made in the field of manufacturing numerically controlled, precision and high efficient forging presses during the Sixth Five-Year Plan period. These machines are relatively advanced technically.

The automobile industry

Auto-making did not exist in old China. There were only some small automobile repair and fittings workshops in Shanghai, Beijing, Tianjin, Chongqing and some other cities. All the motor vehicles then available were imported. The commissioning and operation of No. 1 Motor Vehicle Works at Changchun in 1956 ended the history of China's incapability of making motor vehicles and laid the foundation for the development of China's automobile industry. The period from 1956 to 1966 was a decade of comprehensive transformation and development. Some major auto repair and fittings workshops began copying foreign models in making motor vehicles. In 1964, China pooled an enormous fund in

starting the construction of a number of large basic auto-making enterprises in the interior areas. The No. 2 Motor Vehicle Works, which was designed and built by China, went into operation in 1977. Since 1979 China's automobile industry has entered a new period of development. The China Motor Vehicle Industrial Company was established in 1982, and together with several major auto plants formed some joint motor vehicle industrial corporations and promoted the further development of the auto industry. A number of motor vehicle enterprises have co-operated with foreign auto companies and firms. The Beijing Motor Vehicle Plant and the American Motors Company (AMC) formed a partnership in making jeeps. The Shanghai Heavy Motor Vehicle Plant and the American WAB Company are engaged in a co-operative project to make 32-ton heavy duty trucks for use in the mines. All this has played an important role in raising the standards of the motor vehicles.

China is now capable of making six major categories of motor vehicles, namely, heavy duty trucks, jeeps, passenger vehicles, limousines and sedans, tip lorries and tractors. They cover 82 kinds of motor vehicles and over 200 types of special purpose refitted vehicles. There were originally 23 types of six tonnage-class trucks, namely, below 2.5 tons, 2.5–6 tons, 6–9 tons, 9–15 tons, 15–22 tons and upwards of 22 tons, but a number of new products have recently been made, such as Model CA 141 5-ton trucks of the No. 1 Motor Vehicle Works, *Huanghe* Model JN 162 10-ton trucks of the Jinan Motor Vehicle Plant and *Yuejin* Model NJ 131 3-ton trucks of the Nanjing Motor Vehicle Plant. This shows that a new generation of the three major models of vehicles, namely, *Jiefang, Huanghe* and *Yuejin*, will be produced. These motor vehicles were the earliest produced and are the most widely used in China. Their output is the biggest in the country. There are also 10-ton, 12-ton and 18-ton heavy duty diesel trucks. The performance of these models is aimed at achieving the international standards of similar vehicles of the late 1970s and early 1980s. China also makes 4–5-ton, 7-ton, 10–15-ton, 20-ton, 32-ton and 68-ton dump trucks. There are 27 types of passenger vehicles. To meet the growing need for passenger transport, vehicles with emphasis on safety, comfort, high speed and low energy consumption have been trial-produced and put into operation in the past few years. Model CA 630 tourist cars of the No. 1 Motor Vehicle Works and Model TJ 621 cars of the Tianjin Passenger Car Plant are advanced vehicles. China now mainly produces two types of sedans, *Shanghai* and *Hongqi* sedans. The Shanghai Motor Vehicle Plant has begun assembling *Santana* sedans from Federal Germany.

The shipbuilding industry

China's shipbuilding industry has a long history. The

Jiangnan Manufacturing Bureau was created in Shanghai in 1865, making munitions and ships, and the Fuzhou Shipping Administration was set up at Mawei in 1866, but the average annual output was then only 1,000 dwt. The shipbuilding industry has made big strides since the founding of New China.

In 1965, the *SS Dongfeng*, a 10,000-ton-class ocean-going freighter, was launched in China. The freighter, first of its kind ever designed and made in China, was built with Chinese materials and equipment. In the early 1970s, Chinese shipyards began manufacturing in serial number 13,000-ton cargo vessels, 16,000-ton freighters, 22,000-ton cargo ships, 15,000-ton to 24,000-ton oil tankers as well as 7,500-ton passenger and cargo ships. The *Xihu* (West Lake), a 50,000-ton oil tanker, was launched in 1976. In 1983 the annual output of steel-hulled ships for civilian use reached 1,294,000 tons. It rose to 1,665,000 tons in 1985. Thus Chinese shipyards are able not only to supply various kinds of ships for use for domestic shipping purposes, fishery, agricultural and other departments, but also to compete in the international shipping market. In 1977, for the first time in history, China exported a 3,700-ton cargo vessel. In 1979, it adopted a policy of "excellent quality, fair price, delivery in time and good service" for administering the shipping enterprise, thus opening up more outlets for its export of ships.

During the Sixth Five-Year Plan period, China built ships totalling 1,200,000 dwt for shipowners in the United States, Italy, Federal Germany, Norway, Romania, Singapore, Bangladesh and Libya, as well as Hong Kong. Among the vessels exported by China were 36,000-ton cargo ships, 11,000-ton container ships, 17,500-ton multiple purpose ships, 7,200-ton bulk carriers, 69,000-ton oil tankers and 50-ton floating cranes as well as a 115,000-ton shuttle oil tanker. The Chinese ships for export were designed and built according to international standards. They were commended by shipowners and international shipping associations for their advanced technology and good quality. International shipping circles generally believe that the technology and experience of the Chinese shipping industry are reliable and trustworthy.

The aircraft industry

China's aircraft manufacturing industry was set up in 1951. The first Chinese-made aircraft, a trainer plane, was put into service in July 1954, thus ending the history of China's inability to make aircraft. In July 1956, the first Chinese-made jet fighter was trial-produced successfully. In the following year, the first Chinese-made aircraft for civilian use, the *Yun-5* transporter, was assembled. Then the *Zhi-5* helicopter completed its test flights satisfactorily in December 1959. The latter two types of aircraft are used for transporting passengers and cargoes and flying special

missions on agriculture, forestry and animal husbandry and are available for export.

To promote the development of the aeronautics industry, the Third Ministry of Machine Building was established in 1963. It was renamed the Ministry of the Aviation Industry. Designed and built by China, the *Yun-11*, a light agricultural plane, was put into service in March 1977 and produced in batches. This type of aircraft is known for its high manoeuvrability and great climbing capacity at low altitude and can take off from and land on makeshift runways. The *Yun-5* and *Yun-11* aircraft display great advantages in rendering service to agriculture and forestry. Since 1979 the Ministry of the Aviation Industry has carried out a policy of serving both the people and army and meeting the needs of peace or war, and has made great efforts to develop civilian aircraft. China is now capable of making *Yun-5, Yun-6, Yun-7, Yun-8* and *Yun-12* aircraft for transporting cargoes and passengers and flying special missions, as well as making *Zhi-9* helicopters.

The *Yun-12* is a geological survey plane. It was designed and built in accordance with US Federal Aviation Regulations. Equipped with Canadian-made turboprop engines, it performs satisfactorily and is able to carry 1.7 tons of cargo and 17 passengers. Its maximum range is 1,440 kilometres. The *Yun-12, model 112* aircraft is up to international standards and will shortly make its debut at the international market for civilian aircraft.

The *Yun-7* aircraft, a short-range passenger and cargo plane, is able to carry 48–52 passengers and a maximum commercial payload of 4.7 tons. It cruises at 480 kilometres per hour with a range of 1,900 kilometres. It is equipped with two home-made turboprop engines of 2,900 hp each. It revs up easily, has a short taxiing range and is able to take off at a high temperature of 38°C at an altitude of 2,000 metres. China has decided to fly *Yun-7, model 100* aircraft on its domestic feederline within or between provinces.

The *Yun-8*, a medium-sized transport plane, is used to carry cargoes, air-drop goods and make parachute landings. It can be converted into a drone and used for geological surveys, maritime patrols and air refuelling. It is capable of carrying a maximum payload of 20 tons and has a maximum range of 5,463 kilometres. It cruises at 516 kilometres per hour. It can take off from and land on some third-class airports because of its strong adaptability to domestic low-class airstrips.

The *Zhi-9* helicopter, a light multi-purpose plane, was built after the French model *Dolphin* aircraft. It is an advanced fourth generation helicopter and can be used for carrying passengers and cargoes and flying off-shore oil exploration missions.

China has also designed and built many models of ultralight planes, such as *Bee-1, Bee-2, Bee-3, Dragonfly-5, Dragonfly-5A* and *Dragonfly-6* aircraft. Small and delicate, this kind of aircraft is easy to maintain, cheap, safe and reliable. It does not require a special runway. It has attracted great interest from the Chinese and foreign quarters concerned. Businessmen from the United States, Great Britain and Hong Kong have signed contracts for the purchase of more than 100 ultralight planes. Some rural communities and peasants at home have placed similar orders.

The heavy machine-building and mining equipment industry

The heavy machine-building industry was also non-existent before Liberation. It has now grown into an important industry, providing the metallurgical industry with nine sets of major equipment, including 30,000-ton die-forging hydraulic presses, and 2,800 mm aluminium plate cold rolling and hot rolling mills. It has also supplied the Panzhihua Iron and Steel Company with complete sets of equipment as well as a 1,700 mm continuous rolling mill and a 4,200 mm special steel plate rolling mill. Advanced heavy machines have also been designed and made in the past few years. The Taiyuan Heavy Machinery Plant and a Federal German company co-operated in building the complete set of equipment for the 140 seamless steel tubing mill of the Baoshan Iron and Steel Complex near Shanghai. Steel tubes made by this rolling mill are up to the advanced standards of the 1980s. The No. 1 Heavy Machinery Plant and the Shenyang Heavy Machinery Plant jointly made a 2,800 mm aluminum plate cold rolling mill which applies such new techniques as silicon-controlled exciter and silicon-controlled battery charge, hydraulic press and automatic thickness regulator. The rolling speed is six metres per second, with precision reaching ±0.01 mm. The production of a 2,030 mm continuous cold rolling mill, a 2,050 mm continuous hot rolling mill and a 1,900 mm continuous casting machine and technical preparations for the second-phased project of the Baoshan complex are under way.

China's mining machinery industry has made great progress in the past few years. A complete set of equipment for a large open-cut mine with an annual capacity of 10 million tons of mineral ores has been put into production. It consists mainly of 10–12 cubic metre excavators produced by the Taiyuan Heavy Machinery Plant, 100-ton power-driven motor vehicles produced by the Xiangtan Electrical Machinery Plant and ϕ 250 mm gear wheel drills made by the Jiangxi Mining Machinery Factory. This has laid the foundation for making 2,000-ton class large open-cut mining equipment. The Taiyuan Heavy Machinery Plant has used imported techniques to produce 16 cubic metre excavators, each weighing 730 tons. Its aggregate installed capacity is 23.65 million kilowatts and it has an annual capacity of excavating 12.20 million cubic metres of mineral ores – equivalent to the annual amount of labour of over 40,000 workers. It is a component of the complete set of equipment for large open-cut mines and reaches the world advanced level of the 1980s. In mining equipment, a ϕ 9 m shaft drill has been designed and made. A shaft mine with the longest diameter in the world has been dug. The quality of roller produced by the Luoyang Mining Machinery Plant is up to international standards and has had access to the international market.

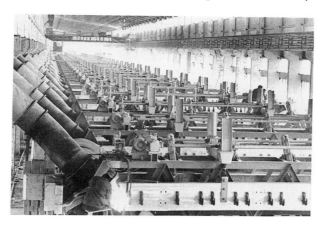

Building the Qinghai aluminium factory, the largest electrolysis aluminium factory in China, was begun on 5 April 1985 in Datong county, Qinghai province. This is the 985 m long electrolysis shop. *(Photo by Wang Jingye)*

The first continuous production line for opencast coal in China, which went into use in Yunnan. *(Photo by Min Fuquan)*

The petrochemical equipment manufacturing industry

The petrochemical equipment manufacturing industry is a new industry established at the start of the First Five-Year Plan period. Up to now, a petrochemical equipment manufacturing system has been set up with Lanzhou and Shanghai as bases and covering six major regions of the country. In oil drilling and mining equipment, products that are being supplied in batches include 1,500-metre, 3,200-metre, 4,500-metre drills, 500 kg/cm² solid well cracking equipment, various types of pumps of less than 12 tons of load, and 210 and 350 kg/cm² oil (gas) well-head equipment. The 4,500-metre drill designed and made by the Lanzhou Petrochemical Machinery Works is close to the international standard of the early 1980s. The quality of three-gear bits produced by the Shanghai No. 1 Petroleum Machinery Factory is close to the advanced international standard. China is able to produce most of the drilling and mining equipment needed for the petroleum industry. Some drilling accessories, pumps and three-gear drill bits have had access to the international market. The production of oil refining equipment mainly started in the early 1960s. China can now provide equipment for refineries with an annual capacity to treat one million tons and 2.5 million tons of crude oil, and most of the equipment for refineries to treat five million tons of crude. The production of chemical equipment started in 1953.

Equipment in the Dalian oil refinery, Liaoning province.

China can now provide complete sets of equipment for making 1,000 tons, 60,000 tons, 300,000 tons of synthetic ammonia a year, 115,000 tons of ethylene a year as well as sulphuric acid, nitric acid and hydrochloric acid, soda and caustic soda, medicine, dyestuffs, agricultural chemicals and synthetic rubber. A 320-ton synthetic urea tower with a diameter of 2.8 metres and a high-pressure urea washing tower were made in 1983. They reach advanced international standards.

The electrical power equipment manufacturing industry

The electric power equipment manufacturing industry has grown apace since Liberation. In hydroelectric generation, 800 kilowatt water turbines were made in 1952. Then came the 10,000 kilowatt, 72,500 kilowatt, and 100,000 kilowatt turbogenerator units. Later, 225,000–300,000 kilowatt turbogenerator units were made. China is now able to provide the power industry with 500 types of 10,000–300,000 kilowatt unit capacity and 10–460-metre water head turbogenerator units. Recently the Gezhouba Hydroelectric Power Station has been installed with seven 125,000 kilowatt and 170,000 kilowatt low-head turbogenerator units. The diameters of the runners are 10.2 metres and 11.3 metres respectively. Compared with similar generating units in the present-day world, they are the largest rotating oar hydroelectric power generators. The Longyangxia Hydroelectric Power Station has been installed with a 320,000 kW mixed-flow water turbine, the biggest unit capacity turbine ever made in China. Its external diameter is 6.44 metres and its runner weighs 150 tons.

The making of thermal power generating equipment began with the production of a 6,000 kW thermal power generator in 1955. China is now able to produce a 300,000 kW thermal power generator. Recently three major power plants in Shanghai jointly trial-produced successfully a 300,000 kW thermal power generator by applying imported and more advanced technology. With the improvement in the technical level, China has become one of the world's foremost producers of large thermal power generators.

The research and manufacture of steam turbine generators has achieved notable successes. A 50,000 kW hydrogen-cooling steam turbine generator and a 125,000 kW turbogenerator with a double internal water-cooling system were made in 1959. China now is able to make a 200,000 kW steam turbogenerator by applying the hydrogen-cooling and water-cooling methods. China has produced 110,000–220,000-volt and 330,000-volt transmission transformers. It has recently made a 500,000-volt super transmission transformer and a complete set of ±100,000-volt direct current powerlines.

China's electrical products and power generators have had access to the international market. Many

This 500 kV disconnector, made by the Xi'an Electrical Machinery Company, is employed in the first 500 kV ultra-high voltage transmission lines in China. *(Photo by Zhang Yuquan)*

products enjoy good international credit. The products of the Tianjin Rods Plant, the suspension insulators of the Dalian Porcelain Insulator Factory, the unipolar small switch of the Tianjin Low Voltage Switch Factory and the switchboards of the Xiamen Electric Control Equipment Plant have received certificates of quality from the Lloyd's Register of Shipping of the United Kingdom, Sweden's Allmanna Svenska Elektriska Aktiebolaget (ASEA) and Britain's Association of Short Circuit Testing Authorities (ASTA) respectively. For the first time China exported a 210,000 kW thermal power generating unit to Pakistan's Guddy Power Station. This was the biggest complete set of power equipment ever exported by China. It went into operation on 9 January 1986.

The farm machinery industry

Farm machinery is another new industry established after the founding of New China. There are now more than 2,800 items of farm machinery products. The output of tractors of more than 20 hp reached 125,600 in 1979. During the Sixth Five-Year Plan period, efforts were made to readjust the development programme and make many new products to meet the structural reform of the rural economy and its need for development. For instance, contracts were signed to make 3–18 hp walking tractors for peasant households, poultry cages, complete sets of battery houses for poultry farms in urban and suburban districts, 50–100 watt wind power generators and complete sets of 10,000-ton-class feeds processing plants. Walking tractors and the number of machines for processing agricultural and sideline occupation products as well as for animal husbandry, transport and feeds processing are increasing by a big margin. The annual output of walking tractors reached 689,000 units in 1984 and rose to 823,000 units in 1985, and 41,000 farm

transport vehicles, 84,000 sets (units) of machines for feeding poultry and domestic animals and 800,000 pumps were produced in that year. *Model 504* wheeled tractors produced by the Qingjiang Tractor Works and the Shanghai Tractor Plant won first prize respectively in pull tests at the exhibitions of farm machinery field operations held in Australia in 1984 and 1985.

Initial success has been reported in the use of imported technology in the past few years. This has made it possible for a number of enterprises to renew products or replace the old ones with new models and thus narrow the gap between their products and those of advanced international standards. After digesting and absorbing the imported technology of 1,000 series combined harvesters, the Jiamusi General Combine Harvester Plant has the annual capacity to make 1,000 harvesters of the advanced standards of the early 1980s, thus ending China's history of importing combine harvesters in units.

Thanks to the development of the farm machinery industry, China had 852,000 large and medium-sized tractors, 3,824,000 walking tractors and 6,163,000 units of power-driven farm irrigation and drainage equipment at the end of 1985. In the main, China had achieved mechanization or semi-mechanization of operations on the threshing ground and in the sugar, cotton, edible oil and feeds processing industries. Walking tractors, diesel engines and pumps have had access to the international market.

The bearings-making industry

In the early post-Liberation years, the gross annual output of bearings in China came only to 138,000 sets. It rose to 277 million sets in 1984 and 310 million sets in 1985, and China now ranks sixth in the world output of bearings. There are 720 size series, 6,000 varieties and 13,000 specifications of bearings (excluding those for military use). China is now able to produce large ball bearings with an outer diameter of five metres (each set weighs nine tons) and micro-bearings with an inner diameter of 0.6 mm. In addition to massive production of general and standard bearings, China also produces such special purpose bearings as high speed, high temperature, high vacuum, low temperature, low friction, low noise, magnetic-proof, corrosion-proof and radiation-proof bearings. These products can, in the main, meet the needs of the various industries for national economic and defence construction. Many new series and varieties of bearings have been produced over the past few years to meet the need for maintenance and repair of advanced equipment imported by the Baoshan Iron and Steel Complex and other key projects and for the production of household electrical appliances. They include sealed bearings, joint bearings, rectilineal motion bearings and ball bearings. These greatly exceed the older products in both novelty of structure and degree of difficulty of manufacture, and completely fill the gap in the bearings industry at home. Chinese-made bearings enjoy good credit on the international market and about 10% of the gross national output is for export.

The manufacture of instruments and meters

The Sixth Five-Year Plan period recorded a rapid growth of the instruments and meters making industry in China. With the development of the applied technology of the microcomputer, a large number of aptitude instruments and meters were trial-produced successfully. More than 120 kinds of such meters were produced in the five years, accounting for one-tenth of all meters developed during the Sixth Five-Year Plan period. The micro-test viscosi-meter made by the Chengdu Instrument and Meter Plant is used for precision measurement of liquid viscosity. It can be used extensively in the biological, medical, electronics, chemicals, petroleum and food departments. Its various performance indices attained the advanced standards of similar products of other countries in the early 1980s. The micro-computer ultra-violet far infra-red spectrophotometer produced by the Shanghai No. 3 Analysis Instrument Plant is a product attaining the technical standards of the late 1970s.

In the field of automatic meters and equipment, a large number of important new products have been made in recent years. They include components assembly meters, crude oil measurement instruments with 4 per thousand accuracy, large numerically controlled drafting instruments and Chinese characters encoding typewriters. The technical level of China's automatic meters and equipment has advanced in big strides alongside the development of the applied technology of micro-computers. Some items are close to or attain the international standards of the late 1970s and early 1980s. Thirteen major categories of automatic meters and instruments embracing 200 series and over 6,000 varieties have now been produced in serial numbers. They range from temperature gauges, pressure gauges, flowmeters, mechanical meters, regulating meters and electrodynamic modular unit instruments to centralized control equipment. China is also able to provide complete sets of automatic meters and control equipment for certain major projects of the various ministries and departments of the national economy. These projects include plants with an annual capacity of making 300,000 tons of synthetic ammonia and 110,000 tons of ethylene, refineries for handling 2.50 million tons and 5 million tons of crude oil, 300,000 kW thermo-power generators, and blast furnaces with a volume of 2,000 cubic metres.

In addition, the machine-building industry has also provided equipment for making atomic reactors, accelerators and nuclear raw materials, as well as power equipment, ground facilities and various necessary accessories and fittings for the space industry and naval vessels.

Current problems in the machine-building industry

The following are the problems existing in the machine-building industry:

– Irrational infrastructure

There are too many coarse processing machines and too few fine processing machines; too many cold processing machines and too few heat processing machines; too many unit machines and too few transfer machines and assembly lines.

– Backward basic technology

Forging, casting and sheet forming technologies are mainly done by hand.

– Irrational mix of products

Products are mainly to serve the iron and steel industry and other heavy industrial sectors. No adequate attention is paid to the development of mechanical and electrical products necessary for agriculture, light industry, science and culture, and for people's livelihood as well as export trade. There is also a great gap in the varieties of mechanical and electrical products compared with those of the developed countries.

The prospects for the machine-building industry

In the years to come, China's machine-building industry will give top priority to improving quality, increasing the varieties of products and developing mechanical and electrical products in demand on the international market, while increasing quantity. Efforts should be made to improve the quality as quickly as possible and to increase the variety of main products so that they will reach the level attained by the industrially developed countries in the late 1970s or the early 1980s. Energetic efforts will also be made to open up international markets and increase the export of mechanical and electrical products. The specific requirements are:

– To enhance the development of production of equipment for the electrical engineering, mining and petroleum industries

During the Seventh Five-Year Plan period, it is necessary to increase the annual capacity for making 10 million kilowatt generators and the corresponding capacity of equipment for power transformation and

Plate 33

1. Advanced control devices at the Baoshan steelworks.

2. Chinese textiles at the Fourth International Trade Exhibition of the Asia-Pacific region.

3. Gold produced at Yantai, Shandong.

4. The first heat of steel in the Baoshan steelworks in Shanghai.

5. Jacquard cloth produced in a polyester fibre plant in Heilongjiang.

6. Edible fungus production in Yanbian, Jilin.

Plate 34

1. Sheep on the grasslands of Nagqu county, Tibet.

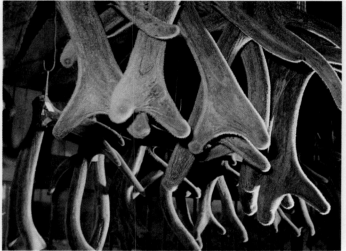

2. Pilose antlers for use as medicine from the Sanjiang plain in North-East China.

3. Pearls from the Beihai sea, Guangxi.

4. Jackfruit from Hainan Island.

5. Hami melons from Xinjiang.

6. The apple harvest in Taiyuan, Shanxi.

Plate 35

1. A section of the North China shelter belt.

2. High tension wires on the North-East China plain.

3. A CAAC helicopter used for oil prospecting in the Bohai Sea.

4. Logs on the move from Mount Zhang Guangcai in North-East China.

5. A container wharf at Shanghai.

Plate 36

1. Beijing roast duck, a traditional dish famous throughout the world.

2. A drilling platform in the South China Sea.

3. Nanyang cattle in Henan.

4. The office of the China International Trust and Investment Co. (CITIC) in Beijing.

5. The joint China–Federal Republic of Germany Santana car factory.

6. Chinese fashion models.

transmission, to manufacture complete sets of equipment for 20 million-ton class open-cut mines, to increase in serial numbers the production of oil drilling and extraction machines, and to conduct research on the making of in-depth oil processing facilities.

— To expand the production of transport facilities and make the auto manufacturing industry a major basic industry

— To accelerate the development of the metallurgical, chemical and building materials industries

To produce complete sets of major metallurgical equipment, advanced continuous casting and rolling machines and blast furnaces, and to provide the chemical industry with complete sets of equipment for processing ethylene as well as for industrial branches making fertilizer, urban coal gas, soda and fine chemicals.

— To make plans for the construction and production of farm machines and various special-purpose machines

— To speed up the development of basic machinery, instruments and meters and mechanical bases

— To increase the output of mechanical and electrical products necessary for the improvement of people's livelihood and social development

The Electronics Industry

The foundation of the electronics industry in old China was very weak. In 1949, there were only a dozen or so small factories in the whole country. Their equipment was simple and their technology backward. They were mainly engaged in assembly and maintenance and produced a small quantity of electronic components, magnets, common-battery telephones, switchboards and other simple communications equipment. These factories employed 4,106 people and had a total output value of 4.95 million yuan.

After the founding of New China, the electronics industry rapidly expanded, from making repairs to manufacturing and from copying foreign products to designing by Chinese engineers and technicians. Today a new industry with quite comprehensive branches and with products for both military and civil use has been set up, and its technology has also reached a fairly high level.

— The scale of production has steadily expanded and the technological basis has been gradually strengthened

During the period of the First Five-Year Plan, while old electronics industry enterprises were rebuilt or expanded, a number of key enterprises were built. These include the Beijing Electron Tube Plant, the North China Radio Equipment Plant, the Beijing Wire Plant, the Changling Machinery Plant in Baoji, the Huanghe Machinery Plant in Xi'an, the Jinjiang Machinery Plant in Chengdu and the Hongming Radio Equipment Plant in Chengdu. In this way, the groundwork was laid for the development of the electronics industry, and between 1958 and 1965 it expanded considerably. Concentrating on the weak links in the industry, the country carried out large-scale capital construction and technological transformation. Meanwhile, the local electronics industry in Shanghai, Jiangsu, Tianjin, Beijing, Liaoning, Shandong and Hubei also developed considerably. After eight years' construction work, the electronics industry further expanded its scale, raised its technological level and grew into an independent new industry. In 1963, the State Council set up the Fourth Ministry of the Machine Building Industry to strengthen leadership over the electronics industry and accelerate its growth. Electronics industry bureaux were set up by various provinces, autonomous regions and municipalities directly under the Central Government. During the ten-year Cultural Revolution, the development of the electronics industry was seriously disrupted and sabotaged and the gap between China's electronics industry and the international level was widened. However, the industry advanced in a number of areas. At that time, several scientific research and production bases were built in the inland areas and branches of the electronics industry were set up in all provinces, autonomous regions and municipalities directly under the Central Government throughout the country.

After 1978, the development of the electronics industry was integrated with technological import and the construction and technological transformation of key projects were speeded up. During this period, a number of large and medium-sized projects were completed, such as the Shaanxi Colour Television Picture Tube Plant; the black and white picture tube assembly line of the Hongguang Electron Tube Plant in Chengdu; the linear integrated circuit project of the Jiangnan Radio Equipment Plant; the colour television set projects in Shanghai, Tianjin and Beijing; the mini-computer production line of the Guangzhou Computer Plant; and the magnetic storage discs production line of the Jiannan Machinery Plant in Hunan. Many projects are now under construction. In the field of computers, there are Chinese–foreign joint-stock and joint operation projects for mini-computers and their external equipment. Up to 1985, 50 mini-computer production (assembly) lines had been imported or transformed, with a total production capacity of 400,000 computers. In the field of communication navigation, imported technological projects include the random access discrete address radio communication system, the satellite communication station, the thermal recording head of a facsimile printer, the automatic testing system of a microwave antenna, millimetre wave testing instrument, ultrashort wave mobile radio station, comprehensive communication system for shipping, ultra-high-frequency radio station for aircraft, and electronic countermeasures. When these projects are completed, the technical and technological level and the self-supporting capacity of China's electronics industry will be raised immensely.

By 1985, after more than 30 years of construction work, China had over 4,100 electronics industrial enterprises with a gross industrial output value of 29.72 billion yuan. By relying mainly on electronic components made in China, the country could produce more than 20 kinds, 2,000 varieties and several thousand types of electronic equipment, supplying large quantities of electronic products for national defence, national economic construction and the people's daily life.

– The research, manufacture and development of electronic products have achieved steady progress and their output has increased substantially

During the period of national economic rehabilitation, from 1950 to 1952, China began to mass produce radios, microphones, electric gramophones and electronic surveying instruments, and manufactured and developed a great variety of communications equipment such as shortwave walkie-talkie and small radio stations. By 1957, through the construction work of the First Five-Year Plan period, the country was able to produce various kinds of radar and navigation equipment, broadcast transmission equipment, radio communication equipment, automatic exchanges, electronic instruments and other electronic equipment for military use, and the means of producing electronic products, as well as consumer electronic products such as tape recorders. In the field of basic electronic products, the country was able to produce many key components such as electron tubes and condensers.

In early 1956 China drew up a 12-year plan for the development of science and technology, listing computers, semiconductors and other typical products of the electronics industry as urgent items in the research and development plan. Under the impetus of this plan, important achievements were scored in the research, manufacture and development of products in all areas of the electronics industry.

In the field of computers, China manufactured its first miniature electron tube computer in 1958. In the following year, it successfully produced a large-type electron tube computer which ranked next only to that of the United States and the Soviet Union throughout the world. In 1965 and 1971, the second generation transistor digital computers were made, and in 1978, large computers capable of five million

calculations were manufactured. In the Sixth Five-Year Plan period, remarkable results were obtained in computer research, manufacture and development. The country successfully manufactured the *Great Wall 0520*, *Zijin-II* and other micro-computers, 8030 medium-sized general-purpose computers, 2780 super-miniature computers and 2701 array processors. In addition, large "757" computers capable of 10 million calculations and the huge *Yinhe* (Milky Way) computers capable of 100 million calculations per second were produced. These were indications that China's computer manufacture and development had attained a new high level.

In 1984 China produced 381 large and medium-sized computers and 27,088 micro-computers; in 1985 the output of the former dropped slightly because of excessive amounts of imported products while the output of the latter went up, reaching 35,715. The work of popularizing the use of computers also made much headway during this period. Computer-using items in the country increased to 1,500 from about 100 in 1981, and are widely used in all sectors of the national economy. In particular, the application of micro-computers has begun to penetrate all trades and professions, achieving visible economic results. By 1985, more than 5,500 large, medium-sized and small computers had been installed in the country as against 2,928 in 1980 and the number of micro-computers increased to 130,000 from 600 in 1980.

In the field of broadcasting and television equipment, 1,000 kW medium-wave broadcast transmission stations, 10-channel television transmission stations and black and white TV sets were manufactured in 1958. Since 1978, on the basis of integrating the import of foreign technology and research at home, the manufacture of broadcast and television products has made progress unknown before. At present, UHF colour TV transmitting stations and retransmitters have been successfully made and mass produced. Frequency-modulated stereo broadcasting transmitters, with a maximum power of 10 kW, have also been manufactured. Pick-up cameras, video recorders and applied televisions are all becoming colour models, and in consumer electronic products, more television receivers with large and medium-sized screens and colour sets are being produced. Colour TV sets with infra-red remote-control devices have been put on the market. Radios and tape recorders are developing in the direction of frequency-modulated stereo sets. Multifunction portable radios with medium wave, frequency and amplitude modulation portable radios, radio/stereo/2-channel/double cassette tape recorders and high-grade tape recorders with the functions of receiving, recording, automatic music selection and music pre-selection have been put on the market in quantities. The output of such products has increased steeply, at an unprecedented rate: 16.677 million TV sets were produced in 1985,

Table 7: The Installation of Computers in the Sixth Five-Year Plan Period

	1980	1981	1982	1983	1984	1985
Large, medium-sized and small computers	2,928	3,210	3,819	4,269	4,769	5,500
Micro-computers	600	10,892	18,020	30,000	75,800	130,000

Table 8: The Output of TV Sets, Tape Recorders and Radios

Item	1952	1957	1965	1975	1978	1980	1984	1985
TV sets,	—	—	0.44	17.78	51.73	249.20	1,003.81	1,667.66
Of which:								
Colour sets	—	—	—	0.29	0.38	3.21	133.95	435.28
Radios	1.7	35.2	81.5	935.6	1,167.7	3,003.8	2,220.3	1,600.3
Tape recorders	—	0.11	0.46	3.17	4.73	74.34	776.42	1,393.05

an increase of 32 times that of 1978. The annual output of colour TV sets reached 4,353,000 – more than 1,100 times that of 1978. The output of tape recorders was 13,931,000, an increase of 296 times that of 1978. In 1952 only 17,000 radios were produced but the number shot up to 11.677 million in 1978 and further climbed to 22.20 million in 1984. As market demand has reached saturation point, the output in 1985 dropped to 16.003 million.

China's consumer electronic products entered the international market in 1958, when only a small number of radios were exported. Since 1980, radio-tape recorders, black and white TV sets and colour TV sets have successively entered the world market, exported mainly to Hong Kong, Macao, South-East Asia, the Middle East, Africa and North America.

In the field of communication navigation, China carried out the policy of serialization and the general use of semiconductors in communication products in the 1960s. It produced semiconductor shortwave single sideband communication equipment, automatic telephone exchanges, cable carrier equipment and microwave relay communication and scatter communication equipment. At the same time, radio navigation technology was put to wider use. In the 1970s, the country manufactured 320-channel small-diameter coaxial cable carrier systems, 960-channel carrier communication equipment, and 120-channel microwave digital communication equipment, and manufactured and built five satellite communication ground stations. New advances were made after 1978: successful trial operation of the 480-channel microwave communication system was carried out in 1983; 100-watt civil radio stations reached the technical standard of similar products in the United States; experiments on and application of optical fibre communication were successful; the satellite communication ground station in Lhasa, Tibet, was designed, built and set up in 1984. In the field of radio navigation equipment, there are now 20 varieties of equipment in the short distance, medium distance, long distance and extra-long distance directional

navigation and instrumental landing systems for aviation and navigation, and new varieties of small-size, lightweight, multi-functional and high precision equipment are being developed. In April 1984, China launched an experimental earth satellite for the first time. The communication navigation industry provided a whole set of communication ground station equipment, communication control equipment and secure terminal equipment for satellite launching and communication testing. The output of main products of the communication navigation industry in 1984 was as follows: 106,000 units of 76 varieties of land radio communication equipment, 3,483 units of 25 varieties of aviation communication directional navigation equipment, 1,678 units of 34 varieties of shipping communication directional navigation equipment, 769 units of 18 varieties of microwave communication equipment, 5,688 units of 29 varieties of carrier communication equipment and 1.154 million telephones of 13 varieties.

In the field of electronic components, China made a breakthrough in semiconductor technology in 1958; in 1962 it imported integrated circuit technology and organized research in this field; in 1966 it manufactured the country's first integrated circuit and put it into mass production. The manufacture and mass production of semiconductors and integrated circuits gave impetus to the miniaturization of electronic equipment. Since 1980, new advances have been made in the research and development of integrated circuits. A number of large-scale integrated circuits of fairly high level have been manufactured, such as 16-k dynamic memory and 4-k static memory, high speed 1-k static memory and large-scale integrated circuit for 4-digit and 8-digit micro-computers. By 1984 the output of integrated circuits had reached 39.279 million pieces. The output of other electronic components also increased rapidly. A total of 16.037 million pieces of vacuum components and 105,000 pieces of semiconductor discrete components were produced in 1984.

– The quality of products has improved markedly

Since the introduction of all-round quality control in 1978, the product quality of China's electronics industry and the reliability of components have improved markedly. More than 100 kinds of semiconductor components have met the technical requirement of resistance to high and low temperatures. The service life of electronic vacuum components has risen generally. The service life of black and white TV picture tubes has exceeded 8,000 hours and that of colour TV picture tubes has surpassed 15,000 hours – up to the international level of similar products. Meanwhile, the quality of TV sets has also risen steadily. The main qualifications of the country's 12-inch and 14-inch black and white TVs have attained or approached the international level. The average faultless operating time of certain brands has exceeded 10,000 hours. Many products have won state quality awards. Among those which have been awarded gold medals are the *Rainbow* brand colour TV picture tube produced by the Shaanxi Colour TV Picture Tube Plant and the *Electrician* brand wide band oscillograph tube produced by the East China Electron Tube Plant. Bentonite, optical fibre prefabricated components and NTD silicon were awarded the Golden Dragon Award at the national new products exhibition. The microwave acupuncture instrument produced by the

Technicians examining the quality of the products at the Dongxiang motor factory in Deyang county, Sichuan province.

Hongdu Radio Plant was awarded a gold medal at the Plovdiv international machinery fair in Bulgaria. The chromium plate produced by the Changsha Integrated Circuit Plant has reached the advanced international level in property and its price is lower than that of the world market. Electronic equipment manufactured for the launching of carrier rockets in the Pacific, for underwater rocket launching and communication satellite experiments have reliable performance, which ensured the success of the experiments. They were awarded prizes by the Chinese government.

Future prospects

In the coming fifteen years, the increase in the total output value of the electronics industry will be much faster than that of the gross industrial output value. The major products and production technology of the electronics industry will reach the level of the advanced industrialized countries of the world in the late 1980s and early 1990s, and certain technologies will attain the advanced world level then. This will be 10 years in advance of the target set for all branches of the national economy by the State by the year 2000.

During the Seventh Five-Year Plan period, the average annual growth rate of the electronics industry will be about 100% higher than that of the gross industrial output value. This will pave the way for the industry's faster growth in the 1990s. The development of integrated circuits, computers, communication equipment and software industry will be speeded up. The building of integrated circuits research and production bases will be accelerated and the application of integrated circuits will be popularized. Stress will be laid on developing micro-computers and external equipment. Large, medium-sized and miniature computers and industrial control machines will be developed correspondingly. The development and production of modern communications equipment will be strengthened and the research, manufacture and development of optical fibre equipment and terminal equipment will be stepped up. Specific requirements in this connection are as follows:

– Adherence to the principle of quality first

The products' safety and adaptability to environment should be up to general international standards, and their performance and stability should reach the level of the same kinds of products of the developed countries in the late 1970s and early 1980s.

– Continuous efforts to develop consumer electronics products

Efforts will be made at the same time actively to develop investment products, so as to gradually increase the currently small proportion of the latter.

*— Strenuous efforts to develop the software industry,
systems engineering and consultative services*

As a result the electronics industry will become one in which manufacture is integrated with service and material production with the development of intellectual faculties.

*— Attention to the development of electronic
components*

There will also be efforts to provide the necessary accessories for the production of colour TV sets in China.

— Moves to develop the supporting system

This refers to electronic surveying instruments, special-purpose technological equipment and special-purpose electronic materials, coordinating the machine building and electronics industries and stimulating the entire machine-building industry to develop special-purpose electronic equipment and testing and experiment instruments. Meanwhile, efforts should be made to integrate closely with various new industrial departments, so that the development of electronic components is built on a reliable basis.

*— Endeavours to expand export and participate in
international competitions*

To set up an export production system and lay stress on promoting the establishment of export production bases and strengthening key export enterprises; to apply the principle of giving equal attention to product export, technology export, service export and contracted engineering projects; to open up more channels of export.

The Building Materials Industry

For several thousand years China had been using natural resources to make building materials, but the industry had long been in a state of stagnation. After the establishment of a modern building materials industry at the end of the nineteenth and beginning of the twentieth centuries, its development was still very slow. The equipment was outdated, relying mainly on manual labour. The output was low, the quality poor and there were very few varieties. In 1949, the country had only about 40 small building materials enterprises, producing 660,000 tons of cement, 1.08 million standard crates of plate glass and about 4,000 pieces of ceramic bathroom fixtures, with a total output value of only 50 million yuan. Many building materials relied on import.

After the founding of New China, the building materials industry developed considerably. In 1985 the country had more than 60,000 building materials enterprises, which produced building materials, non-metallic minerals and inorganic non-metallic materials in more than 80 kinds and over 1,000 varieties. The total output value of the building materials industry reached 35.06 billion yuan, which represents an increase of 38 times over that of 1952 or an average annual increase of 11.7% – faster than the development of industry as a whole. Its proportion in the gross industrial output value rose to 4.2%, from 3% in 1952. Major features of its growth are as follows:

*— The output of building materials products has
increased, their quality has improved and there are
more varieties*

The output of all building materials has gone up substantially and the increase has been more rapid since 1979. In 1985 the output of cement reached 145.95 million tons and plate glass 56.06 million standard crates – an increase of nearly 120% and 180% over 1978, and respectively 51 times and 263 times that of 1952.

In addition, the 1984 output of ceramic bathroom fixtures was 7.32 million pieces, glass fibre 66,555 tons, and clay brick 249.8 billion pieces – all showing a remarkable increase. The output of glazed brick and floor tile showed a three-fold and a four-fold increase over that of 1978 respectively.

New varieties and new materials have been manufactured and developed steadily since the founding of the People's Republic. In the cement industry these include slag silicate dam cement used for the building of dams, sulphate-resistant cement used in oceaneering projects and railway tunnel building projects, oil well cement used for exploiting oilfields and strengthening drilling wells, fast-solidifying cement used in rush repair and casting sand mould, high-alumina cement used in industrial boilers and refractory

Table 9: Gross Output Value of the Building Materials Industry and the Output of Cement and Plate Glass

Item	Unit	1952	1957	1965	1975	1978	1980	1984	1985
Gross output of building materials industry	100 million yuan	10.3	22.7	39.6	100.0	153.9	181.5	287.3	350.6
Cement	10,000 tons	286	686	1,634	4,626	6,524	7,986	12,302	14,595
Plate glass	10,000 standard crates	213	462	687	1,453	2,004	2,771	4,830	5,606

concrete products, No. 800 high-strength cement used for making high strength concrete, and white cement used for decorating purposes. Among the cement products are: pre-stress concrete pressure pipes, self-stressing concrete pipes and pre-stress concrete poles. China is now in the front rank of the world in terms of its great variety of cement products and their wide application.

The plate glass industry has developed from making glass for windows only to producing large and special-shaped toughened glass, polished glass, laminated glass, wired glass, electrical heating glass, tank glass and bullet-proof glass. In the ceramic sanitary-ware industry, energetic efforts are being made to change the backward state in which the products are monotonous in variety, dull in colour, unattractive in design and poor in performance. There are now more than 50 kinds of products and about 10 kinds of colour products. In addition, nearly 300 new varieties of glazed bricks have been produced. In the past few years, a number of new-type building materials have been manufactured, such as composite wallboard, plaster products, mineral wool and vermiculite products, powdered coal dust blocks, hollow brick, waste residue brick, aerated concrete, rubber asphalt felt, decorative stone and chemical building materials.

After the mid-1950s, a new area of inorganic non-metallic minerals was opened up in the building materials industry. In 1958 the glass fibre industry came into being. Later, efforts were made to develop from sole non-alkali glass fibre products alone to a variety of medium-alkali and non-alkali glass fibre products, and the glass fibre reinforced plastics industry gradually took shape. Moreover, synthetic crystal, special ceramics, cast stone, asbestos sealing and other new industries were set up and developed. Many parts of the satellites, guided missiles and rockets launched by China were made of inorganic non-metallic materials manufactured in China.

– Significant achievements have been made in developing the building materials industry

From 1953 to 1985, China allocated 20.75 billion yuan as capital construction funds for the building materials industry. During this period, 138 large and medium-sized projects and more than 2,000 small projects were completed and commissioned. While most of these projects are located in the inland areas, some were built in the coastal cities. A fairly large number of these are large enterprises with advanced equipment, such as the cement plants in Yongdeng, Datong, Luoyang, Yaoxian, Kunming and Jiangyou, built in the First Five-Year Plan period. During the 1960s and 1970s, cement plants in Handan, Emei, Shuicheng, Yingde, Xiangxiang, Xizhuozi; glass factories in Zhuzhou, Luoyang, Lanzhou and Hangzhou; the Mangya Asbestos Mine and the Sichuan asbestos mine were completed one after another. Since 1979, a

A pipe which transports raw materials to the Jidong Cement Plant in Hebei province. *(Photo by Gao Shan)*

number of large and medium-sized key cement plants have been built or expanded, such as the Jidong, Ningguo, Huaihai, Liuzhou, Litang, Changxing, Baimashan and Qujiang cement plants. The Jidong and Ningguo cement plants have adopted the new pre-calcining process which was up to international level in the late 1970s. The Jidong Cement Plant is the first big plant in China to have used computers to control the production process and has a high level of automation: it has an annual capacity of 1.55 million tons. The Luoyang Glass Plant has a capacity of producing 2.6 million standard crates of plate glass annually, and built China's first float glass production line. A number of large float glass production lines have been built in its wake.

Since 1980, nine new-type building materials bases have been built in Beijing, Harbin, Shenyang, Wuhan, Suzhou, Wuxi, Shijiazhuang, Hengyang and Chongqing. The Beijing New-Type Building Materials Plant can produce annually 20 million square metres of thistle board, 16,300 tons of rock wool thermal insulation materials and 65,000 cubic metres of light components.

While new building-materials enterprises were set up, attention was also paid to the transformation of old plants. After transformation and expansion, the Yaohua Glass Factory in Qinhuangdao, the earliest glass factory in China, has become an important base, with a big output, a fairly comprehensive variety of products and an annual capacity of 3.4 million standard crates. Further expansion is under way, and when the whole project is completed, the factory's production capacity will exceed 8 million standard crates.

In addition, many small factories and mines have been built by various localities and departments. They play an important role in the country's building materials production. In 1983, 75% of the cement and 50.5% of the plate glass in China were produced by small factories. In the production of clay brick, the proportion of output by small enterprises was still larger and three-quarters of the products were turned out by township collective enterprises.

Table 10: Output of Major Non-Metallic Minerals
(unit: 10,000 tons)

Product	1949	1980	1984
Asbestos	500 tons	13.2	15.6
Gypsum	9,800 tons	334.8	574
Graphite	900 tons	16	16.54
Talcum	2,300 tons	91.5	134.7
Porcelain clay		40	64.8
Asbestos products		5.9	7.8

– As China has rich natural resources of non-metallic minerals used for building materials, the output of non-metallic products has increased rapidly

There are more than 100 kinds of non-metallic minerals widely used in the world. China has proved reserves of 80 kinds widely scattered in more than 4,700 places of production. Up to the end of 1983, the ascertained reserves of non-metallic minerals in the country were: gypsum, 10.62 billion tons – ranking first in the world; bentonite, 630 million tons – taking second place in the world; talcum, 89.72 million tons, asbestos, 55.19 million tons, and plaster, 108.45 million tons – all taking third place in the world. The reserves of pyrite, magnesite and borax all rank first in the world, and phosphate rock takes second place. In addition the reserves of porcelain clay, barite, diatomaceous earth, zeolite and pearlite all occupy important places.

In old China, except for a few pyrite and phosphate rock mines which produced limited amounts of asbestos, gypsum and talcum, non-metallic mineral mining was virtually non-existent. Today the output of several major non-metallic minerals is ten to several hundred times that of 1949.

Apart from supplying minerals to national economic departments, the non-metallic mineral mining industry has also turned out products and developed in the direction of intensive and comprehensive processing. The varieties of products have also increased notably. For instance, there are 200 kinds of asbestos products with more than 3,000 specifications.

Existing problems and prospects of development

Although China's building materials industry has developed rapidly, it is still far behind the actual demand. Building materials products, both in quantity and quality, are far from meeting the demand; the product mix is not sufficiently rational, and the use of new technologies, equipment and materials is inadequate. The Chinese Government has decided to speed up the development of the building materials industry. In 1986 the State Council made public an outline for the development of the building materials industry, setting forth concrete policies and major steps for invigorating the industry in order to realize strategic changes in its development. Hereafter, China will implement the policy of "fully arousing the masses to run the building materials industry", switching from backward traditional technology to advanced technology; from producing mainly traditional materials to mass producing new materials; from producing high energy and water consumption products to turning out energy and water conserving products; from producing mainly low grade products to turning out an assortment of high, medium and low grade products; from chiefly producing raw and semi-finished materials to vigorous development of intensive processing, and from easily damaged packing to low consumption packing.

During the Seventh Five-Year Plan period, while developing plate glass for windows, China will develop new varieties of intensive processing glass such as large-type toughened glass, stained glass and heat-absorbent glass. Efforts will be made to upgrade ceramic sanitaryware and increase the varieties and designs. Stress will be laid on developing new varieties of new-type building materials for decoration, remodelling, panelling and ceilings. Efforts will also be made to popularize the demonstrative production lines of energy-conserving panelling materials, such as aerated concrete and building blocks. The exploitation and use of silicate and non-metallic mineral resources will be promoted.

The Textile Industry

China's textile industry has a long history of development and a good foundation. The country's first woollen textile mill, The Gansu General Bureau of Woollen Fabrics, was set up in 1876, and the first cotton textile mill was set up in Shanghai in 1890. By the time of national liberation in 1949, the country had 130,000 wool spinning spindles, 1,950 wool weaving machines, 5 million cotton spinning spindles, 63,900 looms and a total printing and dyeing capacity of 1.3 billion metres.

After the founding of New China, through more than three decades of construction work, the textile industry has gained new successes. A system of textile industry with complete branches, rational distribution, a fairly large scale of production and basic self-sufficiency in raw materials and equipment has been set up:

– The textile industry has complete branches

In old China, of all branches of the textile industry, only the cotton textile industry was large in scale and had a good foundation. After the founding of New China, the policy of laying stress on developing the cotton textile industry while actively promoting the wool, linen and silk industries was adopted to solve the problem of clothing the people and to ensure the supply of cotton, woollen, linen and silk textiles. Major changes have taken place in the structure of the textile industry. In the early days of the People's Republic, the proportion of output value between the cotton textile industry, on the one hand, and the woollen, linen, silk and knitwear industries, on the other hand, was 88:12, but in 1983 the proportion had changed to 71:29. China's textile industry has complete branches. It is mainly composed of eight sectors: cotton spinning, printing and dyeing, woollen textile, silk textile, linen textile, knitwear, textile machinery and equipment, and chemical fibre.

The **cotton spinning, printing and dyeing industry** has the largest scale and the best foundation in China's textile industry. From 1950 to 1980, 61.49 million cotton spindles were added by all countries of the world, of which China's increase was 13.94 million spindles, leading the world in the growth rate. By 1980, the numbers of cotton spindles in the world had reached 161.85 million: India, China, the United States, the Soviet Union and Japan had more than 10 million spindles each; China had 17.82 million spindles – ranking second in the world. By the end of 1984, the country's cotton spindles had reached 22.196 million, together with 634,000 looms and a printing and dyeing capacity of more than 9 billion metres, representing an increase of 4.4 times, 9.9 times and 7 times that of 1949 respectively.

By the end of 1984, the **woollen textile industry** had 1.205 million wool spinning spindles and 17,121 wool weaving machines – an increase of 9.3 times and 8.8 times that of 1949 respectively. A total of 18,049 metres of woollen fabrics, 110,000 tons of knitting wool, 17.454 million blankets and 11.29 million metres of artificial fur were produced in 1984.

The development of the **silk industry** has been fairly rapid. China was the first country in the world to produce silk. As early as 2,000 years ago, China's silk products were transported to Western countries along the "silk road" and became world famous. But before Liberation, production gradually declined. The output of silks in 1949 was only about a quarter of the highest level in Chinese history. After Liberation, the industry was gradually rehabilitated and developed. By 1984 the country already had 1.311 million reeling frames and 98,400 silk weaving machines, representing an increase of respectively 14.5 times and 2.4 times that of 1949. In 1984 a total of 37,600 tons of silk and 1.178 billion metres of silk fabrics were produced: China's silk output already topped the list in the world.

In the field of the **linen textile industry,** there were only 23,000 jute spindles and 7,760 ramie spindles at the time of Liberation in 1949. Since the founding of New China, the jute and ramie industries have grown rapidly and the flax textile industry has been set up. By 1984, the country had 190,500 linen spindles and 15,754 linen weaving machines. Today, China has become one of the big exporters of jute and ramie and their fabrics, occupying an important place in the primary market of these products in the world.

The increase in the production capacity of the **knitwear industry** is the fastest of all the textile processing industries. Its gross output value in 1952 was 360 million yuan and its proportion in the total output value of the textile industry was 3.8%, but by 1984 the figure had shot up to 8.22 billion yuan – an increase of 23 times. Its proportion in the textile industry rose to 9.6%.

The **chemical fibre industry** is a new industrial sector. In the readjustment of the national economy in the early 1960s, China diverted its efforts in building up the textile industry to developing synthetic fibres. Soon afterwards, it imported two synthetic fibre technologies from abroad, to give a flying start to the chemical fibre industry. In the early 1970s, whole sets of technological equipment were imported from abroad and the construction of four large petrochemical fibre enterprises started in Shanghai, Liaoyang and other places. In the building of these chemical fibre enterprises, supplementary equipment made in China made up a considerable proportion of the total equipment supply, thanks to adherence to the principle of making whatever supplementary equipment that can be made at home. This not only laid the groundwork for the development of China's chemical fibre industry but increased the country's ability for self-reliance and ensured the industry's rapid growth. By 1983 the country's chemical fibre production capacity had approached 770,000 tons and in the following year an additional capacity of 26,000 tons was added. This played an important role in pushing ahead the growth of the entire textile industry and solving the Chinese people's clothing problem.

– One billion people's demands for clothing are basically met

By 1985, after more than 30 years of construction work, the country had 22,000 textile industrial enterprises with a total output value of 127.32 billion yuan – 13.7 times that of 1952. During this period, the output of major products increased rapidly.

In the early 1970s, China's output of cotton yarn and cotton cloth had already occupied first place in the world. Today the problem of clothing one billion people has been basically solved. When the People's Republic was founded in 1949, the average per capita consumption of cotton cloth was only a little over 2.3 metres and in the rural areas it was only about 1.7 metres. What the peasants wore was mostly homespun cloth and coarse cloth woven by themselves. The colours and designs were very monotonous, mostly in "blue, black and white" colours. In 1985, the country's population was more than double that of the early Liberation days, but the average per capita consumption of cotton cloth (including chemical fibre-cotton blend cloth and pure chemical fibre cloth) went up to 11.67 metres, an increase of twice that of 1952. Beginning from December 1983, textiles were

Table 11: Increase in Output of Major Products

Product	Unit	1952	1957	1965	1975	1980	1984	1985
Cotton yarn	10,000 tons	65.6	84.4	130.0	210.8	292.6	321.9	353.5
Chemical fibre	10,000 tons		0.02	5.01	15.48	45.03	73.47	94.78
Cloth	100 million metres	38.3	50.5	62.8	94.0	134.7	137.0	146.7
Knitting wool	10,000 tons	0.20	0.57	1.10	2.66	5.73	11.0	12.6
Woollen fabrics	10,000 metres	423	1,817	4,240	6,943	10,095	18,049	21,816
Gunny bags	100 million pieces	0.67	0.83	1.25	1.91	4.10	5.48	6.27
Silk	10,000 tons	0.56	0.99	0.91	2.31	3.54	3.76	4.22
Silk fabrics	100 million metres	0.65	1.45	3.42	4.54	7.59	11.78	

supplied in unlimited quantities throughout the country. Coarse woollen fabrics, pure knitting wool and silk quilt covers were all supplied in unlimited quantities.

China has always attached great importance to raising the quality of textiles and increasing their colours and designs, and in the past three decades or so, these have increased considerably. The country has produced large quantities of durable traditional products with new designs, and high-grade textiles, as well as many brand name products. The *Fenghe* brand 4040 poplin and *Golden Mountain Cup* brand printed silk of Shanghai, the *Fallen Flower Lantern Dance* corduroy of Changzhou, the *White Lotus* cashmere sweater of Beijing and the *Flying Child* artificial silk tapestry satin of Hangzhou are of high quality and enjoy brisk sales at home and abroad.

China's textile industry has not only met one billion people's demand for clothing but has supplied large quantities of special-purpose textiles to various national economic departments and provided military supplies for national defence. For instance, it has supplied canvas, cord fabric in tyres, woollen fabrics and felt rugs for industrial use, filter cloth, gunnysacks and sackcloth as well as cloth for sanitation and labour protection. These supplies make up about 10% of the country's total output value of textiles.

China's textiles have a great influence in the world textile market. The country has become one of the major textile exporters, with its products sold in more than 160 countries and regions of the world. China's cotton cloth export surpassed that of Japan and the United States and jumped to first place in the world in 1969. Its exports accounted for one-sixth of the total cotton cloth export of the world. In 1985, the country exported a total of 2.55 billion metres of cotton cloth. Chinese silk products enjoy brisk sales in the world market. Beginning from 1979, the country's export of real silk also took first place in the world. By the early 1980s, it had already accounted for 60% of the world's total export. In 1984 the country's total export amounted to 100 million metres. China's exports of cotton yarn, woollen fabrics, cashmere sweaters, cotton knitwear and bed sheets also have a significant place in the total world exports. Moreover, beginning from 1954, whole sets of Chinese textile machinery

were supplied as aid to foreign countries. Starting from 1973, whole sets of textile machinery were exported, and altogether nearly two million spindles of whole set equipment have been supplied to 36 countries and regions in Asia, Africa, Latin America and Europe.

— The distribution of the textile industry has been improved

In old China, most of the textile industry was concentrated in a few coastal port cities and their neighbouring areas. Of the major production equipment, 87% of cotton spindles and 90% of woollen spindles were concentrated in the coastal areas and only 13% and 10% respectively were in the inland areas. After the founding of New China, the Government adopted the policy of making full use of and actively developing old industrial bases in the coastal areas, while making vigorous efforts to build new industrial bases in inland areas. In the raw materials producing areas and vast consuming areas in the hinterland, large numbers of cotton, woollen, linen and silk textile factories were set up and a number of new textile industry bases were built. This made it possible for the distribution of the textile industry to become gradually rationalized. Today, textile industrial enterprises have spread to all parts of the country. The proportion of cotton spindles in various inland provinces and autonomous regions has gone up from 13% to 43%, and that of woollen spindles from 10% to 35%. The number of cotton and woollen spindles in the cotton and wool producing areas makes up two-thirds and one-half of the nation's total respectively. A modern textile industry has been set up and developed in the frontier autonomous regions of Xinjiang, Ningxia, Guangxi, Inner Mongolia and Tibet, where national minorities live in compact communities. The existing textile industry bases in the coastal areas have also been strengthened and improved. In particular, Shanghai's textile industry has been orientated to turn out advanced, high-grade and high-precision products. It has become the country's largest textiles export base, a base of high and medium-grade products and of textile industrial technology. It is playing a leading role in the development of the country's textile industry.

– The production of raw materials and equipment of the textile industry has been promoted vigorously

In old China, the raw materials and equipment of the textile industry relied heavily on imports. After its founding, New China rapidly took the road of depending on domestic resources. A series of policies and measures were taken to restore and develop agricultural production and animal husbandry in an effort to solve the problem of acquiring agricultural raw materials for the textile industry. By 1984, China's cotton output had amounted to 6.258 million tons, ranking first in the world. China's output of silk, cashmere and jute take up large proportions of the total world output, taking first or second place. In addition, the country also has rich resources of animal hair, such as yak hair and rabbit wool. While the output of natural fibre was increased, energetic efforts were made to develop chemical fibres. By 1983, the self-sufficiency rate of domestic raw materials in the cotton spinning industry had gone up to 91% from 50% in 1949, and there was a surplus in cotton supply. In the woollen textile industry, the self-sufficiency rate of domestic raw materials had risen to 70% from 20%. The rate of self-sufficiency of raw materials in the jute industry had exceeded 90%. In the silk industry the raw materials were not only self-sufficient but were exported in large quantities. In old China, whole sets of equipment required for the development of the textile industry entirely relied on import, and after they were commissioned, the supply of many parts and accessories also depended on foreign countries. Today, except for the import of a number of pieces of up-to-date equipment from abroad, China can design and manufacture whole sets of textile equipment for the cotton, woollen, linen, silk, knitwear, printing and dyeing, and chemical fibre industries and has developed much original technological equipment. It is now able to equip itself mainly with domestically made textile machinery.

Current problems and prospects of development

The main problem in China's textile industry at present is that the industry's structure and product mix have still to be further rationalized. Today the Chinese not only demand greater quantities of textiles but, which is more important, they have ever higher demands on the quality, colours, designs, varieties, grades, and packing of textiles and the development of new products. Textiles will have ever wider use: thus the demand on the textile industry has shifted from increasing quantity to raising quality, and to the development of high-grade fur, woollen and silk products. In the United States, Japan and Federal Germany, knitwear accounts for more than 40% of

the textiles output. In recent years, knitted goods have been much in fashion in China but their output is limited. In industrially developed countries, cloth for decoration and industrial use accounts for 50% of the consumption of textiles, but its proportion in China is still rather low. With the improvement in the people's standard of living, the demand for textiles in this respect will further develop. In 1984 China's export of textiles and clothing accounted for 17% of total exports, constituting China's main export products. However, the proportion of China's export volume in the world textiles trade is still very small. There is great potential for export, but efforts must be made to improve the quality and increase the varieties of textile exports. The second problem in China's textile industry is that proportions between the output of cotton yarn and that of grey cloth and printed and dyed cloth are not sufficiently harmonious. The third problem is that part of the equipment of the textile enterprises is outdated and cannot meet the requirements for developing new products, increasing colours and designs and improving the quality of the products.

The main discrepancies between the supply and demand for textiles have shifted from insufficient quantity to how the quality and varieties of products can better meet market demand. The Chinese Ministry of the Textile Industry has consequently shifted the stress from attention to the rate of development, output and expansion of production capacity to quality, economic result and technological transformation. While developing the cotton textile industry, strenuous efforts will be made to develop the chemical fibre, woollen, silk and linen textile industries. Efforts will be made to solve the problem of imbalance between processing and the capacity of finishing after printing and dyeing in the textile industry and to increase the latter capacity. Technological transformation of the existing enterprises will be carried out in a planned way and step by step. Meanwhile, new channels will be opened up to increase the supply of raw materials.

During the Seventh Five-Year Plan period, the building and production of the chemical fibre industry will be accelerated; the number of airstream spinning machines and new-type looms will be increased and technological reform of cotton spinning equipment will be carried out; the stress of development will be laid on union woollen textiles and coarse woollen textiles; the varieties of silk industry products will be increased and the quality and intensity of processing will be raised; efforts will be made to produce more pure cotton and cotton blend knitwear and to increase the proportion of knitwear in the textile industry.

Light Industry

China's light industry, which produces mainly consumer goods, covers a wide scope. Its products include not only manufactured goods for daily use and durable consumer goods, but stationery and sports articles and articles for artistic appreciation, both traditional products and products of contemporary new creations. At the same time, a part of the means of production is also produced.

After the founding of New China, light industry traversed a tortuous road of development. During the First Five-Year Plan period, it developed rapidly and was basically in keeping with the social purchasing power. Later, owing to one-sided stress on the development of heavy industry under the slogan "taking steel as the key link", light industry could not develop healthily. After 1979, a readjustment of the national economy was carried out and the principle of "six priorities" was applied to light industry, i.e., "priority in the supply of raw and semi-finished materials, fuel and power; in adopting measures for tapping potentials, renovation and transformation; in capital construction; in getting bank loans; in obtaining foreign exchange and importing new technologies; and in communication and transport." This and the formulation of a series of correct policies enabled light industry to develop swiftly. The supply of consumer goods for daily use visibly turned for the better and the people's life improved notably.

After more than three decades of construction work, light industry has taken on a new look:

– New industries have increased steadily and basic sectors are now complete

Since the founding of New China, new industries have developed steadily, simultaneously with the development of traditional industries. These include mainly the watch, photosensitive materials, plastics, synthetic detergents, synthetic perfume and household electrical appliance industries. Today there are 44 major industries under the jurisdiction of the Ministry of Light Industry. They include the industries concerned with paper making, bicycles, sewing machines, clocks and watches, ceramic items, enamel products, glassware, photosensitive materials, light bulbs, lamps and lanterns, dry batteries, detergents, cosmetics, plastics, leather and fur and their products, clothing, hats and footwear, arts and crafts, carpets, toys, household electrical appliances, stationery, furniture, miscellaneous goods for daily use and various industries under the food industry.

China can now produce special-purpose materials and components required by many industries. In the clock and watch industry, for instance, all the necessary materials and components (gem bearings, hairspring, clockwork spring, shockproofing) up to special-purpose machine tools can be made. In the electric lighting industry, a complete production system including tungsten and molybdenum materials, lamp holders, phosphor powder and all kinds of lamps and lanterns has been set up. In the

Manually knotted silk carpets produced at the Minzhong silk carpet factory in Sichuan province won a National Silver Cup. *(Photo by Sun Zhongjing)*

photosensitive materials industry, departments making photographic gelatine and photographic paper have become self-sufficient. The machinery industry can provide special-purpose equipment to nearly 40 branches of light industry.

– The output of products has increased considerably

In 1949 the total output value of light industrial enterprises under the Ministry of Light Industry was only 4.28 billion yuan (counted in terms of the constant price of 1980). By 1984 it had shot up to 132.55 billion yuan, an increase of 31-fold, with an average annual increase of 10.3%. In 1985, it further went up to 157.38 billion yuan, an increase of 18.7% over the preceding year.

During this period, traditional light industrial products increased by ten or even a hundred times.

Starting from scratch, new products developed at a rate faster than that of traditional products. The production of washing machines, for instance, started in 1978 but by 1985 its output had reached 8.872 million. The annual output of electric fans reached 31.746 million, taking front rank in the world.

Table 12: Output of Major Traditional Products

Product	Unit	1952	1957	1965	1975	1980	1984	1985
Machine-made paper and paperboards	10,000 tons	37	91	173	341	535	756	911
Sewing machines	10,000	6.6	27.8	123.8	356.7	767.8	934.9	991.2
Bicycles	10,000	8.0	80.6	183.8	623.2	1,302.4	2,861.4	3,227.7
Enamel products	10,000 tons	0.9	1.8	5.0	9.5	15.1	14.7	15.5
Thermos flasks	10,000	856.1	3,097	4,583	6,870	12,985	14,937	15,541
Electric bulbs	100 million	0.26	0.69	1.92	5.20	9.46	14.12	15.3
Soap	10,000 tons	9.7	26.3	31.5	61.1	85.2	94.3	99.6
Leather	10,000 pieces	330	956	713	2,453	4,145	3,819	4,164
Leather shoes	10,000 pairs	1,200	2,529	1,808	6,646	15,745	19,676	

Table 13: Output of New Products

Product	Unit	1952	1957	1965	1975	1980	1984	1985
Watches	10,000	—	0.04	108.3	809.0	2,267.5	3,807.1	5,447.1
Synthetic detergent	10,000 tons	—	—	3.0	22.3	39.3	81.0	100.5
Refrigerators	10,000	—	0.16	0.30	1.80	4.90	54.74	144.81
Washing machines	10,000	—	—	—	—	24.53	578.06	887.2
Electric fans	10,000	—	—	—	—	723.7	1,770.7	3,174.6
Cameras	10,000	—	0.01	1.72	18.49	37.28	126.18	178.97
Plastics	10,000 tons	0.2	1.4	13.0	60.7	114.4	215.3	248.0
Refined aluminium products	10,000 tons	—	0.28	1.14	3.98	5.80	7.34	7.26

– The varieties of products have increased greatly

In old China there were few varieties of light industrial products that could be produced domestically. In the 1950s and 1960s, scores and even hundreds of new products were added every year, and since 1979 also thousands of new products have been added annually.

Analysis of several main industries shows that in the early period of Liberation there were only 30 varieties of paper and paperboards, but now there are more than 500 kinds. Among these, all kinds of paper for technical use, such as electric insulating paper and 500,000-volt ultra-high voltage cable paper, are well up to advanced world technological level. Paper for all kinds of recording instruments and electrostatic recording paper used on computers, oil prospecting plotting instruments and telecommunication facsimile printers have been awarded the state invention prize. Paper for medical use can be used to make disposable operation overalls, surgical towels, caps and gauge masks which are strong, airy, humidity-absorbing and safe for use. There are also various kinds of paper for agricultural use, such as for transplanting sugarbeet seedlings.

Whereas China could only produce mechanical wooden clocks and mechanical alarm clocks in the past, it can now produce more than 30 kinds of clocks, such as transistor quartz clocks, torsional pendulum quartz desk clocks, console model art pendulum clocks and all kinds of clocks for industrial and other departments, including aviation clocks, car clocks, earthquake clocks and oil drilling well clocks. For watches, the country could at first produce only mechanical men's watches, but now it can produce not only women's watches but also calendar, double-calendar, automatic watches, thin-type watches and quartz and digital watches. In the photosensitive materials industry, colour film, colour photographic paper, printing film and microfilm have been developed. In the electric lighting industry, China could only produce ordinary electric bulbs and assemble a small number of fluorescent lights, but now it can turn out 50 kinds and more than 3,000 specifications of lamps, including tungsten halogen lamps, short arc xenon lamps and metallic halogenide lamps for cinematographic filming and projection, photographic plate making and medical use. In the hardware industry, the country has developed not only multiple-safety spring door locks, but also electronic door locks with electronic frequency conversion devices which can be unlocked only in response to the right message from a special electronic key. In the musical instrument industry, China could only produce ordinary, national musical instruments and a small number of Western musical instruments, but now it can produce whole sets of Chinese and Western musical instruments as well as electronic musical instruments. In the plastics industry, China has produced a great variety of new-type consumer goods, such as film for preserving fruit freshness, polyester containers for storing food, and polyvinyl chloride clothing and gloves. The country has also developed ground cover film and ageing-resistant, low-density film for agricultural use; cables, plates, tubings, plastic woven bags, tote boxes, hollow containers and foamed plastics for industrial use; plastic floors, doors and windows, decorative plates, sewer pipes, sculptured wall paper and synthetic leather for building use. In the field of household electrical appliances, China has developed semi-automatic two-cylinder washing machines, two-door refrigerators, electronic masseurs, single-phase air-conditioners, cleaners and electric cookers.

While restoring long lost varieties, China's traditional light industry has made new advances. For instance, the ceramics industry has restored a number of old kiln varieties and at the same time developed many new ones with distinct local colours. These include the high-grade bone ash porcelain and talcum porcelain of Tangshan, in Hebei and Zibo, in Shandong, and the ivory porcelain of Handan, in Hebei.

– The quality of products has improved markedly

Before Liberation, only handicraft products had a fairly high technological level, while the technical level of modern industrial products was rather backward and their quality was poor. This situation has changed immensely today. The whiteness and smooth finish of newsprint, the service life of batteries and light bulbs, the degree of heat preservation of thermos bottles, the performance of sewing machines and bicycles, and the precision of weighing apparatuses have all improved noticeably. The improvement in the product quality of certain new industries, such as the precise and continuous operation of watches and the cleaning capacity of synthetic detergents, has been particularly striking.

Since the promulgation of the *State Regulations on Awards for Quality Products*, many products have been awarded state gold and silver medals and many arts and crafts have won gold cup and silver cup prizes. Among the products which have won state gold medals in the field of ceramics are the underglazed dinner and tea sets produced by the Qunli Porcelain Factory of Liling and the exquisite blue and white porcelain produced by the People's Porcelain Factory of Jingdezhen; in the field of chemicals for daily use are *White Bear* menthol, and *Maxim* and *Blue Sky* toothpaste; in the field of stationery there is *Xuan* paper; in sports equipment are *Red Happiness* and *Double Fish* table tennis balls, *Friendship* table tennis bats, *Golden Ring* footballs, *Train* volleyballs; in the field of arts and crafts are *Hongmian* and *Xinghai* high-grade violins, lace from Xiaoshan, embroidered tablecloths from Changshu, *Fengchuan* woollen carpets and *Penglaige* lace; there are also *Ship* condenser paper, *Crystal* brand crystal glassware, *Tiger Head* flashlights and *Temple of Heaven* and *Conch* men's shirts. Most of these quality products have approached or reached advanced international level. The *Hongmian* brand

high-grade violin won a gold medal at the Fourth International Violin-Making Competition held in the United States in 1980. The high-grade violin made by technician Dai Hongxiang of the Beijing Musical Instruments Plant was awarded the gold medal at the International Violin-Making Competition in Federal Germany in 1983. Blue and white porcelain produced in Jingdezhen, in Jiangxi, and a dinner set made in Yixing, Jiangsu, were awarded gold medals at the Leipzig Spring Fair in the German Democratic Republic in March 1984. The blue and white porcelain made in Jingdezhen, Jiangxi, once again won a gold medal at the Fifteenth International Consumer Goods Fair held in Czechoslovakia.

– Large quantities of light industrial products with Chinese characteristics have been provided for the international market

The export volume of China's light industrial goods has increased steadily. The amount of foreign exchange earned by export products made by enterprises under the Ministry of Light Industry accounts for about 20% of the total exports. These products are an important prop of China's export trade. Chinese light industrial products are sold in more than 160 countries and regions throughout the world.

In 1954 China had only about 280 kinds of light industrial products for export, but in 1984 the number exceeded 1,000. Among the traditional export products were arts and crafts, porcelain and brand-name liquors and wines, and their amount increased markedly. Among the newly added export products, watches, alarm clocks, bicycles, sewing machines, detergents, leather shoes, hardware and plastics also enjoy brisk sales. In 1985, the total amount of clothing exported was 1.2 billion $US, canned goods 400 million $US, drawn work 200 million $US, toys 79 million $US, carpets 200 million US$, all kinds of shoes 170 million $US, ceramic items 110 million $US, furniture 11 million $US and locks 49 million $US.

Some light industrial products have established themselves as brand-name products in the international market. Among these are many arts and crafts, such as carpets from Tianjin, cloisonné ware from Xiaoshan, embroidered clothes from Shanghai, flannelette toys from Yangzhou, stone carvings from Qingtian in Zhejiang, bodiless lacquerware from Fuzhou, straw articles from Shandong, shell pictures from Dalian and kites from Tianjin. Also included are many articles of daily use, such as blue and white porcelain from Longquan, in Zhejiang, *Phoenix* and *Everlasting* brand bicycles, *White Cat* detergent, *White Bear* menthol, extra white typing paper and *Swan* brand R-20 high performance batteries, as well as table tennis balls, bats, high-grade volleyballs and footballs for international sports competitions.

545

Problems and prospects for light industry

The major problems existing in the light industry are:

– The development of light industrial production cannot catch up with the growth of people's demand

The changes in the product mix fall behind demand in the changes of consumer patterns; there are outstanding contradictions between the supply and demand of a considerable number of products: in particular, the supply of brand-name quality products, high- and medium-grade products and durable consumer goods lags far behind the demand.

– The supply of major raw and semi-finished materials required in the production and building of light industrial enterprises is inadequate

Examples of shortages are rolled steel, pig iron, non-ferrous metals, timber and chemical industry raw materials.

– The management of various enterprises is backward

There is high consumption of materials and energy in production, the quality of products is not very stable and the economic results are low.

During the Seventh Five-Year Plan period, vigorous efforts will be made to develop light industry, to bring about an all-round growth of various kinds of consumer goods and to lay stress on improving the product mix. Efforts will be made to increase the production of people's daily necessities, readily marketable products and high- and medium-grade durable consumer goods. Production of all kinds of small commodities will be promoted to meet market demand. All these measures are designed to promote the sustained, stable and coordinated development of the national economy.

– The regulating role of the price policy will be brought into better play

The price differences between quality products and ordinary products will be gradually widened to promote the increase in the varieties of products, the improvement of their quality and the development of new products. Priorities in loans, the use of foreign exchange, the supply of energy and raw and semi-finished materials and transport facilities will be given to the production of those products badly needed in the market.

– Efforts will be made to organize the association of related enterprises

The coastal areas and advanced enterprises with good technological equipment will play a leading role.

They should actively work for the proliferation of their brand-name quality products as a link in promoting lateral economic associations.

The Food Industry

China's modern food industry was born in the late nineteenth century and the early twentieth century. By 1949 it had gone through half a century but its development was extremely slow because of the people's low purchasing power. At that time, only in big and medium-sized cities were there a number of grain processing, vegetable oil pressing, animal slaughtering, cigarette making and other primary processing factories. Most of the other industries were handicraft industry in workshops. There were only a few small branches of food industry, with low technology and distributed irrationally. The highest annual output of flour was only 1.6 million tons, accounting for 7–8% of the wheat output. The highest annual output of sugar was 410,000 tons, that of salt was 3.92 million tons, and cigarettes 2.36 million crates.

After the founding of New China, a series of measures were adopted to develop the food industry. Between 1953 and 1985, a total of 15.573 billion yuan was invested in the capital construction of the food industry, making up 23.3% of the total investment in light industry. A number of large and medium-sized modern food processing factories were built. In the field of sugar refining, six large sugar refineries were built in the First Five-Year Plan period, with whole sets of equipment imported from a number of East European countries. Later, China itself designed and manufactured whole sets of advanced equipment with which scores of large and medium-sized sugar refineries were built or reconstructed. In the field of tinned food industry, advanced equipment was imported from Britain, France, Japan, Italy and Federal Germany in the 1960s, and renovation and transformation of the existing enterprises in technology, equipment and packing were carried out. As a result, the production capacity of the industry rapidly increased. Moreover, tens of thousands of small food processing factories were built by various localities in accordance with the characteristics of local resources and the people's habits of consumption. Through the above-mentioned construction, big changes have taken place in China's food industry:

– Various branches of the industry have expanded visibly

After more than 30 years of effort, the backward state of a food industry with very few branches has been changed. In the field of agricultural produce processing, in addition to considerable expansion of the existing rice husking, flour milling and oil and fats industries, new industries have been set up, including starch making, sugar refining, confectionery, cake, soybean protein, garden-produce processing (including tinned fruit, tinned vegetables, jam, fruit juice beverages, carbonic acid beverages, preserved fruit, dehydrated vegetables and fruits) and tea making industries. In the field of animal products processing, in addition to the expansion of the existing slaughtering industry, new industries have been set up, such as meat products, dairy products processing (including sterilized milk, sour milk, milk powder, condensed milk, butter, cheese and casein) and milk substitute industries. In the field of aquatic products processing, in addition to the development of the existing salt industry, aquatic animal and plant processing industries have been set up. In the field of fermented food, the handicraft trades of wine, condiments and pickle making have been developed into industrial production through technological transformation and furthermore, new industries such as yeast, amino acid and enzyme have been set up. At present, all the major branches of the food industry have been established in China, laying a solid groundwork for the further advance of this industry.

— The scale of production has been expanded conspicuously

By 1985 China already had 79,800 enterprises in the food industry. Their total output value came to 95.17 billion yuan (counted in terms of the constant price of 1980), an increase of 9.08 times that of 1952, with an average annual growth rate of 6.9%, accounting for 11.5% of the country's gross industrial output value. Counted in terms of output value, the food industry is the third largest industry in China, next only to the machine-building and textile industries.

The development of various branches of the food industry was as follows: The output value of the grain and oil processing industry was 1.25 billion yuan in 1949 and by 1985 it had reached 26.52 billion yuan. The output of the country's sugar refining industry in 1949 was only 200,000 tons, but by 1985 it had reached 4.51 million tons, an increase of 22.6 times. The salt industry was a major industrial sector before Liberation: its output in 1949 was 2.99 million tons. After the founding of New China, it further developed and by 1985 its output had reached 14.79 million tons, an increase of more than 4.9 times. The tobacco industry produced 1.6 million crates of cigarettes in 1949 but by 1985 the output had reached

23.70 million crates, an increase of 14.8 times, with a total output value of 14.47 billion yuan. There were more than 10,000 wine-making enterprises in 1985, producing 8.51 million tons of wine, representing a 31-fold increase over 1952, of which the output of beer was 3.10 million tons as against 50,000 tons in 1957. There were only a few enterprises in the tinned food industry before Liberation and the national output in 1949 was only 484 tons. By 1985 the industry already had more than 1,700 factories with their output reaching 1.425 million tons and their total output value coming to 4.41 billion yuan, becoming an important branch of the food industry. In the field of slaughtering and meat-packing industry, there were only five large slaughterhouses in the early days of the People's Republic, with a daily capacity of slaughtering 10,000 pigs, and 23 cold storages, with a storage capacity of 30,000 tons. By 1985, the country already had more than 4,000 slaughtering and meat-packing enterprises with a total output value of 11.67 billion yuan. With regard to the newly established industries, the dairy products industry has developed rapidly. Beginning with the production of milk powder in Shanghai in 1950, hundreds of dairy products processing factories of considerable size have been built, handling several thousand tons of fresh milk daily. As to the beverage industry, there were only a few small factories before Liberation, with negligible output. By 1982, 130 beverage factories of considerable size had been built with their output reaching 440,000 tons, producing liquid as well as solid beverages.

The output of all major products of the food industry has increased fairly swiftly. Particularly since 1980, with the exception of the output of crude salt, which dropped somewhat, the growth rate of all other products has been very high. The output of sugar and cigarettes increased more than 50%, tinned food and beverages doubled, and beer more than quadrupled.

The varieties of food industry products have also increased greatly. In addition to processing edible refined salt, the salt industry also produces table salt, washing salt, and pulverized washing salt. The production and supply of iodine salt has produced good results in preventing and curing the endemic disease of goitre. Aside from turning out ordinary cigarettes, the cigarette industry also produces cigarettes with filter tips, cigars and medical cigarettes. The tinned food industry produces several hundred

Table 14: Output of Foodstuffs and Cigarettes

Product	Unit	1952	1957	1965	1975	1980	1984	1985
Crude salt	10,000 tons	495	828	1,147	1,481	1,728	1,642	1,479
Sugar	10,000 tons	45	86	146	174	257	380	451
Cigarettes	10,000 crates	265	446	478	992	1,520	2,132	2,370
Tinned food	10,000 tons	1.3	6.2	12.2	35.1	57.2	109.0	142.5
Wine	10,000 tons	23	67	89	212	368	711	851
Beer	10,000 tons		5	9	27	69	224	310

The National Economy

The salt works equipped with machines with an annual output of 300 thousand tons at Caka Salt Lake in the Qaidam basin in Qinghai province – an oval-shaped lake covering an area of 105 square kilometres. *(Photo by Li Jingrei)*

kinds of tinned food which are sold in various Asian, African and Latin American countries as well as in Hong Kong and Macao. The quality of these products has also improved considerably. The *Meilin* brand tinned mushroom enjoys high prestige in the international market. China produces a number of brand-name liquors and wines: Guizhou *Maotai*, Sichuan *Wuliangye* liquor, Shanxi *Zhuyeqing* liquor, Shaoxing *Jiafan* wine, the *Great Wall* brand Fen liquor, Xinluo-quan *Chengang* wine, Luzhou *Tequ* liquor, Qingdao beer, Yantai *Sunflower* brand red grape wine, Shacheng white grape wine and Yantai *Gold Medal* brandy have all won state gold medals and enjoy brisk sales at home and abroad. The dry white grape wine produced by the Great Wall Brewing Company of Shacheng won a silver medal at the 14th International Grape Wine competition held in London in 1983.

– The technological level has improved noticeably

Industries which were operated fully or mainly with manual labour in old China have now basically realized mechanization or semi-mechanization. Taking the salt industry as an instance: today, the level of mechanization or semi-mechanization in the production of sea salt is nearly 80% and the evaporation technology has been adopted in producing more than 80% of the well salt, in place of the old method of boiling in big bowls. A number of industries which were semi-mechanized in old China have now achieved basic mechanization. The degree of mechanization of large sugar refineries has risen from

50–60% to 90% and part of the production process has realized automatic control. Much progress has also been made in multi-purpose utilization: examples include the extraction of rice chaff oil, fatty acid, oryzanol and inositol from rice chaff; the extraction of perfume oil and pectin from oranges; the extraction of insulin, adrenaline, protease and spirit from the internal organs of domestic animals; the use of soy sauce residue, leftover bits of aquatic products and the hair, feet, bones and blood of domestic animals and fowl to make mixed feed; using sugarcane residue in sugar refinery to cultivate the fungus mushroom; and using rice husk to make heat-insulating materials. Breakthroughs have been made in these fields and products have been turned out in a number of factories.

Existing problems and prospects

Although China's food industry has registered big advances, it remains a weak link in the national economy and lags far behind the needs of economic development and the people's rising standard of living. The average per capita output of various kinds of major food items is still very low: The average per capita output of sugar in 1985 was only 4.3 kilograms; of wine, 8.2 kg; and of tinned food, 1.37 kg. The major problems at present are:

– The scope of processing is small

Most of the foodstuffs consumed by the Chinese

548

people come from primary agricultural produce and only a small part are products processed by the food industry. The output value of China's food industry amounts to only 30% of the agricultural output value, and products of the food industry account for only about 30% of the total volume of food consumption.

– The degree of processing is low

The multi-purpose utilization of food materials has failed to create more edible resources and more varieties of food.

– The structure is irrational

This finds expression, firstly, in the larger proportion of food materials provided for primary processing and the smaller proportion of finished products or semi-finished products provided for reprocessing; and secondly, in the fact that in the total output value of the food industry, the proportion of addiction industry, i.e., the cigarette industry, is relatively high while the proportion of processed food necessary for daily life is relatively low.

To change the backward state of the food industry, China has taken the development of this industry as a major task. In July 1984 the State Council approved and made public the *National Programme for the Development of the Food Industry from 1981 to 2000*. It called for the adoption of effective measures and for bringing into full play the advantages of abundant natural resources, excellent traditional technology and a wide market to build the food industry into an important industrial department that meets demand and has a rational distribution and co-ordinated development. By the end of this century, the total output value of the food industry will amount to 300 billion yuan—an increase of more than 5 times over 1980. Its proportion in the total industrial output value will rise to about 15%. The ratio between the output value of the food industry and that of agriculture will rise from 0.28:1 in 1980 to 0.5:1. The consumption of processed food industry products in the total amount of food consumption of the urban and rural residents will rise to more than 50%. Compared with 1980, the planned output of sterilized milk, dairy products, bean products and egg products in 2000 will increase by 20-fold; baby food, beer and beverages more than 15-fold; meat products, refined flour, bread and other flour products, fruit and vegetable products more than 10-fold; starch and aquatic products more than 6-fold; condiments, tinned food and sugar more than 3.5-fold; and cakes, sweets, salt, cigarettes, vegetable oil, the amount of slaughtering and meat packing will increase more than 100%. Food will be diversified to meet the different needs of various quarters.

5. COMMUNICATIONS AND TRANSPORT

SINCE the founding of New China, communications and transportation have undergone enormous development, ultimately forming a comprehensive transport system, with the railways and the water-borne transport of the Yangtze river and coastal region as the backbone of the system, together with various other types of transport including highways, civil airways and pipelines. Remarkable changes have been made in the layout of the communications and transportation network. Technical equipment has been introduced and transport efficiency raised. An army of designers and construction workers, equipped at quite a high technical level, has been organized to deal with passenger and cargo transport, which is now expanding.

RAIL TRANSPORT

THE history of railway construction in China goes back to 109 years ago, when British businessmen built the 15 kilometres of narrow-gauge line from Shanghai to Wusung in 1876. During the 73 years from 1876 to 1949, a total length of 21,800 km of railways was built on the mainland of China. However, owing to the destruction caused by wars, in 1949 there were not more than 11,000 km of railway tolerably capable of going into operation. After the founding of New China, efforts were made to rebuild and almost all the railway lines on the mainland were basically reconstructed and put into operation by the end of 1950. The construction of the Chengdu–Chongqing railway began in June 1950. Between 1950 and the end of 1985, the length of main-line railway in service reached 52,100 km. In addition, there was a total of 3,100 km in service on local lines in the provinces of Henan, Hebei, Guangdong, Guangxi, Liaoning and Hunan, as well as in the autonomous regions. A further 7,790 km of special railways belonged to the factories and mines responsible for coal, oil, electricity, the chemical industry and the construction industry, and railways in forest areas were some 11,000 km long.

The Development of the Railway System

Railway construction and layout

Before the founding of New China, the 21,800 km of railway line on the mainland were distributed in an uneven and unbalanced manner, as shown by the fact that railways were built mostly in the north-eastern areas and sea-coastal regions, and there were almost no railways at all in the south-western and north-western areas. In the north-eastern areas alone there were already 10,000 km of railway – some 45% of the total length of railway in China – while in the areas west of the Beijing–Guangzhou (Canton) railway line, the length of railway was only 19.5% of the country's total. The vast areas of Xinjiang, Qinghai, Gansu, Ningxia and Shaanxi provinces and the autonomous regions comprise 32% of the country's total land area, but there was only one railway line between Tongguan and Tianshui – a short line which often got disconnected because of the very poor quality construction. The three south-western provinces of Sichuan, Yunnan and Guizhou and the Tibet (Xizang) autonomous region constitute 24% of the country's total land area; they had only a few narrow-gauge railways, including the Kunming–Hekou railway. The two areas were very isolated and their railway mileage was not more than 4% of the country's total.

Railway lines built from 1950 to 1985 in South-West and North-West China respectively run from Chengdu to Chongqing, Baoji to Chengdu, Guiyang to Kunming, Chengdu to Kunming, Zhuzhou to Guiyang, Xiangfan to Chongqing, Tianshui to Lanzhou, Lanzhou to Xining, Lanzhou to Urümqi and Lanzhou to Baotou. The Qinghai–Xizang railway line stretching west from Xining now has a through service as far as Golmud, at the foot of the Kunlun mountains, while the line in southern Xinjiang has reached as far as Korla. Communications in North-West China have acquired an entirely new look today, as the proportion of mileage in service has increased to 25% of the total railway lines. In other words, with the exception of the Tibet autonomous region, there

A 3,000 metre ultra-long railway and highway bridge crossing the Huaihe river in Anhui province. *(Photo by Kang Shiwei)*

are railway services all over the provinces and autonomous regions, as well as the municipalities under the Central Government.

Over the Yangtze river three double-track rail and road bridges have successively been built. The first was the Yangtze River Bridge, built in 1957, which connects the Guishan mountains at Hanyang city and the Sheshan mountains at Wuchang city in Hubei province, with a total length of 1,670 metres. Its main body comprises a length of 1,156 metres, connecting the Jinghan railway (from Beijing to Hankou) and the Yuehan railway (from Guangzhou to Wuchang) to form the line at present known as the Jingguang railway (from Beijing to Guangzhou). The second, built in 1959 at Chongqing in Sichuan province, is the 820 metre bridge linking the through service of the Chuanqian railway (from Chongqing to Guiyang) and the Chengyu railway (from Chengdu to Chongqing). The third is the 6772 metre bridge, with a 1577-metre main body, built in 1968 at Nanjing in Jiangsu province. It connects the Jingpu railway (from Tianjin to Pukou) and the Huning railway (from Shanghai to Nanjing), which are the two trunk lines between North and South China, tremendously increasing transport capacity between Beijing and Shanghai. The three steel-built giant bridges over the Yangtze have made a thoroughfare between North and South China – since the river itself has from ancient times been known as the north–south dividing line – thus transforming the backward state of earlier times, when trains could not cross the river without a ferry and cargoes could not be shipped without lighterage.

4,386 railway tunnels have been bored, with a total length of 2,009 km, among which ten are more than 5 km long. The length of the Yimaling tunnel on the Yuanping–Beijing railway is 7 km, making it the longest tunnel today, while the Dayaoshan tunnel, the boring of which is still being carried out on the Hengyang–Guangzhou section of the Beijing–Guangzhou line, is as long as 14.3 km. This tunnel was scheduled for completion in 1988. The

Hengyang–Guangzhou section is a double-track line and the tunnel is a double-lined sectional one.

Raising the technical level

In old China almost all the railways were single-track lines. There was only one double-track railway line, this being just 866 km long and comprising only 3.9% of the mileage in service. There were no electrified railways; all carriages were pulled by steam locomotives. The number of both passenger trains and goods trains was very small, and they were of ramshackle construction. After the founding of New China, while new lines were being built, technical reforms were made in the old railways by increasing the proportion of double-track and electrified lines. By 1985 the mileage of double-track railway lines increased to 9,989 km, comprising 19% of the lines already in service. There were already 4,150.5 km of electrified lines, 8% of the mileage of all the lines in operation. Electrical and diesel locomotives were 34.8% of the total. Railway lines installed with automatic blocks and semi-automatic blocks were over 95% of the mileage in service. As compared with 1980, the number of locomotives on the country's railway network in 1985 had increased 1.74 times; passenger trains, 3.09 times; and goods trains, 4.46 times. The proportion of goods trains with 50 d.w.t. had reached 92.3%.

Railway lines constitute the main force undertaking the nation's chief transport tasks. The 1985 freight volume by rail amounted to 1,307,000,000 tons and the turnover volume of freight 812,600,000,000 tons/km, an increase of 17.5% and 42.1% respectively, compared with 1980, and 12 times and 20.6 times respectively more than in 1950. Of the freight

Logs being transported by train from the Da Hinggan mountains in Inner Mongolia. *(Photo by Yang Shenhe)*

transported by rail, 40% was coal, reaching 518,000,000 tons in 1985. Of this amount 126,000,000 tons were transported from Shanxi province to other localities. The number of passengers transported totalled 1,121,100,000 and the turnover reached 241,600,000,000 men/km, an increase of 21.6% and 74.7% respectively on 1980 and 7 times and 11.3 times respectively on 1950. In the first four years of the Sixth Five-Year Plan period (1980–1985) the passenger-carrying capacity showed an annual increase of about 52,000,000. To ease the heavy load on railway carrying capacity, measures were taken in 1985 to bring highway transport into play by raising the price of a rail ticket by 36% for passenger transport on journeys of less than 100 km. The passenger-carrying demand over short distance journeys as a result was alleviated. The total count of passengers was reduced by 12,430,000 in 1985 as compared with 1984.

The passenger and freight capacity, as well as the turnover volume of the railway service, became the largest in the whole of the nation's transport system. In 1985 the volume of passenger transport was 20%; the turnover volume of passengers 56%; the volume of goods transport 48%; and the turnover volume of goods 49%.

The efficiency of railway transport is comparatively high in China. Transportation efficiency as a comprehensive target is reflected by the turnover time of goods carriers. In 1985 this was 3.48 days, the fastest turnover time in the world. The turnover volume of both passenger transport and freight in 1985 per km was 20,150,000 tons/km, second only to the Soviet railway service. The total average weight of goods trains had always been more or less below 2,000 tons during the 20 years before 1984, but it reached 2,211 tons in 1985, an increase of 13.8% compared with 1984. The time interval of double-track trains was on average 8 to 10 minutes. The average technical speed of the passenger trains was 55.1 km per hour in 1985, 57.9% more than the 34.9 km per hour of 1949.

Consolidation of productivity

Except for some repairs facilities, there was almost no railway industry at all in China before Liberation, but now there is a fully-fledged railway industry which can produce whole-set equipment and has the capability of building as well as repairing. Not only steam locomotives but also electrical locomotives and diesel locomotives can be built. The number of electrical locomotives and diesel locomotives made in 1985 was 1.3 times more than in 1980, surpassing the number of steam-locomotives. Freight car production in 1985 was 83% more than in 1980, and production of passenger cars increased by 44%.

The Administration of the Railway System

All railways are without exception under the administration of the Railway Ministry. Railways belonging to the Central Government are built on state investments and run by the Railway Ministry; while local railways, built by investments chiefly from the provinces, autonomous regions and municipalities under the Central Government but subsidized by the State, are run by the local governments themselves. The railways controlled by the Central Government are a state-owned enterprise and the local railways are local state-owned enterprises, both being part of the whole people's ownership system.

There are 12 railway administrative bureaux, in Harbin, Shenyang, Beijing, Hohhot (Huhehot), Zhengzhou, Jinan, Shanghai, Guangzhou, Liuzhou, Chengdu, Lanzhou and Ürümqi. Branch bureaux

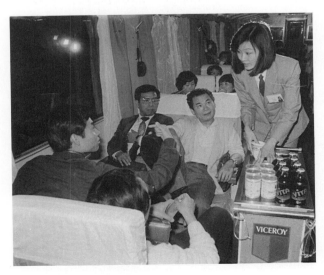

On the Guangzhou–Hong Kong through train. *(Photo by Lu Xiaohua)*

The marshalling yards of the North Zhengzhou railway in Henan. *(Photo by Li Yongtan)*

come under the above-mentioned administrative bureaux, totalling 62 all over the country. Local railways under the control of the provinces, autonomous regions and municipalities under the Central Government all have their respective administrative mechanisms.

There are 68 railway plants directly under the control of the Railway Ministry, responsible for tasks of producing and repairing locomotives, carriages and the various items of equipment of all the country's railways. Under the Ministry there are also 15 engineering bureaux, 5 planning institutes and 5 corporations in charge of electrification, communication signals, bridges, plant-building and tunnel construction. They undertake railway building and plant construction as well as prospecting and designing. Under the Ministry there are a further 8 research institutes, 8 colleges and 41 specialized course middle schools, 32 technical schools and some 1,500 railway middle and primary schools.

The 14,295 km long Dayaoshan double-track electric railway tunnel in Guangdong was completed after 8 years excavation. This is one of the longest tunnels in China and one of the ten longest tunnels in the world.

Problems and Prospects

The present principal problems in connection with railway transport are the shortage of railway lines and the lack of equipment. In China's land areas there are on average only 54.27 km of railway lines per 10 thousand square km. There is also a shortage of locomotives, goods wagons and passenger trains. Even the increasing transport equipment appears unlikely to meet the demands of national economic and social development. The utilization rate of a quarter of the railway sections and one-third of the main marshalling yards has already reached saturation. In some sections the transport capability can only fulfil 50–70% of the volume needed and on some trunk lines, passengers are usually 30–50% beyond the quota.

During the Seventh Five-Year Plan period (1986–1990), railway carrying capacity is to have an annual average increase of 65,000,000 tons, reaching 1,600,000,000 tons in 1990 – a 25.5% increase compared with 1985, passenger carrying capacity is to have a total annual increase of 58,000,000, reaching a total of 1,400,000,000 in 1990, a 36.4% increase over 1985, and railways in China are obviously confronting a much heavier freight demand.

To solve these problems and adapt railway transport to the requirement of the four modernizations, China is building the necessary new lines and at the same time trying to raise the overall transport capability by speeding up the progress in technology. Technical

reform is to be reinforced on railway trunk lines, especially those in the eastern part of the country. In particular, double-track lines are to be constructed and electrification carried out, appropriately adopting diesel locomotives and building new lines and connecting lines. The marshalling yards of the passenger trains are to be further expanded and goods trains developed for heavy load transport, which is to play the leading role in modernizing all the various technical equipment and transportation work. The locomotive building industry is to be renovated to improve productivity and quality. All old locomotives are to be replaced by new ones. Electrical and internal combustion locomotives are to be employed as the main tractive force. The construction of local railways is to be developed more quickly.

Reformation is to be given top priority. The economic-contract-responsibility system is to be implemented in managing the railway business for lines belonging to the Central Government. All the railway departments concerned are to make responsible contracts on the carrying capacity of passenger and goods transport, on the transport of such staple supplies as coal, on the increase of carrying capacity and on the fulfilment of capital construction in accordance with the target stipulated by the Railway Ministry on the orders of the Central Government. In this way, the departments concerned are able to promote a brisk growth of the railway business by using their funds accumulated through raising their self-development and self-reform.

HIGHWAY TRANSPORT

IN the 43 years since the construction in 1906 of the highway between Zhennanguan (known today as Friendship Pass) and Lungzhou in Guangxi province, with a length of 50 km, up to 1949, highways totalling 130,000 km had been built in old China. However, they were in very poor condition. Some of them were without bridges or tunnels and had been for years without repair. Those tolerably open to traffic totalled not more than 80,000 km because of war damage and the lack of repair. Since the founding of New China, through a 36-year effort, highways built and open to traffic have reached 940,000 km, among which there are over 193,000 km with a high-class or sub-high-class surface.

A store-on-yakback in Tibet. *(Photo by Wang Jingye)*

General Development

Highway construction

In old China, most of the highways were constructed in coastal areas. In the vast hinterland and frontier areas there were almost no highways at all. In the south-western and north-western regions, comprising 56% of the country's land area, the mileage of highways open to traffic was only 23% of the total. Since the founding of New China, efforts have been made to rebuild the highways destroyed by the protracted wars, resulting in the restoration of up to 127,000 km by the end of 1952. In the meantime new highways have been built, including the Chuanzang highway (from Chengdu to Lhasa), the Qingzang highway (from Xining to Lhasa), the Xinzang highway (from Ürümqi to Lhasa), the Chengdu–Aba highway, the Wenzhou–Fuzhou highway, the Shenyang–Dandong highway and the Tianshan highway. There are also highways leading to the Wuchihshan mountains and Taxinanling mountains in the frontier areas and the minority nationality regions. There are now roads all over the counties and towns of the whole country. In some localities there are first-class highways, while motorways are being constructed from Beijing to Tanggu via Tianjin and from Guang-

554

The Sichuan–Tibet highway in snowy and icy mountains.   *(Photo by Le Jinxiong)*

zhou to Shenzhen. Changes have taken place also in layout. By the end of 1985, the highways in the south-western and north-western areas open to traffic were 33% of the country's total. Whereas before there were no highways in the Xizang (Tibet) autonomous region, there is already a highway network with Lhasa as the centre and there are five main highways leading towards Sichuan, Qinghai, Yunnan and Xinjiang provinces and autonomous regions as well as to the neighbouring country of Nepal, a total of some 21,000 km. The Tianshan highway, which runs across the Tianshan mountain range, when completed and open to traffic, will have connections with the northern and southern Xinjiang areas. Therefore with the exception only of the Metuo county in the Xizang autonomous region, motor vehicles are running on highways throughout all the counties and 93% of the country's towns and villages.

Increased construction of the highway network obviously calls for fast development in the construction of bridges. In the pre-Liberation period not a single bridge was built over the River Yangtze. Since the founding of New China, however, 3 double-deck rail and road bridges and over 10 highway bridges have been built. In the past, over the 5,400 km-long

Yellow River there was only one bridge (on the Lanzhou highway), built in the Qing dynasty by a foreign construction company and able to accommodate only light motor vehicles and carts drawn by men and animals. Now there are already nearly 40 bridges over the Yellow River. The 2,023 km-long bridge at Jinan, built in 1982, has a width of 19.5 metres and a span of 220 metres. It is an obliquely-drawn pre-stressed concrete bridge, which in design, capacity and structure has attained world advanced standards. By the end of 1985 there were more than 130,000 permanent bridges, either built or rebuilt. Bridges completed in the Sixth Five-Year Plan period (1980–1985) numbered more than 15,000.

The growth of the motor-vehicle manufacturing industry

Old China depended entirely upon the import of automobiles and accessory parts, tyres and oil from foreign countries. The very first car was imported to Shanghai in 1901. Later, in 1917, some Chinese businessmen ran an automobile company at Zhang-jiakou, Hebei province – the very first company that managed an automobile traffic service between

Zhangjiakou and Kulun (Ulan Bator). On the eve of the liberation of the mainland, there were only shaky vehicles, numbering not more than 51,000, with a cargo-transport capacity of 79,630,000 tons and a passenger transport capacity amounting to 18,090,000. The birth of New China began to witness the establishment of the automobile transport business as a state-run enterprise, resulting in the acceleration of the development of a motor vehicle industry. The No. 1 Automobile Manufacturing Plant and the No. 2 Automobile Manufacturing Plant were set up in 1956 and 1975 respectively. Some provinces and cities followed suit, building their own plants and passenger car assembly factories. At present there are 37 car-engine manufacturing plants, some 200 rebuilding plants for civilian use and some 2,400 spare parts factories. All of them are capable not only of producing passenger cars and lorries of large, middle and small sizes but also of producing special-purpose cars, container cars, oil-tank cars and heavy vehicles with a tonnage of 400–500 tons.

The development of highway transport

The growth of highway transport in China has paved the way for developing highway construction, motor-vehicle building and the oil industry. Up to now there are some 1,800 local state-owned highway transport enterprises throughout the country. In counties where there are highways, there are automobile transport

A highway in the Liupan mountains in Gansu province.
(Photo by Shi Guanda)

service offices, and in 90% of the villages also there is a motor vehicle transport business.

The economic target for automobile transport techniques is now raised. Comparing 1985 with 1950, the annual yield of automobile tonnage has been raised from 6,400 tons/km to 39,000 tons/km; the rate of completion of automobiles has increased from 63.7% to 87%; the mileage for requiring regular major servicing has advanced from 14,000 km to 62,000 km. Consequently the transport cost has been reduced by a little more than a half.

Highway transport is becoming more and more important in China, and the responsibility for passenger and goods transport heavier and heavier. The volume of goods transport made by motor vehicles exclusively belonging to the communication departments was 762,270,000 tons in 1985, an increase of 7.85 times and 0.3%, compared with 88,870,000 tons in 1950 and 760,170,000 tons in 1980 respectively. The volume of passenger transport amounted to a total count of 4,270,000,000 persons, an increase of 184.6 times and 91.6% compared with the total count of 23,010,000 persons in 1950 and the total count of 2,227,990,000 in 1980.

Among the diversified types, road transport has gained much in importance in volume and turnover of passenger and goods. In 1985 the volume of passenger transport by road was 75.34%; the turnover volume of passengers, 36.75%; the volume of goods transport, 28.2% and the turnover volume of goods, 2.12%.

In addition to the communication departments which have possessed their own motor vehicles for transportation, other departments, such as the different production organizations, foreign trade, commercial transport, enterprise and administrative departments and even others all have either passenger or goods transport vehicles. Motor vehicles are also owned by individual businessmen or jointly by businessmen who are engaged in the transport business all over the country. Some 290,000 vehicles were owned by the end of 1985, surpassing the amount of motor vehicles possessed by the communication and transportation departments exclusively doing transport business. Such vehicles have been active in all the cities and villages, playing an important part in promoting industrial and agricultural production and in speeding up the exchanges of supplies.

Highway transport has also helped the railways by sharing the short-distance passengers and goods transport successfully. By the end of 1985 there were some 2,300 highway sections that shared the load with railway passenger transport. The mileage in service amounted to 500,000 km and the daily volume of passenger transport 750,000 persons, so that the heavy load of railway short-distance transport has been relieved. In short-distance freight, highway transport departments in different localities have opened the LCL (less than one car-load) freight service. There are already over 2,500 highway sec-

A butterfly-shaped three-dimensional flyover in Tianjin. *(Photo by Yang Baokun)*

tions throughout China doing LCL freight service, the mileage being 680,000 km, beginning to form two highway transport networks with LCL freight service – the eastern Chinese network, with Shanghai as the centre, and the network connecting the northern and north-eastern Chinese provinces and cities, with Beijing and Shenyang as centres. Highway transport is a step further toward playing the major part in short-distance transport.

Highway containerized transport has developed fast. By the end of 1985 there were about 1,000 motor vehicles engaged in international containerized transport at the ports, handling an annual volume of 234,600 standard containers with a tonnage of 2,304,500 tons, an increase of 21 times more than that of 1980. Highways handled 4,910,000 containers at home, with a total tonnage of 5,360,000 tons, four times more than in 1980.

The Administrative System of Highway Transport

The work of Chinese highway construction and transportation is under the leadership and control of the Communications Ministry. Under this ministry there are Highway Bureaux, responsible for making development plans, putting forward policies and stipulating regulations. Under the governments of provinces, autonomous regions and cities under the

Central Government, there are Communication Divisions (bureaux) or Communication Committees (offices), exerting control over highway construction and highway transportation as well as the administrative work. Most of these bureaux have highway transport enterprises directly under their control. Since 1983, some bureaux in certain areas have separated the control of enterprise from administration. Through such a measure the power of running the highway transport enterprise was handed down to the central cities, turning them into an economic entity with self-management, responsible for their own profit and loss. All the highway offices in the provinces, autonomous regions and cities under the Central Government, counties and towns now hold the responsibilities for highway management and maintenance.

Problems and Prospects

The main problems at present are: First, the number of highways is still small and the techniques remain at a low level. Second, the carrying capacity of motor vehicles is far from efficient. There is also a scarcity of heavy trucks above 8 tons and of light trucks below 3 tons. The number of passenger cars, particularly motor coaches, is far from sufficient. There are only 979 km of highways in each 10,000 square metres of the country's land areas, on the average. Again, of the total of 940,000 km of loads, only 63.8% qualify for

557

classification. There are only 400 km of highway classified as first class (4-lane) and only 19,000 km classified as second class. Highways with special-class surface and those with second class surface make up about 20.5% of all highways.

In future China is to speed up developing highway transport by laying the stress on building economical arterial highways, port highways, the transport of energy resources and key tourist highways planned by the Government. During the Seventh Five-Year Plan period new highways to be built are expected to reach 60,000 km and the present highways to be rebuilt by raising their classification are to reach 80,000 km. As a result, by 1990 the total highway mileage open to traffic is expected to reach 1,000,000 km. Of these 680,000 km are expected to be qualified for classification. Included above is an increase of 2,000 km of superhighway, highways only for motor vehicles, as well as first class highways altogether. There is also to be an increase of 30,000 km of second class highways. The growth of highway transport naturally leads to the development of the automobile industry; accordingly, new products are being sought and ways of speeding up renovation. And in order to strengthen self-reliance in handling the automobile industry so as to raise both the quality and quantity of products in China, measures such as joint ventures, co-operative production, technique-trade combination, purchase of patent and other business forms are to be taken in order to import key techniques from foreign countries in a selective and planned manner.

Highway transport departments concerned are to reform their management systems, implement the separation of administration from enterprise, and carry out the simplification of administration and transfer of management powers. Expansion of the self-governing powers of the highway transport enterprise and reinforcement of control over the highway transport professions are to be carried out. The policy of "Let as many as possible carry out the business by encouraging emulation among them" is to be implemented in highway transport for the purpose of rallying all positive factors in running the business. The policy of "Let the people run the business with government assistance" is also to be carried out in highway construction. In other words, the construction of highways is to rely on the local governments and the mass of people, while the Central Government provides subsidies. Foreign funds are to be drawn in as much as possible.

INLAND RIVER TRANSPORT

In 1949 the navigation mileage on China's inland rivers was not more than some 70,000 km. However, in 1985 there were already 109,000 km of waterways, of which 57,000 km had a depth of over 1 metre and 18,000 km were open to steamship traffic. Rivers south of the Qinling mountain ranges and Hui river are ice-free all the year round and therefore open to shipping in the four seasons, while rivers to the north are not open to shipping in the freezing period.

Main Inland Rivers and Inland Ports

The Yangtze is the longest inland river in China, and the mileage open to steamship traffic in its main course amounts to 2,995 km. The part of the shipping route from Chongqing to Yichang (also called the Chuanjiang shipping route) passes through high mountain gorges, full of dangerous rapids and hence was not navigable by night. Dredging work on the dangerous rapids started in 1953; the installation of electrical beacons was finished in September 1959 and steamships going up the upper reaches have hence found it possible to pass at night time. Steamships with a tonnage of 5,000 tons pass day and night in the part from Yichang to Hankou and from Hankou onward steamships of 10,000 tons pass freely. At the 6 km-long arterial waterway of the River Yangtze's upper reaches, along Yichang in Hubei province, a huge 2,561 m-long dam has been built, known as the Gezhouba Water Conservancy Pivot Work. Its lock-gate admits the passage of passenger steamships and freighters of 3,000 tons and 20,000-ton lighter fleets. The Yangtze has several tributaries – the Jialingjiang, Hanjiang, Xiangjiang, Yuanjiang and Ganjiang rivers, and there are also medium and small river branches. The total navigational mileage of the Yangtze amounts to over 70,000 km, the largest inland transport network in China.

Ships at the Gezhouba Dam lock on the Yangtze river in Hubei.

The other important inland rivers are the Zhujiang, Heilungjiang and Huaihe rivers and the Jinghang Canal (between Beijing and Hangzhou). With the exception of the Heilungjiang river, which has a navigable period of only six months per year, all these rivers are navigable throughout the year. Along the Jinghang Canal (also called the Grand Canal) there are two sections – that between Beijing and Tianjin and that between Linqing and the Yellow River – which are not yet open to navigation. The Yellow River is 5,464 km long, very shallow and full of mud and sand. The navigation mileage is 52 km over the upper reaches, 493 km over the middle reaches and 940 km over the lower reaches. Only small steam-lighters pass the river along the three different sections separately.

There are some 2,000 inland ports, of which 300 are relatively large. The Yangtze has 26 main ports, among which the Nanjing port, Zhenjiang port, Zhangjiagong port and Nantong port all have anchorage not only for large-size inland fleet ships but also for ocean-going ships of over 10,000 tons. Those already open to foreign ships are the Nanjing port, Nantong port and Zhangjiagong port.

Other inland river ports have only very simple equipment and some are still in a primitive state.

Inland River Passenger and Cargo Transport

Dating back some 2,500 years, China already started inland river transportation on a wide scale. However the form of transport remained very backward. There were wooden sailing vessels, relying upon sails, oars and tow-ropes. It was not until 1872 that the China Merchants' Steamship Company was set up along the Yangtze river. At the time of the founding of New China, the ships plying the River Yangtze did not total 200,000 tons, and ships on other inland rivers were even fewer. The tonnage of wooden sailing boats was 93% of the total. The volume of cargo transport accomplished in the whole year of 1950 in inland rivers was 25,510,000 tons and that of passenger transport at the same period, 23,010,000 persons. However, in 1980 the cargo transport volume increased to 310,000,000 tons and the turnover volume of cargoes was 57,150,000,000 tons/km; the volume of passenger transport increased to 260,000,000 persons and the turnover volume of passengers was 12,910,000,000 men/km. In 1985 the volume of cargo transport by steam lighters on inland rivers reached more than 330,000,000 tons. Inland river lighters constitute a predominant force in developing inland river transport. The volume of freight traffic at all the ports of the Yangtze was 114,000,000 tons, a 27.3% increase compared with that of 1980.

There were 240,000 ships totalling 3,200,000 tons, belonging to individual businessmen running inland river transport businesses, being one half of the state-owned and collectively-owned ships combined at the end of 1985. Evidently such an individual business constitutes an important supplementary force in the growth of inland river transportation.

Transporting logs by river. *(Photo by Yan Haosheng)*

When the policy of giving more freedom to navigation transport was officially made known, some 800 steamship companies were established immediately along the River Yangtze waterways. The volume of goods shipping showed an annual increase of 10,000,000 tons and the turnover volume of cargoes, an increase of 50% in the Sixth Five-Year Plan period.

The Administrative System of River Transport

Inland river transport is under the leadership and administration of the Communications Ministry. With the exception of the Yangtze and Heilongjiang rivers, both of which are directly managed by the ministry, all the inland rivers are under the management and administration of the provinces (or autonomous regions). The Inland River Administrative Bureau is set up by the Communications Ministry, while the Communications Divisions (bureaux) are set up by each province (autonomous region).

For a time, the Yangtze River Shipping Administrative Bureau exercised administrative leadership and business management over affairs connected with the Yangtze. The Bureau is under the direct control of the Communications Ministry. Beginning in 1984, a structural reform was started by separating the administration from the enterprise and by separating port control from navigation control. As a result the Yangtze River Shipping Administrative Bureau was abolished and replaced by the Yangtze River Shipping Affairs Control Bureau, which is supposed to be an organ charged by the Communications Ministry to exert administrative control over the Yangtze river affairs, while the General Administration of the Yangtze River Steamship Corporation is the shipping enterprise directly under the control of the Communications Ministry running the transport business. There are 5 branches under the Corporation: the Chongqing branch, Wuhan branch, Wuhu branch, Nanjing

A goatskin raft. *(Photo by Shi Guanda)*

branch and Shanghai branch. The Yangtze River Shipping Affairs Control Bureau exercises temporary control over the 14 main ports of the river, while the local governments concerned exercise control over all the ports, port affairs stations and the loading-unloading posts.

Problems and Prospects

The main problems existing on inland river shipping are: First, there are dams or flood-gate buildings of a permanent nature set up in the navigable waters, causing a deduction of the mileage by 63,000 km, as compared with the 172,000 km in 1961, seriously affecting the growth of inland river transport. Second, almost all the inland river ports are simply equipped, without machines for loading and unloading. Some even have no wharves at which ships can anchor. Third, the shipping cost is high while the price is low; as a result some enterprises, especially those collectively-owned, suffer losses in business.

In the Seventh Five-Year Plan period, a 5,000 km waterway is to be dredged by spending funds (limited as they are) on dredging the Yangtze, Zhujiang, and Heilongjiang rivers and the JingHang Canal, as well as a few of their main tributaries. The construction of the ports along the Yangtze river main waterway is to be strengthened as a priority task and stress is to be laid on rebuilding the old wharves. Foreign trade

wharves are to be built at Wuhan, Huangshih and Wuhu ports. Deep water berths are to be constructed speedily for the ports of Zhangjiagong and Nantong. For the Zhujiang (Pearl River), the main task is to continue dredging the shipping route of the section of the Xijiang river from Gueixian to Guangzhou to establish the Gueixian port so as to raise the capability of coal transport. Regarding the Heilongjiang river, the main job is to strengthen the construction of the ports open to trade with the Soviet Union, as well as the transportation system. The shallow rapids of the Sunghuajiang river and the Jiamushih port are to be dredged to expand their cargo-handling capacity. As to the JingHang Canal, the main job is to continue dredging its shipping route and building a port for coal-shipping so as to increase its coal-shipping capability.

The problem of the dams and flood-gates blocking the navigation should be gradually solved. Stress should be placed on dredging the shipping routes with a depth of over one metre. The construction of waterways on local inland rivers is to be handled mainly by the local governments and the people, under a unified plan and with funds supplied by the Central Government.

The raising of transport capability and efficiency relies on the progress of techniques. Loading and unloading in inland ports should be mechanized. The shipping routes should be improved so as to raise their classification. Different kinds of goods need different types of ships. Accordingly, advanced special ships, multi-purpose ships and dump ships are to be chosen for diversified use. For rivers having better conditions, group lighters, a pusher fleet and self-navigation lighters should be popularized.

The administrative system of inland river shipping should be further improved. Control should be exerted over the different professions; administration should be separated from enterprise; administration should also be simplified and management powers shifted to expand the self-governing powers in business management. Policies concerned should not be so strict, giving more freedom in inland river shipping, so that the state-owned shipping, collectively-owned shipping and individually-owned shipping concerns may conduct their business at the same time. Only in this way can inland river shipping business be promoted. Control over all the inland ports, including the Yangtze river ports, is to be handed down to the cities in which they are located. All ports should be open to whatever ships there are. Through shipping should be expanded to all main and branch waterways of the inland rivers by eliminating all the divisions artificially made by man.

COASTAL TRANSPORT

By coastal transport is meant transportation in areas along the Chinese seacoasts, including areas between islands as well as areas between islands and the mainland. The Chinese mainland seacoast stretches a continuous distance of more than 18,000 km from north to south. This coastline connects provinces, autonomous regions and municipalities under the Central Government which are comparatively flourishing in economy and which possess a number of good harbours.

The General Development of Coastal Transport

Coastal transport was not well developed and well utilized before the liberation of the mainland. In 1949 the volume of freight was no more than 1,330,000 tons, and in 1952 the freight-handling capacity in the main ports along the coast was no more than 14,400,000 tons. Since the founding of New China, there has been a fast growth: the cargo-handling capacity in the main ports along the coast has reached more than 350,000,000 tons, a 23-fold increase compared with 1952.

Ships engaged in coastal transport were mainly designed in China, including bulk carriers of the 50,000-ton class, oil tankers also of the 50,000-ton class and passenger-cargo ships of the 3,000-ton and 7,000-ton classes. Some of the coastal freighters, while assuring the domestic shipping tasks, have also taken part in foreign trade transport by sailing in international shipping waters.

Along the seacoast there are 58 larger ports, of which Shanghai, Dalian, Qinhuangdou, Tianjin, Qingtao, Lianyungang, Huangpu and Zhanjiang are of large-size, while the ports of Yinkou, Yantai, Ningpo, Xiamen (Amoy), Fangcheng, Haikou, Basuo as well as the recently built Shijiu and Beilun are medium-sized. The Shanghai port is the largest in China, having an annual volume of freight traffic of more than 100,000,000 tons and also having 50 deep-water berths. A constant business pursued by Shanghai port is transit-lighterage over water. The volume of transit-lighterage in 1985 scored the highest monthly record of 2,200,000 tons. The construction of the Tianjin port began in September 1951; the first stage was finished and the port was put into operation in October 1952; construction of the second stage was continued from 1957 to 1961, and since the 1970s a

Diesel locomotives made in the USA being unloaded from the ship directly to the railway on the wharf at Shanghai port. *(Photo by Zhang Ping)*

deep-water berth and a dock for container ships have been built. As a result, Tianjin port has become the most important foreign trade port in North China. Preparation for building Zhangjiang port started in August 1954, construction work began in 1955 and the port was open to service the following year. It was successively extended after 1958 and hence became one of the foreign trade ports in South China. Deep-water berths for ocean-going ships in the main ports along the coast were 61 in number in 1952 and reached 89 in the early 1970s. In 1973 the Chinese government decided to refurnish and speed up the construction of deep-water berths in all ports. After 13 years of effort, 200 deep-water berths were built by the end of 1985, an increase of 2.3 times compared with 1952 and 1.2 times compared with the early 1970s. Medium-class deep-water berths totalled 156.

Modernized docks have been specially built for oil, coal, ores, timber and containers. The development in the construction of coastal ports has not only provided an important guarantee to seacoast shipping, but has paved the way for developing ocean-shipping.

The Administrative System of Coastal Transport

Seacoast transportation is under the leadership and management of the Communications Ministry. An Ocean Shipping Administrative Bureau is set up under the Communications Ministry, exerting administrative control over coastal transportation. Under the leadership of the ministry are the Shanghai Ocean Shipping Bureau and the Guangzhou (Canton) Ocean Shipping Bureau, managing the coastal transport tasks. A demarcation line is drawn between the northern and southern coastal shipping areas: the area from the north of Xiamen (Amoy) up to the mouth of the Yalujiang river, known as the northern coastal shipping area, is controlled and managed by the Shanghai Ocean Shipping Bureau, whereas the area from the south of Xiamen down to the mouth of Beilunhe river, known as the southern coastal shipping area, is controlled and managed by the Guangzhou Ocean Shipping Bureau. Coastal provinces (or autonomous regions) also have their own ocean-shipping bureaux, mainly responsible for managing the business of coastal transportation of a local nature.

All main coastal ports were once under the direct administration of the Communications Ministry. To date, the ports of Shanghai, Tianjin and Dalian have been brought under the dual leadership of both the Communications Ministry and the local governments. However the local governments hold most of the leading powers.

Problems and Prospects

The main problems in coastal transportation in China are: the cargo-handling capacity in the seacoast main ports is far from sufficient; the construction of medium-sized and small ports, particularly construction of unloading ports, is not able to keep up with the demand of the development of transportation; transit-lighterage over water is not sufficiently popularized. The lack of capacity in the ports has a tremendous effect on the development of coastal transportation and affects the expansion of ocean shipping as well.

Coastal transport is intended to be the main traffic artery between North and South China. Following the development in the national economy and society, especially as the coastal cities are now open to the world, transport is growing busier daily: there must therefore be an increase in the capacity of transportation, and the need for port construction has become even more pressing. In the Seventh Five-Year Plan period 120 more deep-water berths and 80 more medium-sized and small berths are to be built. The volume of freight traffic is to be increased to 200,000,000 tons. In order to answer the demand of energy resources for transport and the shipping of coal to East China from Shanxi province, coal-loading ports connecting with railways are to be built along the seacoast. Docks, especially for loading coal and for electricity works are also to be built. At the same time large crude-oil berths are to be built for expanding the capability of loading. To satisfy the requirement for developing foreign trade, special berths needed for containers, timber and grains are to be expanded. In those seacoast ports which have better working conditions, transit-lighterage over water is to be encouraged by increasing such equipment as anchorages, buoys, floating transit-platforms and whole-set ships, so as to increase the cargo-handling capacity. To share the heavy burden of the large ports and promote the seacoast economy as well as transport between islands and the mainland, a number of all-purpose berths capable of passenger-cargo transport are also to be built. By 1990 the berths along the seacoast ports are expected to reach some 1200, among which deep-water berths are to be some 320 with a total volume of freight traffic up to 550,000,000 tons. Cargo-owners are encouraged to build docks and berths themselves.

China depends mainly upon self-reliant efforts to speed up the construction of ports and docks. However foreign funds are to be made use of in a positive manner, including low-interest loans and interest-free loans from foreign governments, loans from the World Bank, and approved international commercial loans. At the same time, China also extends a welcome hand to companies, enterprises and even individuals from foreign countries, Hong Kong and Macao to handle joint ventures with their investments in co-operation with Chinese companies and enterprises in the territory of the People's Republic of China in an effort to build ports and docks. China will give favourable treatment to all of them.

Coastal transport ships, such as large-size ships, containerized ships and liquid-cargo vessels are to be increased. Ocean-going passenger ships are also to be increased gradually.

Self-management powers are to be expanded to the ocean-shipping enterprises. Powers are to be gradually handed down to all other main seacoast ports by drawing on experience acquired from the system-reform practice in port control in Tianjin, Dalian and Shanghai.

MARINE SHIPPING

MARINE shipping has a long history in China. As early as the Western Han dynasty (206 BC–AD 23) maritime ties were established with Korea and Japan and they were expanded to the countries in the South Seas. In the Ming dynasty (1368–1644) Zheng He, the famous navigator, and his fleet sailed seven successive times to some 30 countries in Asia and Africa. It is through him that maritime ties were set up with Asian and African countries, establishing the "Silk Routes" over the sea.

Nevertheless, ocean shipping remained for a long time in a fragile state in old China, since it had so long submitted to the feudal system and suffered aggression and oppression from foreign countries. At the time of the liberation of the mainland there was almost nothing. The rebirth of ocean shipping began only after the founding of New China. The "Sino-Polish Steamship Company Limited" was set up between China and Poland in 1951, from which China began to enter the sphere of the international ocean shipping business. The General Administration of the China Ocean Shipping Company (COSCO) was inaugurated in 1961, having in its possession 25 ships, with a total tonnage of 220,000 d.w.t. at the initial period. Through a 25-year effort, the ocean-going fleet in China had some 600 ships with 12,700,000 d.w.t. by the end of 1985. Of the 600 ships, 12% were container ships and roll on/roll off ships and 28% were automatic ships. This ocean-going fleet has now begun calling at some 600 ports in over 150 countries. In addition to taking up the tasks allotted for the shipping of import–export goods of China, it has also carried out goods shipping tasks for some other countries. To date, the Chinese ocean-going fleet occupies eleventh place in the world's ocean-going fleets.

Besides COSCO, the General Administration of the China Foreign Trade Shipping Corporation (SINOTRANS) is also engaging in ocean shipping. The Corporation started organizing an ocean-going fleet in 1980 and by 1985 it possessed ships with a total tonnage of 1,000,000 tons. Local foreign trade departments have also organized their fleets engaging in ocean shipping business.

The volume of ocean shipping has witnessed an annual increase. The volume of import–export goods by ocean shipping was 130,000,000 tons (including the volume of chartered ships) in 1985, a 64% increase on 1980.

In China, ocean shipping is under the leadership and management of the Communications Ministry, which sets up the Ocean Shipping Administrative Bureau. COSCO handles the ocean shipping business. In accordance with the different areas in the economy and the development in foreign trade, COSCO has established branch corporations in Guangzhou, Shanghai, Tianjin, Qingtao and Dalian, each handling the ocean shipping business by their respective fleets. SINOTRANS is under the leadership and management of the Ministry of Foreign Economic Relations and Trade (MOFERT).

Both COSCO and SINOTRANS are economic entities, having independent powers in handling their business. The Communications Ministry does not interfere in the enterprise management of COSCO, including the Foreign Steamship Agency, nor does the Ministry of Economic and Trade Relations with Foreign Countries in the enterprise management of SINOTRANS, including the Ship Chartering Corporation. The two ministries, however, retain the power of administrative leadership.

The main problems existing in ocean shipping are that there are very few specialized ships in the ocean-going fleet. The types of ships are relatively out of date and are especially heavy in fuel-consumption. And as there are not enough deep-water berths, ships are usually kept waiting too long for unloading, a fact which seriously affects the rate of navigation efficiency.

In China, 90% of the import–export goods are shipped through maritime transport. In the Sixth Five-Year Plan period (1981–1985) the total value of goods from the import–export trade was $US230,000,000,000, while the volume by ocean shipping was 130,000,000 tons. In the Seventh Five-Year Plan period (1986–1990) China is to further expand its international trade through still stronger effort. By 1990 the total volume of export-import trade is expected to reach $US83,000,000,000, a 40% increase on 1985. The volume of ocean shipping is to be further increased. China's ocean-going fleet is a prominent force in the field of international trade. It is therefore indispensable to further enlarge the scale of the fleet, raise the technical level and improve the fleet structure.

Stress should be laid on the development of specialized ships, such as container ships, RO/RO ships, timber-carrying vessels, bulk carriers, coal-and-ore automatic unloading ships, oil-tankers and bulk ships for grains and fertilizer. Meanwhile, positive measures are to be taken to improve the ships by eliminating the used ships, so that the average age becomes much younger. Advanced techniques are to be adopted to improve the power source of the ships and the automation of the mechanized holds. Signals and pilotage are to have new techniques. Equipment is to be replaced by new models. The traffic control system is to be strengthened.

Demurrage of ships and delays of cargo-shipping in ports are to be improved. The construction of berths, especially deep-water berths, is to be strengthened. In addition, comprehensive and balanced work in connection with plans in shipping foreign trade cargoes is to be carried out. The policy of "two-level balance and centralized management", namely, the level of the Central Government and the level of provinces (municipalities), is to be strictly implemented. A planned management is to be strengthened so that ships for foreign trade are expected to make a smooth arrival in keeping with well-arranged plans.

CIVIL AVIATION

THE development of civil aviation was progressing at a snail's pace in old China: within the 20 years beginning 1929, when an aviation company was opened by joint venture with foreign funds, the total turnover volume of air transport was no more than 200,000,000 tons/km. In November 1949 the Civil Aviation Administration of China (CAAC) was set up and 12 air routes were opened the following year, carrying a total of 10,000 passengers with a total turnover volume of 1,570,000 tons/km. In 1978, 162 air routes were opened, carrying a total of 2,310,000 passengers, with a total turnover of nearly 300,000,000 tons/km. Since the policy of opening to the world and making the economy active at home is being put into practice, civil aviation is undergoing an enormous and speedy growth. By the end of 1985 there were already 267 air routes with an air traffic mileage of over 277,200 km; the volume of passenger transport totalled 7,470,000 seats; the volume of goods and mail transport, over 195,000 tons; and the total turnover volume, over 1,270,000,000 tons/km.

General Development of Civil Aviation

Today, an air transport network leading in all directions has already been formed, with Beijing as the centre. There are 78 airports and 233 routes and there are some 600 scheduled flights each week. Except for Taiwan province, all the provincial capitals, autonomous regional capitals and other main cities have through flights or connecting flights to and from Beijing. CAAC has paid great attention to developing a superior air transport system between the interior and remote frontier areas as well as between the interior and areas where traffic is difficult, so as early as 1950 air routes were opened to the Uygur autonomous region in Xinjiang and to Sichuan province. The air route to Lhasa in the Xizang (Tibet) autonomous region was opened in 1965. After 1961 scheduled through flights were opened between Chengdu and Lhasa and between Xi'an and Lhasa. At present there are also air routes from Beijing, Shanghai and Lanzhou to Ürümqi. There is a local airport in the Xinjiang Uygur autonomous region, forming a local airline network with Ürümqi as the centre. To meet the needs of the developing tourist industry, a number of airports are being either newly built or expanded in the tourist cities. Some 30 more routes have been opened and flights increased. Air transport between the mainland and Hong Kong is also in a period of fast growth: scheduled flights are already open from Beijing, Guangzhou (Canton), Shanghai, Hangzhou, Tianjin and Kunming, and also charter flights from Xi'an, Fuzhou, Xiamen (Amoy) and Guilin.

While developing domestic civil aviation transport, the China Civil Aviation Bureau has been gradually working on the development of the international air traffic business. An international air route was opened to the border cities of the Soviet Union in 1950; in the 1960s the overseas air service began; a maiden flight was made to the Middle-East and Africa in 1965; in 1974 a global flight around the world was made from west to east, while a trial flight was made to New York. International air routes were increased to 12 in 1978, and in 1981 the permanent scheduled flights on the Sino-American airline began. By the end of 1985 aviation agreements were signed between China and some 40 foreign countries and business ties established with aviation corporations in more than 180 countries and in Hong Kong and other areas. International air routes now total 27. Flights have been made to 26 cities in 22 countries. The mileage of air flights has reached 105,959 km and there are 17 aviation corporations from 16 countries with flights to China.

To meet the demands for developing civil aviation since the founding of New China, over 70 airports have been newly built, rebuilt or expanded. The Capital International Airport in Beijing has now been built into the largest in China, capable of handling large-sized and broad-bodied planes and having ad-

A CAAC Airbus A-310.

The cabin being cleaned before passengers board.

vanced equipment for automatic air traffic control. Around the two satellite halls there is sufficient room for parking 16 planes simultaneously, with a passenger flow of 1,500 per hour. Airports in Shanghai, Guangzhou, Ürümqi, Harbin, Tianjin, Hefei, Hangzhou, Nanjing, Chengdu, Chongqing, Lanzhou, Xi'an, Taiyuan, Fuzhou, Gueilin, Xiamen and Lhasa are capable of handling jet passenger planes of modern types. The Civil Aviation Authority is also trying to update and increase the types of planes. In the 1950s there were only a small number of Li-11 and Il-14 light passenger planes; in the 1960s An-24 planes and Il-18 planes were put into service; in the 1970s the Trident III-62 and Boeing 707 jet planes were adopted for service. By the end of 1985 all such new models as Boeing 747, Boeing 767, A-310 and Boeing 747–200B broad-bodied passenger-transport jet planes were already flying on domestic airways, and medium-sized transport planes were playing their part in the cargo-shipping business.

Special aviation business has also been set up. Beginning in 1951, the Bureau started servicing industrial and agricultural production and national defence as well as the scientific and technical fields. By 1985 there was an Aviation Service Corporation for industry and 20 special fleets and independent subfleets, possessing some hundred planes of over ten different types with their corresponding instruments and equipment. Their working bases number around 500 and the business items handled include aerial photography, air remote sensing, air reconnaisance, maritime service, air investigation, agricultural seed-sowing, weed-killing and fertilizer spraying, prevention and treatment of insects, fertilizer spraying and defoliation, artificial rain making, forestry sowing, fire prevention and forest protection, chemical fire-extinguishing, air sowing of pasture, fish reconnaisance and first aid in calamities.

The Administrative System of Civil Aviation

Civil aviation is under the control of CAAC, which not only exerts control over the administrative affairs of civil aviation but also handles the enterprise directly. Also under it are six local bureaux (Beijing,

Shenyang, Shanghai, Guangzhou, Chengdu and Lanzhou) and one corporation – the Industrial Aviation Service Corporation. Under the six local bureaux are the civil aviation bureaux in the 23 provinces, autonomous regions and municipalities under the Central Government, and 78 civil aviation stations, all being the basic transport units. All these bureaux are under the dual-leadership of both CAAC and the local governments. However, CAAC is the main authority.

To satisfy the requirements of the development of the civil aviation business, China Air Appliances Corporation was established in 1980, responsible for placing orders for purchasing appliances and ground equipment, including planes and engines, at home and abroad, and selling domestic-made civil aviation appliances to foreign countries and home consumers. It also serves as an agency to purchase or sell such appliances. Under the Corporation there are six local offices in North-West China, North China, East China, Central South China, South-West China and North-East China, responsible for ordering, purchasing and supplying air aviation appliances needed by these different localities.

Under the civil aviation system there are also plane repairing bases and factories for building and repairing signal and other equipment. There are universities, colleges, technical schools and hospitals. The Beijing Aviation Food Corporation was set up in 1980 by joint venture between the Beijing Administrative Bureau of China Aviation and the Hong Kong China Aviation Food Company.

To rally all available forces to develop communications and transportation business, the China Air-Land Coordinated Transport Corporation was set up by the China Communication and Transportation Association and Kai Li Industrial Co. Ltd, and began operations in December 1984. It manages the business of passenger and goods transport through chartered planes, and the ground transport business connected with air transport. By the end of 1985, nine air routes

A Chinese-designed and produced Y-8 airplane which has just arrived in Lhasa.

were opened: Beijing–Wuxi, Beijing–Hangzhou, Beijing–Fuzhou, Beijing–Huiyang (Shenzhen), Beijing–Jilin, Beijing–Yinchuan, Hangzhou–Huiyang, Huiyang–Lushan and Huiyang–Nanchang. Some 80,000 passengers, Chinese as well as foreign, and over 4,000,000 tons of precious goods were transported in the year. At the same time, official approval was granted to such areas as the Xinjiang Uygur autonomous region, Xiamen in Fujian province, Yunnan province, Heilongjiang province and Shanghai Municipality to set up their own aviation corporations.

Problems and Prospects

The main problems in the civil aviation transport at present lie in the shortage of transport capacity. The quantity of planes is small, the airports in operation now are technically inferior and some of them are not yet capable of landing large and medium-size planes. The service leaves much to be desired and hence needs improving.

Following the development in the national economy and society as well as the expansion of international friendly exchanges and tourism, the ever-growing demand for air transport is daily increasing, particularly with the setting up of special economic zones and the opening of cities with coastal ports and of Hainan Island. In the Seventh Five-Year Plan period (1986–1990) the increase in the capacity of civil aviation transport is to double the speed of national economic development. In 1990 the total turnover of transport is expected to reach 2,500,000,000 tons/km; the volume of passenger transport, a total of 16,000,000 persons; the volume of cargo transport including postal matters, 380,000 tons; respectively 1.96 times, 2.13 times and 1.95 times those of 1985.

The following improvements therefore appear very necessary:

– *The transport capacity is to be raised further*. The number of planes is to be increased by means of channels such as international lease and loans of funds raised through self-effort, so that the transport capacity can be reinforced. The transport capability in 1990 is expected to rise to over 1.75 times that of 1985.

– *Airport construction is to be strengthened*. In addition to building a number of new airports in the coastal cities already opened to the world, emphasis is to be laid on the improvement and rise in the handling capability of existing airports. Simultaneously, attention is to be paid to the improvement of the conditions for landing. In the same way the signals installations and pilotage of the main air routes are to be built up to international standards.

– *The management institutions of civil aviation are to be reformed*. Instead of the present 4-level management, a 3-level management is to be introduced, namely: the civil aviation bureau, the bureaux of provinces (and autonomous regions and municipalities under the Central Government), and the air stations, in accordance with the reform plans approved by the Central Government. Administration is to be separated from enterprise, administrative control simplified and powers shifted. As an organ in the State Council for controlling civil aviation affairs, the China Civil Aviation Bureau controls the administration of the aviation enterprise without directly managing the air transport business. The readjustment is to be worked out by combining the six administrative bureaux (Beijing, Shanghai, Guangzhou, Chengdu, Xi'an and Shenyang) into two international aviation corporations and four home aviation corporations, as well as several local aviation corporations in accordance with the network of air routes and the installation of bases. All these corporations are to be economic entities, keeping independent accounts and having responsibility for their own profit and loss.

– *Aviation enterprise groups are to be organized in a planned manner*. Business is to be managed by all the groups so that they can make emulations themselves. As a result there will be not only state-run aviation corporations but also locally-run corporations, as well as corporations run by the different official departments and corporations that run coordinated air–land transport business through chartered planes. The air stations are to be separated from the corporations and they should also carry out enterprise management. In such a manner all the airports are to be gradually left in the control of the cities in which they are located.

PIPELINE TRANSPORTATION

ALTHOUGH as early as over 1,000 years ago bamboo-pipes were installed as a means for transporting salt liquid and natural gas in the Zigong county, Sichuan province, the modern pipeline as means of transport remained non-existent in old China.

General Development of Pipelines

Pipeline transportation is an entirely new means, only lately developed in China following the increase of production of oil and natural gas. In the early 1950s China began building pipelines in the oilfields themselves. In 1958 the first trunk pipeline for transmitting crude oil was built in Xinjiang, leading from the Karamai oilfield to the oil refinery at Dushanzi. Ever since the 1960s, and particularly in the 1970s, pipeline construction embarked on a new stage of development. The building of pipelines has made tremendous strides, following the successive opening of oilfields in Xinjiang, Daqing, Shenli, Dagong, Renqiu, Liaohe, Jianghan, Henan and Ningxia, as well as the building and putting into production of oil refineries in the consuming areas. In the early 1970s, in North-East China, a long, large calibre pipeline was built from the Daqing oilfields to the refinery at Fushun. Then within 10 years a total length of more than 4,000 km of oil pipeline was constructed. Long oil and gas transmitting pipelines built in the Sixth Five-Year Plan period totalled over 2,000 km, comprising lines between Puyang and Loyang and between Shenli and Huangdao for transmitting oil, and lines between Puyang and Cangzhou, between Panjing and Anshan and between Weiyuan and Chengdu for transmitting natural gas. In the same period technical reforms on different scales were made of the 14 pipelines, including those between Daqing and Tieling, between Tieling and Dalian, between Puyang and Linyi and between Nanyang and Jingmen. Finally, during the whole period of the three Five-Year Plans, China set up a crude oil transmission pipeline network over North-East China, North China and East China. By the end of 1985 there were some 11,000 km of pipelines for transmitting crude oil and natural gas with a comprehensive transmission capacity of 100,000,000 tons.

Crude oil is now mainly transmitted through pipelines. There were already some 7,000 km of pipelines for transmitting crude oil, a fact which has removed the dependence on the railroads. In the mid-1960s the proportion of crude oil transported by railroad was 66%; by boat, 9%; and through pipelines, 25%; but by the early 1980s, the proportion of crude oil transmitted through pipelines was 61%; by boat, 25%; and by railroad, 14%.

Refined oil is chiefly transported by train and by boat and rarely through pipelines. There is a 1,000-km pipeline between Golmud and Lhasa for the transmission of gasoline, kerosene and diesel oil. This line is the only exception, because all the other pipelines for refined oil transmission are laid only from the refineries to the factories or between the commercial storages. These pipelines, being short and small in calibre, are used to transport gasoline, kerosene, diesel oil, fuel, liquefied hydrocarbon and other chemical-industrial products. To date, 65% of refined oil is being transported by rail; 20% by ocean-going steamships; 5% by boat on the Yangtze river; and 10% through pipelines.

Sichuan province is known as the native place principally for producing natural gas. Since 1963 some 1,650 km of trunk pipelines and branches have been laid. In addition, some pipelines of short distance and smaller calibre have been laid in the oilfields at Daqing, Shenli, Renqiu and Dagong to transmit oilfield gas.

As for the transmission of solid materials, only short pipelines are laid, exclusively in metal mining areas, for transmitting refined mineral powder. The construction of pipelines for coal transport is still at an exploratory and research stage.

The Administrative System for Pipelines

Pipeline transmission is under the control of the Pipelines Bureau of the Ministry of the Oil Industry. Under the Pipelines Bureau there are two administrative bureaux – the North-East China Oil Pipeline Administrative Bureau and the East China Pipelines Administrative Bureau. In North China there are two pipelines administrative offices, exerting control over the trunk pipelines located in the respective areas under their control. Under the Pipelines Bureau of the Ministry of the Oil Ministry, there is a Research Institute for prospecting and planning, responsible for the research and design of long pipelines. There are also four engineering corporations, responsible for construction work on the pipelines, as well as the

567

transport and repairing systems which service the long pipeline construction.

The pipelines in the oilfields themselves and the short crude-oil pipelines are as a rule managed by each oilfield. Short pipelines for refined oil are managed by the refineries or the commercial departments. The long oil pipelines between Golmud and Lhasa are managed by the departments that themselves utilize the pipelines. Pipelines for solid materials are as a rule laid, managed and made use of by the ore mines themselves.

Problems and Prospects

The principal problems in pipeline transmission at present are: there is a shortage of pipelines, especially those for refined oil; the transmission techniques of the present oil pipelines are not advanced enough because they are not airtight in transmission and are low in pumping pressure and pipe pressure; the utilization rate of the basic equipment is not sufficiently effective.

In the Seventh Five-Year Plan period, pipeline construction is expected to grow significantly in keeping with the development of the oilfields and gasfields. In this period, the pipelines to be laid for oil and gas are expected to reach some 3,000 km, having a transmission capacity of 150,000,000 tons per annum. Selected priority pipelines for the transmission of refined oil are expected to be laid so as to ease the heavy burden undertaken by the railway, to reduce the loss of oil and to raise economic efficiency. At the same time, maritime pipelines for oil and gas transmission are to be developed.

The efficiency of pipeline transmission is to be raised by technical progress. An advanced temperature-increasing technique, a constant-temperature technique, automatic control process systems and the mechanization of pipe-laying are to be adopted in both newly-laid pipelines and existing pipelines. The technical processes of the existing pipelines are to be reformed in accordance with the principle of economizing in energy resources and of security in oil transmission. Regarding the technique of transmitting fluid coal, including dehydration and handling of polluted water, research and experimental work is to be strengthened and when conditions are ripe, coal transmission pipelines are expected to be laid accordingly.

FUTURE DEVELOPMENTS

THOUGH China has built up a communications and transportation network and has contributed quite a lot towards the national economy by accomplishing the heavy tasks in the fields of passenger and cargo transport, the growth of communications and transportation remains as yet far behind the requirements of national economic and social development, as may be deduced from the backwardness in techniques, poor equipment, grave scarcity of transport capacity, irrationalities of transport structure and inflexible nature of the management system. These facts have arrested the attention of the Central Government. As a result, in the stipulation of strategic targets for developing the national economy, both communications and transportation have been given priority status. When the Sixth Five-Year Plan began, the proportion of investment for communications and transportation was further increased and the investment system reformed, and construction funds were collected through various channels to raise the efficiency. In future, a comprehensive national transportation system is to be established in a logical progression, chiefly by giving economic efficiency priority as the prerequisite. Such a system is not only appropriate to the Chinese national situation but is also reasonable in structure, so that the strengths of the different modes of transport can be brought into full play. Meanwhile in the construction of new communication–transportation routes, technical progress is required for the realization of the modernization of communications and transportation. Emphasis is also to be placed on technical reform, the pace of which is to be speeded up. The management system of the communications and transportation business is to be reformed and the professional management strengthened. Self-governing powers are to be expanded. Through these measures, communications and transportation are expected to adapt fundamentally to the demands of the national economy and social development by the end of the twentieth century.

6. ENERGY RESOURCES AND THE ENERGY INDUSTRY

Resources

Coal

CHINA abounds in coal resources. According to the 1982 *Yearbook of the Chinese Coal Industry*, which was the first ever published in China, the estimated reserves within a depth of 1,500 metres amount to 3,200,000 million tons.

Most of the reserves are in the northern and western parts of China, Shanxi and Inner Mongolia in particular, though other places have reported rich coal deposits. Of the proven reserves, 64% are in North China, 12% in the north-west, 10% in the south-west, 7% in the east, 4% in the south and 3% in the north-east. The proven reserves in Shanxi, Inner Mongolia, Ningxia, Anhui, Shaanxi and Guizhou account for 80% of the national total. The proven recoverable reserves in the western part are many times more than those being mined in the eastern part. The Ordos Basin, covering Shanxi, Shaanxi, Gansu, Ningxia and Inner Mongolia, is a coal basin of a richness rare anywhere in the world, with the largest deposits verified around Shanxi province. The coking coal and anthracite reserves there have been verified to account for 50% of the national total. The coal seams, buried between 300 and 400 metres, have small inclination with little geological hindrance. Construction of such mines costs at least one-third less than those elsewhere and production cost is only about 33–50% that in southern China.

China's coal resources are distributed mainly in the north-west and north, far from the east, where industries are concentrated. There are few reserves in the nine provinces south of the Yangzte river, where the ratio is 1 to 86 in comparison with that in the north. This adds to the difficulties in coal development and transportation. The situation is expected to last.

Petroleum

China has a large oil and natural gas potential. A general geological survey shows that there are 340 sedimentary basins in China, promising large oil reserves. The Songhuajiang–Liaohe River Basin (in the north-east) is a large continental lake depression of the Mesozoic Era (70 million to 170 million years ago) covering 270,000 km². It is believed to have rich oil resources. The North China Basin (including the Bohai Sea), which covers 380,000 km², is the most promising oil-rich sedimentary basin in China, as it has a sedimentary layer of 8,000 metres deep. It is there that the Dagang and Renqiu oilfields have been opened along the shores of the Bohai Sea and on the Central Hebei Plain, and recoverable oil reserves have been found also in the Bohai Bay. The proven reserves in the area account for about 15% of the national total. In South-West China's Sichuan province, China's major gas producer, 250 gas-entrapped structures have been found in addition to the 40 gas fields in operation. Also promising are the Junggar, Tarim and Qaidam basins in North-West China, especially the 130,000 km² Junggar Basin, where more than 170 oil-bearing structures and six fairly large oilfields have been located, and the Tarim Basin in southern Xinjiang, where oil and gas reserves are believed to be larger than the oilfields in the eastern part of China.

Morning in the South China Sea.

569

However, since the areas are sparsely populated and have poor communications facilities, it is difficult to develop the resources, more difficult than in the eastern part of the country. But from a long-term point of view, the western part, Xinjiang in particular, will be China's focus of onshore oil and gas exploration and development.

Chinese territorial seas cover 2.85 million km². About 1.30 million km² are continental shelves with a water depth up to 200 metres. The ten sedimentary basins of the Mesozoic and Cenozoic Eras (between 170 million and one million years ago) cover 1.2 million km², all promising oil potential. With excellent geological conditions, the South China Sea abounds in oil and natural gas resources. The basin of the Zhujiang (Pearl River) mouth, which covers 150,000 km², more than half the size of the whole Guangdong province, boasts more verified oil reserves than any of the known offshore oilfields.

In addition, China has a proven recoverable reserve of oil shale.

Hydropower

The topographic differences, plentiful rainfall and many rivers on the vast land of China promise abundant water power reserves. A general survey shows that theoretically China has water power resources up to 676 million kW, of which 379 million kW are exploitable. Fully developed, they would provide energy equal to 700 million tons of standard coal a year. At present, however, only 4% of the resources are utilized, far less than in industrially developed countries.

Distribution of water power resources differs greatly, as the land tips from the south-west Qinghai–Tibet plateau toward the eastern coast, while precipitation becomes less and less from south-east to north-west. Some 68% of the exploitable water power resources are in the south-west, 16% in central and southern China, and 10% in the north-west. Crisscrossed by water systems, with the Yangtze as the largest, South-West China will be the country's largest hydro-electric power supplier. The Jinsha river (upper part of the Yangtze) and its tributaries alone have an estimated water power reserve of well over 100 million kW. Good geological and topographic conditions and abundant water flows make it easy to develop water power and the construction of dams causes little losses. But at present, only 0.6% of the region's water power resources are being utilized, far below the national average of 4%.

This is because in South-West China transport facilities are poor; high mountains and deep valleys make engineering work difficult; the long distances from electricity users pose the problem of putting up large capacity and super-tension power transmission lines. In addition, backward industry and agriculture in the area can do little to support construction of hydropower stations.

The first 500 kV direct current lines from the Gezhou dam to Shanghai. A helicopter was used to draw the wires across the Yangtze river.

North-West China provides a bigger portion of hydro-electricity. The Yellow River system and the Hanshui and Bailong rivers of the Yangtze river system in southern Gansu and Shaanxi provinces are the main sources of water power in the area. The upper reaches of the Yellow River, with a big gradient and many gorges, are ideal for cascade hydropower stations. Sixteen hydro-electric power stations could be built along the section from the Longyang gorge in Qinghai to the Qingtong gorge in Ningxia, across Gansu. Construction of the hydro-power stations requires small amounts of work and investment and smaller flooded areas, and the reservoirs built may be used for irrigation and flood control. This area will be the focus of hydro-electric power development.

Nuclear and alternative forms of energy

The development of nuclear energy in China has a bright future because of its potential uranium resources.

Located in the northern zone, China is rich in the sources of known alternative forms of energy, such as solar and biological power, wind, geothermal power

Hai'an county in Jiangsu province is one of the regions where solar energy is used most widely.

A wind-driven water pump in Inner Mongolia.

and tidal waves. Preliminary surveys show that areas with more than 2,000 hours of sunshine annually and 140 kilocalories per sq cm of solar radiance account for two-thirds of the total land mass, and especially in the Qinghai–Tibet plateau where the solar radiance is 220 kilocalories per sq cm.

Geothermal power is found in many areas in China. Geothermal sources of steam are located mainly in Tibet, Yunnan and Taiwan. A geothermal field being exploited in Yangbajain, Tibet, has a terrestrial temperature of 171°C at a depth of 200 metres from ground surface. Medium- and low-temperature geothermal water resources are spread throughout the provinces in the south-east coastal areas.

Exploitable wind power is estimated at 100 billion kW. Rich areas include the south-east coasts, the Qinghai–Tibet plateau, North-West and North China, and parts of the north-eastern region, where more than 200 days in a year have a wind with a force of three metres per second at a height of 10 metres above the ground.

With 18,000 km of coastline, China boasts a tidal wave energy reserve of 110 million kW, which could generate 275,000 million kWh of electricity a year. At present only 3,850 kW are being utilized to generate 87,000 million kWh of electricity annually. As the seas are located mainly at low latitudes, the

temperature of the water differs greatly at the surface and at depth, by about 20°C. These are exploitable reserves in three million sq km of the seas, with an estimated 120 million kW. The average height of waves on the Yellow and East China seas is between 1 and 1.5 metres and that on the South China Sea, 1.5 metres. The wave power reserve is estimated at 150 million kW. Abundant though the oceanographic energy resources are, exploitation is restricted by many factors, including both technical and economic. It is impossible at present to invest heavily in the projects. At the moment, the main task is to conduct research and build experimental projects in places where conditions permit.

On the whole, energy resources are abundant in China, but the absolute amount per person is lower than the world average level. Coal is the main source of energy; the proven oil reserves are limited. This determines that coal will remain the principal form of energy for China for quite a long time to come.

Achievements in Energy in New China

In 1949, the annual output of raw coal was 32 million tons, crude oil – 120,000 tons, natural gas – seven million cubic metres and electricity – 4,300 million kWh. The country had to depend on foreign countries for oil supply.

With the large-scale socialist economic construction, China's energy industry has developed fast. The State has not only invested heavily in building and rebuilding coal mines in North and North-East China, but also made energetic efforts to develop oil and water power resources. From 1953 to 1985, the state capital construction investment in energy industry amounted to 180,907 million yuan, adding 135,217 million yuan of fixed assets in the coal, oil and electricity sectors. Through construction over the past three decades, energy has assumed a considerable scale, with a complete range of production and improved distribution. By 1985, the output of primary energy was equivalent to 855.38 million tons of standard coal, 36.1 times that in 1949 or increasing at an annual rate of 10.5%. During the period, raw coal

Herdsmen on the grassland use a solar stove.

571

Table 1: Changes in Primary Energy Output and Energy Structure

Year	Primary energy output (in standard fuel, million tons)	Percentage in the total energy production			
		Raw coal	Crude oil	Natural gas	Hydropower
1949	23.74	96.3	0.7	–	3.0
1952	48.71	96.7	1.3	–	2.0
1957	98.61	94.9	2.1	0.1	2.9
1962	171.85	91.4	4.8	0.9	2.9
1965	188.24	88.0	8.6	0.8	2.6
1970	309.9	81.6	14.1	1.2	3.1
1975	487.54	70.6	22.6	2.4	4.1
1980	637.21	69.4	23.8	3.0	3.8
1984	778.47	72.4	21.1	2.1	4.4
1985	855.38	72.8	20.9	2.0	4.3

output soared 26.3 times to make the country the second largest coal producer in the world, as opposed to ninth in 1949; crude oil output shot up 1,040 times, placed sixth from 27th, and electricity went up 94.5 times, placed fifth from 25th. At the same time, remarkable changes took place in the energy structure. The proportion of coal decreased while that of crude oil, natural gas and hydropower rose. Table 1 shows the changes in the primary energy output and energy structure.

The coal industry

The Chinese coal-mining industry dates back more than 70 years if counted from the time when the first mechanized colliery began operation in the 1870s up to the time of Liberation, with 1942 being the best year, with an output of 61.88 million tons.

Rapid progress has been made in the industry since the founding of New China in 1949. Output topped the pre-Liberation record to reach 66 million tons in 1952. It exceeded 100 million tons in 1956 and 600 million tons in 1978, and came to 8.72 million tons in 1984. Between 1949 and 1985, raw coal output increased at an average annual rate of 9.6%. Over the past 30 years and more, large coal-mining centres have been built in Shanxi, eastern Heilongjiang, the eastern part of Inner Mongolia, south-western Shandong, northern Jiangsu, the Huaihe river valley in Anhui, western Henan and western Guizhou. There are 36 coal-mining administrations whose annual output exceeds three million tons. Of these, 26 boast an annual output of more than 5 million tons each, 10 have an annual output of more than 10 million tons, and two (Datong and Kailuan) each turn out more than 20 million tons a year. In 1985, large and medium-sized coal mines under state administrations cut 406 million tons of coal and local collieries (owned by the public, rural collectives and individuals) reported a combined output of 466 million tons.

The rapid development of the mining industry was attributable to the following measures:

First, the huge investment made by the State. From 1953 to 1985, the state investment in coal mine construction totalled 61,871 million yuan, accounting for 11.3% of the total capital investment in industry. Of this, 43.4% or 26,865 million yuan were invested in the short span of six years from 1979 to 1985. The new production capacity added in the 32 years from 1953 to 1985 went up to 532.35 million tons, averaging 16.13 million tons annually.

Second, technological progress. The Chinese coal industry developed mainly by relying on its own technical forces, which are capable of solving any problem in the designing and construction of large and medium-sized mines. The machine-building industry is now able to design and manufacture a whole range of equipment for mines with an annual capacity of three million tons, open-cast mines with an annual capacity of 5 million tons and coal washing plants with an annual handling capacity of 3 million tons. Up to 1984, 42.62% of coal cutting work had been mechanized as against only 4.12% in 1957. Coal combines were used in 20.73% of the mines.

Third, local initiatives. The State set great store by bringing the initiative of localities into full play. The Central Government provided technical, financial and material aid to local mines. Since 1972, the central authorities earmark a certain amount of funds every year for the technical transformation of local collieries. In recent years, the State has introduced a new policy, encouraging collectives and individuals to open large, medium-sized and small mines at the same time as those sunk by the State. The State has also allocated parts or the edges of proven coalfields to localities. This has brought the initiative of both the collectives and individuals into full play. By the end of 1984, the number of coal pits run by rural collectives and individuals topped 60,000.

On coal marketing, the Central Government has relaxed the rigid control, allowing collective and private mines to sell their products on the market and state mines to sell their above-quota output locally or to wherever it is needed, at prices that float with market demand. The State also encourages all units

Huge coal-mining machines at work underground. *(Photo by Li Yongtan)*

and people, coal producers and consumers, to transport coal by whatever means available. These measures have aroused the enthusiasm of local authorities, towns and townships, and individuals in coal mining and transportation and greatly spurred the development of local mines.

The petroleum industry

There were only three oilfields in 1949 when the country was liberated – Laojunmiao, Yumen (in Gansu province), Dushanzi (in Xinjiang) and Yanchang (in Shaanxi province); two gas fields – Shengdengshan and Shiyougou (in Sichuan province), and two oil shale refineries in Fushun (Liaoning province). The record output in the pre-Liberation days was some 320,000 tons (1943). For oil exploration there were only three drilling rigs, manned by some 20 geologists. The annual drilling footage was less than 4,500 metres.

The oil industry has developed the fastest since the founding of New China. During the First Five-Year Plan period (1953–1957), efforts were focused on exploration and development of natural oil while developing man-made petroleum from oil shale and coal. Oil prospecting was done mainly in North-West China. The Karamai oilfield in Xinjiang and Lenghu oilfield in Qinghai were discovered and developed

The Central Plains oilfield in Henan, with many derricks.

and the existing oil and gas fields, including Yumen, were expanded.

Following the theory developed by noted geologist Li Siguang, the focus of oil exploration was shifted in 1958 to the north-east and north, which were considered by foreign experts as oil-poor. In 1959, oil reservoirs were found in the Songhua–Liaohe river basin in North-East China. In the following year, concentrated efforts were organized to search for oil at Daqing, under extremely difficult conditions. Con-

Table 2: Output of Oil and Natural Gas

Year	Crude oil		Natural gas	
	Output (million tons)	Increase over 1949 (times)	Output (million cubic metres)	Increase over 1949 (times)
1949	0.12	–	7	–
1957	1.46	11	700	99
1962	8.75	47	1,210	172
1965	11.31	93	1,100	156
1970	30.65	254	2,870	409
1975	77.06	641	8,850	1,263
1978	104.05	866	13,730	1,960
1984	114.61	954	12,430	1,775
1985	124.90	1,040	12,930	1,846

siderable reserves were verified and large-scale development began. In 1965, the output of crude oil reached 11.31 million tons, enough for home consumption and with some to spare for export.

Beginning from 1965, the focus of oil exploration has moved to areas around the Bohai Bay, where a number of oilfields have been discovered and developed, including Shengli in Shandong, Dagang in Tianjin, Liaohe in Liaoning and Jizhong in Hebei. Meanwhile, efforts were made to explore and develop gas fields in Sichuan and other parts of China. Exploration of the continental shelves did not start until 1966, and since 1979 foreign co-operation has been sought in the exploration and development of offshore oil resources. Now oil has been found in the Bohai Sea and the Beibu Gulf, the Yingge Sea and the sea off the Zhujiang (Pearl) river mouth.

China's major oilfields now include Daqing, Shengli, Renqiu, Liaohe, Zhongyuan, Xinjiang, Dagang and Gansu and the Sichuan natural gas field. By the end of 1985, the country had established 27 oil extraction enterprises and verified 219 oilfields and 74 gas fields. Table 2 shows the oil and natural gas output from 1949 to 1985.

The rapid increase in oil output has stimulated the refining industry. At the time of Liberation the country had only several small refineries, in Yumen, Gansu, and Liaoning. The oil refining capacity, including that of oil shale processing, reached 2.45 million tons by 1957. With the development of the Daqing oilfield, the refining capacity rose rapidly to 14.23 million tons in 1965 and 92.91 million tons in 1978. Between 1965 and 1978, the refining capacity increased nearly 5.5 times, averaging 15.5 million tons annually. Now refineries have been built in 21 provinces, autonomous regions and municipalities. Of these, 33 have an annual capacity of more than 500,000 tons and nine boast an annual capacity of more than four million tons. They produce nearly 700 kinds of oil products.

Remarkable progress has also been made in oil-connected research and technology. A competent oil exploration contingent of considerable size has been formed. By the end of 1984, 281 geophysical pros-

The oil refinery ship *South China Sea Expectation*, equipped with modern devices. *(Photo by Lu Xiaohua)*

pecting teams were operating, formed by 58,000 people, 12% of which were engineers and technicians. Oil searching equipment has also been improved to a considerable extent. The continental oil formation theory has been confirmed and developed following the discovery of a number of oilfields and oil reserves under the buried hills. China is now able to produce most of the oil drilling, extracting and refining equipment and has become one of the few countries that are able to drill wells up to 7,000 metres deep. The Daqing oilfield, which was discovered and built in 1959 by China's own efforts, developed a technique and corresponding devices to inject water into oil wells to increase the recovery rate. It went on to develop a technology for stabilizing output and raising recovery rate when the oil reservoirs contain excessive water. In oil processing, the country is able to design and build large oil refineries independently.

The power industry

China's power generating units in 1949 totalled only 1.85 million kW and annual electricity output was 4,310 million kWh. From 1950–1985 electricity output increased at an average annual rate of 13.5%, faster than the industrial growth, which averaged

Table 3: Electricity Output in Selected Years

| Year | Output (million kWh) | Of which (million kWh): | |
		Thermal power	Hydropower
1949	4,300	3,600	700
1952	7,300	6,000	1,300
1957	19,300	14,500	4,800
1965	67,600	57,200	10,400
1970	115,900	95,400	20,500
1978	256,600	211,900	44,600
1984	377,000	290,200	86,800
1985	410,600	318,200	92,400

12.8%. Table 3 shows electricity output in selected years:

From 1953 to 1985, the State invested a total of 88,614 million yuan in building power stations, accounting for 16.2% of the total industrial investment. Now an electricity generating and supply network has been formed, consisting of both hydro- and thermal-power stations of all sizes. By the end of 1985, the power generating capacity totalled 87.05 million kW, 47.1 times as much as in 1949, increasing annually by 2.42 million kW. From being 21st in 1949, China's world ranking moved up to eighth place. By the end of 1984, China had 28 power grids, each with a capacity of more than 100,000 kW. Of these, 12 have a capacity of more than one million kW. Six trans-provincial power grids were formed in North-East, North, East, Central, North-West and South-West China. The capacity of the 12 principal power grids made up three-quarters of the country's power generating capacity.

The Qingtongxia hydropower station in the Ningxia autonomous region.

Technicians test the safety door of a nuclear island at the Qinshan nuclear power station in Zhejiang province.
(Photo by Lu Ming)

China's policy is to develop thermal and hydro-electric power simultaneously. In the early post-Liberation days, efforts were concentrated on building coal-fired power stations in power load areas and preparations were made for building hydro-electric power stations. Later, a number of large and medium-sized hydro-electric power stations, including Xin'an-jiang, Liujiaxia and Danjiang, were built. The percentage of hydro-electric power rose from 16.3% in 1949 to 30.4% in 1985. Particularly noteworthy is the development of small hydro-electric power stations over the past decade. By the end of 1985, the small hydropower stations had a combined capacity of 3.802 million kW, satisfying three-quarters of rural needs.

Nuclear power plant construction has just begun in China. Two plants are under construction, one at Qinshan in Haiyan county, Zhejiang province, with a designed capacity of 300,000 kW and one in Guang-dong province. The Qinshan N-power plant is exploratory in nature, mainly for the purpose of training Chinese technicians. The plant was scheduled for completion before October 1989.

The Guangdong N-power plant is a joint venture between the Guangdong Electric Power Company and the China Light and Power Company Ltd. of Hong Kong. Located on the Daya Bay in Shenzhen, Guangdong province, the plant will use two imported reactors, each with a capacity of 900,000 kW.

The development of alternative forms of energy

Developing alternative forms of energy is part of China's energy policy. Some of the new forms of

Table 4: Alternative Forms of Energy (to 1984)

Type of alternative energy devices	Quantity	Energy output (annual)
Solar stove	over 40,000	40,000 kW
Solar heater	200,000 m²	equivalent to 50,000 tons of standard coal
Solar house	30,000 m²	equivalent to 600 tons of standard coal
Solar cell	150 kW	300,000 kWh
Wind-power generator	over 6,000	700 kW
Wind-power pump	over 8,000	24,000 hp
Methane gas pit	4,000,000	800 million m³ gas
Tidal power plant	7	5,000 kW
Geothermal power station	4	7,500 kW
Other uses of geothermal power	over 300 projects	seedling nursing, aquatic product breeding, medical treatment, heating

energy have already entered the market. Specialized research institutions and factories are increasing in number. Thanks to the policy of "developing multiple forms of energy according to local conditions and making comprehensive utilization of resources, with emphasis on practical results", the new forms of energy have developed especially fast in the rural areas, where local people are encouraged to pool funds for developing alternative forms of energy while the State provides aid.

Table 4 shows the development of alternative forms of energy up to 1984.

The alternative sources of energy are developed mainly in remote rural areas, especially those beyond the reach of conventional forms of energy or suffering an acute shortage of conventional forms of energy.

Since the beginning of the 1980s, China's research in alternative forms of energy has been shifted to establishing comprehensive demonstration projects, namely, to establish villages and experimental centres to demonstrate the use of alternative forms of energy. Alternative energy researchers have also carried out international co-operation, introduced advanced foreign technology and equipment, and developed serial products. They have built solar cell production factories, developed small wind-power generators and wind-power pumps, formulated design standards for building solar houses, built geothermal power stations and tidal power stations and spread the use of methane gas in rural areas. The most fruitful is the research in the technology for developing the passive type of solar houses, solar heaters, solar cells, wind-power generators and pumps, methane gas for household use and the utilization of industrial wastes in generating methane gas.

The Jiangsha tidal power station in Zhejiang.

The Quantity and Structure of Energy Consumption

Elastic co-efficiency of energy consumption

Energy consumption in China has continued growing since the founding of New China in 1949. The total annual amount of energy consumed in 1985 increased by 13.1 times over 1953, from 54,110,000 tons of standard coal to 764.26 million tons, averaging an annual increase of 8.6%. During the same period, the total value of all goods and services produced grew by 11.1 times, averaging an annual increase of 8.1%. The elastic co-efficiency of energy consumption averaged 1.1 for the entire period, 1.63 for the First Five-Year Plan period (1953–1957), 2.59 in the Second Five-Year Plan period 1958–1962 (as the result of the development of energy-consuming heavy industry) and 0.29 in the 1963–1965 period, a period of economic readjustment when heavy industry was

Energy Consumption

Table 5: Energy Consumption and Output of Goods and Services (1953–1985)

Year	Total energy consumption (in standard coal, ton)	Gross output value of social product (million yuan)	% of total amount			
			Coal	Oil	Natural gas	Hydro-electricity
1953	54,110,000	124,100	94.33	3.81	0.02	1.84
1957	96,440,000	160,600	92.32	4.59	0.08	3.01
1962	165,400,000	180,000	89.23	6.61	0.93	3.23
1965	189,010,000	269,500	86.45	10.27	0.63	2.65
1970	292,910,000	380,000	80.89	14.67	0.92	3.52
1978	571,440,000	537,900	70.67	22.73	3.20	3.4
1980	602,750,000	853,100	72.10	20.85	3.06	3.99
1984	709,040,000	1,314,700	75.31	17.45	2.33	4.91
1985	764,260,000	1,630,980	75.85	17.09	2.25	4.81

cut and efficient use and management of energy was encouraged. But energy consumption began to rise again after 1965, reaching an average of 1.1 in the following 11 years up to 1977. From 1979 to 1985, thanks to an overall readjustment of the economic development and attention to energy conservation, the elastic co-efficiency of energy consumption dropped sharply to 0.41, since energy consumption increased at an average annual rate of 4.2% while the gross value of all goods and services (including industry, agriculture, construction, transportation and commerce) grew at an average annual rate of 10.3%.

Structure and characteristics of energy consumption

Table 5 (above) shows the amount and structure of the energy (commercial) consumed and the gross value of all goods and services produced from 1953 to 1984.

The table indicates that coal is still the principal form of energy in China. As the petroleum industry develops, the consumption of oil and natural gas have risen steadily. Such a consumption pattern is not likely to change within the twentieth century. This will add to the difficulties in extraction, processing, transportation and environmental protection. At present, the railways devote one-third of their handling capacity to transporting coal and the limited transport capacity causes a shortage in supply of coal to the consumer but accumulation of coal at the mines.

Apart from the huge quantities of energy consumed by urban industries, the rural areas also consume a considerable amount of energy locally produced. It has been estimated that the rural areas burn 180 million tons of firewood and 230 million tons of crop stalks every year, an equivalent of 230 million tons of standard coal, which supplies 85% of the energy needs of the 800 million peasants. In 1984, the consumption of primary energy (including commercial and non-commercial energy) in the whole country was 937,320,000 tons of standard coal, of which non-commercial energy accounted for 24.5%.

In China, productive units consume 3.3 times more energy than non-productive units. Of production

Table 6: Energy Consumption by Department (1980)

Department	Consumption (ton)	% of total
Production dept.:	489,230,000	81.2
Industry	406,330,000	67.5
Agriculture	52,240,000	8.6
Construction	6,170,000	1.0
Transport	22,640,000	3.8
Commerce	1,550,000	0.3
Non-productive departments:	113,520,000	18.8
Social consumption	11,650,000	1.9
Residents	101,870,000	16.9

units, industry is the biggest energy consumer, followed by agriculture, transport, construction and commercial departments. Among the non-productive sectors, the bulk of energy is consumed by residents, which is 8.7 times that by other social groups (See Table 6).

Energy consumption assumes the following characteristics:

– Industrial consumption is on the high side, about 67.5% of the total. The consumption ratio between heavy and light industries is 83.7:16.3, leaving a gap of 5.1 times.

– Energy consumption by the energy industry itself is a little too high. The 1980 figure showed that the amount of energy consumed (including losses) by the energy industry itself accounted for 17.4% of the total energy consumption. The coal used by coal mines accounted for 4% of the total; oil used by oilfields and oil refineries and pipeline losses accounted for 10%; the electricity used by power plants themselves and line loss accounted for 16.7% of the total electricity generated. Therefore, China has a big gap to bridge with regard to energy production, processing, storage and technical equipment, and management as compared with some developed countries such as the Soviet Union, the Federal Republic of Germany and the United States, whose energy industries consume 12.6%, 5.9% and 6% of their total energy output, respectively.

– The energy consumption by agriculture, transportation, construction and commerce and non-productive departments is on the low side. Household energy consumption in urban areas averaged 20 kWh of electricity a year, not only lower than developed countries but also lower than many other developing countries.

The Shortage of Energy Supply and its Causes

Although China is the third biggest energy consumer in the world, the per capita average is the lowest. In 1985, for example, the average per capita consumption of commercial energy was only 700 kilogrammes, only one-fourth of the world average. As in many other developing countries, shortage of energy has become a major factor restricting economic development. It is estimated that about 20% of the country's production capacity is lying idle through shortage of energy, which would otherwise generate more than 70,000,000,000 yuan in output value. Factories in some places have to stop production for some time every year in order to save electricity for agricultural use, thus wasting a lot of manpower and materials.

Energy shortage is also an outstanding problem for the rural areas. Of the 170,000,000 households, about 100,000,000 suffer from fuel shortage for four to five months of the year. In the countryside, 41.3% of the energy comes from crop stalks and 38.1% from firewood. As there are not enough crop stalks, people turn to forests, thus worsening the ecological balance, which in turn causes water loss and soil erosion. The organic matters have also been reduced, making the soil lose fertility.

The main causes for the shortage of energy supply are:

– *China has too large a population.* Though the absolute amount of energy produced by the country is among the biggest in the world, the average amount per capita is among the lowest.

– *Technological processes and equipment are backward and the industrial structure is irrational.* These, plus bad management of energy resources, cause the low utility rate of energy and great waste. According to statistics, the utility rate of primary energy in China averages 28%, far lower than that of industrialized countries, which ranges from 40 to 50%. But the energy consumption per unit output value is much higher than in major industrialized countries. In 1980, China consumed 213,000 tons of standard coal for every 100 million US dollars of goods produced, while the United States used only 92,000 tons, Japan 35,000 tons, and the Soviet Union 123,000 tons.

The efficiency of energy consumed has been dropping since the founding of New China. In 1959, the country used 96,000 tons of standard coal for generating every 100 million yuan of national income, but in 1978, the figure reached 167,800 tons. Though less coal has been consumed in recent years,

the 1985 figure was still 125,300 tons, 33.3% more than that of 1957. Allowing for changes in the industrial structure and other incomparable factors, this still indicates serious waste.

– *Transport facilities fall short of demand.* There are many bottlenecks in railway transport. Owing to insufficient transport capacity, many coal mines in Shanxi, Inner Mongolia, Ningxia, Shaanxi and Guizhou have to limit their coal output, thus aggravating the strained situation in energy supply.

Energy Development Strategy

Forecast of energy demand

Demand forecast provides the basis for formulating development strategy. The major factors affecting energy demand are growth of the national economy, changes in the economic structure, technological progress and energy conservation measures, and changes in resources and policies.

The Twelfth National Congress of the Communist Party of China held in 1983 laid down as the strategic goal for economic and social development the need to quadruple the 1980 total output value of industry and agriculture by the end of this century and to raise the material and cultural living standards of the people to that of the well-to-do family. According to the requirements for this general goal, there are the following options in energy needs by the year 2000:

– To keep the growth of energy consumption in step with that of the growth of total industrial and agricultural output value, that is, at an average annual rate of 7.2%, with the elastic co-efficiency of energy consumption at 1. This would call for a rise in energy demand from 1980's 603,000,000 tons of standard coal to 2,410,000,000 tons, which is the most conservative forecast, supposing that the economic structure will remain unchanged and technology will remain what it is today. This goal is very difficult to achieve, given the present material and financial resources the State is able to put into energy development and the amount of reserves ready for development.

– An analysis of the growth in energy consumption and in economic development between 1981 and 1985 indicates that the elastic co-efficiency of energy consumption in the next 15 years will be far lower than the 30-year average before 1980, that is, at about 0.5 to 0.6, which may basically meet the demand of economic growth. This would mean that the total energy demand by the year 2000 will be 1,223,000,000 to 1,400,000,000 tons, which would require energy output to increase at an annual rate of 3.6 to 4.3%.

This forecast is based on three propositions: the fact that China will further adjust the economic structure to reduce the size of energy consuming industry, especially heavy industry, and increase the proportion

Table 7: Primary Energy Output by the Year 2000 (Forecast)

Form of energy	Low prediction			High prediction		
	Actual amount	in standard coal (million tons)	Growth rate 1986–2000 %	Actual amount	in standard coal (million tons)	Growth rate 1986–2000 %
Coal	1,200 million tons	856.8	2.4	1,300 million tons	928.2	2.9
Petroleum	200 million tons	285.8	3.2	250 million tons	357	4.8
Natural gas	40,000 million m³	53.2	7.9	50,000 million m³	66.5	9.5
Hydro-electricity	250,000 million kWh	90	6.1	280,000 million kWh	101	6.9
Atomic power	50,000 million kWh	18		75,000 million kWh	27	
Sum total		*1,303.8*	*3*		*1,480*	*3.9*

of high-tech industries and service trades, a move that will save energy indirectly; the fact that China is unfolding a technical transformation drive, principally for the purpose of conserving energy, and will carry out a massive scale equipment renewal when conditions are ripe to discard energy-inefficient out-of-date equipment and add more that is energy-efficient. These moves will upgrade the technological equipment in the industrial and transportation departments, thus achieving energy conservation purposes in a direct manner; the fact that China will rely on alternative forms of energy to ease the rural energy shortage within this century instead of increasing the supply of commercial energy.

According to expert predictions, the energy output and structure of China's primary energy by the year 2000 will be as shown in Table 7.

Objectives and Measures for Energy Development during the Seventh Five-Year Plan Period (1986–1990)

During the 1986–1990 Seventh Five-Year Plan period, China will continue to implement the principle of giving equal stress to development and conservation. The State will muster the necessary amount of financial and material resources and adopt measures in price, tax and credit to speed energy production and lower energy consumption so as to ease the shortage and prepare for further development in the 1990s. The State plans to produce 990 million tons of standard coal by 1990, 150 million tons more than in 1985, averaging an annual increase of 3.4%.

The power industry

Priority will be given to the power industry, with hydro- and thermal-electricity developed simultaneously. While great efforts will be made to develop hydro-electric power in areas rich with water-power resources, nuclear power stations will be built in energy-short East China and in southern China.

A 300-thousand therm generator set made in Shanghai with imported techniques. *(Photo by Feng Peishan)*

It is planned to generate 550,000 million kWh of electricity by 1990, increasing at an average annual rate of 6.2%. Within the five years, power stations with a combined generating capacity of 60 to 65 million kW will be under construction, of which 18.8 million kW will be hydro-power and scheduled for completion in this period will be 30 to 35 million kW.

Thermal Power Stations: A number of coal-fired power stations will be built in mining areas in Shanxi, Inner Mongolia, Heilongjiang, Anhui, Shandong, Henan and other major coal-producing provinces and regions. A number of thermal-power plants will be built in some big and medium-sized cities and industrial centres.

Hydropower Stations: Efforts will be focused on the development of water-power resources on the upper reaches of the Yellow and Yangtze rivers and the Honghe river in Yunnan province. In North-East and East China, where the water-power resources are easily developed, a number of medium-sized hydro-power stations will be built. Work will continue to prepare for the construction of the water conservancy and hydropower project at the Three Gorges on the

579

A corner of the construction site of the Longyangxia hydropower station in Qinghai province. *(Photo by Wang Jingye)*

The Qinshan nuclear power station near Hangzhou in Zhejiang province under construction.

Yangtze river. In addition, efforts will be made to support localities to develop small hydro-electric power stations.

Nuclear Power Plants: Follow-up work will be done on the Guangdong nuclear power plant at Daya Bay, the first phase of the nuclear power plant at Qinshan in Zhejiang province will be completed, and preparations will be made to start the second phase.

Power Grid Construction: A power grid network, principally the 500,000 V power transmission lines, will be put up in North, North-East and East China and work on the 500,000 V direct current power transmission and transformation project from Gezhouba, one of the largest hydropower projects, to Shanghai will be completed, linking up the power grids in Central and East China. At the same time, work will be accelerated to build the 330,000 V power transmission lines.

To fulfil these plans, the following major policies will be adopted:

– To encourage local governments, State departments and enterprises to pool funds to build power projects. The investors will share the electricity and reap the profits. This policy will remain unchanged for 20 years.

– To improve the pricing system. Different prices will be fixed for electricity supplies at peak and non-peak hours for thermal electricity and between periods when water is abundantly available and when it is scarce for hydro-electric power.

– To contract out the power projects arranged by the State at a fixed amount of investment, with the Ministry of Water Resources and Electric Power guaranteeing the planned power output, generating capacities in operation and scale and speed of construction.

– To strengthen the management and regulation of power grids, and to check and service the equipment at scheduled intervals so as to ensure safe and full-capacity operations and the rational allocation and use of electricity.

Coal production

Construction of coal production centres will be stepped up to make fuller use of the rich coal resources.

The first generator in the Gezhou dam hydropower station in Hubei province being put in place. *(Photo by Li Zuogao)*

It has been planned to produce 1,000 million tons of coal by 1990, 150 million tons more than in 1985. The average annual growth rate is 3.3%. Within the five years, projects with a designed production capacity of 318 million tons will be undertaken and 167 million tons will be completed. They will mainly be in Shanxi, Inner Mongolia, Henan, western Shaanxi and the Ningxia Hui autonomous region. At the same time, efforts will be made to rebuild or expand the old mines in North-East and North China.

The country will adopt the following major policies to accelerate the construction of the coal industry:

– The State will give a fixed amount of investment to big and medium-sized mines managed by the State, who are required to ensure a fixed amount of output, with the surplus investment and above-quota output retained by themselves. This policy is designed to encourage mines to tap their production potential to the full and strive to use the minimum investment for maximum output.

– To put the emphasis of coal mine construction on the technical transformation, rebuilding or expansion of existing mines in order to improve investment returns. In building new mines, big, medium-sized and small mines will be built, giving emphasis to medium-sized and small ones.

– To encourage local governments and State departments to pool funds to open coal mines.

– To promote technological progress for higher productivity and better resource recovery.

– To increase transport capacity to keep pace with the development of the coal industry.

Petroleum resources

Exploration of petroleum resources will be stepped up to verify more reserves while speeding oil production.

The planned crude output by 1990 is 150 million tons or 1,050 million barrels, 25 million tons or 175 million barrels more than in 1985. The projected average annual increase is 3.7%. The output of natural gas is planned to reach 15,000 million cubic metres, 2,140 million cubic metres more than in 1985. The projected average annual increase rate is 3.1%. Exploratory drilling of 60 million metres will have to be completed within the five years and 60 million tons or 420 million barrels of crude oil production capacity and 3,000 million cubic metres of natural gas extraction capacity will have to be added.

Efforts will be concentrated on the eastern part of China in the near future, in both exploration and production. In the western part and offshore, efforts will be focused on exploration to verify more reserves for future development.

The major policies and measures to accelerate the development of petroleum and natural gas are:

– The State will continue to follow the practice of contracting for a fixed amount of annual increase in output, with the above-quota output and oil conserved

Marsh gas is used for lighting in a rural area of Hunan province.

retained by oilfields as development funds for further exploration and development.

– To improve, renovate, equip and expand the existing oilfields and adopt advanced technology and effective measures to control and slow down the annual decrease rate at the Daqing, Shengli, North China and Liaohe oilfields. At the same time, efforts will be made to develop thick oil or heavy crude to tap the potentiality.

– To import advanced foreign management skills and experience, and sum up and spread experience in the foreign co-operation in developing offshore oil resources in order to strengthen research and management of onshore oil and natural gas exploration and development. Efforts will be made to study the formation and distribution of oil and natural gas and assess the resources and improve the technology for seismic exploration, data processing and logging.

– To step up exploration and development of natural gas to make it keep pace with oil development.

Rural energy

The rural energy problem will be solved according to the principle of developing multiple forms of energy and comprehensive utilization in the light of local conditions and practical results. Within this century, the rural areas will still mainly use bio-energy instead of mineral energy, for mineral energy such as coal and oil cannot meet the huge demand of the 800 million peasants and, as they are distributed unevenly, cannot reach all parts of the country for lack of sufficient transportation facilities. The rural areas have to rely on themselves to solve the energy problem by developing firewood forests, methane gas, small hydropower stations and small coal pits, as well as other alternative forms of energy, such as solar, wind power and geothermal power systems. In addition, efforts will be made to spread the use of firewood saving or energy-efficient stoves to raise the utility rate of the available fuel.

A wind power station in Anxi county, Gansu province.
(Photo by Zhou Guohua)

Conservation of Energy

Waste is another reason for the shortage of energy. Output of the energy consuming units is lower not only than in many of the industrialized countries but also lower than what they achieved themselves in the First Five-Year Plan period (1953–1957). To achieve the end of the century goal, it is not enough to increase output. Greater efforts should be made to encourage economical use of energy, which is of great strategic importance. Measures adopted by China to conserve energy include:

– Strengthening energy management, mainly the basic work, such as the establishment of management organizations and systems, including a metering system, a fixed assessment system, and a punishment and reward system, so as to make energy conservation work institutionalized and systematized. At the same time it is necessary to balance the energy supply to various areas, departments and major enterprises strictly according to the energy use plans. Fixed amounts of energy should be supplied to energy consuming enterprises which should not be allowed to increase energy consumption at will.

– Promoting technological transformation centring round energy conservation. In the near future, main efforts will be made to spread the use of technologies that require little investment but are energy-efficient in the power, metallurgical, chemical, building materials, petroleum, railways and transportation industries. At the same time, efforts will be made to renovate industrial kilns and electrical equipment that are energy-inefficient and raise the efficiency of heating by spreading central heating systems. The machine-building industry will study, trial-produce and manufacture energy-saving and highly efficient motive power equipment and machines, such as internal combustion engines, boilers, steam turbines, automobiles, pumps, blowers, compressors and motors.

– Continued efforts will be made to improve the economic structure, product mix and enterprise organizational systems. While maintaining a balanced development of heavy and light industries, efforts will be made to develop energy-efficient and profitable technology-intensive industry so as to produce energy-saving products to replace the energy-consuming ones. Small enterprises, especially those which are energy-consuming, loss-making and technically backward will be overhauled and reorganized and a number of them that share the same energy sources will be ordered to stop production. Coordination among enterprises according to specialization will be encouraged and ties among enterprises will be developed to end the situation in which every enterprise, big or small, tries to be self-sufficient in everything.

– Well-run factories and enterprises will be given priority in the supply of energy and a fixed amount of energy will be allocated to each factory. Factories that use more energy than they are allowed will pay more and those which conserve energy will be rewarded. Electric machinery will be priced according to their energy efficiency. The pricing of energy products will also be gradually changed so as to encourage enterprises and departments to conserve energy.

7. POSTS AND TELECOMMUNICATIONS

A Historical Survey

CHINA has a long history in posts and telecommunications. It had postal delivery stations as early as the Warring States period (475–221 BC). In the Han dynasty (206 BC–AD 220) lodging houses were built every 15 kilometres along roads for the use of postmen and officials, and in the Tang dynasty (618–907) water post delivery stations were set up along the rivers, supported by growing crops on both banks. The heads of these stations had horses, carriages and boats ready for delivering letters and arranged with local people to distribute them. In the Song dynasty (960–1279) the number of post delivery stations increased, averaging one for every five or ten kilometres, and soldiers were commanded to deliver documents and letters, instead of the local people. In the Yuan dynasty (1206–1368) this delivery route was extended throughout China and connected with European and other Asian countries. This system was still in use even in the Ming (1368–1644) and Qing (1644–1911) dynasties.

Urgent military messages were delivered in a different way, by lighting beacons. In the Han dynasty the people of the Xiongnu nationality in North-West China had many battles with the Han government, which sent soldiers to the north-west border areas (in today's Gansu province and the Xinjiang Uygur autonomous region) to defend the frontier. They built beacons at certain distances, and when soldiers on duty encountered the enemy they lit their beacons to signal to their neighbours, who would immediately do the same. In this way, news could be delivered to the capital Chang'an (today's Xi'an) in two or three days. At the same time all the frontier soldiers were warned by the signals and ready for battle.

After the Opium War in 1840, modern post and telecommunication facilities including cables and telephones were gradually introduced into China. But posts and telecommunications developed slowly and equipment and technology were backward before Liberation in 1949 because of the slump in the economy and long and frequent warring. The long-distance circuits were above-ground, open audio-frequency lines and used single or three-circuit carrier frequency telephones. Local public calls were handled by magneto switchboards and operated by hand. The relay system and the rotatory automatic switchboards were only used in a few big cities. In rural and border areas the posts and telecommunications were even more backward. In 1949, when the People's Republic was founded, China had 700,000 kilometres of postal routes, 400 postal cars, 2,800 long-distance circuits, 310,000 local telephone switchboards and 63,000 rural phones. The government departments had only 35 broadcasting stations, with a total transmitting power of 107 kilowatts. Most telecommunication facilities were concentrated in Nanjing and its surrounding areas, in cities along the south-east coast and in a few medium-sized and big cities in the hinterland. Their distribution was unbalanced.

The founding of the People's Republic opened a new chapter in the development of posts and telecommunications. Especially since the implementation of the policy of opening to the outside world and revitalizing the national economy in the late 1970s, posts and telecommunications have registered a swift development. In 1985 China had 930,000 post and telecommunications workers, as opposed to 100,000 in 1949. Most post and telecommunication facilities are designed and produced by China itself and the practice of relying on imports has been changed. Capability and business volume have markedly increased. Compared with 1949 the capacity for handling letters had increased by 6.8 times in 1985, the press distribution volume went up by 58 times, public telegram business volume rose by 18 times, long-distance telephones by 41.6 times and local public calls by over 9 times. Thirty years of effort have resulted in the establishment of a post and telecommunications network centred on Beijing, which connects various cities and townships through all kinds of communication means. Now China has more than 53,000 post offices, 5 million kilometres of postal routes, 500 postal trains, 8,237 postal cars, 39,000 long-distance circuits, 3.3 million telephone switchboards in the cities and 2.7 million in rural areas. China has also built 14,000 kilometres of microwave trunk lines and 179,000 kilometres of underground long-distance cables which connect Beijing with 20 cities by long-distance dial phones and transmit Beijing's television programmes to 27 provinces, municipalities and autonomous regions. Moreover, Beijing can deliver its TV programmes through communication satellites to more than 50 ground stations in remote and border areas, and facsimile *People's Daily* and other newspapers to 19 provinces, municipalities and autonomous regions. Beijing, Tianjin, Guangzhou, Fuzhou and Shenzhen have also used imported programme-controlled electronic switchboards. China has applied the cables made by itself to switch local public calls and used 4,380-channel medium-sized concentric cables and 7,800-channel microwave carrier systems.

Three decades of effort also saw a swift development in China's international post and telecommunications business. By the end of 1985, China had established postal relations with more than 120 countries and regions and opened international express special delivery services in Beijing, Shanghai and other big cities. It has established direct circuits with 45 countries and regions through communications satellites and other means, and indirect circuits with 170 countries and regions through tie stations. In addition to telephones and a telegram business China has also opened other services including facsimile transmission of newspapers, photos and reference materials and transmission of data at middle and low speed.

The Current Situation

Communications in China consist of posts and telecommunications systems. The telecommunications system is mainly composed of the state post and telecommunications offices which supplement each other with various kinds of exclusive communication networks, including those used by the state broadcasting stations, TV stations, newspapers, state meteorological observatories and marine communications, as well as those used by railways, road traffic, airlines, petroleum exploitation, water conservation and water-power, and in governmental departments. All these communication facilities are used under the principle of "independence and coordination". The communication networks managed by the post and telecommunication offices are used by the public.

Postal services

The post offices mainly handle the delivery and collection of domestic and international letters, newspapers, magazines, parcels and printed matter. They also handle the domestic post of banking and remittances.

Today, in addition to postal cars and automatic and mechanized machines used in some links of the production chain, most work is operated by hand. Some machines have been introduced for sorting, differentiating, stamping, conveying and binding letters. The binding and conveying machines are used more in handling newspapers and magazines. Big post offices in most provincial capitals use machines to unbind, sort and convey printed matter and parcels. An automatic machine is available in most post offices to weigh parcels and to calculate and show charges.

The international post communications mainly handle mail, collection and delivery of international letters, parcels, newspapers, magazines and printed matter.

Telecommunications

Telecommunications mainly handle public telegrams, telephones, newspapers, facsimile, transmission of TV programmes, low-speed data, and lease of circuits.

The main method China has adopted in its long-distance communications is the analogue mode; the digital mode is now being developed. Long-distance communications are mainly transmitted by open wire. Since the early 1960s China has built a 60-channel symmetry cable carrier system and 120-channel and 600-channel microwave systems. In the 1970s a 1,800-channel medium-sized concentric cable carrier system and 600-channel and 960-channel microwave systems were built between Beijing, Shanghai and Hangzhou. The medium-sized concentric cable carrier system from Beijing to Wuhan and Guangzhou has been officially put into use. A 14,000-kilometre microwave system for transmitting TV programmes, transmitting facsimile newspapers and broadcasting news and making calls has been set up to connect 26 provinces, municipalities and autonomous regions. A nationwide network for transmitting TV programmes has been formed. A digital transmission system for public long-distance communications and an optical fibre telecommunication system for local public telephones have been introduced and partially put into use. A communications satellite was successfully launched in 1986 for transmitting TV programmes to remote areas and for improving the communication systems.

Most telephone exchanges now in use in China are electro-mechanical. The new telephone offices in urban areas are equipped with vertical and horizontal systems. Some big and medium-sized cities have imported programme-controlled exchanges. The calls in big and medium-sized cities are exchanged by automatic devices, but in small cities they are still handled manually. Long-distance telephone calls in the country are mainly operated manually, but some calls between Beijing, Tianjin, Jinan, Hefei, Shanghai, Hangzhou, Shijiazhuang, Zhengzhou, Wuhan, Changsha, Guangzhou and nine other cities are dialled directly or by operators. The programme-controlled telegram transmission equipment is only used in a few big and medium-sized cities, and most telegrams are still handled manually.

Before the 1970s, international communications were mainly transmitted by radio shortwave, but since then they have been transmitted through international satellites and other communication facilities. By the end of 1985 China had built 1,500 circuits for transmitting international telegrams and phone calls with an annual business volume of 2.6 million characters of telegrams and 3.9 million characters of public telegrams, 11 million phone calls and 1,606 TV programmes. The turnover reaches 231 million yuan a year.

Problems and Prospects

Although the posts and telecommunications industry has registered great progress in the last three decades, it cannot yet meet the needs of national economic and social development.

The main problems are:

– The post and telecommunications facilities are in short supply and cannot meet the demand of increasing business volume. The communications network cannot reach the remote areas. Each post office in the country has to serve as many as 20,000 people on average and its service area covers 190 square kilometres. At present, telephones are available in half of the villages in the country. Long-distance circuits are also in short supply. An average of 0.6 per cent of the population have phones, a ratio of 200 people per phone, which is lower than the world average of 13 per cent. International post and telecommunications business volume is increasing at a rate of 50 per cent a year. Shortage of facilities causes many problems in international post and telecommunications, and the connection rate is quite low.

– The contradiction between supply and demand is acute. People find it difficult to make a local call and have to wait a long time to make a long-distance call. Long-distance dial phones are not popular in China. The shortage of transport vehicles and the low handling capacity delay the delivery of postal matter.

– Slow development is reported in the new-style post and telecommunication facilities. These new means of post and telecommunications, such as digital telecommunications, photo telecommunications and high-speed digital transmission, are in their trial stage. The movable telecommunications, video digital telecommunications and multi-function comprehensive telecommunications systems have not been put into use.

– Bad services. It is common to find phones unclear, wrongly connected or cut off half way through calls, and telegrams are often delayed or wrongly deciphered.

In order to reduce the strain on post and telecommunications and to meet the needs in carrying out the policy of opening to the outside and revitalizing the national economy, great efforts have been devoted to enabling the development of the post and telecommunications industry to outstrip that of the national economy as a whole. The general plan shows that only by increasing the handling capacity and volume of post and telecommunications by seven

times can the realization of the target of quadrupling the 1981 agricultural and industrial output value by the year 2000 be guaranteed. Its main targets are: the ratio of phones to the population in urban areas will increase to 10 per cent: in cities such as Beijing, Tianjin, Shanghai and Guangzhou it will be 25 per cent, and 20 per cent in the provincial capitals, economic centres and 14 coastal cities. It will be 5 per cent in medium-sized cities and county seats and more than 1 per cent in rural areas. In 2000 China will have 39.6 million phones, the telecommunication network throughout the country will be automatic and dial phones will be used in cities above county level. The optical fibre and satellite telecommunications systems and a wide-band video frequency transmission network will be popularized in big cities. For business, such devices as visual telephone meetings, video telephone and high-speed facsimile will be available. Mobile telephones will be installed on some trains, buses and steam boats for public local, long-distance and international calls. A post communications network will gradually be established, based on central offices, to cover a vast territory through air, land and sea routes in order to shorten delivery time. Post offices will be basically equipped with automatic and semi-automatic facilities, and an electronic post communication business will be opened. The handling capacity of the mails will reach 160 billion pieces a year.

The Chinese government has decided to list the development of the post and telecommunications as one of the main projects to be developed in the Seventh Five-Year Plan period (1986–90). The main target in this period is that the total business volume of post and telecommunications in 1990 will be 5 billion yuan, or an average annual increase of 11 per cent.

Telecommunications

During the Seventh Five-Year Plan period, China will gradually popularize the use of programme-controlled exchanges, optical fibre telecommunications, PCM and satellite communications systems and other new technologies and facilities. China will establish a group of telecommunications receiving stations and a domestic satellite communication system. Dial toll domestic and international phones will be installed in provincial capital cities (except a few), economic centres and opened coastal cities. A digital communication network will be established in the Yangtze river delta and Zhujiang (Pearl River) delta and in the Beijing–Tianjin–Tangshan area. The main targets are: to install 3 million more local phones, to add 100,000 circuit terminals for long-distance calls, to increase long-distance phone circuits by 60,000 and to build international telecommunication bureaux in Shanghai and Beijing in order to meet the needs of the development of international communications.

Postal services

According to the needs of the increasing volume of business, it is necessary to readjust the postal delivery network and steadily increase the delivery capacity as set out in the plans. Mails will be handled by automatic and semi-automatic machines. Businesses will be opened for handling express, registered, insurance and personally delivered letters, printed matter, newspapers, magazines, remittances and parcels. China will open new services for electronic post and postal banking and sell stamp-collection goods. To increase the delivery capacity, China will add 150 postal trains, 5,000 postal cars and 10 postal boats and will install other necessary accessories.

Posts and telecommunications scientific research and production

China will devote great efforts to scientific research in posts and telecommunications and the improvement of technology and equipment.

It will also develop new technologies such as programme-controlled exchanges, satellite communications, digital, microwave and optical fibre communication systems, which will be continuously supplied to post and telecommunication departments.

8. COMMERCE AND SERVICES

Commerce in Ancient Times

THE ancient Chinese created a flourishing commerce as well as a brilliant culture. Exchange of commodities began in China in about the 21st century BC during the Xia dynasty, and commerce as an independent profession took shape around the 16th century BC during the Shang dynasty, when some people of the Shang family clan specialized in this trade. From that period up to 1840, Chinese commerce underwent tremendous development despite changes of rulers, natural disasters and wars. Several factors contributed to this development.

– There were great varieties and quantities of commodities and the area for commodity circulation was large.

China has a vast, richly-endowed territory, with each area having its own special product that can be put on the market for exchange. During the Xia and Shang dynasties, goods available on the market covered such things as porcelain, silk fabrics, bronze ware, cereals, domestic animals, feathers, fur and leather. During the Han dynasty (206 BC–AD 220), when the country was unified and there was social stability, commerce experienced a boom. According to the *Shi Ji* (Historical Records), at that time "rich businessmen and big merchants travelled everywhere in the country, versed in the skills of trading everything available for exchange." The silk road, opened up in the Han dynasty and developed in the Tang dynasty (618–907), linked Asia with Europe. Zheng He (1371–1435), a eunuch of the Ming dynasty (1368–1644), sailed down the Indian Ocean and reached the eastern coast of Africa, taking along with him huge quantities of silks, porcelain and tea.

– There were many people engaged in commerce and commercial cities were flourishing. As far back as the Spring and Autumn period (770 BC–476 BC), business people were counted among the four professions – official, farmer, worker and businessman. By the Han dynasty, Chang'an (Xi'an), Luoyang (in Henan), Nanyang, (Linzi, in Shandong), Handan (in Hebei) and Chengdu (in Sichuan) had developed into big commercial cities. During the Ming dynasty, commerce became increasingly more flourishing, with the number of industrial and commercial cities growing to more than 50, including Shanghai, Tianjin, Hankou (in Hubei), Suzhou (in Jiangsu), and Hangzhou (in Zhejiang).

– There were a variety of forms of commerce and there was a division of labour in handling commodities. In ancient China, the main form of commerce was traffic trade, by which people carried goods from one place to another for sale. Itinerant traders and shopkeepers appeared during the Warring States period (475 BC–221 BC). During the Tang dynasty (AD 618–916) there were further divisions of different trades according to their commodities and a large number of brokers, known at the time as *Yalong*, appeared.

– Commercial capital increased fast and there were many big businessmen. In ancient China, merchants could get fat profits by transporting goods for sale and their capital multiplied fast. This gave rise to numerous big merchants in all dynasties. Zi Gong (520 BC–?), a student of Confucius, was one of them. He became so wealthy by engaging in commerce that his property was comparable to that of kings and nobles. The big merchant, Lu Buwei (?–235 BC), was the Prime Minister of the State of Qin.

– Business people accumulated a wealth of experience and developed a systematic theory. Commerce occupied an important position in ancient Chinese economics. Big merchant, Bai Gui, said, according to the *Historical Records*, that trading was very complicated and it required courage, resourcefulness and the ability to make decisions, as in managing a State or commanding a battle.

However, ancient Chinese commerce was not all plain sailing. Beginning from the Qin dynasty (221–207 BC), many feudal rulers pursued the policy of ostracizing commerce and even taking measures against middle and small business people. At the same time, the feudal monarchy often monopolized the marketing of major commodities such as salt and iron, thus making it difficult for commerce to develop as it should. But social development is inseparable from the development of commerce, and ancient Chinese commerce, too, developed along with the self-supporting feudal economy.

Modern Commerce

The Opium War in 1840 marked the beginning of China's transition from a totally feudal society into a semi-feudal, semi-colonial society, and its commerce was tinged with the same colours. Commercial capital was divided into bureaucratic and national. Bureaucratic capital held over 80 per cent of the country's commercial capital. The China Tea Company, the China Cereals Company, the China Import and Export Trade Corporation and the Yangtze Building Materials Company were among the big commercial trusts that monopolized the markets of all major commodities. The national commercial capital was in the hands of smaller tradesmen who, though indispensable to economic life, were weak in strength and often landed themselves in difficult positions. As the country kept its door open to imperialist countries and tariffs were controlled by foreigners, China's commerce and industry also suffered heavy blows by a great influx of exotic commodities.

Contemporary Commerce

The establishment of socialist commerce

Socialist commerce is based on the ownership of the commercial capital by the public. Such commerce came into being as early as during the revolutionary war years. At that time there were two main forms: one was the publicly-owned shops, with funds provided by the government of the revolutionary base areas, and the other was co-operatives, with funds pooled by local people. These were the embryonic form of the present Chinese socialist commerce.

After the People's Republic of China was founded on 1 October 1949, the Administrative Council of the Central People's Government established a Ministry of Trade to take charge of domestic and external trade. In various provinces, autonomous regions and the centrally administered municipalities there were commercial bureaux or departments and at county level there were commercial sections. These formed a nationwide network for administering the country's commercial affairs. Later, the Ministry of Food was set up to administer trading activities in cereals. In July 1950 the Administrative Council set up a bureau to administer the nation's marketing and supply, consumption, credit and handicrafts producers' co-operatives.

There was a great development in state commerce after Liberation. First, the imperialist and bureaucratic bourgeoisie capital was confiscated, with the commercial capital absorbed as funds for state commerce. Then the State went on to appropriate funds to finance the state commerce. From March 1950 to 1951, the Ministry of Trade established specialized corporations to deal in cereals, native produce, coal, building materials, petroleum, daily necessities, table salt, cloth and industrial supplies. These corporations were headquartered in Beijing, with branches and subsidiaries in various provinces, autonomous regions and municipalities. They formed a strong state commercial network to handle wholesale and retail sales.

The co-operative commerce consisted mainly of supply and marketing co-operatives and consumer co-operatives. The consumer goods co-operatives in urban areas played a positive role in supplying the needs of the urban population, but with the growth of the state commerce, they were gradually phased out. The rural supply and marketing co-operatives served mainly the rural population. The number of such co-operatives grew to 35,096 in 1952, with a total membership of 147.96 million, a working staff of 1,002,000 and an operating fund of 664 million yuan. It has become a vast commercial network that links town and country.

Having a strong state commerce and strong co-operatives, the State proceeded to transform the capitalist and private commerce along socialist lines. Toward private wholesalers, the State adopted the policy of trying to push them aside and taking their place, forcing them to become agents of state wholesale commerce. As to private retailers, they were encouraged to form joint enterprises with the State.

The socialist transformation drive reached its peak in 1955 when large numbers of pedlars were organized into small co-operatives or co-operative shops and most of the private commerce became joint state–private enterprises. In the following year, the joint state-private enterprises were mostly turned into part of the state commerce, thus ending the socialist transformation drive. By the end of 1957, the retail sale volume in the whole country was 47,420,000,000 yuan. Of this, state retail sales were 29.43 billion yuan, accounting for 62.1 per cent; that of collective commerce was 7,780,000,000 yuan, accounting for 16.4 per cent; that of joint commerce was 7,600,000,000 yuan, accounting for 16 per cent; and that of private commerce was 1,290,000,000 yuan, accounting for 2.7 per cent.

The development of socialist commerce

Following the 1957 socialist transformation drive, socialist commerce in China developed into a massive commercial network, with the state commerce as the main body, assisted by the collective commerce and supplemented by the private sector. But under the influence of the "Leftist" deviation line, the socialist transformation drive went much too fast, with all the collective commerce nationalized and the number of private shops and retailers drastically reduced. This caused the initiative of commercial workers to fall and the quality of services to deteriorate. The cutting down of the numerous small shops made it inconvenient for the people. This situation continued until 1978, when the error was corrected at the Third Plenary Session of the Eleventh Central Committee of the CPC. Table 1 (see next page) shows the changes of the various sectors of socialist commerce over the past three decades.

As shown in Table 1, the retail sales increased by 4.6 times from 1952 to 1978, but the number of shops was reduced by three-fourths and employees by 37 per

Table 1: Changes in Socialist Commerce

Sector	1952		1957		1965		1978		1985	
	No.	%	No.	%	No.	%	No.	%	No.	%
Number of retail sale organizations (1,000)	4,200	100	1,953	100	881	100	1,048	100	7,783	100
State	130	3.1	521	26.7	346	39.3	357	34.1	229	2.9
Collective	–	–	1,019	52.2	249	28.3	583	55.6	1,362	17.5
Joint ownership	–	–	–	–	–	–	–	–	3	0.04
Private	4,070	96.9	413	21.1	286	32.4	108	10.3	6,189	79.5
Staff (retail) (1,000)	7,095	100	5,689	100	3,359	100	4,474	100	17,960	100
State	1,200	16.9	3,472	61.0	1,902	56.6	2,586	57.8	2,908	16.2
Collective			1,750	30.8	1,122	33.4	1,752	39.2	6,654	37.2
Private	5,895	83.1	467	8.2	355	10.0	136	3.0	8,369	46.6
Joint retail volume (million)	27,680	100	47,420	100	67,030	100	155,860	100	430,500	100
State	9,530	34.4	29,430	62.1	55,850	83.3	141,010	90.5	174,000	40.6
Collective	–	–	7,780	16.4	8,630	12.9	11,530	7.4	160,030	37.2
Joint ownership	110	0.4	7,600	16.0	–	–	–	–	1,270	0.3
Private	16,860	60.9	1,290	2.7	1,250	1.9	210	0.1	66,100	15.4
Farmer to non-farmer	1,180	4.3	1,320	2.8	1,300	1.9	3,110	2.0	29,190	6.8

cent. In 1978, the retail sales by state commerce accounted for 90.5 per cent, almost a state monopoly. From 1965 to 1978, the number of state retail staff rose from 1,902,00 to 2,586,000, an increase of 36 per cent, while the population of the country increased by 32.7 per cent during the same period, and the consumption level of residents rose by 33.39 per cent and the total industrial and agricultural output value rose by 190.3 per cent. Before 1957, there were a great number of small shops situated close to each other. But after 1957, the shops became bigger, fewer and further between. From 1978, the State encouraged all the collectives and individuals to go in for commerce, resulting in a fast development in the collective and private sectors. Though the percentage of state commerce dropped, it in no way affected its leading position, because all the major wholesale organizations belonged to the State and private wholesalers handled only small articles such as needles, thread and buttons. Most of the big and medium-sized shops were owned by the State.

The collective commerce, mainly the commercial co-operatives, constitutes an important part of socialist commerce. But this sector of commerce developed slowly under the influence of the notions that "private and co-operative enterprises are inferior to state-owned ones, and the higher the level of public ownership, the better". Many co-operative shops and groups became state shops, or shops owned by supply and marketing co-operatives, which were twice swallowed up by state commerce, in 1958 and 1969. This sector of commerce did not pick up speed in development until 1978.

The private sector of commerce is operated by individual labourers independently. Though privately owned, they are not capitalist in nature, but a useful supplement to the socialist commerce. In 1952, private commercial organizations accounted for 96.9

per cent of the total retail organizations, with the number of employees accounting for 83.1 per cent and total retail turnover accounting for 60.9 per cent. By the end of 1978, the number of private commercial organizations, employees and business turnover dropped to next to nothing. The percentage of this sector of the commerce began to rise only in recent years when the State adopted the policy of supporting its development. But the total business turnover of this sector accounted for only 15.4 per cent in 1985 and greater efforts are needed to encourage its development.

The jointly-owned commerce refers to the state–private joint enterprises before 1957. This sector began to expand from 1978 to cover enterprises formed by different departments, regions and ownerships. There are also joint ventures using Chinese and foreign investment. But such joint ventures are still small in number, with employees and business turnover accounting for less than three per cent. Such enterprises hold out great promise.

Mode of Operation of Chinese Commerce

Commerce is a tool to amass and distribute social wealth. The superiority of the socialist planned economy lies in its being able to utilize social wealth in a planned and effective way, to promote a rapid development of social production and to satisfy as much as possible the material and cultural needs of the people. Therefore, it is necessary for the State to provide direct or indirect guidance to the development of commerce through controlling different categories of commodities by different methods (including price control) and through the organization and reorganization of commercial establishments. The management policy and methods determine the mode of operation of Chinese commerce.

Tiered management system: Commodities are divided into three categories according to their importance to the national economy and the people's living and managed at three different levels. The first category, which has a great bearing on the national economy and people's living, is purchased and marketed in a unified manner by the State. Included in this category are mainly grain, edible oil, cotton and cotton cloth. The second category of commodities are secondary in importance, and include pigs, tea, cured tobacco and wool, and are managed by departments under the State Council. The third category covers those not covered by the first two categories. These goods are traded freely and managed by the State only indirectly. Such three-level management may ensure that the limited amount of commodities is fairly distributed and put into use in a balanced manner. The defect is that the management of the first two categories is too rigid to bring the initiatives of producers and shops into full play. Now, with the development of production, the State has gradually reduced the number of commodities covered by the first two categories. The number of goods under the planned management of the Ministry of Commerce has been reduced to 23. They include nine farm products: cereals, edible plant oil, cotton, cotton staple yarn, hemp and ramie, pigs, tea, sheep's wool and cowskin; and 14 manufactured goods: sugar, brand-name wine and liquors, cotton cloth, polyester-cotton fabrics, medium-long fibre cloth, woollen goods, detergent, rubber shoes, iron pots, round nails, zinc-plated lead wire, chemical fertilizer, pesticides and iron scraps.

Purchase of farm and sideline produce: Since the mid-1950s China has put major farm and sideline products under strictly planned management. By the end of 1959, the number of farm and sideline products under state unified purchase reached 222, divided into three categories, which were either purchased under unified planning or by imposing purchasing quotas, or purchased at negotiated prices. This system played its due role in ensuring the needs of the people and national construction in times of insufficiency of farm produce. But its defects began to show up later on: The too rigid control of too many products resulted in keeping the prices too low, so that there were not enough funds for development; the range or number of products covered by imposed quota purchase and unified planned purchase was so large (80 per cent of the total farm and sideline produce) that the initiative of the peasants was adversely affected; nearly all farm and sideline products were purchased and marketed by state commerce or by supply and marketing co-operatives, thus resulting in a monopoly which obstructed the smooth flow of commodities.

Since 1978, the State has drastically readjusted the policies and systems for purchasing farm and sideline produce.

– It has raised the purchasing prices for cereals and other farm and sideline products by a big margin. In 1979 alone the purchasing prices of grain rose by 20 per cent and 50 per cent more for the part exceeding the required amount. At the same time, the State has on several occasions readjusted the relative prices of grain, cotton and other farm and sideline produce to make them more reasonable.

– It has instituted the award system. Awards include payment in advance (a kind of support to agricultural production), purchase with awards (to supply sellers with some commodities in short supply), and extra prices for above-quota sales (extra prices are offered for the part above the required amount purchased by the State).

– It has allowed free trading in products covered by the third category and those of the first two categories above the required quotas at negotiated prices and through a variety of channels, including the state commercial departments, grassroots supply and marketing co-operatives, other collective commercial establishments, licensed private retailers and individual peasants.

– It has loosened control over rural market trade, opened peasant markets in cities and allowed free long distance haulage of goods for sale, by any state and collective commercial units or individuals without restrictions in administrative regions or distances.

– The State ceased to impose quotas on peasants, except for a few special varieties of goods, as of 1985. Instead, the State will buy farm and sideline produce from peasants by signing contracts in advance and from the market. The state monopoly of farm and sideline produce purchase that had been in force for more than three decades has come to an end. The contracts include short-term and long-term ones as well as purchasing and purchase-marketing ones. For products bought from the market, the State may offer either the listed prices or the market prices, and when the market prices are lower than the listed prices, the State will offer the listed prices.

Purchase of manufactured goods: Manufactured goods in China are purchased and marketed through two channels: the state materials allocation and supply department and the commercial department. The former handles mainly raw materials, machines and equipment needed in industrial production and capital construction; and the latter handles everyday consumer goods, some primary industrial and mineral products, subsidiary materials and equipment, parts, small tools and farm implements, pesticides and chemical fertilizer. Some of the products may be marketed by the producers themselves. The manufactured goods purchased by the commercial department account for one-third of the total industrial output value and two-thirds of the light industrial goods in terms of value, or about 70 per cent of the total retail sales of manufactured goods.

The purchase by the commercial department, known as unified purchase and exclusive sale, played a positive role in the course of economic development in China, but it has its defects: producers went on producing regardless of the needs of the market, while purchasers went on purchasing in disregard of the market demand. This method of purchase was changed, beginning from January 1981. While some products are still purchased exclusively by the commercial department, others are allowed to be bought in a planned manner, by contract or by selection. Products covered by unified purchase and marketing are produced according to state plans and bought at state listed prices. The planned purchase means that producers may sell their products according to pre-arranged plans, with the above-quota products sold by themselves. Purchase by contract requires producers and purchasers all to perform their duties according to contract. Other products will be bought by commercial departments on a selective basis. Industrial enterprises may entrust commercial departments to market their products. The reform provided incentives to both the commercial departments and manufacturers and stimulated the flow of manufactured goods. In the future, the number of products covered by unified purchasing and marketing and by planned purchasing will gradually be reduced, and the number of products covered by other methods of purchase will be increased. Both the purchasers and producers will behave according to market demand.

Commodity supply: The method of commodity supply hinges on market demand. During the 1950s, when China began to go in for large-scale economic development in a planned way and employment in urban and mining areas soared, plus the increases in the purchasing prices of farm and sideline produce and in the purchasing power of the people, many commodities were in short supply and a ration system was introduced in the supply of some commodities, especially grain, cotton, edible oil and cotton cloth. During the 1960s and 1970s, as China's economic development slowed down and commodities were in short supply, some special measures were taken in order to ensure the necessary needs of the people. The measures included: *issuance of tickets, ration books and coupons* for buying grain, edible oil, cloth, non-staple food and manufactured goods. The tickets and ration books were issued on an individual and a household basis respectively, while coupons were issued to urban workers and staff members for buying rationed manufactured goods. The number of commodities sold against tickets and coupons came to about 100 in 1962; *supply at high or negotiable prices.* While keeping the prices of most of the commodities stable, the State sold some commodities at higher than normal prices so as to meet the needs of some high-income families; *supply for special needs.* This was designed to ensure the needs and health of people engaged in special work. Commodities so supplied included mainly non-staple food.

After 1978, as the economy developed and farm and sideline produce increased, the shortage of commodities was eased and the number of tickets and coupons was gradually reduced. Now the ration system has basically been cancelled, except for grain and edible oil, for which the coupon system is still retained as a measure to prevent fraudulent purchase, because grain and edible oil are exclusively purchased and marketed by the State, with the purchasing prices higher than the selling prices.

Types of Chinese Commercial Enterprise

Chinese commercial enterprises are divided into state, collective, private and joint enterprises according to the nature of ownership of their capital. Functionally, they are divided into wholesale, retail and service enterprises. A company is formed by a number of commercial enterprises and there are a variety of companies according to what they handle, such as department store companies, fruit companies, hardware and electrical product companies, etc. which are referred to as specialized companies.

Specialized companies: The development of China's socialist commerce began with the establishment of specialized companies. When the Ministry of Trade was set up under the Administrative Council of the Central People's Government, it began to set up specialized companies, with their headquarters at the central level and subsidiaries at the provincial and county levels.

A specialized company is usually formed by all kinds of commercial enterprises, covering such work as wholesale, retail sale, storage, transportation, warehouses and trading centres. With strong economic power, it may plan and undertake the development of national or regional commercial networks and direct the flow of commodities.

Wholesale enterprises: Chinese wholesale enterprises form a three-tier system. Those set up by national companies are the top level wholesalers, known as the procurement and supply stations. Those belonging to provincial subsidiary companies are at the second level, called the second level procurement and supply stations. And those affiliated to county or city companies, which have direct business relations with retailers, are the third level procurement and supply stations. Such a three-tiered wholesale system was deemed necessary as China has a vast territory and production, especially of everyday necessities, during the 1950s was concentrated in a few big cities such as Shanghai, Tianjin, Beijing and Guangzhou.

But gradually, the defects of the system began to reveal themselves. As each specialized company has its own wholesale stations, they have to handle too many products to ensure meticulous management. At the same time, the specialized companies are administered by commercial administrative departments and each level of administration has a wholesale organization. This results in a circuitous movement of commodities, which causes a great waste in manpower and material resources. These problems are being solved in the course of the current economic reforms.

Retail sale enterprises: Chinese retail sale enterprises are divided into large, medium-sized and small ones according to the size of their staff, annual turnover and profits. They are further divided into all-inclusive shops and specialized shops. Generally, large shops are set up in city centres, medium-sized shops are established in places where purchasing power is concentrated, and smaller ones are sited in places nearest the consumers for their convenience. Large shops play the backbone role in the whole retail network, while the medium-sized and small shops, which are extensively distributed, are the priority for development, especially at present, when the number of shops is too few to meet the growing needs. All efforts – state, collective or private – are being encouraged to run medium-sized and small retail shops.

Trading warehouses: These are the middlemen or intermediaries that act as agencies for purchasing, marketing, storing and transportation to help enterprises or units accomplish the procurement and marketing tasks in the fastest possible time. Such establishments date back to ancient times. In the Han dynasty (206 BC–AD 220), there was *Zang Kuai*, which acted as a broker in the animal trade. During the Sui dynasty (581–617), there appeared *Di Dian*, which provided warehouses and lodgings for merchants. Up to the late Qing dynasty (after 1840) such establishments appeared in large numbers and became independent commercial enterprises. After New China was founded, the rural supply and marketing co-operatives set up a large number of trading warehouses for transporting and marketing farm and sideline produce, playing a positive role in facilitating the flow of commodities between town and country. At present, there are more than 1,000 trading warehouses in China and the number is still growing.

Trading centres: These are new, coming into being only from 1984. They mainly serve the needs of enterprises and units engaged in bulk trade. The

The supermarket run by Guangzhou Friendship Store.
(Photo by Chen Yusi)

centres provide: counters, halls and other facilities and sites for displaying products; facilities for keeping and transporting commodities; meeting rooms for business negotiations; information and consulting services; food and lodging. The trading centres are usually financed by rural supply and marketing co-operatives and various specialized companies. Most of the farm and sideline produce trading centres are established by the supply and marketing co-operatives and all the industrial goods trading centres are set up by specialized companies. The centres are still doing wholesale business instead of solely providing service, because their service facilities are inadequate and the service skills of the staff are not high enough. They are mostly situated in commodity collection and distribution centres near hubs of communications. All major cities, such as Chongqing in Sichuan, Wuhan in Hubei province and Guangzhou, Shanghai and Tianjin, have trading centres.

Catering and Service Trades

Catering and service trades are an ancient industry in China. The ancient *Yi Zhou Shu* (Book of Zhou) records that in about the 11th century BC King Wen of Zhou put up a notice to the effect that all business people were welcome to Western Zhou, and that Western Zhou would provide vehicles, boats and lodging and other conveniences so that business people would feel at home. *Zhou Li* (The Rites of Zhou), the writings of the Warring States period (475 BC–221 BC), records that along all roads, there was an inn every ten *li* (about half a kilometre) which provided food, a lodging place with rooms and grain storage every 30 *li*, and a marketplace every 50 *li* which provided lodging and food. This service and catering trade underwent some development in the protracted feudalistic society after the Qin dynasty, though people tended to serve themselves. At that time there were tea houses, restaurants and small hotels, as well as *Ya Hang* (places provided by the brokers), *Di Dian* (hostels) and warehouses to serve the needs in the flow of commodities. But they operated on a small scale, offering a limited number of service items.

After the founding of New China, the State did not pay enough attention to the development of commerce and many catering and service establishments merged or shifted to other trades in the course of the socialist transformation drive. The industry did not pick up until 1979. Table 2 (see next page) shows changes in the catering and service trades:

The service trades cover hotels, baths, barber's shops, laundry, photographic studios and repairs, which are closely related to the people's life. Before 1978, the number of catering and service units and staff members plummeted, creating difficulties in finding a hotel, eating out, having one's hair dressed and one's clothes washed in many major cities. The

Table 2: Changes in the Catering and Service Trades (Unit: 1,000)

Year	Total		Catering		Service trades	
	Number	Staff	Number	Staff	Number	Staff
1952	1,300	2,434	850	1,454	450	980
1957	750	1,925	470	1,155	280	770
1965	405	1,762	217	1,022	188	740
1978	207	1,604	117	1,044	90	560
1979	281	2,278	145	1,394	136	884
1980	559	2,891	299	1,765	260	1,126
1981	915	3,596	477	2,113	438	1,483
1982	1,225	4,212	628	2,388	597	1,824
1983	1,817	4,987	877	2,713	940	2,274
1984	2,435	6,196	1,141	3,221	1,294	2,975
1985	2,887	7,303	1,353	3,764	1,534	3,539

State made little investment and fixed very low prices for the services and labour. The trade as a whole could make little profit or was even running at a loss. The income of the workers was too low to provide adequate incentives for quality service.

After the Third Plenum of the Eleventh Central Committee of the Communist Party of China was held toward the end of 1978, the State put on the agenda the problems of how to solve the difficulties encountered by people in their daily life. At the same time, the State recognized that the socialist economy was also a commodity economy, which calls for the development of the catering and service trades that will provide a better living environment for people to exchange commodities. Therefore, preferential treatment was granted as part of the State's efforts to support the development of the catering and service trades. Income tax was reduced to 15 per cent, the ceiling on prices was raised, catering and service enterprises were allowed to fix their own prices, and the self-employed, collectives and state enterprises were encouraged to go in for catering and service trades. These changes accounted for the big development in this sector of the economy after 1979.

Development trend of catering and services

The traditional service trades, such as catering, hotels, baths, hairdressing, laundry, photography and repairs, are small in number and poorly equipped and managed, and need further development and improvement in service quality. With the development in production and technological progress, the rising service trade, such as tourism, information and consultation will also be developed.

While the traditional service trade must add more enterprises and people, it should be equipped with modern technology and equipment. Modern kitchen utensils serve both to improve productivity and economic results and also to ensure hygienic operations and nutritious food while helping retain and develop the traditional Chinese cuisine. For other services, modern equipment is also a major factor in high level service. In recent years, the service trade has imported some modern technology and equipment.

Service management should also be modernized for higher work efficiency and economic results. This has been done over the past few years, with some advanced managerial experiments introduced into Chinese service enterprises. While it is important to introduce advanced foreign technology and equipment, it is more important to develop China's own research to catch up with the rest of the world. Chinese service trade, a part of the cultural heritage of the nation, is noted for its wealth of experience, especially in the catering trade. If properly summed up and developed with modern science and technology, it would make a major contribution to the people of both China and the rest of the world.

The development of new items of services must suit the actual needs of the country. A technological consulting service, for instance, should be so developed as to make it possible to organize all the possible technical forces and to provide practicable and efficient services for society and its enterprises.

The catering and service trade should gradually be spread from urban to rural areas where most of the population lives. According to 1984 statistics, there were 1,499,000 catering and service organizations in the countryside, with a total employment of 2,577,000 people. This meant that each organization had to serve 470 people and each employee had to serve 273. This situation calls for a bigger development in the rural catering and service trade.

Ways to expand the catering and service trade

The Chinese government has adopted the following policies to support the catering and service trade:

– *To encourage all sectors – state, collective and private – to go into this trade.* The State, with more financial resources, may run bigger and better-equipped enterprises to satisfy the needs of large consumers. Collectives and individual persons are encouraged to concentrate their efforts on running small or mobile enterprises to take their service centres near to the consumers in order to satisfy the needs of ordinary consumers. Most of the hairdressing shops, repair centres, bathhouses, laundries and photographic studios are run by collectives and individuals and

The First National Technical Achievement Fair.　*(Photo by Yang Wumin)*

scattered throughout the whole city. The small catering and service establishments run by the State are being shifted to collective ownership and management and some have been leased or contracted to individuals. This policy also encourages joint ventures with foreign investors and domestic partners, irrespective of regions, trades and nature of ownership.

 – *To support the trade to support itself.* After the completion of the socialist transformation of private enterprises, the State began to levy low taxes on the catering and service trade so that it would have more money to sustain development. From 1985, the State went further to relax control over prices and allow the catering and service enterprises to fix their own prices according to market demand so that they would not suffer losses owing to the fact that the State had fixed the prices subjectively.

 – *To allow a special wage system to provide more incentives to the service workers.* From 1956, the State instituted the wage system in the service and catering trade owned by private–state enterprises, and later in state-owned enterprises, by which the workers got the normal wages plus bonuses or time rate plus dividends of profits. Each service enterprise is allowed to retain part of its profits according to the size of the profit it makes, which is divided up among the workers as a reward for more work done.

 – *To encourage factories and government offices to open their own services.* In China, many factories, enterprises and government institutions have their own service organizations, which are better equipped. They include hostels, hotels, barber's shops, nurseries, kindergartens, hospitals or clinics, canteens or food shops and baths. These often operate under capacity: the Government therefore encourages them to open these services to the public so as to ease the strain on public services.

 – *To train competent personnel.* The catering and service trade requires its personnel to have a high level of technology. A chef, for instance, is required to have the skills of mixing the raw ingredients, cutting, cooking and the making of food with excellent colour, taste, smell and shape. A television repairman has to master all the necessary skills in the making of a television. Therefore, the training of personnel is the key to better catering and services. Apart from the institutes of higher learning and the intermediate professional schools, which train senior and intermediate levels of special personnel, in-service training is also necessary.

The catering and services trade is only part of tertiary industry. In promoting tertiary industry, China not only concentrates its efforts on catering and services, but it is also committed to the development of services to facilitate the flow of commodities.

Reform of the Commercial and Service Management System

The reform of the commercial and service management system is part of the overall economic reform in China. The focus of the reform is to relax control and change the rigid pattern characteristic of the past so as to inject greater vigour into the industry.

Separating administration from business operation

This aims at invigorating the commercial and service establishments. The commerce and service trade in China is socialist in nature. Over the past three decades and more, there have been twists and turns with regard to the relationship between administration and business operations, but basically the two were combined into one, which resulted in the weakening of the functions of the enterprises and the growing strength of administrative organs, this leading in turn to official commerce, bottlenecks in the flow of commodities and a decline in the development of the commerce as a whole.

To separate administration from business operation is to change the nature of the Ministry of Commerce and local commercial departments and bureaux, making them purely administrative organs for managing domestic commerce, instead of directing and managing specific enterprises, that is, of interfering in the operational activities of commercial organizations. Nor will they collect profits from them. On the other hand, the commercial and service establishments are given more decision-making powers to make them independent, with the status of "legal persons", instead of being appendages of administrative organs. Specific measures to this end include:

– *Gradual reduction of the mandatory targets and an increase in the range for guidance plans.* In the past, mandatory targets were imposed on commercial enterprises for purchase, marketing, storage, profits and losses, working capital and expenses, which had to be fulfilled regardless of the actual circumstances of the enterprises themselves. Often the targets for profits were imposed before those for purchase and marketing, thus placing enterprises at a loss as to what to do. Now this has been changed. Apart from a few major categories of commodities, which still require mandatory plans, all the rest may be managed by the enterprises themselves under the guidance of the State.

– *Relaxation of price control.* In the past, all prices were fixed by the State. Now a variety of prices are allowed. They include the state listed prices for some major products, basic prices with a floor and ceiling and negotiated prices. Under this price system, commercial enterprises have the power to fix prices on most of their commodities for sale, thus paving the way for letting enterprises be responsible for their own losses and profits.

– *Changing profit delivery into tax payment.* Commercial enterprises used to deliver both taxes and profits to the State. Now they are required to deliver tax only; profits after tax are left to their own discretion. With the financial power, the enterprises will be able to seek their own survival and development.

– *Allotting more power to enterprises in employment, wages and bonuses.* In the past, all these decisions were made by state administrative departments. Now enterprises have the power to appoint their own personnel, recruit or dismiss their own workers and issue wages and bonuses according to the performances of the workers and the operation of the enterprises.

Institution of the management responsibility system

This system was introduced from 1981 in both state and collective enterprises. At first, the enterprises contracted for profit targets, which are contracted to groups or individuals. If they succeeded in fulfilling the targets, they were rewarded; should they fail, they were punished. The same is true of the subcontractors within the enterprises. Bonuses were drawn from the after-tax profits. The more they drew, the more bonuses each worker got. But this proved to be not so successful, because it was difficult to set the targets for profits and it did not define the responsibilities shared by the enterprises for the capital and assets they possessed, and was liable to create a false impression of fulfilling the profit targets. Later, it was changed into a system with the size of capital as the yardstick for profits, a system that encourages enterprises to seek profits by rationally utilizing the capital, thus preventing the seeking of profits at the expense of socialist public funds and property. In carrying out the responsibility system, the administrative department in charge or other units responsible are required to make a comprehensive assessment of the enterprise.

Assessment includes statistics, supervision and analysis of various economic indices for all aspects of business operations and disciplinary and behavioural conventions, such as the observation of rules of services and operational rules. The assessment is done on a yearly or monthly basis and measures for punishment and reward are taken. The clear distinction between punishments and rewards and linking economic benefits with responsibilities provides the motive force for the smooth implementation of the responsibility system, which is, in essence, to tie responsibility, terms of reference and interests of the business executives and workers together.

Removing the barriers between cities and the countryside and promoting the free flow of commodities

From 1982, China changed the old commodity handling system characterized by a clear distinction between state commerce and the rural supply and marketing co-operatives and introduced a new system in which state commerce is allowed to do business in the countryside and rural supply and marketing co-operatives are allowed to come to cities. Some cities also decided to allow rural marketing co-operatives to open shops in cities and city shops to be leased or sold to rural supply and marketing co-operatives. The state commercial organizations are allowed to set up subsidiary wholesale organizations in the countryside or form joint enterprises with supply and marketing co-operatives or make the co-operatives as their agencies. Many places engage in mobile trade, sending carts loaded with goods to trade fairs, or ask rural co-operatives to sell and store their goods to stimulate the flow of commodities to the countryside.

Promoting lateral ties

This practice has caught on only in recent years and has developed very rapidly. Ties assume a variety of forms: among commercial enterprises; between commercial and industrial, agricultural enterprises; between wholesalers and retailers; among big enterprises; or among big, medium-sized and small ones; among enterprises of different ownerships or among enterprises in different regions. The co-operation is carried out on a voluntary basis, each maintaining its own independence. Such co-operation has resulted in a variety of enterprise groups which have played a positive role in knocking down administrative and regional barriers, smoothing out the flow of commodities, expanding markets and rational utilization of capital, technology and economical use of working capital and, above all, bringing convenience to the people.

Reform of the wholesale system

This is the focus of China's commercial reform. Major steps have been taken over the past few years. These include: disbanding commercial companies which are administrative in nature and establishing a wholesale network between cities, leaving the original top-level and second-level procurement and marketing stations to related cities to become local wholesale organizations; establishing wholesale fairs and trading centres to put an end to the former fixed purchasing and marketing relationships and the restrictions between regions, thus changing the closed-type operations into the open type. This makes it possible for wholesale enterprises to enter the market as equals with others in trading; allowing industrial and agricultural enterprises (including individual peasants) to sell their own products and encouraging collective commercial enterprises to engage in wholesale. Even private pedlars began to go into wholesale of small commodities, thus ending the state monopoly, forming a commodity flow system with the participation of all sectors through a variety of channels and fewer intermediate links while maintaining the dominant position of the state wholesale commerce.

A livestock fair in Yao'an county, Yunnan province. *(Photo by Zhou Zhongyao)*

But still the responsibility of commodity handling seems roughly divided and there are too few wholesale enterprises with too few people to offer efficient services for production and retail sales. Statistics showed that in 1984 there were only 239,000 wholesale organizations, 3.6 per cent of the 6,715,000 retail shops, and the number of people in the wholesale trade was only 2,618,000, as against 15,330,000 in the retail trade, and some wholesale organizations also undertake retail sales. All this calls for further reforms and the solution to the problem of rationalization of the operational organizations and the mode of operation.

Reform of the retail system

Much has been done over the past few years to add more retail shops, invigorate shop operations and open up more channels for the flow of commodities. Measures taken include: encouraging all quarters to open retail shops, including collectives, individuals and various other enterprises and factories; instituting a management responsibility system in big and medium-sized enterprises to tie economic interests to the performance of individual workers and the enterprises themselves while shifting the management of small commercial enterprises from the hands of the State to those of collectives, or transferring their ownership from that of the State into that of collectives or contracting out or leasing them to individuals or groups; lifting the restrictions on the places and wholesalers from which the grassroots shops get their goods. This makes it possible for shops to choose their wholesalers without being restricted by administrative divisions or the range of goods.

Reform of the rural supply and marketing co-operatives

The Chinese rural supply and marketing co-operatives were formed by peasants who contributed their funds as shares and with the support of the Government, that is, their funds came from both individual peasants

Shops in Guangzhou: Huangshanghuang Cured Food Store (1) and (2); a pork market (3); a seafood store in Zhuhai (4).

and the State. In the 1950s they were collectively owned economic organizations, but in 1958, under the influence of the "Leftist" deviation line, the co-operatives were shifted to public ownership, becoming in fact part of the state commerce. This lasted until January 1983, when the Central Committee of the Communist Part of China reaffirmed in its document "Problems of the Present Rural Economic Policies" that the grassroots supply and marketing co-operatives should regain their collective nature and expand the range of their operations and scope of services to become comprehensive service centres capable of providing services in supply and marketing, processing of farm and sideline produce, storage and transportation techniques, and the county supply and marketing co-operatives should become federations of grassroots supply and marketing co-operatives. Steps were then taken to restore the mass character organizationally, democracy in management and flexibility in operations. Organizationally, stocks were taken to reaffirm the shares of each member and recruit new members. This brought the share capital of national co-operatives to 2,200,000,000 yuan by the end of 1985 from about 350,000,000 yuan, which had remained unchanged from 1954 to 1981. The number of members soared to 140,000,000 and working staff members to four million. The number of grassroots supply and marketing co-operatives came to 35,000, with a combined capital of 30,000,000,000 yuan, and their annual sales volume was about 100,000,000,000 yuan.

In management, they resumed the democratic practices. Members are free to join and leave, and grassroots co-operatives are also free to join county co-operatives according to the principle of mutual benefit. The leading bodies of the national, provincial and county co-operatives, as well as grassroots co-operatives, are elected through congresses, which also elect councils and supervisory bodies.

Much has been done in recent years to restore flexible business operations according to the needs of their members. Now the supply and marketing co-operatives actively promote sales of farm and sideline products for the peasants. It was estimated that about 20 to 30 per cent of the goods purchased are farm and sideline produce, and that the amount of major farm products, such as cotton, tea, cured tobacco, ramie and hemp, accounts for over 90 per cent of the country's total purchase. The supply and marketing co-operatives sell most of the manufactured goods in the countryside, about 40 to 50 per cent of the total rural retail sales.

In many ways, such co-operatives have broken with the old practice with regard to division of labour. They have knocked down the barriers between the city and the countryside, organizing the supply of farm and sideline produce to cities and taking manufactured goods down to the countryside. In the past they refused to engage in wholesale of manufactured

Dried salted ducks from Nan'an in Jiangsu province.

everyday-use goods. Now the restrictions have been lifted and they also invest in farm and sideline processing factories, building farms, developing foreign trade and helping rural areas to develop commodity production and opening up markets, and providing services in processing, transportation, storage, repairs, technical guidance and delivery of information.

Prospects for the Development of China's Commerce and Service Trades

Important as they are, the Chinese commerce and service trades make up a very small proportion of the national economy. In 1984, for instance, the total value of commercial services (including catering, supply and marketing of materials, but not hairdressing, baths, photography and hotel services) accounted for only 5.2 per cent of the total value of all trades and services. The major task for the future, therefore, is to concentrate on the development of commerce and services.

The general goal

As the goal of the total industrial and agricultural output value is to quadruple that of 1980 by the end of this century, the total retail sales will have to reach 1,000,000,000,000 yuan, with the midway goal of 600,000,000,000 to 700,000,000,000 yuan by 1990 when the Seventh Five-Year Plan period ends. The structure of the people's consumption will also change. In 1980, of the 179,400,000,000 yuan in retail sales, 51.2 per cent were food, 23.1 were clothing, 22 per cent were articles for daily use, 3.8 per cent were fuel and the rest were non-commodity articles. By the end of the century, the average per capita income is expected to increase more than twofold. By then, expenditure on food will drop to 45 per cent, on clothing it will rise to 24 per cent and on articles for everyday use it will be up to 27 per cent. This will require tremendous changes in the scale and structure of commodity circulation on the market. Yet the present capacity of Chinese commerce and services is only slightly bigger than one-sixth of what is required by the end of this century. So the volume of domestic trade and services from 1980 to 2000 has to be doubled and redoubled and the commerce and services have to be developed ahead in order to pave the way for the development of commodity production.

Measures for attaining the goal

First of all, it is necessary to solve the financial resources problem. While making investment itself, the State will encourage collectives and individuals to pool funds. In addition, the Government will support some commercial and service enterprises in issuing stocks. This has already been done by the Tianqiao Department Store in Beijing, which has become a joint stock company, with shares held by the State, the bank, the department store and individuals in the ratio of 50.97 per cent, 25.8 per cent, 19.68 per cent and 3.46 per cent. The Wuhan Zhongnan Department Store issued bonds with interests and prizes, which is also a way to collect idle funds. The Chinese government will continue to encourage foreign businessmen to run joint ventures or co-operative enterprises with Chinese commercial and service enterprises or run their own commercial and service enterprises. This is a long-term policy of the Chinese government.

Secondly, it is imperative to accelerate the pace of modernization of commerce and service trades. At present, most of the commercial and service enterprises use manual labour. Therefore, the government will require all industrial departments to produce more and better machinery and equipment for commercial and service enterprises and at the same time import some new technology and equipment best suited to Chinese conditions to accelerate technological transformation. During the Seventh Five-Year Plan period, the State will commit itself to transforming a number of large and medium-sized commercial enterprises step by step. This will also include introduction of modern methods of management to replace the present management by rule of thumb.

Thirdly, efforts will be made to build more commercial and service establishments. It is expected that by 1990, the number of retail shops, restaurants, hotels and other service facilities will come to 25 million, double the 1985 figure, and the number in employment will reach 50 million, nearly double the 1985 figure.

Fourthly, great efforts will be made to train personnel and raise the quality and competence of the workers in the commercial and service trade, who are required to master modern technology and equipment and management. The Government is making great efforts to expand higher, secondary education and on-the-job training while sending students abroad to pursue further studies and inviting foreign experts to China on lecture tours.

Fifthly, efforts are being made to deepen the present reform of the management system in commerce and services, which is the key to a big development in commerce and services. The objective is to lay a sound foundation for an economic management system with distinct Chinese characteristics during the Seventh Five-Year Plan period (1986–1990) aimed at invigorating and revitalizing commerce and services, promoting the flow of commodities and production to meet the needs of a planned commodity economy.

9. ENTERPRISES

Enterprises in Old China

IN old China enterprises were underdeveloped. In 1949, when the People's Republic was founded, there were only 250,000 in the whole country, with fixed assets and circulating funds totalling less than 40 billion yuan. Since most of them were under the control of bureaucrat capitalists, they were marked by poor equipment, backward technology, low output, unbalanced product mix and irrational geographical distribution. As regards product mix, the proportion of consumer goods and mineral products outstripped that of means of production and manufactured goods. Of the total industrial output value in 1949, light industry accounted for 73.6 per cent while heavy industry stood at only 26.4 per cent. Of the heavy industrial output value, machine building – mostly repairing – accounted for two per cent, with the rest mainly coming from minerals. Seventy per cent of the enterprises were located in the cities on the east coast and the Yangtze river valley. In the vast area of China's west there were only some 300 factories and mines, whose output value accounted for 10 per cent of the national total.

Enterprises in the People's Republic

Since its founding in 1949 New China has gone through six five-year plans, during which time its enterprises have developed in quantity and quality. By the end of 1985 China had 463,200 industrial enterprises. In commerce and service trades there were 288,000 units engaged in wholesale of industrial goods and purchase of farm and sideline products, 7.783 million retail enterprises, 1.353 million catering enterprises, and 1.534 million enterprises engaged in other service trades, altogether making the social retail value up to 430.5 billion yuan. As for the agricultural sector, there were 2,055 state-owned enterprises engaged in farming, in addition to 1.569 million township enterprises employing local peasants. There were also a large number of enterprises related to posts and telecommunications, construction, banking, foreign trade, tourism, culture and public health. All these constitute the essential part of China's socio-economic life and undertake the bulk of commodity production, circulation and services. Enterprises owned by the whole people had fixed assets worth 800.49 billion yuan in 1985, 32.3 times the 1952 figure.

Among the various kinds, industrial enterprises are the most outstanding in strength and growth rate. They came to 463,200 by the end of 1985, with a total output value of 875.6 billion yuan, which accounted for 53.7 per cent of the national social product and showed a 3,000 per cent increase over the national industrial output value in 1952.

In economic construction, the People's Republic has attached importance to rationalizing geographical distribution and industrial structure. Over the past 30 years or more, while bringing the old enterprises in the coastal areas into full play and constantly expanding and upgrading them, the Government has built up industrial bases in North-East, Central, North, North-West and South-West China, and since 1967 industrial development has also been stepped up in the inland provinces. Meanwhile, there has been a remarkable development in transport, posts and telecommunications, commerce and service trades in those areas. By 1985, industrial enterprises in China's hinterland had surpassed the coastal areas in terms of number, fixed assets and employees. In terms of industrial output value, however, the interior areas, marked by a high proportion of semi-finished products and heavy industry and by lower productivity in the new industrial bases, accounted for about 40 per cent of the national total, lower than the coastal areas benefiting from better technology and more finished products and light industries. There is also a gap between the two areas in commerce, transport, telecommunications and services. But the gap, by and large, has been narrowed.

Types of Ownership

Enterprises under ownership by the whole people

The means of production and funds are owned by the whole of the people, and managed by the State on behalf of the people through administrative and economic organizations at different levels. Therefore they are also called state-owned enterprises which, as China's economic backbone, form the overwhelming majority in all sectors except agriculture. By the end of 1985, the state-owned enterprises had fixed assets worth 800.49 billion yuan – 32.3 times more than in 1952, a year marking the nation's economic recovery. Altogether they employed 89.9 million workers, accounting for 72.7 per cent of the national total.

Gross industrial output value for the same year from state-owned enterprises amounted to 584.02 billion yuan, about 70.4 per cent of the national total. The retail value of the state-owned commercial enterprises was 174 billion yuan, or 40.4 per cent of the nation's social commodity retail value. All turnover of the posts and telecommunications services and 95 per cent of the turnover of the transportation business also came from the state-owned enterprises. Thus production and circulation of all the major products vital to the national economy and people's life are done by state-owned enterprises, which are in the leading and dominant position in the national economy.

Enterprises under collective ownership

These are economic organizations set up during the period of socialist transformation of the individual agricultural economy, the individual handicraft industry and small businesses in the 1950s. They are also organizations of urban and rural working people on the basis of voluntary participation and mutual benefit. Therefore, side by side with the state-owned enterprises, they are called enterprises under public ownership. Their means of production and funds are owned by groups of working people who have the freedom to independently allocate the property and products of their own enterprises and independently conduct economic activities, under the leadership of the government departments concerned and the guidance of the state plan, assuming sole responsibility for profit or loss. They are usually small, labour-intensive and varied in business, and need less funds. The material interests of the workers are closely related to the economic performance of the enterprises. As a result, they can organize production flexibly in accordance with social needs and with the local resources and labour force, and effectively enlarge employment and bring the initiative of the workers into full play. The Government therefore protects and encourages collective-owned enterprises, providing them with guidance and help. In China today there are urban and rural collective enterprises. By the end of 1985, urban collective enterprises employed 33.24 million people, accounting for 26.9 per cent of the national total and playing an important role in urban employment and economic life. The rural collectively-owned enterprises are established mainly by peasants who are no longer farming but still stay in the countryside; by the end of 1985, there were 1.569 million rural township enterprises employing 41.52 million people and producing 182.7 billion yuan worth of goods. The development of these enterprises has promoted the growth of the rural commodity economy and of rural science and education. Moreover, they have increased the rural ability for self-development and helped narrow the difference between town and country. This has helped keep large numbers of peasants from going to the cities as surplus labourers, a possibility which would have led to the lopsided expansion of the urban areas.

Enterprises under private ownership

These are small businesses owned by individual working men and women and are based on households which own the means of production as well as possessing the necessary funds. They have the freedom to allocate products and earnings after taxation. Most are involved in commodity production, circulation and service trades. At present, this sector embraces mainly rural households specializing in one occupation or another or in side-line production, urban households engaged in industry and handicraft, and small businesses – including private stores and peddlers in the street. These enterprises, within the framework of law, are a necessary and useful supplement to the state-owned and collectively-owned enterprises. The State provides guidance, help and supervision of their operation through administrative means. By the end of September 1985, there were 11.224 million households engaged in private industry and commerce, with a total of 16.697 million employees. Of these, 2.67 million households with 3.626 million employees were in the cities and towns, and 8.554 million households with 13.071 million employees were in the countryside. Altogether they had 15.06 billion yuan of funds, with an average of 1,342 yuan for each household. The total turnover amounted to 176.3 billion yuan, an average of 1,570 yuan for each household. Their annual retail volume was 28.81 billion yuan, accounting for 8.6 per cent of China's total retail of social product.

Joint ventures

Joint ventures are jointly run by two or more units under different types of ownership, with funds, equipment and technology from each in accordance with agreements. There are such joint ventures between state-owned enterprises and collectively-owned enterprises, and between Chinese and foreign businesses. Joint ventures between state and collective enterprises are usually operated under the leadership of the government departments concerned. Based on joint operation and accounting, some of them share profits according to the amount of each partner's investment. Others, based on joint operation but independent accounting, divide profits between partners after each paying profits or taxes to the State according to requirements. They represent a developing trend, although there are not yet very many and their output is very limited. Sino-foreign joint ventures are enterprises in China with investment from Chinese concerns and foreign economic organizations or individuals. Based on equality and mutual benefit, the investors share profits in accordance with the relevant Chinese laws or regulations and agreements signed by the two sides. Joint operation binds together the Chinese and foreign investors, who have to share both risks and outcome – profit or loss. The foreign investors' legitimate rights and interests are protected by Chinese law. These enterprises have been increasing every year in number and scale.

Enterprises with exclusive foreign investment

These are set up in China by foreign enterprises and other economic organizations or individuals in accordance with Chinese law. Foreign investors are responsible for their investment, operation and accounting, as well as for profits or losses. Their property is owned by the foreign investors. This is a form China has been using to attract foreign investment since its opening to the rest of the world. Most such enterprises are located in China's special economic zones, especially in Shenzhen (Guangdong province). It seems certain that the continuous implementation of China's open policy will bring more and more such enterprises.

In a country like China, with a vast territory, backward economy, regions with different levels of development, complicated social needs and a multi-layer productivity structure, a variety of kinds of ownership, with ownership by the whole people playing the leading role, will co-exist for a long time to come.

Classification of Industrial Enterprises According to Size

Industrial enterprises are classified as large, medium and small according to the capacity of production and equipment and the value of their fixed assets. The standards of classification, however, have varied in different periods. According to those worked out by the State Planning Commission in April 1978 and partly revised in December 1979, by the end of 1985 China had 2,300 large industrial enterprises, account-

The auto-control centre in the project to make 300,000 tons of ethylene in Daqing, Heilongjiang province. When the project is running, 17 varieties of chemical materials amounting to 500 thousand tons, with a value of over one billion yuan, will be produced here each year.
(Photo by Hu Wei)

ing for 0.5 per cent of the total; 5,600 medium-sized ones, 1.2 per cent; and 455,300 small ones, 98.3 per cent. Of these, the large and medium-sized enterprises produced 46.2 per cent of the national industrial output value, and handed over to the State over 60 per cent of the country's total industrial taxes. This shows that these two types of enterprise play a decisive role in the national economy. However, not all the enterprises are well equipped. In every business trade there are a number of small enterprises with advanced equipment. Adjustments made to the enterprises since 1980 have brought about a situation in which large enterprises continue to play the key role, but enterprises of all three sizes co-operate with and supplement each other.

Management of Enterprises through the State

Functions of the State

To lead and organize economic construction is one of the functions of the socialist state. The state institutions exercise the necessary control, through economic, administrative and legal means, over state-owned and collectively-owned enterprises and other economic sectors in accordance with the needs of developing the national economy in a planned and proportionate way. This aims to ensure coordinated and effective operation of the enterprises, avoid or diminish oversight, and create even more social wealth to meet the requirements of socialist construction and the people's growing material and cultural needs. State control over enterprises through the established managerial system reflects the relations between the State and the enterprises in responsibilities, powers and interests.

Forms of state management

State management can take any one of four forms:
– Management of state-owned enterprises is exercised either by the central or the local government. An alternative is joint management by the central and local governments with one of the two playing the leading role, depending on precise circumstances.
– Management of collectively-owned enterprises is conducted through different levels of authorities. Bigger and better-equipped enterprises in the cities are under the management of relevant government departments of provinces, municipalities, and autonomous regions and counties. The departments of urban districts or town governments look after smaller ones run by communities. The rural township enterprises are under the control of an office at the appropriate government level, called the rural industry administrative bureau. Handicraft enterprises under collective ownership are submitted to the control of the

handicraft administrative bureaux or the second light industry bureaux of local governments.

– Private enterprises are under the management of the local administrations for industry and commerce.

– Sino-foreign joint ventures and enterprises with sole foreign investment are under the management of relevant government departments of the special economic zones (if they are located there). In other areas they are directed by the foreign economic relations and trade department of the local government. The central responsibility is that of the Ministry of Foreign Economic Relations and Trade or departments authorized by the State Council.

State institutions in charge of economic management

The number and functions of ministries and commissions set up by the Central Government after the founding of the People's Republic vary in different periods. According to the organizational system adopted in June 1983 at the Sixth National People's Congress, China's legislature, the country has 45 ministries and commissions. Among these are administrative organizations that lead, control and supervise the country's enterprises of all kinds, including the ministries of metallurgy, petroleum, coal, chemicals, machine-building, nuclear power, aviation, electronics, ordnance, textiles and light industry; ministries of water resources and electric power, astronautics, geology and minerals, railways, communications, posts and telecommunications, agriculture, animal husbandry and fisheries, forestry, commerce, foreign economic relations and trade, and urban and rural development and environmental protection; the state planning, economic, science and technology commissions, the state commission for restructuring the economy, the commission for science, technology and industry for national defence, as well as the ministries of labour and personnel and finance, the auditing administration and the People's Bank of China. In the provinces, municipalities and autonomous regions there are departments and bureaux corresponding to the central ministries and commissions. Responsible for local enterprises, they are under the guidance of the relevant ministries or commissions. There are also a number of national and regional companies involved in such trades as ship-building, automobiles, petrochemicals, non-ferrous metals, tobacco, salt, silk, packaging and fodder processing. As enterprises themselves, they lead and supervise enterprises subordinate to them.

Coverage of state management

Owing to different tasks and circumstances, the management of enterprises by the State has varied in content from one period to another. In the present system, state management covers the following fields:

Deciding on the establishment of new enterprises on the basis of the requirements of the national economy; Deciding on their closing down, suspension of operations, merger with others, switching over to other lines of products and their removal to other places; Deciding on the orientation and scale of production; Assigning planned quotas and checking whether the quotas are fulfilled; Examining and approving long-term programmes and projects for expansion and major technical renovation, and supervising how these are implemented; Appointing, dismissing, checking, rewarding or punishing, within the limits of its power in the management of cadres, such leading officials as factory director/manager, deputy director/deputy manager, marketing officer, chief engineer and chief accountant; Examining and supervising them in implementing the country's established guidelines, policies, laws, regulations, institutions and discipline.

Managerial Reform and its Development

Since 1954, when the establishment of greater administrative regions was dissolved, China has practised a centralized system under which ministries of the Central Government make unified plans for the nation's economic construction. After 1958, enterprises under central control were twice placed under the administration of local governments at provincial and municipal level, but twice the local powers were again centralized. This process involving centralization and decentralization proved ineffective in meeting the needs of economic development. Since the Third Plenary Session of the Eleventh Central Committee of the CPC in 1978, a series of reforms have taken place in China. These include extending the decision-making powers of the enterprises, replacing profit delivering with tax payments, separating government administration from enterprise management, separating ownership of the means of production from the power of operation and giving scope to the role of cities in economic management. These reforms have improved relations between the State and enterprises in terms of duties, rights and interests. The too rigid state control over enterprises has begun to change. The enterprise is no longer an appendage of the state institutions and becomes an independent producer as well as being engaged in socialist commodity production, responsible for its own profit and loss. This has brought the initiative of the enterprise into play in improving its management and economic performance.

Extending decision-making powers

After experiments were made, beginning in 1978, and initial results were achieved, the State Council issued provisional regulations in May 1984 on giving more decision-making powers to state-run enterprises. Key points included in the regulations are: enterprises have

A ZJ-20c truck-mounted drilling rig.

the freedom to increase products needed by the State or the market as long as mandatory state quotas and goods supply contracts are fulfilled; they can sell above-quota products, new products on small trial production and above-quota portions of the products monopolized by the State, with exceptions defined by the State; prices can be set by the enterprises within the limits prescribed by the State or decided upon by the seller and buyer; enterprises have the freedom to choose suppliers for materials and equipment under unified allocation of the State; they may retain 70 per cent of their depreciation funds and dispose of income after paying taxes to the State; they may lease or make over their idle fixed assets with the income used in technical upgrading or renewal of equipment; within the framework set by the government agencies concerned, they can decide on the establishment of organizations and arrangements for their personnel; they can appoint or dismiss middle-level cadres, take on technical and managerial personnel, and reward and punish workers and staff members; they may set their own wage scales, distribute bonuses and raise the wages of those who have done outstanding service; and they can also decide on joint management with other enterprises, including those in other departments or regions.

Separating ownership of means of production from the power of operation

According to the conventional concept of a socialist economy, enterprises under ownership by the whole people must be managed by the State on behalf of the whole people. They must organize their production in accordance with mandatory state quotas and the purchase and marketing of their products must also be monopolized by the State. In such a system, the enterprises lack an incentive to improve their management and product quality and feel no pressure from outside because there is no competition. As a result, an enterprise can produce the same kind of products for decades without any change, hence achieving very poor economic results. These conventional concepts are being broken through. Based on the belief that the socialist economy is a planned commodity economy, the economic theory circles in China are studying ways of ensuring that enterprises operate as independent economic entities and separating ownership of means of production from the power of operation, and this idea is being experimentally tested in many places. They agree that even within the enterprise under ownership by the whole people, elements of collective and private ownership should be allowed to exist. An inevitable outcome of this change will be the introduction of shares in the enterprises. In a socialist enterprise made up of shares, the State is still the biggest shareholder, while the workers and staff members hold part of the rest. The board of directors, the highest decision-making body, will represent the shareholders. It makes decisions on such major issues as appointing or dismissing a factory director/manager, working out operational or financial plans and examining disputes between management and workers. The director/manager is responsible for the operation and management of the enterprise, carrying out the decisions made by the board of directors and having the right to appoint managerial personnel below deputy managers. The presentation of shares in the socialist enterprises is required by the nature of a commodity economy. However, it is different in nature from the joint-stock enterprises under the capitalist system. First of all, they have different ownership, which determines the form of distribution. The State, as the owner of the enterprise, uses taxation to concentrate in its treasury that part of the enterprise's profits which are to be used in the development of the economy and people's welfare. The dividends and bonuses paid to the enterprise are owned by it and used for its own development and collective welfare. The dividends and bonuses paid to the workers are a kind of reward for their contribution of offering funds – they are in fact the part of the value, created by their labour, which is meant for their own consumption at present or in the future; they are similar to the interest from bank savings. All these are different from capitalist enterprises under capitalist ownership and from their way of distribution. The presentation of shares in the enterprises will be a principal form of separating ownership of means of production from the power of operation. The shareholders, including workers and other investors, will be concerned with and will take an active part in the management of the enterprise, since its performance has a direct bearing on their own material benefits. Under the conditions of a socialist commodity economy the joint-stock enterprises will become vigorous economic entities.

Since 1983 China has contracted or leased a number of small state-owned enterprises to collectives or individuals. Some of them have been made over to collectives by hire purchase. Meanwhile, the Government has adopted the policy of allowing co-operative operation between enterprises under ownership by the whole people and collectively-owned ones, and of encouraging economic co-operation among enterprises by breaking through the blocks of regions and departments.

Re-apportioning risk and responsibility

Under the old system of "eating from the common pot" prevailing in the relations of enterprises with the State, factory leaders have no risks to take in operation and no legal responsibilities to bear for loss or even bankruptcy. To change this practice, which has brought serious consequences, at its Eighteenth Session in November 1986 the Standing Committee of the Sixth National People's Congress approved for trial implementation the bankruptcy law governing state-owned enterprises. According to this law, a state enterprise that has serious deficits due to poor management and is unable to clear its debts in a set time will be declared bankrupt. As bankruptcy affects everyone in the enterprise, the possibility will stimulate both enterprise leaders and workers to become concerned with production, management and productivity.

Reform of terms of employment

In the past, once a worker was employed he got an "iron rice bowl" – a permanent job on fixed income, regardless of his performance. This is another kind of practice of "eating from the common pot" prevailing in the relations of workers with their enterprise. The initiative and creativity of the workers and staff members have, as a result, been seriously dampened. In 1986 the Government issued provisional regulations on a contract labour system in state-owned enterprises. This and several other government rulings have put an end to the old system of employment. The contract labour system breaks through the concept of lifelong employment. As the enterprise has the power to recruit or dismiss workers and staff members, who also have the freedom to change jobs, both are given the opportunity to choose each other. This change invigorates the enterprise and puts it in a better position in competition with others. Also, the choice given to both the employer and employee will promote rational flow of work forces. The new system will inevitably create a limited number of people

An open pit at the Jinduicheng molybdenum company in Shaanxi province.

without jobs and this will also help raise the quality of the work force. To guarantee the basic living expenses of the unemployed workers, a labour insurance will be set up, by which they will get unemployment payments for a limited period of time in accordance with their length of service and previous wages.

The Leadership System in Enterprises

A system under which factory directors assume responsibilities and workers' congresses function, all under the leadership of the Communist Party committees, has been practised in enterprises since 1956. It was interrupted during the decade-long Cultural Revolution (1966–76) but resumed after that period. At present, a new system with directors/managers in full control of the plants is being tried out in a number of enterprises according to the decision of the Party Central Committee on reform of the economic structure adopted in 1984, and the results are inspiring.

The Factory Director responsibility system and Workers' Congress system under the leadership of Party Committees

This system involves collective leadership by the Party committee, democratic management by the workers, and administration by the factory director/manager. It provides that the Party committee (or its general branch or branch – this applies also below) is the leading core of the enterprise, which exercises unified leadership of the enterprise's administrative body, workers' congress, trade union, youth and militia organizations. The director/manager puts forward proposals for policy decisions on operation, long-term programmes, annual plans, major technical renovation projects, training programmes, wage readjustments, setting up and changes of offices, establishment of important rules and regulations and revision of them, and other matters of major importance. The proposals are submitted to the Party committee for deliberation and after decisions are made, the director/manager sees to it that they are implemented. He serves as the administrator of the enterprise who, entrusted by the State, exercises unified leadership of operations and management and is responsible to the Party committee. The deputy directors/deputy managers, marketing officer, chief engineer and chief accountant are under the authority of the director/manager, to whom they are responsible. The workers' congress, which functions also under the leadership of the Party committee, is meant to correctly handle relations between the State, the enterprise and the workers in accordance with the Party's principles and policies and government ordinance, dealing with contradictions within the enterprise and guaranteeing fulfilment of the state plans and tasks set by the enterprise.

The director responsibility system

After 1980, when China's modernization process was going faster and economic reform was developing in depth, the defect inherent in the system under which directors were responsible for production and management only under the leadership of Party committees was more and more evident: very often the Party committees totally monopolized the daily administrative affairs, making no distinction between Party leadership and enterprise management or between their responsibilities, and this led to low efficiency. The system became all the more unadaptable to the needs of enterprise management. In 1984, the State Council decided to experiment with a director responsibility system in all the enterprises in Dalian, a port city in Liaoning province, and Changzhou in Jiangsu province, as well as a number of separate enterprises in Beijing, Tianjin, Shanghai and Shenyang.

The decision on the reform of the economic structure, adopted at the Third Plenary Session of the Twelfth Party Central Committee of the CPC in

A numerically-controlled auto cutter-changing boring and milling machine designed and made in Shenyang, Liaoning province. *(Photo by Xiao Ye)*

October 1984, pointed out: "Modern enterprises have a minute division of labour, a high degree of continuity in production, strict technological requirements and complex relations of co-operation. It is therefore necessary to establish a unified, authoritative and highly efficient system to direct production and conduct operations and management. This calls for a system of the director or manager assuming full responsibility." Since then, the experiment of the new system has undergone wider application. Based on new experience drawn from practice and combined with other reforms, the system is being perfected. Essentials of the new system include: full authority of the director/manager in the enterprise's production, operation and administrative management; democratic management by workers and staff; and supervision by the Party committee.

Under the new system, the director/manager is invested with the following powers: Making policy-decisions on production, operation and administrative management; Directing production, operation and administrative management; Deciding on matters concerning labour and personnel; Signing economic contracts on behalf of the enterprise with other organizations at home and abroad and deciding on economic co-operation projects with them; Deciding on the use of funds retained by the enterprise.

While exercising these powers, the director/manager is responsible to the State, society and the workers and staff of the enterprise. He/she must bear the responsibility for the following: the consequences of incorrectly implementing the principles, policies and regulations of the Party or the State; failure to improve the enterprise's economic performance; loss of the enterprise's property and accidents causing death or injury and damage to equipment (except those caused by overpowering factors); failure to fulfil the mandatory state plans according to the required quality and quantity and on schedule; false reports on economic and technological quotas, accounting and statistics; failure to fulfil economic contracts with other organizations at home and abroad; and major waste of material and operational losses.

With the director in full control, the participation of the workers' congress is still the basic form of democratic management. According to the provisional regulation for the workers' congresses in the state-owned industrial enterprises published by the State Council in July 1981, the organization has the power to examine and adopt resolutions on the work report, production and construction plans, budget and final accounts, and major plans concerning technical innovations and management submitted by the enterprise director; discuss and decide the funds for labour protection, welfare funds for the workers and staff and funds for bonuses, and other issues of vital interest to the workers and staff, such as regulations for rewards and punishments and allocation of housing; discuss and adopt resolutions on matters related to the reform

Ma Shengli, a well-known manager of a paper mill in Hebei province, examines the quality of a paper tablecloth.
(Photo by Liu Zhiwei)

of the enterprise's set-up, plan for wage adjustment, vocational training for the workers and staff and major rules and regulations to be applied on an enterprise-wide scale; supervise the leading cadres and other managerial personnel at all levels of the enterprise, recommend those cadres who work hard and have a record of success to the higher authorities for commendation or – in the case of those who have made outstanding achievements – promotion, and propose to the higher authorities that those cadres who cause losses as a result of negligence of their responsibility be criticized, punished or removed from office; elect enterprise administrators in accordance with the arrangements by the higher authorities (the election results are subject to approval and appointments are made by the proper higher authorities). The provisional regulations also provide that the delegates to the workers' congress are selected by direct election in the enterprise and that the grassroots trade union committee serves as the executive body of the workers' congress.

In an enterprise where the director is in full control, the Party committee no longer directs production, operation or administrative work nor examines issues of major importance concerning production and operation. It only supervises these activities and guarantees their smooth progress. Specifically, its main tasks are: to give active support to the director in directing production, operation and administrative

work; to guarantee and supervise the implementation of the policies of the Party and State; to strengthen the ideological and organizational work of the Party organs in the enterprise; to strengthen leadership of the trade union, youth and other mass organizations; and to conduct political and ideological work among the workers and staff. These, if well done, reflect Party leadership in the enterprise. The Party organizations in the enterprises where the directors are in full control are now making adjustments toward this end.

The Operation and Management of Enterprises

The management of enterprises in China involves control of planning, technology, labour, materials, and finance and costs. The form of management has varied from one period to another. Since 1978, when the country was opened to the rest of the world, methods of foreign scientific management that suit Chinese conditions have been introduced, and these have helped to modernize the management of the enterprises in the country.

Plan control

All kinds of work in the enterprise are effectively organized through the process of working out, carrying out and checking plans. This ensures the

607

development of the enterprise's production in line with the fulfilment of the state plan and goals set by the enterprise. Planning includes long- and medium-term plans, an annual plan and quarterly, monthly or daily production plans.

Technological control

This aims to implement the technological policies of the State, to develop new products and technology and skills by making full use of the existing material and technological conditions, promote technical progress, increase the variety of products and improve product quality, ensure safety in production and prevent and solve problems of environmental pollution.

Labour control

This involves hiring; assigning jobs; distribution and checking the performance of workers, technicians and managerial personnel; deciding their wages, rewards, and punishments; and labour organization and protection. The enterprise's labour and wage office is responsible for workers, while technicians and managerial personnel are taken care of by the personnel department. In the past, the workers were assigned to the enterprise by government labour departments: the enterprise had no right to reject the assigned workers or conduct the necessary examinations of them. Now many enterprises are free to select their workers and staff according to their own needs and the workers can begin only after the necessary training. The technicians mainly come from college and technical school graduates, from outstanding workers of the enterprise or from other enterprises and institutions. A few enterprises may advertise for professional people from China and abroad upon approval of higher authorities. The State Economic Commission has set up a special office to invite technical and managerial personnel from abroad and introduce them to proper enterprises and institutions.

Materials control

This refers to the management of raw materials, fuel, power, tools and other means of production. In the past, the supply of materials and marketing of products was under the control of the enterprise's supply and marketing office. Now most enterprises separate supply from marketing in a bid to strengthen materials control.

Financial and cost control

This involves the supply of funds; use of fixed, floating and special funds; cost accounting in accordance with state regulations and control of production cost; regular payment of taxes and depreciation funds

to the State; cash control and financial supervision strictly in accordance with the discipline set by the State; and efforts to raise the utilization rate of funds by practising economy. The accounting results are a comprehensive indicator of the enterprise's expenditure and cost of production in order to strengthen the competitiveness of the products and bring about higher profits.

The provisional regulations on further extending decision-making powers to state-owned enterprises published by the State Council in May 1984 have brought a certain flexibility to enterprise management. The decision-making powers for the industrial enterprises defined in the regulations cover production and operation planning, the marketing of products, pricing of products, purchase of materials, use of funds, disposal of property, establishment of organizations, labour and personnel, wages and bonuses, and joint operation among different enterprises. The exercise of these powers will inevitably bring about changes in enterprise management, changes that will loosen the rigid control by the nationwide conventional systems and invigorate the enterprises.

Business Funds Established in Enterprises

These comprise fixed funds, current funds and special funds.

Fixed funds

These are the enterprise's fixed assets in the form of currency, including those used for production and non-productive purposes, assets not yet put to use, and unnecessary assets such as those purchased unseen, equipment no longer useful as a result of changes made to the production line or replacement with new equipment, and unserviceable equipment. For decades ever since the founding of the People's Republic, the State has allocated fixed assets to enterprises for use without compensation. The funds for new enterprises to buy fixed assets all come from State investment, which also covers the expenses of renovation, expansion and technical upgrading of projects of existing enterprises. In fact, the enterprises are not answerable economically to the State for their use of fixed assets. This encourages the enterprises to ask for as much investment as possible, and as a result, the utilization rate of fixed assets is usually low. As an experiment, beginning in 1980, a number of enterprises have to pay the State for use of their fixed assets, and the new practice has yielded encouraging results.

Current funds

These are working capital used during the process of production and circulation to purchase raw materials, fuel and easily-consumed goods and as advance money for products to be marketed and to pay the workers and staff members. In the process of reproduction the working capital manifests itself as money capital, reserve funds, production funds, finished product funds and funds for settling accounts. An experiment beginning in 1980 which aims to raise the utilization rate of current funds has made enterprises pay the State for the use of working capital.

Special funds

These refer to funds established in the enterprises for special purposes that neither fixed nor current funds cover. According to present practice, these funds include: Fixed assets depreciation fund, which is divided into funds for basic depreciation and funds for major overhauls. The money is used to compensate for wear and tear of the fixed assets. The funds for basic depreciation are taken from sales income every month or every quarter and included in production costs. It is calculated on the basis of the original value of the equipment and its depreciation period defined by the State, deducting its remaining value at the time of discard and adding the expense of dismantling and clearing it. Seventy per cent of the money which is retained by the enterprise may be used, together with the production development fund and new product development fund, for renovating equipment, expanding premises and dormitories, introducing new technology, controlling the "three wastes" (gas, water and industrial residue) and adopting safety measures. The remaining 30 per cent of the money is under the control of higher authorities and put to compensated use by other enterprises. In order to promote technical upgrading and equipment renewal a new method of depreciation has been practised since 1985, which shortens the depreciation period of equipment from an average of 30 years to 20. The Government is also considering the possibility of leaving all the basic depreciation fund to the enterprise, which can use it to renew its equipment. The fund for major overhauls is calculated according to the total cost of such overhauls during the depreciation period and taken every month and included in the production costs. The money belongs to the enterprise; production development fund, collective welfare fund and workers' bonus fund, making up, respectively, 40, 30, and 30 per cent of the part of profit the enterprise retains; science and technology fund, which covers expenses for trial production of new products, experiments and scientific research. The State is responsible for the expenses of major scientific projects it assigns to the enterprise. The expenses for scientific and trial-production projects designated by the enterprise come from the enterprise's production development fund.

Political Parties in Enterprises

The Communist Party, China's ruling party, has more members in the enterprises than any other Chinese political party and sets up grassroots organizations in almost every enterprise. The members of the non-communist parties are mainly distributed in administrative organizations and institutions related to scientific research, culture, education and public health. These parties have very few members in the enterprises and usually set up no branches there.

As their tasks, the Communist Party organizations in the enterprises propagate and implement the Party's principles and policies and see to it that their members play an exemplary role in production and other work and strictly observe Party discipline, state laws and the regulations of the enterprises. Therefore, they play an important role in helping the enterprises to fulfil production targets and maintain good order.

Mass Organizations in Enterprises

These are set up by workers and staff members on the basis of voluntary participation. Different in aims and objectives, they vary from one another in organizational forms. Most of them are in fact grassroots units of the national or regional mass organizations such as trade unions, the Communist Youth League, militia and associations of enterprise management, science and technology, and sports. The trade unions and Communist Youth League and militia organizations in the enterprises are under the leadership of the Communist Party committees and the guidance of their respective organizations at a higher level, while the associations are led by the trade unions in the enterprises and guided by their respective organizations at the higher level.

Trade Unions

Accepting the leadership of the Communist Party, the trade unions are based on voluntary participation and represent the interests of the workers and staff members. Specifically, they take the following as their tasks: to safeguard the fundamental interests of the workers and staff members; to express their just demands, protect their democratic rights as masters of the enterprises and work in coordination with enterprise authorities to improve the working and living conditions for workers, as well as their cultural life; to supervise the performance of the enterprise cadres at all levels, organize workers to take an active part in democratic management and urge them to make concerted efforts for the fulfilment of production targets; to launch socialist labour emulation drives and encourage workers to take part in technical innovation and raise rationalization proposals; and to organize activities in education, sports and recreation for workers, with the aim of raising the quality of the work force.

Communist Youth League

A mass organization of advanced youth, the Commu-

609

nist Youth League is an assistant and reserve force of the Communist Party. The League organizations in the enterprises observe the constitution of the Communist Youth League of China and accept the leadership of the Party organizations in the enterprises and the League committees at higher levels. They lead young workers in fulfilling the tasks set by the enterprises by bringing their initiative and creativeness into play and resisting wrong ideas and pernicious trends, and protect their legitimate rights and interests. They are concerned about every aspect of the young workers – their work, education, well-being and rest – and they organize cultural, recreational and sports activities which appeal to young people.

The Militia

China's militia, an armed mass organization of members actively engaged in production, is an important component of the country's armed forces. Its main task is to help relevant government departments to maintain social order and guarantee enterprises normal production and security. Militia organizations are under the leadership of the Party committees of the enterprises and local military authorities. Workers do not usually leave production to take part in military training or fulfil duties as militiamen and militiawomen.

Science Associations

As grassroots units of the China Association for Science and Technology, these are mass organizations of the scientific and technical workers in the enter-

prises. Their main tasks are: to unite scientific and technical workers, to organize academic activities, to spread scientific and technological knowledge, and to raise the scientific level of both technicians and workers in order to better serve production and the development of the enterprises.

Management Associations

As grassroots units of the China Enterprise Management Association, these are mass organizations in which workers and staff members study problems concerning business management. They aim to study and popularize theories, systems, techniques and methods of business management in China and other countries, spread management knowledge, train managerial personnel and try to improve the management of the enterprises. They help enterprises to meet production targets and modernize their management.

Sports Associations

As grassroots units of the All-China Sports Association, these are amateur sports organizations of workers based on voluntary participation. They aim to spread and implement state policies on sports and physical culture, spreading sports knowledge, organizing regular sports activities, including sports meetings and other competitions, in order to encourage active use of spare time and to build up the workers' health. (For information on labour insurance and collective welfare etc. see Part VI, **Living Standards and Social Welfare**.)

10. URBAN CONSTRUCTION

THE vast land of China is dotted with cities of different sizes and styles, which are the crystallization of the cultures and wisdom of the Chinese people of various nationalities.

Since the founding of New China in 1949, all the old cities have undergone a process of transformation and modernization under an overall plan of the People's Government. New public utilities have been built and streets widened, while attention has been paid to protecting cultural relics, controlling pollution and beautifying the urban environment. With the development of China's economy, some cities have been rapidly expanded, small towns have grown into cities, and new ones have emerged in outlying or formerly poverty-stricken areas. Urban modernization has been accelerated since 1980 thanks to the new economic reform programme aimed in part at enabling cities to fully realize their roles as local economic, political, cultural and scientific centres and to bring along China's rural development by extending their jurisdiction to surrounding counties.

Population Centres in Urban China

Broadly speaking, a city is the political, economic and cultural centre and hub of communications in a given area, a place where non-farming population concentrates. Urban China is divided into cities, county seats, towns and *ji* (market places), forming a four-tier administrative division system.

Cities

Cities are divided into three tiers: Centrally-administered cities, which enjoy the same status as provincial and autonomous regional governments (at present, there are three such cities, usually referred to as municipalities – Beijing, Tianjin and Shanghai); Cities under the direct administration of provincial or autonomous region governments, which enjoy the same status as prefectures; and county level cities under the administration of prefectures, which have the same status as counties.

County seats

These are the sites of county governments or the political, economic and cultural centres of counties.

Most of the county seats are ancient towns with a history of a thousand years. A county seat is administered by what is known as town government, which operates under the county government.

Towns

A town is the political, economic and cultural centre of a designated area outside the county seat. The town government, which operates under the county government, has the same status as the township government.

Ji

A *ji* is a market place, an economically developed residential area for non-farming population within a township. With at least 1,000 residents, it has permanent shops and service centres and regular fairs.

A Chinese city, in its narrowest sense, refers to a place administered by any of the three tiers of municipal government. The area governed by a city government is divided into two parts, namely, the city proper and outskirts. The areas surrounding the city centre with a population less than 40% of the city's total are called inner suburbs, which are administered as the city proper. Part of the city's surrounding areas are delimited as "outer suburbs" or "outskirts" if the percentage of the population there exceeds 40% of the urban population. The outer suburban areas, like the counties and townships under the jurisdiction of the city government, are not considered as part of the urban sector, so policies for rural administration are practised there. The following parts of this chapter refer to cities in the narrowest sense of places where there are city governments, excluding county seats, towns and *ji*. (Hong Kong, Macao and cities in Taiwan province will not be discussed.)

The Development of Chinese Cities

China was impoverished as a result of the feudal rule over the centuries. The situation went from bad to worse when it came to be ruled by imperialism and the bureaucrat – compradore class. Because of this, Chinese cities used to develop only very slowly and their distribution was irrational.

In 1949, there were 69 cities, including 16 with a

The Huangpu river at Shanghai.

population exceeding 500,000, which were mostly in coastal areas in the eastern and southern parts of the country. Cities in the vast hinterland, especially in western China, were much fewer in number and smaller in size. There were only some 20 cities with a population of more than 50,000 in the Inner Mongolia, Ningxia Hui, Xinjiang Uygur and Tibet autonomous regions and the provinces of Qinghai, Gansu, Shaanxi, Sichuan, Yunnan and Guizhou. In some of these areas, towns and cities were so scarce that often not a single one could be found over an area of several hundred square kilometres.

By the end of 1985, however, the number of cities had grown to 324, with a combined area of 2,250,000 square kilometres, including 820,000 square kilometres for the city centres. These had a total population of 554,710,000. Of all the Chinese cities, 21, or 6.5%, had a population of more than 1,000,000; and 31 had a population of 500,000 to 1,000,000 – 9.6%. The corresponding figure for cities with a population of 200,000 to 500,000 was 94 – 29%; for cities with a population of less than 200,000, 178 – 54.9%. In 1984, the four autonomous regions and six provinces mentioned in the preceding paragraph had 27 cities with a combined population of at least 200,000, including five – Xi'an, Lanzhou, Chengdu, Chongqing and Kunming – whose population exceeded 1,000,000. Nevertheless, urban development still varies from area to area due to both natural and historical reasons.

The Chinese cities have played an increasingly important role in the country's economic and social development. According to incomplete statistics, they furnish 69.7% of the nation's total industrial output value, 70.5% of the industrial fixed assets of state-owned enterprises in terms of their original value, and 79.5% of the industrial profits and taxes the State receives every year. Some 68.3% of China's industrial labour force is employed in cities, which also handle 42.9% of the nation's retail sales and 95% of exports. In addition, schools of higher learning in the cities have 95.4% of the country's total student population. In 1985, 7 cities each yielded at least 10,000 million yuan in industrial output value. These were Shanghai, Beijing, Tianjin, Shenyang, Nanjing, Wuhan and Guangzhou.

Urban Planning

With the founding of New China work began to institutionalize urban planning which, by making overall arrangements for the construction of various projects in cities, has helped to promote urban prosperity and social development, to improve the people's life, and to raise the economic, social and environmental benefits of cities.

During the First Five-Year Plan period (1953–1957), urban planning and designing institutions were set up, marking the beginning of the endeavour to develop China's cities in a planned way. Not long

The city of Guangzhou.

afterwards, these institutions very successfully completed the planning for the development of a number of cities to facilitate the building of the 156 key capital construction projects included in the plan. These cities included Lanzhou, Xi'an, Luoyang, Baotou, Wuhan, Chengdu, Taiyuan, Datong, Zhanjiang, Zhuzhou, Changchun, Jilin, Zhengzhou, Shijiazhuang and Anshan. By 1956, urban planning had been finished for more than 150 cities. At that time, the State attached great importance to integrating industrial and urban development, calling for overall arrangements through planning for the building of industrial, communications, housing, infrastructure and service projects. Cities built in accordance with these requirements have proved to be better able to serve the needs of production while making life easier for the residents. In addition, the rational distribution of various projects was the basis for the future development of the cities.

Unfortunately, China's urban development began suffering setbacks as of 1958 due to the influence of "Leftist" ideas on China's economic guidelines and policies. In fact, urban planning was brought to a halt when in the early 1960s a wrong decision was made to suspend it for a time. During the Cultural Revolution (1966-76), urban planning institutions were dissolved, planning workers transferred to other jobs and archives destroyed, causing disaster to the work as a whole.

Urban planning was suspended for a time after the beginning of the 1960s and did not resume and pick up speed until December 1978 when the Third Plenary Session of the Eleventh Party Central Committee was held. The State then formulated a new guiding principle for urban development, namely, the principle of "controlling the sprawl of large cities and developing medium-sized cities and energetically boosting the development of small ones". It also called for revision or drawing up of construction and development plans for all cities. By 1984, overall planning had been completed for 273 cities, or 84.2% of the country's total. Of these, the overall planning for 184 has been approved by the State Council or the provincial, municipal or autonomous regional governments.

In July 1983 the State Council approved Beijing's overall plan for urban development. It defined the city as the national political and cultural centre and proposed that the city subordinate the development of its economy and all other undertakings to serving its function as such.

On 5 January 1984 the State Council published the *Regulations Concerning Urban Planning*, the first ever promulgated in New China for urban construction and management. Local regulations and decrees for urban planning and management were also published by the other two municipalities as well as by many provinces and autonomous regions to illegalize wilful use of land and construction of buildings in violation of the related rules. Thanks to improved legislation, urban construction in China is now proceeding in an orderly manner.

As China has a long history, most of its cities, which date back one or even several thousand years, are renowned for innumerable cultural relics and places of historical interest. In urban planning, China has all along paid attention to protecting these relics and places and to preserving the historical and cultural tradition of the cities. In February 1982 the State Council designated 24 cities as nationally important cultural, historical cities. They include Beijing, Chengde, Datong, Nanjing, Suzhou, Yangzhou, Hangzhou, Shaoxing, Quanzhou, Jingdezhen, Qufu, Luoyang, Kaifeng, Jiangling, Changsha, Guangzhou, Guilin, Chengdu, Zunyi, Kunming, Dali, Lhasa, Xi'an and Yan'an. At the request of the State Council, authorities in these cities are drawing up plans to preserve the cities' original style and salient national, local and historical features. These plans are an important part of the effort to modernize.

The past few years have also witnessed fairly good progress in research on urban building. In addition to the Chinese Academy of Urban Planning Research operating under the Ministry of Urban and Rural Construction and Environmental Protection, institutions with the same function have been set up in nearly a dozen provinces, including Liaoning, Heilongjiang, Jilin, Hubei, Hunan, Shandong, Jiangsu, Zhejiang, Guizhou, Sichuan and Shaanxi. Meanwhile, academic exchanges in this field of work have been on the increase. One example is the Urban Planning

Committee of the Chinese Architectural Engineering Society, which has sub-committees for studying transit systems in big cities, residential area planning, famous historical cities, regional planning and urban economy, and environmental planning for scenic spots. The committee has conducted academic exchanges with its counterparts in Great Britain, the Federal Republic of Germany, the Netherlands, Japan, the United States and Australia, as well as in many Third World countries.

China is paying increasingly greater attention to the training of urban planners. A dozen institutions of higher learning, as well as some secondary technical schools, offer urban planning courses. They include Tongji University, Qinghua (Tsinghua) University, Beijing (Peking) University, Nanjing University, Chongqing Institute of Architectural Engineering and Wuhan Institute of Urban Construction.

Public Utilities

Great efforts have been made since the founding of New China to improve the supplies of water, gas and heat, drainage, roads, bridges, public transport, flood-prevention and other public utilities on which cities depend for survival and development.

Water supply

In 1949 there were only 72 cities which had waterworks. Through 6,500 kilometres of pipelines, they supplied a daily average of 2,400,000 tons of water, benefiting only 9,600,000 people.

By 1985 some 300 cities in China had waterworks, which produced a daily average of over 40,000,000 tons – nearly 20 times more than the pre-Liberation figure – 60% of which was meant for use by industries. In addition, major industrial and mining enterprises drew some 70,000,000 tons of water per day from their own sources. Running water reached the homes of 80% – in some large and medium-sized cities 100% – of the city residents.

Chinese engineers have constantly improved the techniques for building water supply facilities. The country now has fairly strong task forces capable of designing and building large, difficult projects. Examples include the project diverting water from the Luanhe river to Tianjin, a major North China industrial city and port; the project diverting water from the Bihe river to Dalian, the leading port in the north-east; and the Niangziguan water diversion project in Yangquan city, Shanxi province, a major coal producing base. Scientific research results achieved so far have helped waterworks to raise their capacity to purify water from natural sources and accelerate the mechanization and automation of water supply. Significant results have also been achieved in

Xiamen city in Fujian province.

economical use of water and in recycling industrial water for re-use.

Drainage and treatment of urban sewage

In 1984, Chinese cities had some 30,000 kilometres of sewers, five times the 1949 figure. There were 50 sewage treatment plants, able to treat over 1,500,000 tons per day, more than 80 times the early 1950s figure. In addition to dredging and widening the rivers that snake through the cities, many pumping stations have been built to drain off floodwater in low-lying areas. Before 1949, the biggest sewage treatment plant in China had a daily capacity of 20,000 tons. By contrast, sewage treatment plants designed and built by the country itself over the past three decades and more have a daily capacity of up to 260,000 tons. Drainage facilities built over the years have played a big role in the protection of the environment and prevention of flooding and pollution in Chinese cities.

Urban gas supply

Gas supply to cities has steadily increased over the years along with the development of China's metallurgical and petroleum industries. In 1976, 55 cities had gas supplied, accessible to some 10,000,000 residents. Such a supply included an annual average of 298,000,000 cubic metres of natural gas, 133,500 tons of liquefied petroleum and 1,460,000,000 cubic metres of gas obtained from coal gas.

Following the Third Plenary Session of the Eleventh Party Central Committee, the country adopted a new energy policy, encouraging the use of gas in cities. Under a national plan drawn up in accordance with official policy, authorities in Chinese cities have worked hard to enable more families to use liquefied petroleum gas and natural gas instead of coal by tapping the existing supply potential (recycling diffusing gas, for example). Meanwhile, new gas plants have been built wherever possible. In 1985, nearly 100 cities had installed gas facilities, reaching 27,000,000 residents – 22.4% of the urban population, a yearly average of 2,370,000,000 cubic metres of coal gas, 602,000 tons of liquefied petroleum and 1,600,000,000 cubic metres of natural gas. The efforts to spread the use of gas in cities have bought remarkable economic, social and environmental benefits. Use of such an amount of gas as China is able to supply at present would reduce the consumption of energy by something equivalent to 3,200,000 tons of standard coal a year, in addition to making air in cities cleaner, cutting the volume of transport of coal and refuse, improving the living conditions of residents and helping them save the time spent on cooking.

Heat supply centres

Practically all the heat supply centres in China have

been built since 1949. As far back as early 1950s, the country built a number of heat and power plants, which were the basis for developing concentrated supplies of heat in its cities. The work has been speeded up since 1978, when China began regarding concentrated heat supplies as an important energy conservation measure. In 1985, 25 northern cities had heat supply centres, which annually produced 9,000,000 tons of steam and hot water with 5,205,344 million kilocalories of heat to service areas totalling 27,420,000 square metres.

Public transport in cities

In 1949, bus services were available in only 26 cities,

Fuximen underground railway station in Beijing. *(Photo by Wang Lianfeng)*

The cableway across the Jialing river in Chongqing, Sichuan. *(Photo by Chen Jie)*

with a total of 2,292 worn-out buses and tram-cars running almost exclusively along town centre thoroughfares.

In 1985, all the 300 cities had bus services. Of these, 26 had both buses and trolleybuses, and tramcars were still used in Dalian, Anshan, Changchun and Harbin. All in all, China's urban public transport facilities handled 25,500 million passengers that year. Taxis were available in 166 cities, and there were ferry services in 27 cities which are either coastal or have lakes or rivers in their areas. Beijing and Tianjin had each built an underground railway, the total length being 29.6 kilometres. Shanghai was building its first underground railway, 13 kilometres long. In the mountain city of Chongqing, a 740-metre suspension cableway has been thrown across the Jialing river. Some major Chinese cities now have fairly good public transport networks consisting predominantly of buses and trolleybuses, with taxis playing a supplementary role. Efforts have begun to develop public high-speed rail transport.

Inter-city communications

A network of communications consisting of highways, railways, water transport and civil aviation established since 1949 now covers all Chinese cities. In 1984 some 4,000 million passengers and 800,000,000 tons of cargo were handled by highways between cities, ten and 100 times more than the 1974 figures, respectively. In 1985, railways had reached 215 cities, handling 1,040,000,000 passengers and 1,110,000,000 tons of cargo that year, also ten and 100 times more than the 1949 figures. Inland river shipping service between cities transported 270 million passengers and 500 million tons of cargo, 18 and 17 times more than in 1949, and there were scheduled voyages between all coastal cities. Air services had extended to some 40 cities, handling an annual average of 7,470,000 passengers and 195,000 tons of cargo and mail.

Inter-city telecommunications

In 1949, there were only some 5,000 post offices in all China, with postal routes totalling 707,000 kilometres and air mail routes, 1,400 kilometres. Telegraph offices were found in more than 30 cities and there were 902 long-distance lines and 218,000 sets of urban telephones.

By 1985, the number of post offices had increased to 53,000 and the total length of postal routes to 5,000,000 kilometres and of air mail routes to 180,000 kilometres. The country had 32,000 trunk lines, 10,000 telegraph service routes and 3,800,000 sets of urban telephones.

Wuhan city on the banks of the Yangtze river is a hub of aquatic transportation. *(Photo by Bai Liansuo).*

Beginning from 1979, China has begun to install semi-automatic exchanges for international calls. By the end of June 1986, programme controlled telephone exchanges were scheduled to have been put into service in Beijing and Shanghai for the handling of international calls. That meant direct dialling between seven Chinese cities – Beijing, Tianjin, Shanghai, Fuzhou, Xiamen, Guangzhou and Qinghuangdao – and cities in some 170 countries and regions. By 1987, direct dialling with foreign cities should have been available to a total of 40 cities which are either coastal or provincial capitals.

Urban roads and bridges

In 1984, paved roads in Chinese cities totalled 38,282 kilometres, three times the 1949 figure. They covered 358,720,000 square metres, 4.5 times the 1949 figure. There were 7,436 bridges in the urban areas, of which 6,945, or 93.4%, were permanent ones. The quality and techniques of road and bridge construction have constantly been improved. Model projects completed so far include Tian'anmen Square and the second city ring road in Beijing, a boulevard along the Yellow River in Lanzhou, a boulevard running north to south across Chengdu, Yingze Road in Taiyuan, May 1 Road in Changsha, a cable-braced bridge at Liugang and the second tunnel under the Huangpu river in Shanghai, the Yangtze river bridges at Wuhan, Nanjing and Chongqing, and the Yellow River bridges at Lanzhou and Jinan. These make life easier for local residents and provide fairly advanced, reliable transport for the development of production in these cities.

Street lighting

The past three decades and more have also witnessed remarkable improvements in street lighting. By 1985, high-voltage sodium lamps – a third-generation source of illumination – had replaced the old mercury lamps along the streets in cities. Illuminated by street lamps casting pearly radiance of different colours, Chinese cities now look even more magnificent at night than during the daytime.

Urban flood-prevention projects

Chinese cities have become much more secure against flooding, thanks to continual efforts to build water control projects. Since 1949 the majority of cities have emerged safe and intact when heavy flood waters have passed through their rivers in rainy seasons. Examples include Wuhan, Harbin and Tianjin, which conquered the greatest flood peaks ever recorded for their rivers. Wuhan fought successful battles to ensure its safety from flooding by the Yangtze river in 1954 and 1958; Harbin, from flooding by the Songhua river in 1957; and Tianjin, from flooding by the Haihe river in 1962.

Environmental sanitation

In old China, street sweeping and refuse collection were done almost exclusively by hand, and transport of dirt and garbage by animal-drawn or even hand carts.

By 1985, however, the country had already been mass producing motor vehicles with vacuum suckers for collecting human excrement, watering cars, road sweepers and self-unloading refuse transport vehicles with enclosed containers. Thanks to the use of these and other machines in all the cities, almost half of the refuse and human excrement collecting and transport operations had been mechanized. Altogether, some 10,000 refuse disposal stations had been built or expanded, and 14 refuse fermentation plants were in operation that year in some cities, with a combined treatment capacity of 2,000 tons per day. In 1982, the Ministry of Urban and Rural Construction and Environmental Protection published the *Regulations Concerning the Maintenance of the Appearance and Sanitation of Cities*, to systematize and standardize urban sanitation work throughout China.

Urban Housing Construction

Investment in urban housing construction

The Chinese government has all along paid great attention to improving the living conditions of urban residents. It has managed to raise funds to build houses for the people despite the limited financial resources at its disposal. Between 1953 and 1978, the State and the state-owned units spent more than 36,000,000,000 yuan building housing, accounting for 5.8% of the country's total capital investment for the same period. Housing construction has gained momentum since the Third Plenary Session of the Eleventh Party Central Committee: between 1979 and 1984, an annual average of some 13,000,000,000 yuan or 20% of the nation's total capital investment was used to build urban housing.

Achievements of urban housing construction

Housing built between 1950 and 1984 totalled 1,100,000,000 square metres in floor space. This meant 22,000,000 flats, if calculated on a 50 square metre per flat basis. Of this, more than 600,000,000 square metres (including those built by co-operative units) were built between 1981 and 1985, equivalent to the total for the previous 15 years (1966 – 1980). In terms of floor space, housing built since 1949 in many cities doubles or even more than doubles the pre-Liberation figure. One example is Beijing, which in 1985 had 70,000,000 square metres of housing, some five times the 1949 figure of 13,540,000 square metres. Tianjin achieved a 300 per cent increase, from 10,200,000 square metres to 37,490,000 square metres during the same period. The 1949 – 1985 period also saw a 2.5-fold increase in Shanghai, from 23,590,000 square metres to some 64,460,000 square metres. Large numbers of residential estates with different styles and layouts came into being. Among these, the most publicized are Hepingli, Sanlihe, Tuanjiehu, Jinsong, Zhongguancun, Shuanyushu and Shijingshan residential estates in Beijing; Dingzigu, Beicang and Jianchangdao in Tianjin; and Caoyang and Pengpu in Shanghai. Large residential estates have also sprung up in new industrial and mining zones, such as those built for Beijing's Yanshan Petrochemical Works; the Dagang oilfield near Tianjin; the Jinshanwei petrochemical centre in Shanghai; the No. 2 Motor Vehicle Plant in Shiyan city, Hubei province; the Dukou iron and steel centre in Sichuan province; and the Liaoyang Petrochemical Complex in Liaoning province.

Methods of urban housing construction

In order to build as much urban housing as possible, China encourages initiative from four quarters – the State, local authorities, enterprises and individual citizens. The State and local governments are obliged through planning to earmark a certain proportion of their capital construction funds for housing construction. Thanks to China's economic system restructuring since 1980, large numbers of enterprises now have more money at their disposal than ever before, and fairly large proportions of the money are used to build new housing for their own workers. Between 1980 and 1984, enterprises throughout China spent about 50,000,000,000 yuan on housing construction, accounting for 67% of the country's total.

The Government now encourages individual citizens to build or buy homes. In some 100 cities, individual citizens are allowed to build homes exclusively with their own funds or with funds raised through mutual help. Private housing may also be built with assistance from local government departments, while citizens may contribute to local housing construction projects for priority in getting the government-built flats. In addition, the method of encouraging people to buy government-built flats with subsidies from their work units is being tried out in the four cities of Changzhou, Zhengzhou, Shashi and Siping.

Housing construction in Chinese cities has proceeded at a fast speed, but also fast is the growth of the urban population. This explains why each member of the urban population had only 5.2 square metres of housing space at the end of 1985.

New Cities

Large numbers of new cities have sprung up since 1949 along with the development of China's economy and industry in particular.

Zhanjiang, a petroleum city on the South China Sea.

These can be divided into the following categories according to their economic functions:

Oil cities: such as Karamai in the Xinjiang Uygur autonomous region, Daqing in Heilongjiang province and Maoming in Guangdong province. There used to be vast expanses of cobble-strewn Gobi desert in what is now Karamai – a city with a population of 10,000. Daqing, population 270,000, is located in formerly almost uninhabited marshland. Both cities are now thriving centres of oil production and refining, Daqing being China's largest oil centre which provides half of the national output.

Coal cities: These include Jixi, Hegang and Shuangyashan in Heilongjiang; Jiaozuo, Hebi and Pingdingshan in Henan; Huaibei in Anhui; and Liupanshui in Guizhou, which now have a population of less than 200,000 each. These used to be small towns or mountain villages.

Hydro-electric power cities: These include Qingtongxia in the Ningxia Hui autonomous region, Laohekou and Danjiangkou in Hubei, and Sanmenxia in Henan. Mountain villages in the past, these have become cities with tens of thousands of residents. Their coming into being was the result of the construction of reservoirs and hydro-electric power stations as well as the conveyance projects for irrigation, which has boosted local industrial and agricultural production and caused a concentration of population.

Metallurgical cities: These include Dukou in Sichuan, Jinchang in Gansu, Ma'anshan in Anhui and Sanming in Fujian. Dukou city used to be a village with a few dozen families by the Jinsha river. The local population has snowballed to half a million since the discovery of large iron ore deposits, the building of a large iron and steel complex and the completion of the Chengdu–Kunming Railway.

Automotive cities: Shiyan city in Hubei, where China's No. 2 Motor Vehicle Plant is situated, was a village nestling in mountains before construction of the plant started in late 1960s. It now has a population of 300,000. There are other, similar examples.

Machine-building cities: These include Chaoyang in Liaoning; Hanzhong in Shaanxi; Daxian, Deyang and Wanxian in Sichuan; and Anshun and Zunyi in

Guizhou. These are medium-sized cities with a population of some 200,000 each, except for Deyang, which has 700,000 residents. In contrast, their predecessors were county seats or small towns.

Electronics cities: These include Xianyang in Shaanxi, Mianyang in Sichuan, Duyun and Kaili in Guizhou, and Hongjiang in Hunan. Xiangyang is where China's largest colour TV picture tube factory is located.

Chemicals cities: These are Liaoyang in Liaoning and Zigong in Sichuan.

Tourist cities: These include Wudalianchi in Heilongjiang, Jiayuguan and Yumen in Gansu, Yan'an in Shaanxi, Jinggangshan in Jiangxi, Huangshan in Anhui and Dali in Yunnan.

Cities of minority ethnic groups: These include Hami, Aksu, Korla, Kuitun, Shihezi, Hetan and Turpan in the Xinjiang Uygur autonomous region; Golnud in Qinghai province; Baoshan and Chuxiong in Yunnan; and Wuhai, Wulan Hot, Yakshi, Chesheng, Zhalandun, Xilin Hot and Linhe in the Inner Mongolia autonomous region. Although they do not yet qualify for acquiring city status in terms of population and economic development, they have been designated cities to better serve the needs of developing the local natural resources and economy.

Border cities: These serve the needs of improving China's international links. They include Yining in Xinjiang, Erlianhot in Inner Mongolia, Manzhouli in Heilongjiang, Tumen in Jilin and Pingxiang in the Guangxi Zhuang autonomous region. These have been designated as cities on account of their importance to China's links with foreign countries, although they are not important economic centres and have small populations. An example is Erlianhot on the border of China and the People's Republic of Mongolia. Although it has a population of only 6,800, it was given city status because it serves the needs in handling railway passengers and goods between China and the Mongolian People's Republic, the Soviet Union and East European countries, as well as entry and exit procedures.

Altogether, 231 cities have been added since 1949. Of these, two-thirds have been developed on the basis of former county seats or towns, and the rest built almost entirely on empty sites. All these were constructed in accordance with sound planning which included measures for greening and prevention of pollution and construction of public utilities. The industrial and energy development centres among them have played an increasingly great role in China's endeavour to modernize. Still greater numbers of new cities will rise along with the development of China's national economy.

The New Tangshan – a City Built out of Earthquake Ruins

Situated in the north-east and Hebei province, Tangshan municipality is about 160 kilometres east of Beijing and about 100 kilometres north-east of Tianjin, with a population of around 1,000,000 people. It is a well-known northern Chinese industrial city noted as "Coal City" and the "Ceramic City of North China". It has a very developed power industry and there are also several important enterprises including metallurgical, textile, cement, motor vehicles and machine-building industries.

Tragically, this unfortunate city was hit by a strong earthquake, which measured 7.8 on the Richter scale (fracture degrees 11) at 03:42 on 28 July 1976. The earthquake's impact strength was felt by a number of seismic observatories throughout the world. Even more disastrous is that in the following 48 hours intermittent tremors continued to rock the city area: some 900 times registering above 3 and some 16 times above 5 on the Richter scale. The quake killed 242,769 people and seriously injured 164,851. The city was all of a sudden turned into a complete sea of ruins. Of the total 682,267 urban and rural civilian dwellings (10,932,272 square metres), some 656,136 (10,501,056 square metres) were either toppled or heavily damaged. This was over 96% of the buildings. Over 97% of the plants of the city's industrial and mines enterprises as well as over 50% of mechanical equipment were destroyed. Not a single chimney was seen in an upright state after the earthquake. Direct losses estimable in the calamity approached more than 3,000 million yuan.

After the quake urgent measures were taken by the People's Government, who quickly mustered 100,000 men from the army, 50,000 cadres and workers and some 10,000 medical personnel who actively joined in the rescue and rehabilitation work. Through the co-operative endeavours of the Tangshan people themselves, as well as the army-men and civilians from different sources, a first heat of steel was produced on 25 August, less than one month after the quake; the power generated was restored to the level of the pre-quake period in less than four months after the calamity and the 1977 national production plan for rough coal output was fulfilled 24 days ahead of schedule, in just over one year. By the end of 1978 the value of industrial output achieved amounted to 270,000,000 RMB dollars, which was fundamentally the production level before the quake.

In the following years the city was rebuilt entirely in keeping with the overall plan of the new municipal construction. The Kai Luan Coal Mines imported and popularized a new coal-exploiting technique with combined mechanization, and the annual production capacity reached 20,200,000 tons of coal, becoming one of the country's six major coal mines. The Tangshan Power Plant, by the continued construction of the Dou He Power Station, which is already the most up-to-date, and of the Feng Run Thermo-Electricity Plant, has achieved a capacity of 1,500,000 kilowatts from all the generators of the city, over three times more than before the quake. Through adopting new techniques and expanding rolling capability, the Tangshan Iron–Steel Corporation has achieved a 50% rise in steel production over the pre-quake time. It is now one of the country's 10 biggest iron–steel corporations. While efforts are being made to restore the Qi Xin Cement Plant, the Ji Dong Cement Plant, a new plant with imported advanced equipment, was set up to become the most modernized in China with an annual production capacity of 1,500,000 tons, giving an increase in cement output of 1.5 times more than in the pre-quake period. The capacity of production of the ceramic industry also surpassed that of the pre-quake time to a very large extent. There is an installation with an 80,000 square-metre production line for enamelled brick – the first of its kind in China – whereby the enamelled brick production now accounts for more than one-quarter of the country's total production. Enamelled bricks are being exported to 25 countries and areas. The production capability of the machine industry, such as mining machines, cement-producing machines, engine vehicles and heavy trucks, and that of the consumer goods industry, such as textiles, clothing, plastics, bicycles and TV sets, have surpassed by a wide margin the level attained in the pre-quake period. In 1985 the total output value in agriculture and industry was 7,839,000,000 yuan, an increase of 114.12% more than that of 1975, one year before the quake. The city's rough coal output is now 18,580,000 tons; steel, some 1,270,000 tons; cement, some 2,740,000 tons; power supply, more than 10,000,000,000 kilowatts; and grain output, 2,290,000 tons. Thus the city of Tangshan, with only about 1/100,000 of the country's land area and only about 1/1,000 of its population, has achieved a gross production value of nearly one per cent of the total of the whole country's industry.

The newly built Tangshan municipality has a total area of 73.24 square kilometres, 2/5 larger than before the earthquake. The area of the whole city's dwellings

A bird's-eye view of new Tangshan. *(Photo by Liu Zhiwei)*

amounts to more than 17,700,000 square metres, of which 11,270,000 square metres are for residential buildings, an increase of more than 25% and 44% respectively over those before the calamity. The city is no longer a simple restoration of what it was before but appears entirely new, having most of a modern city's character and facilities: a reasonable overall layout, a clear distinction in the distribution of different functions and complete facilities through the municipal construction. The whole city's production areas are away from the residential areas, so that the latter are not disturbed by industrial noise. An average of 6 square metres of grassland is shared by each person. This is double the grassland occupied by each before the quake in the whole city. The waste gases and polluting dust for years deeply hated by the people of Tangshan have now begun to disappear. Their living conditions have now been ameliorated, and they have an average of more than 7 square metres for their housing per head – the most that anybody in the big cities of the country has ever enjoyed. There are one-roomed, two-roomed and three-roomed houses in the residential buildings, with a front hall and a kitchen as well as a lavatory owned by themselves, and other facilities such as water, light, radiators and cooking gas are installed. The municipal construction is also the best in the whole country, with a central heating system and gas supplies provided. In view of the fact that the city is situated in an earthquake-prone zone, every preventive measure has been taken in the construction of the industrial as well as the residential buildings. Particular attention has been paid to the structure of the buildings so that they are capable of withstanding a fracture of even 8 degrees. Even if there should be a quake registering 6 on the Richter Scale, all the buildings would remain intact, as steady and stable as they are now.

Urban Greening and Scenic and Historical Places

New China has paid great attention to preserving

The city of Tangshan in Hebei province after the violent earthquake of 1976. *(Photo by Liu Donghao)*

open spaces in its cities and made great achievements in this respect. According to statistics available at the end of 1985, such spots, including parks, totalled 159,000 hectares in 324 cities. There were 978 parks, covering 20,000 hectares, and 48 zoos, occupying 940 hectares.

Trees and lawns

In 1981, the Standing Committee of the National People's Congress adopted a resolution calling on all citizens of the age of 12 and above to plant one tree per year on a voluntary basis. In response, the Chinese people, old and young, men and women, have taken an active part in the voluntary tree planting drive and in various activities to protect trees and forests. This has ushered in a new stage in the effort to beautify the cities. In addition to planting trees, people are encouraged to grow flowers and lay lawns. One of the most successful examples is Beijing, where many streets are now decorated with lawns, neat lines of trees and bushes alongside them, as well as flowers blooming in three seasons – spring, summer and autumn.

Some tree-lined streets in Chinese cities have salient features. The Dr Sun Yat-sen Road in Nanjing is practically a green corridor, shaded by the elaborate crowns of French parasol trees on both sides. The Beijing Road in the same city is noted for the tall snow pines standing majestically along it. The Jiang-

A Beijing street, with high-rise buildings, trees and lawns. *(Photo by Vaughan James)*

nan Road in Nanning city skirts a long strip of land covered with almond trees, bamboo and cattail grooves, which present a sub-tropical scene. When Beijing is covered with snow in winter, the numerous Chinese pines along the Sanlihe Road look even more magnificent. The most beautiful street in Harbin is the five kilometres long, 58 metres wide Stalin Street. The sidewalks, bicycles and vehicle lanes are separated by winding strips of lawns with trees and flowers. Along the pavements there are lines of white poplars, black pines and other trees. In addition, there are six parks. The streets look even more beautiful in spring, when winter jasmines, oriental cherry, roses and lilacs bloom.

Factories, government organizations and schools are also working hard to beautify their compounds and the surrounding areas. An outstanding example is the Changchun Railroad Car Factory, which is like a garden with lush green and luxuriant trees. Other models in greening include the Zigong Hard Alloys Mill, Xiangtan Textile, Printing and Dyeing Mill, North-East China Light Alloys Mill, Beijing Teachers' University and Guangxi Nationalities' Institute. Good results have also been achieved in the greening and beautification of the residential estates in Xianyang Road (N) of Tianjin and Gucheng in the Shijingshan district of Beijing.

Gardens and parks

China has numerous gardens, distinct in their national style, beauty and artistic value. Some ancient gardens, including imperial gardens in the north and gardens in ancient courtyards in the south, are the cream of the Chinese garden designing and building. Since 1949, the Government has spent huge sums of money repairing and protecting these gardens. Between 1980 and 1984, the municipal government of Beijing completed major repairs to the Tanzhe and Tietai temples and some ancient buildings on the slopes of Wanshou (Longevity) Hill in the Summer Palace, as well as to Zhaigong and Qinian Halls in the Temple of Heaven. (Qinian Hall was where emperors prayed for good harvests every year and Zhaigong was where they fasted to show their sincerity before performing the annual ritual.) Authorities in Suzhou, Yangzhou and Wuxi in Jiangsu province have also done major repairs to their ancient courtyard gardens in an effort to restore them to their original beauty.

Most of the parks in Chinese cities have, however, been built during the last three decades. Guangzhou, for example, in 1949 had four parks, which covered three hectares. In 1985, the city had 18, totalling 735 hectares. There are 21 parks in Wuhan with a combined area of 474 hectares, compared to only two of 29 hectares 35 years ago. In building parks, stress is laid on creating natural scenery with trees and other plants to charm the eyes of visitors, beautify the cities and improve the ecological balance in an attempt to

621

The statue of "Peace" in Beijing. *(Photo by Xiao Yinzhang)*

inherit and carry forward China's tradition of gardening. One example is a park in Beijing which is actually a reproduction of the residence of a prince or high-ranking official in the Qing dynasty (1644–1911). The park was designed and built by referring to descriptions of Daguanyuan – the garden in an official residence – in the ancient classic novel *A Dream of Red Mansions*.

Before 1949, practically none of the zoos in China was presentable. The country now has 42 zoos, the biggest being Beijing Zoo, with some 590 species of animals. The zoos in Hangzhou, Shanghai and Chongqing are also famous for the construction, layout and design of their animal sheds and for the disposition of the plants.

City gardening authorities are also running botanical gardens, some of which, such as those in Beijing, Hangzhou, Shanghai, Lushan and Kunming, are open to the public. Displaying several thousand rare species, these help to promote research and spread knowledge of botany.

China now contracts for building gardens in foreign countries. The Mingxuan Garden built by Suzhou experts in the Metropolitan Museum of New York and the Fangcaoyuan Garden by Guangzhou experts in Munich have attracted large crowds since they were opened. Visitors have spoken highly of their artistic beauty.

China has a long history and magnificent mountains and rivers, hence the existence on its land of innumerable scenic spots and places of historical interest, including ancient towns and sites of cultural relics. While striving to modernize the country, the Government has tried its best to preserve the original style of these ancient sites. In Beijing, for example, the old outer city walls have been demolished to help expand the city's public transport, but the city gates and towers between sections of the walls remain intact. These include the Qianmen Gate and Arrow tower facing the Tian'anmen Gate – the main entrance to the imperial palace – to the north, the Drum Tower in the centre of the old town and the Deshengmen Gate where emperors greeted troops returning from victorious battles. In addition, all these models of ancient Chinese architectural engineering have been restored and repaired again and again, while work has been done to make them blend well with the surrounding modern buildings.

In line with the open policy, the State Council in 1979 designated Shenzhen, Zhuhai and Shantou in Guangdong and Xiamen in Fujian as Special Economic Zones, where flexible policies are pursued to attract foreign investment. In 1984, 14 coastal cities – Dalian, Qinhuangdao, Tianjin, Yantai, Qingdao, Lianyungang, Nantong, Shanghai, Ningbo, Wenzhou, Fuzhou, Guangzhou, Zhanjiang and Beihai – and the Hainan Island were opened to foreign investors. As part of the effort to create an environment attractive to foreign investment, the State has arranged the construction of a host of infrastructural facilities in these zones and open cities including ports, posts and telecommunications facilities, railways, air services and facilities for electric power and water supply. Shenzhen, which used to be a small town bordering Hong Kong, is now a thriving modern city with a population of 232,000, complete with all kinds of public utilities and a large number of high-rise buildings. By the end of 1985, work had been completed on the construction of buildings totalling 11,570,000 square metres in floor space, sewage totalling 281 kilometres and roads 127 kilo-

Hefei, the capital of Anhui province.

metres. The city is already a local hub of communications, linked with Guangzhou, the provincial capital of Guangdong, by an expressway and an electrified railway. Moreover, it is becoming international, its ports handling ships sailing 12 ocean-going routes to Hong Kong, Macao, Singapore, Malaysia, Yugoslavia and Japan. It is also linked with all of China's major coastal cities by regular shipping services and with Beijing by a newly-opened air route. An automatic urban direct dialling telephone system handles 8,000 telephone lines, in addition to some 100 lines for automatic dialling to Hong Kong, 100 telex lines and 10,000 computer-controlled radio intercoms. The development of the Zhuhai special economic zone has also been fast: it is now linked by roads with all cities in the province and has opened a regular tourist bus service in Macao, in addition to passenger shipping services with the territory, and cargo and hovercraft shipping services with Hong Kong. The Xiamen special economic zone now has four berths able to accommodate 10,000 d.w.t.-ships, and construction is underway on the Dongbo port designed to handle 1,000,000 tons of cargo a year. A programme-controlled system for 10,000 telephones and a 960-path microwave communications system are already in operation, making it possible for people in the zone to dial directly to Hong Kong and some cities in the United States.

Development of other special economic zones and open areas has proceeded equally fast and well. It is now foreseeable that in the next five years these will become economically advanced cities and areas attractive to foreign investors, with up-to-date technology for producing goods catering to the needs of the Hong Kong, Macao and world markets, while helping promote the development of the Chinese mainland as a whole.

New China has made great achievements in urban construction as in all other fields of work over the past three decades and more. As a developing country, however, it still lags behind developed countries in this respect. For Chinese cities, the most prominent problem is their underdeveloped tertiary trade and inadequate transport, communications, telecommunications and other public utilities. To tackle this and other problems, the Chinese government is striving to modernize its cities, the order of priority being the three municipalities, the coastal cities open to foreign investment, and provincial and autonomous regional capitals. The urban modernization endeavour will proceed in step with the modernization of the national economy. The country now envisages modernization of its major cities and marked improvements in public utilities in less important cities and county seats, towns and *ji*. It is also foreseeable that along with the country's economic system structuring, still greater numbers of peasants will leave their land for rural towns and *ji* where they will make a living by engaging in industry and tertiary trade. This will mean that more cities will spring up as a result, and that cities will play a still greater role as local political, economic, scientific, technological and cultural centres. This will give fresh impetus to rural development and will be conducive to the effort to narrow the differences between town and country and enable all corners of the country to prosper.

11. FINANCE AND BANKING

Circumstances under the Kuomintang Government

In 1927 the Kuomintang government was established in Nanjing (Nanking). To control national finance it set up the Central Bank, and from then on finance and banking fell in the hands of bureaucratic-capitalists.

During the period between 1927 and 1949 economic conditions in the Kuomintang area became more unfavourable with each passing day: industrial production withered and the agricultural economy was depressed. During this period, especially after 1946, the Kuomintang allocated an enormous military expenditure to wage the Civil War and to meet other demands. Internal and external debts increased rapidly, galloping inflation appeared, prices skyrocketed and the financial deficit became astonishingly great.

Military expenditure and internal and external debts

It was characteristic of the Kuomintang government that military expenditure occupied the first place while expenses for paying debts took second place. The sum of these two items accounted for 75 to 90 per cent of the total expenditure. To pay the enormous military expenditure the Kuomintang government had to issue government bonds and contract an external loan. The bonds issued in 1949 alone totalled 2 million taels of gold, and 136 million US dollars were borrowed, mostly from the United States.

Inflation

The Kuomintang government announced that silver dollars would be withdrawn from circulation on 4 November 1935 and replaced by the *Fabi* (legal money) issued by its bank. At that time the financial deficit was enormous; it reached 90 billion yuan in 1948. Therefore the bank issued banknotes recklessly, which increased by geometric progression. In August 1948 they accumulated 663,694.6 billion yuan, that is, 470,705 times that of June 1937.

This is also reflected in the purchasing power of 100 yuan:
- In 1937 one hundred yuan could buy 2 oxen;
- In 1945 it could buy 2 eggs;
- In 1946 it could buy one-sixth of a cake of soap.
- In 1947 it could buy a small piece of coal;
- In 1948 it could buy 0.1 gramme of rice;
- In 1949 it could buy 0.00000001 grammes of rice!

Taxes

The tax income of the Kuomintang government was about two-thirds of its revenue. According to the statistics between 1927 and 1936 the accumulative income from taxes accounted for 65 per cent of the revenue. Urban and rural people had to pay exorbitant taxes and levies. In Sichuan province, according to the statistics, there were almost two hundred such taxes and levies.

Circumstances in Revolutionary Bases under the Communist Party of China

After 1927 the Communist Party of China began to found the Central Soviet Revolutionary Regime and established more than ten revolutionary bases, including the Jiangxi Revolutionary Base and Hunan–Hubei Border Revolutionary Base. The object of economic development in these areas was to break the economic blockade, ensure supplies, support the war and promote production. Soviet local banks were set up to issue money, absorb deposits, run the treasury, grant credits, support and develop the Soviet economy, etc.

After the outbreak of the War of Resistance against Japanese Aggression in 1937, the Eighth Route Army and the New Fourth Army, under the leadership of the Chinese Communist Party, set up and expanded a number of anti-Japanese revolutionary bases. In finance the aim was "to develop the economy and guarantee the supply." Nearly all the scattered revolutionary bases had their own banks, whose main functions were to issue paper money so as to set up their own currency market and stabilize commodity prices; and to grant loans with lower interests so as to support production and promote the economy. The purpose of the financial policies was not only to meet the needs of the anti-Japanese war, but also to lighten the burden on the people and improve their life by developing production, improving staff and simplifying administration.

During the War of Liberation between 1945 and 1949, along with the continuous expansion of liberated areas, new financial and banking organs were set up, the property owned by enemy and puppet regime and individuals was confiscated and the unified management of currency was adopted. As a result production advanced. In the financial field, the principle of broadening sources of income and reducing expenditure was carried out, especially the strict implementation of efficient and simple administration and thrift. After taking over the big cities in 1949, the financial and banking organs undertook strict control over the money market and stabilization of commodity prices, taking effective measures to recover and develop industrial production so as to support the Liberation War. The financial and banking system constituted during this period was the starting point of New China's financial and banking system.

Financial System and Achievements of New China

The financial system in New China was established and has developed on the basis of its socialist economy, on the principle of taking money from the people and spending it in the interests of the people. In the planned economic and social construction it relies on the strength of the Chinese people and maintains the initiative in their own hands.

Since the founding of the People's Republic in 1949, the financial and tax organizations of the Kuomintang have been abolished and new ones set up by the central and local people's governments. The Central People's Government has set up the Ministry of Finance, which is the supreme organ to administrate the affairs of finance and taxes, while provinces, autonomous regions and municipalities have their own financial departments (bureaux) and tax bureaux. The authorities in cities and counties establish financial and tax bureaux respectively, and financial sectors, teams or offices are set up by townships.

China's finance is brought under unified leadership and controlled by the authorities at different levels. The state budget and final accounts have to be examined and approved by the National People's Congress. The composition of the state budget is determined by the state power structure and according to the administrative regions, and has to suit the needs of the economic administrative system. The state budget comprises the budgets of both the central and local governments, the latter including the budgets of the provincial, municipal, autonomous regional, county and city governments.

The state budget is the main component of the state financial system because it reflects the distribution relationship of various kinds within the socialist financial system. The collection and distribution of the bulk of funds are fulfilled through the state budget. The state enterprises are the foundation of China's financial system not only because the bulk of state revenue comes from them, but also the bulk of state expenditure is used in their economic construction.

The central budget comprises the budgets of all central ministries and departments, including the financial income and expenditure plans of enterprises and institutions directly under the Central Government, and occupies the dominant position in the state budget. Its main duties are: to guarantee the expenditure and expenses for various kinds of items, such as the construction of major projects, culture, education, science, public health, national defence, the development of relations with other countries and the reserve of the state goods and materials; to be responsible for the redistribution of local budgets used to support construction in minority nationality regions and border areas to develop their economy and culture or to provide relief to the people in severely stricken areas; and to concentrate the bulk funds of the state budget.

The local budget comprises the budgets of departments directly under the jurisdiction of provinces, municipalities or autonomous regions and their governed cities and counties. Related to the extension of local authorities, the local budget becomes more and more important, because the bulk of state revenue is levied by the local authorities and the bulk of state budgeted expenditure allocated according to the local budget. The local budget plays an important role in the development of the economy and culture. The policies for the development of the national economy, which are stipulated by the Central People's Government, should be carried out in the local budget.

In the over thirty-six years since the founding of the People's Republic the financial work has played a significant role in the socialist construction, and especially since 1979 the financial strength and vitality have made rapid progress. The state revenue of 1985 amounted to 188.64 billion yuan, which was an increase of 36.45 billion yuan or 24.3 per cent more than the previous year, while during the period of the Sixth Five-Year Plan between 1981 and 1985 it totalled 683.08 billion yuan, with a yearly average increase of 11.5 per cent.

Analysis of state revenue and expenditure illustrates the main features of state financial policy.

Balance between revenue and expenditure

China insists on the principle of "balancing between its revenue and expenditure but allowing a little surplus each year", and was successful in most years from 1950 to 1985: on the whole the total revenue of the 36 years exceeds the total expenditure. Nevertheless deficits did occur in certain of the 16 years due to the political and economic conditions. In the period of the Great Leap Forward between 1958 and 1961, for instance, due to the defects of setting extremely high targets and carrying on too many construction projects, the construction investment in major projects was too much, and demand surpassed the supply. As a result deficits appeared successively in these years. Afterwards, because of the serious damage caused by the ten years of the Cultural Revolution, comparatively great financial deficits occurred in 1967 and in the three successive years after 1974. In 1979–1980, to develop the economy in rural areas the Government raised the prices for purchasing agricultural products while the prices for selling remained the same, so the Government had to make up the price difference. It also granted awards for overfulfilling production quotas, extended the range of agricultural products purchased with negotiated prices and raised the standards of wages and bonuses of workers and staff. As a result, over 10 billion yuan more had to be paid. Due to the above payment plus the excessive construction investment in major projects (52.3 billion yuan in 1979 and 55.9 billion yuan in 1980), comparatively great deficits occurred in those two years, amounting to 17.06 billion yuan in 1979 and 12.75 billion in 1980. These deficits are quite different from those that appeared before: the former were caused by paying the accumulated "debts", that is, to raise the prices for purchasing agricultural products and the wages, while the latter were caused by defects in economic policy decisions. Through the adjustment between 1981 and 1982 the proportional relationship in the national economy was gradually corrected, the accumulation rate began to fall and the financial deficits decreased greatly. In 1985 China's finance regained a balance between revenue and expenditure and had some surplus. Moreover, the funds beyond the budget increased rapidly to over 140 billion yuan. In 1985 these and the funds within the budget reached over 320 billion yuan, twice that of 1980. The national economy grew much stronger and a critical turn was achieved in China's finance.

Improvement in income structure

The increase in state revenue relies mainly on the development of socialist economy and the increase in national income. Since the founding of the People's Republic in 1949, the revenue structure has undergone great changes, in which the income from industrial enterprises and the proportion of industrial and commercial tax has gradually extended. The excessively high proportion of agricultural tax income in the budgeted revenue as a whole, which appeared in the early years after the founding of the People's Republic (e.g., 29.3 per cent in 1950) has changed completely. The proportion of the income from enterprises and the tax income of industry and commerce and others (not including agricultural tax income) in the total revenue as a whole changed to 60 per cent between 1950 and 1952; 77 per cent between 1953 and 1957; 90 per cent between 1963 and 1965; and some 90 per cent between 1981 and 1984. The change of income structure reflects the development of China's industrialization and socialist commercial economy and the rise in economic benefit in enterprises.

In spite of the rapid development of China's agriculture during the Sixth Five-Year Plan from 1981 to 1985, with the total output value (excluding that of village-run industrial enterprises) increasing by the yearly average rate of 8.2 per cent, the proportion of agricultural tax income in the total revenue as a whole grew less and less: 18 per cent in the economic rehabilitation period between 1950 and 1952; 11.1 per cent in the First Five-Year Plan period; 6.2 per cent between 1963 and 1965; and 2.4 per cent between 1981 and 1985. In the past 36 years the absolute sum from the agricultural tax has increased slightly: it was 2.7 billion yuan in 1952 and 3.28 billion yuan in 1983, an increase of only 21.5 per cent within some 30 years, while the output of major grain in 1983 was 387.25 million tons, an increase of 136 per cent over 1952, which was 163.92 million tons. To advance agricultural production and agricultural modernization, the Chinese government has adopted the policy of lightening the burden of the peasants and increasing their income, which is very important and successful to the economic development of socialist China, since of 1 billion Chinese people, 800 million are peasants.

Since 1980 the economic reform in cities centres round galvanizing management of enterprises and extending the independent right of enterprises to mobilize their initiative. Before the reform started the overwhelming majority of profits gained by state-owned enterprises had to be handed over to the State, and most enterprises kept a small fund to improve the

Table 1: Revenue and Expenditure (billion yuan)

Year	Total revenue	Total expenditure	Difference
1950	6.52	6.81	−0.29
1951	13.31	12.25	+1.06
1952	18.37	17.60	+0.77
1953	22.29	22.01	+0.28
1954	26.24	24.63	+1.61
1955	27.20	26.93	+0.27
1956	28.74	30.57	−1.83
1957	31.02	30.42	+0.60
1958	38.76	40.94	−2.18
1959	48.71	55.29	−6.58
1960	57.23	65.41	−8.18
1961	35.61	36.70	−1.09
1962	31.36	30.53	+0.83
1963	34.23	33.96	+0.27
1964	39.95	39.90	+0.05
1965	47.33	46.63	+0.70
1966	55.87	54.16	+1.71
1967	41.94	44.19	−2.25
1968	36.13	35.98	+0.15
1969	52.68	52.59	+0.09
1970	66.29	64.94	+1.35
1971	74.47	73.22	+1.25
1972	76.66	76.64	+0.02
1973	80.97	80.93	+0.04
1974	78.31	79.08	−0.77
1975	81.56	82.09	−0.53
1976	77.66	80.62	−2.96
1977	87.45	84.35	+3.10
1978	112.11	111.10	+1.01
1979	110.33	127.39	−17.06
1980	108.52	121.27	−12.75
1981	108.95	111.50	−2.55
1982	112.40	115.33	−2.93
1983	124.90	129.25	−4.35
1984	150.19	154.64	−4.45
1985	186.64	184.48	+2.16

Table 2: China's Revenue in Detail (billion yuan)

Year	Total[2]	Income from industrial enterprises	Total	Industrial and commercial taxes	Agricultural taxes	Income from debts[1]	Income from other items
1950	0.87	0.44	4.90	2.36	1.91	0.30	0.45
1951	3.05	1.21	8.11	4.75	2.17	0.82	1.33
1952	5.73	2.15	9.77	6.15	2.70	0.98	1.90
1953	7.67	2.78	11.97	8.25	2.71	0.96	1.69
1954	9.96	4.01	13.22	8.97	3.28	1.72	1.34
1955	11.19	4.88	12.75	8.73	3.05	2.28	0.99
1956	13.43	5.26	14.09	10.10	2.97	0.72	0.51
1957	14.42	5.93	15.49	11.31	2.97	0.70	0.41
1958	18.92	9.41	18.74	14.18	3.26	0.80	0.31
1959	27.91	15.44	20.47	15.70	3.30	–	0.33
1960	36.58	21.58	20.37	16.06	2.80	–	0.28
1961	19.13	8.04	15.88	12.05	2.17	–	0.60
1962	14.62	8.51	16.21	12.49	2.28	–	0.53
1963	17.27	12.96	16.43	13.10	2.40	–	0.53
1964	21.29	16.43	18.20	14.53	2.59	–	0.46
1965	26.43	21.65	20.43	16.55	2.58	–	0.47
1966	33.33	26.80	22.20	17.93	2.96	–	0.34
1967	21.85	16.32	19.66	15.74	2.90	–	0.43
1968	16.67	12.00	19.16	14.74	3.00	–	0.30
1969	28.67	20.31	23.54	19.13	2.96	–	0.47
1970	37.90	28.06	28.12	23.21	3.20	–	0.27
1971	42.84	31.64	31.26	26.82	3.09	–	0.37
1972	44.57	32.78	31.70	27.51	2.84	–	0.39
1973	45.70	34.64	34.90	30.14	3.05	–	0.37
1974	40.73	29.80	36.04	30.70	3.01	–	1.54
1975	40.02	33.31	40.28	34.80	2.95	–	1.26
1976	33.81	29.63	40.80	35.37	2.91	–	3.05
1977	40.24	32.63	46.83	40.09	2.93	–	0.38
1978	57.20	44.04	51.93	45.13	2.84	–	2.98
1979	49.29	45.12	53.78	47.27	2.95	3.53	3.72
1980	43.52	44.82	57.17	50.14	2.77	4.30	3.53
1981	35.37	41.59	62.99	53.84	2.84	7.31	3.28
1982	29.65	39.71	70.00	60.00	2.94	8.39	4.36
1983	24.05	39.86	77.56	64.38	3.28	7.94	15.35
1984	27.68	38.53	94.74	75.75	3.46	7.73	20.04

Notes: [1] Income from debts consists of foreign debts and government bonds.
[2] In the years between 1980 and 1983 the total sum of income from enterprises was lower than that from industrial enterprises because great losses were incurred in enterprises engaging in foreign trade and grain.

well-being of workers and staff members. Since the reform the enterprises have handed their profits in the form of tax according to the appraised and decided rate, thus keeping comparatively more profits to develop production, improve the life and well-being of their workers and staff members, and distribute bonuses. With their extended financial right, enterprises begin to change from their old practice of engaging in production only to becoming engaged in both production and management, thus mobilizing the initiative of the workers and staff members. Moreover, the handing over of their profits in the form of tax guarantees the State an income and the effective collection of funds.

Expenditure on economic and cultural construction

The structure of China's financial expenditure provides favourable conditions for economic, scientific and cultural construction. In the past 36 years this expenditure (including construction investment in major projects, circulating funds and expenses) accounted for 60 per cent of the total expenditure. In 1984 the expenditure on economic, scientific and cultural construction amounted to 77.7 billion yuan – 11 per cent more than the accumulated sum of the First Five-Year Plan period (1953–57), which was 72.88 billion yuan.

In the past 36 years the expenditure on national defence accounted for only 17.4 per cent of the total state expenditure, and it has declined gradually. Between 1950 and 1952 to meet the needs of the expenses for the Korean War and for the fight to eliminate the bandits and local despots, 37.8 per cent of the total expenditure was allocated for national defence.

Between 1953 and 1957 the proportion of national defence expenditure in the total expenditure as a whole declined to 23.4 per cent and it continued to decline. Between 1981 and 1985 the expenditure for national defence per year averaged 13.1 per cent of the

Table 3: China's National Expenditure (billion yuan)

Year	Total	Allocated fund for major construction	Expenses for innovation and manufacture of new products	Addition to circulating funds	Expenditure for Culture, Education, Science and Public Health	Expenditure for war preparedness and National Defence	Expenses for administration
1950	6.81	1.25	–	–	0.50	2.80	–
1951	12.25	2.70	–	–	1.06	5.26	–
1952	17.60	4.67	–	1.86	1.35	5.78	1.45
1953	22.01	7.03	–	1.38	1.90	7.54	1.75
1954	24.63	8.43	0.18	2.63	1.97	5.81	1.83
1955	26.93	8.85	0.31	3.08	1.98	6.50	1.87
1956	30.57	13.96	0.25	1.08	2.39	6.12	2.42
1957	30.42	12.37	0.23	2.08	2.78	5.51	2.17
1958	40.94	22.94	0.08	2.57	2.86	5.00	2.16
1959	55.29	30.23	0.22	5.43	3.65	5.80	2.66
1960	65.41	35.45	0.26	6.75	5.05	5.80	2.80
1961	36.70	11.02	0.27	2.94	4.12	5.00	2.68
1962	30.53	5.57	1.47	4.78	3.67	5.69	2.17
1963	33.96	8.02	1.83	3.67	3.80	6.64	2.35
1964	39.90	12.38	2.09	2.34	4.33	7.29	2.52
1965	46.63	15.85	2.52	2.76	4.56	8.68	2.53
1966	54.16	19.10	2.75	4.03	5.17	10.10	2.59
1967	44.19	16.13	1.03	2.91	4.86	8.30	2.28
1968	35.98	11.79	0.57	1.20	4.10	9.41	2.29
1969	52.59	20.62	1.07	2.66	4.10	12.62	2.48
1970	64.94	29.84	1.48	3.12	4.37	14.53	2.53
1971	73.22	30.96	2.64	3.53	5.23	16.95	3.09
1972	76.64	30.91	2.55	4.30	6.20	15.94	3.46
1973	80.93	31.72	2.55	5.38	6.99	14.54	3.56
1974	79.08	31.20	2.72	4.48	7.65	13.34	3.69
1975	82.09	32.70	3.15	4.18	8.13	14.25	3.88
1976	80.62	31.13	3.43	4.54	8.55	13.45	4.10
1977	84.35	30.09	3.95	6.57	9.02	14.90	4.33
1978	111.10	45.19	6.32	6.66	11.27	16.78	4.90
1979	127.39	51.47	7.20	5.21	13.21	22.27	5.69
1980	121.27	41.94	8.05	3.67	15.63	19.38	6.68
1981	111.50	33.06	6.53	2.28	17.14	16.80	7.09
1982	115.33	30.92	6.90	2.36	19.70	17.64	8.16
1983	129.25	38.28	7.87	1.29	22.35	17.71	10.22
1984	154.64	48.89	11.18	1.00	26.32	18.08	13.73
1985	184.48	58.38	10.34	1.43	31.67	19.15	14.36

Note: Since 1984, the circulation funds have been put under unified control by the bank.

total expenditure, while in 1985 it was 10.3 per cent of the total. Since 1979 even in the absolute sum of national defence, expenditure showed some reduction. For example, the national defence expenditure of 1979 amounted to 22.27 billion yuan and it decreased by 14 per cent to 9.15 billion in 1985. In contrast with countries which build up their armed forces and military capabilities, national defence occupies only a small part of China's total expenditure.

In over 30 years of socialist practice China has undergone a zigzag course in the financial field and accumulated both positive and negative experience. The basic principles are summarized as follows:

– Comprehensive balance must be constantly maintained so as to put state finance on a solid foundation. Only by balancing revenue and expenditure, credit and deposit, and the supply and demand of materials can the national economy develop in proper proportion. Hence, it is very important to act according to the country's economic strength, and the most important principle is to maintain strict control of the whole scale of investment in fixed assets and the total sum of consumption funds within the limits allowed by the nation's economic strength.

– Stress should be put on the economic benefit of the whole society so as to make the finance serve economic development. Without the development of the economy and an increase of economic benefit, financial resources can never flourish. The task of the Ministry of Finance, the supreme financial organ of the State, is to learn how to produce, collect and spend the revenue. It should overcome its one-sidedness in considering the finance as it stands.

– The financial administrative system should be actively reformed and stabilized to realize the organic combination of strengthening control over the macro-economy without making the micro-economy too lively. The Ministry of Finance should strengthen control over the macro-economy and make skilful use of tax, subsidy, investment, profit, credit, price and wage as an adjustable lever. At the same time it should hand over necessary independence to enterprises and add vitality to them.

Financial Management and the Reform of the System

The essence of financial management in China is to

distribute and redistribute, by applying state power, some parts of the social aggregate product. It includes the management of budget, taxation, investment in capital construction, enterprise financial affairs, the financing of social culture and education, and the management of funds excluded by the budget. The core of all these is to establish a financial management system that would combine macro-control with micro-control and be dynamic in promoting a planned commodity economy.

A number of previous reforms in financial management systems were characterized by centralization and random decentralization, with the tendency to gradual transformation of the highly centralized management system into one managed by various localities, each of which bore its own economic responsibility.

From 1950 to 1952, China was facing difficulties in finance and in the economy. In order to balance revenue with expenditure, and to stabilize the market, all the financial power was concentrated within the Government, which took charge of the unified revenue and payment, and this helped to improve the conditions of finance and economy in a fundamental way.

From 1953 to 1957, though the central and local governments divided the boundaries of the responsible revenue and expenditure, the emphasis was on the unified financial management system.

From 1958 to 1960, a number of enterprises were put under the lower administrative levels and the reform was carried out by giving some power to enterprises and to local governments in financial matters. This also played a positive role in arousing the initiative of both the local governments and the enterprises, but neglect of the overall balance gave too great a power to the local governments, with the result that for some time there was no macro-control over the economy.

In the national economic readjustment of 1961–1965 the State Council took back from the lower levels the excessive power until then permitted, turned its attention to centralization and decentralization, and let the market regulate the economy under the guidance of the state plan. This helped to restore and promote the national economy.

During the Cultural Revolution (1966–1976) production stopped or stagnated, national income was falling and the financial system changed frequently. In the period from 1971 to 1973, the financial revenue directly under the control of the Central Government yielded only just over 10 per cent of the total because of the overdone decentralization and granting of too high a percentage of the profit to the lower levels. The Central Government then restored the excessive centralization of finance again.

Since 1979, reform of the overall economic system has been sweeping across the whole country, from rural to urban areas, and a series of reforms are being carried out in the financial system. Fairly good results have been achieved in mobilizing the initiative of the

enterprises in production and trading, with an increase in government revenue. The decision-making power in finance given to the enterprises was enlarged and the economic responsibility system was introduced. These experiences may be categorized under three main headings and six particular items. The headings are: to reserve a portion of the profit; to be responsible for one's own profit and loss; and to replace handing over profit by paying taxation. The six items are: to reserve some part of the total profit; to keep some portion after meeting the basic profit target plus taking a share from the additional profit; to reserve a certain proportion after fulfilling the plan; to keep the remaining profit after handing over the part due or to keep the excess after meeting the due target progressively increased year by year; to be responsible for losses; and finally to replace handing over profit by paying taxation. All these reforms enhanced enterprise initiative to a certain extent and increased government revenue.

In the urban reform experiment of devolving decision-making powers to the enterprises, the State Council approved the successful method used in the Capital Iron and Steel Works, i.e., of keeping the remaining profit after handing over a fixed sum, which would be progressively increased. In the seven years of the reform (1979–1985), the Capital Iron and Steel Works increased its profit by 20 per cent per year, and in the first three years of employing the method (1979–1981), it handed over 730 million yuan from this profit, keeping the remainder after meeting the profit target. In the next three years of using the method (1982–1984), when the profit progressively increased, it turned over to the Government a total of 902 million yuan (calculated in comparable terms), i.e., 24 per cent more than in the previous three years. Before the reform, the net income of the profit and tax received by the Government from the Capital Iron and Steel Works was 531 million yuan in the 30 years from 1949 to 1978, after deducting the government investment from the profit. In the seven years from 1979 to 1985, when the economic reform was under way, the Government had an income of 2.9 billion yuan net of profit and taxation from the Capital Iron and Steel Works, and it did not basically need to invest any longer, since according to the regulations, the enterprise could keep some of the profit. The government income in the seven years after the beginning of the economic reform was 450 per cent higher than that in the previous 30 years, and productivity had increased by a big margin. The material and cultural life of the workers also improved considerably.

Financial management in China consists basically of two parts: government financial management and the financial affairs management of the enterprises. The focus of the former is on budget, taxation and financial supervision.

– *The Government strictly carries out the budgeting, examining and approving procedures and the checking of the final accounts*. Every year the Ministry of Finance compiles a budget and final accounts, as do the local authorities. The budget compiling procedure is implemented by combining the opinions formed at the upper level with those formed at the grassroot levels. The budgets of the central and local governments are collected and submitted to the State Council for examination and approval after examination and verification by the Ministry of Finance, and then presented to the National People's Congress for final ratification. Both central and local governments receive their revenues according to the established policy, use their budgets and make a supplementary budget according to the procedures if necessary.

– *The national management of taxation is a tool in readjusting production, guiding consumption and rationalizing distribution.* The profit and taxation system was adjusted and reformed in the period of the Sixth Five-Year Plan. From 1980 to 1981, China gradually introduced personal income tax and income tax on joint-venture enterprises and foreign firms in China. China also regulated and reduced taxation on agriculture, co-operative shops in towns and the private sector of the economy, and began taxation on the value of machines added in order to promote specialization of production. The special tax on consumption of oil was started in 1982, and in 1983 the tax on construction to control the scale of fixed assets and accumulated funds for key constructions in energy and transportation on the income excluded by the budget. The tax on maintaining urban construction was started in 1985.

– *Financial supervision is essential for the financial departments at all levels to guarantee the implementation of the state budget, tax income and income of other kinds.* Such supervision is realized mainly through examination of the financial activities and of income and expenditure on the basis of the state plan, policy and regulations. The Government carries out the necessary and effective supervision of various economic departments, enterprises and institutions which have violated the state financial and economic plans, laws, etc. by frequent or shock examinations.

The national and local people's congress at all levels is authorized to check and supervise the financial affairs of the governments, enterprises and institutions. This is a good method to mobilize the masses for financial supervision through democratic management within the trade unions.

Anyone guilty of a serious economic crime, such as sabotaging the socialist economy, corruption, embezzlement, bribery, graft and stealing state or collective property, speculation, smuggling, and illegally buying and selling foreign exchange, is heavily punished.

The management of the enterprises' financial affairs is the base of the national management in finance. The major aspects of state management of enterprise finance comprise:

– The distribution and management of the reproduction capital of the fixed assets;
– The management of circulating funds;
– The management of the special funds;
– The management of the cost and profit.

Banking Achievements and the Reform of the Banking System

In December 1948, on the eve of the Liberation of the whole of China, the People's Bank of China was officially established. This marked the start of financial enterprise in New China. Since that time, financial enterprise in China has won great achievements.

Stabilizing the currency

Throughout this period the value of Renminbi has remained essentially stable. This stems primarily from the fact that market prices, on the whole, have remained stable, and this results from the consistent policy China follows to stabilize the currency. It plays a very important role in the normal development of the national economy and the stability of the people's life.

During the early years after the founding of New China, the Chinese government strengthened the management of finance to curb the problem of inflation left over by old China. Within less than half a year, the financial and economic conditions were radically improved. In the early years of the 1960s, China's economy was plagued with temporary difficulties, and in 1979 and 1980 the state budget projected a deficit. These two years witnessed the over-issue of currency in circulation and the fluctuation of prices. After the fourth quarter of 1984 there appeared, for a time, the single-minded pursuit of high speed, and as a result, fixed capital investment and consumption capital increased rapidly. However, for more than three decades since the founding of New China the relevant departments of the Government have made decisions promptly and resolutely adopted effective measures to maintain the continuous stability of the currency. The measures taken were mainly to: Strengthen the centralized and unified management of banks; Withdraw the excessive power transferred to the lower levels; Exercise strict control over investment and the issue of currency; Organize the withdrawal of currency from circulation; Readjust industry through economic means and force enterprises lacking in ability to continue production to be closed down, halted, merged or transferred to other enterprises; Actively provide reasonable funding for industry and agriculture to motivate the development of production and increase the supply of materials for society.

The fundamental currency control policy of China is to stabilize the value of its currency and develop the economy. As long as the economy develops, it is possible for the currency to remain essentially stable and thus ensure the smooth development of the economy.

The development of economic construction and the structural reform

For more than three decades, financial enterprise has done much to support large-scale economic construction and structural reform throughout the period of six Five-Year Plans carried out by the State.

Through the collection, distribution and supervision of funds, banks perform their functions in aiding and adjusting production, in regulating markets and in developing the economy so as to contribute to socialist construction. And by means of the administration of allotment and application of credit funds, banks foster the highest economic efficiency to speed up the process of economic construction. The chief roles of the banks are to:

– *Allot capital construction funds and control the application of them.*

Before 1980 capital construction funds in China used to come from the state appropriations. From 1954 to 1980, state budgetary appropriations amounted to about 80 per cent of the total investment for capital construction. All these appropriations were from banks and their applications were under the banks' control. Each unit had its part of self-collected funds for capital construction. This part totalled about 18 per cent of the investment and was managed by the banks, which also supervised the application of these funds.

– *Collect funds for socialist economic construction and sensibly allot loans.*

Banks perform a special function in the collection of funds. They collect the idle capital and reserve funds of enterprises and institutions as well as urban or rural savings deposits so as to serve socialist construction through credit. The circulating capital of state-run enterprises in China comes primarily from bank loans. The loans provided by the banks for the circulating funds of state-run enterprises amount to 30 per cent of the total; the remaining 60 per cent are for commercial enterprises. Banks also provide loans for

The new office of the Bank of China. *(Photo by Wang Lei)*

township enterprises and individual industrialists and businessmen throughout the countryside. One part of capital for renewal and transformation of fixed assets in state-run enterprises comes from bank loans and the applications are kept under the supervision of banks.

– *Readjust the monetary credit policy to promote the rationalization of the national economic structure.*

In 1979, in order to develop the production of consumer goods and speed up the development of agriculture, banks adjusted their credit policy, giving priority to loans for light and textile industries. Since the State has systematically lowered the output of heavy industry, the output of light and textile industries and agricultural products have increased year after year. The national economic structure has therefore been gradually rationalized.

– *Support rural commodity circulation in order to develop rural co-operative financial organizations.*

Since the rural economic reform in 1979, the contracted household responsibility system has been perfected. The agricultural economy is moving towards specialization, socialization and merchandization. To adjust to the rapid development of rural reform and commodity production, the organization at all levels of the Agricultural Bank of China has been reshaped. The focus has been shifted to support for rural commodity circulation. The rural credit co-operatives have also undergone restoration and development, being turned into mass co-operative financial organizations with independent handling of business.

– *Expand the credit business to invigorate national economy.*

In order to make effective use of construction funds, the State's interest-free appropriations for capital construction were replaced mostly by bank loans. Since the cut-down of circulating funds, banks shoulder the responsibility not only of supplying circulating funds for industrial and commercial enterprises, but also of helping outdated enterprises to adopt new technology and to accelerate the transformation of technology. The items and amount of investment in 1984 ranked the highest in the history of China.

To revitalize the economy, the banks no longer confine credit business to the fields of production and circulation, extending it now to all trades. They also provide loans for such non-productive trades as travel, service, science and technology, culture and education and public health. Apart from loans mainly for state-run or collectively-owned enterprises, communes and villages, banks also allot loans for other parts of economy, including individuals. The single-channel system of bank loans is replaced by diversified routes such as commission loans, rental and credit business.

– *Reform the interest rate system to promote economic efficiency.*

During the period of the Sixth Five-Year Plan, banks enlarged the scope of interests, increased grades of saving deposits and raised the interest rate three times to absorb more saving deposits.

An office in the Bank of China.

The average interest rate of deposits increased from 3.6 to 5.84 per cent. At the end of 1985, urban residents' saving deposits amounted to 105.78 billion yuan, 3.7 times the figure at the end of 1980. The interest rate for the fixed deposits of government offices, enterprises and institutions has accordingly been raised.

In January 1986, in accordance with the provisions of the State Council, the People's Bank of China worked out the differential interest rate in terms of state economic policy. Each specialized general bank has some right to float the interest rate. The range of floating interest rate was stipulated by the People's Bank of China. In this way, interests come to be linked with the welfare of enterprises, staff and workers. The State also provided a preferential interest rate for loans to enterprises which needed help, for measures to develop and save energy resources and for national trade enterprises in the minority-inhabited areas. The reform of interest rates has played an active role in invigorating the micro-economy and strengthening the control of macro-finance.

The reform of banking administration

Since 1979, the Agricultural Bank of China has been reworked. The Bank of China, the People's Insurance Company of China, the International Trust and Investment Corporation, and the Investment Bank of China have been successively established. According to the decision made by the State Council, the People's Bank of China can exercise the functions and powers of central bank. Subsequently, the Industrial and Commercial Bank of China was founded to deal with industrial and commercial loans and deposits. Thus banks have fulfilled the goal of specialization. The *Interim Regulations on Foreign Exchange Control* has been issued enhancing the centralized management of foreign exchange. The management system of circulating funds has undergone reform: the circulating funds of state-run enterprises, all provided by bank loans, are subject to interest. The *Preliminary Regulations on Economic Accounting* of the People's Bank of

China has been put into effect: business management and economic accounting within banks have been comprehensively instituted. The check-out standards and ways of drawing the funds of enterprises have been settled. Credit plan management has been changed: credit is planned in a unified way and managed by different levels. The link between deposits and investment has been established, and the deficiency is divided up and assigned to each group. On the premise of no violation of the plan to assign the deficiency to each group, the norms of various investment can be used as regulations. The remaining deposits can be used to increase investment. In order to regulate deficiency, each branch bank of the People's Bank of China can allocate additional funds to the banks of relevant provinces, autonomous regions and municipalities directly under the Central Government, within the range of the plan, to assign the deficiency to each group clarified by the People's Bank of China. The People's Bank of China is in charge of clarifying each specialized bank's total revenue and expenditure of the credit plan. Each specialized bank should strictly control the sum. It is forbidden to exceed it.

The development of foreign economic relations

Since China implemented the open policy to the outside world, the People's Bank of China has taken on the important task of attracting and making systematic use of foreign capital and selectively importing the advanced technology and equipment needed by the State. During the period of the Sixth Five-Year Plan, the bank has done much in the collection and use of foreign capital, enabling foreign economic relations to develop in depth. The total foreign capital China has drawn from various sources amounted to $US 38.26 billion, of which, $US 21.8 billion has been used. 2,300 Chinese–foreign joint ventures and 3,800 co-operative enterprises have been established and more than 10,000 projects of foreign technology imported.

Notable results have been achieved in absorbing foreign capital. It has promoted the development of energy resources and the construction of communications and transportation – such as the Guangdong Nuclear Power Station, the Pingshuo Coal Mine in Shanxi province, the Daqing peripheral oilfields, offshore oilfields, etc. Through the use of foreign capital, four extra berths for the Shijiusuo and Qinhuangdao ports have been built to enlarge the capacity for exporting coal. The technical transformation of outdated enterprises has also been accelerated: the textile industry in Beijing has obtained good results through importing key equipment and transforming the whole industry.

Banks have also achieved remarkable economic results in the constant reform of foreign exchange credit management and allocation of foreign loans.

For example, $US three billion were utilized by the Ministry of Transportation to buy ships for the ocean-going fleet. In the early years of 1960s this fleet had only about 20 ships, totalling little more than 200,000 in tonnage, but now more than 500 ships are available, totalling nearly 10 million in tonnage. With the help of the banks, another ocean-going fleet has been established, which in 1981 ranked fourteenth in size among the ocean-going fleets of the world. Its transportation quota annually amounts to $US one billion. As a result, it not only saved rental expenses totalling several billion US dollars, but also increased foreign exchange earnings. Opening to the outside world is China's firm and unshakeable policy. Banks should continue to take it as a long-term, hard but worthwhile task to make use of foreign capital, and to work to absorb more capital for the realization of the four modernizations in China.

China's Banking System

The current financial system in China includes: the People's Bank of China (which exercises its functions and powers as the central bank), the Industrial and Commercial Bank of China and the Agricultural Bank of China. Besides these, there are the People's Insurance Company of China, the China International Trust and Investment Corporation, and credit co-operatives in the countryside. The organizational principle of the current financial system in China is unified leadership and division of specialism. The overall financial system implements the unified policy, plan and system which are stipulated by the State. Each specialized bank has its special responsibility in its own field. Thus a socialist multi-level financial system with Chinese characteristics has been established, with the central bank as its core and specialized state banks as its main body, and with co-existing diversified forms of financial organization. To further strengthen the management of finance, the *Interim Regulations on Management of Banks of the People's Republic of China* was issued on 7 January 1986, stipulating that the central bank, specialized banks and financial organizations should meticulously observe and carry out state policy. Their business is to pursue the goal of developing the economy, stabilizing the currency and raising the social economic results.

The People's Bank of China

The People's Bank of China is the central bank directly under the State Council. It is the government department in charge of the financial business of the whole country. It concentrates on the study and making of major State policy. It exercises its authority to strengthen the management of credit funds and stabilize currency. It does not handle credits to enterprises or individuals. Its main obligations are to:

– Study and make State financial policies and implement them when approved.

– Study and make drafts for financial laws and regulations.

– Work out the basic regulations for financial business.

– Take charge of the issue of currency, regulate the circulation of currency and stabilize it.

– Control the interest rate of deposits and loans. Work out the rate of exchange between Renminbi and foreign currency.

– Draft the state credit plan. Practise centralized management of credit funds and unified management of the circulating funds of state-run enterprises.

– Control foreign exchange, gold, silver and the State's foreign exchange reserve and gold reserve.

– Examine and approve the establishment, dissolution and merging of specialized banks and other financial organizations.

– Direct, manage, coordinate, oversee and check the business of specialized banks and other financial organizations.

– Take charge of the state treasury and issue government bonds on behalf of the State.

– Manage the stocks, bonds and other securities of enterprises and control the financial market.

– Take part in relevant international financial activities on behalf of the Government.

The People's Bank of China has an authoritative council as its decision-making organ, with the President of the Bank holding the post of Director. The council is made up of relevant experts and leaders of the Ministry of Finance, the Planning Commission, the Economic Commission, specialized banks and insurance companies, etc. The branches of the People's Bank of China are established, in principle, according to the respective economic zones. The State Foreign Currency Control Administration is under the leadership of the People's Bank of China, and they share the management of the State's foreign exchange.

The first automatic cash-points have begun operation in the Bank of China Zhuhai branch and three other branches.

The president of the board of the People's Bank of China is concurrently the director of the board of the State Foreign Currency Control Administration. The board of the State Foreign Currency Control Administration handles official business, together with the People's Bank of China.

The Industrial and Commercial Bank of China

Under the leadership of the People's Bank of China, the Industrial and Commercial Bank of China, an economic body directly under the State Council, is the specialized bank which is responsible for handling industrial and commercial credits and deposits. Its major services include:
- Handling industrial and commercial credits.
- Handling the deposits of urban residents, enterprises and institutions.
- Taking charge of the accounting of industrial and commercial enterprises.
- Managing the circulating funds of state-run industrial and commercial enterprises.
- Taking charge of loans for the common technical transformation of industrial and commercial enterprises.

The General Industrial and Commercial Bank of China is situated in Beijing. Under the vertical leadership of the General Industrial and Commercial Bank of China, the other branches are coordinated, guided, supervised or checked by the branches of the People's Bank of China.

The Agricultural Bank of China

Under the leadership of the People's Bank of China, the Agricultural Bank of China, an economic body directly under the State Council, is the specialized bank responsible for rural financial work. Its major services include:
- Handling the deposits of rural communes and villages, township enterprises, agriculture–industry–commerce co-operative enterprises; handling loans for them and exercising control over rural cash.
- Examining, checking, allotting and paying the appropriations of financial departments for agriculture; issuing forward purchasing advances and managing the funds to support agriculture collected by business departments; overseeing the utilization of these funds.
- Controlling cash and helping to transfer accounts and settle accounts for rural state-owned or collectively-owned enterprises and institutions.

The General Agricultural Bank of China is situated in Beijing; provinces, autonomous regions and municipalities directly under the Central Government have branches. Localities have central sub-branches and counties (cities) have sub-branches. These organs are in charge of business offices and credit co-operatives in the countryside.

Credit co-operatives in the countryside are the socialist collectively-owned financial organizations. They are the basic-level organizations of the Agricultural Bank. Under the leadership of the Agricultural Bank, they are responsible for absorbing the idle funds in the countryside, aiding agricultural production and helping peasants to solve difficulties in production, etc. They have the duty of combatting usury. In addition, they deal with various business mandated by the Agricultural Bank.

The Bank of China

Under the leadership of the People's Bank of China, the Bank of China, an economic body directly under the State Council, is a specialized bank designated by the State to deal with foreign exchange. It is the centre of China's international accounting, foreign exchange credits and receiving and paying out foreign exchange. Its main services include:
- Dealing with the transaction of foreign exchange in a unified manner.
- Dealing with international accounting for all trading or non-trading foreign exchange.
- Dealing with the deposits and loans among banks throughout the world.
- Dealing with deposits of foreign exchange, including remittances from overseas Chinese.
- Handling foreign exchange credits and foreign trade credits.
- Making studies of international or domestic financial tendencies.

The General Bank of China is situated in Beijing, with branches in ports and cities, all with a large work load. It has a board of directors and a supervisory committee – both being consultative organizations. The overseas organizations of the Bank of China can also deal with loans within the permission of local government laws.

The People's Construction Bank of China

The People's Construction Bank of China is the specialized bank dealing particularly with the financial business of capital construction. An economic body directly under the State Council, its appropriations for capital construction are under the control of the Ministry of Finance. Its policies and plans concerning credits are subject to the decisions made by the People's Bank of China. Its main services include:
- Allotting loans for capital construction and some special projects related to capital construction.
- Helping to settle accounts for the units of capital construction, mainly including accounting on money for projects and for loans.
- Handling the deposits of capital construction.
- Managing the expenditure budget for capital construction and overseeing the financial plans and final accounts of each capital construction unit.

The People's Insurance Company of China

Under the Management of the People's Bank of China, the People's Insurance Company of China, an economic body directly under the State Council, is the specialized company dealing with insurance and re-insurance at home and abroad.

China International Trust and Investment Corporation (CITIC)

China International Trust and Investment Corporation is the socialist state-owned enterprise directly under the State Council. Its duty is to direct, absorb and make use of foreign capital, to import advanced technology and equipment, and allot loans for on-going construction in China. The Corporation is situated in Beijing and has branches in Hong Kong and Tokyo and also in provinces, autonomous regions and municipalities directly under the Central Government.

Management of International Banking

International finance management mainly concerns the management of foreign exchange, rates of foreign exchange, international settlements, international credit and allotment.

Foreign exchange control

In March 1979, in order to strengthen the management of foreign exchange, the State Council agreed that the Bank of China be its directly governed organ. Meanwhile the Foreign Currency Control Administration under the leadership of the People's Bank of China was established.

On the premise of independence and self-reliance, the Bank of China makes systematic use of foreign capital and selectively absorbs the advanced technology badly needed. The Bank of China takes it as its

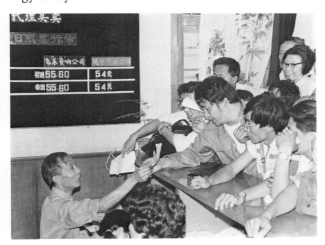

The stock exchange has reappeared in Shanghai. The financial market is very active. (Photo by Liu Zhong-yang)

prime task to collect foreign capital and it is in charge of financing and paying according to the state plan. The prime principle in the use of foreign exchange is based on the reliable capacities of repaying, forming a complete set and digesting advanced technology. Most of the foreign capital China uses is absorbed from the international financial markets through the Bank of China. The main channels include:

– Maintaining the relations of capital accommodation with the foreign banks, including 220 major banks throughout the world.

– Engaging in investment or arranging with banks to allot loans in world financial and capital markets.

– Making use of relevant countries' buyer's credits and mixed loans.

– Issuing public bonds in foreign countries.

– Providing joint investment for domestic projects with the foreign banks and enterprises, etc.

The foreign exchange control system in China implements the policy of "unified management and administration". The main regulations in foreign exchange control include:

– All foreign loans and expenditures in government offices, military establishments, educational institutions, groups, enterprises and institutions should be systematically controlled.

– All foreign loans should be kept under centralized management: all units in China which are going to receive foreign loans should go through formalities in accordance with the procedure of examination and approval.

– Some enterprises should be allowed to keep part of the foreign exchange. But the preserved foreign exchange and free foreign exchange borrowed should be used to open a foreign-exchange account with the Bank of China as special deposits. All foreign exchange should be used under the supervision of the Bank of China.

– The foreign exchange belonging to personal income (i.e., contributors' fees, money paid for giving lectures and money awards, etc.) should be kept in the Bank of China. This foreign exchange still belongs to the individual and can be remitted abroad: it can also be exchanged for Renminbi.

– All foreign revenue and expenditure of foreign organizations in China, overseas Chinese-funded, exclusively foreign-funded and Chinese–foreign joint enterprises should be treated in terms of foreign accounts. Their foreign exchange earnings must be deposited in the Bank of China. All expenditure of foreign exchange should be paid from the deposits. All foreigners, overseas Chinese, compatriots from Hong Kong and Macao who come to China for short-time travelling and visits should declare their foreign exchange, gold and silver, etc. at the Customs when they enter China. If they are going to take gold and silver out of China, the amount should be limited according to the Customs Regulations. When they leave China, the gold and silver they have brought with them can go through the Customs with their transit declarations, and residual foreign exchange can be carried out of China.

– No foreign currency is allowed to circulate in China. It is forbidden to evade paying in foreign exchange or to engage in speculation by means of foreign currency.

– It is forbidden to carry, mail or ask a third party to take Renminbi out of or bring them into China.

Rates of exchange control

The rate of exchange of Renminbi is settled, readjusted and issued to the outside world by the Foreign Currency Control Administration authorized by the State. It is reported daily, both at home and abroad, in Chinese, English and French through the Xinhua News Agency. The current rate of exchange of Renminbi totals 17 different sorts. The rate of exchange between Renminbi and one foreign currency falls into two prices: the buying price and the selling price. The price differential between them is 5 per cent.

The rate of exchange between Renminbi and foreign currencies is settled through a comparison of domestic and world prices, with account also of the balance of payments and other factors.

Transactions between China and the capitalist countries are calculated in Renminbi, and the rate of exchange is flexibly adjusted in the light of changes of prices in the financial markets of some of the main capitalist countries. (After 1970, trading payments between China and the Soviet Union were settled in Swiss francs.) In 1980, it was agreed that non-trading payments between China and the Soviet Union and other Eastern European countries should be paid in currencies which can be freely exchanged. Trading payments are settled with the rate of exchange between Renminbi and rubles.

International accounting

International accounting mainly requires quick and accurate withdrawal of the foreign exchange which should be obtained and prompt payment of the foreign exchange needed for export according to trading or non-trading plans, contracts and agreements. Attention must also be paid to the discrepancy between revenue and expenditure of foreign exchange and full play given to the bank's role in regulating capital.

Since 1970, the Bank of China has done much to strengthen the checking of foreign exchange and adopt flexible accounting measures. It has, by and large, safely drawn back the foreign exchange in time. In 1980, the Bank of China started a trial business of fast postal remittance and exporting bills of exchange at a discount. In 1983, it worked out the accounting method for Chinese–foreign joint ventures, banks and foreign trade departments. It handled buying list documentary bills and acceptance of bills of exchange. In 1984, the Bank of China joined SWIFT. Thus the telecommunications business of China became an integral part of the international global telecommunication network, which provided favourable conditions for raising the efficiency of international accounting.

To foreign countries, the non-trading settlement on account was changed in 1979 and 1980 into settlement on a cash basis. The way of settlement was therefore based on equality and mutual benefit.

Bank notes of different denominations issued by the People's Bank of China (reduced sizes).

International credit management

According to the state plan, the Bank of China provides foreign exchange loans with its own foreign exchange capital for departments or enterprises to import advanced technology and equipment, etc.

The Bank of China reformed the system of foreign exchange credit in 1980 to make good use of foreign exchange loans.

The foreign exchange is categorized into two parts: state-owned foreign exchange and that absorbed. They are controlled separately. The foreign exchange used for importing large-scale projects is provided by the State. If it is not enough, the Bank of China will finance the rest. Borrowing and paying back the loans is under the overall direction of the departments designated by the State. The Bank will:

– Take charge of deposits and loans in foreign exchange and Renminbi. Resolve the problem of divorce between loans of foreign exchange and that of Renminbi.

– Support the manufacture of export commodities. Focus on the export of industrial and textile products. Invest capital in projects which need comparatively little capital but can achieve great economic results and are quick in capital turnover. Support such non-productive departments as travelling services, which have the ability to pay back and offer favourable conditions for loans.

– Give full play to the initiatives of the Central departments and localities. The branches of the Bank of China in each province, autonomous region and municipality directly under the Central Government control and make use of foreign exchange loans within the set quota. 70 per cent of the foreign exchange deposits absorbed by each branch can be used as short-term foreign exchange loans according to the rules.

To improve credit business, the Bank of China initiated "special foreign exchange investment" as an experiment in 1982. It is called "two sorts of investments" for short. The first kind is for those units which have the ability to pay back foreign exchange. These units exchange Renminbi for foreign exchange in the Trust Department of the Bank of China, and when the investment becomes due, they have to pay back the capital plus interest in foreign exchange. The second kind of investment is for those units which have no channel to get foreign exchange. The Bank of China can allot foreign exchange loans to import equipment, raw material and technology, and when the investment becomes due, these units have to exchange foreign currency with Renminbi in the Trust Department of the Bank of China and they pay back the capital, plus interest.

After the reforms, the foreign exchange investments amount to more than ten different kinds and Renminbi investments more than six different kinds. These two major kinds of investments are closely related to each other and complement each other. They have been the main channels through which the State makes use of foreign capital.

International trust and investment management

It is the firm and unshakeable policy of the Chinese government to draw in foreign capital so as to speed up the construction of modernization in China. The China International Trust and Investment Corporation was established to absorb foreign capital and give impetus to the development of trust and investment.

Since 1979, the corporation has been absorbing foreign capital and investing it in enterprises at home. It deals with short-term or long-term investment, establishing contact with relevant foreign organizations and signing agreements or contracts for joint investment on behalf of the domestic units. It affords recommendatory or consultative services for the establishment of joint ventures or technical cooperation. It also takes charge of the advanced technology and equipment, etc. on behalf of foreign enterprises and businessmen. It is starting a rental business: the China Rental Company and China Oriental Rental Company have been set up in Beijing to engage in rental services at home and abroad.

Auditing

There were no formal auditing organizations in China before 1982. The new Constitution adopted at the Fifth Session of the Fifth National People's Congress held in 1982 stipulates that an auditing body should be constituted in the State Council to audit and supervise the financial revenue and expenditure of all departments under the State Council and local governments at all levels. It also exercises its authority to audit and supervise the revenue and expenditure of state financial organizations, enterprises and institutions. The auditing organizations at all levels must conduct their audits and supervision in accordance with the law. The Auditing Bureau of the People's Republic of China was officially set up according to the decision of the First Session of the Sixth National People's Congress held in June 1983. The establishment of the government organization was aimed at enforcing financial discipline, urging all enterprises to raise their economic efficiency and strengthening the control and management of finance so as to ensure the smooth development of the reform of the structure of the economy.

The state auditing services mainly include the auditing of financial revenue and expenditure, special cases of financial rules and regulations, and economic efficiency. The main tasks of audit organizations are:

– To audit and supervise the implementation of

financial plans and credit plans and their results.

– To audit and supervise the revenue and expenditure and the economic efficiency of state-run enterprises, institutions' capital construction units and financial insurance organizations.

– To audit and supervise the revenue and expenditure of administrative departments, military establishments and those units which have state funds or receive state subsidies.

– To audit special cases of bad behaviour, serious infringement of state interests or violation of financial disciplines, such as illegally seizing, damaging or wasting state assets.

– To audit the revenue and expenditure of the construction projects which use loans from world financial organizations and those aided by the special organizations of the United Nations.

– To implement state audit laws and regulations, draw up audit rules and regulations, and join in drawing up important financial and economic laws.

With the establishment of the State Auditing Bureau, many auditing organizations have been set up and auditing staffs rapidly assigned to these organizations, and they have been working hard, so that auditing and supervision of all departments and units have been strengthened and notable results achieved. Moreover, China also takes part in world auditing activities and has become a member state of the international auditing organization.

Insurance Business

After the founding of the New China, the insurance business of old China was readjusted and transformed. In 1949, with the approval of the State Council, the People's Insurance Company of China was established. The company has successively taken charge of fire, life and agriculture insurance business. It has also provided the mandatory insurance service for the assets of the government agencies and state-run enterprises. In addition, it offers an insurance service for transport and transportation vehicles and accident insurance for passengers on trains, ships and planes. It handles external insurance including transportation of export goods, ocean-going ships, international airline planes and the assets of foreigners in China, to meet the demand of foreign trade and economic co-operation with foreign countries. It has exerted an effective role in compensating for the economic or property losses of all units or individuals and amassing construction capital and strengthening links with the world insurance business.

The People's Insurance Company of China has set up branches or liaison offices both at home and abroad. These include: the Hong Kong Branch of the Insurance Company of China Ltd; the Macao Branch of the Insurance Company of China Ltd; the Singa-

Table 4: The Bank of China Overseas Branches

Hong Kong Branches;	
	Western Sub-Branch
	Sheung Wan Sub-Branch
	Wanchai Sub-Branch
	Harbour Road Sub-Branch
	Shau Kei Wan Sub-Branch
	Mongkok Sub-Branch
	Yaumati Sub-Branch
	Cheung Sha Wan Sub-Branch
	Tsim Sha Tsui Sub-Branch
	Yuan Long Sub-Branch
	Sheung Shui Sub-Branch
	Tsuen Wan Sub-Branch
	Shatin Sub-Branch
Other Branches;	
	West End Office, London Branch
	Manchester Sub-Branch
	Glasgow Sub-Branch
	Luxembourg Branch
	New York Branch
	Chinatown Branch
	Grand Cayman Branch
	Singapore Branch
	Dapo Sub-Branch
	Xiaopo Sub-Branch
	Jiadong Sub-Branch
	Paris Branch
	Sydney Branch
	Representative Office, Tokyo

pore Branch of the Insurance Company of China Ltd; the Singapore Branch of the Life Insurance Company Ltd; the Hong Kong Branch of the Taiping Insurance Company Ltd; the Singapore Branch of the Taiping Insurance Company Ltd. and the London Liaison Office of the Insurance Company of China.

In the early 1980s, the People's Insurance Company of China offered building and installation insurance. It also offered insurance according to agreements, insurance for political stability and offshore oil exploration and overall insurance of material processing. The managerial forms of insurance can be divided into voluntary and mandatory insurance. The voluntary insurance is done through signing insurance contracts, making clear the categories, volumes, premium and sum of compensation. The mandatory insurance refers to life insurance for passengers on trains, ships and planes, etc. by compulsory means. It is unnecessary to sign contracts for this kind of insurance, which comes into effect automatically when passengers start their travelling. The premium on insurance is settled in accordance with the unified standard stipulated in the state law. The insurance is carried out through state legal effect.

Table 5: China International Trust and Investment Corporation Overseas Branches

Hong Kong Branch
CITIC Representative Office, Paris
CITIC Representative Office, Japan
CITIC Representative Office, New York

Table 6: The People's Insurance Company of China Overseas Branches

Hong Kong;

    Insurance Company of China
    Taiping Insurance Company of China
    Life Insurance Company of China
    Reinsurance Company of China
    Sino-American Joint Insurance Company, Hong Kong Branch
    Baolian Investment Company
    New Epoch Stock Company

Singapore;

    Insurance Company of China
    Taiping Insurance Company of China
    Life Insurance Company of China

Macao;

    Insurance Company of China

United States;

    Sino-American Joint Insurance Company, New York Branch

United Kingdom;

    Insurance Company of China, London Liaison Office

Bermuda;

    General Sino-American Joint Insurance Company

12. PRICES AND PRICE CONTROL

General Information

THE Chinese government has always attached much importance to prices and price control. Its consistent policy is to keep the market situation and prices basically rationally stable.

In the early post-Liberation days, the market situation was chaotic, with vicious inflation and rocketing prices, a problem left over from the old society. At the time, the war was still going on. The huge military expenditure, plus hoarding and cornering by speculators, caused the prices to fluctuate violently on five occasions, that is, in January, April, July and November 1949 and February 1950, in all parts of the country except North-East China. In Shanghai, for instance, the wholesale price rose about 20 times from June 1949 to February 1950. This brought tremendous pressure to bear upon the national economy and the people's livelihood. To stabilize the market and bring the prices under control, the People's Government issued a decision to unify the state financial and economic work, thus bringing the state income and expenditure, allocation of materials and cash management under a unified direction. In addition, the Government adopted measures to tighten the circulation of currency, put taxation in order and strengthen market control. These included control over the purchasing power of state enterprises, government offices, military establishments and other social organizations; issuing bonds; ensuring an open-ended supply of grain, cotton cloth, coal, salt and other major commodities in major cities; and dealing with speculation that jeopardized the national economy. The measures worked and soon inflation and market prices were brought under control. Prices stabilized in 1952 when the whole national economy had been rehabilitated and developed and there had been a fundamental turn for the better in the financial situation, thus winning a great victory on the economic front.

During the First Five-Year Plan period, from 1953 to 1957, the Government went on to transform agriculture, the handicrafts industry and capitalist industry and commerce along socialist lines. To achieve this goal, the State began to monopolize the purchasing and supply of grain, oil-bearing crops and cotton, while imposing quotas for unified purchase on such crops and farm products as pigs, cured tobacco, sugar-bearing crops and other major agricultural produce. For the private sector of industry, the State placed orders and monopolized the purchase and sales of their products. On prices, the State fixed the prices of farm produce covered by the State's monopolized purchase plan, thus holding in check the law-breaking businessmen's rush for much-wanted commodities at high prices and contributing to stabilizing the market prices and promoting the socialist transformation of agriculture, and private business. In addition, the State examined and reset prices for processing and selling industrial products by private industrialists for the purpose of restricting and transforming this sector of the industry. Next, the State adopted the policy of replacing private wholesalers by systematically reducing price differentials among different regions in order to check the long distance hauling of major commodities and cut off their ties with capitalist industry and commerce and with small farming economy, forcing most of the private businesses to order goods from state-owned commerce. The State also tried to bring into play the positive roles of private retailers in the flow of commodities and to restrict their speculation activities by setting different price differentials between wholesale and retail sales for different categories of goods, so as to guide them onto the road of socialism. Meanwhile, the State systematically raised the purchasing prices for grain, oil-bearing crops, pigs and tobacco while maintaining the retail prices in the market basically stable. The prices for some light industrial and textiles goods, coal and farm-use diesel oil were also readjusted one after another in order to narrow the price differentials between industrial goods and farm produce and to promote production. Comparing 1957 with 1952, the purchasing prices for farm and sideline produce were raised by 20.2 per cent while the retail prices of manufactured goods in rural areas rose by only 2.2 per cent, thus narrowing the price differences by 18 per cent, which means that peasants could exchange 17.6 per cent more manufactured goods for the same amount of farm produce.

At the beginning of the 1960s, owing to errors during the Great Leap Forward and serious natural disasters, the development of the various sectors of the national economy was thrown into imbalance and industrial and agricultural production dropped continuously, causing a serious shortage of many major consumer goods and inducing the prices on the free markets to soar. In 1960 the supply of consumer goods could only meet 87.9 per cent of the demand, and in the following year the market prices were at least twice as high as the state listed prices.

To cope with the difficulties in the financial and economic situation, the State set out to readjust the national economic development and further strengthened its control over prices and the market. Major measures taken included the following:

– To stabilize the prices of 18 major commodities. In September 1961, the Central Government adopted a decision to maintain the prices of the basic daily necessities which claimed 60 to 70 per cent of the living expenditure of the workers and staff members. In February 1963 the National Price Committee announced the list of 18 commodities: grain, cotton cloth, knitwear, cotton fluff, table salt, shoes, soy-sauce, thick soybean sauce and vinegar, the rationed part of meat, fish, edible oil and pastries, sugar and sweets, common vegetables, matches, coal, kerosene, stationery and textbooks, major Western medicine, and enamel ware, aluminium ware and rubber products that were made by using raw materials supplied by the State, house rents, electricity and water charges, transportation fees, mail charges, medical fees and tuition. The measures were of extreme importance in ensuring the basic needs of the people and promoting social stability.

– To allow the prices of part of the commodities to float according to market demand. In early 1961, the Central Committee of the Communist Party of China decided to sell a dozen consumer goods at high prices. They included sweets, pastries, brand name wines and liquors, imported cigarettes, knitwear, bicycles and wrist watches. Meanwhile, the State opened luxury hotels in big and medium-sized cities and industrial and mining areas, all for the purpose of withdrawing currency. These helped to narrow the differences between supply and demand, increase the state revenue, keep the market and prices stable and bring convenience to the people. As the state financial and economic situation improved and the amount of currency in circulation was reduced, the prices of the listed products began to drop in the latter half of 1962 and gradually returned to normal.

– To tighten the purchasing power of social organizations, control the currency issue and strengthen centralized control over prices. At the same time, steps were taken to extend the scope of rationed goods in order to ensure a rational distribution of goods in short supply.

– To readjust the prices of commodities that were either too low or too high. From 1961, the State raised the purchasing prices for grain, oil-bearing crops, pigs, poultry and eggs and other farm and sideline produce while maintaining the sales prices of

these products. It also raised the prices of some coal, concentrated tungsten ore and gold and lowered the prices of metal cutting machine tools, mercury rectifier and tractors, diesel engine, chemical fertilizer and pesticides and other capital goods for farm production. The prices of some manufactured daily necessities were also lowered. Comparing 1965 with 1957, the general purchasing price index of farm and sideline produce (including listed prices, negotiated prices and additional charges for above-quota purchase) rose by 28.5 per cent. Of this, the purchasing prices for grain rose by 46.3 per cent; of cash crops, 22.2 per cent; of other products, 19.6 per cent. The retail price index rose by 11 per cent, of which the listed price index rose by 9 per cent while the market price index rose by 59.0 per cent.

The catastrophic ten-year Cultural Revolution that began in 1966 brought great damage to industrial and agricultural production, resulting in very scarce market supplies and an almost total collapse of the national economy, nearly paralysing leading organizations at all levels and in all economic management departments. Some of the effective price control systems were cast away and there was a general price rise and raising of prices in disguised form. The market prices had gone nearly out of control. Facing this situation, the Party Central Committee and the State Council issued regulations in August 1967, calling for "further practising economy in making changes and controlling purchases by social organizations and strengthening the management of funds, materials and prices." In 1970, the State Council issued a circular banning raising prices without approval. The regulations and the circular brought to a halt the rational adjustment of prices and in fact froze them. This had a positive effect in maintaining order in the market, checking the price rises and ensuring a secure life for the people, but the situation lasted too long to do any good to the development of the economy. The prices of many commodities did not keep up with the changes in production, circulation, consumption and supply and demand. Problems began to pile up, making it very difficult to readjust the prices and carry out reforms later on.

However, the facts showed that it was hard for the freezing of prices to last long. With the improvement in the economic situation, the Chinese government began to adjust the prices of some industrial and agricultural products from 1971. This included raising the purchasing prices of fat, oil-bearing crops, sugar-bearing crops and *Mao* bamboo and reducing the sales prices of chemical fertilizer, pesticides, diesel oil, internal combustion engines, motor vehicles and parts and electronic elements. Then in 1973, the State went on to raise the purchasing prices of hemp, cotton yarn, raw lacquer, goatskin and sheep's wool and to raise the factory and the sales prices of iron, wooden and bamboo farm tools. At the same time, it raised the prices of some industrial products and reduced the prices of others.

During the ten-year Cultural Revolution the general price index dropped slightly as a result of the price freeze, with the prices of paper and some other products even reduced, though the commodities were in acutely short supply. Taking the 1965 price index as the base figure 100, the price index in 1976 was 98.3 per cent (5.7 per cent up for urban areas and 6.7 per cent down in rural areas) and the price index of purchasing prices of farm and sideline produce rose by 11.6 per cent, with grain rising the fastest, at about 25.2 per cent.

The victory in overthrowing the Jiang Qing clique in October 1976 marked a new period of historical development in China. Pricing policy was freed from the bondage of prolonged "Leftist deviation" and began a change of historic importance. The work was reoriented onto a correct course especially after late 1978 when the Third Plenary Session of the Eleventh Central Committee of CPC was held, passing the resolution to shift the focus of work to economic construction and to developing commodity production and the exchange of commodities, consciously applying the law of value. The guiding principle for pricing policy began to change: firstly, it was made to work to serve the needs of socialist economic construction, instead of being a tool for class struggle; secondly, to clarify the idea that the socialist economy is a planned commodity economy, the means of production is also a commodity and price is one of the important economic levers, and to correct the erroneous ideas that ignored the roles of the law of value; thirdly, to break away from the idea that price adjustment is opposed to stability and make it clear that price adjustment is an important condition to keep prices stable; fourthly, to implement and strengthen the principle of market regulation and change the sole form of planned prices. The major changes in the guiding principles helped open up a new situation for carrying out price reforms.

In 1977 and 1978, the national economy was rehabilitated and gained momentum for development, and price work begun to embark on a road of healthy development. The State Council made a number of major policy decisions on prices and price control, which led to active but cautious readjustment of prices of major commodities in a planned and stage-by-stage manner, beginning from 1979.

– *Purchasing prices for farm and sideline produce raised by a big margin.* Agriculture is the foundation of the national economy. It also suffered from the Cultural Revolution. Its cost kept rising, due to the increased application of chemical fertilizers and pesticides, but the purchasing prices of grain and other major farm produce had not been raised for years. Many production teams did not get more income from increased production and some even suffered from decreased income though their production went up. The living standards of the peasants were not at all improved. Many villages had no accumulation funds for ex-

panded production and some even had barely enough to maintain simple production. That was why the State Council decided to raise from 1979 the purchasing prices of grain, oil-bearing crops, castor oil, cotton, pigs, beef cattle and sheep, fresh eggs, aquatic products, sugar beet, sugar cane, hemp, jute, yellow ox skin, silk cocoons, timber in the southern part of China and *Mao* bamboo. The prices for above-quota sales of grain and oil-bearing crops were also raised from the original 30 per cent to 50 per cent. For the above-quota sales of cotton, an additional 30 per cent of the prices was given as an award. The general price rise for these products was 25.7 per cent, with the price of grain raised by 30.5 per cent, oil-bearing crops 38.7 per cent and cotton 25 per cent. The general index of the purchasing prices of farm produce rose by 22.1 per cent in 1979 over the preceding year, giving the peasants an additional income of nearly 10,000 million yuan.

In the following year, the State raised the prices of cotton again, by another 10 per cent in general, with 30 per cent more added for above-quota sales and five per cent more for northern China cotton-producing areas as subsidies. At the same time, the purchasing prices of tung oil, raw lacquer, hemp and cured tobacco were also raised in the country as a whole. The purchasing prices of certain medicinal herbs were also raised or reduced.

From 1981, the State began to take steps to reduce the range of products that would get additional award prices for above-quota sales so as to reduce the income parities between different regions and production units because of the differences in the quota set for them. First of all, the State cancelled the award prices for soybean purchase by raising the purchasing price by 50 per cent to the level of the award price and cancelling the quota system. In the same year, the prices of soybean oil, cured tobacco, timber in the south and *Mao* bamboo were also raised.

During the three years from 1979 to 1981, the purchasing prices of farm and sideline produce were raised by a range that had never been witnessed since the founding of New China. For instance, such prices were raised by only 117.4 per cent during the 28 years from 1950 to 1978, averaging 2.8 per cent annually. But in the three years from 1979 to 1981, they were raised by 38.5 per cent, averaging 11.5 per cent a year. The raising of the purchasing prices of farm produce, plus the award prices for above-quota sales and the expansion of the range of products that could be sold at negotiable prices, gave the peasants an additional benefit of 20,000 million yuan during the three years.

Some smaller changes were made from 1982 to 1984 in the purchasing prices of some farm produce. But the general level of purchasing prices of farm produce continued to rise.

– *Sales prices of eight major non-staple foods raised and price subsidies provided.* As the sales prices of major farm products remained unchanged following the rise in purchasing prices from March 1979, the commercial departments found that the more they sold the greater loss they suffered. The State had to spend huge amounts of money to subsidize the commercial departments. As the purchasing prices were high and sales prices were low, this gave rise to speculation, thus doing harm to the national economy. This led to the decision by the State Council to raise the sales prices of pork, beef, mutton, poultry, eggs, aquatic products, vegetables and milk beginning from November 1. This enabled commercial departments to get a marginal profit and checked the speculation activities, thus ensuring a normal social and economic life.

In order that the workers and staff members in urban areas should not be affected by the price rise, a subsidy of 5 yuan per person was provided to offset the price increase.

The price rise resulted in the rise of the general price index for retail sales, which was 2 per cent in 1979, 6 per cent in 1980 and 2.4 per cent in 1984, which was 10.7 per cent higher than in 1978. During this period, the State also raised the wages for part of the workers and staff members, instituted the award system and opened more avenues for employment and tightened the control over family planning. These changes enabled the average per capita monthly income to rise by 45 per cent or 29 per cent in real terms.

– *Heavy industrial goods prices and transportation fees readjusted.* Over the past three decades, heavy industrial goods had been produced and allocated according to plan, with the prices put under unified control. The policy of keeping the prices of capital goods low resulted in a serious deviation of prices from value, especially during the Cultural Revolution, when the prices were frozen. In general, prices in the mining and raw materials industries were much too low while the prices in the processing industries were relatively high, thus widening the profitability gaps between different departments, trades and enterprises and affecting the balance of development of the various sectors of the economy. To change all this, the State Council decided in 1979 to raise the price of coal by 32 per cent. This put an end to the long loss-making situation and supported its further development.

To encourage more output of coal, the State decided to grant award prices for output of coal above their production quotas to 22 major coal mines whose products were allocated by the State. The award price was usually 25 per cent higher than the state listed prices for the output of 1982 and 50 per cent starting from 1983. These measures had a positive result in increasing production and economical use of coal.

During this period, the State also raised the factory prices of iron ore, coke, pig iron, steel ingots and blooms, rolled steel, non-ferrous metals, cement and plate glass, while lowering the prices of motor vehicles, general machinery and parts, instruments and meters, measuring and cutting tools, thus making the price relations between the mining and raw material industry more rational.

The problems with transportation were that the transport charges were too low, the price relations between the various means of transport were irrational as also were the shipping charges and port fees. These held up the development of shipping and road transport and the improvement in efficiency. But as raising the transport charges would cause a chain reaction, the first step to solve the problems was to resolve the problems of the part of transport charges that were too low and the price relations that were too irrational. With the approval of the State Council, a surcharge was added to the transport fees for short-distance railway freight from 1 August as a provisional measure in order to pave the way for further price readjustment. At the same time, water transport charges were readjusted and port fee collection methods were revised.

– *Prices of light industrial goods and textiles readjusted.* This involved the lowering of the prices for polyester-cotton blended fabrics and the raising of the prices for some cigarettes and wines. The costs of polyester-cotton fabrics had been lowered consistently with the multiplication of the output, which was more than 30 times that of 1960, but the sales prices were on the high side, not in keeping with the purchasing power of the people. In order to expand sales and encourage people to buy more polyester-cotton fabrics, the State Council decided to lower the sales prices of such fabrics as of 18 November 1981 by an average of 13 per cent in general. Meanwhile, the prices for wines, liquors and cigarettes were raised, since the prices of brand name wines and cigarettes were too low to enable producers to make a profit, thus causing a short supply on the market. The move gave an impetus to production and helped improve the supply, benefiting both the State and producers and consumers.

The second step was the raising of the prices of cotton textiles while lowering the prices of chemical fabrics. After 1978, the State raised the purchasing prices of cotton on three occasions and by a margin of about 50 per cent, whereas the sales prices remained intact, thrusting the burden onto the State. The too low price held up the initiatives of cotton textile producers, who often failed to meet their production targets. On the other hand, the prices for chemical fabrics were a bit too high and the goods stockpiled. From 20 January 1983 the prices of chemical fabrics were cut by a big margin while the prices of cotton cloth were raised to an appropriate extent. To balance the rise and fall of prices, the State decided to reduce the prices of wrist watches, alarm clocks, cloth and rubber shoes, photographic films, electric fans and colour television sets. The price readjustments achieved the anticipated results.

– *Price reforms carried out in steady and cautious steps.* 1985 marked the beginning of an overall reform of the price system. The decision was made by the State

Council in the light of the guidelines on the restructuring of the economy set out by the Third Plenary Session of the Twelfth Central Committee of the CPC and by taking into consideration the ability of the State, enterprises and individuals to bear it. The principle was to make cautious, steady steps by combining relaxation of price control with price readjustments. The reform was done mainly by the following means: cancelling the monopolized and compulsory purchase of farm and sideline produce and introducing the system of contractual purchase; derestricting the prices for pork and other live and fresh non-staple foodstuffs; readjusting the purchase and sales prices for grain in the countryside; relaxing the control over the prices of capital goods not covered by state plans; widening the regional price differences for coal; allowing light industrial departments to fix prices for part of their products and raising the charges for short-distance railway freight.

Derestriction of prices

Derestricting the prices for pigs, vegetables and other live and fresh non-staple foodstuffs was the main task for price reform in 1985. The aim was to stimulate the production of pigs to meet the needs in the restructuring of the rural economy and rising living standards of the people. This mainly involved policy changes, which included the replacement of compulsory purchase with contractual purchase and the replacement of unified prices with providing guidance in fixing the prices. The move began in the spring of 1985. Both the purchasing prices and sales prices rose by about 30 per cent and there were big price differences between regions, seasons, lean and fat pork and fresh and frozen pork, which changed with the market demand. The result was that pig raising in the country as a whole began to pick up; all the state enterprises, collectives and individuals became involved in the purchasing and selling of pigs; there was a free supply of pork in both urban and rural areas, with fresh pork visibly on the increase. To offset the increases in family expenditure, a certain amount of subsidies was provided to urban residents by local governments according to actual conditions.

The readjustment of vegetable prices mainly concerned large and medium-sized cities because in smaller cities such prices had always been left to market forces. This was done mainly because there had been too rigid control over vegetable prices and the enthusiasm of vegetable growers was seriously affected. The relaxation of control over vegetable prices, which began in 1985, gave free rein to the initiative of vegetable growers and marketing agents. More and better vegetables became available on the market and the situation on the whole was good, except in certain places where the prices rose too fast and too high, and this caused a strong repercussion. This was because these cities took too big a step and

no follow-up measures were taken. After remedial measures were taken, the situation was much improved.

Readjustment of prices

Readjusting the purchasing and pricing policies on grain mainly involved the abrogation of the monopolized purchasing system and introduction of contractual purchase, allowing more decision-making powers to the peasants. The purpose was to prepare the rural areas for commodity production, stimulate the rationalization of the rural economic structure and invigorate the rural economy as a whole. Under the new system, 30 per cent of the contractual amount would be bought by the State according to the listed prices, while the remaining 70 per cent would be given an additional price, doing away with the multiple forms of prices that had made the purchasing prices of grain unstable and brought about differences between different regions. Meanwhile, the grain sales prices in the rural areas were also raised to the level of the purchasing prices, while the State continued to subsidize the peasants' operational expenses. This put an end to the situation in which the State had to buy grain at a high price and sell it at a lower price.

Raising railway charges

For a long time, the freight charges for short distance haul were on the low side, thus increasing the burden on railways, which would otherwise be shared by road transport. Increasing the short-distance rail freight charges removed some of the burden on railways and stimulated the development of road and water transport.

1985 saw a big rise in the general index of retail prices. In May of that year, when most places began the price reform, the general index of retail prices rose by 9.3 per cent over the same period of the preceding year. Most places adopted stop-gap measures of one kind or another. The result was that the general index of retail prices rose by 8.8 per cent in the country as a whole, 12.2 per cent for urban areas and 7 per cent for rural areas. As the prices rose by a big margin, part of the increased income of the people was written off. A survey conducted by the State Statistics Bureau showed that the average per capita net income in rural areas in 1985 was 11.8 per cent higher than in 1984, and allowing for a price rise factor, the real increase was only 8 per cent. In urban areas, the average income rose by 23.8 per cent from 1984, and allowing for price rise factor, the real income rose by only 10.6 per cent. The life of some people whose income did not increase or increased only a little was adversely affected. But taken as a whole, the increase in income was bigger than the increase of prices and the overwhelming majority of the people improved their living standards to varying degrees.

Price Control Organizations and Terms of Reference

Price control is a major part of economic management in a socialist country and the task is entrusted to a corresponding organization. The price control organizations in New China were formed in the course of socialist economic construction and with the changes in the whole economic management system.

From 1949 to 1952, the work was put in the charge of the Finance and Economic Commission under the State Administrative Council and its affiliated organization – the Ministry of Trade, which exercised overall leadership and formulated policies to be executed by trade departments and other related business sections. The main tasks were to check inflation and deal with speculation and profiteering to pave the way for stabilizing the market, rehabilitating and developing the national economy and making the life of the people secure.

Later the tasks were entrusted to the Ministry of Commerce and the National Federation of Supply and Marketing Co-operatives. During the 1960s, a National Price Control Committee was formed, with corresponding organizations in various provinces, municipalities and autonomous regions. But all these organizations were almost dissolved during the ten years of the Cultural Revolution from 1966 to 1976. After the "Gang of Four" was overthrown in October 1976, the State Council decided in August 1977 to set up the State Administration for Price Control and corresponding organizations in various regions and departments. Similar organizations in provinces, autonomous regions and municipalities as well as in prefectures, cities and counties were also reinstated and resumed work.

The State Administration for Price Control mainly undertakes to draft principles, policies, decrees and plans and have them carried out throughout the country after getting the approval of the State Council. It is also responsible for the overall balance of prices in the whole country and sketches long- and medium-term and annual plans; under the direct leadership of the State Council, it fixes or adjusts prices of commodities that have a great bearing on the national economy and the people's life, including transportation charges and postal charges, and examines and approves price differences between marketing and sales, wholesale and retail sale, between different regions, seasons and degrees of quality, and the prices for commodities allocated or supplied by the State. Moreover, it undertakes to provide professional guidance to departments in charge and to corresponding organizations at provincial, municipal and autonomous regional governments and to supervise and check the implementation of price policies and rules and regulations.

Local price control organizations are charged to ensure that pricing principles, policies and rules and regulations promulgated by the State are carried out in their own region and to exercise supervision over their implementation; execute the price fixing and adjusting plans worked out by the State Council and the State Administration for Price Control; formulate pricing principles and methods for commodities within their terms of reference; formulate and adjust prices for industrial and farm products, transportation charges and fee collection standards for services; and arrange or examine and approve price differences and allocation and supply prices for major commodities. The local price organizations are also charged with the tasks of providing guidance to operational departments or subordinate organizations, and exercising supervision over the implementation of price policies and rules and regulations, coordinating and settling pricing disputes.

Enterprises are empowered to fix prices on the following: commodities with floating prices; farm and sideline products on the free markets; small commodities; commodities on trial sales; commodities produced in co-operation with other enterprises; rejected or substandard products; commodities without state listed prices and non-commodity items and technological co-operation; and food on which the State has not fixed prices. The pricing must be done according to relevant state regulations.

Forms of Pricing

China for a long time practised a highly centralized, planned pricing system, with all major commodities purchased and sold by the State according to prices set by the State. This situation began to change after the beginning of 1978, allowing floating prices, negotiable prices, coordination of pricing by industrial and commercial units and market prices in addition to the unified prices of the State.

State unified prices

These are compulsory and planned. They cover industrial and farm products that have a great bearing on the national economy and the people's livelihood. But the coverage has become smaller and smaller since 1980 in order to meet the needs of commodity production and changes in the supply and demand on the market. The specific items include grain, oil-bearing crops and cotton, which are purchased by contract; table salt, sugar, cotton cloth, major light industrial goods closely associated with the people's life, coal, electricity, petroleum, steel, cement and other major means of production, which are produced according to state mandatory plans and allocated by the State; as well as fee collection standards for rail, shipping on the Yangtze river, marine shipping, and civil aviation and postage.

Floating prices

These float on the basis of state listed prices, covering only part of industrial goods. This is a flexible form of price, aimed at providing guidance to the market. It bears the characteristic of both administrative and economic measures and both planned regulation and market regulation. While keeping the price control power in the hands of the State, it allows enterprises a certain measure of flexibility so that the prices may float according to changes in supply and demand.

There are now three types of floating prices in force: one is downward-floating prices, with the ceiling or floor prices set by the State. This applies to products in excessive supply whose prices are on the high side and whose costs are low. The second is the free-floating price, with the state listed prices as the median. It applies to light industrial goods and textiles which are available in greater varieties and specifications and whose demand and supply change fast. The third is upward-floating prices, with state listed prices as the floor prices. This applies to some low-priced industrial and farm products. It is protective in nature.

Giving more decision-making powers to enterprises on pricing has enabled them to act consciously according to economic law and, under the guidance of state plans, to carry out competition and specialized co-operation. It also encourages the go-ahead enterprises to advance and the less advanced ones to catch up, and stimulates enterprises to improve operations and management, upgrade product designs and technology, and improve quality and lower costs. These have made enterprises more responsive to market changes by adjusting price differentials between different categories of goods and different specifications, qualities and grades, thus doing away with the defects as manifested in state unified pricing.

Negotiable prices

This applies to part of farm and sideline produce. The prices are set through negotiation with producers according to market demand and the principle of protection and rational utilization of resources and by taking into consideration the prices of similar products. The prices are regulated by market forces. The negotiable sales prices are based on the negotiable purchasing prices and fixed according to the principle of more sales at slim profits and according to the direction of the flow of commodities and the expenses. The sales prices are usually lower than the free market prices.

Facts have proved that the purchase and sales of farm and sideline produce at negotiable prices under the guidance of state plans have a positive role to play in promoting rural production, enlivening the market, increasing supplies and regulating the market prices, provided the range of products covered by such prices is properly controlled and management strengthened.

Negotiated prices for small commodities

Small commodities cover small articles for daily use, stationery, small knitted articles, hardware, electrical supplies, sundry goods for daily use, small farm implements, food and small articles for minority ethnic groups. As these are produced in a great variety and the prices are low and the service life short, it is impossible and unnecessary to include them in state plans.

From 1982 to 1984, the prices for all everyday small commodities were left free to the market forces, allowing producers, mostly collective and individual handicraftsmen, to price the commodities through consultation with commercial departments. This helped promote production and flow of commodities, benefiting the State, producers and marketing agents and individual consumers.

Free market prices

This is entirely left to the market forces, rising and falling according to market trend, but within the range allowed by the state policies and decrees. In order to protect legitimate deals, the State provides necessary guidance and control: The State determines the range of products for the market. Commodities outside the range are strictly forbidden; the State forbids illegal deals, cracking down on such illegal acts as bulling and milking the market and speculation; the State intervenes when necessary by buying in and selling goods in short supply in order to keep the market stable.

The volume of market transactions has kept increasing since 1979, with prices stable, playing a useful supplementary role to the unified market.

Price Supervision and Inspection

Price supervision is a major link in the socialist control of prices, and price inspection is a major means to this end. The purpose is to bring the market activities into line with the state price policy and decrees, protect the legitimate rights and interests of all parties, maintain the normal economic order and stimulate enterprises to improve management.

The work began in the 1960s and it has become more complicated and demanding as the country begins to pursue the open policy and introduce reforms of the economic management system. To strengthen price control, price supervision and inspection organizations were set up in all price control departments at all levels, with the highest price inspection authorities instituted at the State Administration for Price Control.

In 1982, the State Council issued *Regulations on Price Control* (*Provisional*). It provides that all enterprises, undertakings and self-employed persons of all trades and services, regardless of ownership, are the main subjects of supervision, and that the State exercises supervision over the prices of their commodities and services *vis-à-vis* state prices and related policies. The departments in charge of enterprises and undertakings are obliged to keep a watch over the price movements of the enterprises and undertakings under their administration, and accept supervision and inspection by the Government and its price control departments over their pricing, price readjustment and measures for price control.

In March 1985 the State Council issued a circular calling for efforts to strengthen price control and supervision. The circular pointed out that severe punishment would be meted out to any units or individuals who tried to take advantage of the economic reforms to raise prices of commodities and services or raise prices in disguised form, buy in and resell goods in short supply for exorbitant profits or disrupt the market by other means in disregard of the interests of the State and the people.

Price supervision and inspection are carried out mainly in three forms:

– *Supervision by the State.* This is the principal form, in addition to what is done by governments at all levels, permanent organizations of the National People's Congress and government price organizations, by planning, statistics, financial auditing departments and banks and the State Administration for Industry and Commerce, within the framework of their own businesses. The discipline inspection departments of Party organizations at all levels are also responsible for handling cases that violate price policies and discipline.

– *Supervision by the public.* All trade union organizations, women's federations, urban neighbourhood community centres as well as retired workers and government employees and teachers are encouraged to participate in price inspection by issuing them with price inspection certificates. Neighbourhood communities, factories and mines are required to set up price inspection stations or posts and to put up consumer hot-lines and opinion boxes to collect complaints from consumers. In the marketplaces and shops, additional weighing and measuring instruments are provided for consumers to check against short weight or measures. Price departments also call regular meetings of consumers to hear their complaints and comments and handle letters and personal calls by consumers. The press and other media are also mobilized to publish prices of major consumer goods.

– *Supervision within enterprises.* Many enterprises and services have set up their own price supervision system, with special or voluntary personnel to inspect the implementation of the state price policies within the enterprises and services. This serves not only as an effective measure to strengthen price control but also as an important means to help enterprises and services improve management and economic performance.

To ensure better price supervision and inspection,

the State has adopted encouragement measures, including commendation, material or cash reward and protection for units and individuals who provide models in observing the state price policies and market discipline or who report and expose cases violating the price rules and discipline. At the same time, punishment is meted out to those who violate state price policies and discipline. Punishments include criticism, confiscation of illegal proceeds, docking of bonuses or part of wages, fines and even punishment by law, depending on the seriousness of the cases.

Reform of the Price System and Price Control

Fair prices are a major condition for a balanced development of the national economy and the reforms of the price system constitute the key to the success of the economic reform as a whole. The *Decision on Restructuring the Economy*, adopted at the Third Plenary Session of the Twelfth Central Committee of the Communist Party of China, set out clearly the theories and policies for establishing a rational price system.

Necessity for price reform

The socialist economy of New China is a planned commodity economy based on public ownership. If the socialist planned commodity economy is to develop, it is imperative to apply the law of value so as to make prices basically reflect the value of the commodities and the changes in market supply and demand.

But for a long time, the law of value and the market role were ignored in China's economic work. This, plus other historical reasons, resulted in a very irrational price system under which prices are distorted. This mainly manifests itself in several aspects:

– The comparative prices of different commodities are irrational, with prices of many products not reflecting their value nor the relationship between supply and demand. Mineral products and other primary products such as raw materials and energy are typical examples. Their prices are too low to provide enough incentives for development and improving economic results. This seriously affects the investment structure and the structure of products and consumption and therefore the healthy and balanced development of the national economy.

– There is not much difference between the same categories of goods of different quality, resulting in a short supply of many brand name products and stockpiling of inferior goods, and thus aggravating the conflict between supply and demand.

– The purchasing prices of grain, oils and other major farm products are higher than their sales prices. The more of such goods the State purchases, the greater the losses and the greater the burden on the

State. This situation is harmful to adjusting the structure of agricultural production and stimulating the conversion of grain into other products.

– The prices of services and repairs are too low to provide incentives for development and some trades have even shrunk.

– Over-centralization of price control over too many commodities and too rigid management have made it impossible to respond to the changes in the consumption of social labour and market demand and supply. Price has thus lost its due role as a lever for regulating the economy.

Principles of price reform

Without changing the price system, the relationships of different kinds in the national economy would never be smoothed out, which would make it impossible for the economy to develop healthily. So the success of the reforms in every area depends on the reform of prices. For instance, without reforming the price system, it would be impossible to reduce the range of products covered by the state mandatory plans and enlarge the range covered by guidance plans, displaying the regulatory role of the market. Furthermore, as enterprises will have larger decision making powers to become relatively independent, responsible for their own profits and losses, this calls for a bigger role of prices in regulating the operational activities of enterprises and other economic activities.

The principles for price reform are:

– Readjust the irrational comparative prices according to the requirements of equal exchange and the changes in supply and demand.

– Following the raising of the prices for part of minerals and raw materials, the increase in cost will be partly offset by the enterprises themselves through lowering consumption and partly by reduction in taxes, so that the market sales prices will not be raised for those products.

– While raising the purchasing prices of major farm and sideline produce, it is necessary to adopt practical measures to ensure that the real income of urban and rural residents is not lowered because of the rise in prices.

– The reform of the price control system must go hand in hand with the reform of prices, gradually reducing the range of products whose prices are fixed by the State and enlarging the range of products whose prices are fixed by enterprises or through negotiations.

In 1985 China achieved its goal of a fundamental improvement in the financial and economic situation. The national economy began to develop steadily and in a sustained and harmonious manner. This helped to pave the way for creating a favourable environment for carrying out the reform of price and price control systems.

The emphasis of price reform during the Seventh Five-Year Plan period (1986–1990) is to solve the problem that the target prices of energy and raw materials and other means of production are too low, striving to make the target prices closer to the market prices. While readjusting the wage scales, steps will be taken to fix the rational prices of housing and rents to facilitate commercialization of urban housing. The prices of services will be gradually readjusted so as to promote the development of the service industry. The ultimate goal is to establish a price system with only a small number of major commodities and services priced by the State and the overwhelming majority of goods and services regulated by the market under the guidance of the State. Such a price system will enable prices to display more fully their role in regulating the market. Price reform should be carried out in cautious but steady steps, combining relaxation of control with price readjustment and taking into full consideration the ability of the State, enterprises and the people, with the general price level maintained basically stable.

13. LABOUR AND WAGES

Labour Resources and Structure

As the most populous country in the world, China has abundant resources of labour. According to 1985 statistics, it had 498,730,000 urban and rural labourers, accounting for 47.7% of its population. Of every 10,000 people, 1,790 were in school, indicating the existence of rich labour reserves. In cities and towns, an average of 3,000,000 people enter the workforce every year.

The bulk of the Chinese population live in the countryside, and this determines the labour force structure. In 1985, 25.7% of the labourers were in cities and towns while the other 74.3% were in the countryside. Women accounted for about half the labour force in rural areas and over 36% in cities and towns. For a long time in the past, heavy industry took in the bulk of the added industrial labour force as it was given priority in development. During the 30 years between 1949 and 1979, the total output value of heavy industry increased 97.8 times, that of light industry increased 21.8 times and that of agriculture, 2.7 times. Over the three decades from 1949 to 1979, 50% of the new labourers were recruited by industry, of which 70% went to heavy industry.

This state of affairs did not change until 1979, when China set about readjusting its economic structure. According to 1985 statistics, 18% of the social labour force were employed by state-owned units, 6.7% by urban collectively-owned units, 0.9% were urban self-employed, and 74.3% were in rural areas as either collective or individual labourers.

Workers and staff members

China established the socialist relations of production and abolished the wage labour system not long after New China was founded. Since then, the contingent of its workers and staff members has grown in number and strength. At the end of 1985, China had 15.3 times as many workers and staff members as in 1949, and the proportion of these to the total number of labourers rose from 4.47% to 24.8%. In addition, the composition of this contingent had undergone constant, profound changes along with the changes in the ownership of the means of production and the development of culture and education, as well as the establishment and growth of new industries. Table 3 shows the changes in the proportionate relations of workers and staff members working in different sectors of the economy.

Table 1: Total Civil Labour Force (Year-end figure) (Unit: million)

	1952	1965	1985
Total	207.49	286.70	498.73
Workers and staff members	16.03	49.65	123.58

Source: *Extracts from Chinese Statistics* (*1986*), Chinese Statistics Publishing House, July 1986.

Table 2: Civil Labour Force Structure (Year-end figures) (Unit: million)

Year		Social group		
	Total	Workers & staff members	Urban self-employed	Rural collective & individual labourers
1952	207.29	16.03	8.83	182.43
1965	286.70	49.65	1.71	235.34
1985	498.73	123.58	4.50	370.65

Source: *Extracts from Chinese Statistics* (*1986*), Chinese Statistics Publishing House, July 1986.

Table 3: Employment by Sectors (Unit: %)

Sector	1952	1957	1965	1978	1983	1985
State	74.1	67.8	75.3	78.4	76.2	72.7
Urban collective	1.4	21.0	24.7	21.6	23.8	26.9
Joint state-private	1.6	11.1	–	–	–	0.4
Private	22.9	0.1	–	–	–	–

Source: See Table 2.

Table 4: Employment in Different Departments (Year-end figures) (Unit: thousand)

	1952	1965	1985
Total	16,030	49,650	123,580
Industry	5,330	17,430	55,560
Construction & resources prospecting	1,050	4,770	10,400
Agriculture, water conservancy, meteorology	240	4,950	8,340
Transport & posts, telecommunications	1,130	4,180	7,670
Commerce, catering & service trade, marketing & supply	2,920	7,500	15,760
Scientific research, education, culture, public health & social welfare	2,390	6,510	14,340
Party & government offices, mass organizations	2,596	2,930	7,180
Other	380	1,380	4,330

Note: "Other" includes urban public utility and financial departments.
Source: See Table 2.

Management of Labour and Wages

After the founding of the People's Republic in 1949, labour and wage departments were set up in governments of all levels and in all enterprises and institutions. The Ministry of Labour and Personnel is responsible for the overall management of the country's labour and wages. Its earliest predecessor, the former Ministry of Labour, was later replaced by the General Administration of Labour, which functioned until 1982. Operating under local governments are labour departments or bureaux which have subordinates right down to grassroots units.

Tasks of labour and wages management institutions

Such institutions assign labourers to where they are needed and systematically regulate their use by making proper arrangements in accordance with the needs of social and economic development. They also look after the interests of labourers, and help to improve their competence and to implement the socialist principle of distribution, namely, "from each according to his ability, to each according to his work", and to get labourers actively involved in social production to which their immediate material interests are tied. The specific tasks for these institutions are:

– To ensure rational deployment and economical use of labour;

– To provide employment to the youth and other able-bodied people in cities and towns;

– To organize vocational and technical training to help enhance the political awareness of workers and staff members and improve their competence;

– To ensure correct handling of the relations of distribution between the State, the collective and the individual and to balance the wage scales in different regions and departments and among different professions in line with the principle "to each according to his work" and improve the life of the workers and staff members on the basis of increased production;

– To pay labour insurance and welfare benefits;

– To ensure the safety and health of workers and staff members;

– To promote social labour productivity and productivity of all trades and services.

Urban Employment Policy

China has pursued different employment policies in different historical periods. In the early post-Liberation period, the policy was to provide jobs to the four million unemployed people left over from old China. While recommending some unemployed people to places where jobs were available, government labour departments gave others vocational and technical training to prepare them for new jobs. People were also encouraged to provide for and help themselves by engaging in production or public services or doing temporary work provided by the Government as a form of relief. In just a few years, all the unemployed got jobs. By the end of 1957, the country had twice as many urban workers as in 1949.

The Cultural Revolution (1966–76) caused great

damage to China's economic development, leaving large numbers of urban youth jobless. By the end of 1978, an estimated 5,300,000 urban young people were waiting for jobs.

A national conference on labour and employment held in 1980 formulated a new policy, encouraging jobless young people to organize themselves on a voluntary basis to create job opportunities or start their own businesses while the State continued its job arrangements.

The past few years have also witnessed experiments with the practice of allowing state-owned enterprises to recruit workers directly from the labour market through examinations. This has made it possible for enterprises to increase or cut their labour force as production demands and for labourers to choose jobs that suit their abilities and wishes to the needs of the country.

Ways to Create Job Opportunities

The on-going economic restructuring and the new employment policy have opened up all avenues for employment.

Expanding the collective and private sectors

More jobs were made available by expanding the collective sector of the economy and allowing the private sector to grow to a proper extent, while keeping the public sector predominant.

According to 1984 statistics, the proportion of collective and private sectors in the total industrial output value rose to 25.2% from 1978's 19.2% and the proportion of retail sales of the two sectors rose to 49.2% from 7.5% in 1978. These two sectors have become major areas for employment, ending the almost sole dependence on state-owned units for jobs.

Statistics show that of the 26,600,000 jobs created in cities and towns between 1979 and 1983, at least 50% came from urban collective and private businesses.

Developing labour-intensive industries

Developing labour-intensive industries increases job opportunities. Since 1979, great efforts have been made to develop commerce, services, catering, repairs

and other tertiary industries as well as light industry. The State has increased its investment in light industry and given it priority in the supply of raw and semi-processed materials, fuel and electricity needed for its development. Of the 8,700,000 workers employed between 1979 and 1983, 64% were recruited by light industrial enterprises. In 1983, China's commerce and service trades employed a total of 16,000,000 workers and staff members, over one-third more than in 1978. Of the 2,000,000 self-employed during the same 1978–83 period, more than 80% were in commerce, catering and other service businesses.

Setting up labour service companies

Such companies are a new type of social labour organization which have sprung up everywhere in China in recent years as a new channel for solving the unemployment problem. They organize, regulate and arrange jobs for the social labour force, train labourers and build factories and open businesses to absorb idle labourers. By the end of 1984, the number of such companies had grown to 38,674, of which 3,220 were run by government labour departments at various levels, 7,176 by township governments and urban district offices, and 28,278 by enterprises, institutions, people's organizations and People's Liberation Army units. The number of production, marketing, supplies and service units run by these companies came to 210,000, employing more than 5,000,000 people; their total business turnover ran up to 25,700,000,000 yuan, profits 2,270,000,000 yuan, and taxes 1,070 million.

The specific functions of the urban labour service companies, which are found almost everywhere in China, are:

– Organizing jobless youths into collective economic organizations. These are responsible for their own profits and losses and operate under the principle of voluntary participation and democratic management, with the collective income distributed according to the contributions made by each worker. Using flexible, diversified methods of business operations, they are keen to market information in arranging their production and willing to make good what is badly needed in society but state-owned enterprises are

Table 5: Employment of Jobless Youth (Unit: %)

Year	Percentage of employed	Percentage of jobs provided by different sectors of the economy			
		State	Collective	Private	Temporary jobs
1979	100	10.8	59.6	0	29.6
1980	100	37.0	42.9	6.1	14.0
1981	100	29.0	49.1	5.4	16.5
1982	100	20.9	50.4	5.5	23.2
1983	100	29.7	47.9	10.5	11.9

Table 6: Employment between 1979 and 1984 (Unit: thousand)

	1979	1980	1981	1982	1983	1984	1985
Total	9,026	9,000	8,200	6,650	6,283	7,215	8,136
Sources of employed:							
Urban labourers	6,885	6,225	5,343	4,081	4,065	4,497	5,023
Rural labourers	708	1,274	920	660	682	1,230	1,502
Graduates of colleges, secondary vocational & technical schools	334	800	1,079	1,174	934	817	885
Others	1,099	701	858	735	602	671	726
Employers:							
State-owned units	5,675	5,722	5,210	4,093	3,737	4,156	4,991
Urban collective units	3,181	2,780	2,671	2,223	1,706	1,973	2,038
Self-employed	170	498	319	334	840	1,086	1,107

Source: *Extracts from Chinese Statistics* (1986) Chinese Statistics Publishing House, July 1986.

reluctant to do. They are also noted for their quick responsiveness to market demand, which enables them to achieve high efficiency and fast capital turnover with relatively limited investment, and the income for their workers is considered fairly good.

– Co-operating with rural collectives and state farms on the outskirts of their cities in establishing agriculture–industry–commerce enterprises in line with the principle of achieving economic development through the joint efforts of the worker and the peasant, and of town and country.

– Setting up retail shops and eating houses to make life easier for the people. At present, these constitute the bulk of the businesses set up by such companies.

– Developing repairs and other services. Through local labour service companies, the authorities in some cities have managed to organize scattered labourers into a reserve force for planned use in the cities' economic construction.

– Establishing training centres for jobless youths. Such centres provide vocational and technical training to prepare senior and junior middle school graduates for jobs. They recommend trainees to units which offer jobs, or give guidance or assistance to those who want to start their own businesses.

Labour Employment

Thanks to the policy of diversifying the channels for creating job opportunities, 54,510,000 people got jobs between 1979 and 1985 (the figure includes those who were assigned jobs by the Government according to state plans). In other words, an average of 7,790,000 people came to be employed annually during this six-year period. At the end of 1978, there were 5,300,000 people waiting for jobs, and by the end of 1985 the figure had been reduced to 2,385,000. This period saw greater numbers of people employed than in any previous period of the same length since New China was founded. The problem of unem-

ployment has now been greatly eased for the entire nation and almost completely solved in a number of small and medium-sized cities, including Changzhou, Wuxi, Nantong, Suzhou and Taizhou in Jiangsu province; Weifang, Yantai and Weihai in Shandong; Foshan in Guangdong; and Shashi and Xiangfang in Hubei.

Wage Systems

At the time of the foundation of New China, there was no uniform wage system. The necessities supply system, by which the People's Government provided simple food, clothes, accommodation and a small financial allowance, existed side by side with a wage system. During the take-over period of the national economy, a wage equal to certain material objects was paid so as to protect employees from the effect of changes in prices. The method used to calculate the material content of wages was through "wage points": one wage point was equal to 0.4 kilos of grain, 0.066 metres of calico, 0.025 kilos of cooking oil, 0.01 kilos of salt and 1 kilo of coal. The necessities supply system was abolished in 1955 and the monetary wage system was made universal. The whole country underwent a uniform wage reformation. A positional level wage system in 30 levels was adopted in the administrative bodies and institutions, and an eight-level wage system was practised among blue collar workers, but some enterprises chose a seven or six-level wage system, a post wage system or other wage systems. A system similar to that used in the administrative bodies and institutions was put into effect for the administrators and technicians of the enterprises. There was a thirteen-level wage system in the scientific research institutes, colleges and universities, a twenty-one level for medical workers, a ten-level for middle school teachers and an eleven-level for primary school teachers. Such a mode of wage systems remained unchanged until the end of the

653

1970s. In the 1980s, the wage systems are gradually being modified in the wake of the economic structural reforms so as to end the egalitarianism among both enterprises and workers in a factory. The reform has brought some positive achievements.

Wages policy

With the institution of socialist public ownership, the following principles came to be applied to the handling of questions concerning the wages of workers and staff members:

– *"From each according to his ability, to each according to his work."* This is the basic socialist principle for distributing social wealth to individual labourers. Under this principle, distribution is made according to the quantity and quality of labour each contributes to society, with more for those who work more, less for those who work less, and no pay for those who can, but do not work. Workers and staff members receive monetary rewards from the State for their labour, and wages are the major embodiment of the principle "to each according to his work". Meanwhile, the State provides social security to those who have lost their ability to work.

– *Coordinating the interests of the State, the collective and the individual.* At present, the guiding principle for handling the relations among the three is one of striving to ensure the essential needs of the people while accumulating some funds for the country's economic construction.

– *Combining ideological and political work with material benefits.* Integrating the principle of material benefits with ideological and political work among workers and staff members is another guideline for implementing the policy "to each according to his work". This calls for continuously improving the life of workers and staff members, along with the development of production, to boost their enthusiasm for production while strengthening ideological education to enhance their socialist consciousness and their enthusiasm for socialist construction.

– *Opposing both egalitarianism and unreasonably wide income gaps.* Egalitarianism in the distribution of consumer goods makes no distinction between good and bad work performances, thus failing to arouse the enthusiasm of labourers for production. Nevertheless, too wide a gap in individual incomes is hazardous to the unity of workers and staff members. Moreover, the income of peasants must be taken into account when work is done to improve the life of workers and staff members, and so must the relations between town and country, and between worker and peasant.

The Wage System For Enterprises

The wage system for enterprises, which is based on the principle "from each according to his ability, to each according to his work", covers wage grades, bonuses and allowances. The wage paid to each labourer according to his wage grade is called the "standard wage" and constitutes the bulk of his monetary income. The labourer's total wage is made up of his standard wage plus any bonuses and allowances that he is entitled to, which are of a supplementary nature.

Under the grade wage system, work is divided into different categories, or "types of work in production", as in the case of workers. In the case of staff members, however, there are different titles of duty. What is known as "work grades" are then fixed according to the technical complexity and labour intensity of each type of work in production, and to the degree of responsibility for each title of duty.

After undergoing a process of overall balance, the work grades, also known as "technical grades", are included in unified wage tables, which specify the standard wage for each grade according to pre-fixed differentials between grades. For state-owned enterprises, wage tables are worked out and issued by the State, and tables are worked out with reference to those practised in state-owned enterprises for workers and staff members in collectively-owned enterprises.

Grade wage systems for workers

There are specific systems for workers in different industries, but an 8-grade system is the most prevalent. Exceptions include the construction industry, which practises a 7-grade system. The systems for workers consist of three parts, namely, technical grade standards, wage grade tables and wage standards (also known as "wage rates"). Technical grade standards are actually the number of grades for a specific type of work filled according to its technical complexity, sophistication and responsibility, as well as its technical grade line in the wage table. For each technical grade, there are specific stipulations on the technical and vocational knowledge and the ability of operations required of the worker. The wage table specifies the number of wage grades and the grade index – the wage grade lines, i.e. the lowest and highest grades for every type of work. The wage standard specifies the standard amount of money paid to the worker for a certain period of time. Chinese workers are usually paid on a monthly basis, grade one being the lowest and grade eight the highest. In enterprises where the eight-grade wage system is practised, in 1984 the ratio between the highest and lowest wages was 3:1, and the wage was 17% higher for each successive grade.

While the eight-grade wage system is practised in most enterprises or industries, some use the piecework system or a system under which the workers are paid at different rates according to their specific jobs or duties in production.

Grade wage system for staff members

The technical and managerial personnel (otherwise called "staff members") of enterprises are paid according to their posts or duties. For each post, there are several grades which may overlap with grades for the next higher or lower post.

The bonus system

While reflecting the complexity and intensity of the labour done by the worker and his ability to perform production tasks, wage grades nonetheless fail to sufficiently reflect the actual amount of labour he has used to perform production tasks or the results of his work. A bonus system is therefore practised to supplement the grade wage system so that the principle "to each according to his work" can be better implemented. At present, the prevalent way of practising this system is to pay workers bonuses or incentive wages on a regular basis in order to encourage higher output, better quality of products and economical use of raw and semi-processed materials. Going hand-in-hand with material incentives are a variety of morale-boosting methods, such as issuing certificates of honour, medals and silk banners to outstanding units or individuals and conferring on them titles of honour such as "advanced worker", "model worker", "pace-setter for quality control", "advanced work group", "advanced workshop" and "advanced enterprise".

The allowance system

Allowances are supplementary wages paid to the workers. At present, these fall into the following categories:

– Allowances for those working under exceptionally harsh conditions, such as in underground operations in the mining industry, and allowances given in hot seasons to metallurgical workers.

– Allowances for workers to make good the extra cost of living resulting from work under special conditions, such as field operations.

– Payment made for the labour contributed by workers in excess of their regular work, such as overtime pay and night shift allowances.

– Allowances to workers engaging in operations hazardous to their health or working in poisonous environments, such as health care benefits and allowances for medical and public sanitation workers.

– Extra cost allowances, such as for those working in remote, outlying and border regions where prices are relatively high.

Since the beginning of the 1980s, efforts have been made to transform the wage system for enterprises along with the on-going restructuring of China's economic system. Beginning as of 1985, the State has been taking initial steps to change the current wages administration system. As a result, the power of enterprises with regard to distribution has been expanded through a process of enabling the authorities at different levels to share the authority for the overall control of wages and separating government administration from economic management. The State, central departments and local governments are assigned specific responsibility to keep the total amount of wages for the nation under control by balancing the increase of the funds for wages at the disposal of different enterprises. Enterprises will have to pay taxes at progressive rates for the part of the wage increases which exceed the percentages fixed by the State.

As regards the relations between the State and enterprises, all enterprises are allowed to retain a bonus fund at a percentage calculated according to the taxes and profits they contribute to the State. The State will collect a bonus tax at progressive rates if their annual bonus funds exceed a pre-fixed amount which, according to a July 1985 government decision, should be equivalent to no more than four months' standard wages for their own workers and staff members. Such funds may be distributed as bonuses or used to increase the wages of all or a few of their workers and staff members whose work is outstanding. Nevertheless, the wage increases realized by enterprises with their own funds do not hold for life for workers and staff members, who will automatically lose the increased part when they are transferred to other places. When conditions permit, enterprises may also let the total wages of their workers and staff members float at a ratio that corresponds to that for the decrease or increase in their own economic results. This will mean still greater decision-making power for enterprises in distribution.

In handling their relations with their staff, enterprises are now free to practise the kind of wage system best suited to their own conditions. Now in force in China are the 8-grade wage system, the piece work system, and the system of paying workers according to their specific responsibility, and the system of allowing part, the bulk or even all of the workers' standard wages, plus the bonus funds, to float along with the changes in the overall economic results of the enterprises and the economic results of individual workers. In addition, there is a structural wage system under which total wages are divided into the basic wage, responsibility or duty wage, seniority wage and bonus. Another system, practised mainly in the catering and service trades, calls for division of profits between the State and the staff according to pre-fixed proportions. There is also a package contract system under which the wages are contained in per unit output or output value. One example is the mining industry, in which the total wage for a production unit is calculated according to the amount of coal produced and then distributed among the members of the unit. In short, wage systems for Chinese enterprises have been experiencing lively transformations never seen before, and gone forever are days when only one system was practised.

Collectively-owned enterprises in cities and towns mostly use the piece work system and the system of allowing the worker to retain a pre-fixed portion of the profits or draw dividends according to the amount of labour he contributes. Work is now under way on the gradual introduction of a system of contract responsibility for business operations, a floating wage system and a system of dividing the net income among members of a collective.

Rural enterprises run by townships or villages pay their workers a basic wage plus bonuses, the total slightly higher than the income for farm labourers in the same localities.

The Wage System for Government Institutions and Offices

In accordance with a 1985 decision of the Communist Party Central Committee and the State Council, work has been done to transform the wage system for functionaries at government institutions and offices. The country instituted a new structural wage system under which the official post held by each functionary is the major factor that determines his wage. In other words, the wage of a functionary is linked to his position, responsibility and performance in work. The structural wage consists of:

– *The basic wage.* This is meant to cover the minimum cost of living for the functionaries themselves. At present, it is calculated according to the functionaries' actual basic cost of living, and the same rate is practised for all functionaries, including the top leaders of the State.

– *The official post wage.* This is fixed according to the official post and responsibility of each functionary and the nature of his work. In his total wage, this part is the major embodiment of the principle "to each according to his work". A functionary draws a wage that corresponds to his official post, and the wage automatically changes when his position changes. For people holding the same official post, there are several scales, so that in the future he may have his wage raised without necessarily being promoted to a higher post.

– *Seniority allowances.* These are designed to enable all functionaries to have their wages automatically increased a little every year, whether they are promoted to a higher post or have their wage scales raised or not. This benefits especially those who have acquired the highest wage scales for their posts. In addition to seniority allowances, nurses and teachers in kindergartens, primary and middle schools and secondary technical and vocational schools are entitled to benefits calculated according to the duration of their service.

– *Bonus wages.* Instead of being divided equally among all functionaries of a unit, these are awarded for excellence in work and may be higher for those who have worked better.

To sum up, this kind of structural wage system, with the wages corresponding to people's official posts playing the predominant role, breaks away from the traditional wage system. It is much more flexible and practical, in that it divides the wage of a functionary into several parts meant to perform different functions, thus making it possible to increase or decrease a certain part of the wage when necessary in the light of the changes in China's social and economic development and in the performance of the functionaries in work. This reform has proved to suit the conditions in government offices and other institutions.

Welfare Benefits

As a developing country, China has all along practised a high employment and low wage policy. Meanwhile, it has instituted a system of social security (see Part VI in this volume: "Living Standards and Social Welfare") and a welfare system in order to make the life of wage earners secure. The Government and enterprises undertake to start public service facilities for their staff members and workers, including residential buildings, mess halls, nurseries, kindergartens, bath houses and barber's shops. The rent is nominal for housing allocated to wage earners by local governments or their work units. Enterprises and institutions provide a special allowance to their staff who need to send their children to nurseries or kindergartens. The staff mess halls in work units operate on a non-profit making basis, with deficits made good by the units out of the administrative funds.

Other benefits include:

– *Home leave benefits.* Entitled to these are persons who are separated from their spouse or parents. During their home leaves, they draw their full pay and have all or part of their travel expenses reimbursed.

– *Winter heating allowances.* These are issued to individual workers and staff members in regions and at rates fixed by the Government according to weather conditions.

– *Allowances for commuters.* These are available in cities with a population of at least 500,000, to those who live at least two kilometres away from a workplace which does not provide transport to take them to and from their work.

– *Family allowances.* Regular aid is given to families with a per capita income lower than the protected minimum determined by the local governments; temporary aid is given to those who happen to run into financial difficulties.

There are also benefits for bathing and hair-cutting, for buying books and periodicals, and for extra cost of food for those eating out while on business. Muslim workers and staff members receive special food subsidies if there are no special canteens for them in their work units.

All these benefits are meant to help overcome extra burdens or special difficulties caused by external factors. As a supplement to their regular wages, the benefits help workers and staff members to enjoy a secure life. In 1984, state-owned units throughout China spent 21,040 million yuan on welfare and labour insurance for workers and staff members, accounting for 24% of their total wages and averaging 243.6 yuan per person.

Industrial Health and Safety

In old China, industrial enterprises and mines lacked the basic safety and health protection facilities. The working conditions were notoriously bad, resulting in frequent accidents and deterioration in the health of workers, women and child labourers in particular.

Institution of the labour protection system

Things began to change immediately after New China was founded in 1949. In explicit terms, the *Common Programme* of the Chinese Political Consultative Conference adopted on the eve of national Liberation called for "instituting an inspection system for industrial enterprises and mines to improve safety and health protection facilities there" and for "work to protect the special interests of women and young workers". Since then, the State has always sought to ensure the safety and health of labourers in production, improve their working conditions and prevent accidents and occupational diseases, regarding this as a basic policy and an important guarantee for the smooth development of the nation's economy. In order to improve labour protection, state departments concerned have done a lot of work, including drawing up laws, decrees and regulations to improve labour protection legislation and legally establish such methods as are conducive to the protection of the labour force. Work has also been done to spread knowledge of production safety and industrial health through various forms, including safety classes and training for workers engaged in work of special types, establishing labour protection education centres, showing educational films and publishing charts of safe operations. Safety inspection systems have been instituted in accordance with the relevant state legislation, as has a national network of labour protection research which undertakes also to exchange and disseminate research results.

Labour protection policies

There are two guiding principles for such policies, the principle "safety first" and the principle of "rationally balancing work and rest". The first is the fundamental principle for labour protection, as it upholds safety as a

must – in and for production. The second calls for fixing an appropriate number of work hours to ensure that labour intensity is reasonable and the labourer has enough time to rest after work. In general, China practises the 8-hour working day system, but workers engaged in heavy labour or working in hazardous or poisonous environments have shorter working hours. In a textile mill, for example, workers are divided into four groups, and every day only three of them work (on 8-hour shifts) so that each group has one day off in every four. One labour system being tried out in coal mines calls for dividing the labour force into four groups, with each group working six hours per day. Another experiment being carried out in mines calls for recruiting peasant labourers, by rotation, each working for a period of three to five years before being replaced by another and this has proved to be good for the health of the labourers. As regards women during pregnancy and menstrual periods, the State has special regulations to protect their health.

Major Labour Protection Systems

The responsibility system

In March 1963 the State Council published *Regulations on Improving Production Safety in Enterprises*. The document specified the responsibility for leaders at all levels in a given enterprise, as well as for each workshop, functional office, functionary and man on the factory floor.

The system for planning technical measures

Enterprises are required to work out technical measures to ensure production safety when drawing up production and financial plans. These include technical and organizational measures to improve working conditions and prevent accidents, occupational diseases and poisoning, as well as industrial health measures, steps to obtain the buildings and other facilities for labour protection and publicity, and education measures. The funds needed to put the technical measures for production safety into practice are defrayed from the funds earmarked by the Government to enterprises for their own technological upgrading.

The system of production safety education

All newly-recruited workers are obliged to receive what is called "three-level" safety education. Factory officials are required to provide them with the most essential information about production safety in the factory, about particularly dangerous places, and some general knowledge of protective facilities available. After they are assigned to a workshop, the workshop leadership will tell them the nature and responsibility of the specific work they are going to do, as well as its operational rules and safety requirements, and the use in emergency of the protective facilities at the workshop. Before they begin independent operations, they have to take examinations on safety rules and regulations and other relevant knowledge. Special technical training will be provided to those who are going to engage in work of special types. In all cases, only those who have passed the examinations are allowed to work independently. Production safety education is a regular feature in all Chinese factories, where such activities as the "safety day" or "safety month" are often observed.

The production safety inspection systems

These are designed to draw timely attention to factors liable to cause accidents or endanger workers' health and propose measures for improvement. Such inspections are organized by the safety divisions in enterprises, with the participation of other divisions concerned. Local labour administrative departments and departments of industry also send people to enterprises on inspection tours.

Handling accidents involving deaths or injuries

Such accidents must be reported to the higher authorities, and investigations must be made before they are handled in accordance with the relevant stipulations.

Labour protection articles and health care benefits

There are regulations specifying the categories and quantities of labour protection articles to be issued to individual workers in all major types of work in all industries. Such articles include work overalls, gloves, caps and shoes. Health care benefits are issued either in cash or in kind, to those doing exceptionally heavy work. The expenses of labour protection articles and health care are defrayed from the enterprises' labour protection funds, which are excluded from the total wages of the staff.

Vocational and Technical Training

Basic principles

– *Channels for providing such training should be diversified through various forms and for people with different lengths of schooling.* Government offices, enterprises, institutions and mass organizations should all undertake to organize such training. On the precondition that the quality of training is guaranteed, there should be training programmes suitable for people with different educational levels and able to produce qualified personnel for jobs with different vocational requirements in the spirit of combining popularization with the raising of standards.

– *In line with the principle of combining education with production, most training programmes should be arranged on a part-work, part-study basis.* This is an important measure to guarantee the quality of such training and an important principle for advancing the training itself.

– *Overall planning should be strengthened and attempts made to boost the enthusiasm of all sides so as to coordinate different forms of training and align them with employment.* Government offices in charge of vocational and technical training are required to provide services and guidance and to coordinate the work of all sides with regard to the arrangement of training programmes and courses, the training of teachers, compilation of teaching materials and research on teaching methods, as well as the provision and exchange of scientific, technological and other information and the transfer of personnel.

– *The irrational training systems and contents and methods of teaching must be transformed in order to produce more qualified personnel in the fastest possible time.* To transform the traditional apprentice system, work is now under way to try out a new practice of selecting apprentices through examinations. Before they are assigned jobs, they have to receive technical training for a fixed period of time to acquire a qualification for the work. Such training is arranged on a part-work, part-study basis to combine classroom teaching with field practice.

Categories of vocational and technical training

In China, such training falls into two major categories: on-job training and training of a reserve labour force.

From the early post-Liberation period to the mid-1960s, China formed an on-job training system offering a complete range of courses, from literacy classes right up to college programmes. During this period, more than 8,700,000 formerly illiterate workers were helped to learn to read and write.

Such training virtually stopped during the Cultural Revolution (1966–1976) and did not resume until 1978. Over the past few years work has been concentrated on training cadres and helping workers in their late 20s or early 30s to make up for the lessons and technical training they missed during the Cultural Revolution, when practically all schools were closed down. These years have also witnessed a rapid development of secondary and higher technical education for workers and staff members. All this has helped many enterprises to improve their management and raise their general technological level. On-job training now assumes the following forms:

– *Television universities.* The length of schooling ranges from two to three years, and the trainees may choose all the subjects offered and study full-time or opt for two or more subjects and study part time, depending on the needs of their work. People who opt for only one subject are required to study in their spare time.

Table 7: Job Training in China

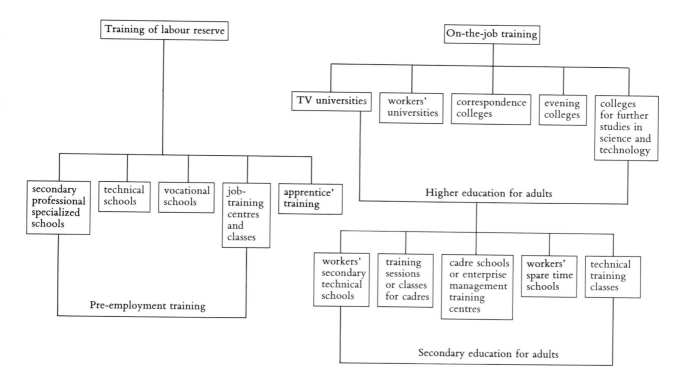

– *Workers' universities.* The length of schooling is three years for full-time courses and four to five years for part-time courses.

– *Correspondence and evening schools.* These offer 3–5 year courses. All students are required to study in their spare time.

– *Three-year secondary vocational or technical schools or classes.* There are some 10,000 such schools and classes, with more than 1,000,000 students attending.

– *Special courses for cadres and cadre training classes.* These are held by colleges or technical schools at the request of responsible authorities. The special courses, with school for two or three years, train reserve leaders for state-owned enterprises at and above the county level. The training classes, with the length of schooling not exceeding two years, are for leaders in reserve for workshops and functional offices at major state-owned factories or leaders at smaller enterprises.

– *Cadre schools and enterprise management training centres.* These are run by economic departments at the central and provincial, municipal and autonomous regional levels to train by rotation enterprise leaders currently in office for a period from three to six months.

– *Colleges and schools for further studies in science and technology.* These are sponsored by national and local science and technology associations.

– *Spare time schools.* These are mainly run by enterprises. Students are young and middle-aged

workers and staff members who need to improve their general knowledge or make up for the technical training they had missed.

– *Short-term training classes.* These offer courses closely connected with production and other tasks.

Technical schools and apprentice training are the two major forms for training a labour reserve. Technical schools which have developed fast along with China's rapid economic construction in recent years produce workers with an intermediate level of skill who, armed with both technical theories and operational skills, are quick to adapt themselves to production and become key members on the shop floor. Apprentice training, also known in the Chinese terminology as "training through production", is a time-honoured practice. After Liberation, the Government abrogated all regulations and labour contracts permitting maltreatment of apprentices and instituted new regulations, encouraging any method proven to be effective in training skilled workers through production.

Prospects

China is seeking its own road to modernization, a road with distinct Chinese characteristics, instead of following the beaten track traversed by some economically developed nations, which has resulted in an over-concentration of population in urban areas. To prevent a massive influx of rural population into major cities, China will go ahead with the policy of what is known as "encouraging peasants to leave the land but not their native places" by vigorously developing forestry, fisheries, animal husbandry and rural industries in order to provide jobs for rural labourers no longer needed on the land.

Employment in urban areas will remain a major problem. An estimated 30,000,000 labourers in the urban areas will enter the labour market between 1986 and 1990. This calls for opening up more avenues for creating jobs by vigorously promoting the development of the collective and private sectors of the economy and the tertiary trade.

The wage system for workers and staff members will be further improved to make it better reflect the principle "to each according to his work". Enterprises of different types will find the kind of distribution methods best suited to their own conditions, methods which will allow the total wages to float along with the decrease and increase of the economic results and correctly reflect the results of labour contributed by each worker and staff member without being influenced by non-labour factors. Still greater efforts will be made to eliminate the remnants of the egalitarian practice and raise the payment for mental labour, which is on the low side. The State will further improve its overall control over payrolls to ensure that wages increase in proportion to the improvement of labour productivity and the growth of the national income. With the increase in the wages level, the government welfare payments will drop slightly.

The State will continue improving labour protection to ensure safety in production, further reducing the hidden hazards and the incidence of occupational diseases.

14. FAMILY PLANNING AND POPULATION POLICY

THANKS to the establishment of the socialist system and economic expansion since the founding of New China in 1949, people's living standards have risen steadily and medical and health services improved markedly, resulting in a much lower death rate and longer life expectancy of the entire population. However, the birth rate has constantly remained at a high level; hence the fast growth of the population. Population dynamics has changed from the pattern of high birthrate – high mortality – slow growth before Liberation in 1949 to that characterized by high birthrate – low death rate – fast growth after Liberation. But this pattern began to change again from the beginning of the 1970s, when the country began to adopt a clear and firm population policy which encourages family planning in order to control fast population growth. The rate of natural growth has now dropped to such an extent as to be closer to the pattern of low birthrate – low death rate – slow growth rate.

Changes in Population Reproduction Patterns

The country's population grew from 541.67 million at the end of 1949 to 1,045.320 million at the end of 1985 (excluding Taiwan province, Hong Kong and Macao) – a net increase of more than 503 million persons in 35 years and a rise of 91.03 per cent from 1949. Table 1 shows changes in birthrate, death rate and growth rate after the founding of New China.

Table 1: Birthrate, Death Rate and Natural Growth Rate
(Unit: per thousand: %$_{00}$)

Year	Birthrate	Death rate	Natural growth rate
1950–1957	35.56	14.21	21.35
1958–1961	23.25	16.58	6.67
1962–1971	36.19	8.99	27.19
1972–1979	21.89	7.02	15.65
1980	18.21	6.34	11.87
1981–1984	19.53	6.70	12.83

(Based on a sample survey. Figures exclude Taiwan, Hong Kong and Macao.)

Source: Economics Department of Beijing University, *Economics* p.54, issue No. 3, 1980; *China Economic Yearbook*; III-5, 1985 edition; *China Statistics Yearbook 1985*, p.186.

The natural growth rate as shown in the table experienced two peaks, one decline, one period of rapid decrease and one period of stability.

1950–1957

The 1950–1957 period is the first peak of population growth. Birthrate in this period fluctuated between 32 and 38 per thousand, with five years staying above 37 per thousand. Meanwhile, the death rate dropped slowly to keep the natural growth rate at a fairly high level. The population increased by 100 million in the eight years.

One of the reasons for the high birth rate and high natural growth rate in the period is that the land reform was completed and peasants received land and shook off the heavy burden of land rent. As a result, production developed rapidly and living standards also improved markedly, and this created favourable material conditions for raising more children. Another reason is that since there were no radical changes in the traditional agricultural production methods based on manual labour, peasants still regarded an increase in the number of labourers as a source of increase in wealth.

1958–1961

The 1958–61 period experienced the lowest population growth. This is a special period in China, when the "ultra-Leftist" line of economic development and certain natural disasters caused production to drop; without enough grain supplies, the people lived in difficulties, hence the slow growth in population. Birthrate dropped drastically and the death rate visibly increased. The natural growth rate dropped 14.67 per thousand from the preceding period and in some years it experienced negative growth.

1962–1971

The 1962–71 period is one of rapid population growth. In the ten years, China's population grew by more than 190 million – an average annual increase of 19 million or above 27 per thousand in terms of natural growth rate. This is the second peak of population growth, which lasted for a decade.

The second peak differs from the first in nature. It is the product of a specific historical period. The growth is temporary and compensatory in nature as the economic situation and living conditions improved rapidly immediately following a period of depressed population growth, thanks to the implementation of the policy of "re-adjusting, consolidating, filling out and improving the national economy" from 1962. For example, during the 1962–65 period, the average birthrate topped 38 per thousand and the average natural growth rate exceeded 28 per thousand. From 1966, when the Cultural Revolution began, population growth shot up. About 150 million babies were born in the six years that followed. Deducting the number of deaths, the net increase was 121.2 million.

The second peak period can be divided into two sub-peaks: the 1962–65 compensatory peak in rebound, and the 1966–76 chaotic peak.

1972–1979

1972–79 is a period of gradual slowing-down. During this period family planning achieved notable successes. On the personal direction of the late Premier Zhou Enlai, the State Council Family Planning Office resumed work in 1973. The birthrate began to drop, though the natural growth rate still remained at over 20 per thousand from 1971 to 1973 as the result of the growth peak caused by the Cultural Revolution. By the end of 1979, the birthrate dropped to 17.82 per thousand from 1971's 30.65 per thousand and the death rate was kept at seven per thousand, causing the natural growth rate to drop to 11.61 per thousand from 1971's 23.33 per thousand.

1980–1985

The 1980–85 period is one of gradual stability. According to a sample survey, the birthrate was 21.09 per thousand in 1982, 18.62 per thousand in 1983, 17.5 per thousand in 1984 and 17.8 per thousand in 1985; the death rate was 6.6, 7.8, 6.69 and 6.57 per thousand, respectively; and the natural growth rate was 14.49, 11.4, 10.81 and 11.23 per thousand.

The changes in population growth reveal the following characteristics:

– *Population development changed from unchecked growth to gradual decline.* Before the 1970s China's population development was virtually in a state of anarchy, with the birthrate kept at above 30 per thousand, because there was a lack of appreciation of the seriousness of the population problem. The birthrate did not drop until the 1970s, when the family planning policy was pursued. It went down to 17.5 per thousand in 1984 – lower than the 1965 levels of Canada and the United States and almost 100 per cent lower than in most other developing countries.

– *The death rate slowed down to stability.* In 1936 the death rate was as high as 27 to 28 per thousand; it has kept dropping since the founding of New China. It was 18 per thousand in 1950, 13.18 per thousand in 1954, 10.8 per thousand in 1957, around 10 per thousand throughout the 1960s and 6.2 per thousand in 1979, which is lower than the death rate of many developed countries and among the lowest in the world.

– *Average life expectancy was prolonged.* The average life expectancy in old China was 35 years in 1936. Since Liberation in 1949, it has gradually lengthened until it reached 67.88 years (66.43 for males and 69.35 for females) as shown by the 1982 national population census.

Analysis of Factors in Changes in Population Growth

Natural population growth is decided by two factors – birthrate and death rate. The birthrate dropped from 21.1 per thousand in 1982 to 17.5 per thousand in 1984; the death rate rose from 6.6 per thousand in 1982 to 6.7 per thousand in 1984; the natural growth rate thus fell from 14.5 per thousand in 1982 to 10.8 per thousand in 1984. It follows that birthrate is the deciding factor in population growth.

Birthrate and natural growth rate are decided by women's fertility rate as well as the proportion of women of child-bearing age in the total number, since the number of births each year is the product of the number of women of child-bearing age multiplied by the fertility rate. Based on this understanding, the Chinese government vigourously advocates late marriages and encourages married couples to have fewer but healthier babies, so that the factors contributing to fewer births act simultaneously. This family planning policy has been a great success as shown by a sample survey conducted by the State Statistics Bureau in Hebei and Shaanxi provinces and Shanghai Municipality in April 1985.

Delayed marriage age of women

Early marriage (before 20) has dropped sharply, while the median marriage age has moved upward. In Shanghai the number of marriages below 20 accounts for 42.2 per cent of women aged between 45 and 49, 33.6 per cent in the 40–44 age group, 10.3 per cent in the 30–39 group, and 4.2 per cent in the 30–34 group, 1.2 per cent in the 25–29 group and 2.8 per cent in the 20–24 group. In Hebei and Shaanxi provinces, early marriage in the 45–49 group is 59.2 per cent and 79.7 per cent, respectively, and 13.8 and 19.3 per cent in the 20–24 age group. Though early marriage is very common among women born in the 1930s and 1940s in the two provinces, it has dropped considerably among young women. The survey also indicates a sharp rise in the number of late marriages in Shanghai, with women staying unmarried even at the age of 30 increasing from 2.3 per cent in the 45–49 age group to 9.2 per cent in the 30–34 age group. The median marriage age also serves as a useful general index. Taken every five years as an age group, the median marriage age rises gradually from the older age groups down to younger age group in the five age groups from 45–49 down to 25–29. It is 20.7, 22, 23.7, 25.6 and 25.3 in Shanghai, increasing by nearly five years; 17.9, 18.3, 19, 20.3 and 22.3 in Shaanxi, increasing by 4.4 years; and 19.4, 19.7, 20.9, 22.4 and 22.8 in Hebei, increasing by 3.4 years. This reflects what has been achieved in the two provinces and one municipality by advocating late marriage.

The study of the average age of first marriage indicates the trend. Investigations in Hebei and Shaanxi show that there are still one-fifth of the women aged between 20 and 24 who got married under the legal age over the last decade, a fact that calls for greater efforts to encourage late marriage in the hinterland and the rural areas. The standard first marriage age in Shanghai, however, was 24 in the mid-70s and it rose to 25 and over in the 1980s, and to 26 in 1984, though the legal marriage age set by the new marriage law promulgated in 1981 is much lower. The women's average first marriage age in Shaanxi was over 21 in the mid-70s, but rose to 22.5 in 1975 and fell to around 22 again in 1981. The average first marriage age in Hebei was 22.9 in 1976 and gradually dropped to 21.7 in 1982, with a slight rebound in 1983 and 1984. The survey shows that the average first marriage age has risen by more than one year in Shanghai, fluctuated in Shaanxi, but slightly dropped in Hebei over the past decade.

Reduction in the number of births per woman

Reduction in the number of births per woman shows that the government policy of encouraging couples to have only one child has received widespread response. The average number of births for women of child-bearing age surveyed is 2.45 in Hebei, 2.8 in Shaanxi and 1.54 in Shanghai. Women of the 45–49 and 40–44 age groups have virtually stopped giving birth. Of the two groups of women, the latter, with a peak child-bearing period in the late 1960s, have fewer children than the former, whose peak child-bearing period was in the early 1960s. The number of children for each women in the second group averages 3.85 in Hebei province, 14 per cent less than in the first group, which averages 4.46. In Shaanxi, the figure drops 13 per cent from 4.94 to 4.3 and in Shanghai, it drops 17 per cent, from 2.76 to 2.29.

The survey in the three areas indicates that the age at which the first birth is given has been greatly delayed since the founding of New China. Early birth is very common among women aged between 45 and 49, who entered the child-bearing period in the 1950s. The number of women in this group who gave birth to the first baby under 22 accounts for 51 per

Honours are presented to young couples who have only one child each, in Henan province. *(Photo by Beijing Family Planning Centre)*

cent of the total in Hebei, 67.6 per cent in Shaanxi and 43.8 per cent in Shanghai; and those giving birth to the first baby under 20 account for 29.2, 43.8 and 23.3 per cent, respectively. But among women aged between 25 and 29, those giving birth to the first baby under 22 account for 13.7 per cent, 23.3 per cent and 2 per cent, respectively; and those giving birth to the first baby under 20 account for 3.1, 7.6 and 0.2 per cent.

Fertility rate and development trend during the 1975–1984 period

The gross fertility rate in Shaanxi dropped from 3.24 in 1975 to 2.31 in 1984, with the lowest at 2 in 1980, a decrease of 0.93 or 28.7 per cent. The gross fertility rate in Hebei was 2.761 in 1981 and 2.776 in 1982 and went down to 2.037 in 1984 – 16 per cent less than in 1975. In Shanghai the gross fertility rate was 1.194 in the late 1970s and 1.332 in the early 1980s, rising 11 per cent. The lowest year is 1975, with 1.04, and the highest year is 1982, with 1.6, which fell to 1.14 in 1984.

Meanwhile, the average primiparous age has dropped somewhat over the past ten years, while the interval between the first marriage and first birth has been shortened. In 1984, the standard average primiparous age was 26.8 in Shanghai, 26 in Shaanxi and 24.9 in Hebei.

Between January 1980 and April 1985, the first birth accounted for 80.6 per cent of the newborn in Shanghai, 46.8 per cent in Hebei and 44.3 per cent in Shaanxi; the second birth accounted for 13.9 per cent in Shanghai, 29 per cent in Hebei and 28.5 per cent in Shaanxi; and multiple births accounted for 5.5, 24.2 and 27.2 per cent, respectively.

The improvement in hygiene, medical and maternity care has helped bring down the mortality rate of the newborn. During the 1980–83 period, the mortality rate of the newborn was 19.3 per thousand in Shanghai, 34.1 per thousand in Hebei and 34.3 per thousand in Shaanxi.

The National Economy

Table 2: Birthrate, Mortality and Natural Growth pre-1980 (Unit: per thousand)

Year	Cities (excluding city admini-stered counties)			Counties (including towns)		
	Birth rate	Mortality	Natural growth rate	Birth rate	Mortality	Natural growth rate
1954	42.45	8.07	34.38	37.51	13.71	23.80
1957	44.48	8.47	36.01	32.81	11.07	21.74
1962	35.46	8.38	27.18	37.27	10.37	26.95
1963	44.50	7.13	37.37	43.19	10.49	32.70
1964	32.17	7.27	24.90	40.27	12.17	28.10
1966	20.85	5.59	15.25	36.71	9.47	27.24
1971	21.30	5.35	15.95	31.86	7.57	24.29
1973	17.35	4.96	12.39	29.36	7.33	22.03
1975	14.71	5.39	9.32	24.17	7.59	16.58
1977	13.38	5.51	7.87	19.70	7.06	12.64
1979	13.67	5.07	8.60	18.43	6.39	12.04

Characteristics of Changes in Population Reproduction

A thorough analysis of the characteristics of changes in reproduction of urban and rural populations will help to give a clearer picture of what has happened since the founding of New China. Table 2 shows the situation before 1980.

The table shows that 1964 marks the turning point in the reproduction of urban and rural population. Before 1964, the urban areas had a higher birthrate but lower death rate than rural areas, hence the higher natural increase rate, about 3.5 to 11 per thousand higher. It is natural for cities to have a lower death rate because urban residents at the time enjoyed better living and hygienic conditions than their rural counterparts. But the higher birthrate in urban areas is due to the then historical conditions. Specifically: the cities outpaced the countryside in the early 50s in improving the people's living standards and medical and hygienic conditions; and large numbers of rural youth moved into cities. It was estimated that the number of immigrants from rural to urban areas accounted for 56 per cent of the increased urban population before 1957. The influx swelled the child-bearing population.

The factors causing urban birthrate to rise temporarily began to fade after 1964, while the factors causing the birthrate to drop became stronger. For example, city residents had spent three times more money than rural residents in bringing up a child; urban employees did not have to worry about their old age because they may receive pensions after retirement; more and more women were given jobs and they had to spend more time on work and study; with a higher educational level, urban people were quicker to overcome the influence of the feudal marriage and birth concepts than rural people; and cities enjoyed better medical and hygienic conditions, including more adequate supplies of contraceptives. Hence, since 1964 the birthrate and natural growth rate in urban areas have been much lower than in the countryside. As more than 80 per cent of the Chinese people live in the countryside, where the birthrate and natural growth rate are higher, the focus of family planning to reduce growth rate has fallen on the countryside.

Population Policy

There was a long period of deliberation before the policy of systematically controlling the population growth was instituted. A similar concept was mooted in the early post-Liberation days. The celebrated scholar Ma Yinchu, for instance, published his *New Population Theory* in 1957, which expounds the interactions of birth control, population growth control and economic construction. But his correct ideas have failed to come to pass. On the contrary, experts in population studies, including Ma, were criticized. The family planning effort, therefore, suffered a severe set-back and population studies became almost a forbidden area. Population growth control efforts began again in 1964, when the State Council set up a family planning office, but soon these efforts were thwarted when the Cultural Revolution began in 1966, with family planning organizations paralysed and their staff members attacked. In a state of anarchy, the population increased at a rapid rate.

In 1971, Premier Zhou Enlai took upon himself to get family planning work started. In August 1973 the State Council established a family planning leading group with an office affiliated to it. Family planning was then included in the country's Fourth (1971–75) and Fifth Five-Year (1976–80) Plans. In 1974, Chairman Mao Zedong also came out to say: "We cannot do without controlling the population growth." Marked progress was made in family planning after that and a fairly complete policy on population control began to take shape. After the Third Plenary Session of the Eleventh Central Committee of the Communist Party of China in late 1978, when it was decided to shift the focus of the Party's work to economic construction, family planning was elevated to such a high plane as to be regarded as something of strategic importance to China's four modernizations. The family planning policy has become more and more specific to cover encouragement of late marriage, late child bearing, longer birth spacing and related socio-economic policies.

The objective basis for formulating the current population policy

From the angle of population economics, the question is whether population development keeps in step with economic growth, as material production is closely related to human reproduction. Experience in China has proved that population growth has a direct bearing on national economic development, living standards and the quality of the entire population.

One of the major reasons for China's low productivity and slow improvement in people's living standards is the size of its population. Of the more than one billion Chinese residents at present, 63 per cent were born after the founding of New China in 1949. The population increase is so rapid and so big that it is bringing great difficulties upon the economic development.

– *It has increased the burdens of the State, collectives and families, and obstructed the increase in state accumulation funds.* Though the cost of rearing one child is not very high in China, the cost of raising more than 600 million children since the founding of the PRC would add up to a huge amount. If population control policy had been adopted from the 1950s, there would have been 150 to 200 million less children and the State would have saved a huge amount of funds for developing production and improving people's living standards. But the fact is that the bulk of products turned out every year were consumed by the increased population, and the funds which should have been used as accumulation had to be used to meet the rising need, thus greatly limiting the accumulation of funds and retarding the progress of industrial and agricultural production and of the national economy as a whole.

– *It has aggravated the unemployment problem.* The too rapid and too large increase in population brings great pressure to bear upon employment, which is limited by the unsteady and slow growth of production. It has been estimated that in the 80s the number of young people entering employment age has been increasing at an annual rate of 10 million, about 3 million in urban areas, far exceeding what society could cater for.

If one industrial worker employed needs 10,000 yuan worth of technical equipment, 10,000 million yuan would be required to employ one million people, which is over half the value of fixed assets added annually between 1952 and 1976. Therefore, funds available for recruiting new workers are limited.

Even the countryside, which absorbs about 90 per cent of the country's new labourers each year, feels the pinch because of limited farmland and the need for mechanization.

China's total arable land averaged 2.71 *mu* (about 0.18 hectares) per person in 1949, but it dropped to 0.17 hectares in 1957, 0.105 hectares in 1977 and further down to 0.103 hectares in 1979 – among the lowest in the world (at present the world average is about 0.33 hectares but it is 0.66 hectares in most countries).

While the total acreage of farmland has remained at 97.33 million to 100 million hectares, the rural workforce soared 65.8 per cent, from 180 million in 1952 to 300 million in 1977. This problem of surplus labour would be further aggravated by progress in farm mechanization. That is why there is now a practical problem of finding a way out for the huge amount of surplus labour.

– *It has delayed the improvement in people's material welfare.* There have been substantial increases in national income and supplies of grain, cotton, cotton cloth, light industrial goods and housing since the founding of New China. But the bulk of increased national income each year has to be used to meet the needs of the increased population. What is available for improving the people's life is relatively reduced and the absolute increase on a per capita basis is quite small.

The amount of grain in China averaged 396 kilos in 1984, close to the world's average, but its per capita national income is far behind that of developed countries. The amount of cotton cloth per capita fell from 8.6 metres in 1956 to 8 metres in 1978, although the total cotton cloth output rose. The housing problem is even worse. Statistics from 190 cities showed that the average living space per person was only 3.6 square metres in 1977, or a decrease of 0.9 square metres from 4.5 in the early 50s. Despite the large numbers of apartment buildings completed between 1977 and 1985, the average living space per person was still around six square metres, among the smallest in the world. As the rural population has increased even faster than the urban, a large part of the increased grain is used to feed the new mouths.

– *It has impeded improvement in education.* Fast developing as it is, China's education is unable to keep pace with the faster growth in its population. The number of people demanding learning opportunities, especially at middle schools and colleges, far exceeds what the State is able to provide. According to the 1978 statistics, there are 370.93 million children under the age of 15. But shortage of educational funds, teaching equipment and teachers has denied a considerable number of children and youth a better education. That is one of the reasons why there are still about 230 million illiterates and semi-illiterates at the age of 12 or above.

The number of college students in every 10,000 persons is much smaller than in many countries. The following is a table showing the comparison in 1980:

Table 3: College Students per 10,000 Persons

	China	India	Japan	United States	Soviet Union	Canada	Yugoslavia
Number	11.6	57.3	210.4	523	190.8	295	156.8

Source: Beijing University Publishing House, *Population Economics*, 1983 edition, p. 461.

General population policy

China's population policy, in general, is to control the number of births and improve the quality, so as to meet the needs of economic growth and the modernization programme, both quantitatively and qualitatively.

The policy has two aspects: to strive to reduce mortality on the basis of improved medical care and living standards and to encourage family planning in order to control the birthrate. Family planning is, in essence, intended to bring child-bearing into line with the interests of the State and the needs of social development. China's family planning programme includes encouragement of late marriage and birth control, which has been specified as late marriage, fewer births and longer birth-spacing, with emphasis on later and fewer births. The People's Government has set the goal of limiting the country's total population to at most 1,200 million by the end of this century. To achieve this end, the Government encourages one couple to have only one child. Couples who do have difficulties may have two. At the same time, it encourages healthier babies and better upbringing.

The fundamental aim of family planning is to make population growth tie in with socio-economic plans and to harmonize with resources and the environment, which conform to the fundamental interests of both the State and the people themselves. It also takes into full consideration people's personal interests, allowing some to have two babies and treating those suffering from infertility.

The State's advocacy and pursuance of family planning have been written into Article 35 of the *Constitution of the People's Republic of China* passed in March 1978. Article 49 of the Constitution, amended in December 1982, provides for obligations of married couples to practise family planning. The new Marriage Law passed in 1980 also stipulates: (1) both the husband and the wife are obliged to practise family planning; (2) the minimum age for marriage is 22 for males and 20 for females, as against 20 and 18 provided in the old Marriage Law, though later marriage is encouraged; (3) marriage between blood relatives or collateral blood relatives within three generations is prohibited and people suffering from or chronically affected with leprosy and certain other diseases are not allowed to marry, in order to ensure better births and healthier children.

In short, the success of family planning is a matter of major importance to socio-economic development

An instructor teaching young women how to use the contraceptives at Shuangqi town in Fujian province. *(Photo by Beijing Family Planning Centre)*

in China. China's population policy will eventually be perfected on the basis of the experience accumulated in all parts of the country.

Population policies toward minority nationalities

There are 55 minority nationalities in the PRC in addition to the majority Han people, with a combined population of 67.23 million as shown by the 1982 population census, accounting for 6.7 per cent of China's total. They occupy 50 to 60 per cent of the country's land areas.

Owing to differences in history, geography, economic development, culture and medical facilities, before the 1970s the minority population increased slower than the Han people, but it has subsequently accelerated until the growth rate has outpaced the Han, who had begun to practise family planning. Moreover, many minority nationalities are young in age structure, as in the case in multi-national Qinghai province, whose population under the age of 14 accounts for 38 per cent, higher than the nation's average.

This determines the need for encouraging family planning among the minority people. But as they differ from the Han in economic and geographic conditions and size of population, different policies are being pursued in different areas:

– Minority nationalities with an exceeding small population are encouraged to keep an appropriate population growth.

– A similar policy applies to minority nationalities living in sparsely-populated pastoral, forestry and border regions, such as the Tibet plateau (one person

666

A propagandist disseminates knowledge about contraception in the field. *(Photo by Beijing Family Planning Centre)*

A doctor gives a lecture on the topic of health in puberty for young women in Liaoning province. *(Photo by Beijing Family Planning Centre)*

per square kilometre) and Qinghai province (five persons per square kilometre).

– Minority nationalities living in densely-populated areas, including the Zhuang in the Guangxi Zhuang autonomous region (averaging 1,158 persons per square kilometre and with a population growth rate faster than the nation's average or the local Han people), the Koreans in Yanbian Korean autonomous prefecture in Jilin province and the Hui and Miao people in Guizhou province, are required to control their population growth, with specific measures differing from those for the Han.

– For minority people living in mixed communities with the Han in cities and towns, things are more complicated and policies are more flexible.

Progress in Establishing Special Organizations and Training Family Planning Workers

The State Family Planning Commission was set up in May 1981 to exercise unified management of family planning work. Its specific tasks are to oversee the implementation of family planning principles, policies and government decrees; co-operate with the State Planning Commission in drawing up China's long-term and annual plans for population growth; co-operate with other departments in carrying out publicity and education and training personnel; co-operate with the public health and pharmaceutical departments to ensure adequate birth control measures and arrange for scientific research and contraceptive production and supplies; and to handle foreign affairs relating to family planning. Moreover, family planning departments at the county, city and provincial levels have all set up subordinate organizations and employed more people to form a nationwide family planning organization network.

There are about 100,000 people working in family planning departments at all levels. Retraining of these personnel began in 1983. Undertaking the task are the Nanjing Training Centre for Family Planning Administrative Personnel and the Chengdu Training Centre for Family Planning Technical Personnel, two co-operative projects between China and the United Nations Fund for Population Activities. The Central Party Schools of the Communist Party Central Committee and at other levels have all opened courses on population theories. Institutes of social sciences and colleges and universities in all provinces, municipalities and autonomous regions have set up population research institutes or offices.

Strengthening publicity to make family planning a conscious popular activity

The Chinese government has always given top priority to publicity for family planning and to popularization of family planning knowledge to ensure that the policy is more acceptable on a voluntary basis. Many newspapers devote space to family planning stories and articles. More than 20 newspapers and journals are devoted entirely to population policy and family planning; many films and television plays have been made to publicize family planning, and even performing arts troupes, full-time or part-time, include family planning themes in their programmes. Since the beginning of the 1980s, the China Population Society has organized regular population symposia, which have enabled more and more people to understand the necessity and urgency to control population growth and improve the quality of the population. Meanwhile, mass organizations at all levels, including women's federations, the Communist Youth League committees and trade unions, have all joined in the publicity effort.

Providing incentives to promote family planning

Encouragement measures include honouring or awarding units performing well in family planning, granting regular childcare fees for couples who have promised to have one child and allowing longer maternity leaves (from the original 56 days to three

Young mothers received certificates of honour of "one couple, one child" at Yinkou township in Fujian province. *(Photo by Beijing Family Planning Centre)*

The United Nations Populations Award of 1983 was conferred on Qian Xinzhong, Chairman of the China State Family Planning Commission for the achievements of the commission under his guidance. *(Photos by Beijing Family Planning Centre).*

months or 100 days) for those determined to practise family planning. All places have laid down work rules and regulations, which have a positive effect on population control.

Providing free contraceptives and free sterilization operations

One of the principles for family planning is to combine the guidance of the State with people's willingness to comply. In both urban and rural areas, people receive free contraceptives from women cadres, medical workers, family planning activists and drug stores, in accordance with the related rules. They may also be given free sterilization operations if they so wish and enjoy post-operational leaves of varying lengths with full pay, or receive allowances for better food or other benefits as in some factories, mines, townships and villages. Research projects, such as the application of intrauterine devices (IUD), the long-acting contraceptives, prostaglandin (PG), contraceptives for external use and other items urgently needed in family planning, have been included in the state science and technology research plans.

Promoting better maternal and child care and home care for the aged

All provinces, municipalities and autonomous regions have health centres or maternity and child care stations, gynaecology and obstetrics hospitals and children's hospitals; prefectures and counties have health maternity and child care stations; and townships and villages have rural doctors and midwives. There are nurseries and kindergartens in cities and in the countryside, government organizations, factories, mines and neighbourhood communities. Some areas have child care outpatient departments or offer outpatient services for only children, which give them regular health check-ups. Moreover, all babies and infants are given free inoculations to prevent and control infectious diseases.

Urban workers and other employees draw pensions when they retire, while in the vast countryside there are different measures to see that all childless old people are well looked after, including the drawing of pensions in some townships and villages.

Carrying out international exchanges and co-operation in family planning

Chinese family planning departments have carried out exchanges and co-operation with international population and birth control organizations and family planning departments of several countries. Co-operative projects between China and the United Nations Fund for Population Activities are well under way;

An exhibition of birth control in China. *(Photo by Beijing Family Planning Centre)*

China takes an active part in international conferences on population and exchanges visits with other countries. The China Family Planning Association has forged ties with the International Planned Parenthood Federation and carried out non-governmental co-operation with the Japan International Consortium for Co-operation in Family Planning, the International Committee for the Administration of Popula-

tion Plans and the Japan Association for the Development of Asian Population. The China Family Planning Association became a full member of the International Planned Parenthood Federation at a conference called by the federation in November 1983. The United Nations issued the first population award to Qian Xinzhong, former Minister of China's State Family Planning Commission, for China's achievements in controlling population growth. These activities have promoted China's family planning work.

Prospects

To sum up, there are many favourable conditions for China to control population growth: the inherent nature of the socialist system, correct population and family planning policies, and voluntary support by the public. China's Seventh Five-Year Plan (1986–90) for social and economic development calls for greater attention to family planning and persistent efforts to limit the average annual population growth rate to around 12.5 per thousand within the five years, so that the total population should be controlled at about 1,113 million by the end of 1990.

15. TOURISM

TOURIST contacts and associations between China and the West may be traced to the period before the opening up of the "Silk Road" by Emperor Wu Di of the Han dynasty (156–87 BC) more than 2,000 years ago, but as an economic and integrated business undertaking, tourism began only as recently as the 1920s. The first Chinese travel service, the tourist department of the Shanghai Commercial Savings Bank, was inaugurated in 1923 and began to undertake the business of a travel agency (in 1927 the name was changed to "China Travel Service") engaged in the administration of international and domestic tourist undertakings. This is considered to be the beginning of China's international tourist trade.

The founding of the People's Republic of China opened up broad prospects to the tourist trade. Thanks to the concern of Premier Zhou Enlai, the head office of the Chinese International Travel Service was established in Beijing on 15 April 1954, with 14 branch offices set up in succession in Shanghai, Hangzhou, Nanjing, Hankou, Guangzhou, Shenyang, Harbin, Andong, Dalian, Manzhouli, Tianjin, Pinxiang, Nanning and Nanchang. After a development of more than 30 years, there are at present more than 100 branches and sub-offices. The main task of the Chinese International Travel Service is to coordinate matters concerning the board, lodging, travel and sight-seeing of foreign guests touring China and the booking and sale of international train-and-plane coordinated transport passenger tickets. The principle countries of origin of the tourists used to be the Soviet Union and the various East European countries, but since 1957 connections with other foreign travel agencies have gradually increased. In 1959 the Chinese International Travel Service received 8,172 foreign tourists, for whom the Soviet Union and East European countries remained the principal source, but since 1960 tourists from the Western countries have increased year after year, bringing about a radical change in the source of international tourism in China.

After the visit of Premier Zhou Enlai to 14 countries in Asia, Africa and Europe in 1964, more and more foreigners expressed their wish to visit China. The change in the objective situation has speeded up the development of China's tourist trade. In the same year, the Administrative Bureau of China's Travel and Tourist Trades (which in 1982 was renamed National Tourist Bureau of the PRC) was set up directly under the State Council, which strengthened the direction of the tourist trade throughout the country. In 1965 foreign tourists numbered 12,877 persons, the highest number received by the Chinese international tourist services for ten years, but the number of tourists in China sharply declined during the Cultural Revolution.

The opening of the Third Plenary Session of the Eleventh Central Committee of the CPC in 1978 instilled new vigour into the development of China's tourist trade. The number of tourists (including those from Hong Kong and Macao) has mounted significantly year after year since 1978 (see Table 1.)

With the continued growth of the tourist trade, the administrative systems of China's tourist services are being constantly improved. Since 1978, local tourist bureaux have been set up in the various provinces, autonomous areas and municipalities directly under the Central Government. From 1981 onwards, the National Tourist Bureau started sending representatives of organs of tourism abroad, with the successive establishment of Chinese tourist offices in Tokyo, Paris, New York, Los Angeles, London, Frankfurt and Sydney. The Hong Kong Chinese International Tourist Co. Ltd. was set up in the Hong Kong area.

According to 1986 statistics, the tourist system of China now has staff and workers amounting to about 276,000 persons. The numerous people engaged in the trade have rendered warm and good services to tourists, and their work has won the commendation of many.

There are in China 974 guesthouses and hotels with toilets attached, a total of about 330,000 beds; 94 of these guesthouses and hotels with 35,000 beds were constructed with foreign capital.

China has opened 27 international air routes, with flights to 26 cities in 22 countries, and in order to keep up with the growth of tourism the civil aviation service has added more than 20 domestic tourist routes, so that these now total 286. Air transport between the interior of the country and Hong Kong has also been developed. There is now air traffic between Hong Kong and Beijing, Tianjin, Shanghai, Guangzhou, Hangzhou and Kunming. There are chartered flights between Hong Kong and Xi'an, Nanjing, Guilin, Xiamen and Fuzhou.

There are in China more than 70 tourist car companies (motor transport corps) under the direct administration of the tourist department, owning

Table 1: Numbers of Tourists in China (Unit: 10,000)

	1978	1979	1980	1981	1982	1983	1984	1985	1986
No. of tourists entering China	180.9	420.3	570.3	776.7	792.4	947.7	1285.2	1783.3	2281.9

15,000 cars of all descriptions for tourist purposes. For pleasure cruising, five first-class pleasure boats have been put into service for tours along the three gorges of the Changjiang (Yangtze) river – *Kunlun, Shengnu, Sanxia, Yangzijiang* and *Emei*; there is also a fleet of well-equipped yachts now on tourist service on the Taihu, Lijiang, Zhujiang (Pearl River) and Huangpujiang and on the Grand Canal. The luxury passenger ships *Xinghu* and *Tianhu* and speedboats ply between Guangzhou (Canton) and Hong Kong.

The Development of the Tourist Industry Today

The tourist resources of China are notable in three respects; first, in the distribution throughout the country of places of historic interest and scenic beauty; second, in the abundance of protected regions of primitive natural scenery; third, in the existence of numerous minority nationalities with their diversified local traditions and customs. To the tourist all of these are alluring and fascinating. In the Seventh Five-Year Plan (1986–1990), the Chinese government has decided to concentrate its manpower, material and financial resources to systematically increase the comprehensive capability of several key tourist cities and regions, such as Beijing (including a part of Hebei province), Shanghai, Xi'an, Guilin, Hangzhou, Jiangsu (including Suzhou, Wuxi, Changzhou, Zhenjiang, Yangzhou and Nanjing), Guangzhou and Hainan Island to receive tourists. To this end, a number of specific measures have been undertaken.

Beijing Great Wall Hotel, equipped with computer-controlled room-status display system and other advanced devices. *(Photo by Wang Lei)*

Beijing: The construction of an international conference centre; the completion of the renovation of the Great Wall at Jinshanling; the reconstruction and transformation of the Beijing–Dongling (East Tombs), Tianjin–Dongling, Beijing–Xiling (West Tombs) highway and the Beijing–Chengde, Beijing–Shanhaiguan air routes.
Shanghai: The construction of tourist shopping and exhibition centres; the extension of the Shanghai–Suzhou, Shanghai–Hangzhou highways as express or first-class highways; the building of 13,000 new guest rooms.
Xi'an: The construction of an all-weather airport and of a new highway leading to the city centre; the extension of a highway connecting Xi'an with the museum of the terracotta figures of warriors and horses buried with the dead during the Qin dynasty; the building of 4,000 new guest rooms.
Guilin: The harnessing of the Lijiang river, and work to raise the water level, improve the water quality, take further steps in the renovation of the landscapes of Guilin's hills, rivers and gardens, expand the capacity of sightseeing in pleasure boats, improve facilities and reduce noise; to construct a second Ludiyan (grotto at Ludi) scenic spot, take further steps to develop the scenic beauties of Yangshuo; to construct 5,000 new guest rooms; to construct and perfect the international communications apparatus of Guilin.
Hangzhou: The construction of silk and tea museums; to extend the Hangzhou–Shaoxing–Ningbo highway; to build 3,000 new guest rooms.
Jiangsu: The harnessing of the Qinhuaihe river and restoration of the old shops and houses along the river; to repair the old site of Tianwangfu and construct it as the museum of Nanjing's modern history; to expand the Hanshan Temple in Suzhou, to construct more buildings for exhibiting historical relics, to repair and maintain the old, small streets on the right side of the temple, forming a scenic area with Hanshan Temple as its centre; to extend the Suzhou – Wuxi – Changzhou – Zhenjiang – Yangzhou – Nanjing highway; to build 3,000 new guest rooms.
Guangzhou: to build 6,200 new guest rooms. The tropical sights of Hainan Island and the Li nationality villages and Miao nationality stockades are amongst China's unique tourist resources. The construction of tourist winter resorts with the bathing beaches of San Ya city at the southern tip of Hainan Island as their centre.

There are many other unique tourist areas and

routes in China, such as the Wulingyuan scenic region in Hunan province, the tourist areas in Zhongyuan (Central Plain), Shandong, Yunnan and Guizhou, the tourist routes of Lhasa in Xizang (Tibet) and the three gorges of the Changjiang (Yangtze) river, and the tourist route of the "Silk Road". Tourist routes with outstanding features include the route of *Sanguo* (Three Kingdoms); the Jinan–Taishan–Qufu route; the West Sichuan route; the Fuzhou–Quanzhou–Xiamen (Amoy)–Wuyishan route; the Huangshan–Jiuhuashan–Hefei route; the Yungang of Datong–*Xuankongsi* (Temple Hung in the Air) of Hunyuan–*Muta* (Wooden Pagoda) of Ying Xian county–Wutaishan–Taiyuan route; the Nanchang–Lushan–Jingdezhen route, etc. Plans are under way for the construction of highways and the development of air or shipping routes in all these scenic spots and places.

At the same time, the Seventh Five-Year Plan calls for the stepping up of the training of specialist tourist personnel, the improvement of services and the enhancement of service levels, the expansion of the production of tourist commodities and the strengthening of external propaganda work. All these are intended to enable the country to receive 3 million foreign tourists into the country in 1990. While in 1986 the figure was about 1,500,000, the general target for the year 2000 is to achieve the plan of receiving 7–8 million foreigners, making China one of the most developed countries of the tourist world.

The Chinese government attaches great importance to tourism. In order to achieve still greater developments in tourist trade, the State Council of China has decided to form a tourist coordination group, with a member of the council acting as group leader. The deputy secretary-general of the State Council and the vice-minister of the State Planning Commission will act as deputy group leaders. Members of the group include the head of the State Tourist Bureau and the responsible officials of the various ministries, commissions and bureaus of the State Economic Commission, the Finance Ministry, the People's Bank of China, the Ministry of Urban and Rural Construction and Protection, the Ministry of Light Industry, the Railway Ministry, the Ministry of Communications, the Civil Aviation Bureau of China, the State Prices Bureau and the Ministry of Culture.

The Nature and Variety of China's Tourist Resources

China extends across the cold-temperate, temperate, warm-temperate, sub-tropical and tropical zones. Its natural conditions are complex and diversified, with tourist resources richly endowed by nature and beautiful landscapes and scenic spots spread all over the country. Cultural relics and places of historical interest abound.

Natural tourist resources

China's topography is high in the west and low in the east. It is noted for its many **mountains**, with its mountainous regions accounting for more than two-thirds of the general area of the nation's land. The lofty mountains are mostly found to the west of a line from Lanzhou to Chengdu and Kunming. Here lies the highest peak in the world, Mount Qomolangma (Everest) of the Himalayas; it is one of the eight peaks opened in 1980, the other seven peaks being the Xixiabangma peak in Tibet, the Mushitage and Gongge'er mountains and Gonggejiubie and Bogeda peaks in Xinjiang, the Gonggashan mountain in Sichuan and the Animaqing peak in Qinghai. These perennially snow-capped mountain peaks are famous scenic spots cherished by mountaineers and scientists.

There are, in addition, the famous Wu Yue (Five Sacred Mountains): Dongyue Taishan (East Mountain) in Shandong, Xiyue Huashan (West Mountain) in Shaanxi, Zhongyue Songshan (Central Mountain) in Henan, Beiyue Hengshan (North Mountain) in Shanxi and Nanyue Hengshan (South Mountain) in Hunan).

There are also four famous mountains honoured as the holy lands of Buddhism; these are Wutaishan mountain (in Shanxi province), Emeishan mountain (in Sichuan province), Putuoshan mountain (in the Zhoushan archipelago in Zhejiang province) and Jiuhuashan mountain (in Anhui province). They are respectively the ritual places of Buddhism–Wenshu, Puxian, Guanyin and the four Bodhisattva of Dizang.

There are more than 90 peaks in the summer resort of Lushan mountain known as "The elegance and wonders of Kuanglu, the finest under heaven." Not only is the climate here pleasant, its natural scenery bizarre and changeable, but it is said that when you look from afar at the sea of clouds, or sit and watch the waterfalls tumbling down the cliffs, you will enjoy it so much as to forget to go home!

China abounds with **rivers**, and more than 1,500 of them have drainage areas exceeding 1000 square kilometres. The whole length of China's longest river, the Changjiang (Yangtze), is 6,300 kilometres. It flows through the famous three gorges, long known as a natural barrier, the river water meandering out of the gorges, with mountain peaks rising one higher than another, covering the skies and smothering the sun. Important tourist cities like Chongqing, Wuhan, Nanjing, Shanghai, etc. are located along the river.

The whole length of China's second largest river, the Huanghe (Yellow River), is 5,464 kilometres, and tourist cities like Lanzhou, Zhengzhou, Jinan, etc. are situated along it. Heshui county in Gansu province in the Huanghe river valley is the site where the fossil of an ancient elephant from the early Pleistocene Epoch of the 4th Quaternary was excavated. This fossil is the remains of a stegodon, the biggest known so far which has been preserved intact.

Moya Stele on Mount Taishan in Shandong province. Cut into it is a text marking Mount Taishan written by Emperor Xuanzong of the Tang dynasty in 727. *(Photo by Chen Zhiping)*

high concentrations of minerals and chemical elements. The five Dalian ponds in Heilongjiang have already set up health-care tourist facilities. The mineral spring of Laoshan in Qingdao is noted for water quality, both at home and abroad. Huaqing Pond in Lintong, Shaanxi, is the place where more than 1,000 years ago, Emperor Xuan Zhong of the Tang dynasty brought his favourite concubine, Yang Yu-huan, every winter to pass the cold days and to bathe. The "first spring under heaven" in Jinshan (Zhenjiang), the "second spring under heaven" in Huishan (Wuxi), the Hupao spring at the foot of Dacishan mountain in Hangzhou and the Baotu spring in Jinan are the most famous springs in China, of which the Baotu spring ranks first among the 72 springs of China's famous "Spring City" of Jinan. The spring waters of Jinan differ from the others in style; some may assume the likeness of streams of gold rushing down the mountain, or the shapes of silvery flowers with jade pistils; some may appear like a drizzle or the low note of a stringed instrument, or be compared to the roar of dragons and tigers, assuming an infinite variety of fantastic phenomena unfolding in all their majesty.

There are also many **waterfalls** in China. The Huangguoshu Cataract of Guizhou province is a cluster of waterfalls, with 18 above-ground and 4 underground. The Longtan falls of Laoshan mountain in Shandong, the cataract of Bijiashan mountain in

In Guilin where "the mountains and waters are the finest under heaven", Lijiang is compared with a "blue silk girdle", with elegant and beautiful peaks dotting both of its banks, assuming the shape of an "emerald hairpin". Here we have the four "uniques": the green hills, the clear waters, the exotic caves and the beautiful stones.

Lakes and **ponds** of all kinds and of every description are scattered all over China: large lakes exceeding 100 square kilometres in area number more than a hundred. West Lake in Hangzhou was compared in older times to the famous beauty, Xishi. The Italian, Marco Polo, in his travel notes written in the thirteenth century, wrote of heavenly West Lake in glowing terms.

Shouxihu (Gaunt West Lake) in Yangzhou, Taihu in Wuxi, Xuanwuhu in Nanjing, Dianchi in Yunnan, Wuchang and Shaoxing, each having its own Donghu (East Lake), Xinjiang and Jilin, each having its own heavenly pond, Jingpohu in Heilongjiang, and Riyuetan (Sun Moon Pond) in Taiwan, etc., are all wonderfully pretty. The five large freshwater lakes (Dongtinghu, Poyanghu, Taihu, Hongzehu and Chaohu) are famous "areas of abundance"; the landscapes of hills and waters in these regions intoxicate visitors with their charm.

China is also very rich in **hot springs**, over 2000 of which have already been discovered, among them more than 1,000 mineral springs containing quite

The Xiaolongdong waterfall in west Henan. *(Photo by Yan Haosheng)*

The National Economy

Hubei and the waterfall of the Huanghe Hukou are well known.

The appearance of karsts in China is singular and their distribution extensive. Karsts are distributed over an area of 3.44 million square kilometres, which is more than one-third of the whole area of the country's territory, among which over 900,000 square kilometres, or 9.4% of the area of the nation's territory, are exposed on the ground. Tourism in **caves** and **grottoes** in China may be dated back to 1,000 years or more, and more than 140 of them have already been or will be opened. They include mainly two kinds; one is intended for views and admiration, which is divided again into two large categories, the first of which includes karst grottoes divorced from or above the underground water level, examples of which may be seen in the Qixing (Seven Star) and Ludi grottoes in Guilin, Boyuedong at Lengshuijiang city in Hunan, and Yunshuidong at Shangfangshan mountain in Beijing municipality. The other category includes caves created by contemporary underground rivers or streams. The Xiejiaweizi water cavern in Benxi city in Liaoning province, the Shanjuan cavern in I'xing in Jiangsu province, the Longgong cavern in Pengze in Jiangxi province, the Lingxiao grotto in Yangchun in Guangdong province, the Longgong (Dragon Palace) in Anshun in Guizhou province, etc. are typical representatives of this category. The second kind is valuable for archaeological studies, represented by the ape-man cavern in Zhoukoudian in Beijing municipality, the Zengpi grotto in Guilin and the ruins of Bailian cavern in Liuzhou. They are the cultural remains of the caves where our forefathers lived.

There are also a group of karsts and grottoes suitable for scientific investigation, such as the Yanzi (Swallow) grotto of Hubei's Shennnongjia and the Bianfu (Bat) cavern at Raoping in Guangdong.

China has a very long **coastline**; the continental coastline alone stretches well over 18,000 kilometres. There are altogether more than 5,000 offshore islands, and many smooth beaches can be found on the winding coasts, with little harbours which became the nucleus of today's well-known seaside tourist resorts such as Beidaihe, Dalian, Qingdao, Lianyungang, Gulangyu in Xiamen and Hainan Island. The delightful weather of these places, their soft sands and clear water make them ideal summer resorts and bathing beaches.

China has a great variety of **biological resources**; there are at present nearly 30,000 species of higher plants in the whole country, including 2,100 species of brophytes, 2,600 species of pteridophytes, almost 300 species of gymnosperms and 25,000 species of angiosperms. More than 50 of these species, such as *Pseudolarix kaempferi*, Taiwan fir, camphor trees, etc. can be found only in China; tree species that grow only in China also include metasequoia, *Cathaya argyrophylle* and ginkgo, etc. There are numerous

Yungang grottoes at Datong, Shanxi province, built over 1,500 years ago.

varieties of flowers and plants, among which the most popular include the tree peony of Luoyang (Henan), the camellia, the azalea and the winter jasmine, etc. (Yunnan).

Animal varieties in China include 450 species of beasts, 1,186 species of birds, 320 species of reptiles and 210 species of amphibians. The Giant Pandas of Shaanxi and Sichuan already enjoy a high reputation at home and abroad. The "horned monster" in Wuyishan mountain in Fujian is one of the rarest animals in the world; red-crowned cranes, red-billed leiothrixes and mandarin ducks are also rare birds.

For the protection of rare species and the typical natural ecosystem, China has to date set up 274 nature reserves (not including Taiwan province), with a total area of 16,260,000 hectares – 1.69 per cent of the nation's territory. These include the nature reserves of Shennongjia, Hubei (forest ecosystem and rare animals and plants); Suoxiyu, Hunan (typical karst vegetation, forest scenery); Zhalong, Heilongjiang (rare water fowls like red-crowned cranes); Jiuzhaigou, Sichuan (rare animals like Giant Pandas, etc. and forest ecosystem); and that of the Chinese alligators of Anhui (China's characteristic reptiles), etc. etc.

The manifold climatic types in China afford favourable conditions for diversified tourist activities; for example, ice sculpture, ice skating, skiing, etc. in the mountains, in contrast to the seashores of the south, with their warm sunshine and radiant and enchanting sea beaches.

Human tourist resources

On a territory of 9,600,000 square kilometres and with an age-old history of 5,000 years or so, China has carried within itself the heritage of a resplendent culture which goes back to ancient times. The remains of the Zhoukoudian "Peking Man" in Beijing; the ruins of the villages of the primitive matrilineal communes in Banpo, in Xi'an; the fossils of the Yunnan "Yuanmou Apeman" and of the Shaanxi "Lantian Apeman", etc. present visible evidence of the course of human development.

The graves of many emperors of China, their empresses and imperial concubines, generals, ministers and other eminent persons reflect social development in the various historical periods. The excavation of the pit containing terracotta figures of warriors and horses buried with the dead in the mausoleum of the Qin dynasty in Lingtong, Shaanxi, and of the tombs of the Han dynasty at Mawangdui in Changsha, Hunan, have authentically shown the political, economic and cultural achievements of China during the times of the Qin dynasty (221–206 BC) and Han dynasty (206 BC–AD 220) and furnished us with precious historical materials and tourist attractions. Others, like the tombs of the 13 Ming emperors in Beijing, Ming Xiao

Ling (tomb of Ming emperor *Zhu Yuan Zhang*) in Nanjing, the east and west mausoleums of the Qing dynasty in Hebei province and the Confucian woods in Qufu, Shandong are well-known repositories of China's ancient past.

China has a large number of Buddhist monasteries, pagodas and grottoes; the Luoyang *Baimasi* (White Horse Temple); the Songshan *Shaolinsi*; Nanjing *Qixiasi*; Zhenjiang *Jinshansi*; Suzhou *Hanshansi*; Hangzhou *Lingyinsi*; the Potala Palace of Xizang (Tibet), etc. are all very famous. Mogaoku in Dunhuang (Dunhuang caves), the rock caves of Yungang, Datong and the Longmen Grottoes in Luoyang etc. are the prime of the world's art in grottoes.

China's ancient architecture has had glorious attainments, like the Great Wall, which winds through a distance of 6,700 kilometres, and the Grand Canal, more than 2,000 kilometres long, the earliest and the longest in the world, dug through human labour, are both "Wonders of the World." China's biggest cluster of buildings intact, the Imperial Palace (Forbidden City), has a total of about 10,000 rooms. The famous ancient irrigation works of Dujiangyan in Guanxian county, Sichuan province, was built in 256 BC; Zhaozhou Bridge in Hebei has a history of more than 1,300 years; others are the well-known gardens at the Beijing Summer Palace and *Beihai* Park, the Chengde *Bishushanzhuang* (Summer Mountain Villa) and the Suzhou *Zhuozhengyuan, Wangshiyuan, Liuyuan, Shizilin*, etc. – all outstanding among world gardens and parks.

China has a glorious revolutionary tradition; numerous traces have been left, from the peasant uprisings of ancient times to the Revolution of 1911 and the revolution led by the Chinese Communist Party, such as the site of the Jintian uprising in Guiping county in Guangxi, the site of the Military Government of the Wuchang uprising in Hubei, the ruins of Tianwangfu of the Taiping Heavenly Kingdom in Nanjing in Jiangsu, the site of the general headquarters of the "August 1" Nanchang uprising in Nanchang, Jiangxi and the historic sites in the Jinggangshan mountains at Ruijin, Zunyi, Yan'an, etc.

The achievements in construction in the more than thirty years since the founding of the People's Republic of China, such as the Changjiang (Yangtze) river bridges at Nanjing and Hankou, the Gezhouba key water control project, the Xinanjiang river hydropower station and the Great Hall of the People in Beijing, have attracted many tourists.

China is also a multinational country: all its 56 nationalities have characteristics and traditions peculiar to themselves. Their festivals, in particular, are rich and colourful, displaying an infinite variety of unusual phenomena most appealing to sightseers. Among festival activities which have aroused the enormous interest of domestic and foreign tourists are the Nadamu Mass Rally of the Mongolian nationality, the Water-Sprinkling Festival of the Dai, the Sanyue-

Roast mutton – a picnic for tourists from Taiwan.

jie (Street of March) of the Bai, the Song Market of the Zhuang, the Festival of Fireworks and Firecrackers of the Dong, the Torch Festival of the Yi, the Bathing Buddha Festival of the Zang, the Festival of Fast-Breaking of the Uygur, the Kuerban Festival of the Kazaks and the Jiusan Festival of the Chaoxian (Koreans). (See also **Appendix 2**.)

Chinese culinary art enjoys a high reputation the world over: special flavour dishes number more than 5,000 and may be divided into eight great systems of Chinese cuisine – Shandong, Sichuan, Jiangsu, Zhejiang, Guangdong, Fujian, Hunan and Jiangxi – each with its own local characteristic in colour, fragrance, taste and shape and all considered to be delicacies by the vast number of tourists. (See also **Appendix 3**.)

Also worth mentioning are China's numerous unique handicraft articles, which have become famous both at home and abroad. Beijing cloisonné, jade and ivory sculptures; Jingdezhen porcelain; Guangzhou *Guangcai* (coloured silk), Yixing pottery, the satchels of Yunnan's Sani nationality, Nanjing *yunjing* (brocade), Hangzhou brocade, Jiading bamboo engravings, Chaozhou wood carvings, Huishan clay sculptures, Fuzhou lacquer wares, Changzhou combs, Luoyang tri-coloured glazed pottery in the style of the Tang dynasty, Xi'an miniature figurines from the Qin dynasty, Tianjin cloth toys, as well as the famous embroideries of Jiangsu, Hunan, Sichuan and Guangdong, etc., are all articles of superb workmanship, a feast for the eyes and ideal tourist souvenirs.

MAJOR TOURIST AREAS

THE vast expanse of China's territory, her age-old history, the numerous new and old architectural monuments and the fruits of culture and the arts, as well as the natural scenery, with its famous mountains and great rivers, lakes, beaches, gorges, grottoes, springs, waterfalls, forests and plains have become the favourite haunts and scenic spots of tourism. The few districts introduced below comprise only a small part of the 436 opened to foreigners, including the first group of key scenic spots of the country nominated by the State Council.

Beijing

The capital of China, Beijing, is situated on the northern part of the North China plain, with its suburban areas surrounded by undulating hills and winding waterways. Five feudal dynasties down the ages made Beijing their capital, and the numerous imperial buildings have made it a typical city with the distinguishing features of traditional Chinese architecture. The vast number of cultural relics and places of historical interest, the beautiful scenic landscapes, the magnificent examples of culture and the arts, and the modern features offer great attraction to vast numbers of tourists from both home and abroad.

The Imperial Palace and Tian'anmen

The Imperial Palace, situated in the centre of the city, was the palace of the Ming dynasty (1368–1644) and the Qing dynasty (1644–1911). Twenty-four emperors, one after another, were at the helm of State here. It is the biggest and the most complete ancient architectural complex of palaces now existing in China, occupying an area of 72 hectares with 150,000 square metres of building area and more than 9,000 rooms, magnificent and resplendent. This "Forbidden City" is surrounded by ten-metre high walls and a 52-metre wide moat. The Imperial Palace is now a museum, and in addition to its buildings there are exhibitions of China's ancient porcelain, jewellery and various kinds of art treasures.

Tian'anmen (Gate of Heavenly Peace) was formerly the main entrance of the imperial city. On 1 October 1949, Chairman Mao Zedong announced the founding of the People's Republic of China from the rostrum of Tian'anmen, and since then it has become the symbol of China. Tian'anmen Square covers an area of 44 hectares (100 acres) and is one of the largest in the world.

Tiantan Temple

Tiantan, the Temple of Heaven, situated in the southeast corner of the city, is the largest temple now existing in China. It is the place where the emperors of the Ming and Qing dynasties offered sacrifices to Heaven and prayed for bumper harvests. It was built in the 18th year of Yongle of the Ming dynasty (1420), occupying 273 hectares of land and incorporating the Hall of Prayer for Good Harvests, the Imperial Vaulted Temple, the Echo Wall and the Round Altar as its main buildings. The Hall of Prayer for Good Harvests is 38 metres high and 30 metres in diameter. The architecture of its resplendent gilded roof is a typical example of the art unique to China, and is constructed entirely of wood. The Echo Wall of the Imperial Vaulted Temple is circular, and a person who

The Angle Terrace *(Diao Yu Tai)* is a luxurious Guest House where Queen Elizabeth II stayed during her visit in Beijing. This is the Honoured-guest Building. *(Photo by Li Shixin)*

stands on one side of the wall speaking softly can be heard distinctly a long distance away. Sightseers marvel at the wonders of this locality.

The Summer Palace

Situated 20 kilometres away in the north-west suburb of Beijing is the Summer Palace (Yiheyuan), which covers an area of 290 hectares and was used in the past by the imperial family of Qing dynasty, in particular Dowager Empress Ci Xi (1835–1908), as a temporary imperial palace for passing the summer. The layout of the palace is broad in scale and is an excellent model of the classical garden architecture of China. The lakes and hills here complement each other delightfully. With Wanshoushan (the Hill of Longevity) as the centre, the major buildings include Paiyundian, Foxiangge (Pavilion of Buddhist Fragrance), the Long Corridor, the Marble Boat, the Seventeen-Arched Bridge, Xiequyuan (Palace of Virtue and Harmony), etc. From the top of Wanshoushan, there is a panoramic view of the vast Kunminghu lake, as smooth as a mirror, with thirteen pavilions and towers along the banks. (For the **Great Wall** and **Ming Tombs** see Part 1, **Chapter 13**.)

The scenic spots of Beijing also include Jingshan (Coal Hill), Beihai Park, Tuancheng (Round City), Guozijian, Yonghegong Lamasery (Palace of Harmony and Peace), the zoo, Taoranting Park, Zhongshan Park, Xiangshan Park, Yingtaogou (Cherry Valley) Garden, Lugouqiao (Marco Polo Bridge), Biyunsi (Azure Cloud Monastery), the Tantuosi and Jietaisi temples, Dazhongsi (Big Bell Temple), Wofosi (the Temple of the Reclining Buddha),

Zhoukoudian (the home of Peking Man), the ancient observatory, the Han Tombs at Dabaotai, etc. A large, modern, pleasure garden is being constructed at Longtanhu in the south-east of Beijing city.

● Tourist spots in the neighbourhood include the east and west mausoleums of the Qing dynasty. **Dong Ling** (East Mausoleum) of the Qing dynasty is situated in the county of Zunhua of Hebei province, 125 kilometres east of Beijing. The underground palace of Emperor Qianlong (1736–1795) Yuling has already been opened to the public. The walls and ceilings of arches in the palace are covered with sumptuous reliefs. Among the various mausoleums in Dongling, the most gorgeous architecture is in the mausoleum of Dowager Empress Ci Xi, the transparent sculpture of dragon and phoenix marble steps in front of Longen Hall at the mausoleum having a style of its own, with the phoenix, the symbol of an empress, above that of the dragon, the symbol of an emperor. This underground palace is now also open to the public.

Xiling (West Mausoleum) is situated at the foot of Yongning Hill in Yi county in Hebei, over 120 kilometres to the south-west of Beijing. The area encompassed by the mausoleum is more than 100 kilometres, where the tombs of four emperors, three empresses, three imperial concubines and four lords and princesses can be found, the floor space of the entire architecture reaching 500,000 square metres. The area is covered with luxuriant growths of flowers and trees, with birds singing on broad hillsides and water flowing in murmuring streams.

● Beijing is the general hub of air and railway traffic of the whole country. The Civil Aviation Administration of China (CAAC) runs 27 international air routes and the planes on 126 international scheduled flights take off and land in Beijing every week, connecting 26 cities of 22 countries and districts in the five continents of the world. There are 153 domestic air routes, flying 660 scheduled flights each week, connecting 83 cities. There are

also daily flights between Beijing and the Hong Kong region.

The main railway lines of the whole country converge on Beijing; through trains reach the provincial capitals, the capitals of autonomous regions and municipalities directly under the Central Government and the various major and medium-sized cities (with the exception of Xizang). There are international through trains twice weekly between Beijing and Pyongyang, Ulan Bator and Moscow.

Beijing city at present has more than 140 bus and trolleybus lines which greatly facilitate visiting, sightseeing and shopping. The subway between Beijing railway station and Pingguoyuan (Apple Garden) is 24 kilometres long; a round-the-city subway is now in operation.

There are, in addition, more than 200 passenger transport services such as the Capital Car Co., the Beijing Tourist Car Co., etc., which have set up service networks at the various big hotels, undertaking taxi or car-hiring business.

Shanghai

Shanghai is one of the three municipalities directly under the Central Government. At the beginning of the last century, it was already one of the most prosperous and flourishing cities in the south-eastern part of the country. Not only is it an important industrial base, but it is also the most prosperous commercial city of the country, one of the ports for foreign trade and a hub of communications. It is a busy metropolis with numerous sightseeing places famous for their scenery or historical relics.

Yuyuan Garden

This is one of the most famous gardens south of the Yangtze, built in the 38th year of Emperor Jiajing of the Ming dynasty (1559), covering an area of over 20,000 square metres. There are more than 30 delightful sights in the garden, the cream of all the buildings being Dianchuntang, in the north-east corner, which was the site of the headquarters of the Xiaodaohui (Small Sword Society) Uprising in Shanghai in 1853, the historical relics of which are now on exhibition.

Yufosi (Jade Buddha Temple)

This is located at 170 Anyuan Road. The monk Huigen brought back the white jade figure of Buddha from Burma in the 8th year of Tongzhi of the Qing dynasty (1869), and a temple for its worship was subsequently built in Jiangwan in 1882, from which the name of Yufosi was derived. It was moved to the present site in 1918.

Foreign tourists tasting traditional Chinese snacks in Beijing.

678

Longhua Pagoda and Temple

Longhua Pagoda is situated in the south-western suburb and close to the old county of Longhua. The building of the pagoda was begun in the 8th year of Zhengshi of the Wei dynasty (AD 247), during the period of the Three Kingdoms. It is an octagonal brick and wood structure, 40.40 metres in height and beautifully shaped.

Longhua Temple is said to have been built at the same time as the pagoda, but had been neglected for years and was rebuilt in 977. It comprises the Hall of Buddha Maitreya, the Hall of Tian Wang (Heavenly King), and the Daxiongbaodian, the Hall of Three Saints and Abbot, with the Hall of Arhats and the Bell and Drum Tower on its sides. Alongside the monastery is the Longhua park.

Guyiyuan Garden

One of Shanghai's five age-old gardens, Guyiyuan is located in the county of Nanxiang of Jiading. The construction of the garden was started in the 31st year of Emperor Shizong of the Ming dynasty (1552). Precious cultural relics, like a Buddhist sutra and stone pillars inscribed with Buddha's names, and Buddhist scriptures from the Tang dynasty, etc., can be seen there.

Shanghai Museum

Built in 1952, the museum has a collection of more than 100,000 items of various kinds of historical relics and exhibits of bronze wares, pottery and paintings. A shop for the sale of replicas of cultural relics has also been set up there.

Shanghai Exhibition Centre

This centre, which occupies 11.4 hectares, was completed in 1955. The Shanghai Industrial Exhibition Association has set up permanent halls for metallurgy, machines and electricity, the chemical industry, meters, telecommunications, light industry, spinning and weaving, and handicrafts in order to exhibit new industrial products and exchange new technologies.

The House, Memorial Hall and Tomb of Lu Xun

Situated at Daluxincun in Shanyang Road is the former residence of Lu Xun, a great thinker and writer, who lived there from 1933 to 1936. On exhibition are some of his original belongings, just as they were during his lifetime. The Memorial Hall was completed in 1951 and is located in Hongkou Park. Over 1,200 exhibits showing the development of Lu Xun's thoughts and his fighting career are on display.

Lu Xun's tomb, a granite structure in the park, was moved there from the International Cemetery in the western suburbs on the 20th anniversary of his death. The statue of Lu Xun sitting was cast in 1961 in commemoration of his eightieth birthday.

● Shanghai has, moreover, the site of the first national congress of the Chinese Communist Party, the former residence of **Sun Zhong-san** (Sun Yatsen), the former residence and grave of **Song Qingling**, the **Zhou Enlai residence**, the **Tao Fen Memorial Hall**, the **Children's Palace**, the **Shanghai Botanical Garden**, the **Shanghai Zoo**, etc.

● Regular air services and trains connect Shanghai with the various major cities of the country. International lines fly direct to New York, San Francisco, Tokyo, Osaka, Nagasaki and other cities. There is a regional service between Shanghai and Hong Kong. Passenger steamers on the Changjiang (Yangtze) river reach Nanjing, Wuhan, Sanxia (Yangtze Gorges), etc. Regular steamship services operate between Shanghai and Hong Kong. In the city proper, there are more than 200 bus and tram lines, which greatly facilitate communications. There are, in addition, a large number of taxis and first-class tourist cars for the service of the public.

Tianjin

One of the three big municipalities in China directly under the Central Government, Tianjin is a well-known seaport in the north, and the gateway of the capital to the sea. It is the second largest industrial and commercial city of the whole country, second only to Shanghai, as well as the centre of industry and foreign trade of North China. The Tianjin new harbour situated in Bohai Bay is the largest man-made harbour in the northern part of China, the construction of which was completed in 1952. Some 24 big liners of over 10,000 tons can berth at the docks in the new harbour at the same time.

The Park on the Water

This is situated in the south-western part of the city proper, occupying 200 hectares, with the water surface of the lake taking up almost half of its area. There are 13 islets, connected with each other by bridges and causeways. The willows on the embankments are particularly alluring in the spring.

Dulesi (Temple of Solitary Enjoyment)

Situated inside the western gate of Jixian county in Tianjin municipality, the temple was built at the beginning of the Tang dynasty (618–907). The principal parts of the building, the gate of the temple and the *Guanyin* Pavilion were rebuilt in the second year of Tonghe of the Liao dynasty (984). The former has a corridor roof which is the earliest of its kind now existing in China; the latter is one of the oldest wooden constructions now existing, and also one of the tallest two-tiered pavilions now extant in the country and a representative work of China's ancient wood construction.

Panshan Mountain (Winding Mountain) Excursion Centre

Mount Panshan is one of China's 15 great famous mountains. It is located 12 kilometres north-west of Jixian county and has several major scenic spots, which include the Dongwutai, or the "Five Mountain Peaks in the East" – the highest peak in the mountain range; the Guayue (Hanging Moon) peak, with Zigai (Purple Cover) peak in front and Zilai (Original) peak behind it; Jiuhua peak to its east and Wujian (Sword-Dance) peak to its west; and the Wonders of Sanpan (Three Bends) – the upper bend, the middle bend and the lower bend. Handrails have been installed along Babuxian (Eight Perilous Steps) and the dangerous and difficult paths up the Guayue peak. The Woyunlou (Building Reclining on the Clouds), where Emperor Qianlong of the Qing dynasty (1736–1795) used to come to watch opera performances, has been rebuilt. There is a snack-bar for the convenience of sightseers.

Tianjin Art Museum

Situated in Jiefangbeilu (North Liberation Road), the museum has a collection of rare works of art handed down from ancient times, which include ceramics, bronze wares, ancient jades, ancient seals and royal seals, as well as the paintings and calligraphies, seal cuttings and handicraft articles of contemporary masters and works of folk art of pronounced local colour, such as the Spring Festival pictures of Yangliuqing, the painted figurines of Niren Zhang, Tianjin brick engravings and dolls carved in wood, etc.

● One may also travel from Tianjin to its adjoining city, the municipality of Tangshan in the province of Hebei, often called the "Coal Capital" as well as the "porcelain capital of the north" for sightseeing tours.

● Tianjin is the communication hub of China's northern regions. Regular air services make non-stop flights between Tianjin and Beijing, Shanghai, Guangzhou, Nanjing, Changsha, Guilin, etc. Through trains travel to the various major cities of the country, and passenger steamships ply between Tianjin and Dalian, Yantai, Longkou and other ports.

Shijiazhuang

Shijiazhuang is the junction of three railway lines, the Beijing–Guangzhou, the Shijiazhuang–Dezhou and the Shijiazhuang–Taiyuan lines.

Great Zhaozhou Stone Bridge

45 kilometres away from Shijiazhuang and 2.5 kilometres south of Zhao county stands the Great Zhaozhou Stone Bridge (or Anji Bridge). Built in the years 500–610, the bridge was designed and constructed by the great architect Li Chun of the Sui dynasty (581–618). One of the oldest stone bridges in China, it is 64.4 metres long, 9 metres wide, built of 28 independent stone arches with a net span of 37.35 metres. It is a single-hole, curved, open shoulder arch stone bridge, kept intact to this day, and the earliest bridge in the world built with such a big span. Highly artistic and scientific, it is a great pioneering achievement in the history of bridge construction, particularly for the "open shoulder arch" technique.

Longxing Monastery

Also called Dafosi (Temple of Great Buddha), this is a group of temples of massive scale and long history. Located inside the county town of Zhengding, 15 kilometres north of Shijiazhuang, the construction was begun in the 6th year of Emperor Wendi Kaihuang of the Sui dynasty (586), occupying 5 hectares of land. Moni Hall, in the monastery, is a plane architecture in the shape of a cross with an imposing layout and an unusual appearance and shape, which stands out as unique in the ancient architecture of China. The principal building of the monastery is Dabeige, a three-storeyed structure with 5 eaves, 33 metres in height, inside which stands the 42-arm Dabei Buddha cast in bronze (also called *Guanyin* of a Thousand Hands and Eyes), 19.2 metres high, the tallest of its kind in the country. There are also stone inscriptions, wood engravings, murals, hanging sculptures, etc., all of them of very high artistic value.

Cangyanshan Mountain

Stituated among the mountains of the Taihangshan mountain group 78 kilometres south-west of Shijiazhuang, Cangyanshan enjoys the reputation from time immemorial of being "a mountain that monopolizes the bizarre beauties of Wuyue (the Five Mountains)". After a climb of some 300 stone steps, one reaches an arched stone bridge stretching across the western wall of a steep precipice, with a large, beautifully shaped hall constructed on the bridge. High upon the mountain is the Qingfusi which, according to legend, was the temple where princess Nanyang, the eldest daughter of Emperor Yangdi of the Sui dynasty, cut off her hair to become a nun. Other buildings on the mountain include the Cangshan Academy of Classical Learning, the Wanxiantang (Hall of 10,000 Celestial Beings), the Fenghuixuan, the Cangjinglou (a building housing a collection of Buddhist scriptures), and the Hall of the Real Looks of the Princess, etc.

The Cemetery of Revolutionary Martyrs

The cemetery of the revolutionary martyrs of the North China military area, occupying an area of 21 hectares, is situated in the western part of the city of Shijiazhuang. Here rest some of the cadres of the Liberation Army and combat heroes of the North China region, a total of more than 700, who sacrificed their lives during the anti-Japanese war and the War of Liberation. On the western side of the cemetery is the tomb of the great internationalist, Dr Norman Bethune, while on the eastern side lie the tomb of Dr Ke Di-hua of the International Red Cross Medical Team in Aid of China, and the monument to the memory of Dr Edward, the Indian doctor and leader of the medical team.

● Shijiazhuang is one of the communication hubs of the North China region. Scheduled CAAC flights connect Shijiazhuang every week with Beijing, Changsha, Guangzhou, Shanghai, Qinhuangdao, etc. About 60 trains arrive, start from or pass through every day to all major cities of the country.

Chengde

Chengde is located between the North China plain and the Mongolian plateau, 256 kilometres from Beijing, being the latter's gate to the north-east. The Yanshan mountain range lies across the Chengde region, providing a natural defence for Beijing. There is no sweltering heat here in the summer nor bitter cold in the winter. In Changde are the classical gardens and parks of the imperial families, the biggest extant in China; the most concentrated group of ancient monasteries; a wooden Buddha image of one thousand hands and one thousand eyes (the biggest of its kind in the world); and the world's shortest river, Rehe. Also there is the rarely seen *yardang* landform of Hebei.

Bishushanzhuang Palace

The "Mountain Hamlet for Escaping the Heat", Bishushanzhuang, also called Chengde Temporary

A hotel in a rural area in Inner Mongolia. *(Photo by Yang Shenhe)*

Palace, or the palace for short stays of the emperor in Rehe, was a large imperial garden built by Emperors Kangxi and Qianlong of the Qing dynasty (1644–1911), in the northern part of Chengde city. It covers an area of 5,640,000 square metres, with the wall enclosing it as long as 10 kilometres – a rare spot for natural scenery in the northern part of China. The construction of this mountain resort was begun in the 11th year of Kangxi (1703) and completed in the 55th year of Qianlong (1790), encompassing 119 groups of buildings which included the 36 views of Kangxi and the 36 views of Qianlong, known as the 72 views of Bishushanzhuang. In those years, celebrations and ceremonies for audiences by Qing emperors were mostly held here. The area of the mountain chain accounts for four-fifths of the resort, with more than forty courtyards and temples scattered in it.

Twelve imperial temples were built one after another by Emperors Kangxi and Qianlong in the east and north of the mountain resort. They were called the *Waibamiao* (Eight Outer Temples) because they were located outside the metropolitan capital. Seven of them, the Anyuan Temple, the Xumifushoumiao, the Shuxiang Temple, the Puningsi (Temple of Universal Peace), the Pulesi (Temple of Universal Happiness), the Putuozongshengmiao and the Purensi, are still standing. The impressive architectural styles of Han, Mongolian and Zang (Tibetan) nationalities, with their gilded tile roofs of a dazzling brilliance, are of high scientific and artistic value. Together with Bishushanzhuang they have become an integral whole, adding radiance and beauty to each other.

Scattered on a vast plain to the north of the temporary palace, are 31 spotlessly white *yurts*, the largest of which used to be the place where Emperor Qianlong granted audience to Mongolian princes and foreign envoys. 28 yurts have now been opened up as guest rooms for tourists, all of them equipped with toilets, air-conditioning, telephones, coloured TV sets and carpets, etc. Here visitors may enjoy not only the cuisine of the imperial courts of the Qing dynasty but typical Mongolian dishes as well.

● Through trains run between here and Beijing; there are also through services to Jinzhou, Fuxin, Longhua, etc. During busy tourist seasons, 9 trains travel daily between Chengde and other parts of the country. Six major lines of the highway bus service connect the Mountain Resort with Beijing, Tianjin, Tangshan, Lingyuan, Chiefeng and Qinglong, totalling 120 runs daily.

Qinhuangdao

Situated in the north-eastern part of Hebei province and bordering on the Bohai Sea, the city of Qinhuangdao is divided into three districts: Shanhaiguan, the city of historical fame; Qinhuangdao harbour, the natural ice-free port; and Beidaihe, the famous summer resort.

Shanhaiguan is located 15 kilometres north-east of Qinhuangdao. It is an important mountain pass on the eastern part of the Great Wall where the "First pass of the world", a place contested by all strategists in the history of China, is located. The pass was named Shanhaiguan because it is situated between the mountain and the sea.

Beidaihe is a famous summer resort and a scenic spot for convalescence. (See Part I, **Chapter 13** in **Volume 1**.)

● It has convenient communications; through trains leave for various major cities like Beijing, Tianjin, Nanjing, etc., and during tourist seasons there are through bus services from Qianmen, Chongwenmen, etc. in Beijing for trips to Beidaihe.

Taiyuan

Taiyuan is an important industrial city in the north of China. Situated in the central part of Shanxi province, it is hedged in the east, west and north by mountains. Its southern side is flat, open terrain, with the water of Fenhe river flowing southward from the north, irrigating it. The history of Taiyuan city dates back more than 2,400 years and many scenic spots and places of historical interest can be seen inside and outside the city.

Jinci (Ancestral Temple of the King of Jin)

Situated in the south-western suburb of Taiyuan city, the ancestral temple has a history of over 1,500 years. In its nearly 100 buildings, the principal structure, the Yijiang (Goddess Hall), is the oldest extant building of wooden construction in Taiyuan, grand in scale and elegant in architecture. In the middle of the hall is the statue of the goddess, said to have been erected by the wife of King Wu of the dynasty of Western Zhou (*ca.* 11th *ca.*–771 BC); on two sides are the statues of 42 maidens, almost life-size, vividly realistic in shape and individual in bearing. They are one of the treasures of ancient Chinese sculpture.

Taiyuan's sightseeing spots also include **Dafosi** (Temple of the Great Buddha); **Taishansi** temple; **Shuangtasi** (Temple of Twin Pagodas); **Shuanlingsi** temple; **Tianlongshan Grotto** and **Longshan Grotto**; **Chunyang Palace**; the **Xuanzihongse, Chongshansi** and **Duofusi** temples; the ancient **mosque**; the **Tongzisi** (Boy Temple); the **Randengta** (Lamp-Lighting Pagoda) and the Shanxi Museum.

355 kilometres away from Taiyuan is the city of Datong, where lies one of China's biggest complexes of grottoes, the **Yungang Grottoes**. (See Part I, **Chapter 13.**)

Jiulongbi (Nine-Dragon Wall)

The nine glazed-tile dragons on this wall are beautiful in colour and vivid in shape. The wall was originally the screen wall facing the gate of the house of Zhu Gui (Prince Dai), the third son of Emperor Zhu Yuanzhang, the founder of the Ming dynasty more than 500 years ago. A pool at the foot of the wall reflects the dragons in apparent movement.

Bojiajiaozang Hall

The Bojiajiaozang (Hall for Keeping Buddhist Scriptures) in the Huayansi temple in Datong city is one of the two biggest Buddhist halls still existing (the other being the great hall of Fengguosi in Yi county, Liaoning province). The 31 statues from the Liao dynasty (916–1125) in the hall constitute a treasure of ancient Chinese clay sculpture.

Yingxian Muta Pagoda

This wooden pagoda is located in Yingxian county, about 70 kilometres away from Datong city. It was built in the second year of Qingning of the Liao dynasty (1059) and is 67 metres in height and 30 metres in diameter. This ingeniously constructed pagoda is imposing and majestic in appearance, having been in its time the site for publicizing Buddha *dharma* as well as an observation tower for watching the progress of battles and for conducting them during a war. It is the oldest and tallest pagoda made of timber now existing in China, and despite almost a thousand years of weather and wars, it still stands lofty and firm, providing precious material for research in pagoda construction in China's ancient architecture.

Xuanggongsi (Temple Suspended in Mid-Air)

In Hunyuanxian county, adjacent to Ying county, is the famous Xuanggongsi, built in the last stage of Northern Wei dynasty (420–534). Overlooking a deep valley and with a precipitous cliff above it, the temple faces the mighty North Mountain, Mount Hengshan. In perilous and unusual conditions, the workers of that time cut and hammered stones for the foundation and erected structures moulded to the rocky cliffs. In 1958 the Hunyuan people built a big reservoir in the neighbourhood, where the examples of the wonderful workmanship of old and new architecture form a delightful contrast.

● There are also many scenic spots on the Hengshan and Wutaishan mountains in the vicinity of Taiyuan city. (See Part I, **Chapter 13.**)

Scheduled flights connect Taiyuan with Beijing, Shanghai, Guangzhou and other cities. Trains passing through or leaving Taiyuan run daily direct to Beijing, Xi'an, Jinan and Shijiazhuang, as well as Dezhou, Baoding, Datong and other places. There are also long-distance buses running to Changzhi Yangquan, Wutaishan, etc.

Hohhot

Hohhot, the capital of the Autonomous Region of Inner Mongolia on the northern border of China, is a city with a strong flavour and features of the Mongolian nationality. Crossing the mountain of Daqingshan, sightseers will find three grassland tourist spots, the Gegentala, the Bulamuren, and the Huitengxile. They will have opportunities to live in yurts, ride on horses and camels and on Lele carriages, take a drink of tea with milk and savour the flavour of Mongolian food.

Zhao Jun's Tomb

This is situated on the southern bank of the Daheihe river, 9 kilometres from the southern suburb of Hohhot. The 33 metres high, dark and gloomy tomb occupies an area of more than 30,000 square metres, and has been known through the ages as the "Green Tomb". Wang Zhaojun, who was named Wang Qiang and styled herself Zhao-jun, was a native of Xingshanxian county in Hubei province and a *Dai Zhao* (lady-in-waiting) in the inner court of Emperor Yuandi of the Western Han dynasty (48–33 BC). In 33 BC she was married to Hu Han-xie Chanyu, a chieftan of the Xiongnu – the minority nationality in the north at that period. She had a deep respect for the people and their customs and habits and did much that contributed to friendly and harmonious relations between the Han and Xiongnu nationalities, which won her the love and esteem of the local people. Zhao Jun's tomb has now become a symbol of the unity of the two nationalities.

Wutasi (Five Pagoda Temple)

This temple is located in the south-eastern part of the old city of Hohhot. Its original name was the "Stupa of the Pedestals of Buddha's Warrior Attendants". The 16.5-metre high pagodas were built between 1727 and 1732. The base of the pagodas is in the form of an elevated square platform with an arched door, and towering above the platform, tall and graceful, are five pagodas built in the courtyard of CiDeng (Lantern of Mercy) temple, which is why the temple is popularly called the Five Pagoda Temple. The pagodas were built of brick and decorated mainly with small carved tiles. A total of 1,563 small gilded figures of Buddha with scriptures carved in Mongolian, Tibetan and Sanskrit can be seen all over these pagodas. The screen walls are inlaid with three fine line sculptures and carved stones – an astronomical map in Mongolian, a picture of the six lines of samsara and a distribution map of Xumishan mountain to the north of the pagodas are very precious cultural relics, among which the astronomical map, in particular, is invaluable. Because it is the only astronomical map with indications and annotations in Mongolian so far

discovered, it is considered to be of very high scientific research value.

Wanbuhuayanjing (White Pagoda)

Wanbuhuayanjing pagoda is located to the south-west of Baita (White Pagoda) village in the eastern suburb of Hohhot city, 18 kilometres away. The construction of the pagoda was begun during the Liao dynasty (11th century). It is an octagonal, 7-tiered pavilion-style brick pagoda, 43 metres in height, and the only architectural monument in Fengzhou city from the Liao dynasty preserved intact to this day. Vivid relief sculptures of heavenly kings, strongmen, Bodhisattvas, etc., in various postures, may be found on the walls.

● Hohhot is the communications hub of the autonomous region of Inner Mongolia. There are regular flights direct to Beijing, Chifeng, Hailaer, Tongliao, Xilinhaote and other localities every week, and through trains connect Hohhot with Beijing, Yinchuan, Lanzhou and other cities.

Shenyang

Shenyang is a famous city with a long history and the communications hub of China's north-eastern region, with many historical remains and sites of the Qing dynasty.

The Imperial Palace

The Shenyang Imperial Palace was the residence of Nu Er Ha Chi, leader of the Nuzhen nationality (predecessors of the Man (Manchu) nationality) and founder of the Qing dynasty (1644–1911), and of his successor, Huangtaiji, until the dynasty had become established. It incorporates over 70 buildings with more than 300 rooms, occupying altogether an area of over 60,000 square metres. The spacious halls and tall pavilions, sumptuously decorated and furnished, may be divided into three parts: the middle part, with Chongzheng Hall as its centre; the eastern part, with Dazheng Hall as its centre; and the western part, with Wensu Pavilion as its centre. All these structures are noted for their strong national characteristics, which embody the cultural exchanges between Han, Man and Meng (Mongol) nationalities in palace architecture. Among extant architectural complexes of royal palaces preserved intact, they are second only to the imperial palace in Beijing, and are now open to the public as a museum of the history and arts of the Qing dynasty.

Dongling (East Tombs) or Fuling

Situated in the eastern suburb of Shenyang is the huge mausoleum of Qingtaizu, Emperor Nu Er Ha Chi, the founder of the Qing dynasty, and his empress and concubines, covering 500 hectares of land, of which 16 hectares are the sites of the tombs. The great mausoleum is surrounded by rectangular red walls. Inside the gate entrance, stone animals stand on each side of the paved path, and at the top of the 108 brick steps, behind the pavilion with a stone tablet erected inside, is the square wall of the tombs. Beyond the square wall are the crescent wall, the treasure wall and the treasure roof. Below is the subterranean palace where the inner and outer coffins of Nu Er Ha Chi and his empress and concubines were laid.

Beiling (North Tombs) or Zhaoling

The tombs of Emperor Taizhong, Huangtaiji of the Qing dynasty (1627–1643) and his empress are located in the northern suburb of Shenyang. The area of the cemetery occupies 330 hectares (of which 16 hectares are occupied by the tombs). The layout is in the main the same as that of Dongling. The area in front of the mausoleum has been opened up as a park, with a forest at the back.

Qianshan Hill

Qianshan Hill (Hill of a Thousand Lotus Flowers), known as the "Jewel of the North-East", is situated 18 kilometres south-east of Anshan city to the south of Shenyang city. Xianrentai (Terrace of the Gods), the highest peak, is 708 metres above sea level. Trees grow luxuriantly on the hill, on which many temples and places of historical interest can be found. There are almost a hundred kinds of precious birds and animals living among the trees.

Dalian

Travelling southward from Qianshan, one reaches the seaside city of Dalian on the southern tip of Liaodong peninsula. The locality is characterized by oceanic climates and is variously dubbed "Gem of North Sea", "Garden City" and "Home of Apples". Famous scenic spots include the Laohutan (Tiger Beach) Park, the Xinghai Park, the Fujiazhuang Tourist Centre, the bathing beach at Bangchuidao (Wooden Club Island), Baiyushan Hill (White Jade Hill), the Wanzhong Tombs, the Northern Fortress of East Jiguanshan Hill (East Cockscomb Hill) and the newly opened scenic seaside roads, etc.

Jinzhou

Situated to the south-west of Shenyang city, Jinzhou has always been the place contested by strategists. For a one-day tour, one may visit the grotto of Wanfotang (Hall of 10,000 Buddhas) and Fengguosi temple, etc.; for a two-day tour, one may also visit the *Guanyin* cave and the memorial hall of the Liao-Shen Campaign etc.; for a three-day tour one may, besides the

above, travel to Xingcheng by the shore of the Bohai Sea to see a typical ancient town which has been preserved intact to this day, a "Ming dynasty street", the Hot Spring Sanatorium, etc. The bathing beaches here may accommodate as many as 200,000 people.

● From Shenyang, scheduled flights leave every week for Beijing, Shanghai, Tianjin, Guangzhou, Changchun, Yanji, Dalian, Harbin, Mudanjiang, Qingdao, Hangzhou, Nanjing, Xi'an, Chengdu and other cities. Five railway trunk lines connect Shenyang with various parts of the country, and some 60 long-distance bus lines are in operation. There are also tourist buses travelling straight to Qianshan scenic spots.

Changchun

The young and beautiful city of Changchun in China's north-east is referred to as the "Spring city beyond the Great Wall".

Nanhugongyuan (South Lake Park)

Occupying an area of 2,220,000 square metres and brimming with outdoor life, the Nanhu Park is the largest park in Changchun, the water surface of its artificial lake reaching 930,000 square metres. There is an islet in the centre of the lake, and on the northern side of the islet are the jade ribbon and the quadrangular pavilion bridges. Tourists may enjoy rowing boats on the lake, and in the winter, when the lake freezes, it becomes an ideal skating rink.

Children's Park

In the Hall of a Hundred Flowers in this park, flowers blossom all the year round in a riot of colour, with a sweet smell to greet all sightseers. The "Exhibition of a Hundred Flowers", "Flower Exhibition for the Lunar New Year", "May Day Flower Exhibition" and the "Exhibition of Chrysanthemums", etc. are held here.

Jingyuetan Forest Park

The park, with green hills and exuberant foliage, elegant and secluded, is situated on the southern outskirts of the city. The water of Jingyuetan (Clear Moon Pond) is as clear as a mirror. The seclusion of the place and the clarity of the lake tend to make tourists reluctant to leave.

In the city itself, sightseeing spots include the **Changchun Studio**, the **First Changchun Automobile Factory**, the **Embroidery Arts and Crafts Factory** and the former **Imperial Palace** of the bogus Manchuguo, or puppet state of Manchuria.

Jilin

Jilin city, situated due east of Changchun, is well known in China as a city of chemical industries.

The vortex flow of the turbo unit of the Fengman hydroelectrics station south of the city has caused the temperature of the water in the more than two hundred *li* (*ca.* 100 km) of the Songhua river under the dam to rise and the current velocity to quicken. Due to the same effect, the river water does not freeze, despite the bitter cold of the winter, and the mists steaming above the river upon contact with the cold air make the condensation on the pine needles and willow twigs on the causeways freeze into beautiful frosty shapes, like silver chrysanthemums in full bloom. This is the marvellous spectacle of the famous "tree hangings" which make the 10-*li* causeway silvery white, winning for it the name of "Causeway fontanesia" and giving the Jilin landscape a style of its own in the winter season.

The exhibition hall in the Jiangnan park in the city has on display the material objects of the world's largest stone meteorite shower.

The ski slopes of Songhua Lake, 30 kilometres away from Jilin city proper, form an urban skiing ground hard to better. A manned cableway 1,776 metres long, with 86 suspension supports, can lift a number of tourists up to the hilltop in 18 minutes. There are two 3,000-metre long and 50-metre wide ski tracks and a cross-country track 5 kilometres long, which are looked upon as paradise by skiing enthusiasts.

● There are regular weekly air services between Jilin and Beijing, Shanghai, Dalian, Guangzhou and other important cities. Trains travel daily to various major cities throughout the country.

Harbin

Harbin has a very long winter and a pleasantly cool summer, as well as a magnificent northern scenery. It enjoys the reputation as the "Ice city" and the "Home of music of the north".

Taiyang (Sun) Island

This is a famous scenic spot for convalescing in north-eastern China. In the park on the island, the landscapes at the Sun Hill and the Sun Lake are especially pleasant. The Youth Home at Jile village caters to the public with rich and colourful programmes of entertainment. The sandy beaches at the bank of Songhua river are natural swimming places on the island.

Children's Park

This is located in the centre of the city. There is a miniature railway two kilometres long with two stations, the Beijing Station and the Harbin Station, and seven carriages attached to the mini-train, driven by an internal-combustion engine, which provides seats for 320 children. A round trip takes twelve minutes and the railway is staffed by primary school students in turn.

Zhalong Nature Reserve

The reserve is situated on the lower reaches of Wuyuerhe river, south-east of Qiqiha'er city to the north-west of Harbin. Here is a vast world of marshes, with numerous lakes that send up bubbles, and abundant growths of reeds. Red-crowned cranes, precious birds of world renown, fly here from the south in March every year to spend the summer, returning to the south in November. Tourists enjoy the landscapes of the vast expanse of lakes and swamps in this region and the charms of the fluttering, red-crowned cranes.

Wudalianchi Springs

Situated in Wudalianchi City, this medicinal springs convalescent district has more than 30 sanatoria within it. The medicinal spring-water is especially efficacious in treating indigestion and skin diseases. (See Part I, **Chapter 13** of this volume.)

Jingpohu Lake:
See Part I, **Chapter 13**–Taoshan.

This scenic spot is 238 kilometres away from Harbin and within the boundaries of Tieli county in Ichun City. In this region of undulating hills and dense forests, a hunting field, the first one in China, has recently been opened to foreigners, and guesthouses, villas, kiosks, terraces and pavilions have been newly constructed for the development of tourist programmes with distinctive local features such as skiing, walking and sightseeing in virgin forests.

● Regular direct flights and trains go to Beijing, Shanghai and other major cities of the country.

Xi'an

Xi'an is the ancient city of Chang'an, which in its day enjoyed equal fame with imperial Rome. Chang'an

Yumen Gate, an important pass on the ancient Silk Road, built in the Han dynasty (206 BC–AD 220) in the north-west of Dunhuang county, Gansu province. *(Photo by Cheng Dalin)*

was the starting point of the age-old "Silk Road" and an important centre, from which China carried on economic and cultural exchanges with the different countries of the world. Since the 11th century BC, eleven dynasties had their capitals here or in its vicinity. Xi'an has a history of more than 3,000 years and places of historical interest and scenic beauty abound inside and outside the city.

The Forest of Steles

The Shaanxi Provincial Museum in the city keeps more than 30,000 items of cultural relics and of handicraft art. A second section of exhibits on display is the Forest of Steles, the construction of which was begun in the 5th year of Yuanyou of the Northern Song dynasty (1090). This comprises over 2,300 steles and epitaphs, including the famous "Filial Inscriptions" of Shitai (Stone Terrace) and the Stone Inscriptions of Kaicheng, etc. The museum also keeps a collection of stone tablets bearing the original engravings of noted calligraphers like Ouyang Xun Yu Shinan, Liu Gongquan and others.

Dayanta and Xiaoyanta Pagodas

Dayanta (Great Wild Goose Pagoda), situated in the courtyard of the Ciensi (Temple of Maternal Kindness) to the south of the city, was constructed for the storage of scrolls and pictures brought back from India in the 3rd year of Yonghui of the Tang dynasty (652) by the famous monk, Xuan Zang (602–664). The pagoda assumes the shape of a square pyramid, 7-tiered and 64 metres high. Xiaoyanta (Small Wild Goose Pagoda) is in the grounds of the Jianfusi temple, also to the south of the city, and had a similar function. The construction of the pagoda was begun in the first year and completed in the 3rd year of Jinglong of the Tang dynasty (707–709); 13 tiers of it, at a height of 43.3 metres, are still standing, though the top two storeys were toppled by the earthquake of 1555.

Banpo (Slope Halfway up a Hill) Museum

The museum is located in Banpo Village in the eastern suburb, where lie the ruins of matrilineal commune villages of the Neolithic Age, about 6,000 years ago. The extant area of about 50,000 square metres (to date about one-fifth of the area has been excavated) had been divided into sections for residences, for making earthenware and for burials. There are the ruins of 45 houses, over 200 pits and caves, 6 earthenware kilns and 177 graves, as well as up to 10,000 articles for production and for daily use.

The Terracotta Army

The Qinshihuang Ling Bingmayong terracotta figures of warriors and horses in the mausoleum of the first emperor of the Qin dynasty now constitutes one of the Wonders of the World. The mausoleum of Qinshihuang (259–210 BC) is situated on a site 5 kilometres east of the county town of Lingtong to the north-east of Xi'an city, where Emperor Qinshihuang spent more than 30 years on its construction. Excavations made in 1974 and 1976 unearthed pits of terracotta figures of warriors and horses buried with the dead on the east side of the imperial mausoleum of Qinshihuang. No. 1 vault, the biggest, contains 6,000 figures of warriors and horses in battle order and countless numbers of weapons, intended to protect the tomb from attack from the east. A museum 16,300 square metres in area was allocated in 1979 for these figures, which are almost of the same size as real men and real horses (the height of the figure of a warrior is about 1.82 metres). The large bronze carriages, horses and men discovered in 1980 were the earliest and biggest yet discovered. The museum has become famous as the greatest archaeological discovery of the twentieth century.

Huaqing Pool

Five kilometres away from the mausoleum of the first emperor of Qin is Huaqing Pool, located at the northern foot of Lishan mountain. The now famous hot spring pool was constructed on the foundation of Tangquan Palace in the 18th year of Zhenguan of the Tang dynasty (644) and extended in the 6th year of Tianbao (747). To the north of the ruins of Efanggong of the Qin dynasty (built in 212 BC) is Guifeichi (the pool of the highest-ranking imperial concubine), which is the place where Yang Yuhuan, the favourite concubine of Emperor Xuanzong (685–762) of the Tang dynasty took her bath. The five rooms south of Guifei Pool were the temporary residence of Jiang Jie-shih (Chiang Kai-shek) at the time of the Xi'an Incident in 1936. (see Part I, **Chapter 13** in **Volume 1.**)

● The scenic spots of Xi'an also include the **Bell Tower**, the **Drum Tower**; the Maoling, Zhaoling and Qianling tombs; the Xingjiaosi, Xiangjisi and Huayansi temples; **Qingzhensi** (Great Mosque); Xingqinggong Park; the Museum of Xianyang Municipality, etc. The old **city wall** of Xi'an is believed to be one of the biggest still preserved intact anywhere in the world.

Huashan Mountain is another scenic spot in the neighbourhood. (see Part I, **Chapters 12** and **13** in **Volume 1.**)

● There are regular air and train services between Xi'an and all other major cities of the country. There are also buses running to the Huaqing Pool, the Museum of the Terracotta Army, the Zhaoling, Qianling and Maoling tombs, Huashan mountain and other places.

Lanzhou

Lanzhou city in Gansu province is a large city in China's north-west and the inland hub of air and land communications for Ningxia, Qinghai and Xizang. In the distant past it served as the only route for the exchange of friendly visits between China and various Asian, African and European countries. The long "Silk Road"; the expedition to the Western Regions by Huo Qubing, the great general of the Han dynasty; the pilgrimage of Monk Xuan Zang of the Tang dynasty to India for Buddist scriptures; all these passed through Lanzhou. By virtue of its long and extraordinary history, this beautiful, long and narrow belt-shaped city has left many scenic spots and places of historical interest.

Wuquanshan (Hill of Five Springs)

Situated at the northern foot of Gaolanshan mountain south of Lanzhou city, the Wuquanshan hill, with an elevation of more than 1,600 metres, got its present name by virtue of its five springs, the Ganlu (Sweet Dew) Spring and others. From the top of the hill, tourists may enjoy wonderful sights of the Chongqingsi temple, Qianfoge (Pavilion of a Thousand Buddhas), the Manisi and Dizangsi temples, Sanjiaodong (Cave of Three Religions) and other scenic spots and historic sites. Forest trees hide the skies; looking down, one has a bird's eye-view of Lanzhou city.

Baitashan (White Pagoda Hill)

Situated to the north of the Yellow River, which flows past Lanzhou city, there is a 7-tiered white pagoda with 8 facets and about 17 metres in height, set on the hill. Other architectural monuments there include Baitasi (Temple of the White Pagoda), Yunyuesi (Temple of Cloud and Moon), Luohandian (Hall of Arhats), Sangongdian (Three-Palace Hall), Sanxingdian (Three Star Hall), Zhudiange, etc. Climbing up Zhudiange, tourists will be able to enjoy the sights of sunrise and the nine bends of the Yellow River.

Yantan (Wild Goose Beach)

The north-eastern corner of Lanzhou city was formerly the site of eighteen sandy islets in the Yellow River and the habitat of wild geese from which the name of the place was derived. There is a beach 20 kilometres long. The western part of Yantan has now been converted into a park, with an artificial lake and a swimming pool.

First Bridge of Huanghe (Yellow River)

Situated on the foot of Baitashan hill, the bridge was built during the reign of Hongwu of the Ming dynasty (1368–1398), at first as a pontoon bridge linked by 24 big vessels, which were untied in winter and linked up again in spring. In the 33rd year of Guangxu of the Qing dynasty (1907), the pontoon bridge was replaced by an iron bridge. Since the Liberation, the iron bridge looks more resplendent and beautiful than ever after renovation, becoming one of the scenic spots of Lanzhou. Eight bridges now span the Yellow River in the municipality of Lanzhou.

Gansu Museum

Situated on the southern side of Qilihe (Seven *li* River) in Lanzhou city, the museum keeps a collection of ancient painted pottery of many varieties with distinctive local features. The more than 20,000 Ju Yan bamboo slips from the Han dynasty are precious materials for the study of the history of the Han. Cultural relics of national minorities are very much in evidence. The precious art collections in the museum also include the restored frescoes of the tombs of the Wei and Jin dynasties at Jiayuguan, and the books of calligraphy models and carved stones of Chunhuage, including the calligraphies of Ou-yang Xun, Yan Zhen-qing, Liu Gongquan, etc.

Binglingsi Grotto

The grotto is located in Xiaojishishan mountain on the northern bank of the Huanghe river, west of Yongjingxian county to the south-west of Lanzhou city. The grotto is divided into three parts, the upper temple, the cavern ditch and the most magnificent of the three, the lower temple. The grotto still preserves historical relics from the various dynasties of Western Qin, Northern Wei, Sui, Tang, Song, Yuan, Ming and Qing. It has 183 niches, 694 large and small statues of stone, 82 statues of clay and more than 900 square metres of frescoes.

● Other scenic spots in Lanzhou city include **Xinglongshan Hill, Baiyisi Tower**, the **Great Wall** of the Han dynasty at Yongdeng county, the **Liujiaxia Hydroelectric Station**, etc.

For Maijishan Grotto see Part I, **Chapter 13** in **Volume 1**. The grotto is located in Tianshui county, south-east of Lanzhou city.

● In Lanzhou there are regular air and train services to major cities of the country. Long-distance coaches travel to the various counties in the province; also there is a highway connecting Gansu with Sichuan.

Yinchuan

A folk saying has it: "The Yellow River sows a hundred disasters but brings riches in its bends". Yinchuan, which is fortunate to be situated on the Great Bend of the Yellow River, is very rich in resources and enjoys the reputation of being the

"Jiangnan of the North" (Jiangnan is a fertile area of the lower reaches of the Changjiang river – a land of plenty). Numerous historic sites and scenic spots may be found here.

Haibaota (Pagoda of Sea Treasures)

This is located in the northern outskirts of the old city of Yinchuan and is popularly called North Pagoda. The construction of the pagoda was said to have begun in the Han and Jin dynasties and it was renovated in the Ming and Qing dynasties. It is 54 metres high, with 9 tiers and 11 divisions. With its front in the shape of a square and its sides that of an elegant written Chinese character, it is grand and austere, with a peculiar style of its own. The architectural modelling and the technique in the treatment of space are of a quality rarely seen in the architecture of old Chinese pagodas. From the top storey, one can enjoy the scenes of "Jiangnan of the North".

Mausoleum Region of the Western Xia Dynasty

Situated at the eastern foot of Helanshan mountain about 30 kilometres to the west of the city, the mausoleum occupies about 40 square kilometres, with 9 imperial tombs and over 140 tombs of people buried with the dead during the Western Xia dynasty (1038–1227). Each of the imperial tombs occupies upwards of 10 hectares, forming an independent and integrated architectural complex. The above-ground architecture in the mausoleum region has long been in a state of ruin, but the large quantities of remains of stone pillars meticulously carved with dragons, the vividly modelled green coloured glaze and the grey owl's tail demonstrate the luxurious trappings of the Western Xia cemetery. Up to the present, the No. 8 imperial tomb and three tombs of people buried with the dead have been excavated.

Helanshan Mountains

Located in the western suburb of Yingchuan city, the mountains in general are 2,000 metres above sea level, though the main peak soars to 3,556 metres. The fault has become the natural barrier of the western part of Yingchuan. At the mouth of the little Rolling Bell at the foot of the mountains over 40 kilometres away from Yingchuan city stand Bijiafeng (Pen Rack Peak), Helan Temple, the mosque and other scenic places, forming one of the best landscapes in the Helanshan mountain area.

Yuhuangge (Pavilion of the Jade Emperor)

The pavilion is situated in the street east of the Drum Tower of the old city. Its construction was begun in the Ming dynasty. Its platform base is rectangularly shaped (19 metres high, 37.6 metres long and 25 metres wide). Below it is an archway passing north to south, 4.5 metres in width – wide enough for the passage of cars. Kiosks, halls and several storeyed houses and pavilions with upturned eaves are built at the base, the embodiment of ancient architecture with consummately skilful structure. At present it houses the Yinchuan Library.

● Sightseeing spots which may be added to a tourist's itinerary include the great mosque at **Nanguan** (Southern Pass), the **Zhongshan Park** (the former site of the Summer Palace of the Western Xia dynasties), the age-old **ferry crossing**, the gate tower of **Nanxun Gate**, the **Drum Tower** and the hydroelectric station of **Qingtong (Bronze) Gorge** and the **Baibata** (Hundred and Eight Pagodas), etc.

● Ningxia is situated on the vital communications line of Nei Monggol (Inner Mongolia), Shaanxi and Gansu, whereas Yingchuan is the communications hub of Ningxia itself.

Scheduled flights go to Beijing, Taiyuan and other cities. The Baotou–Lanzhou railway runs through the urban district from north to south of the new city. Through passenger trains run direct from Yinchuan to Beijing, Lanzhou and other cities.

Xining

The beautiful old city of Xining is located in a narrow valley on the eastern part of the Qinghai–Xizang (Tibet) plateau and surrounded by hills. The city is 2,276 metres above sea level, with the Huangshuihe river flowing through it. From the time when Emperor Wudi of the Han dynasty (156–87 BC) built "Lingjuzhai", the city has a history of more than 2,100 years, the present city having been rebuilt during the Ming dynasty. It is on the vital communications line between the interior and Xizang, as well as being a city of commercial importance in its own right.

Taersi Lamasery

This lamasery is located in the town of Lushaer in Huangzhongxian county, 25 kilometres from Xining city, and is one of the six great monasteries of the Huangjiao (Yellow Sect) of Lamaism (the other five monasteries are Selasi, Zhebangsi, Zhashilunbusi and Gandansi in Xizang and Labulengsi in Gansu), the construction of which was started in the 39th year of Jiajing of the Ming dynasty (1560).

This imposing ancient architectural complex occupies upwards of 122,000 square metres and incorporates Dajinwasi (Great Gold Tile Temple), Xiaojinwasi, Dajingtang (Great Hall of Scriptures), Jiujiandian (Nine Halls), Babaoruyita (Eight Treasures Pagoda of Good Fortune), etc., an embodiment of the coordinated style of architecture of the Zang and Han nationalities.

Dongguan (Grand Mosque)

To the east of Xining city there is one of the grandest mosques of north-west China. Built in the Ming dynasty and rehabilitated in 1917, it has a history of more than 500 years. The great hall of the mosque has a capacity of 3,000 for believers to carry on religious services. The mosque is Xining's major leading Islamic temple.

Qinghai Lake, Bird Island

The lake, occupying an area of 4,583 square kilometres (its western extreme is about 300 kilometres from Xining), is the largest salt-water lake in the inland plateau of China. Bird Island is one of the many islands in the lake to which more than 100,000 birds of different species migrate from the south every year when spring is changing into summer, taking the island as their temporary habitat. They include wild geese, cormorants, herring gulls and brown-headed gulls.

Princess Wen Cheng's Temple

Travelling southward along the Qinghai–Xizang highway, one reaches the capital of the autonomous region of the Zang (Tibetan) nationality of Yushu, the site of a Tibetan style, flat-roofed building of three storeys, Princess Jia Sha's Temple (Jia Sha in Tibetan means of Han nationality). Princess Jia Sha was the Princess Wen Cheng, who married Tubozanpusongzanganbu in the 15th year of Zhenguan of the Tang dynasty (641). The statue of Princess Wen Cheng may be seen inside the temple, and there are some stone figures on its outside walls, which, according to legend, are carved in the likeness of Princess Wen Cheng and her retinue.
● There is a regular air service running to Beijing, Taiyuan, Xi'an and Lanzhou. Train services operate between Xining and Beijing, Shanghai, Xi'an and other cities. Long-distance buses connect Xining with the various administrative divisions and counties of Qinghai province.

Ürümqi

This important city on the north-western frontier of China is situated at the northern foot of the Tianshan mountains on the south-eastern fringe of Zhung'er Basin. Capital of the Xinjiang Uygur autonomous region, Ürümqi is a city 900 metres above sea level where 13 nationalities – Uygur, Kazak, Han, Hui, Mongol, Kirghiz, Tatar, Tajik, Xibe, Ozbek, Man, Daur and Eluosi (Russian) – live in compact communities.

Yanerwo (Swallow's Nest)

This famous scenic spot in the southern outskirts of Ürümqi is commonly known as Wulapo (Excellent Ground for Hunting Competition). With hills behind and the river in front, its landscape is really alluring. A sanatorium and a cemetery for revolutionary martyrs have been built there since Liberation, and the Wulapo Reservoir is also in the neighbourhood.

Hongshan Hill (Red Hill)

The hill, located inside the city, is starkly precipitous, with jagged rocks of red hues. On top of the hill there is a nine-storeyed pagoda and a kiosk from which tourists can observe the scenes of Ürümqi city from far off.

Baiyang (White Poplar) Ditch Summer Resort

Situated in a Tianshan mountain valley in the southern outskirts, about 60 kilometres away from the city proper, is a natural pastureland with dense forests, luxuriant flowers and sweet and refreshing springs. Picturesque spots like Gangou (Sweet Ditch), Miaoergou, Dengcaogou, Daxigou and white poplar line the ditches here and there.
● There are other sightseeing spots in Ürümqi, such as the ancient city of **Wulabo** (Water Mill Ditch), the **Muguomu** (Tomb of the Wooden Coffin) at **Yuergou** (Fish Ditch), **Jianhu** lake and the pastureland at **Nanshan** (South Hill).

Tianchi (Heavenly Pond)

The pond is located half way up the mountain northwest of the peak of Bogeda, 100 kilometres to the east of Ürümqi. This famous summer resort is more than 1,900 metres above sea level and has an area of two square kilometres. The clear blue ripples of Tianchi, with green pastures and luxuriant growths of flowers around and green pines covering the slopes, contrasting with the expanse of white snow on the summit of Bogeda, add radiance and beauty to each other. The landscape is intoxicating.
● A regular air service operates from Ürümqi to Beijing, Shanghai, Lanzhou, Xi'an and other cities. Through trains run to Beijing, Shanghai, Nanjing, etc., and long-distance buses connect Ürümqi with the various counties inside the province, as well as with Qinghai, Gansu and Xizang.

Jinan

Jinan is a famous city with a long history. It borders on the Yellow River in the north and rests on Taishan mountain in the south. The city has had many springs since ancient days and is traditionally called the "City of Springs".

Baotu Spring

Located in the city centre, this is the biggest gushing spring and the most important of the 72 springs in Jinan. One of the 16 springs in Baotu Spring Park, Shuyu Spring, is in the vicinity of the former home of Li Qingzhao (1084–*ca.* 1151), the famous poetess of the Southern Song dynasty, whose works were published in the *Shuyu Collection*.

Heihuquan (Black Tiger Spring)

Situated to the east of Baotu Spring, this is one of the four principal groups of springs in Jinan, the water of which comes from deep hollow grottoes, gushing out of the mouths of three tiger heads carved of stone, tempestuous and violent, a grand sight.

Daminghu Park

North of Baotu and Heihu springs, the lake in this park occupies an area of 46 hectares. The sights of poplars and willows on the banks, lotuses everywhere, and kiosks and pavilions setting each other off will long linger in one's mind. Lixiating, Beijige (North Pole Pavilion), Xiaocanglang and Xiayuan, etc. are the main attractions.

Qianfoshan (Lishan) (Hill of a Thousand Buddhas)

Located to the south of the city centre and at an elevation of 285 metres, Qianfoshan has several scenic spots, such as Yilanting, Longquandong (Dragon Spring Cave), Xingguosi (Temple of National Prosperity), etc. Up on Yilanting, sightseers have a view in the foregound of the whole city and Daminghu lake, and a distant view of Huanghe river and Qiyanjiudian – the nine solitary hills of the Woniushan range close to the northern side of Jinan.

Other scenic spots in Jinan include **Zhenzhuquan** (Pearl Spring), **Wulongtan** (Five Dragon Pond), the historic sites at **Liufu**, the cultural ruins of **Longshan Hill** (Dragon Hill) and the **Shandong Provincial Museum**.

There are also other famous scenic spots near Jinan city:

Taishan Mountain:

See Part I, **Chapter 13** in **Volume 1**.

Qufu

This was the capital of the State of Lu during the period of Zhou (1120–221 BC) and also the native place of the famous thinker and educator in ancient China, Confucius (551–479 BC).

The long history of China has left large quantities

Listening to the sound from the heart of a dragon – French President François Mitterrand at Qufu in Shandong province, the home town of Confucius.

of cultural relics and places of historical interest in Qufu. Among the more than 200 places of attraction, perhaps *Sankong* – the Confucian Temple, the Confucian Mansion and the Confucian Forest, are the most famous.

The **Confucian Temple** is the place for offering sacrifices to Confucius, its principal architectural feature being the Dacheng Temple, which incorporates 466 halls, rooms, pavilions and corridors. There are 54 memorial archways stretching out in three directions, the east, the west and centre, glistening in gold. With a forest of stone tablets and steles, the magnificent scale is second only to the Imperial Palace of Beijing.

The **Confucian Mansion** used to be the living quarters of the direct descendants of Confucius. It comprises 9 courtyards, incorporating 463 several-storey buildings, halls, rooms with verandas, and many other big and small rooms. With its row upon row of serene and winding architecture, the mansion will not fail to impress the visitor.

The **Confucian Forest** is in the north of the city. It is the cemetery of Confucius and his descendants, and occupies more than 200 hectares of land, with towering old trees and over a thousand stone tablets

Riding on imitation ancient carts and sightseeing in the Confucius forest *(Konglin)* at Qufu, Shandong.

and steles, and Confucius's tomb in the centre. The Confucius Forest is the site of a cluster of ancient tombs of clan society and of an artificial garden, the biggest in China, which has survived for the longest period and is preserved intact.

● Regular flights connect Jinan with Beijing, Shanghai, Nanjing, Qingdao and other cities. Through trains run to all major cities of the country. Jinan is the hub of highway communication of Shandong province; long-distance buses travel from Jinan to every county of the province. Tourist buses go direct to Qufu, Taishan Mountain and other places.

Qingdao

Situated on the border of Jiaozhou Bay at the southwestern tip of Shandong peninsula, Qingdao is one of the summer convalescent resorts of China known as the "Switzerland of the East". The harbour inside the bay is broad and the water deep, calm and tranquil, making one of the best seaports of China, ice-free and silt-free.

Qianhaizhanqiao (Landing Stage Sea Front)

The landing stage was constructed in the centre of Qingdao Bay, south of Qingdao city, originally as the garrison commander's jetty. It dates from the 17th year of Guangxu of the Qing dynasty (1891) and was supplemented and renovated in 1931. The landing stage is 440 metres long and 10 metres wide and on its northern tip is the Zhanqiao Park.

Xiao Qingdao (Small Qingdao)

This small island and the landing stage face each other across the sea, with a long causeway connecting the island with the mainland. At the highest spot of the island, a white octagonal lighthouse, 15.5 metres in height, towers above the green grove, giving guidance to ships sailing in and out of the harbour.

Laoshan Mountain

The mountain covers an area of 300 square kilometres and is located on the eastern part of the urban district of Qingdao. The water quality of the mineral springs here is excellent and known far and wide both at home and abroad. (See Part I, **Chapter 13** in **Volume 1**.)

Badaguan (Eight Great Passes)

Badaguan is the name of a locality by the sea on the eastern part of the city proper. It received its present name because of the streets which bear the names of eight different strategic passes in China, criss-crossing each other in this locality. Their names are: Shanhaiguan, Zhengyangguan, Jiayuguan, Wushengguan, Zijingguan, Ningwuguan, Juyongguan, and Shaoguan. In this locality there are more than 80 villa-style houses setting each other off among thickets of flowers and trees, with seaside sanatoria scattered at the foot of the hill. There is also a beach for sea bathing.

Qingdao Museum of Marine Products

The museum is located in Lu Xun Park in Huiquan Bay, incorporating an exhibition hall and an aquarium. With more than 600 specimens of different kinds of organisms, the exhibition hall introduces the public to the evolution, properties, shape and ecology, etc. of marine organisms. The aquarium is equipped with over 60 glass show-pools in addition to three open-air pools linked with the sea for raising different kinds of fish, shrimps, turtles, crabs, shellfish, etc.

● Qingdao is one of the 14 coastal ports of China open to foreign countries, having convenient communications. Scheduled flights of seven airlines go direct to Beijing, Shanghai and other major cities. Through trains travel to Beijing, Shanghai, Wuchang, Shenyang, Lanzhou, etc. Coastal passenger steamers sail direct to Dalian, Shanghai and Guangzhou. Qingdao beer and the mineral water of Laoshan mountain are the special products of Qingdao.

Nanjing

Nanjing, a famous cultural city situated on the lower reaches of the Changjiang river, has a history of more than 2,400 years. With its eastern suburbs surrounded by the Zijingshan hills and a stone fortress towering on the western part of the city, Nanjing is often likened to a coiling dragon and a crouching tiger. From the third to fifteenth centuries eight feudal dynasties one after another had their capitals there. The historical remains of six dynasties (beginning of the third century to the end of the sixth century) and the architecture of the Ming and Qing dynasties are fascinating.

Nanjing Museum

On display in the museum are important historical relics and art treasures of Jiangsu province over the past 5,000 years. There are frequent exhibitions of archeological finds, books and paintings, ceramics, arts and crafts, as well as items of science and technology.

Mochouhu (Don't Be Distressed Lake)

The lake covers an area of more than 49 hectares and is about 5 kilometres in circumference. Located outside Shuiximen gate, it is commonly called the "First Scenic Spot of Jinling" (another name for Nanjing). Multi-storeyed houses were built on the lake in the first year of the Ming dynasty (1368–1644). It was said that the first Ming emperor, Zhu Yuan-zhang, once had a game of chess with his senior general Xu Da, and when the latter won the game, the emperor gave him the lake. Thus one of the pavilions got its present name of Qishenglou, or the house where chess was won.

Xuanwuhu (Black Dragon Lake)

The lake is located outside Xuanwumen gate and is 444 hectares in area and 15 kilometres in circumference. There are five islets, of which the one called Liangzhou is the best in scenic beauty and was also the first one opened to the public. There are scenic spots on the islet like Hushenmiao (a temple worshipping the god of the lake), Lanshenglou, Shangheting (Kiosk for Watching Lotuses), Taoranting, Tonggoujing (Copper Hook Well), etc. The other four islets are Huanzhou, Yingzhou (Cherry Islet), Cuizhou (Green Islet), and Lingzhou (Water Chestnut Islet). There are bridges and causeways linking up all the five islets, and with the blue water of the lake rippling all the year round, the scenery is just like a picture.

Yuhuatai Terrace

The terrace, situated outside Zhonghuamen, is a low hill of about 100 metres in height and 3,000 metres in length. It abounds in colourful agate stones, popularly called Yuhua stones, which look beautiful, strange and lovely. For many centuries, heroes and revolutionary martyrs of the Chinese nation have left heroic and moving relics, which are now on display in the exhibition hall of the historical materials of revolutionary martyrs.

Sun Yat-sen Mausoleum (The Mausoleum of Sun Zhong-shan)

The Mausoleum of Sun Zhong-shan was constructed in the years between 1926 and 1929 on the southern

Visitors at the Mausoleum of Dr Sun Yat-sen.

foot of Zijinshan hill (Zhongshan). It occupies more than 130 hectares of land and the area of the tomb covers upwards of 80,000 square metres. With its back against the hill, the terrain of the mausoleum rises by degrees from south to north, with the sites of the following in order of precedence; the ancient bronze cooking vessel, the memorial archway, the tomb passage, the gate, the kiosk of the monument, the platform, the sacrificial altar and the coffin chamber (158 metres in elevation). In the sacrificial altar there is a stone sculpture of Sun Zhong-shan in sitting posture, surrounded by relief sculptures of his revolutionary deeds.

Mingxiaoling

Situated on the south-western slope of Zijinshan hill, Mingxiaoling was the tomb of the first emperor of the Ming dynasty, Zhu Yuan-zhang. It was built between 1381 and 1383, with a depth of about 2.5 kilometres. Historical sites still existing include Baocheng (City of Treasure), Minglou (Bright Building), Shengongshengdebei monument, the eight stone sculptures of civil officials and military generals, and twelve pairs of stone animals on the two sides of the tomb passage.

Linggusi Monastery

Situated to the east of Sun Yat-sen Mausoleum, this is one of the 48 beauty spots of Jinling (Nanjing). Surrounded by towering old trees and deep and serene paths of pines, it is reputed to be the most enchanting, tranquil place in the Zhongshan scenic region. Among the scenic spots in the monastery are the Beamless Hall, Songfengge (Pavilion of Wind and Pines), Lingguta pagoda, etc.

Nanjing Changjiang (Yangtze) River Bridge

This bridge stretches across the Changjiang river at a point between Xiaguan and Pukou. It is a railway-highway double-deck dual-purpose bridge built between 1960 and 1968. The double-track railway bridge on the lower deck is 6,772 metres long and 14 metres wide and the highway bridge on the upper deck is 4,589 metres long and 19.5 metres wide. The main bridge has 9 piers and the span between them is 160 metres.

• Other scenic spots and places of historic interest include **Qixiashan Hill, Qianfoyan** (Thousand-Buddha Cliff). **Shelita** (stupa), the **Astronomical Observatory**, the ruins of the **Imperial Palace** of the Ming dynasty, the ruins of the **Heavenly King's Mansion** of the Taiping Heavenly Kingdom, the **Qinghuaihe River, Zhanyuan, Fuzimiao** (Confucian Temple), **Egret Islet, Chaotiangong** (Palace for Making Pilgrimages to Heaven), the **Stone Fort, Qingliangshan Hill** (Cool and Refreshing Hill), **Yanziji** (Swallow Rock), **Fuzhoushan** (Capsized Boat Hill), the **New Villa of Plum Garden**, the **Memorial Tower** in memory of the victorious river crossing of the Chinese People's Liberation Army, etc.

• Nanjing has convenient communications by water, land and air. Regular flights and trains run direct to various major cities throughout the country. Nanjing is the centre of the highway network of Jiangsu province, with buses running in all directions. In the busy tourist seasons there are long-distance buses travelling to Huangshan mountain.

Nanjing is also one of the hubs of inland navigation in the Changjiang river valley. Large river steamers make regular runs to Yangzhou, Shanghai, Wuhan, Chongqing and other cities. Tourists may enjoy pleasure tours in luxury steamers to the three gorges of the Changjiang.

Suzhou

The beautiful city of Suzhou is situated in a region of rivers and lakes south of the Changjiang river and was the capital of the state of Wu more than 2,000 years ago. There are many lakes and marshes on the eastern side of the city and numerous hills and mounds on the western side. Outside the city, river courses criss-cross each other like nets, and lanes and alleys along canal banks intersect one another throughout the length and breadth of the city, which is often called "Venice of the East". 1986 was the 2,500th anniversary of the founding of the city.

The Gardens of Suzhou

Suzhou ranks first in China for its gardens, since it still preserves famous gardens in the different styles of the Song, Yuan, Ming and Qing dynasties. People praise it as "the city of gardens", saying "Up above is Paradise, down below are Suzhou and Hangzhou."

Canglangting (Dark Blue Wave Pavilion)

This is located on the southern side of Suzhou city. It is one of the oldest extant gardens south of the Changjiang river, having a history of about a thousand years. The building of Canglangting was begun in the dynasty of Northern Song. The layout is clear, spaced and open, making use of the natural landscape but forming a pattern of its own, and a stream of limpid water passes round it. The central hill is densely wooded, with many winding paths. There is a pavilion for admiring the beauty of the hill and a memorial temple for the worship of 500 sages called Mingdaotang (Hall of Bright Ways) south of the hill.

Zhuozhengyuan (Humble Administrator's Garden)

Located inside Loumen, this is one of the four great gardens of Suzhou, dating from 1513 and occupying 5 hectares of land. There are 31 views in the garden, of which the aquatic scenery, however, is celebrated most. The water surface takes up almost three-fifths of the total area of the garden, with most of the buildings set along the banks of the lake. It is typical of the gardens south of the Changjiang river, with courtyards, corridors and multiple pavilions.

Liuyuan (Garden to Linger In)

The garden is located outside Changmen. It occupies about 3 hectares of land and is one of Suzhou's four great old gardens. The eastern part, in which buildings predominate, is sumptuous and splendid. The middle part has a pond at its centre, surrounded by kiosks, pavilions, pagodas and rockeries. The western part is a landscape of hills alternating with rocks, winding walls and stretches of maple forest. On the northern side there are the small, sunken bed of peach trees and a little stream with peach and willow trees lining both its banks, emanating the delightful serenity of seclusion. It is one of the gardens most typically representative of the style of the Qing dynasty.

Shizilin (The Forest of Lions)

Located on Yuanlinlu (Garden Road), this is another of Suzhou's four great old gardens, occupying one hectare in area. The garden was built by the Buddhist Monk Tian Ru in the 10th year of Zhizheng of the Yuan dynasty (1350); the principal part consists of a rockery built with stones from Taihu lake. The unusually shaped stones are so arranged as to appear like lions in ever-changing postures, and in the rockery there are tortuous caves and gullies, deep and serene, like a maze.

Wangshiyuan (Master of the Nets Garden)

The garden occupies an area of a little over half a hectare and is located on Shiquanjie (Street of Perfection). Although it is the smallest garden in Suzhou, it has maintained a series of integrated residential complexes of old and well-known families. The layout exploits to the full the use of the water of the pond to set off the buildings. The garden is typical of the style of the Ming dynasty, with winding paths leading to secluded spots, compact and natural.

Huqiu (Tiger Mound)

This hillock is located at San Tang Street outside Changmen gate. According to legend, Fu Cha, the king of Wu, buried his father He Lu, the former king, here. The Huqiu Pagoda (also called Yunsita – Pagoda of Cloud Cliff Temple) on the top of the hillock was built in 959 and completed in 961. It is a seven-storeyed octagonal brick pagoda with a tilt of 15 degrees as a result of subsidence and has now become an extraordinary sight.

Hanshansi (Cold Hill Temple)

The temple is situated on the south of Fengqiao (Maple Bridge) to the west of Suzhou city. It became famous thanks to the poem "Anchor Alongside Fengqiao at Night" by Zhang Ji, a poet of the Tang dynasty. The words of the poem are: "The crows caw when the moon goes down in a sky of frost, travellers sleep in anxiety amidst maple leaves on the river and lights on fishing boats, from Hanshan Temple outside Gusu (Suzhou) city the sound of a midnight bell reaches passenger boats." Tradition has it that it was because two monks of the Tang dynasty had lived in this temple that Hanshansi got its present name. There is a stele of the temple in the compound.

● There are numerous other sightseeing spots in Suzhou, including: **Shangfangshan Mountain, Keyuan, Heyuan** (Crane Garden), **Yiyuan, Xiyuan, Wufengyuan** (Five-Peak Garden), **Yipu, Wen Miao, Xuanmiaoguan, Kuanggongci, Yunyansi Pagoda, Beisita** (North Temple Pagoda), **Huanxiushanzhuang** (Mountain Hamlet of Elegant Surroundings), **Jianchi** (Sword Pond), **Tangyin's Tomb**, etc.

● Suzhou's Shuofang airport operates regular air services to Beijing. Through trains leave for Beijing, Shanghai, Nanjing and other major cities of the country. Long-distance buses run to Shanghai, Nanjing, Zhenjiang, Hangzhou and other cities. The Beijing–Hangzhou Grand Canal passes through the city and passenger boats sail from here for Hangzhou direct.

Wuxi

The city of Wuxi borders on Taihu lake in the south and Huishan hill in the west, and the Beijing–Hangzhou Grand Canal passes through it. Wuxi is a city of mountains and rivers; it has a beautiful landscape and very rich resources, which has won for

it the name of "land of fish and rice". It is an ideal place for admiring the beautiful scenery of Taihu lake. (See Part I, **Chapter 13.**)

Yuantouzhu Park, Liyuan, Meiyuan Gardens

All these famous gardens are located along the shores of Taihu lake. If you climb up to **Yuantouzhu**, you will command a broad view of the wide expanse of misty Taihu lake and the beautiful sight of sails skimming over the water. Liyuan depends on water to adorn its scenery, in combination with the hills in the distance. According to legend, Liyuan got its name from General Fan Li who resigned after victory and lived in seclusion in the garden, where he often went boating with Xishi (a famous beauty) on the Taihu lake. Scenic spots in the garden include a cluster of rockeries, the Sijiting (Kiosk of Four Seasons), the Long Corridor, Baojieqiao, etc. Meiyuan (Plum Garden) was built at the foot of the hill: it has 10,000 plum trees, and in early spring the plum blossom makes a sea of flowers, with its fragrance filling the air.

Xihui Park

The excavation of Yingshanhu lake in 1958 joined together the Huishan and Xishan hills on the western suburbs of Wuxi, and the area was opened as Xihui Park. Huishan hill is famous for its springs, like Dragon Eyes Spring, etc. In the eastern foot hills, there is **Jichangyuan**, a classical garden unique in style, and in this vicinity there are other scenic spots like **Huishan Monastery, Longguang Pagoda**, etc.

Wuxi's newly opened tourist spots include the former residence of Xu Xia-ke (1586–1641), noted geographer of the Ming dynasty, who wrote the *Travels of Xu Xia-ke*. There are also Yunushanzhuang (Mountain Hamlet of Jade Girl), the Fortress of Huangshan mountain, the Taihu Amusement Garden, Ludingyinghui and Kaiyuan Temple, etc.

Grottoes

Yixing's karst grottoes complex is a tourist spot in the neighbourhood of Wuxi. Zhanggongdong, about 22 kilometres south-west of Yixing county town, has 72 caves of different sizes with one cave linking with another, tortuous and deep, presenting a strange landscape. Together with two other grottoes, **Shanjuandong** and **Linggudong**, the three are jointly called the "Three Wonders of Yixing". Shanjuandong is divided into three interconnected levels; the water cave at the bottom is 120 metres long and has boating services of a distinctive kind. Linggudong has more than 30 strange sights: stalactites, stone pillars, stalagmites, stone flowers, stone screens, etc., gleaming brightly in a mysterious fairy world.

● There is a regular air service plying between Wuxi

and Beijing. Through trains travel to 20 major cities including Beijing, Shanghai, and Tianjin, and long-distance buses connect Wuxi with Yixing, Suzhou, Nanjing and other localities. Special tourist buses run direct from Wuxi to the Shanjuandong and Zhanggongdong grottoes. Passenger steamers sail direct to Hanzhou and Suzhou.

Yangzhou

Situated on the northern bank of Changjiang (Yangtze) river and by the western shore of the Beijing–Hangzhou Grand Canal, the urban architecture of Yangzhou is strongly characteristic of regions south of the lower reaches of the Changjiang river. Emperor Yangdi of the Sui dynasty (569–618) made three special trips here on dragon boats for sightseeing. Emperor Qianlong (1711–1799) visited regions south of the Yangtze river on six occasions, three of which he spent in Yangzhou. Eight artists, including the well-known painter Zheng Ban-qiao, founded a new school of painting at that time, known through generations as the "Eight Eccentrics of Yangzhou", which has influenced the art of Chinese painting to a considerable degree.

Damingsi Temple

This temple was constructed in the fifth century in the period of the Southern dynasties. In the 8th year of Qingli of Emperor Jenzhong of the Song dynasty (1048), the famous writer and historian Ouyang Xiu (1007–1072) came to take up a post in Yangzhou. He built a hall called Pingshantang to the west of the temple for pleasure and feasting. The Ouyang Memorial Hall, behind Pingshantang, was built by Ouyang Xiu's student, the famous man of letters Su Dong-po (1037–1101), in memory of his teacher. At the northeastern corner of the temple is the memorial hall of Jian Zhen (native of Yangzhou 688–763), an eminent monk of the Tang dynasty.

Shouxihu (Thin West Lake)

The lake is winding, narrow, long and elegant. The sights of poplars and willows on both banks of the lake are captivating and the trees and flowers are luxuriant and well-spaced. Beautiful scenic spots include the spring willows on the long causeway, Chuitai, White Pagoda, Rainbow Bridge, Xiaojinshan Hill, Wutingqiao (Five Kiosks Bridge), etc.

There are in Yangzhou City, moreover, several small and exquisite gardens – **Geyuan, Heyuan** and **Yechunyuan**, compactly laid out, quiet, beautiful and unconventional. Other scenic spots include **Tianningsi** temple, **Xianhesi** (Red-Crowned Crane Temple), **Wenfengta, Wenchangge, Siwangting**, the age-old **Grand Canal**, the **Mausoleum of Emperor Yangdi** of the Sui dynasty and the memorial temple and tomb of **Shi ke-fa**, etc.

Zhenjiang City

Zhenjiang City, in the neighbourhood of Yangzhou, is surrounded by hills on three sides. Its fourth side faces water and the view is gorgeous and enchanting. There are four caves, Fahai, Bailong (White Dragon), Chaoyang (Morning Sun) and Luohan (*Arhat*), on the Jinshan hills outside the town. On the top of the hill, there is a pagoda named Cishouta and on its west a spring called Zhonglengquan. The Jinshan Monastery built along the foot of the hill has an individual appearance peculiar to itself, exquisite and magnificent.

Beigushan Hill

By the shore of the river and on the east side of the city proper stands Beigushan hill, where many places of historic interest and scenic beauty are located, including the iron pagoda of Northern Song, the old Ganlusi (Sweet Dew Temple), Duojinglou (Building of Many Views), Jijiangting (Worship River Kiosk), etc. It is the setting of many popular legends, such as the story of Liu Bei's marrying into and living with his bride's family in Eastern Wu in the period of the Three Kingdoms (220–280). There are also historical places, like Shijianshi (Touchstone for Swords), Henshi, Zoumajian (Trotting Horse Ravine), etc.

Jiaoshan Hill

Towering aloft on an island in the middle of the Changjiang river is Jiaoshan hill, which stands facing Xiangshan hill on the southern bank. There are many steles and stone tablets on Jiaoshan, which is an impressive sight on its background of a chain of beautiful hills.

Yangzhou is located on the confluence of the Changjiang and the Huaihe rivers, with its south facing the Changjiang and its north bordering on the Huaihe.

● The age-old Grand Canal flows through the city of Yangzhou, which thus has convenient communications by land and water. Yangzhou is the hub of communications of northern Jiangsu province; its long-distance buses travel direct to Beijing, Shanghai, Hangzhou, Jinan, Nanjing, Lianyungang, Wuxi and many other cities. The construction of Yangzhou's harbour on the Changjiang river is now in full swing.

Hangzhou

Hangzhou, the provincial capital of Zhejiang province, has long been famous for its scenic beauty and enjoyed equal popularity with Suzhou in Jiangsu province. Marco Polo, the Italian traveller, recorded in his travel notes: "This city is stately and beautiful and may be rated as the first city in the world. There are very many places of historic interest and scenic beauty here, which make people imagine themselves living in Paradise . . . ."

Xihu (West Lake)

This famous lake got its present name because of its location in the western part of Hangzhou city. Its circumference is 15 kilometres and its area 6 square kilometres. Here the scenery is extremely beautiful with its combination of hills and waters, and all the four seasons are suitable for sightseeing.

The West Lake is surrounded by many scenic spots and places of historic interest, such as Liuheta and Baoshuta pagodas, the Wushan and Yuhuangshan hills, Feilaifeng (Peak Flown Here), Yanxiasandong (The Three Caves of Mist and Rosy Clouds), the Nine Brooks and Eighteen Ravines, Yuewangmiao (Temple for Worshipping Yue Fei) – the national hero, Lingyinsi, Xilengyinshe, etc., among which Lingyinsi is one of the ten Buddhist monasteries of the Chan sect in China. (See Part I, **Chapter 13** in **Volume 1.**)

Ningbo

Tourist sites in the vicinity of Hangzhou include Ningbo, a city 208 kilometres east of Hangzhou. The two cities are linked by railroad and highway. **Tianyige** in Ningbo city is the oldest library building now existing in China. The **Tianfeng Pagoda** was built during the reign of Empress Wu of the Tang dynasty (695–696). From the top of the pagoda, there is a panoramic view of the whole city. **Baoguosi** (Defend the Country Temple) is the oldest extant building with a timber structure in the regions south of the Changjiang river, dating from the period of the Eastern Han dynasty (25–220). **Tiantongsi** (Temple of Boy from Heaven), situated on the rural area east of Ningbo, is a famous Buddhist monastery, with "ten great landscapes" in its vicinity, which for years has been an attraction to tourists. The "relics of the true self of Sakyamuni Buddha" kept in **Ayuwangsi** (The Temple of King A Yu) is a rare treasure of Buddhism.

Putuoshan and Yandangshan mountains

See Part I, **Chapter 13.**

Moganshan

Moganshan mountain is 84 kilometres from Hangzhou. According to legend, in the last years of Chunqiu, or the Spring and Autumn period (770–476 BC), Mo Xie and Gan Jiang, husband and wife, cast a sword for the king of Wu. They died after the sword was cast, hence the origin of the mountain's name.

The main peak, Tashan (Pagoda Mountain), is 719 metres high and the circumference of the mountain is more than fifty kilometres. The clear springs and tall bamboos scattered in places on the mountain make good locations for summer resorts. Other scenic spots include the Sword Pond, the Celestial Pond, the Celestial Bridge, the Shady Hill, etc.

For scenic regions of the Fuchunjiang and Xinanjiang rivers see Part I, **Chapter 13**.

Yaolin Grotto

Yaolin Grotto is another scenic spot 120 kilometres from Hangzhou. The main cavern is about 1 kilometre long and the area more than 27,000 square metres. There are six halls in the cavern, high, open and cool, with the running water in limpid springs, tortuous, deep and serene. Numerous stalactites and stalagmites in thousands of unique postures and shapes are found inside the cavern, which is often referred to as a fairyland.

● Regular air services connect Hangzhou with Beijing, Nanjing, Shanghai, Xiamen and other major cities; there is also a local airline which links Hangzhou with Hong Kong. Through trains travel to the various major cities of the country. Hangzhou is the centre of the highway network of Zhejiang province, with buses linking it with Shanghai, Nanjing, Huangshan mountain and other places. The whole length of the Beijing–Hangzhou Grand Canal is more than 1,700 kilometres: passenger steamers now travel to and fro between Hangzhou and Suzhou.

Shaoxing

Shaoxing is a city of green hills and clear water, rich and fertile, which has produced many eminent persons and has many places of historical interest. Shaoxing has altogether 54 big and small stone bridges, which causes it to be called a "museum of old stone bridges". It is a historically famous old cultural city rich in mythical flavour.

Donghu (East Lake)

The lake is situated 3.5 kilometres east of the city, and together with the West Lake of Hangzhou and the South Lake of Jiaxing, it is one of the three great lakes of Zhejiang. Donghu was originally a hill of dark green rocks, and due to the superior quality and hardness of the rocks which serve wide-ranging purposes, they were quarried and exploited generation after generation. The place became a lake after long digging, producing steep precipices and deep caves. The water here is deep and the rock formation strange, with the lake and caves linked with one another forming a river outside the causeway and a lake inside it, which brings a unique scene. It is especially interesting to take a black-sail boat and go into the "cave of celestial peaches" to "look at the sky from the bottom of a well".

King Yu's Tomb and Temple

Both the tomb and the temple are located at the foot of Huijishan mountain about three kilometres outside Jishanmen gate to the south-east of the city. According to legend, King Yu's tomb was actually the mausoleum of Da Yu, the first monarch of the Xia dynasty, about 21st century BC. King Yu's temple was located on the right side of the mausoleum, the construction of which was begun in the beginning of Liang of the Southern dynasties. Historical monuments such as the statue of Da Yu, the Goulu stele or King Yu's stele, engraved during the Ming dynasty, and burial stones, etc. may be found inside the temple.

Lanting (Orchid Pavilion)

The pavilion is located 12 kilometres south-west of the city. It is the ruins of the site where Wang Xi-zhi (321–379), the great calligrapher of the Jin dynasty, wrote the Lantingjixu (Preface of Lan Ting Collections), and is also the place of pilgrimage for China's famous calligraphers. The pavilion contains the "ink pond", the goose pond and the kiosk of an imperial stele, etc. The views here are very charming; green peaks rising one higher than another, and winding streams meandering through dense forests and tall bamboos. The traditional calligraphy fair, started over 1,600 years ago, is mounted here at the Qingming terminal – the 3rd day of the 3rd month of the lunar calendar – every year.

● There are other scenic spots and historic sites in Shaoxing, namely, the ancestral home of Premier **Zhou Enlai**; the **Lu Xun Memorial Hall** (including Lu Xun's former home, San Wei Study); the former home of **Qiu Jin** (1879–1907), the woman revolutionary during the Chinese Revolution of 1911; and **Shenyuan**, a garden which became famous following the matrimonial tragedy of Lu You (1125–1210), a patriotic poet in the times of Southern Song. **Jianhu Lake** outside Shuipianmen, located in Keqiao town 11 kilometres west of Shaoxing city, is another scenic spot as beautiful as a picture. Traditionally it is said: "A walk in the shady paths of the mountain is like wandering in a mirror."

● Shaoxing has convenient communications. Trains connect it with Ningbo, Hangzhou, Shanghai and other cities. Every day there are long-distance buses running between Shaoxing and Hangzhou and between Shaoxing and Suzhou.

Hefei

Hefei is an old city with a history of more than 2,000 years. It is strategically located in the middle of Anhui province, between the Changjiang and Huaihe rivers and is difficult to reach. Several places of historical interest may be found inside the city, such as those connected with Bao Zheng, the upright official in the period of Northern Song, and Cao Cao of the Three Kingdoms.

Xiaoyaojin Battlefield

Located in the north-eastern corner of the urban district, this was originally a ferry on the Feishui river, and according to legend, it was the site of an old battlefield during the period of the Three Kingdoms (220–280) and the place where Cao Cao's famous general Zhang Liao fought a big battle with Sun Quan – the very place where "Zhang Liao's military prowess shocked Xiao Yao Jin" in the classical novel *The Romance of the Three Kingdoms*. It has been opened up since Liberation as the biggest and most handsome park in the city.

Mount Huangshan.

Baogongci Temple

This memorial temple in comemoration of the famous official of Northern Song, Bao Zheng (990–1062), is located on a mound of fragrant flowers in Baohe Park on the southern side of the central district of the city. The mound is said to be the place where Bao Zheng used to study. Inside the temple there is a pavilion called Lianquan (Honest Spring) and Bao Zheng's statue. The Baohe Park, with the pond covered with water chestnuts and lotuses and the banks dotted here and there with poplars and willows, is a pleasant place for strolling and relaxation. The tomb of Bao Gong, which has been rebuilt, now lies on an elevation at the east side of the memorial temple. The watch pillars, stone men, stone animals and the subterranean palace which has in its custody the remains of Bao Gong, have all been rebuilt in accordance with the style of the Song dynasty.

Jiaonutai (Crossbow Teaching Terrace)

Also called the terrace used by Cao Cao for calling the muster roll of officers and assigning them tasks, this is located by the side of Xiaoyaojin Park, and is 5 metres in height and 3,700 square metres in area. It was built by Cao Cao (155–220) of the Eastern Han dynasty, who trained 500 picked archers here for defence against the navy of Sun Quan. There is a well on the terrace which, since its mouth is higher than the roofs of single-storey houses on the streets, is called the "housetop well".

● Tourist spots in the neighbourhood of Hefei include **Jiuhuashan Mountains**. (See Part I, **Chapter 13**.)

● Hefei's Luogang airport is one of China's large, modern airports which has enough room for giant passenger planes to take off and land. Regular planes connect Hefei with Beijing, Shanghai, Guangzhou, Tunxi (going to Huangshan mountain), etc. Trains run regularly to Beijing, Shanghai, Tianjin, Nanjing and other major cities. Tourist buses operate to Huangshan, Lushan, and the Jiuhuashan mountains. There are also boats for travel to the various scenic spots of Caohu lake during tourist seasons.

Huangshan (Yellow Mountains)

These mountains, which are located on the south-eastern part of Anhui province (see Part I, **Chapter 13** of this volume), got their present name from popular legends which claimed that this was the place where Emperor Huangdi (The Yellow Emperor) made pills of immortality 5,000 years ago. They cover an area of 1,200 square kilometres, including about 154 square kilometres of scenic spots. They have concurrently the distinguishing features of all the various famous great mountains of China and are especially well known for their "four unique characteristics" (strange pines, grotesque stones, a sea of clouds and hot springs).

In 1985 the *China Tourists* organization sponsored a programme for choosing China's ten great scenic spots through public appraisal. More than 370,000 votes were cast and Huangshan mountains was chosen as one of the ten, the other nine being The Great Wall, the Hills and Waters of Guilin, the Hangzhou West Lake, Beijing Imperial Palace, Suzhou Gardens, the Three Gorges of the Changjiang river, the Sun and Moon Pond of Taiwan, Bishushanzhuang, and the Terracotta Warriors and Horses buried with the dead in the mausoleums of the Qin dynasty at Xi'an.

Hot Springs

This scenic area is located between the two peaks of Ziyun (Purple Cloud) and Taohua (Peach Blossom). The spring water flowing out of the foot of Ziyun peak is clean and drinkable, maintaining a temperature of 42°C all the year round. The water is also good for bathing and has a curative effect in the treatment of stomach and skin troubles and rheumatoid arthritis. There are a hot springs bathhouse and a swimming pool in the vicinity of the Huangshan Guesthouse. There are also more than ten other beauty spots such as **Baizhangquan**, etc., in the area.

Yupinglou (Jade Screen Building)

Yupinglou, located between the Tiandu (Celestial Capital) and Lianhua (Lotus) peaks, which, together with Guangmingding (Bright Summit) are the three main peaks of the Huangshan mountains, is the former site of Wenshuyuan (Temple for Worship of the Wenshu Buddha), 1,680 metres above sea level and the western route from the hot springs area to the Beihai Sea. The landscape here is extremely beautiful, affording views of the various peaks, such as Tiandu, Lianhua, "Donghai" (East Sea), Huanghai, Houhai, etc.

Beihai (North Sea)

On top of the hill opposite the Beihai Guesthouse is a pavilion called Shuguangting (Dawn Pavilion) where one may enjoy the sunrise. One may also enjoy the sunset or look far into the distance at the marvellous spectacle of mountainous landscapes from the Xihai (West Sea) Paiyunting (Pavilion Pushing into the Clouds). Towards the east, one sees three peaks – the Shixin, the Shisun (Stalagmite) and the Shangsheng (Rise) – which stand like the three legs of a tripod. The Shixin peak is an overhanging cliff of a great height, with strange-looking pines in great numbers and wonderful stones in a riot of colours and forms. On the summit there is a bridge called Duxianqiao (Bridge for the Crossing of Fairies).

Yungusi (Cloud Gorge Temple)

The temple is located at the foot of Buoyu (Alms Bowl) peak at an elevation of 890 metres and was called Zhibuo (Throw Alms) Buddhist Temple in the olden days. The temple is surrounded by peaks and ridges, with green pines, green bamboos, yellow firs, grotesque-looking rocks, streams and gulleys setting each other off among clouds and mists, a spot which tends to make tourists feel as though they were in a landscape painting, rich in poetic flavour. Stone epitaphs to famous people through the ages stand like trees in a forest. A guesthouse has been built on the site of the former Yungusi to enable sightseers ascending the hill from the east to take a little rest and enjoy a cup of tea.

Songguan (Pine Valley Thatched Hut)

The hut is located at the foot of Diezhang peak in the northern part of the Huangshan mountains. In the early years of Bao You of the Song dynasty (1253–1258), it was the hermitage of Taoist priest Zhang Yi-fu. The surroundings here are secluded and quiet, planted all around with green bamboos, and with the Wulongtan (Five Dragons Pond) and Feicuichi (Jadeite Pool). The *Songguyuqian* tea produced here is known far and wide. The cableway, built in 1986, stretches more than 2,804 metres and is at present the longest mountain cableway in Asia, the drop between the upper and lower stations being 772 metres. Tourists may take a ride to Yungusi from the Huangshan Guesthouse, and thence to Beihai on a cable car to enjoy the wonderful sights.
● Facing the Huangshan mountains across the Changjiang river is **Tianzhushan Mountain**, a mountainous scenic region formed of granite, with a summer resort and rest home. The region has an area of 54 square kilometres. (See Part I, **Chapter 13** in **Volume 1**.)
● The Huangshan mountains may be reached by bus and train, but there is no direct air service. However, tourists may fly to Hefei on scheduled flights and go thence to the Huangshan mountain by bus or train.

Nanchang

Nanchang is a famous old city in the southern part of China. On 1 August 1927 an armed uprising broke out there under the leadership of the Chinese Communist Party which shocked the country and the whole world. The day has subsequently been fixed as the Army Day of the Chinese People's Liberation Army.

The Nanchang Memorial Hall of the August 1st Uprising

Located at Ximachi (Pond for Bathing Horses), Zhongshan Street, in the city proper, the memorial hall is an old style four-storeyed building, formerly the Jiangxi Hotel. This was the site of the General Headquarters of the Nanchang Uprising. Zhou Enlai's office, the office of the Staff Officers Group and the office of Lin Boqu, Chairman of the Financial Commission, have all been restored to their former state. Historical relics and photographs concerned with the uprising are on display.

Qingyunpu Temple

The former home of Ba Da Shan Ren – Qingyunpu is a Taoist temple with a very long history located in the vicinity of Dingshan Bridge, 5 kilometres south of Nanchang city. The halls and courtyards, with their winding corridors and paths, and the towering old trees combine to make the environment quiet and beautiful. Ba Da Shan Ren (*ca.* 1626–*ca.* 1705) was an outstanding painter towards the end of the Ming and the beginning of the Qing dynasties. His original name was Zhu Da and he was the grandson of the ninth generation of Zhu Quan, the 16th son of the founder of the Ming dynasty, Zhu Yuanzhang. After the Ming dynasty was overthrown, he led a hermit's life for many years at Qingyunpu. His paintings have had considerable influence over painters of later generations (such as Qi Baishi, Wu Changshuo, Pan Tianshou, etc.)

August 1st Park, the Islet of Hundred Flowers

This islet is located in Donghu (East Lake) in the city proper, with an area of 26 hectares. The scenic area comprises the East Lake, Baihuazhou (Isle of a Hundred Flowers), Su Garden, Su Causeway, etc. Among the kiosks, pavilions and pagodas, the flowers and trees are luxuriant and well spaced, giving expression to the style of a classical garden.
● Tourist spots nearby include the **Lushan** and **Jinggangshan Mountains** (See Part I, **Chapter 13** in **Volume 1**.)
● Nanchang is the hub of communications of Jiangxi province with scheduled flights to Beijing, Shanghai, Guangzhou, Wuhan, Fuzhou, Hangzhou, Hefei, Jingde and other cities. Regular air services operate every week to Shenzhen (Huiyang). A railway crosses the urban district from north to south, and through trains connect Nanchang with Beijing, Shanghai, Hangzhou, Guangzhou, Wuhan, Nanjing and other cities. During tourist seasons, regular services of buses and tourist buses leave Nanchang every day for Lushan mountain.

Fuzhou

Fuzhou is a famous old city along the south-eastern coast of China located on the southern part of the central sub-tropical zone, with no winter and the trees always green and produce in abundance all the year round. Three hills stand towering over the city like the three legs of a tripod and there are many places of historical interest. In the urban district, there is a distribution zone of hot springs with an area of 5 square kilometres, which supplies more than 14,000 tons of spring water daily. The water quality of the spring is excellent and the temperature high. In addition to being suitable for bathing, the water is also good as a cure for many ailments.

Gushan Mountain

Towering aloft on the northern bank of the Minjiang river on the eastern suburb, about 12 kilometres away from the centre of Fuzhou city, this mountain rises nearly 1,000 metres above sea level. It got its present name because of a huge rock on the summit which looks like a drum. The peak of Gushan mountain is the highest point in Fuzhou city, where one may enjoy the sight of sunrise. An age-old temple Yongquansi (Temple of Gushing Springs), the building was begun in 908, is the "Crown of all Fujian Monasteries". There are two pottery pagodas of one thousand Buddhas from the Song dynasty in front of the temple. The Reclining Buddha carved of white jade, the Buddhist scriptures of past ages in the temple, the several thousand volumes of scriptures and classics, and the prints and carvings, in particular, are all very precious historical relics. To the east of the temple is a pavilion called Shuiyunting (Water and Cloud Pavilion), where Zhu Xi (1130–1200), the philosopher and educator of the Southern Song dynasty, used to give lectures. Over two hundred stone carvings on precipitous cliffs may be found concentrated in an area around the middle part of Lingyuan; among them, carvings made in the Song dynasty period alone account for as many as 109. There are 18 caverns to the west of the temple.

Yushan Hill

Located in the centre of the city, this hill is 58.6 metres high. For over a thousand years it has been a famous scenic spot on which the people of Fuzhou love to stroll and relax. Upon the hill is a memorial temple in worship of Qi Jiguang (1528–1587), a famous general and strategist of the Ming dynasty, who defended the country against the harassing of Japanese pirates. Stone carvings on towering cliffs, from the Song, Yuan, Ming, and Qing dynasties, as well as some of modern day, which are of value as art and as historical data, may also be seen.

Wushishan Hill

Also called Wushan hill, this is located in the south-west of the old city, facing Yushan hill from east to west. Up on the hill are two huge rocks standing very close to each other, with a third one, a rectangular slab of stone, lying naturally across the tops of the two. This is one of the 36 wonders of Wushishan hill – the Sky Terrace Bridge. The spring water of the Yayuchi (Bathing Pond of Ducks) on the hill is cool and chilly, excellent for making tea. The most ancient stone cliff carvings dating from the Tang dynasty, *Bo Re Tai Ji*, may be found on the southern side of the hill. This was the writing of Li Yangning, the well-known calligrapher of the Tang dynasty.

Xihu Lake (West Lake)

This lake is in the north-western suburb of the city and was dug in the 3rd year of Taikang of the Jin dynasty (282). There are two islets, linked up with each other by a long causeway, and three bridges – the Feihong, Buyun and Yudai bridges – to form an integrated whole.

Maweigang (Horse-Tail Harbour)

The harbour is located in the south-eastern part of Fuzhou, at the confluence of the Minjiang and Wulongjiang rivers, about 21 kilometres from the city centre. In the harbour at present there is a 10,000-ton dock with two 10,000-ton and one 5,000-ton berths. Luoxingta pagoda at Mawei was built in the Song dynasty period. Thirty metres high, it is a symbol of the gate of Fuzhou.

Wuyishan Mountain

Also in the vicinity of Fuzhou, this mountain is part of the high range in the southern part of Chongan county in Fujian province. It is a famous scenic area (see Part I, **Chapters 12** and **13**).

There is a snake garden located between the Nature Reserve and the scenic region of Wuyishan mountain, which has a general area of about 30,000 square metres. The garden raises 33 kinds of snakes – the number successfully raised has exceeded 10,000. The showroom in the garden has on display a specimen of China's most precious animal, the "horned monster", and specimens of the various kinds of snakes of Wuyishan mountain, which are a great attraction to tourists.

● In 1986 Fujian province chose through public appraisal the "ten best scenic spots" in the province: they are **Gulangyu, Wuyishan Mountain**, the Fuzhou **Gushan Mountain**, the Xiamen **Jimei**, the Fuzhou **West Lake**, Quanzhou **Kaiyuan Temple**, Jinmen **Taihurongyan Garden**, the site of the **Gutian Conference** in Shanghang, **Guanghua Temple** of Putian and **Guanzhishan Hill**.

● Fuzhou is the hub of communications of Fujian province and an important harbour on the south-eastern coast of China. There are regular flights to Beijing, Shanghai, Guangzhou and Xiamen; through trains leave for Beijing, Shanghai, Tianjin, Nanjing and other major cities and long-distance buses connect Fuzhou with Xiamen and Zhangzhou.

Xiamen (Amoy)

The island of Xiamen is blessed with scenery of enchanting beauty throughout the four seasons. It is said that in the past the island used to be the habitat of egrets and it is therefore sometimes called the Egret Island. A long causeway built of granite connects it with Jimei and Xinlin. The south-western corner of the island is the urban district of Xiamen. It is one of China's special economic zones open to foreign countries.

Gulangyu (Kulangsu) Island

This is a small, beautiful, quiet and secluded island situated on the south-western seaboard of Xiamen with an area of 1.71 square kilometres. Taking a ferry from Xiamen, one reaches Gulangyu in 5 minutes. The island is green all the year round, which wins for it the name of a "Garden on the Sea". The peak of Longtoushan (Dragon Head Hill) towers magnificently over the centre of the island, facing Hutoushan (Tiger Head Hill) in Xiamen, a situation which gives rise to the story of "A dragon and a tiger defending Xiamen harbour". More than 300 years ago, at the end of the Ming dynasty and the beginning of the Qing dynasty, the national hero Zheng Chenggong (1624–1662) stationed troops on Sunlight Rock on the top of Dragon Head Hill and the ruins of the camp gate can still be seen today. The memorial hall of Zheng Chenggong on the island has on exhibit the historical relics concerned. Situated at the foot of a hill and beside the sea are the Shuzhuang garden and a bathing beach.

Nanputuosi Temple

The temple built at the foot of the Xiamen Wulaofeng (Peaks of Five Old Men) has a history of more than 1,000 years. It has a large number of jade Buddhas in the Yufobaodian (Hall of Jade Buddhas) including the bearing of Sakyamuni's nirvana carved out of a piece of white jade from Burma. The Overseas Chinese Museum, the only one in China, and the Anthropological Museum are located in the vicinity of the temple – the latter on the campus of Xiamen University.

Jimei Peninsula

Jimei is a small peninsula on the sea wall of Xiamen, with three sides surrounded by the sea. Jimei school, the architecture of which is majestic and graceful, was built by a patriotic overseas Chinese, Chen Jiageng (Tan Kah-kee). Aoyuan (Turtle Garden) on the southern tip of the peninsula is linked with the land

Foreign tourists visiting the Jimei school established by Chen Jiageng *(Tan Kah-kee)* in Xiamen (Amoy), Fujian province.

by a stone-laid causeway. The tomb of Chen and the Guilaitang (Return Hall) in his memory are in the garden.

There are altogether 24 well-known scenic spots in this beautiful seaside city.

Quanzhou

Quanzhou, in the vicinity of Xiamen, built in the sixth year of Kaiyuan (718) of the Tang dynasty, is historically one of the 24 famous cultural cities of China. Quanzhou Bay is a good natural bay and was one of the biggest commercial ports of China in the Song dynasty (960–1279). By the Yuan dynasty (1271–1368), Quanzhou's trade contacts with overseas had reached an unprecedented scale and the city was exceedingly prosperous, having been mentioned on a par with Egypt's Alexandria as "the biggest commercial port of the world." It was then also the starting point of China's "Silk Road of the Sea". It still maintains the styles and features of an ancient city, and places of historical interest and scenic beauty abound both within the city and in the surrounding countryside. Famous historical sites here include Kaiyuansi (which, together with Guangjisi in Beijing and Lingyingsi in Hangzhou, forms the three great Buddhist monasteries of China) – the Double Pagoda

Foreign visitors on Mount Jiuhua in Anhui province watching Li Guozhen, vice-chairman of the Chinese Calligrapher's Association, writing with a piece of bamboo. *(Photo by Zhang Yikuan)*

in the temple courtyard is China's biggest extant stone pagoda; Tianhougong (Palace of the Empress of Heaven), the former dwelling of Li Zhi (thinker and man of letters (1527–1602) of the Ming dynasty); the memorial temple of Cai Xiang, calligrapher of the Northern Song dynasty (1012–1067); the Moslem Sacred Tombs on Lingshan mountain; Qingyuanshan mountain; Luoyang Bridge; etc. Laojunyan in Quanzhou is the biggest stone statue of Taoist Lao Jun in China. The Moni thatched hut here is the only extant ruins in China of the Moni religion and there are also ancient Hindu and Christian ruins. In the Quanzhou museum of the history of overseas communications there are seagoing vessels from the Song dynasty unearthed at Quanzhou Bay in 1974 and various other artefacts.

● Xiamen has regular air services to Beijing, Shanghai, Guangzhou, Hangzhou, Xi'an, etc., and there are also regional chartered planes flying to Hong Kong. Trains connect Xiamen with Fuzhou, Yingtan, Hangzhou and Shanghai; long-distance buses operate to Fuzhou, Quanzhou, Shenzhen and other places, and passenger steamers run between Xiamen and Hong Kong.

Zhengzhou

Zhengzhou is a famous city in the Central Plains with a long history. It is strategically located and has very rich resources, besides numerous cultural relics and places of historic interest.

Inside the city proper there are ruins of an important metropolis of the earlier stage of the Shang dynasty (16th to 17th century BC), which are even earlier than the Anyang Yin dynasty ruins, and are of extremely significant archaeological value. In the central part of the ruins a city wall with a circumference of 7 kilometres still remains. Large quantities of precious historical relics have been unearthed, which include two square, bronze cooking vessels – things

rarely seen – left behind by the royal family among the bronze wares of the earlier stage of the Shang dynasty, and a green porcelain wine vessel believed to be the earliest porcelain discovered in China so far.

Dahecun Village

The ruins located at Dahecun village in the northern suburb, 12 kilometres away from the city proper, are the sites of ancient cultural remains of the Neolithic Age, especially the Yangshao and Longshan cultures of more than 5,000 years ago. The cultural layer is from 4 to 7 metres thick, with large quantities of graves, foundations of buildings, potteries, jadeware and bone implements, which serve now as precious materials for the study of the culture of China's primitive societies. The wall of No. 1 Foundation measures one metre in height and is the only one discovered so far among the foundations of that period excavated.

Dahutinghanmu Tomb

Located within the boundaries of Mixian county, south-west of Zhengzhou city, this is one of the biggest ancient tombs excavated and has a history of more than 1,800 years. The tomb is side by side with another; one with Han dynasty paintings, the other with Han dynasty murals. The drawings and carvings depict the life of the deceased in his manor and the coffin chamber is a vault in the form of a mat roofing, more than 20 metres both in length and in width, very grand in scale.

February 7th Memorial Tower

The tower stands on the February 7th Square in the centre of the city and was built to commemorate the great strike of the Beijing–Hankou railway workers led by the Chinese Communist Party on 7 February 1923. The tower is 63 metres high, 14 storeyed, and the tower body is of double pagoda style. The revolutionary relics of the period of the great strike are on display inside the tower. From the top of the tower, one is able to have a bird's eye view of the whole city.

Henan Provincial Museum

The museum is located on the intersection of Jinshui and Renmin (People) streets and exhibits precious historical relics, excavated and collected from the various places of the province, which vividly reflect the general history and culture of the Central Plains in ancient times. Among them are a green porcelain wine vessel of the Shang dynasty and the *Si Mu Wu* big, square, cooking vessel, etc.

● Besides the above, there are such scenic spots as the **Huanghe River Sightseeing Area** (30 kilometres north-west of the city proper) and **Shaolinsi** temple,

Talin (Pagoda Forest), **Zhongyuemiao** temple, **Songyang Academy**, etc., Dengfengxian county. Tourist spots in the vicinity include the Songshan and Jigongshan mountains. (See Part I, **Chapter 13** in **Volume 1**.)

● Scheduled flights go direct from Zhengzhou to Beijing, Shanghai, Guangzhou and other major cities. Through trains leave here for Beijing, Shanghai, Nanjing, Shenzhen, Ürümqi and about 20 other cities of the country.

Kaifeng

Kaifeng was a famous city in history where seven feudal dynasties had their capitals. It has a very rich legacy of culture and art.

Tieta (Iron Pagoda)

Located in Iron Pagoda Park on the north-eastern corner of the city proper, the pagoda was constructed in 1049. Its former name was Youguosita (Help the Country Temple), but is commonly called the Iron Pagoda because the glazed bricks on the outer wall of the pagoda are iron brown in colour. It is octagonal in shape, 13 storeyed and 54.66 metres high, a master-piece of ancient Chinese tall brick architecture.

Longting (Dragon Pavilion)

The pavilion is located on the northern tip of the middle axis of the city on the ruins of the Imperial Palace of the Northern Song dynasty. The existing great hall of Longting was built in 1734. The hall foundation is 13 metres high, with 72 stone steps. At the sides of the pavilion and in front of it are two lakes, the Pan and the Yang.

Xiangguosi Temple

Situated on the western section of Ziyoulu (Freedom Street) in the southern part of the city, Xiangguosi is one of China's famous Buddhist monasteries, the construction of which was begun in 555. Its former name being Jianguosi, Emperor Xuanzhong of the Tang dynasty changed its name to Great Xiangguosi to commemorate his ascension to the throne after Prince Xiang. There is a huge statue carved of wood of a four-sided *Guanyin* with one thousand hands and one thousand eyes. The statue is about 7 metres high, gilded all over. It is exceedingly beautiful and said to be carved out of a single ginkgo tree.

Yuwangtai Park

The park is located on the south-eastern part of the urban district. Its original name was Chuitai (Wind Music Platform), since according to legend it was the place where the great musician Shi Kuang of the State of Jin during the Spring and Autumn period (770–476 BC) played. It was a sightseeing area as early as over 1,000 years ago. In the Ming dynasty, a temple called Yuwang (King Yu) Temple was constructed on Chuitai to commemorate Yu Wang for his work on water control, and the name of Chuitai was changed to Yuwangtai. A huge statue of Yu Wang can be seen in the temple and there are halls, corridors, several-tiered pagodas and pavilions compactly laid out and long famous for being so small and exquisite.

● Through trains operate to Shanghai, Nanjing, Xi'an, Wuhan and other major cities. Buses from the city travel to all tourist spots.

Luoyang

Luoyang is traditionally called the "Ancient Capital of the Nine Dynasties". It is located on the northern bank of the Luohe river. In ancient China, all places on the southern side of a hill or the northern side of a river are called *Yang*, hence the name Luoyang. The city has many scenic spots and places of historical interest.

Longmen Grottoes

The grottoes, situated 12 kilometres south of the city, are among the three great grottoes of China. They contain more than 100,000 Buddhist images of different sizes and postures, carved of stone, with heights varying from 2 cm to 17.14 m. The construction of the Longmen Grottoes was started in the fifth century and completed in the period of the Northern Song dynasty (960–1127). Exquisitely carved and with substantial content, these grottoes offer important materials for the study of China's ancient history and art. (See Part I, **Chapter 13**.)

Baimasi (White Horse Temple)

This temple is 10 kilometres east of Luoyang. Erected in the 11th year of Yongping of the Eastern Han dynasty (AD 68), it was the first monastery built after Buddhism spread to China. Constructed at first in accordance with Indian styles, after restoration through the ages it gradually evolved as a Chinese-style monastery. Buildings still standing include Tianwangdian (Hall of the Heavenly King), Dafodian (Hall of Great Buddha), Daxiongdian, Jieyindian, Pihuge, etc. The Buddhist scriptures and stone pillars inscribed with Buddha's names or scriptures of the Tang dynasty, as well as steles and carvings of the Yuan dynasty kept in the monastery, are all articles of high artistic attainment.

Luoyang Museum

About 2,000 cultural relics are displayed in chronological order in the museum, including numerous rare

The National Economy

unearthed objects and artefacts such as the fossils of elephant tusks 580,000 years old, ceramics of the Shang dynasty (*ca.* 16th–11th century BC), bronze-wares of the Zhou dynasty (*ca.* 11th century–22nd year BC) and handicrafts of the Tang dynasty (618–907), etc.

● Besides these, tours may be arranged for visiting the tomb of **Bai Ju-yi** (772–846), a great poet of the Tang dynasty; the tomb of **Liu Xiu** (6 BC–AD 57), **Emperor Guangwu** of the Han dynasty; the native place of **Du Fu** (712–770), a great poet of the Tang dynasty; **Wangcheng Park**, etc.

● Luoyang has good transport facilities; through trains operate to Beijing, Tianjin, Shanghai, Nanjing and other major cities. The six tricoloured steeds produced in Luoyang, the imitation of unearthed artefacts, the black horse, the tricoloured glazed pottery of the Tang dynasty, etc. are exquisite works of handicraft and ideal tourist souvenirs.

Wuhan

The city of Wuhan is in the centre of Hubei province, on the confluence of the Changjiang and Hanshui rivers. It is the hub of land and water communications of the middle part of China. Wuhan municipality is made up of three parts, Wuchang, Hankou and Hanyang, traditionally called the "Three Garrison Posts of Wuhan". Wuchang is where the Revolution of 1911 led by Sun Zhong-shan (Sun Yat-sen) won its success; Hankou is where merchants and travellers gathered in the olden days; and Hanyang is said to be the place that King Yu visited when he was making efforts to regulate rivers and watercourses during the Xia dynasty (*ca.* 21st to 16th century BC).

Donghu (East Lake)

The lake is located in the eastern suburb of Wuchang, its surface covering an area of 73 square kilometres. The Xingyinge pavilion on a round islet on the north-western part of Donghu lake was built to commemorate Qu Yuan, the well-known poet of ancient China (*ca.* 340–*ca.* 278 BC). Climbing up to the third storey of the tall pavilion, one has a splendid panoramic view of Donghu lake. (See Part I, **Chapter 13**.)

Huanghelou (Yellow Crane Pavilion)

This pavilion is located on Huangheji by the riverside in Wuchang. Mounting the building to look into the distance, one sees the great river flowing east, on and on for a thousand *li*. Since ancient times, this has always been a scenic spot which poets and writers frequent to make inscriptions and write poems.

The Wuhan Changjiang River Bridge

This stretches across the river between Sheshan (Snake Hill) and Guishan (Tortoise Hill). It is the first great double-deck bridge of steel structure thrown across the Changjiang river. The whole length is 1,670 metres; its upper deck allows the passage of six lorries running parallel and its lower deck is a double-track railway. It is a railway and highway dual-purpose bridge, under which large steamers may pass freely. One can enjoy the full view of Wuhan city from either end of the bridge.

Guqintai (The platform where musical instruments are played)

Guqintai or Bo Ya's *qintai*, is located on the shore of Moon Lake in Hanyang and was said to be the place where Bo Ya, a famous musician of the State of Chu in the Spring and Autumn period (770–221 BC), played his *guqin* (a kind of zither). According to legend, it was here that Bo Ya met woodcutter Zhong Zi-qi, his admirer and close friend. A portrait of Bo Ya and an inscription may be seen engraved on the monument on the *Guqin* platform.

● Scenic spots of Wuhan also include the former sites of the **Peasant Movement Institute** and the **Military Government** of the Wuchang Uprising, **Jiunudun** (Nine Girls Mound) in Wuchang, the **Monument of February 7th Martyrs** in Hankou, etc.

The scenic spot of **Wudangshan Mountain** lying north-west of Wuhan Municipality is located in the south-west of Junxian county. (See Part I, **Chapter 13** in **Volume 1**.)

● There are regular services from Wuhan to Beijing, Shanghai, Nanjing, Chengdu and other major cities, and through trains to Beijing, Zhengzhou and other major cities.

Water transport and communication are very convenient in Wuhan. On the 2,500-kilometre shipping line from Chongqing to Shanghai, Wuhan is one of the biggest transfer ports. When the water rises, 10,000-ton river steamers may travel to places below Wuhan, whereas 1,000-ton steamers may run all the year round, past the three gorges up to Chongqing.

Changsha

Located on the shore of the Xiangjiang river, Changsha is a city with a long history of glorious revolutionary traditions. The woman's corpse excavated from the Han Tombs at Mawangdui, Changsha and the large quantities of precious historical relics unearthed in 1972 have added interest to Changsha as a tourist region.

The Hunan Provincial Museum

The museum, located on the bank of Liuyanghe river, keeps a wealth of materials of local revolutionary history. On exhibition are artefacts unearthed from the tombs of the Han dynasty at Mawangdui, Changsha. It shows the graves of Li Chang, Changsha's Minister and Marquis of Dai, together with his wife and son, from the period of the Western Han dynasty (206–24 BC) more than 2,100 years ago. The woman's corpse is preserved in good condition, and there are also more than 3,000 items of precious cultural relics.

Yuelushan Mountain

This mountain towers on the west bank of the Xiangjiang river. The exuberant foliage of the dense forests on the mountain is green and luxuriant, with old trees including yew podocarpus, ginkgo, maple, pine, camphor and chestnut. Gulushan Temple was built in the 4th year of Taishi of the Western Jin dynasty (268) and Yuelu Academy was one of the four great academies of classical learning of the Song dynasty (960–1127). The pavilion of Aiwanting at the foot of the mountain was built in the Qing dynasty (1792). The surroundings here are quiet and secluded. Mao Zedong was active here in his youthful days. Python Cavern is one of the many scenic spots. Climbing up Wangxiangting Pavilion on Yunlu Peak, one has a full view of Changhsa from afar.

Juzizhou (Orange Islet) Park

Located on the Xiangjiang river, the island park is about 5 kilometres long and at the broadest part about 300 metres. It is also called Changdao (Long Island) and abounds in mandarin oranges. The landscape here is elegant and there is a natural swimming beach at the southern tip of the park.

Places of historic interest and scenic beauty in Changsha include also the exhibition hall and the memorial tower of the former site of the Hunan District Council of the Chinese Communist Party, and the former dwelling of Jia Yi (200–168 BC), the political commentator and man of letters of the Western Han dynasty. There are also other scenic spots in the vicinity.

Yueyanglou

This is one of China's three most famous tiered buildings south of the Changjiang river (the other two are Huanghelou at Wuchang and Tengwangge at Nanchang). It towers over the western city gate of Yueyang city, which has long been praised: "Dongting tops all waters under heaven, whereas Yueyang tops all the tiered buildings beneath the sky." In the fifth year of Qingli of the Song dynasty (1045), when Teng Zijing was an official here, he invited the great writer Fan Zhongyan to write the *Chronicle of Yueyanglou*. The chronicle contained the famous sentences: "Be concerned about the anxieties of all others before being concerned about your own, and enjoy yourself only after all others have enjoyed themselves," which have been read with admiration by people through the ages. In the years that followed, Yueyanglou experienced several vicissitudes; the present building was built in the 6th year of Tongzhi of the Qing dynasty (1867) and rebuilt in 1984 according to the original design. It is a 15-metre high, three-storeyed building of pure wooden construction, with three eaves and a helmet roof. From the top floor, one is able to command a broad view of Dongtinghu lake.

Yueyangleyuan Park

This is one of China's up-to-date pleasure gardens, offering 27 attractions, including expeditions on the rapids, etc.

Dongtinghu Lake

With an area of about 3,900 square kilometres, this is China's second largest freshwater lake. The Junshan mountains in the lake, with an area of 94 hectares, are made up of 72 big and small mountain peaks, about which beautiful and touching stories are told. The famous tea "Junshan Silver Needle" prepared here won a gold medal in 1956 at the Leipzig World Fair.

Zhangjiajie

The Zhangjiajie scenic spot lies in the area of Wulingyuan on the western edge of the Dongtinghu lake, about 30 kilometres north of the county town of Dayong. The locality has many strange, precipitous mountain peaks and the landscapes there are enchanting.

Shaoshan Mountain

The mountain is 40 kilometres west of the county town of Xiangtan and is one of the 72 peaks of the Nanyue (Southern Mountains). One can reach it by taking a train at Changsha. At the foot of the mountain is the former dwelling and exhibition hall of Mao Zedong, which has an exhibition of the historical relics and materials of his revolutionary activities.

Hengshan Mountain: See Part I, **Chapter 13**.

● Planes and trains leave Changsha regularly for Beijing, Shanghai, Guangzhou, Chengdu and other cities. Long-distance buses operate services to the various scenic spots at Zhangjiajie, Shaoshan mountain, etc.

Guangzhou (Canton)

Guangzhou is a famous city with a history of more than 2,800 years; it is also known as *Yangcheng* (City

Guangzhou is also called the "City of Rams". This is the statue of Five Rams which symbolizes the city.
(Photo by Zhou Youma)

of Rams), or *Suicheng* (City of Ears of Corn). There is a beautiful legend which says that, in the old days, five celestial beings were seen coming to Guangzhou, each riding on a ram of five colours and carrying ears of corn with them and blessing the inhabitants of Guangzhou with ample food and clothing. Afterwards, the celestial beings rose to the sky and flew away, but the five rams were turned into stone and remained in Guangzhou. The granite image of five rams on Yuexiushan hill in Guangzhou has now been made the emblem of the city.

Zhenhailou Hall

Yuexiushan hill on the north side of the city is a part of the Baiyunshan mountain range and its seven hillocks very close to the urban district of Guangzhou have formed a landscape which has become the head of the "eight beauty spots of the Ram City". It is now open to the public as Yuexiu Park. Occupying 92.8 hectares in area, the park contains the historic site of Zhenhailou, a hall built during the Ming dynasty, more than 600 years ago. The Guangzhou Museum is located here. The orchid garden on the west side of the park has on display about 10,000 pots of different kinds of orchids.

Chenjiaci Temple

The ancestral temple is a noted hall-type building in

Guangzhou city, with an area of more than 10,000 square metres, an embodiment of the traditional style of Chinese architecture with the distinguishing features of local technological decoration. It has now been opened as the "Hall of Guangdong Folk Technology".

Liurongsi and Huata (Six-Banyan Temple and Flower Pagoda)

This is a famous old Buddhist monastery built in the 3rd year of Datong of the Liang dynasty (537). The architectural complex of the monastery includes the Flower Pagoda, Liuzhutang (Hall of Six Ancestors), Burongting and Guanyin Hall. The Flower Pagoda is 57.6 metres high and octagonal in shape, and looks like a flower soaring into the sky. It has an outer appearance of nine storeys but is actually 17-storeyed inside.

Guangxiaosi Temple

The temple was the former dwelling of the king of Nanyue in the second century BC. In the years of Longan of the Eastern Jin dynasty (397–401), a famous Indian monk came to Guangzhou to spread the idea of Buddhism and built a temple there. In the Song dynasty the temple was named Guangxiaochansi.

Huaishengsi and Guangta Temples

Huaishengsi is one of China's earliest Islamic monasteries and was built in the first year of Zhenguan of the Tang dynasty (627). Guangta (so named because the main part of the pagoda is smooth) is 36.3 metres high and has the Moslem architectural style.
● The six great historic sites of Guangzhou, besides those mentioned above, include also the tomb of the **King of Yue**. Besides **Yuexiu Park**, the other five famous parks are **Liuhua, Donghu** (East Lake), and **Liwanhu** parks, the **zoo** and the **botanical garden.** There are also pleasure resorts in Guangzhou, namely **Dongfang, Nanhu** (Southern Lake) and **Taiyang-dao** (Sun Island).

Revolutionary Monuments

The former site of the Peasant Movement Institute directed by Mao Zedong, the cemetery of revolutionary martyrs of the Guangzhou Uprising, the cemetery of the 72 revolutionary martyrs at Huanghuagang, the Zhongshan Memorial Hall, the memorial hall of the anti-imperialist struggle of Sanyuanli and the former dwelling and memorial hall of Hong Xiu-quan (1814–1864), the revolutionary leader of Taiping Heavenly Kingdom etc., are all located inside the city. Humen (Tiger Gate) Park, not far south of Guangzhou city, was where Lin Ze-xu (1785–1850) burnt the foreign opium and a hall was built there in his memory.

Zhaoqing's Xinghu

This scenic spot is located at Zhaoqing city, 110 kilometres away from Guangzhou. (See Part I, **Chapters 12** and **13**.)
● Airlines from Guangzhou fly to over 30 major cities of the country. International airlines link Guangzhou with Bangkok, Manila and Singapore, and Guangzhou operates a regular regional air service to Hong Kong. Through trains link the city with Beijing, Shanghai and other major cities and there are trains to Hong Kong and Kowloon. Long distance buses travel to Zhaoqing and other localities and there are also tourist buses going to the special economic zones of Shenzhen and Zhuhai. A regular coastal steamship service operates to Shantou, Haikou and Hong Kong.

Nanning

The subtropical climate has made this old city of more than 2,000 years history, capital of the Guangxi Zhuang autonomous region, evergreen in the four seasons, with the air heavy with the aroma of flowers and fruits.

Yilingyan

This is a grotto located to the north-west of Nanning city. It is a huge cavern of calcareous sandstone with an area of 24,000 square metres. The interior of the grotto is warm in winter and cool in summer, and it has tortuous pathways with stalacites, stone posts, stone flowers and stalagmites which – under the illumination of coloured light – seem to change themselves into the wonderful landscapes of thickly forested mountains, airy corridors, the marvellous spectacles of the seabed, the night view of the mountain area and the happy village of the Zhuang nationality, making tourists feel as though they are being led into a miraculous world of crystal.

The Museum of the Guangxi Zhuang Autonomous Region

This museum, located inside Nanning city, is a comprehensive topological museum occupying 12,900 square metres. It was built according to the national architectural style of the southern part of China and has at present the biggest and most complete collection of bronze drums in the whole country. It has concurrently gathered data on the origins of the 1,388 bronze drums preserved at the various places of China.

● At the scenic spots of **Zuojiang River** and **Huashan Mountain**, 188 kilometres away from the urban districts, tourists will be able to admire the rugged shorelines; and at **Damingshan Mountain** about 100 kilometres away from the city they may enjoy the scenery of virgin forests.
● One may reach Beijing, Guangzhou and other cities direct by plane or train.

Guilin

Guilin is famous in China for its scenery, with hills and waters, and for its historical relics. It is situated on the upper reaches of the Guijiang river in the northeastern part of the Kwangxi Zhuang autonomous region. It is named *Guilin* on account of the exuberant growth of sweet-scented osmanthus in the city.

The essence of Guilin's hills and waters may be represented by a river (Lijiang), two grottoes (Ludi Grotto and Qixing "Seven Star" Grotto) and three hills (Diecai, Fubo and Duxiu hills).
Lijiang River, Ludi and **Qixing Grottoes:** (See Part I, **Chapter 13**.)
The China **Karst Geological Museum**, built in 1982, and located 5 kilometres south-west of Guilin city, is the only one of its kind in the world.
● Regular flights and train services connect Guilin with various major cities such as Beijing, Shanghai, Hangzhou, Guangzhou, etc. Guilin is also linked with Hong Kong through a service of chartered planes. A regular steamship service connects Guilin with Guangzhou, Zhaoqing and other places.

Chengdu

Chengdu, also named Rongcheng (Lotus City), is an old historical city more than 2,000 years old. The great poet of the Tang dynasty, Du Fu (712–770), lived in this city for about four years. There are many scenic spots and places of historic interest here.

The Straw Hut of Du Fu

Located in the western suburbs of Chengdu, the hut is the former dwelling of Du Fu where he wrote more than 240 poems, and to commemorate him a hall named Dugongbuci was later built. The official name of Du Fu was "Jian Jiao Gong Bu Yuan Wai Lang".

Wuhouci Temple

This memorial temple was situated on the southern outskirts of Chengdu and built in the period of the Western Jin dynasty (265–316) to the memory of the

Prime Minister of the Shu Han dynasty (221–263), Zhuge Liang (181–234). Inside the temple there are the halls of Liu Bei, the emperor of Shu Han, and Zhuge Liang, with their statues enshrined at their respective halls. Liu Bei's tomb is also located here.

Dujiangyan Weir

The weir located on the west of Guanxian county town, 57 kilometres away from Chengdu, was constructed in the years 306–251 BC and was one of the famous irrigation works of ancient China which today still irrigates several million *mu* of land on Chengdu plain. Hence Chengdu won its name of "land of abundance". The Erwangmiao (Two Kings' Temple) here was for the commemoration of the founder of Dujiangyan, Li Bing, and his son. (See Part I, **Chapter 13** in **Volume 1**.)

Baoguangsi Temple

This temple, the construction of which is believed to have started during the Eastern Han dynasty (25–220), is situated in Xinduxian county, 18 kilometres away from Chengdu. A complex of statues of 500 *Arhats* sculptured in the Qing dynasty may be found inside the temple.
● Scenic spots in the vicinity of Chengdu include **Emeishan Mountain**, the **Big Buddha** at Leshan hill, **Shudao** at Jianmen (Sword Gate) and **Jiuzhaigou**. (See Part I, **Chapters 12** and **13**.)
● There are regular flights and trains for Beijing, Chongqing, Shanghai, Nanjing and other major cities. Long-distance buses operate to Leshan hill, Emeishan mountain, Jiuzhaigou and other scenic regions.

Chongqing

Surrounded by hills, Chongqing is situated in the eastern part of Sichuan province on the confluence of the Changjiang and Jialingjiang rivers. It is an inland river port for foreign trade and the economic centre of China's south-west region, as well as a gate in the upper reaches to the three gorges of the Changjiang river, long famous for their grandeur.

The scenic spot of **Jinyunshan Mountain** at Chongqing is one of the famous tourist resorts. (See Part I, **Chapter 13**.)

Dazhushike (Stone Inscriptions of Dazhu)

Located 162 kilometres north-west of Chongqing, Dazhuxian county is famous for its carved stones. There are more than 40 places with stone inscriptions

in which were carved upwards of 50,000 statues. Among these, the places in the Beishan and Baodingshan hills are the most famous. The stone statues there are very finely carved and the figures vivid, containing many interesting stories of Buddhism, such as the "Picture of the Birth of Sakyamuni", "Herd Cows Buddhist Rites", etc. A most magnificent sight is the statue of the one-thousand-hand Guanyin, which has in fact 1,030 hands and dainty and delicate lines and very graceful carriage which make it a quite uncommon work.
● Regular flights and trains connect Chongqing with Chengdu, Shanghai, Wuhan, Beijing and other major cities. Passenger steamships sailing along the river call at all ports.

Kunming

Kunming is located in a long and narrow basin on the plateau of Yunnan and Guizhou. The city is surrounded by hills on three sides, with its southern side facing Dianchi. The views there are elegant and beautiful and all the four seasons are like spring; it is therefore also called "Spring City". Marco Polo praised it as a "Magnificent City".

Dianchi Lake and Daguanlou Park

Dianchi is a highland lake of about 340 square kilometres in area. Longmen (Dragon Gate), which towers more than 300 metres over the water surface, was dug out of the sheer precipice and overhanging rocks of Xishan mountain. It is an ideal place for enjoying the view of Dianchi. Up on a bank of Dianchi is Daguanlou Park.

Qiongzhusi Temple

The temple is located in the north-western suburb of Kunming city and was the first to be built after Buddhism was spread to Kunming from China's interior. The plain and vivid 500 *Arhats*, each of a peculiar bearing, were sculptured in the years 1883–1890 by folk sculptor Li Guangxiu of the Qing dynasty.

Jindian (Gold Hall)

This is also called Tongwasi (Bronze Tiles Temple) and is located on Mingfengshan mountain in the north-eastern suburb of Kunming. The main hall was built of bronze, dazzlingly brilliant, in the 30th year of Wanli of the Ming dynasty (1602) and was cast after the model of the Jindian at Wudangshan mountain, Hubei. It was moved to Jizhushan mountain in Binchuan in the 10th year of Chongzhen (1637). The present Jindian was modelled by Ping Xi Wang (Prince who Subjugates the West) Wu Sangui in the 10th year of Kangxi (1671). Jindian is square shaped, 6.7 metres high, with each side 6.2 metres long. The beams, columns, inscribed boards, painted wall screens, Buddhist statues, etc., were all cast in bronze and the stone steps, floors and balustrades were all inlaid with or built of marble.

● The scenic spots inside and outside Kunming City are scattered all over the area, and include **Yuantongshan Mountain, Yuhuashan Mountain, Heilongtan** (Black Dragon Pond), **Sanqingge** (the tomb of the famous musician Nie Er is close by), **Cuihu Park, Anning** hot spring, etc.

There are also other famous scenic spots in the vicinity of Kunming which are attractive to tourists, such as **Lunanshilin** (Stone Forest), **Dali, Xishuangbanna.** (See Part I, **Chapters 12** and **13**.)

● Besides regular flights to Beijing, Shanghai, Guangzhou and other major cities, there is also a regional air service operating regularly to Hong Kong and an international air line which connects Kunming with Bangkok and Rangoon. Trains travel to all major cities of the country and highway communications are also very well developed, linking Kunming with any major city of Yunnan province, as well as with Guiyang city in Guizhou province and other places.

Guiyang

The urban district of Guiyang is a basin surrounded by hills on all four sides. It is a city where people of various nationalities (Han, Miao, Puyi, Hui, etc.) live in compact communities.

Qianling Park

The park is located in the north-western corner of the city proper. Green peaks rise one higher than another and old trees soar into the sky, where pavilions and terraces set each other off and tortuous paths lead to secluded spots. The old Buddhist temple Hongfusi on the mountain top has a history of over 300 years. Kanzhuting pagoda in the temple courtyard is an ideal place to get a full bird's-eye view of the mountain city. Qianlinghu lake is behind the mountain.

Nanjiao (Southern Suburb) Park

The park is situated on the southern suburb by the bank of the Xiaochehe river. It is also called the underground park and is actually a subterranean corrosion cavern of about 500 and more metres long. Inside the cavern one sees strange and beautiful stalacites, stalagmites, stone flowers, stone canopies, etc.

Jiaxiulou Hall

The building is constructed on Fuyu (Floating Jade) Bridge across the Nanminghe river south of the city and contains numerous written couplets, inscribed boards, poems and steles. The scenery here is elegant and beautiful, which has won for it the melodious name of *Xiaoxihu* (Small West Lake).

Huangguoshu Waterfall

The waterfall is on Baishuihe river, 15 kilometres south-west of the autonomous region of the Puyi and Miao nationalities at Zhenning, in the vicinity of Guiyang city. This zone is a mountainous region of calcareous sandstone, with peaks rising one over another and many torrential waterfalls among strange looking crags and grotesque rocks. The Huangguoshu waterfall cluster is one of the strange sights in this locality. (See Part I, **Chapter 13**.)

Wen Temple

The temple is located at Anshun, 100 kilometres away from Guiyang. In the architectural complex of Wen Temple are stone dragon posts of cloud lines of penetration sculpture which are rarely seen in China. Here also grows a 300-year-old osmanthus tree that yields tricoloured flowers for as long as 50 days or more.

● There are regular flights to Beijing, Shanghai, Guangzhou and other cities, and through trains travel to various major cities of the country.

Lhasa

Lhasa, the capital of the autonomous region of Xizang (Tibet), is an old city having a history of more than 1,300 years, situated on the "Roof of the World" on the Qinghai–Xizang plateau. It is 3,500 metres above sea level and is one of the cities with the most hours of sunshine, being often called "Sunlight City."

Budalagong (Potala Palace)

The palace is located on Maburishan hill at the north-western corner of the urban district. Construction of the palace begun in the seventh century, and it was originally built to welcome Princess Wen Cheng of the Tang dynasty to an arranged marriage with Tubozanpusongzanganbu. It has 13 storeys and is 117.19 metres high, with more than one thousand rooms of various sizes, all of stone and wooden construction. The walls are about 3 metres thick – some over 5 metres. The palace is divided into two parts, the white palace and the red palace. The white palace is where the Dalai Lama leads his daily life or carries out political activities; in the red palace there are pagodas and halls preserving the remains of deceased Dalai Lamas of past dynasties and various halls for worshipping Buddha. The pagodas for the remains of the fifth and the thirteenth Dalai Lamas are the biggest: for the fifth, the pagoda is 14 metres high and covered with gold leaves, made up from a total of more than 119,000 *liangs* (1 *liang* = 50 grams) of gold, 230,000 *jins* (1 jin = $\frac{1}{2}$ kilogram) of copper, over 4,000 large and small pearls and innumerable jewels. Though the pagoda for Dalai Lama the thirteenth is smaller, it is mounted with over 2,000 pearls. In the palace there are large quantities of historical relics and murals of very high artistic value. Budalagong is a famous complex of palatial fortresses and the essence of the ancient architectural arts of the Zang nationality.

Luobulinka Garden

This name means "Garden of Treasures" in Tibetan. The palace is located in the western suburb of the city and about one kilometre away from Budalagong. The construction of the palace was started in 1755 and it was used by Dalai Lamas in past dynasties as their summer palace. It occupies an area of 32 hectares, of which 15 are forest. Every year, from the 4th to the 9th moon of the lunar calendar used by the Zang nationality, the Dalai Lama would come here to attend to government affairs and hold celebrations (from the 10th moon to the third moon of the next year, the same duties would be performed at Budalagong). In the garden there are palaces and halls for worshipping Buddha, kiosks and waterside pavilions, lakes and ponds, and tortuous paths leading to secluded spots. Famous in Lhasa for its flowers and scenery, the garden has now been opened as a public park. At festival time, the Zang people gather in the Linka to sing and dance.

Dazhaosi Temple

This temple, the construction of which was begun in 647, is located in the centre of Lhasa's old city. It is one of the oldest buildings in Xizang, having been extended in the later dynasties of Yuan, Ming and Qing. It covers an area of 25,100 square metres; the hall is 4-storeyed, with its upper part covered by a gold roof, in the style of the architecture of the Tang dynasty. Enshrined in the temple is a gilded bronze statue of Sakyamuni at the age of 12, brought from Chang'an by Princess Wen Cheng. Statues of Song Zan Gan Bu, Princess Wen Cheng and Princess Ci Zun of Nepal are also enshrined in the temple. Outside the temple are willows from the time of the Tang dynasty, said to be planted by the hands of Princess Wen Cheng herself, and a stele erected in 823, symbolizing the formation of the alliance between the Tang dynasty and Tu Bo and the close, friendly relations between the Zang and Han nationalities.

Zhebangsi Temple

The temple is located half-way up a mountain slope 5 kilometres north-west of the urban district. It was built in 1416, occupying 25 hectares in area. The temple is grand in scale, with halls linking up with one another. It houses four academies devoted to the studies of Buddhist scriptures and the number of resident monks is set at 7,700. It is the greatest monastery of Lamaism, and together with Gandansi and Selasi, constitutes the "Three Great Monasteries".

Selasi Temple

This temple, built in 1418, is located in a valley at the foot of a hill three kilometres from the northern suburb. Inside the temple, which also keeps large quantities of historical relics, there are close to 10,000 statues of Buddha's warrior attendants, manufactured locally in Xizang, and many bronze statues of Buddha brought from the interior and from India.

● From other places of the country to Lhasa, people travel mainly on scheduled flights. The highway network with Lhasa as its centre is basically in shape, and the mileage inside the boundary of Xizang open to traffic reaches more than 21,000 kilometres.

See also Part I, Chapters 12 and 13 in Volume 1.

CHINA'S TOURIST ROUTES

THE tourist areas introduced above comprise many tourist routes interlocking with each other. Introduced below are some of the most essential routes on which tourists may make their choices according to their own wishes. Before coming to China, consultation with Chinese tourist bureaux will provide tourists with specific routes.

(1) Beijing, Jiangsu Zhijiang route

Beijing – Nanjing – Suzhou – Hangzhou (including Shaoxing) – Shanghai

(2) Beijing, Jiangsu route

Beijing – Nanjing – Zhenjiang (or Yangzhou) – Wuxi – Suzhou – Shanghai

(3) Beijing, Huangshan Mountain route

Beijing – Hefei – Huangshan Mountain – Hangzhou – Shanghai

(4) Beijing, Shandong route

Beijing – Jinan – Qufu, Taishan Mountain (or Qingdao) – Suzhou – Shanghai

(5) Guangdong and Guangxi, Guizhou route

Guangzhou – Nanning – Guilin – Guiyang (including Huangguoshu) – Beijing (or Shanghai)

(6) Guilin, south-west route

Guangzhou – Guilin – Kunming – Chongqing (or Chengdu) – Beijing (or Shanghai)

(7) Guilin, Central China route

Guangzhou – Guilin – Changsha – Wuhan – Shijiazhuang – Beijing

(8) Shanghai, Fujian route

Shanghai – Fuzhou – Xiamen – Hangzhou – Beijing (or Guangzhou)

(9) Old capitals route

Beijing – Zhengzhou – Kaifeng – Luoyang – Xi'an – Hangzhou

(10) Beijing, north-east route

Beijing – Chengde – Shenyang – Dalian – Changchun (or Jilin) – Harbin

(11) Beijing, Lhasa route

Beijing – Xi'an – Lhasa – Chengdu – Shanghai

(12) The Changjiang (Yangtze) River Three Gorges route

(13) The "Silk Road" route

Tourist Routes to the Three Gorges of the Changjiang (Yangtze) River

Tourists may take a river steamer at Chongqing in Sichuan province for a tour of the Changjiang river of from 3 to 4 days (a distance of 1,370 kilometres) to Wuhan in Hubei province. This is considered to be the ideal route for touring China.

The section of three gorges in this route is a gallery of hills and waters concentrated in strange and elegant landscapes along the scenic path of the Changjiang river. It starts from Baidicheng (City of the White Emperor) in Sichuan's Fengjie county, moving east to Nanjinguan in Yichang city, Hubei – a distance of 192 kilometres – and takes in three great gorges, the Qutang Gorge, the Wu Gorge and the Xiling Gorge, formed by the water of Changjiang river cutting across the Wushan mountain range, which stretches along the borders of Sichuan and Hubei provinces. The river surface in the three gorges is tortuous and narrow and the flow rapid, which produces a grand sight, with towering peaks confronting one another and tall, serene and precipitous cliffs and gorges on both banks.

This area was the cradle of the culture of the ancient country of Chu, a country of long history where people of talent assembled. In the period of the Northern Wei dynasty, the Chinese geographer Li Daoyuan, in his famous work *Shuijingzhu* (Notes on Water Classics), wrote vivid descriptions of the three gorges. The great poet of the Tang dynasty, Li Bai, toured the three gorges three times, leaving many famous poems which have been circulated far and wide through the ages. The age-old city of Baidicheng is the entrance to the gorges. In Baidimiao (Temple of White Emperor) one can see the statues of Emperor Liu Bei, Prime Minister Zhuge Liang and generals Guan Yu and Zhang Fei of the State of Shu during the period of the Three Kingdoms (220–280). Guanxingting (Star Observation Kiosk), according to legend, was the place where Zhuge Liang watched the stars at night.

The whole length of **Jutang Gorge** is about eight kilometres, with high mountain ridges and precipitous cliffs towering above both banks and where, looking up between the two cliffs, one sees only a gleam of the sky, particularly at Kuimen, at the western entrance, where the cliffs rise steeply to a great height and the space between them is often less than a hundred metres, so that they look like two skyscrapers.

Wu Gorge is located between Sichuan's Wushan mountain and the county of Badong in Hubei province, with a length of about 40 kilometres. Wushan mountain has 12 peaks, among which the Shennu (Fairy) Peak is the subject of many touching legends. The Shoushutai at the foot of Shennu Peak, according to legend, was the place where the Fairy gave books to Da Yu (King Yu). Kongmingbei at the foot of Jixian (Gathering of Fairies) Peak, has six written characters *Chong Ya Die Zhang Wu Xia* (Peaks Rising one Higher than Another at Wu Gorge) engraved on a stone tablet, said to be the original handwriting of Zhuge Liang.

Xiling Gorge is the longest of the three gorges, the whole length of it being 120 kilometres. There is a canyon inside the gorge called Bingshubaojianxia (canyon where books on the art of war and a double-edged sword were kept), said to be the place where Zhuge Liang kept his books on the art of war. There are many other places of tourist interest, such as the "canyon of cow's liver and horse's lungs" (so called because of the shapes of the rocks there), Konglingtan (one of the dangerous shoals of the three gorges), and other famous canyons, as well as Huanglingmiao, Sanyoudong and Luyouquan.

The high, misty scenic region on this route has been praised as the "twin sister of Guilin". It is located inside the boundary of Xingshan county in Hubei province on the northern bank of Xiling Gorge, not far from the native places of both Qu Yuan and Zhao Jun, the virgin forest area of Shennongjia and the big dam at Gezhouba.

The Tourist Route of the "Silk Road"

The so-called "Silk Road" has a history of more than 2,000 years. The name refers to a route of more than 7,000 kilometres which started in those years from the capital of the Western Han dynasty (206–24 BC), Chang'an, extending westward, through Central Asia and the Middle East and reaching Anduaoke on the eastern coast of the Mediterranean Sea. The Han dynasty lands abounded with silks, and the merchants of those days used to transport them westward along this route for trade contacts with other countries. The missions of Zhang Qian and Ban Chao of the Han dynasty to the Western Regions and the pilgrimage westward of Master Xuanzang of the Tang dynasty all took this route.

For thousands of years the Chinese people cultivated friendship and carried out economic and cultural exchanges with peoples of various countries by way of this route and, with the discovery of new sea routes to the east from Europe in the Middle Ages, the route has become the symbol and historical witness of friendly contacts between Chinese and foreign peoples. The scenic spots and places of historical interest along this route have also become mysterious places in the minds of many tourists, who are eager to see them with their own eyes.

On the eastern section of the "Silk Road", a beacon tower 9.1 metres high, used by the garrison troops of the Western Han dynasty for raising the alarm outside Yumenguan (Pass at Jade Gate), can still be seen. It showed Master Xuanzang, the famous monk of the Tang dynasty, his way back home and has remained till today a landmark in the Gobi Desert.

The old strategically important city of Shangchang on the "Silk Road" is located in the south-east of Xinjiang's Tulufan county (Turpan). Though this old city of more than 1,000 years was eventually abandoned, its streets and houses built of rammed earth have been miraculously preserved and now serve as ideal places for those wishing to explore secluded spots and places of historic interest.

The "Silk Road" traverses a vast territory. Its routes incorporate many different ruins and abound in rich and colourful sights. To travel along these routes would be most rewarding for either tourists or archaeologists.

712

NOTICE TO PERSONS WISHING TO TRAVEL IN CHINA

Formalities for Travelling in China

ALL foreign travellers (missions) wishing to travel in China may make direct contact with the relevant tourist bureaux in China. They may also make contacts through the various Chinese embassies and consulates in the different countries, Chinese tourist offices abroad, organizations of friendship with China or foreign tourist bureaux having business relations with Chinese tourist organizations.

When agreement about the proposed travel in China has been made with the Chinese travel services concerned, foreign travellers (missions) may enter and travel in China on the production of valid entry visas.

China's Main Travel Services

China International Travel Service (CITS)

Known inside China as LÜXINGSHE (International), this service, set up in 1954, is the biggest nationwide international travel enterprise and the earliest establishment in China specially responsible for the reception of foreign visitors. At present it has business contacts with 600 foreign travel services throughout the world, with over 4000 interpreters and guides who understand more than twenty languages, including English, Japanese, French, German, Spanish and others. All have received higher education and are well-trained. The head office is in Beijing, with 180 branch and sub-offices in various places throughout the country.

China Travel Service and Overseas Chinese Travel Service

This is a special organization for rendering services to overseas Chinese – compatriots in Hong Kong and Macao and those in Taiwan, and Chinese of foreign nationality coming home to visit their relatives and for sightseeing, as well as to foreign friends touring in China. The head office is in Beijing and a total of more than 270 China Travel Services have been set up in the various big cities and scenic regions and in some counties and municipalities of the native places of overseas Chinese, forming a comparatively integrated system of nationwide tourist services. China Travel Services have also been set up in Hong Kong and Macao.

The China Youth Travel Service

The above belongs to the tourist department of the Chinese All-Nation Youth Union set up in 1980. Its chief objectives are to develop friendly intercourse between Chinese youth and the youth of the various countries of the world, to promote mutual understanding and friendship, and to maintain close ties with Chinese youth living in Hong Kong, Macao and Taiwan and with overseas Chinese youth. The head office is in Beijing, with branch organizations in different tourist cities all over the country and an agency in the Hong Kong region.

Visas

Foreigners wishing to travel to China must hold valid visas issued by the Chinese authorities, those belonging to mutual-exemption countries excepted.

Persons applying for visas for China may do so themselves directly or through foreign travel agencies, with a letter or cable confirmation by LÜXINGSHE (International). Those who are in Hong Kong may apply for visas to the Visa Office of the Ministry of Foreign Affairs of the People's Republic of China in Hong Kong (address: 26 Harbour Road, Wanchai, Hong Kong) or through LÜXINGSHE, Hong Kong (address: 6th Floor 1, Tower II, South Seas Centre, 75 Mody Road, Tsim Sha Tsui, East Kowloon, Hong Kong) or at the Visa Office of the Public Security Bureau of Guangdong Province in Shenzhen.

Foreigners who have received approval to visit China may choose an itinerary prepared by the relevant travel agencies in China.

Ports of Entry and Exit for People of Chinese and Foreign Nationalities

In accordance with the Administrative Laws of the People's Republic of China governing the entry and exit of foreign persons, the Administrative Laws on the entry and exit of the citizens of the People's Republic of China and the regulations on Frontier Inspection Rules promulgated by the State Council of the Central People's Government of the People's Republic of China, the Ministry of Public Security has officially published the names of the ports of entry and exit of people of Chinese and foreign nationalities (see below).

Regions Open to Foreigners in China

At present, there are 436 regions in China open to foreigners. In accordance with the Administrative Laws of the People's Republic of China governing the entry and exit of foreign persons, foreigners holding valid visas or residence permits may visit the open regions without applying for travel permits (see below).

Foreigners touring other regions in China must apply for travel permits. They may themselves apply for these permits upon entry or through LÜXINGSHE, with departments connected with the administration of foreigners of local public security bureaux.

Quarantine

1. Passengers arriving in the People's Republic of China should have their health certificates ready before the landing of the plane or the arrival of the train or the ship.

(a) Passengers travelling from or via areas where yellow fever is prevalent are requested to show their valid yellow fever inoculation certificates, otherwise, they should have their health checked for 6 days in China. No yellow fever inoculation certificates are required for passengers from areas not susceptible to yellow fever.

(b) Incoming passengers should fill in the Health Declaration and abide by the frontier quarantine regulations of the PRC and other rules pertaining to their implementation.

2. If passengers have infectious diseases such as psychosis, leprosy, AIDS, venereal diseases, open-lung tuberculosis, etc. they should be cured before coming to China.

3. Should passengers feel indisposed on the way to China, they should report to the Chinese frontier quarantine personnel at the airport, seaport or railway station of arrival.

Airlines

The development of Chinese civil aviation services has been very fast in recent years. Civil airports in China now total 90, eight of which are capable of handling the taking-off and landing of Boeing 747 planes, 13 are capable of handling the taking off and landing of Boeing 707 and MD-82 planes, and 32 are able to handle the taking off and landing of Boeing 737 and Tridents. Beijing is the centre of the domestic aviation network which has scheduled flights every week to various tourist spots. Its international routes cover the five continents of the world, with air services to more than 26 cities of 22 countries and regions, including Tokyo, Osaka, Nagasaki, New York, San Francisco, Los Angeles, Pyongyang, Rangoon, Bangkok, Manila, Karachi, Sharjah, Bagdad, Teheran, Moscow, London, Bucharest, Paris, Belgrade, Zürich, Frankfurt, Addis Ababa, Sydney, etc. There are also about 20 foreign airlines which have opened routes to China.

Railways

The railway is the backbone of China's communication and transport system; the distance open to traffic has reached more than 50,000 kilometres. Railways radiate in all directions. All major sightseeing cities and tourist centres of the country are linked by railways. The whole journey of the 13/14, 21/22 through-express between Beijing and Shanghai requires only 17 hours to reach its destination. The technical equipment of Chinese railways is constantly being improved and perfected. Long-distance trains are all equipped with dining cars and snack counters which supply tasty food, good wines and pastries. It is safe and comfortable to travel by Chinese trains.

There are international trains travelling twice weekly between Beijing and cities like Pyongyang, Ulan Bator and Moscow. There are also many express trains daily between Guangzhou and Kowloon and between Guangzhou and Shenzhen, which greatly facilitate passengers entering or leaving China by way of Hong Kong.

Table 2: International Trains Departing from Beijing

Destination	Whole journey (kilometres)	Travel time	Fare (Renminbi, yuan)		
			Box	Soft sleeper	Hard sleeper
Beijing – Pyongyang	1,347	about 23 hours		248.90	177.60
Beijing – Xinyizhou	1,122	about 17 hours		203.80	144.90
Beijing – Ulan Bator	1,561	30–39 hours	315.20	275.10	196.80
Beijing – Moscow (via Er lian, Ulan Bator)	7,865	5 mornings and nights and 3 hours	1056.00	894.60	660.60
Beijing – Moscow (via Manzhouli)	9,001	about 6 mornings and nights	1016.90	709.70	506.50

Note: The above table is for reference only. For specific fares, consult the appropriate booking office.

REGIONS OF CHINA OPEN TO FOREIGNERS

Counties, Cities, etc.

Beijing Municipality

Shanghai Municipality

Tianjin Municipality

Hebei
Qinhuangdao, Shijiazhuang city, Chengde city, Baoding city, Tangshan city, Handan city, Zhuo Xian county, Xingtai city, Langfang city, Cangzhou city, Botou city, Zhaoxian county, Luanping county (Great wall of Jinshanling).

Shanxi
Taiyuan city, Datong city, Yangquan city, Linfen city, Yuncheng city, Changzhi city, Pingyao county, Hongdong county, Ruicheng county.

Neimongol (Inner Mongolia)
Hohhot city, Baotou city, Erlianhaote city, Manzhouli city, Tongliao city, Hailaer city, Dongsheng city, Xilinhaote city, Zhalantun city, Wulanhaote city, Dalate banner, Chifeng city.

Liaoning
Shenyang city, Dalian city, Anshan city, Fushun city, Dandong city, Jinzhou city, Yingkou city, Fusin city, Liaoyang city, Benxi city, Tieling city, Chaoyang city, Panjin city.

Jilin
Changchun city, Jilin city, Yanji city, Siping city, Liaoyuan city, Tonghua city, Baicheng city, Hunjiang city, Gongzhuling city, Meihekou city, Tumen city, Longjing county, Antu county (Changbaishan Mountain Nature Reserve).

Heilongjiang
Harbin city, Qiqihar city, Daqing city, Jiamusi city, Mudanjiang city, Jixi city, Hegang city, Qitaihe city, Yichun city, Wudalianchi city, Shuangyashan city, Anda city, Suihua city, Bei'an city, Hailun County, Shuangcheng county, Fangzheng county, Nenjiang county, Zhaodong county, Jiagedaqi district (in the Daxinganling area).

Jiangsu
Nanjing city, Suzhou city, Wuxi city, Liangyungang city, Nantong city, Changzhou city, Yangzhou city, Zhenjiang city, Xuzhou city, Huaiyin city, Yiancheng city.

Zhejiang
Hangzhou city, Ningbo city, Shaoxing city, Wenzhou city, Jiaxing city, Huzhou city, Jinhua city, Jiaojiang city, Putuo county (Putuo Mountain Scenic Spot), Quzhou city, Lishui city, Tiantai county, Qingtian county, Jinyun county.

Anhui
Hefei city, Wuhu city, Huangshan city, Bengbu city, Tunxi city, Ma'anshan city, Anqing city, Huainan city, Huaibei city, Chuzhou city, Chaohu city, Shexian county, Fengyang county, Jingxian county, Fuyang city, Suzhou city, Liu'an city, Bozhou city, Fuyang county, Jiuhuashan Mountain Scenic Spot.

Fujian
Fuzhou city, Xiamen city, Quanzhou city, Zhangzhou city, Chong'an county, Putian city.

Jiangxi
Nanchang city, Jiujiang city, Jingdezhen city, Yingtan city, Jinggangshan city, Ganzhou city, Pingxiang city, Xinyu city, Yichun city, Fuzhou city, Ji'an city, Wuyuan county, Dexing county, Yiyang county, Qianshan county, Nanfeng county, Chongren county, Le'an county, Yihuang county, Ji'an county, Ganxian county, Quannan county, Xunwu county, Wanzai county, Shanggao county, Yifeng county, Fengxin county.

Shandong
Jinan city, Qingdao city, Yantai city, Tai'an city, Weifang city, Zibo city, Jining city, Zaozhuang city, Dongying city, Rizhao city, Dezhou city, Linyi city, Weihai city.

Henan
Zhengzhou city, Kaifeng city, Luoyang city, Anyang city, Xinxiang city, Xinyang city, Nanyang city, Puyang city, Pingdingshan city, Wenxian county, Sanmenxia city, Jiaozuo city, Hebi city, Shangqiu city, Xuchang city, Zhumadian city, Zhoukou city, Luohe city.

Hubei
Wuhan city, Yichang city, Shashi city, Xiangfan city, Xianning city, Danjiangkou city, Huangshi city, Jinmen city, Ezhou city, Shiyan city, Jiangling county, Puqi city, Huanggang county, Honghu county, Jianli county.

Hunan

Changsha city, Hengyang city, Yueyang city, Xiangtan city, Zhuzhou city, Changde city, Jinshi city, Yiyang city, Chenzhou city, Zixing city, Jishou city, Dayong city, Shaogyang city, Loudi city, Lengshuijiang city, Yongzhou city, Lengshuitan city, Taoyuan county, Linli county, Lixian county, Anxiang county, Hanshou county, Nanxian county, Taojiang county, Yunjiang county, Chenxian county, Anren county, Yongxing county, Guiyang county, Rucheng county, Sangzhi county, Fenghuang county, Yongshun county, Lianyuan county, Yuanling county, Zhijiang county, Xupu county, Dongan county, Qiyang county, Changde county, Xinhuang Dong Autonomous county, Jianghua Yao Autonomous county, Yizhang county, Guidong county.

Guangdong

Guangzhou city, Fushan city, Zhaoqing city, Shenzhen city, Zhuhai city, Shantou city, Haikou city, Zhanjiang city, Zhongshan city, Jiangmen city, Shaoguan city, Maoming city, Huizhou city, Chaozhou city, Sanya city, Meixian city, Dongguan city, Gaoyao county, Qiongshan county, Dingan county, Qionghai county, Wanning county, Tunchang county, Chengmai county, Lingao county, Danxian county, Wenchang county, Baoting county, Baisha county, Qiongzhong county, Lingshui county, Ledong county, Dongfang county, Changjiang county, Xingning county, Huiyang county, Boluo county, Heyuan county, Lufeng county, Haifeng county, Huidong county, Xinxing county, Yunfu county, Sihui county, Fengka county, Deqing county.

Guangxi

Nanning city, Guilin city, Beihai city, Liuzhou city, Wuzhou city, Binyan county, Guiping county, Rongxian county, Guixian county, Beiliu county, Xingan county, Luchuan county, Yulin city, Qinzhou city, Longan county, Hepu county, Linshan county, Rongshui Miao Autonomous County, Sanjiang Dong Autonomous County, Jinxiu Yao Autonomous County, Longsheng county.

Sichuan

Chengdu city, Chongqing city, Leshan city, Wanxian city, Yunyang county, Fengjie county, Wushan county, Zhongxian county, Zigong city, Dukou city, Luzhou city, Deyang city, Mianyang city, Guangyuan city, Neijiang city, Fuling city, Yibin city, Nanchong city, Xichang city, Wuxi city, Fengdu county, Jiangan county, Changning county, Gongxian county, Xingwen county, Songpan county, Ma'erkang county, Nanping county, Maowen Qiang Autonomous county.

Guizhou

Guiyang city, Anshun city, Zunyi city, Kaili city, Liupanshui city, Shibing city, Qingzhen county, Zhenyuan county, Huangguoshu Scenic Spot (great water fall).

Yunnan

Kunming city, Dali city, Yuxi city, Chuxiong city, Qujing city, Tonghai county, Jinghong county, Menghai county, Simao county, Lijiang Naxi Autonomous County.

Xizang (Tibet)

Lhasa city, Rikaze county (Rikaze town), Naqu county (Naqu town), Naidong county (Zedang town), Nielamu county (Zhangmu district).

Shaanxi

Xi'an city, Xianyang city, Yanan city, Baoji city, Hancheng city, Tongchuan city, Hanzhong city, Huayin county, Pucheng county, Huangling county, Nanzheng county, Mianxian county, Liuba county, Lüeyang county.

Gansu

Lanzhou city, Baiyin city, Jiayuguan city, Tianshui city, Linxia city, Yongjing county, Dunhuang city, Xiahe county, Jinchang city, Yumen city, Zhangye city, Wuwei city, Pingliang city, Xifeng city, Minqin county, Qingyang county, Minxian county, Wudu county, Dangchang county, Chengxian county, Wenxian county, Diebu county, Zhouqu county, Anxi county, Jiuquan city.

Qinghai

Xining city, Huangzhong county (Ta'ersi), Ge'ermu city, Gonghe county, Gangcha county (Qinghai Lake Birds Island).

Ningxia

Yinchuan city, Zhongwei county, Wuzhong city, Qingtongxia city, Lingwu county, Yanchi county, Zhongning county, Pingluo county, Tongxin county, Guyuan county, Xiji county, Haiyuan county.

Xinjiang

Ürümqi city, Shihezi city, Turpan city, Kashi city, Hami city, Ku'erle city, Akesu city, Atushi city, Changji city.

Ports of Entry and Exit

Airports

Beijing, Hongqiao (Shanghai), Zhangguizhuang (Tianjin), Harbin, Shenyang, Zhousuizi (Dalian), Xi'an, Kunming, Ürümqi, Nanning, Guilin, Chengdu, Nanjing, Hangzhou, Gaoqi (Xiamen), Yixu (Fuzhou), Baiyun (Guangzhou), Haikou.

Seaports

Shanghai (including the docks of Baoshan and Shihua)
Tianjin
Liaoning: Dalian (including the new harbour), Yingkou
Hebei: Qinhuangdao
Shandong: Qingdao (including Huangdao), Yantai, Shijiu, Weihai, Huangxian, Longkou
Jiangsu: Nanjing, Lianyungang, Nantong, Zhangjiagang
Zhejiang: Ningbo, Wenzhou

Fujian: Fuzhou, Xiamen, Quangzhou
Guangdong: Guangzhou (including Zhoutouzui), Huangpu (including Fangcun), Shantou, Shanwei, Haikou, Zhanjiang (including Xiahai, Nanyou Dock), Shekou (including Zhiwan), Huiyang Aotou, Taiping, Basuo, Kaiping, Sanfu, Sanya, Zhuhai, Jiuzhou, Zhongshan, Jiangmen, Zhaoqing, Panyu, Lianhuashan, Taishan, Guanghai, Shenzhen Dayia Wan, Shenzhen Meisha
Guangxi: Beihai, Fangchen, Wuzhou

By Land

Liaoning: Dendong
Jilin: Tumen
Inner Mongolia: Manzhouli, Erlan
Tibet: Nielamu
Xinjiang: Hongqilapu
Guangdong: Shengzhen Luohu, Shenzhen Wenjindu, Shenzhen Shatoujiao, Zhuhai Gongbei, Guangzhou (railway station)

APPLYING FOR A VISA; CUSTOMS REGULATIONS

Visa Application

FOREIGNERS wishing to travel to China must hold valid visas issued by Chinese diplomatic missions or consulates, or any other offices stationed in foreign countries which are authorized by the Chinese Ministry of Foreign Affairs.

Tourists who are to be received by LÜXINGSHE may apply for confirmation from the Head Office of LÜXINGSHE or through foreign travel agencies which have business relations with LÜXINGSHE. With the letter or cable confirmation by LÜXINGSHE, the applicant may apply for visas for China through the above-mentioned Chinese offices situated in foreign countries. Individual tourists travelling to China in non-peak seasons may apply for visas directly through the above-mentioned Chinese offices. Those who are in Hong Kong may apply for visas to the Visa Office of the Ministry of Foreign Affairs of the People's Republic of China in Hong Kong (address: 26 Harbour Road, Wanchai, Hong Kong) or ask LÜXINGSHE (International) Hong Kong Ltd. to apply for a visa on their behalf.

The length of validity of a visa is generally the tourist's duration of stay in China. In case of a need to extend the period of stay, an application must be filed prior to the expiration of the visa in the entry and exit office of the public security authorities.

Foreigners who have been approved to visit China may choose an itinerary prepared by LÜXINGSHE. A special permit is needed for travel to any of the non-open cities. Travel permits can be obtained through application at the entry and exit office of the local public security bureau by tourists themselves upon their arrival in China or by LÜXINGSHE on their behalf.

Importation of the following articles is prohibited

1. Arms, ammunition and explosives of all kinds.
2. All counterfeits of currencies and securities.
3. Manuscripts, printed matter, films, photographs, gramophone records, cinematographic films, loaded recording tapes and video-tapes, compact disks and data media for computers etc. detrimental to Chinese political, economic, cultural or moral interests.
4. Deadly poisons of all sorts.
5. Opium, morphia, heroin, marijuana and other habit-forming drugs.
6. Animals, plants and products thereof infected with or carrying disease germs and insect pests.
7. Foodstuffs, medicine, etc. coming from infected areas, carrying germs, or being unhealthy to human-beings and animals.
8. Renminbi (with the exception of those according to monetary agreement; foreign exchange certificates refer to the regulations concerned).

Exportation of the following articles is prohibited

1. All articles prohibited for import into China;
2. Manuscripts, printed matter, films, photographs, gramophone records, cinematographic films, loaded recording tapes and video-tapes, compact disks and data media for computers etc. which contain state secrets.
3. Valuable cultural relics and other relics prohibited for export.
4. Rare animals, rare plants and those in danger of extinction (including specimens and seeds or reproducible material).

Customs Regulations for Foreign Tourists

(1) Foreign visitors on entering into China shall fill in a "Baggage Declaration Form for Inward Passengers" and submit it to the Customs for inspection.

(2) Foreign visitors may bring in duty-free personal belongings in reasonable quantity for personal use during the journey, including two bottles of wine (not more than 750 g for each) and 400 cigarettes. Wristwatches, recorders, cameras, cine-cameras and video-cameras may be allowed in by the Customs with a registration provided that they are to be taken out of the country when the visitors leave China.

(3) Foreign visitors are not allowed to carry any articles into or out of China on behalf of others.

(4) Invoices bearing the stamp of "Bought with Foreign Currency" for the purchase of jewellery, jade, gold and silver ornaments, works of arts, handicrafts, calligraphy, etc. at such shops as the Friendship Stores or Antique Shops in China should be kept by foreign visitors for the Customs inspection on exit.

(5) Foreign visitors shall present to the Customs at the time of exit a certificate issued by the authorities in charge of cultural relics for export of cultural relics (including ancient books, paintings or calligraphy). Without the above-mentioned certificates, no cultural relics shall be taken out of China.

RMB, arms and ammunition, narcotics, deadly poisons and radio transmitter-receivers are prohibited to be carried into and out of China.

Customs Regulations of the People's Republic of China Governing Control over Outward Cultural Relics Carried or Shipped by Passengers and Posted by Individuals

Enacted by the Customs General Administration of the People's Republic of China and effective as of 15 February 1985.

(1) The present Regulations are enacted in accordance with Articles 2.27 and 28 of the "Cultural Relics Preservation Act of the People's Republic of China".

(2) Outward cultural relics (including products by late modern famous painters and calligraphers) which are carried or shipped by passengers and posted by individuals shall be declared to the Customs. The Customs shall examine and release them against the verifying marks affixed to them and invoices for selling cultural relics abroad, or against the export certificates issued by the cultural administrative departments designated by the Ministry of Culture.

(3) Any cases in which the cultural relics are carried, shipped or posted abroad without being declared to the Customs, whether concealed or not, shall be treated as smuggling. The Customs shall deal with them in accordance with the relevant regulations.

(4) Cultural relics which have been declared to the Customs without submitting for Customs examination Export Certificates for Cultural Relics and affixed verifying marks given by the cultural administrative departments or invoices for selling cultural relics abroad shall not be permitted for export but returned. They shall be taken back by the involved person or his or her agent within three months (or within one month for passengers coming from and going to Hong Kong or Macao); if not, they shall be dealt with by the Customs in accordance with the relevant regulations.

(5) The present Regulations shall enter into force on 15 February 1985.

CURRENCY REGULATIONS

Chinese Currency

THE Chinese currency is called Renminbi and is issued by the People's Bank of China. The principal unit of Renminbi is *yuan* and the sub-units are *jiao* and *fen*. A yuan is made up of 10 jiao while a jiao is equal to 10 fen. Yuan notes are in denominations of 1, 2, 5, 10, 50 and 100 yuan; jiao notes are in denominations of 1, 2 and 5 jiao, and fen, either in the form of notes or coins, are in denominations of 1, 2 and 5 fen. The symbol for Renminbi yuan is ¥. For instance, the amount of one thousand two hundred and thirty-four yuan five jiao and six fen is expressed as ¥ 1,234.56.

Sets for numismatists

With a view to promoting the economic and cultural exchange between China and other countries, enhancing friendship among peoples the world and meeting the requirements of those, both Chinese and foreigners, who have the hobby of collecting currencies, the China Mint Company has issued two sets of Renminbi banknotes and coins currently in circulation. One of them contains the Renminbi banknotes

in ten denominations: 10-yuan, 5-yuan, 2-yuan and 1-yuan; 5-jiao, 2-jiao and 1-jiao; and 5-fen, 2-fen and 1-fen, and the other set includes the Renminbi coins in seven denominations: 1-yuan, 5-jiao, 2-jiao, 1-jiao, 5-fen, 2-fen and 1-fen. They are presented in beautifully designed and exquisitely decorated albums, available at the Bank of China and its branches in hotels and guest houses in Beijing, Shanghai, Xi'an, Nanjing, Hangzhou, Kunming, Xiamen, Shenyang, Dalian, etc. Both the banknote album and coin album are a must for connoisseurs and hobbyists and also can be taken as precious gifts for relatives and friends.

Foreign Exchange Certificates and Renminbi Travellers Cheques

Foreign Exchange Certificates

Foreign Exchange Certificates, equal to Renminbi in value, are issued by the Bank of China for foreign visitors, overseas Chinese and Chinese compatriots from Hong Kong and Macao on short visits to China, and diplomatic corps and foreign representative offices and their permanent staff to make payments in place of foreign currencies, or to make purchases in the designated stores where only Foreign Exchange Certificates are accepted. They are issued in seven denominations, ranging from 100-yuan, 50-yuan, 10-yuan, 5-yuan, 1-yuan to 5-jiao and 1-jiao.

Renminbi Travellers Cheques

For the convenience of travellers from abroad, Renminbi travellers cheques are sold at the Bank of China branches in China and in London, Singapore, Luxembourg and Hong Kong. The Renminbi travellers cheques are in two denominations of 50-yuan and 100-yuan, valid for six months from the date they are bought in. Foreign travellers may convert them into Foreign Exchange Certificates or Renminbi at the Bank of China and its foreign exchange counters in various cities in China, and make payments direct in Renminbi travellers cheques at the designated stores where Foreign Exchange Certificates are accepted.

Conversion of Foreign Currencies

1. Rules governing the carrying of foreign currencies and payment instruments in convertible currencies into/out of China

No limit is imposed on the amount of foreign currencies and payment instruments brought into China by travellers from abroad, but they must be declared to Chinese customs at the point of entry. The circulation and unauthorized sales or purchases of foreign exchange among individuals in China are prohibited. In case of need, the travellers must convert their foreign currencies and payment instruments in convertible currencies into Renminbi at the Bank of China and its exchange counters at the official rate quoted on the day of conversion. An exchange memo valid for 6 months will be issued to the travellers after conversion.

Renminbi is prohibited to be taken out of or brought into China. Against the valid exchange memo the travellers may reconvert the remaining Renminbi or foreign exchange certificates before leaving China. However, foreign exchange certificates are permitted to be taken out of China.

2. Foreign banknotes which are acceptable and convertible in China

Foreign banknotes of the following 18 countries and regions can be converted into Renminbi or foreign exchange certificates: Australian dollar ($A), Austrian Schilling (Sch), Belgian franc (BF), Canadian dollar ($Can), Danish krone (DKr), Dutch guilder (Fl), French franc (FF), West German Mark (DM), Hong Kong dollars ($HK), Japanese yen (¥), Malaysian Ringgit ($M), Norwegian Krone (NKr), Pound Sterling (£), Singapore dollar ($S), Swedish Krona (SKr.), Swiss franc (SF), and US dollar ($US).

3. Travellers cheques of issuers who have previously agreed paying arrangements with the Bank of China are widely acceptable and encashable. There are almost 600 locations throughout China where travellers cheques in international currencies are accepted. Most hotels, Friendship Stores and tourist locations are included in this list. Travellers cheques from the leading institutions are recommended. Refunds for these companies can be arranged by contacting any branch of the Bank of China.

4. Credit cards which are acceptable in China

At present, the following credit cards are acceptable in China: Federal Card, Visa, Mastercard, American Express Card, Million Card, JCB Card and Diners. Cardholders may present their credit cards for cash advances at the Bank of China and its foreign exchange counters, or make payments by presenting their credit cards to the designated agents. Credit cards are legal; they enjoy less acceptance than travellers cheques but may be presented in Bank of China branches where cash advances are obtainable. Some direct acceptance in Friendship Stores has just commenced, but this is limited to major cities only.

5. Payment instruments in convertible currencies which are payable in China

A. Renminbi Travellers Letters of Credit bought with foreign currencies, drafts and other payment instruments in convertible currencies issued by the Bank of China branches in London, New York, Singapore, Luxembourg and Hong Kong and the banks maintaining accounts in convertible Renminbi with the Banking Department, Bank of China, Head Office.

B. Other payment instruments in convertible currencies are payable in China. Although these are less popular, arrangements can be made with the Bank of China. It is, however, recommended that the acceptability in China of such instruments be checked in advance of purchasing to avoid possible disappointment.

FLYING TO CHINA

Timetable

CIVIL Aviation Administration of China (CAAC) flight schedules are arranged according to the time-table published by CAAC, but if the occasion requires, CAAC may change flights, schedules, stopover points or aircraft without prior notice.

Reservations

Passengers can reserve their seats in advance at CAAC booking offices or CAAC booking agents according to CAAC regulations. Domestic passengers having reserved their seats should purchase their tickets at the appointed time or not later than 12 o'clock noon the day before the flight, after which time their reservations will automatically be cancelled. The ticket for which a seat has been reserved is valid for the flight, date and route specified on the flight coupon. If domestic flight group-passengers cancel or change their reservations, CAAC will collect a service charge according to relevant regulations.

Reconfirmation of Reservations

Domestic route passengers having reserved seats on connecting or return flights should reconfirm their reservations not later than 12 o'clock noon the day before the date of flight, otherwise their reservations will automatically be cancelled. Passengers holding open-date tickets must reserve their seats before taking a flight. This kind of ticket has no priority in reservation. International route passengers having reserved their seats on connecting or return flights should reconfirm their reservations at the connecting or return point not later than 72 hours before the connecting or return flights, if they stay at such points for more than 72 hours. Failure to make such reconfirmation will result in the cancellation of the space reserved. International passengers staying at the connecting or return points less than 72 hours do not have to reconfirm their reservations. This provision does not apply to travel wholly within Europe.

Tickets

Any ticket is valid only for the passenger whose name is on the ticket and is not transferable. The ticket will be void if it has been mutilated or altered. Domestic passengers buying tickets must hold valid certification and identity cards. Foreign passengers, overseas Chinese passengers and Xianggang (Hong Kong) and Macao compatriots must hold valid travel documents.

Validity Periods of Tickets

The validity period of the domestic route ticket is 90 days. The international route ticket is valid for one year from the date of commencing the travel. The validity period for the special fare ticket will be fixed according to CAAC regulations governing special fare tickets.

Fares

Fares are one-way fares from the airports of origin to the airports of destination, not including ground transportation fares between airports and town centres. For information about domestic, international and regional fares and rates, enquire at the nearest CAAC Booking Office or CAAC Representative Office or CAAC agent.

Children's Fares

A child under 8 years of age must travel in the company of an adult passenger. An infant under 2 years of age not occupying a separate seat and accompanied by an adult passenger is charged at 10% of the adult fare.

Infants under 2 years of age in excess of one accompanied by an adult passenger and children between 2 and 12 years of age are charged at 50% of the adult fare and may occupy separate seats. Children 12 years of age or over will be charged the adult fare.

Health

Passengers suffering from serious illness must hold a certificate issued by a medical unit certifying their fitness to travel by air, and require approval by CAAC before they can buy their tickets.

Check-in Procedure

Passengers must arrive at the designated airport at the designated time. Domestic passengers should produce their identity cards and tickets for check-in procedure. International passengers should produce their tickets and travel documents for exit and check-in procedures. If passengers fail to arrive at the airport at the designated time or if their travel documents do not conform with regulations, resulting in their not being able to complete the necessary exit and check-in procedures, any loss or responsibility will be borne by the passengers themselves.

Airport Fee

Each international passenger of Chinese or foreign nationality leaving the territory of China from any international airport in China, whether such passenger travels by CAAC or foreign air service, is required to pay an airport fee of RMB 5 yuan before departure. Diplomats holding diplomatic passports, transit passengers stopping at the transit point within 24 hours and children under 12 years of age will be exempt from the airport fee.

Changes

If a passenger having purchased a domestic ticket wishes to change the flight, date or route specified in his ticket, he should return his original ticket and purchase a new ticket. If he wishes to change the passenger, he should produce a letter from the original unit testifying the matter, and such change is allowed only once. If he wants to make another change of passenger, the matter will be treated as refund. If a passenger holding an international ticket wishes to make any such change, CAAC international passenger traffic regulations will apply.

Cancellation and Refund

Domestic Ticket If owing to CAAC's reason the passenger asks for refund of his ticket, full refund will be made. If owing to the passenger's reason, the passenger asks for refund, the following cancellation fees will apply:
(1) If the passenger asks for refund 24 hours before flight departure, the cancellation fee is 10% of the original fare.
(2) If the passenger asks for refund between 24 hours and 2 hours before flight departure time, the cancellation fee is 20% of the original fare.
(3) If the passenger asks for refund within 2 hours before flight departure, the cancellation fee is 50% of the original fare.
Infant passengers are not subject to the cancellation fee.
International Ticket If either owing to CAAC's or the passenger's own reason, the passenger is unable to take the flight specified in his ticket, refund will be made according to CAAC refund regulations, but the passenger should complete the refund procedure

within 30 days after the validity period of his ticket. Such a refund can only be made at the place where the ticket was bought or at a place approved by CAAC.

Non-Appearance

If a passenger holding a domestic ticket fails to appear for departure, his ticket will be regarded as void and no refund will be made.

Safety Inspection

According to government regulations, CAAC stations have the right to inspect a passenger's person and baggage. If any passenger or his baggage is found during inspection to be a danger to safety, CAAC will behave according to relevant government regulations. If any passenger refuses to be inspected, CAAC will not allow him to take his flight.

Baggage

(A) Free baggage allowance in weight

The free baggage allowances for each published adult-fare or half-fare passenger are as follows:
Domestic service

Published fare	First class	30 kg
	Economy	20 kg
Discounted fare	First class	20 kg
	Economy class	15 kg

International service

First class	30 kg (66 lbs.)
Economy class	20 kg (44 lbs.)

No free baggage allowance is granted to infants paying 10% of the adult fare.

(B) Free baggage allowance by piece

Free baggage allowance by piece is applicable only to CHINA – USA flights. According to the class of ticket, the free baggage allowance for each full-fare or half-fare passenger is two pieces, the sum of the length, width and height of each piece must not exceed 158 cm (62 in.), and the weight of each piece must not exceed 32 kg, but for each economy-class passenger, including discounted tourist-class tickets, the sum of the length, width and height of the two pieces of baggage must not exceed 273 cm (107 in.).

Aside from the above free baggage allowance, each international passenger may carry one piece or several pieces of free hand baggage, the total length, width and height of which shall not exceed 115 cm (45 in.)

Baggage in excess of the free baggage allowance in pieces, or if the sum of the length, width and height of each piece exceeds 203 cm (80 in.), or if the weight of each piece exceeds 32 kg, may be shipped as baggage only upon approval by CAAC and excess baggage charge should be paid.

An infant paying 10% of the adult fare is allowed one piece or two pieces of hand baggage, the total length, width and height of which must not exceed 115 cm. In addition, it is also allowed a collapsible perambulator, to be carried free.

Baggage Compensation

In the event of any passenger travelling on CAAC domestic service suffering loss of or damage to his checked baggage, compensation will be made by CAAC according to the actual value of the checked baggage, but the amount of compensation shall not exceed RMB 10 yuan per kg and the baggage charge already paid will be refunded. Passengers are advised not to pack in their checked baggage such valuable articles as cash, negotiable securities, pearls, jewellery, gold and silver articles as well as fragile articles, since CAAC will not be liable to compensate for the loss of or damage to such articles in their checked baggage.

Baggage Declared Value

A passenger travelling on a CAAC domestic service may declare the value of his checked-baggage. If the value exceeds 10 yuan per kg, CAAC will collect a declared value surcharge at 0.5% of the value exceeding the free baggage value. If such baggage is lost or damaged, compensation will be made according to its declared value.

Hand Baggage

Each domestic flight passenger may carry in his own custody articles which are required for use en route or which need his personal care, but such articles are limited to 5 kg and the volume of each piece may not be more than $20 \times 30 \times 50$ cm³. Hand baggage in excess of the limit must be shipped as checked baggage or cargo according to regulations. Each international passenger may carry in his own custody the following articles without charge:

A lady's handbag, an overcoat or a raincoat or a travelling blanket, an umbrella or a walking stick, a small camera, small binoculars, a small amount of reading material for the trip, infants' food for consumption en route, an infant's carrying basket, a fully collapsible invalid chair or a pair of braces or artificial limbs.

Articles which Cannot be Shipped as Baggage

Passengers are not allowed to carry in their checked baggage or hand baggage dangerous articles, such as inflammables, explosives, corrosive, poisonous, radioactive, polymerizable, magnetized materials and other dangerous articles. Passengers are not allowed to carry in their checked baggage or hand baggage articles which the law, orders or regulations of the People's Republic of China or the countries en route prohibit for export or import or transit through their countries. Passengers are not allowed carry arms or sharp or lethal weapons on their person.

Meals and Hotel Accommodation

Meals for passengers during the flight will be catered free of charge by CAAC according to relevant regulations; meals served on the ground are at the expense of the passengers. At scheduled overnight stopovers, charges for hotel accommodation will be borne by passengers. If it is due to CAAC's reason that passengers have to stay overnight at a scheduled stopover, hotel accommodation will be arranged by CAAC free of charge.

Meals and hotel accommodation for passengers holding international tickets with confirmed space on connecting flights will be arranged at the connecting point by CAAC according to regulations.

CLIMATE AND CLOTHING

MOST of China's territories lie in the North Temperate Zone, with four distinct seasons. The climate is suitable for travelling all the year round, but as China is a vast country, it varies greatly from place to place. On the whole, it is temperate and humid in the southeast and South China, and rather dry in the north and the north-east.

In spring (March – May) and autumn (September – November) light clothes (such as jackets and woollen sweaters) are appropriate in most of the areas. In summer, a shirt or blouse is enough. A heavy woollen overcoat is needed outdoors in winter. A raincoat will come in handy at the turn of spring and summer and that of summer and autumn, when rainfall is frequent.

Based on weather observations, Chinese climatologists determine that if the mean temperature of every five days is higher than 22 degrees C., it is summer; lower than 10 degrees C., winter; somewhere between 10 and 22 degrees C., spring or autumn. The four seasons of different areas listed below are calculated by the above standards. The summer and autumn records of Kunming are lacking. This shows that autumn in Kunming comes immediately on spring's heel, with no summer throughout the year. The records of spring and winter are lacking for Guangzhou. That means when summer is over, autumn and spring are connected, with no winter at all. The rest may be inferred by analogy.

Table 3: The Four Seasons

City	Spring			Summer			Autumn			Winter		
	First date	Last date	Total days	First date	Last date	Total days	First date	Last date	Total days	First date	Last date	Total days
Harbin	26/4	25/6	61	26/6	15/8	51	16/8	10/10	56	11/10	25/4	197
Shenyang	21/4	15/6	56	16/6	31/8	77	1/9	20/10	50	21/10	20/4	182
Dalian	16/4	25/6	71	26/6	5/9	72	6/9	5/11	61	6/11	15/4	161
Hohhot	26/4	15/7	81	16/7	25/7	10	26/7	30/9	67	1/10	25/4	207
Taiyuan	21/4	10/6	51	11/6	20/8	71	21/8	20/10	61	21/10	20/4	182
Beijing	1/4	25/5	55	26/5	5/9	103	6/9	25/10	50	26/10	31/3	157
Qingdao	11/4	5/7	86	6/7	15/9	72	16/9	15/11	61	16/11	10/4	146
Jinan	26/3	15/5	51	16/5	20/9	128	21/9	15/11	56	16/11	25/3	130
Nanjing	21/3	25/5	66	26/5	20/9	118	21/9	20/11	61	21/11	20/3	120
Shanghai	26/3	5/6	72	6/6	25/9	112	26/9	25/11	61	26/11	25/3	120
Hangzhou	21/3	25/5	66	26/5	30/9	126	1/10	30/11	61	1/12	20/3	110
Wuhan	16/3	15/5	61	16/5	30/9	138	1/10	30/11	61	1/12	15/3	105
Changsha	6/3	10/5	66	11/5	30/9	143	1/10	30/11	61	1/12	5/3	95
Chongqing	21/2	5/5	74	6/5	30/9	148	1/10	5/12	66	6/12	20/2	77
Chengdu	26/2	10/5	74	11/5	15/9	128	16/9	30/11	76	1/12	25/2	87
Kunming	1/2	10/12	313							11/12	31/1	52
Guangzhou				21/4	5/11	199	6/11	20/4	166			
Guilin	21/2	30/4	69	1/5	20/10	173	21/10	5/1	77	6/1	20/2	46
Nanning				16/4	10/11	209	11/11	15/4	157			
Xi'an	21/3	25/5	66	26/5	5/9	103	6/9	10/11	66	11/11	20/3	130
Ürümqi	16/4	5/7	81	6/7	20/7	15	21/7	5/10	77	6/10	15/4	192

Table 4: Mean Monthly Temperatures (°C)

City	Jan	Feb	Mar	Apr	May	June	July	Aug	Sept	Oct	Nov	Dec
Harbin	−19.7	−15.4	−5.1	6.1	14.3	20.0	22.7	21.4	14.3	5.9	−5.8	−15.5
Dalian	−5.3	−3.5	1.8	8.9	15.5	19.3	22.9	24.1	20.0	13.8	5.6	−1.5
Hohhot	−13.5	−9.3	−0.4	7.7	15.2	20.0	21.8	19.9	13.8	6.5	−3.0	−11.4
Shenyang	−12.7	−8.6	−0.3	9.1	17.0	21.4	24.6	23.7	17.2	9.6	−0.3	−8.7
Tianjin	−4.2	−1.6	4.7	13.0	20.0	24.0	26.5	25.8	20.8	13.6	4.9	−1.7
Beijing	−4.7	−2.3	4.4	13.2	20.2	24.2	26.0	24.6	19.5	12.5	4.0	−2.8
Taiyuan	−7.0	−3.3	3.6	11.2	17.5	21.7	23.7	21.9	16.1	9.8	1.8	−5.1
Jinan	−1.7	0.9	7.3	15.1	21.9	26.3	27.6	26.3	21.7	15.8	7.8	0.8
Qingdao	−2.6	−0.5	4.6	10.9	16.7	20.9	24.7	25.4	20.5	14.3	7.4	0.5
Zhengzhou	−0.3	2.1	7.7	14.8	21.1	26.3	27.5	25.9	21.0	15.1	7.8	1.6
Nanjing	1.9	3.8	8.4	14.7	20.0	24.5	28.2	27.9	22.9	16.9	10.7	4.5
Wuxi	2.4	3.8	8.4	14.2	19.5	23.8	28.3	28.0	23.3	17.0	11.4	4.9
Suzhou	2.8	4.2	8.6	14.2	19.6	23.6	28.2	28.1	23.5	17.6	12.1	5.5
Shanghai	3.3	4.6	8.3	13.8	18.8	23.2	27.9	27.8	23.8	17.9	12.5	6.2
Hangzhou	3.6	5.0	9.2	15.1	20.3	24.3	28.7	28.2	23.5	17.4	12.1	6.1
Fuzhou	10.4	10.6	13.4	18.1	22.2	25.3	28.7	28.2	26.0	21.6	17.8	13.1
Nanchang	4.8	6.3	10.9	17.0	22.0	25.7	29.7	29.4	25.1	18.9	13.1	7.3
Wuhan	2.8	5.0	10.0	16.0	21.3	25.8	29.0	28.5	23.6	17.5	11.2	5.3
Changsha	4.6	6.2	10.9	16.7	21.7	26.0	29.5	28.9	24.5	18.2	12.5	7.0
Guangzhou	13.4	14.2	17.7	21.8	25.7	27.2	28.3	28.2	27.0	23.8	19.7	15.2
Guilin	8.0	9.0	13.1	18.4	23.1	26.2	28.3	27.8	25.8	20.7	15.2	10.1
Nanning	12.9	13.9	17.3	21.9	26.0	27.4	28.3	27.9	26.7	23.3	18.9	14.8
Chongqing	7.5	9.4	14.0	18.8	22.2	25.2	28.6	28.4	24.0	18.4	13.9	9.4
Chengdu	9.1	11.4	16.6	22.0	25.3	28.1	29.7	30.1	24.9	20.8	15.4	11.1
Kunming	7.8	9.8	13.2	16.7	19.3	19.5	19.9	19.2	17.6	15.0	11.5	8.3
Lhasa	−2.3	0.8	4.3	8.3	12.6	15.5	14.9	14.1	12.8	8.1	1.9	−1.9
Lanzhou	−7.3	−2.5	5.3	11.7	16.7	20.5	22.4	21.0	15.9	9.4	1.6	−5.7
Turpan	−9.5	−2.0	9.6	18.9	25.9	31.2	33.0	30.7	23.6	12.6	1.5	−7.2
Ürümqi	−15.2	−12.2	0.7	10.8	18.9	23.4	25.7	23.8	17.4	8.2	−2.6	−12.0

Table 5: Mean Monthly Precipitation (mm)

City	Jan	Feb	Mar	Apr	May	June	July	Aug	Sept	Oct	Nov	Dec	Total
Harbin	4.3	3.9	12.5	25.3	33.8	77.7	176.5	107.0	72.7	26.6	7.5	5.9	553.7
Dalian	7.3	8.6	12.9	35.4	41.2	81.8	188.5	143.1	68.0	36.3	24.2	8.7	656.0
Hohhot	2.4	6.1	10.1	19.9	28.4	46.2	104.4	136.9	40.4	24.1	5.9	1.4	426.2
Beijing	2.6	7.7	9.1	22.4	36.1	70.4	196.6	243.5	63.9	21.1	7.9	1.6	682.9
Taiyuan	2.9	5.3	9.9	25.7	37.0	46.5	124.6	99.3	65.8	32.4	14.8	2.3	466.5
Jinan	6.2	10.4	16.1	36.1	36.8	73.7	214.0	147.9	60.9	33.0	28.9	8.2	672.2
Qingdao	7.8	11.4	12.5	33.3	48.7	92.2	209.7	155.2	108.2	45.5	34.8	9.7	768.8
Zhengzhou	8.8	12.6	29.2	50.8	46.4	68.3	134.8	135.2	67.2	40.6	34.4	7.8	636.1
Nanjing	31.8	52.9	78.6	98.3	97.3	140.2	181.7	121.7	101.2	44.1	53.1	30.2	1031.1
Shanghai	44.3	63.0	80.5	111.1	129.3	156.6	142.4	116.0	145.9	46.8	54.3	39.2	1129.4
Hangzhou	64.3	84.4	116.7	130.4	185.8	191.6	131.6	135.5	183.0	67.0	61.2	49.1	1400.6
Fuzhou	52.6	79.9	121.4	136.2	210.0	223.5	118.5	142.2	155.3	31.0	28.8	28.7	1328.1
Nanchang	59.1	93.8	170.2	221.1	306.5	277.3	127.0	93.8	85.1	57.2	62.2	44.9	1598.2
Wuhan	35.5	60.5	104.5	144.4	161.2	218.0	119.0	133.4	80.6	53.2	56.6	33.5	1200.4
Changsha	53.1	87.2	152.3	199.2	244.5	184.5	123.2	106.3	69.3	84.8	69.9	48.1	1422.5
Guangzhou	39.1	62.5	91.5	158.5	267.2	299.0	219.6	225.3	204.4	52.0	41.9	19.6	1680.6
Guilin	55.6	76.0	133.8	279.7	318.7	316.2	224.0	167.2	65.7	97.3	83.1	56.4	1875.7
Nanning	40.0	41.6	62.8	84.0	183.1	241.3	180.0	203.5	109.6	66.6	43.5	24.9	1280.9
Chongqing	18.8	20.9	43.2	72.3	155.4	165.4	156.0	141.0	132.3	99.2	51.2	24.7	1081.1
Chengdu	5.0	11.4	21.8	51.1	88.3	119.4	228.9	265.8	113.5	47.9	16.5	6.4	976.0
Kunming	10.0	9.8	13.6	19.6	78.0	181.7	216.4	195.2	122.9	94.9	33.7	15.9	991.7
Lhasa	0.2	0.1	1.5	4.4	20.6	73.1	141.7	149.1	57.3	4.8	0.8	0.3	453.9
Xi'an	7.6	10.3	24.7	53.0	62.3	57.6	105.9	80.1	100.2	61.5	34.0	7.1	604.3
Lanzhou	1.4	1.8	7.4	19.0	40.0	33.0	59.3	85.6	51.0	26.9	4.9	1.5	331.8
Ürümqi	5.6	4.0	18.8	22.6	25.1	29.1	16.4	18.9	14.2	17.2	15.2	7.4	194.6
Turpan	1.0	0.1	1.7	0.4	0.6	3.6	2.5	3.7	0.9	0.5	0.5	1.1	16.6

FOREIGN AIRLINES IN BEIJING

Airline	Address	Telephone No.
AEROFLOT (USSR)	Diplomatic Apartments 5–53, Jianguomenwai	5323581
Air France	Diplomatic Apartments 12–71, Jianguomenwai	5323894
All Nippon Airways	Beijing Hotel	5125551
British Airways	Room 210, Noble Tower, Jianguomenwai	5122288–210
CAA (DPRK)	Embassy of the Democratic People's Republic of Korea, Ritan Bei Road, Jianguomenwai	5323981
Cathay Pacific	Jianguo Hotel	5003339
Ethiopian Airlines	Diplomatic Apartments 12–32, Jianguomenwai	5323285
IRANAIR	Diplomatic Apartments 12–65, Jianguomenwai	5323843
Iraqi Airways	Diplomatic Apartments 7–1–54, Jianguomenwai	5321379
Japan Airlines	Hotel Beijing-Toronto	5002221
LUFTHANSA	Great Wall Sheraton Hotel 338–340,	5002626
North-West Airlines	Room 101, Jianguo Hotel	5004334
Pakistan International Airline	Diplomatic Apartments 12–43, Jianguomenwai	5323975
Philippine Airlines	Diplomatic Apartments 12–53, Jianguomenwai	5323992
QANTAS	Hotel Beijing–Toronto	5002235
Romanian Airlines	Embassy of the Socialist Republic of Romania, Ritan Dong'er Road	5323552
Singapore Airlines	1/F International Building, Jianguomenwai	5004138
SWISSAIR	2/F Noble Tower, Jianguomenwai	5123555
Thai International Airways	Great Wall Sheraton Hotel 343	5001978
United Airlines	2/F Noble Tower, Jianguomenwai	5128888

DISTANCES IN CHINA

Distance Between Main Tourist Cities
(Shortest distance between cities by rail in kilometres)

	Beijing	Shanghai	Tianjin	Guangzhou	Nanning	Changsha	Shaoshan	Wuchang	Nanjing	Wuxi	Suzhou	Hangzhou	Jinan	Qingdao	Xi'an	Kunming	Chengdu	Chongqing	Zhengzhou	Shijiazhuang	Dalian	Shenyang	Changchun	Harbin
Beijing	Beijing																							
Shanghai	1462	Shanghai																						
Tianjin	137	1325	Tianjin																					
Guangzhou	2313	1811	2450	Guangzhou																				
Nanning	2565	2063	2702	1334	Nanning																			
Changsha	1587	1187	1724	726	978	Changsha																		
Shaoshan	1718	1216	1855	755	1007	131	Shaoshan																	
Wuchang	1229	1534	1366	1084	1336	358	489	Wuchang																
Nanjing	1157	305	1020	2116	2368	1492	1521	1229	Nanjing															
Wuxi	1334	128	1197	1939	2191	1315	1344	1406	177	Wuxi														
Suzhou	1376	86	1239	1897	2149	1273	1302	1448	219	42	Suzhou													
Hangzhou	1651	189	1514	1622	1874	998	1027	1356	494	317	275	Hangzhou												
Jinan	494	968	357	2284	2536	1558	1689	1200	663	840	882	1157	Jinan											
Qingdao	887	1361	750	2677	2929	1951	2082	1593	1056	1233	1275	1550	393	Qingdao										
Xi'an	1165	1511	1302	2129	2381	1403	1534	1045	1206	1383	1425	1700	1177	1570	Xi'an									
Kunming	3179	2677	3316	2216	1501	1592	1503	1950	2982	2805	2763	2488	3119	3512	1942	Kunming								
Chengdu	2048	2353	2185	2544	1829	1920	1831	1887	2048	2225	2267	2542	2019	2412	842	1100	Chengdu							
Chongqing	2552	2501	2689	2040	1325	1416	1327	1774	2552	2729	2771	2312	2523	2916	1346	1102	504	Chongqing						
Zhengzhou	695	1000	832	1618	1870	892	1023	534	695	872	914	1189	666	1059	511	2453	1353	1857	Zhengzhou					
Shijiazhuang	283	1266	420	2030	2282	1304	1435	946	961	1138	1180	1455	298	691	923	2865	1765	2269	412	Shijiazhuang				
Dalian	1238	2426	1101	3551	3803	2825	2956	2467	2121	2298	2340	2615	1458	1851	2403	4417	3286	3790	1933	1521	Dalian			
Shenyang	841	2029	704	3154	3406	2428	2559	2070	1724	1901	1943	2218	1061	1454	2006	4020	2889	3393	1536	1124	397	Shenyang		
Changchun	1146	2334	1009	3459	3711	2733	2864	2375	2029	2206	2248	2523	1366	1759	2311	4325	3194	3698	1841	1429	702	305	Changchun	
Harbin	1388	2576	1251	3701	3953	2975	3106	2617	2271	2448	2490	2763	1608	2001	2553	4567	3436	3940	2083	1671	944	547	242	Harbin

CHINA TOURIST OFFICES

CHINA TOURIST OFFICE, FRANKFURT

Eschenheimer Anlage 28,
D-6000 Frankfurt A.M.1
Tel.: 069–555292, 069 5973412
Telex: 417 0360 FAC D

LÜXINGSHE (International), HONG KONG

6th Floor, Tower II,
South Seas Centre,
75 Mody Road,
Tsim Sha Tsui East,
Kowloon, Hong Kong
Tel.: 3–7215317 (6 lines)
Telex: 38449 CITS HX
Cable: 2320 Hong Kong

CHINA TOURIST OFFICE, LONDON

4 Glentworth Street,
London NW1
Tel.: 01–9359427/8/9; Dormitory: 429539
Telex: 291221 CTCLONG

CHINA TOURIST OFFICE, LOS ANGELES

303 W. Broadway, Suite 201,
CA 91204
Tel.: (818) 545–7505
Telex: 9102508906 TOLACN
Fax: (818) 545–7506

CHINA TOURIST OFFICE, NEW YORK

Suite 465, Lincoln Building,
60 East 42nd Street, NY 10165
Tel.: (212) 867–0271, (202) 564–8615
Telex: 662142 CITSNY
Cable: LUXINGSHE NEW YORK

OFFICE DE TOURISME DE CHINE, PARIS

51 Rue Saint-Anne,
75002 Paris
Tel.: 42969548, Dormitory 45254415
Telex: 612866 F OTCHINE

CHINA TOURIST OFFICE, SYDNEY

Floor 11, 55 Clarence Street,
Sydney, NSW 2000
Tel.: (02) 294057
Telex: AA 1778806 CHTOS

CHINA TOURIST OFFICE, TOKYO

6F Hanchidai Hamamatsu Cho Bl.,
1–27–13 Hamatsu-Cho,
Manato-Ku, Tokyo
Tel.: (03) 433–1461 (Office)
　　　(03) 452–6266 (Evening)
Fax: (03) 433–8653

PROCEDURES FOR ALIEN ENTRY INTO AND EXIT FROM THE PEOPLE'S REPUBLIC OF CHINA

(adopted at the Thirteenth Session of the Standing Committee of the Sixth National People's Congress on 22 November 1985); **Order of the President of the People's Republic of China (No. 31), Li Xiannian,** 22 November 1985 (unofficial translation)

The Procedures for Alien Entry into and Exit from the People's Republic of China, adopted by the Standing Committee of the Sixth National People's Congress at its Thirteenth Session on 22 November 1985, to take effect as of 1 February 1986, are hereby promulgated:

Chapter 1: GENERAL PROVISIONS

Article 1 The present procedures are formulated in order to safeguard the sovereignty and maintain the security and social order of the People's Republic of China and facilitate international exchange. They are applicable to aliens who desire to enter into, exit from and transit the territory of the People's Republic of China and to those who desire to reside and travel in China.

Article 2 Aliens must have prior permission from competent authorities of the Chinese Government to enter, transit and reside in China.

Article 3 For entry, exit and transit aliens must use

ports declared open to aliens or specially designated ports and accept inspection at border checkpoints. Alien means of transport must also proceed through ports declared open to aliens or through designated ports and accept inspection and supervision at border checkpoints.

Article 4 The Chinese Government protects the legitimate rights and interests of aliens on Chinese territory.

The personal freedom of aliens shall not be infringed, and without a warrant or decision by a people's procuracy or decision by a people's court and the execution of such a warrant or decision by a public security organ or state security organ aliens shall not be liable to arrest.

Article 5 Aliens in China must abide by Chinese law and not jeopardize the national security of China, harm public interest or undermine social order.

Chapter Two: ENTRY

Article 6 For entry into China, aliens shall apply for visas from Chinese diplomatic or consular missions or from other foreign-based agencies authorized by the Ministry of Foreign Affairs. In specific situations and in compliance with the stipulations of the State Council, aliens may also apply for visas from visa issuing agencies at ports designated by competent authorities of the Chinese Government.

The entry of nationals from countries having visa agreements with the Chinese Government shall be handled in accordance with the agreements.

In cases where another country has special regulations for the entry and transit of Chinese citizens, the competent authorities of the Chinese Government may assume similar measures contingent on the situation.

Aliens who transit China on international flights and spend no more than 24 hours entirely within airport boundaries do not need visas. Anyone desiring to leave the airport temporarily may obtain permission from border checkpoints.

Article 7 When applying for visas, aliens shall present valid passports and, if necessary, provide pertinent evidence.

Article 8 Aliens invited or hired to work in China shall, when applying for visas, produce evidence of invitation or hire.

Article 9 Aliens desiring to reside permanently in China shall, when applying for Chinese visas, present status-of-residence identification forms. Applicants may obtain such forms from public security organs at the intended place of residence.

Article 10 Competent authorities of the Chinese Government shall issue visas according to the particulars of alien application for entry into China.

Article 11 When aircraft or vessels navigating on international routes arrive in Chinese ports, the captain or his agent must submit a passenger list to border checkpoints; alien aircraft or vessels must also provide a list of crew members.

Article 12 Aliens considered a possible threat to China's national security and social order shall not be permitted to enter China.

Chapter Three: RESIDENCE

Article 13 For residence in China aliens must possess identification cards or residence certificates issued by competent authorities of the Chinese Government.

The term of validity of identification cards or residence certificates shall be decided according to the reasons for entry.

Aliens residing in China shall submit their certificates for examination to the local public security organs within the prescribed period of time.

Article 14 Aliens who, in compliance with Chinese law, desire to establish prolonged residence in China for the purpose of investing in China or engaging in co-operative projects with Chinese enterprises or government institutions in such fields as economy, science and technology, and culture as well as other undertakings may be eligible for prolonged or permanent residence in China upon approval by competent authorities of the Chinese Government.

Article 15 Aliens who seek political asylum shall be permitted to reside in China upon approval by competent authorities of the Chinese Government.

Article 16 Aliens who fail to abide by Chinese law may have their period of stay in China curtailed or their status of residence in China annulled by competent authorities of the Chinese Government.

Article 17 For a temporary overnight stay in China aliens shall be registered pursuant to stipulations.

Article 18 If aliens holding residence certificates desire to change their place of residence in China, they must undergo removal procedures pursuant to stipulations.

Article 19 Aliens who have not obtained residence certificates or are on a study programme in China shall not seek employment in China without permission of competent authorities of the Chinese Government.

Chapter Four: TRAVEL

Article 20 Aliens who hold valid visas or residence certificates may travel to places declared open to aliens by the Chinese Government.

Article 21 Aliens who desire to travel to places closed to aliens shall apply for travel permits from local public security organs.

Chapter Five: EXIT

Article 22 For exit from China, aliens shall present valid passports or other valid certificates.

Article 23 Aliens who fit one of the following cases shall not be permitted to exit China:

(1) A defendant in a criminal case or a criminal suspected of having committed a crime under the jurisdiction of a public security organ or people's procuracy or people's court.

(2) Anyone under notice from the people's court to be denied exit for an unsettled civil case.

(3) Anyone awaiting decision for other contravention of Chinese law, whose case is up for investigation by relevant competent authorities.

Article 24 Border checkpoints shall have the power to prohibit exit to aliens who come under one of the following conditions and to handle them according to law:

(1) Those who hold invalid exit certificates.

(2) Those who hold exit certificates other than their own.

(3) Those who hold forged or altered exit certificates.

Chapter Six: ADMINISTRATIVE ORGANS

Article 25 China's diplomatic and consular missions and other foreign-based agencies authorized by the Ministry of Foreign Affairs are the agents of the Chinese Government abroad to handle aliens' applications for entry and transit.

The Ministry of Public Security, departments in charge of exit and entry matters in local public security ogans authorized by the Ministry of Public Security, the Ministry of Foreign Affairs and local foreign affairs departments authorized by the Ministry of Foreign Affairs are agents of the Chinese Government in China to handle aliens' applications for entry, transit, residence and travel.

Article 26 The authorities handling aliens' applications for entry, transit, residence and travel shall have the power to refuse to issue visas and certificates or to cancel or annul visas and certificates already issued.

The Ministry of Public Security and the Ministry of Foreign Affairs may, if necessary, alter decisions made by their respective authorized agencies.

Article 27 Aliens who enter China illegally or establish illegal residence may be detained by public security organs above county level for examination or be subjected to supervised residence or deportation.

Article 28 Policemen in charge of foreign affairs at public security organs above county level shall have the power to examine aliens' passports and other certificates. When conducting such examination, the policemen in question shall produce their own work certificates, and the relevant organizations or individuals shall be under obligation to offer assistance.

Chapter Seven: PENALTIES

Article 29 Those who enter or exit China illegally, establish illegal residence or make an illegal stopover, travel to places closed to aliens without valid travel documents or forge, alter, misuse or negotiate entry or exit certificates in contravention of the provisions of the present procedures shall be subjected by public security organs above county level to such penalties as warning, fine or detention for less than ten days, and if violations are serious enough to form a criminal case, to criminal prosecution according to law.

If aliens being fined or detained by public security organs do not agree with the penalty, they may, within fifteen days of receiving the notice, appeal to the next higher public security organ, which shall make the final judgment; they may also file a suit directly in a local people's court.

Article 30 In cases where contravention of present procedures is serious, such as those listed in Article 29, the Ministry of Public Security may order those involved in such contravention to leave the country within a certain time limit or may expel them from the country.

Chapter Eight: ANCILLARY PROVISIONS

Article 31 The term "aliens" used in these procedures shall mean any person not having Chinese nationality, according to the Nationality Law of the People's Republic of China.

Article 32 Transitory entry into and exit from China by citizens of countries adjacent to China who reside in contiguous areas shall be handled pursuant to agreements between the two countries; if no such agreements exist, transitory entry and exit shall be handled in accordance with the stipulations of the Chinese Government.

Article 33 Rules for implementation of the present procedures shall be formulated by the Ministry of Public Security and the Ministry of Foreign Affairs and come into force upon approval by the State Council.

Article 34 After their entry into China, affairs of staff members of foreign diplomatic and consular missions to the People's Republic of China and of other aliens who enjoy diplomatic privileges and immunity shall be administered in accordance with the pertinent stipulations of the State Council and its competent authorities.

Article 35 These procedures shall take effect as of 1 February 1986.

16. PROSPECTS FOR THE NEXT TWO DECADES

THE Twelfth Congress of the Chinese Communist Party held in September 1982 approved the strategic objective, priorities and steps and a series of policies for China's economic construction for the next two decades.

The general objective of China's economic construction for the two decades between 1981 and the end of this century is, while steadily working for more and better economic results, to quadruple the gross annual value of industrial and agricultural production – from 710 billion yuan in 1980 to 2,800 billion yuan or so in 2000. This will place China in the front rank of the countries with major industrial and agricultural products; it will represent an important advance in the modernization of her entire national economy; it will increase the income of her urban and rural population several times over; and the Chinese people will be comparatively wealthy, both materially and culturally.

From an overall point of view, what is most important in the effort to realize this objective in economic growth is to properly solve the problems of agriculture, energy and transport and of education and science. Effective solution of these problems will lead to a fairly swift rise in the production of consumer goods, stimulate the development of industry as a whole and of production and construction in other fields and ensure a betterment of living standards.

In order to realize her objective for the next two decades, China must take the following two steps in strategic planning: in the first decade, aim mainly at laying a solid foundation, accumulating strength and creating the necessary conditions; and in the second, usher in a new period of vigorous economic development.

In accordance with this important political decision, in the later period of the Sixth-Five Year Plan the Chinese Government began to organize the departments and specialists concerned to draw up the Seventh Five-Year Plan (1986–1990).

Major Tasks and Strategic Steps for Economic Development in the Seventh Five-Year Plan

The guidelines of the Seventh Five-Year Plan are: in the first two years, to carry out the policies of consolidation, digestion, replenishment and improvement, while stabilizing the economy, and to balance economic relations so as to create conditions for further reforms and construction in the coming three years.

Principles and policies

The programme contained in the Seventh Five-Year Plan comprises a number of clear steps:

– Give priority to reform and make sure that reform and development are adapted to and promote each other;

– Keep a basic balance between total social demand and supply and maintain a balance within state finance, credits, materials and foreign exchange and a general balance among these different sectors;

– Give priority to improving economic results and especially the quality of products, and maintain a proper relation between economic results and growth rates and between quality and quantity;

– Further rationalize the industrial structure so as to keep pace with the people's changing patterns of demand and with the modernization of the national economy;

– Keep total investment in fixed assets within proper limits, rationalize investment patterns and accelerate the development of the energy, transport, telecommunications, and raw and semi-finished materials industries;

– Shift the emphasis of development to the technological transformation, renovation and expansion of existing enterprises and have them expand reproduction chiefly by internal means;

– Attach strategic importance to the advance of science and education, promote scientific and technological progress and speed up the development of intellectual resources;

– Open wider to the outside world and link the development of the domestic economy more closely with expanded economic and technological exchange with other countries;

– Further improve the material and cultural lives of both urban and rural residents on the basis of increased production and better economic results;

– Promote the cultural and ideological advance of socialist society while furthering its material progress;

– In all the efforts to build up the country, maintain the tradition of hard work and thrift.

Major tasks and strategies

These may be summarized under three aims:

– To create a favourable economic and social environment and maintain a basic balance between total social demand and supply, so as to facilitate the reform and to lay most of the groundwork for a new type of socialist economic structure with Chinese characteristics within the five years or a little longer.

– To maintain a steady growth of the economy and, while controlling the scale of investment in fixed assets, vigorously push forward the construction of key projects, the technological transformation of enterprises and the development of intellectual resources, so as to prepare the materials, technology and trained personnel required for continued economic and social development in the 1990s.

– To further raise the living standards of the people in town and country on the basis of increased production and better economic performance.

Of these three closely-interrelated tasks, the first is the most important. With a view to creating a sound environment for economic reforms and ensuring a steady growth of the economy, the economic growth rate and construction should be proportionate in order to avoid too much tension in economic life, while steps and measures to be taken in economic reforms should be concentrated on gaining all-round economic stability and a rise in economic performance.

The work of the Seventh Five-Year Plan period can be divided into two stages: the first two years constituting the first stage and the last three years the second. In the first stage, efforts in economic construction will be focused on reducing excessive investment in fixed assets and checking the precipitous rise in consumption funds, so as to strike a basic balance between total supply and demand. In economic structure reform, efforts will be made to enhance macro-economic control in order to stabilize the economy and at the same time to further invigorate the large and medium-sized state enterprises and to develop lateral economic ties among them. In the second stage, these tasks having been accomplished, China will push forward economic structural reform and step up production and construction to fulfil all the other tasks set forth by the Plan.

Objectives for Economic Development

Economic performance

The amount of energy required to produce each 10,000 yuan of national income will be reduced from the 1985 figure of 12.9 tons to 11.4 tons by 1990. National labour productivity is expected to rise by an average of 3.8 per cent annually. In state enterprises and institutions, the proportion of investment in fixed assets for capital construction projects which will go into operation will increase from 73.6 per cent in the period of the Sixth Five-Year Plan to 75 per cent in the period of the Seventh. The average turnover period for budgetary circulating funds of state-owned industrial enterprises will be shortened from 101 days in 1985 to 96 days in 1990. By the year 1990, 40 per cent of major industrial products are expected to measure up to international standards of the late 1970s and early 1980s in both quality and service. About 3,000 kinds of machinery products and 6,000 light industrial products will be manufactured.

National income

In 1990, national income will reach 935 billion yuan, an increase of 38 per cent over 1985, or an average annual increase of 6.7 per cent. In 1990, the amount of the national income spent (the amount produced plus the difference between import and export of foreign trade and expenditure on foreign aid) will top 952 billion yuan, an increase of 232.5 billion yuan, or an average annual increase of 46.5 billion yuan. The total amount of national income spent for the five years is set at 4,322 billion yuan. Total consumption funds for the five years are set at 3,007 billion yuan, the average annual rate of consumption being 70 per cent of national income. Total accumulation funds are set at 1,315 billion yuan, the average annual rate of accumulation being 30 per cent of national income.

Scale of investment in fixed assets

The fixed assets of state enterprises are to grow by more than 600 billion yuan in five years.

State finance

State revenues in 1990 are expected to come to 256.7 billion yuan, an increase of 71.3 billion yuan over 1985, or an average annual increase of 6.7 per cent. Total revenues for the five-year period are expected to be 1,119.4 billion yuan, an increase of 437.6 billion yuan or 64 per cent over the previous five-year period. Of the total revenues for the five years, domestic revenues will amount to 1,078.2 billion yuan and income from foreign loans to 41.2 billion yuan, the average proportion of state revenue in the national income in the five years being 26 per cent.

State expenditures in 1990 are expected to amount to 256.7 billion yuan. Total expenditures for the five-year period are expected to be 1,119.4 billion yuan; thus the budget will be balanced.

The major purposes of state expenditures will be as follows:

– The appropriations for capital construction in the five years will be 349.9 billion yuan, representing 31.3 per cent of the total state expenditure.

Table 1: Output of Major Products

	Unit	1990	Increase over 1985 (%)
Sugar	1,000 tons	5,500–6,000	33.6–34.8
Cigarettes	1,000 packets	26,000	10.6
Beer	1,000 tons	6,500	110
Drinks	1,000 tons	3,000	200
Chemical fabrics	1,000 tons	1,450	52.6
Yarn	1,000 pieces	21,500	10
Cloth	1 billion metres	16.2	13.5
Clothes	1 billion articles	2.8	65
Television	1,000 sets	15,000	7.5
Colour TV	1,000 sets	5,000	22
Refrigerators	1,000	6,500–7,500	370–440
Washing machines	1,000	12,000	36
Machine-made paper and paper plate	1,000 tons	10,000	21
Synthetic detergents	1,000 tons	1,400	40.6
Crude coal	1 billion tons	1.0	17.7
Coal under unified distribution	1 billion tons	0.5	20
Petroleum	1 billion tons	0.15	20
Natural gas	1 billion cubic metres	15	16.6
Power generating capacity	1 billion kWh	550	35
Steel	1,000 tons	55,000–58,000	17.9–24.3
Steel materials	1,000 tons	44,000–46,500	19.16–26.4
Chemical fertilizer	1,000 tons	16,300	22.1
Soda (ash)	1,000 tons	3,500	75
Ethylene	1,000 tons	1,200–1,400	84.3–115
Timber	1,000 cubic metres	68,180–72,000	8–14
Cement	1,000 tons	180,000	26.4
Vehicles	1,000	560	27.6
Volume of railway freight	1,000 tons	160	25.5
Volume of railway passenger transport	1 billion people	1.4	36.4
Volume of marine freight	1 billion tons	0.6	23.2
Volume of marine passenger transport	1 billion people	0.299	12.3
Handling capacity of ports	1 billion tons	0.5	51.3
Volume of highway freight	1 billion tons	0.9	38.5
Total rotation volume of transport of CAAC	1 billion tons/kms	2.5	100
Volume of postal business	1 billion yuan	5	70.1

Table 2: Economic Growth Rate (Unit: 100 million yuan)

	1990	Increase over 1985 (%)	Average annual growth rate (%)	
Total Output Value of Industry and Agriculture	16,770	38	6.7	Calculated in terms of 1980 constant prices, the average annual growth
Of which:				
Agriculture	3,530	21.6	4	rate will be 6 per cent if village-run
Industry	13,240	43.4	7.5	industry is included; otherwise it will
Light industry	6,610	40	7.5	be 7 per cent. By 1990 the proportion
Heavy Industry	6,630	40.3	7.5	of agriculture, light and heavy industries will be 21% : 39.4% : 39.6%.
Gross National Product	11,170	44	7.5	Calculated in terms of 1985 prices.
Of which:				By 1990, tertiary industry will
Primary Industry	3,060	22.9	4.2	make up 25.1 per cent of GNP.
Secondary Industry	5,300	45.2	7.7	
Tertiary Industry	2,810	71.3	11.4	

Table 3: Output Index of Major Agricultural Products (Unit: 10,000 tons)

	1990	Increase over 1985 (%)	Average annual output	Average annual increase of output over the Sixth Five-Year period (%)
Grain	42,500–45,000	11.8–18.4	41,500	12
Cotton	425	2.4	425	relatively low
Oil crops	1,825	15.6	1,712	42
Sugar crops	6,875	23.4	6,385	40
Meat	2,275	19.7	1,984.4	
Dairy products	625	110	363	
Eggs	875	65	599.2	
Aquatic products	900	29	738.2	

Table 4: Consumption Level of Citizens (Unit: yuan)

	1985	1990	Average annual increase (%)
Average consumption level of citizens throughout the country	404	517	5
Urban residents	736	903	4.2
Rural residents	325	416	5.1

Table 5: Scale of Investment in Fixed Assets

Total amount for the five years	Investment in fixed assets in state enterprises and institutions				Investment in collectively-run enterprises	Investment in private enterprises in town and country
	Amount	Investment on capital construction	Investment in updating equipment and technological transformation	In other projects		
12,960	89.60	5,000	2,760	1,200	1,600	2,400

– In the five-year period, operating expenses for education, science, culture, public health and sports will total 201.6 billion yuan, an average annual increase of 8 per cent, which exceeds the growth rate of revenues from regular items representing 18 per cent of total state expenditure.

– Expenditure for promoting reform of the price structure and wage system will be increased accordingly. Expenditures for administration and national defence will experience drops over the previous five-year period, occupying 6.3 per cent and 9.1 per cent respectively of total state expenditure.

Foreign exchange receipts and payments

The nation's total turnover of import and export in 1990 will reach $US 83 billion, a 40 per cent increase over 1985, among which, the turnover of exports will amount to $US 38 billion, a 47 per cent increase over 1985 and that of imports to $US 45 billion, a 35 per cent increase over the previous year. While trying to earn more foreign exchange through export, China will increase the amount earned from sources other than trade and economize on the use of all foreign currencies.

Objectives for the Development of Science and Technology, Education and other Social Programmes

Scientific research and technological progress

In the five years, the State will concentrate on 76 major scientific and technological research projects and 200 projects designed to develop technology and spread the use of significant research achievements. China will try to attain major successes in new technological research projects that are of crucial importance for progress in the application of new technology to transform traditional industries. Vigorous efforts will be made to open up areas in new and high technology, gradually forming new areas of technology.

Education

A system of nine-year education will be gradually introduced. In 1990 China will make primary school education universal throughout the country and make junior middle school education universal in cities, developed areas in the coastal provinces and a few developed interior areas. In the next five years, the number of graduates from institutions of higher learning will reach 2.6 million, rising by 70 per cent as compared to the preceding period, and the number of those who have completed postgraduate work is expected to be 180,000 or 4.5 times the figure of the preceding five-year period. Various forms of adult higher education will see 2.1 million specialized personnel with college level education, 2.5 times the figure of the preceding five-year period.

Other social programmes

About 29 million new jobs will be provided in cities and towns in the five years. More effective measures will be taken in occupational health and safety to gradually introduce or improve systems of social benefits to meet the needs of the new situation. 400,000 beds in hospitals will be added above county level. China will further improve the use of land, exploit and utilize natural resources more rationally and control pollution more effectively, and will continue to expand cultural and sports undertakings.

Capital Construction in the Seventh Five-Year Plan Period

In the next five years, the State will concentrate on 925 large and medium-sized projects, of which 350 are started-up, renovated and expanded projects, and the rest left over from the previous five-year period. In the five years, 450 projects will be completed and put into operation. The equity of the 925 projects is estimated at 200 billion yuan, representing 40 per cent of the total investment in capital construction in the next five years.

In the five-year period, power generating capacity will be increased to 60–65 million kW. A number of thermal power plants will be built in the major coal producing areas and coastal areas. In connection with hydropower construction, efforts will be concentrated on exploiting water resources along the upper reaches of the Huanghe (Yellow River), the major tributaries of the Yangtze river in its upper and middle reaches and along the Hongshui river. Large and medium-sized hydropower stations will be built in these regions. In the coal industry, China will accelerate the construction of coal producing bases in Inner Mongolia, Henan, and west of Shaanxi and Ningxia, with Shanxi as its centre. In the petroleum industry, efforts will be made to renovate and expand old oilfields such as Daqing, Shengli, North China and Liaohe oilfields and to provide them with supporting facilities.

In transportation, priority will be given to the construction and revamping of a number of railways so as to increase the freight capacity of coal carried from Shanxi to other parts of the country. In addition, a number of water berths will be built, renovated and expanded in order to expand transportation of foreign trade.

In posts and telecommunications, the State will continue to give priority to increasing telephone capacity in large and medium-sized cities and coastal cities opening to the outside world; and to installing new high-capacity digital microwave trunk-lines between Beijing and Shanghai, where two international telecommunication bureaux will be set up.

In developing the raw materials industry, China will upgrade a number of key enterprises and special steel plants, while carrying out the construction of the first two stages of the Shanghai Baoshan Steel Plant. With regard to the petroleum and chemical industry, the State will continue the construction of Daqing, Qilu and Yangtze ethylene projects, and three large alkaline plants of Nanbao in Hebei, Shouguang in Shangdong and Lianyungang in Jiangsu, etc.

Import and Export

China will continue to increase exports of petroleum, coal, non-ferrous metals, grain, cotton, etc. In addition, it will gradually increase the proportion of manufactured goods, especially of light and textile products and machinery and electronics products in the total volume of export. China is traditionally strong in light and textile industries, and the production capacity of the machinery and electronics industries is large. Further efforts will be made to update the technology of the light and textile industries and the machinery and electronics industries to increase the varieties of products and improve their quality, thus causing an obvious rise in the volume of export.

So far as imports are concerned, priority will be given to computer software, advanced technologies and key equipment, as well as to certain essential means of production that are in short supply in order to raise the economic efficiency of utilizing foreign exchange earned through imports, as well as to guarantee the country's technological progress to enhance capacity to earn foreign exchange through export. China will strictly control the import of ordinary processing equipment and durable consumer goods. In assembly-line industries which use imported spare parts and accessories, the approval procedure should be tightened, with a reduction in the proportion of imported components and avoidance of imports.

In using foreign funds, China will give first priority to construction projects in such areas as energy, transport, communications, and raw and semi-finished materials, and especially to projects for power generating, port facilities and the petroleum industry, and also to the technological transformation of the machine-building and electronics and industries. It will give second priority to projects that will increase ability to earn foreign exchange through export and to produce substitutes for imports. China will further expand and utilize foreign funds.

In introducing foreign technology, China will give priority to the transformation of existing enterprises. It will first import technology and equipment that will help increase capacity to export and to produce substitutes for imports.

Forms of introduction are various, including licensing trade and supply of specialized technology, construction projects and technological services. Ways of introducing technology are determined by the characteristics of different trades and conditions of projects. Any way that may help China achieve a balance in foreign currency and integration of foreign trade with technology is welcome.

While expanding the influx of technology and equipment, China will, in more ways and through more channels, expand the introduction of foreign intellectual resources with emphasis on opening up new products, technological design, business management and project construction, etc. It will enhance co-operation with foreign engineers and technicians and invite foreign experts to China to advise and consult.

Under the guidance of the state plan, special economic zones and open coastal cities should systematically carry out the construction and development. Greater efforts will be made to improve the existing infrastructure and develop supporting industries for projects that use foreign capital. China will concentrate on completing construction in those areas where development has already begun. It will actively solicit more foreign investment, open up productive projects, especially knowledge- and technology-intensive projects, to bring out as early as possible exported products that are more competitive on the international market, gradually building an export-orientated economy that is based on industry and advanced technology and earns foreign exchange through export.

In the light of their own conditions and characteristics, the 14 open coastal cities and Hainan Island should exploit their advantages to introduce investment from abroad and establish lateral ties at home. In this way they will systematically expand economic and trade relations and technological exchanges with other countries.

In the open areas such as the Yangtze river and Zhujiang (Pearl River) deltas and the triangular area in southern Fujian province, China will gradually build an economic structure in which agriculture serves the processing industry and the processing industry serves trade. In these areas it will rely on technological transformation and the introduction of advanced technology and renovation of products to expand export and earn more foreign exchange, thus making those economic open areas into foreign trade centres, which may bring along the interior regions in economic development.

In co-operating with other countries China will call for a further development by contracting for more construction projects and labour services abroad. It will continue to offer possible economic and technological aid to underdeveloped Third World countries and do its utmost to offer or receive international multilateral or bilateral aid. Emphasis in receiving assistance lies on projects of technological and intelligence development.

To increase foreign exchange earnings and promote friendly contacts between people of different countries, China must fully exploit her rich tourist resources and expand the tourist industry. It plans to receive 5 million tourists from abroad in 1990.

Living Standards and Social Security

At the end of 1990 China's total population should not exceed 1.113 billion and the average annual growth rate of population will be controlled at around 12.4%.

With regard to employment in rural areas, China will continue to encourage peasants to leave the land but not the village, drawing surplus labour out of agriculture by developing forestry, animal husbandry, fishery and township enterprises. In cities and towns, it will explore all possibilities of employment for urban people. It will carry out the policy of employment through assignment by labour departments under the unified plan and guidance, while at the same time, employees are encouraged to organize themselves into business voluntarily and to take up self-employment.

With regard to personal income and patterns of consumption, it is anticipated that in 1990 the average per capita net income of peasants will be 560 yuan, an increase of 41.1 per cent over the 1985 figure of 397 yuan, or an average annual increase of 7 per cent. It is expected that in 1990 total wages of workers and other employees will be 190 billion yuan, 54.4 billion more than in 1985. This figure represents an average annual growth rate of 7 per cent.

With regard to distribution of income, China will continue to follow the principle of distribution according to work and encourage some areas, enterprises and individuals to become prosperous first. It will lay stress on overcoming egalitarianism but at the same time guard against excessive discrepancies in income between trades and enterprises and among people. As the income of the people everywhere increases, the pattern of consumption will change for the better and there will be more consumer goods of greater variety and better design. Of total personal expenditure, the proportion that goes on housing, articles for daily use, cultural and recreational activities and daily services will grow, while the amount spent on food and fuel will decrease.

The next five years will witness a dramatic growth in public health and health care, to enhance the health level of the whole nation. By 1990, safe drinking water will be available for 80 per cent of the rural population, and over 85 per cent of the total

Foreign tourists purchasing traditional Chinese medicine – *Qingchun Bao* (Youth Keeper) in Hangzhou No.2 Traditional Chinese Medicine plant. *(Photo by Lu Ming)*

population will have received inoculations against major diseases. China will build more key hospitals. The State will allocate funds to build 16 general hospitals, each specializing in one or more branches of medicine, and two modern hospitals with advanced equipment and techniques. China will develop traditional Chinese medicine, with emphasis on the construction of research centres of Chinese pharmacology in Shanghai, Tianjin, Sichuan and Jilin.

During the period of the Seventh Five-Year Plan, in accordance with its actual conditions and national power and the principle of benefiting production and ensuring people's life, China will try to gradually put in place a socialist social security system with Chinese characteristics which conforms to China's policy of invigorating the domestic economy and opening to the outside world.

Perspectives for Further Economic Structural Reform

Objective of the reform

In the Seventh Five-Year Plan, the Chinese government has determined to try to lay an essential foundation for a socialist economic system which has Chinese features and is full of vitality.

Major contents of the reform

There are three main aspects of economic structural reform during this period: China will further invigorate enterprises, especially large and medium-sized state-owned enterprises; further expand the socialist commodity market and gradually improve the market system; and shift state control of enterprises from direct to indirect means, in order to establish a socialist macro-economic control system. These three aspects of the reform are closely interrelated and inseparable. Bearing these three tasks in mind, China will restructure the planning, pricing, financial, monetary, labour and wage systems, so as to develop a whole set of mechanisms which will integrate planning with marketing, micro-economic flexibility with macro-economic control and centralization with decentralization.

To fulfil the above-mentioned tasks and lay the foundation of a new economic structure, China will carry out the reform in three stages. In the first stage, that is, during the next year or two, it will continue to invigorate enterprises, especially large and medium-sized ones, and to expand lateral economic associations while strengthening indirect macro-economic control. In the second stage, it will develop the socialist commodity market by gradually reducing the scope of mandatory planning, reforming the pricing system and the price control system for means of production, improving the taxation system and reforming the financial and monetary systems. In the third stage, it will establish a new organizational structure to deal with the question of subordination of enterprises to proper authorities, eventually separating the functions of government from those of enterprises, thus putting the economic structural reform on a sound path.

The Seventh Five-Year Plan sets an ambitious goal. The task is arduous, but it can be accomplished through hard work. The Plan offers the people of the whole country an inspiring prospect for the future. When this Plan is fulfilled, China will have basically rationalized the economic relations of all sectors, built a new framework for the economic structure, increased economic strength and greatly raised the country's level of science and technology. Thus, important progress will have been made in the modernization of the entire economy, and the living standards and quality of life in both the cities and the countryside will have been improved. China will then be in a better position to bring about an economic upsurge and prosperity in the 1990s, and it will have even more assurance that it will reach its great goal by the end of this century.

PART V

FOREIGN TRADE AND FOREIGN ECONOMIC RELATIONS

THE DEVELOPMENT OF FOREIGN TRADE

As a semi-feudal and semi-colonial country, old China was economically backward and its major trading ports and foreign trade were in the hands of foreign powers. Starting from the 1870s, the country suffered from an unfavourable balance of trade every year for seventy years in succession. The markets then were flooded with foreign goods and its national industry and commerce were rudely trampled upon.

The founding of New China brought the country political and economic independence, and the Government began to exercise control over foreign trade. During the restoration period of the national economy (1950–1952), China's major trade partners were the Soviet Union and Eastern European countries, with whom the volume of trade accounted for 50–60 per cent of the national total. It also established trade relations with countries like India, Pakistan, Burma, Indonesia and Sri Lanka on the basis of mutual benefit.

During the period of the First Five-Year Plan (1953–1957), China imported from the Soviet Union 156 complete sets of equipment, which played an important role in the building of China's industry at its initial stage. At the same time, China supplied the Soviet Union with a vast amount of agricultural products and foodstuffs, non-ferrous metals, rare metals, etc. In addition, economic relations between China and some 54 Asian countries and regions were established, together with the establishment of government-to-government relations between China and

Customers from neighbouring countries shopping at the border trade fair held in Tibet.   *(Photo by Qun Sang)*

some Northern European countries. China also signed people-to-people economic contracts with quite a number of organizations of industry and commerce in many countries. In 1957, the first Chinese Export Commodities Fair was held in Guangzhou (Canton) with the purpose of expanding trade with the Hong Kong–Macao area and the Western countries.

In the early 1960s, when China's national economy was afflicted with great difficulties, importation of grain was given the top priority in foreign trade. Next to grain came such items as chemical fertilizer, pesticide and some industrial raw materials, which were urgently needed for restoring and developing production.

In 1962, China began importing Japanese technology and equipment, and established economic ties with Western European countries. By the year 1968, 84 technical projects and types of equipment had been introduced to China. These were soon put into full operation and raised China's technical level in the fields of petrochemicals, mining and soil amelioration and the electronics industry.

The early period of the Cultural Revolution saw the volume of trade decline year after year. In the early 1970s, however, foreign trade began to show a sign of improvement as the result of the restoration of China's legitimate seat in the United Nations and the revival of Sino-American and Sino-Japanese relations.

The Third Plenary Session of the Eleventh Central Committee of the Communist Party of China, in December 1978, pushed foreign trade into a new phase of development as the policy of opening to the outside world and invigorating the domestic economy was put into effect. The actual calculation of the total volume of foreign trade in 1985 reached $US 602.5 hundred million, a figure registering a 190 per cent

increase over the total volume of $US 206.4 hundred million in 1978: the average annual increase was as much as 16.5 per cent. China now has economic relations with over 170 countries and regions all over the world.

Table 1: Development of China's Foreign Trade

Year	Total volume of trade	$US 100m	
		Export	Import
1950	11.3	5.5	5.8
1952	19.4	8.2	11.2
1957	31.0	16.0	15.1
1962	26.6	14.9	11.7
1965	42.5	22.3	20.2
1970	45.9	22.6	23.3
1975	147.5	72.6	74.9
1978	206.4	97.5	108.9
1980	378.2	182.7	195.5
1984	497.7	244.2	253.6
1985	602.5	259.1	343.4

In addition to the remarkable increase in the volume of foreign trade, the structure of import and export commodities has also changed considerably. Among export commodities, the proportions of industrial and mining products rose from 17.9 per cent in 1953 to 55.6 per cent in 1985 (products of energy, light industry, textile industry and engineering industry increased especially drastically); processed agricultural products and foodstuffs rose from 22.8 per cent to 26.9 per cent, while the proportion of agricultural products and foodstuffs dropped from 59.3 per cent to 17.5 per cent. Among import commodities, the proportion of means of production dropped from 89.4 per cent in 1952 to 82.8 per cent, whereas the proportion of means of subsistence rose from 10.6 per cent to 17.2 per cent.

THE ADMINISTRATIVE BODIES OF FOREIGN TRADE AND ECONOMICS

In China, organizations concerning foreign trade comprise two kinds: governmental and non-governmental. The main such bodies are as follows:

The State Planning Commission

This formulates the long-term, medium-term and annual plans of revenue and expenditure of the whole country, the total volume of foreign trade and the trade volume of certain major commodities. It decides the extent to which foreign investments should be utilized, new technology should be introduced and complete sets of equipment be imported. It works out plans of priority and above-norm projects and other projects where foreign exchange is used. It checks

these plans and, when necessary, adjusts them jointly with the State Economic Commission and the Ministry of Foreign Economic Relations and Trade.

The State Economic Commission

The function of this body is, among other things, to participate in the formulation, checking, coordination and adjustment of the annual plan of foreign trade.

The Ministry of Foreign Economic Relations and Trade

This is an administrative body which controls affairs concerning foreign trade and economic relations and

Accompanied by Li Zewang, Chinese Ambassador to the USSR, Soviet Premier Nikolai Ivanovich Ryzhkov (third from right) and Vadim Andreevich Medvediev (second from right), Secretary of the Central Committee of the CPSU, visited the exhibition of Chinese Economy and Trade opened in Moscow on 25 July 1986.

foreign trade enterprises all over the country. Its main functions include: drafting and implementing policies and regulations for foreign trade; co-operating with the State Planning Commission to formulate, assign and check long-term, medium-term and annual foreign trade plans; using various kinds of economic measures to readjust foreign trade; deciding countries and regions with which foreign trade should be carried out; organizing government-to-government trade negotiations, signing trade agreements and putting them into effect; examining and approving the setting up, merging and withdrawal of foreign trade enterprises operating domestically and overseas; examining, approving and administering foreign resident offices in China; controlling Chinese commercial and economic administrative organizations abroad; examining, approving and granting import and export licences; controlling and distributing quotas and limits of foreign trade commodities, and formulating and adjusting the inventory of foreign trade commodities under centralized management; examining and approving, in accordance with the relevant regulations of the country, major contracts for import and export of technology; controlling trademarks of all exporting commodities. It is also in charge of world market investigation and information exchange and provides timely information and prediction to foreign trade enterprises and other institutions throughout the country.

The State Administration for Industry and Commerce

The duties of this organization concerning foreign trade are: handling the registration of joint-ventures, co-operative ventures, enterprises of sole foreign investment and foreign resident offices in China;

handling the registration of foreign trademarks and protecting the exclusive right to use of them; controlling trade contracts and advertisements, protecting legal business, banning illegal trade and maintaining a good commercial atmosphere in the market place.

The administration has a branch in each province, autonomous region and municipality directly under the Central Government.

Customs General Administration

This is the headquarters of customs posts throughout the country. Its functions are: supervising and managing the legal entry and exit of conveyances, cargo and non-trading articles; levying customs duty and other duties which, by law, should be levied by customs; stopping smuggling, and safeguarding and promoting the country's socialist construction for modernization. China pursues the policy of protective tariffs in order to achieve equality and mutual benefit, to protect production, to introduce advanced technology and to encourage export. The administration has 117 subsidiary bodies in 22 provinces, autonomous regions and municipalities directly under the Central Government.

Administration of Foreign Exchange Control

This manages the country's foreign exchange and foreign exchange reserve, formulates and carries out governmental decrees and policies concerning foreign exchange and, in coordination with the State Planning Commission, collects and makes the country's plan of revenue and expenditure of foreign exchange and the plan of international revenue and expenditure; formulates and publishes the exchange rate between Renminbi (RMB) and foreign currencies; controls the borrowing of foreign capital by domestic institutions and the issuing of foreign exchange bonds domestically and overseas; examines, approves, allocates, checks and supervises the revenue and expenditure of trading and non-trading foreign exchange of domestic institutions; examines, approves and manages foreign exchange transactions conducted by overseas Chinese banks, banks of foreign capital, joint-venture banks, the China International Trust and Investment Corporation and other domestic institutions handling international financial affairs; investigates and handles violations of the country's regulations concerning foreign exchange control.

The administration has its branches in every province, autonomous region and municipality directly under the Central Government, and the main economic areas and areas where people have close kinship with the overseas Chinese.

Bank of China

This is the government appointed bank dealing exclusively with foreign exchange affairs. According to the policy of putting foreign exchange under the unified control and management of the Government, the Bank of China looks after China's international settlement, international credit, foreign trade credit and the buying and selling of foreign exchange. In China, the accounts of all foreign trade transactions payable and receivable in foreign exchange must, without any exception, be settled through the Bank of China and the foreign banks concerned. The total capital of the Bank of China in 1985 reached over RMB 200,000,000,000. The Bank of China has branches in all trading ports, areas where overseas remittance is used, areas where bills of purchase are used and main border areas. Overseas branches and offices of the Bank of China in countries and regions like Hong Kong, London, New York, Singapore and Luxembourg amounted, by the end of 1984, to over 293, with a total staff of more than 9,500. Capital in these branches and offices totalled $US 18,300,000,000, where deposits amounted to $US 9,600,000,000 and investment $US 4,700,000,000. As their financing ability is strengthening and prestige grows, people working in these branches and offices are making an effort to render better service so as to back China's foreign trade effort.

Commodity Inspection Bureau

This supervises and manages the inspection of the country's foreign trade commodities and deals with notary appraisal. Only the most important foreign trade commodities are inspected by the bureau and its branches; other commodities are checked by each

Soviet visitors looking at a high speed automatic industrial sewing machine operated by a Chinese worker.

institution concerned. The inspection includes a check on quality, weight, quantity and packing. Commodities imported without inspection are not allowed to be installed and put into operation, sold or used; commodities without inspection or considered below standard by the inspection cannot be exported.

There are Commodity Inspection Bureaux in 29 provinces, autonomous regions and centrally administered municipalities. In addition, 78 commodity inspection offices have been set up in major trading ports and foreign commodity distribution centres.

China Council for the Promotion of International Trade

This is a non-governmental organization whose main task is to promote the development of economic and trade relations between China and the rest of the world. It is in charge of forming economic liaisons with foreign countries, holding exhibitions of products for export, staging foreign exhibitions and organizing seminars on foreign trade relations. It also settles disputes between parties through the Foreign Trade Arbitration Commission and the Maritime Arbitration Commission – two organizations attached to the Council. It often holds technical exhibitions to promote exchange of technology between China and other countries. It runs several journals, such as *China's Foreign Trade* and *China's Exports*. These journals help to publicize China's foreign trade policies and promote sales of Chinese products.

The Council has branches in more than 20 provinces, autonomous regions and municipalities directly under the Central Government.

China International Trust and Investment Corporation (CITIC)

This is a ministerial-level enterprise which, under the direct leadership of the State Council of the People's Republic of China, is engaged in economic and technical co-operation with foreign enterprises. Its main business activities are: organizing economic co-operation in the form of joint ventures, production in co-operation, compensation trade, etc.; investment in China and abroad; promoting technical co-operation between China and foreign institutions; managing the foreign exchange banks; handling international finance and investment by import and export companies; dealing with leasing and real estate business; acting as an advisory body for Chinese and foreign customers; providing insurance for foreign investors in China; and handling mandatory affairs concerning the above business activities.

	19 Jianguomenwai Dajie
	Beijing, China
Tel:	5002255
P.O. Box:	6200
Telex:	22305 CITIC CN

Beijing Ever Bright Industrial Company

Entrusted by governmental organizations of provinces, autonomous regions and municipalities directly under the Central Government, this company imports technology and equipment with rationed or self-raised foreign exchange (including foreign exchange as payments for goods and the utilization of foreign investment). It helps its customers to purchase desirable "second hand" equipment in the world market. It manages affairs of joint ventures, compensation trade and the processing of imported material. In line with government policy and in co-operation with the Ministry of Foreign Economic Relations and Trade, the company handles foreign trade, the export of labour and engineering project contracts.

	Chang Guan Lu
	143 Xizhimenwai Dajie
	Beijing, China
Tel:	89.8574
Cable:	Beijing 5503
Telex:	20023 BEBIC CN

EMBASSIES AND COMMERCIAL DEPARTMENTS OF THE PEOPLE'S REPUBLIC OF CHINA IN FOREIGN COUNTRIES

I. ASIA

Embassy of the People's Republic of China in Japan

	4–33, Motoabazu 3-chome, Minato-ku,
	Tokyo, 106
Tel:	444–6577 (Commercial Department)
Telex:	Chinaemb J 28705
	Chicotel J 28506

Consulate-General of the People's Republic of China in Osaka

	9–2, Jinmoto-cho 3 chome, Nishi-ku, Osaka
Postal Code:	550
Tel:	06–445–9471 (Commercial Department)
Telex:	J 64201

Foreign Trade and Foreign Economic Relations

Embassy of the People's Republic of China in the Democratic People's Republic of Korea

        Kinmaeuldong, Pyongyang
Tel: 390275 (Commercial Department)
Cable: Ctatpr Ioritc 6787, Pyongyang

Embassy of the People's Republic of China in Pakistan

        Diplomatic Enclave, Ramna 4, Islamabad
Tel: 21115 (Economic Counsellor's Office)
Cable: Chinembasy, Islamabad, Pakistan

Consulate-General of the People's Republic of China in Karachi

        207 Aziz Bhatti Shaheed Road, Karachi
Tel: 510425, 514934 (Commercial Department)
Cable: Chinconsul, Karachi

Embassy of the People's Republic of China in India

        50–D, Shantipath, Chanakyapur,
        New Delhi–21
Tel: 608944 (Commercial Department)
Cable: Chinembasy, New Delhi
Telex: 3162250 Sino IN

Embassy of the People's Republic of China in Sri Lanka

        191, Dharmapala Mawatha, Colombo 7
Tel: 580912 (Commercial Department)
Cable: Chinembasy, Colombo
Telex: 22408 Chincoce Colombo

Embassy of the People's Republic of China in Bangladesh

        Ne(L)6, Road No. 83, Gulshan, Dhaka
Tel: 603491 (Commercial Department)
Cable: Chinemba, Dhaka

Embassy of the People's Republic of China in Burma

        1 Pyidaungsu Yeiktha Road, Rangoon
Tel: 77526, 75865 (Commercial Department)
Cable: Chinembasy, Rangoon
Telex: 21346 Chicomoff (Commercial)

Embassy of the People's Republic of China in Afghanistan

        Sardar Shah Mahmoud Ghazi Wat, Kabul
Tel: 25552 (Commercial Department)
Cable: Chinemba, Kabul

Embassy of the People's Republic of China in Iran

        53 Golestan First, Pasdaran Ave.,
        Tehran
Tel: 283783 (Commercial Department)
P.O. Box: 11365–7744
Cable: Chinaemba, Teheran
Telex: 213237 Como IR (Commercial)

Embassy of the People's Republic of China in Turkey

        Golgeli Sor 34, Gazi Osman Pasa, Ankara
Tel: 280813 (Commercial Department)
Cable: Chinaemba, Ankara
Telex: 42420 Cham TR

Embassy of the People's Republic of China in Syria

        83, Rue Ata Ayoubi, Damascus
Tel: 330845, 333559 (Commercial Department)
P.O. Box: 2455 Damascus
Cable: Chinaemba, Damascus

Embassy of the People's Republic of China in Iraq

        Saddam International Airport Road New
        Embassy Arer, Al-Armiria District, Baghdad,
        Iraq
Tel: 5562740 (Economic & Commercial Department)
P.O. Box: 225, Baghdad
Cable: Chinembassy, Baghdad
Telex: 2195 Chincom IK

Embassy of the People's Republic of China in the State of Kuwait

        Sheikh Ahmad Jaber Building 4, Dasman
        District, Kuwait
Tel: 423815 (Commercial Department)
P.O. Box: 2346, Kuwait
Cable: Chinaemba Al, Kuwait
Telex: 22688 KT Chinaem

Ambassade de la République Populaire de Chine au Liban

        Rue 72, Nicolas Ibrahim Sursock, Bamlek–
        Baida, Beyrouth
Tel: 830318 (Commercial Department)
P.O. Box: 8928, Beyrouth
Cable: Chinaemba, Beirut
Telex: 21344 LE Chinco

Embassy of the People's Republic of China in Cyprus

27 Clementos Street, Nicosia
Tel: 73044 (Commercial Department)
P.O. Box: 4531 Nicosia
Cable: Chinaemba, Nicosia
Telex: 4910 Chinacof CY (Commercial)

Embassy of the People's Republic of China in Jordan

Shmeisani–Beside Ambassador Hotel,
Amman
Tel: 817186 (Commercial Department)
P.O. Box: 7365 Amman, Jordan
Telex: 21770 Chinem JO

Embassy of the People's Republic of China in Oman

Ruwi, Muscat, Sultanate of Oman
Tel: 704343 (Commercial Department)
P.O. Box: 3315, Ruwi, Muscat, Sultanate of Oman
Cable: Chinaemba, Muscat
Telex: 3125 Chinaemb ON

Embassy of the People's Republic of China in the People's Democratic Republic of Yemen

145, Andalas Garden Street, Khormarksar,
Aden
Tel: 42468 (Commercial Department)
P.O. Box: 5213, Aden
Cable: Chinaemba, Aden

Embassy of the People's Republic of China in the Arab Republic of Yemen

Al–Zubeiri Street, Sana'a
Tel: 72026 (Commercial Department)
P.O. Box: 482, Sana'a
Cable: Chinembassy, Sana'a
Telex: 2548 CCCOFF

Embassy of the People's Republic of China in United Arab Emirates

Bateen Area, Abu Dhabi
Tel: 321677 (Commercial Department)
P.O. Box: 2741 Abu Dhabi, U.A.E
Cable: Chinemba, Abudhabi
Telex: 23829 Chinco EM (Commercial)

Embassy of the People's Republic of China in Thailand

57 Rachadapisake Road, Bangkok
Tel: 2457038 (Commercial Department)
Cable: Chinaemba, Bangkok

Embassy of the People's Republic of China in Malaysia

229, Jalan Ampang, Kuala Lumpur
Tel: 428585 (Commercial Department)
Cable: Chinaemaba, Kualalumpur
Telex: Chinem MA 30488

Embassy of the People's Republic of China in the Philippines

4896 Pasay Road, Dasmarinas Village,
Makati, Metro–Manila, Philippines
Tel: 572555 (Commercial Department)
P.O. Box: 7328 Airmail
Exchange Office, Manila International Airport, 3120, Philippines
Cable: Chinaemba, Manila
Telex: 27682 EPRCC PH (Commercial Department)

Ambassade de la République Populaire de Chine au Vietnam

So Nha 46, Pho Hoang Dieu, Hanoi, Vietnam
Tel: 3955 (Commercial)

Office of the Commercial Representative of the People's Republic of China in Singapore

70–76 Dalvey Road, Singapore 1025
Tel: 7343360, 7343307
Cable: Chicomer
Telex: 36878 Chicro RS

II. AFRICA

Ambassade de la République Populaire de Chine au Maroc

16 Charia Alfahssouissi, Rabat
Tel: 54940 (Commercial Department)
Cable: Chinambassade, Rabat
Telex: 32698 Comchine (Commercial Department)

Ambassade de la République de Chine en Algérie

34, Boulevard des Martyrs, Alger
Tel: 605362 (Commercial Department)
Cable: Ambachine, Alger
Telex: 53233 BCCAC DZ (Commercial Department)

Ambassade de la République Populaire de Chine en Tunisie

41, Avenue de Lesseps, Tunis
Tel: 286192 (Commercial Department)
Cable: Comchine, Tunis (Commercial Department)
Telex: 155221 Ambchi TN

Foreign Trade and Foreign Economic Relations

Embassy of the People's Republic of China in Libya

Gargaresh M 486
Tel: 74664 (Commercial Department)
P.O. Box: 5329
Cable: Chinaemba, Tripoli
Telex: 20790 Chineme LY

Embassy of the People's Republic of China in Egypt

No. 14 Bahgat Aly Street, Zamalek, Cairo
Tel: 417423, 416561 (Commercial Counsellor's
        Office)
Cable: Chinembassy, Cairo
Telex: Chemb UN 93216

Embassy of the People's Republic of China in the Sudan

93, 22nd Street, Riad Town, Khartoum
Tel: 222041 (Commercial Department)
P.O. Box: 1425 Khartoum
Telex: 24205 KHXIN SD

Embassy of the People's Republic of China in Ethiopia

Jimma Road, Higher 24, Kebele, Addis
Ababa
Tel: 201959 (Commercial Department)
        160337 (Residence of CAAC)
P.O. Box: 5643 Addis Ababa
Cable: Chinaemba, Addis Ababa
Telex: 21145 Chinaemba Addis

Embassy of the People's Republic of China in Somalia

Zai–39, Via Scire Warsame,
Mogadishu
Tel: 21823 (Commercial Department)
P.O. Box: 548, Mogadishu
Telex: 642 Hsinhua MOG
Cable: Chinemba, Mogadishu

Embassy of the People's Republic of China in Kenya

Woodlands Road, Kilimani District,
Nairobi
Tel: 26396 (Commercial Department)
P.O. Box: 30508, Nairobi
Cable: Chinaemba, Nairobi
Telex: 23011 CECOM KE

Ambassade de la République Populaire de Chine au Burundi

Sur la Parcelle 675, A Vugizo, Bujumbura
Tel: 2558 (Commercial Department)
P.O. Box: 2550 Bujumbura
Cable: Chinaemba, Bujumbura

Ambassade de la République Populaire de Chine au Rwanda

Rue de la Chanson, Parcelle, No. 663, Kigali
Tel: 5629 (Commercial Department)
P.O. Box: 1345, Kigali
Cable: Chinaemba, Kigali
Telex: 599 Ambachine RW

Embassy of the People's Republic of China in Uganda

37 Malcolm Avenue, Kololo Kampala
Tel: 259881 (Economic and Commercial Depart-
        ment)
P.O. Box: 4106 Kampala
Cable: Chinemba, Kampala
Telex: 61383 Chinac UGA

Embassy of the People's Republic of China in Tanzania

No. 2 Kajificheni Close, Touré Drive,
Dar–es–Salaam
Tel: 21517 (Commercial Department)
P.O. Box: 1649, Dar–es–Salaam
Cable: Chinembassy, Daressalaam
Telex: 41036 Chinemba

Embassy of the People's Republic of China in Zambia

7430 Haile Selassie Avenue, Lusaka
Tel: 235601 (Commercial Department)
P.O. Box: 1975, Lusaka
Cable: Chinemb, Lusaka
Telex: ZA 41360 Chineb

Embaixada da Republica Popuvar da China em Moçambique

1309 Av. Dos Martires da Machava, Maputo
Tel: 741462 (Commercial Department)
P.O. Box: 4668 Maputo
Cable: Chinaemba, Maputo
Telex: 6–449 HNALM MO

Ambassade de la République Populaire de Chine en Madagascar

Ancien Hôtel Panorama, Route d'Andrinar-
ivo, Tananarive
Tel: 44126 (Commercial Department)
P.O. Box: 1658 Analakely–Tananarive
Telex: 22360 Chinaemba Tananarive
Cable: Chinaemba, Tananarive

Embassy of the People's Republic of China in Mauritius

Royac Road, Belle-Rose Hill, Mauritius
Tel: 43074 (Commercial Department)
Cable: Chinaemba, Port Louis

Ambassade de la République Populaire de Chine en Mauritanie

Nouakchott
Tel: 52347 (Commercial Department)
P.O. Box: 257, Nouakchott
Cable: Chinaemba, Nouakchott
Telex: 541 Hsinhu MTN

Ambassade de la République Populaire de Chine au Sénégal

Avenue des Ambassadeurs, Fann–Residence
Tel: 230541 (Commercial Department)
P.O. Box: 342 Dakar
Telex: 3188 Sinocomsg

Ambassade de la République Populaire de Chine au Mali

Bamako
Tel: 223919 (Commercial Department)
P.O. Box: 112, Bamako
Cable: Chineamba, Bamako
Telex: 455 Xinhua BKO

Embassy of the People's Republic of China in Gambia

6A Marina Parade, Banjul, The Gambia
Cable: Chinaemba, Banjul
P.O. Box: 784, Banjul
Tel: 9–8595 (Commercial Department)
Telex: 2299 CHCMRCL GV

Ambassade de la République Populaire de Chine en Guinea–Bissau

35'Rua Eduardo Mondlane,
Bissau
Tel: 3970 (Commercial Department)
P.O. Box: 141 Bissau
Cable: Chinaemba, Bissau

Ambassade de la République Populaire de Chine en Guinee

Donka, Conakry
Tel: 461340 (Commercial Department)
P.O. Box: 714 Conakry
Cable: Chinamba, Conakry
Telex: 2128 Hsinhua Conakry

Embassy of the People's Republic of China in Sierra Leone

29 Wilberforce Loop,
Freetown
Tel: 40490 (Commercial Department)
P.O. Box: 778, Freetown
Cable: Chinaemba, Freetown
Telex: 3318 Sinhua SL

Embassy of the People's Republic of China in Liberia

65 Tubman Boulevard, Sinkor, Monrovia
Tel: 261294 (Commercial Department)
P.O. Box: 3001 Monrovia
Cable: Chinaemba, Monrovia

Embassy of the People's Republic of China in Ghana

House No. 14, Botswe Dzorwulu Street, Achimota Forest Residential Area, Accra
Tel: 77462 (Commercial Department)
P.O. Box: 3356, Accra, Ghana
Cable: Chinaemba, Accra

Ambassade de la République Populaire de Chine au Togo

Toroin–Ouest, Prés de l'Hôpital de Lomé
Tel: 5243 (Commercial Department)
P.O. Box: 2690, Lomé
Cable: Chinaemba, Lomé
Telex: 5070 Sinocom TO

Ambassade de la République Populaire de Chine au Benin

No. 2, Zone des Ambassades, Route de l'Aéroport de Cotonou, en face de l'hôtel Sheraton, Benin
Tel: 301097 (Commercial Department)
P.O. Box: 196, Cotonou
Cable: Chinaemba, Cotonou

Embassy of the People's Republic of China in Nigeria

Plot 161A Idejo Street,
Victoria Island Lagos, Nigeria
Tel: 612404 (Commercial Department)
P.O. Box: 70510, Lagos
Cable: Chinaemba, Lagos

Ambassade de la République Populaire de Chine au Cameroun

Rue Joseph Omgba Nsi, Yaoundé
Tel: 223191 (Commercial Department)
P.O. Box: 1307, 4019 Yaoundé
Cable: Chinaemba, Yaoundé
Telex: 8294 Hsinhua KN

Ambassade de la République Populaire de Chine au Congo

Boulevard de Maréchal Lyautey,
Brazzaville
Tel: 811121 (Commercial Department)
P.O. Box: 213
Cable: Chinaemba, Brazzaville
Telex: 5230 Hsinhua KG

Ambassade de la République Populaire de Chine en
République Centrafricaine

> Rue des Missions, Bangui
Tel: 613230 (Commercial Department)
P.O. Box: 1430 Bangui
Cable: Chinaemba, Bangui
Telex: 5217 Public E.C.A. Bangui Extension
        Chinaemba

Ambassade de la République Populaire de Chine en le
Burkina–Faso

> Quartier Rodonde, Ouagadougou
Tel: 334411 (Commercial Department)
P.O. Box: 538 Ouagadougou
Cable: Chinaemba, Ouagadougou

Ambassade de la République Populaire de Chine au
Niger

> Quartier Plateau, Niamey
Tel: 723380 (Commercial Department)
P.O. Box: 725 Niamey
Cable: Ambachine, Niamey
Telex: 5452 BCAC NJ

Embassy of the People's Republic of China in
Zimbabwe

> 30 Baines Avenue,
> Harare, Zimbabwe
Tel: 83616 (Commercial Department)
P.O. Box: 4749 Harare
Cable: Chinaemba, Harare
Telex: 2310 Xinhua ZW

III. EUROPE

Embassy of the People's Republic of China in the
United Kingdom

> 49/51 Portland Place,
> London W1N 3AH
Tel: 01–858 6901 (Commercial Department)
Cable: Chinaemba, London (Ldn)

Ambassade de la République Populaire de Chine en
France

> 11 Avenue George V,
> Paris, 8ème
Tel: 6871901 (Commercial Department)
        5001994 (CAAC Office)
Cable: Chinaemba, Paris
Telex: 270114 (Embassy)

Botschaft der Volksrepublik China in der Bundes-
republik Deutschland

> Kurfuerstenallee 12,
> 5300 Bonn–Bad Godesberg
Tel: 353622, 353628 (Commercial Department)
        CAAC Office in Frankfurt:
        06174–63188 (Residence)
        0611–6905214 (Airport)
Telex: 885672 (Commercial Department)

Embassy of the People's Republic of China in Austria

> 1030 Wien, Metternichgasse 4
Tel: 753140 (Commercial Department)
Cable: Chinb, Wien
Telex: 135794 Chinb A

Ambassade de la République Populaire de Chine en
Belgique

> 19, Boulevard Général Jacques,
> 1050 Bruxelles
Tel: 6404006, 6404210 (Commercial Depart-
        ment)
Cable: Ambachin, Bruxelles
Telex: 23328 Amchin B

Embassy of the People's Republic of China in the
Netherlands

> Adriaan Goekooplaan 7,
> The Hague
Tel: 541170 (Commercial Department)
Cable: 32108 Chiem, NL
Telex: id

Ambassade de la République Populaire de Chine en
Suisse

> Kalcheggweg 10,
> 3006 Berne
Tel: 031/521401 (Commercial Department)
Cable: Ambarpchine, Berne
Telex: 32203(33562) Chiam CH

Ambasciata della Repubblica Populare Cinese nella
Repubblica Italiana

> Via Bruxelles 56,
> 00198 Roma
Tel: 865475 (Commercial Department)
Cable: Ambachina, Roma
Telex: 680159 Cina 1

Embajada da la Republica Popular China en España

> C. Arturo Soria, No. 111–113,
> Madrid–33
Tel: (91)4135892 (Commercial Department)
Cable: Chinaembaco, Madrid
Telex: 22808 Emchi E Madrid

Embassy of the People's Republic of China in Hellenic Republic

Athens 10210, Greece
Tel: 6723281 (Commercial Department)
P.O. Box: 65188 Athens 15410, Greece
Cable: Chinaemba, Athens
Telex: 214383 PRC GR

Embassy of the People's Republic of China in Malta

"Karmnu Court", Lapsi Street, St. Julian's, Malta
Tel: 513280 (Commercial Counsellor's Office)
P.O. Box: 432, Valletta
Cable: Chinaemba, Malta
Telex: 1385 MW Chinew Malta

Embassy of the People's Republic of China in Sweden

Bragevagen 4,
11426 Stockholm
Tel: 7674083, 7654588 (Commercial Department)
Cable: Hoplazatine
Telex: 19608 Hoatine S

Embassy of the People's Republic of China in Denmark

Oregards Alle 25, 2900 Hellerup, Copenhagen
Tel: (01)611013 (Commercial Department)
Cable: Chinem 27019, Copenhagen
Telex: 27019 Chinen DK

Embassy of the People's Republic of China in Iceland

Vidimelur 29, Reykjavik
Tel: 26322 (Commercial Department)
P.O. Box: 1393(513) Reykjavik
Cable: Chinaemba, Reykjavik
Telex: 2418 Kinemb IS

Embassy of the People's Republic of China in Finland

Vanha Kelkkamak 11 (Kulos Aari), Helsinki 57
Tel: 688416 (Commercial Department)
Cable: Kengplatine, Helsinki
Telex: 124661 China SF

Embassy of the People's Republic of China in Romania

Sos Nordului Nr. 2,
Bucuresti
Tel: 335040, 797204 (Commercial Department)
         662180(CAAC)
Cable: Chinamb, Bucharest
Telex: 11324 Chiab R

Embassy of the People's Republic of China in Yugoslavia

Kralja Milutina 6, Belgrade
Tel: 337246 (Commercial Department)
Cable: Chinemb, Belgrade
Telex: 1146 Yu Kinamb

Embassy of People's Republic of China in Albania

Bruga "Skenderbej" Nr. 57,
Tirana (Tirane)
Tel: 2118 (Commercial Department)
Cable: 503, Tirana

Embassy of the People's Republic of China in the Soviet Union

Ul. Druzhby, 6, Leninskie Gory, Moscow
Tel: 1431544 (Commercial Department)
         1431560 (CAAC)
Cable: Chinaemba, Moscow
Telex: 413981 China SU
         413982 China SU

Embassy of the People's Republic of China in Bulgaria

Bul. Rouski, 18, Sofia
Tel: 882080 (Commercial Department)
Cable: Chinese Embassy, Sofia
Telex: 22545 Took BG

Embassy of the People's Republic of China in Poland

00–203, Warszawa, Ul Bonifraterska 1
Tel: 313861 (Commercial Department)
Cable: Sinoembassy, Warszawa
Telex: 813589 China PL

Embassy of the People's Republic of China in Czechoslovakia

Majakovskeho 22,
Praha 6–Bubenec
Tel: 326143 (Commercial Department)
Cable: Chinaemba, Prague
Telex: 121417 (Chiem C)

Botschaft der Volksrepublik China in der Deutschen Demokratischen Republik

111, Berlin, Niederschönhausen,
Heinrich–Mann Strasse 9
Tel: 4828045 (Commercial Department)
Cable: Chidimi, Berlin
Telex: 112474 Berlin Chidi DD

Embassy of the People's Republic of China in Hungary

Benczur Utca 17,
Budapest 1068
Tel: 425724 (Commercial Department)
Cable: Sinoemb, Budapest
Telex: 227733 Chibe H

IV. AMERICA

Embassy of the People's Republic of China in the United States

2300 Connecticut Avenue N.W.,
Washington, DC 20008
Tel: (202)328-2520 (Commercial Department)
Cable: Chinembasy, Washdc
Telex: 440038 PRC JI

Consulate General of the People's Republic of China in San Francisco

1450 Laguna St.
San Francisco, CA 94115
Tel: (415)563-4853 (Commercial Department)
Telex: 4970121 CCSF

Embassy of the People's Republic of China in Canada

415, St Andrew Street, Ottawa, Ontario, Canada K1N 5H3
Tel: (514)2342718 (Commercial Department)
          2858313, 9370692 (CAAC office in Montreal)
Cable: Chinaemba, Ottawa
Telex: 0533770

Embajada de la Republica Popular China en los Estados Unidos Mexicanos

Avenida Rio Magdalena 172,
Colonia Villa Alvaro Obregon,
Mexico 20 D.F. Mexico
Tel: 5482821 (Commercial Department)
Cable: C & Q Chinaemba, Mexico
Telex: 01773907 Echime

Embajada de la Republica Popular China en Cuba

Calle 13, No. 551, E/C. Y. D.,
Vedado, La Havana
Tel: 328749 (Commercial Department)
Cable: Chinaemba, Havana
Telex: 511692 Sinjua CU

Embassy of the People's Republic of China in Jamaica

8 Seaview Avenue, Kingston 10, Jamaica
Tel: (92)70723 (Commercial Department)
P.O. Box: 232 Kingston 6
Cable: Chinaemba
Telex: 2202 Chinaemb JA

Embassy of the People's Republic of China in Guyana

108 Duke Street,
Kingston, Georgetown
Tel: 71652 (Commercial Department)
Cable: Chinaemba, Georgetown–Guyana
Telex: 2251 Chinamemba GY

Embajada da la Republica Popular China en el Peru

Jiron Jose Granda, 150,
San Isidro, Lima
Tel: 405509 (Commercial Department)
P.O. Box: Z. P. 2547, Lima
Telex: 25283 PE Chilima
Cable: Chinaemba, Lima

Embajada de la Republica Popular China en Chile

Av. Pedro de Valdivia 550,
Santiago
Tel: 239988 (Commercial Department)
P.O. Box: Casilla 3417
Telex: 240863 EMBCH CL

Embajada de la Republica Popular China en la Republica del Ecuador

Avenida Atahualpa No. 349 y
Avenida Amazonas
Tel: 458128 (Commercial Department)
P.O. Box: 5143 Quito
Telex: 2614 Echina ED

Embajada de la Republica Popular China en Colombia

Calle 71, No. 2A–41
Bogota, Colombia S.A.
Tel: 2115411 (Commercial Department)
Cable: Embachina, Bogota
Telex: 45387 China CO

V. OCEANIA

Embassy of the People's Republic of China in Australia

247 Federal Highway, Watson,
Canberra, A.C.T. 2602
Tel: 412449 (Commercial Department)
Cable: Chinaemba, Canberra
Telex: Chiem AA 62489

Consulate General of the People's Republic of China in Sydney

539 Elizabeth Street, Surrey Hills, Sydney,
N.S.W. 2010, Australia
Tel: 698-7373 (Commercial Department)
Cable: Chiconsus, Sydney
Telex: Chisyd AA 127931

Embassy of the People's Republic of China in New Zealand

    2-6, Glenmore Street,
    Wellington
Tel: 721383 (Commercial Department)
Cable: Chinaemba
Telex: Chinemb NZ 3843

Embassy of the People's Republic of China in Fiji

    147, Queen Elizabeth Drive,
    Suva, Fiji
Tel: 25391 (Commercial Department)
P.O. Box: Private Mail Bag
Cable: Chinaemb, Suva
Telex: 2136 Chinaemb FJ

ORGANIZATIONS DEALING WITH FOREIGN TRADE

Foreign Trade Policies

FOREIGN trade in China is carried out under the guidance of state policies. First of all, foreign trade business has been undertaken in accordance with state policies in different periods and with regard to the needs of domestic economic development, on the basis of equality and mutual benefit, with different strategies towards different nations and regions. In the fifties, confined by the international situation at that time, China undertook her foreign trade mainly with the Soviet Union and other people's democracies. Today, in the eighties, China carries out a policy of opening to the outside world and develops her trade with all countries, irrespective of their being socialist or capitalist nations, developed or developing countries, on the basis of supplying what she has in return for what she has not.

Economic and trading relations between China and Japan have been developing increasingly since the normalization of their diplomatic relations. Japan is now China's biggest trade partner, with a trade volume of $US21.14 billion in 1985, which accounted for 30.4 per cent of China's total foreign trade volume. Hong Kong and Macao are two regions which have very close trade relations with the mainland of China. A great amount of fresh and live goods and daily consumer commodities needed locally are supplied mainly by the latter. China's trade volume with them in 1985 was $US12.3 billion, which made up 17.9 per cent of her total volume, with the export volume accounting for 27.2 per cent of the total. Western Europe is one of the main areas with which China conducts trade traditionally. China's trade volume with this area in 1985 reached $US7.05 billion, which made up 9.5 per cent of her total value. China's main trade partner in Western Europe is the Federal Republic of Germany, and the next are Italy, Britain, France, Holland, Belgium and Switzerland. China's trade relations with the United States have undergone fairly fast development since 1978, and the trade volume in 1985 reached $7.44 billion, making up about 10.7 per cent of the total. In recent years, China's trade with the Third World nations and regions, including ASEAN countries, Middle Eastern oil-producing countries and Latin American countries, as well as with the Soviet Union and other Eastern European countries, has continued to develop. In the coming years, in accordance with her policy of opening up to the whole outside world, China will carry out her foreign trade on a basis of equality and mutual benefit in opposition to any kind of trade barrier, not only making great efforts to extend her market share in developed countries, but also exploring markets in developing nations in a positive way and quickly resuming her trade relations with the Soviet Union and other Eastern European nations – especially trade with the Soviet Union, which shows a promising prospect.

Secondly, so far as the import and export business is concerned, China will enlarge her export capacity actively in order to earn more foreign currency and to increase her importation for the purposes of strengthening her capacity for self-reliance and accelerating her progress in socialist modernizations: these are the most significant policies of China's foreign trade development. In order to export more, China must organize and extend her resources of goods for export. When problems of contradictions between her domestic and foreign trade over goods resources occur, China will make a unified plan and proper arrangements for both sides. The exportation of commodities necessary to the national economy and people's livelihood is limited in order to meet domestic needs first; priority is given to export of a certain amount of general goods of limited resources but needed by both home and foreign markets; the commodities that are not in great demand in the home market will be exported as much as possible.

Processing zones for export goods have gradually been set up in places with the required conditions, and the construction of export bases will be continued further. The system of sharing retained foreign currency will be put into practice and award funds for foreign trade development established to encourage the regions, departments and enterprises which have

751

Japanese Prime Minister Yasohiro Nakasone and his wife visited a demonstration of the laser composition system for Chinese characters displayed in the China Hall at Tsukuba Expo '85. *(Photo by Qian Sijie)*

done especially well in exporting more goods for foreign currency. Economic levers, such as prices, exchange rates and tariffs, are utilized to stimulate the production of exports. In her import business, China will carry on her consistent policy of self-reliance and not import products that can be manufactured at home, in order to protect and promote national industry. The structure of import commodities is under rational readjustment and the stress is laid on the import of software, advanced technology and key equipment. Raw materials in short supply at home will be imported appropriately, and the import of the instruments and equipment that cannot be made at home but are needed for the development of scientific research, education and industry will be increased. As for consumer goods, a limited amount of those that are in short supply at home may be allowed to be imported at certain times; expensive consumer goods are, however, not imported in excessive quantity and frequency as domestic market incentives. China's purpose of introducing advanced technology is to absorb, assimilate and renovate it. The import of the components and parts for assembling lines to produce tape recorders, refrigerators and coloured television sets will be cut down gradually and replaced by home-made parts as soon as possible, thus to use foreign currency where it is most needed for better economic results.

Patterns of Foreign Trade

In the past, China's foreign trade was carried out exclusively by national specialized import and export corporations with less trade patterns. Today, various general international trade patterns are adopted widely and flexibly.

Trade by Cash

This refers to the trade by means of payment accepted internationally, that is, in US dollars, GDR marks, UK pounds, Japanese Yen, Hong Kong dollars, etc. This is common pattern in international trade nowadays and is adopted by China in her trade transactions with Western developed countries, most Third World nations and with Hong Kong and Macao. Currently, trade by cash accounts for over 90 per cent of China's foreign trade total volume.

Trade on Account

This applies to transactions according to the trade and payment agreements between the Chinese and foreign governments, which is why it may also be referred to trade on agreements. Adopting this pattern, both parties make an annual agreement on their trade volume and types and quantity of staple imports and

The production line of refrigerators imported from Singapore in operation in Guizhou province produces a hundred thousand refrigerators per year.

exports, and both sides open accounts at the other's banks. The payment of each transaction is charged to the accounts and settled at the end of the year. China undertook her foreign trade mainly on the basis of trade on account in the fifties, and it was the principal way of trading with the Soviet Union, other Eastern European nations and some Third World countries. Today, this pattern of trade makes up less than 7 per cent of the total value of Chinese foreign trade.

Compensation Trade

This refers to absorbing foreign investments in a credit way to import advanced equipment, technology and certain raw materials, and reimbursing the principals and the interest in the form of products by instalments. If the foreign businessmen do not wish to accept the compensated products made directly by the imported technology and equipment, compensation can be made up by other products through a bilateral agreement.

Processing Trade

This is a pattern in which China accepts partly or wholly the raw materials, accessories, components and

parts and, in some cases, technical equipment necessary to the processing and assembling, supplied by foreign firms, to manufacture export-oriented products for them according to their requirements. This is a form adopted mainly in business with some developed nations, and can be classified as processing with supplied materials and samples and assembling with components provided, of which processing with supplied materials is the main operation to be undertaken in textiles, machine-building, electronic and light industries as well as agriculture, fishery and breeding, with textiles and light industry taking the lead.

Leasing Trade

This refers to the pattern in which equipment is supplied to Chinese clients by foreign businessmen directly or through leasing companies on a basis of collecting rent. When the leases expire, the equipment is either sold to the clients or shipped back by the lease holders. China did not adopt this trade pattern until 1981, but it is widely welcomed in China because in this way advanced technology and equipment can be obtained to promote her economic development without making any investment first or causing any problem of shortage of funds.

Trading Companies by Joint Venture or Co-operative Management

This refers to trading companies run jointly by Chinese foreign trade corporations and foreign firms outside China. They deal mainly in the marketing of the products made abroad or in China, and some of them act as sales agents abroad for Chinese products in the local markets.

Chinese Export Commodities Fairs

This is one of the most important ways adopted by China in her foreign trade business, and the export value made in the fairs accounts for 20 to 25 per cent of the total current volume of exports to Western countries. A fairly large number of import transactions also are made at the fairs. The Chinese Export Commodities Fair (Guang Jiao Hui) which began in 1957, is held in Guangzhou twice a year, in spring and autumn. Up to 1985 there had been altogether 56 sessions. The fair has become one of China's most significant business channels towards all the nations and regions in the world.

The Administrative System of Foreign Trade

China's foreign trade was formerly administered by a system of being undertaken exclusively by specialized departments, with the State responsible for the overall

The International Mercury Gold Medal delegation visiting Guangzhou Trade Fair. *(Photo by Huang Jianqiu)*

profits and losses. This system once played a useful role, but it now no longer fits the new situation of opening to the outside world. In late 1984 the State Council of the People's Republic of China approved the plan for foreign trade system reform submitted by the Ministry of Foreign Economic Relations and Trade. According to the plan, reform experiments have been made in some departments and are to be extended step by step to the whole nation. The gist of the plan is as follows:

The leadership of foreign trade is unified by the State, while the administration is carried out by specialized departments, according to their different business scopes. The Ministry of Foreign Economic Relations and Trade takes charge of the administration of China's foreign trade as a whole, so that administrative and economic means can be put into effect in order to exercise fully the State's administrative functions in foreign trade, to eliminate the unfavourable situation in which the same business is undertaken by many departments or companies individually and less profit is gained, and to obtain a favourable position of competition in international trade. Meanwhile, full play is given to the initiative of local authorities, departments and enterprises to make their foreign trade management more flexible in order to promote foreign trade.

There is separation of governmental responsibilities from managerial duties: the Ministry of Foreign Economic Relations and Trade and its local administrations in all provinces, autonomous regions and municipalities only oversee the administrative work of foreign trade, being principally engaged in overall planning, coordination, service supply, supervision and programming. Enterprises dealing in foreign trade handle their import and export business on their own, keeping their accounts independently and assuming sole responsibility for their profits and losses. In the planning and administration of foreign trade, the State is gradually reducing the range of instruction and enlarging the scope of guidance. The national specialized foreign trade corporations are the main force in undertaking foreign trade, but they cannot take the shape of monopolies; they need supplementation from a considerable number of middle and small-sized companies which have the right to deal in foreign trade. A few large qualified enterprises can undertake foreign trade directly, once approved by the State.

An import and export agent system is adopted. In principle, the agent system should be adopted in all import transactions, with the profits and losses being assumed by the clients themselves. In export business, the agent system is basically adopted, with the profits and losses assumed either solely by the manufacturing enterprises or jointly by producers and foreign trade enterprises. Foreign trade establishments act as import and export agents for manufacturing departments and end users, charging fees for all services, with the profits and losses assumed by those who entrust the business to them.

There is integration of foreign trade with industry and scientific and technological undertakings. According to the peculiarities of different commodities, foreign trade enterprises co-operate with manufactur-

ing enterprises and scientific institutes in helping them to obtain current information about foreign markets promptly, in order to produce more market-oriented export commodities. In this way, foreign trade establishments will share the same interest with producers and thus will introduce advanced technology to promote the technical retooling of manufacturing enterprises.

ENTERPRISES DEALING WITH FOREIGN TRADE

THE enterprises dealing in foreign trade in China can be classified into four types:

Type 1. Specialized import and export corporations

CHINA NATIONAL CEREALS, OILS AND FOODSTUFFS IMPORT AND EXPORT CORPORATION

Scope of business:

Mainly dealing with the marketing of rice, wheat, maize, soyabean, flour, cereals, beans and peas, peanuts and peanut products; tung oil, edible vegetable oils and animal oils, table salt, livestock and live poultry, frozen meat, eggs and egg products; fresh fruit, dried fruit and fruit products, fresh and dried vegetables, aquatic and marine products, sugar and candy, biscuits and cakes, wines and liquors, beverages, canned food, condiments, etc.

82, Dong'anmen Street, Beijing, China
Tel: 55.5180
Cable: Ceroilfood, Beijing
Telex: 22281 CEROF CN   22111 CEROF CN

CHINA NATIONAL NATIVE PRODUCE AND ANIMAL BY-PRODUCTS IMPORT AND EXPORT CORPORATION

Scope of business:

Undertaking the import and export of native produce, animal by-products and teas, as well as the import of foreign technology, utilisation of foreign funds; handling China–foreign joint venture, co-production and compensation trade related to the trade business of the goods mentioned above.

82 Dong'anmen Street, Beijing, China
Tel: 55.4124, 55.3808
Cable: Chinatuhsu, Beijing
Telex: 22283 Tuhsu Ch

CHINA NATIONAL TEXTILES IMPORT AND EXPORT CORPORATION

Scope of business:

Principally engaged in the import and export of textile raw cotton, wool and man-made fibres, as well as products, ready-made goods and accessories made of the above materials.

82 Dong'anmen Street, Beijing, China
Tel: 55.3793
Cable: Chinatex, Beijing
Telex: 22280 CNTEX CN, 22468 CNTEX CN

CHINA NATIONAL LIGHT INDUSTRIAL PRODUCTS IMPORT AND EXPORT CORPORATION

Scope of business:

Sewing machines and spare parts, bicycles and cycle parts, enamelware, glassware, aluminium utensils, vacuum flasks, sports shoes, cloth shoes, rubber-soled shoes and leather shoes, leather articles, leatherette suitcases and bags, locks, clocks and wrist watches, toilet soap, detergents, plastic products, paper, pencils, leather balls, glass, glazed wall tiles, bakelite products, flashlights, dry batteries, electric fans, fluorescent lights and fittings, etc.

82 Dong'anmen Street, Beijing, China
Tel: 55.6749
Cable: Industry, Beijing
Telex: 22282 LIGHT CN

CHINA NATIONAL ARTS & CRAFTS IMPORT AND EXPORT CORPORATION

Scope of business:

Mainly exporting pottery and porcelain, hand-drawn works, diamonds, pearls and gems, jewellery, ivory carvings, jade carvings, mahogany articles, lacquered furniture, antiques, hand-woven bamboo and straw articles, steel and wooden furniture, um-

Hanging carpets entitled "Beijing Amorous Feelings" and "The Six Steeds of the Zhao Tomb" designed by young artists of the Beijing Carpet Institute.

brellas, artificial flowers, etc.; importing elephant tusk, various jade, jadeite, rosewood, teak, sandalwood, blackwood, glass beads, rattan cane, organdy, linen cloth and added-yarn cloth, etc.

82 Dong'anmen Street, Beijing, China
Tel: 55.2187
Cable: Artchina, Beijing
Telex: 22155 CNART CN

CHINA NATIONAL CHEMICALS IMPORT AND EXPORT CORPORATION

Scope of business:

Engaged mainly in the export of crude oil, various kinds of kerosene, gasoline, diesel oil, lubricant oils and greases, liquefied petroleum gas, paraffin wax, petroleum coke, naphtha, toluene, ethyl alcohol, methyl alcohol, furfural, ammonium molybdate, agricultural chemicals, plastics, dinaphthol, oxalic acid, white oil, tyres, anhydrous sodium sulphate, lithopone, calcium carbide, diosgenin, etc., as well as the import of chemical fertilizers, farming chemicals, rubber, chemical materials, dyestuffs, medical apparatus, etc.

Erligou, Xijiao, Beijing, China
Tel: 89.1289
Cable: Sinochem, Beijing
Telex: 22243 CHEMI CN

CHINA NATIONAL MACHINERY IMPORT AND EXPORT CORPORATION

Scope of business:

Dealing in the import and export business of equipment for transportation and communications, equipment and machinery for power, mining, metallurgical and petroleum industries, agricultural machinery, construction machinery, tool and machine manufacturing machinery, textile, chemical, foodstuff and light industrial machinery and other electrical and mechanical products, instruments and meters, industrial and agricultural tools and graphite electrodes, etc.

Erligou, Xijiao, Beijing, China
Tel: 89.1974
Cable: Machimpex, Beijing
Telex: 22242 CMIEC CN

CHINA NATIONAL METALS AND MINERALS IMPORT AND EXPORT CORPORATION

Scope of business:

Mainly importing various kinds of steel products, pig iron, ferro-alloys, steel scrap, iron ore; non-ferrous metal minerals, semi-products and finished products, rare and precious metals; cements, refractory materials, other non-metallic minerals; exporting mainly tungsten, antimony and its products, tin, graphite, firebricks, cements, pig iron, steel billets, steel products, cast iron products, hardwares for construction, standardized fasteners, etc.

Erligou, Xijiao, Beijing, China
Tel: 89.2376
Cable: Minmetals, Beijing
Telex: 22241 MIMET CN, 22190   MIMET CN

CHINA NATIONAL INSTRUMENTS IMPORT AND EXPORT CORPORATION

Scope of business:

Handling the business of electronic computers and peripheral equipment, television broadcasting centre equipment, modernized telecommunications and broadcasting equipment, geological and mine prospecting equipment, and up-to-date products needed by various science and production fields, such as electronics, optics, physics, chemistry, marine and biological engineering, etc.

Erligou, Xijiao, Beijing, China
Tel: 89.0931 (operator)
Cable: Instrimpex, Beijing
Telex: 22304 CHEC CN

CHINA NATIONAL MEDICINES AND HEALTH PRODUCTS IMPORT AND EXPORT CORPORATION

Scope of business:

Dealing with the business of Chinese medicinal herbs, Chinese patent drugs, medicated wine, healthcare products, pharmaceuticals and their main preparations, chemcal intermediates and reagents, medical instruments and supplies, pharmaceutical manufacturing machines, medical glassware, surgical dressings, biochemical pharmaceuticals, biopreparations, etc.

Building 17, Yongandongli, Jianguomenwai, Beijing, China
Tel: 59.4761
Cable: Meheco, Beijing
Telex: 20046 MEHEC CN

CHINA NATIONAL PACKAGING IMPORT AND EXPORT CORPORATION

Scope of business:

Importing and exporting various packaging materials and accessories, containers, printing equipment and products, machinery and equipments for packaging and food processing and relating technology.

28 Donghouxiang, Andingmenwai, Beijing, China
Tel: 46.2124, 46.2677, 46.4273
Cable: Chinapack, Beijing
Telex: 22490 CPACK CN

CHINA NATIONAL TECHNICAL IMPORT CORPORATION

Scope of business:

In accordance with the state plan, inter-governmental trade agreements, credit agreements and in the light of domestic market demand, importing advanced technology (including technology transfer of processes, equipment-manufacturing, etc.), purchasing various kinds of complete plants, production lines, key equipment and their spare parts, unit equipment and raw materials necessary for the imported projects; entrusting overseas manufacturers and companies with engineering design, technical consulting and factory revamping; handling compensation trade, co-operative production and joint ventures with foreign enterprises; inviting from abroad, or dispatching from China, technical personnel for the imported projects, dealing in the business activities of exporting Chinese technology licences and acting as agent for foreign enterprises in China.

Erligou, Xijiao, Beijing, China
Tel: 89.2116
Cable: Techimport, Beijing
Telex: 22244 CNTIC CN

CHINA NATIONAL COMPLETE PLANT EXPORT CORPORATION

Scope of business:

As entrusted by the Chinese government, being in charge of implementing all the Chinese-aided complete projects abroad in various fields, such as textile, building materials, food processing and light industries, agriculture, fishery and animal husbandry, constructional engineering, water conservancy and electric power, petrochemical industry, communication and transportation, metallurgy, machine building, radio, telecommunication and broadcasting, geological survey and drilling; conducting contract business for designing, construction and installation of projects and technical training in accordance with international commercial practices, and handling joint ventures with either public or private foreign companies; exporting various kinds of complete plants, unit equipment and spare parts; providing special technical or labour services in various fields, particularly in manufacturing enterprises.

28 Donghouxiang, Andingmenwai, Beijing, China
Tel: 44.5678, 46.1742, 46.1796
Cable: Complant, Beijing
Telex: 22559 COMPT CN

Most of these corporations have their own branches in all provinces, autonomous regions and municipalities (except Taiwan province), agencies in Hong Kong and Macao and representative offices in some of the world metropolises, including New York, London,

Foreign Trade and Foreign Economic Relations

Paris, Hamburg and Tokyo. These corporations are mainly engaged in the import and export of the relevant commodities in bulk quantities. Meanwhile, they undertake import and export on a commission basis, providing services to different regions and productive enterprises for the development of local foreign trade. They also take charge of coordinating the prices, clients and markets of the same commodities exported locally, and implementing the policy of unifying the operation of home enterprises in their foreign trade business.

Type 2. Import and Export Corporations under Various Departments of the State Council

CHINA SILK CORPORATION

Scope of business:

Dealing in the export business of white steam filature, tussah silk, spun silk; pure silk satin, spun silk satin, noil poplin, synthetic fibre fabrics, rayon, blend and mixed silk fabrics as well as ready-made embroidered shirts, blouses and other articles of the satins; importing rayon, synthetic fibres; handling processing with supplied materials, joint venture and compensation trade.

> 82 Dong'anmen Street, Beijing, China
> Tel: 55.8831 (operator)
> Cable: Chinasilk, Beijing
> Telex: 22552 CSCBJ CN

CHINA NATIONAL MACHINERY AND EQUIPMENT IMPORT AND EXPORT CORPORATION

Scope of business:

Exporting machinery, electrical and instrumental products manufactured by the Chinese machine-building industry; importing technology required by machinery industrial enterprises and handling co-production or joint venture; importing various mechanical, electrical and instrumental products, components and parts and raw materials; undertaking the business of processing according to clients' designs, samples or with their materials, assembling with clients' components as well as compensation trade; providing technical and labour services for foreign clients.

> 12 Fuxingmenwai Street, Beijing, China
> Tel: 36.6462
> Cable: Equimpex, Beijing
> Telex: 22186 EQUIP CN

CHINA SHIP-BUILDING TRADING COMPANY

Scope of business:

Exporting various ships for civil or military use and

758

necessary equipment, other machinery and electrical products; importing materials and equipment for ship-building; undertaking technology transferring, compensation trade, co-operative production, joint venture, processing with supplied materials and assembling with supplied parts; providing labour and technical services; contracting for the various construction projects of shipyards and ship equipment factories, heavy-duty steel structures, industrial complete plants, high buildings, etc.

> 10 Yuetan Beixiaojie, Beijing, China
> Tel: 89.5947, 89.3038
> Cable: CSTC, CN
> Telex: 22335 CSSC CN
> P.O. Box: 2123 Beijing, China

CHINA NATIONAL COAL IMPORT AND EXPORT CORPORATION

Scope of business:

Unifying the management of the nation's coal import and export business, managing overall local export plans and business; coordinating and conducting coal compensation trade, joint venture, development co-operation, import of advanced foreign technology and equipment; introducing and making use of loans from abroad; organizing sales-oriented technology exchanges and technology and production co-operation within the coal industry.

> 3A Huangsi Street, Deshengmenwai, Beijing, China
> Tel: 46.1223
> Cable: CNCDC, Beijing
> Telex: 22494 CNCDC CN, 22008 CNCDC CN

CHINA METALLURGICAL IMPORT AND EXPORT CORPORATION

Scope of business:

Exporting metallurgical products; importing iron, manganese and chrome ore, pig iron, steel billets and scrap; undertaking compensation trade, joint venture; importing metallurgical special equipment, spare parts, instruments and meters for iron and steel plants, metal and non-metal mining; importing and exporting metallurgical technical patents and know-how; conducting co-operative production of metallurgical and mining equipment, processing of machinery parts, various cast iron and steel products and other metallurgical products with materials supplied or according to clients' samples.

> 46 Dongsixi Street, Beijing, China
> Tel: 55.0197
> Cable: 2250, Beijing
> Telex: 22461 MIEC CN, 22604 MIEC CN

CHINA NATIONAL NON-FERROUS METALS IMPORT AND EXPORT CORPORATION

Scope of business:

Handling on a unified basis the import and export of non-ferrous metal products; undertaking the business of absorbing foreign investments, joint venture, compensation trade and processing with materials, designs and samples supplied by foreign clients, as well as importing complete sets of equipment, technical equipment and technical reform projects.

9 Xizhang Hutong, Xizhimennei Street, Beijing, China
Tel: 65.7031 ext. 233
Cable: 5330, Beijing
Telex: 22086 CNIEC CN

CHINA ELECTRONICS IMPORT AND EXPORT CORPORATION

Scope of business:

Exporting complete sets of electronic equipment and know-how, undertaking radio electronic engineering projects abroad; providing labour services; exporting various kinds of radars, telecommunication equipment, computers and peripheral devices, electronic measuring instruments, special radio equipment, consumer electronics, as well as electronic components, assemblies, modules, vacuum and semiconductor devices, ICs, special materials, wires, cables; importing electronic technology and production lines; handling the processing of imported materials according to clients' samples and designs, compensation trade, co-production and joint ventures, as well as unit electronic equipment, instruments, components and devices, special materials, etc.; implementing governmental trade agreements, handling comprehensive trade items, acting as sales and/or service agents for clients at home and abroad; carrying out market development and research; holding electronic product exhibitions abroad and providing services to foreign electronic exhibitions and technical seminars in China, etc.

49 Fuxing Road, Beijing, China
Tel: 81.1188
Cable: 1284, Dzjsjck
Telex: 22475 CEIEC CN

CHINA NATIONAL AERO-TECHNOLOGY IMPORT AND EXPORT CORPORATION

Scope of business:

Importing and exporting various kinds of aero-products and non-aero products, including aircraft for various purposes, engines, aviation instruments, accessories, electronic appliances and spare parts, air-borne devices, various special and general machinery and equipment, tools, measuring and cutting tools, automobiles, bicycles, motorcycles, household electrical appliances, forgings and castings, electronic instruments and computers; handling the processing and assembling of aero-products and other machinery, equipment and electrical products of imported materials or according to clients' samples and designs; providing maintenance service for aeroplanes, engines and other products and accessories; undertaking design and construction of aero and non-aero projects, providing labour service, engineering machinery, equipment and materials; importing advanced foreign aviation technology, complete plants and single-piece equipments, air-borne components, spare parts and materials; conducting co-operative research and development, designing and production of aero-products and other machines, equipment and electrical products; handling joint ventures and compensation trade with foreign firms.

67 Jiaonan Street, Beijing, China
Tel: 44.2444
Cable: Caid, Beijing
Telex: 22318 AEROT CN

CHINA PRECISION MACHINERY IMPORT AND EXPORT CORPORATION

Scope of business:

Exporting precision machinery products including automatic piloting instruments, controllers, radar equipment, remote measuring equipment, navigation equipment, detonating devices, various testing equipment, instruments and meters; optical machinery products including infra-red, laser, optical instruments and other comprehensive products and electron microscopes with a magnification of 800,000 times; electrical products including various micromotors, alternators, chargers, transformers, message sources; electronic products including computers, facsimile equipment, television sets, wired broadcast equipment and stereo record players; general machinery products including medical devices, light industrial machinery, construction machinery, food processing machinery; chemical products including various chemical power sources; organizing the export of technology and labour service, handling compensation trade, joint venture, co-operative production, processing with materials, designs or samples supplied by clients and assembling with supplied components; importing advanced technology and various advanced precision machinery.

2 Yuetan Beixiaojie, Beijing, China
Tel: 89.5012
Cable: CPMIEC, Beijing
Telex: 22484 CPMC CN

CHINA XINSHIDAI COMPANY

Scope of business:

Importing and exporting aircraft products, electronics, ships, vehicles and some general and precision

759

machinery, chemical products and light industrial products; and providing maintenance services and spare parts for the products mentioned above.

P.O. Box 511, Beijing, China
Tel: 66.4714
Telex: 22338 XSDCO CN

CHINA NORTH INDUSTRIES CORPORATION

Scope of business:

Importing and exporting various types of heavy-duty machinery, custom-made equipment, construction equipment, heavy-duty vehicles and other machinery and electrical products, hardware and tools, chemicals, high polymer materials, paints and coatings, chemical processing equipment, explosives and related items, plastic products, labour safety devices, various light-industrial products, precision machinery, optical glass, optical instruments, photographic equipment, testing and measuring instruments, etc.; accepting orders of special technical equipment, processing materials and assembling components supplied by foreign clients; undertaking compensation trade and joint ventures with foreign companies, contracting for the design of engineering projects and supplying engineering consultation services, etc.

7A Yuetan Nanjie, Beijing, China
Tel: 86.2254
Cable: Norinco, Beijing
Telex: 22339 CNIC CN

CHINA NUCLEAR ENERGY INDUSTRY CORPORATION

Scope of business:

Importing and exporting uranium products for peaceful applications, various kinds of isotopes, calcium metals, nuclear electronic instruments, neutron monitoring equipment, instruments for radioactive ore exploration and mining, radioactive protection devices, nuclear medical facilities and nuclear detecting elements, etc.; undertaking the processing of imported materials, assembling of supplied kits, compensation trade, co-operative production and joint ventures.

21 Nanlishi Road, Beijing, China
P.O. Box 2139, Beijing
Tel: Export Department: 86.7717;
Import Department: 86.6930
Foreign Liaison Department: 86.7657
Cable: CNEIC, Beijing
Telex: 22240 CNEIC CN

CHINA GREAT WALL INDUSTRY CORPORATION

Scope of business:

Exporting various special precision machinery, elec-

tronic instruments and mechanical products, including gyroscopic meters, various special purpose machines and tools, measuring tools, moulds, refuelling trucks, tunnel borers, electronic computers and peripheral devices, flight simulators, radar equipment, satellite navigation equipment, remote measuring and controlling equipment, ICs, conductors, accelerometers, strain gauges, crystal, various testing instruments and meters; handling joint ventures with foreign firms, compensation trade, processing of supplied materials and assembling with imported parts, agent of maintenance service; contracting for the technical designing for foreign relating engineering projects as well as the construction designing and other technical services for them.

P.O. Box 847, Beijing, China
Tel: 89.3175
Cable: GWIC, Beijing
Telex: 22651 CGWIC CN

CHINA SCIENTIFIC INSTRUMENTS AND MATERIALS CORPORATION

Scope of business:

Exporting novel instruments and materials for metallurgy, building materials, chemical, petroleum, textile and light industries.

75 Dengshikou Street W., Beijing, China
Tel: 55.0951
Cable: CSIMC, Beijing

CHINA XIAO FENG TECHNOLOGY AND EQUIPMENT COMPANY

Scope of business:

Dealing in the business of importing and exporting instruments, equipment, devices and apparatus for scientific research, education, production and experiment; undertaking technical services, acceptance testing, training, maintenance, measurement and technical consultation for imported and domestic instruments and equipment; handling processing and assembling operations.

92 Dongzhimennei Street, Beijing, China
Tel: 44.7079
Telex: 22499 CIFEC CN

CHINA NATIONAL NEW BUILDING MATERIALS CORPORATION

Scope of business:

Engaged mainly in the manufacture and sales of various new building materials, including gypsum plasterboard with paper facings, gypsum compound board, gypsum for whitewashing, mineral wool board, pipe section and lamellar mat, gas concrete, PVC floor tiles, glass fibre wall fabrics, concrete fibre board, acoustic sheet, complete houses and buildings; undertaking design and construction of hotels, dwelling houses, schools and hospitals with new building materials; dealing in import and export of the technology of new building material production, complete sets of equipment, raw materials and products.

Zizhuyuan Road, Beijing, China
Tel: 89.1260
Cable: 4554, Beijing

CHINA NATIONAL OFFSHORE OIL CORPORATION

Scope of business:

According to the Regulations of the People's Republic of China on the Exploitation of Offshore Petroleum Resources in Co-operation with Foreign Enterprises, undertaking petroleum resources exploration, exploitation, production operations in areas and blocks of sea waters approved by the Chinese government in co-operation with foreign companies and conducting the marketing of petroleum derived therefrom and other related operations.

31 Dongchangan Street, Beijing, China
Tel: 55.5225
Cable: 3113, Beijing
Telex: 22611 CNOOC CN

CHINA PETROCHEMICAL INTERNATIONAL COMPANY

Scope of business:

Unifying for all the enterprises of China Petrochemical Corporation (SINOPEC) the management of the import business of technology and complete plants, special unit processing equipment and spare parts needed by the petrochemical industry in production, scientific research, construction and technical revamping of existing plants; undertaking various kinds of economic and technical co-operation with foreign firms; handling the export of special complete sets of equipment made by SINOPEC; contracting for engineering and construction projects and providing labour service abroad; undertaking bilateral and multilateral aid projects according to governmental agreements as well as economic and technical aid projects sponsored by foreign governments and international organizations, including the United Nations.

2 District 5, He Ping Li, Beijing, China
Tel: 48.5531
Cable: 4270, Beijing
Telex: 22655 CPCCI CN
P.O. Box: 4713 Beijing

CHINA NATIONAL CHEMICAL CONSTRUCTION CORPORATION

Scope of business:

Exporting complete chemical plants and special equipment; providing various technical services; un-

dertaking construction work of bilateral or multilateral chemical projects for assisting foreign countries; importing advanced foreign technology, special equipment and spare parts for chemical production; engaging in various types of economic and technical co-operation with foreign enterprises; contracting for overseas chemical projects and providing labour service abroad.

Building 16, District 7, He Ping Li, Beijing, China
Tel: 46.4043
Cable: CNCCC, Beijing
Telex: 22492 CNCCC CN

THE ORIENTAL SCIENTIFIC INSTRUMENTS IMPORT AND EXPORT CORPORATION

Scope of business:

Undertaking import and export of various kinds of instruments and equipment, components and devices, materials, reagents and new technology for scientific research and education.

The Chinese Academy of Sciences, 52 Sanlihe Road, Beijing, China
Tel: 866119
Telex: 22474 ASCHI CN

CHINA NATIONAL SEED CORPORATION

Scope of business:

Importing and exporting the seeds and saplings of all kinds of crops producing cereal, cotton, oil, vegetable, green manure, bast fibre, tea, tobacco, melon and fruits; undertaking seed production for overseas businessmen and seed companies, including the production of hybrid seeds; handling compensation trade, joint venture and marketing on a commission basis.

16 Donghuanbei Road, Beijing, China
Tel: 59.3169
Cable: CNSC, Beijing
Telex: 22233 MAAF CN CNSC

CHINA NATIONAL TREE SEED CORPORATION

Scope of business:

Undertaking the import and export of tree breeding materials, including seeds and seedlings, cuttings, scions and roots of trees and shrubs for propagation.

He Ping Li, Beijing, China
Tel: 46.4717
Cable: CNTSC, Beijing
Telex: 22237 CFFC CN CNTSC

CHINA NATIONAL ANIMAL BREEDING STOCK IMPORT AND EXPORT CORPORATION

Scope of business:

Specialized in the import and export of all kinds of breeding stock, including cattle, sheep, goats, pigs, horses, donkeys, camels, rabbits, bees, dogs, breeding poultry stock as well as pasture seeds.

He Ping Li, Beijing, China
Tel: 46.4344
Cable: CNABSIEC, Beijing

The corporations listed above are authorised to undertake import and export business directly with foreign firms or countries within their respective scopes of business.

Type 3. Local import and export companies

By the end of 1985, provincial import and export companies had been set up all over the country; for instance, Beijing, Shanghai, Tianjin, Guangdong, Fujian, and Liaoning had established their own import and export corporations. Under the guidance of the State's unified foreign trade policies and plans, these corporations administrate and coordinate the local foreign trade, undertake import business entrusted by local entities or other entities in China, and handle business entrusted by foreign manufacturers, such as sales, agency, consignment sale, sales on exhibition, maintenance service, etc.

Type 4. Enterprises combining industrial production with foreign trade and integrated complexes

Practically, these can be classified into:

– large industrial enterprises

e.g. Anshan Iron and Steel Company, the Capital Iron and Steel Company, Wuhan Iron and Steel Company, Ma'anshan Iron and Steel Company, and a group of industrial enterprises affiliated with the Ministry of Machine Building and its branches. They are allowed to deal with export business directly.

– industry and trade combined enterprises run unifiedly on a national level

e.g. the China Silk Corporation takes the charge of overall planning and developing the production of white steam filature, tussah silk, rayon, synthetic fibre and various satins, as well as handling the import and export of silk and satin, satin garments and other silk and satin manufactured products.

– united foreign trade establishments run jointly by industrial enterprises

e.g. China United Electric Export Corporation, China Electro-Ceramic Export Allied Corporation, China National Electric Wire and Cable Export Corporation, China Abrasives Export Corporation, China National Bearing Joint Export Corporation, China Packaging Company, etc.

– foreign trade enterprises of joint venture of domestic enterprises

e.g. China Yanshan United Foreign Trade Company, Ltd. is a joint venture of China National Chemicals Import and Export Corporation, China National Technical Import Corporation, Beijing Foreign Trade Corporation and Yanshan Petrochemical Corporation.

– foreign trade enterprises run by one local region, or jointly by different regions

e.g., for the former, Shanghai Toys Import and Export Corporation, Shanghai Handkerchiefs Import and Export Corporation, Qingdao Associated Textile Import and Export Corporation, Changzhou Agricultural Machinery Import and Export Corporation; for the latter, Shanghai United Embroidered and Drawn Works Export Corporation, which is an economic complex with independent accounts settlement, a specialized foreign trade corporation taking Shanghai port as its trading centre, and was set up in 1984 and run jointly by Jiangsu, Zhejiang and Shanghai.

– industrial enterprises authorized to undertake foreign trade directly

e.g. the Beijing Silk Flowers Factory undertakes the export of various silk flowers made in the factory, such as flowers in bouquets, cases and gift packs, flowers for wedding ceremonies and paper products; it also imports necessary raw materials.

There are also various service corporations for foreign trade, such as companies undertaking foreign trade storage, transportation, export base construction, foreign trade and economic consulting, import and export commodity inspection, etc.

UTILIZATION OF FOREIGN CAPITAL AND INTRODUCTION OF FOREIGN TECHNOLOGY

General Development and Major Achievements

SHORTLY after the founding of New China, the Chinese government laid down the policy of building up the country mainly through self-reliance and seeking foreign aid as a supplementary source for the construction. Under this policy, China started to utilize foreign capital and introduce foreign technology to facilitate its socialist construction. In 1950, China signed its first loan agreement with the Soviet Union. During the 1950s, China introduced technology and equipment from the Soviet Union by means of loan and credit account, having successively signed and introduced 304 items of complete sets of equipment and 64 sets of individual workshop equipment. During the 1950s, China also introduced complete sets of equipment and individual machinery from the six East European socialist countries by means of loan and credit account.

Since the late 1970s, China has made further headway in the utilization of foreign capital and introduction of foreign technology. Most of the means by which to absorb foreign capital now employed internationally are being used by China. Among the various contracts signed between China and other countries over the past few years for the introduction of foreign technology, those concerning licensed trade, co-operative production, counselling and technical service account for about 60 per cent. There are now more and more businesses and industries in China engaged in the introduction of foreign technology, covering dozens of areas such as machinery, electronics, chemicals, light industry, oil, coal, building material, metallurgy, automobiles, hydropower, the textile industry and so on. The source countries of the technology are also becoming multiple. In 1985, China absorbed a record amount of foreign capital, having signed foreign loan agreements totalling $US3.53 billion, registering an increase of 84.4 per cent over the previous year. Among these loans, $US2.51 billion has been actually used. The direct foreign investment contracts signed between China and foreign businesses in 1985 totalled $US6.33 billion, registering an increase of 120.3 per cent over the previous year; $US1.96 billion of this total has been actually used. The commodity credit contracts between China and foreign countries in 1985 totalled $US360 million, an increase of 62.8 per cent over the previous year, with $US300 million having been actually used.

Within the seven-year period between 1979, when China started to implement the open policy, and 1985, China signed foreign loan agreements that accumulatively totalled over $US22.18 billion, and actually used $US15.3 billion out of these loans. Within the same period, the direct foreign investment contracts between China and foreign businesses totalled over $US16.08 billion, with over $US6.06 billion having been actually used. By the end of 1985, more than 2,300 Sino-foreign joint ventures, over 3,700 Sino-foreign co-operative enterprises and 120 fully foreign-owned enterprises had been successively set up in China. 35 ocean oil exploration projects had been ratified. Already under way are projects such as the Guangdong Nuclear Power Station, Pingshuo Opencut Coal Mine in Shansi province, Shanghai-Volkswagen Car Factory, Beijing China International Trade Centre, etc., all of which involve large amounts of investment and new technology, and are of special significance for China's economic construction. Encouraging results have also been achieved in the joint ocean oil exploration projects.

Foreign governments, regions and international financial organizations that have provided China with loans for its construction projects or have directly invested in China include Japan, United States, Great Britain, France, Switzerland, Belgium, Federal Republic of Germany, Canada, Singapore, Sweden, Brazil, Malta, Denmark, Argentina and Spain, as well as Hong Kong, Macao, the World Bank, the International Monetary Fund, the UN Agricultural Development Fund, etc.

Utilizing foreign capital and introducing foreign technology have been greatly conducive to supplementing China's lack of funds for its internal construction projects and to facilitating China's economic construction. The major achievements of this policy are manifest in the following aspects:

Reinforcing the country's major construction projects

In the field of agriculture, 129 construction projects using foreign capital have been contracted by the Ministry of Agriculture, Animal Husbandry and

The production line in the Beijing Jeep Company Ltd. managed by Beijing Automobile Factory and American Motors Corporation.

Fishery alone with other countries, totalling more than $US400 million. Within the energy industry, over $US1 billion has been channelled into the construction of the oil industry in the past few years. And by using foreign capital, the coal industry has increased its production capacity by more than 20 million tons in recent years. During the first phase of construction of Baoshan Iron and Steel General Plant at Shanghai, foreign capital amounting to RMB¥8.8 billion has been used and 22 sets of advanced equipment have been introduced. When the project is completed and the projected production capacity reached, 500,000 tons of seamless steel tubes will be produced annually, including 210,000 tons of oil pipes and 60,000 tons of boiler pipes, which at present are in short supply domestically and have to be imported in large quantity. These products will help fill a gap in the domestic raw and semi-finished materials industry. In the area of transportation, a group of projects have been constructed by using foreign capital, which are now helping to alleviate the inadequacy of the domestic transportation facilities.

Facilitating the improvement of the industry's technical level

In the past few years, China has introduced several thousand pieces of advanced technology and equipment from other countries. Among these items more than 900 have been introduced by using the country's

foreign currency alone. Most of these items of technology and equipment are up to the level of the 1970s or 1980s. Now the emphasis is being gradually shifted from introducing large and complete sets of equipment to introducing specific pieces of technology, particularly a greater amount of software technology, and from building up new enterprises to transforming the technology of the old enterprises. The introduction of technology is gradually being combined with digesting and assimilating the introduced technology and with inventing and independently developing new technology and products. This has brought about a manifest improvement of economic benefit.

Promoting the development of production and increasing the country's capacity to export and to earn foreign currency

The establishment and operation of the joint ventures and co-operative enterprises have created new sources of exporting commodities and have increased the competitiveness of China's products on the international market.

Principle of the Policy and Methods of Management

Since 1979, on the basis of the past experience and with reference to other countries' practices, China has

The passenger plane MD-82, manufactured by Sino-American joint venture.

successively formulated Legal Provision for Sino-foreign Joint Ventures, Regulations for Sino-foreign Joint Exploration of Ocean Oil Resources, Income Tax Law Concerning Joint Ventures, Income Tax Law Concerning Foreign-owned Enterprises, and Personal Income Tax Law, as well as laws and regulations regarding foreign economic relations such as planning, labour, finance, foreign currency, insurance, etc. These laws and regulations have laid down a series of policies and principles for the utilization of foreign capital and the introduction of foreign technology. The essence of these policies is that the Chinese government will protect foreign business participants in terms of their investment, profits, and other legal rights according to the agreements, contracts, and regulations ratified by the Chinese government. In May of 1983, the State Council of the People's Republic of China convened the First National Conference on the Utilization of Foreign Capital and appropriately liberalized the policies regarding the utilization of foreign capital in order to step up progress in this area. Later, the State Council made a number of amendments to the policies aiming for further liberalization in the utilization of foreign capital. The main principles for China's present policies concerning the utilization of foreign capital are:

1. Foreign businessmen investing in China in joint

ventures do not have to run the risk of having to pay high taxes and will be given preferential treatment. In the first place, with regard to taxes, foreign businessmen will enjoy tax reduction, better preferential treatment and simplified formalities. Preferential treatment will be given to joint ventures regarding income tax, i.e., the tax rate will be reduced to a lower level of 30 per cent, with another 10 per cent to be levied as local income tax according to the actual amount of the income. The two amounts will account for 33 per cent of the total income, which is below the middle level compared with other countries. On the basis of this reduced tax rate, China has made some additional stipulations regarding tax reduction and exemption. For instance, newly established joint ventures with a stipulated term of more than 10 years will enjoy a tax exemption in the first two profit-making years, and a 50 per cent tax reduction during the following 3 years. With those joint ventures in agriculture and forestry where profit is relatively low, and with those joint ventures set up in the remote and economically underdeveloped areas, in addition to a tax exemption and reduction in the first 5 years, there will be a continued 15–30 per cent reduction of·income tax during the following 10 years. If the foreign participant uses his profit derived from the joint venture to reinvest in China, with a term of

765

not less than 5 years, he is entitled to apply for a 40 per cent return of the income tax levied on his reinvested capital.

Foreign businessmen will enjoy preferential treatment regarding the tax on their capital investment. Their machines, equipment, parts, components and other materials imported into China as investment or additional investment will be free from customs duty and the industrial and commercial consolidated tax on imports. Regarding the fixed assets derived from the capital investment, especially regarding the ocean oil exploration involving greater investment and longer time, foreign investors will be allowed, after proper application and approval, an accelerated period of years for depreciation so as to speed up the return of the capital.

With respect to the preferential treatment regarding industrial and commercial consolidated taxes on joint ventures, the tax rate will be fixed with reference to the lower level, rather than the higher level. If the tax rate is lower than that for other enterprises in China, it will be kept unchanged; if it is above the level for other domestic enterprises, the tax rate will be reduced to the level equal to that for other domestic enterprises in China. The products of the joint ventures, except those limited by the State for export, will be free from the industrial and commercial consolidated tax. The raw materials, parts and components imported by joint ventures for the production of export goods will be free from customs duty and the industrial and commercial consolidated tax on imports. The essential instruments and equipment imported into China along with the technology still non-existent in China will be free from the import duty and the industrial and commercial consolidated tax on imports. On instruments and equipment imported into China that are suitable for domestic use but cannot be produced or supplied in China, a 50 per cent customs duty will be levied, and the industrial and commercial consolidated tax on imports.

Preferential treatment will be given to foreign businessmen regarding their personal income tax. The excessive progressive tax rate is applied to wage and salary, starting with RMB¥800, the tax rate being 5–45 per cent. Income from service payment, privilege charge, or property lease is eligible for proportional tax rate, which starts with RMB¥4,000, the tax rate being 20 per cent. Profits, interests, dividends and other incomes are taxed according to the specific amount of income each time, the tax rate being 20 per cent. Foreign businessmen's income derived from their profit and lease in China will be given a 10 per cent tax reduction; this provision, as had been stipulated, was to expire in 1985, but it has now been extended to the end of 1990. All types of income shall be calculated in terms of reminbi. Incomes in the form of foreign currency must be converted into reminbi according to the exchange rate issued by the State

General Administration of Foreign Currency Control of the People's Republic of China for taxation.

Secondly, with regard to the revenue and expenditure of foreign currency, joint ventures are allowed to make adjustments or use other methods to achieve a balance in the revenue and expenditure of foreign currency. It had been stipulated earlier that joint ventures should generally maintain a balance in their revenue and expenditure of foreign currency. In January 1986, it was decided by the State Council of the People's Republic of China that for those joint ventures established through the approval of a competent authority of the State, if an adjustment of the revenue and expenditure of foreign currency is needed, it will fall within the responsibility of that competent authority and shall be settled with recourse to the foreign currency revenue of the other joint ventures across China. With those joint ventures established by the approval of a local government or a government department, the adjustment will fall within the responsibility of the local government or the government department concerned and shall be settled with recourse to the foreign currency revenue of the newly approved and established joint ventures. For those highly sophisticated products or those products having a competitive power on the international market that are produced with advanced or crucial technology provided by the foreign business participant, if these products are really badly needed domestically, arrangements can be made, after proper approval, to increase – through contract – the proportion of their sale in China. The foreign currency balance plan concerning the sale of these products can be settled by being incorporated into the foreign currency plan of the State.

Foreign business participants working for a balance of the revenue and expenditure of the joint venture can, after proper approval, make use of the mechanism of joint sale to market certain domestically produced products abroad for a comprehensive compensation. When a foreign business participant runs two or more joint ventures in China and has surplus and deficit at the same time in his legitimate revenue of foreign currency, he can, after proper approval, make complementary adjustment between his enterprises.

Thirdly, foreign business participants will enjoy the same treatment regarding material supply as China's state-run enterprises. Resources like machinery, equipment, raw material and fuel needed by joint ventures, when belonging to the category for planned distribution, will, as is the case with state enterprises, be incorporated into the supply plan of the competent department of the enterprise and will enjoy, according to contract, a guaranteed supply from the related commercial or material supplies department or the manufacturer. Regarding the price of goods and materials, only six types of raw materials, i.e., gold, silver, platinum, petroleum, coal, and timber, when used directly for the manufacture of exporting products, will be priced according to the international market price level. Other goods and materials, including water, electricity, gas, heat, transportation and other services that are provided to joint ventures, will, as is the case with state enterprises, be priced and charged according to the current domestic market price. Payment for the above-mentioned domestically supplied materials should all be made in renminbi.

Fourthly, with regard to the marketing of products, a certain portion of China's domestic market will be left specially to the joint ventures as a favour. In the past there was an over-rigid control of the domestic market, and joint ventures were required to sell most or all of their products abroad without discrimination, even though some of these products were badly needed domestically and had to be imported in large quantities. Since March 1983, the country has appropriately liberalized the relevant policy. Now, while joint ventures are still encouraged to sell their products abroad, they are allowed to increase the proportion of the domestic sale of those products that are badly needed in China or have to be imported into China. Some of these products can even be given a major share of the domestic market to replace imports.

2. *Measures have been taken to expand the authority of the local administrations and government departments to ratify the utilization of foreign capital and introduction of foreign technology while strengthening the function of the state plan to provide macro guidance on the utilization of foreign capital.* For some time, only in Fujian and Guangdong provinces had special policies been implemented and flexible measures taken, allowing the two regions greater self-determination in utilizing foreign capital. In October 1984, a new decision was made by the State that grants the administrations of Beijing municipality, Liaoning province, Guangdong province, Fujian province, the Shenyang municipality, and the China National Corporation of the Nonferrous Metal Industry a greater authority to ratify foreign investment for productive capital construction

Chinese and American technicians check the preparation work carefully before the trial flight of the MD-82.

projects and technological transformation projects, with the ceiling of the amount raised to $US10 million for an individual project. The decision also allows the other provinces, autonomous regions, and Chongqing and Wuhan municipalities as well as the Ministries of Industry, Transportation, Agriculture and Forestry and the general industrial corporations under these ministries, a greater authority to ratify foreign investment, with the ceiling of the amount raised to $US5 million for an individual project. This authority is given provided that the funds (including the foreign currency and the supplementary funds in reminbi), energy, transportation, raw materials and the miscellaneous production conditions involved in the investment project can be balanced by the relevant administration itself. The coastal seaport cities are given an even greater authority to ratify foreign investment. The total amount of foreign investment in an individual project that may be ratified is up to $US30 million for Shanghai and Tianjin municipalities, up to $US10 million for Dalian and Guangzhou municipalities, and up to $US5 million for the other coastal cities, provided that the construction and production conditions do not involve a comprehensive balancing by the State, that the products do not require the State for marketing, that the export of the products does not involve state quota, and that the borrowed foreign funds can be returned by the relevant administration itself. As for those nonproductive construction projects that utilize foreign investment, they can be ratified by the local administrations, government departments or the coastal seaport cities themselves, so long as these projects can be carried out mainly with foreign funds to be borrowed and returned by the relevant administration itself, or with self-raised funds, self-collected materials and self-imported equipment without involving general balancing by the State. Meanwhile, a greater authority is given to the local administrations and government departments to ratify the usage of the state and self-owned foreign currency to introduce foreign technology; the minimum amount of the foreign currency to be submitted to the State Planning Commission for ratification of use has been raised to $US5 million. Any project involving an amount below this level can be ratified by the relevant local administration or government department itself.

While expanding the power of the local administrations and government departments to utilize foreign capital, the State has strengthened its planning and guidance for the utilization of foreign capital. When the planning administrations at the various levels make drafts for annual, medium and long-term plans for national economic and social development, the utilization of foreign capital, including an appropriate utilization of foreign commercial loans, is incorporated as an important component into the plan. Directive planning is used by the State to supervise the general volume of foreign capital used

Packages of Chinese goods won 22 gold medals when participating for the first time in an international package competition: (upper left to right) Hunan spirit of the Western Han, Anhui tea from Mount Huangshan, crystal glassware from Chongqing; (lower left to right) Maotai spirits from Guizhou, coffee set from Hunan, Jilin cosmetics with ginseng.

by the whole country. The local administrations and government departments are required to report the volume of foreign capital to be used to the State Planning Commission, for checking and ratification. The local administrations and government departments should also report to the State Planning Commission, for the record, the total volume of self-possessed foreign currency they use for the introduction of foreign technology. Thus, through the macro guidance of the state planning and a comprehensive balancing, the construction conditions for joint ventures and for introduced foreign technology can be guaranteed.

3. *The utilization of foreign capital and introduction of foreign technology are chiefly supervised by the State Planning Commission, the State Economic Commission, and the Ministry of Foreign Economic Relations and Trade.* The State Planning Commission is responsible for working out the scale, volume and priority for the utilization of foreign capital, introduction of foreign technology and import of complete sets of equipment, as well as for drawing up plans for projects involving an amount of foreign capital above the maximum that can be ratified by lower administrations. It is also responsible for drawing up plans concerning miscellaneous projects requiring foreign capital and for the supervision of the execution of these plans. The State Economic Commission is responsible for drawing up

plans for projects involving an amount of foreign capital below the maximum that can be ratified by the lower administrations, and for the digestion, assimilation and popularization of the introduced foreign technology as well as the reproduction of the imported equipment by China's own industry. The Ministry of Foreign Economic Relations and Trade works according to the state plan to organize and coordinate negotiations and conclusions of agreements with foreigners concerning projects using foreign loans, introduction of foreign technology and import of complete sets of foreign equipment. It is also responsible for the examination and ratification of agreements and contracts for those projects involving the utilization of foreign capital and the introduction of foreign technology.

According to China's present administrative system, the utilization of foreign capital is managed through unified planning and stratified administrations. With those local units and organizations, the plan for the utilization of foreign capital will be drawn up by the planning committees of the respective province, autonomous region or the municipality directly under the Central Government. With those units and organizations under the various ministries of the State, the plan for the utilization of foreign capital will be drawn up by the respective ministry itself. The local administrations and government departments should report their plan for the utilization of foreign capital to the State Planning Commission and submit a copy of the plan to the Ministry of Foreign Economic Relations and Trade. After a comprehensive balancing and an integrated ratification by the State Planning Commission, the plan will be incorporated into the state plan for national economic and social development. With regard to those foreign investment projects involving an amount above the maximum quota a particular department is allowed to ratify the recommendation instrument and the feasibility study report of the project should be subjected to examination and ratification by the State Planning Commission, along with the State Economic Commission, the Ministry of Foreign Economic Relations and Trade, and other departments concerned. If the project involves a total investment of more than $US200 million, it will undergo a preliminary examination by the State Planning Commission and the other departments mentioned above before it is submitted to the State Council for examination and approval. Projects with a total value below the maximum quota set by

the State will be examined and ratified by the proper local administration or the competent department according to the stratification of responsibility and administration and will be reported to the State Planning Commission, the State Economic Commission, the Ministry of Foreign Economic Relations and Trade and other departments concerned for the record. However, if the project requires a comprehensive national balancing regarding fuel, power, raw material, transportation, etc., it must be reported to the State Planning Commission, the State Economic Commission, the Ministry of Foreign Economic Relations and Trade, and other relevant departments for examination and approval. For all the projects using foreign funds to be undertaken, the supplementary funds in terms of reminbi must be arranged and settled at the same time according to the stratification of responsibility and administration. The Ministry of Foreign Economic Relations and Trade will provide counsel and professional guidance to government departments, administrations and business enterprises concerning the utilization of foreign capital.

SPECIAL ECONOMIC ZONES AND OPEN COASTAL CITIES

SPECIAL policies are being implemented and flexible measures taken in Guangdong and Fujian provinces in the development of foreign trade, the utilization of foreign capital and the introduction of foreign technology. The special economic zones and open coastal seaport cities, as well as the deltas of the Zhujiang (Pearl River) and the Yangtze River, the triangle area of the south of Fujian province, the East Liaoning Peninsula and the East Shandong Peninsula are the frontier areas of China as the country opens up to the outside world and are thus charged with specially important tasks to perform.

Special Policies and Flexible Measures Granted to Gaungdong and Fujian Provinces in their External Economic Activities

Both Guangdong and Fujian provinces are situated in China's south-eastern coastal areas, bordering Hong Kong and Macao. The two provinces face Taiwan across the sea and enjoy convenient sea transport links with Japan and South-East Asian countries. They have a long history of foreign trade. For example, the Quanzhou Port in Fujian province was described by Marco Polo as the second largest port in the world at the time, following the port of Alexandria in Egypt. There are about 13 million overseas Chinese living

abroad who have origins in the two provinces, amounting to two-thirds of the country's total number of overseas Chinese. With a mild climate, abundant rainfall and rich products, the two provinces boast the excellent natural conditions of sub-tropical zones.

In July 1979, the Party Central Committee and the State Council granted more initiative to the two provinces, authorizing them to take special policies and flexible measures in their external economic activities and to bring into full play their local advantages in attracting capital from both the overseas Chinese and foreign enterprises, importing advanced technology and managerial experience from abroad, so as to expand their foreign trade and speed up their economic development. This marked an important decision in China's opening up to the outside world, and has an important significance in accelerating China's socialist modernization process.

In accordance with that decision, the two provinces have taken the following special policies and flexible measures in their external economic activities:

More planning power for the local authorities

Under the guidance of the State's long-term plans and policies for economic construction, the provincial authorities have more power in planning their production, capital construction, technological transformation, finance, goods and materials, foreign trade, commerce, labour wages, science and technology, culture, education, public health and tourism. All the enterprises and institutions in agriculture, industry, transportation, commerce, culture, education, science and technology, and public health have since been under the administration of the provincial authorities, except those in the sectors of railway, port, post and telecommunications, civil aviation, customs, banking and national defence.

More power to the local authorities in foreign trade

Under the overall guidance of the State's foreign trade policies and planning, the provincial authorities have planned and conducted their own foreign trade. There has been no restriction on their export products normally imposed on different commodities according to different port locations. The two provinces have been permitted to conduct foreign trade directly from their local ports. The provincial authorities decide on the evaluation of foreign exchange for imported goods. The provincial foreign trade corporations are under the dual administration of the State's head corporations and the provincial authorities concerned, with the latter as the main administrators. Meanwhile, some provincial specialized companies have been set up to conduct the production, marketing and export of special products, on the principle of combining production with marketing, industry with foreign trade, and domestic trade with foreign trade. Thus, the surplus from foreign trade earnings is distributed in the ratio of 30 per cent to the State and 70 per cent to the local authorities.

Fixed amount responsibility in the financial sectors

Since 1980, a planned payment has been in effect in the two provinces, which specifies that Guangdong province submit a fixed amount of profit to the State and that Fujian province receive a fixed amount of subsidies from the State within five years. The surplus from the payment falls into the budget plans of the respective provinces. This method is still being enforced today.

More flexibility in the monetary system

Under the State's overall policies and planning, the provincial authorities design their plans for foreign exchange earnings and report them to the State for the record. All such earnings should be deposited with the Bank of China and used under its supervision. The two provinces have set up investment companies, which secure investment by both overseas Chinese and foreign businessmen. Such companies conduct all their business entirely at their own risk and profit. At

the same time, the State allocates a certain amount of loans in RMB and foreign currencies so as to help develop local production, processing and assembling of export commodities, as well as compensation trade.

More local power in other economic sectors

For example, all the goods and materials needed by the enterprises and institutions in the two provinces have been allocated by the provincial authorities after careful consideration. A certain quota is imposed on such goods and materials when they are allotted in and out of the provinces. In commerce, the provincial authorities have taken up the main administration work, and the wholesale offices set up by the state ministries at provincial level are also administrated by the provincial authorities. The provincial authorities have made their own plans on labour wages and reported them to the state authorities concerned for the record. Such plans are not subject to restriction under the state quotas for labour and wages. With regard to prices, more power has also been accorded to the local authorities in fixing the price. For instance, the provinces have been allowed to adjust prices for products made in their own provinces. The prices of those locally-made commodities that are sold locally are fixed by the provincial authorities in the light of the production cost; the prices for those commodities that are allotted in or out of the provinces by the State are fixed by the State.

Setting up special economic zones as an experiment

Shenzhen, Zhuhai and Shantou, in Guangdong province, and Xiamen in Fujian province have been selected as special economic zones with a view to drawing capital from both the overseas Chinese and foreign enterprises, importing advanced technology and equipment from abroad, setting up Sino-foreign joint ventures or enterprises with sole foreign investment, and developing tourism.

In the past few years, the above-mentioned special policies and flexible measures carried out in the two provinces have produced good results in speeding up utilization of overseas Chinese and foreign capital, expanding foreign trade, increasing local foreign exchange earnings, developing labour export and processing industry, strengthening the construction of an infrastructure and therefore laying down a sound foundation for further opening up to the outside world and revitalizing domestic economy. In the meantime, the special economic zones have also experienced a remarkable development.

Special Economic Zones

The setting up of special economic zones is an important measure in China's opening up to the outside world. In July 1979, the Party Central Committee and the State Council decided to set up four special economic zones (referred to hereafter as SEZ) in Shenzhen, Zhuhai and Shantou, in Guangdong province, and Xiamen in Fujian province. The geographical locations and the limits of administration of these four SEZ are as follows:

Shenzhen SEZ

Situated in the south of Shenzhen city in Guangdong province, it is bordered by Baoan county along the Wutong Mountain and Yangtai Mountain on the north, Hong Kong along the Shenzhen River on the south, Dapeng Bay on the east and Houhai Bay on the west. It extends for 49 kilometres from east to west, and for 7 kilometres from north to south, covering an area of 327.5 square kilometres, of which 100 square kilometres are suitable for construction.

Zhuhai SEZ

Situated in the south of Zhuhai city in Guangdong province, it borders on Macao and covers an area of 15.6 square kilometres, of which 10 square kilometres are suitable for construction.

Shantou SEZ

Situated in the Longhu area in the eastern suburbs of Shantou city in Guangdong province, in the vicinity of Shantou New Port, it initially covered an area of 1.6 square kilometres. In 1984, the area was expanded to 52.6 square kilometres, including 22.6 square kilometres in the Longhu area, and the rest in the Guang'ao area.

Xiamen SEZ

Situated in the north-west of Xiamen Island of Xiamen city in Fujian province, it initially had an area of 2.5 square kilometres. In 1984, the area was expanded to include the whole of Xiamen city, with a total area of 1,516 square kilometres.

All these four SEZ are richly endowed by nature in their geographical location, climate, products and resources. The purpose of setting them up is to make the most of their local advantages, so as to make use of preferential policies to draw capital from foreign businesses, overseas Chinese and compatriots in Hong Kong, Macao and Taiwan; to conduct various forms of economic co-operation with foreign counterparts; to import advanced technology and draw on the positive managerial experience from abroad; to keep abreast with international markets, promote production and increase export earnings. In this way, the SEZ will become "windows" for technology, management, knowledge and foreign policies, and so play a central role as "radiating sector" both at home and abroad.

According to the objectives for the SEZ, Shenzhen and Zhuhai shall become comprehensive SEZ dealing in industry, commerce, agriculture, livestock breeding, residence and tourism, whereas Shantou and Xiamen shall become SEZ dealing mainly in processing industry and tourism.

The economic policies and economic management system as practised in the SEZ are different from those carried out in the hinterland. The differences can be summed up as follows:

The SEZ economy is an entity which deals mainly in Sino-foreign joint ventures, Sino-foreign co-operation enterprises and enterprises wholly owned by foreign investment while retaining various forms of economy

With support and guidance by the country's socialist economy, the SEZ economy relies mainly on foreign investment for its development. The products made in the SEZ are mostly for export.

Full play is given to market regulation in SEZ economic activities

Enterprises in the SEZ enjoy decision-making power in their production and management, so long as they abide by China's relevant laws and acts

Special preference and facilities are accorded to businessmen who invest in the SEZ with regard to tax and entry/exit visa procedures

Other preferential treatment granted to such businessmen under the Interim Regulations of the State Council Concerning the Reduction and Exemption of Enterprise Income Tax and Consolidated Industrial and Commercial Tax on the Special Economic Zones and the 14 Coastal Port Cities mainly includes:

For incomes derived from production, business and other sources by SEZ enterprises operating in the SEZ, an enterprise income tax at the reduced tax rate of 15 per cent shall be levied. For enterprises engaged in industry, communications and transport, agriculture, forestry and livestock breeding, which have a contract life of 10 years or longer, a two-year tax holiday commencing from the first profit-making year is allowed, followed by a 50 per cent reduction in the three following years (third to fifth year). Enterprises engaged in the service trade, which have overseas investments exceeding $US5 million and a contract life of 10 years or longer, shall be exempted from income tax in the first profit-making year, followed by a 50 per cent reduction in the two following years (second and third year).

Foreign participants in a joint venture in the SEZ are exempted from individual income tax when repatriating their profits derived therefrom. Income tax at the reduced rate of 10 per cent shall be levied on income derived from dividends, interest, rentals, royalties and other sources in the SEZ by foreign investors who have no establishments in China, except when a tax exemption is granted according to law. Where further preferences in tax reductions or exemptions are to be given to foreign investors who have provided investment and equipment on favourable terms or transferred truly advanced technology, they shall be decided by the people's governments of the SEZs.

Consolidated industrial and commercial tax shall be waived for SEZ enterprises importing taxable machines, equipment, raw materials, spare parts and accessories, means of transport and other means of production that are needed for production, before the SEZ control border lines are completed. Consolidated industrial and commercial tax shall be waived for export products made by SEZ enterprises, except a small number of products whose export is restricted by the State or otherwise provided.

Since 1980, the four SEZ have gone into capital construction with the focus on infrastructure. The investment environment has been steadily improving, which has resulted in rapid development of industries and of the whole economy. By the end of 1985, the accumulated investment in capital construction in the SEZ had amounted to ¥7.63 billion, of which Shenzhen SEZ accounted for nearly ¥6 billion. Capital construction carried out in the SEZ mainly includes roads, water carriage, power transmission, post and telecommunications, sea ports and airports, factory buildings, department stores, residential quarters and tourist facilities, totalling a construction area of 45 square kilometres. As a result, nine industrial areas have been set up in Shekou, Shangbu, Shahe, Bagualing and Shuibei in Shenzhen, Jida and Nanshan in Zhuhai, Longhu in Shantou and Huli in Xiamen. Special mention should be made of Shenzhen, where 8.08 million square metres of building area have been completed, which has made this once little border town into an economic entity well known in the world for its modern outlook.

From 1980 to 1985, foreign capital actually used by the four SEZ amounted to $US1.17 billion, chiefly in the form of direct investment, which was about a fifth of the international investment in the country. This amount includes $US800 million in Shenzhen, $US200 million in Zhuhai, $US140 million in Xiamen and $US30 million in Shantou. Some advanced technology and equipment have been imported from abroad by the SEZ, such as Philips laser TV disc technology imported from the Netherlands and special glass-making technology imported from Austria by Shenzhen; multi-layer circuit board technology imported from the United States by Zhuhai; Kodak sensitive material technology imported from the United States and Sony video-tape recorder manufacture technology imported from Japan by Xiamen. The total industrial output value of the four SEZ in 1985 was ¥9.696 billion, 5.3 times more than in 1979. Of

this total amount, the industrial output value of Shenzhen was ¥2.758 billion, 43 times more than in 1979. Specifically, of that total amount, 67.8 per cent comes from Sino-foreign joint ventures, Sino-foreign co-operation enterprises and solely owned foreign enterprises. At present, the Shenzhen SEZ (including Shekou) makes about 600 kinds of industrial products, of which 200 are for export. The percentage of earnings from direct export in total sales increased from 33.4 per cent in 1984 to 43 per cent in 1985 (of which Shekou Industrial Area takes about 68 per cent). Therefore, the SEZ have begun to serve as the "window" and "pivot" in China's economic and technological exchanges with foreign countries and regions. They are now developing towards an export-oriented economy.

Note: At the Thirteenth Congress of the CPC in October 1987 it was decided that Hainan Island would be made a province and a Special Economic Zone. (See Part II, **Chapter 4**, final section.)

Open Coastal Port Cities

In order to speed up utilization of foreign capital and import of technology, the Party Central Committee and the State Council decided in April 1984 to open the following 14 coastal port cities to the outside world: Dalian, Qinhuangdao, Tianjin, Yantai, Qingdao, Lianyungang, Nantong, Shanghai, Ningbo, Wenzhou, Fuzhou, Guangzhou, Zhanjiang and Beihai, and the whole of Hainan Island. The State Council further decided in March 1985 to accord Yingkou City some of the powers that have been accorded to those open coastal cities. Thus, China has opened 15 coastal port cities and Hainan Island to the outside world. These cities enjoy the advantages of convenient transport, a sound industrial foundation, high levels of technology, management, science, culture and education. With the support of the hinterland, they constitute frontier areas from the north to the south of mainland China for economic exchanges with the outside world. The following is some key information about these open port cities.

Dalian

Situated at the southern tip of the Liaodong Peninsula, and bordered by the Yellow Sea on the east and the Bohai Sea on the west, it enjoys excellent geographical and natural conditions. Administratively, it has 5 counties and 5 districts under it, covering an area of 12,600 square kilometres, including 1,062 square kilometres of urban area. Its population in 1985 was 4,850,000, including 1,630,000 in the urban area. Rich in agricultural resources, the city produces large quantities of fruit, rice, peanuts and aquatic products. Among its specialities which enjoy a high reputation in world markets are apples, sea cucumbers and prawns. Dalian is also an industrial city with comprehensive industrial sectors, including machinery, metallurgy, petrochemicals, light and textile industries, some of which have sold their products in the world market. In 1985, its industrial output value totalled about ¥10.6 billion, an increase of 15 per cent over 1983. As a pivot of sea transport linking China's north-eastern part with Asian and American countries, the port of Dalian provides convenient sea and land transport. An ideal ice-free port, it has ocean transport links with more than 140 countries and regions of the world. In 1985, it handled 43,810,000 tons of cargo. The Nianyu Bay petroleum port, which is China's biggest deep-water petroleum port, can berth oil-tankers of up to 50,000 and 100,000 tons. In addition, the city also boasts a dozen scenic spots for sightseeing.

Yingkou

Situated on the western shore of the Bohai Gulf, the city has 2 counties and 4 districts under it, covering an area of 5,401 square kilometres, with a population of 1,930,000. The city is rich in mineral resources, including petroleum and 27 kinds of mineral pro-

Coal loaded onto a ship at Qinhuangdao Coal Wharf in Hebei province. *(Photo by Liu Zhiwei)*

ducts. Among them, the deposits of magnesite, talcum and borax rank first in the country. It is also a production base in the eastern part of the Liaodong Peninsula for fruit, aquatic products and rice. It has relatively comprehensive industrial sectors, and with its well-developed commodity economy, it is among the most developed cities in the province of Liaoning. The Yingkou port has a long history. Recently, the Bayu New Port has been built, about 45 kilometres away from the city centre. In 1985, the port handled 980,000 tons of cargo.

Qinhuangdao

Situated in the east of Hebei province, it is also on the Bohai Sea. The Shanhaiguan Pass, which marks the beginning of the Great Wall, is in the eastern part of the city, and in the western part there is the famous summer resort of Beidaihe. It has 4 counties and 3 urban districts, covering an area of 7,523 square kilometres, including 363 square kilometres in the urban area. In 1985, its population was 2,280,000, including 440,000 in the urban area. In industry, it chiefly makes plate glass, which is sold in more than 70 countries and regions of the world. In 1985, its industrial output value totalled ¥1.19 billion, an increase of 16 per cent over 1983. The city became a trading port with other countries in the 19th century and has since had good transport facilities. This ice-free port handled 44,190,000 tons of cargo in 1985. It is a key port for the export of coal, produced in Shanxi province, and petroleum, produced in Daqing in the north-east.

Tianjin

Situated on the mouth of the Haihe river, the city is bordered by the Bohai Sea on the east and the Yanshan mountains on the north, and is 137 kilometres from Beijing. One of the three municipalities under the direct administration of the central government, it has under it 9 coastal districts, 4 suburban districts and 5 counties, covering an area of 11,300 square kilometres. In 1985, its population was 8,080,000. As an important industrial base, the city has well-developed industrial sectors, which include petrochemicals, ocean chemicals, machinery, electronics, medical, automobile, bicycle, sewing-machine, home appliance, textile, clothing, carpet, metallurgy, electric power, building material and other industrial sectors, which employ more than 1.43 million workers. In 1985, its industrial output value totalled ¥28.6 billion, an increase of 13 per cent over 1983. It is also the pivot of transport linking the Beijing–Shenyang railway and the Beijing–Shanghai railway. It used to be the economic centre for the whole of the North-East, North-West and North China regions. The Tianjin port is the biggest trading port in North China. It is equipped with the biggest container dock in the country, extending for about 6,100 metres. It has 34 berths, including 20 for ocean-going ships of 10,000 tons or above. In 1984, the port handled 16,110,000 tons of cargo; in 1985, it handled 18,560,000 tons of cargo. The Tianjin airport is one of the biggest in the country. The city is also developed in foreign trade and has established trade and economic relations with more than 140 countries and regions of the world, its commodities for export covering more than 1,000 varieties.

Yantai

Situated at the eastern tip of the Shandong Peninsula, the city faces Dalian across the sea. It has a coastline of about 1,300 kilometres. The city has two districts under it, 12 counties and Weihai city, covering an area of about 18,900 square kilometres, including 835 square kilometres in the urban area. In 1985, its population totalled 8,200,000 including 720,000 in the urban area. With its developed agriculture, it is an important production base in Shandong province for grain, vegetable oil and fruit. The city is also rich in aquatic products, its prawn output being the first in the country. The city has more than 30 kinds of mineral resources, with its gold output making one-quarter of the country's total. As a newly developed industrial city, it has machinery, electronics, chemical, textile and light industries. In 1985, its industrial output value totalled ¥6.8 billion, an increase of 25 per cent over 1983. For land transport, it has the Qingdao–Jinan railway, extending for 393 kilometres, which is the key transport line in the province. There are 13 ports of varying sizes along its coastal line, linking the city with other big ports in the country and more than 100 ports in the world. In 1985, the Yantai port handled 13,630,000 tons of cargo. The city has foreign trade transactions with more than 90 countries and regions of the world.

Qingdao

Situated in the south-east of the Shandong Peninsula, the city is bordered by the Yellow Sea and Jiaozhou Bay. It comprises 6 counties and 6 districts, covering an area of 10,700 square kilometres, including 244 square kilometres in the urban area. In 1985, its population was 6,270,000, including 1,250,000 in the urban area. In agriculture, it produces grain, cotton, peanuts and fruit; in industry, it is well developed in light industry and textiles, in addition to rubber, chemical, electronics, machinery, metallurgy, building material and other industrial sectors. In 1985, its industrial output value totalled ¥9.9 billion, an increase of 16 per cent over 1983. The port of Qingdao, which is ice-free, has sea transport links with more than 140 countries and regions of the world. In 1985, it handled 26,790,000 tons of cargo.

Lianyungang

Situated in the north-east of Jiangsu province, the city is bordered by the Yellow Sea on the east, and by the Subei Plain on the west. It has under it 3 counties and 3 districts, covering an area of 6,327 square kilometres. In 1983, it had a population of 3,000,000. It has rich fish and salt resources along the coastal area, and is one of China's bases for deep-sea fishing and offshore breeding. It is also one of China's four major production bases for salt. The city has quite well developed industry and agriculture. In 1985, its industrial output value totalled ¥1.98 billion, an increase of 26 per cent over 1983. The city has convenient land transport links, with the Long-Hai railway (Lianyungang–Lanzhou) going through the central plain and the north-west, and the Tianjin–Pukou, Beijing–Guangzhan and Baoji–Chendu railways. The port is a good ice-free port in the coastal area of the province, and with its inland navigation canal, it is linked with the Beijing–Hangzhou Canal and the Yangtze River system. In 1985, it handled 9.29 million tons of cargo.

Nantong

Situated on the northern bank of the mouth of the

A Buddhist bell made in Shanghai for a Buddhist temple in Hawaii. (*Photo by Yao Zongyi*)

Yangtze River, this is a newly developed city. It has 6 counties and 2 districts, covering an area of 9,140 square kilometres, including 244 square kilometres in the urban area. In 1985, its population was 7,450,000, including a 410,000 urban population. Rich in agricultural product and by-product resources, the city is a major production base for such famous products as cotton, silkworm mulberry, peppermint, spearmint and jute. In addition, it also produces many sea and fresh-water aquatic products. In industry, it has textiles and light industry, food, machinery, electronics, chemicals, medicine, building construction, building material, ship-building, electrical power and other industries. In 1985, its industrial output value totalled ¥8.5 billion, an increase of 23 per cent over 1983. The city has a construction contingent with relatively high skill, which not only takes up building projects in more than 20 provinces in China, but also provides labour service abroad. The Nantong port is the pivot of water transport in the Yangtze River area. Being free from ice and typhoons, it can provide navigation to ocean-going ships of up to 10,000 tons. It has become an important key port linking other ports both at home and abroad. In 1985, it handled 25,260,000 tons of cargo.

Shanghai

Situated in the central part of China's coastal line, and on the southern bank of the Yangtze River mouth, the Shanghai Municipality, directly under the central government, is China's biggest industrial city and economic centre. It comprises 12 districts and 10 counties, covering an area of 6,186 square kilometres, including 351 square kilometres in the city proper. In 1985, its population was 12,170,000, including 6,980,000 in the urban area. In 1984, the city's total social output value reached ¥87.6 billion and its income reached ¥34.1 billion; both represented an increase over 1982. There are 10,656 industrial enterprises in the city, which provided a total of ¥83.23 billion worth of industrial products in 1985, an increase of 12 per cent over 1983, accounting for about 10 per cent of the country's total. Of this figure, the output of light industrial products accounted for more than 11 per cent of the country's total, and that of heavy industrial products accounted for about 9 per cent of the country's total. Industry is highly developed in machinery, textiles, chemicals, metallurgy, food, sewing, paper-making and other industries. The city links the Beijing–Shanghai railway with Shanghai–Hangzhou railway, and from these it is linked with other parts of the country. The port of Shanghai is China's biggest port and has 96 berths, including 45 for 10,000-ton ships. The dock extends for 13,500 metres. In 1985, it handled 112,910,000 tons of cargo, with its imported cargo ranking the first in the country. For air transport, there are 37 domestic lines from the city and 7 international lines. Shanghai has

A berth in Beilun Port for ships of 100,000 tons at Ningbo, Zhejiang province. *(Photo by Lu Ming)*

developed trade relations with more than 166 countries and regions of the world, dealing in more than 3,000 kinds of commodities, which are handled through more than 20 navigation lines.

Ningbo

Situated in the north-eastern coastal area of Zhejiang province, the city is bordered by Hangzhou Bay in the north, by Sanmen Bay in the south and by the East Sea in the east, with the Zhoushan Islands serving as its natural defence. The city covers an area of 9,365 square kilometres, including 1,033 square kilometres in the urban area. In 1985, its population was 4,880,000. In agriculture, it relies mainly on grain and cotton, with all-round development in agriculture, forestry, livestock breeding, side products and fishing. In industry, the city is developed in light industry and textile industry, and has recently developed machinery, electronics and other modern industries. In 1985,

A foreign ship being unloaded at a wharf at Wenzhou Port in Zhejiang province. *(Photo by Wang Jinqiu)*

its industrial output value totalled ¥8.91 billion, an increase of 34.2 per cent over 1983. The city provides convenient transport through sea, railway, highway and inland river navigation. Ningbo's foreign trade has experienced a rapid growth, its import and export volume being more than half the province's total. In 1985, the port handled 10,410,000 tons of cargo.

Wenzhou

Situated in the south-eastern coastal area of Zhejiang province, the city is surrounded by mountains on three sides, with the East Sea to its east. The city covers an area of 11,800 square kilometres, including 187 square kilometres in the urban area. In 1985, its population was 6,290,000, including 530,000 in the urban area. The city is rich in more than 40 varieties of mineral resources; among them the deposits of alumstone are estimated at more than 300 million tons. Taking advantage of its geographical location, the city produces large quantities of rice, wheat, tangerines, sugarcane, rapeseed, mat straw, jute and natural spice in the eastern plains, and timber, bamboo, tung tree, tea, tallow tree and tea-oil tree in the western and southern plains. The Zhoushan Islands are a famous fishing base. Historically, Wenzhou has been a commercial city with skilled handicraft industry, and has recently developed machinery, electronics, light industry, textile and building material industries. In 1985, its industrial output value totalled ¥3.27 billion, an increase of 39.1 per cent over 1983. The city's handicraft articles sell quite well both at home and abroad. In 1985, the port handled 3,590,000 tons of cargo.

Fuzhou

Situated in the eastern coastal area of Fujian province, Fuzhou is on the lower reaches of the Minjiang river, facing Taiwan province across the sea. As the provincial capital, the city comprises 3 urban districts, 8

Sheep of fine breed to be exported to the Middle East. (*Photo by Wang Gangfa*)

counties and 2 suburban districts, covering an area of 11,968 square kilometres, with an urban population of 1,190,000 in 1985. Rich in fishing and agricultural resources, it produces tangerines, olives, sugarcane and peanuts. In industry, it has machinery, chemicals, light industry and textiles and electronics. In 1985, its industrial output value totalled ¥3.79 billion, an increase of 14.8 per cent over 1983. Its famous arts and crafts include stone seals, stone carving and bodiless lacquerware made in Shoushan. In 1985, the port handled 3,880,000 tons of cargo.

Guangzhou

Situated in the middle of Guangdong province and on the northern bank of the Zhujiang river, the city is at the confluence of the Dongjiang, Xijiang and Beijiang rivers. Guangzhou is the provincial capital, having under it 8 districts and 8 counties, covering an area of about 16,600 square kilometres, including 1,444 square kilometres in the urban area. In 1985, its population was 7,100,000, including 3,290,000 in the urban area. In agriculture, the city produces large quantities of rice, sugarcane, litchi, bananas, longan, flowering quince and tangerines. It has quite comprehensive industries, including ship-building, machinery, textiles, knitting, sugar refining, refrigerators, computers, other home appliances, bicycles, sewing machines, wrist watches, petrochemical, rubber and other industries, in important portions of the country's total output. In 1985, its industrial output value totalled ¥16.1 billion, an increase of 2 per cent over 1983. The city provides convenient water, land and air transport, with the Beijing–Guangzhou and Guangzhou–Hongkong railways, linking the south with the north. The port at Guangzhou includes Guangzhou Port and Huangpu Port, which link the city with the hinterland through inland navigation and with other ports in China through the domestic sea lines, and with other major ports in the world through the international ocean lines. In 1985, the port handled 25,810,000 tons of cargo. The Baiyun Airport provides domestic airlines to other major cities in China and international airlines to Hong Kong, Bangkok, Manila and other foreign destinations. Having been one of the first of China's cities to open trade with foreign countries, the city has well-developed commerce and banking. It has established trade relations with more than 140 foreign countries and regions of the world.

Zhanjiang

Situated in the south-west of Guangdong province, the city is at the north-eastern tip of the Leizhou Peninsula, bordered by the South Sea. It comprises 5 counties, covering an area of 12,500 square kilometres, including 1,460 square kilometres in the urban area. In 1985, its population was 4,770,000. In agriculture, it produces large quantities of rice, sugarcane, peanuts, jute and bluish dogbane. The city is a production base in the province for peanut oil, cane sugar and other tropical cash crops. Its industrial sectors include light industry, food, building material, home appliances and other industries. In 1985, its industrial output value totalled ¥1.5 billion, an increase of 33 per cent over 1983. With its coastal line extending for more than 1,300 kilometres, the city has abundant aquatic resources. Having been China's first deep-sea fishing base, it has recently become an important petroleum development centre in the western part of the South Sea. Zhanjiang Port is a natural deep-water port, which is also China's nearest trade port on the shipping lines to South Asia, Europe and Africa. It has trade relations with more than 70 countries and regions of the world. In 1985, the port handled 13,960,000 tons of cargo.

Beihai

Situated in the south of Guangxi Zhuang autonomous region and bordered by the Beibu Gulf, the city is a peninsula surrounded by the sea on three sides. It has an area of 275 square kilometres, with a population of 176,000 in 1985. It has abundant fishing resources, among which its South Sea Prawn is famous in the world market for its large size, tender meat and delicious taste. Its offshore natural resources along the Beibu Gulf include petroleum, natural gas and quartz ore. Its industries include machinery, building material, sugar refining, food, and arts and crafts industries. In 1985, its industrial output value totalled ¥220 million, an increase of 37.5 per cent over 1983. The Beihai Port has trade relations with more than 40 countries and regions of the world. In 1985, it handled 550,000 tons of cargo.

Hainan Island

Situated in the South Sea, the island faces the Leizhou Peninsula across the Qiongzhou Strait. The island is an administrative region of Guangdong province. With 17 counties and cities, it covers an area of 34,100 square kilometres, with a population of 5,800,000 in 1983. There are more than 20 kinds of rare trees in the island, which produces large quantities of natural rubber, pepper, sugarcane, coffee, pineapple and coconut. The island also offers abundant mineral resources, which include more than 50 kinds, among them the Shilu iron ore, with a high grade of 50 per cent. The island has a coastal line of 1,528 kilometres, with a fishing area of 78,000 square kilometres, which provide excellent breeding conditions for shellfish, sea cucumber, prawns and pearls and other aquatic products. Major ports in the island include Haikou and Yulin Ports.

Policy toward Coastal Open Cities

China has designed a series of policies and administration principles for coastal open cities. These policies and principles include:

More local authority over the examination and approval of projects involving foreign investment
These projects can be divided into two categories

First, with regard to production-oriented projects which do not need state overall consideration in either construction or production, market their own products, export their products free from the state quota and are able to pay back the foreign loans, more decision-making power has been accorded. Tianjin and Shanghai are entitled to approve projects with a total investment of less than $US 30 million; Dalian and Guangzhou are entitled to approve such projects with a total investment of less than $US 10 million, while the limit for other coastal open cities is $US 5 million. Second, with regard to non-production-oriented projects which are self-sufficient in securing and paying back their foreign loans, and do not need state overall consideration in securing capital, material or importing equipment, all the coastal open city authorities are entitled to approve these projects, regardless of the amount of investment. In this way, the decision-making process in approving such projects can be speeded up.

Setting up economic and technological development zones

In accordance with the local situation, coastal cities have permission to set up economic and technological development zones to attract foreign investment and high technology. Foreign businessmen, overseas Chinese and Hong Kong, Macao and Taiwan compatriots are encouraged to come to these zones for joint ventures or wholly foreign-owned enterprises. The preferential treatment they enjoy includes: (a) Chinese–foreign joint ventures, co-operatives and wholly foreign-owned productive enterprises in the development zones enjoy a reduced rate of 15 per cent in income tax. Those enterprises whose contract is for more than 10 years can be exempted from income tax for two years, beginning from the first profit-earning year, and have a 50 per cent reduction in income tax between the 3rd and 5th years. (b) When remitted overseas, the legitimate profits shared by foreign businessmen from their enterprises in these zones will be duty free. According to relevant regulations, foreign businessmen can be exempted from income tax on certain parts of their dividends, interests, rentals, royalties and income from other sources and also enjoy a reduced rate of 10 per cent in income tax on the rest. Apart from these, there are additional reductions and exemptions for those businessmen who offer funds and equipment on favourable terms or provide advanced technology. (c) Enterprises in development zones can be exempted from industrial and commercial consolidated taxes on their products for export (except state-embargoed export products). The exemption also applies to the materials, equipment, spare parts, vehicles and office equipment such enterprises import for their own use.

Encouraging old enterprises to seek foreign capital for the purpose of technical transformation

Whatever their sources of foreign exchange might be, old enterprises engaged in technical transformation are exempted, until 1990, from custom tariffs and industrial and commercial consolidated taxes when they import key equipment, apparatus, instruments, etc. which China is at present unable to produce or cannot ensure a sufficient supply of. If necessary, these enterprises have permission to use the additional profits resulting from the technical renovation to pay off debts prior to paying taxes. The enterprises which practise the system of paying taxes instead of turning profits over to the State can pay off debts prior to paying enterprise income tax. As regards the following three types of projects: i. those which mainly improve the quality of products instead of increasing enterprise productivity; ii. those which create good economic results but do not bring in foreign exchange; iii. those which have good social economic effects but do not increase the enterprise income; coastal cities are allowed to use the income from other enterprises in the same trade or local revenue to pay off their debts. Municipal governments can also adjust the production quota and reduce the income tax of those enterprises which experience a temporary decrease in productivity and profit during the period of technical transformation.

Promoting projects involved in importing materials for producing export products

Municipal governments can choose a few suitable enterprises and allocate to them the production of goods with a long-term international market. The recommended practice is to import materials to process and then export the products. These enterprises will gradually adopt a new system of integration of industry with trade and import with export. They must use foreign exchange for quoting prices and settling accounts according to quotations on the international market, and assume sole responsibility for their profits or losses.

Laying emphasis on improving essential equipment and public utilities

The State has allocated some investments in such

projects as ports, postal services, railways and air transportation, supply of electricity, water and gas, etc., of which a few have already started. To secure sufficient capital for these projects, these cities are also tapping local resources and pooling funds through developing economic relations with other regions of the country. Foreign investment is regarded as another source. Upon approval from the authority, they can issue bonds abroad.

Encouraging municipal authorities to benefit from the experiences gained from the administration of the economy in the special zones

They can adopt policies made for special zones, for example, the system of bidding and contracted responsibility, contract labour system, cadre engaging system, floating wage system, various contracted responsibility systems in practice for enterprise administration, and the practice of establishing trade centres.

With the further implementation of the open policy, the 14 coastal cities have made gratifying achievements in securing foreign capital and introducing advanced technology. In 1984 alone they signed over 200 agreements on Chinese–foreign joint ventures, Chinese–foreign co-operative enterprises and wholly foreign-owned enterprises involving as much as $US900 million in foreign investment. They also signed more than 800 contracts on introducing advanced technology, with a total value of 740 million. The total number of agreements and contracts made in 1984 equalled that of several previous years. While carrying out the open policy, the coastal cities have been making efforts to expand economic relations with hinterland areas. The increased exchange of funds, equipment, technology and human resources between coastal and inland areas has considerably quickened the development of inland economy. For example, Dalian has reached agreement with three provinces in North-East China and eastern Inner Mongolia on over 180 co-operative projects in industry. In 1984, Shanghai was involved in 779 economic and technical co-operative projects at provincial level, a 53 per cent increase over the previous year.

To implement the open policy on a broader scale, the State Council decided, in January 1985, to open three more coastal economic zones – the Changjiang Delta, the Zhujian Delta and the Xiamen–Zhangzhou–Quanzhou triangle area.

Since 1979 China has issued a series of laws, rules and regulations concerning commerce and business with foreign countries to ensure the implementation of the open policy. By the end of 1985 these laws and regulations amounted to about 200, among which 21 were promulgated by the National People's Congress, over 40 by the State Council, some by relevant central government departments and the rest were issued by the Guangdong and Fujian provincial governments to suit local conditions. China's new constitution, ratified in 1982, stipulates that foreign enterprises and other economic institutions or individuals have permission to invest in China or conduct economic co-operation of various forms, in accordance with Chinese laws and regulations, with Chinese enterprises or other economic institutions. It also stipulates that Chinese–foreign joint ventures as well as foreign enterprises and other foreign economic institutions should abide by the laws of the People's Republic of China. Specific laws and regulations have been issued concerning Chinese–foreign joint ventures, Chinese–foreign co-operative enterprises and wholly foreign-owned businesses.

On 8 July 1979 the Law on Joint Ventures Using Chinese and Foreign Investment was issued and went into effect. This law, which provides a guideline for Chinese–foreign joint ventures, stipulates that Chinese–foreign joint ventures should be an economic institution jointly sponsored, upon approval by the Chinese government, by Chinese and foreign partners within the boundaries of China. The major feature of such an institution is that as both sides are involved in its administration and management, they also share the risks, profits and losses. September 1980 saw the promulgation of two more laws: Personal Income Law Concerning Chinese-Foreign Joint Ventures, and the Personal Income Law. While firmly safeguarding the state sovereignty and interests, the two laws also stipulate the principle of reducing duties and taxes and providing additional preferential treatment with the purpose of attracting more foreign funds. To facilitate the implementation of these laws, the State Council has drawn up a series of additional regulations, such as Regulations for the Implementation of the Law on Joint Venture Using Chinese and Foreign Investment, Rules for the Implementation of Registration and Administration of Chinese–Foreign Joint Ventures, Regulations on Labour Managements in Joint Ventures Using Chinese and Foreign Invest-

ment, Interim Regulations on Foreign Exchange Control, etc. The Law on Foreign Enterprises was ratified during the sixth session of the National People's Congress in 1986. These laws and regulations enable foreign investors to gain a good understanding of China's open policy and provide a legal basis for the establishment and management of Chinese–foreign joint ventures, Chinese–foreign co-operative enterprises, etc.

To obtain a proper solution of the problems arising in the field of foreign investment, China has signed agreements on the protection of investment with 16 countries: Sweden, Romania, Federal Republic of Germany, France, Belgium–Luxembourg Economic Union, Finland, Norway, Italy, Thailand, Denmark, the Netherlands, Austria, Singapore, Kuwait and Sri Lanka. China has also signed agreements on avoidance of double taxation and prevention of tax evasion with such countries as Japan, USA, France, Great Britain, Belgium, Federal Republic of Germany, Malaysia, etc.

With reference to technological co-operation and transference, China has promulgated a Patent Law and a Trade Mark Law. The first Patent Law of the People's Republic of China was ratified at the National People's Congress on 12 March 1984, and with its coming into effect on 1 April 1985 the legal rights of those foreigners who have applied for and been granted a patent right for their invention, utility model and industrial design are protected by Chinese law.

The Law on International Economic Contracts was issued in March 1985. It is expected that the legislation concerning economic relations with foreign countries will be completed in the near future. Before the promulgation of the relevant laws and regulations those involved in the business had to try to reach agreement, through consultation on the basis of equality, on the rights and duties of both sides. Once the contract is ratified by the government department concerned, it will take effect and be binding on all parties.

INTERNATIONAL ENGINEERING CONTRACT AND LABOUR SERVICE CO-OPERATION AND INTERNATIONAL AID

International Engineering Contract and Labour Service Co-operation

RECENT years have witnessed great development in engineering contract and labour service co-operation – a new undertaking China is engaged in to promote economic relations with foreign countries. In this market China has already secured initial success and won a good reputation.

The business scope of China's contracting corporations which undertake projects abroad has been expanding steadily and is experiencing changes from mainly exporting labour service to exporting package-contracted projects. Among over 60 corporations, several have emerged as the backbone: the China State Engineering Construction Corporation, which enjoys a good reputation for the quality of its work, was awarded the International Mercury Gold Medal for

1984 by Italy, and the Grand Medal of the International Garden Festival of Liverpool. Two other corporations, the China Civil Engineering Construction Corporation and the China Geological Prospecting and Drilling Corporation, had the honour of winning International Commerce Prizes offered by Spain in 1984.

By 1985 China's international contracting corporations and labour service co-operation corporations numbered 64. They contracted over 2,600 projects, including housing, road construction, water conservancy, factory building, etc. The value of these projects, which involve as many as 59,000 staff and workers, reaches $1,265 million, an over 17-fold increase over the $69 million for 1979, the year when China first entered the market. During the 7 years between 1979 and 1985, the value of the contracts these corporations signed for labour and engineering service totalled 5,230 million, with a turnover of approximately $2,430 million. Their achievements have opened a new way for China to earn foreign exchange, promoted "South–South" co-operation and helped to strengthen the friendship between the people of China and those of other countries.

In the market of engineering contract and labour service co-operation China has the advantages of sufficient technology, rich human resources and abundant materials. Chinese workers are hardworking, industrious and able to work in difficult conditions. Moreover, they are highly responsible and have a strong sense of discipline. All this put together makes Chinese corporations desirable partners in the market.

China plans further expansion of the export of labour and engineering services in the years to come. Contracting corporations must stick to the principle of abiding by contracts, guaranteeing quality, seeking low profits and stressing obligations. They should be even better prepared for the sharp competition in the world market so that they can not only keep their present share of the market but break into new areas. To ensure success, they will adopt a series of flexible strategies in management and put the emphasis on practical results. If need be, they can accept either foreign exchange or barter compensation. China's export of services will include both the physical labour force and intellectual and technical services, and will be steadily expanded to include prospecting, designing, programming, etc. It can contract to send either all the staff and workers needed by a project or only individuals. While continuing business in engineering construction, it may also export third industry services as seamen, cleaners, attendants, gardeners, cooks, etc. All contracting corporations will continue improving their administration and management to achieve better economic results so that they will be more competitive in market.

The following is some brief information about the China State Engineering Construction Corporation and its agencies abroad:

780

China State Construction Engineering Corporation (CSCEC)

The lines of business of the China State Construction Engineering Corporation include

– construction of industrial and office buildings for the chemical industry, machinery, light industry, textile, postal and telecommunication services;
– erection of meeting halls, office buildings, residential houses, apartments, hotels, cinemas, hospitals, schools, stadiums, railway stations, airports, docks, power stations, reservoirs, high-voltage grid systems, railways, highways and bridges;
– contracting projects concerning water-supply, drainage, sewage treatment, well-digging and civil engineering;
– municipal works and infrastructure construction, sculpture and mural creations, garden construction and afforestation, as well as plumbing and equipment installations.

Forms of business

Contracting whole or part of the survey, design, construction and installation of a project; contracting projects by the item; contracts for a job; Providing labour services, technicians and consultation services for technological problems; supplying equipment and materials; participating in joint contracts or joint ventures.

The CSCEC headquarters in China

China State Construction Engineering Corporation

Baiwanzhuang Street, Xijiao, Beijing, China
Tel: 891293, 892368
Cable: 2368, 2046, Beijing
Telex: 22477 CSCEC CN, 22038 CSCEC CN

CSCEC branches abroad

China Overseas Building Development Co. Ltd.

21/F China Resources Building,
26 Harbour Road, Hong Kong
Tel: 5–8938339
Cable: 7787
Telex: 60960 COBDC HK

China Construction Engineering (Macao) Co. Ltd.

1/F Hang Chang Building No. 9
Nan Wan Street, Macao
Tel: 557455/555062/555063
Cable: 4591
Telex: 88732 CCECM OM

The Branch Office of CSCEC in Thailand

114/6–7 Soi Prasoet Dis
Sukhumvit 63, Bangkok, Thailand
Tel: 3900661–1125
Telex: 82014 HSHUABK TH C/O CSCEC

The Branch Office of CSCEC in Yemen

Hada Road, San'a, Yemen
Tel: 248410 248411
Cable: Chinegco
Telex: 2660 CSCEC YE

The Branch Office of CSCEC in Kuwait

P.O. Box 66289, Bayan, Kuwait
Tel: 5314499
Cable: Chinaemba, Kuwait
Telex: Chianem 22688 KT C/O CSCEC

The Branch Office of CSCEC in Libya

Gargarish, Near Abonoas Restaurant,
Tripoli, Libya
Tel: (021)832758
Telex: 20924 CSCEC LY

The Branch Office of CSCEC in Algeria

29 Lotissement Cadat Ben Omar Kouba,
Algiers, Algeria
Tel: 580121
Telex: 54116 CSCEC DZ

The Branch Office of CSCEC in the United Arab Emirates

P.O. Box 111, Abu Dhabi, UAE
Tel: 727138 727139
Telex: 23273 CCEC EM

The Branch Office of CSCEC in South Yemen

P.O. Box 4592, Aden, South Yemen
Tel: 41560
Telex: 2500 YTCTA C/O CSCEC

The Branch Office of CSCEC in Egypt

35 Iraq Street, Engineer City, Cairo
Tel: 480234
Telex: 93180 Chico UN C/O CSCEC

China State Construction Engineering Corp. (Guam) Inc.

P.O. Box 8052, Tamuning, Guam
96911, USA
Telex: 6113 Guam

The Representative Office of CSCEC in Europe

Weserstr. 41, D–6000 Frankfurt 1, Federal
Republic of Germany
Tel: 251426
Telex: 416066 CSCEC D

The Representative Office of CSCEC in Japan

Aurora Heights 301 Shitsu,
(12) Bashi, Shitadai, Shihjuku-ku,
Tokyodo
Tel: 03–359–6988
Telex: 28506 Chico TELJ C/O CSCEC

The Office of CSCEC in the Philippines

Suite B–2 Sinagoga Bldg.,
481 Sinagoga Street,
Malate, Metro, Manila
Tel: 58–16–11
Telex: 27682 Prochi PN C/O CSCEC

China Civil Engineering Construction Corporation

The lines of business of the China Civil Engineering Construction Corporation (CCECC) include

– construction of railways (including subways and stations), roads, bridges, tunnels and other civil works;
– construction of workshops, industrial and civilian buildings;
– undertaking product processing with drawings, samples and/or materials from customers; assembling with imported parts from customers; exporting all types of railway equipment and parts;
– providing technical and labour services;
– establishing joint ventures with foreign firms and carrying out economic co-operation in various forms.

In its overseas operations, CCECC may act as prime contractors, sub-contractor, partner in a joint venture or as a supplier of engineering personnel, consultants and skilled workers.

CCECC headquarters in China

10 Fuxing Street, Beijing, China
Tel: 8642714
Cable: Chicicon, Beijing
Telex: 22471 CCECC CN

CCECC branch and representation offices

CCECC Representative Office in Libya

P.O. Box 75091, Tripoli, Libya
Tel: 76046
Telex: 20862 CCECCR LY

CCECC Branch Office in Kuwait

    Dahia Abdula Al Salem Nosef
    Al Yousef St., Villa No. 18
Tel: 2543788
Telex: Chinaemb 22688 KT (to CCECC)

CCECC Branch Office in Tanzania

    P.O. Box 1291, Dar es Salaam, Tanzania
Tel: 50568 DSM (Kurasini)
Telex: 41036 Chinemba DSM (to CCECC)

CCECC Branch Office in Guam

    845 N. Granada, Dededo, Guam
    96912, USA
Tel: 632–9726
Telex: 6611 Midcat GM

CCECC Branch Office in Algeria

    No. 12C Zouaou Cheraga Street,
    Algiers, Algeria
Tel: 814628
Telex: 53233 BCCAC DZ (to CCECC)

CCECC Representative Office in Europe

    62 Haeberlin Str., Ginheim
    D–6000 Frankfurt Main, Federal Republic
    of Germany
Tel: 069520148
Telex: 176997187 Rofed

CCECC Representative Office in Japan

    3F Kyodo Bldg. No. 3–1,
    Nihonbashi–Honcho
    Chuo-Ku, Tokyo 103, Japan
Tel: (03)270–4501/4505
Telefax: (03)270–4504
Telex: Jinglian J 33250

CCECC Representative Office in the United Arab Emirates

Telex: 23928 Chinem EM

International Aid

Ever since its founding, the People's Republic of China has offered economic aid and made efforts to develop international economic and technological co-operation. In 1954, China began to provide other countries with complete sets of equipment. Over the past thirty years and more, China has assisted and helped more than eighty Third World countries and regions in carrying out over 1,000 aid projects from the beginning to the end, and sent abroad a total of more than 100 thousand engineers and technicians. Since 1979, China has readjusted and improved its aid efforts and diversified its economic and technological co-operation with foreign countries. The aid and assistance China have rendered in the past five years totalled 5.61 billion yuan and the number of recipient countries increased from 74 in 1980 to 90 in 1985. 70 more agreements on aid projects have been signed and 175 projects completed. These projects have produced good economic results and the governments and people of the beneficiary countries have thus spoken highly of them. Meanwhile, China has also enjoyed multilateral and bilateral technical assistance gratis, rendered by UN agencies and a number of friendly countries, and those projects have yielded good social-economic results.

China will continue to make efforts to aid and assist other countries to the best of its ability in the spirit of "equality and mutual benefit, stress on practical results, diversity in forms and attainment of common

Chinese and Kenyan workers working to complete a stadium in Kenya built with aid from China.

progress." With regard to economic aid projects, efforts will be mainly concentrated on small and medium projects with small investments, big impact, easy management and close linkage with the people's life of the recipient countries, while trying to consolidate already completed projects. At the same time attention must also be given to a moderate increase of material and intellectual investment and other types of aid. China will continue actively to develop multilateral and bilateral co-operation with UN agencies and the countries concerned, on the basis of equality and mutual benefit.

BALANCE OF PAYMENTS AND EXCHANGE CONTROL

Balance of International Payments

THE recording of statistics of international payments was first introduced in the PRC in 1981. The Table of China's International Payments (1982–1984) was first made public in October 1985 by the People's Bank of China. At present, the State Planning Commission, together with the Ministry of Finance, the People's Bank of China, the State General Administration of Exchange Control and other institutions concerned, is trying to work out an international payments budget and control the overall development in its foreign economic and trade relations with other countries in a planned way.

During the years from the founding of the People's Republic of China to the 1970s, the proportion of trade and economic exchanges with foreign countries in China's national economy remained rather small. Plans were made and statistical data were collected only on foreign exchange receipts and disbursements. The statistics about foreign exchange payments at that time mainly covered foreign exchange involving imports and exports, non-commercial foreign exchange payments and aid given in foreign exchange. The foreign exchange budget was drawn up in accordance with development of national economy and in the spirit of keeping revenue and expenditure in balance with a slight surplus. Since 1979 changes have taken place in the composition of China's foreign exchange receipts and disbursements, with the introduction of the policy of opening up to the outside world and expanding China's foreign trade. In recent years, the structural reform in the field of foreign trade has helped bring into full play the enthusiasm of local and departmental authorities to increase exports. As a result, the figure for foreign exchange earnings from exports has ballooned. Moreover, with the increase in international contacts and the development of tourism, earnings and expenditure concerning labour service have undergone a steady rise. Non-commercial foreign exchange payments are becoming an increasingly important item in China's international payments. In the past few years, China has actively utilized foreign capital and intensified contacts with

Table 2: Schedule of China's Balance of Payments (1982–1984)

Items	1982	*Unit: million US dollars* 1983	1984
Current Items	5,674	4,240	2,030
Trade	4,249	1,990	14
Export F.O.B.	21,125	20,707	23,905
Import F.O.B.	−16,876	−18,717	−23,891
Labour service	939	1,739	1,574
Receipts	3,604	4,028	4,819
Disbursements	2,665	2,289	3,245
Transfer gratis	486	511	442
Private	530	436	305
Official	−44	75	137
Capital Items	338	−226	−1,003
Long-term capital	389	49	−113
Inflow	3,312	2,702	4,128
Outflow	−2,923	−2,653	−4,241
Short-term capital	−51	−275	−890
Inflow	244	59	223
Outflow	−295	−334	−1,113
Errors and Omissions	279	−366	−932
Reserve Assets	−6,291	−3,648	−95

the UN, international financial institutions and economic organizations, which has resulted in a marked increase in capital interflows. China possesses a certain amount of gold reserve and foreign exchange reserves. It has special drawing rights, reserve position and the right to utilize credits, etc. in the International Monetary Fund (IMF), as reserve funds to balance its international payments.

Table 1 is the Schedule of China's Balance of Payments (1982–1984). This table gives a general picture of China's balance of international payments in the recent three years: three years' favourable balance of payments for current items; a shift from a favourable balance of payments to an unfavourable one for the capital items and a steady yearly increase of foreign exchange reserves.

Current items include trade, labour service, transfer gratis and other items in China's foreign contacts. The current items enjoyed a favourable balance of $US5,674 million for 1982, 4,240 million for 1983 and 2,030 million for 1984. The favourable balance of payments can be attributed mainly to the following reasons: a decrease of imports coupled with an increase of exports resulted in a trade surplus of $US4,249 million in China's favour for 1982; a slight reduction in China's exports due to slow world economic recovery and its increased imports encouraged by an improved foreign exchange reserve position contributed to a drop of its favourable balance of payments to $US1,990 for 1983; a steady development of domestic production, sufficient supply of goods for foreign trade and rising exports of suitable commodities brought about a record year in exports for 1984. Meanwhile, imports for the year were also a record high, due to the policy of opening coastal port cities to the outside world and acceleration of the speed of technical transformation of small and medium enterprises. The surplus was thus further reduced to $US14 million. As a result of expansion of non-commercial businesses such as banking, tourism, transportation, insurance, post and telecommunications, the surplus in non-commercial sectors amounted to $US939 million for 1982, increased to 1,739 million for 1983 and 1,574 million for 1984. With regard to transfer gratis, overseas remittance at private level decreased year after year, while aid gratis and grants given to China by international organizations and other countries increased steadily.

Capital items reflected changes in the positions of the debtors and creditors or the debt relationship between China, on the one hand, and other countries and Hong Kong and Macao, on the other. In view of long-term capitals, the payment of loans obtained previously and purchase of foreign bonds reduced China from a surplus position to a deficit one within three years. For short-term capitals, the unfavourable balance became increasingly serious, mainly because provinces and municipalities offered foreigners deferred payment and prepayment for goods.

For reserves items, increase of reserve assets is indicated by negative signs. Therefore, the table shows an increase of $US6,291 million in foreign exchange reserve for 1982, 3,648 million for 1983 and 95 million for 1984.

In a word, the favourable balance in three successive years shown in the Schedule of China's International Payments during the period from 1982 to 1984 reflects continued, steady and coordinated development of China's national economy. However, the foreign exchange reserves were reduced in 1985 due to the fact that imports outgrew exports.

The trend of reducing China's foreign exchange reserves has been basically brought under control by strengthening foreign exchange control, restraining non-commercial foreign exchange expenditure and cutting the number of people going abroad. As its economy and exports further expand, China will definitely earn more foreign exchange and achieve balanced international payments.

Foreign Exchange Control

Foreign exchange control has been put into practice ever since the founding of the PRC. The promulgation of the Provisional Regulations for Exchange Control of the PRC by the State Council in December 1980 has since introduced a stricter system governing exchange control.

China is a developing, socialist country with a not fully developed economy and a shortage of foreign funds. To further open itself to the outside world, it needs foreign exchange to pay for imports and for advanced foreign technology, to repay capital with interest for utilizing foreign capital, to extend aid to other countries and to cover all kinds of international contacts. Therefore, China has adopted the policy of centralized control and management of foreign exchange. It has strengthened its planning and control of foreign exchange so that limited foreign funds can be pooled together by the State to be used in economic and trade exchanges with foreign countries in a planned way, and that foreign exchanges can be appropriated according to plans. Moreover, efforts will be made to increase revenue and save expenditure in order to achieve a balance of foreign exchange receipts.

The principal organs in China in charge of foreign exchange control are the State General Administration of Exchange Control and its branches in all provinces, autonomous regions, municipalities directly under the central government, important economic regions and key regions where most people have relatives residing abroad. These organs have centralized control of China's foreign exchanges and foreign exchange reserves. China follows the following process in determining its plan for foreign exchange receipts and expenditure. The Ministry of Foreign Economic Relations and Trade draws up plans for imports and exports, for trade incidental expenses, for contracted projects, for aid to other countries and for inflow and outflow of capital. The Ministry of Finance is responsible for mapping out non-commercial foreign exchange plans covering operational income and expenditure of various ministries and departments under the State Council and their work concerning foreign personnel and foreign visitors. The State General Administration of Exchange Control and its branches are instrumental in formulating local non-commercial foreign exchange payments plans, and plans for overseas remittance and private exchanges. All the above-mentioned plans concerning foreign exchange are collected by the State General Administration of Exchange Control and sent to the State Planning Commission to be incorporated into a national foreign-exchange revenue and expenditure plan, with a view to achieving an overall balance. Finally, the national plan is submitted to the State Council for approval.

China undertakes all kinds of exchange business including international settlement, international transfer, purchase and sale of foreign exchange, deposits in foreign exchange and foreign exchange loans. The Bank of China is designated by the State as the exchange bank. Other banks or financial institutions are not allowed to conduct foreign exchange business unless authorized by the State General Administration of Exchange Control of the PRC. So far, only the branches of the Overseas–Chinese Banking Corporation in Shanghai and Amoy, the Bank of East Asia, the Hong Kong and Shanghai Banking Corporation, the Standard Chartered Bank, Nanyang Commercial Bank–Shen-zhen Branch, the China International Trust and Investment Corporation and some provincial or municipal trust and investment companies have permission to do foreign exchange business in China.

Institutions, organizations and individuals, within the Chinese territories, whether Chinese or foreign, must all sell their earned foreign exchanges to the Bank of China unless otherwise stipulated by the state regulations concerned; and they must buy any foreign exchange they need from the Bank of China, which sells it according to state-approved plans or other regulations concerned. The circulation, utilization and mortgage of foreign currencies, transactions of foreign exchange without permission, arbitrage and evasion of declaring foreign currencies are all forbidden in China. The Bank of China has implemented new deposit regulations since November 1985 and has offered the residents throughout China deposit business in foreign currencies which can be drawn in foreign currencies as well.

Administrative offices, army units, mass organizations, schools, state enterprises, institutions and collective economic organizations both in urban and rural areas within the Chinese territory shall all plan and manage their foreign exchange receipts and expenditures, report their plans to the authorities in charge of exchange control every season and every year to be incorporated into the state plan, and spend foreign currencies on earmarked projects within the framework of the state plan approved by the Central Government.

Chinese people and foreign nationals living in China must sell to the Bank of China the foreign

Table 3: Average Annual Exchange Rates of Foreign Currencies against the Renminbi of the PRC

Foreign currencies	Unit	1981		1982		1983		1984	
		Buying	Selling	Buying	Selling	Buying	Selling	Buying	Selling
Australian dollar	100	195.09	196.07	191.69	192.65	177.99	178.80	203.18	204.20
Austrian schilling	100	10.70	10.76	11.08	11.14	11.01	11.07	11.58	11.64
Canadian dollar	100	147.73	142.44	152.68	153.44	159.84	160.65	178.59	179.49
Swiss franc	100	86.88	87.32	93.15	93.62	93.97	94.36	98.50	99.00
German deutschmark	100	75.45	75.82	77.75	78.14	77.41	77.80	81.35	81.76
Danish krone	100	23.97	24.08	22.70	22.82	21.65	21.76	22.35	22.46
Finnish markka	100	36.69	39.89	39.46	39.62	35.53	35.71	38.40	38.59
French franc	100	31.43	31.59	28.78	28.93	26.02	26.15	26.49	26.63
Dutch guilder	100	68.31	68.65	70.63	70.98	69.34	69.68	72.14	72.51
Norwegian krone	100	29.66	29.80	29.39	29.54	27.01	27.15	28.36	28.51
Singapore dollar	100	80.41	80.81	88.12	88.57	93.22	93.69	108.53	109.13
Swedish krona	100	33.80	33.97	30.30	30.46	25.75	25.88	27.99	28.13
UK pound sterling	100	343.86	345.59	330.28	331.94	298.85	300.35	307.79	309.33
US dollar	100	170.08	170.93	188.78	189.73	197.07	198.06	232.12	232.28
Hong Kong dollar	100	30.33	30.49	31.07	31.23	27.28	27.44	29.64	29.78
Italian lira	10,000	15.03	15.11	13.98	14.05	13.04	13.10	13.18	13.24
Japanese yen	100,000	771.58	775.44	758.81	762.61	829.85	833.68	975.05	980.39
Belgian franc	10,000	458.94	491.23	414.77	416.85	387.14	389.08	400.91	402.91

currencies remitted from foreign countries and from Hong Kong and Macao, except those which they are allowed to keep by the State. If they are in need of foreign exchange, they must apply to the departments in charge of exchange control which may sell them foreign exchange only after getting approval.

Foreign missions and their staff stationed in China may keep the foreign exchange remitted to them or brought in by themselves from abroad or from Hong Kong and Macao, or sell or deposit it in the Bank of China, and may also remit it back or take it out of China. All the foreign exchange earnings from enterprises with Overseas Chinese capital or foreign investment and Sino-foreign joint ventures must be deposited in the Bank of China, while all their foreign exchange expenditures shall be paid from their foreign exchange deposit account. The foreign partners of these enterprises can, after payment of taxes according to the laws concerned, apply to the Bank of

China and remit their net profits and other lawful earnings to be deducted from the foreign exchange deposit accounts of their enterprises. If the foreign staff, or staff from Hong Kong and Macao, of these enterprises desire to transfer or take foreign exchange out of China, no more than 50 per cent of their lawful net income including their salaries or wages after paying taxes is allowed to be taken out. If an individual wants to take out foreign exchange, the customs will issue clearance on the evidence of the certificate issued by the Bank of China or the original entry declaration forms.

The regulations governing exchange control in China are appropriate to the development of its national economy and its profound economic structural reforms. China is adhering to the principle of centralized management and gradually perfecting the control system to further promote the development of its economic contacts with foreign countries.

Chinese models at the Second Paris International Fashion Festival, 9 September 1987.

PROSPECTS

THE policy of opening to the outside world is China's fundamental state policy. In the spirit of independence and following the principle of equality and mutual benefit, China will further increase its economic and commercial contacts and expand economic and technical co-operation with various countries all over the world, both developed and developing countries, so as to promote China's socialist modernization.

China's Seventh Five-Year Plan has envisaged expansion of its import and export to as much as $US83 billion by 1990. This means an annual average trade growth rate of 7 per cent compared with its foreign trade in 1985. Past experience shows that the trade target set in the Seventh Five-Year Plan is attainable. The two-way trade increased by 80.1 per cent in five years from $US37.82 billion in 1980 to 69.61 billion in 1985, with an average annual growth rate of 13 per cent, more than the growth rate of 51.8 desired in the Sixth Five-Year Plan.

China has realized the urgency of increasing exports to earn more foreign exchange, since the key to expansion of foreign economic and trade relations and of technical co-operation lies in more exports and hence more foreign exchange. At present, efforts are being made to build an export-oriented production system and various types of bases for export-oriented agricultural and industrial commodities in coastal and other regions with favourable conditions. While China will continue to actively pursue an increase in its exports of petroleum, coal, non-ferrous metals, grain, cotton and other products, the proportion of manufactured goods in the overall exports will also go up as it improves its processing capability and raises its technological level. China has its own strength in the traditional light and textile industry and the newly-rising food-processing industry. Therefore, there is a good prospect of increasing export of light and textile products and processed food. If appropriate measures are taken, export of machinery and power-generating equipment will be marked by a substantial increase. In addition, the Government will introduce a series of policy measures to encourage export: to continue and improve the foreign exchange sharing system; to establish an export development fund; and to capitalize the economic leverage such as pricing, exchange rate and tariff and tax in encouraging export-oriented production. As far as import is concerned, with experiences accumulated during the Sixth Five-Year Plan in mind China will, during the Seventh Five-Year Plan, maintain a rational balance in importing commodities and try in every way to use foreign exchange sparingly in considering imports, with emphasis on importing software, advanced technology, key equipment and means of production in short supply but in urgent need in China, so as to accelerate technological advance at home and enhance capabilities of self-reliance.

In the period of the Seventh Five-Year Plan, China will further increase the use of foreign capital and import of advanced technology. Foreign investors are welcome to set up enterprises with sole capital or joint ventures in China. Efforts will be made to develop Sino-foreign co-operative production, joint development projects and research work. China, for its part, will actively pursue contracting projects abroad and co-operation in labour service, and continue to do its best in providing aid to foreign countries. At the same time, China will strengthen its economic and technological co-operation with UN agencies for development and other international institutes, and endeavour to make proper use of the multilateral and bilateral aid given to China. In short, there is a broad prospect for developing foreign economic relations and trade in China on the basis of a fairly rapid growth of its national economy. As time goes by, the policy of opening China to the outside world will be implemented even more thoroughly and extensively.

PROVISIONS OF THE STATE COUNCIL OF THE PEOPLE'S REPUBLIC OF CHINA FOR THE ENCOURAGEMENT OF FOREIGN INVESTMENT

(Promulgated on 11 October 1986)

Article 1

These provisions are hereby formulated in order to improve the investment environment, facilitate the absorption of foreign investment, introduce advanced technology, improve product quality, expand exports in order to generate foreign exchange and develop the national economy.

Article 2

The State encourages foreign companies, enterprises and other economic entities or individuals (hereinafter referred to as "foreign investors") to establish Chinese–foreign equity joint ventures, Chinese–foreign co-operative ventures and wholly foreign-owned enterprises (hereinafter referred to as "enterprises with foreign investment") within the territory of China.

The State grants special preferences to the enterprises with foreign investment listed below:

(1) Production enterprises whose products are mainly for export, which have a foreign exchange surplus after deducting from their total annual foreign exchange revenues the annual foreign exchange expenditures incurred in production and operation and the foreign exchange needed for the remittance abroad of the profits earned by foreign investors (hereinafter referred to as "export enterprises").

(2) Production enterprises possessing advanced technology supplied by foreign investors which are engaged in developing new products, and upgrading and replacing products in order to increase foreign exchange generated by exports or for import substitution (hereinafter referred to as "technologically advanced enterprises").

Article 3

Export enterprises and technologically advanced enterprises shall be exempt from payment to the state of all subsidies to staff and workers, except for the payment of or allocation of funds for labour insurance, welfare costs and housing subsidies for Chinese staff and workers in accordance with the provisions of the State.

Article 4

The site use fees for export enterprises and technologically advanced enterprises, except for those located in busy urban sectors of large cities, shall be computed and charged according to the following standards:

(1) Five to twenty RMB yuan per square metre per year in areas where the development fee and the site use fee are computed and charged together.

(2) Not more than three RMB yuan per square metre per year in site areas where the development fee is computed and charged on a one-time basis or areas which are developed by the above-mentioned enterprises themselves.

Exemptions for specified periods of time from the fees provided in the foregoing provision may be granted at the discretion of local people's governments.

Article 5

Export enterprises and technologically advanced enterprises shall be given priority in obtaining water, electricity and transportation services, and communication facilities needed for their production and operation. Fees shall be computed and charged in accordance with the standards for local state enterprises.

Article 6

Export enterprises and technologically advanced enterprises, after examination by the Bank of China, shall be given priority in receiving loans for short-term revolving funds needed for production and distribution, as well as for other needed credit.

Article 7

When foreign investors in export enterprises and technologically advanced enterprises remit abroad profits distributed to them by such enterprises, the amount remitted shall be exempt from income tax.

Article 8

After the expiration of the period for the reduction or exemption of enterprise income tax in accordance

788

with the provisions of the State, export enterprises whose value of export products in that year amounts to 70 per cent or more of the value of their products for that year may pay enterprise income tax at one-half the rate of the present tax.

Export enterprises in the special economic zones and in the economic and technological development zones and other export enterprises that already pay enterprise income tax at a tax rate of 15 per cent and that comply with the foregoing conditions shall pay enterprise income tax at a rate of 10 per cent.

Article 9

After the expiration of the period of reduction or exemption of enterprise income tax in accordance with the provisions of the State, technologically advanced enterprises may extend for three years the payment of enterprise income tax at a rate reduced by one-half.

Article 10

Foreign investors who reinvest the profits distributed to them by their enterprises in order to establish or expand export enterprises or technologically advanced enterprises for a period of operation of not less than five years, after application to and approval by the tax authorities, shall be refunded the total amount of enterprise income tax already paid on the reinvested portion. If the investment is withdrawn before the period of operation reaches five years, the amount of enterprise income tax refunded shall be repaid.

Article 11

Export products of enterprises with foreign investment, except crude oil, finished oil and other products subject to special State provisions, shall be exempt from the consolidated industrial and commercial tax.

Article 12

Enterprises with foreign investment may arrange the export of their products directly or may also export by consignment to agents in accordance with State provisions. For products that require an export licence, in accordance with the annual export plan of the enterprise, an application for an export licence may be made every six months.

Article 13

Machinery and equipment, vehicles used in production, raw materials, fuel, bulk parts, spare parts, machine component parts and fittings (including imports restricted by the State) which enterprises with foreign investment need to import in order to carry out their export contracts do not require further applications for examination and approval and are exempt from the requirement for import licences. The customs department shall exercise supervision and control, and shall inspect and release such imports on the basis of the enterprise contract or the export contract.

The imported materials and items mentioned above are restricted to use by the enterprise and may not be sold on the domestic market. If they are used in products to be sold domestically, import procedures shall be handled in accordance with provisions and the taxes shall be made up according to the governing sections.

Article 14

Under the supervision of the foreign exchange control departments, enterprises with foreign investment may mutually adjust their foreign exchange surpluses and deficiencies among each other.

The Bank of China and other banks designated by the People's Bank of China may provide cash security services and may grant loans in Renminbi to enterprises with foreign investment.

Article 15

The people's governments at all levels and relevant departments in charge shall guarantee the right of autonomy of enterprises with foreign investment and shall support enterprises with foreign investment in managing themselves in accordance with international advanced scientific methods.

With the scope of their approved contracts, enterprises with foreign investment have the right to determine by themselves production and operation plans, to raise funds, to use funds, to purchase production materials and to sell products; and to determine by themselves the wage levels, the forms of wages and bonuses, and the allowance system.

Enterprises with foreign investment may, in accordance with their production and operation requirements, determine by themselves their organizational structure and personnel system, employ or dismiss senior management personnel, increase or dismiss staff and workers. They may recruit and employ technical personnel, managerial personnel and workers in their locality. The unit to which such employed personnel belong shall provide its support and shall permit their transfer. Staff and workers who violate the rules and regulations, and thereby cause certain bad consequences may, in accordance with the seriousness of the case, be given differing sanctions, up to that of discharge. Enterprises with foreign investment that recruit, employ, dismiss or discharge staff and workers shall file a report with the local labour and personnel department.

Article 16

All districts and departments must implement the "Circular of the State Council Concerning Firmly Curbing the Indiscriminate Levy of Charges on Enterprises." The people's governments at the provincial level shall formulate specific methods and strengthen supervision and administration.

Enterprises with foreign investment that encounter unreasonable charges may refuse to pay and may also appeal to the local economic committees up to the State Economic Commission.

Article 17

The people's government at all levels and relevant departments in charge shall strengthen the co-ordination of their work, improve efficiency in handling matters and shall promptly examine and approve matters reported by enterprises with foreign investment that require response and resolution. The agreement, contract and articles of association of an enterprise with foreign investment shall be examined and approved by the departments in charge under the State Council. The examination and approval authority must within three months from the date of receipt of all documents decide to approve or not to approve them.

Article 18

Export enterprises and technologically advanced enterprises mentioned in these provisions shall be confirmed jointly as such by the foreign economic relations and trade departments where such enterprises are located and the relevant departments in accordance with the enterprise contract, and certification shall be issued.

If the actual results of the annual exports of an export enterprise are unable to realize the goal of the surplus in the foreign exchange balance that is stipulated in the enterprise contract, the taxes and fees which have already been reduced or exempted in the previous year shall be made up in the following year.

Article 19

Except where these provisions expressly provide that they are to be applicable to export enterprises or technologically advanced enterprises, other articles shall be applicable to all enterprises with foreign investment.

These provisions apply from the date of implementation to those enterprises with foreign investment that have obtained approval for establishment before the date of implementation of these provisions and that qualify for the preferential terms of these provisions.

Article 20

For enterprises invested in and established by companies, enterprises and other economic organizations or individuals from Hong Kong, Macao, or Taiwan, matters shall be handled by reference to these provisions.

Article 21

The Ministry of Foreign Economic Relations and Trade shall be responsible for interpreting these provisions.

Article 22

These provisions shall go into effect on the date of issue.

PART VI

LIVING STANDARDS AND SOCIAL WELFARE

LIVING STANDARDS

CHINA's nationwide liberation in 1949 has brought about fundamental changes in the life and social security of the people, for the aim of the Chinese revolution and the current modernization programme is to make China a socialist country with a high level of culture and democracy to meet, to the maximum, the growing needs of the people in their material and cultural life. Soon after New China was founded, the Chinese people, under the leadership of the People's Government, threw themselves into an unremitting struggle against poverty and underdevelopment. Now the problem of food and clothing has basically been solved. The people's living standards are much higher than in the pre-Liberation days and a social security system has been set up extensively. The people's life is secure and a fledging prosperity has appeared throughout the nation.

Living Standards before and after Liberation

In old China, production was backward and the people lived in dire poverty; wages were often at such a low level that they were barely enough to support the maintenance of a family sufficient to reproduce itself. The 1931 statistics released by the Ministry of Industry and Commerce of the Kuomintang Government showed that the monthly living expenses needed by a family of five was 27.2 yuan. But statistics in Shanghai, the largest industrial city in China, indicated that only printing, machine building and shipbuilding workers, who accounted for only six per cent of the total workforce in the city at the time, reached such a standard in the second half of 1928. The 1930 monthly salary survey conducted in 29 cities indicated that the average monthly salary was about 15 yuan in most places, with none reaching the 27.2 yuan level. The Kuomintang Government adopted an inflationary policy from 1937 to 1949, subjecting the common people to invisible but very cruel plunder. Taking the total amount of money issued in June 1937 as the base figure, it rocketed 266,000 fold in the following 11 years up to July 1948 and the rise in prices far outpaced inflation. The wholesale price index of major consumer goods in Shanghai is an instance. In the same period, it soared by 2,606,000 times. By the end of August 1948, inflation and prices in Shanghai had risen by 455,000 and 4,721,000 times, respec-

tively. As a result, workers' real income plummeted. The real wage of the workers in the Tianjin Qixin Cement Company provide an instance. Suppose the average monthly wage was 100 between July 1936 and June 1937: it dropped to 26.47 by April 1946, to 20.34 by April 1947, further down to 17.14 by April 1948 and still further down to 14.77 by the end of September of the same year. Life in the rural areas was even worse. With little food and clothing, countless peasants were struggling to stave off starvation. Many had to go begging or even sell their children in the hope that they would survive. The national industry and commerce could hardly manage to continue and, one after another, businesses went bankrupt. On the eve of the nationwide liberation in 1949, the value of industrial output was only about half that in 1936; grain output had dropped by 25 per cent and cotton by 48 per cent.

The ditch full of dirty water, with huts, of the past (above) is now a broad street with flowers (below).
(Photo by Xia Daoling)

Living Standards and Social Welfare

The Chinese people did not begin a new life until October 1949 when New China was declared founded. In just six months, or by the end of March 1950, the country succeeded in checking the 12-year-long vicious inflation, stabilizing the circulation of currency. In 1952, land reform was completed, with 46 million hectares of farmland (about 50 per cent of China's total) distributed among the landless, together with large quantities of farm tools and implements and other things necessary for farm production. The peasants no longer had to pay the landlords rent in kind that used to amount to 30 million tons of grain. They at last became masters of the land, a goal they had sought for many thousands of years. The total output value of farm and sideline produce in 1952 amounted to 48,400,000,000 yuan according to constant price, 48.5 per cent more than the 32,600,000,000 yuan of 1949. The peasants' living standards improved strikingly. By 1957, when the First Five-Year Plan was fulfilled, the peasants' income had risen 28 per cent over that of 1952.

In cities, not only had the millions of unemployed in the old society been given jobs, but more people were recruited into the workforce. By 1957, the average consumption level of urban residents was 46.4 per cent higher than in the pre-Liberation peak year of 1936.

Consumption Level of Chinese Residents

The overall consumption level of Chinese residents is reflected in the amount of national income used as consumption funds. The average annual consumption level refers to the per capita average of the residents' consumption funds from the year's total national income. In 1952, the last year of the three-year rehabilitation period following Liberation in 1949, the average annual consumption level of Chinese residents was 76 yuan – 62 yuan for rural residents and 148 yuan for the non-agricultural population. This figure rose to 330 yuan in 1984 when the country celebrated its 35th anniversary, 2.8 times that of 1952, allowing for the price rise factor. The breakdown is 268 yuan for peasants, increasing by 1.6 times, and 592 yuan for non-agricultural residents, increasing by 1.7 times. In 1985, the figure rose to 407 yuan, with rural residents accounting for 324 yuan and non-agricultural residents 754 yuan.

The average per capita consumption of food also increased markedly. Comparing 1985 with 1952, food grain consumption rose from 197.7 kg to 254.4 kg; of vegetable oil, from 2.1 kg to 5.1 kg; of pork, from 5.9 kg to 14 kg; of eggs, from 1 kg to 5 kg; of sugar, from 0.9 to 5.6 kg; of wines and liquor, from 1.1 kg to 7.7 kg; and of garment cloth, from 5.7 m to 11.7 m.

The rise in the consumption level of Chinese residents is also seen from the rapid growth in their purchasing power, which manifests itself in part in the

growth in their bank savings. From 1957 to 1985, the amount of urban and rural bank savings jumped by 45 times from 3,520,000,000 yuan to 162,260,000,000 yuan (equal to 86.9 per cent of the year's state revenue). In terms of per capita average, it rose by 28.7 times from 5.4 yuan to 155 yuan.

Income and Expenditure of Urban Families

Wages are the principal source of family income for workers and other employees in cities. The total payroll, including fixed rate (time wage), piece rate (including above-quota payment), extra wages, bonuses, allowances, overtime pay and non-staple food subsidies, was 138,300,000,000 yuan in 1985 as against 77,250,000,000 yuan in 1980, a rise of 79 per cent.

Over the past three decades since the founding of New China, the total payroll of Chinese workers and other employees has grown at an average annual rate of 8.3 per cent. Correspondingly, the total agricultural and industrial output value increased at an average annual rate of 8.4 per cent. Such well coordinated growth ensured a steady increase in the average amount of wages and the number in employment, the two key factors for improving the living standards of the families of workers and staff members.

In 1985, the last year of the Sixth Five-Year Plan period, the average annual wage income of Chinese employees reached 1,148 yuan, 386 yuan more than in 1980, increasing at an average rate of 4.2 per cent in real terms. The average annual wage of employees in enterprises and undertakings run by the State reached 1,213 yuan – 767 yuan or 62 per cent more than 1952's 446 yuan.

Table 1: Average per capita Monthly Cash Income and Expenditure of Urban Employees' Families (RMB)

	1985	Percentage in living expense
Total income	68.45	
Income disposable on living	62.70	
1. Non-elastic spending	36.81	58.7
Food, of which:	32.53	51.9
Grain	5.19	8.3
Non-staple food	18.91	30.2
Cigarettes, wine and tea	3.17	5.1
Other foods	5.26	8.4
Rent	0.66	1.1
Fuel	0.84	1.3
Water and electricity	0.63	1.0
Medical expenses	0.46	0.7
Tuition and school service	0.58	0.9
Child care	0.34	0.5
Transportation	0.70	1.1
Posts and telecommunications	0.07	0.1
2. Flexible spending	25.89	41.3

Note: Figures are based on sampie survey data by the State Statistics Bureau.

794

Table 2: Income and Expenditure of Urban Families

Item	1964	1985
Number of households surveyed	3,537	17,143
Average number of people in a family	5.30	3.82
Average number of people employed in a family	1.58	2.20
Number of people a job-holder has to support (including himself)	3.35	1.74
Average per capita monthly income	20.29 yuan	68.45 yuan
Income disposable on living	18.92 yuan	62.70 yuan
Percentage of different income group (grouped according to the amount of per capita monthly income disposable on living):	100	100
less than 20 yuan	59.74% ⎫	0.91
20–25 yuan	17.19% ⎬	
25–35 yuan	16.03%	4.34
35–50 yuan	5.77%	22.22
50–60 yuan	⎫	20.92
more than 60 yuan	⎬ 1.27%	51.61
Average per capita monthly expenditure	18.39 yuan	61.02 yuan

Note: The income disposable on living refers to the amount of real income after deduction of maintenance and bonuses.

Source: State Statistics Bureau, *China Statistics Yearbook 1986*. Page 667.

Table 3: Income and Expenditure of Peasant Families

Item	1978	1985
Number of families surveyed	6,095	66,642
Number of residents of the families surveyed	34,961	341,525
Average number of residents of a family	5.74	5.12
Average number of able-bodied and half labour power of a family	2.27	2.95
Average number of people a labourer has to support	2.53	1.74
Average annual net income per capita:	133.57 yuan	397.60 yuan
income derived from collective undertakings	88.53 yuan	33.37 yuan
income derived from economic co-operatives		3.69 yuan
net income from family businesses	35.79 yuan	322.53 yuan
income other than loans	9.25 yuan	38.01 yuan
Percentage of incomes from different sources:		
income from collectives	66.3	8.4
income from economic co-operatives		0.9
income from family businesses	26.8	81.1
income other than loans	6.9	9.6
Percentage of different income groups (grouped according to average per capita net income):		
under 100 yuan	33.3%	1.0
100–150 yuan	31.7%	3.4
150–200 yuan	17.6%	7.9
200–300 yuan	15.0%	25.6
300–400 yuan	⎫	24.0
400–500 yuan	⎬ 2.4%	15.8
above 500 yuan	⎭	22.3
Average per capita living expenses	116.06	317.42

Source: The State Statistics Bureau, *China Statistics Yearbook 1986*. Page 673.

According to sample surveys conducted by the State Statistics Bureau, the number of people employed in each urban family was 1.33 in 1957 and rose to 2.20 in 1985, rising from 30.4 per cent to 57.6 per cent. This means that the number of people each employee had to support (including himself) was reduced from 3.29 to 1.74. Although the average wage did not rise quickly and in some years even dropped over the past three decades, the rapid increase in employment still contributed to an improvement in the living standards of employees' families.

According to sample surveys, the monthly income available for living expenses in urban families averaged 62.7 yuan per capita in 1985, 43.08 yuan more than 1957's 19.62 yuan, a 108 per cent growth in real terms. The average per capita cost of living was 61.02 yuan a month in 1985, 42.52 yuan more than the 1957 figure of 18.5 yuan. Of the 106 cities surveyed, Fushan, Guangdong province enjoyed the highest cost of living per capita, which was 101.20 yuan, followed by Guangzhou, 87.21 yuan; Shanghai, 84.17 yuan; and Beijing, the 8th, 75.64 yuan.

As the sample survey showed, of the amount 62.7 yuan, the per capita monthly living expenses of urban employees' families in 1985, 32.53 yuan was spent on food, which included 15 kilogrammes of rice (5.19 yuan), 15 kilogrammes of common vegetables (6 yuan), three kilogrammes of eggs (7 yuan), 1.5 kilogrammes of pork (5.91 yuan), and some cigarettes, wine and tea (3.17 yuan): 5.26 yuan was paid for other

An ordinary worker's family. With the development of the economy, the standard of living of Chinese people has gradually improved. *(Photo by Yang Futao)*

foods; 0.66 yuan was paid as rent; 0.84 yuan was spent on fuel; 0.63 yuan on running water and electricity; 0.46 yuan on medical care; 0.58 yuan on tuition and school expenses; 0.34 yuan on child care; 0.70 yuan on transportation, and 0.07 yuan on posts and telecommunications. The above non-elastic spending totalled 36.81 yuan, accounting for 58.7 per cent, and the remaining flexibly disposable amount was 25.89 yuan, accounting for 41.3 per cent.

The surveys also showed that low-income families with a per capita monthly income disposable on living on less than 25 yuan accounted for 76.93 per cent of the total number of families surveyed in 1964. The percentage dropped to 1.67 per cent in 1984, 0.91 per cent in 1985, ranking last of various income groups. The number of high-income families with a per capita monthly income above 50 yuan made up only 1.27 per cent in 1964, the last of all income groups. But in 1984, the number of families in this group accounted for 48.92 per cent; in 1985, 72.53 per cent. In 1985, the number of middle income families with a per capita monthly income of 30–50 yuan accounted for 22.22 per cent. The last two income groups made up 94.75 per cent of the total.

Income and Expenditure of Peasant Families

There are 800 million people living in rural areas, accounting for about 80 per cent of China's population. Their living conditions by and large reflect those of the whole nation.

There has been remarkable progress in China's rural economy since the Third Plenary Session of the Eleventh Central Committee of the Communist Party of China in December 1978. The rural average per capita annual income rose from 134 yuan in 1978 to 398 yuan in 1985, increasing at an average annual rate

An unforgettable moment. *(Photo by Chai Gengsheng)*

A peasant brass band at Pingxiang, Jiangxi province.

of 14.8 per cent in real terms, an increase never witnessed before (the average annual growth during the previous five Five-Year Plan periods was about 3–4 per cent).

The rural economic reforms instituted since 1979 have reduced the part of the rural economy operated by collectives and increased the part operated by contract on a household basis, thus bringing about great changes in the sources of peasant income. A sample survey (see Table 3) by the State Statistics Bureau showed that in 1978 peasants derived 66.3 per cent of the net income from the collectives and 26.8 per cent from household sideline occupations, but the reverse was the case in 1985, when they derived only 8.4 per cent of their net income from the former collectives and 81.1 per cent from household economy, and the rest, about 0.9 per cent, from economic co-operatives organized by themselves.

According to the living cost and other conditions in rural China in the 1980s, a rural peasant generally needs some 200 yuan a year to maintain the lowest living standards and simple reproduction. Families with a per capita annual income of less than 200 yuan are considered to be in poverty; those with a per capita annual income of 200–500 yuan are rated as basically solving the food and clothing problem; those with a per capital income of 500–1,000 yuan are regarded as being well-off; and those with an average annual income above 1,000 yuan are considered better off. A sample survey conducted by the State Statistics Bureau showed that the number of poor families in 1978 accounted for 82.6 per cent of the families surveyed and in 1984, the figure dropped to 14 per cent; the number of families with just enough to feed and clothe themselves increased from 17 per cent in 1978 to 67.8 per cent in 1984; the number of well-off families with a per capita annual income of over 500 yuan rose from almost zero to 16.8 per cent; and there have been some better-off families with a per capita

annual income of more than 1,000 yuan, accounting for about 1.4 per cent.

According to the survey, the real per capita net annual income of poor families averaged 158.8 yuan, barely enough to sustain simple reproduction. They usually need state relief or loans. Most of these families were in remote, mountainous areas and some were poor because of large families but not enough labour power, a low level of education and poor production skills.

The real per capita annual net income of the 200–500 yuan group averaged 323.1 yuan, with 258.3 yuan spent on living. In normal circumstances, they have food and clothes enough and to spare. But as they had little to start out with and had limited power to resist natural disasters or accidents, their life is not secure enough. The real per capita net annual income of the 500–1,000 yuan group averaged 644.6 yuan, with living expenses amounting to 432.8 yuan. They lead an easy life, with a marked improvement in food, clothing, housing and daily necessities. With a better education and production skills, most of them have great potential for expanding production and further improving their living standards. The real per capita annual net income of the more than 1,000 yuan group averaged 1,311 yuan, with 693.6 yuan spent on living. They have improved their life in every aspect.

Viewing rural life as a whole, the majority of the rural residents have solved the problem of food and clothing and the number of well-off and better-off families is growing. But the 1985 sample survey showed that there were still about 12.2 per cent of the peasant families (mainly in mountainous and remote areas where the natural conditions are harsh) who have not yet shaken off poverty, and the life of families with enough food and clothing is still unstable. But the People's Government has adopted all kinds of measures to help them out of poverty. Better-off regions and all trades and services are all lending a helping hand, striving to help them put an end to poverty once and for all. All these have helped boost their confidence in the future of their life.

Consumption Patterns

The consumption pattern mirrors roughly the level of development of production and the living standards. The living costs of the Chinese people cover mainly the following five items: food, clothing, housing, fuel and daily necessities. The following tables show the rough 1985 consumption patterns of urban and rural families.

Analysis of consumption patterns

—As consumption patterns show, spending on food takes the biggest proportion of the total living expenditure, 58–59 per cent since the beginning of

Citizens can purchase fresh aquatic products at any time at peasants' markets in Guangzhou. *(Photo by Liu Yusheng)*

Table 4: Consumption Pattern of Chinese Families (1) Urban

Order of priority: Item:	1 Food	2 Clothing	3 Daily necessities	4 Housing	5 Fuel
Percentage	53.31	15.34	22.22	1.08	1.38

(2) Peasant

Order of priority: Item:	1 Food	2 Housing	3 Daily necessities	4 Clothing	5 Fuel
Percentage	57.7	12.4	11.4	9.9	5.7

(Data provided by the State Statistics Bureau, *China Statistics Yearbook, 1986*)

Table 5: Consumption Pattern of Urban Families (%)

Item	1957	1985
Food	58.43	53.31
Clothing	12.00	15.34
Housing, water, electricity and fuel	7.67	3.49
Of which: rent	2.32	1.08
fuel/gas	3.89	1.38
Medical fees	1.84	0.75
Child care	1.30	0.56
Education, culture and entertainment	2.32	2.25
Of which: tuition and stationery	0.65	0.95
subscription to books, newspapers and journals	0.59	0.94
recreational activities	1.08	0.36
Utility goods	7.62	18.64
Of which: articles for recreational activities		7.50
articles for daily use		11.14
Transportation	} 2.38	1.15
Posts and telecommunications		0.11
Other	6.44	

Source: Compiled based on data released by the State Statistics Bureau.

Table 6: Consumption Pattern of Peasant Families (%)

Item	1957	1985
Food	65.8	57.7
Clothing	13.5	9.9
Fuel	10.0	5.7
Housing	2.1	12.4
Daily necessities and other	6.9	11.4
Culture, services	1.7	2.9

Source: The State Statistics Bureau, *The China Statistics Yearbook, 1986,* "Statistics of the National Economy".

the 1980s, which doubles that in developed countries. This indicates that China is a developing country, with a low level of economic development and low living standards. As the Chinese people had always been looking forward to sufficient food and clothing, it is natural that they give them top priority. From 1957 to 1984, spending on food remained about 58 per cent of the total family expenditure in urban areas; in 1985, however, it dropped to 53.3 per cent. But the peasants' spending on food dropped by 6.8 percentage points from 65.8 per cent in 1957 to 59 per cent in 1984, to 57.7 per cent in 1985, a drop of 8.1 per cent, with the biggest drop registered since 1978. In the two years from 1978 to 1980, it dropped astonishingly from 67.7 per cent to 61.8 per cent, a drop of 5.9 percentage points. Compared with urban families, the gap was

only 4.40 percentage points. The change shows how rapidly the rural living standards have improved.
—Spending on articles of clothing accounted for 13.5 per cent of consumer spending in 1957, the second largest family expenditure. The gap between urban and rural areas was 1.5 percentage points in 1957 and narrowed to 0.65 percentage points in 1981. Beginning from 1981, urban families began to spend more on articles of clothing and by 1981, the percentage of such spending reached 14.79 per cent, and by 1985,

A new residence at Datang, a suburban district of Maoming City, Guangdong province. *(Photo by Li Changyong)*

Table 7: Comparison between Chinese Consumption Patterns and Those of Other Countries (%)

Country	Spending on food	Spending on clothing	Rents, water and electricity charges	Medical expenses	Transportation	Spending on education and entertainment	Others
USA	16.5	6.9	27.1	11.8	16.4	8.6	12.7
Britain	31.4	8.2	27.2	1.0	13.2	10.0	9.0
France	23.5	7.2	25.6	11.6	12.8	6.6	12.7
Canada	20.9	8.0	27.2	3.1	15.6	10.1	15.1
India	62.6	7.8	11.9	2.3	8.0	3.3	4.1
Japan	25.2	7.2	23.6	9.8	9.6	9.0	15.6
China	56.7	14.8	4.3	0.6	1.3	1.8	20.5

Notes: (1) Figures for China are the 1981 statistics on urban families, based on data released by the State Statistics Bureau.

(2) Figures for other countries are for 1977, taken from the 1981 supplement to the Japanese Economic Statistics Yearbook.

15.34 per cent, showing a trend of caring for better appearance as the urban living standards improved. In rural areas, however, such spending was reduced from 12.35 per cent in 1981 to 9.9 per cent in 1985, becoming the fourth largest family expenditure. This is because during this period a housing construction fever gripped the countryside as the peasants were eager to improve their living conditions and buy high level consumer durables after they had enough food and clothing. But, in terms of absolute value, the spending on articles of clothing had kept growing.

—The spending on house rent, water, electricity and fuel shows a declining trend, dropping from 8.59 per cent in 1964 to 4.3 per cent in 1981 and staying at about 5 per cent after that. This is because spending on these is fixed, with little change, while the income grew by a big margin, thus bringing down the relative proportion of such spending in the total family expenditure. Peasants used only 2–3 per cent of family expenditure on housing before 1978. But after 1978, such spending grew rapidly as they began to build new houses, thus bringing the proportion of such spending up to 12.4 per cent, much higher than urban families' 1.08 per cent.

—Spending on articles of daily use shows an upward trend, with that in urban areas rising from 10.93 per cent in 1964 to 22 per cent by 1985, with about one-third on articles for recreational activities and entertainment. Such spending in rural areas rose from 6.9 per cent in 1957 to 11.4 per cent in 1985, as this is also an area in which the peasants are trying to improve.

—Expenditure on education is relatively small, because tuition at universities and colleges is usually covered by the State, and many college and university students are given grants-in-aid, while finance for tuition in primary and middle schools is very low. The low expenditure on recreational activities and entertainment shows the monotonous after-work life of Chinese residents. The proportion of such spending on cultural activities and services in rural families rose from 1.7 per cent in 1957 to 2.9 per cent in 1985, which was only 0.2 per cent higher than in 1978. This shows a lack of effective measures to improve the cultural life in the countryside.

—Medical expenses take up a very small proportion of the urban families' spending, less than one per cent, much lower than in developed countries, thanks to the free medicare system, which is one of the outstanding features of the socialist society.

—Expenses on transportation also take up a very small proportion of family expenditure in urban areas, never exceeding 1.5 per cent, because urban residents travel mainly by bicycle or public buses and enjoy allowances for travelling to work. (See Part IV, Chapter 13, **Labour and Wages**.)

—Merchandise spending in rural families rose from 39.7 per cent in 1978 to 60.2 per cent in 1985, becoming a principal part of family expenditure. Their self-supporting expenditure dropped from 60.3 per cent to 39.8 per cent, signifying the transition of China's rural economy from partly self-supporting to a commodity producing pattern.

To sum up, the consumption pattern of the Chinese people has the following characteristics: (1) spending on food takes the largest part of family expenditure, still too large; (2) the order of spending in urban families has basically been food, clothing, articles of daily use and housing; (3) the order of spending in rural families has shifted from food, clothing, daily-use articles and housing to food, housing, daily-use articles and clothing; and (4) the spending on daily-use articles has increased the fastest of all family spending in cities. For instance, such spending in 1985 doubled that of 1964. Next comes spending on articles of clothing, which increased by 4.4 percentage points, comparing 1985 with 1964. In rural areas, housing spending rose time and again until it jumped from fourth to second place in the list of family expenditure.

Table 7 shows the comparison between the consumption pattern of urban Chinese residents in 1981 and those of other countries in 1977. Statistical methods are different from country to country; for instance, the real consumption of urban Chinese residents cannot be fully reflected in their cash expenditure because most of the expenses on housing, medical care, education and other welfare facilities and social services are not included in personal expenditure. The comparison is therefore extremely rough and can only serve to show the general differences.

Food, Clothing, Everyday Articles, Housing and Transportation

The following is an examination of the Chinese people's life from the five aspects of food, clothing, articles of daily use, housing and transportation.

Food

Marked changes have taken place since the beginning of the 1980s in the food situation of the Chinese people – changes from quantitative satisfaction to seeking quality. More and more people are seeking high protein food, food with rich nutrients and less fat. Statistics showed that urban families reduced their spending on cereals from 22.8 per cent in 1957 to 8.5 per cent in 1985 while increasing their spending on meat and vegetables from 26.8 per cent to 31.0 per cent. The ratio of the two categories of spending changed from 1:1.2 to 1:3.6.

The average per capita daily intake of calories, protein, and fat measures up to the internationally recognized standard – 2,400 kilocalories, 75 grammes of protein, and 65 grammes of fat. The ratio of carbohydrates, protein and fat, the three sources of energy in the diet, recommended by Chinese nutritionists is 5:1:0.8. A 1984 survey showed this ratio to be 5.4:1:0.8, close to that recommended by nutritionists. But of the total number of families surveyed, about 12 per cent were in the low income group whose intake of nutrients fell short of the standard.

In rural areas, the average daily intake of energy and protein was above the internationally recognized

Table 8: Per capita Daily Intake of Nutrients by Chinese Residents in 1983

	Energy (kilocalories)	Protein (g)	Fat (g)
Average	2,877.4	82.8	47.2
Urban residents	3,182.5	87.5	74.9
Rural residents	2,805.9	81.7	40.7

Source: The State Statistics Bureau, *China Statistics Yearbook, 1984*

general standard and that of fat was below the standard.

The nutritional level of different income groups varies greatly. In 1984, families with a per capita income of 200–500 yuan consumed 270.5 kilogrammes of grain, 141 kilogrammes of vegetables and 17 kilogrammes of meat, eggs, milk and aquatic products per person per year, drawing 2,415 kilocalories of energy and 73 grammes of protein, close to the optimum amount. For well-off peasant families, i.e., the 500–1,000 yuan income group, each person takes in 2,712 kilocalories of energy and 83 grammes of protein a day, which is sufficient. The better-off families, i.e., the above-1,000 yuan income group, are almost the same as urban families in terms of nutritional intake. But poor families with a per capita annual income of less than 200 yuan take in 20 per cent less calories and 22.7 per cent less protein than the recommended allowances.

Taken as a whole, the Chinese people have sufficient calorie intake in terms of absolute amount. The intake of protein, carotene, thiamine, nicotinic acid and vitamin C is enough to meet the bodily needs. The nutritional pattern is also rational, with less than 20 per cent of calories coming from fat and the rest from course fibre food. But the absolute

Beijing roast duck is a dish famous both at home and abroad, with more than 100 years of history. Zhang Wenzao, an old cook, has over 50 years of experience of roasting duck. *(Photo by Yu Yongfu)*

Roast sucking pig, a famous and delicious Guangdong dish. *(Photo by Bi Yuenian)*

Chinese passers-by stopped to watch when these furs in SAGA mink and SAGA fox were photographed outside the Forbidden City in Beijing. *(Photo from China Daily)*

amount of protein taken in is not sufficient and the protein derived from meat is even less (only about 30 per cent). The food is therefore inferior in quality. Also insufficient is the intake of minerals and vitamins and still less is the intake of calcium and riboflavin. It is, therefore, necessary to increase meat, beans and dairy products in the diet.

Clothing

For a long time after the founding of New China, people took pride in dressing simply, with the one-colour uniforms predominant. Approaching the 1980s, production began to pick up speed and economic reforms have also brought about changes in the people's attitude toward clothes. They not only demand warmer clothes but have come to care about the colour and style that will bring out the beauty of the body and temperament of the person. Big cities began to hold exhibitions and fashion shows and published magazines to introduce fashionable clothes. People all try to beautify themselves within their means.

As demand for garments diversifies, styles change frequently. More and more people have taken to western style suits, jackets, skirts, tight-trousers, *Qipao*

(a close-fitting woman's gown with high stiff collar and slit skirt), sports wear, wind-cheaters, quilted coats, woollen overcoats and fur coats. Grey, blue and black have fallen into disfavour. Most attractive are women's dresses, which have appeared in an array of changing colours. Men's suits are becoming more natural, soft and bright.

Everyday articles

What Chinese residents wanted before the 1980s were such consumer durables as bicycles, sewing machines, radios and wrist-watches. Sample surveys showed that in urban areas there were 163.72 bicycles for every hundred families in 1985 while in rural areas there were 80.64. This is why China is known as the "Kingdom of Bicycles". Peasants also use bicycles to transport goods, while better-off families have begun to buy motorcycles.

Since the beginning of the 1980s, Chinese residents have turned their eyes to electric fans, domestic washing machines, black-and-white television sets and record players. Since 1983, colour television sets and refrigerators have become things much sought-after. China is still a developing country, yet high-level electrical appliances have already found their

801

A traditional fair in the Spring Festival at Ditan, Beijing.
(Photo by Xiao Yinzhang)

way into Chinese homes. As the economy develops, more and more people can afford to buy high-level consumer durables. Already some of them have fallen short of demand in some places and people, money in hand, are waiting for supplies. It was estimated that by the end of 1985, every hundred urban families owned 79.17 electric fans, 53 washing machines, 74.9 black-and-white television sets and 48.41 record players, increasing 85.8 per cent, 736 per cent, 31.3 per cent and 273 per cent, respectively, over those in 1981. But there were only 18.43 colour television sets and 9.57 refrigerators in every hundred urban families. In the vast countryside, however, the use of consumer durables has just begun; in 1985, there were only 11.74 television sets in every hundred families. Other much sought-after consumer durables include high-grade furniture, which has become a must for newly-

weds. Now young people buy a complete range of furniture and household electrical appliances before their wedding instead of having to save up for these things after marriage as in the 1950s and 1960s. Such articles prepared for weddings are becoming more and more exquisite and fashionable.

Young people's favourites also include cameras. As was estimated by the end of 1985 every hundred families owned 12.09 cameras. Urban people have begun to favour 135 mm cameras instead of 120 mm and to take colour pictures instead of black and white.

The use of clocks and wrist-watches has spread rapidly throughout the countryside since 1979. Surveys showed that every hundred peasant families owned 163.64 clocks and wrist-watches in 1985, as against 51.75 in 1978.

As China has a vast territory and a large population, economic development is uneven. On average, the number of consumer durables possessed per one hundred families is still rather small. A 1985 survey showed that every hundred persons owned 9.4 sewing machines, 21.4 bicycles, 34.5 wrist-watches, 23.1 radios and 6.7 television sets.

Since the downfall of the "Gang of Four" in 1976, the cosmetics market has gradually become brisker. Since the beginning of the 1980s, the variety of cosmetics has developed from a few dozen kinds into nearly one thousand, falling into scores of categories. Some women are beginning to wear lipstick and use nail polish, eyebrow pencil and eye shadow, things

A refrigerator arrives at a peasant's family in a mountain village.

they dared not use in the past. Medicated cosmetics are becoming more and more popular.

Gold and silver ornaments and jewellery have been listed as consumer goods again, as more and more young women are wearing earrings, finger rings and other gold and silver ornaments.

Housing and transportation

Housing is an important part of the means of subsistence. In the cities and towns housing construction is mainly financed by the State and enterprises. During the First Five-Year Plan period (1953–57), state housing investment accounted for 9.1 per cent of the total investment in capital construction. Housing completed totalled 94,540,000 square metres in floor space, averaging 18,910,000 square metres a year. Many workers who used to live in wornout and dilapidated bungalows, makeshift huts or small log cabins have moved into new housing estates. During the 23 years from 1953 to 1975, 427.1 million square metres of housing were completed, averaging 18,570,000 square metres a year. But, owing to over-rapid growth of population, as the 1978 sample survey showed, the average living space per person was 20 per cent less than the 4.5 square metres in 1952.

Peasants' residences in Dongguan County, Guangdong province. (See also next column) *(Photo by Lu Xiaohua)*

The dwindling living space has spurred a housing construction boom which began in 1979 when the State devoted 14.8 per cent of its total capital investment to housing construction. By the end of 1980, when the Fifth Five-Year Plan was fulfilled, 234.86 million square metres of housing were completed, averaging 46,972,000 square metres a year. Housing construction went even faster during the Sixth Five-Year Plan period which began in 1981. During this period, the State devoted 20–25 per cent of its total capital investment to housing construction. At the end of this period, the housing completed in cities and towns totalled 630 million square metres in floor space, averaging 126 million square metres a year, or 2.3 times the total (54 million square metres) completed in the Third Five-Year Plan period (1966–70), and 112.9 million square metres more than, or 1.2 times, the total completed during the previous 29 years from 1950 to 1978. By the end of 1985, the living space per person averaged 6.1 square metres in Chinese cities and towns.

During this period, the Government readjusted the policy on urban housing. Under the new policy, free trading in houses is allowed, the state constructs and sells houses to urban residents, and individuals are encouraged to build their own houses. In 1984, 274,000 urban households built their own houses,

16.6 per cent more than in the preceding year. Such houses completed totalled 16,720,000 square metres in floor space, 21.1 per cent more than in the preceding year.

The most outstanding problem with urban housing is that the rent system is not rational enough. Under this system, the State provides "invisible subsidies" to occupants of state houses. The more floor space one occupies, the more subsidies one gets. Moreover, the rent is not collected according to progressive rates, resulting in a certain degree of inequality, with some people occupying more space than others. This is detrimental to mobilizing private efforts to building houses and suppresses the development of the civil construction trade. The State is also overburdened and therefore the development of the whole national economy is adversely affected.

Peasants are also eager to improve their living conditions. A guiding principle was laid down at the first national work conference on rural housing construction held in December 1979. From 1979 to 1985, the rural areas constructed 4,100 million square metres of houses (3,200 million square metres between 1981 and 1985), boosting the average living space per person from 8.1 square metres to 14.7 square metres. The number of two- or three-storeyed build-ings accounts for 13 per cent of the total. Some well-off peasants have decorated their buildings with marble flooring, insulation ceiling, plastic wallpaper and sanitary porcelain. In Inner Mongolia, herdsmen used to rove on the pastures, but now 90 per cent of them have settled down in permanent houses. While building new houses, rural peasants have made great efforts to improve the sanitation and appearance in the environment. About 40 per cent of the villages and towns now have clean tap water supply. In 1985, a programme for the construction of villages and towns was worked out, covering the construction of peasant housing. It is expected that construction will be faster and layout more rational.

As the income level of Chinese residents is low and roads and housing are inadequate, public transit and bicycles have to be the chief means of transportation. Only very few people can afford cars. The number of buses and other public motor vehicles in all cities was 6,174 in 1957 and increased to 45,155 in 1985, 6.3 times that in 1957. The number of such vehicles per 10,000 people averaged one in 1957, but 3.9 in 1985. The total road mileage was 18,259 kilometres in 1957, 38,282 kilometres in 1985, increasing by 109 per cent. Most of the workers working in the city proper go to work by bicycle.

A stream of vehicles in Chang'an Avenue, Beijing. *(Photo by Wang Wenbo)*

SOCIAL WELFARE

IN old China, people's life was insecure. It was very hard to find jobs. Even if a man had a job, he would run the risk of losing it at any time. Poor people in both urban and rural areas often had to go without food and clothing, struggling on the verge of starvation. Soon after New China was founded, the State set about solving the unemployment problem and introduced a free labour insurance scheme for workers when the economic situation was still very harsh. In the vast rural areas, when the agricultural co-operation movement was still going on, a mutual medicare programme was gradually introduced and a system was set up to insure the life of childless and aged people and orphans.

Social insurance for Chinese workers covers births, old age, sickness, death, injuries and disabilities and medical treatment. Chinese employees can be classified into five categories according to what industries they serve: Government functionaries, workers in state-owned enterprises, in collective enterprises, contractual workers and employees of Sino-Foreign joint ventures or enterprises with exclusive foreign capital. Social insurance for different categories of workers is different, and in some cases varies greatly. Workers' social insurance is managed by the Government's labour and personnel department and social insurance for rural residents is run by townships, villages or production teams.

Social Insurance of State-Owned Enterprises and Government Offices and Institutions

All state-owned enterprises should comply with the "Labour Insurance Regulations of the People's Republic of China" promulgated in February 1951. Government offices and institutions implement separate regulations. The two sets of regulations are by and large the same in content. The items of insurance coverage and payments are completely the same in some cases, basically the same in others and different in still others.

The following are the rough contents of various kinds of insurance:

Medical treatment

The medical expenses of workers, including fees for treatment, examination, operations, in-patient services and medicines (except tonic drugs), are covered by the enterprises or the State. The registration and travelling fees for treating work-connected injuries, and travelling fees for seeing doctors other than in the work places for workers of government institutions are also covered by enterprises or by the State.

The direct relatives of factory workers and staff members enjoy the benefit that covers 50 per cent of the fees on drugs or operations.

For workers hospitalized for work-connected injuries and those who enjoy preferential labour insurance, one-third of their hospital food expenses are covered by themselves and two-thirds are covered by their enterprises or the State. They receive full pay during their sick leave.

Injury and disability

When an employee retires due to work-related injuries or disabilities, he receives 80 or 90 per cent of his standard pay according to the degree of disability, with a minimum protection of 40 yuan a month. If nursing is needed, a nursing fee amounting to an ordinary worker's wage is added.

Work-connected disability benefits

A factory worker who becomes disabled from industrial injury but can still do some jobs receives a subsidy amounting to 10–13 per cent of the original pay according to the degree of disability. Those who work in government offices and institutions and become disabled at work receive a lump-sum subsidy of 50–120 yuan annually if they continue to work or stay in homes for the disabled, and 140–518 yuan if they return home.

Sick leave benefits

Factory workers asking for sick leave extending to six months receive 60–100 per cent of their original wages. If the duration of sick leave exceeds six months, they receive 40–60 per cent of their wages. For employees working in government offices and institutions, full pay is given for the first two months, and 90–100 per cent of wages are given beginning from the third month, provided the duration of sick leave does not exceed six months. If the duration of sick leave exceeds six months, 70–80 per cent of their

A kindergarten in the Panzhihua steelworks in Sichuan province. *(Photo by Xiong Ruqing)*

original wages will be given, but full pay must be given to those who began to work for the Revolution before New China was founded.

Maternity leave benefits

Maternity leave is 56 days, in normal circumstances; 14 more days for those in difficult labour, or giving birth to twins; and no more than 30 days for a miscarriage. Full pay is given during maternity leave. Many regions and units have now extended maternity leave to three months or even six months with full pay for those conforming well in family planning. Maternity allowances for factory workers are 4 yuan in normal circumstances and eight yuan for each baby in cases of twins or multiple births. To encourage family planning, a monthly health care fee of five yuan is given to an only child until he or she is 14 years of age.

Retirement benefits

Retired employees who retire at the prescribed age receive 60–80 per cent of their original pay, according to the length of their services, with a minimum protection of 30 yuan a month. Officials and workers who began to work for the Revolution before 1949,

Children of Hangzhou spend their holiday happily in the park. *(Photo by Wu Yuanliu)*

when the People's Republic of China was founded, may leave their jobs with full pay, and some of them may receive additional subsidies amounting to one to two months of their original wages upon leaving their jobs if their circumstances meet related state regulations.

For national model workers and those with special contributions, the pension may be 5–15 per cent higher, but no more than their original standard wages.

Retirement age

The prescribed retirement age is 60 for men, 50 for women workers and 55 for women clerks, if the duration of their services exceeds 10 years; for those working for at least ten years in coal mines, in high temperatures or doing very heavy physical labour or work harmful to health, the retirement age is 55 for men and 45 for women. Men at 50 and women at 45 certified by hospitals (confirmed by the labour assessment committees in cases of workers) as having lost the ability to work may also retire.

Resignation

Employees who have completely lost the ability to work before the prescribed retirement age may quit their jobs, with 40 per cent of their original standard wages or no less than 25 yuan a month, and continue to enjoy free medical care.

Death and survivors' benefits

Burial expenses: when a worker dies, funeral expenses amounting to two to three months of the deceased's average wage are given. For employees in government offices and institutions, the prescribed burial expense is a lump sum of 240 yuan. Survivors' benefits for factory workers who die in industrial accidents will be 25–50 per cent of the original wage of the deceased, according to the number of survivors, until they lose eligibility. If a worker dies of illness, the survivors will get a lump-sum amounting to 6–12 months' wages of the deceased. If an employee of a government office or institution dies in employment, his survivors will receive a lump sum of between 500 and 700 yuan; if he is killed in the course of duty, they will receive a sum equivalent to 40 months' wages of the deceased; and if he dies of illness, they will receive 400–600 yuan. If the survivors have difficulties, they may be subsidized by the work-units of the deceased. Burial subsidies for direct relatives above one year-old of factory workers will be one-third or half of the average wage of the unit, according to the age of the deceased. High insurance standards are set for those who are wounded or disabled in war and for families of soldiers and people who died in the cause of Revolution.

Special benefits for returned overseas Chinese and their working family members

Returned overseas Chinese or their working family members are given leave on private business, apart from leave to see relatives. The duration of private business leave is less than three months to Hong Kong

and Macao, and they are permitted six months to foreign countries. Extension of the leave should not exceed one month. During their leave, they will receive the amount of pay for absence leave. They are required to cover their own medical expenses outside the territory. They are also eligible for burial expenses should they die. If the extension of private business leave exceeds six months, their wages will be stopped but their jobs will be retained; if the leave extension exceeds six months, they are deemed to have quit their jobs. If they have permission to settle outside China, they will be given an amount of money which will not exceed 24 months of their original wages.

Returned overseas Chinese retirees and people who have quit their jobs and their working family members are given leave to travel abroad, with full pension or living expenses. The duration of such leave allowed is three months if they go to Hong Kong and Macao and one year if they go to foreign countries. Medical expenses incurred abroad are to be covered by themselves. Should they die, burial expenses will be paid to the survivors. If their leave is over-stayed, the pensions for retirees and living expenses for job-quitters will be stopped until they return (there are separate stipulations). If they obtain permission to settle abroad, the pensions of the retirees and living expenses for job-quitters will be issued in full.

Sources of security funds

Social insurance payments for state-owned enterprises are borne completely by the enterprises. According to the insurance regulations, an enterprise is required to pay a monthly social security contribution equivalent to three per cent of its total payroll. Of this, 30 per cent goes to the All-China Federation of Trade Unions as the national social security fund and the remaining 70 per cent is kept by the enterprise's trade union, which pays security benefits. The accounts of the insurance funds of an enterprise are settled on a monthly basis, with the balance carried over to the accounts of the trade union at the next higher level as insurance regulatory funds; if an enterprise's insurance funds are not enough to cover the payments, the trade union may apply for regulation with the trade union at a higher level. This practice was discontinued from 1969 owing to the Cultural Revolution. Insurance payments were then listed as extra-operational expenses instead of being fixed amounts of contributions. The method was introduced only as expedient and proved to have many drawbacks; some areas and departments have begun to change it.

Insurance funds of government offices and institutions come mainly from two sources: (1) Expenses for free medical care appropriated from state revenue and allocated by public health departments; (2) expenses on other insurance items paid by various units as their administrative or operating expenditure.

Social Insurance for Employees in Collective Enterprises

Social insurance in collective enterprises (mostly operating under district or county authorities or above) is similar to that of state-owned enterprises.

Some collective enterprises (mainly those operating under authorities below the district or county level) have instituted their own social insurance systems, according to their financial situation. The system chiefly covers old age and medical care. Standards of payments vary. They chiefly fall into three categories: (1) a certain amount of medical expenses are pre-paid, with overruns to be reimbursed and remainders partly retained by the employees themselves at the end of the year; (2) most of the medical expenses are reimbursable (with the ceiling set) and only a small part is borne by the employees themselves; (3) different set proportions are shared by the enterprises and workers according to out-patient and in-patient services. Retirement benefits vary from enterprise to enterprise, depending on the regulations worked out by the enterprises themselves or by the departments in charge.

Social Insurance for Contractual Workers

Contractual workers enjoy the same medical care benefits as non-contractual workers (with some slight differences in some places). The insurance coverage is determined by provincial, autonomous regional or municipal authorities. Current practices in different regions show that most places cover retirement and unemployment insurance. Insurance funds are mainly contributed by enterprises. In some places, subsidies are given from local revenue.

Social Insurance for Employees in Sino-foreign Joint Ventures or Foreign Enterprises in China

In providing social insurance, Sino-foreign joint ventures and foreign enterprises in China usually follow the regulations governing state-owned enterprises. If any provision is deemed inapplicable, new provisions must be submitted for approval by the departments in charge of provincial, autonomous regional or municipal governments and trade union organizations at the corresponding level before they are implemented.

Social Insurance for Rural Labourers (including employees in rural enterprises)

A limited social security system was introduced in the Chinese rural areas in the mid-1950s. This is known as the "Five guarantees", which covers food, clothing, daily necessities, medical and burial expenses for childless old people, the weak (including the disabled) and orphans (whose education is guaranteed). Some townships and villages have set up "old people's homes" to take care of childless old people. By the end of 1985, China had 2,747,000 people covered by the "Five guarantee" system, and by the end of 1985, there were well over 20,000 childless old people's homes, with 240,000 inmates.

There were only a few places in the rural areas that introduced the pension system before the Third Plenary Session of the Eleventh Central Committee of the Communist Party of China held in December 1978. But progress has been made since then. The system had been introduced in 9,410 villages and 1,330 townships in 23 provinces, autonomous regions and municipalities by the end of 1984. But, considering the vastness of China, the number is still very small.

At present, the rural social insurance items are mainly the following:

Co-operative medical care system

This is covered by a co-operative medical care system commonly practised in the vast rural areas. The specific practices vary according to the economic situation in each township or village. They fall mainly into three types: (1) all or part of medical fees are reimbursable; (2) fees for house calls, injections, dressings and other hospital services are free while the cost of medicines is paid by patients; and (3) out-patient service fees are paid by the patients while all or part of in-patient service fees are reimbursable.

Retirement and old-age benefits

Specific regulations concerning such benefits are worked out by townships and villages according to their own economic conditions. Most townships and villages stipulate that male field labourers may retire at the age of 65 and women at 55 or 60. Some townships and villages stipulate that field labourers of both sexes may retire at 60. Those engaging in industrial or sideline production may retire five years earlier. Labourers, men at 50 and women at 45, or both at the age of 55, may receive pensions, if they become disabled from illness. Some townships or villages stipulate that any one who loses the ability to work may enjoy a pension, without age restrictions, while others provide only for those who become disabled from work-related injuries or accidents before the prescribed retirement age.

Retirement payments

The amount of payment in most townships and villages is a basic amount plus a subsidy according to the length of service. The basic sum varies according to economic situation. It is 20–40 yuan per person in some areas, and 10–30 yuan in others, with the minimum at 4–8 yuan and the maximum ranging up to 60 yuan. Labourers doing industrial and sideline production usually get 5–10 yuan more pension than those engaged in farming. An additional amount is given to retired cadres holding the posts of production team leaders and higher, model labourers and those holding professional titles or making special contributions to their collectives.

Pension funds are raised by different methods in different places. There are two main ways: one is that townships, villages and production teams share – with townships contributing 50 per cent, villages 30–40 per cent, and production teams 10–20 per cent; the other is that they are borne entirely by the township, village or production team and in both circumstances no personal contributions are required.

Other insurance benefits

Some economically developed townships and villages provide the following additional benefits: (1) Disability benefit. This includes a daily allowance of 0.60 yuan for those disabled from illness and a monthly allowance of 22–35 yuan for those disabled from work-related injuries or accidents, with a certain amount of nursing fees added if nursing is required. (2) Death benefits. When a labourer dies, a burial expense of 40–100 yuan is given and a monthly subsidy of 15–18 yuan is added for survivors unable to work. (3) Maternity benefits. Maternity leave ranges from 50 to 70 days. Those participating in collective labour after the maternity leave is due are assigned light jobs.

Social Security for the Handicapped

Handicapped people, such as the blind, deaf-mutes and disabled, were discriminated against and led a most bitter life in old China. Since New China was founded, a security system has gradually been set up for them. The State has also established schools for handicapped children and given them professional training. Colleges and universities are also open to those meeting the requirements in physical conditions. The number of schools for the blind and deaf-mutes has increased from 42 in the early 1950s to 375 in 1985 and the enrolment has grown from 2,000 to 41,706. The number of professional teachers in these schools has reached 7,300. The state education department has a special section to take charge of the education of the blind and deaf-mutes. Braille, which was not unified or scientifically designed in old China, was recreated and unified in 1953. From 1958, the country began to use the nationally unified finger scheme for the Chinese phonetic alphabet. The schooling for the blind and deaf-mutes used to be 8 years: for some it is now 9 or 10. Graduates receive two years professional training before being assigned jobs in enterprises specially set up for them. Such schools set great store by classes in handwork. Students reaching 15 years of age begin to learn some professional skills as part of their courses. Some older students are required to enter technical classes to take up full professional training courses. These schools are run by educational and civil affairs departments, while jobs are assigned by the latter, which have set up social welfare factories for the handicapped and massage clinics. Job arrangements for other handicapped people are made by the civil affairs departments and by labour departments, neighbourhood communities and factories, mines and other enterprises. By the end of 1985, the civil affairs departments had opened 1,600 welfare factories for the handicapped and 194 massage clinics manned by the blind. In addition, neighbourhood committees, big factories, mines and other enterprises established 8,500 work units, including 4,200 factories, to provide employment opportunities for the handicapped. The State has also established prosthesis factories and accelerated studies of the manufacture of prostheses and rehabilitation. Progress has also been made in helping deaf people to restore hearing and in treating deaf-mutes. Braille books have been

A table-tennis match at the 1st National Disabled Games held in October 1984. *(Photo by Cheng Zhishan)*

A basketball match on wheelchairs at the 1st National Disabled Games. *(Photo by Song Qingtao)*

published and all kinds of cultural and sports activities organized for them. The first national invitation games for the handicapped were held in October 1983. Many performing art troupes give charity performances to collect welfare funds for the handicapped. Help has also been given in marriage arrangements and in resolving family problems. Handicapped people who are too old to work and have no relatives to turn to are put in welfare homes or homes for the aged, or are looked after by designated families. The China Welfare Fund for the Handicapped, the national non-governmental organization for the handicapped in China, has branches in all provinces and cities to promote welfare undertakings for the handicapped.

Social Security Benefits for Single Old People and Orphans

Childless old people and orphans are mostly looked after at welfare homes run by the state civil affairs departments. Some are looked after by neighbourhood committees or their neighbours. The number of such urban welfare homes in 1985 was 952 with 35,000 inmates. The welfare homes have professional doctors and nurses, and during festivals they are visited by Party and government leaders. Well fed and well looked after, the old people generally live longer, 62.5 per cent to over 70, with the oldest at 110.

Retired Old People

The Constitution of the People's Republic of China approved at the National People's Congress in 1982 stipulated: "The livelihood of retired persons is ensured by the State and society." China had 14 million retired people by the end of 1984.

Students of the painting and calligraphy class practising at the Luwan Arts School of Shanghai for Older People, which opened in November 1985 with 150 enrolled in the classes of literature and arts, painting and calligraphy, photography, medical exercises, etc. *(Photo by Ren Long)*

Respecting and looking after the old is a traditional virtue of the Chinese nation and this virtue has been elevated to a new height by the social security system introduced since the founding of New China. The old people are not only well looked after at home by their children, but also meticulously attended to by their former work units and Party and government departments and respected in society. They are offered a variety of services. "Recreational centres for the aged" set up in various places provide them with social, recreational and study facilities to enrich their life and promote their physical and mental health. Lectures on health care and current affairs are organized for them to hear. The Government has set up a geriatric sports association and stations for teaching *taijiquan* (shadow boxing) and *qigong* (deep breathing exercises). People who enjoy performing arts are helped with rehearsals for regional art festivals. Some local hospitals and clinics have arranged for regular home visits to old people with chronic diseases. Young workers in commerce and service trades often cut hair for the aged and send vegetables, food grain and daily necessities to the homes of old people who have no children or live far from their children. Old people's former work units organize regular service teams to serve or nurse the retirees at their homes. In Beijing municipality, for instance, 2,641 enterprises organized 12,219 such teams with a total membership of 110,000 between 1981 and 1985. Primary and middle school pupils also do whatever they can to help the retirees.

Since the beginning of the 1980s, a learning craze has spread all over the country. By the end of 1985, 61 universities for the aged had been opened in the

Old but vigorous retired women exercise with swords for early morning training. *(Photo by Cheng Zhishan)*

country and more than 30,000 old people of about 65 on average and even at 90 had gone back to the classroom. Courses offered by the universities include health care, nutrition, art and literature, history, drama, music, composition, painting, calligraphy, photography, cooking, tailoring, cultivation of flowers, goldfish rearing, *taijiquan* and *qigong*. Numerous books and journals have appeared to provide guidance on retired life or health care.

Some retired cadres who are in good health and wish to continue their contributions to society have offered to go down to the grassroots to carry out investigations and study, research into policy problems, run technical classes for jobless young people and help them start their own factories or businesses, or to be technical advisors to factories or rural work units. The 1984 statistics showed that more than one million retired people volunteered to serve in all types of posts for the good of the people.

Convalescent and Rest Homes

Many convalescent and rest homes have been built by health departments, trade unions and industrial enterprises since the founding of New China. Some mines and factories have also set up spare-time sanitoria. Up

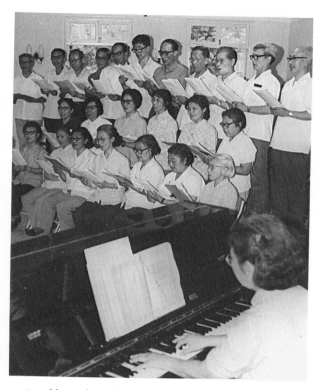

An old-people's choir singing in Wuhan, Hubei province. *(Photo by Li Yifang)*

A peasants' sanatorium situated on the bank of picturesque Taihu lake in Jiangsu province. *(Photo by Gao Meiji)*

811

Patients fishing. *(Photo by Wang Xinmin)*

to 1985, the number of such rest homes came to 632, with 95,000 beds.

In China, there are scores of convalescent areas with beautiful scenery and pleasant weather. They include Beidaihe and Qingdao, noted for their beaches; the Lushan and Huangshan mountains; the Taihu and Dianchi lakes; the hot springs at Tanggangzi, Conghua and Wudalianchi; and picturesque Hangzhou and Guilin, as well as the Tianshan, Nyingchi and Altai mountains, inhabited by people of minority nationalities. Each year, they receive tens of thousands of model workers and other workers with chronic or occupational diseases. The convalescent homes offer physiotherapy, physical exercise therapy, psychological and other therapies, with medicines and food as ancillary treatment. Principal kinds of physiotherapy include electrical, light, magnetic, hydropathic, mudbath, paraffin and ultrasonic. Traditional methods often used include acupuncture and moxibustion, massage and *qigong*. Life in rest homes is interesting: walking, boating, swimming, mountain-climbing, ball games, evening parties, sightseeing tours and visiting places, plus a better diet go a long way toward improving the health of the residents.

China's first peasant rest home appeared in 1982 in the scenic spot by Taihu lake, Wuxi city, Jiangsu province. Run by local peasants, it caters for rural factory workers and local peasants.

Prospects

The people's living standards have improved greatly since the founding of New China, though the wage level is not high. To ensure continued improvement in the people's life, the Central Government has adopted the policy of extensive employment, providing welfare benefits (such as housing at nominal rents), and setting up subsidy systems, especially non-paying social security systems (such as a free medical care system). Supported by state subsidies, the commercial departments have for long maintained the selling prices of such daily necessities as food grain, oil, meat, eggs, vegetables, cotton and cloth at a very low level, often lower even than the purchasing prices. But the price policy gradually changed after 1978. The selling prices of all foodstuffs, except grain and oil, have been raised, while the State has raised the wages of employees and provided price subsidies ranging from several yuan to over a dozen yuan a month to urban residents in order that their living standards should not be affected by the reform. This has ensured peace and good public order, except for a few periods, and the people in the country as a whole have been progressing well, except in some backward areas and poor households. However, compared with developed countries, China still has a big gap to bridge. A long-term economic and social development programme worked out by the Central Government has set as its goal for the end of this century to quadruple the 1981 gross national product from 710,000 million US dollars to 2,800,000 million US dollars and to increase the mean annual per capita national income at an average annual rate of about 5 per cent, from 300 to 800 US dollars.

To attain the goal, the State has to ensure the necessary funds for construction. This calls for the implementation of the following principles in improving the life of the people: consideration must be taken for the needs of both production and consumption, so that they develop in a well coordinated manner; the living standards of the people have to be improved together with the country's capability and on the basis of developed production, ensuring that consumption does not outpace production.

With regard to the distribution of social wealth, China should still continue the policy of allowing some of the people to become prosperous first, avoiding egalitarianism. At the same time, efforts should be made to see that the gap in the incomes of the various categories of people is not irrationally over-widened, by applying taxation and other economic regulatory means. To bring about a steady improvement in the material and cultural life of the people on the basis of developed production and to enable all members of the society to achieve prosperity has always been, and will continue to be, the starting point in China's socialist modernization drive.

According to the general goal for the end of the

century, the net income of Chinese peasants will have to increase at an average annual rate of seven per cent during the Seventh Five-Year Plan period (1986–90). The average per capita income for peasants will have to reach 560 yuan by 1990, 41.1 per cent higher than in 1985; the total payroll of the workers and staff members in China will reach 190,000 million yuan, 39 per cent more than in 1985. The average real wage of the employee will increase at an average annual rate of four per cent. When the increase in employment is taken into consideration, the annual growth rate of the average income of urban residents will be higher. The real consumption level in both urban and rural areas will increase by 27 per cent in five years.

As the living standards will improve markedly with the development of the national economy and growth of people's income, the State has to ensure that the consumption pattern is appropriate to conditions in China. China is a country with a large population but a relatively small amount of arable land and pasture. A rapid improvement in the food structure will be impossible for quite a long period to come. The increase in the consumption of meat, poultry and eggs has to be gradual. With regard to clothing, cotton cloth and chemical fibre or blended fabrics should be encouraged, while gradually increasing the supply of pure wool, leather and fur. As electricity is still in short supply, priority will be given to developing household electrical applicances that lighten household labour and enrich cultural life. The use of air-conditioners and other high power appliances is discouraged. Public buses and bicycles will remain the main means of transportation and the development of motorcycles will have to be restricted. A great effort will be made to improve housing conditions; the old methods of allocating houses by the State will be gradually changed; and commercialization of urban

housing will be promoted to distract overconcentrated attention from durable consumer goods. Even so, the average per capita living space will still remain at a low level, increasing by about one square metre per person in the 1986–90 period. It was estimated that by 1990, when the Seventh Five-Year Plan is fulfilled, food consumption expenditure will drop to 55 per cent from the 58 per cent in the Sixth Five-Year Plan period; the expenditure on clothing will be kept at 12 per cent of the total family expenditure; spending on articles of daily use will rise to 15 per cent from 13 per cent; expenditure on housing will grow from 8 to 10 per cent; and that on leisure and services will rise to 5 per cent.

The existing social security system will be improved to keep it in line with the situation brought about by the policy of invigorating the domestic economy and opening to the outside world. This will include the establishment of and improvement in the unemployment insurance and the social insurance system for workers of collective enterprises, Sino-foreign joint ventures and businesses with exclusive foreign capital, as well as in the social insurance system for urban and rural self-employed and rural labourers. The establishment and improvement of these systems are of vital importance to the success of the current economic reforms and are an important guarantee for maintaining social stability. While carrying out economic reforms, steps will also be taken to overcome the shortcomings of the existing social security system, such as waste entailed by the free medical care system. The aim is to develop a social security system with distinct Chinese characteristics which puts social insurance, social welfare and social relief under an overall, coordinated and unified management by both the society and work units, with the society as the main administrator.

PART VII

THE ARMED FORCES

GENERAL INFORMATION

THE armed forces of the People's Republic of China comprise the Chinese People's Liberation Army (PLA), the Chinese People's Armed Police Forces and the People's Militia, which constitute an organic armed body. The mainstay of China's armed forces is the Chinese People's Liberation Army. According to the 1982 statistics, the PLA was about 4.238 million strong, of which over 108,000 were armywomen. Since June 1985 the PLA has been carrying out a structural reform to streamline its administrative structure and reorganize the troops with a view to reducing its number by one million. This reorganization has not yet been completed. After the reform, the PLA will be somewhat more than 3 million in size, which means one soldier in about three hundred people of China's 1.03 billion population, making the

PRC one of those countries whose army is relatively small in proportion to the population.

Since the founding of New China in 1949, along with the gradual reduction of the size of the army, the proportion of China's defence expenditure in the national budget has declined year by year. In 1985 its defence expenditure of 19.148 billion yuan accounted for 10.5% of its total expenditure.

The Chinese People's Armed Police Forces, numbering over 500,000, are responsible for the country's domestic security. The People's Militia, who do not withdraw from production, are the auxiliary and reserve force of the PLA, with registered members totalling about 100 million.

The armed forces of the People's Republic of China belong to the people.

Table 1: China's Defence Expenditures and their Proportions of the Total State Expenditures (1950–1985)

Year	Total state expenditure (in 100 million yuan RMB)	Defence expenditure (in 100 million yuan RMB)	The proportion of defence expenditure to state expenditure (%)
1950	68.1	28.0	41.1
1952	176.0	57.8	32.8
1957	304.2	55.1	18.1
1962	305.3	56.9	18.7
1965	466.3	86.8	18.6
1970	649.4	145.3	22.4
1975	820.9	142.5	17.4
1976	806.2	134.5	16.7
1977	843.5	149.0	17.7
1978	1,111.0	167.8	15.1
1979	1,273.9	222.7	17.5
1980	1,212.7	193.8	16.0
1981	1,115.0	168.0	15.1
1982	1,153.3	176.4	15.3
1983	1,292.5	177.1	13.7
1984	1,515.0	180.7	11.9
1985	1,844.8	191.5	10.5

The Armed Forces

Deng Xiaoping, Chairman of the Central Military Committee, declared on 4 June 1985 at an enlarged meeting that the People's Liberation Army would be reduced by one million. *(Photo by Wu Senhui)*

The Chinese people love peace. The arduous task of China's modernization calls for an international environment that is both stable and peaceful. China follows a strategic principle of active defence, neither encroaching an inch upon foreign soil nor stationing any soldier there. The Chinese armed forces serve to oppose aggressive wars and safeguard world peace.

More specifically, their tasks, as stipulated by the Constitution of the People's Republic of China, are: "to strengthen national defence, resist aggression, defend the motherland, safeguard the people's peaceful labour, participate in national reconstruction and work hard to serve the people."

THE BIRTH AND GROWTH OF THE PEOPLE'S LIBERATION ARMY

THE Chinese People's Liberation Army is a people's army of a new type under the leadership of the CPC. It was set up and developed in the course of protracted revolutionary struggles. It has traversed, since its establishment, a hard, tortuous and victorious road through four historical periods: the Second Revolutionary Civil War (or the Agrarian Revolutionary War, 1927–37), the War of Resistance Against Japan (1937–45), the Third

Revolutionary Civil War (or the War of Liberation 1945–49) and Socialist Construction (1949–   ).

The Chinese Workers' and Peasants' Red Army during the Second Revolutionary Civil War Period

After the failure of China's First Revolutionary Civil War (1924–27) against imperialism and feudalism,

818

and faced with the mass slaughter of revolutionary activists by the Kuomintang (KMT) reactionaries, the Chinese Communist Party was made painfully aware of the extreme importance of having its own armed forces. It decided to stage armed uprisings and build a people's army.

On 1 August 1927, the Front Committee of the Chinese Communist Party, with Zhou Enlai as its secretary, together with He Long, Ye Ting, Zhu De, Liu Bocheng and others, took the lead in launching and directing the armed uprising in Nanchang, Jiangxi province, with 30,000 troops of the Northern Expeditionary Army who were under the influence of the Communist Party. The Nanchang Uprising fired the first shot in the armed resistance against the Kuomintang reactionaries, marking the birth of the Chinese PLA and the beginning of the Party-led armed struggles. In the years that followed, 1 August was named PLA Army Day, while the Chinese characters for "August 1st" became the symbols on the army flag and emblem.

Following the Nanchang Uprising, on 9 September 1927 Mao Zedong launched and led the Autumn Harvest Uprising of the peasants' armed forces on the Hunan–Jiangxi border. On 11 December of the same year Zhang Tailei, Ye Jianying and Ye Ting led the workers and revolutionary soldiers in Guangzhou in an armed uprising. Between August 1927 and late 1929 the Chinese Communist Party staged and led more than 100 armed uprisings in the Hunan, Hubei, Jiangxi, Fujian, Guangdong, Guangxi, Jiangsu, Anhui, Henan and Shaanxi provinces. The armed forces survived these armed uprisings, becoming the initial source and basis of the Workers' and Peasants' Red Army in various parts of the country.

In October 1927 Mao Zedong led the troops organized during the Autumn Harvest Uprising to the Jinggangshan mountains on the Hunan–Jiangxi border and set up the first rural revolutionary base. In April 1928 Zhu De, Chen Yi and others led the withdrawal of the remaining troops of the Nanchang Uprising to southern Hunan via Jiangxi, and together with the peasant army there joined Mao Zedong's forces in the Jinggangshan mountains. The two forces, numbering some 10,000, were merged and became the Fourth Army of the Chinese Workers' and Peasants' Revolutionary Army, with Zhu De as Army Commander and Mao Zedong as Party Representative. Beginning in late May 1928, the workers' and peasants' revolutionary armies and other revolutionary armed forces were renamed the Chinese Workers' and Peasants' Red Army.

During the initial period of building the Jinggangshan Mountains Base Area, the Red Army in the Jinggangshan mountains, commanded by Mao Zedong and Zhu De, repulsed many enemy attacks by following the tactics of guerrilla warfare: "divide the forces to arouse the masses; concentrate the forces to deal with the enemy" and "the enemy advances, we retreat; the enemy camps, we harass; the enemy tires, we attack; the enemy retreats, we pursue." The victories of the Red Army greatly consolidated the base area and expanded its forces. In December 1928 Peng Dehuai and Teng Daiyuan led the main forces of the Fifth Army of the Red Army, formed by the troops of the Pingjiang Uprising, to the Jinggangshan mountains. Thereafter, the main forces of the Fifth Army and part of the Fourth Army of the Red Army remained there to carry on armed struggles while the main part of the Fourth Army marched into the southern Jiangxi–western Fujian border area and carried on guerrilla operations there. Later the two areas joined together and became the Central Base Area.

In December 1929 the Ninth Party Congress of the Fourth Army of the Red Army was held in Gutian, in the Shanghang county of Fujian province, with Mao Zedong presiding. The congress summed up the experience of building the army since the Nanchang Uprising and adopted a resolution drafted by Mao, which was to be known as the Gutian Congress Resolution. The resolution formulated a series of principles in building the army. It stipulated: Being an armed body for carrying out the political tasks of the revolution, the Red Army must be placed under the absolute leadership of the Party; it must strengthen Marxist–Leninist education, conduct criticism and self-criticism to overcome unhealthy tendencies and ensure democracy under centralized guidance; it should, besides fighting, do propaganda work among the masses, organizing, arming and helping them to establish revolutionary political power; it should correctly handle internal and external relations, achieving unity between officers and men, and between the army and the people, firmly observing revolutionary discipline and carrying out the policy of lenient treatment of prisoners of war, etc. Later, the other Red Armies, learning from their own experience, applied the above principles, thereby building the Workers' and Peasants' Red Army, composed in the main of peasantry, into a new type of people's army.

Under the impact of the armed struggle in the Jinggangshan mountains, the revolutionary armed forces in various parts of the country gradually set up their rural base areas after the Autumn Harvest Uprising. By late June and early July 1930, the many small guerrilla base areas scattered across more than 100 counties of 10 provinces had gradually expanded and joined to form a number of relatively large rural revolutionary base areas. Besides the Central Base Area in Jiangxi province, the major ones were the Hubei–Henan–Anhui Base Area, the Hunan and Western Hubei Base Area, the Hunan–Jiangxi Base Area, the Hunan–Hubei–Jiangxi Base Area, the North-eastern Jiangxi Base Area and the Zuojiang River and Youjiang River Base Area in Guangxi. Meanwhile the Workers' and Peasants' Red Army had developed to 100,000 strong. With a view to strategical concentration, the Red Armies scattered in various

Red Army men helping peasants to harvest wheat during the Second Civil War.

Table 2: The Composition and Chief Commanders of the First Front Army of the Chinese Workers' and Peasants' Red Army

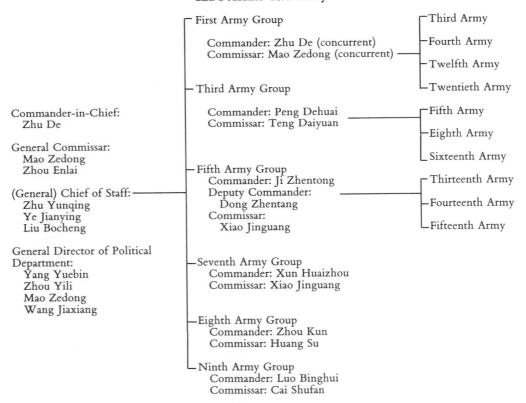

Commander-in-Chief:
  Zhu De

General Commissar:
  Mao Zedong
  Zhou Enlai

(General) Chief of Staff:
  Zhu Yunqing
  Ye Jianying
  Liu Bocheng

General Director of Political Department:
  Yang Yuebin
  Zhou Yili
  Mao Zedong
  Wang Jiaxiang

First Army Group
  Commander: Zhu De (concurrent)
  Commissar: Mao Zedong (concurrent)
    Third Army
    Fourth Army
    Twelfth Army
    Twentieth Army

Third Army Group
  Commander: Peng Dehuai
  Commissar: Teng Daiyuan
    Fifth Army
    Eighth Army
    Sixteenth Army

Fifth Army Group
  Commander: Ji Zhentong
  Deputy Commander:
    Dong Zhentang
  Commissar:
    Xiao Jinguang
    Thirteenth Army
    Fourteenth Army
    Fifteenth Army

Seventh Army Group
  Commander: Xun Huaizhou
  Commissar: Xiao Jinguang

Eighth Army Group
  Commander: Zhou Kun
  Commissar: Huang Su

Ninth Army Group
  Commander: Luo Binghui
  Commissar: Cai Shufan

Note: The above table shows the situation between 1930 and 1934. When two or more names appear for the same post, they are arranged in order of succession.

Table 3: The Composition and Chief Commanders of the Fourth Front Army of the Chinese Workers' and Peasants' Red Army (October 1930)

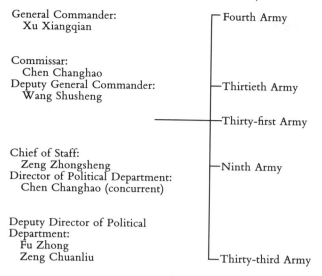

General Commander:
  Xu Xiangqian
┌─ Fourth Army

Commissar:
  Chen Changhao
Deputy General Commander:
  Wang Shusheng
├─ Thirtieth Army

├─ Thirty-first Army

Chief of Staff:
  Zeng Zhongsheng
Director of Political Department:
  Chen Changhao (concurrent)
├─ Ninth Army

Deputy Director of Political
Department:
  Fu Zhong
  Zeng Chuanliu
└─ Thirty-third Army

places were regrouped into regular forces, with guerrilla detachments organized into army groups, armies and divisions, while in terms of strategy and tactics the shift from guerrilla warfare to mobile warfare was also effected.

Meanwhile, the KMT reactionaries did not stand idle. Between the winter of 1930 and the spring of 1933 they launched four campaigns of "encirclement and suppression" against the Red Army in the Central Base Area, committing, respectively, 100, 200, 300 and 500 thousand troops. Forestalling these campaigns, in August 1930 the First and Third Army Groups merged into the First Front Army of the Red Army (also known as the Central Red Army) with Zhu De as Commander-in-Chief and Mao Zedong as General Commissar. By the strategy of luring enemy troops deep into the base area so as to annihilate them there, the First Front Red Army defeated these offensives one after another, while the Red Army itself expanded from 30,000 to 140,000 men.

In November 1931 the Red Army troops in the Hubei–Henan–Anhui Base Area were organized into the Fourth Front Army of the Red Army, with Xu Xiangqian as General Commander and Chen Changhao as Commissar, defeating at about the same time the first, second and third KMT "encirclement and suppression" campaigns. Later, because it failed to smash the enemy's fourth campaign, the Fourth Front Army was evacuated to the Sichuan–Shaanxi border and set up its base area there. The total force increased to over 80,000 by the autumn of 1934.

In September 1933 the Kuomintang concentrated one million troops to launch its fifth campaign of "encirclement and suppression" against the Red Army in the Central Base Area in Jiangxi province. Wang Ming and his followers, who at the time constituted the Party's leadership, discarded the tactics of "luring the enemy troops in deeply" and "crushing the enemy forces one by one" successfully employed in previous operations, adopting instead the mistaken policy of "scattering troops to defend all positions" and "engaging the enemy on the frontiers", and lost the struggle against the enemy's fifth campaign. Leaving behind some units commanded by Xiang Ying and Chen Yi to operate as guerrillas in the south, in October 1934 the main forces of the First Front Army of the Red Army forfeited the Central Base Area and began their strategic retreat, thus starting on the 25,000-*li* Long March.

In January 1935, an enlarged meeting of the Political Bureau of the CPC Central Committee was convened in Zunyi, Guizhou province; it put an end to Wang Ming's mistaken leadership, established Mao Zedong's leading position in the Party Central Committee and set up a three-man command group made up of Mao Zedong, Zhou Enlai and Wang Jiaxian to conduct the operations of the Red Army. From then on the First Front Army, under the leadership of the Central Committee of the Party and Mao Zedong, made a series of thrusts, penetrating the several hundred thousand enemy troops who were surrounding them, and constantly harried, obstructed and intercepted them. Four times they crossed the Chishuihe, forced the Jinshajiang and Daduhe rivers and traversed the perpetually snow-capped Jiajin Mountain and trackless grasslands, finally arriving at Wuqizhen in the Northern Shaanxi Base Area on 19 October 1935.

In March 1935 the Fourth Front Army set off on the Long March from its base in the Sichuan–Shaanxi border area. In June it joined forces with the First Front Army in Maogong in western Sichuan and the two armies continued northward together. Later, because Zhang Guotao, who had been in charge of work in the Fourth Front Army, insisted on retreating in the face of enemy attack and ordered his troops to march southward, the Fourth Front Army suffered heavy losses. In March 1936 they withdrew to Ganzi, Xikang province (now under the jurisdiction of Sichuan province).

The Sixth Army Group of the Red Army in the Hunan–Jiangxi border area started the long march in August 1934. In October it arrived in the eastern Guizhou base area and there joined forces with the Second Army Group coming from the Hunan–western Hubei border area. Together they set up a general headquarters, headed by He Long and Ren Bishi, and created the Hunan–Hubei–Sichuan–Guizhou Base Area with troops totalling over 17,000. In November 1935, starting from their base area, the two army groups fought their way via Hunan, Guizhou and Yunnan provinces, forced the Jinsha River and climbed over the greater snowy Daxueshan mountain. In June 1936 they reached the Ganzi area and joined forces with the Fourth Front Army, who had arrived there earlier. Then the two Army Groups and their general headquarters, together with the Thirty-Second Army, were merged to form the Second Front Army, with He Long as General Commander and Ren Bishi as Commissar.

Table 4: The Composition and Commanders of the Second Front Army of the Chinese Workers' and Peasants' Red Army (July–December 1936)

General Commander:
  He Long
Commissar:
  Ren Bishi
Deputy General Commander:
  Xiao Ke
Deputy Commissar:
  Guan Xiangying
Chief of Staff:
  Li Da

Second Army Group
  Commander: He Long (concurrent)
  Commissar: Ren Bishi (concurrent)
            Guan Xiangying (concurrent)

Sixth Army Group
  Commander: Chen Bojun
  Commissar: Wang Zhen

Thirty-Second Army
  Commander: Luo Binghui
  Commissar: Yuan Renyuan

The Second and Fourth Front Armies continued their long march and in October they reached the Huining–Jingning area of Gansu province. When the three main forces of the First, Second and Fourth Front Armies of the Chinese Workers' and Peasants' Red Army joined forces, the famous 25,000-*li* Long March came to a victorious end.

Having grown to a force of 300,000 men during the Second Revolutionary Civil War Period, the Chinese Workers' and Peasants' Red Army had dwindled to about 30,000 by the conclusion of its Long March in northern Shaanxi. Nevertheless, these constituted the core and backbone of the Red Army, who led and fought the War of Resistance Against Japan which was to begin two years later.

Militia men laying mines to support the main troops in the War of Resistance Against Japan.

The Eighth Route Army and New Fourth Army in the Period of the War of Resistance Against Japan

On 18 September 1931 the Japanese imperialists launched a sudden attack on Shenyang and soon occupied the three provinces in North-East China. The Communist Party and the Workers' and Peasants' Red Army, who were being encircled and attacked by the Kuomintang, raised the banner of national unity and issued declarations calling for a halt to the civil war and for united efforts to resist Japanese aggression. At the same time they organized the Anti-Japanese Allied Army in the North-East and sent the Northward Anti-Japan Vanguard from south of the Yangtze river to fight the Japanese. In December 1936, Generals Zhang Xueliang and Yang Hucheng, both of the Kuomintang troops stationed in Xi'an, arrested Chiang Kai-shek to admonish him and ask him to co-operate with the Communists to resist the Japanese; this event came to be known as the Xi'an Incident. The Central Committee of the CPC sent Zhou Enlai and others to Xi'an to take part in the negotiations that followed. Thanks to the efforts of the CPC, the incident was peacefully resolved, laying the basis for the realization of co-operation between the Kuomintang and the Communist Party for a united front to resist Japan.

On 7 July 1937, Japanese invading forces attacked the Chinese garrison at Lugouqiao, south-west of Peiping (now Beijing), and the KMT 29th Army stationed there put up resistance. On 9 July the Chinese Workers' and Peasants' Red Army sent a cable offering to march to the anti-Japanese front to fight the enemy. Soon after Chiang Kai-shek, as the Generalissimo of the Military Committee of the Kuomintang Government, announced in a public statement its formal recognition of the legal status of the CPC, and the Anti-Japanese National United Front was established, based mainly on the CPC and the KMT. Thus, with resisting the Japanese invading troops at Lugouqiao as a starting point, the national anti-Japanese and self-defence war commenced and opened up the Eastern Front in the worldwide anti-fascist war.

In August 1937, under an agreement between the CPC and the KMT, the main forces of the Chinese Workers' and Peasants' Red Army were reorganized as the Eighth Route Army of the National Revolutionary Army (abbreviated as the Eighth Route Army), with Zhu De as General Commander, Peng Dehuai as Deputy General Commander, Ye Jianying as Chief of Staff, Zuo Quan as Deputy Chief of Staff, Ren Bishi as Director of the Political Department and Deng Xiaoping as Deputy Director of the Political Department. There were three divisions under their command: the 115th Division, with Lin Biao as Commander and Nie Rongzhen as Deputy Commander; the 120th division, with He Long as Commander and Xiao Ke as Deputy Commander; and the 129th Division, with Liu

Table 5: The Composition and Chief Commanders of the Eighth Route Army of the National Revolutionary Army (August 1937)

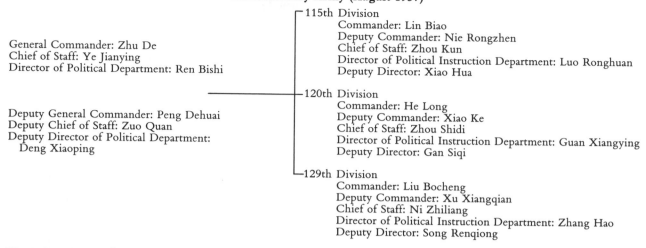

General Commander: Zhu De
Chief of Staff: Ye Jianying
Director of Political Department: Ren Bishi

Deputy General Commander: Peng Dehuai
Deputy Chief of Staff: Zuo Quan
Deputy Director of Political Department:
   Deng Xiaoping

115th Division
Commander: Lin Biao
Deputy Commander: Nie Rongzhen
Chief of Staff: Zhou Kun
Director of Political Instruction Department: Luo Ronghuan
Deputy Director: Xiao Hua

120th Division
Commander: He Long
Deputy Commander: Xiao Ke
Chief of Staff: Zhou Shidi
Director of Political Instruction Department: Guan Xiangying
Deputy Director: Gan Siqi

129th Division
Commander: Liu Bocheng
Deputy Commander: Xu Xiangqian
Chief of Staff: Ni Zhiliang
Director of Political Instruction Department: Zhang Hao
Deputy Director: Song Renqiong

Note: On 12 September 1937 the Military Committee of the National Government sent a cable asking that the designation of the Eighth Route Army be changed to the Eighteenth Group Army, and its General Commander and Deputy General Commander to Commander in Chief and Deputy Commander in Chief. Upon the order of the Central Committee, CPC, in October 1937 the Group Army reinstituted a commissar system, with the political instruction department changed into the political department.

Table 6: The Composition and Chief Commanders of the New Fourth Army of the National Revolutionary Army (February 1938)

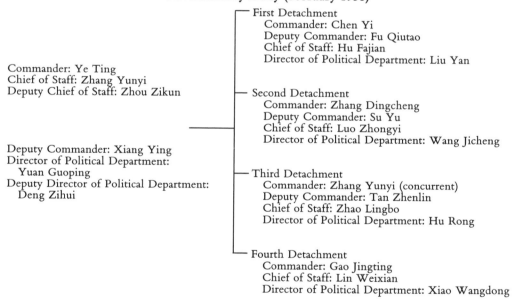

Commander: Ye Ting
Chief of Staff: Zhang Yunyi
Deputy Chief of Staff: Zhou Zikun

Deputy Commander: Xiang Ying
Director of Political Department:
   Yuan Guoping
Deputy Director of Political Department:
   Deng Zihui

First Detachment
Commander: Chen Yi
Deputy Commander: Fu Qiutao
Chief of Staff: Hu Fajian
Director of Political Department: Liu Yan

Second Detachment
Commander: Zhang Dingcheng
Deputy Commander: Su Yu
Chief of Staff: Luo Zhongyi
Director of Political Department: Wang Jicheng

Third Detachment
Commander: Zhang Yunyi (concurrent)
Deputy Commander: Tan Zhenlin
Chief of Staff: Zhao Lingbo
Director of Political Department: Hu Rong

Fourth Detachment
Commander: Gao Jingting
Chief of Staff: Lin Weixian
Director of Political Department: Xiao Wangdong

Bocheng as Commander and Xu Xiangqian as Deputy Commander. Later, when the commissar system was reinstituted in the Eighth Route Army, Nie Rongzhen, Guan Xiangying and Zhang Hao became commissars of the above divisions respectively. The three divisions, with their general rear headquarters (later renamed the rear army group), numbered over 46,000.

The guerrilla forces of the Red Army that had remained in the eight provinces in south China in October 1937 were grouped and reorganized into the New Fourth Army of the National Revolutionary Army (abbreviated as the New Fourth Army), with Ye

Ting as Commander, Xiang Ying as Deputy Commander, Zhang Yunyi as Chief of Staff, Zhou Zikun as Deputy Chief of Staff, Yuan Guoping as Director of the Political Department and Deng Zihui as Deputy Director of the Political Department. The army, totalling over 10,000 strong, was divided into four Detachments, with Chen Yi, Zhang Dingcheng, Zhang Yunyi and Gao Jingting as commanders.

At about the same time, the invading Japanese army drove deep into north and central China. The Chinese Eighth Route Army immediately marched eastward across the Yellow River and advanced into northern

(From left to right) Chen Yi, Su Yu, Fu Qiutao, Zhou Enlai, Zhu Kejin and Ye Ting at the headquarters of the New Fourth Army in 1939.

China, and the New Fourth Army advanced to southern Jiangsu and central Anhui, opening up the battlefields in north and central China. On 25 September 1937, the 115th Division of the Eighth Route Army wiped out more than one thousand men of the crack Itagaki division at the Pingxingguan pass in north-eastern Shanxi, winning the first victory in the war against Japan. From then on the Eighth Route Army and New Fourth Army, seeking opportunities in the rear areas of the enemy, fought and won many battles. By late 1938, the two armies had recovered large areas of Chinese territory and set up many anti-Japanese base areas, such as the Shanxi–Chahar–Hebei, Shanxi–Suiyuan, Shanxi–Hebei–Henan, Hebei–Shandong–Henan, Shandong, southern Jiangsu, northern Jiangsu, northern Anhui and central Anhui areas. The Eighth Route Army grew to over 156,000 and the New Fourth Army to more than 25,000 strong. Thus two theatres of war were developed in the national war of resistance against Japan: the front theatre of the KMT troops and the rear theatre of the troops of the CPC. And while victories won at the front, like the victory in the Taierzhuang battle, inspired the operations in the enemy's rear, the operations in the rear area pinned down large numbers of the Japanese forces, making it impossible for them to be deployed on the battlefields at the front.

After their occupation of Guangzhou and Wuhan in October 1938, the Japanese invaders halted their thrust, and the war against Japan entered a stage of stalemate. The Japanese gradually transferred their forces from the fronts to unleash mopping up and harassment campaigns against the anti-Japanese base areas of the Eighth Route and New Fourth Armies. The minority group in power in the KMT government also stepped up their political suppression of and military attacks on the Communist Party and the two people's armies. In January 1941, 80,000 KMT troops ambushed the headquarters of the New Fourth Army and some 9,000 troops under its command when the latter were moving to the rear of the Japanese invaders, staging the Southern Anhui Incident, which shocked the world. Thus, the Eighth Route Army and New Fourth Army were forced to fight simultaneously against KMT "friction" as well as Japanese mopping up battles. Under these conditions, the two armies resorted to the policy of "fewer and better troops and simpler administration" and launched a great production drive. Overcoming many political, economic and military difficulties, they achieved remarkable military successes by smashing repeated attacks and mopping up campaigns of the Japanese and puppet troops. For instance, in October–December 1939, the troops in the Shanxi–Chahar–Hebei

Peasants transporting arms and ammunition to the people's troops deep behind the enemy's lines in the anti-Japanese war.

border area smashed the winter mopping up campaign of the Japanese army, annihilating over 3,600 enemy troops and killing a Japanese Lieutenant General commander, Abe Norihide, the so-called flower of the elite generals. In August–December 1940 the Eighth Route Army employed the forces of 105 regiments to wage the famous "One-Hundred Regiment Operation" in North China, captured 2,993 strongholds from Japanese and puppet troops, killed and wounded over 40,000 enemy troops, including 21,000 Japanese soldiers, and destroyed 470 kilometres of railway and 1,500 kilometres of highway held by the Japanese. For a time the enemy's communications in North China were at a standstill.

Beginning in 1944, the Japanese army resumed its attacks at the Kuomintang troops in the field in an attempt to open up a continental communication line from Peiping to Guangzhou (Canton), so as to avert a crisis in the Pacific theatre of war. The panic-stricken Kuomintang troops retreated in a series of defeats, leaving to the enemy vast areas of land in central and south China. Taking advantage of the situation, the Eighth Route Army and New Fourth Army began a partial counter-offensive. They marched into areas newly occupied by the Japanese army, setting up the western Henan, Zhejiang–Anhui border, southern Anhui and Hunan–Hubei–Jiangxi base areas.

In May 1945 troops of the Soviet Union, United States and Great Britain defeated Hitler in Germany. In August the Soviet Union declared war on Japan and its troops marched into North-East China. On 10 August, acting on the orders of Commander in Chief Zhu De, the Eighth Route Army, New Fourth Army, North-Eastern Allied Anti-Japanese Army and the guerrilla forces in south China speedily launched an all-out counter-attack in co-operation with the Soviet troops and liberated the entire territory of the north-east and vast regions south of Shanhaiguan from the Japanese and puppet troops. On 14 August Japan surrendered unconditionally, and the eight-year anti-Japanese war came to a victorious end with the help of the allied forces of the USSR, USA and Great Britain. During the war,

the Eighth Route Army, the New Fourth Army and guerrilla forces in various parts of the country engaged large numbers of Japanese troops and almost all the puppet armies, and fought more than 125,000 engagements, annihilating 1,714,000 Japanese and puppet troops. They had grown to a force of 1.2 million, with a liberated area of over 1,000,000 square kilometres, covering parts of 19 provinces and with a population of 130 million.

During the Second World War, China was the major power fighting against the Japanese fascists on the Asian continent. The CPC-led Eighth Route Army, New Fourth Army and the guerrilla forces, fighting in the rear of the enemy in co-ordination with Kuomintang troops at the front, wiped out large numbers of Japanese troops, dealt the enemy heavy blows and greatly weakened the fascist forces. They made their own contributions to the victory.

The Chinese PLA in the Third Revolutionary Civil War Period

On the conclusion of the War of Resistance Against Japan, Kuomintang leaders, relying on their superior military forces, planned to launch another civil war in an attempt to seize all the fruits of the victory. In order to gain time for war preparations, the KMT started peace talks with the CPC and in an attempt to achieve domestic peace, the CPC sent Mao Zedong, Zhou Enlai and others to Chongqing for negotiations with the KMT. On 10 October 1945 the two parties signed an agreement known as the "October 10 Agreement". The CPC carried out the agreement to the letter and evacuated its troops from eight of their base areas in Guangdong, Zhejiang, southern Jiangsu, southern Anhui, central Anhui, Hunan, Hubei and Henan provinces. At about the same time, the Eighth Route Army and New Fourth Army, as a precautionary measure, made the necessary preparations to cope with any national civil war that the Kuomintang might unleash. They adjusted their strategic dispositions, reorganized their troops, and built up a base area in the north-east by transferring over 100,000 troops and cadres from south of the Great Wall. In the meanwhile, a reduction of rents and interest and a production drive were under way in the base areas all over the country. The field armies, local troops and militia also stepped up training to improve their combat effectiveness.

On 26 June 1946 the KMT tore up the truce agreement signed with the CPC and launched a nationwide civil war against the liberated areas, and the people's armies were forced to fight. This marked the beginning of an all-out civil war, i.e., the Third Revolutionary Civil War, also known as the War of Liberation. At that time the KMT troops, who were given huge military and financial aid by the US government and had taken over all the munitions and equipment of the million-strong Japanese invaders, totalled some 4.3 million and controlled most of the

825

Table 7: The Formation of the Field Armies of the Chinese PLA (April 1949)

**The Revolutionary Military Commission,
Central Committee, Communist Party of China**

Chairman: Mao Zedong
Vice-Chairman: Zhu De
Vice-Chairman and Director
    of General Political Department: Liu Shaoqi
Vice-Chairman and Acting General
    Chief of Staff: Zhou Enlai
Vice-Chairman: Peng Dehuai
Deputy General Chiefs of Staff: Nie Rongzhen
                         Ye Jianying
Deputy Director of General
    Political Department: Fu Zhong
Secretary-General: Yang Shangkun

The Chinese People's Liberation Army
    Commander-in-Chief: Zhu De
    Deputy Commander-in-Chief: Peng Dehuai

North-West Military Region
Commander: He Long
Commissar: Xi Zhongxun
Deputy Commander: Wang Weizhou
Chief of Staff: Zhang Jingwu

1st Field Army
Commander and Commissar: Peng Dehuai
Deputy Commander: Zhang Zongxun
                Zhao Shoushan
Chief of Staff: Yan Kuiyao
Director: Gan Siqi

Central Plains Military Region
Commander: Liu Bocheng
Commissar: Deng Xiaoping
Deputy Commander: Li Xiannian
Deputy Commissar: Deng Zihui

2nd Field Army
Commander: Liu Bocheng
Commissar: Deng Xiaoping
Deputy Commissar and Director: Zhang Jichun
Chief of Staff: Li Da

North China Military Region
Commander: Nie Rongzhen
Commissar: Bo Yibo
Deputy Commander: Xu Xiangqian
Chief of Staff: Tang Yanjie
Director: Luo Ruiqing

East China Military Region
Commander: Chen Yi
Commissar: Rao Shushi
Deputy Commanders: Zhang Yunyi
                  Su Yu
Deputy Commissar: Tan Zhenlin
Chief of Staff: Zhang Zhen
Director: Shu Tong

3rd Field Army
Commander and Commissar: Chen Yi
Deputy Commander and Second Deputy Commissar: Su Yu
First Deputy Commissar: Tan Zhenlin
Chief of Staff: Zhang Zhen
Director: Tang Liang

North-East Military Region
Commander and Commissar: Gao Gang
Deputy Commissar: Li Fuchun
Chief of Staff: Wu Xiuquan
Director: Zhou Huan

4th Field Army
Commander: Lin Biao
Commissar: Luo Ronghuan
Deputy Commissar and Director: Tan Zheng
First Chief of Staff: Xiao Ke
Second Chief of Staff: Zhao Erlu

18th Army
Commander and Commissar: Zhou Shidi

19th Army
Commander: Yang Dezhi
Commissar: Li Zhimin

3rd Army
Commander: Chen Xilian
Commissar: Xie Fuzhi

4th Army
Commander and Commissar: Chen Geng

5th Army
Commander: Yang Yong
Commissar: Su Zhenhua

20th Army
Commander: Yang Chengwu
Commissar: Li Tianhuan

7th Army
Commander: Wang Jian'an
Commissar: Tan Qilong

8th Army
Commander: Chen Shiju
Commissar: Yuan Zhongxian

9th Army
Commander: Song Shilun
Commissar: Guo Huaruo

10th Army
Commander: Ye Fei
Commissar: Wei Guoqing

12th Army
Commander and Commissar: Xiao Jinguang

13th Army
Commander: Cheng Zihua
Commissar: Xiao Hua

14th Army
Commander: Liu Yalou
Commissar: Mo Wenhua

15th Army
Commander: Deng Hua
Commissar: Lai Chuanzhu

827

big cities and railways of the country, whereas the CPC-led field armies and local troops which numbered only some 600,000, were totally without any outside help and had far inferior arms and rear areas which were not very well consolidated.

During the initial period of the War of Liberation the Kuomintang employed 80 per cent of its regular armies of 1.6 million men to wage all-out attacks on the liberated areas, proclaiming that they were going to wipe out the Communists and overrun all the base areas within three to six months. For their part, the troops led by the CPC followed the principle of concentrating their forces to wipe out the enemy's effective strength, not to hold or seize cities, towns or localities. Guided by this principle, they annihilated large numbers of enemy troops in their mobile warfare on various battlefields. In only eight months up to February 1947, the KMT lost some 710,000 men and were forced to cease their general offensive. During this period, in the light of the changes in their strategic task, the Eighth Route Army and New Fourth Army were renamed the Chinese People's Liberation Army (PLA), and Zhu De and Peng Dehuai were appointed as its Commander in Chief and Deputy Commander in Chief.

Starting from March 1947, the KMT changed its all-out offensive against the liberated areas into "concentrated offensives," i.e., concentrating its forces for offensives against the Shaanxi–Gansu–Ningxia Liberated Area and the Shandong Liberated Area. KMT troops in the former theatre were more than 230,000 strong, while the PLA there had only some 20,000. In the early stages of the campaign the PLA lured the enemy troops deep into the region, abandoning Yan'an, seat of the Party Central Committee, and the region's other county towns. In four major campaigns the PLA annihilated over 20,000 of the enemy troops, while the PLA in Shandong wiped out over 60,000 enemy troops in their three-month operation. Thus, the Kuomintang's so-called "concentrated offensives" ended in defeat. Moreover, during this period the troops of the PLA in the north-east, Rehe, eastern Hebei, northern Henan and southern Shanxi began their strategic counter-offensive. In the first year of the war the PLA annihilated 1.12 million enemy troops and itself grew to a force of 1.95 million.

In June 1947 the Shanxi–Hebei–Shandong–Henan Field Army, commanded by Liu Bocheng and Deng Xiaoping, broke the KMT Yellow River defence line and made a thrust into the Dabie mountains. In August the Field Army under the command of Chen Geng and Xie Fuzhi forced a crossing of the Yellow River to the southern bank and thrust into western Henan. In September the East China Field Army led by Chen Yi and Su Yu thrust into south-western Shandong and from there advanced to the Henan–Anhui–Jiangsu area. These three columns of the PLA swept across the Central Plains and areas along the Yangtze, the Huai river, the Yellow River and the Han river, igniting the flame of war in the hinterland of the KMT-controlled area. Thereafter, the PLA shifted its strategy from defence to strategic attack.

Between the winter of 1947 and spring of 1948 the PLA unfolded a new type of ideological education movement, its content being "to pour out grievances" (of the wrongs done to the labouring people by the old society and by the reactionaries) and "three checks" (on class origin, performance of duty and will to fight) of each PLA member, heightening the troops' ideological consciousness and sense of discipline. Alongside this, a movement of tactical training and manual exercises was launched and carried out. At a meeting in December 1947 Mao Zedong, basing himself on the past experience of the war, put forward the ten major military principles, with the stress on concentrating superior forces for annihilation operations, further elucidating a whole set of major principles to guide the PLA in its operations, its basic tactics, methods and fighting style, and its provisions and supply. All these were of great significance for victory in the Third Revolutionary Civil War.

The time of decisive campaigns between the CPC and KMT armies came in the second half of 1948 when the KMT was caught up in some hesitation about whether to evacuate the north-east so as to secure their defence of central China. The PLA grasped the opportunity to wage three great and resolute campaigns—the Liaoxi–Shenyang, the Huai–Hai and the Peiping–Tianjin campaigns. In the 52-day Liaoxi–Shenyang Campaign, starting from September 1948, the North-East Field Army of 700,000 men annihilated over 470,000 of the enemy troops and liberated the entire territory of the north-east. The Huai–Hai Campaign, which began in November 1948 and lasted 65 days, was fought jointly by the Eastern China and Central Plains Field Armies and regional troops totalling some 600,000. Over 550,000 Kuomintang troops were wiped out, the vast area between the Yangtze and Huai Rivers was liberated, and PLA troops drew close to Nanjing, capital of the Kuomintang regime. The 64-day Peiping–Tianjin Campaign, timed almost simultaneously with the Huai–Hai Campaign, was fought by the North-East Field Army and two armies of the Northern China People's Liberation Army and regional forces, totalling one million men. It started with the liberation of Zhangjiakou, Xinbao'an and Tianjin. Under the military and political pressures of the PLA, the Peiping Garrison commanded by Fu Zuoyi, Commander in Chief of the KMT Northern China "Bandit Suppression" Headquarters, accepted the peaceful reorganization of his troops, and Peiping was liberated. In the course of the 64 days of this campaign, over 520,000 KMT troops were either annihilated or reorganized. After these three decisive campaigns, the main forces which the KMT had relied on to launch the civil war and maintain its rule were in the main disposed of.

In the spring of 1949 the PLA troops were reorganized on a nationwide scale into the four Field

Armies and five Military Regions of the First Level: The First Field Army, reorganized from the North-West Field Army, with Peng Dehuai as Commander and Commissar; the Second Field Army, from the Central Plains Field Army, with Liu Bocheng as Commander and Deng Xiaoping as Commissar; the Third Field Army, from the Eastern China Field Army, with Chen Yi as Commander and Commissar; and the Fourth Field Army, from the North-East Field Army, with Lin Biao as Commander and Luo Ronghuan as Commissar. The five military regions were: the North-West Military Region, with He Long as Commander and Xi Zhongxun as Commissar; the North-East Military Region, with Gao Gang as Commander and Commissar; the Northern China Military Region, with Nie Rongzhen as Commander and Bo Yibo as Commissar; the Eastern China Military Region, with Chen Yi as Commander and Rao Shushi as Commissar; and the Central Plains Military Region, with Liu Bocheng as Commander and Deng Xiaoping as Commissar.

On 20 April 1949 the KMT finally refused to sign an agreement on internal peace. On the morning of 21 April the Second and Third Field Armies and part of the Fourth Field Army forced the Yangtze river on a front extending more than five hundred kilometres, from Hukou (north-east of Jiujiang) in the west to Jiangyin in the east; the KMT defence line along the Yangtze, which it had painstakingly been building up for three and a half months, collapsed in total confusion. On 23 April the PLA liberated Nanjing, the centre of the Kuomintang regime for 22 years. On 27 May Shanghai, China's biggest city, was liberated. In these campaigns over 430,000 of the Kuomintang troops were wiped out. Thereafter the forces of the PLA successfully marched to the regions which up till then had not been liberated in the south-east and in Central-South, South-West, North-West and North China. KMT governors and commanders in Hunan, Xinjiang, Yunnan and Xikang provinces and other regions renounced their allegiance to the Kuomintang, and these provinces and areas were peacefully liberated. In April and May 1950 parts of the Fourth and Third Field Armies crossed the sea to liberate Hainan Island and the Zhoushan Islands. In the spring of the same year parts of the First and Second Field Armies advanced to Tibet. In May 1951, an agreement was reached between the Central People's Government and the Tibetan local government, and Tibet was peacefully liberated. From then on the whole territory of China was liberated, except Taiwan and a few small islands.

In the War of Liberation from July 1946 to June 1950, the Chinese PLA, with inferior arms but supported by the people throughout the country, defeated the KMT troops armed with superior weapons, annihilating 8.07 million men, killing and capturing 1,600 KMT high-ranking officers (divisional commanders and major generals and above). The PLA developed from 1.2 million in the early period of the war to a mighty army of over 5 million.

From 5 December 1948 to 31 January 1949, the PLA carried out the Ping-Jin (Beiping–Tianjin) Campaign, captured Zhangjiakou and Tianjin and liberated Beiping (Beijing) peacefully. The PLA soldiers entered the city of Beiping to the cheers of thousands of people.

The Chinese PLA in the Period of Socialist Construction

Since the founding of the People's Republic of China in 1949 the historical mission of the PLA has changed from the seizure of political power to consolidating national defence, safeguarding national territorial integrity, and defending and participating in socialist construction. To fulfil these missions, the PLA entered a new phase of building itself into a regular and modernized army.

In June 1950 the Korean War broke out. In October US troops, flaunting the flag of the United Nations, pushed up to China's north-eastern frontier near the Yalu and Tumen rivers, gravely menacing the security of New China. The Chinese People's Volunteers were then organized, with Peng Dehuai as Commander and Commissar, and crossed the border to fight shoulder to shoulder with the Korean army and people. Under extremely hard and bitter conditions the Chinese and Korean armies fought five successive campaigns, driving the enemy back to near the 38th Parallel, from where they had first set out. This was followed by two years of positional warfare, including the battles known as the Sanggamryong Range and the Gim Seng Campaign. Finally the US troops were forced to sign the Korean Armistice Agreement. From 25 October 1950, when the Chinese People's Volunteers crossed into Korea, to 27 July 1953, when the armistice agreement was signed, the Chinese and Korean armies killed, wounded and captured 1.09 million of the enemy troops, of whom over 390,000 were Americans. Their victory frustrated the US attempt to further expand its war of aggression against Korea, safeguarded the national security of China and Korea, and defended world peace. Through this war the Chinese People's Volunteers also gained new experience in the operation of a

Zhou Enlai, Zhu De, He Long, Liu Bocheng and Ye Ting in the Nanchang Insurrection of 1 August 1927. *(Oil painting)*

Mao Zedong and Zhu De joined forces in the Jinggang-shan mountains in 1928. *(Oil painting)*

composite army with multiple arms and learned how to defeat an enemy with much superior weapons and equipment.

After the founding of New China the PLA was also engaged in the task of suppressing bandits and hidden agents of the Kuomintang. By 1953 it had wiped out bandits and armed KMT agents totalling over 2.4 million, basically eliminating harassment by bandits throughout the country. Between 1953 and 1955 the PLA smashed the attacks by KMT troops at Dongshan Island and liberated Yijiangshan, Dachen, Yushan and Pishan Islands in the coastal waters of the country. In March 1959 the Tibetan upper strata tore up the agreement reached by the Central People's Government with the Tibetan local government and staged an armed rebellion, based in Lhasa. With the help of the Tibetan ecclesiastical and secular masses the PLA troops rapidly put down the rebellion. In operations with convoys escorting fishing boats and in air defence, since the founding of the People's Republic, the naval and air forces of the PLA have shot down or damaged 488 invading enemy planes and sunk, damaged or captured 404 enemy warships, thereby defending China's air space and territorial waters.

During the same period the PLA fought also in self-defence on the frontier. In October 1962 Indian troops launched a large-scale armed invasion of China after the Indian government refused several times the proposal put forward by the Chinese government to come to a negotiated settlement of boundary questions left over from history. The PLA were forced to strike back in self-defence. When the invading Indian troops were repulsed, the PLA, taking the initiative, ceased fire, withdrew, repatriated Indian prisoners of war and returned to the Indian government the munitions and military supplies captured in the conflict. In March 1969, when Soviet troops invaded Zhenbao Island in Heilongjiang province, in spite of repeated warnings from China, the PLA troops

rose to repulse and beat back their attack. In January 1974 the Vietnam authorities sent their warships to invade the waters of the Yongle Islands in the Xisha Islands and occupied the Chinese islands of Gangquan, Shanhu and Jinyin, etc. The Chinese PLA navy struck back in self-defence and recovered the islands. After the conclusion of their War of Resistance Against the USA, the Vietnamese authorities sought regional hegemony. At the same time as they overran Kampuchea by force, they also sent troops to carry out provocations on the Chinese frontier, occupying Chinese territory, bombarding Chinese villages and killing and wounding Chinese citizens. To relieve the serious threats to China's security, the situation being no longer tolerable, PLA troops in Guangxi and Yunnan struck back in self-defence in February and March 1979, successfully repulsing the attacks of the Vietnamese troops at the Faka mountain in Guangxi, in the area of the Koulin mountain in Yunnan in May 1981 and the Laoshan and the Zheyin mountain in Yunnan in April–May 1984. At the time of writing (June 1986), the Chinese PLA troops on the frontier were still fighting against Vietnamese incursions. Through these actions the PLA has safeguarded China's territorial integrity and defended its frontier and coastal security.

Since the founding of New China, the Party and the State have established and gradually perfected the leading bodies of the PLA and several times readjusted the division of the strategic regions. The PLA's structural system has constantly been reformed and perfected, while its navy, air forces, artillery corps, armoured corps, engineer corps, railways corps, anti-chemical warfare corps, signal corps and strategic guided missiles corps have been set up one after another, making it a comprehensive army of multiple services and arms. In the meantime, the PLA has been paying close attention to training and setting up all sorts of military academies and institutes, while at the same time improving its arms and equipment. It also constantly sums up the experience gained in decades of building the army and in fighting, works out and

Red Army soldiers forcing the Dadu river during the Long March. *(Oil painting)*

publishes regulations on routine service training, discipline, combat, political work and cadre service, etc. In this way the PLA has greatly improved itself in terms of modernization and regularization and in heightening its combat effectiveness.

For the last thirty years and more the PLA, like the country as a whole, has traversed a zigzag road in terms of construction. During the period starting from 1959, Lin Biao was in charge of the daily work of the CMC; he spared no effort to pursue a policy of the "Left", which seriously affected the army's regularization and modernization. In the period of the Cultural Revolution, PLA officers and men were ordered to carry out "three support and two military tasks" in various places, which meant supporting industry, supporting agriculture and supporting the broad masses of the Left; military control of political organs, enterprises and institutions; and political and military training among the students and teachers of universities, colleges and middle schools. This practice – necessary at the time when the country was in chaos – played an active part in stabilizing the situation, but it was not without certain negative consequences. Since the Cultural Revolution, and especially since the time when Deng Xiaoping began to take charge of the PLA, the PLA has been engaged in readjustment to eliminate Leftist influence and strengthen its education and training. Things have taken on a new aspect. In order to adapt the armed forces to the needs of an anti-aggression war under modern conditions, from June 1985 the PLA began to streamline its organization, reduce its number of troops, and organize and set up group armies with composite arms. Attention has also been paid to strengthening technical units and reserve forces.

Marshal Nie Rongzhen (front, in dark spectacles) inspecting a missile base in 1966.

LEADING MILITARY BODIES, SERVICES AND ARMS, MILITARY EDUCATIONAL INSTITUTIONS

Major Leading Military Bodies of the PRC

The Central Military Commission (CMC)

THIS is the supreme leading military body of the country; all the country's armed forces are under its leadership.

In September 1982, the First Plenary Session of the Twelfth Central Committee, CPC, elected Deng Xiaoping to be the Chairman of the Party's Central Military Commission (CMC), and Ye Jianying, Xu Xiangqian, Nie Rongzhen and Yang Shangkun to be its Vice-Chairmen. Later, in December of the same year, the Fifth Session of the Fifth National People's Congress adopted the new *Constitution of the People's Republic of China*, stipulating that the Central Military Commission, PRC, was to be set up, with one Chairman and several Vice-Chairmen and members. The Chairman of the Central Military Commission has overall responsibility for the Commission. The Chairman would be elected by the NPC and be responsible to the NPC and its Standing Committee. The Vice-Chairmen and other members were to be determined by the NPC or its Standing Committee on the nomination of the CMC Chairman. The term of office of the Commission was to be the same as that of the NPC representatives. In June 1983, Deng Xiaoping was elected CMC Chairman by the First Session of the Sixth NPC and, on his nomination, Ye Jianying, Xu Xiangqian, Nie Rongzhen and Yang Shangkun were appointed the Commission's Vice-Chairmen.

The People's Committees of the Armed Forces (PCAF)

The PCAFs are specialized bodies established at various administrative levels, from the Central Government to county government, and are put under the leadership, respectively, of the CMC and Party committees at different levels. They take charge of work of a mass character concerning the armed forces, i.e., the reserves and the militia. Specifically, they study and solve problems arising in these fields and, by mobilizing and organizing social forces in all quarters, they build up these armed forces of the masses.

The highest of these organs is the National People's Committee of the Armed Forces, which is made up of responsible persons from the headquarters of the PLA'S different services and arms, related government departments and mass organizations, and has its offices in the Mobilization Department of the Headquarters of the General Staff, PLA. PCAFs at lower levels – provincial (municipal and autonomous regional), prefectural and county (district) committees – are made up of responsible persons from local Party committees, governments, related departments of the armed forces and mass organizations at corresponding ranks, with local Party committee secretaries as chairmen and offices set up in the headquarters of the Provincial Military Region commands, Military Sub-area Commands, or the county (district) government Departments of People's Armed Forces.

The Ministry of National Defence, PRC

This is the military department of the National Government under the State Council; it was established by a decision adopted in September 1954 by the First Session of the First NPC.

Headquarters of the General Staff, PLA

This is the supreme military body that assists the CMC to lead and command the armed forces of the country, to organize and build the services, and to conduct operations.

The General Political Department, PLA

An organ for political work under the CMC, this is responsible for conducting Party affairs and political work in the armed forces, and is the top leading body of political work in the PLA.

The General Department of Logistics (GDL), PLA

This is the top organ under the CMC responsible for all logistics services to the armed forces.

The Commission for Science, Technology and Industry for National Defence (CSTIND), PLA

Also known as the Commission for Science, Technology and Industry for National Defence, PRC, this is concurrently under the CMC and the State Council and is the leading body responsible for defence science and technology for the services and the various defence industry ministries. It is made up of a Committee of Science and Technology and a number of specialized departments and bureaux.

Leading Bodies of the Military Region Command (MRC)

The MRCs are the top military organizations set up in the seven strategical regions of the PRC – Shenyang, Beijing, Jin'an, Nanjing, Guangzhou, Chengdu and

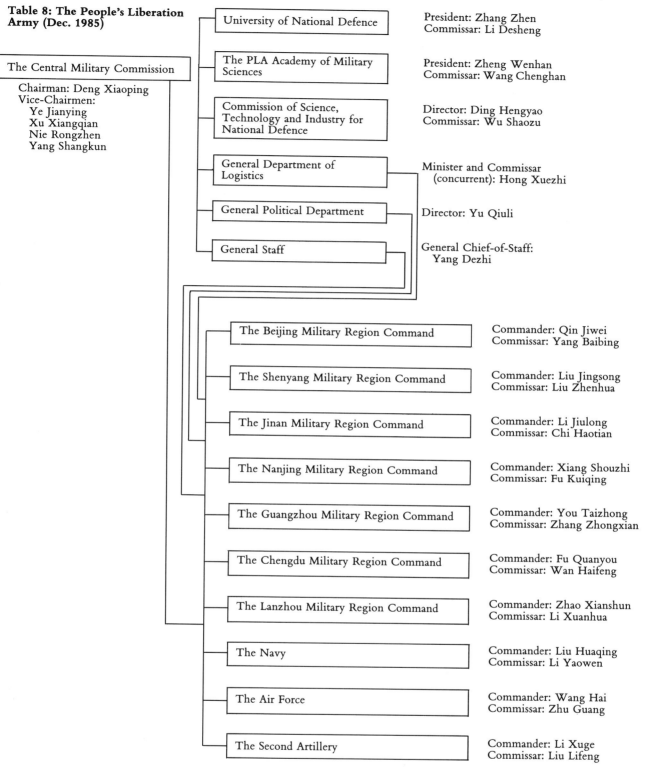

Table 8: The People's Liberation Army (Dec. 1985)

The Central Military Commission

Chairman: Deng Xiaoping
Vice-Chairmen:
Ye Jianying
Xu Xiangqian
Nie Rongzhen
Yang Shangkun

University of National Defence — President: Zhang Zhen / Commissar: Li Desheng

The PLA Academy of Military Sciences — President: Zheng Wenhan / Commissar: Wang Chenghan

Commission of Science, Technology and Industry for National Defence — Director: Ding Hengyao / Commissar: Wu Shaozu

General Department of Logistics — Minister and Commissar (concurrent): Hong Xuezhi

General Political Department — Director: Yu Qiuli

General Staff — General Chief-of-Staff: Yang Dezhi

The Beijing Military Region Command — Commander: Qin Jiwei / Commissar: Yang Baibing

The Shenyang Military Region Command — Commander: Liu Jingsong / Commissar: Liu Zhenhua

The Jinan Military Region Command — Commander: Li Jiulong / Commissar: Chi Haotian

The Nanjing Military Region Command — Commander: Xiang Shouzhi / Commissar: Fu Kuiqing

The Guangzhou Military Region Command — Commander: You Taizhong / Commissar: Zhang Zhongxian

The Chengdu Military Region Command — Commander: Fu Quanyou / Commissar: Wan Haifeng

The Lanzhou Military Region Command — Commander: Zhao Xianshun / Commissar: Li Xuanhua

The Navy — Commander: Liu Huaqing / Commissar: Li Yaowen

The Air Force — Commander: Wang Hai / Commissar: Zhu Guang

The Second Artillery — Commander: Li Xuge / Commissar: Liu Lifeng

Lanzhou – and are named after them. Each of these commands has its commander, political commissar and other commanding officers in charge of its various organs, which include the Headquarters, Political Department, Department of Logistics, etc.

Under the direct command of the CMC, it is the military region command which in turn commands all the PLA units in the region: group armies, provincial military area commands (garrison commands and fortification commands), and military academies and schools. It is responsible for the operation, training, political work, administration and logistics services of the region's ground, navy and air forces, as well as for taking charge of the area's work on the militia, military service, mobilization and fortification. In order to be differentiated from the provincial military area and the military sub-area commands, it is also known as the Greater Military Region Command.

833

The Armed Forces

Services and Arms of the PLA

The PLA is made up of four services: the ground force, the navy, the air force and the strategic guided missiles unit.

Ground Force

As the major branch of the PLA and the main force in ground warfare, the ground force is designed for operations either independently or jointly with the navy and the air force.

During the war years before Liberation, the PLA ground force consisted chiefly of foot troops. Gradual development since the founding of the PRC in 1949 has seen it turning into an army of various arms and specialized units. These include infantry (foot infantry and motorized infantry), artillery (ground artillery, anti-aircraft artillery, and strategic and tactical guided missiles units), armoured corps (tank corps, self-propelled artillery corps, etc.), engineering corps (general engineers, pontoon bridge units, construction service, camouflage service, water-supply units, etc.), signal corps (communication units, communication engineers, radio-interference units, army post service). There are also specialized units and detachments for reconnaissance, electronic countermeasures, motor transportation, mapping, etc.

The ground force's organizational system consists, in general, of the following units: group army, division, regiment, battalion, company, platoon and squad and, in the case of some arms, brigade.

Along with defence research and development and industrial growth, the weaponry and equipment of the PLA ground force are becoming increasingly modernized. Having now at its disposal large quanti-

ties of new types of artillery pieces, tanks, infantry combat vehicles, anti-tank firearms, anti-aircraft firearms, tactical guided missiles of different sorts and some new types of electronic communication, engineering and anti-chemical warfare equipment, and with more and better equipment to come, the ground force has been considerably strengthened in terms of firepower, mobility, defence and assault capability, and the capability for instant response.

The Navy

Main force of the PLA for submarine, surface and aerial combat at sea, the navy is made up chiefly of naval troops, and is capable of operating either independently or in co-operation with the ground and air forces.

The first naval force of the PLA came into being on 23 April 1949 at White Horse Temple in Taizhou, Jiangsu province, when a navy detachment for the East China Military Region Command was founded with those craft that had either come over to the PLA towards the end of the Third Revolutionary War (which included the KMT cruiser *Chungking*, ships and boats from the KMT Second Fleet for Naval Defence and the China Merchants' Steam Navigation Company), or had been captured during the war. This was followed by the founding of the River Defence Command in Guangdong and a naval base in Qingdao. After the founding of the PRC, leading bodies of the navy were set up on 14 April 1950, by order of the CMC. The navy then became a service branch of the Chinese PLA.

Inheriting and giving full play to the excellent traditions of the ground force, the navy has grown and has won remarkable victories. Its first engagement was fought in May 1950, when it joined the ground force in the campaign to liberate the Wanshan Islands off the Guangdong coast. This 71-day operation, fought with small gunboats, wooden vessels and refitted merchantmen against a regular KMT fleet many times its superior in terms of tonnage, terminated with the liberation of all the islands along the Guangdong coast

A PLA signals station in the Xisha Islands.

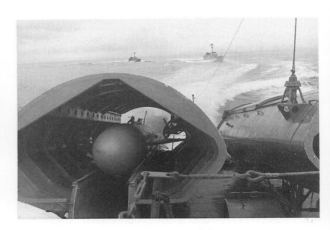

Training missile destroyers of the PLA Navy.

834

and removal of the KMT blockade of the Zhujiang (Pearl River) estuary. Soon after, relying on river gunboats with a draught of 30 cm and a displacement of only 25 tons, the infantry turned sailors forced their way to the East China Sea through the Yangtze river estuary and engaged KMT warships with infantry weapons plus satchels of dynamite. In close coordination with ground forces they landed on the islets of Tanhushan and Shengsi, smashing the KMT blockade of the Yangtze river estuary, and followed up the victory by liberating all the islands along the coast from southern Jiangsu to eastern Zhejiang except Taiwan, Penghu, Jinmen and Mazu.

In fulfilling its various tasks of liberating coastal islands, suppressing and eliminating pirates, protecting sea transportation and defending territorial waters and air space during the period from 1949, when the first detachment was formed, to 1974 the people's navy fought altogether 1,263 engagements, sinking, crippling or capturing 404 enemy ships and boats, downing or crippling 204 enemy planes, and killing or wounding 7,530 enemy troops. In recent years it has shared in maritime scientific experiments by providing protection on the sea to ships sailing to the Antarctic Ocean and Antarctica for scientific exploration, as well as performing other missions.

The leading body of the people's navy is comprised of Headquarters, Political Department, Logistics Service, Equipment and Technology Department, Repair Service, Naval Air Force Command, etc. There are three fleets along the coast from north to south: the North China Sea, East China Sea and South China Sea Fleets, a number of naval bases and task forces, and many naval–civil defence units. The main arms of the navy are: submarine forces (including conventional and nuclear torpedo and guided missile submarine units), surface forces (including combat units and tender and supply units), naval air force (including bomber, fighter, attack plane, anti-submarine plane, reconnaissance, air transportation groups, and anti-aircraft artillery, radar, and ground-to-air guided missiles units), naval coastal defence forces (including coastal artillery and coastal guided missile units), and a

marine corps. The navy's organizational system consists of: fleet, naval base (corresponding to the ground force army), naval garrison command (corresponding to the division), sub-fleet (corresponding to the division), flotilla (corresponding to the regiment), and boat squadron (corresponding to the battalion).

The navy is developing its weapons and equipment along the line of maximum employment of missile and electronic technology, and automating its command mechanism. Its surface forces are already equipped with guided missile cruisers and guided missile escorts and boats; the submarine fleets have nuclear-powered as well as conventional submarines. On the whole, the people's navy has emerged from the single arm force with only surface vessels, primitive weaponry and equipment of its initial days to become a fully fledged sea force with numerous technological arms, considerable in scale and capability in attack and defence.

The Air Force

This is the PLA service devoted chiefly to aerial, air-to-ground and ground-to-air combat. Highly mobile and capable of long distance operation and powerful strikes, it operates either independently or in coordination with the ground force and the navy. It is the main force for territorial air defence and for supporting the ground force and the navy.

During the First Revolutionary Civil War period and even before the PLA came into being, a group of CPC members already started to study and engage in aviation. In the period of the War of Resistance Against Japan, some 40 officers of the Red Army were formed into a group and sent to Xinjiang to participate in an Aviation Training Course there. In 1946, after the Third Revolutionary Civil War had broken out, the PLA set up its first aviation academy in the north-east, making use of planes and equipment left by a Japanese air group when Japan surrendered. Liu Shanben, a KMT pilot who came over in June 1946, became its Deputy Commandant. In November, following a decision of the CPC Central Committee adopted earlier in July of the same year to set up an air force, the leading body was established, and the air force became a regular service of the Chinese PLA.

The backbone of the new-born air force was made up of units and large numbers of officers transferred from the ground force and the first batch of graduates from the aviation school in the north-east, plus a contingent of intellectuals and former KMT aviation technicians. Under extremely difficult material conditions, several aviation schools and a composite brigade comprising fighter, bomber and attack plane units were soon organized. Subsequently, they served as a foundation for setting up fighter, bomber, attack plane, reconnaissance and transport plane divisions and regiments, and to provide personnel for the air

Training missile speedboats of a unit of the PLA Navy.

The Armed Forces

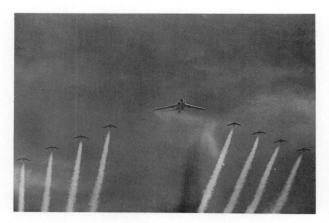

Formation flight training for bombers of the PLA Air Force.

An H6-A bomber produced by Xi'an Aircraft Company, the manufacturing base for large planes with advanced technology in China.

force leading bodies in the various military region commands.

The War to Resist US Aggression and Aid Korea began soon after the PLA air force came into existence. Pilots, technicians and other personnel joined the Chinese People's Volunteers (CPV) in large numbers. Once in Korea, the young CPV pilots found themselves face to face with the air superiority of the major air power in the world. Undaunted, they plunged into large scale air battles against the USAF, weakening its air superiority north of the Chong Chon Gang and safeguarding the communication and transportation lines in Korea. The CPVAF war record in Korea, from December 1950 to July 1953, was 330 enemy planes downed and 95 damaged.

Tasks fulfilled by the PLA air force after the founding of the PRC included the air defence of Beijing, Shanghai and other major Chinese cities, support for the ground force and navy in mopping up remnant KMT troops, air transportation and air drops in support of the ground force's march into Tibet, etc. In defending territorial sovereignty, the PLA air force encountered US and KMT war planes of various types – F–86, F–104, RF–101, P–2V, RB–57D, U–2, F–4B, etc. – that had invaded China's air space, bringing down 99 and damaging 184 of them.

Through some 30 years of hard work, the Chinese PLA air force has been built into a composite force of multiple arms with comparatively modern equipment. Its leading body is comprised of the Headquarters, Political Department, Logistics Service, Aeronautical Engineering Department and other organs. Its major arms are: air units (including fighter, bomber, attack plane, reconnaissance plane, transportation plane units and other specialized air units), anti-aircraft artillery, ground-to-air guided missile units, radar units, airborne troops, etc. Its organizational system is made up of the military region command air force, air army, air force division, air force regiment, air group and air squadron.

In the early years of the PRC, the equipment of the PLA air force was chiefly either captured from the enemy or bought from the Soviet Union. From the mid-50s planes made in China began to be used, and since the mid-60s all the main equipment has been developed and produced in China. This includes supersonic fighters and attack planes, jet bombers and other comparatively sophisticated planes.

The Strategic Guided Missiles Unit

Designed for nuclear counterattack in case of foreign aggression, this is the PLA unit equipped with ground-to-ground guided missiles to achieve strategic goals by instant and direct elimination of enemy strategic targets. It constitutes China's chief means of nuclear counterattack to realize its positive strategy for self-defence. It is capable of operating independently or in coordination with other armed services.

The Chinese PLA set up its first guided missiles battalion in the 50s. Then in the 60s, with a material basis provided by the successive and successful tests of China's atomic bomb, guided missiles with nuclear warheads and the hydrogen bomb, the strategic guided missiles unit and its commanding body were organized by order of the CMC and put under its direct command. The unit is made up of intermediate, long-distance and intercontinental missiles units, engineering units, specialized safety units, and military academies and schools and research institutes. Armed with numerous types of intermediate and long-distance missiles, it has attained considerable combat capability.

China has developed its nuclear weapons and established a strategic guided missiles arm; this has been done with a view to improving self-defence, breaking the nuclear monopoly, opposing nuclear blackmail and, ultimately, eliminating nuclear weapons. The Chinese government has repeatedly declared that under no circumstances will it be the first to use nuclear arms, and it has pledged uncondition-

A new type of missile is fired.

means for training military personnel in order to upgrade the quality of the armed forces. Dating as far back as the war years, when it was constantly engaged in one campaign after another, the PLA successively set up the Red Army School, the Red Army University, the Anti-Japanese Military and Political College, the University of Military Affairs and Politics, and numerous military academies and schools in the fields of communications, artillery, engineering, aviation, logistics, military sanitation, etc., which turned out hundreds of thousands of military, political and technological personnel for the armed forces.

After the founding of the PRC, with the establishment of the PLA Military Academy and the PLA Political Academy by Marshals Liu Bocheng and Luo Ronghuan respectively, many high-ranking generals, rich in operational experience and military scholarship, were at first engaged in setting up and running various regular military academies, schools and research institutes. These included academies and schools for training army, navy and air force commanding officers and specialized personnel in different fields, and the Academy of Military Sciences.

ally not to use nuclear arms against non-nuclear countries or areas.

China's efforts will continue with the specific goal of building up a strategic guided missiles unit that is limited in size but capable of effective nuclear counterattack when subjected to a nuclear raid.

Military Academies, Schools and Research Institutes

The PLA has always regarded these as important

When Deng Xiaoping took charge of the day-to-day work of the CMC, the practice that had come down from the war years to directly select and appoint officers from among privates was stopped, to be

Deng Xiaoping inspecting the three armed services of the PLA at the 35th Anniversary of the PRC on 1 October 1984.

gradually replaced by a new system by which no private can be promoted to become a commissioned officer without being trained by a military institute or academy, nor can any be assigned to a commanding post without first receiving training in an academy of the corresponding level.

In April 1986, a new decision on the reform of education in the military academies and schools was adopted by the CMC. Because of the rather low level of the instructors, relatively backward teaching facilities and the repetition and overlapping of programmes and subjects, appropriate measures were adopted for readjustment, including improving the training and academic structure of the academies and schools, upgrading the quality of the instructors, and revising course contents and teaching methodology. The object of these measures is to establish, by the end of the present century, a systematic military education that is modern, caters to the country's conditions and has characteristics specific to the PLA. At the same time, adapting to the reduction of the PLA by one million men and officers, a number of military academies and schools were replaced by others, to meet the needs of modernization, while new departments and specialities were added in other institutes. As a result, the number of military academies and schools decreased to just over 100. Throughout the years since the founding of the PRC, these institutes have trained more than one million cadres, including a great many high-ranking commanding officers for the armed forces and war offices.

The PLA military academies and schools fall into two categories according to their training objectives: institutes for commanding officers, and institutes for technological specialists: the former are further divided into senior, intermediate and junior levels, while the latter are further divided into senior and intermediate grades.

Academy for senior commanders

So far, only the University of National Defence has been set up. Established by merging the three institutes of the Military, Political and Logistics Academies in November 1985, it is also the single highest-level composite military institute under the direct leadership of the CMC. Its students are enrolled from among outstanding officers at the level of division and brigade who have graduated from academies for intermediate commanding officers. The university offers them a comprehensive high-level education, preparing them chiefly for composite commanding duties in the military, political and logistics departments of the services at the grade of group army and above. Other students are to be trained to serve as high-ranking staff officers, researchers and leading cadres for relevant government departments. The university is also engaged in research programmes on strategy and studies problems in the modernization of national defence. Another of its duties is to provide consultation and advice for the CMC and the General Headquarters of PLA on decision-making. To fulfil these latter tasks, the University has its own Science Department, Strategy Institute, Institute of Marxism, Institute on the Construction of the Armed Forces, etc. It aims at making full use of the latest information and research results in the fields of natural and military sciences from all over the world in order to enrich the contents of its programmes and courses. The university is open to the outside world: to promote academic exchange, foreign specialists as well as leaders of foreign governments and armed forces are invited to lecture or teach courses. At the same time, cadres, instructors and researchers and students of the university will be selected to lecture or conduct investigations abroad.

The University of National Defence began to recruit its first batch of students in the summer of 1986 and classes began on 1 September.

Academies and schools for intermediate and junior commanding officers

These include the whole array of the academies and professional schools of the ground force, navy, air force, and the Strategic Guided Missiles Unit that are put under the charge, respectively, of the General

A squad formation drill of the students in the Shijiazhuang Army School.

Headquarters of the PLA, the various services and arms, and the major military region commands.

These intermediate academies and schools recruit battalion and company officers who have graduated from a junior academy or school, and prepare them to undertake command duties in military, political or logistics posts at regimental level. They offer advanced courses in different fields, aiming at converting the students from commanders of single detachments to commanders of composite forces. They also train departmental and section heads, staff members for relevant offices, and instructors and administrators for the academies and schools.

The junior academies and schools enrol current graduates of senior middle schools and privates who have passed through a training centre in their respective units. They offer basic military, political and general cultural courses, preparing them for duties as platoon leaders, ship's captains, pilots, etc. Besides giving the students an educational qualification corresponding to that of a professional school, college or university graduate, these academies and schools aim also at transforming them from young students or privates to commanders of military detachments.

Senior and intermediate professional academies and schools of technology

These include the University of National Defence Science and Technology, the Medical University of the Armed Forces, various engineering and technological institutes for communication, topography, ordnance, radar, meteorology, etc., and different professional and technical schools. They are put under the

charge of respective general headquarters, services and arms, and major military regional commands. Their students, enrolled from current year graduates of senior or junior middle schools and privates with the same educational level, are trained to become technicians of different specialisms and grades for the services. Some of these academies offer postgraduate courses for master's or doctor's degrees.

The PLA Academy of Military Sciences

This is the research centre for military sciences that serves the armed forces as a whole and is under the direct leadership of the CMC. Inaugurated in March 1958, its first director and concurrent political commissar was Ye Jianying. Its research departments cover the following fields: military theory, strategy, campaign tactics, military institutions, history of the PLA and its operations, operational programming and analysis, political work in the armed forces, military sciences of foreign armies, etc. The academy possesses a research staff with appropriate academic levels and experience of operational practice. During the last 20 years or so, the academy has produced large quantities of research papers, military decrees, regulations, manuals, translations and annotations to well-known foreign and ancient Chinese military works, and dictionaries and reference books; it also publishes, among other learned periodicals, the journal *Military Sciences*. The academy attaches great importance to exchanges with military academic circles at home and abroad; activities in this respect will be further extended in the near future.

MILITARY TRAINING

DURING the war years the PLA, limited by objective conditions, upgraded the combat capabilities of its troops by relying in the main on learning in actual fighting, i.e., learning warfare through warfare. Even so, full use was made of the intervals between campaigns for "training and drill before taking up positions", taking into consideration the specifics both of the immediate assignment and of the enemy troops confronted. To make up for the lack of professional instructors, a mass line approach to training was adopted, in which "officers teach soldiers, soldiers teach officers and the soldiers teach each other", that is, "let those who know teach". After the birth of the PRC in 1949, the CMC drew up an outline for the training programme and started regular military training for the entire army to help it quickly master the modern arms and equipment and learn new techniques. War exercises on land, sea and in the air

were repeatedly organized, centring on different themes and on different scales, including exercises in nuclear counterattack, so as to raise the army's combat effectiveness in joint operations under conditions of modern warfare.

In the late 1970s new thinking in building the armed forces emerged. Instead of stressing constant readiness for war at any given moment, as was the case in the past, emphasis has since been shifted to building the army in times of peace; military education and training were elevated to the plane of strategy and efforts were devoted to introduce reforms. Under the general policy of a strategy for positive defence, the following have been stressed: Study and solve the strategy and tactics of a people's war under modern conditions; basing this on existing equipment and taking into account future developments, probe and practice new ways to overpower better-equipped enemies; recognize in full the importance of joint campaign operations and, while laying a solid foundation for the combat effectiveness of individual service branches, step up training for fighting in coordination; conduct training vigorously and strictly to meet the imperatives of actual combat by taking into consideration the enemy's conditions as well as the tasks assigned and the particularities of the war zones.

After the reforms during the last few years, three major shifts have been initially effected in terms of the main focuses of training: from training soldiers to training commanding officers; from training chiefly to fight enemy infantry to fighting its tanks, aircraft and airborne troops; from training single arms to training for coordinated actions by the services and arms in joint campaigns and operations. In terms of content, it has been definitely established that the capabilities of the armed forces must be upgraded in five respects: 1) The capability for instant response, so as to meet the increased firepower, power for shock assaults and mobility of modern troops, and to meet the objective situation of increased suddenness of a modern war. Only in this way will it be possible for the army to win the initiative and frustrate the enemy in cases of anti-aggressive war in the future. 2) The capability for coordinated action, so as to adapt to the characteristics of modern warfare – three-dimensional, extensive in operational space and participated in by multiple arms, and to give full play to the combined power of the various service branches and arms. 3) The capability

for electronic confrontation, so as to adapt to the drastic innovations in reconnaissance, information services and the automatic control of weapons brought about by the application of electronic technology, the PLA being still relatively backward in this respect. 4) The capability for guaranteeing supply from the rear, which, as demanded by a modern war, is large in quantity and high in standard, a situation the PLA logistics service departments are not yet adapted to. 5) The capability of the army to survive in field operations so as to meet the exacting demands of a modern war, which includes the ability of the troops to disperse, take shelter and camouflage themselves, and the will-power, physical fitness and stamina of both men and officers, to guarantee that the forces will not be exhausted or shattered under any conditions.

In terms of training organization, training of new recruits is gradually being separated from that of the units as a whole. At present, the units are each setting up their own training regiments, where all the recruits are concentrated, modelled on military academies and schools and achieving unprecedentedly good results in recruit training. Alongside large-scale development and universal application of electronic and laser simulators and audio-visual educational programmes, grounds for training emphasizing combined tactical operations are being systematically constructed. Reform of the military training of the PLA is in full swing.

POLITICAL WORK IN THE ARMED FORCES

POLITICAL work is the life-blood of the PLA, an important factor by which the people's army unites to defeat the enemy. Why has the PLA been able, throughout its history of more than half a century, to grow from being small and weak to being big and strong, overpowering one after another enemies superior in equipment? This has been inseparable from the leadership of the CPC and the vigorous political work it developed in the armed forces.

Basic Principles of Political Work

The political work of the PLA, which dates back to the earliest days when the army was first established, has developed a whole set of systematic and comprehensive policies and principles during the past decades. The following are included:

Persist in upholding the purpose of whole-hearted service to the people

All members of this army are requested, on the one hand, to come together and fight solely for the

interests of the people and, on the other hand, to share fortune and misfortune with the masses. The PLA is not allowed to separate itself from or to place itself above the people. It must, in accordance with the general task of the Chinese revolution in its different historical periods, engage itself in the triple tasks of fighting, mass work and production. In the new historical period at present, the PLA must function not only as the Great Wall of iron and steel defending the socialist motherland, but also as an important force for the construction of socialist material and spiritual civilization.

Guarantee the CPC's absolute leadership over the PLA

Political work must, through ideological–political education and by strengthening the construction of Party organizations and giving full play to the leading role of the Party committees as the core at different levels, with Party members acting as vanguards and models, guarantee that the PLA as a whole will obey the Party's command.

Take ideological–political education as the core of political work

This means persisting in educating the troops in proletarian thinking, theories and spirit and in the Party's programme and general line. Help officers and men to form a Marxist world outlook and a Marxist outlook on life; to increase their ability to understand and reform the objective world, and to cultivate in themselves the dedication to serve the people whole-heartedly; to develop patriotism, internationalism and revolutionary heroism; and to strive to make themselves members of a revolutionary army with high ideals, moral principles, knowledge and a sense of discipline.

Implement the principles of unity between officers and men, and between the army and the people, and of respect for the dignity of capitulating enemy troops

The people's army must respect its own soldiers, respect the people, and respect the human dignity of prisoners of war once they have laid down their arms.

Practice democracy in the three main fields of politics, the economy and military affairs

Cadres and superiors should respect the democratic rights of soldiers and subordinates and, by giving full play to democracy under centralized leadership, achieve the three major objectives of a high degree of political unity, better living conditions, and better military techniques and tactics.

Enforce the Three Main Rules of Discipline and the Eight Points for Attention

The Three Main Rules of Discipline are as follows:

(1) Obey orders in all your actions.
(2) Do not take even a single needle or piece of thread from the masses.
(3) Hand in everything captured.

The Eight Points for Attention are as follows:

(1) Speak politely.
(2) Pay fairly for what you buy.
(3) Return everything you borrow.
(4) Pay for anything you damage.
(5) Do not hit or swear at people.
(6) Do not damage crops.
(7) Do not take liberties with women.
(8) Do not ill-treat captives.

Unity between the government and the armed forces

The troops are requested to support the Government and protect the people. They must abide by the law and follow Party and government policies as well as obeying the discipline on relations with the masses; they must also respect local authorities and cadres, and modestly learn from the people and listen to suggestions and criticism from them and from the Government. In the present new historical period, they must co-operate with local government and people to build a socialist spiritual civilization and establish a new-type relationship between the army and the people.

During the long years of practice, PLA political work has come to form a style and methods unique to itself. The most fundamental of these are: To seek the truth by setting out from the basis of reality and to handle all tasks according to the facts by going to the grassroots to investigate and study, integrating theory with reality; to follow the mass line, trust the masses and rely upon them, integrate leadership with the masses and a general appeal with personal guidance; to persist in the guiding principle that political work must implement and execute the Party's general task, must serve to enhance the troops' fighting effectiveness and must be carried out in close association with the units' combat missions and various other activities; to give full play to the exemplary roles of the political departments and organs and of all political workers, etc.

The chief contents of the PLA's political work can be divided, in terms of specialism, into education and propaganda, building the Party and Communist Youth League organizations, political work concerned with cadres, security, cultural activities, the masses, enemy troops, political work concerned with the militia and the reserve forces, etc. In terms of its aim and scope, it can be divided into wartime political work, political work during the process of military training, defence science research, construction, production and the execution of other duties; political work in services in the rear, in military academies and schools, etc.

The chief institutions and organs of the PLA's political work are:

The Party committee system

Party organizations are set up in each of the units at different levels. For regiments and other units of the same level and above, there is the Party committee; for battalions and other units at the same level – the Party's primary committee; and for companies and other units at the same level – the Party branch. Each of these provides a core of leadership and cohesion for its unit.

The political commissar system

Regiments and other units at higher levels each have a political commissar, each battalion has a political instructor, and each company – a political director. These officers share the leadership with the unit's military commander and are responsible for organizing and leading the unit's political work. Usually they are also in charge of the day-to-day work of the unit's Party committee or branch.

Political organs

These refer to the political sections or departments set up in regiments or units at higher levels. Of equal rank with the corresponding Headquarters, they take charge of the Party's affairs and political work of their respective units under the leadership of the political organ higher up, the unit's Party committee, and its political commissar.

Other political bodies include branches of the Communist Youth League in units below the regiment, and the Revolutionary Soldiers' Committee and Club in the company. The main functions of these bodies are to organize study groups, encourage reading and creative writing in spare time, and promote cultural and sports activities so as to enliven daily life in the army.

The PLA's military propaganda, which constitutes a major content of its political work, has always been highly valued by the Party and the army's political organs. During the war years, the General Political Department of the Chinese Workers' and Peasants' Red Army published its own paper *The Red Star*, which was succeeded by the *Journal of Military and Political Affairs of the Eighth Route Army*, published by the army's political department. Then, during the period of the Third Revolutionary Civil War, all the field armies, army corps and columns, and the majority of divisions and regiments all produced their own papers or magazines. After the founding of the PRC, the PLA General Political Department inaugurated successively the *PLA Daily, PLA Pictorial, PLA Life*, and other papers and periodicals. The organ of the CMC, the *PLA Daily*, has a circulation of 1.5 million and the *PLA Pictorial* distributes some 400,000 copies at home and abroad. Publishers working under the armed forces totalled eleven by the end of 1985, including the PLA Publishing House, the PLA Art and Literature Press, the Military Translation Publishers, etc., covering the fields of politics, military science, economics, history, science and technology, art and literature, journalism, industrial and agricultural production, medicine and sanitation, sport, education, etc. The Chinese People's Revolutionary Military Museum, located in Beijing, undertakes military propaganda among the masses and serves international exchange by briefing foreign visitors in the history of the Chinese people's revolutionary armed struggles. The majority of the service branches and arms, major military region commands, institutes for higher military education, etc., all have their papers or journals.

One of the important tasks of PLA political work is to organize science and culture education and train people for military and non-military departments to serve the country's construction as well as defence. The project has since been included in the PLA's general plan for training and education. By the end of 1985, more than 539,000 officers had participated in educational courses of different types and at different levels; of these, 244,000 had received their senior middle school or professional school certificates, while 7,100 had finished their college or university courses. More than 1,700,000 soldiers had participated in military and non-military study programmes, of which more than 600,000 had learned one or more professional skills or specialized knowledge. The drive to study science and culture has helped update arms and equipment, encouraged technical transformation, and raised the quality of training. At the same time, it has provided the country with persons with specialized knowledge and skills. The 1986 statistics from the Ministry of Civil Affairs report that 1,959 counties and cities in the country's provinces and autonomous regions had set up new service business with demobilized soldiers, and had recommended over 1.05 million of them from the countryside to work in different professions and trades.

In the PLA's political work, cultural and artistic undertakings have always been regarded as very important. During the periods of the Second Revolutionary Civil War, the War of Resistance Against Japan and the Third Revolutionary Civil War, artists and writers in the army created many artistic and literary works reflecting the life and struggles of the troops, which constituted an important part of the army's military propaganda in promoting the troops' morale and fighting effectiveness. After the founding of the PRC, writers in the army produced large numbers of literary works portraying the revolutionary wars and life in the people's army in the new era. Among the more prominent of them are the reportage *Who Are Our Most Beloved Ones?*, the drama *Sentinels Under the Neonlights*, the novels *Defend Yan'an* and *Garland Below the Tall Mountains*, the scenarios *The Sanggamryong Ridge* and *The Red Women's Detachment*. There were also poems, paintings, songs and music, dances, and also many pieces for artistic folk performances, including story-telling, singing, comic dialogues, clapper talks, cross talks, etc., which found warm echoes in the hearts of the troops and the masses of people. Some of these works were translated into various foreign languages and distributed abroad. The PLA General Political Department set up its art troupe, the August the First Sports Team and the August the First Film Studio. It inaugurated the art and literature periodicals *PLA Literature, The Kunlun, PLA Art, PLA Songs, PLA Films*, etc., and published a library of PLA literature. All the military region commands and service branches, and some of the PLA arms, have their own art troupes and sports teams. The PLA's undertakings in culture and art have become an important part of the country's general effort in these fields.

THE PLA'S MASS WORK

THE army's mass work, to which the People's Liberation Army has paid great attention ever since the Jinggang Mountains days, is of paramount importance, since it best displays the PLA's essence and characteristics as an army that exists to serve the people's interests.

During the Second Revolutionary Civil War period, in addition to fighting against the enemy the Red Army also undertook to do propaganda work among the masses, to organize and to assist them to build revolutionary political power and new branches of the CPC. During the War of Resistance Against Japan, the Army launched the movement of supporting the Government and caring for the people. They opened up waste land and engaged in production in order to reduce the economic burden on the masses. In the period of the Third Revolutionary Civil War, the Army helped peasants in carrying out land reform and did much to promote what was beneficial and eliminate what was harmful to the people. All these activities worked to develop a relationship between the army and the people as inseparable as fish and water. In the revolutionary wars that determined the future of China, the broad masses of the people firmly supported the people's army, vied with one another to join the army and other war efforts, and actively supported troops fighting at the front, thus swamping the enemy in the vast ocean of a people's war. Since the founding of the PRC, the PLA has carried forward the fine tradition of being a work team and production team as well as a fighting force, and has taken part in socialist reconstruction and public welfare undertakings, rushing to deal with emergencies or to help overcome natural disasters. In recent years, the army has been co-operating with local people to build a socialist spiritual civilization, and has further developed the army's mass work.

Taking part in socialist reconstruction

The PLA is a powerful reinforcement in China's construction projects in water conservancy and power generation. Soon after the founding of the PRC, the PLA despatched more than 100,000 troops almost straight from the battle field to take part in the two major water conservancy projects – the Jing River (*Jingjiang*) Flood-Division Project and the Project to Harness the Huai River (*Huaihe*). In places where they

were stationed, army units joined in the building of more than 100 reservoirs, such as those at Foziling, Ming Tomb, Miyun and Guanting reservoirs. They also took part in bringing the Haihe river (*Haihe*), Ziya river (*Ziyahe*) and Liao river (*Liaohe*) under permanent control and the rebuilding of the Dujiang weir and other water conservancy and power projects such as diverting the Luan river (*Luanhe*) to Tianjin, the expansion of the Zhanjiang Harbour, diversion works in Dalian and the putting up of the power station in Xuzhou. In all these projects they made tremendous efforts to alleviate natural calamities and to improve the people's livelihood. In diverting the Luan river to Tianjin, which was started in May 1982, the army undertook to cut a 10 km-long tunnel, which constituted the principal part of the project. Officers and soldiers alike worked with dauntless heroism. They made more than 908,000 blasts, dug

A tunnel excavated by PLA soldiers to divert the water of the Luanhe river to Tianjin.

through 239 fault zones, overcame cave-ins and other dangerous situations on more than 5,100 occasions, making it possible for the arduous project to be completed ahead of schedule, channelling water to Tianjin only 16 months after it was started. Leaders of the Central Party Committee and Government commended the army for their good example in getting better, faster and more economic results in the country's key construction projects. To mark the occasion and thank the troops, Tianjin set up the Monument to Diverting the Luan River to Tianjin.

The PLA has also rendered great help in the construction of other industrial and communication and transportation projects. In the 1960s, it concentrated a fairly large number of troops in the wilderness of the valley of the Songhua river (*Songhuajiang*) and Liao river (*Liaohe*) to help open up the Daqing oilfield, thus bringing an end to China's dependence on imported petroleum. PLA railway troops working in high mountains and along precipitous gorges and rivers built 52 railway trunk lines as well as branch lines, totalling over 13,000 kilometres, equivalent to one-third of the railroad built since 1949. In many of the country's capital construction projects, large and small, PLA commanders and soldiers willingly took the most difficult part, such as in the Beijing underground railway, Nanjing Yangtze river bridge, the international airport in Amoy and the cableway for sightseeing on Mount Tai. In more than five years – from 1978, when the Central Committee of the CPC decided to shift the priority of their work to socialist modernization, to 1984 – the PLA took part in 8,200 national or local key projects of large or medium size.

The PLA has also made major efforts to support the construction of special economic zones, economic development areas, and cities and towns being opened to the outside world. In the Shenzhen SEZ alone, for example, PLA troops have completed up to the present more than 160 construction projects. Meanwhile the whole army, by rearranging over one thousand of its military installations, has handed over a total of more than 130,000 square metres of land and over 200,000 square metres of barrack buildings in different camp areas for economic use. It has also thrown open 59 military airfields, more than 300 military railway lines and many military docks to help civilian transportation.

Troops stationed in different localities always support local public undertakings and actively take part in afforestation. Since 1979, units in various parts of the country have planted 201,450,000 trees, afforested a total area of 11,300 hectares by manual labour and another 700,000 hectares by sowing by aircraft. In the same period, they assisted in constructing some 20,000 bridges, roads, theatres, cinemas, parks and children's gardens, as well as renovating historic relics.

Dealing with emergencies and disaster relief

Catastrophic floods have taken place one after another since 1954 in the middle and lower reaches of the Yangtze river and the Huai river, and in Tianjin, Henan, Sichuan, Shaanxi and Liaoning. Altogether about one million PLA men have been sent to fight the floods alongside local people, safeguarding big cities in those regions and rescuing millions of people. In the summer of 1985, when North-East China, especially Liaoning province, was hit by the worst flood in decades, threatening lives and state property like oilfields, factories and mines, PLA ground, navy and air forces in the area were mobilized and rushed to 64 endangered places to fight the flood, employing altogether 80,700 men, 3,892 vehicles, 351 ships and a number of aircraft. In Liaoning alone more than 52,000 people were rescued, and 13,000 tons of materials were transported during the emergency. When the flood had receded, the troops aided the masses to repair more than 3,000 damaged houses.

Since 1949 disastrous earthquakes have taken place in the Yunnan province, and the Xingtai, Ganzi, Yingkou, Tangshan and other regions. Each time the PLA was the first to set off to provide relief at the forefront. After the first violent quake in Tangshan and Fengnan, in July 1976, when the whole region was still heaving underfoot with frequent aftershocks, more than 100,000 PLA men had already rushed to the area for rescue and relief work. Many worked very hard for days and nights in succession, and quite a few died saving other people. In 1983, when the year's ninth typhoon hit the mouth of the Pearl River, more than 700 metres of dyke were wrecked and the nearby area very quickly flooded. Some 800 officers and men of the navy were rushed to the spot. They fought continuously for over 10 hours and, while all the endangered civilians – about 1,200 – were rescued, seven sailors died in the struggle. According to statistics, in over three decades since 1949, the PLA has taken part in 342,700 disaster relief operations of various kinds by contributing 12,290,000 units of

Doctors and nurses of the PLA rescue injured people in a seriously damaged area after an earthquake in Yunnan province on 18 April 1985. *(Photo by Chen Haining)*

PLA soldiers rebuilding a dyke to defend Panjin city in Liaoning province from flood in October 1985. *(Photo by Miao Ming)*

men/time, and has rescued a total of 3,700,000 people.

Building socialist spiritual civilization together with the civilians

This means that the PLA and the local people cooperate, under the unified leadership of the local government and the Party, to build up civilized units. Specifically, the troops help local organizations or institutions to carry on ideological education for the youth and children, to maintain public security and to develop good social customs. They also provide assistance in cultural activities, such as recreational entertainment and sports, in order to enrich people's cultural life. In addition, they explain to the masses the principles and policies of the Party and Government and disseminate scientific and technological

knowledge, so as to promote production and enable the masses of the people to become materially better-off as soon as possible. This activity started in autumn 1981, when troops taking part in a military manoeuvre in North China came into contact with the people in places where they were stationed and started to jointly build more sophisticated villages. Fully affirmed by the CPC Central Committee, the State Council and the Central Military Commission, and encouraged by the General Political Department of the PLA, these activities have been popularized from villages to cities, from the hinterland to border areas. It started with establishing more sophisticated villages, and has now been developed to building streets, townships, factories, shops, hospitals and stations, etc. By 1985, 49,000 of such PLA–civilian jointly established civilized units had emerged, involving a total population of over 100 million.

Many "stinking ditches" or "muddy ponds" have been eliminated, making the localities habitable, even pleasant. Squabbles and quarrels between neighbours or between mothers- and daughters-in-law, gambling, thefts and robbery, as well as feudal superstitions, have been markedly reduced in many places, and replaced by new customs of respecting the old and caring for the young, and of mutual help within neighbourhoods. Wedding ceremonies and funerals have been simplified. The spiritual change in people has brought about improved developments in production. A survey of more than 21,000 PLA–civilian jointly established units shows that wherever a good job has been done in the joint effort, there is a noticeable increase in per capita income and a considerable improvement in the people's livelihood.

LOGISTICS

THE logistics of the PLA has gradually expanded and strengthened alongside the development of the army in its frequent battles.

In the 28 years before the founding of the People's Republic, owing to the lack of a unified government, the army's supplies were ensured mainly with local sources and captured enemy goods. "Millet plus rifle, our warehouses are at the front"; "we have neither rifles nor guns, the enemy build them for us" – the state of the PLA's logistics so vividly portrayed by these sayings took a historical turn with the coming into being of the People's Republic: changing from the decentralized approach into one of a centralized and unified supply system relying mainly on the State; from a logistics department serving only the ground force into one that serves the ground, naval and air forces as well as other technical army forces; from being mainly responsible for providing materials and

medicine to being responsible for providing transportation and technology as well, and organizing – as well as commanding – the fighting in the rear. In accomplishing these transformations, the PLA logistics department has met the needs of building a modernized and regular army, while achieving its own modernization and regularization.

To undertake the development of the role of the rear services into that of a composite armed force, separate logistics commands, organs and units were set up for the different services and their various arms on the basis of the original logistics service for just the ground force, forming a logistics network covering both the universal needs of the armed forces as a whole and the individual needs of specialized units. The air force logistics command has built a nationwide airfield network and corresponding facilities and defence works, making it possible for the air force to make sorties continuously and for many different types of aircraft to land, station and take off simultaneously. The naval logistics service has constructed bases for various types of warships, built supply anchorages and developed auxiliary fleets to supply ships at sea. The supplies command of the strategic guided missiles unit has set up specialized units and installations to store and transport supply and fuel, maintain equipment and site facilities and provide special health care, etc., enabling the troops to shelter or fight whenever necessary. The logistics departments of the PLA, with their many units and sophisticated technology, have for the first time become a systematic force to serve a composite army.

In accordance with the strategy of active defence and in order to meet the needs of battlefield construction for a future anti-aggression war, strategic as well as campaign bases in the rear and first line supply depots have gradually been set up, and quantities of war reserves have been stored. Meanwhile, in coordination with relevant government departments, logistics departments have developed military transportation, set up hospitals, warehouses, factories and stud farms, and organized rear engineering and transportation units. Now a comprehensive logistics service has been formed comprising networks of materials supply, equipment maintenance and repair, communications and transportation, and medical services, as well as military factories.

The technical equipment and means of maintenance of the logistics department have been continuously improving in step with the improvement in the combat equipment of the armed forces. In place of the primitive smithies, capable only of simple repairs in the war years, a maintenance and repair system linking army repair shops and plants with state-run industrial departments has now been developed, with sophisticated instruments and tools for checking and repairing, guaranteeing high quality repair work and ensuring a high ratio of readiness of the army's equipment. Shipment and distribution of petrol are increasingly being mechanized and automated. The oil pipeline laid from Gohrmu to Lhasa on "the roof of the world" goes through 560 kilometres of frozen zones with pingoes and ice hillocks. Completion of the project not only relieved many motor regiments from year-round transportation, but also developed the necessary new techniques in oil-piping in China. Work in the rear services is being computerized, and plans are under way for an automated command network for logistics departments above the level of the military regional command.

In line with the policy of giving priority to prevention, integrating prevention with treatment and combining traditional Chinese with Western medicine, medical work in the army has made great advances. In 1949, PLA troops entered the river and the lake districts of East China south of the Yangtze river. There they found schistosomiasis to be endemic.

Army paramedics implemented urgent measures for universal screening and treatment, designed to benefit civilians as well as troops. As a result, the disease was soon brought under control. These efforts served as the prelude to the government's large-scale battle against this parasitic fluke disease in the years which followed. In 1950 the PLA entered western Yunnan province, an area known to have been plagued by malaria for thousands of years. Evidence for this is suggested by the fact that no army was able to maintain a permanent garrison there. Bai Juyi, the Tang dynasty poet, described the malaria-like conditions in these lines:

> Of Yunnan's Lu River, it is said
> Miasmas rise from its steaming surface
> At the time when pepper blossoms fade,
> Two or three troops die in every ten, fording.

Certainly, when the PLA first arrived in this area of Yunnan, the incidence of malaria among some units was as high as 99.78 percent. Special army contingents for malaria prevention and cure were organized to cooperate with civilian medical workers and a large-scale campaign was launched against the disease. With their efforts, the incidence in the army dropped to 0.5 percent by 1954, while the incidence and mortality rate among the civilians also fell by a big margin. The technical level and quality of treatment of the disease gradually improved, and there was a marked development of specialized treatment with the setting up of 54 special medical centres. Health conditions of the army kept improving, with the daily incidence of contagious and other diseases dropping continuously.

As regards the military medical scientific research, major progress has been made in research into the prevention and cure of injuries by nuclear, chemical and biological weapons, and in research on field surgery, medical equipment, medical science pertaining to aviation and navigation, the prevention and cure of diseases peculiar in torrid and frigid areas and in high altitude areas, and the application of genetic engineering. PLA medical experts are now among the most advanced in China in curing burns, reattaching severed limbs, microsurgery, liver and gall surgery, heart surgery and neuro-surgery.

The logistics department has provided ever improving accommodation and supplies for troops at the frontiers and on the coasts, on highlands and in the desert, where conditions are very hard. The example can be cited of Tibet, 4000 metres above sea level on average, where many places are bitterly cold, short of oxygen and sparsely populated. To guarantee the material supply of the army stationed in Tibet and support Tibetan construction, the logistics department successively built several highways (Sichuan–Tibet, Qinghai–Tibet, Xinjiang–Tibet and Yunnan–Tibet) as well as airfields. A number of depots, motor transport regiments, hospitals, storehouses and repair plants were put up along the roads.

Another example is the Xisha Islands, where there is no fresh water and there are no trees, flowers or grass. To allow the troops to perform their duties, the army logistics built not only defence works, but also garrison constructions, desalination plants, sun-tracking solar ovens and other services essential to life, like water storage, power stations, refrigerators and medical facilities. Thousands of tons of soil were transported to the islands, enabling the troops to produce their own fresh vegetables and meat and to plant trees in the barracks area. After many years of effort, the housing, drinking water, lighting, medical care and transportation conditions of all the coastal defence forces have greatly improved.

Considerate of the nation's needs and limits in its socialist construction, and carrying on the tradition established during the war years of working hard "with both hands to provide ourselves with enough food and clothing", the PLA has developed agricultural and sideline production as well as practising frugality so as to reduce the budget for national defence and lessen the people's financial burden. During the period 1958–1985, it produced 14,000,000 tons of grain, 1,050,000 tons of soya beans, 1,150,000 tons of meat, 19,000,000 tons of vegetables, 175,000 tons of aquatic products, and sugar, fruits, tea, rubber and herbs, totalling 12.2 billion yuan. By careful calculation and strict budgeting, as well as by broadening sources of income and reducing expenditure, from the 1950s to the 1970s the army saved and handed over a total of 14.3 billion yuan of military expenditure and production income to the State. In 1981 and 1982, the PLA bought more than 600 million yuan of state treasury bonds to support the economic readjustment now in progress.

THE CHINESE PEOPLE'S ARMED POLICE

THE fundamental mission of the Chinese People's Armed Police is to safeguard the country's sovereignty and dignity, guard targets important to the Party and the State, protect the security of the people's lives and property and maintain social security.

Following a decision of the Central Committee of the CPC made in June 1982, that the part of the PLA responsible for domestic security be transferred to the public security department of the Government and merged with the three police forces existing therein – the armed police, the border guard and the fire brigade – to form the Chinese People's Armed Police, the CPAP came into existence after a year's preparation in April 1983.

As part of the public security establishment of the state, the Chinese People's Armed Police has headquarters at national level, an army for each province, autonomous region and municipality directly under the jurisdiction of the Central Government, a regiment for each prefecture, municipality, autonomous prefecture (or *meng*), a battalion or company for each county (or city or banner), and corresponding leading organs for the armies and regiments.

As a component part of the armed forces of China, the Chinese People's Armed Police is subject to the leadership of the CMC in terms of general policies and principles. It follows the Military Service Law of the People's Republic of China and the manuals and regulations of the PLA; at the same time, as a component part of the public security system, it is controlled and commanded by the public security departments at various levels in terms of its administrative affairs and duties.

The Chinese People's Armed Police consists of three branches: security guard, border guard and fire brigade. Their basic tasks are, respectively:

The security guard

To safeguard Party and government organs, foreign embassies and consulates in China, airports, broadcasting stations, state treasuries and scientific research institutions; to protect important bridges and tunnels; to guard and escort criminals; to carry out public security patrols in large and medium-sized cities and specially designated areas; and to deal with major emergencies.

The border guard

To maintain public security in border areas; to conduct border control of incoming or outgoing people and vehicles at harbours, airports and border railway stations and bus terminals open to the outside world, and at tunnels, routes, harbours and other places subject to special permission; to perform security check-ups on passengers and their luggage on international and domestic air flights; and to patrol China's territorial waters.

The fire brigade

To propagate and popularize fire prevention measures, to assist related units to set up fire prevention facilities and, of course, to put out fires when they occur so as to protect the country's economic construction and the people's lives and property.

The Chinese People's Armed Police pays attention to building up its educational institutions. Under the headquarters there are an officers' college and a number of polytechnic colleges and professional schools. Under the general brigades there are usually elementary commanders' colleges and schools and related professional polytechnic schools.

The Chinese People's Armed Police aims at its own revolutionization, modernization and regularization. Upholding the principle of strictness in running the police, it gears all its work to the fulfilment of its duties. Strict attention is paid to this aspect, beginning with education and training, which is required to be scientific in order to raise the quality of the personnel with emphasis on the ability to make instant re-sponses. Integrated closely with its active duties, training in military techniques, professional skill and basic tactics at different levels is carried out in a carefully planned way. Meanwhile, law and a professional knowledge of public security are designated as obligatory courses for every cadre and soldier in order to qualify them as guardians of the people, who understand, abide by, enforce and protect the law. Serving the people whole-heartedly is the sole objective of the People's Armed Police; it gives priority to political ideological work and pays constant attention to education in political theory, ideology and discipline, current affairs and science and culture, so that the quality of the cadres and soldiers will be constantly improved.

THE MILITIA

CHINA's militia came into being under the leadership of the CPC in the upsurge of the revolutionary movement of the Chinese workers and peasants. It has developed in the long revolutionary struggles into a new type of armed organization of the masses of the people not withdrawn from production.

As early as in the First Revolutionary Civil War, a Peasants' Self-defence Army and Worker Pickets were organized in villages and cities under the control of revolutionary forces to co-operate with the Northern Expedition Army. These may be seen as the forerunners of the contemporary Chinese militia. During the Second Revolutionary Civil War, the Provisional Central Government of the Republic of China organized the armed forces of workers and peasants in the many revolutionary base areas into Red Guards and Young Pioneers, which developed into the militia and self-defence corps in the War of Resistance Against Japan. By the time China was liberated, the militia and the self-defence corps had expanded into forces of 5.5 million and dozens of millions of men respectively. After the founding of the People's Republic, the militia as a state military system was given a good overhaul, which improved its organization and reformed its training. Thus it has become an indispensable part of China's armed forces.

The militia made historical contributions in the revolutionary wars by making full use of its familiarity with both the local people and conditions to operate on the spot in a scattered way. They supported the field army by providing recruits, protecting and building up the rear areas, transporting food to the front, evacuating the wounded to the rear and doing other war service.

Since the founding of New China, the militia has again played an important role in co-operating with the PLA and public security departments in putting down bandits and suppressing local despots, maintaining order, guarding the borders on land and at sea, and supporting counterattacks in self-defence against invaders, as well as in building up a socialist material and spiritual civilization.

The present militia is divided into two categories—the core militia and the ordinary militia. The core militia members consist of those who have been discharged from active service or have had military training and are under 28 years of age, and civilians who are selected to take part in military training. They are the core members constantly at the ready to join the army, take part in fighting and carry out emergency tasks. Other male citizens from 18 to 35 who are qualified to enlist in the army are enlisted in the ordinary militia. Neither category withdraws from production. The tasks of the militia in the new period are: to take active part in the national effort for socialist modernization, taking the lead in performing efficiently in production and other work; to undertake services for preparations against war, safeguarding the borders and maintaining local order; and to be always ready to join the army and take part in combat, resisting foreign aggression and defending the motherland.

THE SYSTEM OF MILITARY SERVICE

FROM the time when the PLA was founded till the first years after the founding of New China, PLA men were recruited from volunteers. The practice was replaced by the system of compulsory military service after the promulgation of the first military service law of the People's Republic of China in July 1955. Then the Military Service Law of the People's Republic of China passed by the Second Plenary Session of the Sixth National People's Congress in May 1984 stipulates that China practises a military service system which, while chiefly compulsory in nature, combines compulsory service with voluntary service as well as militia and reserve service. Corresponding stipulations for the implementation of this military service system were also laid down in the law.

A system combining compulsory service with voluntary service

The compulsory military service system keeps the army healthy and vital by constantly recruiting new members and, at the same time, it also keeps a large number of well-trained soldiers in reserve. However, the service period is too short for the armed forces to train and retain technical personnel. Hence the integration of compulsory service with voluntary service. Under the new system, rational compulsory service periods are set, i.e., three years for the ground force and four years for the navy and air force. These terms can be extended for another one to two years in the ground force and one year in the navy or air force according to the need of the unit and the soldiers' own wishes. Thus the compulsory servicemen are guaranteed sufficient time to learn and master complicated weapons and equipment. On the other hand, it is also stipulated that those servicemen who have served on active duty for five years and mastered their respective profession or technique can, with their personal application approved by leading organs above the division level, continue their active duty by eight to twelve years until they reach the highest age limit for soldiers – 35. The army is thus able to maintain a stable contingent of volunteers to serve as core among its rank and file.

A system combining militia with reserve service

The Chinese militia has always been the main source of China's military forces. Nevertheless, under the conditions of modern warfare, it cannot meet the needs of the army for officers and technically proficient servicemen, or meet by itself the need for the quick mobilization, if war suddenly breaks out, of a composite army with all its organic units. To solve this problem, the new military service law establishes a reserve force system integrated with the militia system. It stipulates a unified age limit for members of the militia and the reserve service and a unified organizational form. In non-military units where a militia is to be set up, all those who are qualified for reserve service are enlisted in the militia unit as members of the reserve service. Core militia members belong to the reserve service, first class, and ordinary members of the militia belong to the reserve service, second class. The militia is thus a well-organized, well-equipped, well-trained, combat-effective reserve force. Meanwhile, rules and regulations have been established to determine, examine and register respective members of the soldiers' and officers' reserve. There are regulations for giving military training to students in higher educational institutions and high schools, and for training reserve officers among college and university students. Thus both officers and soldiers are reserved among the civilians, so that the country – while supporting the fewest possible servicemen in peacetime – will have a great number of troops at its disposal in time of war.

System of military ranks

The PLA introduced the following system of military ranks in September 1955: generalissimo, marshal; senior general, general, lieutenant general and major general; senior colonel, colonel, lieutenant colonel and major colonel; senior captain, captain, lieutenant, second lieutenant and warrant officer; sergeant first class, sergeant second class and sergeant third class; as well as private first class and private. The title of marshal was then conferred on Zhu De, Peng Dehuai, Lin Biao, Liu Bocheng, He Long, Chen Yi, Luo Ronghuan, Xu Xiangqian, Nie Rongzhen and Ye Jianying. The system of military ranks was abolished in May 1965 on the proposal of Mao Zedong, but was restored by the new military service law of 1984. The new law also stipulates that non-military personnel will be assigned to the troops according to need. A plan to put this into practice is being drawn up.

Rehabilitation of veterans

Many measures to rehabilitate veterans were adopted by the State after the founding of New China. Appropriate measures were also stipulated in the new military service law of 1984. These are, mainly: 1. *Demobilization*: Volunteer servicemen and certain officers will, after they have served their terms and left active service, return to the places where they joined the army. They will be paid a certain sum of money as production subsidy, and local governments will make arrangements for them to take part in production or assign them suitable jobs, but generally not as cadres. 2. *Transference to civilian work*: Officers and volunteer servicemen withdrawn from active duty will be assigned jobs in a unified way by the Government in state organs, enterprises or institutions. The State will also see to their livelihood and professional or vocational training so that they will play an active part in socialist construction. 3. *Discharge*: Compulsory servicemen will return to places where they enlisted in the army after they are discharged from active service. Local governments are responsible for making arrangements for their livelihood and work. Those who were regular workers or staff members will be reinstated to jobs or positions they held before joining the army; others will have priorities when state organs, enterprises, institutions and other units recruit new employees. Colleges, universities or intermediate professional schools will also give them preferential treatment in being enrolled if they are equally qualified with other candidates.

SCIENCE AND TECHNOLOGY AND THE DEFENCE INDUSTRY

NEW China's science and technology and industry for national defence had to start from scratch, since the few munitions factories of old China were able to produce only certain simple light arms. In the 30 years and more since the founding of New China, a whole system combining scientific research, experiment and production covering almost all fields and with a rational distribution has been built up through self-reliance and hard work. Now the PLA, the People's Armed Police and the Militia are equipped with weapons developed and made in China. Industries for conventional weapons have produced advanced rifles, machine guns, specialized guns and tanks of different types to serve different purposes, radar communication systems, etc. The aeronautics industry has successively developed and produced supersonic fighters, bombers, attack planes, airfreighters, helicopters, ground-to-air and air-to-air missiles, etc. The shipbuilding industry has developed and produced surface and underwater ships such as guided missile destroyers and escorts, torpedo boats, high-speed gunboats, submarines and coastal defence missiles.

China has also developed and produced its strategic weapons, as marked by successive events: making and testing its first atom bomb and medium- and short-range guided missiles in 1964; launching its intermediate ground-to-ground missile and guided missile with a nuclear warhead in 1966; exploding its hydrogen bomb in 1967; launching its long-range ground-to-ground missile in 1969; building an advanced surveying fleet in 1979, thus providing the facilities for carrying out important tests in the sea; accurately hitting the target with its long-range carrier rocket in the South Pacific in 1980. Then it launched three satellites aboard one carrier rocket in 1981, and in 1982 it launched a carrier rocket from a submerged submarine, the warhead of which splashed accurately into the target area. At the same time, China has developed a relatively complete nuclear industry system that encompasses geological prospecting, mining and the production of nuclear fuel, as well as safety techniques and facilities.

On the basis of carrier rocket technology, China has developed its space technology, set up a complete system for launching, monitoring and controlling, and tracking and has built up a nationwide satellite observation network. Eighteen satellites were launched successfully from 1970, when it sent its first man-made satellite into the space, to March 1986. Among them, the scientific exploration and technique experiment satellite launched on 26 November 1975 shows that China has mastered the satellite retrieval technique. The experimental communications satellite launched on 8 April 1984, positioned at 125 E over the equator, has been the subject of successful experiments and trials for communications and radio and television broadcasting. A communications and broadcasting geostationary satellite for practical use was launched on 1 February 1986 and has since been working regularly. China's carrier rocket and man-made satellite technology has passed through the experimental stage into the application stage. China is now able to launch satellites for foreign customers for practical purposes.

Corresponding to the development of weapons and equipment, China has made great progress in its electronics technology. In recent years, it has developed and produced various electronic equipment for aircraft, warships, carrier rockets and satellites. Electronic computers are widely used for computing, control, display, navigation and survey. Its 100 million calculations per second computer has passed the appraisal of the State. Rigorous work is being done to develop microcomputers.

Following the policy of "serving the civilian as well as the army and catering to the needs of both peace and war, giving priority to military goods and maintaining defence production with civilian goods production", the defence industry has gained promising results in applying its technical know-how to produce goods for civilian use. Various defence industries, research institutes and centres have been adapted and reorganized to produce goods for both military and civilian use instead of focusing exclusively on military equipment. Applying their technology and production capacity to the full in common or approximate fields, the defence industry enterprises are now producing capital goods for coal-mining oil, communications and transportation industries; helping textile, food and other light industries to carry out the technical transformation of their operations; or directly producing durable consumer goods to help meet the needs of people in the countryside and urban areas. By 1985, the defence industry's output value for civilian products constituted 40 percent of its total output, four times the 10 percent level of 1978. The defence science and technology institutes and indus-

tries developed and produced the *YUN*-7, *YUN*-11, and *YUN*-12 civilian aircraft and some light aircraft for agricultural use. These are important contributions to the development of civil aviation. The defence industries also help civilian enterprises with technological transfer, consultation services, technical transformation and training of personnel, as well as solving key problems in production and organizing joint ventures.

The Jialing Machines, a defence plant in Chongqing, Sichuan province, joined two other military and five civilian factories to form a Jialing Motorcycle Combination. It has become the first example of an economic combination of military and civilian enterprises. By the end of 1985, more than 400 production lines had been set up to produce more than 300 varieties of civilian goods in military enterprises in nuclear, aeronautic, weaponry and space industries. A number of defence industrial enterprises have accepted contracts to co-operate with and provide technical services to many countries in Europe, Asia, America and Oceania. To promote technical exchanges with foreign business and enterprises, a large export trade fair displaying military technologies for civilian use was held in Shenzhen Special Economic Zone in April 1986. The first of its kind, it exhibited more than 1,700 civilian technologies and products.

THE MODERNIZATION OF NATIONAL DEFENCE

AN important component part of China's ongoing four modernizations, the modernization of national defence, is also an indispensable guarantee for the modernization of industry, agriculture, and science and technology, since China's socialist construction is taking place in a not-so-peaceful world where its national security is sometimes threatened. A powerful modernized national defence is of significance both in ensuring a long, stable period for China's modernization construction and in safeguarding world peace.

The modernization of China's national defence encompasses the building up of a modernized and regularized revolutionary army with Chinese characteristics; it has to raise its national defence science and technology and industry to the world's most advanced level as soon as possible; to develop advanced military science and improve the strategy and tactics of the people's war under modern conditions; to strengthen battlefield construction against the needs of an anti-aggression war in the future; to perfect various military facilities, communications and transportation as well as the storage of wartime materials; and to

build a strong civil defence system, etc. The most important of all these is to speed up the modernization of the PLA and to raise the level of science and technology of the national defence industry.

Revolutionization, modernization and regularization of the PLA – these three links are interconnected and promote each other. The PLA's superiority lies in its revolutionization, while its weakness lies in the fact that it is not sufficiently modernized – the relatively low level of its cadres in terms of science, culture and professional qualifications, and the relative backwardness of its weaponry and equipment. Modernization therefore must be stressed while all the three links must be constructed as a whole. To strengthen the PLA's modernization and regularization, building it into a well-trained army high in combat effectiveness under modern conditions, coupled with a modern system of defence industry, and science and technology capable of continuously supplying the army with excellent weapons and equipment – this will be like giving wings to a tiger, adding to national security and the peace of the world.

PART VIII

SPORT

A BRIEF OUTLINE

CHINA has a time-honoured tradition in physical culture and sports. After thousands of years of changes, this rich heritage handed down from ancient times has developed into the colourful and lively sports of today.

Ancient Sports

As far back as the later stage of the New Stone Age (about 4,000 to 10,000 years ago), embryonic forms of sports such as dances, *jirang* (hitting a stake), *wuyi* (fighting arts) and *shiqiu* (stone ball game) began to appear in some tribes which were more advanced in production. These were created and developed in conjunction with production, medical treatment, military affairs, recreation and religious activities. Dancing, for instance, was not only a kind of art in ancient times, but also a form of culture related to *daoyin*, an ancient exercise combining regulated breathing with bodily movements. Vivid pictures of three groups of dancers are found on the inner surface of a painted pottery of the New Stone Age which has been unearthed in Datong county, Qinghai province.

A greater variety of sports came into being in the slave society during the Xia, Shang and Western Zhou dynasties (*ca.* 21–*ca* 8 BC). Physical education was taught at schools. *She* (archery) and *yu* (charioteering) were among the six courses given in schools of the Zhou period. The Spring and Autumn and the Warring States periods (770 BC–221 BC) witnessed a widespread growth of sports, including *quandou* (fist fighting), *jianshu* (swordsmanship), *jueli* (contest of strength), *xiangbo* (grappling), *juding* (lifting a bronze tripod), *benzou* (running), *yugao* (high jump), *toushi* (stone throwing), *chaoju* (jumping), *saima* (horse-racing), *tianlie* (field hunting), *youyong* (swimming), *gouqiang* (tug-of-war), *shejian* (archery), *touhu* (throwing at a kettle), *taju* (ball kicking), *nongwan* (pellet playing), *qiuqian* (swing), *weiqi* (go) and *xiangqi* (Chinese chess). Competitions were held and prizes were awarded to the winners. Early writings on sports theories were published. In his *Tian Lun (On Heaven)*, the well-known philosopher Xun Zi (298–238 BC) wrote: "If you take good care of yourself and do exercises regularly, heaven can't make you ill. If you don't do so, heaven can't make you healthy."

Sports continued to flourish along with the economic and cultural growth in the feudal society. During the Qin, Han and Three Kingdoms periods (221 BC–AD 265), medical progress spurred the ad-

A picture teaching people how to do exercises, painted on a piece of silk in the Western Han dynasty (206 BC–AD 24).

855

vancement of *daoyin*, as is evidenced by the 44 figures of *daoyin* performers painted on a silk scroll which has been unearthed from a Western Han tomb at Mawangdui on the outskirts of Changsha, Hunan province. This is the earliest and most complete set of ancient gymnastics exercises yet to be discovered. Stone carvings of the Eastern Han period show vivid scenes of *cuju* (ball-kicking). *Jiju*, which resembled the modern game of polo, was played in those times. In the popular *baixi*, a kind of variety show, many sports items were performed, including tight-rope stunts, pole climbing, tripod lifting, stone turning, jumping through hoops, skimming over water, horse-riding, juggling and wrestling. There were sports exchanges with the Western Regions and foreign countries.

The Sui and Tang dynasties (581–907), especially the years of Kaiyuan and Tianbao (713–756), saw a new upsurge in sporting activities. The invention of inflated balls and the substitution of goals for old-fashioned pits gave a great fillip to the *cuju* (ball-kicking) game. Thus as far back as more than 1,200 years ago a sport similar to modern soccer in equipment and playing methods had already come into practice in China. The "15 pins" invented by China then was also very much like the bowling game introduced from the West in modern times. With the restoration and development of folk sports, there was an unprecedented increase of *baixi* (variety shows). Even women were involved in such sports as *jiju*

(polo), *cuju* (ball-kicking) and *weiqi* (go). Among the international sports activities were the Brahman Dancing Exhibition held in Chang'an (Xi'an) during the years 710–712, and the China–Japan Weiqi Contest in 848.

During the Song, Liao, Jin and Yuan periods (960–1368) much importance was attached to archery on horseback, about which many works were written. Aquatic sports developed in the Song dynasty as never before. There were rowing exhibitions in which the boats were arranged in battle formations, boat races which offered prizes to winners, a peculiar kind of diving performance called *shuiqiuqian* (swing on water), swimming competitions, "riding the waves" on the Qiantang river, and so on, all held on a large scale. Women's *sumo* also appeared during this period.

Wushu made rapid development during the period from the Ming dynasty (1368–1644) up to the Opium War (1840), which took place during the Qing dynasty. It was in the Ming dynasty that *wushu*, which had previously been practised as a fighting art, was established as a sport. An outstanding example of the development of *wushu* during the Ming and Qing dynasties was at the Shaolin Monastery in Songshan, Henan province, where the monks paid great attention to practising the art and were very skilful at it. Other activities like wrestling and sports on ice (mainly skating, ball games and acrobatics) were also very popular in those days.

Modern Sports

During the period from the Opium War (1840) to the establishment of the People's Republic in 1949, China was a semi-colonial, semi-feudal country with waning economy, backward science and culture, and declining sports. Although Euro-American systems and methods of physical education were introduced, they were mainly practised at schools, while the sports and physical culture of the Chinese nation as a whole were underdeveloped. Chinese athletes reached the front ranks only on rare occasions at the Far Eastern Games, but never at the Olympics. Living a miserable life, the Chinese people suffered from poor health and were scornfully called "The sick man of East Asia".

Contemporary Sports

The founding of the People's Republic of China in 1949 opened up a broad vista for political, economic, scientific and cultural development and instilled new life into physical education and sports. For the first time ever, an article on "the promotion of national sport" was written into the first supreme law promulgated by New China – the Common Programme of the Chinese People's Political Consultative Conference. A call was issued by the then Chairman Mao Zedong: "Promote physical culture and sports and build up the people's health." Sports administrative

A female go-chess *(weiqi)* player painted on a piece of silk in the Tang dynasty (618–907)

A rubbing from the "Hundred Games" stone tablet unearthed in an Eastern Han dynasty tomb (AD 25–220) in Yinan county, Shandong. This is a precious historical relic showing artists of that period dancing, performing acrobatic and circus tricks, and playing musical instruments.

bodies were quickly set up in the government at all levels. During his long years of premiership, Zhou Enlai paid great attention to the development of physical culture and sports in the whole country. In spite of certain setbacks and difficulties, China has in the past 36 years achieved brilliant successes in the field of sports. Initial results have been gained in her effort to find a distinctly Chinese way of developing physical culture and sports, one that may be outlined as follows:

Under the leadership of the Chinese Communist Party and the People's Government, and taking Marxism-Leninism and Mao Zedong Thought as guide, it arouses the enthusiasm of the whole society in developing physical culture and sports in a planned and structured way and according to the laws and characteristic features of sports, so as to raise the general fitness level of the people, improve sports performances, contribute to the building of spiritual civilization and serve the interest of socialism.

Physical culture and sports in New China have gone through four stages of development, as outlined below.

Laying the foundation (1949–1956)

Soon after the founding of the People's Republic, the Central People's Government entrusted the Youth League with the work of administering physical culture and sports throughout the country. In the meantime, the All-China Sports Federation was formed. In November 1952, the Physical Culture and Sports Commission of the Central People's Government was established. The first national leading body ever set up for sports in Chinese history, it was headed by He Long, who made important contributions to the rapid progress of physical culture and sports in New China. Sports bodies were also established or strengthened in the government at all levels, and in trade unions, Youth League organizations, army units and many industries. Sports grounds were built in various localities for public use. Six physical culture institutes and 11 sports schools were started in different cities, while sports departments or specialisms in 28 teachers' colleges or schools were restored or newly established. Seventy-seven spare-time sports schools for juniors were opened. The "System of Physical Training for Labour and National Defence" ("Labour and Defence System" for short) was instituted and enforced. Regulations for the grading of athletes and judges were promulgated. Various kinds of keep-fit exercises, notably those synchronized with broadcast music, were popularized in offices, factories, mines and schools throughout the country. These were usually done during work breaks or between classes. Mass sports were steadily restored and developed.

He Long with outstanding athletes in January 1960.

Two high tides (1957–1966)

With the advent of the era of socialist construction, China began to make great strides in sports endeavours. In the wake of the first two National Games came two high tides in sporting development. At the first Games in 1959, four world records were smashed by seven persons on four occasions, while 106 national records were renewed by 664 persons on 844 occasions. At the second Games in 1965, nine world records were rewritten by 24 persons on 10 occasions and 130 national records were toppled 469 times by 331 persons. During the 10 years from 1957 to 1966, a total of over 42 million people reached the standards set for the Labour and Defence System and the Standards of Physical Fitness for Young People. More than 1.47 million people underwent training at one time or another in spare-time sports schools for juniors. Over 10 million persons qualified as ranking athletes. National records were improved over 5,000 times and world records were broken or surpassed 142 times. A total of 13 world titles went to China in table tennis and speed skating competitions.

Setbacks during the ten chaotic years (1966–1976)

Physical culture and sports suffered a severe setback during the 10 years of the Cultural Revolution. Sports administrators at all levels were removed in large numbers. Many sports institutions were closed down. Sports colleges and schools stopped enrolling students, while sports facilities lay idle or were damaged. Most sports teams were paralysed. Nevertheless, the masses of the sports organizers and athletes were not to be daunted, and they struggled against the extreme difficulties confronting them. In 1971 the late Premier Zhou Enlai unequivocally affirmed the successes achieved in the field of physical culture and sports during the 17 years preceding the Cultural Revolution. Consequently, most of the dismissed sports organizers were restored to their former posts, regular training was resumed in certain sports, athletic grounds were re-opened to the public, and national sports competitions were held in addition to the First Asian–African–Latin American Table Tennis Invitational Tournament staged in Beijing in 1973. After Deng Xiaoping's reinstallation as a vice-premier of the State Council, he took charge of physical culture and sports and gave more effective guidance to the work in this field. In 1974 China participated in the Seventh Asian Games and the First World Middle School Games, both times with good results. However, Deng Xiaoping was once again overthrown in the movement to "counter the 'Right' deviationist trend to reverse correct verdicts," and the sports organizers as well as all the sports people were again reduced to an extremely difficult situation.

A historic breakthrough (1976–1985)

The counter-revolutionary group headed by Jiang Qing was smashed in October 1976. In the spring of 1979, with the approval of the Chinese Communist Party's Central Committee, the sports people repudiated all the slanders directed against them by the two counter-revolutionary cliques headed by Lin Biao and Jiang Qing, thus shattering the mental shackles that had been imposed on them. At the National Sports Conference in 1983, a programme of development was drawn up for turning China into a sports power in the world by the end of this century. The Fifth National Games staged in Shanghai that year was an unprecedentedly great event. President J. A. Samaranch of the International Olympic Committee, who attended the Games by invitation, highly praised the Chinese government for attaching importance to both athletic performance at a high level and sports for all the people. During this period, a new prospect was opened up for China's involvement in international sports activities. The Chinese Olympic Committee's representation on the International Olympic Committee was settled in 1979. China's international sports exchanges were progressively widened. Her

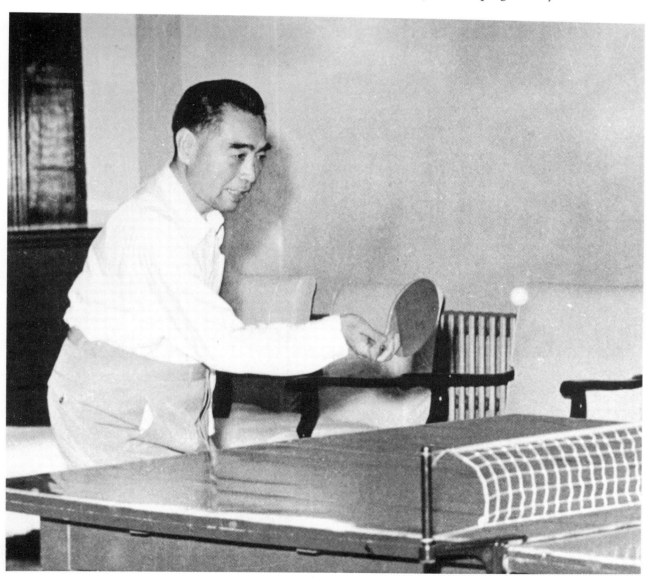

Premier Zhou Enlai playing table tennis in a break.

athletes achieved good results in international competitions, winning a total of 183 world titles in 15 events, and smashing or bettering world records on 138 occasions. Among the most heartening successes were:

Li Ning, after bagging six gold medals at the Sixth World Cup Gymnastics Tournament, claimed five medals at the 23rd Olympic Games;

Zhu Jianhua three times renewed the world record in the high jump;

The table tennis team made a clean sweep of all the seven titles on offer at the 36th World Championships;

The women's volleyball team registered five straight wins – at two World Cups, two World Championships and the 1984 Olympics – and followed up with a victory over a world all-star team;

The men's gymnastics team, the men's and women's badminton squads, and the women's walking race contingent captured many titles in world tournaments;

China topped the gold medals table at both the Ninth and the Tenth Asian Games;

At the 23rd Olympics China gained 15 golds, eight silvers and nine bronzes to take fourth place in gold medals;

In the year 1985, Chinese athletes earned 46 world titles – more than in any other year in Chinese history, and five world records were broken or surpassed by nine persons on nine occasions.

Table 1: World Records Broken or Surpassed by Chinese Athletes (1956–1985)

	No. of events		No. of athletes		No. of times records broken	
	Total	Women's	Total	Women	Total	Women
Total	*119*	*40*	*254*	*81*	*295*	*112*
Track & Field	4	3	5	3	8	4
Swimming	1		3		5	
Weightlifting	12		12		36	
Shooting	28	13	53	28	56	38
Archery	13	11	13	12	41	40
Speed skating	1		2		2	
Skydiving	25	13	79	37	44	29
Aeromodels	24		61	1	64	1
Model ships	9		23		36	
Underwater swimming	1		1		1	
Motorboating	1		2		2	

Table 2: World Titles Won by Chinese Athletes (1959–1985)

	No. of events		No. of titles		No. of winners	
	Total	Women's	Total	Women's	Total	Women
Total	*87*	*31*	*205*	*83*	*195*	*93*
Table tennis	7	3.5	52	24	46	21
Badminton	6	3	28	17	24	13
Weightlifting	10		15		6	
Weiqi (go)*	1		6		6	
Diving	7	3.5	14	9	10	5
Model ships	10		13		10	
Speed skating	1		1		1	
Sports acrobatics	16	7	24	9	30	12
Shooting	7	5	10	8	11	9
Volleyball	1	1	4	4	22	22
Gymnastics	9	1	23	2	8	1
Skydiving	3	2	4	3	7	3
Aeromodels	4		4		7	
Track & Field	2	2	4	4	4	4
Fencing	1	1	1	1	1	1
Windsurfing	2	2	2	2	2	2

*Go is a kind of chess.

THE SIXTH NATIONAL GAMES OF THE PRC

THE Sixth National Games of the PRC was held in the city of Guangzhou, the capital of Guangdong province, from 20 November to 5 December 1987. More than 7,500 athletes from 37 teams competed in 44 official events at 14 venues. There were also three exhibition matches. Athletes representing provinces, autonomous regions, cities and sports associations competed not only in 27 official Olympic events, but also in 17 Chinese traditional activities such as the martial arts (gongfu), wrestling and go chess.

Table 3: Medals Won by Chinese Athletes at the 23rd Olympics (1984)

	Name	Event	Result	Date
15 GOLD MEDALS	Xu Haifeng	Men's free pistol	566 pts	7.29
	Zeng Guoqiang	52 kg class weightlifting	235 kg	7.29
	Wu Shude	56 kg class weightlifting	267.5 kg	7.30
	Li Yuwei	Men's moving target shooting	587 pts	7.31
	Chen Weiqiang	60 kg class weightlifting	282.5 kg	7.31
	Yao Jingyuan	67.5 kg class weightlifting	320 kg	8.1
	Wu Xiaoxuan	Women's standard small-bore rifle	581 pts	8.2
	Luan Jujie	Women's foil individual		8.3
	Li Ning	Men's floor exercise	19.925 pts	8.4
	Li Ning	Pommel horse	19.950 pts	8.4
	Li Ning	Rings	19.850 pts	8.4
	Lou Yun	Men's vaulting horse	19.950 pts	8.4
	Ma Yanhong	Uneven bars	19.950 pts	8.5
	Women's Volleyball Team	Women's volleyball		8.7
	Zhou Jihong	Women's platform diving	435.51 pts	8.10
8 SILVERS	Zhou Peishun	52 kg class weightlifting	235 kg	7.29
	Lai Runming	56 kg class weightlifting	265 kg	7.30
	Men's Gymnastics Team	Team event	590.80 pts	7.31
	Lou Yun	Men's floor exercise	19.775 pts	8.4
	Li Ning	Men's vaulting horse	19.825 pts	8.4
	Tong Fei	Horizontal bar	19.975 pts	8.4
	Tan Liangde	Men's springboard diving	662.31 pts	8.8
	Li Lingjuan	Women's archery: grand total	2559 pts	8.11
BRONZES	Wang Yifu	Men's free pistol	564 pts	7.29
	Huang Shiping	Men's moving target shooting	581 pts	7.31
	Wu Xiaoxuan	Women's air rifle	389 pts	7.31
	Women's Gymnastics Team	Team event	388.60 pts	8.1
	Li Ning	Men's all-round gymnastics	118.575 pts	8.2
	Women's Basketball Team	Women's basketball		8.7
	Women's Handball Team	Women's handball		8.9
	Zhu Jianhua	Men's high jump	2.31 m	8.11
	Li Kongzheng	Men's platform diving	638.28 pts	8.12

In recent years, attention has been given to applying science to physical culture and training, thus raising the level of competition in China. The spiker completed a super grand slam by winning the World Women's Volleyball Championship (twice), the World Cup (twice), and the Olympics. In the 23rd Olympic Games, in which 140 countries and regions participated, China won its first 15 gold, eight silver, and nine bronze medals. In the ninth and tenth Asian Games, China ranked first in the number of gold medals twice in succession.

Never before have so many world and Asian records been shattered at a national games, the experts pointed out; the 16-day 44-event Games (the preliminaries and some finals were held before the official November opening) saw 19 world and 29 Asian records broken or surpassed, and 3 world records were equalled.

Weightlifter He Zhuoqiang from Guangdong broke two in the 52 kilogram category, snatching 117.5 kilograms and lifting a total of 265 kilograms, thus becoming the first Chinese to hold a world record in snatch, jerk and total. Another strongman, He Yingqiang, snatched 133.5 kilograms and broke the world record in the 56 kilogram category.

There was marked progress in the swimming and

Weightlifter He Zhuoqiang, of Guangdong, in the 52 kg category, snatching 117.9 kg to break the world record.

General Secretary Zhao Ziyang talks with Juan Antonio Samaranch, Chairman of the International Olympic Committee, during the Sixth National Games of the PRC.

Table 4: The 46 World Titles Won by Chinese Athletes in 1985

Winner	Event	Date	Venue	Meeting
Zhang Xiaodong	Windsurfing: Women's triangle	1984.12.26–1985.1.6	Perth, Australia	11th World Championships
Men's table tennis team	Table tennis: Men's team	3.28–4.7	Gothenburg, Sweden	38th World Championships
Women's table tennis team	Women's team	3.28–4.7	Gothenburg, Sweden	38th World Championships
Jiang Jialiang	Men's singles	3.28–4.7	Gothenburg, Sweden	38th World Championships
Cao Yanhua	Women's singles	3.28–4.7	Gothenburg, Sweden	38th World Championships
Dai Lili/Geng Lijuan	Women's doubles	3.28–4.7	Gothenburg, Sweden	38th World Championships
Cai Zhenhua/Cao Yanhua	Mixed doubles	3.28–4.7	Gothenburg, Sweden	38th World Championships
Tan Liangde	Diving: Men's springboard	4.25–4.28	Shanghai	4th World Cup
Tong Hui	Men's platform	4.25–4.28	Shanghai	4th World Cup
Li Yihua	Women's springboard	4.25–4.28	Shanghai	4th World Cup
Men's diving team	Men's team	4.25–4.28	Shanghai	4th World Cup
Women's diving team	Women's team	4.25–4.28	Shanghai	4th World Cup
Men's & women's diving team	Mixed	4.25–4.28	Shanghai	4th World Cup
Wang Jianhong	Weiqi (go)	5.20–5.24	Tokyo	7th World Amateur Go Championships
Wang Guping	Model ships: C_2	5.25–5.31	Rastatt, FRG	3rd World Championship in Model Shipbuilding "C"
Li Jie	C_4	5.25–5.31	Rastatt, FRG	3rd World Championship in Model Shipbuilding "C"
Han Jian	Badminton: Men's singles	6.10–6.16	Calgary, Canada	4th World Championships
Han Aiping	Women's singles	6.10–6.16	Calgary, Canada	4th World Championships
Han Aiping/Li Lingwei	Women's doubles	6.10–6.16	Calgary, Canada	4th World Championships
Zhou Jianming	Model ships: F_1–$V_{3.5}$	8.4–8.11	Rotterdam, Holland	4th World Championships
Tan Lifeng	F_1–$V_{6.5}$	8.4–8.11	Rotterdam, Holland	4th World Championships
Liu Haiqing	F_2–$_A$	8.4–8.11	Rotterdam, Holland	4th World Championships
Liang Yue	Aeromodels: F1A individual	8.14–8.16	Livno, Yugoslavia	22nd World Free Flight Aeromodel Championships
Liang Yue/Kong Kai/Zhou Yaodong	F1A team	8.14–8.16	Livno, Yugoslavia	22nd World Free Flight Aeromodel Championships
Chen Xinhua	Table tennis: Men's singles	8.22–8.25	Foshan, Guangdong	6th World Cup
Liu Ling/Shao Weiping/Wu Jie	Shooting: Women's skeet team	9.1–9.7	Montecatini, Italy	World Skeet Shooting Championships
Li Li/Gao E/Wang Xiaoyan	Women's skeet team	9.1–9.7	Montecatini, Italy	World Skeet Shooting Championships
Li Li	Women's skeet individual	9.1–9.7	Montecatini, Italy	World Skeet Shooting Championships

Table 4: *(continued)*

Li Lingwei	Badminton: Women's singles	9.2–9.7	Jakarta, Indonesia	5th World Cup
Lin Ying/Wu Dixi	Women's doubles	9.2–9.7	Jakarta, Indonesia	5th World Cup
He Xiaohong	Skydiving: Women's individual accuracy jump	8.31–9.8	Siena, Italy	3rd World Cup
Huang Ruifen (co-holder)	Sports acrobatics: Women's tumbling all-round	9.16–9.18	Beijing	5th World Cup
Yao Zhihua (co-holder)	Women's tumbling all-round	9.16–9.18	Beijing	5th World Cup
Huang Ruifen	Women's tumbling routine 1	9.16–9.18	Beijing	5th World Cup
Yao Zhihua	Women's tumbling routine 2	9.16–9.18	Beijing	5th World Cup
Feng Tao	Men's tumbling routine 2	9.16–9.18	Beijing	5th World Cup
Xu Hong/Hu Bingchen	Men's pairs all-round	9.16–9.18	Beijing	5th World Cup
Xu Hong/Hu Bingchen	Men's pairs routine 1	9.16–9.18	Beijing	5th World Cup
Yang Ping/Li Jun/Lu Haiyqan	Women's trios routine 2	9.16–9.18	Beijing	5th World Cup
Wang Pei/Zhao Jie/Wang Liyou/ Zhou Chuanbiao	Men's fours all-round	9.16–9.18	Beijing	5th World Cup
Women's walking team	Walking: Women's 10 km team	9.28–9.29	Douglas, Isle of Man, Great Britain	World Cup
Yan Hong	Women's 10 km individual	9.28–9.29	Douglas, Isle of Man, Great Britain	World Cup
Tong Fei	Gymnastics: Men's floor exercise	11.4–11.10	Montreal, Canada	23rd World Championships
Tong Fei	Horizontal bar	11.4–11.10	Montreal, Canada	23rd World Championships
Li Ning	Rings		Montreal, Canada	23rd World Championships
Women's volleyball team	Women's volleyball	11.10–11.20	Japan	4th World Cup

Table 5: The Five World Records Broken or Surpassed by Chinese Athletes in 1985

Setter	Event	Result	Meeting
Tan Lifeng	Model ships F_1–$V_{6.5}$	12.7 sec	National Elite Athletes Tournament
Sun Zhiye	Model ships F_1–V_{15}	12.5 sec	National Elite Athletes Tournament
Zhou Jianming	Model ships F_1–$V_{3.5}$	13.8 sec	National Elite Athletes Tournament
Zhou Jianming	Model ships F_1–$V_{3.5}$	14.5 sec	4th World Championships
Zhou Jianming	Model ships F_1–$V_{3.5}$	13.4 sec	4th World Championships
Tan Lifeng	Model ships F_1–$V_{6.5}$	12.9 sec	4th World Championships
Li Xin	Shooting: Women's standard small-bore rifle prone	599 pts	Beijing International Invitational
Wu Hangjian	Model ships F_1–$V_{6.5}$	12.7 sec	National Championships
Shang Biao	Model ships F_3–V	144.2 pts	National Championships

Table 6: Chinese Winners of 94 Gold Medals at the 10th Asian Games (21 September–5 October 1986)

Event	Gold Medallists	Results
Ball Games		
Men's basketball	Men's basketball team	
Women's basketball	Women's basketball team	
Men's volleyball	Men's volleyball team	
Women's volleyball	Women's volleyball team	
Tennis: Women's team event	Women's tennis team	
Tennis: Women's singles	Li Xinyi	
Table tennis: Women's singles	Jiao Zhimin	
Table tennis: Men's doubles	Teng Yi, Hui Jun	
Table tennis: Women's doubles	Dai Lili, Geng Lijuan	
Table tennis: Mixed doubles	Teng Yi, Dai Lili	
Badminton: Women's team event	Women's badminton team	
Badminton: Men's singles	Zhao Jianhua	
Badminton: Women's singles	Han Aiping	
Badminton: Women's doubles	Lin Ying, Guan Weizhen	
Men's water polo	Men's water polo team	
Track & Field		
Decathlon	Chen Zebin	7255 pts
Women's heptathlon	Zhu Yuqing	5580 pts
Men's high jump	Zhu Jianhua	2.31 m
Women's long jump	Liao Wenfen	6.37 m
Men's 20 km walk	Sun Xiaoguang	1:25:45.72
Women's 10 km walk	Guan Ping	48:40
Women's 10000 m	Wang Xiuting	32:47.77
Men's 110 m hurdles	Yu Zhicheng	14.07
Women's 100 m hurdles	Chen Kemei	13.78
Men's pole vault	Ji Zebiao	5.40 m
Men's 4 × 100 m	Cai Jianming, Li Feng, Yu Zhuanghui, Zheng Chen	39.17
Women's 4 × 100 m	Pan Weixin, Shao Liwei, Luo Xin, Tian Yumei	44.78
Men's discus	Li Weinan	58.28 m
Women's discus	Hou Xuemei	59.28 m
Men's shot put	Ma Yongfeng	18.30 m
Women's shot put	Huang Zhihong	17.51 m
Women's javelin	Li Baolian	59.42 m
Gymnastics		
Men's team event	Men's gymnastics team	291.10 pts
Women's team event	Women's gymnastics team	195.05 pts
Men's individual all-round	Li Ning	117.80 pts
Men's floor exercise	Li Ning	19.60 pts
Rings	Li Ning	19.60 pts
Women's individual all-around	Chen Cuiting	78.75 pts
Women's floor exercise	Chen Cuiting	19.90 pts
Horizontal bar	Yang Yueshan	19.80 pts
Pommel horse	Yang Yueshan	19.75 pts
Men's vaulting horse	Lou Yun	19.30 pts
Uneven bars	Huang Qun	19.80 pts
Women's vaulting horse	Ma Ying	19.75 pts
Swimming		
Women's 400 m IM	Yan Ming	4:52.43
Women's 400 m freestyle	Yan Ming	4:15.61
Women's 800 m freestyle	Yan Ming	8:43.42
Men's 100 m breaststroke	Jin Fu	1:04.02
Men's 400 m freestyle	Xie Jun	4:00.35
Women's 100 m breaststroke	Huang Xiaomin	1:12.70
Women's 100 m butterfly	Qian Hong	1:01.36

Table 6: *(continued)*

Events	Gold Medallists	Results
Swimming *(continued)*		
Women's 4 × 100 m freestyle	Xia Fujie, Huang Hong, Zhou Xun, Qian Hong	3:52.21
Men's 4 × 100 m freestyle	Shen Jianqiang, Yang Qing, Mulati, Feng Qiangbiaol	3:27.51
Men's 1500 m freestyle	Wang Dali	15:50.93
Diving		
Men's springboard	Tan Liangde	678.24 pts
Men's platform	Tong Hui	656.58 pts
Women's springboard	Zhang Yuping	589.17 pts
Women's platform	Lu Wei	460.02 pts
Rowing		
Men's single sculls	Liu Qun	7:48.77
Women's single sculls	Chen Changfeng	9:02.27
Men's coxed pair	Yan Jun, Wang Hongbing, Chen Lianjia	7:35.21
Women's coxless pair	Zhang Xiuying, Yang Xiao	8:11.97
Men's coxed four	Li Jianxin, Gao Yuhua, Wang Hongbing, Yan Jun, Chen Zhiqiang	6:59.74
Women's coxed four	Li Hongbing, Zhou Xiuhua, Ma Yumin, He Li, Li Ronghua	7:41.78
Men's eight	Li Jianxin, Yu Hanqiao, Gao Yuhua, He Dongjiang, Zhu Ledan, Wang Xinle, Xu Quan, Zheng Bingsheng, Chen Zhiqiang	5:56.46
Yachting		
Division II class	Qi Jianguo	14.4 pts
470 class	Chen Hongtai, Lin Jiacheng	14.7 pts
Weightlifting		
52 kg class	He Zhuoqiang	247.5 kg
56 kg class	He Yingqiang	265 kg
60 kg class	Lai Runming	285 kg
67.5 kg class	Yao Jingyuan	307.5 kg
75 kg class	Cai Yanshu	340 kg
Fencing		
Men's sabre team event	Wang Xingqi, Wang Zhiming, Chen Jinchu, Huang Weixiong, Zheng Zhaokang	
Women's foil team event	Luan Jujie, Zhu Qingyuan, Zhang Jianqiu, Li Huahua	
Men's sabre individual	Wang Xingqi	
Women's foil individual	Li Huahua	
Archery		
Women's 70 m double round	Ma Xiangjun	628 pts
Shooting		
Men's air rifle team event	Qiu Bo, Xu Xiaoguang, Zhang Yingzhou	1739 pts
Men's air rifle individual	Qiu Bo	685.3 pts
Men's small-bore standard rifle team event	Qiu Bo, Xu Xiaoguang, Qiu Zeqing	1727 pts
Men's small-bore standard rifle individual	Qiu Bo	576 pts
Men's free pistol team event	Xu Haifeng, Wang Yifu, Liu Jingsheng	1680 pts
Men's free pistol individual	Xu Haifeng	660 pts
Men's air pistol team event	Xu Haifeng, Wang Yifu, Zuo Pei	1721 pts
Men's air pistol individual	Xu Haifeng	678.8 pts
Men's rapid-fire pistol individual	Li Zhongqi	694 pts
Women's standard rifle team event	Zhou Danhong, Zhang Qiuping, Jin Dongxiang	1735 pts
Women's small-bore standard rifle individual	Zhou Danhong	682.4 pts
Women's small-bore pistol team event	Wen Zhifang, Zhu Yuqin, Qi Chunxia	1748 pts
Women's small-bore pistol individual	Wen Zhifang	687 pts
Men's skeet team event	Wang Zhonghua, Yue Ming, Zhang Weigang	432 pts
Men's skeet individual	Zhang Weigang	214 pts
Cycling		
Men's 100 km team time trial	Han Shuxiang, Guo Longchen, Zhang Zhonglu, Wu Weipei	2:08:28.462
Women's 1000 m sprint	Zhou Suying	

track and field, which were regarded as weak events in Chinese sports. In the Sixth National Games, nine Asian and national records of swimming were topped. Huang Xiaomin clocked the year's second best time of two minutes 27.78 seconds in the women's 200-metre breaststroke, only 0.38 seconds outside the world record. An outstanding showing, led by Huang, brought some light to China's swimming, which had been at a low ebb for 30 years.

The track and field highlight came in the women's middle and long distance hurdles and shotput: Wang Xiuting, holder of three Asian records, broke two of her own, one in the 5,000 metre (15'27"44), the other in the 10,000 metre (31'27"00). Liu Huajin shattered the 17-years-old women's 100-metre hurdles mark with a time of 13″03, and shot putter Li Meisu neared the 21-metre mark with a throw of 20.95 metres. In the track and field events, the most exciting news was that Chen Yaoling and her friend Xu Yongjiu both broke the world record for the women's 10,000-metre walking race event in times of 43′52″1 and 44′19″5 respectively.

As expected, Guangdong, Shanghai, Liaoning and Beijing were the first, second, third and fourth in total points.

China's goal is to build itself into a strong sports nation of advanced world level by the end of the century. The level and scale of China's development are still behind those of the world's stronger nations. The range of activities is somewhat uneven around the country. Sports are more popular in the coastal areas, where living standards are usually higher than inland. Of the top 10 teams at the Games, only two were from inland areas: Hubei, the sixth, and Sichuan, seventh. Another problem is that of the shortage of young and promising newcomers, especially in gymnastics and men's and women's volleyball and soccer. There is still a long way to go for the Chinese people and athletes to climb to new heights.

Party and State leaders, including Party General Secretary Zhao Ziyang, acting Premier Li Peng and Vice-Premier Wan Li, attended the opening and closing ceremonies. VIPs of the International Olympic Committee, headed by Juan Antonio Samaranch and other international sports organizations leaders and officials, overseas Chinese and noted personages or compatriots from Hong Kong and Macao were also invited to the ceremonies.

Table 7: Asian Records Broken at the 6th National Games

	Event	Athlete	Result	Previous Asian Record
Track & Field	Men's 110 m Hurdles	Yu Zhicheng	13″72	13″82
	Women's 5000 m	Wang Qinghuan	15′29″91	15′37″17
	Women's 5000 m	Hou Juhua	15′33″73	15′37″17
	Women's 5000 m	Wang Xiuting	15′27″44	15′29″91
	Women's 10000 m	Wang Xiuting	32′36″52	32′44″17
	Women's 10000 m	Wang Xiuting	31′27″00	31′48″88
	Women's 10000 m	Hou Juhua	31′27″99	31′48″88
	Women's 10000 m	Wang Qinghuan	31′44″73	31′48″88
	Women's 4×100 m Relay	Tian Yumei, Huang Peilan, Cao Liling, Pan Weixin	44″61	44″77
	Women's 100 m Hurdle	Liu Huajin	12″89	12″93
	Women's 10 km Walk	Chen Yueling	43′52″1	44′26″5
	Women's 10 km Walk	Xu Yongjiu	44′19″5	44′26″5
	Women's Shot Put	Li Meisu	20.30 m	19.87 m
	Women's Shot Put	Li Meisu	20.87 m	20.66 m
	Women's Shot Put	Li Meisu	20.95 m	20.87 m
	Women's Javelin Throw	Zhou Yuanxiang	65.28 m	65.16 m
	Women's Javelin Throw	Zhou Yuanxiang	65.50 m	65.28 m
	Women's Heptathlon	Dong Yuping	5968 pts	5611 pts
	Women's Heptathlon	Dong Yuping	5896 pts	5611 pts
	Women's Heptathlon	Dong Yuping	5715 pts	5611 pts
	Women's Heptathlon	Dong Yuping	5648 pts	5611 pts
Weightlifting	Up to 52 kg Snatch	He Zhuoqiang	117.5 kg	116.5 kg
	Up to 52 kg Total	He Zhuoqiang	265 kg	257.5 kg
	Up to 56 kg Snatch	He Yingqiang	133.5 kg	130 kg
	Up to 56 kg Clean & Jerk	He Yingqiang	160.5 kg	160 kg
	Up to 60 kg Snatch	Liang Shaofeng	133.5 kg	133 kg
	Up to 67.5 kg Snatch	Li Jinhe	145.5 kg	145 kg
	Up to 82.5 kg Snatch	Li Guangshun	165.5 kg	165 kg
	Up to 90 kg Snatch	Yang Bo	167.5 kg	166 kg

Table 8: World Records Broken or Surpassed at the 6th National Games

	Event	Athlete	Result	Previous World Record
Track & Field	Women's 10 km Walk	Chen Yueling	43′52″1	44′26″5
	Women's 10 km Walk	Xu Yongjiu	44′19″5	44′26″5
Weightlifting	Up to 52 kg Snatch	He Zhuoqiang	117.5 kg	116.5 kg
	Up to 52 kg Total	He Zhuoqiang	265 kg	262.5 kg
	Up to 56 kg Snatch	He Yingqiang	133.5 kg	133 kg
Shooting	Men's Small Bore Free Rifle English Match Final	Li Chaoyang	705.3	704.9
Parachuting	Men's Four-Way Rotation	Wang Yongli, Chen Li, Zhang Lin, Han Yiqiang	24 Formations	22 Formations

Table 8: (*continued*)

	Event	Athlete	Result	Previous World Record
Underwater swimming	Men's 100 m Immersion	Qiu Yadi	35″42	35″54
	Women's 50 m Immersion	Zheng Shiyu	17″63	17″79
	Women's 100 m Immersion	Zheng Shiyu	39″55	39″90
	Women's 4 × 200 m Surface Relay	Liu Huizhang, Lin Xiaomei, Fu Xiaoyun, Huang Shaohuan	6′32″57	6′34″21
Model ship	F1 – V3.5	Tan Lifeng	12″3	13″1
	F1 – V6.5	Wu Hangjian	11″6	12″5
	F1 – V15	Hu Shenggao	11″4	11″7
	F1 – E>1 kg	Tan Lifeng	12″1	12″8
	F1 – E>1 kg	Tan Lifeng	11″5	12″1
	F3 – V	Chen Zhaolun	18″5 (146.30 pts)	19″8 (146.04 pts)
	F3 – E	Chen Zhaolun	21″3 (145.74 pts)	29″1 (144.18 pts)
	F3 – E	Xu Ke	20″5 (145.90 pts)	21″3 (145.74 pts)

Table 9: World Records Equalled at the 6th National Games

	Event	Athlete	Result	Previous World Record
Shooting	Women's Small Bore Standard Rifle English Match	Tian Hong	598	598
	Men's Small Bore Free Rifle 40 Shots Prone	Pang Yonghong	400	400
	Men's Small Bore Free Rifle English Match	Li Chaoyang	600	600

SPORT FOR THE MASSES

THE primary task of sports and physical education in New China is to develop sports activities on an extensive scale among all the people so as to improve their physique and raise the fitness level of the whole nation in the interest of socialist construction. The Constitution of the People's Republic of China adopted by the National People's Congress in 1982 stipulates: "The State develops physical culture and promotes mass sports activities to build up the people's physique," and "The State promotes the all-round moral, intellectual and physical development of children and young people." Since the birth of New China, the people's health has been greatly ameliorated with the improvement in their material well-being and the betterment of the country's cultural, educational and hygienic facilities, and with the extensive development of physical culture and sports. Surveys showed that the average life expectancy of the Chinese people had increased from 35 years before the Liberation to 67.88 in 1983. Tests taken on children and young men and women ranging from seven to 18 years in age in Beijing, Shenyang and nine other cities revealed that they had grown upwards of two centimetres in body height and about one kilogramme in body weight every 10 years since the founding of the People's Republic. It may be noted that young men and women in China today are generally bigger and stronger than their parents.

At present over 300 million people, or 30 per cent of the Chinese population, regularly take part in sports activities, and an aggregate of 120 million have attained various standards for fitness training. A Canadian physical educationist who has been to 67 countries wrote in an article about his visit to China: "The Chinese people are very fond of sports. Multitudes of them, men and women, young and old, engage in sporting activities, presenting a spectacular scene, almost an illusory picture. I have seen three- or four-year-olds swimming, 60-year-olds engrossed in their daily exercises, countless students engaged in different kinds of sports."

Sports Activities among Workers and Employees

There are 110 million workers and employees in China. As early as January 1954, the Central Committee of the Communist Party of China issued a call demanding that "mass sports activities should be seriously carried out, above all in factories and mines, schools and government offices", and that "trade unions should give concrete guidance to sports undertakings in factories, mines and other enterprises." In March of the same year, the then Government Administrative Council of the Central People's Government issued the "Notice on Promoting *Gongjiancao*

Women workers of Beijing No. 1 Cotton Textile Plant doing exercises in their break. *(Photo by Song Lianfeng)*

(limbering-up exercises to be done during work breaks) and other Sports Activities in Government Offices." In the early 1950s over 520,000 people in the railway system regularly took part in various kinds of physical training, while an average of more than 70 per cent of government functionaries in the whole country took to *gongjiancao*. The First National Workers' Games were held in 1955. By the end of 1956, 19 national sports associations for different trades and 25,100 sports associations at the grassroots level had been formed, with a total membership of over 1.68 million. To help the workers and employees keep fit and prevent diseases, the State Physical Culture and Sports Commission and other organizations created and popularized a number of special exercises for iron and steel workers, textile workers, coal-miners, shop assistants and dockers.

By 1985, the number of workers and employees regularly engaged in physical exercises had grown to 40 million (40 per cent of the total), which was double the number registered in 1981. There were more than 230,000 workers' sports teams, with a total of over 2.8 million members. Trade unions in the whole country had at their disposal 223 indoor stadiums and gyms, 894 swimming pools, 16,021 sports grounds, and over 222,400 courts or fields for various ball games. The Second National Workers' Games were staged in 1985.

The Peasants Take to the Sportsground

China has a rural population of 800 million. Sports

began to develop steadily in the Chinese countryside in the 1950s. By 1957 they had attracted over 20 million participants, with the Labour and Defence System enforced in 67 counties and a total of 100,000 people reaching its standards. With the reform of the rural economic system and the improvement of the peasants' livelihood during the past few years, rural sports have entered a new stage of development. By 1985, upwards of 70 per cent of all the townships in the country had set up their own cultural centres where sports formed an important part of their activities. Shandong province alone boasts some 300 cultural centres and over 50,000 Youth Homes, with 58,000 sports teams of various kinds operating under them. Across the length and breadth of the country there have appeared many sports centres – areas which

A motorcycle competition for peasants in Lingbao county, Henan province. *(Photo by Jia Tie)*

have developed one or two kinds of sports in a big way as their traditional specialisms. These include volleyball centres, football centres, swimming centres, track and field centres, *wushu* centres, wrestling centres, etc.

Army Sports

Physical education and sports were included in the training and educational programme of the people's army in the early days of its inception. Sports activities, including multi-event meetings, were organized by the Red Army even in the thick of fighting against the enemy's "annihilation campaigns". During the Long March they managed to find time for basketball games, walking and running races, and other sports competitions. Mao Zedong, Zhou Enlai, Zhu De and other leaders of the Communist Party and the army joined the rank and file in these activities. After the liberation, still greater importance was attached to developing sports in the armed forces. Most companies in the army have their own basketball teams and courts; some of them also have teams for other sports, such as football, volleyball, track and field events, and badminton. In recent years army units across the country have made energetic efforts to popularize the National Standards of Physical Fitness. By 1983 a total of 3,000,000 persons had met the standards for different events and different classes. About a million soldiers and officers regularly took part in long distance runs that year.

Sports in Schools

Sports in primary and middle schools and institutions of higher learning, which have a total enrolment of over 200 million, constitute the key aspect of the national sports programme. According to the "Resolution on Improving the Health Condition of Students in Schools of All Grades" promulgated by the Government Administration Council in 1951, educational departments of the government at all levels and schools of all grades were required to "take effective measures to improve physical education, and to do everything they can to increase facilities for sports and recreation, so as to intensify the students' physical training." The Ministry of Education stipulated that physical training courses be made obligatory for all students from the first grade of primary school up to the second year at college or university. Students in most schools were required to attend two periods of PE classes and to participate in extra-curricular sports activities at least twice each week. In addition, they are expected to take part in morning exercises, exercises during the breaks between classes and eye

Chief Commander Zhu De (jumping smasher) playing volleyball at Yan'an in the 1940s.

Sport

Children of the swimming class training in the Physical Training School for Juvenile Amateurs of Beijing Gymnasium. *(Photo by Wang Hongjun)*

exercises every day. During the 1980s, outlay for sports in schools in all parts of the country has increased. According to statistics taken from 14 provinces, municipalities and autonomous regions, nearly 5,000,000 yuan was allocated for this purpose in 1980. During the period from 1981 to 1983, upwards of 10 million students passed the National Standards of Physical Fitness tests every year.

To popularize sports, improve athletic performance and cultivate sports talent among the children, various forms of spare-time junior sports training have been developed. In 1983, there were 2,672 sports schools of different types, mostly for spare-time training, and 396 selected sports classes, with a total enrolment of 237,031. By 1985, 18,000 schools had been selected for specializing in one or several kinds of sports in which they were traditionally strong, with 2,000,000 students taking part in spare-time training.

Sports among Women and Pre-school Children

The broad masses of women in old China, subjected to centuries-old feudal bondage, were deprived of the opportunity to participate in sports activities. In New China they are provided with favourable conditions and today many of them are regularly involved in sports activities. Moreover, they have displayed their talent in athletic endeavours. During the period from 1949 to 1983, women athletes attained or approached world level in 16 events, or over one-third of the 42 events in which China was involved in world competitions. During the period from 1949 to 1985, Chinese athletes won 205 world titles in major international contests. Of these, 83 (or 40 per cent) were claimed by women.

Children are the hope of the nation and their

physical and intellectual development receives great attention. Sports and physical education for pre-school children consist of three aspects: (1) Activities in the family, which form the basis of sports for children and are given increasing attention along with the improvement of the people's material life and the raising of their educational level; (2) Activities in the kindergarten, which constitute the principal form of children's sports. There are now over 10 million kindergarten children who are gaining all-round physical development through sports, games, sunbaths, airbaths and other activities; (3) Activities in society at large, which are a supplement to, and a development of, sports for children. Many parks, children's palaces and amusement centres have laid out children's playgrounds complete with various kinds of equipment for games and recreation.

Sports for Senior Citizens

With the improvement of the people's material and cultural well-being and the extension of their life span, China has a growing population of aged people. Their sports activities have received ever greater attention and in the past few years they have gradually developed from a scattered state to organized forms. The year 1983 saw the establishment of the Chinese National Committee for the Study of Problems of Old Age and the Chinese Association of Sports for Senior Citizens. Tens of thousands of sports teams have been formed by senior citizens in both towns and countryside for jogging, ball games, cycling and other

Li Chenggang won five gold medals at the 3rd Far East and South Pacific Disabled Games. *(Photo by Ding Putian)*

870

physical exercises. In 1983, some 10 million of the country's 80 million old people persisted in physical training. The first sports meets for elderly people were held in many places in 1978. Sports exhibitions were given by senior citizens at both the Fourth and the Fifth National Games held in 1979 and 1983 respectively.

Sports for the Disabled

Sports of this category are managed by the Chinese Association of Sports for the Disabled. They are given much attention and support from the State Physical Culture and Sports Commission, the Ministry of Education, the Ministry of Public Health, the Ministry of Civil Affairs, the Ministry of Labour and Personnel, the All-China Federation of Trade Unions,

the Central Committee of the Communist Youth League, the Chinese Association of the Blind and the Deaf-Mute, the Red Cross Society of China and other organizations and departments. PE classes and extra-curricular sports activities are arranged at schools for the blind and for deaf-mutes. National tournaments were held in 1957 and 1959 for deaf-mutes in such events as track and field, swimming and basketball. At the Third Far East and South Pacific International Games for the Disabled in 1982, Chinese athletes claimed six gold, 12 silver and seven bronze medals. Li Chenggang, a young man who lost his right arm and right leg in his childhood, gained five golds at the Games, setting a world record in the process. China was represented by 24 athletes at the Third International Games for the Disabled in 1984. They gained 24 silver medals and seven of them surpassed world records in nine events.

NATIONAL TRADITIONAL SPORTS

CHINA is a multi-national country with 56 ethnic groups. In the long course of historical development they have amalgamated as the Chinese nation and by working together they have created a splendid culture, including a wealth of national traditional sports.

Wushu

Wushu, also called *wuyi* (martial arts) or *Gungfu*, is a priceless cultural heritage of the Chinese nation. Evolved through long years of practice, it is the most important of all traditional Chinese sports. With extremely rich contents, it falls into numerous schools and styles. Formerly a *wushu* school or style was named after its founder or the region, mountain or river where it originated and developed, or according to its technical features. Today *wushu* is generally divided into five categories: *quanshu* (barehand exercises), *qixie* (exercises with weapons), *duilian* (dual combats), group performances, and combat using offensive and defensive skills.

After the founding of New China, the ancient art of *wushu* was restored, explored, systematized and improved. Being extensively practised by the people, it regained its brilliance. A national meet was held in 1953, at which 145 athletes demonstrated 332 traditional sports items, including 139 barehand *wushu* exercises. In 1956 the state leader Liu Shaoqi issued the call: "We must study and reform our country's traditional sports such as *wushu* and *qigong*. We must examine their scientific value and popularize them by various means." In 1957 *wushu* was listed by the State Physical Culture and Sports Commission as an event for official competitions. A national *wushu* meet was

An exercise in *qigong* when being stabbed in the throat.
(Photo by Xie Jun)

staged in 1960. *Wushu* and archery championships were held in 1963 and 1964, with competitors coming from 15 and 19 units respectively.

A notice was issued in January 1979 by the State Physical Culture and Sports Commission to explore and systematize the heritage of *wushu*. A national *wushu* exhibition meeting was held in May that year, with 510 *wushu* exercises of different styles performed by 284 athletes from 24 provinces, autonomous regions, municipalities directly under the central government, and the regions of Hong Kong and Macao. By 1982 the number of *wushu* disciplines for competition had increased to 16 for both the men's and women's divisions. These were: group exercises, optional *changquan* routines, *taijiquan*, *nanquan*, broadswordplay, swordplay, spearplay, cudgelplay, traditional barehand exercises (Categories 1–4), traditional single-weapon exercises, traditional double-weapon

A foreigner doing *taijiquan*.

exercises, traditional soft-weapon exercises, and dual combats. (In 1984 all the traditional barehand exercises were listed as "other barehand exercises" and all the traditional exercises with weapons were grouped as "exercises with other weapons".) Since 1977 Chinese *wushu* delegations have visited over 30 countries, and *wushu* experts have been invited to give lectures in many parts of the world. Consultations among representatives from 18 countries and regions during an international *wushu* invitational tournament held in Xi'an in 1985 led to the formation of a preparatory committee for the establishment of an International Wushu Federation. This marked an important step in bringing Chinese *wushu* to the sporting world.

Apart from *wushu*, the Han (the largest ethnic group in China) have such traditional sports as rope jumping, shuttlecock kicking, pole climbing, stone-weight lifting and various kinds of popular games.

Traditional Sports among the Minorities

Since the founding of New China much importance has been attached to developing sports among the minority peoples: e.g., the "pole ball" game of the Gaoshan people; "flowerpot jump" of the Bais; the spinning top played by the Lahus; the Miao sport of shooting with crossbows and special races in which young women run along the course while putting on colourful dress; the Manchu game of "whipping a spinning top on ice"; the Ewenki practice of lassoing

horses; the Dong *huapao* game in which contestants scramble for iron hoops discharged from a cannon; the Xibo art of archery; the horse race, "sheep chase" and "girls give chase" games among the Uygur, Kazak and Tajik nationals; and the Tibetan horsemanship and yak race. Each with its own unique features, these sports and games have a fascination for the people of different nationalities. Traditional sports activities such as shooting with a crossbow, playing the "chicken-feather ball" and "throwing the husk-filled pouch" which used to be popular among the Kucong people, who lived a secluded life deep in the mountain forests in Yunnan before the Liberation, have been revived and developed. Wrestling is now widely practised by the Yi and Hani in Yunnan. The springboard, swing and wrestling activities among the Koreans, which used to serve as performing arts, have now developed into competitive sports.

Some favourite sports and games among the minority peoples have become important features of their traditional festivals. The *Wangguo* (pray-for-a-good-harvest) Festival of the Tibetan people, the "Fair on the Third Day of the Third Lunar Month" among the Zhuang, the Bai people's "Country Fair in the Third Lunar Month" and the Miao "Jamboree on Flower Mountains" are all marked with sports performances and contests. Among the biggest festivals of the minority peoples are the following:

The "Nadam" of the Mongolian people

Taking place in July–August every year, it features wrestling, horse-racing, archery and other sports activities. The size of the competitions varies with the number of entries, a larger one drawing as many as 2,000 adult wrestlers and 800 juniors.

The Torch Festival of the Yi nationality

Starting from the 24th day of the sixth month by the lunar calendar, it lasts 1–3 days with traditional sports like wrestling, horse-racing, archery and bull fights held in the daytime. After nightfall, hundreds of young men and women dressed in their holiday best gather round bonfires to sing and dance. The festivities are highlighted by the burning of pine torches. They also afford the young people a good opportunity for courtship.

The Water-Sprinkling Festival of the Dai

Lasting for three days, this falls around 10 days after the Qingming Festival (or mid-April by the solar calendar). The first day is devoted to dragon-boat races and *yilahe* dances. On the second day, people go about sprinkling clear water on one another to exchange greetings and express their wish for a good harvest. The third day is the New Year's Day of the Dai people, who celebrate it by throwing good luck pouches at each other – practised by the young people also as a means of courtship.

The First National Minority People's Traditional Sports Meeting was held in September 1982 in Huhhot, capital of Inner Mongolia. Over 800 athletes of the country's 55 minority nationalities presented 68 traditional sports items at this extravaganza, which drew an aggregate audience of 800,000. Over the past 36 years the minority peoples have produced a number of fine athletes who have won gold medals or achieved creditable results at domestic and international contests in such events as javelin throwing and archery. Among the competitors at the Fifth National Games in 1983, there were 201 belonging to 23 minority groups, some of them giving outstanding performances. Of the 12 Chinese who conquered Mt. Qomolangma (Everest) – the world's highest peak – on two occasions, nine were Tibetans.

IMPROVING ATHLETIC PERFORMANCE

To improve athletic standards, New China lavishes care on the broad masses of athletes and provides favourable conditions for developing their talent. Applying themselves to close studies of sports techniques and scientific training, Chinese athletes have constantly achieved good results in athletic performance and rid China of the extremely backward status in world sports competitions. In their first-ever full-scale participation in the Olympics – the 23rd Games in 1984 – Chinese athletes won 32 medals to put an end to the humiliating history in which China never made any impression in Olympic competitions. During the period from 1956 to 1985, Chinese athletes broke or surpassed world records on 295 occasions and captured 205 world titles. Altogether 880 persons were involved in these record-breaking or title-winning feats.

So far China has gone in for over 60 sports events, including track and field, table tennis, volleyball, football, basketball, badminton, tennis, field hockey, softball, baseball, handball, bocci, bowling, golf, gymnastics, rhythmic gymnastics, sports acrobatics, weightlifting, swimming, diving, water polo, synchronized swimming, water skiing, motorboating, rowing, canoeing, yachting, windsurfing, model ships, underwater swimming, speed skating, ice hockey, figure skating, skiing, biathlon, mountaineering, shooting, archery, fencing, Chinese-style wrestling, wrestling (free style and Greco-Roman), judo, *wushu*, equestrian sports, modern pentathlon, aero-models, gliding, skydiving, radio transmitting, cycling, motor-cycling, Chinese chess, *weiqi* (*go*), bridge, angling, homing pigeons, roller skating, shuttlecock kicking, dragon-boat racing and military pentathlon. It has reached or approached the world's advanced levels in one-third of these events, namely, table tennis, badminton, volleyball, diving, gymnastics, sports aerobatics, weightlifting, mountaineering, *weiqi*, shooting, skydiving, aeromodels, archery, water polo, women's fencing, basketball, softball, chess, certain disciplines in track and field, and model ships.

Table Tennis

It was in table tennis that China won its first-ever world title, and it has retained its glory for a number of years.

China joined the International Table Tennis Federation in 1953. At the 20th World Table Tennis Championships held in the same year, China's men's team was placed 10th in Category A and its women's team 3rd in Category B. Four years later, both teams were promoted to third place in Category A. At the 25th World Championships in 1959, Rong Guotuan won the men's singles title to earn for his country the first gold medal in a world table tennis competition. At the 26th World Championship in 1961, China

Rong Guotuan won the men's singles title at the 25th World Table Tennis Championships in 1959 in Dortmund in the Federal Republic of Germany. *(Photo by Zhang Hesong)*

At the 36th World Table Tennis Championship in 1981, the Chinese team swept the board, taking all seven gold medals and five silver. Four Chinese players contested the men's doubles title, which was won by Guo Yuehua and Xie Saike.

won three golds in the men's team, the men's and women's singles competitions, and four silvers and eight bronzes, thus putting an end to the Japanese domination over world table tennis. He Long, the then Minister in charge of the State Physical Culture and Sports Commission, urged the Chinese table tennis players to remain sober-minded and go on striving for new victories. "Now that you have got on the back of a tiger," he said by way of analogy, "it will be hard for you to get off – you have no way to back down!" Later, Chinese players maintained their lead by taking three golds at the 27th Worlds and five at the 28th. The table tennis players suffered a heavy loss during the 10 tumultuous years of the Cultural Revolution. Although they still displayed their strength by winning four golds at the 31st Worlds in 1971, three at the 32nd Worlds in 1973 and two at the 33rd Worlds in 1975, much of the edge had already been taken off them by then. It was only after the overthrow of the "Gang of Four" in 1976 that Chinese table tennis gained a new lease of life. At the 34th Worlds in 1977 China came out with four golds (one of them being shared with a foreign player), four silvers and 6 bronzes. At the 35th Worlds the Chinese women's team made a clean sweep of all the women's titles in addition to contributing to the victory in the mixed doubles, but the men players suffered defeats in the team as well as the singles and doubles events. However, at the 36th Worlds China swept all the seven titles on offer in addition to five silvers – a feat unparalleled in all the 55 years of world table tennis. It claimed six gold medals each at the 37th and 38th Worlds.

All in all, Chinese players won 276 medals includ-ing 48 golds, or more than half the total of 84, in the 12 world fixtures they competed in, with a total of 121 players mounting the victor's podium to take the top prizes. In the field of table tennis there have been exchanges with more than 100 countries and regions, involving a total of over 10,000 persons. Nearly 200 Chinese coaches have gone abroad to pass on their skills and knowledge to some 70 countries and regions.

Volleyball

The rules and methods of play for the six-a-side game was introduced in July 1950 and China became a provisional member of the International Volleyball Federation in 1952 and a full member in 1954. It made rapid progress in the game during the first half of the 1960s. Although its men's and women's teams were both placed ninth at the World Championships in 1962, it already boasted world-class players like Li Zongyong on the men's team and Cao Qiwei on the women's, both being honoured as "Outstanding Players". In 1965 China achieved good results in international competitions, both the national and the Beijing men's teams triumphing over the Japanese team in three straight games, and the national team finishing third at an international invitational in Riga in the Soviet Union.

Chinese volleyball suffered a serious setback during the 10 chaotic years of the Cultural Revolution. At the 1974 World Championships, the men's and women's teams finished 15th and 14th respectively. The national team was reorganized in 1976. With things set right after the overthrow of the "Gang of

The Chinese Women's Volleyball team won the title at the 23rd Olympic Games. They won championships at five successive world competitions.

Four," the volleyball game was quickly restored and developed. At the 1977 World Cup, the men's team was placed fifth and the women's team came fourth. At the World Championships in 1978, they ranked seventh and sixth respectively. At the Asian Championships in 1979 and the 1981 World Cup preliminaries, both the men's and women's teams emerged the winners. At the 1981 World Cup finals, the women's team ascended the rostrum while the men's team was placed fifth. The women's squad again won the title at the 1982 World Championship, while its male counterpart finished seventh. The women spikers came off victoriously in the World Super-Three tournament involving China, the United States and Japan in 1983. They remained at the top in the 23rd Olympic Games in 1984 and continued their winning streak at the 1985 World Cup, besides taking a two-match series from a world all-star team. In 1986 they successfully defended their world championship title to register a fifth straight victory in world competitions, thus adding a brilliant page to world volleyball history. Among them have emerged Sun Jinfang, who was named "Best Player," "Outstanding Player" and "Best Setter" at world tournaments; Lang Ping, who was honoured as an "Outstanding Player" and reputed

to be one of the three strongest women spikers in the world; Cao Huiying, who was awarded prizes for her dauntless spirit and as a best player and blocker; and other world-famous stars like Zhang Rongfang, Chen Yaqiong and Chen Zhaodi.

Football

Football standards were steadily improved after the founding of New China and within 10 years China became a leading power in Asia. In 1956 the Chinese team defeated the Indian national squad. Two years later, both the Beijing team and the "August 1" team of the People's Liberation Army managed to tie, at identical scores of 1–1, with the Soviet national team who had triumphed at the 16th Olympic Games. The Chinese team won some of their friendly games with internationally strong teams from the Soviet Union and Hungary during the years 1959 and 1960, and they took the top spot in the four-nation tournament in 1960, which involved China, Korea, Vietnam and Mongolia.

Chinese football experienced several setbacks in the 1960s, particularly during the years of the Cultural Revolution, and was revived only after the downfall

Lang Ping, main attacker of the Chinese volleyball team, making a smash in the finals at the 23rd Olympic Games.

of the "Gang of Four" in 1976. There were increasing contacts with the world soccer community, and good results were achieved in some international tournaments in the 1980s. At the Olympic preliminaries held in Singapore in February 1980, China registered two wins, two draws and one loss. At the World Cup Asia–Oceania Zone Qualifying Tournament, the Chinese side defeated Hong Kong, Japan, Macao and the DPR Korea to emerge the winner of Group 4 and qualify for the Zone final. On that occasion Rong Zhixing was chosen as Best Striker and Li Fusheng as Best Goalkeeper. Then, in their third match in the Asia–Oceania Finals, which lasted from September 1981 to January 1982, China beat Asian champions Kuwait 3–0. In 1984, they were placed second at the 8th Asian Cup and received a special award for good sportsmanship while their full-back Jia Xiuquan was awarded prizes as Best Player and Best Shooter of the tournament. China won the title at the 24th Asian Youth Championship in 1985 and subsequently reached the top eight at the World Youth Championship. A Chinese eleven took third place in the football contest of the World University Games in 1985. Women's football has also been catching on in recent years. In 1983, China for the first time hosted an international women's football invitational tournament.

Basketball

Basketball standards were quickly raised after the birth of New China. During the years from 1953 to 1957, Chinese basketball teams were involved in 283 international matches, in which they registered 163 wins, seven draws and 113 losses. In other words, they won or tied 60 per cent of all the matches they played during this period. In 1958, the Chinese national teams, the "August 1" and the national youth squad registered 30 wins, three draws and five losses during their tours of the then United Arab Republic, Switzerland, France and the Soviet Union. Chinese basketball rose to a new height in 1959, when the men's team scored an 86–77 victory over Bulgaria, placed fourth at the World Championship, and an 82–64 win over European champion Czechoslovakia while the women's team drew twice with European champion Bulgaria and got the better of Hungary. Triumphs over strong European contingents were achieved not only by the national team, but also by the "August 1" and local teams like Beijing, Hebei and Heilongjiang. China's Vanguard Team came first at the first men's basketball tournament among the public security sports organizations of socialist countries. The "August 1" men's team took the title in the basketball tournament for the armed forces of friendly countries in 1961. Both the men's and the women's teams of China came off victoriously in the basketball competitions at the Games of the Newly Emerging Forces (GANEFO) in 1963. China won the four-nation women's basketball tournament in 1964 which involved China, Romania, Hungary and France. In 1966, the Chinese women won all the matches they played during their visit to Romania, Poland and France. They won two and lost one of the three matches they played with the 1965 world runner-up Czechoslovakia.

China's legitimate seats in the International Federation of Amateur Basketball and the Asian Basketball Confederation were restored in 1974 and 1975 respectively. The Chinese men's team made a triumphant debut at the Asian Championship in 1975, while its female counterpart ascended the rostrum at the Asian fixture the following year. The men's team successfully defended its title at the 9th Asian Championship in 1977 to qualify for the 8th World Championship involving the world's top 14. Except in 1982, when they were beaten by the South Koreans and had to settle for second place at the 9th Asian Games, the Chinese men retained their Asian title all through the years from 1978 to 1984. But in 1985 they dropped to third place at the 13th Asian Championship. The women's team, after going through a reshuffle, captured the crown at the 9th Asian Games in 1982 and was placed third after the Soviet Union and the United States at the 9th Worlds in 1983. They defeated the US team by a narrow margin to win the top honour at an international women's basketball invitational held in Shenyang that year.

Badminton and Other Ball Games

Badminton

This game began to gain vigorous development in the 1950s and a national team was set up in 1954. Some good results were achieved in the years following 1963, with China winning four matches and losing one in its encounters with Indonesia, twice Thomas Cup winner. The Chinese team won all the six matches they played with the Indonesian team during their visit to Indonesia in 1964. During their tours of the world's leading badminton powers of Denmark and Sweden in 1965, they won all but one of the 34 matches they played – and all in two straight games. Yet during this period China was excluded from world competitions because her rightful seat in the International Badminton Federation was not restored for more than 20 years. For this reason some of the foreign press regarded the Chinese badminton team as the "uncrowned king" and maintained that "without China's participation, no world championship is worthy of its name."

In 1978 the Chinese Badminton Association joined the World Badminton Federation inaugurated in Hong Kong. The following year, Indonesia challenged China to a match to be held in some neutral place – to settle the question as to who was the *de facto* world champion. Both the men's and women's teams of China accepted the challenge and, fielding young players in the duel, they came out victorious at 6–0 and 5–0. The two men's teams of the badminton powers had another competition in 1980, with China winning 5–4.

After the merger of the International Badminton Federation (IBF) and the World Badminton Federation in 1981, China became a full member of the new

The Chinese Badminton team beat the Indonesian team, the winner of 7 world titles, 5–4 and won the 12th Thomas Cup on 21 May 1982. Han Jian was playing.

The Chinese Women's Badminton Team took the Uber Cup on 17 May 1984 when they participated for the first time in the competition. Li Lingwei taking part in the match.

IBF. At the First World Games for Non-Olympic Sports held in July that year, China won four of the five events contested. In their first-ever appearance at the All-England Open in 1982, China's shuttlers took two titles in the women's section. In the same year the Chinese men's team achieved their first-ever triumph in the 12th Thomas Cup, a world tournament of the highest order, to become a "king with a crown". On this occasion Luan Jin outplayed Rudy Hartono, eight-times All-England champion, while Han Jian defeated "badminton king" Liem Swie King. At both the 1983 All-England and the 3rd World Cup, China accounted for three of the five titles at stake. In 1984 the Chinese women's team gained the Uber Cup. At the 1985 All-England fixture, up-and-coming shuttler Zhao Jianhua won the men's singles while Han Aiping and Li Lingwei took the first two places in the women's singles in addition to sharing the doubles honour. At the 4th World Championships that year, Han Jian and Han Aiping landed the men's singles and the women's singles titles respectively, while Han Aiping in partnership with Li Lingwei captured the women's doubles gold. At the 5th World Cup, the women's singles crown went to Li Lingwei, and the women's doubles title fell to Lin Ying and Wu Dixi. China walked off with both the Thomas and Uber Cups in May 1985.

Tennis

This game began to develop after the birth of New

China, but only on a limited scale. It has made some headway in a number of cities in recent years, with the number of courts increased to over 200, or double what it was previously. In 1980 China hosted its first major international tennis event – the Canton Grand Prix Tennis Classic, which drew well-known players from more than 10 countries. The Chinese women's team took part in the Federation Cup for three years running (1981–1983), each time managing to advance to the second round. The men's team won the title at the Ghafar Cup in 1983.

Softball and baseball

The first national tournaments were held in 1956 for both softball and baseball. Women's softball has made rapid progress in the 1980s. The Chinese team came out the winner in the 2nd Hong Kong International Women's Softball Invitational in 1983. Its captain, Li Nianmin, was honoured as "crack pitcher" and player Hua Jie was awarded the "best batter" prize. In 1985, China asserted her superiority by triumphing in both the China–Japan–USA Women's Softball Championship and the Second Junior Softball World Championship. In 1986 she finished second at the 6th World Women's Softball Championship.

Handball

The first national handball exhibition was held in 1957. The Chinese Handball Association was formed in 1979 and it was affiliated to the International Handball Federation the next year. China's men's team was placed second at the 3rd Asian Championship in 1979. The girls' team defeated all Asian rivals in the Third Junior World Championship preliminaries in 1981 to earn a place in the finals, thus taking the lead in realizing the aim of "reaching the top in Asia and breaking into the front ranks in the world" as cherished by all Chinese athletes, handballers included, and they did fairly well in the finals ending up in sixth place. The Chinese men's team dominated the handball competition in the 9th Asian Games in 1982. Its female counterpart took a bronze medal at the 23rd Olympic Games in 1984.

Track and Field Events

After the founding of New China, this sport was promoted on an extensive scale, with some initial achievements. At the 12th University Summer Games in 1954, Mongolian runner Yitaotege finished fifth in the men's 5000 m, while Yang Shaoshan came sixth in the men's shot put. In 1956 woman thrower Shi Baozhu hurled the discus to 50.93 m, which was the world's seventh best that year. In 1957 Zheng Fengrong cleared 1.77 m to smash the world women's high-jump record. At the GANEFO in 1963, China netted 20 gold and 18 silver medals in track and field

Chinese walking athletes Xu Yongjiu (left, the winner of the World Cup of women's 10 km walking in 1983), Yan Hong (2nd from left) and Guan Ping. *(Photo by Zhang Liure)*

competitions. The year 1965 witnessed three Chinese topping the world in athletics performance: Chen Jiaquan running the men's 100 m in 10 seconds (hand-timing), Ni Zhiqin scaling 2.25 m in the men's high jump, and Cui Lin clocking 13.5 sec. in the men's 110m hurdles. Chinese athletes reached the world's top 10 in such other events as the men's marathon and the triple jump, and the women's 100 m, 80 m hurdles, high jump, long jump, shot put and discus.

At the 8th Asian Games in 1978, China claimed 12 titles in track and field competitions to surpass Japan in gold medal standing. At the Asian Track and Field Meet in 1979, China gained seven golds and eight silvers to take second place in team total. At the Liberty Bell International Track and Field Meet held in Philadelphia, USA, in 1980, China took five golds, one silver and four bronzes to reach third place in team total. In 1981, 12 Chinese athletes were selected for the Asian team for the 3rd World Cup, where they were placed second, fourth, fifth and sixth in different events. At the 11th World University Games held in the same year, Zou Zhenxian snatched the triple-jump title with a performance that placed him third in world ranking, while Zhu Jianhua and Liu Yuhuang were runners-up in the men's high jump and long jump respectively. Primo Nebiolo, President of the International Amateur Athletics Federation (IAAF), pointed out that China had attained the world's advanced level in jumping events. By decision of the IAAF Congress, the Chinese Track and Field Association was promoted from Group B, which had entitled it to four votes, to Group AA in which it had the right to eight votes, thus gaining equal footing in decision-making with other major national associations affiliated to the IAAF. In 1983, Zhu Jianhua twice improved the world men's high jump record with 2.37 m and 2.38 m. A Chinese women's walking team won the 10 km race at the World Cup, with Xu Yongjiu capturing the individual title in the same race. At an international high-jump contest in the Federal Republic of Germany in 1984, Zhu Jianhua cleared 2.39 m to topple the world record for the third time, but he had to settle for a bronze at the 23rd Olympics. Yan Hong and Guan Ping bettered the world marks in the women's 5000 m and 10000 m walks on three occasions. In 1985 the women's walking team successfully defended its 10 km title at the World Cup, with Yan Hong and Guan Ping finishing first and second. That year seven Asian records were smashed by Chinese athletes. At the Sixth Asian Track and Field Meet, China topped the medals table, both in the number of gold medals and the total number of medals, by winning 19 golds, 15 silvers and seven bronzes.

Weightlifting

This was where China made the first-ever breakthrough in her effort to get on a par with the rest of the world in sports. In 1956 Chen Jingkai jerked 133 kg in the bantamweight class to set a world record, the first in Chinese sports history. In the ensuing years, ending in 1964, Chen renewed world records on eight more occasions and collected gold medals in the friendly competition at the Third World Youth Festival and the Moscow Cup weightlifting individual championships. At the GANEFO in 1963, Chinese weightlifters collected four golds and two silvers. World records were rewritten in 1965 by four lifters in four events on six occasions, and in 1966 by four lifters in six events on nine occasions.

In 1977, 18 Chinese weightlifters achieved results equal to those of the top ten in the world championships that year. China won the team title both at the 3rd Asian Weightlifting Championships in 1981 and in the weightlifting contests at the 9th Asian Games in 1982. It was placed sixth in team total at the 36th World Championships in 1982. Chinese strongman Wu Shude thrice bettered world records. At the 23rd Olympics in 1984, Zeng Guoqiang, Wu Shude, Chen Weiqiang and Yao Jingyuan each won a gold medal, while Zhou Peishun and Lai Runming each took a silver. At the 17th Asian Championships in 1985, the Chinese team netted 10 golds, 11 silvers and three bronzes to place first in team total, in gold medal standing as well as in the total number of medals won. At the 39th Worlds that year, China earned two

Cheng Jinkai broke the world record for clean and jerk for the level of 56 kilos with a weight of 133 kilos at the Sino-Soviet Friendship Competition of Weight Lifting in Shanghai on 7 June 1956. This was the first world record set by a Chinese athlete. *(Photo by Bi Pinfu)*

silvers and six bronzes to rank fourth in team total, which was the best result it had ever achieved in a world weightlifting tournament.

Gymnastics and Acrobatics

Gymnastics

This sport has made much progress over the last three decades and more. Particularly in recent years, Chinese gymnasts have achieved repeated successes in international competitions.

The Chinese Gymnastics Association joined the International Gymnastics Federation (FIG) in 1956. Two years later, its men's and women's teams were placed 11th and seventh respectively at the 14th World Championships. They rose to the fourth and sixth places respectively at the 1962 Worlds. At the GANEFO they both finished second in team competitions while taking eight golds, three silvers and 10 bronzes in the all-round and individual events, with woman gymnast Wang Weijian accounting for half of the gold medals. At the Asian GANEFO in 1966, China carried off the team titles and the all-round honours in both the men's and the women's competitions. It repeated its team triumphs at the 7th Asian Games in 1974, in addition to winning six golds, eight silvers and two bronzes for the all-round and individual events. In 1978 China hosted its first

Ma Yanhong, the winner of the women's uneven bars title at the 23rd Olympic Games, performing on the balance beam at the 5th National Games.

international invitational tournament in Shanghai, at which its performers took 12 gold medals. At the 8th Asian Games that year, both the Chinese men's and women's teams ascended the rostrum for the second time while making a clean sweep of the top three places in the men's and women's all-round competitions. All in all they gained 10 golds, eight silvers and five bronzes on that occasion. At the 20th Worlds in 1979, they came fifth and fourth in the men's and women's team events respectively, while Ma Yanhong became a co-champion in the uneven bars event to earn the first-ever world gymnastics title for her country.

Practically all world gymnastics competitions in the 1980s featured successful performances by Chinese gymnasts. At the 5th World Cup in 1980, they snatched two golds, one silver and one bronze. At the 11th Universiade in 1981 they took five golds, three of which went to Li Ning. At the 21st Worlds that year they were third and second respectively in the men's and women's team competitions besides winning two golds and three silvers in individual events. At the Sixth Grand Prix of Paris Gymnastics held in the same year, Tong Fei single-handedly netted six medals, including three golds, two silvers and one bronze. At the 6th World Cup in 1982, China claimed seven titles, six of which to the credit of Li Ning. At the 9th Asiad in the same year, Chinese gymnasts secured 12 titles, including those for the

men's and women's team competitions. The men's team mounted the rostrum at the 22nd Worlds in 1983. At the 23rd Olympics in 1984, the Chinese gymnastics team gained five golds, four silvers and two bronzes. These included a silver for the men's team, a bronze for the women's team, five medals (three golds, one silver and one bronze) captured by Li Ning, a gold and a silver earned by Lou Yun, a gold by Ma Yanhong and a silver by Tong Fei. In the Code of Points issued by FIG for 1985–1988, four unique moves are named after Chinese gymnasts – Floor Exercise "Li Yuejiu", Pommel Horse "Tong Fei", Rings "Li Ning" and Parallel Bars "Li Ning". These make up one-fifth of all the moves named after gymnasts of various countries. At the 23rd Worlds in 1985, China won three gold medals in addition to a silver for the men's team competition. At the 7th World Cup in 1986, Li Ning took the all-round event, while he and his team-mates earned three golds in the men's individual competitions.

Sports Acrobatics

China became a member of the International Sports Acrobatics Federation in 1979. The following year it made its debut at the Fourth World Championships and came out with 11 bronze medals. At the world tournaments in the ensuing years, it registered the following medal counts (in the order of gold, silver and bronze): 4–7–8 at the 3rd World Cup in 1981, 1–5–6 at the 5th Worlds in 1982, 10–8–1 at the 4th World Cup in 1983 and 9–7–7 at the 5th World Cup in 1985.

Aquatic Sports

Swimming

This sport advanced rapidly after the birth of New China. Wu Chuanyu won the 100 m backstroke at the First International Friendly Youth Games in 1953. The next year he finished second in both the backstroke and butterfly events at the 12th World University Games. During the years from 1957 to 1960, world breaststroke records were created five times by Qi Lieyun, Mu Xiangxiong and Mo Guoxiong. At the 1963 GANEFO, the Chinese swimming team came first in total points. Up to 1966, some 20 swimmers had reached the world's top 20.

Liang Weifen won the 100 m breaststroke at the international invitational held in Hawaii in 1980. At the 9th Asiad in 1982, Chinese swimmers took three golds. At the Nanning International Invitational in 1983, they ended up with four golds, 14 silvers and 18 bronzes. In some major national and international competitions in 1985, the results achieved by ten Chinese swimmers in eight events were rated among

Wu Chuanyu, the first Chinese swimming gold medal winner, gained the title for the men's 100 m backstroke at the 1st International Youth Friendship Games in 1953 in Bucharest.

Diving

Chinese divers gained one gold, four silvers and three bronzes at the 1963 GANEFO. At the 1966 Asian GANEFO they took four golds and four silvers. At the 7th Asiad in 1974 they won four gold medals. Up to 1977, at least 28 Chinese divers had produced new, highly difficult stunts not yet included in the international diving table, such as forward $4\frac{1}{2}$ somersaults; backward, reverse or inward dive $3\frac{1}{2}$ somersaults; forward $1\frac{1}{2}$ somersaults 4 twists; backward $1\frac{1}{2}$ somersaults $3\frac{1}{2}$ twists; reverse $1\frac{1}{2}$ somersaults $3\frac{1}{2}$ twists. Not until 1980 were these dives included in the new FINA diving table, which was to become effective as from September 1982. In 1979, after seeing China's woman diver Liu Meichuan perform the backward $3\frac{1}{2}$ somersaults tuck, American diving coach Sammy Lee remarked: "Right now only two men divers in other countries of the world can do this dive. The fact that here in China there are four divers, including the ladies, who can do it should be written into the *Guinness Book of World Records.*" China swept all the gold and silver medals on offer in both the men's and women's diving competitions at the 8th Asiad in 1978. Five Chinese performers entered the top six in the diving competitions at the 10th Universiade in 1979, with Chen Xiaoxia emerging the victor in the women's platform event to win the first-ever world diving title for China.

In 1980, following the restoration of China's legitimate seat in the International Amateur Swim-

the top 50 in the world. Jin Fu's performance in the men's 100 m breaststroke, for instance, was equal to that of the 12th on the world list, while the results in two men's relay events were the best in Asia.

Yan Ming won the gold medal for the women's 400 m freestyle at the 10th Asian Games. *(Photo by Cheng Zhishan)*

Zhou Jihong won the title for women's platform diving at the 23rd Olympic Games. *(Photo by Liu Xinning)*

ming Federation (FINA), there were reciprocal visits between swimmers and divers of China and the United States, with the Chinese side winning 45–43 and 68–65 in two dual meets. At the Martini International Diving Competition held in London in November 1980, China took three golds, including one for their team victory, and a silver medal. At the 2nd World Cup in 1981, Chinese divers earned three golds. They did the same at the 11th Universiade that year, gaining a silver medal into the bargain. At the Canada–USA–Mexico invitational diving tournament in 1982, China came off with nine gold medals. At the 3rd World Cup in 1983, they outscored the US team, which had made a clean sweep of all the gold medals at the 4th World Championships, to come first in the overall team points, in the women's team event and in women's springboard and high diving, in addition to taking two silvers and two bronzes. At the 12th Universiade in the same year, Lu Wei and Shi Meiqin swept the board in the women's diving events. At the 23rd Olympics in 1984, China captured one gold, through Zhou Jihong, one silver, through Tan Liangde, and one bronze, through Li Kongzheng. At the 4th World Cup in 1985 China gave the best-ever performance by carrying off six of the seven titles contested. At the 5th World Swimming and Diving Championships in 1986, Gao Min and Li Yihua took the first two places in the women's springboard diving, while Chen Lin and Lu Wei emerged the top two in the women's platform event.

Water polo

The first national water polo contest was held in 1955. The Chinese team shared honours with the Indonesian team when they played each other in 1964. China won the title at the Asian GANEFO in 1966, finished second at the 7th Asiad in 1974 and came first at the 8th fixture in 1978. It was placed 10th at the 10th Universiade in 1979, first at the Malta Invitational in 1980, 8th at the 11th Universiade in 1981, and 10th at the 1982 World Championships after qualifying through the Asian preliminaries for the first time ever. It retained its title at the 9th Asiad in 1982, finished 7th at the 12th Universiade in 1983, and 9th at the 23rd Olympics in 1984.

Rowing

This sport was initiated in 1953. Chinese rowers won three gold medals at the Asian GANEFO in 1966. China became a member of the International Federation of Rowing Societies (FISA) in 1973. It took one gold, one silver and one bronze at the World University Rowing Competitions in 1981; five golds and a silver at the East Asian Rowing Championships in the same year; four golds and six silvers in the rowing contests at the 4th Universiade in 1982; all four gold medals at stake in the 9th Asiad the same

year; eight of the 10 golds offered at the First Asian Rowing Championships in 1985; and two sixth places at the 14th World Championships.

Canoeing

This sport was started in 1955. At the 14th World Canoeing Championships in 1978, Chinese canoeists reached the semi-finals in three individual events. At the Mexico City International Canoeing Meeting held in the same year, they were placed third in three disciplines. At the 15th Worlds in 1979, they advanced to the semi-finals in all the men's events. At both the 1980 and the 1982 Hong Kong Asian Invitational they won the team title and 14 of the 15 individual events contested. At the East Asian tournament in Japan in 1980 they took five golds, two silvers and one bronze.

Motorboating

The sport was officially listed as a competitive event in 1956. At the First International Navigational Sports Meeting held in Poland that year, China came off the team winner in one event. At the Second International Navigational Sports Meeting in Varna, Bulgaria, in 1957, she carried away one gold, three silvers and three bronzes. At the 1982 World OB Class Motorboating Championships, Chinese athletes were placed fifth in total score. In 1985 two Chinese surpassed a world record in motorboating.

Yachting

This sport was started in 1956. At the 9th Asian Games in 1982 China was sixth in the one-man OK Class and eighth in the two-member crew Fireball Class event. She was placed eighth in the two-member crew 470 Class at the Second Asian Championships in 1983.

Windsurfing

The first national competition was held in 1981. China finished fourth at the windsurfing competition at the 9th Asiad in 1982. In 1983, Chinese women windsurfers took the first two places in overall standing at the 1983 Kent Asian Windsurfing Gold Cup in Hong Kong. At the Hong Kong Open that year, China claimed two golds, three silvers and one bronze. At the 8th Siam World Cup the Chinese women's team took four golds and four silvers, while Tang Qingcai of the men's team was named Best Athlete. At the 11th World Championships in 1985, China was second in total score, with Zhang Xiaodong claiming two golds and one bronze.

Model ships

China took up this sport in 1954 and joined the World Organization for Model Shipbuilding and Model Ship Sport (NAVIGA) in 1981. It won a gold, two silvers and a bronze at the 2nd World Championships that year. At the 3rd World Endurance Championships in 1982, three Chinese advanced to the finals in three categories. At the 3rd World Championships in 1983, Chinese athletes won four gold and three silver medals, breaking two world records in the process. In 1984 China earned one world title and surpassed two world records. At the 4th Worlds in 1985 it took four golds while two Chinese contestants renewed two world records on three occasions. In domestic competitions that year, five hobbyists set four world records on five occasions.

Underwater swimming

A national underwater swimming team was formed in 1959. In its friendly encounters with France and Switzerland in 1982, it won nine of the 16 events contested. At a triangular meeting of the three nations the following year, it accounted for 14 of the 21 titles on offer. Chinese underwater swimmers surpassed one world record in 1983 and two in 1984.

Wang Jinyu, who broke the world record for 5,000 m speed skating on flatlands in the World Tournament in 1965, during a 5,000 m speed skating match. *(Photo by Liu Zhiwei)*

Winter Sports

Speed skating

China became a member of the International Skating Union in 1956 and made its maiden appearance in

Swimming in winter in Harbin, Heilongjiang province.

world championships the next year. It finished second in overall team points, while its male skater Wang Jinyu landed the all-round title at the six-nation invitational held in Alma-Ata in 1959. At the 53rd World Championships that year, Chinese men skaters took a silver and came ninth in the all-round event, and at the 17th World Women's Speed Skating Championships China accounted for the ninth and the 13th places in the all-round competition. At the 1961 Worlds it came fourth and eighth in the women's and men's all-round respectively. At the nine-nation invitational that year, Wang Jinyu beat Holland's world champion H. V. Grift to wrest the all-round title. At the 1962 Worlds, Wang finished third in the 1500 m to earn the reputation as "Asia's best speed skater", while one woman skater was placed fourth and two male competitors came fifth and sixth in the all-round competitions. In a friendly duel with the Soviet Union that year, Wang Jinyu turned in the world's best performance on the flat. At the 1963 World Championships Luo Zhihuan came first in the 1500 m to win the first speed skating gold for China, creating a new Championship record in the process. In addition, both Luo Zhihuan and Wang Jinyu smashed the world record in the men's individual all-round event. The women skaters came away with one silver and a sixth place in the all-round event. Wang Jinyu chalked up another global best for 5000 m speed skating on the flat at the 1965 Worlds. At an international contest in Austria in 1985, Liang Xiaoping had a double win in the women's all-round and the 3000 m race, while Zhang Qing emerged the winner in both the women's 1000 m and 1500 m events.

Ice hockey

The first national tournament was held in 1953 and the first indoor artificially frozen rink was built in 1968. China participated in eight world championships during the period 1972–1983. Except for its promotion to Pool B in 1979 and 1982, it played in Pool C throughout these years. At a world invitational held in the United States in 1982, China beat Japan, drew with the USA and lost to Canada to finish second. At that time both the US and the Canadian teams belonged to Pool A.

Figure skating

China appeared in the world championships for the first time in 1980. At the Budapest International Competition in 1984, Xu Zhaoxiao captured the single skating crown. At the 12th World University Winter Games in 1985, Zhang Shubin carried the day in the men's single skating to earn China's first figure-skating gold in a world tournament.

Skiing

China had its first skiing meet in 1957. Of the 94 entrants in the men's slalom at the 14th Winter Olympic Games in 1984, 47 finished the whole course, including three Chinese who finished 29th, 30th and 33rd respectively. In the women's slalom, China accounted for the 19th and 20th places. To promote the sport, several skiing grounds have been rebuilt and new ones constructed in Jilin and Heilongjiang province in the last few years.

Board Games and Bridge

Weiqi (Go)

As an ancient board game, weiqi has undergone accelerated development since the founding of New China. During the Northern and Southern dynasties (420–589) the game spread to Japan, where playing skills have now reached a very high level. There have been frequent exchanges between the weiqi circles of China and Japan since 1960. Playing 30 handicap games against a visiting Japanese delegation that year, Chinese players holding Black managed only two wins and one draw. In 1965 Chen Zude became the first Chinese to overcome a Japanese 9-dan master in a game played on equal terms. During the years from 1974 to 1979, Nie Weiping played 25 games with 19 Japanese masters including 9-dan players Shukaku Takagawa, Hideyuki Fujisawa, Utaro Hashimoto, Shiro Ishi and Shoji Hashimoto. The results were 16 wins, two draws and seven losses, which meant a winning average of 68%. In the China–Japan Women's Weiqi Duel in 1978, Kong Xiangming beat the well-known Japanese player Kobayashi Chizu with an overwhelming advantage of 3–0. For this the Japanese go players called her "the world's No. 1 woman player de facto." In 1980, Kong beat Japan's Yoshimi Ninami to become the first woman player in the world to get the better of a Japanese 9-dan master. At all the annual world amateur go championships held in the years from 1979 to 1985 with the exception of the 1980 fixture, the titles went to Chinese players

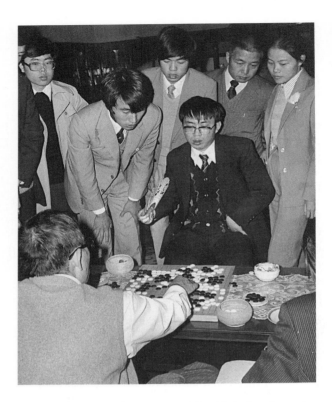

Go-chess (weiqi) player Nie Weiping (sitting) exchanged views with his Japanese opponent Hideyuki Fujisawa after he had won the game. (Photo by Cheng Zhishan)

Nie Weiping, Shao Zhenzhong, Cao Dayuan, Ma Xiaochun, Wang Qun and Wang Jianhong. In the final match of the China–Japan Super Weiqi Series lasting from October 1984 to November 1985, Nie Weiping finished off Hideyuki Fujisawa after having beaten Koichi Kobayashi and Nasao Kato, thus bringing the year-long battle to a triumphant end. The victory over the "super-class" players of Japan was a historical breakthrough; it marked the first step towards realizing China's hope of outstripping Japan in the field of weiqi. After that, in the China–Japan duel in 1986, the Chinese team came off the victor with 31 wins against 25 losses.

Chinese chess

This ancient Chinese game is very popular in Asia, particularly its south-eastern parts. With the establishment of the Asian Chinese Chess Federation in 1978, an Asian Cup Championship has been held once every two years since 1980. China carried off the men's team title in the first two fixtures, while woman player Xie Siming captured the individual title twice in succession.

Chess

The first exhibition matches were played in 1956. Playing 24 matches against a Soviet team in 1963, the Chinese side managed only one win – registered by Huang Xinzhai in his encounter with International

Liu Shilan is the first woman International Grandmaster
of chess in Asia. *(Photo by Chen Jie)*

was placed fourth and the men's team came eighth. Wu Minqian finished second at one of the International Women's Interzonal Tournaments in 1985 to become one of the eight qualifiers for the Women's Candidates Tournament – and to earn the title of International Master.

Bridge

This game was listed as a competitive event in 1980. The next year saw China affiliated to the International Bridge Federation. At the Sixth World Open Tournament in 1982, Wang Junren and Lu Yulin were placed 15th in a field of 360 pairs. The Chinese women's team came fifth at the 28th Far East Team Championship in 1985.

Mountaineering

The modern sport of mountaineering began to develop after the birth of New China. By 1985 Chinese mountaineers had conquered three mountain peaks above 8,000 metres in altitude – Qomolangma, Xixabangma and Cho Oyu; seven peaks above 7,000 m – Mt October, Muztagata, Kongur Tiubie, Gongga, Lenin, Tomur and Naimona Nyi; and over 30 peaks above 6,000 m. Up to 1985, 12 climbers had reached the summit of the "Peak of the Globe" – Mt Qomolangma; 54 had climbed up to 8,500 m and above; 140 had gone upwards of 8,000 m; and many world records have been set by both men and women mountaineers. To mention a few:

At 4:20 hours on the morning of 25 May 1960, Wang Fuzhou, Gongbu and Qu Yinghua reached the top of the world's highest peak Mt. Qomolangma (8,848.13 m) from the north side for the first time in human history.

On 27 May 1975, Sodnam Norbu, Panduo, Lotse, Kunga Pasang, Hou Shengfu, Samzhub, Cering Dorje, Darphuntso and Ngapo Khyen made the second ascent of Mt Qomolangma from the north side. This was the world's largest group of climbers ever to reach the highest peak on earth. Moreover, Panduo was the first woman in the world to get to the top of Mt Qomolangma from its north face.

Since the 1950s China has organized joint expeditions with mountaineers from the Soviet Union, Japan and other countries. It will continue to arrange mountaineering activities in co-operation with other countries.

Mountaineering tourism

A mountaineering tourist organization was set up in 1980 by the Chinese Mountaineering Association to provide foreign mountaineering expeditions with transport, board and lodging, equipment, guides and other services. Up to now 40 peaks in nine mountain areas have been opened to foreign visitors. These

Master Zagorovsky. In 1965 China won two of the nine matches they played against the Soviet team, with both Liu Wenzhe and Zhang Donglu triumphing over International Grandmaster Krogius. Qi Jingxuan gave a good account of himself, managing one win and one draw in his two matches with Soviet International Master Shipov. China was admitted into the Fédération Internationale des Echecs (FIDE) in 1975. In 1977 she was placed second at the 2nd Asian Team Championship. At the 23rd Chess Olympiad in 1978, the Chinese team finished 18th. Liu Wenzhe and Liang Jinrong earned the title of International Master in 1980. In the same year the women's team made its debut at the Olympiad, where it was placed fifth and aroused the attention of the world chess community by forcing a draw on the Soviet world champions. The following year saw Liu Shilan, An Yanfeng and Qi Jingxuan winning the title of International Master. At the FIDE Zone 10 (South-East Asia and Oceania) Ladies' Chess Tournament in 1981, Liu Shilan accomplished a rare feat, notching 14 straight wins to earn the title. At the zonal tournament the following year she was placed third to break into the world's top eight and gain the title of International Grandmaster. China took the top honour at the 5th Asian Chess Championship in 1983. At the 1984 Chess Olympiad the women's team

Wang Fuzhou (right), Gongbu (a Tibetan, middle) and Qu Yinhua.   *(Photo by Chen Jun)*

include the world's No. 1 Mt Qomolangma and its sister peak Mt Zhangzi (North Peak), world No. 11 Mt Gasherbrum No. 1, world No. 12 Mt Broad, world No. 14 Mt Xixabangma, and other mountain peaks like Gongga, Muztagata, Kongur, Kongur Tiubie, Anyêmaqên, Bogda and Siguniang. By the end of 1985, China had received mountaineering tourist groups from Japan, New Zealand, Great Britain, France, the Federal Republic of Germany, Italy, the United States and other countries.

Aeromodels – Amateur Radio – Cycling – etc.

Aeromodels

This sport gained rapid progress after the founding of New China. During the period from 1959 to 1985, 24 world records were broken or surpassed by 61 persons on 64 occasions. In 1981 China was placed second in both the F1B and F1C team events at the World Free-Flight Championships. In recent years Chinese athletes have won four world titles – in the F1B team event at the 1983 World Championships, in the F2B competition at the World Control Line Circular Flight Championships in 1984, and in two events at the 22nd World Free-Flight Championships

in 1985. In 1984 two world records were surpassed in home competitions.

Gliders

The Chinese Gliding Team was set up in 1960. In a dual contest with a team from the Federal Republic of Germany, one of the strongest in the world, China's Zhang Quansheng earned a respectable second place.

Skydiving

China was placed seventh in team total at an international competition held in Bulgaria in 1955. During the years from 1958 to 1965, 22 world records were surpassed by 70 skydivers on 41 occasions, while a number of spectacular items were created for exhibition purposes. At the 3rd World Relative Work Skydiving Championships in 1979, Chinese jumpers finished fourth in two individual events. At the 15th World Championships in 1980, Chinese women parachutists were placed fourth in team total in addition to finishing second in group precision jumps, while their male counterparts were sixth in team total. At the 2nd World Cup in 1983, Li Rongrong captured the all-round crown in the women's competition. All in all, China earned 47 individual titles in

15 international contests during the period 1978–1982.

Amateur radio

This sport got started in 1952 and has since undergone steady development. China collected three golds at the 2nd International Fast Transmitting Friendly Tournament in 1956. At the 1958 fixture it came first in team total as well as in eight of the nine individual events contested. At the 27th Yugoslavia Amateur Radio Direction Finding Championships in 1983, China came off with four titles and five second places. At the 2nd World Amateur Radio Direction Finding Championships in 1984, it was placed second in three events and third in one.

Cycling

This sport is very popular in China. Chinese cyclists won two golds at the 1963 GANEFO; one silver and four bronzes at the 8th Asiad in 1978; and three golds and one silver at the 10th Asian Championships in 1982. At the World Championships in 1982, Zhou Zuohui broke into the top six. In the cycling competitions at the 12th Universiade in 1983, three Chinese riders finished third, fifth and sixth respectively, while two others finished fourth in different disciplines. At the 11th Asian Championships which took place in the same year, China won three gold medals, two of which in the person of Lu Yu'e, who toppled two Asian records. At the World Championsips in 1984, Zhou Suying finished third in the women's sprint.

Motorcycling

The sport was initiated in 1952. The Chinese men's team came third at the 1955 International Moto-cross. At the 1980 All-Japan Moto-cross Grand Prix,

China came second in team total for international "A" class. At the 2nd International Moto-cross in 1982, China finished first in team total in the 125 cc class and claimed the first three individual places in the same event.

Shooting, Archery and Fencing

Shooting

At the Beijing International Shooting Friendly Contest in 1955, China was placed fourth in team total and took one gold, three silvers and five bronzes in individual events. At the 7th Asiad in 1974, Chinese shooters garnered four golds, six silvers and three bronzes while coming third in team total. The year 1975 saw six persons improving on world records on nine occasions. At the 3rd Asian Championships that year, China clinched 13 titles and came first in total score. At the World Clay-Pigeon Shooting Championships in 1981, two gold medals came China's way. At the 43rd World Shooting Championships in 1982, they got one gold, three silvers and six bronzes, surpassing two world records in the process. At the 9th Asiad that year, they gained eight golds and topped the table in team total. Of the 32 gold medals competed for at the 5th Asian Championships in 1983, China accounted for 17 while improving one old world record and creating four new ones. At the 23rd Olympics in 1984, Chinese shooters Xu Hai-

Li Shulan broke the world record for women's 30 m double-round archery with 628 points at the Games of the New Emerging Forces in Djakarta in November 1963. *(Photo by Tang Likui)*

Xu Haifeng at the men's free pistol shooting match at the 23rd Olympic Games. He was the gold medal winner of this event. *(Photo by Guan Tianyi)*

887

feng, Li Yuwei and Wu Xiaoxuan each earned a gold, while Wang Yifu, Huang Shiping and Wu Xiaoxuan each took a bronze, with Wu setting an Olympic record into the bargain. One world record was surpassed in 1985.

Archery

Between 1959 and 1966, seven marksmen and women surpassed 12 world records on 28 occasions. Woman archer Li Shulan alone accomplished the feat 11 times in addition to contributing to team records on six occasions. At the 1963 GANEFO archery competitions, China was the winner in the women's team event and second in the men's team event, while Li Shulan won four individual honours. Six world records were broken 13 times by six persons between 1974 and 1979. At the 1st Asian Cup Championships in 1980, the women's team won five of the six events contested, while the men's team ended up with a bronze. At an international tournament held in Romania that year, China captured both the men's and women's titles as well as five individual events. At the 31st World Championships in 1981, China took a bronze in the women's team competition and won two golds in individual events. At the 23rd Olympics in 1984, Li Lingjuan and Wu Yanan improved seven Olympic records, with Li taking a silver in the process.

Fencing

As a modern sport, fencing is still young in China. At the 32nd World Championships in 1975, Fang Yujie managed a win over 1973 world women's foil champion Nirinova of the Soviet Union. China snatched four golds and four silvers at the 8th Asiad in

Luan Jujie, gold medal winner for women's individual foil at the 23rd Olympic Games.

1978. Luan Jujie picked up a silver at the 29th World Youth Championships that year, then took another silver at the 36th World Championships in 1981, in which China was placed seventh in the women's team event. The women's team came fifth at the 37th World Championships in 1982 and first at the 12th Universiade in 1983. Luan Jujie emerged the winner in the women's foil competition at the 23rd Olympics in 1984.

SPORTS ORGANIZATIONS, PERSONNEL AND FACILITIES

To develop physical culture and sports in New China, organizations for sports administration have been set up in the People's Government at all levels. Meanwhile, many popular sports organizations and institutes for research in sport sciences have been established. Various measures have been taken to step up the expansion of sports contingents, and energetic efforts have been made to increase sports facilities and equipment.

Sports Organizations

These fall into three main categories:

Physical Culture and Sports Commissions of the Government at Various Levels

These function as governing bodies in the field of physical culture and sports. The main tasks of the State Physical Culture and Sports Commission are: to follow the general and specific policies of the Communist Party and the State, exercise unified leadership and supervision over physical culture and sports throughout the country, give guidance to the work undertaken by different kinds of popular sports organizations, and support the activities of the Chinese Olympic Committee. Local governmental commissions in the provinces, autonomous regions, municipalities directly under the Central Government, prefectures, cities and counties are responsible for work in their respective administrative areas. Sports organizations also exist in trade unions, the Communist Youth League system, educational departments and army units.

The All-China Sports Federation and the Chinese Olympic Committee

The former is a national popular sports organization uniting sports people throughout China for the development of physical culture and sports in the country. Formed through the reorganization of the former China National Amateur Athletics Federation (CNAAF), it has its branches in all the provinces, autonomous regions, municipalities directly under the Central Government, prefectures, cities and counties. Sports associations have been formed by people of different trades and at the grassroots level. All the existing national and trade-by-trade associations dedicated to 40 individual sports, as well as the sports commission of the People's Liberation Army, are members of the All-China Sports Federation. The Chinese Olympic Committee is a nationwide popular sports organization whose aim is to publicize and promote the Olympic Movement and its ideal. It is affiliated to the International Olympic Committee as the sole organization representing the Olympic Movement in China. The Taipei Olympic Committee is a local organization representing China's Taiwan Province.

The Chinese Sports Science Society

This is a national popular academic organization formed by those working in the field of sports science and techniques. It is a component part of the Chinese Scientific and Technological Association. Since its establishment in 1980, its membership has grown to over 5,000. Today it has 10 branches specializing in different sciences and 24 local chapters at the provincial level – all actively engaged in academic activities.

Another national sports organization is the Chinese Sports Press Association.

Sports Personnel

In the early days of the People's Republic two major measures were taken to bring up the country's sports personnel. First, to unite the old sports workers and help them master new knowledge and acquaint themselves with the people's sports undertakings so as to give full play to their ability. And second, to draw a large number of cadres from the Youth League and the armed forces who were to serve as the backbone in sports work. In the three decades and more since then, a system for bringing out sports talents has gradually

been established, contributing to the growth of sports contingents in China, in both quantity and quality.

The development of sports contingents in New China has been closely linked with the training of sports talents of various kinds. A three-level training system has begun to take shape, comprising the sports teams at the grass-roots level (primary and middle schools), the spare-time sports schools and the elite teams. The whole structure may be regarded as a "pyramid of sports talents" in China.

The base of the pyramid

This refers to the vast numbers of sports teams and training centres at the grassroots level, primary and secondary schools specializing in one or two sports in which they are traditionally good, and ordinary spare-time schools for children. Since 1980, a total of 23,070 reserve athletes have been produced by schools specializing in certain sports. Among them 15,715 persons have been admitted into key spare-time sports schools (including key classes at ordinary spare-time sports schools) at prefectural or county level, provincial sports schools or sports-oriented middle schools; 1,270 persons have been selected into sports teams of different provinces, autonomous regions, municipalities directly under the Central Government, and the armed forces; and 2,312 have been enrolled at physical culture institutes.

The middle layer of the pyramid

This refers to the sports schools, sports-oriented middle schools and key spare-time sports schools (including key classes at ordinary spare-time sports schools). There are many different kinds of key spare-time sports schools. Some of them provide board and lodging so that the students can live, study and train together, spending half the day on general knowledge courses and the other half on athletic work. Some key spare-time sports schools have developed into sports-oriented middle schools that are jointly run and administered by sports commissions and educational departments, with PE teachers appointed by the former and other teachers supplied by the latter. Up to the end of 1983, 67 sports-oriented middle schools staffed with 790 full-time coaches had been established, with a total enrollment of 7,807 students. In some places there have appeared a form of vocational sports school of the secondary grade, which offers a four-year course for producing reserve forces for elite sports teams as well as PE teachers for primary schools. By 1983 the number of such schools had grown to 27, with 5,710 students and 979 full-time coaches.

The vertex of the pyramid

This refers to the elite sports teams representing the

provinces, autonomous regions, municipalities directly under the Central Government, different trades and the armed forces – the best of them representing the country in international competitions.

The State also attaches much attention to running physical culture institutes at the collegiate level for the training of specialized sports personnel. There were 13 such institutes in the whole country in 1983. These formed a nationwide training network together with the Sports College under the People's Liberation Army, the Beijing PE Teachers College and the PE departments under 116 institutes of higher learning.

By relying on the broadly-based three-level training system and the sports schools mentioned above, New China has trained a growing number of sports talents to augment various kinds of sports teams and achieve better results in athletic performance.

Sports Facilities and Equipment

In old China there were only 26 more or less standard stadiums and gymnasiums. Other sports facilities were also few and far between. Swimming pools, for instance, numbered only 101 and were mostly poorly equipped. China today boasts more than 410,000 sports grounds of various descriptions. These include over 500 standard stadiums and gymnasiums, or about 20 times as many as in old China; and some 2,200 newly built swimming pools and indoor swimming stadiums, more than 20 times the pre-liberation figure. The largest of these new modern sportsgrounds is the Beijing Workers' Stadium, which has a seating capacity of 80,000, and the biggest gymnasium is Beijing's Capital Indoor Stadium seating 18,000 spectators. Eleven sports training centres have been built in different parts of the country to cater to the needs of elite teams.

During the 36 years and more of its existence, New China has made rapid progress in the manufacture of sports equipment. Not a few products have earned a widespread reputation and their supply to the international market often falls short of demand. Quite a number of products have been approved for use in official international competitions. The racket rubbers and sponges approved by the International Table Tennis Federation for use in international matches in the years 1982–1983, for instance, included 17 types of Chinese products. China's FRIENDSHIP brand of rubbers and sponges, regarded as "mysterious weapons" by foreign players, are now available on the world market. Having been acclaimed by ITTF President Roy Evans as "the world's top-class products", they sell extremely well in such countries as the United States, the Federal Republic of Germany, Japan and Australia. Table tennis balls bearing Shanghai's DOUBLE HAPPINESS and Guangzhou's DOUBLE FISH brands were adopted for use in international tournaments as early as the 1970s. Other items approved by the international federations con-

cerned include footballs and basketballs of Dandong's ARROW brand, volleyballs of Shanghai's TRAIN brand and barbells of Shanghai's HERCULES brand. So far, 350,000 footballs of Tianjin's GOLD CUP brand have been sold in 67 countries and regions of the world. During the World Soccer Cup preliminaries in 1981, the Kuwaiti team placed an order for 2,000 GOLD CUP balls. At a Conference of Manufacturers called by the International Weightlifting Federation in 1981, China-made barbells were rated among the world's best; the collars on both ends of the barbell, in particular, were considered most advanced. During a badminton contest in England in 1981, the International Badminton Federation had some English players try out seven famous brands of shuttles. Marks were given to each brand, and finally the AEROPLANE brand made in Shanghai came first with 100 points. Subsequently, IBF President Craig Reedie specially wrote a letter to the Shanghai Shuttlecock Factory to congratulate it for turning out products of the world's top standard. That year, upwards of a million shuttles of the AEROPLANE brand were marketed to 50-odd countries but still they were not enough to meet the demand. Among other world-famous products are traditional Chinese items like *weiqi* (*go*) pieces of Yunnan and *Longquan* swords of Zhejiang, and innovative items like standard sporting pistols, hydraulic foldable basketball stands and volleyball net posts without guys. Some sportswear and shoes of Chinese make also find a market overseas. The QINGTING (DRAGONFLY) brand sports shoes made in Beijing are favoured by shuttlers in Thailand, Indonesia and other countries, and are used as models by Japanese manufacturers.

International Sports Exchanges

Although China went in for modern sports as early as the late nineteenth century, up to the founding of the People's Republic sports exchanges with other countries had been few and far between. The only major international tournaments in which she was involved were ten Far Eastern Games during the period from 1913 to 1934 and three Olympiads between 1932 and 1948. Since the birth of New China in 1949, particularly during the 1980s, there have been frequent exchanges with sporting communities in other lands. These have taken the forms of paying mutual visits, sending people abroad for international sports competitions, training, study or teaching, and inviting foreign experts to give lectures or take up coaching in China. These activities have helped strengthen China's ties with the various international sports bodies and promote its friendship with the sports circles and people in other parts of the world. Up to now China has joined 65 world sports organizations including the International Olympic Committee, and 33 Asian ones. It has carried out over 7,000 sports exchanges with 152 countries and regions, involving a total of

10,000 persons. While attending China's Fifth National Games in September 1983, IOC President J.A. Samaranch pointed out, "China has taken great strides in sports over the last few years. It has become a sporting power commanding worldwide respect."

Developing International Exchanges

As part of the country's foreign relations, China's sports exchanges with other countries are conducted in line with the foreign policies of the State and the needs of sports development in the country. Following this principle and cherishing the hope of promoting friendship and technical exchanges among nations and contributing to the development of world sports and to human progress and peace, the Chinese sports people and athletes have actively increased their contacts with their counterparts in other countries. They have become goodwill envoys of the Chinese people.

During the 1950s, China had frequent sports exchanges with the Soviet Union, Hungary, Czechoslovakia, Bulgaria, Poland, the German Democratic Republic, Romania, Albania and Yugoslavia. The Chinese sports people cherish the memory of this phase of history in which they fulfilled their internationalist duties while receiving support and assistance from their friends. After a break of many years, China's sports exchanges with the Soviet Union and most East European countries have been restored in the 1980s. There were some 50 exchanges of this kind in 1983, involving over 600 people.

China has always maintained close ties with the Democratic People's Republic of Korea in the sports field. In 1983 alone, over 200 people were involved in mutual visits between the sports circles of the two countries.

Sports contacts between China and Japan began quite early. Such contacts have been most frequent in the field of table tennis, contributing to the growth of friendship as well as to common progress in playing techniques.

There have been numerous contacts with Western European countries ever since the 1950s. Sports exchanges with countries like France, Italy, the Federal Republic of Germany and Portugal had begun before the establishment of diplomatic relations. Such exchanges helped increase friendship among the peoples and were conducive to the establishment of diplomatic relations.

In the early 1970s a US table tennis team was invited to China, opening the door to the Sino-American relations which had been severed for over two decades. China's initiative, which eventually led to the normalization of the relations between the two countries, was later acclaimed as "ping-pong diplomacy". Recalling his first reception of the Chinese table tennis team, ex-President Nixon of the United States remarked: "I said then that there are always wins and losses in games but there will be one victor and that is the friendship between the United States and the People's Republic of China.... The ball you play is small but powerful enough to propel the development of Sino-US friendship."

Taking Part in the GANEFO

At the 4th Asian Games in the summer of 1962, the host nation Indonesia upheld justice and refused the sports organization of Taiwan admittance into the Games under the name of "Republic of China". It also refused to grant Israel entry into the event. At this, some people in the governing international sports organization showed their displeasure and arrogantly decided not to recognize the 4th Asian Games. They also withdrew their recognition of the Indonesian Olympic Committee and banned its participation in the Olympic Games for an indefinite period of time. In protest against such a perversity, the then Indonesian President Sukarno initiated the Games of the Newly Emerging Forces (GANEFO). "GANEFO is a world event," he said. "It is demanded not by individual countries but by history." The initiative won widespread support among the Asian, African, Latin American and some European countries. When the big event was held in the Indonesian capital of Jakarta in November 1963, it drew 2,404 entries from 48 countries and regions. China actively supported the idea of holding the GANEFO and sent a sports delegation to it. During the GANEFO competitions Chinese athletes won 66 gold medals and chalked up two world records in the process. Contestants from many other countries displayed their talent by improving their own national records. The Jakarta meet served to promote the friendship and understanding among the newly-emerging countries. Later, in November 1966, the Asian GANEFO was successfully held in Phnom Penh in Kampuchea. Meanwhile, individual sport contests among newly-emerging forces were held in China and some other countries.

Hosting International Tournaments

To promote international sports interflow and raise the level of athletic performance in China, the Chinese government supports the holding of international tournaments in this country and provides them with the necessary facilities. Since its inception, New China has hosted a considerable number of big international events.

International shooting friendly meeting

Held in Beijing in 1955, this involved eight countries: Bulgaria, China, Korea, Mongolia, Poland, Romania, the Soviet Union and Czechoslovakia. To stage the contest a new shooting range covering an area of 250,000 square metres was constructed in Beijing.

The organizational work of the meet and the reception accorded to its participants won the praise of foreign guests.

26th World Table Tennis Championships

Players from 32 countries and regions took part in this world tournament held in Beijing in 1961. To provide for the event, the Beijing Workers' Indoor Stadium seating 15,000 was built and a large amount of organizational work was done. At the end of the championships, Ivor Montagu, President of the International Table Tennis Federation, said: "What really shocked me as something beyond our dream and expectation, and what we really never imagined before coming here, was the profound, genuine feeling of friendship you showed us."

The Afro-Asian Table Tennis Friendship Invitational Tournament

Held in Beijing in 1971.

The 1st Asian Table Tennis Championships

Held in Beijing in 1972.

The Asian–African–Latin American Table Tennis Friendship Invitational Tournament

Held in Beijing in 1973, it was a great, friendly meet for Third World countries, with 569 players from 87 countries and regions participating in it.

Besides, China has hosted international competitions in such events as volleyball, field hockey and archery; world championships in badminton and ice hockey (Pool C); invitationals in track and field, football and swimming; the First Asian Cup Table Tennis Tournament; and invitationals in women's basketball, gymnastics, bridge and other events.

Following an application put forward by the Chinese Olympic Committee on 23 August 1983, a decision was taken by the Olympic Council of Asia (OCA) at its 3rd Congress on 28 September 1984 that the 11th Asian Games be held in Beijing in 1990 and at the 20th Congress of the International Volleyball Federation in 1986, it was decided that the 11th World Women's Volleyball Championship would be held in China in 1990. The Chinese government, sports people and other quarters concerned are now making active preparations for these big sports meetings.

Restoring and Developing Relations with the International Olympic Committee and Other International Sports Organizations

Because of the changes in the international situation, China has traversed a tortuous path in developing its relations with the IOC and other international sports organizations.

The China National Amateur Athletic Federation was recognized by the IOC as early as in 1922. After the founding of New China, the federation was reorganized into the All-China Sports Federation (the Chinese Olympic Committee). Prior to the 15th Olympic Games due to be held in Helsinki in Finland in 1952, the Chinese Olympic Committee declared that it would send athletes to take part in the Games. After some twists and turns, a Chinese sports delegation finally took part in the Helsinki event, with swimmer Wu Chuanyu registering a time of 1:12.3 in the 100 m backstroke. This was the first mark ever left by an athlete of New China in the Olympic Games. In May 1954, at the 49th session of the IOC held in Athens, a resolution was passed, with 23 votes for and 21 votes against, for the continued recognition of the Chinese Olympic Committee. Subsequently, IOC Secretary General Otto Mayer wrote a letter to the COC to notify it of the IOC resolution. However, the local sports organization of China's Taiwan was stealthily listed by Avery Brundage, the American then holding the IOC presidency, among the NOCs recognized by the IOC, without any prior discussions at IOC meetings. Thereafter, the term "two Chinas" appeared again and again in the documents released by the 16th Olympic Games Organizing Committee. A protest raised by the Chinese sports delegation went unheeded. The Chinese Olympic Committee then issued a statement demanding that the IOC and the 16th Olympic Games Organizing Committee correct the above-mentioned mistakes, but the demand was also turned down. To demonstrate its protest, the COC officially declared its non-involvement in the coming games. In 1958, in his reply to a letter from Brundage, China's IOC member Dong Shouyi solemnly pointed out that Taiwan had been Chinese territory ever since ancient times, and refuted Brundage's absurd arguments which were designed to split up Chinese territory. In view of the fact that the IOC and some other international federations – e.g. FIFA (football), IAAF (athletics), IWF (weightlifting), FINA (swimming), FIBA (basketball), UIT (shooting), FIAC (cycling), FILA (wrestling) and the Asian Table Tennis Federation – had accepted China's local sports organizations in Taiwan as "national" bodies in a vain attempt to create a "two Chinas" or "one China, one Taiwan" situation, the Chinese sports organizations declared one after another during the months from June to August of 1958 that they were withdrawing from the respective international federations and that they would sever all relations with those federations until they rectified their errors.

In October 1971 the United Nations Organization decided by an overwhelming majority vote to restore China's rightful seat in the UN. In February 1972 the Sino-US Joint Communiqué was signed, opening a new chapter in the annals of relations between the two countries. In September of the same year, diplomatic relations between China and Japan were restored. Around this time diplomatic relations were established with some other countries as well. In these circumstances, many justice-upholding personalities in the international sports community called for the restoration of China's legitimate seats in international sports organizations. During the years from 1973 to 1978, China's memberships were settled in the Asian Games Federation and the international federations governing fencing, weightlifting, basketball, track and field, gymnastics and wrestling. Meanwhile, China's lawful rights were recognized by 13 Asian sports organizations.

By now the IOC had undergone great changes, its presidency having been taken over by Lord Killanin of Ireland, an international figure enjoying great popularity. He and most IOC members were of the opinion that the question of China's representation in the IOC should be solved and the relations between China and the IOC which had been suspended for over two decades should be restored. The key to solving the problem naturally lay in the Taiwan issue. It is a well-known fact that there is only one China in the world and Taiwan is only a component part of China, and that the sole representative of the Chinese people is the People's Republic of China. Since this fact was recognized by the majority of the IOC leaders, there was room for dialogue. During their visits to China in 1977 and 1978 respectively, the then IOC President Killanin and Vice-President Samaranch further acquainted themselves with the Chinese stand. At the Executive Board meeting of the IOC in March 1979, Killanin pointed out two important facts: First, when the All-China Sports Federation was recognized by the IOC in 1954, it bore the name of "Chinese Olympic Committee". In other words, the All-China Sports Federation was inheriting membership of the past at the time when it was recognized as a National Olympic Committee. Second, in the files of the IOC no record whatsoever could be found about recognizing the "Olympic Committee" of Taiwan. This showed that the thrusting of Taiwan upon the IOC – which had been done by a few people in secret – was illegal. In October 1979, FIFA accepted the Chinese Football Association as its member and decided that the Taiwan football association only use the title "Chinese Taipei" and refrain from using any signs of "Republic of China". Undoubtedly, this fair and reasonable decision produced a positive influence on the IOC in its effort to solve the question of China's representation. In November of the same year, a resolution was passed by IOC members by postal vote, with 62 votes for, 17 votes against and 2 abstentions, recognizing the Olympic Committee of the People's Republic of China as the "Chinese Olympic Committee" whose anthem and flag should be those of the People's Republic of China; while maintaining the recognition of the committee based

IOC President Samaranch (left) awarded Chinese Vice-Premier Wan Li an Olympic gold decoration on 28 April 1986 for his special contribution to the Olympic movement and Chinese sport.

in Taipei under the name of "Chinese Taipei Olympic Committee" whose anthem, flag and emblem should be other than those used then and had to be approved by the Executive Board of the IOC. Thus, after 21 years of struggle, the question of China's representation in the IOC was finally settled.

Opening Up New Vistas in International Sports

Since the settlement of China's representation in the IOC, the Chinese sports people have increased their contacts and exchanges with the international sports community on a still more extensive scale. They have taken part in a series of major international sports activities and opened up new vistas in this domain.

In January 1980, a Chinese sports delegation made its debut at the Olympic Winter Games – the 13th version which took place in the United States. In August of the same year, to demonstrate their opposition to the Soviet invasion of Afghanistan, the Chinese Olympic Committee together with its counterparts in many countries stayed away from the 22nd Olympic Games held in Moscow.

The year 1981 witnessed China's take-off in world sports, with a total of 1,151 Chinese athletes taking part in 55 official competitions at the continental level and above. They won 25 world titles, smashed or surpassed eight world records and equalled three world records. The most noteworthy was the Chinese table tennis team which made history by making a clean sweep of all the seven titles at stake in the 36th World Championships. That year also saw the Chinese women's volleyball team posting their first victory at the World Cup tournament.

In 1982, China achieved its first-ever Thomas Cup triumph at the 12th World Badminton Championship men's team competition. Its women shuttlers

893

made it a double take in the singles and doubles events at the All-England Championships. The women's volleyball team carried off the title at the World Championship. Li Ning gained six golds at the 6th World Cup Gymnastics Tournament – a feat unprecedented in gymnastics World Cup history. China captured 61 gold medals at the 9th Asian Games to top the gold medal standing.

In 1983 China was involved in 73 international contests at continental level and above, winning 39 world titles and breaking or surpassing world records on 17 occasions. The triumph of the men's team in the World Gymnastics Championships and Zhu Jianhua's improvement of the world men's high-jump record on two occasions were something that caused a sensation in the sporting world.

The year 1984 was punctuated with good news about Chinese women race walkers breaking world records one after another. It saw Zhu Jianhua renewing the high-jump world record for the third time, the women's badminton team capturing the Uber Cup, and the Chinese delegation coming home from the Los Angeles Olympic Games with 15 golds, eight silvers and nine bronzes.

A total of 46 world titles went to Chinese athletes in 1985. This was more than they had obtained in any other year before.

International Co-operation in Sports Techniques

Although China is a developing country belonging to the Third World, it has done all it can to help other Third World countries develop their economy and culture, including sports. In the meantime, it has entered into extensive exchanges and co-operation with developed countries in the field of sports techniques.

Up to 1983 China had sent 870 coaches and other sports specialists to 88 countries where they helped promote sporting activities and improve athletic performance. They worked in such fields as table tennis, badminton, gymnastics, volleyball, basketball, football, track and field, weightlifting, cycling, handball, swimming, diving, fencing, *wushu* and judo. Some of the coaches sent abroad were holders of world titles or world records, e.g., table tennis coaches Xi Enting, Liang Geliang and Wang Zhiliang and track coach Ni Zhiqin. After working in France for half a year at the invitation of the French Table

Tennis Association, Xi Enting succeeded in helping the French team, ninth place finisher at the 34th World Championships, to jump to fifth place at the 35th Worlds, the best result achieved by France in international table tennis competitions in 30 years. Xi's contributions won high praise from the French news media.

In its efforts to develop sports and physical culture, particularly to improve the level of technical performance, China has gained support and assistance from many countries. In the 1950s, China received help from the Soviet Union and Hungary in developing such events as football, weightlifting and swimming, and assistance from Poland in advancing the sport of gliding. China has received aid from Japan in developing table tennis, volleyball, *weiqi* (*go*) and judo; from Romania and Poland in rowing and canoeing; from France and Pakistan in fencing and field hockey; and from Japan, Austria and others in skiing. In 1980 alone, experts were invited from The Netherlands, Romania, Japan, Italy, France, the USA, Australia, Pakistan, Switzerland, Venezuela, Spain, Belgium and the Federal Republic of Germany to teach or run coaching clinics in China. That year, Chinese athletes, coaches and judges in such events as basketball, volleyball, track and field, gymnastics, wrestling, motorcycling and skiing were sent to Yugoslavia, Japan, India, Singapore, France, the Federal Republic of Germany, the United States and the Soviet Union to receive training or attend courses run by international sports organizations.

In accordance with agreements on economic and technical co-operation with the governments of other countries, China has, since the 1960s, undertaken to assist in the construction of stadiums, gymnasiums and other sports facilities in these countries. Nineteen projects were completed between 1972 and 1983, including the Mogadishu Stadium in Somalia, the Siaka Stevens Stadium in Sierra Leone, the Nouakchott Olympic Stadium in Mauritania, the Independence Stadium in Gambia, the Damascus Gymnasium in Syria, and sports complexes in Benin, Western Samoa and Morocco. Still under construction are 11 projects in Pakistan, Upper Volta, Burma, Libya and Surinam.

China's aid to other Third World countries also includes sports equipment. Between 1980 and 1982, over RMB¥100,000 worth of balls, rackets, table tennis tables and sportswear of different types was supplied to 30-odd countries for sports development.

LOOKING FORWARD TO THE FUTURE

IN spite of the tremendous progress made over the last 36 years, China is still lagging far behind the world's advanced countries both in the rate of participation in physical training and in the level of performance in most sports. National sports conferences in the last few years have repeatedly discussed plans for sports development in the era of socialist modernization in this country. The objectives to be achieved before the end of this century are: popularizing sports activities in both town and countryside; raising technical performance in sports to the world's top level; building modernized sports facilities; and developing a sports contingent that is both socialist-minded and technically proficient. In a word, China will become one of the leading sporting powers in the world.

Popularizing Sports in Both Town and Countryside

While over half of the population in some economically developed and athletically advanced countries in the world today regularly take part in physical exercises, the proportion in China is only 30 per cent. By the end of the century, this is expected to reach about 50 per cent so that the fitness level of the whole nation will be further improved. There will be marked improvements particularly in the physical shape, quality and functions of young people. The average body height of urban youth is expected to increase by 2–3 cm, their weight by 2–4 kg, and their chest measurement by 2–3 cm. The students' physical qualities and level of sports performance will be the best by Asian standards. To attain these ends, both urban and rural sports will be further communized and spread to all spheres of society and the people's daily life; knowledge of sports will be popularized and athletic standards raised; modern sports will be energetically developed and positive efforts will be made to foster national traditional sports so that China will become a country with the richest and most colourful sports in the world.

Bringing Technical Performance up to the World's Top Level

The Olympic Games are an important stage on which the athletic strength of a country is tested. By the end of this century, China hopes to break into the front ranks in Olympic competitions by attaining or approaching the world's advanced levels in most Olympic events. At present, some of China's strong events (e.g., table tennis and badminton) have not yet been included in the Olympic Games, while athletics and swimming, which account for a large portion of Olympic golds, are the very areas in which China is lagging behind. In order to improve athletic performance quickly, it is necessary to intensify research in the strategies for sports development and to make a good job of sports reform. It is necessary to introduce and utilize in a selective way the world's latest achievements in science and technology, to make full use of electronic computers, to observe and analyse sports training processes through extensive application of new branches of science such as systematology, information theory and cybernetics, and to use advanced ways and means to step up sports training. In doing so, China will give play to its own strong points rather than blindly follow in other countries' footsteps. The three-level sports personnel training system will be steadily perfected, spare-time training will be energetically developed, and the ranks of elite athletes will be expanded and strengthened at various levels, through diversified means and by different forms of training. China will give fuller play to its advantages in sporting events of light categories, in those sports which emphasize dexterity, and in certain female sports. Meanwhile, active measures will be taken to change the backwardness of athletics and swimming within the shortest possible time. As for those sports which are still not very popular in this country, including those which have been newly started here, such as the modern pentathlon, speed skating, figure skating, water polo, handball, tennis, fencing, sports acrobatics and women's softball, necessary means will be provided to speed up their development. Great efforts will also be made to achieve new advances in those sports which do not fetch many gold medals in international competitions, but which – as in the case of soccer – enjoy great popularity both in and outside China.

Building Modernized Sports Facilities

In a circular issued in 1983 by the State Council it was

Sport

pointed out that "the main targets for sports developments, including those for the increase in sports facilities, should be incorporated into plans for social development." The Seventh Five-Year Plan (1986–1990) for National Economic and Social Development adopted at the Fourth Session of the Sixth National People's Congress in April 1986 stipulated that "construction of sports facilities will be properly stepped up. Apart from the key projects undertaken by the State, sports and physical culture facilities should be gradually increased wherever conditions permit." Before the century is out, a number of modernized sports training centres will have been built; in Beijing, adequate facilities will be available for the holding of Asian and Olympic Games. A set of sports complexes for large-scale tournaments will be built in each of those provinces, autonomous regions, municipalities directly under the Central Government – as well as some selected provincial and autonomous regional capitals – which undertake to host the National Games by turns. In North-East China, these complexes will include arenas for Olympic Winter Games.

Developing a Sports Contingent that is Both Socialist-Minded and Technically Proficient

During the remaining years of this century, China will endeavour not only to raise its athletic performance to the world's top level, but also to greatly enhance the ideological consciousness of the athletes and sports workers, increase their cultural and scientific knowledge, and improve their technical and vocational levels. In a word, she will develop a sports contingent with high ideals, moral integrity, general education and a sense of discipline. Intellectual development will be speeded up and great efforts will be made to arm the sports people with modern scientific knowledge. Through various forms of schooling, including refresher courses, training in rotation, correspondence courses and college education, the overwhelming majority of the sports administrators and coaches will attain an educational level corresponding to that of the institutes of higher learning. In the meantime, sports schools and colleges will be developed in order to train specialized sports personnel of a high calibre.

PART IX

MEDICINE AND HEALTH

GENERAL INFORMATION

Since the founding of the People's Republic in 1949, China has taken many measures and effectively transformed the extremely backward medical and health services which had been left over by the old society.

In old China, diseases and epidemics were rampant. The State showed no concern whatsoever for the health of the working people. Various infectious, parasitic and endemic diseases took innumerable lives of the poor. Statistics from 1900 to 1949 revealed 1,160,000 cases of plague, of which 1,030,000 were fatal. Since cholera was first carried into China from abroad in 1820, there had been nearly 100 outbreaks of the disease up to 1948, at least 60 of which were recorded as serious. Smallpox struck every year and epidemics broke out once every few years, taking an annual toll of lives in tens of thousands. Snail fever (schistosomiasis) infested more than two million square kilometres and affected 11 million people. There were frequent epidemic outbreaks of malaria, plaguing many regions in South and South-West China. There were 30 million cases of filariasis, while the incidence of tuberculosis was as high as four per cent of the total population, with a mortality rate of 200 per 100,000. The number of lepers was at least 500,000. Endemic goitre was rife in 1,464 counties of 28 provinces, autonomous regions and municipalities, threatening 278,010,000 people. Keshan disease, an endemic myocardial disorder unique to China, was prevalent in 311 counties in North-East, North-West and South-West China, menacing 82,950,000 people. Other infectious, parasitic and endemic diseases were also widespread and posed a grave threat to the health of the people. Before the founding of New China in 1949, the death rate in the country stood at 25 per thousand, and infant mortality was as high as 200 per thousand. The average life expectancy was approximately 35 years.

The Communist Party of China (CPC) has always been concerned about the health of the working people and had attached great importance to medical and health work. At the time of the founding of the Red Army and the revolutionary bases in the late 1920s, the CPC had started medical and health work amidst the flames of war. Medical workers in revolutionary bases, carrying forward the spirit of revolutionary humanitarianism of healing the wounded and rescuing the dying, accomplished their tasks in extremely arduous conditions. Progressive foreign medical experts and workers, such as Norman Bethune from Canada, Ma Haide (George Hatem) from the United States, and Dwarkanath S. Kotnis from India, arrived in China to offer their services to the Chinese people in their War of Resistance against Japanese Aggression. Apart from treating and saving the lives of large numbers of the sick and the wounded, they also helped train many qualified medical workers.

Since the founding of New China, the People's Government has taken vigorous action to expand the people's medical and health services. The Common Programme of the Chinese People's Political Consultative Conference (CPPCC), approved at the first plenary session of the CPPCC in September 1949, stipulates in Article 48: "National physical culture shall be promoted. Public health and medical work shall be expanded and attention shall be paid to the protection of the health of mothers, infants and children." The 1982 Constitution of the People's Republic of China stipulates in Article 21: "The State develops medical and health services, promotes modern medicine and traditional Chinese medicine, encourages and supports the setting up of various medical and health facilities by the rural economic collectives, state enterprises and undertakings and neighbourhood organizations, and promotes sanitation activities of a mass character, all to protect the people's health." China's health work is aimed at serving the people and socialist construction. In the early 1950s, the People's Government laid down the principles of health work: serve the workers, peasants and soldiers; give priority to prevention; unite practioners of traditional Chinese medicine with those of Western medicine; and combine health work with mass movements.

The principle of "serving workers, peasants and soldiers" clearly stipulates that public health work must serve the majority of the people, thus fundamentally changing the situation in old China, where only a handful of the privileged enjoyed medical and health services. The State has basically solved the problem of medicine and health services for the majority of the people through such measures as free medical service, labour protection and co-operative medical service. The principle of "giving priority to prevention" makes clear the emphasis of China's public health

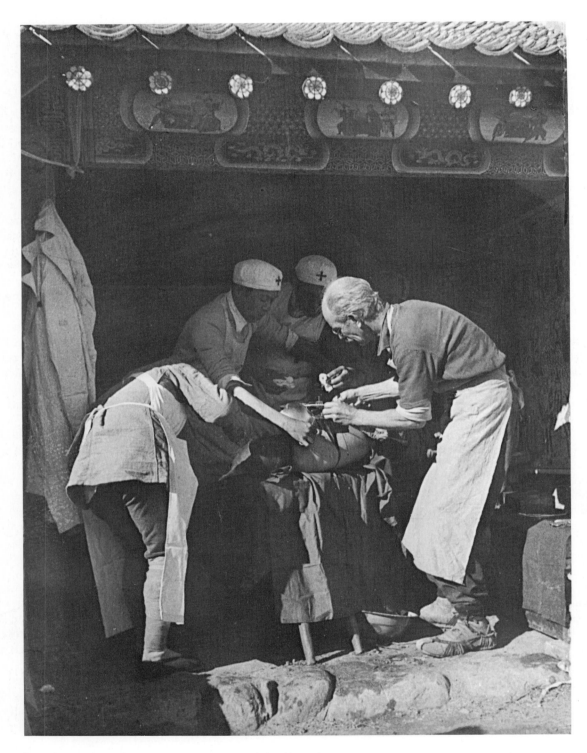

Canadian Dr Norman Bethune operating on a wounded soldier of the Eighth Route Army in the War of Resistance Against Japan.

Preventive inoculation of children in the countryside.   *(Photo from Xinhua)*

work. Effective preventive measures reduce the incidence and spread of diseases, relieve people from the menace of diseases and improve their health steadily. "Unity of practitioners of traditional Chinese and Western medicine" is an important policy in the development of China's medical and health work. Traditional medicine is a great treasure-house of the accumulated experience of the Chinese people of various nationalities in their fight against diseases for thousands of years and has played an important role in the growth of the Chinese nation. Therefore, only by proper handling of the relationship between traditional Chinese and Western medicine and between their practitioners, and by mobilizing all possible technical forces engaged in medical and public health work can China more effectively control diseases and protect the people's health. "Combining public health work with mass movements" is an approach peculiar to China in health work. The broad masses of the people have great interest in and enthusiasm for health work as it has a direct bearing on their well-being. So long as the people understand and master the scientific knowledge of hygiene and throw themselves into the battle with nature and diseases, they will become a powerful force in the control of diseases, transformation of nature and correction of insanitary habits, and

will thus promote the development of public health work. The Patriotic Public Health Campaign has developed on such a basis in New China.

Under the guidance of the principles mentioned above, New China has in the past 37 years established and improved public health institutions from central to local levels, forming a network of medical and health services covering both urban and rural areas; reared an army of medical and health workers consisting of personnel skilled in traditional Chinese medicine, Western medicine, and integrated traditional Chinese–Western medicine, and personnel with higher, secondary and primary medical training and various specialisms; and set up centres for research and education and for the production of pharmaceutical and medical apparatus. Through efforts to control disease in a planned way, some acute infectious diseases have been completely or virtually eliminated, and the state of health of the urban and rural population has improved markedly. The 1982 national census showed a drop in the infant mortality rate from 200 per thousand before 1949 to 34.68 per thousand, and the average life expectancy jumped from 35 to 68 years. Both indicators approached the level of the developed countries.

THE NETWORK OF MEDICAL AND HEALTH SERVICES AND THE PUBLIC HEALTH CAMPAIGN

BEFORE the founding of New China, there were very few public health organizations and facilities in the country. According to statistics, in 1949 China had only 3,670 health institutions, 505,000 doctors and other health workers, 2,600 big and small hospitals, and 80,000 hospital beds. Not only was the number of medical institutions small, but their distribution was also irrational, with the overwhelming majority concentrated in cities and coastal areas. In the vast countryside, where over 80 per cent of the population lived, only a few county seats had hospitals, with poor facilities. Villages had no medical institutions or facilities except a few scattered practitioners.

In order to change the situation, New China has made great efforts in building hospitals and clinics and established a network of medical and health services covering all urban and rural areas of the country (see Table 1). According to 1985 statistics, China had 201,000 health establishments – 54.8 times that in 1949; the number of hospital beds increased to 22,290,000 – 27.9 times that in 1949; medical workers totalled 4,313,000 – an eight-fold increase, including 3,411,000 with lower-level training – 6.7 times that in 1949.

Urban medical insititutions play an important role in China's health services. Since the founding of New China, the State has given priority to the construction and expansion of large numbers of general hospitals

Table 1: Medical and Health Establishments at Different Levels

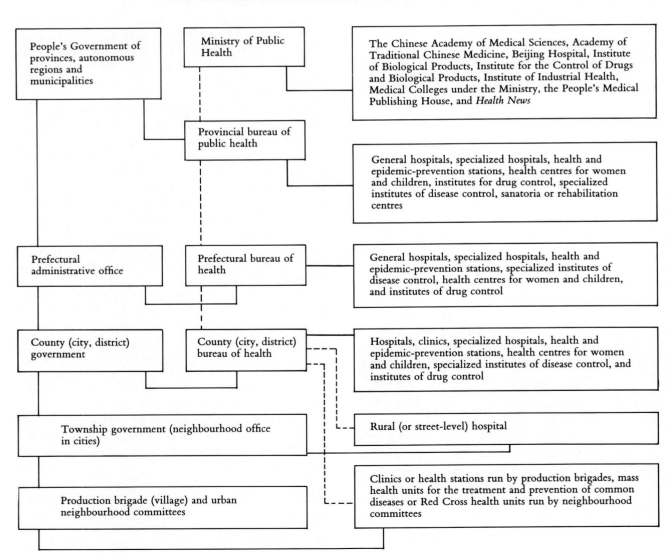

with specialized fields. By 1985, urban hospitals in the country totalled 10,456, with 962,000 beds and 2,242,000 personnel. While building more general hospitals, the State has also set up various specialized hospitals, including those for infectious diseases, tuberculosis, mental disorders, obstetrics and gynaecology, children, stomatology, leprosy, tumours, ophthalmology, chest diseases, and acupuncture and moxibustion. In big and medium-sized cities, in addition to hospitals under municipal and district authorities, there are hospitals and clinics run by sub-district offices or mass anti-epidemic units, or Red-Cross health units under the neighbourhood committees. For example, the capital, Beijing, had 1,178 Red Cross health units in 1985, which treated 928,000 patients from the city proper and the nearby suburbs. Doctors from these health units also regularly attended 15,000 patients with chronic diseases in their homes. These units have played an important role in urban health services at grassroots level.

Over 80 per cent of China's population live in the countryside, and thus the health departments at all levels have always focused their attention on medical and health services in the rural areas. By the late 1950s, medical and health institutions had been set up at county and district (commune) levels throughout the whole country; and the 1960s witnessed the establishment of grassroots health units at most of the production brigades (administrative villages each comprising one or several villages). By 1985, China had 49,158 county and township level hospitals with 1,267,000 beds, 2,032 county health and epidemic-prevention stations, 1,823 county health centres for women and children, 997 county institutes of drug control, and 2,071,000 medical personnel. In addition, 87.3 per cent of the villages throughout the country had set up clinics (health units). The establishment of the health service network has ensured the most needed medical assistance, prevention and health services and family planning for the 800 million peasants.

Tangshan Workers' Hospital is the largest hospital in Tangshan since the earthquake of 1976. It covers 29.72 thousand square metres and has 500 beds. 1,800 patients can be treated every day. *(Photo by Ben Lanwu)*

Ruth and Victor W. Sidel, consultants to the World Health Organisation, wrote in their co-authored book, *The Health of China*, that the outstandingly high life expectancy for a country at China's per capita income level might be attributed to the following factors: 1) a medical service network in both urban and rural areas; 2) a comparatively comprehensive medical and health service system; 3) a great number of health workers who whole-heartedly serve the people; 4) the establishment and development of medical care for the minority nationalities with aid from the State; and 5) the setting up of rehabilitation institutions for the disabled. The integration of these five factors formed a complete medical and health service system, which provided fundamental medical services for the one billion Chinese people.

In order to eliminate diseases gravely menacing the health and lives of the people, New China had made it an important task in the early years to exterminate pests and control diseases. When Mao Zedong issued the call: "Get mobilized, pay attention to hygiene, reduce diseases, improve health conditions" in 1952, a nationwide Patriotic Public Health Campaign was launched to improve environmental sanitation, wipe out pests and control diseases. The Government Administrative Council decided to set up the Central Patriotic Public Health Campaign Committee, with Premier Zhou Enlai as Chairman – a decision illustrating the great importance the People's Government attached to public health work. Local campaign committees were subsequently established throughout the country. The Patriotic Public Health Campaign not only greatly improved the sanitary conditions in urban and rural areas, built up and enhanced the people's strength and confidence to fight against pests and diseases, but it also created a Chinese-style preliminary method of carrying out health work, that is, an effective method for rapidly transforming the backward state of the health services and disease prevention in a vast country with such a large population and relatively backward economy and culture as China.

Under the guidance of the principle of "putting prevention first", the Patriotic Public Health Campaign, which was focused on improving environmental sanitation, wiping out pests and controlling diseases, had greatly brought down the incidence of various diseases and completely or largely eliminated some of the acute infectious diseases severely jeopardizing the health and lives of the people.

The plague, the dreadful acute infectious disease, was basically brought under control by 1955, thanks to the joint efforts of anti-plague personnel and the inhabitants of stricken areas. In the late 1950s, the annual incidence of plague plunged from tens of thousands before Liberation in 1949 to about 40 cases, and further down to less than twenty or several cases after 1964. The epidemic areas have been narrowed down to such sparsely-populated remote places as the

Tibetan-Qinghai Plateau and the Inner Mongolia autonomous region, in contrast with 19 provinces before Liberation. Smallpox was exterminated in China in the early 1960s, a decade or more earlier than its extinction in the world in general. Thanks to planned and free inoculation throughout the country, most of the infectious diseases that can be effectively prevented by biological products have been brought under control. For instance, there is a marked decrease in the incidence of diphtheria, whooping cough, tuberculosis, measles, epidemic cerebrospinal meningitis, poliomyelitis and epidemic encephalitis B. Not long after the founding of the People's Republic, cholera, relapsing fever, typhus and venereal diseases were eliminated or brought under control one after another. The number of lepers in China has also dropped from 500,000 in the early days of the People's Republic to less than 150,000. The Second National Conference on the Control of Leprosy convened by the Ministry of Public Health in 1981 made it an official goal to eradicate leprosy by the end of the century.

Prevalence of schistosomiasis has a long history in China. Schistosome eggs were found in the female corpse of the Western Han dynasty (206 BC–24) unearthed from Mawangdui in Changsha, Hunan province, and in the male corpse of the Western Han dynasty unearthed from Fenghuang Hill in Jiangling, Hubei province. This shows that there were people suffering from schistosomiasis along the middle and lower reaches of the Yangtze river at least 2,100 years ago. In the early 1950s, schistosomiasis was prevalent in 348 counties and cities in 12 provinces, autonomous regions and municipalities, with more than 11 million people suffering from the disease, and oncomelania, which carries the parasite and serves as a vector of the disease, bred in more than 14,000 million square metres and menaced more than 100 million people. Control of schistosomiasis started in 1949. After Mao Zedong issued the call in 1955 for the elimination of schistosomiasis, anti-schistosomiasis leading groups were set up from central to local governments, pooling the efforts of leaders, medical workers and the masses of the people, and coordinating those of various departments concerned with the control of disease. By 1985, among the 12 provinces, autonomous regions and municipalities where the disease had been prevalent, Guangdong province and Shanghai had eradicated schistosomiasis; oncomelania had been exterminated in more than 10,000 million square metres – 80 per cent of its breeding-ground; and over 10 million patients were cured – more than 90 per cent of the total; 161 counties and cities were basically freed of the disease and 110 other counties and cities reached the standard for eradication.

In addition to schistosomiasis, kala-azar, filariasis and malaria were also widespread and serious parasitic diseases in the country. Kala-azar was basically eradicated in most of the epidemic areas in 1958. By 1985,

A patient with schistosomiasis (snail fever) at Ningguo county, Anhui province back at work after treatment.

among the 14 provinces, autonomous regions and municipalities where filariasis was prevalent, Shandong and Guizhou provinces and the Guangxi Zhuang autonomous region had brought it under control, and 645 counties and cities – 75 per cent of those affected by the disease – reached the standard of basic eradication. Before 1949, patients with malaria numbered 30,000,000 annually; the incidence fell to 440,000 cases in 1985, and periodic outbreaks have now been brought under control.

Keshan disease, Kaschin-Beck disease, endemic goitre and endemic fluorosis are serious endemic diseases left over from former times. Endemic diseases occurred in 80 per cent of China's territory, menacing 400 million people, and thirty-six million people were actually afflicted with various such diseases. Thanks to prolonged, unremitting efforts since the founding of New China, there were no outbreaks of Keshan disease for the 12 years up to 1985. Even in Keshan county, Heilongjiang province, the most seriously stricken area, after which the disease was named, there was not a single new case. Twelve provinces and municipalities, including Heilongjiang, Jilin, Liaoning, Shaanxi, Hebei, Tianjin, Qinghai, Shanxi, Henan, Shandong, Gansu and Beijing, have basically brought endemic goitre under control; in fluorosis-prevalent regions, the number of afflicted people has declined steadily, thanks to efforts made in the supply of purified drinking water. The time when fluorosis comes under full control is not far off.

This comprehensive control and prevention of acute and chronic infectious diseases and parasitic and endemic diseases in the past three decades and more have greatly changed the composition of the causes of death. In the past, the main causes of death were infectious, parasitic and endemic diseases, but now they are cerebrovascular and heart diseases and malignant tumours. For example, acute infectious diseases now rank seventh or eighth as compared to second or third in the early years of New China; pulmonary tuberculosis, formerly the main or second most common cause of death, has now become the sixth or seventh. The health level of both the urban and the rural population has been raised markedly, life expectancy has become longer and the mortality rate has dropped conspicuously. The death rate in the whole nation stood between 25 and 33 per thousand before Liberation: it fell to 14 per thousand in the 1950s, 12 per thousand in the 1960s, and seven per thousand in the 1970s. Compared with other continents, China's average life expectancy is higher than that of Africa, Asia and Latin America, and approaches that of Oceania.

PUBLIC HEALTH

Occupational Health

IN the course of productive labour, people are exposed to high temperatures, radiation, dust, toxic chemicals, noise, vibration and other factors affecting health. The tasks of occupational health are to study the effect of occupational factors harmful to the health of the workers, suggest measures for improving working conditions and protect the health of the workers.

In old China, occupational health was utterly ignored, and people worked in abominable conditions with frequent disasters, death and injuries as a result. Since the founding of New China, great concern has been shown for the health and safety of the working people, and a number of measures have been taken to protect their health, improve their working conditions and control occupational diseases.

First, since the 1950s, occupational health sections have been set up in health and epidemic-prevention stations at all levels, and occupational health offices, institutions for the prevention and treatment of occupational diseases, and workshop health care units have been established in factories and mines, all staffed with health personnel of various specialized fields. In order to intensify scientific research on occupational health and on the prevention and treatment of occupational diseases, China's first occupational health laboratory was set up in Tianjin in 1950; the Institute of Occupational Health was established in Beijing in 1953, and the Ministry of Public Health decided in 1983 to set up eight occupational health and occupational disease prevention and treatment centres. In the early 1980s, health departments in all parts of China had established 120 research institutions of occupational health and occupational disease control. In addition, the metallurgical and coal industrial departments had also set up over 60 occupational health and occupational disease control institutions for the prevention and treatment of occupational diseases among their employees.

Second, laws and regulations as well as standards for monitoring occupational health have been worked out. The Industrial Insurance Regulations of the People's Republic of China issued in 1951 and the "Constitution of the People's Republic of China" promulgated in 1954 instituted free medical services and a retirement system. Beginning in 1951, the state departments concerned issued the "Provisional Regulations on Factory Safety and Sanitation (Draft)", "Measures for the Prevention of Bitumen Poisoning", the "Decision on the Prevention of Harm from Silica Dust in Factories and Mines", "Rules on Factory Safety and Sanitation", "Regulations on the Range of Occupational Diseases and Treatment of Patients with Occupational Diseases", "Interim Hygienic Standards for Designing Industrial Enterprises", "Interim Hygienic Standards of Microwave Radiation", "Hygienic Standards of Noise in Industrial Enterprises", and "Standards for the Classification of Physical Labour". The formulation and implementation of these regulations and standards have played a positive role in protecting the workers' health.

Third, in order to get at the root causes of occupational health hazards and provide guidance for the prevention and treatment of occupational diseases, nationwide surveys and studies have been conducted on pneumoconiosis, pesticide poisoning, noise, vibration, high-frequency, microwaves and carcinogens related with occupations. Surveys were made in 1957 among some ten thousand workers operating in high

Table 2: Health Units, Beds and Personnel in Industrial and Other Departments

	1949	1965	1985	Growth rate of 1985 over 1949 (times)
Units				
Hospitals	150	1,748	5,401	36
Sanatoria	5	692	553	110.6
Beds				
Hospitals	9,000	157,849	458,000	50.8
Sanatoria	700	77,474	91,000	130
Personnel	25,880	294,301	1,252,000	48.3

temperatures; a survey on silicosis was made among 2.9 million workers operating in silicious dust surroundings between 1974 and 1976; from 1979 to 1981 check-ups were conducted among nearly one million workers in contact with lead, benzene, mercury, organic phosphorus or trinitrotoluene. In the early 1980s, 138 medical and health institutions were organized by the Ministry of Public Health to conduct a retrospective epidemiological survey for the past decade among 130,000 workers (including control groups) in 456 enterprises in 18 provinces and cities, who were in contact with eight carcinogens – methyl chloride, substances escaping from coke ovens, asbestos, benzidine, benzene, chromium, arsenic and vinyl chloride. These surveys helped make clear the incidence, mortality and distribution of heatstroke, silicosis, occupational tumours and several common occupational toxins; provided a scientific basis for adopting measures of prevention and treatment; and played an active guiding role in occupational health administration.

Environmental Sanitation

Health departments at all levels in China have set up institutions supervising environmental sanitation in order to protect and improve the environment and ecology, and to control pollution and other public nuisances. In line with the principle of "facilitating prevention of diseases and serving the people's life and production", these institutions have carried out extensive supervision and monitoring of environmental questions closely related with the people's life and health.

One such feature closely related with the people's life and health is water supply. In the early 1950s, health departments concentrated their efforts on protecting water sources, improving wells, expanding the supply of running water and sterilizing drinking water. The State promulgated the "Standards for the Quality of Drinking Water" in 1956 and the "Regulations for Drinking Water Sanitation" in 1959. In the early 1980s, 85 per cent of urban residents were supplied with running water and 40 per cent of the rural population had safe and clean drinking water. Especially since China's participa-

tion in the "International Drinking Water and Sanitation Decade" (1981–1990) sponsored by the United Nations, nationwide surveys on rural drinking water have been conducted in the country and efforts made to provide 80 per cent of rural residents with clean drinking water by 1990.

From 1971 onwards, environmental sanitation personnel have monitored and investigated the quality of water of the five major river systems (Yangtze, Yellow, Pearl, Songhua and Xiangjiang), 177 rivers, five lakes (Taihu, Dongting, Poyang, Hongze and Weishan), six bays (Baohai, Dalian, Laizhou, Jinzhou, Hangzhou and Jiaozhou) and the air over 221 cities, obtaining over 730,000 pieces of scientific data. The survey has produced a clear picture of environmental pollution in China and provided a scientific basis for environmental protection. On 1 June 1975 the Monitoring Centre for Environmental Sanitation was set up in Beijing to intensify monitoring of the environment. In April 1979, China joined the global environmental monitoring system sponsored by the United Nations environment programme and the World Health Organisation, and began overall monitoring of the atmosphere and water. In 1983, the Health and Epidemic-Prevention Division of the Ministry of Public Health began to compile a corpus of China's monitoring data as part of the global environmental monitoring system, and the data were provided as reference material for the local health, environmental protection departments and other organizations concerned in the country.

Since the late 1970s, environmental sanitation work in China has been moved from general monitoring of environmental pollution to investigation into the relationship between environmental factors and community health. In 1978, the State organized a number of provincial and municipal health and epidemic prevention stations, medical colleges and research institutes to study the relationship between air pollution and health in 25 cities with a population of more than 500,000. In addition to common indicators, immunology, genetics and other basic medical theories and techniques were applied in observing the effect of environmental factors on human beings. The study involves analysis of multiple factors instead of

Medical officers of the Industrial and Commercial Administration of Wuhan testing the pork at a trade fair. *(Photo by Li Yifang)*

Nanjing Child Mental Health Research Centre is the first institute for children's mental health in China. It was established in Nanjing in 1984. *(Photo by Fang Ailing)*

only the environmental factor, and electronic computer techniques were also used in the investigation.

Food Hygiene

Monitoring food hygiene is a system instituted by the State to ensure the safety of the people's food and drink. New China has formulated a series of standards, decrees, and regulations on food hygiene and trained a technical force for food monitoring and testing.

After health and epidemic prevention stations had been set up at county level and above in 1953, monitoring of food hygiene was developed step by step in the whole country. In addition to health departments, food production enterprises and shops under the light industrial and commercial departments have also established their own food hygiene administration, testing and research institutions to ensure the standard of food hygiene; some big industrial and mining enterprises, transportation and communications departments have installed health and epidemic prevention stations to monitor food hygiene. By 1985, there were about 3,000 food hygiene monitoring institutions operating under health departments in China. In addition, there were 23 food hygiene control posts in all border points and outlets for the monitoring and testing of imported food.

In order to guarantee the safety, hygiene and rational nutrition of food, the departments concerned under the State Council have worked on the basis of scientific experiment and investigation to formulate and publish 75 state standards on food hygiene (57 official and 18 for trial implementation) and 18 methods of food hygiene control. Especially after the Standing Committee of the National People's Congress promulgated the "Food Hygiene Law of the People's Republic of China (for Trial Implementation)", monitoring of food hygiene has entered the stage of control by the legal system. Formulation of decrees and regulations on food hygiene and intensifi-

cation of monitoring have upgraded the hygienic quality of food and greatly reduced the incidence of food poisoning and intestinal infectious diseases.

School Hygiene

Institutes of higher learning and middle and primary schools in China have an enrolment of nearly 200 million students, about 20 per cent of the total population. School hygiene and the protection of the mental and physical health of children and young people therefore have an important bearing on the prosperity and development of the Chinese nation.

The "Constitution of the People's Republic of China" stipulates in Article 46: "The State promotes the all-round moral, intellectual and physical development of children and young people". In the spring of 1951, Mao Zedong put forward the demand of "health first" to the Ministry of Education and called on the young people to keep fit, study diligently and work well, putting good health in the first place. In August of the same year, the Government Administrative Council promulgated the "Decision on Improving the Health of Students in Schools at All Levels", specifically stipulating that school hygiene and the management of student canteens should be improved. In 1979 and 1980, the ministries of education and health jointly promulgated the "Provisional Regulations on Health Work in Middle and Primary Schools (Draft)", and the "Provisional Regulations on Health Work in Institutes of Higher Learning (Draft)". In 1981, the Secretariat of the CPC Central Committee issued the call that "the whole Party and the whole of society must be concerned about the healthy growth of children and young people". According to statistics, the education, health and other departments have jointly issued more than 20 documents over the past three decades on improving school hygiene and health care. The formulation and implementation of these directives, decrees and measures have helped advance

907

the management of school hygiene in a planned and regulated way.

In order to guarantee the healthy growth of children and young people, representatives of the departments of education, health, physical culture and sports, the educational councils of trade unions, the Communist Youth League, the students' federation and medical institutions established the School Health Care Guidance Committee in the early 1950s to offer free direction in and take charge of improving and checking school hygiene and health care. The Ministry of Public Health set up a division supervising school hygiene; provincial, municipal, prefectural and county health and epidemic prevention stations established school hygiene sections to direct and inspect school hygiene. Every institute of higher learning has set up a health unit or clinic, and all college students enjoy free medical services; urban middle and primary schools have clinics; in rural primary schools there are medical kits, and teachers in charge of the kits work under the guidance of health departments. Students in all schools have health cards, health examinations are carried out every year, and new entrants to institutes of higher learning are re-examined so as to have a clear picture of the health of students. Since 1978, China has undertaken three large-scale surveys on physical condition, myopia and dental caries among students under a national unified plan and standard; three national meetings on physical culture and sports, hygiene and control of myopia and dental caries in schools were held, and the "Implementation Methods for Protecting Students' Eyesight" and the "Epidemiological Survey and Control Programme on Dental Caries and Periodontal Diseases Among Students" were promulgated. In July 1982, the State Science and Technology Commission approved the establishment of the "Beijing Institute of Child and Youth Hygiene". Led and managed by the Beijing Medical College, the institute undertakes research, technical guidance, consultation and personnel training for child and youth hygiene.

Thanks to the concern of the State, the incidence of diseases and mortality among children and young people has dropped sharply and their physical fitness has improved markedly. For example, the rate of incidence of tuberculosis among primary school pupils in some districts of Beijing fell from 1,700 per 100,000 in 1949 to 40 per 100,000 in 1979, and that among middle school students from 5,400 per 100,000 to 200 per 100,000. The mortality rate from infectious diseases among children in the age group of five to seven years dropped markedly from 446.2 per 100,000 in 1951 to 3.69 per 100,000 in 1979. At the same time, the physical development of children and young people also improved greatly. For example, nine sample surveys on the physical growth and development of children and young people conducted in Shanghai between 1931 and 1979 showed that the average height of seven-year-old boy pupils in 1979 was similar to that of the 8.5-year-olds in 1931; the average weight of seven- and 13-year-old boy pupils in 1979 was similar to that of eight- and 14.5-year-olds respectively in 1931; the average height of seven- and 12-year-old girl pupils in 1979 matched that of 8.5- and 15-year-olds respectively in 1931; and the average weight of eight- and 13-year-old girl pupils in 1979 equalled that of nine- and 15-year-old ones in 1931. Surveys in Beijing and Shanghai show that the younger generation of today are 3–3.5 cm taller on average than their parents. Between 1978 and 1980, surveys carried out jointly by the State Physical Culture and Sports Commission, the Ministry of Education and the Ministry of Public Health on the physical constitution of 200,000 students in 1,210 colleges, middle and primary schools of 16 provinces and municipalities showed that the physical development of Chinese children and young people was generally up to normal requirements and the height, weight and chest measurements of the majority were above the average normal.

MATERNITY AND CHILD HEALTH

CHILDREN under 15 years of age and women above 16 number 650 million, about two-thirds of the population of China. Maternity and child health services, therefore, are closely related with the happiness of all families and the vital interests of 1,000 million people, the healthy growth of the new generation and the higher health standard of the Chinese nation.

In old China, there were practically no maternity and child health services. In 1949, the country had only 80 maternity and child health centres with 1,762 beds, five children's hospitals with 139 beds and nine

maternity and child health stations with no beds. There was no guarantee of health for the large number of working women and children. As a result, gynaecopathy was widespread and the mortality rate of children was high. Since its founding, New China has attached great importance to maternity and child health services, which have become an important part of the people's health work.

In order to implement state policy on the protection of women and children, specialized institutions have been set up and personnel in charge of maternity and

Doctor Lin Qiaozhi conducting an antenatal examination in the ward.

child health work assigned to the Ministry of Public Health and the people's governments at all levels. The State has also set up specialized institutions, such as women's and children's health care hospitals, centres and stations, children's health care hospitals, centres and clinics, women's health care hospitals and centres, maternity hospitals and children's hospitals. By 1985, China had 2,742 women's and children's health care centres (stations), 272 women's and children's hospitals and maternity hospitals with 24,000 beds, and 26 children's hospitals with 6,000 beds. These specialized institutions, together with the maternity and child health sections of urban subdistrict and rural township hospitals, formed a maternity and child health network for the whole country. Through colleges and training courses, about a million people were engaged in maternity and child health care services in the early 1980s, including personnel with higher and secondary education and part-time health workers with short-term training. They included more than 42,000 gynaecologists and obstetricians, 31,000 paediatricians, 70,000 midwives, and 73,000 health workers in women's and children's health care centres. In addition, 410,000 women doctors and 550,000 midwives in rural areas also devoted time to women's and children's health care work and assisting at deliveries.

In order to protect women's health and reduce the infant mortality rate, China began to popularize modern delivery methods in 1950 to lower the incidence of *tetanus neonatorum* and puerperal fever. By 1985, modern delivery methods were basically popularized in 20 provinces, autonomous regions and municipalities, accounting for 93 per cent of all deliveries in the country and 99 per cent of those in cities. Since 1978, health care for pregnant and lying-in women in cities and the countryside has been expanded from popularization of modern delivery methods to systematic health services. More than 100 institutions in 26 provinces, autonomous regions and municipalities have conducted studies on prenatal diagnosis. More than 200 hospitals affiliated to

medical colleges and provincial hospitals have carried out prenatal diagnosis to prevent congenital and hereditary diseases. By the early 1980s, puerperal fever and *tetanus neonatorum* had been basically eliminated in all cities and part of the countryside; the mortality rate of pregnant and puerperal women dropped from 150 per 10,000 before the founding of the People's Republic to five per 10,000, and perinatal mortality to about 20 per 1,000. In order to control common and frequently-occurring diseases among women, universal surveys and treatment of gynaecological diseases, with emphasis on cervical carcinoma, were carried out in many regions of the country to facilitate their early detection, timely treatment and prevention. Since 1978, rural women suffering from hysteroptosis and urinary fistula have been provided with free treatment. Medical teams were formed in all provinces, autonomous regions and municipalities to tour villages and provide surgical or non-surgical treatment for women patients,. By the end of 1983, 80 per cent of patients with these two diseases had received treatment. The incidence of cervical erosion and vaginitis has also declined year by year. Regular examination and treatment of women with gynaecological diseases have effectively protected the health of women.

Women enjoy equal status with men in New China, and vast numbers of women are actively engaged in productive work with the development of agriculture and industry. The State has formulated and adopted various labour protection measures in consideration of the physiological characteristics and special needs of women. The "Regulations on Labour Insurance of the People's Republic of China" promulgated in 1953 clearly stipulated against specially strenuous work for women workers or any work harmful to their physiological functions. Women after seven months of gestation and those in the first four months of lactation are not allowed to work on night shifts. Women employees enjoy 56 days of maternity leave with full pay. Industrial enterprises with a considerable number of women workers have set up women's clinics, rest rooms for pregnant women, nursing rooms and nurseries.

Healthy babies and good care to promote the healthy growth and development of children are matters vital to the prosperity of the nation. The State has always attached importance to children's health care. In 1949, a maternity and child health college was set up in Shenyang to train paediatricians, gynaecologists and obstetricians; in 1950, the Ministry of Public Health established the Central Maternity and Child Health Experimental Academy. By the early 1980s, eight medical colleges in China had paediatrics faculties, more than 10 provinces and municipalities had child health or paediatric institutes, and 24 children's hospitals had paediatric research departments, all for the purpose of promoting research on children's health care. To upgrade children's health-

909

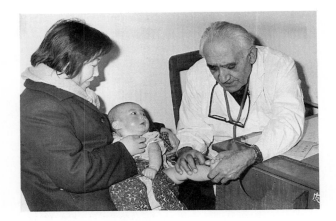

Dr Ma Haide (ethnic Chinese American), adviser to the Public Health Ministry of China, examining a child.

care workers' scientific and technical knowledge, the Ministry of Public Health entrusted the Institute of Paediatrics of the Chinese Academy of Medical Sciences in 1965 to open training classes for children's health-care doctors from 24 provinces, autonomous regions and municipalities. From 1979 to 1982, nationwide training courses for teachers of children's health care were held for four years running. On this basis, a large number of child health-care workers with secondary or primary education were trained in various parts of the country, forming a vast child

health-care force comprising paediatricians, assistant paediatricians, nurses, health-care assistants and kindergarten nurses. In addition, village doctors, part-time medical workers in factories and health-care assistants in neighbourhood committees were trained and engaged in the control of children's diseases and in child health-care services in all grassroots units throughout the country.

Before Liberation, various acute and chronic infectious diseases gravely menaced the lives of infants and children. Shortly after its founding, New China adopted positive measures of prevention and treatment to control infants' and children's infectious diseases. In October 1950, the Government Administrative Council promulgated the "Directions on the Autumn Vaccination Campaign". More than 100 million infants and children were soon vaccinated against smallpox free of charge, and the disease was brought under control. In 1963, the Ministry of Public Health promulgated the "Implementation Methods for Inoculation" to further extend free inoculation, establish a system of children's innoculation cards and intensify planned immunization. Since then, irregular, universal preventive inoculation among children has been replaced by planned inoculation for specific groups and under stipulated immunization programmes. To further extend planned immunization, the Ministry of Public Health promulgated

A Babies Room in the Hubei Women and Children Health Centre.

in 1980 the "Implementation Methods for Preventive Inoculation", stipulating BCG vaccine, measles vaccine, pertussis–diphtheria–tetanus vaccine, OPV (oral poliomyelitis vaccine) and epidemic encephalitis vaccine as basic vaccines for infants and children. Implementation of planned immunization programmes in China has helped to control some infectious diseases and greatly reduce the incidence of diseases among infants and children. According to a 1982 survey made in 1,784 counties (districts) of 24 provinces, autonomous regions and municipalities, 1,041 counties (districts) had not reported a single case of diphtheria for three years from 1979 to 1981, accounting for 58.3 per cent of the surveyed counties; 43.1 per cent of the counties (districts) had no cases of poliomyelitis in these three years; and 295 counties had brought the incidence of measles to below 10 per 100,000. The incidence dropped further after 1983.

China has also adopted measures to control common diseases affecting children's health, such as infantile rickets and nutritional anaemia. The National Anti-Rickets Research Coordinate Group, set up in 1977, formulated standards of diagnosis and drew up measures for the prevention and treatment of the disease. A national meeting on maternity and child health services held at the end of 1980 decided that infantile rickets and nutritional anaemia were focal points in the control of children's diseases. In 1981, a group of medical and health researchers from 17 provinces, autonomous regions and municipalities made a survey of the incidence of nutritional anaemia among children in both cities and rural areas, including those living in dormitories and at home, and those living in the plains and in mountain areas. The group also worked out control measures, the implementation of which yielded marked results in a few years.

Child-care institutions at all levels have conducted systematic health work among children living collectively or otherwise in urban and rural areas to ensure their healthy growth. This includes regular health examinations of new-born babies, guidance on child-care methods, timely correction of malformation and treatment of diseases, systematic observation and caring for weak infants; establishment and improvement of the system of infectious disease control, propagation of knowledge about disease prevention, timely isolation of people afflicted with infectious diseases, carrying out of disinfection, quarantine and treatment; co-operation with epidemic prevention departments to improve planned immunization and raise the inoculation percentage, etc. The "Hygiene and Health-care System in Nurseries and Kindergartens (Draft)", jointly promulgated by the Ministry of Public Health and the Ministry of Education in October 1980, provided detailed stipulations about the style of living, food, physical exercise and health examination of infants and children; regulations about hygiene and disinfection of nurseries and kindergartens; isolation, disease prevention and safety measures; and liaison with parents. Since the Secretariat of the CPC Central Committee called on the whole Party and the whole of society to pay attention to the healthy growth of children and adolescents, child health care has drawn the attention of people of all social sectors and entered a new period of development.

TRADITIONAL CHINESE MEDICINE

TRADITIONAL Chinese medicine has a long history; it is the result of the accumulated experience of the Chinese people of various nationalities in their prolonged fight against disease. It is a science of disease control and health protection with striking therapeutic results, and is in itself an integrated theoretical system, contributing tremendously to the growth and prosperity of the Chinese nation. Traditional Chinese medicine has not only effective drugs made from herbs, trees, fish, shellfish, insects, metals, minerals, fowls and animals, but also unique therapeutic means such as massage, breathing and physical exercise therapy, acupuncture and moxibustion, and qigong (deep-breathing exercises), as well as methods to prolong life and resist diseases and senility. With its rich content and extensive literature, it is really a great treasure-house.

China's earliest extant literature in this treasure-house is The Yellow Emperor's Classic of Internal Medicine (Huangdi Nei Jing), which summed up the medical achievements and therapeutic experience before the Spring and Autumn and Warring States periods (770–221 BC), established the unique theoretical system of Chinese medicine and constituted the basis of development of traditional Chinese medicine. In the late Eastern Han dynasty (25–220), the noted physician Zhang Zhongjing (about 150–219) further summed up the medical achievements of his forerunners and, combining them with his own clinical experience, wrote China's first clinical work, Treatise on Febrile and other Diseases (Shangh Han Za Bin Lun), which was later known as Treatise on Ferer (Shang Han Lun) and The Gold Chest Collection of Prescriptions (Jin Gui Yao Lue). Towards the end of the Eastern Han dynasty (25–220), another noted doctor, Hua Tuo (?–208), invented mafeisan (an oral anaesthetic) for surgery, and was the first in the world to operate on a patient under anaesthesia. Ge Hong (284–364), a

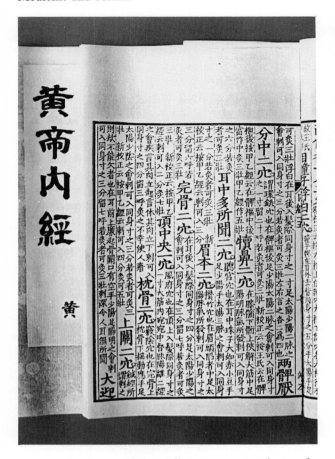

Huangdi Nei Jing (The Yellow Emperor's Classic of Internal Medicine) written in the Warring States period (475–221 BC) was an important classical medical document in China.

noted alchemist in the Eastern Jin dynasty (317–420), wrote the *Master Baopu On Alchemy* (*Bao Pu Zi*), which indicated that he had discovered some important chemical reactions of drugs more than 1,000 years before modern science and technology, and mentioned the effects of *Qigong* (deep-breathing exercises). Cao Yuanfang (sixth to early seventh century), a physician of the Sui dynasty (581–618), wrote *Causes and Symptoms of Diseases* (*Zhu Bing Yuan Hou Lun*), the first pathological work of traditional Chinese medicine which recorded in detail the causes and symptoms of various diseases. Noted doctor Sun Simiao (581–682) of the Tang dynasty (618–907) summed up the clinical experience and medical theories before the Tang dynasty, collected prescriptions and data on acupuncture and moxibustion, and in the course of 60 years completed the works *The Thousand Golden Formulae* or *Precious Prescriptions* (*Qian Jin Yao Fang*) and *Supplement to the Thousand Golden Formulae* (*Qian Jin Yi Fang*). Wang Qingren (1768–1831), a noted physician of the Qing dynasty (1644–1911) and expert on the basics of human anatomy, wrote *The Redress of Medical Books* (*Yi Lin Gai Cuo*), updating the knowledge and understanding of the human body.

912

Li Shizhen was an outstanding medicinalist in ancient China. His tomb is in his home town in Qichun county in Hubei.

In addition, *Shen Nong's Materia Medica* (*Shen Nong Ben Cao Jing*), completed in the late Eastern Han dynasty (25–220), is China's earliest pharmacological work, consisting of three volumes and recording 365 drugs. It is a summation of pharmacological knowledge and experience before the Han dynasty. Li Shizhen (1518–1593), the great pharmacologist of the Ming dynasty (1368–1644), devoted his whole life to sorting out and summing up ancient *materia medica*, and spent 27 years in compiling the great work, *Compendium of Materia Medica* (*Ben Cao Gangmu*). The book recorded 1,892 drugs, 11,096 prescriptions and classified 1,094 plant species. It was the most scientific and detailed classification of plants in the world at that time, and the principles of classification are basically in accord with those of modern botany. *Compendium of Materia Medica*, one of the greatest scientific works in the world, has been translated into Japanese, Latin, French, English, German and other languages.

Works by Chinese physicians in various historical periods are so numerous that there are still some 10,000 titles despite the loss of many with the passage of time. The medical literature includes basic medicine, clinical medicine, pharmacology and prescriptions. The content of each field is rich and detailed,

Some of the precious copies of *Ben Cao Gangmu* (Compendium of Materia Medica) written by Li Shizhen (1518–1593), preserved at Qichun, Hubei.

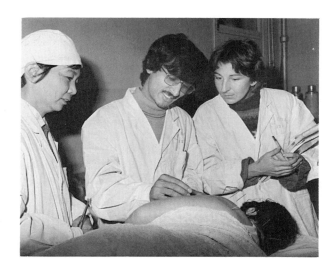

A Bengali student (middle) and a French student (right) practise acupuncture in Beijing Traditional Chinese Medicine College. More than 200 doctors of traditional Chinese medicine from 39 countries have been trained here. *(Photo by Yuan Ruxun)*

and the medical inventions and achievements of the Chinese people are recorded. They are the crystallization of the wisdom of the Chinese people in the fight against diseases for many generations, as well as one of the precious spiritual riches of human civilization.

Since its founding in 1949, New China has

formulated a series of principles and policies on the protection and development of traditional Chinese medicine, and adopted many measures so as to inherit and carry forward the legacy of Chinese medicine and to bring into full play the advantages of traditional medicine and pharmacology.

The People's Government has worked out correct principles to promote the development of traditional medicine and pharmacology, giving equal stress to traditional Chinese medicine and Western medicine, uniting their practitioners, and absorbing and building on the legacy of traditional medicine and pharmacology to protect the health of the people. Beginning in 1954, health departments from central down to local levels have set up administrative organs of traditional Chinese medicine. Meanwhile, the State has organized practitioners of traditional medicine, who were scattered over the country, to form tens of thousands of joint clinics, and has established state-owned or collective clinics and hospitals of traditional Chinese medicine. During this time, 280,000 practitioners of traditional medicine have joined these medical institutions and thus put an end to the discriminating practice of banning practitioners of traditional medicine from working in hospitals. By the end of 1985, China had 1,414 county hospitals of traditional Chinese medicine operating under the authorities of counties or above, with 101,000 beds. In addition, most of the general and specialized hospitals have set

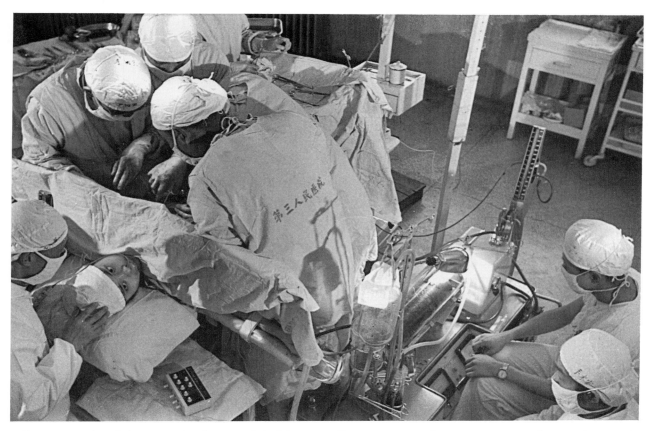

Doctors at Shanghai No. 3 People's Hospital doing a cardiac operation with acupuncture anaesthesia and external circulation. *(Photo by Xia Daoling)*

913

up departments of traditional medicine. Hospitals of traditional medicine at all levels have done a great deal of work in medical and health services. In most provincial and municipal hospitals of traditional medicine, over 2,000 outpatients are attended to daily.

Practitioners of traditional Chinese medicine constitute an important part of China's medical and health workers. They comprise those mastering the art from the family, those acquiring it through apprenticeship, the self-taught and graduates from colleges of traditional medicine. After the founding of New China, the State intensified the training of personnel in traditional Chinese medicine and pharmacology to make up for the lack of successors in that field, while increasing the number of personnel in Western medicine. From the early 1950s to the mid-1960s, 59,000 practitioners of traditional medicine had been trained through apprenticeship, thus injecting new blood into the ranks. The establishment of training schools in traditional medicine and secondary schools in traditional medicine and pharmacology, and the establishment of colleges of traditional medicine played an important role in the training of qualified personnel. Higher education in traditional Chinese medicine started in China in 1956, when the State Council approved the establishment of four colleges of traditional Chinese medicine in Beijing, Shanghai, Guangzhou, and Chengdu. Similar colleges were also opened in some provinces, autonomous regions and muncipalities in the following years. By 1985 there were 24 such colleges in the country, while 10 other medical colleges had set up departments of traditional Chinese medicine. At the same time, there was a rapid increase in the number of secondary schools of traditional medicine and pharmacology, and a great number of traditional medicine personnel were trained. Statistics show that by 1985 China had 336,000 practitioners of traditional medicine, who have become the mainstay in the inheritance and development of traditional Chinese medicine.

Integration of traditional Chinese medicine with Western medicine is a form of therapy unique to China, and the study of traditional medicine by practitioners of Western medicine is an important measure to promote the integration.

Since December 1955, full-time training classes in traditional medicine for practitioners of Western medicine have been held all over China, which has helped to provide the basis for clinical and research work in the field of integrated traditional Chinese–Western medicine. By 1983, more than 130,000 practitioners of Western medicine had completed traditional medicine training courses, and 2,230 had received professional titles of physician-(surgeon-)in-charge and above. They are the basis in clinical practice, teaching and research for promoting the integration of traditional Chinese medicine with Western medicine, and have become one of the three

major forces in China's medical and health services, side by side with the practitioners of traditional Chinese medicine and those of Western medicine.

Researchers in traditional Chinese medicine and integrated traditional Chinese–Western medicine have achieved many unique and important results since the founding of New China, making traditional Chinese medicine shine with new splendour. For example, people with acute abdominal diseases can be cured by means of traditional therapies without the pain of surgery. China's traditional acupuncture and moxibustion therapies have been introduced into more than 100 countries and regions. Acupuncture anaesthesia, developed by medical workers on the basis of acupuncture analgesia, has been applied to more than 100 kinds of operation, including pneumonectomy, thyroid and craniocerebral operations, and Caesarean section. Traditional therapies are safe and reliable in the treatment of intestinal and anal troubles, and are popular among patients. Fractures treated by means of traditional Chinese medicine combined with local fixation with small splints heal faster, have better functions restored and less complications, and the general result is better than those treated by the traditional or Western method alone. Indigo red, a substance extracted from *Indigo naturalis*,

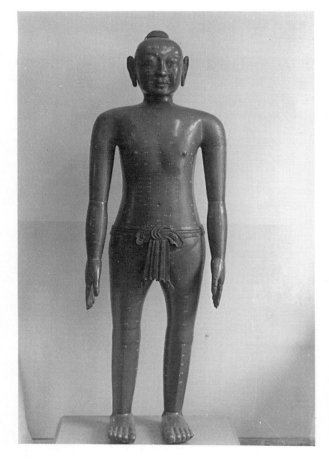

A bronze body for teaching acupuncture, 185 cm high, with 354 acupoints, made by Doctor Wang Weiyi of the Song dynasty in 1027.

has provided a new and safe therapy with reliable results for chronic granulocytic leukaemia. In addition, integrated Chinese–Western therapies have achieved good results in the treatment of kidney, liver and cardiocerebral diseases, scleroderma, leukoma, viral pneumonia, infected compound fractures, burns, shock, acute myocardial infarct, septicaemia, diffuse intravascular clotting, adult respiratory distress syndromes and acute renal failure. Successes have also been made in obtaining musk from musk deer-breeding, in synthetic bezoar and in sexual reproduction of *Rhizoma gastrodiae*.

Analysing and summing up the academic experience of veteran doctors is an important aspect of inheriting and carrying forward traditional Chinese medicine. Since the Ministry of Public Health issued the "Urgent Notice Regarding the Inheritance of the Academic Experience of Veteran Doctors of Traditional Chinese Medicine" in 1958, measures have been taken in all parts of China to classify and publish medical case records and medical notes of some well-known veteran practitioners, including *The Medical Experience of Pu Fuzhou*, *The Collection of Medical Case Records of Yue Meizhong*, *The Collection of Clinical Prescriptions of Shi Jinmo*, *The Collection of Clinical Experience of Zhao Bingnan*, *The Selected Gynaecological Case Records and Notes of Ha Litian*, and *The Medical Case Records of Liu Huimin*. Nearly 500 medical classics have also been photolithographed or reprinted, including the *Classic of Internal Medicine (Nei Jing)*, *Compendium of Materia Medica (Ben Cao Gang Mu)*, *Prescriptions for Universal Relief (Pu Ji Fang)*, *Compendium of Acupuncture and Moxibustion (Zhen Jiu Da Cheng)*, and *Jingui Collection of Prescriptions (Jin Gui Yao Lue)*.

On 4 January 1986 the State Council decided to set up the State Administration for Traditional Chinese Medicine, which is entrusted to the Ministry of Public Health, and to allocate special funds for the undertaking. This important decision promises a still greater development of traditional medicine in China.

MEDICAL RESEARCH

CHINA'S medical research has been conducted in the light of the development of the national economy, the occurrence of diseases among the people, the needs and requirements of the people, and the trends of progress in science and technology. The fundamental principles are: the development of medical science in coordination with social and economic development in the service of disease control and health protection; the emphasis of medical science should be placed on the study and solution of key scientific and technological problems for the control of diseases most harmful to the people's health; the three branches of traditional Chinese medicine, Western medicine and integrated traditional–Western medicine should coexist for a long time to come and develop side by side with a view to absorbing and carrying forward traditional Chinese medicine; a combination of theory with practice, with emphasis on applied research projects and attention to basic theories to increase the resources of science and technology; and vigorous steps to introduce, digest and assimilate advanced foreign science and technology.

Old China left very few medical science research institutions, scientists and researchers. Upon its founding, New China first of all established a number of research institutions, from central down to local levels, and increased the number of scientific and technical personnel. The mid-1950s witnessed the establishment of the Chinese Academy of Medical Sciences, the Chinese Academy of Traditional Chinese Medicine and the Military Medical Sciences Institute of the People's Liberation Army, the three serving as the centre of guidance for scientific research in the country. Two kinds of research institution, the independent and those affiliated to medical colleges or major medical and health departments or hospitals, were set up in the light of Chinese conditions and the distribution of medical personnel. By 1983, the country had 323 independent scientific research institutions.

Under the guideline of "putting prevention first" and by combining science and technology with the efforts of the masses, Chinese medical researchers have concentrated on the study of major scientific and technical problems in respect of the plague, cholera, epidemic encephalitis B, epidemic cerebrospinal meningitis, diphtheria, measles, anterior poliomyelitis, scarlet fever and other infectious diseases, and on the systematic study of the five major parasitic diseases – schistosomiasis, malaria, filariasis, ancylostomiasis and kala-azar. After unremitting efforts, the medical scientists have basically made clear the sources of the plague, the epidemic factors in epidemic sources, seasonal ebb and flow, routes of dissemination and related patterns and characteristics; on this basis they have summed up and worked out a whole set of control measures and brought the plague under control. They have also found out the epidemic range, the rate of infection, incidence, and dissemination routes of the five major parasitic diseases and the

Table 3: Research Institutions and Medical Science Personnel

	1947	1957	1963	1975	1980	1983	Growth rate of 1983 over 1947 (times)
Institutions	4	38	120	141	282	301	75.3
Total number of employees	300	4,512	8,250	12,389	25,107	31,004	103.3
Scientific and technical personnel	–	4,299	5,770	8,140	17,596	21,868	–

habits of the five parasites, and accumulated comparatively complete data about related natural and social factors. All this has provided a scientific basis for classification of epidemic areas and for control measures. New drugs have also been developed for the prevention and treatment of parasitic diseases. Thanks to the close combination of scientific research with disease control, the incidence and mortality rate of various infectious and parasitic diseases have dropped markedly.

Development of medical research has promoted the progress of clinical medicine. China has attained an advanced level by world standards in the treatment of extensive burns, replantation of severed limbs and

Orthopaedists of Shanghai No.6 People's Hospital have done a great many of replantations of severed limbs. This peasant works with a replanted hand.

treatment of chorionic epithelioma. After the Shanghai Guangxi Hospital first succeeded in saving the life of a patient with extensive severe burns in 1958, a Beijing hospital in 1977 successfully saved another patient with burns covering nearly 100 per cent of body surface, including 94 per cent third-degree burns. From 1960 to 1982, the Shanghai Guangxi Hospital treated a total of 34,164 burn cases with a success rate of 93.13 per cent. With the steady rise in the level of burns treatment, China has accumulated rich experience in the treatment of shock and wounds, early removal of scabs and autodermic grafting. In January 1963, Professor Chen Zhongwei of the Shanghai Sixth People's Hospital successfully performed the first replantation of a severed limb in the world. Soon afterwards, many Chinese hospitals and other medical institutions, including some county hospitals, started to perform replantation of severed limbs and microsurgery. They have successfully performed replantation of severed palms, fingers, toes and limbs, as well as of limbs after the removal of a diseased section, transplantation of free skin flaps and free bone grafts with blood vessels. Zhou Lirong, a surgeon in the Dancheng County Hospital, Henan province, replanted and transplanted 62 severed fingers or toes for 55 patients between 1975 and May of 1983, with only two cases of failure, a success rate of 96.7 per cent. Xiu Ruijuan, a woman medical scientist brought up after the founding of New China, found that microvessel movement is carried forward in waves when she was studying at the Microcirculation Laboratory of the Department of Bioengineering, University of California at San Diego. She also discovered that anisodamine hydrochloride (known as 654), a plant-derived drug produced in China, and another vasoactive agent, 703, act to prevent thrombosis by slowing the clumping of platelets and granulocytes (which are the main components of clots), and the production of thromboxane, a compound causing clotting, thus proving the Chinese vasoactive agents 654 and 703 to be "vasomotion enhancers". Under the guidance of Professor Patrick D. Harris, Head of the Physiology and Biophysics Department at the University of Missouri, she completed the academic paper, "Effects of Altered Bath Oxygen on Cremasteric Arteriolar Diameters in Normotensive and Renovascular Hypertensive Rats After Decerebration", which won her a high reputation at the 28th Annual Meeting of the American

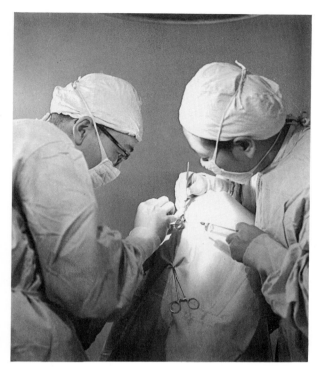

Doctors of Beijing Traditional Medicine Academy doing a cataract extraction with a golden needle. *(Photo by Gu Dehua)*

Microcirculatory Society. Cancer is a disease seriously menacing people's health and the third biggest killer in China. Tumour surveys and small-scale pathogen-

etic investigations were conducted throughout the country step by step from the late 1950s to improve tumour control. The nationwide retrospective survey of fatal cases of malignant tumours in the period 1973–5, which was conducted in 29 provinces, autonomous regions and municipalities between 1974 and 1978, made clear the standard fatality rate and geographical distribution of malignant tumours in the country, and the "Atlas of Malignant Tumours in the People's Republic of China" made on the basis of the survey has won high praise from the medical circles of the world. Among the some 100 types of cancer, the nine leading killers in China in order of fatality rate are cancer of the stomach, oesophagus, liver, cervix, lung, intestine, nasopharynx and breast, and leukaemia.

On the basis of epidemiological surveys of malignant tumours, Chinese medical scientists, with emphasis on the nine leading cancers, have carried out research into anti-cancer drugs, anti-cancer therapies and drugs of traditional medicine, and basic theories on tumours, and have made some progress in the early diagnosis and treatment of liver, oesophageal and nasopharyngeal cancer. The level of China's clinical treatment of cancer shows that the 5-year survival rate of patients with small liver cancer reached 72 per cent, oesophageal and stomach cancer 40 and 30 per cent respectively, and nasopharyngeal cancer 50 per cent (90 per cent among early cases), and early cervical cancer as high as 97 per cent. Good results were also

Table 4: Medical Research Projects which Won International Awards

Projects	Awards	Winners
Isolation and cultivation of chlamydozoon trachomatis	*Ligue Contre le Trachome Médaille d'Or* (Gold Medal) and prizes awarded by the International Organisation Against Trachoma	Tang Feifan, Institute of Biological Products of the Ministry of Public Health
		Zhang Xiaolou, Beijing Tongren Hospital
		Huang Yuantong and Wang Keqian, Institute of Biological Products of the Ministry of Public Health
Research into the serum alpha feto-protein (AFP) in the precancerous and early stages of liver cancer	Gold medal and prizes awarded by the US Cancer Research Institute	Ritan Hospital of the Chinese Academy of Medical Sciences
		Qidong Institute of Liver Cancer, Jiangsu Province
		Tumour Hospital of Nantong Prefecture, Jiangsu Province
Prevention of Keshan disease with oral sodium selenite	Schward Reward presented by the International Association of Bioinorganic Scientists	Institute of Health (now under the Chinese Preventive Medicine Centre) of the Chinese Academy of Medical Sciences; Xi'an Medical College
Chronic allyl chloride poisoning – an epidemiological, clinical, toxicological and neuropathological study	Scipione Caccuri International Prize (Italy)	He Fengshen *et al.*, Institute of Health, Chinese Preventive Medicine Centre
Research on the prevention and treatment of schistosomiasis	Léon Bernard Prize, awarded by the World Health Organisation	Mao Shoubai, Institute of Parasitology, Chinese Preventive Medicine Centre

achieved in the treatment of advanced cases of malignant tumours. For example, the cure rate of metastatic choriocarcinoma reached 78 per cent. The Beijing (Peking) Union Medical College Hospital had treated 392 patients with choriocarcinoma between 1959 and 1975, and the fatality rate plunged from 90 per cent to 20 per cent.

While persisting in research in applied science, China has also intensified work on basic theory. The early 1960s registered developments in biophysics, pathological physiology, biochemistry and virology, and other basic medicine. This was followed by studies on cytobiology, molecular biology, immunology, genetics and such new disciplines as biomedical engineering and social medicine, filling the gaps in medical disciplines in China.

With the increase in international exchange, China has introduced some advanced biotechnologies from abroad and begun studies on cytofusion, monoclonal antibody and genetic technology of recombination of DNA. Introduced technologies are assimilated in the light of China's conditions so as continuously to raise the level of medical sciences at home.

PHARMACY AND MEDICAL APPARATUS

PRODUCTION and circulation of traditional and Western drugs and medical apparatus are part of both China's socialist economy and the people's health and welfare services. The rapid growth of China's pharmaceutics has contributed much to the medical services, immunization and epidemic control, relief work in disaster-stricken areas, family planning, export and aid to foreign countries, and the development of animal husbandry.

Traditional Chinese pharmacology, with a history of several thousand years, is a very precious legacy of the country. The production and application of traditional drugs, which enjoy a good reputation at home and abroad, has a unique history. China now has more than 5,000 varieties of traditional drugs made of herbs, animal by-products and minerals, and 293,000 hectares of medicinal herbs are cultivated. While collecting medicinal herbs and medicinal animal by-products in a planned way and protecting the resources of wild herbal and animal drugs, China has also experimented with artificial breeding and cultivation of 800 plant species and animal breeds. Over 50 species and breeds have been successfully cultivated or bred and put into commercial production. For example, *Rhizoma gastrodiae*, "a herb bestowed by nature", as legend has it, which was believed to be impossible to cultivate, was in fact successfully cultivated and its output increased markedly after Chinese scientists mastered the law governing grafting of *Armillaria mellea*. Cultivation of *Ginseng* and *Notoginseng*, and the gathering of pilose antler from deer breeding have produced enough of each to meet medical needs. Tropical medicinal herbs, including *Aucklandia lappa,* borneol and a score of other species, had in the past to be imported but are now successfully grown in China, and their output not only meets domestic needs but also leaves a surplus for export.

Traditional pharmaceuticals were made by hand with poor and primitive facilities. Production is now mechanized or semi-mechanized after the technological transformation over the past decades. Some pharmaceutical factories of Chinese medicine have adopted such modern technologies as sealed pulverization, decompressed distillation, vacuum drying, reverse-flow extracting, electronic numerical control, microwave and ultra-infrared sterilization. Prescriptions have been improved and varieties increased. In addition to the traditional varieties of pills, powder, ointment, jelly, distillate and wines, pharmaceutical factories have developed soluble granules for oral use, injections, tablets, drops, capsules, aerosols, inunctions and a dozen other new preparations. There are over 480 factories of traditional pharmaceuticals in China, producing 3,800 varieties, including over 100 traditional brand varieties and over 500 new products. Some traditional pharmaceuticals are very popular and sell well in over 80 countries and regions of five

Chinese wolfberry, a special product of Ningxia.

918

Modern techniques used to produce traditional medicine in Hangzhou No.2 Traditional Chinese Medicine Plant. *(Photo by Lu Ming)*

For some hundreds of years the Huqingyu Tang Drugstore in Zhejiang province has specialized in traditional Chinese medicine. *(Photo by Ge Weiwei)*

continents. They include *An Gong Niu Huang Wan* (an anti-pyretic, antidotal and anti-convulsive bolus of *Calculus bovis*) produced by the Tong Ren Tang Pharmaceutical Factory in Beijing, *Liu Shen Wan* (small pills especially effective in the treatment of sore throats) produced by the Lei Yun Shang Pharmaceutical Factory in Suzhou, the Yunnan *Baiyao* (a cimobufotoxin compound in the form of pills or powder used as a highly effective haemostatic and analgesic) produced by the Yunnan Baiyao Pharmaceutical Factory, and medicinal herbs such as *Radix angelica sinenisi*, *Radix astragalus membranaceus*, *Radix codonopsis pilosula*, *Radix ginseng* and *Cordyceps sinensis*.

China's chemical pharmaceutical industry was so weak before Liberation that only a small number of little factories in a few coastal cities could make preparations from imported crude drugs. After the founding of New China, the State invested a great amount of funds in the pharmaceutical industry. In line with the principle of "mainly developing the production of crude drugs", China first of all developed the production of the effective and widely used antibiotics, sulpha drugs and other badly needed medicine for the control of endemic, common and epidemic diseases. During the First Five-Year Plan

period (1953–7), the Huabei (North China) Pharmaceutical Plant, the Taiyuan Pharmaceutical Plant, the DongBei (North-East) General Pharmaceutical Plant and other similar key enterprises were constructed. These plants mainly turned out antibiotics, sulpha drugs and analgesic-antipyretics. At the same time, the existing pharmaceutical enterprises in Shanghai, Tianjin, Guangzhou and other big cities were consolidated and expanded. With the completion and putting into operation of new pharmaceutical plants, the capacity for production of many common drugs increased by tens, even hundreds, of times, thus lifting the country out of the backward situation in which all crude drugs had to be imported. Since the 1960s, the chemical pharmaceutical industry has been put under centralized leadership and specialized management, and the pharmaceutical industry in inland areas has been developed in a planned way. The construction of more than 20 modern pharmaceutical plants in inland areas has preliminarily changed the irrational distribution of the industry. Output and varieties of chemical drugs have increased steadily since 1958. China can now produce 26 categories of chemical drugs including antibiotics, sulpha drugs, vitamins, antituberculotics, anticarcinogens, drugs for cardiovascular diseases, contraceptives and hormones – 1,100 varieties of crude drugs with an annual output of over 47,000 tons, and more than 3,000 varieties of pharmaceuticals and preparations. With the progress in medical science research, China has developed new drugs for the control of cancer, cardiovascular diseases, chronic tracheitis and malaria, and those for birth control. Apart from meeting domestic needs, more than 300 varieties of quality crude drugs and preparations are exported to more than 100 countries and enjoy a good reputation in Europe, the Americas, Africa and South-East Asia. The country has now built up a complete, nationwide pharmaceutical industry system with over 800 plants producing crude and chemical drugs or preparations and employing 350,000 people, a system of considerable scale and technical level – from the production of crude drugs to that of preparations and pharmaceuticals, and from scientific research and design to industrial production.

The medical apparatus manufacturing industry was almost non-existent in old China, when almost all major medical apparatus and instruments were imported except for simple surgical instruments and imitations of hospital equipment. The medical apparatus industry has undergone a comparatively rapid growth in both the coastal and inland areas, especially in Shanghai, Beijing and Tianjin municipalities and in Jiangsu, Zhejiang, Hubei, Sichuan and Shaanxi provinces since the founding of New China. By the early 1980s, a medical apparatus industrial system was basically established with coordinated development between the central and local departments and between the coastal and inland areas, a system with fairly complete categories and varieties and a rational layout.

There are 220 medical apparatus enterprises with over 80,000 employees, mainly producing surgical instruments, apparatus for birth control, X-ray equipment, medical electronic instruments, medical optical instruments, medical nuclear isotope apparatus, medical laboratory equipment, stomatological apparatus, hospital equipment, external circulation apparatus and artificial internal organs, etc., which fall into 20 categories with 1,500 varieties and more than 5,000 specifications. In the production of medical apparatus, common and conventional apparatus is being replaced by specialized and precision apparatus, and manual operation by casting, precision pressing, mechanization and automation processes. The introduction of the vacuum heat treatment process and the use of molybdenum stainless steel have greatly improved the quality of surgical apparatus made in China. Meanwhile, China has begun to adopt such new technologies as electronics, ultrasonic, fibre optical, laser, profound hypothermia, isotope and nuclear processes for the development of large and precision medical apparatus and instruments, including those for multiple-nuclear, isotopic and radiodiagnosis and treatment, electronic scanning instruments and monitoring units, and laser treatment apparatus. The property indicators of some apparatus have reached or approached the advanced levels of similar products abroad. Apart from meeting domestic needs, there is a surplus of medical apparatus for export to more than 70 countries and regions.

INTERNATIONAL MEDICAL CO-OPERATION AND EXCHANGE

MEDICAL co-operation and exchange with other countries constitutes an important way of developing medical and health-care services in New China. In the 1950s, China signed bilateral agreements with the Soviet Union and other Eastern European countries on medical and health sciences, providing for mutual visits and exchange of personnel and data. In the 1960s, China increased her contact with the developed and developing countries and participated in some large international academic conferences on medical and health sciences. With the developed countries, it was mainly friendship exchanges; with the developing countries, emphasis was on offering medical aid. Since the late 1970s, especially after the implementation of the policy of opening to the outside world, China has increased medical co-operation and exchange with the World Health Organisation, the United Nations Fund for Population Activities, the United Nations Children's Fund,

the United Nations Development Programme, and the World Bank. Apart from this, China has carried out extensive exchanges in many forms with over 100 countries and regions, including exchange of data, special surveys, advanced training, exchange of delegations and academic exchanges.

China is a founder member of the World Health Organisation (WHO). In 1978, China and WHO signed a memorandum on medical technical co-operation; by 1982, 91 Chinese medical specialists had been appointed by WHO as members of its expert panels or advisory committees. WHO has also appointed 41 Chinese clinical, teaching and research institutions as its centres of co-operation in Beijing and Shanghai; in Guangdong, Shandong and Jiangsu provinces; and in the Inner Mongolian autonomous region. These institutions have undertaken research projects and technical services assigned by WHO, and the sphere of co-operation covered studies on 26

Table 5: Chinese Medical Teams Abroad (1963–1984)

Recipient country	Date of dispatch	Province, municipality or autonomous region dispatching the teams	Notes
Algeria	April, 1963	Hubei	
Tanzania (Zanzibar region)	August, 1964	Jiangsu	
Laos	December, 1964	Yunna	Suspended in 1974
Somalia	June, 1965	Jilin	
The Yemen Arab Republic	July, 1966	Liaoning	
The Congo	February, 1967	Tianjin	
Mali	February, 1968	Zhejiang	
Tanzania (Tanganyika region)	March, 1968	Shandong	
Mauritania	April, 1968	Heilongjiang	
Guinea	June, 1968	Beijing	
Vietnam	December, 1968	Yunnan	Suspended in 1971
The People's Democratic Republic of Yemen	January, 1970	Anhui	
The Sudan	April, 1971	Shaanxi	
Equitorial Guinea	October, 1971	Guangdong	
Sierra Leone	March, 1973	Hunan	
Tunisia	June, 1973	Jiangxi	
Zaire	September, 1973	Hebei	
Ethiopia	November, 1974	Henan	Suspended in September, 1979, and resumed in December, 1984
Togo	November, 1974	Shanghai	
Cameroon	June, 1975	Shanghai	Suspended in January, 1979
Kampuchea	June, 1975	Shanxi	Suspended in January, 1981
Senegal	July, 1975	Fujian	
Madagascar	August, 1975	Gansu	
Morocco	September, 1975	Shanghai	
Niger	January, 1976	Guangxi	
Mozambique	April, 1976	Sichuan	
Saõ Tome and Principe	June, 1976	Heilongjiang	
Burkina Faso (Upper Volta)	June, 1976	Beijing	
Guinea-Bissau	July, 1976	Guizhou	
Kuwait	November, 1976	Liaoning	
Gabon	May, 1977	Tianjin	
Gambia	October, 1977	Guangdong	
Benin	January, 1978	Ningxia	
Zambia	January, 1978	Henan	
The Central African Republic (Empire)	June, 1978	Zhejiang	
Syria	May, 1978	The Academy of Traditional Chinese Medicine, Ministry of Public Health	Suspended in June, 1981
Iran	August, 1978	Jiangsu	Suspended in February, 1979
Chad	November, 1978	Jiangxi	Suspended in July, 1979
Botswana	January, 1981	Fujian	
Djibouti	February, 1981	Shanxi	
The United Arab Emirates	October, 1981	Sichuan	
Rwanda	February, 1982	Inner Mongolia	
Uganda	January, 1983	Yunnan	
Libya	December, 1983	Beijing	
Malta	April, 1984	Jiangsu	
Cape Verde	July, 1984	Heilongjiang	
Liberia	July, 1984	Heilongjiang	

disciplines, including primary health services, traditional medicine, cardiovascular diseases, tumour control, neurology, mental health, family planning, maternity and child health, disease classification and parasitic diseases. Bilateral co-operation in medical and health services between China and other countries is aimed at finding out each other's strong points and helping each other's needs on the basis of equality and mutual benefit. China receives about 2,000 foreign medical specialists every year, who hold training classes, give lectures, conduct co-operative research and make academic tours and surveys. She also sends about 1,000 people abroad on survey missions, academic visits and scientific exchange and to attend academic meetings. Since 1980, the three international training centres of acupuncture and moxibustion in Beijing, Shanghai and Nanjing have held 43 training courses and trained more than 800 practitioners of acupuncture and moxibustion for more than 100 countries and regions. China has also aided 14 countries, including Mauritania and the Yemen Arab Republic, to build 29 hospitals, health centres and medical apparatus factories.

Dispatch of medical teams is an important form of China's friendship co-operation and technical exchange with other Third World countries. In April 1963, the Chinese government sent a medical team to Algeria under an agreement between the two countries, the first of its kind to another Third World country. Since then, with the development of friendship ties between China and other Third World countries, China has sent 7,400 medical workers to 47 countries and regions in Asia and Africa. These medical teams were selected from 26 provinces, autonomous regions and municipalities. In 1984 alone, China sent 40 medical teams with 1,226 members to 88 medical centres in 40 countries to serve the local people. Over the past 20 years and more, Chinese medical teams, with the support and help of the recipient governments and health departments and working in close co-operation with local medical workers, have treated large numbers of people with common and frequently-occurring diseases, cured many difficult and complicated cases, and saved the lives of many critical patients, thus promoting friendship between China and other Third World countries.

THE CHINA RED CROSS SOCIETY

THE China Red Cross Society has experienced two historical eras – old China and New China – since its establishment on 29 May 1904. In the era of old China, which was ravaged by frequent natural disasters and wars, the China Red Cross Society had carried out huge amounts of relief and rescue work. In New China, it has made its contribution to socialist construction, to protecting the people's health, safeguarding world peace and promoting friendship with the people of other countries.

When war broke out between Japan and Russia in early 1904, North-East China was turned into a battlefield. To relieve the people there from the ravages of war, Shen Dunhe and other public figures in Shanghai established the Shanghai Branch of the International Red Cross on 29 May of the same year. This was the forerunner of the China Red Cross Society. In 1907, the Shanghai Branch of the International Red Cross was renamed the Da Qing Red Cross Society. After the overthrow of the Qing dynasty in 1911, it was again renamed the China Red Cross Society, with Shen Dunhe as its Chairman. On 15 January 1912, the league of Red Cross Societies notified the societies of all countries to recognize the China Red Cross Society as an official member of the league. By 1937, the China Red Cross Society had 464 local branches, 262 medical institutions and 138,000 members. After the outbreak of the War of Resistance Against Japanese Aggression in 1937, the headquarters of the society was moved from Shanghai to Chongqing via Hong Kong. By the eve of the founding of the People's Republic of China on 1 October 1949, the China Red Cross Society had a membership of over 300,000.

On 2 August 1950, the China Red Cross Society was reorganized, and held the first congress in Beijing after the founding of New China. The Constitution of the Society approved at the congress stipulated that the China Red Cross Society is a people's health and rescue organization under the leadership of the Government of the People's Republic of China, and its basic aim is to heal the wounded, rescue the dying and practise revolutionary humanitarianism. At home, it abides by the state policies and principles on health work, and helps the Government to mobilise and

Deng Yingchao, chair of the CPPCC and honorary councillor-in-chief of the China Nursing Society conferring on Wang Xiuying the Nightingale Medal awarded by the Red Cross International Committee.
(Photo by Wang Jingde)

Table 6: Organizational Structure of the China Red Cross Society

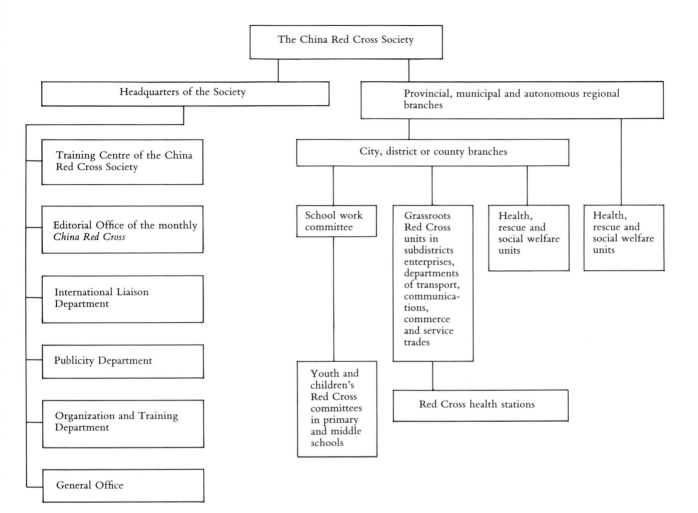

organize the people to develop mass rescue and health campaigns and to improve the people's health. In its activities abroad, it promotes friendship with the Red Cross societies and people of other countries, expands amicable ties, opposes wars of aggression, safeguards world peace and thus makes its contribution to the progress of mankind.

Over the three decades and more since the founding of New China, the China Red Cross Society has improved the structure of its headquarters and expanded its local branches. By 1985, 193 cities and counties (districts) in 26 provinces, autonomous regions and municipalities have set up branches. There are 25,868 grassroots Red Cross units with 1,877,954 members in the country. Red Cross units at all levels have played an active role in mass health and rescue work, medical care, and blood donation, in helping the old and the disabled, giving relief to the sick and the poor, and in foreign relief activities.

Training courses of the Red Cross society include general knowledge of health, prevention and treatment of common diseases, first aid, rescue on the battlefield, first aid in air defence, anti-nuclear and anti-chemical defence and first aid to the drowning. As a spare-time training for the masses, the courses are attended by both members and non-members. By 1983, 5.08 million people had received varied training, and there were 1,006 Red Cross ambulance corps and 10,697 Red Cross health stations in subdistrict committees, factory workshops and mines throughout the whole country.

The ambulance corps and spare-time health workers, in line with the principle of healing the wounded and rescuing the dying, give first aid to the wounded and the sick in neighbourhoods, workshops, mines, fields, school campuses, swimming pools, stadiums, public places, buses and ships. Their work provides a service for the people and helps them avoid serious consequences, such as disability or death from industrial accidents, poisoning, acute diseases, drowning and other incidents. In the event of natural disasters, the Red Cross Society, in co-operation with other departments, organizes temporary Red Cross ambulance corps to help the people in stricken areas.

Mobilizing and organizing citizens to donate blood is an important task of the China Red Cross Society.

Table 7: Foreign Aid Donated by the China Red Cross Society (1985)

Recipients	Funds (US dollars)	Materials	Worth in yuan
Fiji	100,000		
Vanuatu	10,000		
The Comoros	4,000		
Argentina	40,000		
Madagascar		Handicrafts, porcelain, silks and cloth	10,000
Pakistan		Drugs	20,000
		Cotton blankets, towels and stationary	30,000
Chile	40,000		
Nepal		Woollen blankets, drugs and medical apparatus	57,589.81
		50,000 ampoules of tetravalent vaccine	10,749.53
Mozambique	20,000		
Somalia		4,000 ampoules of vaccine Drugs	20,000
Equatorial Guinea		Drugs	2,000
Ethiopia		50,400 farm tools	
		Cotton cloth	75,000
Niger	10,000		
Bangladesh	50,000		
Mali		200,000 tablets of tetracyline and Co. SMZ	
Benin	3,100		
Pakistan		Black tea	300,000
		Medical apparatus	100,000
		Cotton cloth, cotton blankets and plastic sandals	200,000
Sudan		Cotton cloth	150,000
Somalia		Cotton cloth	75,000
Mexico	200,000		
	50,000		
Colombia	150,000		
	40,000		
Saõ Tome and Principe	5,000		

Sixty-five big or small blood donation stations have been set up in 24 provinces, autonomous regions and municipalities and in some prefectures and cities. The number of blood-donors has increased steadily. For example, 116,000 people donated blood at the Beijing Red Cross Central Blood Station in 1983, 15 per cent more than the annual plan target. The China Red Cross Society is also in charge of international technical exchange on blood donation. Between 1979 and 1984, it sent 36 blood transfusion technicians and officials in 12 groups to Switzerland, Japan and Canada on study or survey missions or to attend international blood transfusion conferences. It has also invited 80 foreign blood transfusion experts in 16 groups to give lectures in China. In 1983 the Red Cross societies of China and Japan began a two-year research project on blood transfusion in the Beijing Red Cross Central Blood Station, the Shanghai Central Blood Station and the Institute of Blood Transfusion of the Chinese Academy of Medical Sciences and achieved good results.

Social welfare undertakings of the China Red Cross Society mainly serve the sick, the disabled and the aged living alone. These undertakings include: first,

setting up Red Cross welfare homes, welfare stations or welfare production teams for the disabled, which give equal emphasis to production, education and medical care so as to help the disabled live on their income from production; second, holding lectures on gerontology, opening old people's universities to give lectures on health care, literature, history and the arts, and setting up old folks service stations, health coaching stations and old folks centres, so as to enable the old people to live a healthy and happy life in their remaining years. Apart from the welfare undertakings of the China Red Cross Society and its units, a much greater volume of services for the disabled, the sick and the aged living alone is offered by members of the society. In some places, society members have established networks of such services, which are rendered by specific persons to specific homes at a specific time, including medical assistance for and visits to the needy.

The China Red Cross Society keeps in touch with international Red Cross organizations and the Red Cross and Red Crescent societies in 127 countries. From 1979 to 1983, the China Red Cross Society attended the first, second and third conferences of the

League of Red Cross Societies and congresses of Red Cross societies, the 24th International Conference of the Red Cross and the first world assembly of Red Cross volunteers. During the same period, the China Red Cross Society received 295 people in 65 delegations of Red Cross societies, Red Crescent societies and international Red Cross organizations, and sent 131 people in 44 groups to visit 27 countries and regions or attend meetings. In line with the principle of promoting international friendship, the China Red Cross Society every year provides aid to countries and people suffering from natural disasters. From 1979 to 1984, it offered 10 million US dollars of aid to 66 countries hit by natural disasters. In 1985, it sponsored a donation campaign to aid the African people hit by drought, and collected 13.87 million yuan, all of which was used as relief for the afflicted African people. Following the principle of give-and-take, the China Red Cross Society also began to accept international aid from 1979.

MENTAL DISORDERS: THEIR TREATMENT AND PREVENTION

MENTAL disorders are generally classified into four categories:

1. **Psychoses**, in which bizarre symptoms such as delusions and hallucinations occur and the patient may lose touch with reality. These may be further sub-divided into:

– *Organic psychoses*, in which the illness is due to some identifiable pathology, such as infection of the central nervous system (viral, bacterial, syphilitic, etc.), cerebrovascular disease, brain injury, drugs or degenerative processes such as senile dementia;

– *Functional (or endogenous) psychoses*, which comprise schizophrenia and manic depressive disorder. The aetiology of this group is unclear, although it is evident that both genetic and environmental factors play a role.

2. **Neuroses and reactive states**, a group which includes anxiety, hysteria, phobias, obsessional and compulsive problems, neurotic depression and neurasthenia.

3. **Personality disorder**, in which deeply ingrained maladaptive patterns of behaviour generally recognizable by the time of adolescence or earlier and continuing through most of adult life have adverse effects upon the individual or society.

4. **Mental retardation**, the causes of which may be congenital, pre-natal, peri-natal or post-natal.

The aetiology of mental disorders is often complex. A few disorders have a definable pathology: these include congenital conditions (such as Down's syndrome, phenylketonuria, etc.), infections (e.g., syphilis), drugs and trauma. However, in many disorders the aetiology is uncertain and probably multifactorial. Social and psychological factors may play an essential role in causation in some conditions and indeed are of importance in the treatment and progress of all mental disorders.

Historically Important Mental Disorders in China

Opium

Opium addiction was rampant in China for about 200 years before the founding of the PRC and was once a serious health problem.

The opium trade was forcibly expanded in China by imperialist intervention. Following the Chinese defeat by the British in the Opium War of 1840, the pernicious effect of opium smoking became daily more serious. When North-East China was occupied by the Japanese in the 1930s there was a rampant epidemic of opium addiction as a consequence of imperialist narcotic policies. During the years of Kuomintang rule occasional campaigns against opium addiction and trafficking were launched, but with little success. As the Kuomintang government relied upon opium taxes as a means of control, the results of the policy were the reverse of those intended: heavy taxation increased the profits to be gained by domestic and international opium smugglers from the illegal manufacture, traffic and trade in opium, and this resulted in a rise in the number of opium smokers. The prevalence of opium addiction in pre-1949 China has been estimated to have been as high as 10 million, with an especially high density of addicted in the provinces of South-West China – Yunnan, Sichuan and Guizhou.

On 4 February 1950, just four months after the founding of the PRC, Premier Zhou Enlai issued a decree prohibiting opium and the People's Central Government launched a nationwide campaign to eradicate opium addiction. The cultivation and processing of the opium poppy and other drugs were strictly prohibited, as were the trade in and transportation of opium, and strict penalties were imposed on offenders. A series of health education policies were introduced with the aim of raising popular awareness of the evils of opium addiction and of mobilizing the masses to participate in a campaign against it. Special committees against opium addiction were organized by governments at provincial, municipal and county levels. Health education was promoted by the mass media, including newspapers, posters and street performances. All seized opium and smoking paraphernalia was burnt in public. For instance, in Guiyang municipality in Guizhou province more than 30,000 ounces of opium were burnt at one rally. In 1950 a total of 550,000 ounces of opium was burnt in three provinces of South-West China. Leaders of smuggling gangs were severely punished.

The abrogation of the unequal treaties forced on China in the past and the restoration of tariff autonomy after Liberation effectively put an end to the import of opium from abroad. Internally, its cultivation was prohibited and land formerly used to grow opium poppies was converted to food production. The Government required all drug addicts to register and gave them a set time in which to overcome their narcotic habits. At the same time, it set up medical institutions where opium addicts could receive treatment and instruction and participate in production teams in order to recover their mental and physical health. For instance, in Chongqing city in Sichuan, 3,000 addicts gave up the smoking habit within 6 months and began a new life. Due to the strenuous efforts of the Chinese people, opium addiction was virtually eradicated within the three-year period from 1950 to 1953. Since then, the Chinese government has paid constant attention to the control and management of narcotics and other addictive drugs. Subsequently, only sporadic cases of addiction have been reported.

Venereal disease

Syphilis used to be another important source of mental disorder in the form of general paresis of the insane. Prostitution was a major agent in its spread, and in the early 1950s a campaign against prostitution was launched with the purpose of educating and converting prostitutes to honest labour. Free, obligatory medical care was given to those with syphilis and other venereal diseases, with the result that the incidence of general paresis showed a steady decline. Data from Shanghai Psychiatric Hospital show that cases of general paresis constituted about 12 per cent of the in-patient population before the founding of the PRC: by 1971, this figure had shrunk to 0.16 per cent. In the affiliated psychiatric hospital of Beijing Medical University, general paresis constituted 1.23 per cent of cases in the 1950s, whereas in the past decade no cases were found.

Malnutrition and infectious and parasitic diseases

With social reform and economic development, the living conditions of the population have been much improved and problems of unemployment and starvation no longer exist in China. With the advancement of public health, infectious diseases such as malaria, schistosomiasis and kala-azar have been well controlled. In consequence, mental disorders caused by malnutrition and infectious or parasitic disease have become rare amongst in-patients. A national epidemiological study of 12 districts was conducted in 1982 as a door-to-door survey of 500 households from urban and rural areas. A total of 38,136 inhabitants aged 15 and over were screened and only five psychiatric patients were identified whose conditions were caused by somatic disease or were infective in origin. This constitutes a prevalence of 0.13 per thousand.

The Development of Community Care

The aetiology of mental disorders is complex, and psycho-social factors as well as biological factors play a role in their occurrence. For this reason, prevention and treatment cannot be confined to the hospital alone: community and family support are also important. Whereas drugs are often an effective treatment, especially in the acute stages, the psychological effects of social environment are important, especially in the longer term.

In 1958, the first national workshop on the treatment and prevention of mental illness was held in Nanjing. This national workshop formulated a plan according to which approaches to mental disorders should comprise "active treatment and community-based care, with institutional care only for the severely disturbed". As regards the principles of treatment, a comprehensive approach was emphasized, involving "drug treatment in combination with occupational therapy, recreation, physical exercise and education". Under the influence of these principles, the management of mental patients in psychiatric hospitals was reformed from the old, closed system to an open system, and the environment in psychiatric hospitals was improved, with more social activities for patients to participate in. All this was psychologically beneficial to the psychiatric patient, in particular as regards rehabilitation.

In China, under the principle of prevention, field surveys of psychiatric patients were conducted in many areas even as early as the 1950s. It was estimated in 1959 that field surveys in big cities such as Shanghai, Nanjing, Beijing and Chengdu had covered as many as 18,000,000 inhabitants. These surveys gave a general picture of the distribution of psychiatric disorders in urban and rural areas. Since the 1970s almost all major psychiatric hospitals have sent medical teams to urban and rural communities to train primary health workers, spread knowledge about mental disorders, conduct field surveys and establish community mental health networks at grassroots level. This has promoted psychiatric practice in the community as well as epidemiological study and has benefited patients by early diagnosis and treatment of mental disorder and by prevention of relapse.

As an example, in the urban area of Shanghai psychiatric out-patient clinics have been set up in around 94.1 per cent of street hospitals. One hundred and eighteen rehabilitation centres have been organized for chronic mental patients as part of a joint effort with the civil administrative departments; in these centres 3,227 chronic mental patients have been cared for and have participated in rehabilitation programmes. The results have been successful: readmission rates for relapse have decreased by 77 per cent and accidents caused by psychiatric patients in the community have decreased by 78 per cent. After occupational therapy, around 71.5 per cent of mental patients have been able to participate in daily labour.

In rural areas, community care programmes for mental patients have been developed in which patients receive drug treatment at their own homes and undertake some household or farm work in their communities at the same time. For example, during the period 1974 to 1976, in an agricultural area with a population of 190,000, more than 300 primary health workers were trained by psychiatrists from the Institute of Mental Health at Beijing Medical University. Under the direction of these psychiatrists, mental patients were identified and received treatment at their homes, supervised locally by primary health workers. Some 231 schizophrenic patients who did not exhibit dangerous behaviour were treated at their homes and followed up for about 10 years. The therapeutic affect of drug treatment was found to be similar to that for in-patients who had received their treatment in psychiatric hospitals: 64.9 per cent of schizophrenic patients were markedly improved. The therapeutic effects proved more stable in the community sample, and of the 231 patients treated at home, 67.9 per cent kept in a good state of remission: 47.1 per cent of schizophrenic patients were able to participate in whole-day farm work. The transfer of the care and treatment of mental patients from traditional hospitals to community-based mental health services is a significant development. China is just at the beginning of this shift in the pattern of care. To promote this evolution in mental health, the support and close co-operation of social services and of different branches and departments of the community are essential elements.

The Effects of Economic Advance

In recent years, economic advances and the accompanying urbanization, industrialization and changes in family and population structure have led to the occurence of new psychosocial factors and these have inevitably had an effect on patterns of mental health.

The entrance to the Institute of Mental Health, Beijing Medical University, a WHO Mental Health Collaborating Centre for Research and Training.

As in the developed countries during their periods of urbanization, the incidence of behaviour problems in children and adolescents and of mental health problems in the elderly greatly increased, as did the incidence of psychosomatic disease. This tendency can now be observed in China. The data from a survey on behavioural problems in schoolchildren in Beijing in 1986 showed that the prevalence was 8.4 per cent. Statistical data from several big cities in China in 1983 indicates that cardiovascular disease, cerebrovascular disease and cancer, in that order, were the three main causes of death. Psychosocial factors play an important role in the occurrence of these diseases.

In order to accommodate these social changes, psychological consultation in general hospital settings is stressed. For instance, in the city of Tianjin a system of psychological consultation and biofeedback treatment has been set up in different districts in recent years and a total of 30,000 people have used this service. This indicates an increasing demand from

Lord Skelmersdale (fourth from left), Parliamentary Under-Secretary of State, Department of Health and Social Security, paid a visit to the Institute of Mental Health of Beijing Medical University on 14 September 1987 to meet the Director of the Institute, Dr (Mme) Shen Yucun, on the wards during the 1987 China Medical Exhibition.

society for mental health services. Furthermore, a multidisciplinary academic organization, the Chinese Mental Health Association, was established in 1985, in which psychiatrists, psychologists, sociologists and public health experts have joined hands to promote and collaborate in mental health research.

Recent Developments in Psychiatry

In 1949 there were no more than 100 neuropsychiatrists and 1,000 psychiatric beds in the whole of China. Since the 1950s China has paid special attention to the training of mental health professionals and the establishment of psychiatric institutions. By 1985 there were 348 psychiatric institutions, more than 60,000 psychiatric beds and around 6,000 psychiatrists. Psychiatry as an independent discipline has been taught in medical schools, and the departments of psychiatry in 11 medical universities have their own affiliated teaching hospitals. Specialist textbooks of psychiatry have been published for undergraduate students, and professors and associate professors of psychiatry in medical universities offer postgraduate training courses for psychiatrists for masters degrees and doctorates. To raise the standard of qualifications of mental health workers, seven departments of psychiatry have been designated continuing education centres by the Ministry of Public Health. Since 1982, medical psychology as a premedical subject has begun to be taught in 46 medical schools or universities (the total number of medical schools and universities is approximately 120).

In recent years, many research centres and units have been set up. Among these, three institutes of mental health prominent for their high standards of expertise in research and teaching have been designated as World Health Organisation (WHO) collaborating centres for research and training in mental health. They are the Institute of Mental Health at Beijing University, the Shanghai Institute of Mental Health, and the Nanjing Child Mental Health Centre.

From 1980 to 1982 the Beijing and Shanghai Institutes, in co-operation with 10 other departments of psychiatry, conducted a collaborative programme of epidemiological sampling of mental disorders with the technical support of the WHO. Each of 500 households in urban and rural areas were screened door to door and suspect cases were identified. The results of this investigation gave an indication of the distribution pattern of mental disorders in the urban and rural population and provided the Ministry of Public Health with important information for policy making. The prevalence rate for psychiatric disorder in urban areas was 11.79 per 1000; among these, the highest rate was for schizophrenia at 6.06 per 1000, second was mental retardation at 2.04 per 1000, third came mental disorders secondary to cerebrovascular disease at 0.68 per 1000. In rural areas, the total

Publications and a journal edited by Professor Shen and staff of the Institute of Mental Health, Beijing Medical University: *Psychiatry* for postgraduate students (1980); *Manual of Psychiatric Epidemiology* (1985); *Mental Health*, for non-medical professionals (1985); *Chinese Mental Health Journal*, a bi-monthly multi-disciplinary journal (1987).

prevalence of psychiatric disorder was 9.88 per 1000; the highest rate was for mental retardation at 3.73 per 1000, second was schizophrenia with 3.42 per 1000 and third was mental disorder caused by epilepsy. (In mental retardation only moderate and severe cases are included). Psychiatry reference books for post-graduates were produced by the Institute of Mental Health at Beijing Medical University from 1980. From 1980 to 1986, four volumes of reference books on psychiatry edited by Sichuan, Hunan and two other medical colleges were published.

In recent years, international academic exchanges and collaboration in China have increased day by day. Since 1980 the Ministry of Public Health, in co-operation with the WHO, have conducted a total of 9 workshops and seminars on mental health in China. Topics have included: The Epidemiology of Psychiatry; Clinical Psychopharmacology; The Teaching of Psychiatry in Medical Schools; Minor Mental Health Problems in General Hospitals; Psycho-Social Factors in Primary Health Care; Child Mental Health; Mental Retardation and Geriatric Mental Health Issues. The neuropsychiatric branch of the Chinese Medical Association has developed professional academic exchanges with many foreign countries, such as the USA, Denmark, Norway, Japan and France. Many foreign psychiatrists and psychologists have visited China, given lectures and organized bilateral professional academic exchanges. Many Chinese doctors and experts have also travelled abroad on exchanges and study trips or to participate in conferences and many collaborative projects have been developed. Dr Shen

Yucun was elected member of the Academy of Science and Letters of Norway.

In China, there are four journals of mental health: the *Chinese Journal of Neurology and Psychiatry* (established 1955); the *Chinese Journal of Nervous and Mental Diseases* (established 1975); the *Referential Journal of Psychiatry* (established 1974) and the *Chinese Mental Health Journal* (established 1987).

FUTURE PROSPECTS

MEDICAL and health work in New China has made marked achievements over the past three decades or more, but it still falls short of the needs of economic and social development and those of the people for disease control. After the all-round fulfilment of the Sixth Five-Year Plan (1981–85), China has entered the Seventh Five-Year Plan period (1986–1990), a crucial period of major changes in China's economic and social development. In this period, the general task of China's health work is to further develop medical and health services, increase medical and health facilities in both urban and rural areas, improve urban and rural sanitation, control and reduce the incidence of major diseases, expand the medical and health care forces, and raise the level of medical science and technology – all this with a view to providing the people with more convenient and effective medical and health services and laying a foundation for health services with Chinese characteristics suitable for urban and rural economic development and meeting the people's needs in disease control, as well as laying a solid foundation for further development in the following decade.

In the Seventh Five-Year Plan period, the first task is to further improve the urban and rural medical networks and the health care system, and to provide better medical and health care conditions for the people. The capital, Beijing, the other municipalities and the capitals of most provinces and autonomous regions will establish centres of technical instruction, complete with facilities for the treatment and prevention of diseases and for health care, teaching and research. The cities will place emphasis on the transformation and expansion of existing medical institutions, on medium-sized and small ones, and on improvement of the buildings, equipment and technical forces of district and subdistrict hospitals, so as to provide timely medical care for patients. In order to improve the medical and health services for the 800 million peasants in China, every county is expected to concentrate a considerable amount of manpower, material and funds to build three to five central hospitals, improve their medical and pharmacological

sections and expand their services, while bettering and consolidating county medical institutions. Efforts will be made to see that every village will have at least one doctor with secondary medical education by the end of the Seventh Five-Year Plan. Hospital beds will total 2,590,000–2,640,000 by 1990, with an annual average increase of 70,000–80,000.

Second, an improvement will be made in the prevention and treatment of diseases during the 1986–90 period. The incidence of acute infectious diseases will drop 20 per cent, and epidemic outbreaks of severe infectious diseases will be prevented. Planned inoculation will cover 85 per cent of the children in each province by 1988 and in each county by 1990, so as to bring down sharply the incidence of diseases that can be prevented by inoculation. Efforts will be made to basically eliminate filariasis in the whole country, wipe out leprosy or bring it under control in 75 per cent of former epidemic counties or cities, and basically eliminate pernicious malaria in Jiangsu, Henan and Anhui provinces. Infant mortality will be brought down to 15 per thousand in the cities and 30 per thousand in the rural areas.

Third, existing medical colleges and schools will expand enrolment to increase the number of medical personnel. By 1990, medical colleges or universities are expected to enrol 40,000-43,000 new students and 8,000 postgraduates a year, and secondary medical schools, 90,000–100,000 students a year. The country will try to expand the ranks of medical personnel by 770,000 during the 1986–90 period, an average increase of 150,000 per year.

Fourth, the country will raise the level of medical sciences. Research institutes are expected to accomplish about 100 research projects in medical science and health assigned by the State, and to make breakthroughs in research into malignant tumours, cardio-, cerebro- and pulmonary vascular diseases, viral hepatitis and birth control, and in the development of new drugs and the study of pharmacology. As a result the medical sciences and technology in the whole country will reach the level of the developed countries in the early 1990s.

Map 2.3

IND

Irtysh R.

Uvs Nuur

Chövsgöl

Balkhash L.

Zaisan L.

Ernix R.

Ulungur L.

Altai

Manas L.

Tacheng

Karamai

Ili

Issyk-Kul' L.

Ili R.

Yining (Gulja)

Dushanzi

Urümqi

Barkol

Turpan

Hami (Kumul)

Gaxun L.

Aksu

Korla

Tiemenguan

Bosten L.

Kansu

Kashi (Kaxgar)

Tarim R.

Lop L.

Shule R.

Ruoshui R.

Shache (Yarkant)

Hotan R.

Yumen

Jiuquan

Qarqan R.

Ruoqiang (Qarkilik)

Lenghu

Qilian

Hotan

Minfeng (Niya)

Mangnai

Da Qaidam

Tianjun

Datong

Delingha

Indus

Qarhan

Qinghai L.

Xini

Indus

Golmud

Ngoring L.

Rutog

Gyaring L.

Shiquanhe

Maqên

Moincar

Lhazhong

Siling L.

Tumain

Yushu

Macala

Yalong R.

Qamdo

Garzê

Dar

Jinsha R.

Nagqu

Kangding

Nam L.

Saga

Ngaqen

Lhasa

Nyingchi

Nujiang R.

Shimi

Xigazê

Yarlung Zangbo R.

Yadong (Chomo)

ZayÜ

Ganges

Brahmaputra

Dukou

Dali

Dong

Erhai L.

Yipinglang

Tengchong

Shilong

Lancang R.

Salween

Ku

K

Bay of Bengal

Mojiang

Jinghong

Irrawaddy

Mekong

○ Coal industry	● Chemical industry	Large industrial centre
● Oil industry	○ Building materials industry	Medium-sized industrial centre
● Iron and steel industry	○ Forest industry	Small industrial centre
● Nonferrous metallurgical industry	○ Power industry	• Small local industry
● Machine manufacturing industry	—•— Oil pipeline	

Map 2.4

USTRY 〈
1:18 500 000

Baikal L.

uur

Cher

Bayan Obo

Baotou   Ho

Dengkou
Wuda   *Huanghe R.*

Shitanjing   Wuhai
              Shizuishan
Rujigou

andan Qingtongxia **Yinchuan** Yulin
Wuwei   Wuzhong   **Tai**
zhu Zhongwei   Fuji

              Yanchang
Yaojie Baiyin Jingyuan   Fen
                        Yan'an   Hancheng
        Guyuan   Yan'an Hancheng   Yu
Lanzhou Aganzhen Pingliang
Liujiaxia   Tongchuan
        Weihe R. Yaoxian   Sanmenxia
Tianshui   **Xi'an**
              Lüeyang Shiquan Baoji
Hanzhong   Shiquan   *Hanshui k.*
                        Shiyan

kam Jiangyou
        Jinfang   *Jialing R.* *Changjiang* Gezhout
Chengdu Nanchong   Enshi
Weiyuan Tianfu   Shizitan
Leshan   Changshou
Wutongqiao Zigong Chongqing Fengta
Yibin Luzhou Qijiang Nantong Jishou
        Chishui   Tongren
              Zunyi   Lengshu
Yilihe Shuicheng Qingzhen Kaiyang   Shad
Yangchang Anshun   Kaili
uan **Gui-**   Duyun   Suinin
      yang Langdai   Guilin
              Nandan
unming Guishan   Liuzhou
        Nanpan R. *Hongshui R.* Heshan
yuan Mengzi Bose   **Nanning** Gupi
jiu Pingxiang   Xijin
        Song Hong Dongluo Qinzhou
                    Qiongzhou
Beibu Gulf
Yinggehai

Legend

- ● Textile industry
- ● Silk - spinning industry
- ● Food industry
- ● Sugar - refining industry
- ● Cigarette industry
- ● Tanning industry
- ● Paper - making industry
- ● Ceramic industry

Balkhash L.
Il

Issyk - Kul' L.

PAN

Kashi (Kaxgar)
Shache (Yarkant) *Hotan*
Hotan   *R.*

Indus
Indus

Shiquanhe

Burang

Ganges

Tatar
Str.

SEA OF OKHOTSK

PACIFIC OCEAN

anning ● Shantou
Guangzhou Taiwan I.
        Dongsha Is.
Haikou
Hainan I.
Xisha Is.
        Zhongsha Is.
SOUTH CHINA SEA

Nansha Is.

mu Shoal

SOUTH CHINA SEA IS.
1:37 000 000

Map 2.5

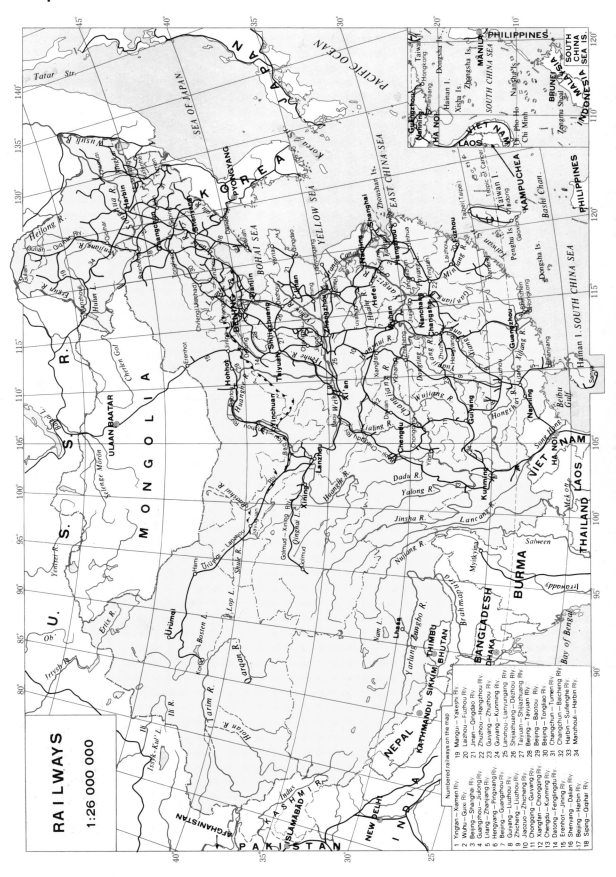

RAILWAYS

1:26 000 000

Numbered railways on the map

1 Yingtan—Xiamen Rly.
2 Wuhu—Guixi Rly.
3 Beijing—Shanghai Rly.
4 Guangzhou—Jiudong Rly.
5 Litang—Zhanjiang Rly.
6 Hengyang—Pingxiang Rly.
7 Beijing—Guangzhou Rly.
8 Guiyang—Luzhou Rly.
9 Guiyang—Luzhou Rly.
10 Jiaozuo—Zhicheng Rly.
11 Chongqing—Guiyang Rly.
12 Xiangtan—Chongqing Rly.
13 Chengdu—Kunming Rly.
14 Datong—Fenglingdu Rly.
15 Erenhot—Jining Rly.
16 Shenyang—Dalian Rly.
17 Beijing—Harbin Rly.
18 Siping—Qiqihar Rly.
19 Mangui—Yakeshi Rly.
20 Laizhou—Fuzhou Rly.
21 Jinan—Qingdao Rly.
22 Zhuzhou—Hangzhou Rly.
23 Guiyang—Zhuzhou Rly.
24 Guiyang—Kunming Rly.
25 Lanzhou—Lianyungang Rly.
26 Shijiazhuang—Dezhou Rly.
27 Taiyuan—Shijiazhuang Rly.
28 Beijing—Taiyuan Rly.
29 Beijing—Baotou Rly.
30 Beijing—Tongliao Rly.
31 Changchun—Tumen Rly.
32 Changchun—Baicheng Rly.
33 Harbin—Suifenghe Rly.
34 Manzhouli—Harbin Rly.

Map 2.6

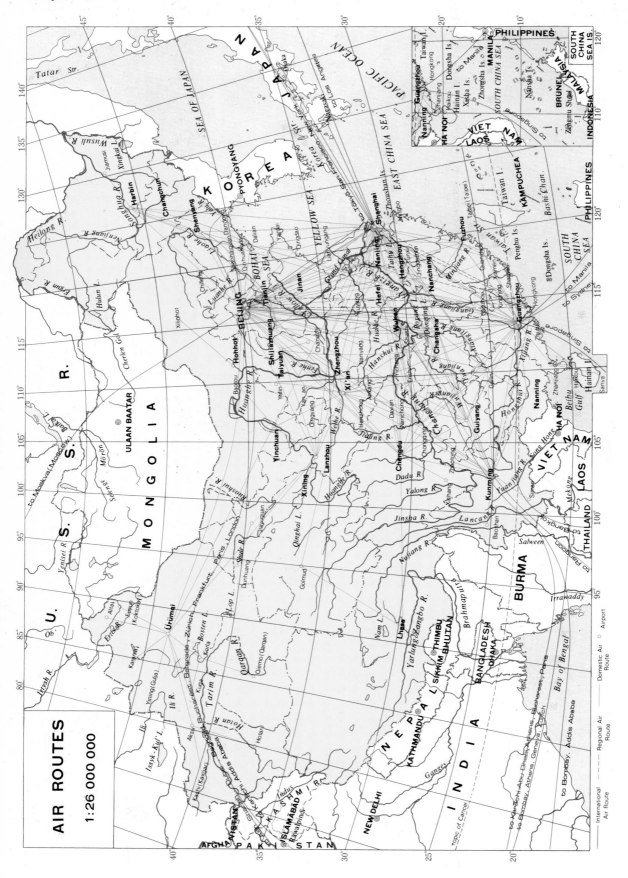

AIR ROUTES
1:26 000 000

International Air Route ——
Regional Air Route ----
Domestic Air Route ——
Airport ○

CHINA NATIONAL TEXTILES IMPORT & EXPORT CORPORATION, HEBEI BRANCH

Mr Xu Rundong
General Manager

MAIN EXPORT ITEMS:

Cotton

Cotton Yarn

Cotton Piece Goods

Spun Rayon Piece Goods

Blended Polyester Polynosic Fabric

Polyester Cotton Fabric

Cotton Ramie Yarn

Polyester Cotton Yarn

Mulberry Silk & Tussah Silk

Pure Silk Piece Goods

Rayon Silk Piece Goods

Embroidered Pure Silk Blouses

Silk Garments

Silk Reproduction

China National Textiles Import & Export Corporation Hebei Branch
8 Jichang Road, Shijiazhuang, China
Tel: 27941 ext. 370
Cable: CHINATEX SHIJIAZHUANG
Telex: 747941-370

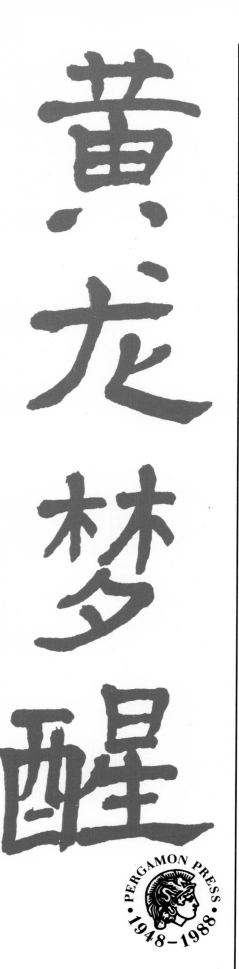

CHINA BUSINESS STRATEGIES

A Survey of Foreign Business Activity in the PRC

NIGEL CAMPBELL and **PETER ADLINGTON,** *China Research Unit, Manchester Business School, Manchester, UK*

China Business Strategies is based on the largest survey of foreign business activity ever undertaken in China, covering over two hundred firms which have representative offices in China and supplemented by extensive fieldwork, desk research and in-depth interviews. The results reveal the current views of the foreign business community on a wide variety of vital topics.

But **China Business Strategies** goes beyond recording survey results. It reveals strategic implications - both for companies already operating in China and for those considering entry to the China market.

China Business Strategies offers a unique and authoritative mix of analysis, information and practical advice on doing business in China which will be of great value to practising managers and China specialists alike.

250x172 mm   272pp approx   November 1988
0 08 0367488 Hardcover

A STRATEGIC GUIDE TO EQUITY JOINT VENTURES IN CHINA

NIGEL CAMPBELL, *China Research Unit, Manchester Business School, Manchester, UK*

A Strategic Guide to Equity Joint Ventures in China draws on detailed studies of 30 equity joint ventures in China, together with an analysis of joint venture statistics between 1978 and 1986. It explains the unique opportunities and difficulties that confront the foreign investor in China and the strategic issues involved. Vital topics covered under "Making the Deal" include the Chinese bureaucratic system, partner selection and negotiations. The chapters on "Making the Deal Work" cover essentials such as management control, factory construction, marketing, and labour and personnel. Appendices include detailed case studies, a feasibility study checklist and equity joint venture regulations.

The practical insights offered in this book make it an indispensable guide both for those already in the China market and for those who are still at the decision stage.

229x152 mm   196pp approx   November 1988
0 08 0367496 Hardcover

PERGAMON PRESS plc, Headington Hill Hall, Oxford OX3 OBW, UK
PERGAMON PRESS INC, Fairview Park, Elmsford, New York 10523, USA

BEST FRIEND OF MACHINERY & EQUIPMENT IMPORTERS & EXPORTERS

Two-Colour Offset Press

Universal Tool Milling Machine Fitted with Digital Display System

Y Series Three-Phase Induction Motors

CMEC Beijing Co., Ltd. practices the integration of industry and trade, technology and trade, import and export. She is a qualified legal person with a high reputation. She has hundreds of manufacturers as her direct suppliers. Her machinery and equipment have been well marketed all over the world. Founded in 1978, she has already established broad connections with trading companies and manufacturers in more than 100 countries and regions. With rapid development of import and export businesses, her prestige in international trade is rising and her trade value is increasing year by year.

CMEC Beijing Co., Ltd. has four export departments. The main business scope is: machine tools and tools, general machinery, engineering machinery, electric motors, electrical apparatus and materials, instruments and meters, agricultural machinery, automoblie parts and accessories, complete sets of plant, etc.

In addition to the general export business, *CMEC Beijing Co., Ltd.* being one of the four corporations appointed by Beijing Municipality, has the right to import technology. Her two import departments are entrusted not only by enterprises from Beijing area, but also from other cities and provinces to undertake technology introduction, co-operation, joint ventures and importation of mechanical, electrical, and instrumental products, parts and materials.

CMEC Beijing Co., Ltd. makes it a point to honour her contracts with high quality, prompt delivery, reasonable prices and good service. Wishing to be the best friend of machinery and equipment importers and exporters, *CMEC, Beijing Co., Ltd.* welcomes businessmen and industrialists the world over to set up and develop trade relations with her.

CMEC Beijing Co., Ltd. has set up an office in Shenzhen which is located at 14/F, East Wing, Shenzhen International Commercial Building, Shenzhen - Tel: 39147

China National Machinery & Equipment Import / Export Corporation
A-3 Jianguomen Wai St., Beijing, China
Tel: 583081 582273 • Cable: CTBC BEIJING • Telex: 210077 CTCBJ CN

CHINA NATIONAL CEREALS, OILS & FOODSTUFFS IMPORT & EXPORT CORPORATION, LIAONING FOODSTUFFS BRANCH

Liaoning is the most southern province in North-East China. It is famous for its mountains, rivers, scenic beauty and rich resources.

In the south of the province, the sea around the Liao Dong Peninsula teems with nutritious fish and shellfish. Sea food from this area has become popular wordwide. We stock a full range of brand name products and guarantee the supply all year round.

The province has fertile mountain areas, dense forests and vast plains. Thus it furnishes fresh fruits which are crispy and colourful and fruit products of Hong Mei brand as well as unblemished fresh or dry vegetables.

Live cows, which we export to Hong Kong are famous for their tender beef and the high rate of beef output. Demand now exceeds supply. The animal products which we export such as force-fed chicken, cut chicken and frozen duck are going to about 30 countries and areas.

Liaoning province is also an advanced industrial province. With advanced technology and the equipment of the food industry, we have produced many export products of excellent quality. The canned foods, sweets, wines, beverages, and Hong Mei seasoning are enjoying a high reputation in the international market.

中国粮油食品进出口公司辽宁省食品分公司

China National Cereals, Oils and Foodstuffs Import & Export Corporation, Liaoning Foodstuffs Branch

145 Stalin Road, Dalian, China

Tel: 236132 233244 • Cable: DALFOOD DALIAN • Telex: 86216 DACOF CN

A Brief Introduction to the China National Chemicals Import & Export Corporation Beijing Branch

The *Beijing Branch* of the *China National Chemicals Import & Export Corporation* is a nationwide, professional and specialized state corporation.

The *Beijing Branch* works in accordance with the business scope laid down by the State, the *China National Chemicals Import & Export Corporation.*

It undertakes unified management in the import and export of chemical raw materials, plastics, resins, dyestuffs, auxiliaries, pigments, intermediates, paints, printing inks, agrichemicals, rubber products and reagent materials. At the same time, it engages in processing with imported materials, compensation trade and joint ventures. The *Beijing Branch* adopts international trade practices in its foreign economic and trade activities.

The Branch was set up in 1958, and traded with the Soviet Union, East European countries and some Asian countries and regions. Since 1973, it has engaged in import and export trade worldwide, and its import and export trade has increased year by year.

The *Beijing Branch* has made useful contributions to the promotion of economic and technical exchanges, China's modernization and friendship with people around the world.

190, Chaoyangmennei Street, Beijing, China.
Tel: 551316 • Cable: SINOCHEMIP BEIJING • Telex 222448 BCIEC CN

CHINESE FOODS TO TAKE AWAY ...

COFCO

China National Cereals, Oils & Foodstuffs Import and Export Coporation, Hebei Branch

Chinese food is renowned the world over. Its exquisiteness is a result not only of masterly cooking, but also of the ingredients used. There is a great variety of top Chinese foods from our Corporation for you to choose from.

Cereals and Beans
Tientsin Small Red Beans • Tangshan Small Red Beans • Zhangjiakou Broad Beans • Zhangjiakou Green Beans • Hebei Green Beans • Red Kidney Beans • Red Coloured Kidney Beans • White Peas • Black Beans • Millet in Husk • Red Millet in Husk • Buckwheat • Yellow Maize • White Maize • Gaoliang (Sorghum) and Millet Sprays.

Oilseeds
Groundnut Kernels • Groundnuts in Shell • Sesame Seeds • Castor Seeds • Sunflower Seeds • Cotton Seeds and Soya Bean Cakes.

Fruit and Vegetables
Tientsin Ya Pears • Tientsin • Tender Pears (Tai Hwang Pears) • Tientsin Hsueh Pears • Chang Ching Apples • Chih Kuan Apples • Red Kuo Kuang Apples • Niu-Nai Grapes • Shenchow Honey • Peaches • Fresh Peaches • Persimmons • Potatoes • Feicui • Capsicums • Red-hearted Turnips • Quick Frozen Garlic Sprouts • Fresh Garlic Sprouts • Quick Frozen Strawberries • Tomatoes • White Garlic • Hebei Preserved Vegetables • Salted Garlic Splits • Salted Bracken and Salted Cucumbers.

Dry and Preserved Fruits
Chestnuts • Dried Pears • Preserved Apricots • Preserved Apples • Preserved Hua Hong (Crab Apples) • Preserved Cherry Apples • Dried Haw Slices and Preserved Dates (Jujube).

Sundries
Tianjin Greenbeans Starch Sheet • Greenbeans Vermicelli • Royal Noodles • Greenbeans Powder • Zhangjiakou Fried Broadbeans • Roasted Peanuts (Salted) and Roasted Peanuts.

Wines and Spirits
Green Bamboo Brand - Liu Ling Tsui Chiew • Yuan Yu Chiew • Guifeizui Chiew • Mi Hou Tao Chiew • Ming Shui Chiew and Dry Red Wine.

Meat, Eggs and Egg Products
Live Cattle • Live Sheep • Frozen Goats with Skin • Frozen Mutton • Frozen Beef • Frozen Rabbit Meat • Frozen Donkey Meat • Frozen Horse Meat • Frozen Pork • Frozen Broilers • Frozen Wild Rabbits • Frozen Wild Boars • Frozen Quails • Frozen Venison • Fresh Eggs and Hebei Preserved Duck Eggs.

Aquatic Products
Frozen Prawn • Frozen Pomfret • Frozen Globe Fish • Frozen Octopus • Frozen Cuttle Fish (Sliced) • Frozen Ark Shell (Shelled) • Frozen Mudsnail • Frozen Periwinkle Meat • Jelly Fish • Jelly Fish Heads • Frozen Blue Crab and Frozen Boiled Clam.

Canned Foods
Greatwall Brand - Pork Luncheon Meat • Pork • Chicken • Beef • Mutton • Fish • Shellfish • Fruits • Vegetables • Fruit Juices and Jam etc.

Your enquires and orders are most welcome.
Please Contact Yang Zhongya
China National Cereals, Oils & Foodstuffs I/E Corp. Hebei Branch
8 Jichang Road, Shijiazhuang, China
Cable: CEROILFOOD SHIJIAZHUANG Telex: 26215 COFHB CN

YOUR IDEAL CHOICE
CHINA NATIONAL LIGHT INDUSTRIAL PRODUCTS IMPORT & EXPORT CORPORATION LIAONING BRANCH

Located in the south of Liaoning Province, China National Light Industrial Products Import & Export Corporation, Liaoning Branch has devoted itself to promoting international trade exchanges since 1960. In pursuit of the principles of equality, mutual benefit and the exchange of each other's needs, the Corporation has developed trade relations with more than one hundred countries and regions, and has done direct business with 2,000 clients around the world.

In recent years, great success has been achieved through increasing the quantity, variety, and quality of our products and packing according to the demands of our international customers. Various flexible trade practices have been adopted, such as processing materials supplied by buyers, production based on a client's sample, assembling parts provided by buyers, compensation trade, co-production and co-management. No doubt, there is a bright future in the export of light industrial products from Liaoning Province. World traders are welcome to visit us.

Main Lines of Business

Glassware
Enamelware
Vacuum bottels
Stainless steel
  tableware
Bicycles
Sewing machines
Leatherette

Watches
Clocks
Shoes
Detergents
Hardware
Constructruction
  materials
Plastic products

Paper
Stationery goods
Sports ware
Travel goods
Musical
  instruments
Household
  appliances

CHINA NATIONAL LIGHT INDUSTRIAL PRODUCTS 1/E CORP., LIAONING BRANCH
110 SI DA LIN ROAD, DALIAN, CHINA
TELEX: 86156 YASHU CN